DogFriendly.com's

EAST COAST
Dog Travel Guide

by
Tara Kain and Len Kain
DogFriendly.com, Inc.

DogFriendly.com's East Coast Dog Travel Guide
by Tara Kain and Len Kain

DogFriendly.com, Inc.
6454 Pony Express Trail #33-233
Pollock Pines, CA 95726 USA
1-877-475-2275
email: email@dogfriendly.com
http://www.dogfriendly.com

PLEASE NOTE
Although the authors and publisher have tried to make the information as accurate as possible, they do not assume, and hereby disclaim, any liability for any loss or damage caused by errors, omissions, misleading information or potential travel problems caused by this book, even if such errors or omissions result from negligence, accident or any other cause.

CHECK AHEAD
We remind you, as always, to call ahead and confirm that the applicable establishment is still "dog-friendly" and that it will accommodate your pet.

DOGS OF ALL SIZES
If your dog is over 75-80 pounds, then please call the individual establishment to make sure that they allow your dog. Please be aware that establishments and local governments may also not allow particular breeds.

OTHER PARTIES DESCRIPTIONS
Some of the descriptions have been provided to us by our web site advertisers, paid researchers or other parties.

ISBN 13 - 978-0-9795551-2-1
ISBN 10 - 0-9795551-2-4

Printed in the United States of America

Photographs taken by Len Kain, Tara Kain and Jodi Kain

Cover Photographs (top to bottom, left to right):
The White House, Washington, DC
Acadia National Park, Bar Harbor, ME
Sunrise at the Beach, St Augustine, FL
A Street Fair in New York, NY

Back Cover Photographs (left to right):
Independence Hall, Philadelphia, PA
Southernmost Point Monument, Key West, FL
The Freedom Trail, Boston, MA

TABLE OF CONTENTS

Introduction

DogFriendly.com's guides have helped over one million dog lovers plan vacations and trips with their dogs. Included in this book are over 8000 truly dog-friendly accommodations including nearly 2000 independent hotels, B&Bs and vacation rentals. The guide gives detailed pet policies, including how many dogs may be allowed per room, weight limits, fees and other useful information. In many cases, toll-free numbers and websites are given. Also very importantly, this dog-friendly lodging guide focuses on those places that allow dogs of all sizes and do not restrict dogs to smoking rooms only. Not included in this guide are places that allow, for example, only dogs up to ten pounds or require that your dog be carried or in a carrier while on the premises. Also, we do not think that places that require dog owners to stay in smoking rooms are dog-friendly and we do not include them. Accommodations in this book have been called by DogFriendly.com to verify pet policies although these policies do change often. There are also helpful road trip tips and airline pet policies. Thank you for selecting our pet travel guide and we hope you spend less time researching and more time actually going places with your dog. Enjoy your dog-friendly travels!

About Author Tara Kain

Tara Kain grew up with dogs and has always loved dogs. When she moved away from home, she discovered a whole new world through traveling. But whenever she traveled, the last thing she wanted was to leave her best friend behind. Tara often spent the whole time worrying about her pooch. So she began taking her dog. It was much tougher than she originally thought. Tara would spend several days researching and planning where her dog would be accepted and what else there was to do with her dog, aside from staying in a hotel room. Unfortunately, many places did not allow dogs, especially a large dog like her standard poodle. Many times when she found a supposedly "dog-friendly" hotel or motel, they would allow pets only in smoking rooms. In her opinion, because one travels with a dog should not limit them to a smoking room. So in June of 1998, she began to compile a list of dog-friendly places, notes and photos and began posting them on a web site called DogFriendly.com. This allowed her to easily keep track of the research and also help other dog lovers know about dog-friendly places. Today she still travels with her family, including the family dog. She is devoted to finding the best pet-friendly places and letting others know about them.

Tara has traveled over 150,000 miles across the United States and Canada with her dog. She serves as DogFriendly.com's President and editor-in-chief. She has written a number of magazine articles. Tara has been interviewed by numerous reporters about dog travel, dogs in the workplace and other issues concerning dogs in public places. DogFriendly.com and Tara have been featured in many articles over the years including in most major newspapers. She has appeared on CNN and CBS Television, did a live on-line forum for USA Today and has been a guest on many radio shows. Tara and her family reside in California, in the Sierra Nevada foothills near Sacramento.

About Author Len Kain

Len Kain began traveling with his dog when he was young. His family traveled with a camping trailer and brought along their standard poodle, Ricky. On trips, he found places and attractions that welcomed his best friend. When Len grew up and got his own dog, he continued the tradition of bringing his dog on trips with him. Len and his family have traveled over 150,000 miles across the country on road trips. Today he continues to travel and find fun and exciting dog-friendly places.

Currently, Len serves as DogFriendly.com's Vice President of Sales and Marketing. Len has been quoted numerous times in print, on radio and television about issues relating to traveling with dogs. Prior to joining DogFriendly.com Len served in various executive and management positions in several Silicon Valley and Internet Companies. Len holds a Bachelor of Engineering degree from Stevens Tech in New Jersey, a Master of Science degree from Stanford University and an MBA from the University of Phoenix. Len resides with his family in the Sierra Nevada foothills of California.

Your Comments and Feedback

We value and appreciate your feedback and comments. If you want to recommend a dog-friendly place or establishment, let us know. If you find a place that is no longer dog-friendly, allows small dogs only or allows dogs in smoking rooms only, please let us know. You can contact us using the following information.

Mailing Address and Contact Information:
DogFriendly.com, Inc.
6454 Pony Express Trail #33-233
Pollock Pines, CA 95726 USA
Toll free phone: 1-877-475-2275
email: email@ dogfriendly.com
http://www.dogfriendly.com

How To Use This Guide

General Guidelines

1. Please only travel with a well-behaved dog that is comfortable around other people and especially children. Dogs should also be potty trained and not bark excessively.

2. Always keep your dog leashed unless management specifically tells you otherwise.

3. Establishments listed in this book should allow well-behaved dogs of ALL sizes (at least up to 75 pounds) and in non-smoking rooms. If your dog is over 75-80 pounds, then please call the individual establishment to make sure they will allow your dog. We have listed some establishments which only allow dogs up to 50 pounds, but we try our best to make a note in the comments about the restrictions. All restaurants and attractions we list should allow dogs of all sizes.

4. Accommodations listed do not allow dogs to be left alone in the room unless specified by hotel management. If the establishment does not allow pets to be left alone, try hiring a local pet sitter to watch your dog in the room.

5. All restaurants listed as dog-friendly refer to outdoor seating only. While dogs are not permitted to sit in a chair at a restaurant's outdoor dining table, they should be allowed to sit or lay next to your table. We do not list outdoor restaurants that require your dog to be tied outside of a fenced area (with you at the dining table on one side and your dog on the other side of the fence). In our opinion, those are not truly dog-friendly restaurants. Restaurants listed may have seasonal outdoor seating.

6. Pet policies and management change often, especially within the lodging and restaurant industries. Please always call ahead to make sure an establishment still exists and is still dog-friendly.

7. After purchasing your book, please visit http://www.dogfriendly.com/updates for FREE book updates. We will do our best to let you know which places may no longer be dog-friendly.

Preparation for a Road Trip

A Month Before

If you don't already have one, get a pet identification tag for your dog. It should have your dog's name, your name and phone number. Consider using a cell phone number, a home number and, if possible, the number of where you will be staying.

Get a first aid kit for your dog. It comes in very handy if you need to remove any ticks. The kits are usually available at a pet store, a veterinary office or on the Internet.

If you do not already have a dog harness for riding the car, consider purchasing one for your dog's and your own safety. A loose dog in the car can fly into the windshield, out of the car, or into you and injure you or cause you to lose control of the car. Dog harnesses are usually sold at pet stores or on the Internet.

Make a trip to the vet if necessary for the following:

- A current rabies tag for your dog's collar. Also get paperwork with proof of the rabies vaccine.
- Dogs can possibly get heartworm from mosquitoes in the mountains, rural areas or on hikes. Research or talk to your vet and ask him or her if the area you are traveling to has a high risk of heartworm disease. The vet may suggest placing your dog on a monthly heartworm preventative medicine.
- Consider using some type of flea preventative for your dog, preferably a natural remedy. This is out of courtesy for the dog-friendly hotels plus for the comfort of your pooch.
- Make sure your dog is in good health.

Several Days Before

Make sure you have enough dog food for the duration of the trip.

If your dog is on any medication, remember to bring it along.

Some dog owners will also purchase bottled water for the trip, because some dogs can get sick from drinking water they are not used to. Talk to your vet for more information.

The Day Before

Do not forget to review DogFriendly.com's Etiquette for the Traveling Dog!

Road Trip Day

Remember to pack all of your dog's necessities: food, water, dog dishes, leash, snacks and goodies, several favorite toys, brush, towels for dirty paws, plastic bags for cleaning up after your dog, doggie first aid kit, possibly dog booties if you are venturing to an especially cold or hot region, and bring any medicine your dog might be taking.

Before you head out, put on that doggie seat belt harness.

On The Road

Keep it cool and well ventilated in the car for your dog.

Stop at least every 2-3 hours so your dog can relieve him or herself. Also offer him or her water during the stops.

Never leave your pet alone in a parked car - even in the shade with the window cracked open. According to the Los Angeles SPCA, on a hot day, a car can heat up to 160 degrees in minutes, potentially causing your pet (or child) heat stroke, brain damage, and even death.

If your dog needs medical attention during your trip, check the yellow pages phone book in the area and look under Veterinarians. If you do not see an emergency vet listed, call any local vet even   during the evening hours and they can usually inform you of the closest emergency vet.

Etiquette for the Traveling Dog

So you have found the perfect getaway spot that allows dogs, but maybe you have never traveled with your dog. Or maybe you are a seasoned dog traveler. But do you know all of your doggie etiquette? Basic courtesy rules, like your dog should be leashed unless a place specifically allows your dog to be leash-free. And do you ask for a paper bowl or cup for your thirsty pooch at an outdoor restaurant instead of letting him or her drink from your water glass?

There are many do's and don'ts when traveling with your best friend. We encourage all dog owners to follow a basic code of doggie etiquette, so places will continue to allow and welcome our best friends. Unfortunately all it takes is one bad experience for an establishment to stop allowing dogs. Let's all try to be on our best behavior to keep and, heck, even encourage new places to allow our pooches.

Everywhere...

- Well-Behaved Dogs. Only travel or go around town with a well-behaved dog that is friendly to people and especially children. If your dog is not comfortable around other people, you might consider taking your dog to obedience classes or hiring a professional trainer. Your well-behaved dog should also be potty trained and not bark excessively in a hotel or other lodging room. We believe that dogs should be kept on leash. If a dog is on leash, he or she is easier to bring under control. Also, many establishments require that dogs be on leash and many people around you will feel more comfortable as well. And last, please never leave your dog alone in a hotel or other lodging room unless you have the approval from the establishment's management.

- Leashed Dogs. Please always keep your dog leashed, unless management specifically states otherwise. Most establishments (including lodging, outdoor restaurants, attractions, parks, beaches, stores and festivals) require that your dog be on leash. Plus most cities and counties have an official leash law that requires pets to be leashed at all times when not on your property. Keeping your dog on leash will also prevent any unwanted contact with other people that are afraid of dogs, people that do not appreciate strange dogs coming up to them, and even other dog owners who have a leashed dog. Even when on leash, do not let your pooch visit with other people or dogs unless welcomed. Keeping dogs on leash will also protect them from running into traffic, running away, or getting injured by wildlife or other dogs. Even the most well-behaved and trained dogs can be startled by something, especially in a new environment.

- Be Considerate. Always clean up after your dog. Pet stores sell pooper scooper bags. You can also buy sandwich bags from your local grocery store. They work quite well and are cheap!

At Hotels or Other Types of Lodging...

- Unless it is obvious, ask the hotel clerk if dogs are allowed in the hotel lobby. Also, because of health codes, dogs are usually not allowed into a lobby area while it is being used for serving food like continental breakfast. Dogs may be allowed into the area once there is no food being served, but check with management first.

- Never leave your dog alone in the hotel room without the permission of management. The number one reason hotel management does not allow dogs is because some people leave them in the room alone. Some dogs, no matter how well-trained, can cause damage, bark continuously or scare the housekeepers. Unless the hotel management allows it, please make sure your dog is never left alone in the room. If you need to leave your dog in the room, consider hiring a local pet sitter.

- While you are in the room with your dog, place the Do Not Disturb sign on the door or keep the deadbolt locked. Many housekeepers have been surprised or scared by dogs when entering a room.

- In general, do not let your pet on the bed or chairs, especially if your dog sheds easily and might leave pet hair on the furniture. Some very pet-friendly accommodations will actually give you a sheet to lay over the bed so your pet can join you. If your pet cannot resist coming hopping onto the furniture with you, bring your own sheet.

- When your dog needs to go to the bathroom, take him or her away from the hotel rooms and the bushes located right next to the rooms. Try to find some dirt or bushes near the parking lot. Some hotels have a designated pet walk area.

At Outdoor Restaurants...

- Tie your dog to your chair, not the table (unless the table is secured to the ground). If your dog decides to get up and move away from the table, he or she will not take the entire table.

- If you want to give your dog some water, please ask the waiter/waitress to bring a paper cup or bowl of water for your dog. Do not use your own water glass. Many restaurants and even other guests frown upon this.

- Your pooch should lay or sit next to your table. At restaurants, dogs are not allowed to sit on the chairs or tables, or eat off the tables. This type of activity could make a restaurant owner or manager ban dogs. And do not let your pooch beg from other customers. Unfortunately, not everyone loves dogs!

- About Restaurant Laws regarding dogs at restaurants
State health codes in the United States prohibit all animals except for service animals inside indoor sections of restaurants. In recent years some health departments have begun banning dogs from some outdoor restaurant areas. It is complicated to determine where dogs are and are not allowed outdoors because most State laws are vague. They state something such as "Animals are not allowed on the premises of a food establishment". These laws also define animals to include "birds, vermin and insects" which are always present at outdoor restaurants. Various health departments have various interpretations of where the premises start and stop. Some allow dogs at outdoor areas where food is served, some allow dogs at outdoor areas only where you bring your own food to the table. Some will allow special pet-friendly areas or will allow dogs on the outside of the outer most tables. Any city or county can issue a variance to State law if it wants to allow dogs into outdoor (or indoor) restaurants. This can be done in two ways, directly by the local health department or through a vote of the local government. If a restaurant that you are visiting with your dog cites some curious requirement it is probably due to the health code. Please also understand that in all places the owner of a restaurant has the choice to not allow dogs with the exception of service dogs. Nationally, Austin, Dallas, Orlando, Chicago, Denver and Alexandria forced law changes to allow dogs at outdoor restaurants when their health departments went too far in banning dogs from outdoor seats. Dogs are now allowed in outdoor areas in these cities through variances (or in Orlando's case) changing Florida state law. For up to date information please see http://www.dogfriendly.com/dining . The laws are in a state of flux at the moment so please understand that they may change.

At Retail Stores...

- Keep a close eye on your dog and make sure he or she does not go to the bathroom in the store. Store owners that allow dogs inside assume that responsible dog owners will be entering their store. Before entering a dog-friendly store, visit your local pet store first. They are by far the most forgiving. If your dog does not go to the bathroom there, then you are off to a great start! If your dog does make a mistake in any store, clean it up. Ask the store clerk for paper towels or something similar so you can clean up any mess.

- In most states dogs are allowed in stores, shops and other private buildings with the exception of grocery stores and restaurants. The decision to allow dogs is the business owner's and you can always ask if you may bring your dog inside. Also in most states packaged foods (bottled sodas, waters, bags of cookies or boxes of snacks) does not cause a store to be classified as a grocery. Even pet stores do sell these items . In many states, drinks such as coffee, tea and water are also allowed. You can order food from a restaurant to a pet-friendly establishment (so long as the establishment is not also the restaurant with the kitchen) in most areas.

At Festivals and Outdoor Events...

Make sure your dog has relieved himself or herself before entering a festival or event area. The number one reason that most festival coordinators do not allow dogs is because some dogs go to the bathroom on a vendor's booth or in areas where people might sit.

Breed Specific Laws and the Effect of These Laws on Travel With Dogs

There has been a trend in cities, counties, states and provinces towards what is known as Breed-Specific Laws (BSL) in which a municipality bans or restricts the freedoms of dog owners with specific breeds of dogs. These laws vary from place to place and are effecting a greater number of dog owners every year. Most people may think that these laws effect only the "Pit Bull" but this is not always the case. Although the majority of dogs effected are pit-bulls other breeds of dogs as well as mixed breeds that include targeted breeds are also named in the various laws in North America. These laws range from registration requirements and leash or muzzle requirements to extreme laws in which the breed is banned from the municipality outright. Some places may even be permitted to confiscate a visitor's dog who unknowingly enters the region with a banned breed.

As of August 29, 2005 the province of Ontario, Canada (including Toronto, Niagara Falls, and Ottawa) passed a very broad breed-specific law banning Pit Bulls and "similar" dogs from the province. The law allows for confiscation of visiting dogs as well as dogs living in Ontario. It is extremely important that people visiting Ontario make sure that they are able to prove that their dog is not a Pit Bull with other documentation. Various cities throughout the U.S. and Canada have muzzle requirements for Pit Bulls and other restrictions on targeted breeds as well. Breed-specific laws do get repealed as well. In October, 2005 the city of Vancouver, BC removed its requirement that Pit Bulls be muzzled in public and now only requires dogs with a known history of aggressiveness to be muzzled.

The breed specific laws usually effect pit bull type dogs but are often vaguely written and may also effect mixed breed dogs that resemble the targeted breeds. These laws are always changing and can be passed by cities, counties and even states and provinces. We recommend that travelers with dogs check into whether they are effected by such laws. You may check www.DogFriendly.com/bsl for links to further information on BSL.

DogFriendly.com does not support breed-specific laws. Most people who take their dogs out in public are responsible and those that choose to train a dog to be viscous will simply choose another breed, causing other breeds to be banned or regulated in the future.

Customs Information for Traveling Between the United States and Canada

If you will be traveling between the United States and Canada, identification for Customs and Immigration is required. U.S. and Canadian citizens traveling across the border need the following:

People

- A passport is now required (or will shortly be required depending on your point of entry) to move between the U.S. and Canada. This is a new policy so be sure to have your passport with you. Children also need a passport of their own now.

Dogs

- Dogs must be free of evidence of diseases communicable to humans when possibly examined at the port of entry.

- Valid rabies vaccination certificate (including an expiration date usually up to 3 years from the actual vaccine date and a veterinarian's signature). If no expiration date is specified on the certificate, then the certificate is acceptable if the date of the vaccination is not more than 12 months before the date of arrival. The certificate must show that the dog had the rabies vaccine at least 30 days prior to entry.

- Young puppies must be confined at a place of the owner's choosing until they are three months old, then they must be vaccinated. They must remain in confinement for 30 days after the vaccination.

Chain Hotel Websites

Best Western	www.bestwestern.com
Candlewood Suites	www.ichotelsgroup.com
Clarion	www.choicehotels.com
Comfort Inn	www.choicehotels.com
Drury Inn	www.druryhotels.com
Hilton	www.hilton.com
Holiday Inn	www.ichotelsgroup.com
Howard Johnson	www.hojo.com
Kimpton Group	www.kimptonhotels.com
La Quinta	www.lq.com
Loews Hotels	www.loewshotels.com
Marriott	www.marriott.com
Motel 6	www.motel6.com
Novotel	www.novotel.com
Quality Inn	www.choicehotels.com
Red Roof Inn	www.redroof.com
Residence Inn	www.residenceinn.com
Sheraton	www.starwoodhotels.com
Sleep Inn	www.choicehotels.com
Staybridge Suites	www.ichotelsgroup.com
Studio 6	www.staystudio6.com
Super 8	www.super8.com
Towneplace Suites	www.towneplaceSuites.com
Westin	www.starwoodhotels.com

Traveling with a Dog By Air

Many airlines allow dogs to be transported with the traveling public. Small dogs, usually no more than 15 pounds and with shorter legs, may travel in a carrier in the cabin with you. They must usually be kept under the seat. Any larger dogs must travel in a kennel in the cargo hold. It can be difficult for dogs to travel in the cargo hold of airplanes. Most airlines restrict cargo hold pet transportation during very hot and cold periods. Most require that you notify them when making reservations about the pet as they limit the number of pets allowed on each plane and the size of the carriers may vary depending on what type of plane is being used. There are no airlines that we are aware of today that will allow dogs larger than those that fit in a carrier under a seat to fly in the cabin. Service animals are allowed in the cabin and are harnessed during takeoff and landing. The FAA is now tracking pet injury and death information from airline cargo section pet travel. Their monthly reports are at the website airconsumer.ost.dot.gov/reports. Below is a summary of the pet policies for airlines at the time of publication of this book.

Airline	Cabin – Small Dogs Allowed	Cargo – Dogs Allowed	Phone	Fees (US) (each way)	Web Link for More Information - May Change
Air Canada	No	Yes	888-247-2262 (US)	$105 US- Can $245 Overseas	No Dogs allowed on flights within Canada aircanada.com/en/travelinfo/airport/baggage/pets.html
Alaska Air / Horizon Air	Yes	Yes	800-252-7522	$75.00 Cabin $100 Cargo	alaskaair.com/www2/help/faqs/Pets.asp
America West/ US Airways	Yes	No	800-235-9292	$80.00	usairways.com/awa/content/traveltools/specialneeds/pets.aspx
American	Yes	Yes	800-433-7300	Cabin - $80 Cargo - $100	aa.com/content/travelInformation/specialAssistance/travelingWithPets.jhtml
Continental	Yes	Yes	Live animal desk - 800-575-3335 reserv 800-525-0280	$95 (Cabin), from $119 (Cargo)	continental.com/travel/policies/animals/ default.asp
Delta	Yes	Yes	800-221-1212	Cabin - $75 Cargo - $150	delta.com/planning_reservations/special_travel_needs/pet_travel_information/pet_travel_options/index.jsp#Cargo
Frontier	Yes	Yes	800-432-1359	$100.00	frontierairlines.com/frontier/plan-book/travel-info-services/family-pets/traveling-with-pets.do
Independence	Yes	No	800-FLYFLYI	$35.00	flyi.com/tools/policies.aspx#traveling_pets
Jet Blue	Yes	No	800-538-2583	$75.00	jetblue.com/travelinfo/howToDetail.asp?topicId=%278%27
Northwest	Yes	Yes	800-225-2525	$80 Cabin $139+ Cargo	nwa.com/services/shipping/Cargo/products/ppet2.shtml
Southwest	No	No			
United	Yes	Yes	800-864-8331	Cabin - $85 Cargo - $100+	united.com/page/middlepage/0,6823,1047,00.html

* We do not recommend that dogs travel in the cargo hold of airplanes unless it is absolutely necessary. Temperatures can range from freezing to sweltering and there can be delays on the runways, at the gates and elsewhere. These varying conditions can cause injury or even death to a pet.

Chapter 1

200 "Must See" Dog-Friendly Places

"Must See" Maine Dog-Friendly Places

Bar Harbor - Acadia

Acadia National Park

Acadia National Park Eagle Lake Road Bar Harbor ME   207-288-3338
http://www.nps.gov/acad/
This National Park ranks high on the tail wagging meter. Dogs are allowed on most of the hiking trails, which is unusual for a national park. There are miles and miles of both hiking trails and carriage roads. Pets are also allowed at the campgrounds, but must be attended at all times. They are not allowed on sand beaches during the Summer or on the steeper hiking trails year-round. Pets must be on a 6 foot or less leash at all times. There is one exception to the leash rule. There is an area in the park that is privately owned where dogs are allowed to run leash-free. It is called Little Long Pond and is located near Seal Harbor. Don't miss the awe-inspiring view from the top of Cadillac Mountain in the park. Overall, this is a pretty popular national park for dogs and their dog-loving owners. There is a $10 entrance fee into the park, which is good for 7 days. You can also purchase an audio tape tour of the Park Loop Road which is a self-guided auto tour. The driving tour is about 27 miles and takes 3 to 4 hours including stops. Audio tapes are available at the Hulls Cove Visitor Center.
Jordon Pond House Restaurant Route 3 Bar Harbor ME   207-276-3316
http://www.jordanpond.com/
This is an extremely dog-friendly restaurant. Dine outdoors at the tables on the lawn with your leashed pooch. The outdoor seating area offers a beautiful view of the pond and mountains. They are open for lunch, afternoon tea and popovers, and dinner. Enjoy entrees like the Grilled Maine Salmon, Steamed Lobster, and Maine Crab Cakes. The restaurant also offers salads, beef, chicken, desserts and a children's menu.
The Ledgelawn Inn 66 Mount Desert Street Bar Harbor ME   207-288-4596 (800-274-5334)
This bed and breakfast inn has a $25 per night pet charge. The B&B is totally non-smoking and there are 8 pet rooms, each with separate entrances.

2

Boothbay

Boothbay Railway Village 586 Wiscasset Road /H 29 Boothbay ME   207-633-4727
http://www.railwayvillage.org/
A village reflecting the rural life of Old New England, an impressive 60 antique vehicle collection, beautiful gardens, and a real steam engine train to ride make this a fun and educational destination. Dogs are allowed throughout the grounds and they may even ride the train. Dogs are not allowed on Special Event days, so they suggest calling ahead. Dogs must be well behaved, under owner's control, leashed, and cleaned up after at all times.
Cap'n Fish Boat Tours 65 Atlantic Avenue Boothbay Harbor ME   207-633-3244
www.capnfishmotel.com
Specializing in whale watch and nature cruises, this company will allow your pooch to come aboard for tours. There is no additional pet fee. Dogs must be under owner's control, leashed, and cleaned up after at all times.

Camden Area

Schooner Olad Camden Harbor/Camden Public Landing Camden ME   207-236-2323
http://www.maineschooners.com/
This water adventure company offers two hour tours along Maine's coastline where visitors can see plenty of marine and bird life and seafaring activity. Dogs are allowed on board for no additional fee. Dogs must be friendly, under owner's control/care at all times, and leashed. They also suggest visitors bring necessary refreshments for themselves and the pet.

Portland

Inn By The Sea 40 Bowery Beach Road Cape Elizabeth ME   207-799-3134 (800-888-4287)
http://www.innbythesea.com/
Thanks to one of our readers for these comments: "This hotel is an amazing place for dog lovers. It's a four star hotel that treats your puppy like any other hotel guest. There are two suites (bedroom, kitchen, living room) that are specifically appointed for dogs. Water dishes, biscuits, towels for paws, and outside hoses are provided. There are four nearby state parks and the hotel itself borders a feral area which my dog spent hours on end exploring. There's even a fenced-in kennel area, complete with a dog house, if you want to leave your pet for an hour and go for dinner. Wonderful place, they love dogs, great recreation, beautiful rooms, great hotel restaurant - truly a superb experience." This hotel also offers dog walking service with 24-hour notification. They even have a special pet menu with items like gourmet chuck burgers, grilled range chicken, NY sirloin strip steak with potatoes and vegetables, and for dessert, vanilla ice cream or doggie bon bons. If you are there during Thanksgiving, Christmas or the Fourth of July, they offer a special pet holiday menu. The hotel asks that all pets be kept on a leash when not in their suite and that pets are not left alone in the suite. When making a reservation, they do require that you tell them you are bringing your pet. There are no pet fees. All rooms are non-smoking.
Bay View Cruises 184 Commercial Street Portland ME   207-761-0486
http://www.bayviewcruises.com
The boat tours are about 1 1/2 hours long. Well behaved dogs on lead are allowed on board.
Old Port Waterfront District Congress Street Portland ME   207-772-6828
Combining a working waterfront with a trendy shopping, dining, and entertainment district with a vibrant nightlife has successfully revitalized this area. Well mannered dogs are welcome. Dogs must be leashed and cleaned up after at all times. It is up to individual stores whether dogs are allowed inside. There are several eateries with outdoor dining that allow pets at the outer tables.
Bayley's Camping Resort 275 Pine Point Road Scarborough ME   207-883-6043
http://www.bayleys-camping.com
Dogs of all sizes are allowed. There is a pet policy to sign at check in and there are no additional pet fees. Dogs may not be left unattended, must be leashed, and cleaned up after. This RV park has many special weekends and events such has Father's Day and Halloween. This RV park is closed during the off-season. The camping and tent areas also allow dogs. There is a dog walk area at the campground.

"Must See" New Hampshire Dog-Friendly Places

Ossipee Lake Region

Lazy Dog Inn 201 White Mountain H/H 16 Chocorua Village NH   603-323-8350 (888-323-8350)
http://www.lazydoginn.com/
This 160 year old New England farmhouse really is a dog friendly place (even the rooms have doggie themed

names), and there are plenty of picturesque walking trails close by too. Included in the rates is a fenced in "Doggie Play Area" with agility equipment and a climate controlled Doggie Lodge providing doggie daycare. They also offer a bottomless treat jar for their canine guests and a like jar of cookies for their owners. Dogs must be at least 12 weeks old, and there are no additional pet fees for one dog. There may be an additional fee of $25 per night per pet for 2 pets or more depending on length of stay. Dogs must be friendly and well mannered with humans and the other pets in residence. Dogs must be leashed and cleaned up after.

King Pine Ski Area 1251 Eaton Road East Madison NH   603-367-8896
http://www.xcskinh.com/king_pine.cfm
Dogs are allowed on this year round recreational mountain. In Spring through Fall dogs are allowed on the trails, preferably on lead; however, if the pet is under good voice control, they may be off-lead. In Winter they ask that dogs are kept on lead and out of the groomed skate tracks. Dogs must be under owner's control and cleaned up after at all times. Dogs are not allowed at the lodge.

Portsmouth

Portsmouth Guided Walking Tours

Portsmouth Guided Walking Tours 500 Market Street Portsmouth NH   603-436-3988
The Chamber of Commerce offers 2 different tours here. The Highlights Tour tells lively and interesting stories relating almost 400 years of history, and the Twilight Tour that tells of its more colorful, bawdy side. Both are outside tours, and your well mannered, quiet pet is welcome to come along. Dogs must be under owner's control, leashed, and cleaned up after at all times.

White Mtns - H-16 Corridor

Bear Notch Ski Touring Center Route 302 Bartlett NH   603-374-2277
http://www.bearnotchski.com
This dog-friendly rental center allows dogs on most of their cross-country ski trails. They have 40 to 65 kilometers of groomed trails. Dogs can be off-leash but need to be under voice control. You need to carry a leash with you just in case. The center rents skis, snowshoes and sleds.

Mount Washinton Auto Road Mount Washinton Auto Road Gorham NH   603-466-3988
http://www.mountwashingtonautoroad.com
Even though self-guided tours are not available in the Winter, the ever-changing weather conditions and outstanding views of this drive to New England's tallest peak is an adventure in and of itself. Due to the climb, there are some automobile make/model restrictions, and there may be times they need to close the road due to

weather, so it is a good idea to check ahead. The fee for 1 driver and the car is $20; $7 for each additional adult; $5 for children 5-12, and pets are free. Dogs must be on a leash at all times when out of the vehicle, and they are not allowed in any park buildings or on any guided tours. Please clean up after your pet.

Adventure Suites 3440 White Mountain H/H16 North Conway NH 603-356-9744 (800-N.CONWAY (606-6929))
http://www.adventuresuites.com/
This inn with various themed rooms offers 16 suites with a variety of adventures from a tree house setting to a unique 2 story cave dwelling, from the penthouse to the jungle, and more, and each suite has a Jacuzzi. Dogs of all sizes are welcome for an additional $10 per pet, and when you reserve ahead of time there is a special treat waiting in the room for them. Dogs must be at least 1 year old, quiet, and very well behaved as there are other animals on site. Dogs must be leashed and cleaned up after at all times, and dog depots are provided. Dogs may not be left alone in the room at any time.

White Mtns - I-93 Corridor

The Hilltop Inn 9 Norton Lane Sugar Hill NH 603-823-5695 (800-770-5695)
http://www.hilltopinn.com/
This 1895 traditional country inn sits on 50 acres in the White Mountains with an impressive array of relaxing and recreational pursuits. There are 20 acres of ungroomed cross-country skiing here and your pooch is welcome to join you on them. They also have a large fenced in yard for pets to run free. Dogs of all sizes are welcome for an additional pet fee of $10 per night per room. They ask that you clean up after your pet if they do their business on the lawns, but it's not necessary in the fields. Dogs must be well behaved and friendly towards the other pets in residence. Dogs only need to be on lead around the house or when felt necessary by the owner, and they may only be left alone in the room if they will be quiet and the front desk is informed.

"Must See" Vermont Dog-Friendly Places

Bennington

Bennington Battle Monument 15 Monument Circle Bennington VT 802-447-0550
This monument pays tribute to a significant 1777 battle with interpretive exhibits, dioramas, statuary, and interpreters who will take visitors to the top of the 1891. You can ride to the top of the 306 foot stone obelisk via an elevator to a view from where three states are visible. They are open 9am to 5pm, 7 days a week from mid-April to October 31st. Pooches who are not elevator shy have been known to go up also as long as no one is allergic; they are allowed throughout the grounds. Dogs must be leashed and cleaned up after at all times.

Brandon

Robert Frost Interpretive Trail H 125 Middlebury VT 802-388-4362
This scenic recreation trail stands as a commemorative to the poetry of Robert Frost, and there are several of his poems along this 1.2 mile loop in addition to a blueberry and huckleberry patch at the far end of the trail. Dogs are allowed on leash. Dogs must be under owner's control and cleaned up after at all times.

Burlington

Burlington Bike Path Lake Champlain Shoreline Burlington VT 802-864-0123
Dogs on leash are allowed to accompany you as you walk or jog this 7.6 mile bike path on the shore of beautiful Lake Champlain. It stretches from Oakledge Park in the south to the Winooski River in the north. Please clean up after your dog.
Lake Champlain Ferries King Street Dock Burlington VT 802-864-9804
http://www.ferries.com/
Leashed dogs of all sizes are allowed on the Lake Champlain Ferry crossing that travels between New York and Vermont. Ferry schedules changes constantly so please confirm the time of your voyage.

Craftsbury Common

Craftsburg Outdoor Center 535 Lost Nation Road Craftsbury Common VT 802-586-7767
http://www.craftsbury.com
This 320 acre four season resort is located beside a secluded lake. They allow dogs in a couple of their non-smoking cabins. There is a $50 one time pet fee. Well-behaved dogs of all sizes are welcome and there is limit of 2 pets per cabin. Summer activities include hiking and mountain biking. Winter activities include dog-friendly cross-country skiing on 7 kilometers of groomed trails.

Hero Islands

Apple Island Marina H 2 South Hero VT   802-372-3922
http://www.appleislandresort.com/
In addition to being a full service marina, they also offer canoe and kayak rentals. Dogs are allowed on the watercraft rentals for no additional fee. Dogs must be well behaved, leashed when not on the boat, and cleaned up after at all times.

Killington

The Paw House 1376 Clarendon Avenue Killington VT   802-438-2738 (866-PAW-HOUSE)
http://www.pawhouseinn.com
The Paw House Inn is a B&B that caters exclusively to dog owners and their pets. Dog care is available on site. Before staying here with your dog you will be required to submit an application in advance.

Rutland

The Nordic Ski Touring Center 195 Mountian Top Road Chittenden VT   802-483-2311
http://www.mountaintopinn.com/
This Nordic center sits amid thousands of acres of forest and mountain lakes, with miles and miles of year round, multi-use trails offering visitors a variety of land and water recreation. Dogs are allowed on select cross country ski trails and on all the hiking trails. There are no additional pet fees. Dogs must be under owner's control, leashed, and cleaned up after. There are some trails where dogs may be off-lead if they are under good voice control, and pet friendly lodging is available on site.

St Johnsbury

Stephen Huneck Gallery at Dog Mountain 143 Parks Road St Johnsbury VT   800-449-2580
http://www.dogmt.com/
This amazing dog friendly estate is the home and showcase of the dog lover,artist and author Stephen Huneck. There is a variety of doggy art, books, gifts, and clothing available, lots of green lawns, a pond, and a Dog Chapel where all denominations are welcome to commune with their pet. Also on site is a Dog Agility Course providing fun romps for the pooch, and the gallery is home to special doggy events through the year. Dogs must be friendly, under owner's control, leashed (unless under good voice control), and cleaned up after at all times.

Warren

Blueberry Lake Ski Area 424 Robinson Road Warren VT   802-496-6687
Called the "Snow Bowl of Sugarbush" this cross-country ski area offers almost 20 miles of groomed trails with some of the trails lit for night skiing. Dogs are allowed on the trails and they may be off leash if they are under good voice control. Dogs must be cleaned up after at all times.

"Must See" Massachusetts Dog-Friendly Places

Berkshires

Natural Bridge State Park Mc Cauley Road North Adams MA   413-663-6392
This 48 acre seasonal park offers many unique geological features, an old marble quarry, a short walkway through a chasm, walking trails, picnic areas, and scenic overlooks. Dogs are allowed throughout the park and on the trails. Dogs must be under owner's control at all times, be on no more than a 10 foot leash, cleaned up after, and have proof of current rabies inoculation.

Boston

Boston Common Park Beacon Street/H 2 Boston MA   617-635-4505
At 350 years old, this is the country's oldest park and it boasts an interesting cultural and natural history. The Freedom Trail Visitor Center is on site, and the park is a hub for the Emerald Necklace system that links several parks and areas of the city. The 50 acre park is also home to many large, public events, a children's play area, a public garden, several memorials, the Frog Pond (skating in Winter and a spray pool for Summer), and the entrance to the oldest subway in America is here as well. Dogs are welcome here, on the trails, and may be present during public events. Dogs must be well behaved, be on no more than an 8 foot leash, and be cleaned

up after. Dogs are not allowed in the community garden. There are off-leash hours in certain areas of the park in the early mornings and evenings.
Boston T   Boston MA   617-222-3200
http://www.mbta.com/
Both small and large dogs are allowed on the Boston T (subway) and the commuter trains run by the T from Boston. Small dogs may be transported in a carrier. Larger dogs may be taken on the T during off-peak hours and must be leashed and controlled at all times. At no time should a pet compromise safety, get in a passenger's way or occupy a seat.

Toby following the Red Line marking the Boston Freedom Trail

Freedom Trail   Tremont and Temple   Boston MA
This 2.5 mile historical tour marked by a red line on the sidewalk takes you by many famous sites including the Boston Common, Faneuil Hall and the Old North Church. Your dog may join you on the self-guided tour.
Nine Zero Hotel   90 Tremont Street   Boston MA   617-772-5800 (866-906-9090)
This boutique hotel located in downtown Boston has all the amenities for the business and leisure traveler and is located across the street from Boston Common, a pet-friendly 50 acre public park. Dogs of all sizes are welcome for no additional pet fee. They offer a pet bed, bowls, and a special treat for all their canine guests. Dogs may only be left alone in the room if assured they will be quiet, well behaved, and the "Dog in Room" sign is put on the door. Dogs must be leashed and cleaned up after at all times.

Boston Area

Normandy Farms   72 West Street   Foxboro MA   508-543-7600
http://normandyfarms.com
This large, full-service RV campground has it all, including an indoor and outdoor pool, restaurant with outdoor seating and a clubhouse. It's kind of like a hotel for your RV. There is also a new off-leash dog park. Well behaved dogs of all sizes are allowed. There are no additional pet fees. Dogs must be quiet, leashed, cleaned up after, and not left unattended at any time.
Dogtown Common   Dogtown Road at Cherry   Gloucester MA
Dogtown Common hosts the remains of an old abandoned town. It is named Dogtown because while the town was decaying only dogs remained. There are boulders with messages written on them throughout the park. Guides to the park are available at the Glouster Tourist Center at Stage Fort Park. Dogtown Common is 3000 acres with trails and historic sites. Dogs on and off-leash under voice control are allowed. To get to Dogtown Commons exit Rt 128 to Washington Street North. Turn right on Reynard, left on Cherry and right on Dogtown Road.

Hawthorne Hotel 18 Washington Square Salem MA   978-744-4080 (800-729-7829)
http://www.hawthornehotel.com/
Keeping in character with its New England charm, this historic hotel has tastefully appointed the rooms with 18th style reproduction furniture. The Salem hotel is within walking distance of several other pet-friendly attractions. Dogs of all sizes are welcome for an additional fee of $10 per night per pet plus a $100 refundable deposit. Dogs must be leashed, cleaned up after, and a contact number left at the desk if they are in the room alone.

Salem Willows Amusement Park 171-185 Fort Avenue Salem MA   978-745-0251
http://www.salemwillowspark.com/
A park since 1858, this scenic wooded and hilly peninsula is the place for great outings with shaded seaside grounds, a public pier, grand ocean views, numerous eateries, activity/gaming areas, an historic 1866 carousel, kiddie rides, a bandstand and seating area for outdoor concerts, and more. Dogs are welcome throughout the park and the water areas; they are not allowed in buildings. Dogs must be friendly, under owner's control at all times, and leashed and cleaned up after.

Sheraton Colonial Hotel & Golf Club Boston North One Audubon Rd. Wakefield MA   781-245-9300 (888-625-5144)
Dogs up to 80 pounds are allowed. There are no additional pet fees. Dogs are not allowed to be left alone in the room.

Cape Cod

Simmons Homestead Inn 288 Scudder Ave. Hyannis Port MA   800-637-1649
http://www.SimmonsHomesteadInn.com
The B & B is at an 1800 Sea Captain's estate in Hyannis Port in the center of Cape Cod. There are 14 rooms in two buildings. They offer a wine hour, beach stuff, billiards and a bunch more. A chance to see the collection of over 50 classic red sports cars behind the Inn at Toad Hall is probably worth the trip by itself.

Cape Cod Canal Cruise Town Pier Onset MA   508-295-3883
http://www.hy-linecruises.com/
This 2 or 3 hour boat cruise starts at the pier in the Victorian village of Onset. The cruise will take you through the Cape Cod Canal to the Sandwich Yacht Basin. You will be able to enjoy live commentary about the history and sights. Some points of interest include Taylor Point, Massachusetts Maritime Academy Training Ship, Vertical Lift Railroad Bridge, Sagamore Bridge and more. Well-behaved, leashed dogs are allowed.

Bay State Cruise Company MacMillan Pier Provincetown MA   617-748-1428
http://www.baystatecruises.com
These ferry rides are about 1 to 1 1/2 hours long and go between Provincetown and Boston. Dogs are allowed, but they must be leashed and cleaned up after, so bring doggy bags.

Cape Cod National Seashore 99 Marconi Station Site Road Wellfleet MA   508-349-3785
The Seashore is a forty-mile long stretch of pristine sandy beach. Dogs of all sizes are allowed. There are no additional pet fees, but they request that guests pick up a pet brochure at the visitor's center when they arrive. Dogs may not be left unattended, and they must be leashed and cleaned up after. Dogs are not allowed on the self guided nature trails, at the fresh water ponds, nor in the the picket fenced areas. Parking lots are open 6 A.M. to midnight, daily, year-round. The Salt Pond Visitor Center is open from 9 A.M. to 4:30 P.M. daily, year-round, with extended hours during the Summer months. The Province Lands Visitor Center is open from 9 A.M. to 5 P.M. daily, early-May through late-October.

Wellfleet Drive-in Movie Theater 51 H 6 Wellfleet MA   508-349-7176
http://www.wellfleetcinemas.com/
This drive-in theater will allow well behaved, quiet dogs to come to the movies too. Dogs must be leashed and cleaned up after at all times. Dogs are not allowed here during flea market hours unless they belong to one of the vendors.

Franklin County - Mohawk Trail

Historic Deerfield Village Old Main Street Deerfield MA   413-775-7214
http://www.historic-deerfield.org/
Dogs are welcome to stroll the streets of this authentic New England Village with their owners. They are just not allowed in any of the buildings. Dogs must be leashed and cleaned up after at all times.

Nantucket

Nantucket Airlines 660 Barnstable Road/North Ramp Hyannis MA   508-790-0300 (800-635-8787)
http://www.nantucketairlines.com
This airline offers daily flights between Hyannis and Nantucket (20 minute flight). Dogs are allowed in the cabin with you on this airline! Dogs under 35 pounds can be carried on your lap and no kennel is required. For dogs over 35 pounds, there is a "shelf" which is just a few inches off the floor, in the back of the plane where your dog

can sit or lay. While you cannot sit next to your dog, you can try to get the seat directly in front of him or her. There is no reserved seating, so you'll need to arrive early to try and make special arrangements to sit in front of your pooch. Large dogs must be properly restrained with a leash, harness or similar device. No kennel is required. You will need to reserve a space for your pet in advance as the airline usually only allows one dog per flight. Their sister airline, Cape Air also allows dogs in the cabin, but most flights require your dog to be in a kennel, and they have a size limit for dogs.

The Cottages at the Boat Basin (Woof Cottages) New Whale Street P.O. Box 1139 Nantucket MA 508-325-1499 (866-838-9253)
http://www.thecottagesnantucket.com
Dogs and cats are welcome in "The Woof Cottages." These cottages are one and two bedroom cottages which include special pet amenities like a welcome basket of pet treats and play toys, a pet bed, food and water bowls, and a Nantucket bandana. When you make a reservation, let them know what size your pet is, so they can have the appropriate size pet bed and bowls in the room. All cottages are non-smoking. There is a $25 one time per stay pet fee.

"Must See" Rhode Island Dog-Friendly Places

Block Island

Block Island Beaches Corn Neck Road Block Island RI 401-466-2982
Dogs are allowed year-round on the island beaches, but they must be leashed and people are required to clean up after their pets. To get to the beaches, take a right out of town and follow Corn Neck Road. To get to the island, you will need to take the Block Island Ferry which allows leashed dogs. The ferry from Port Judith, RI to Block Island operates daily. If you are taking the ferry from Newport, RI or New London, CT to the island, please note these ferries only operate during the Summer. If you are bringing a vehicle on the ferry, reservations are required. Call the Block Island Ferry at 401-783-4613 for auto reservations.

The Blue Dory Inn Dodge Street Block Island RI 401-466-2254 (800-992-7290)
http://www.blockislandinns.com/
This historic 1862 mansion sits at the head of Crescent Beach only a mile from the Atlantic Ocean on 5 rolling acres, and every afternoon guests can meet in the parlor for wine, hors d'oevres and their specialty-Blue Dory cookies. Dogs of all sizes are welcome for an additional $25 one time fee per pet. Dogs must be leashed and cleaned up after.

Newport

Fort Adams State Park Harrison Avenue Newport RI 401-847-2400
http://www.riparks.com/fortadams.htm
In addition to sitting prominently on Newport Harbor with spectacular panoramic views and year round recreation, this historic park is also host to various festivals and concerts. Dogs are allowed for no additional fee; they must have a valid license tag, and owners must carry proof of current rabies inoculation. Dogs must be quiet, well behaved, leashed (6 foot), and properly cleaned up after at all times. They may not be left unattended; with exception for hunting season or dog trials at which time dogs may be left alone in a vehicle. Dogs are not allowed at bathing beaches, or to be washed in any natural body of water.

"Must See" Connecticut Dog-Friendly Places

Berkshire Region

Interlaken Inn 74 Interlaken Road Lakeville CT 860-435-9878
http://www.interlakeninn.com/
This is a charming resort with lakes to swim in, trails to walk and a PUPS amenity package. It's located in the heart of the Berkshires. The hotel offers 30 open acres with a lake shore and is a great property to frolic on. There are off-leash play areas too. There are miles of pet-friendly walking and hiking trails nearby. There is a $15 per day pet fee.

New Haven

Sleeping Giant State Park 200 Mount Carmel Avenue Hamden CT 203-789-7498
Offering scenic vistas from a stone observation tower, nature trails, stream fishing (a designated trout stocked park), and some great hiking trails, this park is also known for the 2 miles of the mountaintop that resemble a large "sleeping giant". Dogs are permitted for no additional pet fees. Dogs are allowed at the picnic areas and on the hiking trails; they are not allowed in park buildings. Dogs must be under owner's control at all times, and be

leashed and cleaned up after.
Thimble Islands Cruise & Charters P.O. Box 3138 Stony Creek CT 203-488-8905
http://www.thimbleislandcruise.com/
Well behaved pooches are welcome aboard the ferry for transport to the islands for no additional fee; they are not allowed on tours. Dogs must be crated or leashed, cleaned up after, and under owner's control at all times.

New London - Mystic

Mystic Seaport - The Museum of America and the Sea

Mystic Seaport - The Museum of America and the Sea 75 Greenmanville Ave Mystic CT 860-572-0711
http://www.mysticseaport.org
Referred to as the Museum of America and the Sea, Mystic Seaport is considered to be one of the nation's leading maritime museums. There is plenty to see in an authentic 19th century village with about 40 buildings complete with storytellers, a waterfront of tall ships and other historic vessels, a preservation shipyard where visitors can watch restoration of antique vessels, several exhibits and galleries, and a lot more. Dogs are allowed throughout the port; they are not allowed in any of the buildings or on the ship. Dogs must be under owner's care, leashed, and cleaned up after at all times.
Olde Mistic Village 27 Coogan Blvd Mystic CT 860-536-4941
http://www.oldmysticvillage.com/
More than 40 unique shops are nestled in this shopping center that is reminiscent of a 1720's era New England village with lots of foliage, flowers, waterscapes, and trees creating wonderful little places to take repose. Your well behaved pooch is welcome to explore this area as long as they are on leash and picked up after. It is up to the individual stores as to whether pets are allowed inside. There is a pet boutique store located here.

"Must See" New York Dog-Friendly Places

Adirondacks

Crowne Plaza Resort & Golf Club 101 Olympic Drive Lake Placid NY 518-523-2556 (877-270-6405)
http://www.lakeplacidcp.com
The cross-country ski rental center at this resort is only open on the weekends. They have over 25km of groomed cross-country and snowshoeing trails. Dogs are allowed on the lower cross-country ski trails which are located south of Route 86. They just ask that dogs walk alongside but not directly on the groomed trails. It is a

short walk from the Golf Course Shop where you rent the skis to the trailhead. This trail system connects up to the 50km Jackrabbit Trail. Dogs need to be leashed at the resort and on the trails. Pets are welcome to stay with you at this resort for an extra pet fee.

St Regis Canoe Outfitters 73 Dorsey Street Saranac Lake NY 518-891-1838
http://www.canoeoutfitters.com/
This outfitters supply company offers canoe and kayak rentals and dogs may accompany their owners on rentals, with no additional fee if there is no additional cleaning is needed. If dogs need to be shuttled between sites the fee is the same as an adult ticket and starts at about $10. Dogs must be under owner's control/care at all times, be leashed, and cleaned up after.

Daggett Lake Campsites & Cabins 660 Glen Athol Rd Warrensburg NY 518-623-2198
http://www.daggettlake.com
Well behaved, leashed pets are welcome in the RV Park and the cabins. There is no additional charge for pets in the campground and a $50 cleaning fee for cabins. Proof of rabies shots are required in the campground and flea control in the cabins. This campground is home of the "DOG BEACH" where dogs can go off leash if they are under voice control. There are 400 acres with hiking and mountain biking trails, canoe, kayak, and rowboat rentals, and a sandy swim beach for people.

Whiteface Mountain Veterans Memorial Highway 5021 RT 86 Wilmington NY 518-523-1655
http://www.whiteface.com/
Grab your leash and hit the trails of Whiteface Mountains Veterans Memorial Highway. Beautiful views are just one of the things you will remember after your trip. Dogs are not allowed inside the buildings or the elevators but are welcome anywhere else on the mountain. The Veterans Highway is closed during the Winter.

Alexandria Bay

Uncle Sam Boat Tours 47 James Street Alexandria Bay NY 315-482-2611
http://www.usboattours.com/
A variety of cruises are featured by this company that cruise the 1000 Islands area daily through the end of October. Your well behaved pooch is welcome to join you on several of the cruises; they are not allowed on lunch or dinner cruises. Dogs must be under owner's control, leashed, and cleaned up after at all times.

Catskills

Ice Caves of the Shawangunks 400 Sams Point Road Cragsmoor NY 518-272-0195
Born of glacial activity, this park features an unusual landscape with miles of hiking trails and impressive geological features, but the ice caves (some rare) are the exciting draw here. A few of the caves may not be pet-friendly, so they suggest using some caution, bring an electric torch light, and dress warm. Dogs are allowed throughout the park and on the trails. Dogs must be under owner's care at all times, be leashed, and cleaned up after.

Woodstock Byrdcliffe Upper Byrdcliffe Road Woodstock NY 845-679-2079
http://www.woodstockguild.org/
Thirty buildings, 300 acres on the slope of a mountain, and listed on the National Register of Historic Places, this scenic art and craft colony offers plenty to see and places to hike, and it is also home to an Artist-in-Residence program hosting various exhibitions and performances for guests. Dogs are allowed to walk through the village and on the trails up the mountain; they are not allowed in buildings. Dogs must be well mannered, leashed, and cleaned up after at all times.

Cooperstown

Glen Highland Farm 217 Pegg Road Morris NY 607-263-5415
http://glenhighlandfarm.com/
This "Canine County Getaway" sits on 175 picturesque acres complete with ponds, a stream, trails, open meadows and forests, and dogs may explore anywhere on the farm off-leash. The farm is home to several dogs but it is also a Border Collier rescue sanctuary that functions as a training/recovery and placement center, and their complete obstacle course is also available to guests and their dogs. There are several mini-activity camps and programs available to help strengthen the bond between dogs and their companions such as the "Canine Discovery" camp to learn about how smart your dog really is and the "Inner Dog" camp for a greater understanding of your dog. There is even a trainer on staff available to work one on one with guests. The getaway lodging for guests and their canine companions include cottages, cabins, rentable RVs, a few RV spaces, and a camping shelter that has all the amenities on hand for meal prep plus private showers and flush toilets are only a few feet away. There are no additional pet fees. Dogs may not be left alone, they just have to be friendly and have a great time.

Elmira

Woodlawn Cemetery - Mark Twain's Burial Site 1200 Walnut Street Elmira NY 607-732-0151
There are several notables buried at this cemetery, but probably the most famous person buried here is Mark Twain. Your pooch is welcome to visit with you. Dogs must be leashed and cleaned up after at all times.

Finger Lakes

Caboose Motel 8620 State Route 415 Avoca NY 607-566-2216
http://www.caboosemotel.net
Small to large dogs are allowed in the 5 cabooses that serve as guestrooms at this unique hotel.
Letchworth State Park 1 Letchworth State Park Castile NY 585-493-3600 (800-456-2267)
This multi-faceted park provides opportunities for a wide range of year-round activities and recreation, and is considered the "Grand Canyon of the East" with 3 major waterfalls, 600 foot high cliffs along the river flanked by lush forests, 70 miles of incredible hiking trails, plenty of food options, and a museum/visitor center that provides the history of the area. Dogs must have proof of rabies inoculation and there are no additional pet fees. Dogs must be crated or leashed (6 foot) and cleaned up after. They are not allowed in buildings, cabins or cabin areas, or swim areas. Dogs are allowed throughout the rest of the park and on the trails.
Cornell Plantations 1 Plantations Road Ithaca NY 607-255-3020
Cornell Plantations is a museum of plants including the arboretum and botanical garden of Cornell University. See the crop garden portraying how technology and other cultures have influenced American gardens. Additionally, plants native to New York grow in the wildflower garden and a number of trails allow for hiking and nature study. The grounds are open free of charge from sunrise to sunset daily. Dogs are allowed on a short lead.
Tiohero Tours Boat Cruises 435 Old Taughannock Blvd Ithaca NY 866-846-4376
http://www.tioherotours.com/
This company offers daily, historically narrated tours on beautiful Cayuga Lake from two locations; the one above and also at Steamboat Landing. Guests are welcome to bring a dog aboard for no additional fee, and they prefer that only 1 hour tours be taken with pets. Guests with dogs are seated in front of the pilot house where they are not under the canopy. Dogs must be under owner's control, leashed or crated, and cleaned up after at all times.
Taughannock Falls State Park 2221 Taughannock Park Road Trumansburg NY 607-387-6739 (800-456-2267)
Taller than Niagara Falls by 33 feet, the namesake waterfall of this park plunges 215 feet over craggy cliffs towering nearly 400 feet above the gorge providing spectacular views from lookout points or along the multi-use trails, and there are planned activities like tours and concerts during the Summer season. Dogs must have proof of rabies inoculation and there are no additional pet fees. Dogs may not be left unattended in cabins, and they must be leashed (6 foot) and cleaned up after. They are not allowed in buildings or swim areas. Dogs are allowed throughout the rest of the park and on the trails.

Hudson Valley

Vanderbilt Mansion - FDR Homesite 4079 Albany Post Road Hyde Park NY 800-337-8474
http://www.nps.gov/vama/
Located in Hyde Park along with 2 other National Historic Sites; F. D. Roosevelt's home and Mrs. Roosevelt's country cottage, Val-Kill, the Vanderbilt Mansion and surrounding property is a significant historic reflection of American industrialization after the Civil War. Although dogs are not allowed in the mansion or any other estate buildings, they are allowed to explore the meticulously kept grounds (open daily from 7 am to sunset), hike along old carriage trails or to the Hudson River, or picnic at the Overlook. Dogs must be leashed and cleaned up after at all times.
Audrey's Farmhouse 2188 Brunswyck Road Wallkill NY 845-895-3440 (800-501-3872)
http://www.audreysfarmhouse.com/
Sweeping manicured lawns, stately trees, an outdoor pool, Jacuzzi, sundeck and a central location to an array of other activities make this 1740's dog-friendly country inn an attractive destination for both people and their dogs. Pets also like the many hiking trails in the area. Dogs of all sizes are allowed for no additional pet fee. Dogs must be well mannered, leashed, and cleaned up after.

Long Island - Nassau

Sagamore Hill Estate 20 Sagamore Hill Road Oyster Bay NY 516-922-4447
http://www.nps.gov/sahi
Home to Theodore Roosevelt, our 26th President, for 34 years, this beautiful estate welcomes guests to tour the mansion, explore the grounds, or hike down a nature trail to the harbor. Dogs are not allowed in the buildings, but they are allowed on the grounds and on the trails. Dogs must be on no more than a 6 foot leash and be

cleaned up after at all times.

Long Island - Suffolk

Bend In the Road Guest House 58 Spring Close H East Hampton NY 631-324-4592
http://www.bendintheroadguesthouse.com/
With a convenient location to the beaches, eateries, and shops, this inn (that also functions as a pottery studio) sits on 22 acres of farmland featuring a driving range for golfers, a private jogging path great for running your pooch, a large lawn area, and a secluded garden with a large swimming pool. Dogs of all sizes are welcome for no additional pet fee. Dogs may not be left alone in the room at any time, and they must be leashed and cleaned up after in common areas.

NYC Boroughs

New York Mets Dog Day at Shea Shea Stadium Flushing NY
http://newyork.mets.mlb.com
The New York Mets Baseball team holds an annual Dog Day Event at the baseball game. The event helps to support the North Shore Animal League which is the world's largest no-kill animal rescue. There is a dog parade on the field before the game and the dogs get to watch the game with you. Check with the Mets for the dates scheduled for these events.

New York

Author Len Kain and dog Toby in New York

Central Park Central Park W & Fifth Ave. New York NY
http://www.centralpark.org/
Central Park, located the heart of Manhattan, is the world's most famous park. This 843 acre park is so nice and refreshing that you'll find it hard to believe it is in the middle of the country's largest city. When we visited Central Park, it seemed very clean and safe, however there are two rules of thumb to follow. Only walk in the park during daylight hours and stay on the main paths. It is best to go on main paths where other people are walking. The park is 6 miles long and has an inner path which is a 4 mile loop. Also inside the park is a popular running track which is a 1.58 mile loop (between 86th and 96th Streets). When inside the park, be sure to stop by the Shakespeare Garden - leashed pooches are welcome on the paths. And don't miss Balto - a bronze sculpture of Balto, the sled dog. Balto is located between the Shakespeare Garden and Fifth Street (around 67th Street). If

13

66th Street were to go through the Park, the statue of Balto would be on 66th Street. Another popular area for dog fanatics is "Dog Hill". On a nice day, you will find dogs of all shapes, sizes and breeds socializing here. It is located near Central Park West and 79th Street (north of 79th Street.) Sections of Central Park now have off-leash hours. Be sure to follow the signs for the correct areas and hours for off-leash activity.

Horse & Carriage Rides 59th Street and Fifth Avenue New York NY
You and your pooch are welcome to hop on the horse and carriage rides for a tour of Central Park and NYC. The carriage driver will also supply a blanket for humans (and possibly your pooch!) if it is a little chilly outside. Carriages are available seven days a week after 10am, weather permitting. The carriages are located at the south end of Central Park, at 59th Street and Fifth Avenue (up to 6th Avenue).

Seastreak Ferry Rides various (see below) New York NY 800-BOAT-RIDE
http://www.seastreakusa.com
Want to enjoy the sights of New York City from the water, including the Manhattan Skyline and the Statue of Liberty? Or maybe you want to stay at a hotel in New Jersey and visit New York City during the day. Well, the nice folks at Seastreak allow dogs onboard their commuter ferries. Here are the rules: Dogs of all sizes must stay on the outside portion of the ferry and they need to be on a short leash. Dogs are not allowed on the inside area regardless of the weather unless you have a small dog and he or she is in a carrier. The ferries operate between Manhattan and New Jersey on a daily basis with up to 11 ferry rides during the weekday and about 4 ferry rides on the weekend. The ride lasts about 45 minutes each way and costs approximately $20 per round trip, half price for children and free for dogs! The ferries depart from Pier 11 (Wall Street) and East 34th Street in Manhattan and Atlantic Highlands and Highlands in New Jersey. Please visit their website for current ferry schedules, times and fares.

The Muse 130 West 46th Street New York NY 212-485-2400 (877-NYC-MUSE)
http://www.themusehotel.com
There are no additional pet fees at this pet-friendly Kimpton boutique hotel. They offer a pampered pooch package for an additional fee.

Time Warner Center 10 Columbus Circle New York NY 212-823-6000
http://www.shopsatcolumbuscircle.com
Time Warner Center is an upscale, indoor shopping mall located on Columbus Circle on the Southwest corner of Central Park. Dogs on leash, if very well behaved, are allowed in the mall. It is up to the stores if dogs are allowed inside the stores. We have seen many dogs here after walks in the park during our previous visits.

William Secord Gallery 52 East 76th Street New York NY 212-249-0075
http://www.dogpainting.com/
The William Secord Gallery, located in Manhattan's Upper East Side, specializes in nineteenth century dog paintings, bronzes and works on paper. The only gallery of its kind in North America, it was established by William Secord in 1990. Since then, it has become a popular destination for those interested in dog art and collectibles. In addition to creating the gallery, William Secord was the founding director of The Dog Museum of America and is the author of Dog Painting, 1840-1940, a Social history of the Dog in Art, as well as European Dog Painting, both books available at the gallery. And of course, your well-behaved dog is welcome inside! If you ask, they will serve your pooch cookies and water. If you want a portrait of your own pooch, this gallery can direct you to several painters like Christine Merrill and Barrie Barnett. Samples of their work are located at the gallery. Merrill has painted several pet portraits for celebrities like Oprah Winfrey and Bob Schieffer. Prices for consignment portraits start at $7,000 and up. The gallery is open Monday - Saturday 10a.m. to 5:00p.m. and by appointment. It is located on the third floor, so when you enter from the street, press the "William Secord" button. One of the staff members will then buzz the door open. Once inside, you can either take the small elevator or use the stairs. The toll free number is 1-877-249-DOGS.

Niagara Falls

Niagara Falls State Park Robert Moses Parkway Niagara Falls NY 716-278-1796
This park surrounds Niagara Falls and is the oldest state park in the United States. It offers beautiful views of the falls and you can expect to get wet with some of the mist from the water if you walk up to the railings at the falls. Dogs on a six foot or less leash are allowed on the hiking and walking trails, but are not allowed on the trolley, inside buildings or on the attractions like the boat rides. Pets must be cleaned up after. From the park you can walk along the water and view Niagara Falls and the gorge. There are miles of trails at the park and some have steep stairs and rocks to climb over. Remember to stay away from the river as it has very strong currents. If all the hiking makes you work up an appetite, the park service has several outdoor snack stands in the park. Stop at the visitor's center for trail details. The center is open daily from 8am to 10pm in the Summer and daily from 8am to 6pm in the Winter and closed Christmas and New Years Day. The park is open year round. To get there, take the Robert Moses Parkway into Niagara Falls.

Niagara Falls State Park

Rome

Erie Canal Village 5789 New London Road /H 46 & 49 Rome NY   315-337-3999
http://www.eriecanalvillage.net/
This reconstructed 19th century settlement is an outdoor living history museum on the site where the building of the canal began, and there are 3 museums; The Erie Canal Museum, The Harden Museum, and the Museum of Cheese in addition to several other typical structures of the era. Well behaved dogs are allowed to explore the grounds, but they are not allowed in the buildings. Dogs must be friendly toward other dogs and people, under owner's control, leashed, and cleaned up after at all times.

Saratoga

Yaddo Gardens H 9P/P. O. Box 395 Saratoga Springs NY   518-584-0746
http://www.yaddo.org
A gift of love, the gardens here are breathtaking as you wind by pools with fountains, statuary, a castle, wide sweeping lawns, tree lined paths bordered by lush greenery, and a rose and rock garden. Only the gardens are open to the public; the rest of the estate is private. Dogs are welcome for no fee. Dogs must be friendly, leashed, and cleaned up after at all times.

Syracuse

Skaneateles Historical Walking Tour The Creamery, 28 Hannum Street Skaneateles NY   315-685-1360
http://www.skaneateles.com/
This lakeside scenic town is home to several carefully restored buildings, some dating back to 1796, and a brochure of the walking tour can be obtained at the above listed address or at the Chamber of Commerce at 22 Jordon Street. Visitors are allowed to bring their dogs on this tour. Dogs must be under owner's control, leashed, and cleaned up after at all times.

"Must See" New Jersey Dog-Friendly Places

Atlantic City

Sheraton Atlantic City Convention Center Hotel Two Miss America Parkway Atlantic City NJ 609-344-3535 (888-625-5144)
Dogs up to 80 pounds are allowed at this resort hotel in Atlantic City. There are no additional pet fees. Dogs are not allowed to be left alone in the room.

Cape May

Cape May Whale Watcher 2nd Avenue & Wilson Drive Cape May NJ 609-884-5445
http://www.capemaywhalewatcher.com/
Dogs are welcome aboard the 110 foot Cape May Whale Watcher for the whale and dolphin tours for no additional fee. Dogs must be well behaved, and under owner's control/care at all times.
Historic Cold Spring Village 720 H 9S Cape May NJ 609-898-2300
http://www.hcsv.org/
This open-air living history museum depicting 18th century life offers a variety of entertainment, recreation, activities, and a trail that meanders through the 22 acres where visitors may take pleasure in the gardens or observe the heritage crops. Dogs are welcome to explore the park. Dogs must be on no more than a 4 foot leash, under owner's control, and cleaned up after at all times. Dogs are not allowed in any of the buildings.
Cape May-Lewes Ferry Sandman Blvd. & Lincoln Drive North Cape May NJ 609-889-7200
http://www.capemaylewesferry.com/
This ferry service provides transportation for vehicles and passengers between Cape May, New Jersey and Lewes, Delaware. The ferry cuts miles off of driving along the Atlantic coast. Pets are welcome but the following rules apply. For the M.V. Cape May, M.V. Delaware and M.V. Twin Cape ferries, pets are welcome on the ferry on exterior decks and any lounge areas where food is not being made, served or eaten. Pets are not allowed in the lounge area whenever there is a private party being hosted. For the M.V. Cape Henlopen and M.V. New Jersey ferries, pets are not allowed in any interior space but are allowed on all exterior decks. For all ferries, dogs of all sizes are allowed but need to be kept under control at all times and leashed or in a carrier. People need to clean up after their pets. Pets are not allowed in the shuttles. Rates start at $20 to $25 for a vehicle and driver. For a foot passenger with no car, rates start at $6 to $8 per person. Larger vehicles can be accommodated but there is an extra charge. The Cape May Terminal is located at Sandman Blvd. and Lincoln Drive in North Cape May, New Jersey. The Lewes Terminal is located at 43 Henlopen Drive in Lewes, Delaware. Rates are subject to change. For reservations or to check rates, call the ferry line toll free at 1-800-643-3779.

Hunterdon County

Liberty Village Premium Outlets One Church Street Flemington NJ 908-782-8550
Enjoy the neatly landscaped and red cobblestones streets of this shopping area that offer 60 stores to explore. Well mannered dogs are welcome. Dogs must be leashed and cleaned up after at all times. It is up to individual stores whether dogs are allowed inside.

New Brunswick

East Jersey Olde Towne Village 1050 River Road Piscataway NJ 732-745-3030
Dedicated to the historical education of the people who founded the area of Raritan Valley, this replicated 18th/19th century village offers a wide variety of activities, educational programs, and entertaining stories of their traditions, folk art, and craftsmanship. Well behaved dogs are welcome throughout the park and on the trails; they are not allowed in any of the buildings. Dogs must be under owner's control, leashed, and cleaned up after at all times.

Newark - NYC Area

Libery State Park Morris Pesin Drive Jersey City NJ 201-915-3440
http://www.libertystatepark.org/
Once the heart of an extensive transportation network for industry, this area served an even bigger role as the passage point for thousands and thousands of immigrants in the 19th and early 20th century, and now it provides over 300 developed acres for public recreation less than 2,000 feet from the Statue of Liberty. This is the closest view from land that your dog can get of the Statue of Liberty. Dogs are allowed throughout the park, on the trails, and at the picnic areas. Dogs must be leashed and cleaned up after at all times.

Newark - NYC Suburbs

Great Falls of the Passaic River McBride Avenue Paterson NJ 973-279-9587
This 89 acre National Historic Site Park boasts a long, rich cultural and industrial history, trails, and a 77+ foot waterfall. Well behaved dogs are welcome. Dogs must be under owner's control, leashed, and cleaned up after

at all times. Dogs are not allowed in buildings.
Long Pond Ironworks Historic District 1304 Sloatsburg Road, c/o Ringwood State Park Ringwood NJ   973-962-7031
Located within the Ringwood State Park, this 175 acre district is rich in historical and natural beauty and stands as an example of pre-independence ironworks plantations. Leashed dogs may also explore this area. Dogs must be under owner's control and cleaned up after at all times.

North Shore

Allaire Village 4265 Atlantic Avenue Farmingdale NJ   732-919-3500
http://www.allairevillage.org/
This living history museum offers more than just a step back in time with beautifully manicured lawns, lots of shaded areas and trails, various special events such as the Spring Planting Festival, flea and craft markets, master craftsmen demonstrations, and a bakery featuring daily, fresh "flat cakes". Dogs are welcome here for no additional fee. Dogs must be under owner's control, leashed, and cleaned up after at all times. Dogs are not allowed in any of the buildings.

Trenton

Trenton Battle Monument N Broad Street/H 206 Trenton NJ 609-737-0623
This monument stands as a testament to an important American victory which occurred here the day after Christmas 1776. Dogs are allowed throughout the park and on the trails. Dogs must be on no more than a 6 foot leash, cleaned up after, and under owner's control at all times. Dogs are not allowed in the buildings.

Vineland

Glasstown Arts District 22 N High Street Millville NJ   800-887-4957
http://www.glasstownartsdistrict.com/
You and your pooch can both enjoy exploring this unique artesian district with its rich architecture, unique shops, eateries, and a 700 foot river walk with a riverfront park. Dogs are welcome along the streets, trails, and at the park. It is up to the individual store whether they are allowed inside. A couple of the eateries have seasonal outdoor seating and allow pets at the outer tables. Dogs must be under owner's control, leashed, and cleaned up after at all times.

"Must See" Pennsylvania Dog-Friendly Places

Bedford Area

Old Bedford Village 220 Sawblade Road Bedford PA   800-238-4347
This living history village offers a rich variety of educational and entertainment activities, including a diverse assortment of military and civilian reenactments, exhibits, festivals, an antique car show, classes to learn the old west way of doing things, holiday themed specials, and a lot more. They are open daily from Memorial Day through Labor Day from 9 am to 5 pm (closed on Wednesday); from Labor Day through October 27 they are open Thursday through Sunday from 9 am to 5 pm, and then open a few days on the holidays. Dogs of all sizes are allowed throughout the village; they are not allowed in the buildings or in any food service areas. Dogs must be leashed and cleaned up after at all times.

Bloomsburg

Ashland Coal Mine and Steam Train 19th and Oak Streets Ashland PA   570-325-3850
http://www.pioneertunnel.com/home.shtml
There are 2 tours offered here; Pioneer Tunnel takes visitors deep into the mountain for a lesson in "hard coal" coal mining, and the Henry Clay is a gauge steam train (once used to haul coal cars), that now take visitors 3,000 feet along side the mountain. Your pooch is welcome on both tours if they are well behaved and comfortable with being in the mine cars or on the train. Dogs must be under owner's control at all times, and be leashed and cleaned up after. Tours last about 30 to 35 minutes.
Knoebel's Amusement Park Route 487 Elysburg PA   800-ITS-4FUN
http://www.knoebels.com
This amusement park is the largest free admission amusement park in the country. From roller coasters to kiddie rides this park has it all. Dogs on leash are allowed in the amusement park and in the camping area. Dogs are not allowed in any of the buildings, on the rides, or in the pool.

Delaware Water Gap

Bushkill Falls P.O. Box 151 Bushkill PA 888-628-7454
http://www.visitbushkillfalls.com
This park features a series of eight waterfalls and natural beauty. Dogs on leash are allowed in the park. Dogs are allowed on most of the trails throughout the park. Dogs are not allowed in the buildings and must be cleaned up after.

Dutch Country

Abe's Buggy Rides 2596 Old Philadelphia Pike Bird-in-hand PA 717-392-1794
http://www.800padutch.com/abes.html
Take a ride in an Amish Horse Drawn Buggy. Well-behaved dogs are allowed to accompany you on these buggy rides through Amish Country.

Erie

Presque Isle State Park Beach PA Route 832 Erie PA 814-833-7424
This state park offers beaches and almost 11 miles of hiking trails. Popular activities at the park include surfing, swimming, boating, hiking, in-line skating and bicycling. Dogs are allowed on a 6 foot or less leash at the park including on the hiking trails and only on beaches that are not guarded by lifeguard staff. Dogs can go into the water, still on leash, but people can only wade in up to their knees since there are no lifeguards in those areas. The unguarded beaches are located throughout the park, but if you want to know exact locations, please stop at the park office for details. The park is located four miles west of downtown Erie, off Route 832.

Gettysburg

Gettysburg National Military Park Gettysburg PA 717-334-1124
http://www.nps.gov/gett/
Probably the most famous American battlefield, Gettysburg marked the turning point in the Civil War. Later, President Lincoln gave his famous Gettysburg Address here. Dogs are allowed to visit the outside portions of the battlefield on leash. They are not allowed into buildings or the cemetery. The battlefield consists of auto touring, walking and you can get tapes or CDs to guide you on your tour.
Jenny Wade House Ghost Tours 528 Baltimore St Gettysburg PA 717-334-4100
Your dog may accompany you on the Candlelit Ghost Tour that leaves from the Jenny Wade House Gift Shop regularly during the Summer. The tour walks around and explores the ghostly history of Gettysburg and includes entry into the Jenny Wade House.

Jim Thorpe

Eckleys Miners Village 2 Eckley Main Street Weatherly PA 570-636-2070
http://www.eckleyminers.org/about.html
This historic village is a museum dedicated to the everyday lives of the "hard coal" miners and their families. Well behaved dogs are allowed on the grounds; they are not allowed in buildings. Dogs must be under owner's control, leashed or crated, and cleaned up after.

Lehigh Valley

Colonial Industrial Quarter 459 Old York Road Bethlehem PA 610-691-6055
http://www.historicbethlehem.org/
It's easy to feel like you have been transported back in time as one walks the historic streets of this colonial town and the surrounding points of interest. The welcome center is a good place to stop first for beginner's information. Dogs are allowed throughout the town; they are not allowed in any of the buildings. Dogs must be well behaved, leashed, and cleaned up after at all times.
Moyer Aviation 3800 Sullivan Trail Easton PA 610-258-0473
http://www.moyeraviation.com/
This aviation company offers a variety of services, including 10 to 40 minute tours with advance reservations (2 person minimum). A dog up to about 50 pounds is allowed for no additional fee. Dogs must be under owner's control/care, and leashed or crated at all times.

New Hope - Washington Crossing

Washington Crossing Historical Park 1112 River Road Washington Crossing PA 215-493-4076
This historic park commemorates where General Washington and his men crossed the Delaware in the dead of Winter to win a major victory towards America's independence. Dogs are allowed throughout the grounds; they must be leashed and cleaned up after at all times. Dogs must be under owner's control and well behaved, and they may not be left unattended anywhere-including vehicles. Dogs are not allowed in the visitor center or in any of the historic structures, including Bowman's Hill Tower.

Perkasie

Our Farm Under the Mimosa Tree 1487 Blue School Road Perkasie PA 215-249-9420
http://www.mimosatreebnb.com/
This scenic 20 acre, 200 year old farmhouse surrounded by mimosa trees, has numerous farm animals, peacocks, 2 ponds, a Japanese garden complete with a koi pond, hiking trails, and many places for picnicking and exploring. Dogs of all sizes are allowed for no additional pet fee. Puppies are not allowed, and dogs must be friendly toward humans and the farm animals. Dogs must be well behaved, leashed, cleaned up after, and they are not allowed on the furnishings.

Philadelphia

Horse and Carriage Rides at Independence Mall At the Liberty Bell Pavilion Philadelphia PA
The horse and carriage rides leave from next to Independence Hall on Independence Mall. The tours are from 20 minutes up and will take you around the Center City and the historical area of Philadelphia. Most drivers will allow well behaved dogs.
Independence National Historic Park Market St and 5th St Philadelphia PA
http://www.nps.gov/inde
Walk your dog through history. You can view all of the historic buildings from the Congress of 1776. You can see the Liberty Bell through the shaded glass windows if you stay outside with your dog. If you would like to see the Liberty Bell from the inside then someone would have to stay outside with the dog. Dogs are also allowed through the security gate to the area behind Independence Hall but are not allowed in any of the historic buildings.
Loews Philadelphia Hotel 1200 Market Street Philadelphia PA 215-627-1200
All well-behaved dogs of any size are welcome. This upscale hotel offers their "Loews Loves Pets" program which includes special pet treats, local dog walking routes, and a list of nearby pet-friendly places to visit. There are no pet fees.
Pat's King of Steaks 1237 E Passyunk Ave Philadelphia PA 215-468-1546
http://www.patskingofsteaks.com
While in Philadelphia you need to try one of the original Cheesesteaks. At Pat's you order food outside at a window and can eat on the tables here or take out.

Philadelphia Area

Valley Forge National Historical Park

Valley Forge National Historical Park 1400 North Outer Line Drive King of Prussia PA 610-783-1077
http://www.nps.gov/vafo/
Dedicated to the education and preservation of the Revolutionary War generation and of the common citizens who overcame great hardships and adversity in the name of freedom, this park offers a variety of ongoing informative programs and special events. Dogs are allowed throughout the park and on the trails; they are not allowed in any of the buildings. This is a large park so you will probably want to take an auto tour and walk to see the attractions from the nearest parking areas. Dogs must be well behaved, leashed, and cleaned up after at all times.

Pittsburgh

Hartwood County Park and Amphitheater 215 Saxonburg Blvd Pittsburgh PA 412-767-9200
This 629 acre park allows dogs on leash in most of the park and off-leash in an unfenced specified off-leash dog exercise area. Off special interest in the park is the outdoor amphitheater and its Summer Concert Series and other musical events. Your leashed dog is allowed to accompany you to listen to the concerts. There is an off-leash area in the park behind the amphitheater
The Duquesne Incline 1220 Grandview Avenue Pittsburgh PA 412-381-1665
http://incline.pghfree.net/
The Duquesne Incline is actually a working museum with 2 original 1877 cable cars that connects the upper and lower levels of the city, and not only does this tram save miles and gives outstanding views of the city, but your pooch can ride too. There is free parking at the bottom, but not at the top. Dogs must be well behaved, under owner's control, leashed, and cleaned up after at all times.

Pittsburgh Area

Air Heritage Museum 35 Piper Street Beaver Falls PA 724-843-2820
http://airheritage.org/
Dedicated to the education and preservation of America's history of flight, this museum will take guests through the challenges and victories leading to today's flight technology. Well behaved dogs are welcome to accompany their owners. Dogs must be leashed and cleaned up after at all times.

Titusville

Oil Creek and Titusville Railroad 409 S Perry Street Titusville PA 814-676-1733
http://www.octrr.org/
Various amenities and activities are offered at this 1892 freight station including picnic areas, water and comfort stations, a river, trails (one is a bypass to the Appalachian Trail), the only railroad post office in the US, and guided tours in open-air rail cars describing the people and places where the US oil history began. Visitors can also get on and off the train at different stops. Dogs are allowed throughout the grounds and on the touring train for no additional fee. Dogs must be under owner's control at all times, and be leashed and cleaned up after. Guests with pets will need to sign a pet responsibility form.

Uniontown

Ohiopyle State Park 171 Dinner Bell Road Ohiopyle PA 724-329-8591
Offering over 19,000 recreational acres, this park's several trails take visitors by waterfalls, unique geological formations, overlook platforms offering stunning views, and more than 14 miles of the Youghiogheny River Gorge running through the heart of the park. Dogs are allowed at the park for day use for no additional fee. Dogs must be quiet, well behaved, under owner's control, leashed or crated, and cleaned up after at all times. Dogs must be licensed and have proof of all vaccinations. Aggressive dogs are not allowed. Dogs may not be left unattended outside at any time and may only be left alone in a vehicle for very short times. Dogs must stay on selected pet routes/trails and areas; they may not be in designated swim areas or in park buildings, and pet food may not be left outside.

West Chester

Brandywine Battlefield Historic Site H 1 Chadds Ford PA 610-459-3342
This historic site depicts the largest encounter of the Revolutionary War (9-11-1777) with permanent and altering interpretive exhibits, special events, a visitor center with a museum and gift shop, and 3 different self-guided driving tours of significant sites. Dogs are allowed throughout the park and on the trails. Dogs must be under owner's control, leashed, and cleaned up after at all times.

"Must See" Delaware Dog-Friendly Places

Lewes

Lazy L at Willow Creek - A B&B Resort 16061 Willow Creek Road Lewes DE   302-644-7220
http://www.lazyl.net
Located on 8 secluded acres overlooking a marsh and creek, the Lazy L offers creature comforts for pets and pet owners. They offer 5 large rooms with Queen sized beds, a swimming pool, hot tub, pool table, guest kitchen and a barbecue. The dogs have a fenced in one acre run area, are allowed to sleep in the guest rooms and stay by themselves while you shop or go to dinner.

Rehoboth - Dewey Beach

Dewey Beach Coastal Highway/Route 1 Dewey Beach DE   302-227-1110
Dogs are allowed on the beach year-round only with a special license and with certain hour restrictions during the Summer season. A special license is required for your dog to go on the beach. You do not have to be a resident of Dewey Beach to get the license. You can obtain one from the Town of Dewey Beach during regular business hours at 105 Rodney Avenue in Dewey Beach. The cost is $5 per dog and is good for the lifetime of your dog. During the Summer, from May 15 to September 15, dogs are only allowed before 9:30am and after 5:30pm. During the off-season there are no hourly restrictions. Year-round, dogs can be off-leash but need to be under your control at all times and cleaned up after.

Greyhounds Reach the Beach The beach Dewey Beach DE   617-527-8843
http://www.adopt-a-greyhound.org/dewey/
For more than 120 years thousands of greyhounds and their owners have gathered to participate in this event held annually on Columbus Day weekend. There are a variety of activities, contests, educational and rescue programs, and plenty of doggy and human shopping available. The town's dog license requirement is covered under a special events license that covers all the dogs registered. Dogs must be leashed and cleaned up after at all times; please bring clean up supplies. Dogs are allowed on Dewey Beach after October 1st; however, Rehoboth Beach has implemented a 4-day permit for the event as they usually do not allow dogs on the beach until after October 31st. Dogs must be attended to at all times. Contact information for the organization is at 295 Tremont Street, Newton MA.

Wilmington

Trolley Square Shopping Center 21A Trolley Square Wilmington DE   302-428-1040
Trolley Square sits amid a lovely Victorian neighborhood and is considered a premium tax-free shopping area with dozens of shops, eateries, galleries, and numerous services. There are a couple of doggy boutiques, and some of the restaurants with outside seating will allow well mannered pooches. Dogs must be friendly, under owner's control, leashed, and cleaned up after at all times.

"Must See" Maryland Dog-Friendly Places

Aberdeen - Havre de Grace

The Skipjack Martha Lewis South end of Union Avenue/Tidings Park Havre de Grace MD   410-939-4078
http://www.skipjackmarthalewis.org/
This 2-sail bateau (skipjack) is one of the few working oyster dredge boats left in the bay, and in addition to being an onboard classroom, it is also a venue for special events or just cruising. Well mannered dogs are allowed on board for no additional fee. They must be under owner's firm control/care at all times, and must remain leashed. Since there is no cover on the sailboat to speak of, they suggest bringing a non-glass water dish for your pet and any protective covering deemed necessary.

Annapolis

Quiet Waters Park Dog Beach 600 Quiet Waters Park Road Annapolis MD   410-222-1777
http://friendsofquietwaterspark.org
This park is located on Chesapeake Bay. Dogs are welcome to run off-leash at this dog beach and dog park. The dog park is closed every Tuesday. Leashed dogs are also allowed at Quiet Waters Park. The park offers over 6 miles of scenic paved trails, and a large multi-level children's playground. People need to clean up after their pets. To get there, take Route 665 until it ends and merges with Forrest Drive. Take Forrest Drive for 2 miles and then turn right onto Hillsmere Drive. The park entrance is about 100 yards on the right. The dog beach

is located to the left of the South River overlook. Park in Lot N.
Watermark Cruises 1 Dock Street Annapolis MD 800-569-9622
Well behaved dogs are allowed on the 40 minute boat tours for no extra charge. The size and/or number of dogs allowed will depend on how full the tour is. It is a narrated tour and it covers the area's history from the 17th century to the present. The tours explore the residential areas of Old Annapolis, the headwaters of Spa Creek, along the banks of the US Navel Academy, and the Severn River where you can catch a glimpse of the Bay Bridge. Beer, non-alcoholic beverages, and snacks are available. Tour times may sometimes vary depending on weather, but they usually run every hour on the hour. Dogs must be leashed, and please bring clean up bags just in case.

Assateague Island

Assateague Island National Seashore 7206 National Seashore Lane Assateague Island MD 410-641-1441 (877-444-6777)
http://www.nps.gov/asis/
This undeveloped barrier island park allots visitors educational as well as numerous land, water, and seaside recreational opportunities. Dogs are allowed in the Maryland portion of the National Seashore for day and overnight use for no additional fee. Dogs are allowed on the many unguarded beaches on the Maryland portion of the National Seashore. They are not allowed in the Maryland State Park, on the Virginia part of the island- (even in a vehicle), or north of the State Park to the Ocean City inlet. They may not be on life-guarded beaches or on nature trails. Dogs may not be left unattended, and they must be on no more than a 6 foot leash and cleaned up after at all times. The camp area includes chemical toilets, cold-water showers, picnic tables, grills, and water. The camping and tent areas also allow dogs. There is a dog walk area at the campground. There are no electric or water hookups at the campgrounds.

Baltimore

The Admiral Fell Inn 888 South Broadway Baltimore MD 410-522-7377
http://www.harbormagic.com
The Admiral Fell Inn is a historic inn in the waterfront village of Fell's Point. All well-behaved dogs are welcome and there no additional pet fees.
The Original Fell's Point Ghost Walk Tour P. O. Box 38140 Baltimore MD 410-522-7400
http://www.fellspointghost.com/
This outdoor tour weaves the history and lore of a city rich with mystery. It was the birthplace of the dangerous Baltimore Clipper ships, was the privateer capital during the War of 1812, and a bohemian enclave during the 60's. They tell fun and spooky stories about this shipbuilding town, the founder of the city, about bars, rough pirates, ladies of the night, typhoid outbreaks, Edgar Allen Poe, and the War of 1812. The tours are one hour long and less then a mile. Tours depart from Max's Darthouse on Broadway, at 731 S. Broadway near the Fell's Point Square in Baltimore, Maryland. The tours run rain or shine (unless dangerous weather), and leave promptly at 7 pm. Since tours sometimes sell out, usually in the Fall-October especially, advance ticket purchases are recommended. Also, parking can be difficult on evenings and weekends, so they suggest the parking garage on Caroline Street as it is very close to the departure point. Well behaved, dogs on leash are allowed to join you on this walking tour, and please be prepared to clean up after your pet.

Ellicott City

Turf Valley Resort 2700 Turf Valley Road Ellicott City MD 410-465-1500 (888-833-8873)
http://www.turfvalleyresort.com
Turf Valley Resort has over 1000 acres of land with golf, spas, meeting rooms, a children's playground, a driving range and more. Pets are allowed for a $150 one time additional pet fee.

Grantsville

Spruce Forest Artisan Village 177 Casselman Road Grantsville MD 301-895-3332
http://spruceforest.org/
Dedicated to the education, preservation, and promotion to the uncommon beauty of the Appalachian culture and their craftspeople, this agency offers a living craft village where visitors can view artisan's studios and their craft up close or purchase handcrafted items. There are also several special events, activities, workshops, music jams, and their "Christmas in the Village" for visitors to enjoy. Your well mannered pooch is welcome in the village. Owners accept 100% responsibility for their pets, and dogs must be under owner's control/care, leashed, and cleaned up after at all times.

Washington Suburbs

Chesapeake and Ohio Canal National Historical Park 11710 MacArthur Blvd, Great Falls Tavern Visitor Center Potomac MD   301-767-3714
http://www.nps.gov/choh
Dedicated to preserving and educating the public about the canal era and America's transportation history, several visitor centers can be found along this 184 mile long canal trail. Dogs are allowed throughout the park and on the canal trail. Dogs must be under owner's control, leashed, and cleaned up after at all times.

"Must See" Washington D.C. Dog-Friendly Places

Washington

National Arboretum 3501 New York Ave NE Washington DC   202-245-2726
http://www.ars-grin.gov/na/
The National Arboretum allows dogs on leash. There are miles of walking trails here through the many beautiful gardens.
National Mall Independence Ave and 14th St. Washington DC
http://www.nps.gov/nama
Dogs are permitted on the National Mall on leash. According to the National Park Service, they are permitted up to the monuments except in indoor or covered areas. The mall is two miles long and is an excellent place for dog walking downtown. You may get up-close views of the Capital, White House and most of the Monuments. Dogs are not permitted on the walkways at the Vietnam or Korean War Memorials or inside the Washington Monument.

"Must See" Virginia Dog-Friendly Places

Charlottesville

Thomas Jefferson's Monticello Estate 931 Thomas Jefferson Parkway Charlottesville VA   434-984-9822
http://www.monticello.org/
This historically significant estate was designed and built by Thomas Jefferson, who also had a love of nature and planted flower, fruit, vegetable, and international gardens, and a wide variety of trees. Guided tours are offered of its vibrant history. Dogs are allowed on the grounds; they are not allowed in buildings. Dogs must be under owner's control, leashed, and cleaned up after at all times.
Montfair Resort Farm 2500 Bezaleel Drive Crozet VA   434-823-5202
http://www.montfairresortfarm.com
Dogs are welcome at these cottages and country retreat. They are located just 15 miles from Charlottesville. There is a $24.00 additional one time pet fee for your first pet plus $5 for any additional pets. Montfair's rustic lodge is available for a variety of pet-friendly events such as weddings, retreats or reunions.

Chincoteague Island

Barnacle Bill's Boat Tours 3691 Main Street Chincoteague Island VA   757-336-5920
This water touring company will allow dogs on board for no additional fee. They also have a bait and tackle shop at this location. There is a 2 person minimum per trip. Dogs must be well behaved, under owner's control/care at all times, and leashed.

Fredericksburg

Fredericksburg Battlefield Park 1013 Lafayette Blvd Fredericksburg VA   540-373-6122
http://www.nps.gov/frsp
The battle here was purportedly one of General Lee's easiest victories of all the battles of the Civil War that occurred in this region. It features exhibits, interpretive programs, and a five mile driving tour that connects this section to the other battlefront areas. Dogs are allowed at all the sites along the way. Dogs must be under owner's control, leashed, and cleaned up after at all times.

Lexington

Hull's Drive-In Rr 5 Lexington VA   540-463-2621

http://www.hullsdrivein.com
This pet friendly drive-in theater allows well behaved pets of all sizes to come to the movies for no additional fee. Dogs must be quiet, and leashed and cleaned up after at all times. The gates open at 7:00pm, and the movie starts at 9:00 - 9:15pm Monday through Saturday. The movie starts sooner on Sundays.

Lynchburg - Appomattox

Appomattox Court House NHP Hwy 24, PO Box 218 Appomattox VA   434-352-8987
http://www.nps.gov/apco/
Steeped in a rich cultural and revolutionary history, in April 1865 this was the site where agreements were made to end the Civil War and the 13th, 14th, and 15th amendments to the Constitution were enacted as a result. Dogs are allowed throughout the property and on the trails. They must be under owner's control, leashed, and cleaned up after at all times. Dogs may never be tied up and left unattended, and they are not allowed in any of the buildings.

Newport News - Hampton

Mariner's Museum 100 Museum Drive Newport News VA   757-596-2222
http://www.mariner.org/
Located on 550 wooded acres on the shores of Lake Maury, this is one of the world's largest international maritime history museums. Here visitors can also see a full-scale replica of the Civil War ironclad USS Monitor and they have an annual 5-week concert series each Summer. Dogs are allowed throughout the park and on the trails; they are not allowed in buildings. Dogs must be under owner's control, leashed, and cleaned up after at all times.

Northern Virginia

Doggie Happy Hour 480 King Street Alexandria VA   703-549-6080
http://www.doggiehappyhour.com
Dogs on leash are allowed at the outdoor tables in the courtyard. Open to dogs of all sizes between April-October 31st on Tuesdays and Thursdays. All they ask is to stay away from bar area and to keep paws off the tables and chairs. Water and gourmet biscuits are served to your pets.
Pat Troy's Irish Pub 111 N Pitt Street Alexandria VA   703-549-4535
http://www.pattroysirishpub.com
This restaurant serves traditional Irish and American cuisine as well as providing an active entertainment calendar of fun events. They also offer a dog friendly patio and a doggylicious menu. The menu for dogs include chopped chicken, chopped burger, beef stew, and lamb stew.
Potomac Riverboat Co. Canine Cruises Cameron and Union Streets Alexandria VA   703-548-9000
Every second Thursday in May through September, Potomac Riverboat hosts a Canine Cruise. This is a 40 minute Cruise in the Potomac River that invites you to bring your dog along. Dogs must be on a 6 foot leash. Canine Cruises leave from the Alexandria City Marina. The price for a tour is $11 per person and the dog rides free. The boats depart at 6:00, 7:00, 8:00 and 9:00pm. Only one dog per person is allowed.
Theodore Roosevelt Island Park and Memorial George Washington Parkway Arlington VA   703-289-2500
http://www.nps.gov/this/
Theodore Roosevelt Island park has nice dirt trails and an impressive memorial to Theodore Roosevelt. Your dog will probably like this memorial the most in Washington as it has many acres of trails and nature. Dogs may accompany you on leash in the park. Parking is on the George Washington Parkway on the north-bound side and you walk to the island over a bridge.
Mount Vernon George Washington Pkwy Mount Vernon VA   703-780-2000
http://www.mountvernon.org/
Your dog is welcome to explore the vast estate that George Washington called home. Your leashed, well behaved dog can accompany you to all outdoor areas of Mount Vernon. If you would like to take the mansion tour then someone will need to watch the dog. Otherwise, most of the site is outdoors.

Richmond

Stony Point Fashion Park 9200 Stony Point Parkway Richmond VA   804-560-SHOP
http://www.shopstonypoint.com/
This open air mall is home to such stores as Nordstroms, Sharper Image and The Banana Republic, and they have recently opened a Three Dog Bakery providing freshly baked treats and foods for dogs. You will find "pit stop" areas for your pet where there are waterbowls and clean up supplies throughout the mall. Many stores allow your pet inside; just look for the large dog sticker in the window. Dogs of all sizes are allowed, and dogs must be friendly, leashed at all times (or in a carrier), and please clean up after your pet. They are open from 10

am to 9 pm Monday through Saturday, and from noon to 6 pm on Sunday.

Shenandoah National Park

Shenandoah National Park 3655 U.S. Highway 211 East Luray VA   540-999-3500
http://www.nps.gov/shen/
Covering 300 mostly forested square miles of the Blue Ridge Mountains the park provides many diverse habitats for thousands of birds and wildlife. The park also provides a wide range of recreational opportunities. There are more than 500 miles of trails, including 101 miles of the Appalachian Trail, Summer and Fall festivals/reenactments, a rich cultural history to share, interpretive programs, and breathtaking natural beauty. There are several highlights along the 105 mile long, 35 MPH, Skyline Drive (the only public road through the park), such as 75 scenic overlooks and Mary's Rock Tunnel at milepost 32. The 610 foot-long tunnel was considered an engineering feet in 1932; just note that the clearance for the tunnel is 12'8". Dogs of all sizes are allowed for no additional fee. Dogs must be under owner's control, on no more than a 6 foot leash or securely crated, cleaned up after at all times, and are not to be left unattended. Dogs are not allowed in buildings or on about 14 miles of the trails; please ask the attendant at the gate for a list of the trails.

Williamsburg

Colonial Williamsburg

Colonial Williamsburg   Williamsburg VA
http://www.history.org
Colonial Williamsburg is a preservation of life in Virginia before the Declaration of Independence. The main park area is about three square miles and there are many historical buildings. Colonial Williamsburg allows dogs in all outdoor areas. If you want to go inside the buildings, then someone will need to stay outside with the dog. Tour materials are available such as tapes, CDs and guide books. There are also horse and carriage tours which may take your dog as it is up to the driver. You can easily spend a full day or even two here with your dog.

Winchester

Pirates of the Shenandoah Treasure Hunt 1360 S Pleasant Valley Road Winchester VA   877-871-1326
Your pup can go with you on this treasure hunting expedition. Dogs are not allowed in the cemetery, so they will need to skip this one spot. Visitors can pick up maps for this interactive family game at the visitor center, and then after the hunt and solving the puzzle, check on the county's web site or at the visitor center to see if the

mission was accomplished. Dogs must be leashed and cleaned up after at all times, and they are not allowed in any buildings.

"Must See" West Virginia Dog-Friendly Places

Berkeley Springs

Berkeley Springs Walking Tour 127 Fairfax Street Berkeley Springs WV   800-447-8797
Home to the country's first spa and believed to have curative powers, this resort town is rich in its history and architecture, and compact enough to make a nice stroll through the streets, as there has been little change to this historic town. Brochures for the walking tour are available at the visitor center or at several of the shops in town. Dogs on leash are allowed throughout the town; they are not allowed in most buildings, and they must be picked up after.

Bluefield

Pipestem Resort State Park H 20 N/ Pipestem WV   304-466-1800 (800-CALL WVA (225-5982))
http://www.pipestemresort.com/
Two golf courses, a Nature Center, an eatery, recreation center with a pool, an amphitheater, a 3600 foot aerial tramway, and 20 different hiking trails are just some of the amenities found at this popular park. Healthy dogs are allowed in camp areas for no charge and the cabins/cottages for a $50 refundable deposit, plus $40 for the first night and $5 for each additional night per pet. A credit card must be on file, and there is a pet agreement to sign at check in. Pets may not be left unattended outside, they must be securely crated when left alone in the cabins or cottages, they are not allowed to be tied/chained on the porch or yard, and their food may not be kept outside. Dogs must have certified proof of inoculations from a veterinarian, be on no more than a 10 foot leash, and picked up after. Dogs are allowed on the aerial tram. The campground offers 82 sites with a heated bathroom, a camp store, laundry, a playground, and other gaming areas. The camping and tent areas also allow dogs. There is a dog walk area at the campground. Dogs are allowed in the camping cabins.

Buckhannon

Audra State Park Rt. 4 Box 564 Buckhannon WV   304-457-1162 (800-CALL WVA)
http://www.audrastatepark.com/
The highlight of this wooded park along the Middle Fork River is the stunning view from the boardwalk that follows along the cave's overhanging ledge. Healthy dogs are allowed for no additional pet fee. Dogs must be restrained on no more than a 10 foot leash, be picked up after, and have certified proof of inoculations from a veterinarian.

Harpers Ferry

Ghost Tours of Harpers Ferry 173 Potomac Street Harpers Ferry WV   304-725-8019
http://www.harpersferryghost.20m.com
Dogs are allowed to go on the ghostly tours to assist you in your search for ghosts from Harpers Ferry's past. The tours are given on Saturdays in April and May and Fridays and Saturdays from Memorial Day to November 8th. Reservations are required for October and November. The tour starts at the Old Towne Cafe.
Harpers Ferry National Historical Park P.O. Box 65 Harpers Ferry WV   304-535-6029
http://www.nps.gov/hafe
According to the National Park Service (NPS), Harpers Ferry was made into a national historical site because of a number of different events. The NPS states "Harpers Ferry witnessed the first successful application of interchangeable manufacture, the arrival of the first successful American railroad, John Brown's attack on slavery, the largest surrender of Federal troops during the Civil War, and the education of former slaves in one of the earliest integrated schools in the United States." Dogs are allowed on leash at all outdoor areas of the park. However, dogs are not allowed on the shuttle buses from the visitors center to the historic area. There is limited parking at the historic area next to the train station for you to park with your dog. Otherwise, you will need someone to stay with your dog while someone parks the car and takes the shuttle bus back. Once at the historical town, you can walk around town, on trails and a pedestrian bridge over the river.

"Must See" North Carolina Dog-Friendly Places

Asheville

Asheville Historic Trolley Tour 151 Haywood Street/Asheville Visitor Center Asheville NC 888-667-3600
http://www.ashevilletrolleytours.com/
Hop aboard this state-of-the-art Touring Trolley for a funny and historically narrated cruise to see the best that Asheville has to offer. Tickets are available at several locations around town including the one listed above. Well mannered dogs are allowed on the trolley for no additional fee. Dogs must be under owner's control/care and short leashed at all times.

Biltmore Estate 1 Approach Road Asheville NC 800-624-1575
http://www.biltmore.com/
This opulent estate of George Vanderbilt is America's largest home covering 4 acres with 250 rooms on 8000 acres. The variety of sites and activities include an interpretive 1890's working farm, an award winning winery, extraordinary formal gardens, a one-of-a-kind shopping center, several eateries, and a variety of festivals and special events throughout the year. Dogs of all sizes are allowed throughout the grounds; they are not allowed in buildings. It is up to individual stores whether a dog is permitted inside. Dogs must be under owner's control, leashed, and cleaned up after at all times.

Blue Ridge Parkway

Blowing Rock H 321 S Blowing Rock NC 828-295-7111
http://www.theblowingrock.com/
Known as the state's oldest travel destination, this 4000 foot cliff overhanging the Johns River Gorge is rich in Native American folklore. There is an unusual atmospheric condition that occurs here that made Ripley's Believe-it-or-Not comment that it is "the only place in the world where snow falls upside down". Dogs are allowed and they must be leashed and under owner's control/care at all times.

Grandfather Mountain near Blue Ridge Parkway Linville NC 828-733-4337
http://www.grandfather.com
This rugged mountain is full of hiking trails and natural beauty. At the top there is a swinging bridge to walk out on as it is usually quite windy. The bridge is quite a spectacle. Dogs are allowed on leash throughout. There is calmer hiking lower on the mountain.

Blue Ridge Parkway Auto Tour Blue Ridge Parkway, Milepost 0 Waynesboro NC 828-271-4779
http://www.blueridgeparkway.org/
Taking more than 50 years to build and setting standards in engineering and design along the way, the Blue Ridge Parkway offers thousands of recreational acres and exceptional scenery to explore as it connects the Shenandoah National Park with the Great Smoky Mountains National Park. The maximum speed limit is 45 MPH on the parkway so this is not the fastest route to take. Its natural and cultural history reveals itself as visitors drive through the 469 miles of the country's first and longest rural parkway, or by hiking its many diverse trails. Visitors will also pass over the Linn Cove Viaduct, considered to be one of the most complicated concrete bridges ever built at Milepost 304.6. From May through October ranger programs are offered, and there are a number of campgrounds, trails, eateries, viewing areas, and historic/interpretive sites along the way. Dogs are allowed at all the camp areas and on all the trails. Dogs must be very well behaved, under owner's control, on no more than a 6 foot leash or securely crated, and cleaned up after at all times.

Cape Hatteras

Cape Hatteras National Seashore 1401 National Park Drive Manteo NC 252-473-2111
http://www.nps.gov/caha/
This National Park offers a captivating combination of natural and cultural resources. The park is rich in maritime history, is stretched over 70 miles of barrier islands and offers a variety of recreational pursuits. Dogs of all sizes are allowed at no additional fee. Dogs may not be left unattended, and they must be on no more than a 6 foot leash or crated, and cleaned up after. Dogs are not allowed in public swim areas, however, they are allowed on the trails. The camping and tent areas also allow dogs. There is a dog walk area at the campground. There are no electric or water hookups at the campground.

Charlotte

Dog Bar NoDa 3307 N Davidson Street Charlotte NC 704-370-3595
http://www.dogbarnoda.com/
Dogs of all shapes and sizes are welcome at this unique, beer, wine, and liquor bar. In addition to being able to hang out at the bar with your pet, they offer special events for dog lovers, free doggy biscuits, and in the warmer months they rent out the Dog Bar for social events, and dog birthday or adoption parties. In the Summer they are closed Mon. and Tue., and open Wed. and Thurs. from 4pm - 11pm, Fri. 4pm - 2am, Sat. 3pm - 2am, and Sun 3pm - 10pm. In the Winter the bar is open on Wed. and Thurs. 7 - 11 pm, Fri and Sat 7 - 2 am, and Sunday from 1 - 10. Dogs must be well behaved, friendly, and have a current rabies certificate (either tags or show papers to staff). Dogs may be leashed or off-leash. They must be cleaned up after; they provide a scooper on the side of the building. While on the Dog Bar premises, owners are solely responsible for their pet.

Cherokee - Smoky Mountain NP

Oconaluftee Cherokee Indian Village 498 Tsali Blvd. Cherokee NC 828-497-2315
http://www.cherokee-nc.com/index.php?page=17
This original 1750's Indian village and grounds are dedicated to living and passing on of the Cherokee's ancestral ways. This region is home to the world's oldest mountains, rich with lush greenery, colorful each Spring with explosion of wildflowers, and numerous waterways, Dogs are allowed on the grounds; they are not allowed in buildings, and they must be under owner's control/care at all times.

Greensboro

Replacements, Ltd. 1089 Knox Road Mcleansville NC 800-REPLACE (737-5223)
http://www.replacements.com/
Well behaved, leashed dogs are welcome to explore this amazing store of almost a half a million square feet that is home to the world's largest selection of replacement and new dinnerware. Dogs must be under owner's control and care at all times.

Hendersonville

Historic Johnson Farm 3346 Hayward Road Hendersonville NC 828-891-6585
Listed on the National Register of Historic Places, this late 19th/early 20th century farm offers mountain farming "hands-on" experiences, a number of historic buildings, and nature trails. Dogs are allowed on the trails and at the farm; they are not allowed in buildings. Dogs must be leashed and cleaned up after.

Sanford

Fearrington Village 2000 Fearrington Village Center Pittsboro NC 919-542-2121
http://www.fearrington.com/village/
In addition of offering a number of unique and eclectic varieties of shops, dining choices, and special events, this shopping center resides in farm country and comes complete with farm animals, folk art, and beautiful gardens that are open daily. Leashed, well behaved dogs are welcome.

Winston - Salem

Old Salem 601 Old Salem Road Salem NC 336-721-7350
http://www.oldsalem.org/
Old Salem is a living history town with restored buildings and costumed interpreters. Dogs are not allowed in the buildings but you can still get a good flavor of the place and most of the buildings are small so you can take a quick look inside if someone can watch the dog.

"Must See" South Carolina Dog-Friendly Places

Charleston

Tour Charleston Ghost Tours 45 Broad Street Suite 200 Charleston SC 843-577-3800 (800-729-3420)
http://www.tourcharleston.com
This ghost tour company not only welcomes dogs on their ghost tours, they have dogs of their own who may be joining the tour from time to time. Other tours may be available as well.
Isle of Palms County Park Beach 14th Avenue Isle of Palms SC 843-886-3863
Dogs on leash are allowed year-round at this beach. People are required to clean up after their pets. The beach is located on the Isle of Palms, on 14th Ave., between Palm Blvd. and Ocean Blvd. Then coming to Isle of Palms from 517, continue straight at the Palm Blvd intersection and then take the next left at the park gate.

Clemson

South Carolina Botanical Garden Perimeter Road Clemson SC 864-656-3405
http://www.clemson.edu/scbg/
This 295 acre site offers a number of attractions and activities; there is a beautiful waterfall flowing into a serene pond of bright Koi fish, 70 acres of demonstration and display gardens, more than 90 acres of woods and waterways with some great hiking trails. Plus they offer a 40 acre arboretum, diverse habitats and their inhabitants, and native plants for sale. Dogs are allowed throughout the park; they are not allowed in buildings.

Dogs must be leashed and under owner's control/care at all times.

Darlington

Kalmia Gardens 1624 W Carolina Avenue/H 151 Hartsville SC 843-383-8145
http://www.coker.edu/Kalmia/index.html
An historic 1820s home and a 35 acre private botanical garden have put his amazingly beautiful location on the National Register of Historic Places. There are trails and boardwalks here that lead visitors to the Black Creek flood plain below with all its unique habitats and inhabitants. Dogs are allowed throughout the park and on the boardwalks; they are not allowed to go swimming in the pond. Dogs must be leashed and under owner's control/care at all times.

Georgetown

Swamp Fox Tours 600 Front Street Georgetown SC 843-527-1112
http://www.swampfoxtours.com
These trollies and tram will take you on a guided tour of Georgetown's historic heritage. Tours depart from 1001 Front Street in front of the Georgetown Chamber of Commerce building. Tours are offered on the hour daily and are about one hour long. The Tram departs on the hour Monday through Friday, 10 AM to 4 PM. Dogs must be well behaved and leashed.

Hilton Head Island

Daufuskie Island Resort & Breathe Spa 421 Squire Pope Road Hilton Head Island SC 800-648-6778
http://www.daufuskieislandresort.com
Daufuskie Island is a family friendly island golf and spa resort located a short ferry boat cruise from Hilton Head Island. They have a "Deluxe Doggie package" for your best friends for $35 per night per dog. They provide a Canine goodie bag at check - in, which includes doggie treats, chew toy, doggie pick-up bags, a Daufuskie Island Resort & Breathe Spa dog tag with phone number and a "Dog Guest in residence" door hanger. Awaiting your friend in the room is a doggie bed, extra towels, food and water bowl with bottled water. The resort has two 18 hole championship golf courses.

Moncks Corner

Old Santee Canal Park 900 Stony Landing Road Moncks Corner SC 843-899-5200
http://www.oldsanteecanalpark.org
In addition to the natural beauty of this 195 acre park, it shares a long cultural, military and natural history, an 1843 plantation home, many scenic trails and waterways, 4 miles of boardwalks, trails, several monthly events, and a museum/heritage center featuring over 12,000 years of the area's past. Dogs are allowed throughout the park and on the boardwalks; they must be leashed and under owner's control and care at all times. Dogs are not allowed in buildings.

Myrtle Beach

Barefoot Landing 4898 H 17S North Myrtle Beach SC 843-272-8349
http://www.bflanding.com/index.html
In addition to over 100 retail and specialty shops, this waterside shopping and entertainment district offers dozens of attractions and activities, plus there is a pet boutique and a pet bakery on site. A crowd favorite is the authentic remake of a Barnum and Bailey carousel with 41 animals cast from the original molds. Dogs are allowed throughout boardwalk and dock; it is up to individual stores whether a pet may enter. Dogs must be under owner's control, leashed, and cleaned up after at all times.

"Must See" Georgia Dog-Friendly Places

Atlanta

Hotel Indigo 683 Peachtree St NE Atlanta GA 404-874-9200 (800-HOLIDAY)
Dogs of all sizes are allowed for no additional fee. This is an especially pet-friendly and high end hotel. The hotel has a weekly Canine Cocktail hour on Tuesdays from 5 to 8 pm. The hotel also provides a doggy menu as well. Please check with the hotel for the day and time and seasonal schedules.

Atlanta Area

Kennesaw Mountain National Battlefield Park 900 Kennesaw Mountain Drive Kennesaw GA 770-427-4686
http://www.nps.gov/kemo
This 2,888 acre National Battlefield preserves an 1864 Civil War battleground. Kennisaw Mountain stood between a large Union force and and a Confederate railroad and manufacturing center. There are many trails, monuments and living history demonstrations and exhibits. This is a very dog-friendly park. Dogs are welcome on the park grounds on a six foot leash. Please clean up after your dog with the "mutt mits" that are provided at the park.

Dawsonville

Amicalola Falls State Park and Lodge 418 Amicalola Falls State Park Road Dawsonville GA 706-265-4703 (800-864-7275)
True to its Cherokee word meaning "tumbling waters", the 729 foot falls at this park are the highest cascading falls east of the Mississippi, and there are numerous trails for exploring this beautiful mountain recreational destination. The park is also host to many special events throughout the year. Dogs are allowed throughout the park and in the campground (2+ dogs) for no additional fee. There is a $40 one time fee per pet for the cabin, and only 2 dogs are allowed. They are not allowed in the Lodge or in any park buildings. Dogs must be leashed and under owner's control/care at all times. The camp area offers 24 sites, 14 cottages (2-pet friendly), picnic areas, restrooms, concessionaires, and a dump station. The camping and tent areas also allow dogs. There is a dog walk area at the campground. Dogs are allowed in the camping cabins.

Fargo

Stephen C. Foster State Park 17515 H 177 Fargo GA 912-637-5274 (800-864-7275)
Some of the most interesting and breathtaking scenery can be found at this park with its moss-laced cypress trees canopying the black waters below, and in addition to a range of recreational activities and the 1.5 mile Trembling Earth Nature Trail, there are environmental and educational programs provided. Dogs are allowed throughout the park and in the campground (2+ dogs) for no additional fee. There is a $40 one time fee per pet for the cabin, and only 2 dogs are allowed. Dogs are not allowed in buildings or on the boats. Dogs should not be close to the edge of waterways because of alligators. The campground offers 66 sites, restrooms, an amphitheater, a dump station, and some food, drinks, and ice can be obtained at the park office. The camping and tent areas also allow dogs. There is a dog walk area at the campground. Dogs are allowed in the camping cabins.

Jekyll Island

Amazing Spaces Tour History Center Jekyll Island GA 912-635-4036
If you want to learn more about Jekyll Island including its history and highlights, you and your pooch can ride the Amazing Spaces Tour. The tram will take you on a forty-five minute narrated tour through the Historic District for a venture into the past. Your pooch can sit on the bench next to you. Because of physical space limitations on the tram, they can only take a dog up to about the size of a lab or golden retriever. Well-behaved leashed dogs are allowed. The tour is offered year round.
Jekyll Island Beaches and Trails off SR 520 Jekyll Island GA 877-453-5955
These beaches look like a Caribbean island setting. It is hard to believe that you just drove here over a causeway. Dogs on leash are welcome year round on the beach and the paved and dirt trails. There are about 10 miles of beaches and 20 miles of inland paved and dirt trails. It is recommended that your pooch stay on the paved trails instead of the dirt trails during the warm Summer months because there are too many ticks along the dirt trails. On warmer days you might choose a beach walk rather than the inland trails anyway because of the cooler ocean breezes.

Savannah

Ghost Talk On Abercorn between Congress and Bryan Savannah GA 912-233-3896
http://www.savannahgeorgia.com/ghosttalk
This is a narrated tour of the ghostly stories and legends of Savannah. The meeting place is at the 20 foot statue of John Wesley in Reynolds's Square. Tours depart at dusk, and times vary through the year. Please call for reservations and departure times. A quiet, well behaved dog on leash is allowed.

Warner-Robins

Museum of Aviation 247 Russell Parkway Warner-Robins GA   478-923-6600
http://www.museumofaviation.org/home.htm
Sitting on 51 scenic acres, this is the second largest museum of Aviation in the US Air Force with hundreds of exhibits and aircraft, plus they are also home to Freedom Park-a beautiful park/play area dedicated to those who have given the ultimate cost for America's freedom. Although dogs are not allowed inside the buildings, there is a large display of aircraft throughout the grounds. Dogs are allowed on leash; they must be well mannered and picked up after.

"Must See" Florida Dog-Friendly Places

Cape San Blas

Cape San Blas Barrier Dunes   Cape San Blas FL
This is one of the nicer pet-friendly beaches in Florida. Leashed dogs are allowed year round on the beach which has a number of stations with clean up bags. Please clean up after your dog.
Port St Joe Marina 340 Marina Drive Port St Joe FL   850-227-9393
http://www.psjmarina.com/
There are some nice walking areas around this marina for you and your pet. There are pontoon boat rentals that dogs are allowed on, or they may join you on the patio at the restaurant, or even in the Ship Store. Dogs must be well behaved, and leashed and cleaned up after at all times.

Fort Myers

Manatee World Boat Tours 5605 Palm Beach Blvd Fort Myers FL   239-693-1434
http://www.manateeworld.com/
These excursions take you on a narrated ecological cruise into a natural wildlife habitat featuring many of Florida's most beautiful birds, plants, and animals in their native surroundings, with focus on the endangered manatees. Up to 2 well behaved, friendly, dogs are allowed for no additional fee. Dogs must be leashed. The tours usually run through the Winter months, and not through the Summer when the manatees are not visible.
Dog Beach Estero Blvd/H 865 Fort Myers Beach FL   239-461-7400
Located just north of the New Pass Bridge, this barrier island beach offers a perfect off-leash area for beach-lov'in pups. This beach is actually in Bonita Beach on the city line with Fort Myers Beach. Dogs are allowed in designated areas only, and they must be licensed, immunized, and non-aggressive to people, other pets, or wildlife. Dogs may not be left unattended at any time, and they must be under owner's control/care at all times; clean-up stations are provided. Two healthy dogs are allowed per person over 15 years old. Dogs on Fort Myers Beach must be leashed at all times.

Jacksonville

Fort Caroline National Memorial 12713 Ft. Caroline Road Jacksonville FL   904-641-7155
http://www.nps.gov/foca/
Fort Caroline National Memorial is located within the Timucuan Ecological and Historic Preserve. The memorial commemorates the short-lived French presence in sixteenth century Florida. French settlers established a colony which comprised of a village and a small earthen and timber fortification. There are no remains of the original fort, but there is a near full-scale interpretive rendering of the fort which provides information on the history of the French colony. Leashed dogs are allowed in the fort area and on the one mile self-guided loop trail (Hammock Trail) which has interpretive placards along the way that focus on the natural and cultural history of the site. Fort Caroline is located in Jacksonville, Florida about 14 miles northeast of downtown.

Key West

Key West Aquarium 1 Whitehead St Key West FL   305-296-2051
http://www.keywestaquarium.com/
This aquarium is the only one we know of that allows you to take your pup along on leash. It has a large unfenced shark tank so please keep your pup under good control. You and your dog will see all sorts of marine life.
Mallory Square 1 Whitehead St Key West FL   305-296-4557
http://www.mallorysquare.com
You and your leashed dog can join other Key West party goers for the Key West Sunset Celebration at Mallory Square. There are numerous street performers, food, drinks, arts and crafts exhibitors, psychics and a lot more. The celebration begins about two hours before sunset nightly. Mallory square is also open for walks or congregating for the rest of the day and evening.

Miami

Catalina Hotel and Beach Club 1732-1756 Collins Avenue Miami FL 305-674-1160
Summer brings about a weekly "Must Love Dogs" brunch every Sunday from 10:30 AM to 2:30 PM where pampered pups may dine alfresco with their human companions. Dogs get personal water bowls and a selection of gourmet treats to make any discerning pup happy. Dogs are not allowed in the hotel. Dogs must be well mannered and under owner's control/care at all times.

Orlando

Portofino Bay Hotel 5601 Universal Blvd Orlando FL 407-503-1000 (800-BEASTAR (232-7827))
Built to resemble an Italian Riviera seaside village, this beautiful bay hotel features 3 themed swimming pools, special privileges to the area's best golf courses, and express access and transportation to the Universal Orlando Theme Park. Dogs of all sizes are welcome for an additional one time pet fee of $25 per room. Guests must have a health certificate for each pet obtained within 10 days prior to arrival. Dogs must be quiet, well behaved, leashed and cleaned up after, and removed for housekeeping. Dogs must be walked in designated areas only, and they are not allowed in the pool/lounge or restaurant areas. Dogs are not allowed in Club rooms.
Sam Sneads Downtown Restaurant 301 East Pine Street Orlando FL 407-999-0109
http://www.samsneadsdowntown.com/
This is the restaurant that became the epicenter of the doggie dining legislation and bill in 2006. It is here that a Florida state health inspector threatened fines for dogs on the patio while dogs were happily dining on patios throughout the state. The restaurant's complaint to the city resulted in governor Jeb Bush signing the doggy dining bill at this restaurant. Now your dog can join you here with his own Furry Friends menu including meals like the Buddy Boy's Burger, Chicken and Kibble, Bow Wow Pizza and other items. The items are served on a complimentary frisbee. We recommend that people who travel with dogs to Orlando as well as locals visit Sam Sneads and show your support as well as enjoy a dog-friendly atmosphere.
Fleet Peeples Park Dog Park South Lakemont Avenue Winter Park FL 407-740-8897
http://www.ffpp.org/
This park is a fenced dog park with a pond for swimming. Dogs are allowed off-leash within the park. There is shade, water, and bags for cleanup. The park is open to Winter Park residents as well as the public at large. The dog park is located in Fleet Peeples Park on South Lakemont Avenue.

Pensacola

Milton Canoe Adventures 8974 Tomahawk Landing Road Milton FL 850-623-6197
http://www.adventuresunlimited.com/
Whether you take two hours or many days, you can experience canoeing here with your dog. The spring fed rivers flow at an average depth of two feet over a soft, sandy bottom. Your pet and you can enjoy a canoe trip together for an additional $10 for the dog. Dogs must be kept leashed at all times, and cleaned up after. They are open year round.

Sarasota

De Soto National Memorial P. O. Box 15390 Bradenton FL 941-792-0458
http://www.nps.gov/deso/
This memorial commemorates the Spanish explorer Hernando de Soto, who landed on the southwest Florida coast in 1539. He brought with him 600 soldiers and was under orders from the King of Spain to explore, colonize and pacify the Indians of the area known as "La Florida". The park depicts 16th century Spanish cultural values and the clash with the native cultures that the expedition encountered. From late December to early April, there is a reproduction of the 16th Century Indian village with park rangers dressed in period costume. They give demonstrations of blacksmithing, cooking, armor repair and military weapons. Dogs are not allowed in the buildings, but they are allowed on the one half mile self-guiding interpretive trail which leads through mangrove and coastal environments. Dogs need to be on a 6 foot leash.

South Florida

Canine Beach East End of Sunrise Blvd Fort Lauderdale FL 954-761-5346
There is a 100 yard stretch of beach which dogs can use. Dogs must be on leash when they are not in the water. The beach is open to dogs only on Friday, Saturday and Sundays. In Winter, the hours are 3 pm - 7 pm and the Summer hours are 5 pm - 9 pm. A permit is required to use the Canine Beach. There are annual permits available for $25 for residents of the city or $40 for non-residents or you can get a one weekend permit for $5.65. Permits can be purchased at Parks and Recreation Department, 1350 W. Broward Boulevard. Call (954) 761-

5346 for permit information.
Jupiter Beach A1A at Xanadu Road Jupiter FL
This is a wide, nice, white sandy beach that stretches 2 miles along the Atlantic Coast. It is one of the nicer beaches that allow leashed dogs in South Florida. Please follow the dog rules requiring leashes and cleaning up after your dog.

St Augustine

Fountain of Youth 11 Magnolia Ave. St Augustine FL   904-829-3168
http://www.fountainofyouthflorida.com/
Tradition has it that The Fountain of Youth is the exact spot where the Spanish Explorer Ponce de Leon landed on April 2, 1513. He met the Timucuan Indians who at the time had an unusually long life span that averaged about 90 years. The Spanish at the time had a much shorter life span average. The water that the Indians drank became known as the "fountain of youth". Of course, the Indians longer life span could have had something to do with their healthy seafood diet and their active lifestyle. Today this park offers exhibits of early Timucuan Indians and Sixteenth Century Spaniards. At the park you can stroll along the gardens, explore excavations, view exhibits, presentations and a planetarium. In the Spring House, both people and pets can take a sip of the famous "Fountain of Youth" water. A guide will hand out samples of the water in little paper cups. The water has a very strong mineral taste. Well-behaved leashed pets are welcome both outside and inside the buildings.
St Augustine Scenic Cruise St Augustine Municipal Marina St Augustine FL   904-824-1806 (800-542-8316)
http://www.scenic-cruise.com/
The Victory III departs daily from the Marina in downtown St Augustine for a one hour and fifteen minute scenic cruise. View the historic St Augustine area from the water and bring your well-behaved, leashed dog with you.

Tampa Bay

Heritage Village 11909 125th Street N Largo FL   727-582-2123
http://www.pinellascounty.org/heritage/
Dogs are allowed at this open-air historical village and museum at no additional fee. There is an art and historical museum, botanical gardens, a gift shop and much more. Dogs must be leashed and cleaned up after, and they are not allowed in the buildings. The village is open Tuesday through Saturday from 10 am to 4 pm, and on Sunday from 1 to 4 pm. They are closed on Monday and major holidays.

Chapter 2

Maine
Dog Travel Guide

Abbot

Campgrounds and RV Parks
Balsam Woods 112 Pond Road Abbot ME   207-876-2731
http://www.balsamwoods.com
Dogs of all sizes are allowed. There are no additional pet fees. Dogs must be leashed and cleaned up after. This
RV park is closed during the off-season. The camping and tent areas also allow dogs. There is a dog walk area
at the campground. Dogs are allowed in the camping cabins.

Augusta

Accommodations
Augusta Hotel and Suites 390 Western Avenue Augusta ME   207-622-6371
There are no pet fees unless you stay more than one week. Then there is a $20 one time pet fee.
Best Western Senator Inn and Spa 284 Western Ave @Turnpike 95 Augusta ME   207-622-5804 (800-780-
7234)
Dogs are allowed for an additional fee of $9 per night per pet.
Comfort Inn Civic Center 281 Civic Center Drive Augusta ME   207-623-1000 (877-424-6423)
Dogs are allowed for no additional pet fee, but a credit card must be on file.
Holiday Inn 110 Community Drive Augusta ME   207-622-4751 (877-270-6405)
Dogs of all sizes are allowed for no additional fee, and they may not be left alone in the room.
Motel 6 - AUGUSTA 18 Edison Drive Augusta ME   207-622-0000 (800-466-8356)
One well-behaved family pet per room. Guest must notify front desk upon arrival. Guest is liable for any
damages. In consideration of all guests, pets must never be left unattended in the guest rooms.

Campgrounds and RV Parks
Augusta West Lakeside Resort 183 Holmes Brook Lane Winthrop ME   207-377-9993
Dogs of all sizes are allowed. There is a $4 per pet per stay additional fee. Dogs may not be left unattended,
must be leashed, and cleaned up after. Dogs are also not allowed at the beach or the pool. This RV park is
closed during the off-season. The camping and tent areas also allow dogs. There is a dog walk area at the
campground.

Stores
Petco Pet Store 10 Whitten Rd, Ste 6 Augusta ME   207-622-2502
Your licensed and well-behaved leashed dog is allowed in the store.

Bangor

Accommodations
Best Western White House Inn 155 Littlefield Ave Bangor ME   207-862-3737 (800-780-7234)
Dogs are allowed for no additional pet fee with a credit card on file.
Comfort Inn 750 Hogan Road Bangor ME   207-942-7899 (877-424-6423)
Dogs are allowed for an additional one time pet fee of $10 per room.
Days Inn Bangor Airport 250 Odlin Rd Bangor ME   207-942-8272 (800-329-7466)
Dogs of all sizes are allowed. There is a $6 per night pet fee per pet.
Motel 6 - Bangor 1100 Hammond Street Bangor ME   207-947-6921 (800-466-8356)
One well-behaved family pet per room. Guest must notify front desk upon arrival. Guest is liable for any
damages. In consideration of all guests, pets must never be left unattended in the guest rooms.
The Phenix Inn 20 Broad Street Bangor ME   207-947-0411
Pets are welcome in the first floor rooms. They have two non-smoking pet rooms. There is a $5 per day
additional pet fee.
Best Western Black Bear Inn and Conf Cntr 4 Godfrey Dr Orono ME   207-866-7120 (800-780-7234)
Quiet dogs are allowed for an additional fee of $3 per night per pet.

Campgrounds and RV Parks

Paul Bunyan Campground 1862 Union Street Bangor ME 207-941-1177
http://www.paulbunyancampground.com
Dogs of all sizes are allowed. There are no additional pet fees. Dogs must be leashed and cleaned up after. This RV park is closed during the off-season. The camping and tent areas also allow dogs. There is a dog walk area at the campground.

Paul Bunyan's Wheeler Stream Campground 2202 H 2 Hermon ME 207-848-7877
Dogs of all sizes are allowed. There are no additional pet fees. Dogs may not be left unattended, must be leashed, and cleaned up after. This RV park is closed during the off-season. The camping and tent areas also allow dogs. There is a dog walk area at the campground.

Pumpkin Patch 149 Billings Road Hermon ME 207-848-2231
http://www.pumpkinpatchry.com
Dogs of all sizes are allowed, and they are greeted here with a bone or other doggy treat when they come. There are no additional pet fees. Dogs must be leashed and cleaned up after. There are some breed restrictions. This RV park is closed during the off-season. The camping and tent areas also allow dogs. There is a dog walk area at the campground. There are special amenities given to dogs at this campground.

Red Barn Campground 602 Main Road Holden ME 207-843-6011
http://www.redbarnmaine.com
Dogs of all sizes are allowed. There are no additional pet fees. Dogs may not be left unattended, be leashed, and cleaned up after. Dogs may not be in any of the buildings. This RV park is closed during the off-season. The camping and tent areas also allow dogs. There is a dog walk area at the campground.

Stores

Petco Pet Store 777 Stillwater Avenue Bangor ME 207-945-0049
Your licensed and well-behaved leashed dog is allowed in the store.

Bar Harbor - Acadia

Accommodations

Oceanside Meadows Inn Prospect Harbor Road Acadia Schoodic ME 207-963-5557
http://www.oceaninn.com/
Oceanside Meadows has been a working inn since 1860 and is also a 200 acre preserve of numerous, carefully maintained habitats and eco-systems. It is also home to the Oceanside Meadows Institute for the Arts and Sciences' located in a restored barn between the inn's two guest buildings where they have a variety of events, classes, and musical performances. There are also gardens, a private beach, hiking trails, and many local recreational pursuits. Dogs of all sizes are allowed for an additional fee of $8 per night per pet. There is only one party with a pet allowed at a time in each of the two buildings. Dogs may not be left unattended at any time, and they must be very well behaved, leashed, and cleaned up after.

Acadia Acres 205 Knox Road Bar Harbor ME 207-288-5055
http://www.acadiaacres.net/
There are now 2 pet friendly, fully equipped homes available here; the Knox House in Bar Harbor that offers its own 150+ yard golf practice area, with 6 acres of open fields for your pup to run, and the Jordan Point House on 23 acres in Lamoine that overlooks the Bar Harbor Golf Course and the water. This house also has a 20 x 50 foot fenced shaded yard with a doggy door so pups can be comfortable inside or out if the owners are away. Dogs of all sizes are allowed for an additional fee of $25 per dog. Dogs must be house trained, well behaved, and cleaned up after inside and out. The phone listed is the daytime number; for calls after 4 pm (to 9 pm) EST the number is 207-288-4065.

Balance Rock Inn 21 Albert Meadow Bar Harbor ME 207-288-2610 (800-753-0494)
The oceanfront inn is within walking distance of many restaurants and shops in downtown Bar Harbor. Choose from fourteen individually decorated rooms at the inn, many of which offer an ocean view and private balcony. They also offer a heated outdoor pool and fitness room. Room rates for this inn average $200 to $300 per night but can start at $95 and go up to almost $600 per night. There is also a $30 per day pet fee.

Days Inn Frenchman's Bay 120 Eden St Bar Harbor ME 207-288-3321 (800-329-7466)
Dogs of all sizes are allowed. There are no additional pet fees.

Hanscom's Motel and Cottages 273 H 3 Bar Harbor ME 207-288-3744
http://www.hanscomsmotel.com/
This vintage motor court is only a 5 minute walk to a private rocky beach, sits among giant oaks, white pines, and landscaped grounds/gardens, has shady picnic areas with barbecues, and an outdoor heated pool with a roomy sundeck. Dogs of all sizes are allowed for an additional fee of $8 per night per pet. Dogs may be left alone

only for short periods and only if they will be quiet and well behaved. Dogs must be leashed and cleaned up after at all times.

Hutchins Mountain View Cottages 286 H 3 Bar Harbor ME   207-288-4833 (800-775-4833)
http://www.hutchinscottages.com/
Trees and grazing fields grace this 20 acre country retreat that is only a mile from the Acadia National Park's Visitor Center. Dogs of all sizes are welcome for no additional pet fee. Dogs must be quiet, well behaved, leashed, and cleaned up after in common areas.

Rose Eden Cottages 864 State Highway 3 Bar Harbor ME   207-288-3038
http://www.roseeden.com
This small cottage complex offers ten non-smoking cottages and some of them have kitchenettes. They are located just 4 miles to the entrance of Acadia National Park and about 10 minutes from downtown Bar Harbor. Harbor Point Beach, which allows leashed dogs, is located within walking distance. Room rates range from about $40 to $80 per night depending on the season and size of the cottage. One dog is allowed per cottage and there is a $10 per day pet charge.

The Atlantic Oakes by the Sea hotel 119 Eden Street Bar Harbor ME   207-288-5218 (800-336-2463)
http://www.barharbor.com
The Atlantic Oakes Hotel has a number of pet-friendly rooms for a $25.00 per night pet fee. There is an exercise room, tennis courts and breakfast is provided.

The Ledgelawn Inn

TOP 200 PLACE **The Ledgelawn Inn** 66 Mount Desert Street Bar Harbor ME   207-288-4596 (800-274-5334)
This bed and breakfast inn has a $25 per night pet charge. The B&B is totally non-smoking and there are 8 pet rooms, each with separate entrances.

Town and Country Cottage 230 H 3 Bar Harbor ME   207-288-3439
http://www.townandcountrycottage.com/
Although only minutes from several other attractions and activities, this nicely appointed cottage features a large furnished deck with a barbecue grill, and a sizable lawn with a woodland meadow beyond. Dogs of all sizes are welcome for no additional pet fee. Dogs must be quiet, leashed, cleaned up after, and crated when left alone in the room. Dogs may only be left alone in the room for a short time and then only if they will be well behaved.

Holiday Inn 215 High Street Ellsworth ME   207-667-9341 (877-270-6405)
Dogs of all sizes are allowed for an additional pet fee of $20 per night for 1 pet; $30 per night for 2 pets, and $40 per night for 3 dogs.

The Crocker House 967 Point Road Hancock ME   207-422-6808 (877-715-6017)
http://www.crockerhouse.com/
Built in 1884 (restored in 1986), this seasonally operating inn sits only 300 feet from the water, offers 11 uniquely

differing rooms, a restaurant and full bar, and they are within easy walking distance to several activities and attractions. Dogs of all sizes are welcome for no additional pet fee. Dogs must be under owner's control at all times and be cleaned up after.

Crocker House Country Inn 967 Point Road Hancock Point ME   207-422-6806
Dogs of all sizes are allowed. There are no additional pet fees.

Flander's Bay Cabins 22 Harbor View Drive Sullivan ME   207-422-6408
Dogs of all sizes are allowed. There is a $35 one time fee if the dogs are under 30 pounds and there is a $35 per pet fee if they are over the 30 pounds. Dogs are not allowed to be left alone in the cabins.

Harbor Watch Motel   Swans Island ME   207-526-4563
To get to this motel on Swans Island, take the ferry from Bass Harbor in Southwest Harbor to Swans Island. Leashed dogs and cars are allowed on the Maine State Ferries. Dogs are allowed for an additional $10 per day pet fee. Rooms rates range from about $60 to $80 per night.

Campgrounds and RV Parks

Spruce Valley Campground 136 County Road Bar Harbor ME   207-288-5139
http://www.barharborkoa.com
Dogs of all sizes are allowed. There are no additional pet fees. Dogs may not be left unattended, must be leashed, and cleaned up after. This RV park is closed during the off-season. The camping and tent areas also allow dogs. There is a dog walk area at the campground.

Lamoine State Park 23 State Park Road Ellsworth ME   207-667-4778 (207-287-3824 (out of state res.))
Dogs of all sizes are allowed. There are no additional pet fees. Dogs may not be left unattended at any time, and they must be quiet, be on no more than a 4 foot leash, and be cleaned up after. Dogs may be off lead on your own site if they will stay on site, and they are well behaved and under voice command. There are no dump stations at this park. This campground is closed during the off-season. The camping and tent areas also allow dogs. There is a dog walk area at the campground. There are no electric or water hookups at the campground.

Timberland Acres Campground 57 Bar Harbor Trenton ME   207-667-3600
Dogs of all sizes are allowed. There are no additional pet fees. Dogs may not be left unattended, must be leashed, and cleaned up after. This RV park is closed during the off-season. The camping and tent areas also allow dogs. There is a dog walk area at the campground.

Vacation Home Rentals

Gale's Gardens Guesthouses Daylily Lane Bar Harbor ME   207-733-8811
http://www.galesgardensguesthouse.com
There are two vacation rentals available that can be rented separately or together. The dog-friendly properties are located one mile from the Acadia National Park Entrance and four miles to the center of Bar Harbor.

Summertime Cottages 1 Bloomfield Road Bar Harbor ME   207-288-2893
http://www.summertimebarharbor.com/
Secluded by giant pine trees and about a block from the ocean, these vacation rentals offer a great starting point for several activities and recreation; 150 miles of hiking trails, 56 miles of carriage roads, and proximity to the tallest summit on the Eastern seaboard where the US gets its first light of sun each day. Dogs of all sizes are welcome for no additional fee; Rottweilers and Pit Bulls are not allowed. Dogs must be well mannered, leashed, and cleaned up after.

Transportation Systems

The Cat Ferry, Bar Harbor Terminal 121 Eden Street Bar Harbor ME   877-359-3760
http://www.catferry.com/
Gaining recognition for its speed and agility on the water, this CAT carries up to 775 passengers and 240 cars (not to mention a few furry friends also) across the Gulf of Maine from June to mid-October. Dogs of all sizes are allowed for no additional pet fee. Dogs must be well behaved, and remain in a vehicle on the auto deck or in a kennel during passage. Kennels are available on a 1st come 1st served basis.

Maine State Ferry Service Bass Harbor Southwest Harbor ME   207-596-2202
Dogs are allowed on the ferries if they are leashed, crated or caged. The ferries closest to Bar Harbor depart at the nearby Southwest Harbor and go to Swans Island. Cars can also be transported on the ferry.

Island Explorer Buses Bar Harbor and Acadia Bar Harbor ME   207-667-5796
http://www.exploreacadia.com/
Leashed dogs are allowed on the Island Explorer buses that take people between Bar Harbor, campgrounds, hotels and Acadia National Park.

Attractions

Acadia Outfitters 106 Cottage Street Bar Harbor ME   207-288-8118
This boat rental company allows dogs on their lake canoes. Rent a tandem canoe for $35. Just make sure your pooch does not rock the canoe enough to tip it over and send everyone into the water!

Maine - Please always call ahead to make sure that an establishment is still dog-friendly

Island Explorer Buses

Bar Harbor Downtown Shopping District

Bar Harbor Downtown Shopping District Downtown Bar Harbor Bar Harbor ME   800-345-4617
http://www.barharborinfo.com/home.html
This quaint shopping district extends about 8 blocks in length and there are a number of interesting stores. A

number of the stores welcome pets and some have signs that pets are welcome. In other stores, you may ask if you can bring your pet inside.

Coastal Kayaking Tours and Rentals 48 Cottage Street Bar Harbor ME   207-288-9605
http://www.acadiafun.com/
This watercraft company offers tours of the Maine coastal area and kayak rentals. Dogs are allowed on the rentals for no additional fee. Dogs must be leashed (until on the kayak) and be cleaned up after at all times.
Downeast Windjammer Cruises Bar Harbor Pier Bar Harbor ME   207-288-4585
http://www.downeastwindhammer.com
Well-behaved, leashed dogs may go with you on the boat tours and ferry rides.

Wildwood Stables Carriage Tours

Wildwood Stables Carriage Tours Route 3 Bar Harbor ME   207-276-3622
Take a horse and carriage ride with your pooch in Acadia National Park. The ride is along carriage roads which do not allow cars. Dogs are only allowed on the private tours which cost about $180 ($90 per hour, 2 hour minimum, holds up to 6 people including dogs). These tours fill up fast each season so book early.
Beal and Bunker Mail Boat Ferry Harbor Drive Northeast Harbor ME   207-244-3575
This family run/owned ferry service carries mail, passengers, and freight for the Great Cranberry, Little Cranberry, and at times, Sutton's Islands. They run year round and leave from the Northeast Harbor Town Dock. Dogs are allowed for no additional fee. Dogs must be well behaved, under owner's control, leashed, and cleaned up after at all times.
Masako Queen Fishing Company Beal's Wharf Southwest Harbor ME   207-244-5385
Take a water excursion on a fishing boat with your dog. This boating company offers five hour deep sea fishing trips. Prices are about $39 per person for a half day, and a little less for children and seniors. The boat goes out eight to twelve miles from the shore to fish for mackerel, codfish and more. You will even be able to bring back your own lobster.

Beaches
Hadley Point Beach Highway 3 Bar Harbor ME
Dogs are allowed on the beach, but must be leashed. The beach is located about 10 minutes northwest of downtown Bar Harbor, near Eden.

Parks

Acadia National Park

TOP 200 PLACE Acadia National Park Eagle Lake Road Bar Harbor ME 207-288-3338
http://www.nps.gov/acad/
This National Park ranks high on the tail wagging meter. Dogs are allowed on most of the hiking trails, which is unusual for a National Park. There are miles and miles of both hiking trails and carriage roads. Pets are also allowed at the campgrounds, but must be attended at all times. They are not allowed on sand beaches during the Summer or on the steeper hiking trails year round. Pets must be on a 6 foot or less leash at all times. There is one exception to the leash rule. There is an area in the park that is privately owned where dogs are allowed to run leash-free. It is called Little Long Pond and is located near Seal Harbor. Don't miss the awe-inspiring view from the top of Cadillac Mountain in the park. Overall, this is a pretty popular National Park for dogs and their dog-loving owners. There is a $10 entrance fee into the park, which is good for 7 days. You can also purchase an audio tape tour of the Park Loop Road which is a self-guided auto tour. The driving tour is about 27 miles and takes 3 to 4 hours including stops. Audio tapes are available at the Hulls Cove Visitor Center.

Off-Leash Dog Parks
Little Long Pond Leash-Free Area near Seal Harbor Bar Harbor ME 207-288-3338
This leash free area is a privately owned section of land bordering the Acadia National Park. The off-leash property is located near Seal Harbor on the east side of Long Pond. Pets must be leashed when on Acadia National Park property while accessing the leash-free area.

Outdoor Restaurants
China Joy Restaurant 195 Main Street Bar Harbor ME 207-288-8666
Dogs are allowed at the outdoor tables.
Cottage Street Bakery & Deli 59 Cottage St Bar Harbor ME 207-288-3010
This is not really a bakery but a breakfast and lunch restaurant. It has a nice patio and dogs are welcome on the patio.
Dog & Pony Tavern 4 Rodick Place Bar Harbor ME 207-288-0900
http://www.dogandponytavern.com
This tavern has an outdoor beer garden. Well-behaved, leashed dogs are welcome to join you in the outside areas. The tavern serves food and drinks and has a takeout window for food that is open until 2 am during the summers.
George's Restaurant 7 Stephens Lane Bar Harbor ME 207-288-4505
http://www.georgesbarharbor.com/
Located in downtown Bar Harbor, this restaurant allows your dog to dine with you at the outside tables. This

Mediterranean restaurant offers nice patio seating which overlooks a garden. Enjoy dinner entrees like the Lobster Strudel, Whole Maine Lobster, Filet of Beef and more.

Cottage Street Bakery & Deli

Jordon Pond House Restaurant

TOP 200 PLACE **Jordon Pond House Restaurant** Route 3 Bar Harbor ME 207-276-3316
http://www.jordanpond.com/
Dine outdoors at the tables on the lawn with your leashed pooch. The outdoor seating area offers a beautiful view of the pond and mountains. They are open for lunch, afternoon tea and popovers, and dinner. Enjoy entrees like the Grilled Maine Salmon, Steamed Lobster, and Maine Crab Cakes. The restaurant also offers salads, beef, chicken, desserts and a children's menu.
Pier Restaurant 55 West Street Bar Harbor ME 207-288-2110
http://www.goldenanchorinn.com/pier.htm
Dogs are not allowed on the outdoor deck, but you can dine with your dog at the picnic tables on the pier.
Rupununi 119 Main St Bar Harbor ME 207-288-2886
http://www.rupununi.com
This restaurant serves American and seafood. Dogs may be tied next to the seating area.

Bath

Accommodations
Fairhaven Inn 118 North Bath Rd. Bath ME 207-443-4391 (888-443-4391)
http://www.mainecoast.com/fairhaveninn
This B&B with 8 guest rooms overlooks the Kennebec River. Your dog is welcome to join you for your vacation here.
The Inn at Bath 969 Washington Street Bath ME 207-443-4294 (800-423-0964)
http://www.innatbath.com/
This well appointed 1800's Greek revival home sits among the trees within easy walking distance to town, and they are also close to two ocean beaches and numerous recreational opportunities. Dogs of all sizes are allowed for an additional fee of $15 per night per pet. Dogs must be quiet, leashed, and cleaned up after. Dogs may not be left alone in the room at any time.

Campgrounds and RV Parks
Meadowbrook Camping 33 Meadowbrook Road Phippsburg ME 207-443-4967
http://www.meadowbrookme.com
Dogs of all sizes are allowed. There are no additional pet fees. Dogs may not be left unattended, must be leashed, and cleaned up after. Dogs are not allowed in the rentals. The camping and tent areas also allow dogs. There is a dog walk area at the campground.

Attractions
Fort Popham State Historic Site 10 Perkins Farm Lane Phippsburg ME 207-389-1335
Although construction began In 1862 and the fort was utilized through the years, it was never completed and now in addition to sharing its history, there are also great ocean views, picnic areas, and trails to enjoy. Dogs are allowed throughout the park; they are not allowed on the beach. Dogs must be well behaved, under owner's control, leashed, and cleaned up after at all times.

Belfast

Accommodations
Comfort Inn Ocean's Edge 159 Searsport Avenue/H 1 Belfast ME 207-338-2090 (877-424-6423)
Dogs are allowed for an additional pet fee of $10 per night per room, and they must be declared at the time of reservations.

Vacation Home Rentals
Day Lily Cottage Call to Arrange Belfast ME 207-342-5444
http://www.landworkswaterfront.com
This vacation rental is a newly remodeled 1920 stone bungalow nestled in country gardens. The cottage sits 20 feet from stairs leading to the beach. There are three bedrooms, two baths and the rental can sleep 6. Pets are welcome with $125.00 non-refundable one time fee. No Smoking is allowed. The rental can be rented with Tranquility Cottage next door to sleep 12.

Bethel

Accommodations

Bethel Inn and Country Club 7 Broad Street Bethel ME   207-824-2175
http://www.bethelinn.com
This country resort allows dogs in some of their rooms. Pets are welcome in some of guest buildings and luxury townhouses, but not in the Chapman Building or the main inn. All well-behaved dogs of any size are allowed in non-smoking rooms and there is a one to two dogs per room limit. There is a $10 per day pet fee. During the Winter, dogs are also allowed on a special 2km cross-country skijoring trail.
Sudbury Inn 151 Main Street Bethel ME   207-824-2174
Dogs of all sizes are allowed. There are no additional pet fees.
The Inn at the Rostay 186 Mayville Road Bethel ME   888-754-0072
Dogs of all sizes are allowed. There is a $10 one time fee per room for small pets and a $10 per pet fee for large pets. They are not allowed on the beds and dogs are not allowed to be left alone in the room. There is a pet policy to sign at check in.

Cross Country Ski Resorts

Bethel Inn and Country Club 7 Broad Street Bethel ME   207-824-6276
http://www.bethelinn.com
Dogs are allowed on one of the cross-country ski trails. Skijoring is allowed on this trail. It is a 2km groomed loop and dogs can be off-leash under direct voice control. Please clean up after your dog. Skis and snowshoes can be rented from their Nordic Ski Center. If you are looking for a place to stay, the Bethel Inn also allows well-behaved dogs in some of their rooms.
Carter's X-C Ski Center Intervale Road Bethel ME   207-824-3880
http://www.cartersxcski.com
The cross country ski trails at this center offer views of the valley and ranges. Dogs are allowed on all of the 55 kilometers of groomed beginner to advanced cross-country ski trails. Dogs need to be well-behaved and either leashed or off-leash under direct voice control. You will need to purchase a $12 dog pass and your dog will need to wear the trail pass. Pets are not allowed in the lodge.
Sunday River Cross Country Ski Center 23 Skiway Road Newry ME   207-824-2410
http://www.sundayriverinn.com
This rental center is located at the Sunday River Inn. They have one short trail that allows dogs. It is about 1km and is called The Farm Loop. Dogs can be off-leash on the cross-country ski trail but need to be under direct voice control. While dogs are not allowed at the inn, they are allowed in one of the rental units across the street called The Farm Cottage (207-824-2410).

Parks

Grafton Notch State Park 1941 Bear River Road Newry ME   207-824-2912
A day use park for all seasons with a variety of recreational pursuits. There are 3000 lush acres to explore here, and picnic grills and tables available. Dogs are allowed for no additional pet fee. Dogs must be on no more than a 4 foot leash, cleaned up after at all times, and never be left unattended. Dogs are allowed throughout the park and on the trails; they are not allowed on the beaches.

Boothbay

Accommodations

Sheepscot River Inn 306 Eddy Road Edgecomb ME   207-882-6343
Dogs of all sizes are allowed. There is a $10 per night per room fee and a pet policy to sign at check in.

Campgrounds and RV Parks

Beaver Dam Campground 551 H 9 Boothbay ME   207-698-2267
http://www.beaverdamcampground.com
Dogs of all sizes are allowed. There are no additional pet fees. Dogs may not be left unattended, must be leashed at all times, and cleaned up after. Dogs are not allowed at the playground or the beach. This RV park is closed during the off-season. The camping and tent areas also allow dogs. There is a dog walk area at the campground.
Little Ponderosa Campground 159 Wiscasset Road Boothbay ME   207-633-2700

http://www.littleponderosa.com
Dogs of all sizes are allowed. There are no additional pet fees. Dogs may not be left unattended unless they are well behaved and will be quiet, and then only inside your unit for short periods. Dogs must be leashed and cleaned up after. This RV park is closed during the off-season. The camping and tent areas also allow dogs. There is a dog walk area at the campground.
Shore Hills Campground 553 Wiscaffet Road Boothbay ME   207-633-4782
http://www.shorehillscampground.com
Dogs of all sizes are allowed. There are no additional pet fees. Dogs may not be left unattended, must be leashed, and cleaned up after. This RV park is closed during the off-season. The camping and tent areas also allow dogs. There is a dog walk area at the campground.

Attractions

TOP 200 PLACE **Boothbay Railway Village** 586 Wiscasset Road /H 29 Boothbay ME   207-633-4727
http://www.railwayvillage.org/
A village reflecting the rural life of Old New England, a 60 antique vehicle collection, beautiful gardens, and a real steam engine train to ride make this a fun and educational destination. Dogs are allowed throughout the grounds and they may even ride the train. Dogs are not allowed on Special Event days, so they suggest calling ahead. Dogs must be well behaved, under owner's control, leashed, and cleaned up after at all times.
Balmy Day Cruises 42 Commercial Street/Pier 8 Boothbay Harbor ME   207-633-2284
www.balmycruises.com
One hour tours of the harbor with its scenic surrounding shores and busy waterfront, or trips to Monhegan Island are some of the services offered by this company, and well mannered dogs are allowed aboard for an additional fee of $5 per pet. Dogs must be under owner's control, leashed, and cleaned up after at all times.
TOP 200 PLACE **Cap'n Fish Boat Tours** 65 Atlantic Avenue Boothbay Harbor ME   207-633-3244
www.capnfishmotel.com
Specializing in whale watch and nature cruises, this company will allow your pooch to come aboard for tours. There is no additional pet fee. Dogs must be under owner's control, leashed, and cleaned up after at all times.
Tidal Transit Kayak Company 18 Granary Way Boothbay Harbor ME   207-633-7140
www.kayakboothbay.com
Since this harbor is one of the most protected and beautiful harbors along the coast, it is a great place for all skill levels for ocean kayaking. Well mannered dogs are allowed aboard watercraft rentals for no additional fee; they are not allowed on tours. Dogs must be under owner's control, leashed, and cleaned up after at all times.

Outdoor Restaurants

Boothbay Lobster Wharf 97 Atlantic Avenue Boothbay ME   207-633-4900
http://www.boothbaylobsterwharf.com/
Whether you choose your own lobster from their tanks or any of the seafood, it is fresh from the sea to you, and they offer indoor or outdoor dining on the wharf where you can watch all the waterway activities. The restaurant is open daily from 11:30 am to 9:00 pm mid-May through mid-October. Dogs are allowed at the outer tables of the outside seating area. Dogs must be under owner's control, leashed, and cleaned up after at all times.
The Lobster Dock 49 Atlantic Avenue Boothbay Harbor ME   207-633-7120
http://www.thelobsterdock.com/
A great view of the harbor and outdoor dining on the wharf has made this a popular eatery. Dogs are allowed at the outer tables. Dogs must be under owner's control, leashed, and cleaned up after at all times.

Bridgton - Lake Area

Campgrounds and RV Parks

Naples Campground 295 Sebago Road Naples ME   207-693-5267
http://www.naplescampground.com
Dogs of all sizes are allowed. There are no additional pet fees. Dogs must be friendly, not left unattended, be leashed, and cleaned up after. Dogs are not allowed in the rentals. This RV park is closed during the off-season. The camping and tent areas also allow dogs. There is a dog walk area at the campground.
Lakeside Pines Campground 54 Lakeside Pines Road North Bridgton ME   207-647-3935
http://www.lakesidecamping.com
Dogs of all sizes are allowed. There are no additional pet fees. Dogs must be up to date on their shots. Some breeds are not allowed. Dogs are not allowed in the rentals or on the beach. Dogs must be leashed and cleaned up after. This RV park is closed during the off-season. The camping and tent areas also allow dogs. There is a dog walk area at the campground.

Cross Country Ski Resorts

Carter's X-C Ski Center 420 Main Street Oxford ME   207-539-4848
http://www.cartersxcski.com
Dogs are allowed on any of the 40 kilometers of groomed beginner to intermediate cross-country ski trails. Dogs need to be well-behaved and either leashed or off-leash under direct voice control. You will need to purchase a $12 dog pass and your dog will need to wear the trail pass. Pets are not allowed in the lodge. Dogs may not be allowed on the trails during a special event, so please call ahead to confirm.
Five Fields Farm Route 106 South Bridgton ME 207-647-2425
http://www.fivefieldsfarmx-cski.com
This 70 acre Apple Orchard Farm offers 12 miles of groomed and backcountry cross-country skiing trails during the Winter. They rent both skis and snowshoes. Dogs are welcome and should be leashed on the trails. There are no extra pet fees. This is a popular spot for skiers with dogs.

Brunswick

Outdoor Restaurants

Fat Boy Drive-in 111 Bath Road/H 24 Brunswick ME   207-729-9431
An eatery with good old American favorites, and they also offer an outdoor area for diners with dogs. Dogs must be under owner's control, leashed, and cleaned up after at all times.

Calais

Accommodations

Calais Motor Inn 293 Main Street Calais ME   207-454-7111
There is a $10 per day pet charge.
International Motel 276 Main Street Calais ME   207-454-7515
Dogs are allowed in the older building only and not in the motel office. There are no additional pet fees.

Camden Area

Accommodations

Blue Harbor House 67 Elm Street Camden ME   207-236-3196 (800-248-3196)
http://www.blueharborhouse.com/
Dogs are allowed in one of the suites in the Carriage House at this Village Inn. There are no additional pet fees.
Camden Harbour Inn 83 Bayview Street Camden ME   207-236-4200 (800-236-4266)
http://www.4chi.com/
The Camden Harbour Inn, built in 1874, overlooks the historic and picturesque Camden harbor. Be sure to ask for their "Pooch Package" which includes dog cookies upon arrival, pet bowls for food and water, cushioned dog bed or bedspread cover, a basket of treats and towels for muddy paws. Thanks to one of our readers who writes "Great hotel and home to a beautiful elderly yellow labrador named Bo. Great lobster restaurant at the marina which on our visit had 7 dogs with owners... beautiful place." There is a $20 one time pet fee.
Camden Riverhouse Hotel & Inns 11 Tannery Lane Camden ME   207-236-0500 (800-755-7483)
http://www.camdenmaine.com
This downtown hotel allows your dog of any size for $15 per night additional pet fee. Dogs may not be left unattended in the room.
Lord Camden Inn 24 Main Street Camden ME   207-236-4325 (800-336-4325)
http://www.lordcamdeninn.com
The Lord Camden Inn is located in the heart of downtown Camden. Many rooms boast ocean views, full balconies and kitchenettes. Dogs are welcome and pampered at the Lord Camden Inn with doggy biscuits and a list of activities and day care options awaiting your arrival in your room. Two well-behaved dogs are allowed per room (no size restrictions), and dogs are not to be left unattended. There is an additional $20 per pet per night fee. The hotel is open year round.
Pine Grove Cottages 2076 Atlantic H Lincolnville ME   207-236-2929 (800-530-5265)
http://www.pinegrovemaine.com/
Offering 9 well-equipped cottages on 3 acres, all with private decks and barbecues, this seasonal retreat is also

close to several other attractions, eateries, shops, and recreation. Dogs of all sizes are welcome for no additional pet fee. Dogs may be left alone only for short periods and only if they will be quiet, well behaved, and crated. Please keep dogs off the furniture, and they must be leashed and cleaned up after at all times. They also invite your pooch in when you register for some water and a cookie, and if OK with the pet owner they would like to take a photo of the pet to go with all the other doggy guest photos.

Old Granite Inn 546 Main Street Rockland ME 207-594-9036
Well behaved pets of all sizes are allowed. There are no additional pet fees. Dogs are not allowed to be left alone in the room, and they must be very good around cats.

The East Wind Inn 21 Mechanic Street Tenants Harbor ME 207-372-6366 (800-241-VIEW (8439))
http://www.eastwindinn.com/
This seasonal Historic Inn sits at the water's edge and has 23 spacious guest rooms, a wrap-around porch for watching all the harbor activity, and a central location to numerous other activities and recreation. One dog of any size is allowed for an additional fee of $15 per night. Dogs may not be left alone in the room at any time, and they must be leashed and cleaned up after.

Campgrounds and RV Parks

Camden Hills State Park 280 Belfast Road Camden ME 207-236-3109
This park is a year round recreational destination providing cross-country skiing in Winter and more than 30 miles of hiking trails that can be accessed from 5 major trailheads at other parts of the year, and there is a scenic auto drive up Mount Battie for some fantastic views. Dogs must be well behaved under owner's control, leashed, and cleaned up after at all times. They are very strict about pets being on leash and dogs may not be left unattended. The 107 site campground offers hot showers, picnic areas, and flush toilets. This RV park is closed during the off-season. The camping and tent areas also allow dogs. There is a dog walk area at the campground. There are no electric or water hookups at the campgrounds.

Camden Hills RV Resort 30 Applewood Road Rockport ME 207-236-2498
http://www.camdenhillsrv.com
Dogs of all sizes are allowed. There are no additional pet fees. Dogs may not be left unattended, must be leashed, and cleaned up after. This RV park is closed during the off-season. There is a dog walk area at the campground.

Megunticook Campground On H 1 Rockport ME 207-594-2428
http://www.campgroundbythesea.com
Dogs of all sizes are allowed. There are no additional pet fees. Dogs must be quiet and well behaved. Dogs may not be left unattended, must be leashed, and cleaned up after. There are some breed restrictions. This RV park is closed during the off-season. The camping and tent areas also allow dogs. There is a dog walk area at the campground. Dogs are allowed in the camping cabins.

Vacation Home Rentals

Fisherman's Cottage 113 Bayview Street Camden ME 207-342-5444
http://www.landworkswaterfront.com
100-year-old fisherman cottage in a deluxe neighborhood. Ocean view from the master bedroom, living room, and kitchen. An easy walk to Camden, easy access to beach and beautiful walking and biking roads. Stone terrace across front of house for ocean harbor viewing. Available year-round. Three bedrooms, two baths, linens provided, telephone, television, cable, VCR, washer/dryer, ocean view. Sleeps six. Pets welcome with non-refundable deposit of $125.00. No Smoking. $1,800 per week.

Transportation Systems

Mohegan Boat Line End of Port Clyde Road/H 131 Port Clyde ME 207-372-8848
http://www.monheganboat.com/
Nature and art lovers from all over come to experience this wonderfully scenic island that provides about 17 miles of trails to explore. It also features a number of shops and artists' studios. This ferry will transport dogs to the island for an additional pet fee of $5 per dog. Dogs must be well mannered, under owner's control, leashed, and cleaned up after at all times.

Maine State Ferry Service (Maine D.O.T.) 517A Main Street Rockland ME 207-596-2202
This state owned/operated year round ferry service provides a fixed route from Bass Harbor to Swans Island and Frenchboro ports. Dogs of all sizes are allowed for no additional pet fee. Dogs must be well behaved, under owner's immediate control, securely leashed, crated, or caged, and cleaned up after at all times. There is a separate room for passengers with pets.

Attractions

Lively Lady Too Boat Tours Bay View Landing Wharf Camden ME 207-236-6672
http://www.livelyladytoo.com/
This water adventure company offers two hour lighthouse, nature, or lobster fishing tours, and on the lobster tour

the captain actually brings up live lobster traps and shares the art of "lobstering". Dogs are allowed on board for no additional fee. Dogs must be friendly, under owner's control/care at all times, and leashed.

Merryspring Nature Park 30 Conway Road Camden ME   207-236-2239
http://www.merryspring.org/
This 66 acre park is home to abundant bird and wildlife, an arboretum with more than 70 labeled native trees and shrubs, numerous trails and meadows, gardens, and several special events throughout the year. Dogs are welcome throughout the park with the exception of the gardens. Dogs must be under owner's control, leashed (except in the North Meadow where dogs can be off lead as long as they are under voice control), and cleaned up after at all times.

TOP 200 PLACE **Schooner Olad** Camden Harbor/Camden Public Landing Camden ME   207-236-2323
http://www.maineschooners.com/
This water adventure company offers two hour tours along Maine's coastline where visitors can see plenty of marine and bird life and seafaring activity. Dogs are allowed on board for no additional fee. Dogs must be friendly, under owner's control/care at all times, and leashed. They also suggest visitors bring necessary refreshments for themselves and the pet.

Stores

Owl and Turtle Bookshop 32 Washington Street Camden ME   207-236-4769
http://www.owlandturtle.com/
This is the city's oldest full service bookstore, and they will allow your house-trained and well mannered pet to browse, too. Dogs must be under owner's control, leashed, and cleaned up after at all times.

Parks

Camden Hills State Park 280 Belfast Road Camden ME   207-236-3109
This park is a year round recreational destination providing cross-country skiing in Winter and more than 30 miles of hiking trails that can be accessed from 5 major trailheads at other parts of the year, and there is also a scenic auto drive up Mount Battie for some fantastic views. Dogs must be well behaved under owner's control, leashed, and cleaned up after at all times. They are very strict about pets being on leash and dogs may not be left unattended.

Outdoor Restaurants

Bayview Lobster Bayview Landing Camden ME   207-236-2005
This restaurant serves seafood. Dogs are allowed at the outdoor tables. They serve frozen paws dog ice cream (soy based) to your pet.

Canaan

Campgrounds and RV Parks

Skowhegan/Canaan 18 Cabin Row Canaan ME   207-474-2858
http://www.smorefuncampground.com
Dogs of all sizes are allowed and they are allowed in the cabins with a credit card on file. There are no additional pet fees. Dogs must be quiet and well behaved. Dogs may not be left unattended, must be leashed, and cleaned up after. Dogs are not allowed in the buildings, the pavillion, the pool or playground. This RV park is closed during the off-season. The camping and tent areas also allow dogs. There is a dog walk area at the campground. Dogs are allowed in the camping cabins.

Castine

Accommodations

Castine Harbor Lodge 147 Perkins Street Castine ME   207-326-4335
http://www.castinemaine.com/
This 1893 waterfront hotel features 250 feet of ocean-facing porches overlooking the bay, clay tennis courts, one of the country's oldest 9-hole golf courses, a steak and seafood restaurant and bar, and access to several historic walking trails. Dogs of all sizes are allowed for an additional fee of $10 per night per pet. Dogs may not be left alone in the room at any time, and they must be very well behaved, always kept leashed, and cleaned up after.

Corinth

Cross Country Ski Resorts
Critterwoods Outdoor Recreation Area 118 O'Roak Road Corinth ME   207-285-0099
http://www.critterwoods.com
This resort offers over 20 miles of groomed trails. Dogs are allowed on about 4 miles of cross-country ski and dog sledding or skijoring trails. Call ahead to confirm trail availability as sometimes only the dog sledding trails are open. Dogs need to be leashed at the resort and on the trails. The center rents skis and snowshoes.

Deer Isle

Accommodations
The Pilgrim's Inn 20 Main Street Deer Isle ME   207-348-6615 (888-778-7505)
http://www.pilgrimsinn.com/
This 1793 restored historic inn overlooks the picturesque Northwest Harbor, features a tavern restaurant, a large mill pond, and offers 3 cottages that are pet friendly. Dogs of all sizes are welcome, but there can only be 1 large or 2 small to medium dogs per room. Dogs may only be left alone in the room while dining on the property, and they must be leashed and cleaned up after at all times.

Campgrounds and RV Parks
Old Quarry Campground 130 Settlement Road Stonington ME   207-367-9877
This camp area gives access to the Maine shoreline and plenty of hiking opportunities. They also offer dog friendly kayak rentals. There are hot showers, a laundry, Wi-Fi (fee), swimming pond, and a camp store in the campground. Responsible owners are allowed to bring their dogs for no additional fee. Dogs must be quiet, well behaved, leashed, and cleaned up after at all times. The camping and tent areas also allow dogs. There is a dog walk area at the campground. There are no electric or water hookups at the campgrounds.

Attractions
Old Quarry Ocean Adventures 130 Settlement Road Stonington ME   207-367-8977
http://oldquarry.com/shop/kayak.php
This water adventure company offers kayak rentals for paddling through some of the most beautiful islands along the coast. There is also a dog-friendly campground on site. Dogs are allowed on rentals for no additional fee. Dogs must be friendly, under owner's control/care at all times, and leashed.

Dennysville

Campgrounds and RV Parks
Cobscook Bay State Park RR#1 Dennysville ME   207-726-4412
This peninsula park offers visitors excellent vantage points to view the ebb and flow of the tides of Whiting Bay, scenic hiking trails, groomed x-country trails in Winter, and it is a popular clamming destination as well. Dogs of all sizes are allowed for no additional fee. Dogs may not be left unattended at any time, and they must be on no more than a 4 foot leash and cleaned up after. Dogs must be quiet and well mannered. There are more than 100 secluded, well maintained sites, and most of the campsites are located along the water's edge. There are picnic sites, restrooms, and hot showers available. This RV park is closed during the off-season. The camping and tent areas also allow dogs. There is a dog walk area at the campground. There are no electric or water hookups at the campgrounds.

Parks
Cobscook Bay State Park RR#1 Dennysville ME   207-726-4412
This peninsula park offers visitors excellent vantage points to view the ebb and flow of the tides of Whiting Bay, scenic hiking trails, groomed x-country trails in Winter, and it is a popular clamming destination as well. Dogs of all sizes are allowed for no additional fee. Dogs may not be left unattended at any time, and they must be on no more than a 4 foot leash and cleaned up after. Dogs must be quiet and well mannered.

Dover-Faxcroft

Campgrounds and RV Parks
Peaks-Kenny State Park 401 State Park Road Dover-Faxcroft ME 207-564-2003
Dogs of all sizes are allowed. There are no additional pet fees. Dogs may not be left unattended, and they must be leashed and cleaned up after at all times. Dogs are not allowed on the beach, the gravel, in the water, or the picnic areas. Dogs can be on the grass at the beach area and on all the trails. This campground is closed during the off-season. The camping and tent areas also allow dogs. There is a dog walk area at the campground. There are no electric or water hookups at the campground.

Eastport

Accommodations
Milliken House 29 Washington Street Eastport ME 207-853-2955
Well behaved dogs of all sizes are allowed. There are no additional pet fees.

Parks
Quoddy Head State Park 973 N Lubec Road Lubec ME 207-733-0911
Located on the easternmost point of land in the US, this 532 acre diversely landscaped and inhabited park offers 5 different trails showcasing the varying features of the park. Dogs are allowed; they must be under owner's control, leashed, and cleaned up after at all times.
Roosevelt Campobello International Park PO Box 97 Lubec ME 506-752-2922
http://www.nps.gov/roca/index.htm
Dogs must be on leash and must be cleaned up after in park. They are not allowed in any buildings. The Visitor Center is open all year 9am-5pm. The park features auto touring, camping, hiking, nature walks, and more. This 2800 acre park is a joint memorial by Canada and the US as a symbol of the close relationship between the two countries.

Freeport Area

Accommodations
Best Western Freeport Inn 31 US Rt 1 Freeport ME 207-865-3106 (800-780-7234)
Dogs are allowed for no additional pet fee.
Harraseeket Inn 162 Main Street Freeport ME 207-865-9377 (800-342-6423)
http://www.harraseeketinn.com/
Whether it's for the perfect vacation package, a shopping adventure (over 170 shops only 2 blocks away), or a romantic getaway, this inn also offers amenities like a live Jazz brunch on Sundays, award winning dining, and an indoor pool. Dogs of all sizes are allowed for an additional fee of $25 per night per pet, and advance notification is required. For their canine guests they place a doggy bed, a small can of dog food, water and food dishes, 4 small clean-up duty bags, and a small treat in the room. Dogs must be kept leashed when out of the room and they must be cleaned up after at all times. Dogs are not to be left alone in the room for more than 2 hours and only then if they will be quiet and well mannered. Dogs must be removed for housekeeping, and they are not allowed in the main building.
The Main Idyll Motor Court 1411 H 1 Freeport ME 207-865-4201
http://www.maineidyll.com/
This motor court features 20 cottages set among a grove of trees with play and barbecue/picnic areas, hiking trails and they provide a doggie comfort station. Dogs of all sizes are allowed for an additional $4 per night per pet. Dogs must be leased and cleaned up after. They may only be left for a short time alone in the room, and then only if they will be quiet and well behaved.

Campgrounds and RV Parks
Freeport/Durham KOA 82 Big Skye Lane Durham ME 207-688-4288 (888-562-5609)
http://www.freeportkoa.com
Dogs of all sizes are allowed, and there are no additional pet fees for tent or RV sites. There is a $10 one time

additional pet fee for cabin rentals. Dogs must be quiet, leashed, and cleaned up after. There are some breed restrictions. This RV park is closed during the off-season. The camping and tent areas also allow dogs. There is a dog walk area at the campground. Dogs are allowed in the camping cabins.

Cedar Haven Campground 39 Baker Road Freeport ME 207-865-6254
http://www.campmaine.com/cedar haven
Well behaved dogs of all sizes are allowed. There are no additional pet fees. Dogs may not be left unattended, must be leashed, and cleaned up after. There is a pond for dogs to swim in at which time they can be off lead if they are under voice control. No excessive barking is allowed. This RV park is closed during the off-season. The camping and tent areas also allow dogs. There is a dog walk area at the campground. Dogs are allowed in the camping cabins.

Blueberry Pond Camping 218 Poland Range Road Pownal ME 207-688-4421
http://www.blueberrycampground.com
Dogs of all sizes are allowed. There are no additional pet fees. Dogs must be well behaved, leashed, and cleaned up after. This RV park is closed during the off-season. The camping and tent areas also allow dogs. There is a dog walk area at the campground. Dogs are allowed in the camping cabins.

Bradbury Mountain State Park 528 Hallowell Road/H9 Pownal ME 207-688-4712
Home to a wide variety of flora and fauna, this 590 acre forested park also features many recreational opportunities, great views from the summit, and a variety of multi-use trails. Dogs are allowed for no additional pet fee. Dogs must be well behaved, on no more than a 4 foot leash, cleaned up after at all times, and never be left unattended. Dogs are allowed throughout the park and on the trails; they are not allowed on the beaches. The camp area offers 41 sites, restrooms, a playground, ball fields, picnic tables, and grills. The camping and tent areas also allow dogs. There is a dog walk area at the campground. There are no electric or water hookups at the campgrounds.

Attractions
Atlantic Seal Cruises 25 Main Street South Freeport ME 207-865-6112
This water touring company offers a 4 hour Eagle Island tour with 3 hours on the water and about 1 hour on the island. Although, dogs are not allowed on the island, they are allowed on the tour and the crew will be glad to doggy sit for the time guests are on the island. There is no additional pet fee. Dogs must be friendly, well behaved, leashed, and cleaned up after.

Parks
Wolfe's Neck Woods State Park 426 Wolfe's Neck Road Freeport ME 207-865-4465
Varied ecosystems and wildlife give visitors a real "back to nature" feel even though this 233 acre park is only a few minutes from a busy city, and they provide interpretive signage, picnic tables and grills, bathrooms, and 5 miles of wooded and shoreline trails. Dogs are allowed throughout the park and on the trails; they are not allowed on the beach. Dogs must be well behaved, on no more than a 4 foot leash, cleaned up after at all times, and never be left unattended.

Bradbury Mountain State Park 528 Hallowell Road/H9 Pownal ME 207-688-4712
Home to a wide variety of flora and fauna, this 590 acre forested park also features many recreational opportunities, great views from the summit, and a variety of multi-use trails. Dogs are allowed for no additional pet fee. Dogs must be well behaved, on no more than a 4 foot leash, cleaned up after at all times, and never be left unattended. Dogs are allowed throughout the park and on the trails; they are not allowed on the beaches.

Houlton

Campgrounds and RV Parks
My Brother's Place Campground 659 North Street Houlton ME 207-532-6739
http://www.mainerec.com/mybro.html
Dogs of all sizes are allowed, however the cabins will only accept 1 dog up to 50 pounds. There are no additional pet fees. Dogs may not be left unattended, must be leashed, and cleaned up after. This RV park is closed during the off-season. The camping and tent areas also allow dogs. There is a dog walk area at the campground. Dogs are allowed in the camping cabins.

Kennebunk

Accommodations
Arundel Meadows Inn 1024 Portland Road Arundel ME 207-985-3770

http://www.arundelmeadowsinn.com
From the months of April through December, this 1800's farm house (renovated in the 1990's) offers it's ambiance to guests and their four-legged companions. Dogs of all sizes are welcome for no additional pet fee, unless extra cleaning is required. Dogs must be well behaved, leashed, and cleaned up after.
The Hounds Tooth Inn 82 Summer Street Kennebunk ME 207-985-0117
http://www.houndstoothinn.biz/#
Sitting on about an acre of landscaped grounds, this 4 bedroom, 1843 farmhouse offers spacious accommodations and a large fenced-in area off the back patio where guests can watch their pooches have a good time. Dogs are allowed for an additional fee of $10 per night per pet. Dogs may not be left alone in the room, and they must be under owner's control/care at all times. Dogs are allowed throughout the grounds and common areas of the house, but they are not allowed in the kitchen.
Captain Jefferds Inn 5 Pearl Street Kennebunkport ME 207-967-2311 (800-839-6844)
http://www.captainjefferdsinn.com/
This historic inn has a $20 per day pet charge. They ask that you please never leave your dog alone in the room.
Lodge At Turbat's Creek Turbats Creek Rd at Ocean Avenue Kennebunkport ME 207-967-8700
There are no additional pet fees.
The Colony Hotel 140 Ocean Avenue Kennebunkport ME 207-967-3331
Dogs of all sizes are allowed. There is a $25 per night per pet additional fee.
The Yachtsman Lodge and Marina Ocean Avenue Kennebunkport ME 207-967-2511
http://www.yachtsmanlodge.com/
Sitting right on the waterfront with all the rooms having its own patio overlooking the river, has inspired the redesign of the rooms to reflect those of a luxury yacht. This seasonal inn also provides a great starting point to several local attractions. Dogs of all sizes are allowed for an additional fee of $25 per night per pet, and they must be declared at the time of registration as pet friendly rooms are limited. Dogs may be left alone only for short periods and only if they will be quiet, well behaved, and a contact number is left with the front desk. Dogs must be leashed and cleaned up after at all times.

Campgrounds and RV Parks
Hemlock Grove Campground 1299 Portland Road Arundel ME 207-985-0398
http://www.hemlockgrovecampground.com/
Dogs of all sizes are allowed. There are no additional pet fees. Dogs can be left unattended only if they are quiet, well behaved, and comfortable with owner's absence. They must be left in the tent or RV. Dogs must be leashed at all times and cleaned up after. This RV park is closed during the off-season. The camping and tent areas also allow dogs. There is a dog walk area at the campground.
Red Apple Campground 111 Sinnott Road Kennebunkport ME 207-967-4927
http://www.redapplecampground.com
Dogs of all sizes are allowed. There are no additional pet fees. Dogs may not be left unattended, must be leashed, and cleaned up after. This RV park is closed during the off-season. The camping and tent areas also allow dogs. There is a dog walk area at the campground.
Sea-Vu Campground 1733 Post Road Wells ME 207-646-7732
http://www.sea-vucampground.com
Dogs of all sizes are allowed. There are no additional pet fees. Dogs must be leashed and cleaned up after. This RV park is closed during the off-season. The camping and tent areas also allow dogs. There is a dog walk area at the campground.
Well Beach Resort 1000 Post Road Wells ME 207-646-7570
http://www.wellsbeach.com
Dogs of all sizes are allowed. There are no additional pet fees for 2 pets per site. There is a $7 per night per pet additional fee if over 2 dogs. Dogs must be leashed and cleaned up after. This RV park is closed during the off-season. There is a dog walk area at the campground.

Attractions
Gallery on Chase Hill 10 Chase Hill Road Kennebunkport ME 207-967-0049
http://www.maine-art.com/
The Sculpture Garden is open throughout the Summer, and your well mannered pet is welcome on the grounds during regular business days. They are not allowed when there is on opening for the season or during an artist showing, so they suggest calling ahead. Dogs must be under owner's control, leashed, and cleaned up after at all times.
World Within Sea Kayaking 746 Ocean Avenue Wells ME 207-646-0455
http://www.worldwithin.com/
This watercraft rental company will allow your well behaved dog to come aboard rentals and explore the tidal Ogunquit River. There is no additional pet fee. They do request that dogs have had prior experience on the water. Dogs must be under owner's control, leashed, and cleaned up after at all times. One of the launch points is located at the Ogunquit River Plantation Hotel; pay inside at the lobby and go around back to the kayaks.

Beaches

Kennebunk Beaches Beach Avenue Kennebunk ME
Dogs are allowed with certain restrictions. During the summertime, from about Memorial Day weekend through Labor Day weekend, leashed dogs are only allowed on the beach before 8am and after 6pm. During the rest of the year, dogs are allowed on the beach during park hours. There are a string of beaches, including Kennebunk, Gooch's and Mother's, that make up a nice stretch of wide sandy beaches. People need to clean up after their pets. The beaches are located on Beach Avenue, off Routes 9 and 35.

Goose Rocks Beach Dyke Street Kennebunkport ME
Leashed dogs are allowed, with certain restrictions. From June 15 through September 15, dogs are only allowed on the beach before 8am and after 6pm. During the rest of the year, dogs are allowed on the beach during park hours. People need to clean up after their pets. The beach is located about 3 miles east of Cape Porpoise. From Route 9, exit onto Dyke Street.

Wells Beach Route 1 Wells ME 207-646-2451
Leashed dogs are allowed, with certain restrictions. During the Summer, from June 16 through September 15, dogs are only allowed on the beach before 8am and after 6pm. The rest of the year, dogs are allowed on the beach during all park hours. There are seven miles of sandy beaches in Wells. People are required to clean up after their pets.

Parks

Rachel Carson National Wildlife Refuge 321 Port Road Wells ME 207-646-9226
This park was established in 1966 for the protection of important salt marshes and migratory bird estuaries, and there are great opportunities for bird and wildlife viewing/photography, picnicking, hiking, and they offer special events throughout the year. Dogs are allowed on site and on the Carson Trail. Dogs must be under owner's control, leashed, and cleaned up after at all times.

Off-Leash Dog Parks

Kennebunk Dog Park 36 Sea Road Kennebunk ME 207-985-3244
This popular, fenced off leash area offers a natural environment setting, benches, and year round accessibility from dawn to dusk. Dogs must be sociable, current on all vaccinations, licensed, and under owner's control/care at all times. Dogs must be leashed when not in designated off-lead areas.

Outdoor Restaurants

Cape Pier Chowder House 84 Pier Road Cape Porpoise ME 207-967-0123
This chowder house features indoor or outdoor dining directly over the water, and great ocean views. Dogs are allowed at the outer tables. Dogs must be under owner's control, leashed, and cleaned up after at all times.

Lewiston

Accommodations

Motel 6 - Lewiston 516 Pleasant Street Lewiston ME 207-782-6558 (800-466-8356)
One well-behaved family pet per room. Guest must notify front desk upon arrival. Guest is liable for any damages. In consideration of all guests, pets must never be left unattended in the guest rooms.

Medway

Accommodations

Gateway Inn Route 157 Medway ME 207-746-3193
Dogs of all sizes are allowed. There are no additional pet fees.

Campgrounds and RV Parks

Katahdin Shadows Campground and Cabins H 157 Medway ME 207-746-9349
http://www.katahdinshadows.com
Dogs of all sizes are allowed. There are no additional pet fees. Dogs may not be left unattended, must be leashed, and cleaned up after. This campground is open through the Winter and closes for only one month in

April. This RV park is closed during the off-season. The camping and tent areas also allow dogs. There is a dog walk area at the campground. Dogs are allowed in the camping cabins.

Milbridge

Attractions
Robertson Sea Tours and Adventures Milbridge Marina Milbridge ME   207-546-3883
This sea tour adventure company offers a variety of 2 to 2 1/2 hour cruises as well as private charters and your friendly, well mannered pooch is welcome aboard for no additional fee. Dogs must be under owner's control, leashed, and cleaned up after at all times.

Moosehead Lake

Campgrounds and RV Parks
Lily Bay State Park Lily Bay Road Greenville ME   207-695-2700
Dogs of all sizes are allowed. There are no additional pet fees. Dogs may not be left unattended, and they must be leashed and cleaned up after. Dogs are allowed on all of the trails. This park has 2 campgrounds, and one usually closes up for the season earlier than the other. This campground is closed during the off-season. The camping and tent areas also allow dogs. There is a dog walk area at the campground. There are no electric or water hookups at the campground.

Attractions
Northwoods Outfitters 5 Lily Bay Road Greenville ME   207-695-3288
http://www.maineoutfitter.com/
Located on the shores of the state's largest lake amid the largest forest in the eastern US, these recreation specialists offer a long list of recreation equipment rentals, a variety of land and/or water guided or self-guided tours, and year round activities for all age and skill levels. Dogs are allowed on the grounds, on the trails (Summer and Winter), and they are allowed on any tour that does not require mechanical movement. Dogs must be well behaved, under owner's control, leashed, and cleaned up after.

Cross Country Ski Resorts
The Birches Ski Touring Center 1 Birches Road Rockwood ME   207-537-7305
http://www.birches.com
This center allows dogs on all of their 40 kilometers of groomed trails. Dogs need to be leashed at the resort and on the trails. The center rents both skis and snowshoes. Pets are not allowed in the main lodge.

Parks
Lily Bay 13 Myrles Way Greenville ME   207-695-2700 (in season)
Over 900 acres and home to the largest lake in the New England with plenty of year round recreation have made this a popular destination. Dogs are allowed for no additional pet fee. Dogs must be on no more than a 4 foot leash, cleaned up after at all times, and never be left unattended. Dogs are allowed throughout the park and on the trail

New Harbor

Campgrounds and RV Parks
Lake Pemaquid Camping 100 Twin Cove Lane Damariscotta ME   207-563-5202
http://www.lakepemaquid.com
Dogs of all sizes are allowed. There are no additional pet fees. Dogs must be quiet, leashed, and cleaned up after. This RV park is closed during the off-season. The camping and tent areas also allow dogs. There is a dog walk area at the campground. Dogs are allowed in the camping cabins.

Attractions

Hardy Boat Cruises 132 H 32 New Harbor ME 207-677-2026
http://www.hardyboat.com/
Puffin and seal watching, lighthouses, and coastal Fall foliage tours are some of the cruises offered by this seafaring company. Dogs are allowed on all the cruises for no additional fee. Dogs must be well mannered, under owner's control, leashed, and cleaned up after at all times.
Salt Water Charters Town Landing Road/Round Pond Dock Round Pond ME 207-677-6229
www.saltwatercharters.com
This custom charter company provides visitors opportunities to lobster or fish or to just explore all that the Muscongus Bay area has to offer. Dogs are allowed aboard for no additional fee. Dogs must be well mannered, under owner's control, leashed, and cleaned up after at all times.

North Monmouth

Campgrounds and RV Parks
Beaver Brook Campground RFD 1 Box 1835 Wilson Pond Roa North Monmouth ME 207-933-2108
http://www.beaver-brook.com
Dogs of all sizes are allowed. There are no additional pet fees. Dogs must be leashed and cleaned up after. Dogs can be off leash to go swimming at the lake as long as they are under owner's control. This RV park is closed during the off-season. The camping and tent areas also allow dogs. There is a dog walk area at the campground.

Old Orchard Beach

Accommodations
Hampton Inn 48 Industrial Park Road Saco ME 207-282- 7222
Dogs of all sizes are allowed. There are no additional pet fees, and there is a pet policy to sign at check in. Pet rooms are on the 3rd floor and dogs are not allowed in any of the food areas.

Campgrounds and RV Parks
Hid'n Pines Family Campground 8 Cascade Road Old Orchard Beach ME 207-934-2352
http://www.hidnpines.com
One dog of any size is allowed. There is a pet policy to sign at check in and there are no additional pet fees. Dogs may not be left unattended at any time and must be leashed and cleaned up after. Dogs are not allowed in the pool or bathroom areas. There are some breed restrictions. This RV park is closed during the off-season. The camping and tent areas also allow dogs. There is a dog walk area at the campground.
Powder Horn Family Camping Resort 48 Cascade Road Old Orchard Beach ME 207-934-4733
http://www.mainecampgrounds.com
Dogs of all sizes are allowed. There is a pet policy to sign at check in and there are no additional pet fees. Dogs may not be left unattended at any time, and they are not allowed at the tents, buildings, or common areas. This RV park is closed during the off-season. There is a dog walk area at the campground.
Wild Acres Family Camping Resort 179 Saco Avenue Old Orchard Beach ME 207-934-2535
http://www.mainecamping.com
Dogs of all sizes are allowed. There are no additional pet fees. There is a pet policy to sign at check in and there are no additional fees. Dogs may not be left unattended, must be leashed, and cleaned up after. This RV park is closed during the off-season. The camping and tent areas also allow dogs. There is a dog walk area at the campground.
KOA Saco/Portland South 814 Portland Road Saco ME 207-282-0502 (800-562-1886)
http://www.sacokoa.com
Dogs of all sizes are allowed, and there are no additional pet fees for tent or RV sites. There is a $15 one time fee plus a $100 refundable pet deposit for cabin rentals. Dogs may not be left unattended, must be leashed, and cleaned up after. This RV park is closed during the off-season. The camping and tent areas also allow dogs. There is a dog walk area at the campground. Dogs are allowed in the camping cabins.

Beaches
Old Orchard Beach City Beach Old Orchard Beach ME 207-934-0860
Leashed dogs are allowed on this beach at all hours from the day after Labor Day to the day before Memorial Day. Dogs are not allowed on the beach from Memorial Day through Labor Day except before 8 am and after 4 pm. People need to make sure they pick up their dog's waste with a plastic bag and throw it away in a trash can.

Off-Leash Dog Parks
Old Orchard Beach Dog Park Memorial Park at 1st St. Old Orchard Park ME   207-934-0860
This fenced dog park is open 24 hours a day. It is located in Memorial Park.

Orrs Island

Campgrounds and RV Parks
Orr's Island Campground 44 Bond Point Road Orrs Island ME   207-833-5595
http://www.orrsisland.com/contact.htm
This full-service coastal campground offers 70 open or wooded sites for RV camping only. One dog is allowed
per site for no additional fee. Dogs must be quiet, leashed, cleaned up after, and they may not be left unattended
at any time. They are allowed throughout the park and on the trails. This RV park is closed during the off-season.
There is a dog walk area at the campground.

Portland

Accommodations
TOP 200 PLACE **Inn By The Sea** 40 Bowery Beach Road Cape Elizabeth ME   207-799-3134 (800-888-
4287)
http://www.innbythesea.com/
Thanks to one of our readers for these comments: "This hotel is an amazing place for dog lovers. It's a four star
hotel that treats your puppy like any other hotel guest. There are two suites (bedroom, kitchen, living room) that
are specifically appointed for dogs. Water dishes, biscuits, towels for paws, and outside hoses are provided.
There are four nearby state parks and the hotel itself borders a feral area which my dog spent hours on end
exploring. There's even a fenced-in kennel area, complete with a dog house, if you want to leave your pet for an
hour and go for dinner. Wonderful place, they love dogs, great recreation, beautiful rooms, great hotel restaurant
- truly a superb experience." This hotel also offers dog walking service with 24-hour notification. They even have
a special pet menu with items like gourmet chuck burgers, grilled range chicken, NY sirloin strip steak with
potatoes and vegetables, and for dessert, vanilla ice cream or doggie bon bons. If you are there during
Thanksgiving, Christmas or the Fourth of July, they offer a special pet holiday menu. The hotel asks that all pets
be kept on a leash when not in their suite and that pets are not left alone in the suite. When making a
reservation, they do require that you tell them you are bringing your pet. There are no pet fees. All rooms are
non-smoking.
Embassy Suites Hotel Portland 1050 Westbrook Street Portland ME   207-775-2200
Dogs of all sizes are allowed. There are no additional pet fees. Dogs are not allowed to be left alone in the room.
Holiday Inn 81 Riverside St Portland ME   207-774-5601 (877-270-6405)
Dogs of all sizes are allowed for an additional one time pet fee of $35 per room.
Howard Johnson Plaza Hotel 155 Riverside Portland ME   207-774-5861 (800-446-4656)
Dogs of all sizes are welcome. There is a $50 refundable pet deposit.
Motel 6 - Portland One Riverside Street Portland ME   207-775-0111 (800-466-8356)
One well-behaved family pet per room. Guest must notify front desk upon arrival. Guest is liable for any
damages. In consideration of all guests, pets must never be left unattended in the guest rooms.
The Inn at St John 939 Congress Street Portland ME   207-773-6481 (800-636-9127)
http://www.innatstjohn.com/index.php
This 1897 inn, originally built to accommodate train travelers, now offers free pick up for plane, train, or bus
travelers, and it has been fully restored in European style with 3 levels of lodging offered. Dogs of all sizes are
allowed for an additional fee of $10 per night per pet. Dogs may not be left alone in the room at any time, and
they have a list of pet sitters if the need arises. Dogs must be well mannered, leashed, and cleaned up after.
Residence Inn by Marriott 800 Roundwood Drive Scarborough ME   207-883-0400
Dogs of all sizes are allowed. There is a $75 one time fee and a pet policy to sign at check in.
TownePlace Suites Portland Scarborough 700 Roundwood Drive Scarborough ME   207-883-6800
Dogs of all sizes are allowed. There is a $75 one time pet fee per visit.
Best Western Merry Manor Inn 700 Main St South Portland ME   207-774-6151 (800-780-7234)
Dogs are allowed for no additional pet fee.
Comfort Inn Airport 90 Maine Mall Road South Portland ME   207-775-0409 (877-424-6423)
Dogs are allowed for an additional one time pet fee of $25 per room.
Holiday Inn Express Hotel & Suites South Portland 303 Sable Oaks Drive South Portland ME   207-775-

3900 (877-270-6405)
Dogs of all sizes are allowed for an additional one time fee of $20 per pet.
Howard Johnson Hotel 675 Main St. South Portland ME   207-775-5343 (800-446-4656)
Dogs of all sizes are welcome. There are no additional pet fees.
Portland Marriott at Sable Oaks 200 Sable Oaks Drive South Portland ME   207-871-8000 (800-228-9290)
Dogs of all sizes are allowed. There is a $35 one time fee per pet. Dogs must be leashed, cleaned up after, crated or removed for housekeeping, and the Do Not Disturb sign is put on the door if they are in the room alone.
Sheraton South Portland Hotel 363 Maines Mall Rd. South Portland ME   207-775-6161 (888-625-5144)
Dogs up to 80 pounds are allowed. There are no additional pet fees. Dogs are not allowed to be left alone in the room.
The Willard Beach House 14 Myrtle Avenue South Portland ME   207-799-9824
http://www.vacationinmaine.net/
Both of their pet friendly rentals, the Willard Beach House condo and the Carriage House with its private back yard, offer views of the ocean and Willard Beach, which has an oceanside walkway connecting a lighthouse and a fort. (Please see our Willard Beach listing for pet restrictions.) Dogs of all sizes are welcome for no additional pet fee. Dogs must be leashed and cleaned up after.

Campgrounds and RV Parks

Bayley's Camping Resort

TOP 200 PLACE **Bayley's Camping Resort** 275 Pine Point Road Scarborough ME   207-883-6043
http://www.bayleys-camping.com
Dogs of all sizes are allowed. There is a pet policy to sign at check in and there are no additional pet fees. Dogs may not be left unattended, must be leashed, and cleaned up after. This RV park has many special weekends and events such as Father's Day and Halloween. This RV park is closed during the off-season. The camping and tent areas also allow dogs. There is a dog walk area at the campground.
Wassamki Springs 56 Soco Street Scarborough ME   207-839-4276
http://www.wassamkisprings.com
Well behaved dogs of all sizes are allowed. There are no additional pet fees. Dogs may not be left unattended, must be leashed, and cleaned up after. There are some breed restrictions. This RV park is closed during the off-season. There is a dog walk area at the campground.

Transportation Systems
Casco Bay Lines 56 Commercial Street Portland ME   207-774-7871

Casco Bay Lines
This year round ferry service carries vehicles, passengers, and freight from Portland to a number of off-shore islands. Dogs are allowed for an additional fee of $3.25. Dogs must be well behaved, under owner's control, leashed, and cleaned up after at all times.

Attractions

Bay View Cruises

TOP 200 PLACE **Bay View Cruises** 184 Commercial Street Portland ME   207-761-0486
http://www.bayviewcruises.com
The boat tours of the Portland Harbor area are about 1 1/2 hours long. Well behaved dogs on lead are allowed on board.
Casco Bay Lines Boats 56 Commercial Street Portland ME   207-74-7871
http://www.cascobaylines.com
The tours are from 1 to 3 hours long. A friendly, leashed dog is allowed. The dog also needs a ticket.
Eagle Island Tours 170 Commercial Street Portland ME   207-774-6498
http://www.eagleislandtours.com
The cruises are about 1 1/2 hours long. Dogs on lead are allowed.
Greater Portland Landmarks Walking Tours 165 State Street/H 77 Portland ME   207-774-5561
Self guided walking tour booklets are available for 4 distinct areas of the city's historical and social history. Dogs are welcome to take the tour too. Dogs must be leashed and cleaned up after at all times. Dogs are not allowed in the buildings.
The Maine Narrow Gauge Railroad 58 Fore Street Portland ME   207-828-0814
http://www.mngrr.org/
Dedicated to restoring, preserving, educating, and entertaining the public about the state's historic narrow gauge railroad, this museum and rail grounds also provides fun train rides that takes visitors along the city's working waterfront, and dogs are allowed on the train too-for no extra fee. Dogs must be well behaved, leashed, and under owner's control/care at all times.

Shopping Centers

Old Port Waterfront District

TOP 200 PLACE Old Port Waterfront District Congress Street Portland ME   207-772-6828
Combining a working waterfront with a trendy shopping, dining, and entertainment district with a vibrant nightlife has successfully revitalized this area. Well mannered dogs are welcome. Dogs must be leashed and cleaned up after at all times. It is up to individual stores whether dogs are allowed inside. There are several eateries with outdoor dining that allow pets at the outer tables.

Stores

Book Etc. Bookstore 38 Exchange Street Portland ME   207-774-0626
http://www.mainebooketc.com
One well behaved dog on lead per person is allowed in the store.
Longfellow Books One Monument Way Portland ME   207-799-2661
From free parking to free doggy biscuits, this book store offers that "bit extra" for their customers and their four-legged companions. Dogs must be well behaved, leashed, and under owner's control at all times.
Petco Pet Store 220 Maine Mall Rd South Portland ME   207-772-9119
Your licensed and well-behaved leashed dog is allowed in the store.

Beaches

East End Beach Cutter Street Portland ME   207-874-8793
Dogs are only allowed on this beach from the day after Labor Day to the day before Memorial Day. Dogs are not allowed on the beach from Memorial Day through Labor Day. During the months that dogs are allowed, they can be off-leash but need to be under direct voice control. People need to make sure they pick up their dog's waste with a plastic bag and throw it away in a trash can.
Old Orchard Cutter Street Portland ME   207-874-8793
Dogs are only allowed on this beach from the day after Labor Day to the day before Memorial Day. Dogs are not allowed on the beach from Memorial Day through Labor Day. During the months that dogs are allowed, they can be off-leash but need to be under direct voice control. People need to make sure they pick up their dog's waste with a plastic bag and throw it away in a trash can.
Willard Beach   South Portland ME   207-767-7601
At Willard Beach there are restrooms, lifeguards, and parking for 75 cars. Dog are allowed on the beach from October 1 through April 30 during all hours. Dogs are not allowed on the beach from 9:00 a.m. to 9:00 p.m. from May 1 through September 30. Dogs must be kept away from bird eggs and out of the dunes. There are dog bag stations at many entrances to the mile long beach. Dogs must be cleaned up after at all times. Dogs must be leashed at all times or off-leash and under excellent voice control within a limited distance of the owner.

Parks

Portland Head Light Park

Portland Head Light Park 1000 Shore Road Cape Elizabeth ME   207-799-266
This park offers 90 acres, spectacular ocean views, picnic facilities, recreation areas, historic structures, plenty of hiking trails, and a lighthouse complex. Dogs are allowed throughout the park; they are not allowed in buildings. Dogs must be under owner's control, leashed, and cleaned up after at all times.
Two Lights State Park 7 Tower Drive Cape Elizabeth ME   207-799-5871
Rocky coastlines, powerful rolling surf, outstanding panoramic Casco Bay and ocean views, and great hiking and picnicking areas have made this 40 acre park a popular destination. Dogs are allowed throughout the park and on the trails; they are not allowed on the beaches. Dogs must be well behaved, on no more than a 4 foot leash, cleaned up after at all times, and never be left unattended.
Mackworth Island Andrews Avenue Falmouth ME   207-624-6076
An area rich in cultural and ghostly lore, this small island is a sanctuary for birds, animals and people with a hundred acres to explore and a 1.25 mile walking trail that takes visitors around the entire island for some great views of harbor activity and bird and marine life. There is also a private walled area to commemorate the 19 Irish Setters who were the "lifelong friends and companions" of the Governor who donated this island. Dogs are welcome here, and they must be leashed and cleaned up after at all times.

Off-Leash Dog Parks
Capisic Pond Park Capisic Street Portland ME   207-874-8793
Dogs can be off-leash in this park but need to be under direct voice control. People need to make sure they pick up their dog's waste with a plastic bag and throw it away in a trash can. There is no fenced off-leash area in the park.
Eastern Promenade Park Off-Leash Area Cutter Street Portland ME   207-874-8793
Dogs are allowed off-leash under direct voice control during certain hours and only within the perimeter bounded by the Portland House Property, the water side of the Eastern Prominade, and Cutter Street following the curve of the parking lot. Fort Allen Park is not part of the off-leash area. Off-leash play is allowed from April 15 to October 15, from 5am to 9am and from 5pm to 10pm daily. From October 16 through April 14, the off-leash hours are from 5am to 10pm daily.
Hall School Woods 23 Orono Road Portland ME   207-874-8793
Dogs can be off-leash in the woods near this school, but need to be under direct voice control. Dogs need to be leashed except for when in this special area. People need to make sure they pick up their dog's waste with a plastic bag and throw it away in a trash can.

Jack School Dog Run North St. and Washington Ave. Portland ME   207-874-8793
Dogs can be off-leash in this area, but need to be under direct voice control. The leash free area is located behind Jack School. Dogs need to be leashed except for when in this special area. People need to make sure they pick up their dog's waste with a plastic bag and throw it away in a trash can.
Pine Grove Park Harpswell Road Portland ME   207-874-8793
Dogs can be off-leash in this park but need to be under direct voice control. People need to make sure they pick up their dog's waste with a plastic bag and throw it away in a trash can.
Portland Arts & Technology School Dog Run 196 Allen Avenue Portland ME   207-874-8793
Dogs can be off-leash in the woods behind this school, but need to be under direct voice control. Dogs need to be leashed except for when in this special area. People need to make sure they pick up their dog's waste with a plastic bag and throw it away in a trash can.
Riverton Park Riverside Street Portland ME   207-874-8793
Dogs can be off-leash in this park but need to be under direct voice control. People need to make sure they pick up their dog's waste with a plastic bag and throw it away in a trash can.
University Park Harvard Street Portland ME   207-874-8793
Dogs can be off-leash in this park but need to be under direct voice control. People need to make sure they pick up their dog's waste with a plastic bag and throw it away in a trash can.
Valley Street Park Valley St. Portland ME   207-874-8793
Dogs can be off-leash in this park but need to be under direct voice control. People need to make sure they pick up their dog's waste with a plastic bag and throw it away in a trash can.

Outdoor Restaurants
O'Naturals 240 US Route 1 Falmouth ME   207-781-8889
http://www.onaturals.com
Located in The Shops at Falmouth Village, this organic and natural food restaurant has a number of outdoor tables where your well-behaved, leashed dog is welcome. There is a pet store next door to the restaurant.
Beals Old Fashioned Ice Cream 12 Moulton St Portland ME   207-828-1335
This homemade ice cream place is located in the Old Port district of Portland. Dogs may accompany you at the outdoor tables.
O'Naturals 83 Exchange St Portland ME   207-321-2050
http://www.onaturals.com
This organic and natural food restaurant has a number of outdoor tables where your well-behaved, leashed dog is welcome.

Rangeley

Campgrounds and RV Parks
Rangeley Lake State Park South Shore Drive Rangeley ME   207-864-3858
Dogs of all sizes are allowed. There are no additional pet fees. Dogs may not be left unattended, and they must be well behaved, leashed at all times, and be cleaned up after. Dogs are allowed on all the trails in the park. This campground is closed during the off-season. The camping and tent areas also allow dogs. There is a dog walk area at the campground. There are no electric or water hookups at the campground.

Parks
Rangeley Lake State Park South Shore Road Rangeley ME   207-864-3858
Located in the scenic western mountains on Rangeley Lake, this 869 acre remote park is popular for a variety of land and water recreational activities. Dogs are allowed for no additional pet fee. Dogs must be well behaved, on no more than a 4 foot leash, cleaned up after at all times, and never be left unattended. Dogs are allowed throughout the park and on the trails; they are not allowed on the beaches.

Outdoor Restaurants
The Gingerbread House 55 Carry Road, Rangeley Lk Oquossoc ME   207-864-3602
This eatery serves breakfast, lunch, and dinner amid beautifully wooded grounds, and in Summer there is a picnic table and benches on the lawn area for guests with dogs. Dogs are allowed at the outer tables. Dogs must be under owner's control, leashed, and cleaned up after at all times.

Richmond

Campgrounds and RV Parks
Augusta/Gardiner KOA 30 Mallard Drive Richmond ME 207-582-5086 (800-562-1496)
http://www.koa.com
Dogs of all sizes are allowed. There are no additional pet fees. There is only one pet friendly cabin available, so early booking would be advised. Dogs must be leashed and cleaned up after. There are some breed restrictions. This RV park is closed during the off-season. The camping and tent areas also allow dogs. There is a dog walk area at the campground. Dogs are allowed in the camping cabins.

Rumford

Accommodations
Linnel Motel 986 Prospect Avenue Rumford ME 207-364-4511 (800-446-9038)
Dogs of all sizes are allowed. There is a $5 per night per room additional pet fee and dogs may not be left unattended. Leash at all times when on the grounds.

Sanford

Accommodations
Super 8 Sanford/Kennebunkport Area 1892 Main St Sanford ME 207-324-8823 (800-800-8000)
Dogs of all sizes are allowed. There is a $15 per night pet fee per pet. Smoking and non-smoking rooms are available for pet rooms.

Campgrounds and RV Parks
Walnut Grove Campground 599 Gore Road Alfred ME 207-324-1207
http://www.walnutgrovecampground.net
Dogs of all sizes are allowed. There are no additional pet fees. Dogs must be leashed and cleaned up after. Visitor pets are not allowed. Dogs must have current rabies records. This RV park is closed during the off-season. Only one dog is allowed per campsite. The camping and tent areas also allow dogs. There is a dog walk area at the campground.

Cross Country Ski Resorts
Harris Farm X-C Ski Center 280 Buzzell Road Dayton ME 207-499-2678
http://www.harrisfarm.com
Dogs are not allowed on cross-country ski trails on the weekends, but are allowed during the weekdays. Pets can be off-leash under direct voice control. This center offers 35 to 40 kilometers of groomed trails and rents both skis and snowshoes.
McDougal Orchards Ski Trails 201 Hanson Ridge Road Springvale ME 207-324-5054
Dogs are not allowed during the weekends but are allowed during the weekdays. This center offers over 17km of groomed beginner to advanced cross-country ski trails. Dogs are allowed on any of the trails during the weekdays and need to be leashed or off-leash under direct voice control. The center rents both skis and snowshoes.

Waterville

Accommodations
Holiday Inn 375 Main Street Waterville ME 207-873-0111 (877-270-6405)
Dogs of all sizes are allowed for no additional fee, and they may not be left alone in the room.

Weld

Campgrounds and RV Parks
Mt Blue State Park 299 Center Hill Road Weld ME   207-585-2347
Dogs of all sizes are allowed. There are no additional pet fees. Dogs may not be left unattended at any time, and they must be leashed and cleaned up after. Dogs are not allowed on Webb Beach, or anywhere on the sand, but they may go up to the tree line at the beach. Dogs are allowed on leash throughout the park, and at the boat launch area for swimming. The camping and tent areas also allow dogs. There is a dog walk area at the campground. There are no electric or water hookups at the campground.

Parks
Mount Blue State Park 299 Center Hill Road Weld ME   207-585-2347
This 5,000+ acre lakeside park is home to a wide variety of natural habitats and wildlife, and it provides many year round recreational activities and some great scenic hiking trails. Dogs are allowed for no additional pet fee. Dogs must be well behaved, on no more than a 4 foot leash, cleaned up after at all times, and never be left unattended. Dogs are allowed throughout the park and on the trails; they are not allowed on the beaches.

York

Accommodations
Enchanted Nights 29 Wentworth Street Kittery ME   207-439-1489
Dogs of all sizes are allowed. There are no additional pet fees. Dogs are not allowed to be left unattended.

Campgrounds and RV Parks
Libby's Oceanside Camp 725 York Street York Harbor ME   207-363-4171
http://www.libbysoceancamping.com
Dogs of all sizes are allowed. There are no additional pet fees. Dogs must be leashed and cleaned up after. Dogs are allowed to go to the beach before 8AM and after 6PM. This RV park is closed during the off-season. The camping and tent areas also allow dogs. There is a dog walk area at the campground.

Shopping Centers
Kittery Premium Outlets 375 H 1 Kittery ME   207-439-6548
www.premiumoutlets.com
This outlet shopping area features 65 stores. Dogs are allowed on the grounds. It is up to the individual stores whether they are allowed inside or not. Dogs must be under owner's control, leashed, and cleaned up after at all times.

Beaches
Long Sands Beach Route 1A York ME   207-363-4422
Leashed dogs are allowed, with certain restrictions. During the summertime, from about Memorial Day weekend through Labor Day weekend, dogs are only allowed on the beach before 8am and after 6pm. During the off-season, dogs are allowed during all park hours. This beach offers a 1.5 mile sandy beach. Metered parking and private lots are available. The beach and bathhouse are also handicap accessible. People are required to clean up after their pets.
Short Sands Beach Route 1A York ME   207-363-4422
Leashed dogs are allowed, with certain restrictions. During the summertime, from about Memorial Day weekend through Labor Day weekend, dogs are only allowed on the beach before 8am and after 6pm. During the off-season, dogs are allowed during all park hours. At the beach, there is a large parking area and a playground. People are required to clean up after their pets.
York Harbor Beach Route 1A York ME   207-363-4422
Leashed dogs are allowed, with certain restrictions. During the summertime, from about Memorial Day weekend through Labor Day weekend, dogs are only allowed on the beach before 8am and after 6pm. During the off-season, dogs are allowed during all park hours. This park offers a sandy beach nestled against a rocky shoreline. There is limited parking. People are required to clean up after their pets.

Chapter 3

New Hampshire
Dog Travel Guide

Bennington

Accommodations
Highland Inn 634 Francestown Rd Bennington NH   603-588-2777
There is a $10 one time pet fee.

Concord

Accommodations
Comfort Inn 71 Hall Street Concord NH   603-226-4100 (877-424-6423)
Dogs are allowed for an additional one time fee of $15 per pet. Dogs may not be left alone in the room.
Red Roof Inn - Loudon 519 SR 106 South Loudon NH   603-225-8399 (800-RED-ROOF)
One well-behaved family pet per room. Guest must notify front desk upon arrival. Guest is liable for any damages. In consideration of all guests, pets must never be left unattended in the guest rooms.

Campgrounds and RV Parks
Bear Brook State Park 157 Deerfield Road Allenstown NH   603-485-9874
With more than 10,000 acres, this is the state's largest developed park offering more than 40 miles of scenic trails, and a wide array of land and water recreation and activities for all ages and interests. Dogs of all sizes are allowed for no additional fee. Dogs must be well behaved, leashed, cleaned up after, and owners are responsible for them at all times. Dogs may not be left unattended in any vehicle, camper, carrier, or enclosure at any time. Dogs are allowed on the trails and in the campground, but not in the day use areas or on the beach. Nestled alone the shore of Beaver Pond, the camp area has 93 reservation only sites (603-271-3628), 2 first come, first served sites, and is located 5 miles from the day use area. There are showers, laundry facilities, and a camp store on site. This RV park is closed during the off-season. The camping and tent areas also allow dogs. There is a dog walk area at the campground. There are no electric or water hookups at the campgrounds.
Circle 9 Ranch 39 Windymere Drive Epsom NH   603-736-9656
http://www.circle9ranch.com
Dogs of all sizes are allowed. There are no additional pet fees. Dogs must be leashed at all times and be cleaned up after. There is a dog walk area at the campground.
Mile-Away Campground 41 Old West Hockington Road Henniker NH   603-428-7616
http://www.mileaway.com
Dogs of all sizes are allowed. There are no additional pet fees. Dogs must be leashed and cleaned up after. This RV park is closed during the off-season. The camping and tent areas also allow dogs. There is a dog walk area at the campground.
Cold Springs RV and Camp Resort 62 Barnard Hill Road Weare NH   603-529-2528
http://www.coldspringscampresort.com
Dogs of all sizes are allowed. There is a $2 per night per pet additional fee. Dogs must be quiet, well behaved, leashed, and cleaned up after. Dogs are not allowed at the beach or pool. Visitor dogs are not allowed. This RV park is closed during the off-season. The camping and tent areas also allow dogs. There is a dog walk area at the campground.

Stores
Charlie's Paw Wash 248 Sheep Davis Road Concord NH   603-225-7297
http://www.charliespawwash.com/
In addition to providing an equipped, professional bathing area for self-serve doggy washes, they also have a training center, boutique, and bakery. Dogs must be under owner's control/care at all times.
Petco Pet Store 35 Fort Eddy Rd Concord NH   603-225-7355
Your licensed and well-behaved leashed dog is allowed in the store.

Parks
Bear Brook State Park 157 Deerfield Road Allenstown NH   603-485-9874
With more than 10,000 acres, this is the state's largest developed park offering more than 40 miles of scenic trails, and a wide array of land and water recreation and activities for all ages and interests. Dogs of all sizes are allowed for no additional fee. Dogs must be well behaved, leashed, cleaned up after, and owners are responsible

for them at all times. Dogs may not be left unattended in any vehicle, camper, carrier, or enclosure at any time. Dogs are allowed on the trails and in the campground, but not in the day use areas or on the beach.
Rollins State Park Kearsarge Mountain Road Warner NH   603-456-3808
There is a scenic auto road from the park entrance that travels 3½ miles through the woodlands to a parking and picnic area in a natural wooded glen setting near the top. From there visitors can take the ½ mile trail to the summit for some more great views. This park is seasonal. Dogs are allowed at this park. Dogs must be well behaved, leashed, cleaned up after, and owners are responsible for them at all times. Dogs may not be left unattended at any time.

Francestown

Accommodations
The Inn at Crotched Mountain 534 Mountain Road Francestown NH   603-588-6840
This 180 year-old colonial house on 65 acres, once a stop for the Underground Railroad, has an amazing view of the Piscatagoug Valley, several hiking or Winter skiing trails, food and flower gardens, an 18 hole golf course, an outdoor pool, and more. Dogs of all sizes are welcome for an additional $5 per night per pet. Dogs must be leashed, cleaned up after, and crated when left alone in the room. This inn closes for the first 3 weeks each April.

Jefferson

Accommodations
Applebrook 110 Meadows Road/H 115A Jefferson NH   603-586-7713 (800-545-6504)
http://www.applebrook.com/
This large Victorian farmhouse is only about a minutes drive away from Santa's Village, which is also open year round. Dogs of all sizes are allowed for a one time additional pet fee of $25 per pet of which 50% is donated to the local humane society. Dogs may only be left alone in the room for short periods and they must be crated. Dogs must be under owner's control/care at all times, and please clean up after your pet.

Campgrounds and RV Parks
Lantern Resort Motel and Campground 571 Presidential H Jefferson NH   603-586-7151
http://www.thelanternresort.com
Dogs of all sizes are allowed. There are no additional pet fees. Dogs must be leashed and cleaned up after. Dogs may be left inside your unit for short periods if they will be quiet and well behaved. Dogs are not allowed at the motel. This RV park is closed during the off-season. The camping and tent areas also allow dogs. There is a dog walk area at the campground.

Keene

Accommodations
Best Western Sovereign Hotel 401 Winchester ST Keene NH   603-357-3038 (800-780-7234)
Dogs are allowed for an additional one time pet fee of $25 per room.
Holiday Inn Express Keene 175 Key Rd. Keene NH   603-352-7616 (877-270-6405)
http://www.keenehi.com
Dogs are allowed in this family style pet-friendly hotel in historic Keene.
Super 8 Keene 3 Ashbrook Rd Keene NH   603-352-9780 (800-800-8000)
Dogs of all sizes are allowed. There is a $20 one time pet fee per visit. Smoking and non-smoking rooms are available for pet rooms.
The Inn at East Hill Farm 460 Monadnock Street Troy NH   603-588-6495 (800-242-6495)
http://www.east-hill-farm.com/
Whether it is a Winter family farm day, a special Caribbean night/dinner, or a special getaway, this inn offers year round events, indoor/outdoor pools, a Winter indoor skating rink, paddle or row boating, and cross-country ski trails. Dogs of all sizes are allowed for an additional $10 per night per pet. Dogs must be quiet and well behaved, and they are not allowed in the dining or public rooms. Dogs must be leashed and cleaned up after at all times.
Chesterfield Inn HCR 10 Box 59 West Chesterfield NH   603-256-3211
http://www.chesterfieldinn.com/

There are no additional pet fees.

Campgrounds and RV Parks

Shir-roy Camping 100 Athol Road Richmond NH 603-239-4768
Dogs of all sizes are allowed. There are no additional pet fees. Dogs may not be left unattended, must be leashed, and cleaned up after. This RV park is closed during the off-season. The camping and tent areas also allow dogs. There is a dog walk area at the campground.
Forest Lake Campground 331 Keene Road Winchester NH 603-239-4267
http://www.ucampnh.com/forestlake
Dogs of all sizes are allowed. There are no additional pet fees. Dogs must be leashed and cleaned up after. There are some breed restrictions. This RV park is closed during the off-season. The camping and tent areas also allow dogs. There is a dog walk area at the campground.

Stores

Petco Pet Store 55-63 Key Rd Keene NH 603-352-7634
Your licensed and well-behaved leashed dog is allowed in the store.

Parks

Rhododendron State Park H 119W Fitzwilliam NH 603-532-8862 (Monadnock St Pk)
There is a trail a little over a half mile long that encircles the 16 acre, fragrant, pink blossomed Rhododendron flower grove, a focal point of this 2,723 acre scenic park, and another trail that winds through forest and wildflowers. Dogs of all sizes are allowed at this park for no additional fee. Dogs must be well behaved, leashed, cleaned up after, and owners are responsible for them at all times. Dogs may not be left unattended at any time.

Outdoor Restaurants

Luca's Mediterranean Café 10 Central Square Keene NH 603-358-3335
http://www.lucascafe.com/
Reflecting the cuisines from North Africa to the Eastern Mediterranean, this eatery offers outdoor dining. Dogs are welcome guests here and receive their own treat and a water bowl, too. Dogs must be under owner's control/care and leashed at all times.

Lake Winnipesaukee Region

Accommodations

The Glynn House Inn 59 Highland Street Ashland NH 603-968-3775 (866-686-4362)
http://www.glynnhouse.com
Pets are allowed in four of the deluxe suites. These have direct access from the room to the gardens. There is a $30 pet fee per visit per dog. There is a $250 fully refundable damage deposit and pets may not be left alone in the room.
Temperance Tavern Old Providence Rd Gilmanton NH 603-267-7349
Owners have a dog and welcome well-trained potty trained dogs only. There is a $5 per day additional pet fee.
Yankee Trail Motel US 3 Holderness NH 603-968-3535 (800-972-1492)
There are no additional pet fees.
The Lake Opechee Inn and Spa 62 Doris Ray Court Laconia NH 603-524-0111 (877-300-5253)
http://www.opecheeinn.com/
This peaceful retreat, on the shores of Lake Opechee, is an historic renovated mill building offering 34 luxury rooms, a steak and seafood restaurant, a conference center, and a full service spa. Dogs of all sizes are allowed for an additional fee of $20 per night per pet. Dogs must be quiet, leashed and cleaned up after, and crated when left alone in the room.

Campgrounds and RV Parks

Jellystone Park 35 Jellystone Park Ashland NH 603-968-9000
http://www.jellystonenh.com
Dogs of all sizes are allowed. There are no additional pet fees. Dogs must have a valid rabies certificate, can not be left unattended, and must be leashed and cleaned up after. This RV park is closed during the off-season. The camping and tent areas also allow dogs. There is a dog walk area at the campground.
Davidson's Countryside Campgrounds 100 Schofield Road Bristol NH 603-744-2403
http://www.worldpath.net/~davcamp/

Dogs of all sizes are allowed. There are no additional pet fees. Dogs must be well behaved, leashed, and cleaned up after. This RV park is closed during the off-season. The camping and tent areas also allow dogs. There is a dog walk area at the campground.

White Mountain National Forest 719 Main Street Laconia NH   603-528-8721
http://www.fs.fed.us/r9/white
Dogs of all sizes are allowed. There are no additional pet fees. Dogs may not be left unattended, and they must be quiet, leashed, and cleaned up after. Dogs are allowed on most trails in the forest. There is a trail map that can be ordered ahead or at seen at the entrances of the park. Since there is private and state owned land, where dogs are not allowed, in the park, they request adherence to the map. There are 22 campgrounds in this national forest. The camping and tent areas also allow dogs. There is a dog walk area at the campground. There are no electric or water hookups at the campground.

Pine Woods Campground 65 Barrett Place Moultonborough NH   603-253-6251
http://www.bearspinewoodscampground.com
Dogs of all sizes are allowed. There are no additional pet fees. Dogs may not be left unattended, must be leashed, and cleaned up after. Dogs are allowed to go to the lake about a 15 minute walk away. This RV park is closed during the off-season. The camping and tent areas also allow dogs. There is a dog walk area at the campground.

Twin Tamarack Family Camping 431 Twin Tamarack Road New Hampton NH   603-279-4387
http://www.ucampnh.com/twintamarack
Dogs of all sizes are allowed. There are no additional pet fees. Dogs may not be left unattended, must be leashed, and cleaned up after. There are some breed restrictions. This RV park is closed during the off-season. The camping and tent areas also allow dogs. There is a dog walk area at the campground.

Attractions
Wet Wolfe Watercraft Rentals 17 Bay Street Wolfeboro NH   603-271-3254
http://www.wolfetrap.com/wetwolfe.html
Dogs are welcome to come aboard these watercraft rentals for no additional pet fee. Dogs must be well mannered, leashed (until on the boat), and cleaned up after at all times. They request visitors with pets bring a blanket or covering of some type to put on the bottom of the boat as it is hard to remove pet hair from the marine type carpet.

Stores
Tanger Outlet Center 120 Laconia Road Tilton NH   603-286-7880
http://www.tangeroutlet.com/
Visitors can buy direct from over 50 brand name manufacturers and designer outlet stores at this open-air mall, and your well behaved dog is welcome to join you exploring the area. It is up to individual stores whether they permit pets inside. Dogs must be under owner's control, be leashed, and cleaned up after at all times.

Lancaster

Campgrounds and RV Parks
Mountain Lake Campground 485 Prospect Street Lancaster NH   603-788-4509
Dogs of all sizes are allowed. There is a $2 per night per pet additional fee, and dogs must have current rabies and shot records. Dogs must be leashed and cleaned up after. There are some breed restrictions. This RV park is closed during the off-season. The camping and tent areas also allow dogs. There is a dog walk area at the campground.

Roger's Campground 10 Roger's Campground Road Lancaster NH   603-788-4885
http://www.rogerscampground.com
Dogs of all sizes are allowed. There are no additional pet fees. Dogs must be leashed and cleaned up after. Dogs are not allowed at the motel or other rentals. This RV park is closed during the off-season. The camping and tent areas also allow dogs. There is a dog walk area at the campground.

Lebanon

Accommodations
Chieftain Motor Inn 84 Lyme Road Hanover NH   603-643-2550
http://www.chieftaininn.com/
Nestled along the banks of the Connecticut River, this scenic inn also offers an outdoor heated pool,

complimentary canoes, barbecue areas, a gazebo, and a variety of land and water recreation. Dogs of all sizes are allowed for an additional fee of $35 per night per pet. Dogs must be quiet, well behaved, leashed, and cleaned up after. Dogs may only be left alone in the room if the owner is confident in their behavior.
Residence Inn by Marriott 32 Centerra Parkway Lebanon NH   603-643-4511
Dogs of all sizes are allowed. There is a $75 one time fee and a pet policy to sign at check in.
Dowds County Inn On the Common, Box 58 Lyme NH   603-795-4712 (800-482-4712)
http://www.dowdscountryinn.com/
This country inn sits on 6 landscaped acres to explore with a natural duck pond, flower gardens, a water fountain, and historic stonework and buildings. Dogs of all sizes are welcome for an additional $10 per night per pet with a credit card on file. Dogs must be well behaved, leashed, and cleaned up after.
Loch Lyme Lodge 70 Orford Road Lyme NH   603-795-2141
Dog of all sizes are allowed. There are no additional pet fees, however you must have up to date vacination information on your dog(s).
Airport Economy Inn 45 Airport Rd West Lebanon NH   603-298-8888
There is a $10 per day pet fee.
Fireside Inn and Suites 25 Airport Road West Lebanon NH   877-258-5900 (877-258-5900)
http://www.afiresideinn.com/
This inn, nestled in the beauty of the River Valley amid numerous educational, cultural, and recreational opportunities, features a garden court atrium, an indoor heated pool and hot tub, and a full breakfast buffet. Dogs must be well behaved, leashed, and cleaned up after. Dogs may not be left alone in the room, and they must be under owner's control/care at all times.

Attractions
Saint-Gaudens National Historic Site 139 Saint-Gaudens Road Cornish NH 603-675-2175
http://www.nps.gov/saga/
Home to one of America's most renowned sculptors with more than 100 of his artworks on display, this park also has 25 acres to explore gardens complete with statuary reminiscent of the gardens of Europe, and nature trails. Dogs are allowed on leash. They must be under owner's control and cleaned up after at all times. Dogs are allowed throughout the grounds and on the trails; they are not allowed in any of the park buildings.

Parks
Cardigan State Park Cardigan Mountain Road Orange NH   603-823-7722, ext. 757
This day use park covers over 5,600 acres and is a favorite among hikers. A mountain road and trails lead to its 3,121 foot summit and a fire tower where visitors can get a 360 degree panoramic view of neighboring states, plus there are plenty of interesting sites along the way. Dogs of all sizes are allowed at this park for no additional fee. Dogs must be well behaved, leashed, cleaned up after, and owners are responsible for them at all times. Dogs may not be left unattended at any time.

Lisbon

Campgrounds and RV Parks
KOA Littleton/Lisbon 2154 Route 302 Lisbon NH   603-838-5525 (800-562-5836)
http://www.littletonkoa.com
Dogs of all sizes are allowed. There are no additional pet fees. Dogs may not be left unattended, must be well behaved, leashed, and cleaned up after. There are some breed restrictions. This RV park is closed during the off-season. The camping and tent areas also allow dogs. There is a dog walk area at the campground.

Manchester

Accommodations
Quality Inn Manchester Airport 121 S River Road/H3 Bedford NH   603-622-3766 (877-424-6423)
Quiet dogs are allowed for an additional pet fee of $25 per room for each 1 to 7 days.
Comfort Inn 298 Queen City Avenue Manchester NH   603-668-2600 (877-424-6423)
Dogs are allowed for an additional fee of $25 per night per pet.
Econo Lodge 75 W Hancock St Manchester NH   603-624-0111
There is a $100 refundable deposit and a $10 per day pet fee.
Holiday Inn Express Hotel and Suites 1298 South Porter St Manchester NH   603-669-6800 (877-270-6405)

Dogs of all sizes are allowed for a $50 refundable pet deposit per room.
Ramada Hotel Manchester 700 Elm Street Manchester NH   603-625-1000
Dogs of all sizes are allowed. There is a $25 one time additional pet fee. Dogs may not be left alone in the rooms unless they are crated.
TownePlace Suites Manchester Airport 686 Huse Road Manchester NH   603-641-2288
Dogs of all sizes are allowed. There is a $75 one time pet fee per visit.

Campgrounds and RV Parks
Friendly Beaver Campground Old Coach Road New Boston NH   603-487-5570
http://www.friendlybeaver.com
Dogs of all sizes are allowed. There are no additional pet fees. Dogs must be leashed, cleaned up after, and brought in after dark. The camping and tent areas also allow dogs. There is a dog walk area at the campground.
Pine Acres Family Campground 74 Freetown Road Raymond NH   603-895-2519
http://www.pineacresrvresort.com
Dogs of all sizes are allowed. There are no additional pet fees. Dogs may not be left unattended, must be leashed and cleaned up after. Dogs are not allowed at the beach or the pavilion This RV park is closed during the off-season. The camping and tent areas also allow dogs. There is a dog walk area at the campground.

Stores
Petco Pet Store 1049 S Willow St Manchester NH   603-666-7387
Your licensed and well-behaved leashed dog is allowed in the store.

Parks
Rockingham Recreation Trail Windham Depot Road Derry NH   603-271-3254
This 18 mile multi-use, easy to moderate trail (with a few sandy spots) is the state's longest rail trail taking visitors through several small towns, past wooded areas, fields, wetlands, and ponds, and connects Derry to Fremont in Rockingham County. Dogs are welcome on this path. They must be under owner's control, leashed, and cleaned up after at all times.

Off-Leash Dog Parks
Town of Derry Dog Park 45 Fordway Derry NH   603-432-6100
This half acre dog park is adjacent to the Derry Animal Control office. To get there from I-93, take exit #4/Route 102 towards Derry(east). Go about 1.5 miles and turn right onto Fordway. Go about 1/2 mile and arrive at the dog park at 45 Fordway.

Nashua

Accommodations
Days Inn Merrimack 242 Daniel Webster Hwy Merrimack NH   603-429-4600 (800-329-7466)
Dogs of all sizes are allowed. There is a $10 per night pet fee per small pet and $25 per large pet.
Residence Inn by Marriott 246 Daniel Webster Highway Merrimack NH   603-424-8100
Dogs of all sizes are allowed. There is a $75 one time fee and a pet policy to sign at check in.
Holiday Inn 9 Northeastern Blvd Nashua NH   603-888-1551 (877-270-6405)
Dogs of all sizes are allowed for an additional one time pet fee of $25 per room.
Motel 6 - Nashua 2 Progress Avenue Nashua NH   603-889-4151 (800-466-8356)
One well-behaved family pet per room. Guest must notify front desk upon arrival. Guest is liable for any damages. In consideration of all guests, pets must never be left unattended in the guest rooms.
Red Roof Inn - Nashua 77 Spitbrook Road Nashua NH   603-888-1893 (800-RED-ROOF)
One well-behaved family pet per room. Guest must notify front desk upon arrival. Guest is liable for any damages. In consideration of all guests, pets must never be left unattended in the guest rooms.

Stores
PetSmart Pet Store 213 Daniel Webster Hwy Nashua NH   603-888-7599
Your licensed and well-behaved leashed dog is allowed in the store.
PetSmart Pet Store 4 Cellu Dr Nashua NH   603-595-6460
Your licensed and well-behaved leashed dog is allowed in the store.
Petco Pet Store 7 East Desilvio Drive Nashua NH   603-897-7387
Your licensed and well-behaved leashed dog is allowed in the store.

Outdoor Restaurants
Michael Timothy's 212 Main Street Nashua NH   603-595-9334
http://www.michaeltimothys.com
Dogs are allowed at the outdoor tables. The restaurant has outdoor tables only in the Summer.

North State Region

Accommodations
Northern Comfort Motel RR 1, Box 520 Colebrook NH   603-237-4440
There is a $5.00 per day pet charge.
The Glen 77 The Glen Rd Pittsburg NH   603-538-6500
Pets are allowed in the cottages only. There are no pet fees. There are no designated smoking or non-smoking cottages.

Orford

Campgrounds and RV Parks
Jacob's Brook 46 Highbridge Road Orford NH   603-353-9210
http://www.jacobsbrookcampground.com
Dogs of all sizes are allowed. There are no additional pet fees. Normally only 2 dogs are allowed per site, but more may be accepted if you let them know in advance. Dogs must be well behaved, leashed, and cleaned up after. This RV park is closed during the off-season. The camping and tent areas also allow dogs. There is a dog walk area at the campground.

Ossipee Lake Region

Accommodations
TOP 200 PLACE **Lazy Dog Inn** 201 White Mountain H/H 16 Chocorua Village NH   603-323-8350 (888-323-8350)
http://www.lazydoginn.com/
This 160 year old New England farmhouse really is a dog friendly place (even the rooms have doggie themed names), and there are plenty of picturesque walking trails close by too. Included in the rates is a fenced in "Doggie Play Area" with agility equipment and a climate controlled Doggie Lodge providing doggie daycare. They also offer a bottomless treat jar for their canine guests and a like jar of cookies for their owners. Dogs must be at least 12 weeks old, and there are no additional pet fees for one dog. There may be an additional fee of $25 per night per pet for 2 pets or more depending on length of stay. Dogs must be friendly and well mannered with humans and the other pets in residence. Dogs must be leashed and cleaned up after.
Tamworth Inn Tamworth Village Tamworth NH   603-323-7721 (800-642-7352)
http://tamworth.com/
Offering 16 rooms and suites all with a private bath, this simple but elegant lodge offers a full country breakfast, an authentic New England Pub, and they are central to various other activities and recreation. Dogs of all sizes are allowed for an additional $15 per night per pet on a space available basis. Dogs must be quiet and well mannered, and they are welcome throughout the inn and grounds, just not in the dining room or breakfast areas. Dogs must be leashed and cleaned up after, and they may only be left alone in the room if they are crated and the owners are on the property.

Campgrounds and RV Parks
Terrace Pines Campground 110 Terrace Pine Center Ossipee NH   603-539-6210
http://www.terracepines.com
Dogs of all sizes are allowed. There are no additional pet fees. Dogs may not be left unattended, must be leashed, and cleaned up after. This RV park is closed during the off-season. The camping and tent areas also allow dogs. There is a dog walk area at the campground. Dogs are allowed in the camping cabins.
Danforth Bay Camping Resort 196 Shawtown Road Freedom NH   603-539-2069

http://www.danforthbay.com
Dogs of all sizes are allowed. There are no additional pet fees. Dogs must have current shot records, and be leashed and cleaned up after. Dogs are not allowed at the pool or beach. There are some breed restrictions. This RV park is closed during the off-season. The camping and tent areas also allow dogs. There is a dog walk area at the campground.
Tamworth Camping 194 Depot Road Tamworth NH   603-323-8031
http://www.tamworthcamping.com/
Dogs of all sizes are allowed. There are no additional pet fees. Dogs must have current rabies and shot records, and be leashed and cleaned up after. There is a river nearby where you can take your pet. This RV park is closed during the off-season. The camping and tent areas also allow dogs. There is a dog walk area at the campground.

Cross Country Ski Resorts

TOP 200 PLACE King Pine Ski Area 1251 Eaton Road East Madison NH   603-367-8896
http://www.xcskinh.com/king_pine.cfm
Dogs are allowed on this year round recreational mountain. In Spring through Fall dogs are allowed on the trails, preferably on lead; however, if the pet is under good voice control, they may be off lead. In Winter they ask that dogs are kept on lead and out of the groomed skate tracks. Dogs must be under owner's control and cleaned up after at all times. Dogs are not allowed at the lodge.

Outdoor Restaurants

Yankee Smokehouse H 16 and H 25W West Ossipee NH   603-539-7427
http://www.yankeesmokehouse.com/
This eatery claims to have the largest open-pit barbecue on their side of the Mason Dixon Line bringing authentic Southern barbecue to this New England area. During the Summer, they offer picnic tables on the lawn out back where you and your pooch can enjoy the fair. Dogs must be under owner's control, leashed, and cleaned up after at all times.

Peterborough

Parks

Miller State Park H 101E Peterborough NH   603-924-3672
This is the state's oldest state park. It is a popular scenic driving/hiking area with great places for picnicking and an operational fire tower at the top of the mountain offers outstanding views. Dogs of all sizes are allowed at this park for no additional fee. Dogs must be well behaved, leashed, cleaned up after, and owners are responsible for them at all times. Dogs may not be left unattended at any time.

Plaistow

Stores

Petco Pet Store 9 Plaistow Rd #125 Plaistow NH   603-382-8600
Your licensed and well-behaved leashed dog is allowed in the store.

Pet Sitters

Calling All Paws Call or Email Plaistow NH   603-475-4810
mailto:callingallpaws@comcast.net
This firm offers pet sitting and dog walking services.

Portsmouth

Accommodations

Hickory Pond Inn & Golf Course 1 Stagecoach Rd Durham NH   603-659-2227
There are several designated pet rooms. All rooms are non-smoking. There is a $10 one time pet fee.
Meadowbrook Inn Portsmouth Traffic Circle Portsmouth NH   603-436-2700 (800-370-2727)

http://www.meadowbrookinn.com/
This inn offers a convenient location for exploring the seacoast and taking advantage of the tax-free shopping. Dogs of all sizes are allowed for an additional $10 per night per pet. Dogs must be leashed, cleaned up after, and they may only be left alone in the room if they will be quiet and well behaved. Dobermans and Rottweilers are not allowed.
Motel 6 - Portsmouth 3 Gosling Road Portsmouth NH   603-334-6606 (800-466-8356)
One well-behaved family pet per room. Guest must notify front desk upon arrival. Guest is liable for any damages. In consideration of all guests, pets must never be left unattended in the guest rooms.
Sheraton Portsmouth Harborside Hotel 250 Market St. Portsmouth NH   603-431-2300 (888-625-5144)
Dogs up to 80 pounds are allowed. There are no additional pet fees. Dogs are not allowed to be left alone in the room.

Campgrounds and RV Parks
Wakeda Campground 294 Exeter Road Hampton Falls NH   603-772-5274
http://www.wakedacampground.com
Dogs of all sizes are allowed. There are no additional pet fees. Dogs may not be left unattended, must be leashed, and cleaned up after. This RV park is closed during the off-season. The camping and tent areas also allow dogs. There is a dog walk area at the campground. Dogs are allowed in the camping cabins.

Attractions

Portsmouth Guided Walking Tours

TOP 200 PLACE **Portsmouth Guided Walking Tours** 500 Market Street Portsmouth NH   603-436-3988
The Chamber of Commerce offers 2 different tours here. The Highlights Tour tells lively and interesting stories relating almost 400 years of history, and the Twilight Tour that tells of its more colorful, bawdy side. Both are outside tours, and your well mannered, quiet pet is welcome to come along. Dogs must be under owner's control, leashed, and cleaned up after at all times.
Granite State Whale Watch PO Box 768 Rye NH   603-964-5545
http://www.granitestatewhalewatch.com/
This whale watch touring company will allow your pet to come on board. They request that your pet has already gotten their "sea-legs", and that it is not a first time trip. There is no additional fee for the dog. Dogs must be under owner's control, leashed, and cleaned up after at all times.

Stores

Tail Waggers Boutique 147 Main Street Newmarket NH   603-659-7077
This pet boutique specializes in pet gifts, clothing, toys, bed, and carriers. They do not carry food items. Dogs must be under owner's control/care and leashed.
Petco Pet Store 1600 Woodbury Avenue Portsmouth NH   603-436-9399
Your licensed and well-behaved leashed dog is allowed in the store.

Parks

Urban Forestry Center 45 Elwyn Road Portsmouth NH   603-431-6774
In the mist of a bustling city, this 182 acre wilderness preserve has much to offer year round; in addition to its marshes, creeks, woodlands, fields, herb garden, and bird observation areas, there are exhibits and educational programs offered at the Forestry Center campus. The real treat here for hikers are the excellent array of easy terrain trails brimming with lush greenery, and self-guided trails like the tree identification trail and the plant/wildlife woodlands trail. Dogs are allowed on leash, and please clean up after your pet.

Off-Leash Dog Parks

Portsmouth Dog Park South Mill Pond Portsmouth NH   603-431-2000
http://www.cityofportsmouth.com
This fenced dog park is located at the South Mill Pond. The South Mill Pond is located near downtown Portsmouth, south of the Pleasant Street and Junkins Avenue intersection. From I-93, take exit #4.

Outdoor Restaurants

Annabelle's Natural Ice Cream 49 Ceres Street Portsmouth NH   603-436-3400
www.annabellesicecream.com
This natural ice creamery offers a take-out window in the Summer where your pooch can order their favorite flavor. Dogs must be well mannered, leashed, and cleaned up after.
Portsmouth (Redhook) Brewery and Cataqua 35 Corporate Drive Portsmouth NH   603-430-8600
www.redhook.com
This brewery offers outside accommodations in the Summer, and your well mannered dog is welcome at the outer tables. Dogs must be under owner's control, leashed, and cleaned up after at all times.

Rindge

Campgrounds and RV Parks

Woodmore Family Campground 21 Woodmore Drive Rindge NH   603-899-3362
http://www.woodmorecampground.com
Dogs of all sizes are allowed. There are no additional pet fees. Dogs must be quiet, well behaved, leashed, and cleaned up after. Dogs may not be left unattended. This RV park is closed during the off-season. The camping and tent areas also allow dogs. There is a dog walk area at the campground. Dogs are allowed in the camping cabins.

Rochester

Accommodations

Days Inn Downtown Dover 481 Central Ave Dover NH   603-742-0400 (800-329-7466)
Dogs of all sizes are allowed. There is a $50 returnable deposit required per room.
Anchorage Inn 80 Main St Rochester NH   603-332-3350
There is a $10 per day additional pet fee.

Campgrounds and RV Parks

Mi-te-jo Campground 111 Mi-te-jo Road Milton NH   603-652-9022
http://www.mi-te-jo.com
Dogs of all sizes are allowed. There are no additional pet fees. Dogs may not be left unattended, must be leashed, and cleaned up after. Dogs are not allowed on the ball field, the playground, or the beach. This RV park is closed during the off-season. The camping and tent areas also allow dogs. There is a dog walk area at the campground.

Outdoor Restaurants
Susty's 159 1st New Hampshire Turnpike Northwood NH   603-942-5862
Dogs are allowed at the outdoor tables. The restaurant has outdoor tables only in the Summer.

Salem

Accommodations
Holiday Inn 1 Keewaydin Drive Salem NH   603-893-5511 (877-270-6405)
Dogs of all sizes are allowed for an additional fee per room of $25 (plus tax) for 1 to 3 nights; 4 to 14 nights is $50 (plus tax).
Red Roof Inn - Salem, NH 15 Red Roof Lane Salem NH   603-898-6422 (800-RED-ROOF)
One well-behaved family pet per room. Guest must notify front desk upon arrival. Guest is liable for any damages. In consideration of all guests, pets must never be left unattended in the guest rooms.

Stores
PetSmart Pet Store 290 S Broadway Salem NH   603-898-8232
Your licensed and well behaved leashed dog is allowed in the store.
Petco Pet Store 92 Cluff Crossing Rd Salem NH   603-890-6922
Your licensed and well-behaved leashed dog is allowed in the store.

Sunapee Region

Accommodations
Mountain Lake Inn 2871 Route 114 Bradford NH   603-938-2136 (800-662-6005)
http://www.mountainlakeinn.com/
This 1760 dwelling sits on 168 acres along the shores of Lake Massasecum and offers 9 guest rooms with private baths, walking trails, and a private beach equipped with a canoe and rowboat. Dogs of all sizes are welcome for an additional $25 one time pet fee per room. Dogs must be well behaved, leashed (at times), and cleaned up after. Dogs must be friendly and very well mannered with children and the other pets in residence.
Claremont Motor Lodge Beauregard St, near SR 103 Claremont NH   603-542-2540
There are no additional pet fees.
Best Western Sunapee Lake Lodge 1403 Route 103 Mount Sunapee NH   603-763-2010 (800-780-7234)
Dogs are allowed for an additional pet fee of $10 per night per room.

Campgrounds and RV Parks
Mt. Sunapee State Park Off Route 103 between Newbury and Goshen Newbury NH   603-763-5561
This beautiful lakeside park features wooded, natural settings and is a major year round recreation destination for a number of activities. Dogs of all sizes are allowed for no additional fee. They must be well behaved, leashed, cleaned up after, and owners are responsible for them at all times. Dogs may not be left unattended in any vehicle, camper, carrier, or enclosure at any time. Pets are permitted at the campground and throughout the park (except during the Arts/Crafts festival), but not in picnic areas, at the beach, or the ski area during the ski operating season. The campground has 5 refurbished lean-to sites available by reservation (603-271-3628) with more lean-to sites in development. There are pit toilets and water on site, and flush toilets and showers are at the State Beach a mile away. This RV park is closed during the off-season. There is a dog walk area at the campground. There are no electric or water hookups at the campgrounds.
Crow's Nest Campground 529 S Main Street Newport NH   603-863-6170
http://www.crowsnestcampground.com/
A location along a scenic river, 120 grassy, wooded, or riverfront sites, a store, laundry, rec hall, and all the amenities for a great camping experience, have made this park a popular camping and recreation destination. Dogs of all sizes are allowed for no additional pet fee. Dogs may not be left unattended, and they must be leashed and cleaned up after at all times. Dogs must be quiet, well behaved, and have proof of current rabies inoculation. The camping and tent areas also allow dogs. There is a dog walk area at the campground.
Pillsbury State Park Clemac Trail/Pillsbury State Park Road Washington NH   603-863-2860
Ponds, wetlands, woods, a diversity of habitats, a network of multi-use trails that also connect up with the 51 mile Mt. Monadnock/Mt. Sunapee Trail, historic niches, and a bit of seclusion make this a popular exploring area. Dogs of all sizes are allowed for no additional fee. Dogs must be well behaved, leashed, cleaned up after, and owners are responsible for them at all times. Dogs may not be left unattended in any vehicle, camper, carrier, or

enclosure at any time. Dogs are allowed on the trails and in the campground, but not in picnic areas or on the beach. The camp area has 34 sites by reservation only (603-271-3628), 7 first come, first served sites, and there are pit toilets, water, a playground, and firewood available. The camping permits here may also be used at the Sunapee State Park for free day use. This RV park is closed during the off-season. The camping and tent areas also allow dogs. There is a dog walk area at the campground. There are no electric or water hookups at the campgrounds.

Vacation Home Rentals
Sunapee Harbor Cottages (Lake Station Realty 1066 H 103 Newbury NH   603-763-3033 (800-639-9960)
http://www.cottagesrus.com/
This multi-listing company has about a dozen of their vacation rentals in the Lake Sunapee area that allow pets and the prices and policies vary per rental. Dogs must be under owner's control/care at all times, and they may not be left unattended in the rentals.

Cross Country Ski Resorts
Norsk Cross Country Ski 100 Country Club Lane New London NH   603-526-4685
http://www.skinorsk.com/
This ski center has about 8km of groomed trails that are open to dogs. Dogs must be leashed at all times. Skijoring is allowed on the dog trails. The dog trails are North Flats, Partridge, Kellom, Sonya, Deer and Moose. Only use trails that have a "Dog Trail" sign. Other dogs rules include the following; dogs are not allowed in the shop, only bring a well-behaved and trained dog, one dog per person at a time, a collar and tags need to be on your dog, dogs must be leashed and under your control at all times, keep your dog on a short leash within three feet of you when on the trail, in the parking lot and at the trailheads, have a proof of current rabies vaccine such as a tag or paperwork, and be sure to clean up after your dog. The ski center is located about 1.5 hours from Boston.

Parks
Mt. Sunapee State Park Off Route 103 between Newbury and Goshen Newbury NH   603-763-5561
This beautiful lakeside park features wooded, natural settings and is a major year round recreation destination for a number of activities. Dogs of all sizes are allowed for no additional fee. They must be well behaved, leashed, cleaned up after, and owners are responsible for them at all times. Dogs may not be left unattended in any vehicle, camper, carrier, or enclosure at any time. Pets are permitted at the campground and throughout the park (except during the Arts/Crafts festival), but not in picnic areas, at the beach, or the ski area during the ski operating season.
Pillsbury State Park Clemac Trail/Pillsbury State Park Road Washington NH   603-863-2860
Ponds, wetlands, woods, a diversity of habitats, a network of multi-use trails that also connect up with the 51 mile Mt. Monadnock/Mt. Sunapee Trail, historic niches, and a bit of seclusion make this a popular exploring area. Dogs of all sizes are allowed for no additional fee. Dogs must be well behaved, leashed, cleaned up after, and owners are responsible for them at all times. Dogs may not be left unattended in any vehicle, camper, carrier, or enclosure at any time. Dogs are allowed on the trails and in the campground, but not in picnic areas or on the beach.

Outdoor Restaurants
Jack's of New London 207 Main Street New London NH   603-526-8003
http://www.jackscoffee.com/
This restaurant features an eclectic variety of foods and wines with indoor or outdoor dining options. Dogs are permitted at the outdoor tables. Dogs must be well behaved, under owner's control, and leashed and cleaned up after at all times.

Weirs Beach

Vacation Home Rentals
Victorian Cottage #30 Veterans Ave Weirs Beach NH   603-279-4583
mailto:captstus@verizon.net
Remodeled antique home located at Weirs Beach, NH. Spectacular view of Lake Winnipesaukee and surrounding mountains from the house and porch. 3 bedrooms/sleeps 6. Pets are welcome to join you.

White Mtns - H-16 Corridor

Accommodations

Foothills Farm P. O. Box 1368 Conway NH   207-935-3799
www.foothillsfarmbedandbreakfast.com
This restored 1820 farmhouse and guest cottage sits on 50 acres of fields, forests, and streams, has close proximity to several other recreational activities and tax free shopping, and much of the food served here comes straight from their on-site organic garden. Dogs of all sizes are allowed for an additional $15 per night per pet. Dogs are usually preferred in the 2-bedroom cottage, but sometimes there may be availability in the main house. Dogs must be leashed and cleaned up after, and crated when left alone in the room.

Tanglewood Motel and Cottages 1681 H 16 Conway NH   603-447-5932 (866-TANGLEWOOD(826-4539))
http://www.tanglewoodmotel.com/
This family recreational destination sits alongside a beautiful mountain stream and offers guests a variety of activity areas, 2 central picnic spots with barbecues, and plenty of hiking trails are close by. Dogs are welcome in the cottages for an additional fee of $10 per night per pet. Dogs must be friendly, well mannered, and leashed and cleaned up after at all times.

Swiss Chalets Village Inn Old Route 16A Intervale NH   603-356-2232 (800-831-2727)
http://www.swisschaletsvillage.com
Swiss Chalets Village Inn offers comfortable lodgings, some with fireplace Jacuzzi suites, plenty of indoor and outdoor activities, and a bit of Swiss charm right in the midst of New Hampshire's White Mountains. Pets are welcome.

Dana Place Inn SR 16 Jackson NH   603-383-6822 (800-537-9276)
http://www.danaplace.com/
There are no additional pet fees.

The Village House PO Box 359 Rt 16A Jackson NH   603-383-6666 (800-972-8343)
http://www.yellowsnowdoggear.com/
This bed and breakfast's rooms are located in a 100 year old barn behind the main house that houses the Yellow Snow Dog Gear collar and lead business. Rooms have kitchenettes, balconies, Jacuzzi tubs, and are decorated in the style of a B&B. There are 15 guest rooms and 13 have private baths. They welcome all well-behaved dogs and there are no size restrictions. Rates range from $65-140 depending on the season. There is a $10 per day pet fee.

TOP 200 PLACE **Adventure Suites** 3440 White Mountain H/H16 North Conway NH   603-356-9744 (800-N.CONWAY (606-6929))
http://www.adventuresuites.com/
This inn with various themed rooms offers 16 suites with a variety of adventures from a tree house setting to a unique 2 story cave dwelling, from the penthouse to the jungle, and more, and each suite has a Jacuzzi. Dogs of all sizes are welcome for an additional $10 per night per pet, and when you reserve ahead of time there is a special treat waiting in the room for them. Dogs must be at least 1 year old, quiet, and very well behaved as there are other animals on site. Dogs must be leashed and cleaned up after at all times, and dog depots are provided. Dogs may not be left alone in the room at any time.

Best Western Red Jacket Mountain View Resort & Conf. Ctr. Route 16 North Conway NH   603-356-5411 (800-780-7234)
Dogs are allowed for an additional fee of $25 per night per pet.

Spruce Moose Lodge and Cottages 207 Seavey Street North Conway NH   603-356-6239 (800-600-6239)
http://sprucemooselodge.com/
This inn, located in the scenic Mount Washington Valley, offers both lodge and cottage accommodations and they are only a short 5 minute walk to the village. Dogs of all sizes are welcome in the cottages and in one of the lodge rooms (breakfast is not included for cottage stays) for an additional pet fee of $10 per night per pet and there may be a $100 cash refundable security deposit required. Dogs must be quiet, well behaved, leashed, and cleaned up after. Dogs may not be left alone in the lodge guest room at any time, but they may be left for a short time in the cottages if the owner is confident in the pet's behavior.

Campgrounds and RV Parks

Jigger Johnson Campground Kancamagus Highway Conway NH   603-528-8721 (877-444-6777)
Located in the White Mountain National Forest, this camp area offers 76 sites on a first-come, first-served basis, picnic tables, coin-op showers, and flush toilets. Dogs of all sizes are allowed for no additional pet fee. Dogs must be well behaved, under owner's control, leashed, and cleaned up after at all times. This RV park is closed during the off-season. The camping and tent areas also allow dogs. There is a dog walk area at the campground. There are no electric or water hookups at the campgrounds.

Dolly Copp Family and Barns Field Group Campground H 16 Gorham NH   603-528-8721 (877-444-6777)
Located in the White Mountain National Forest, this camp area offers 176 sites (69 are on a first-come, first-served basis), picnic tables, and flush toilets. Dogs of all sizes are allowed for no additional pet fee. Dogs must be well behaved, under owner's control, leashed, and cleaned up after at all times. This RV park is closed during

the off-season. The camping and tent areas also allow dogs. There is a dog walk area at the campground. There are no electric or water hookups at the campgrounds.

Moose Brook State Park Jimtown Road Gorham NH   603-466-3860

Located in an area of unsurpassed scenery, this park offers many trails, fishing from the brook that flows through the park, and a variety of other recreational opportunities. The season for the day use area is from about the end of June to about the first week in September from 10 am to 5pm. Dogs of all sizes are allowed for no additional fee. Dogs must be well behaved, leashed, cleaned up after, and owners are responsible for them at all times. Dogs may not be left unattended in any vehicle, camper, carrier, or enclosure at any time. Dogs are allowed on the trails and at the campground; they are not allowed on any beaches or picnic areas. The 59 site campground includes 6 first come, first served sites, and the rest are available by reservation only. There are a variety of camp sites with restrooms, showers, and a camp store close by. The number for campground reservations is 603-271-3628. This RV park is closed during the off-season. The camping and tent areas also allow dogs. There is a dog walk area at the campground. There are no electric or water hookups at the campgrounds.

Beach Camping Area 776 White Mountain H North Conway NH   603-447-2723

http://www.ucampnh.com/thebeach

Dogs of all sizes are allowed. There is a $2 per night per pet additional fee. Dogs may not be left unattended, must be leashed, and cleaned up after. Dogs are not allowed at the river. This RV park is closed during the off-season. The camping and tent areas also allow dogs. There is a dog walk area at the campground.

Saco River Camping 1550 White Mountain H North Conway NH   603-356-3360

http://www.sacorivercampingarea.com

Dogs of all sizes are allowed. There is a $2 per night per pet additional fee. Dogs may not be left unattended, and must be leashed and cleaned up after. Dogs are not allowed at the beach or pool, the playground, or the office. There are some breed restrictions. This RV park is closed during the off-season. The camping and tent areas also allow dogs. There is a dog walk area at the campground.

Timberland Camping Area 809 H 2 Shelburne NH   603-466-3872

http://www.ucampnh.com/timberland

Dogs of all sizes are allowed. There are no additional pet fees. Dogs must be leashed and cleaned up after. There are some breed restrictions. The camping and tent areas also allow dogs. There is a dog walk area at the campground.

Attractions

Saco Bound Canoe Rental 2561 E Main Street Center Conway NH   603-356-5251

This is a seasonal attraction, and friendly, leashed dogs are allowed to canoe with their owner.

TOP 200 PLACE **Mount Washinton Auto Road** Mount Washinton Auto Road Gorham NH   603-466-3988

http://www.mountwashingtonautoroad.com

Even though self-guided tours are not available in the Winter, the ever-changing weather conditions and outstanding views of this drive to New England's tallest peak is an adventure in and of itself. Due to the climb, there are some automobile make/model restrictions, and there may be times they need to close the road due to weather, so it is a good idea to check ahead. The fee for 1 driver and the car is $20; $7 for each additional adult; $5 for children 5-12, and pets are free. Dogs must be on a leash at all times when out of the vehicle, and they are not allowed in any park buildings or on any guided tours. Please clean up after your pet.

Hartmann Model Railroad Museum 15 Town Hall Road/H 16 Intervale NH   603-356-9922

http://www.hartmannrr.com/

There are a variety of sizes (G to Z scales) and in depth miniature train layouts on display at this fun museum. Well trained/behaved dogs are allowed. Dogs must be under owner's control, leashed, and cleaned up after at all times.

Cross Country Ski Resorts

TOP 200 PLACE **Bear Notch Ski Touring Center** Route 302 Bartlett NH   603-374-2277

http://www.bearnotchski.com

This dog-friendly rental center allows dogs on most of their cross-country ski trails. They have 40 to 65 kilometers of groomed trails. Dogs can be off-leash but need to be under voice control. You need to carry a leash with you just in case. The center rents skis, snowshoes and sleds.

Great Glen Trails Outdoor Center 705 Route 16 Gorham NH   603-466-2333

http://www.greatglentrails.com

This rental center allows dogs on one of their trails. The Dog Loop is about 5km. When they have enough snow, it is used as a cross-country ski trail. When there is not enough snow it is used as a snowshoe trail. Dogs need to be leashed when the trail is open for cross-country skiing but can be off-leash under voice control when the trail is being used for snowshoeing. The center rents both skis and snowshoes.

Mt Washington Valley Ski Area 279 H 16-302 Intervale NH   603-356-9920

http://www.crosscountryskinh.com/

This year round recreational mountain offers a variety of activities and numerous trails of varying difficulty. In Winter, dogs are allowed on the trails in Whitaker Woods in the Village of North Conway only. Dogs must be under owners control/care, leashed, and cleaned up after at all times.

Jackson Ski Touring Center 153 Main Street Jackson NH 603-383-9355
http://www.jacksonxc.org
This Nordic center allows dogs on some of their cross-country ski trails. Their web site says they have 5 km of trails for dogs but when we called they only mentioned a small .4 km trail. Availability of trails could possibly be based on snow conditions, so be sure to call before you go. The dog trails are sometimes groomed and pets need to be leashed.

Stores

Four Your Paws Only 2506 Main Street/H 16 N Conway NH 800-327-5957
http://fouryourpawsonly.com/index.html
In addition to providing a wide variety of pet supplies/gifts, breed-specific items, care products, clothing items, and fresh bakery items, this store also offers a number of other special services and special events. Dogs must be current on vaccines, be leashed, and under owner's control/care at all times.

Parks

Moose Brook State Park Jimtown Road Gorham NH 603-466-3860
Located in an area of unsurpassed scenery, this park offers many trails, fishing from the brook that flows through the park, and a variety of other recreational opportunities. The season for the day use area is from about the end of June to about the first week in September from 10 am to 5pm. Dogs of all sizes are allowed for no additional fee. Dogs must be well behaved, leashed, cleaned up after, and owners are responsible for them at all times. Dogs may not be left unattended in any vehicle, camper, carrier, or enclosure at any time. Dogs are allowed on the trails and at the campground; they are not allowed on any beaches or picnic areas.

Outdoor Restaurants

Primo's Cafe 2633 White Mountain Highway North Conway NH 603-356-0078
This restaurant serves deli-type food. Dogs are allowed at the outdoor tables.

White Mtns - I-93 Corridor

Accommodations

Bretton Arms Country Inn Route 302 Bretton Woods NH 603-278-3000 (800-258-0330)
This inn is located less than a five minute walk from the Mount Washington Hotel. Well-behaved dogs of any size are allowed for an extra $30 per dog per day pet fee, up to two dogs per room. During the Winter the Nordic center at the Mount Washington Hotel allows dogs on a special 8km cross-country ski trail. Dogs need to be leashed on the property and on the trail.

Best Western White Mountain Resort 87 Wallace Hill Road Franconia NH 603-823-7422 (800-780-7234)
Dogs are allowed for an additional fee of $15 per night per pet.

Horse & Hound 205 Wells Rd Franconia NH 603-823-5501 (800-450-5501)
There are no designated smoking or non-smoking rooms. There is an $8.50 per day additional pet fee.

Lovetts Inn by Lafayette Brook SR 18 Franconia NH 603-823-7761
There are two pet rooms, both non-smoking. There is a $10 one time additional pet fee.

Westwind Vacation Cottages 1614 Profile Road Franconia NH 603-823-5532
Dogs of all sizes are allowed. There is a pet policy to sign at check in and there are no additional pet fees.

Comfort Inn and Suites 21 Railroad Street Lincoln NH 603-745-6700 (877-424-6423)
Dogs are allowed for an additional fee of $15 per night per pet.

The Beal House Inn 2 W Main Street Littleton NH 603-444-2661 (888-616-BEAL(2325))
http://www.bealhouseinn.com/
Offering fine dining, lodging, and a full bar specializing in martinis (over 250), this inn holds special events throughout the year, and they are central to numerous year round activities and recreation. Dogs of all sizes are welcome for an additional $25 to $35 per night per pet depending on the room/suite, and there may be a $150 refundable deposit. One of the suites has a fenced private yard. Dogs must be leashed, cleaned up after, and they must be crated when left alone in the room.

The Common Man Inn 231 Main Street Plymouth NH 603-536-2200 (866-THE.C.MAN (843-2626))
http://www.thecmaninn.com/
This inn is also home to the Foster's Boiler Room Lounge offering a pub-style menu and unique creations, a full service spa with many amenities including a heated waterfall Jacuzzi, and a great location to several other attractions in the area. Dogs of all sizes are welcome for no additional pet fee. Your pooch is greeted with a personalized treat with food bowls, and pet friendly rooms also provide cushy pet beds. Dogs must be leashed, cleaned up after, and crated if left alone in the room. They also provide a designated pet walking area, and a

separate pet entrance.

TOP 200 PLACE **The Hilltop Inn** 9 Norton Lane Sugar Hill NH   603-823-5695 (800-770-5695)
http://www.hilltopinn.com/
This 1895 traditional country inn sits on 50 acres in the White Mountains with an impressive array of relaxing and recreational pursuits. There are 20 acres of ungroomed cross-country skiing here and your pooch is welcome to join you on them. They also have a large fenced in yard for pets to run free. Dogs of all sizes are welcome for an additional pet fee of $10 per night per room. They ask that you clean up after your pet if they do their business on the lawns, but it's not necessary in the fields. Dogs must be well behaved and friendly towards the other pets in residence. Dogs only need to be on lead around the house or when felt necessary by the owner, and they may only be left alone in the room if they will be quiet and the front desk is informed.

Johnson Motel and Cottages 364 H 3 Twin Mountain NH   888-244-5561 (888-244-5561)
http://www.johnsonsmotel.com/
Located in the White Mountains where there are year round activities, this motel also include a picnic, playground, and campfire area, in addition to a nature trail leading to a pond frequented by numerous birds and wildlife. They also have direct trail access for skiers and snowmobilers. Dogs of all sizes are allowed for an additional fee of $10 per night per pet, and special treats are provided for their four-legged guests. Aggressive dogs are not allowed, and barkers must stay with their owners at all times. They must be friendly to humans and to the other 2 dogs on site. Dogs must be well behaved, leashed, and cleaned up after. Dogs may only be left alone in the room if the owner is confident in the pet's behavior.

Campgrounds and RV Parks

Russell Pond Campground Tripoli Road Campton NH   603-528-8721 (877-444-6777)
Located in the White Mountain National Forest, this camp area offers 86 first-come, first-served sites with flush toilets, coin-op showers, and sinks with hot water. Dogs of all sizes are allowed for no additional pet fee. Dogs must be well behaved, under owner's control, leashed, and cleaned up after at all times. This RV park is closed during the off-season. The camping and tent areas also allow dogs. There is a dog walk area at the campground. There are no electric or water hookups at the campgrounds.

Fransted Family Campground 974 Profile Road Franconia NH   603-823-5675
http://www.franstedcampground.com
Dogs of all sizes are allowed. There are no additional pet fees. Dogs may not be left unattended, must be leashed, and cleaned up after. There are some breed restrictions. This RV park is closed during the off-season. Only one dog is allowed per campsite. The camping and tent areas also allow dogs. There is a dog walk area at the campground.

Handcock Campground Kancamagus Highway Lincoln NH   603-528-8721 (877-444-6777)
Located in the White Mountain National Forest, this camp area offers 56 sites, and in Summer sites are on a first-come, first-served basis. Winter reservations are accepted from December 5th to April 15th, and they plow here in the Winter. They offer picnic tables, vault and flush toilets, and a variety of land and water recreation. Dogs of all sizes are allowed for no additional pet fee. Dogs must be well behaved, under owner's control, leashed, and cleaned up after at all times. The camping and tent areas also allow dogs. There is a dog walk area at the campground. There are no electric or water hookups at the campgrounds.

Crazy Horse Campground 788 Hiltop Road Littleton NH   603-444-2204
http://www.ucampnh.com/crazyhorse
Dogs of all sizes are allowed. There are no additional pet fees. Dogs must have current rabies records, be leashed, and cleaned up after. The camping and tent areas also allow dogs. There is a dog walk area at the campground.

KOA Twin Mountain 372 H 115 Twin Mountain NH   603-846-5559 (800-562-9117)
http://www.twinmtnkoa.com
Dogs of all sizes are allowed. There are no additional pet fees. Dogs must be leashed and cleaned up after. This RV park is closed during the off-season. The camping and tent areas also allow dogs. There is a dog walk area at the campground.

KOA Woodstock 1001 Eastside Road Woodstock NH   603-745-8008 (800-562-9736)
http://www.koa.com
Dogs of all sizes are allowed. There are no additional pet fees. Dogs must be leashed and cleaned up after. This RV park is closed during the off-season. The camping and tent areas also allow dogs. There is a dog walk area at the campground. Dogs are allowed in the camping cabins.

Vacation Home Rentals

Franconia Notch Vacations Call or email to Arrange. Franconia NH   800-247-5536
http://www.franconiares.com/
Vacation rentals in Franconia and the surrounding White Mountains. Some dog-friendly rentals are available.

Cross Country Ski Resorts

Bretton Woods Mountain Resort Route 302 Bretton Woods NH 603-278-1000
http://www.brettonwoods.com
Dogs are allowed on one cross-country ski trail. It is called the Honeymoon Trail which is about an 8km groomed round trip trail. Dogs should be leashed on the resort property and on the trail. This resort has a Nordic center which rents skis and snowshoes. If you are looking for a place to stay, the Bretton Arms Country Inn allows well-behaved dogs for an extra charge. The inn is less than a five minute walk from the Mount Washington Hotel and the ski rental center.

Loon Mountain Ski Resort 60 Loon Mountain Road Lincoln NH 603-745-81111
http://www.skinh.com/loon_mountain.cfm
This Winter sports Mecca was rated one of the top ten ski areas in the east by readers of a popular ski magazine. Dogs are allowed on the West side of the mountain only on the beginner's trail that follows along the river. Dogs are not allowed on the east side of the mountain. Dogs must be under owner's control/care at all times, and please clean up after your pet along the trails.

Stores

Village Book Store 81 Main Street Littleton NH 603-444-5263
http://www.booksmusictoys.com/
For more than 30 years this store has been providing visitors with entertaining, educational toys and games, music, and books for all ages. Your well behaved, house-trained dog is welcome to join you in the store. Dogs must be leashed and under owner's control/care at all times.

Woodsville

Accommodations

All Seasons Motel 36 Smith St Woodsville NH 603-747-2157 (800-660-0644)
http://www.quikpage.com/A/allseamotel/
There is a $6 per day pet fee. Dogs must not be left alone in the rooms.

Chapter 4

Vermont
Dog Travel Guide

Ascutney

Campgrounds and RV Parks

Wilgus State Park On H 5 Ascutney VT   802-674-5422 (888-409-7579)
http://www.vtstateparks.com
Dogs of all sizes are allowed. There are no additional pet fees. Dogs may not be left unattended, and they must be leashed and cleaned up after. Dogs are not allowed on the beach, the picnic areas, the day use area, and they must have proof of rabies shots. This campground is closed during the off-season. The camping and tent areas also allow dogs. There is a dog walk area at the campground.

Ascutney State Park 1826 Back Mountain Road Windsor VT   802-674-2060
http://www.vtstateparks.com
Dogs of all sizes are allowed. There are no additional pet fees. Dogs may not be left unattended at any time, they must be on no more than a 10 foot leash, and be cleaned up after. Dogs are not allowed in any day use areas, including parking lots, picnic areas, beach and swim areas, playgrounds, or buildings. Dogs must be at least 6 months old and have a current rabies certificate and shot records. Dogs on leash are allowed on the trails. The camping and tent areas also allow dogs. There is a dog walk area at the campground. There are no electric or water hookups at the campground.

Bellows Falls

Accommodations

Everyday Inn 593 Rockingham Road Bellows Falls VT   802-463-4536
http://www.everydayinn.com/
Although they are central to many other activities, recreation, and ski areas, each season brings its own beauty to this inn that sits on 7 acres of lawns and woods along the Connecticut River. Dogs of all sizes are allowed for an additional fee of $10 (plus tax) per night per pet. Dogs must be well behaved, leashed, and cleaned up after.

Bennington

Accommodations

Knotty Pine Motel 130 Northside Drive Bennington VT   802-442-5487
Dogs of all sizes are allowed. There are no additional pet fees. Dogs may not be left unattended at any time and they are not allowed on the bed and furniture.

South Gate Motel US 7S Bennington VT   802-447-7525
There is a $6 per day pet fee.

The Vermonter Motor Lodge 2968 West Road Bennington VT 802-442-2529
http://www.thevermontermotorlodge.com
This motor lodge offers one or two bed rooms. There is a $10 per night additional pet fee per pet.

Campgrounds and RV Parks

Greenwood Lodge and Campsites 311 Greenwood Drive Bennington VT   802-442-2547
http://www.campvermont.com/greenwood
Dogs of all sizes are allowed. There are no additional pet fees. Dogs must have their shot records and they may not be left unattended. Dogs must be quiet, leashed and cleaned up after. They are allowed to swim in the lake and be off lead at that time if the owner has voice control, but they may not swim in any of the ponds. This RV park is closed during the off-season. The camping and tent areas also allow dogs. There is a dog walk area at the campground.

Woodford State Park 142 State Park Road Bennington VT   802-447-7169 (888-409-7579)
You'll get great views here; the state's highest park at 2,400 feet sits amid plush vegetation, trees, and bodies of water with 398 recreational acres and plenty of hiking trails. Dogs of all sizes are allowed for no additional pet fee, and they must be declared at the time of reservation. All dogs must have proof of rabies inoculation, be on no more than a 10 foot leash or crated, and cleaned up after at all times. Dogs must be quiet, well behaved, and never left unattended. Dogs are not allowed at beaches, picnic areas, or playgrounds; they are allowed on the

trails and camping areas. The camp area offers 103 sites (including 20 lean-tos), flush toilets, hot showers ($), and a dump station. This RV park is closed during the off-season. The camping and tent areas also allow dogs. There is a dog walk area at the campground. There are no electric or water hookups at the campgrounds.

Green Mountain National Forest On H 7N Rutland VT   802-747-6700
http://www.vtstateparks.com
Dogs of all sizes are allowed. There are no additional pet fees. Dogs may not be left unattended, and they must be well behaved, leashed, and cleaned up after. Dogs are not allowed in the picnic or pond areas. Dogs on lead are allowed on all the trails. There are 7 campgrounds in this national forest, 2 remain open all year. The camping and tent areas also allow dogs. There is a dog walk area at the campground. There are no electric or water hookups at the campground.

Attractions

Apple Barn and Country Bake Shop 604 H 7S Bennington VT   802-447-7780
http://www.theapplebarn.com/
This farm offers 30 varieties of apples plus berries, fruits, maple syrup, homemade specialty products, signature bakery items, picnic areas, and special events throughout the year. Dogs are allowed on the grounds; they are not allowed in the store. Dogs must be under owner's control, leashed, and cleaned up after at all times.

TOP 200 PLACE Bennington Battle Monument 15 Monument Circle Bennington VT   802-447-0550
This monument pays tribute to a significant 1777 battle with interpretive exhibits, dioramas, statuary, and interpreters who will take visitors to the top of the 1891. You can ride to the top of the 306 foot stone obelisk via an elevator to a view from where three states are visible. They are open 9am to 5pm, 7 days a week from mid-April to October 31st. Pooches who are not elevator shy have been known to go up also as long as no one is allergic; they are allowed throughout the grounds. Dogs must be leashed and cleaned up after at all times.

Parks

Woodford State Park 142 State Park Road Bennington VT   802-447-7169 (888-409-7579)
You'll get great views here; the state's highest park at 2,400 feet sits amid plush vegetation, trees, and bodies of water with 398 recreational acres and plenty of hiking trails. Dogs of all sizes are allowed for no additional pet fee, and they must be declared at the time of reservation. All dogs must have proof of rabies inoculation, be on no more than a 10 foot leash or crated, and cleaned up after at all times. Dogs must be quiet, well behaved, and never left unattended. Dogs are not allowed at beaches, picnic areas, or playgrounds; they are allowed on the trails and camping areas.

Bethel

Accommodations

Greenhurst Inn 88 North Road Bethel VT   802-234-9474 (800-510-2553)
This Queen Anne Victorian mansion sits just a short distance from the White River and several other local attractions. Dogs of all sizes are welcome for no additional pet fee. Dogs must be well behaved, leashed and cleaned up after and friendly towards the other pets in residence. Dogs may not be left alone in the room at any time.

Brandon

Accommodations

Lilac Inn 53 Parks Street Brandon VT   802-247-5463 (800-221-0720)
http://www.lilacinn.com/
Whether a vacation getaway or to host your own special celebration, this beautifully restored 1900 mansion has all the amenities, 2 acres of gardens, and a full service English Tavern. Dogs of all sizes are allowed for an additional one time pet fee of $30 per room. Dogs must be well behaved, leashed and cleaned up after at all times, and crated when left alone in the room.

Blueberry Hill Inn 1307 Goshen Ripton Road Goshen VT   802-247-6735 (800-448-0707)
http://www.blueberryhillinn.com/
This early 1800's mountain inn offers traditional country ambiance, a spring fed swimming pond, gardens, gourmet dining for both breakfast and dinner (included in the rates), and plenty of skiing and hiking trails. They offer 1 pet friendly cottage and dogs of all sizes are allowed for no additional pet fee. Dogs are allowed on all of the trails year round except the groomed ski trails in Winter, and they are not allowed inside the inn. Dogs must

be leashed and cleaned up after at all times.
Fairhill 724 E Munger Street Middlebury VT   802-388-3044
http://www.midvermont.com/fairhill/
This nicely restored 1825 farmhouse is surrounded by lush lawns and gardens, and offers a great view of the mountains and valley below. Up to 2 dogs of all sizes are allowed and there is no additional pet fee; however, when they have a full house only 1 dog is allowed per room. Dogs may not be left alone in the room at any time, and they must be leashed and cleaned up after.
Middlebury Inn 14 Courthouse Square Middlebury VT   802-388-4961
http://www.middleburyinn.com
Dogs are allowed and will be given a treat on check-in. There are nearby dog-friendly trails to walk your dog on.
North Cove Cottages 1958 Lake Dunmore Road Salisbury VT   802-352-4236 (711-802-352-9064 (line for deaf))
Quiet, friendly, and well behaved dogs of all sizes are allowed. There is an $18 one time pet fee per room. The owner requests the dogs be walked off grounds and that you bring extra linens to cover the furniture or beds if your pet is used to being on them. She asks to be contacted ahead of time so she knows, and can OK, the number and type of animal. There is also a 2 night minimum stay.

Campgrounds and RV Parks
Smoke Rise Campground 2111 Grove Street Brandon VT   802-247-6984
Dogs of all sizes are allowed. There are no additional pet fees. Dogs may not be left unattended, must be leashed, and cleaned up after. This RV park is closed during the off-season. The camping and tent areas also allow dogs. There is a dog walk area at the campground.
Lake Dunmore 1457 Lake Dunmore Road Salisbury VT   802-352-4501
http://www.kampersville.com
Dogs of all sizes are allowed. There are no additional pet fees. Dogs must have current shot records, be well behaved, and be leashed and cleaned up after. This RV park is closed during the off-season. The camping and tent areas also allow dogs. There is a dog walk area at the campground.

Attractions
TOP 200 PLACE **Robert Frost Interpretive Trail** H 125 Middlebury VT   802-388-4362
This scenic recreation trail stands as a commemorative to the poetry of Robert Frost, and there are several of his poems along this 1.2 mile loop. In addition, there is a blueberry and a huckleberry patch at the far end of the trail. Dogs are allowed on leash. Dogs must be under owner's control and cleaned up after at all times.

Stores
Holy Cow 44 Main Street Middlebury VT   802-388-6737
http://www.woodyjackson.com/
This gift store offers some great cow collectibles, clothing, kitchen and home items, and much more. Your well behaved, house-trained dog is welcome in the store. Dogs must be under owner's control/care and leashed at all times.

Outdoor Restaurants
Cafe Provence 11 Center Street Brandon VT   802-247-9997
This eatery offers more than just gourmet cuisine, such as monthly wine tasting dinners, catering on and off site, cooking classes, and indoor and outdoor dinning options. Dogs are allowed at the outer tables. Dogs must be under owner's control/care and leashed at all times.

Brattleboro

Accommodations
Forty Putney Road 192 Putney Road/H 5 Brattleboro VT   802-254-6268 (800-941-2413)
http://www.fortyputneyroad.com/
This graceful French provincial estate overlooks a wildlife sanctuary and the West River, features individually decorated rooms, beautiful lawns and gardens, and they allow for indoor or outdoor (weather permitting) wining and dining. They are open seasonally. Dogs of all sizes are allowed for an additional fee of $15 per night per pet. Dogs must be friendly towards other animals as there is an older dog on site. Dogs must be leashed and cleaned up after at all times, and may only be left alone in the room if owners are confident the dog will be quiet, well behaved, and a contact number is left at the front desk.
Motel 6 - Brattleboro 1254 Putney Road Brattleboro VT   802-254-6007 (800-466-8356)

One well-behaved family pet per room. Guest must notify front desk upon arrival. Guest is liable for any damages. In consideration of all guests, pets must never be left unattended in the guest rooms.

Campgrounds and RV Parks

Fort Dummer State Park 517 Old Guilford Road Brattleboro VT   802-254-2610 (888-409-7579)
In addition to offering a rich cultural history, this forested park offers 217 acres for recreational use. Dogs of all sizes are allowed for no additional pet fee, and they must be declared at the time of reservation. All dogs must have proof of rabies inoculation, be on no more than a 10 foot leash or crated, and cleaned up after at all times. Dogs must be quiet, well behaved, and never left unattended. Dogs are not allowed in picnic areas or playgrounds; they are allowed on the trails and camping areas. The camp area has 51 sites and 10 lean-tos, restrooms, hot showers ($), a large open grassy field, and a dump station. This RV park is closed during the off-season. The camping and tent areas also allow dogs. There is a dog walk area at the campground. There are no electric or water hookups at the campgrounds.
KOA Brattleboro N 1238 US Route 5 East Dummerston VT   802-254-5908 (800-562-5909)
http://www.koa.com
Dogs of all sizes are allowed. There are no additional pet fees. Dogs must be leashed and cleaned up after. This RV park is closed during the off-season. The camping and tent areas also allow dogs. There is a dog walk area at the campground.

Attractions

Vermont Canoe Touring Center 451 Putney Road Brattleboro VT   802-257-5008
This watercraft rental company will allow your well behaved dog on the rentals for no additional fee. Dogs must be leashed when not aboard watercraft, and cleaned up after at all times.
Harlow's Sugar House 563 Bellows Falls Road Putney VT   802-387-5852
http://www.vermontsugar.com/
This farm offers a variety of pick-your-own or ready picked berries, and a customer favorite-pure maple syrup. Different months bring a variety of new produce. Your well mannered pooch is welcome on the grounds, except in the strawberry fields. Dogs must be under owner's control (especially no digging), leashed, and cleaned up after at all times.

Parks

Fort Dummer State Park 517 Old Guilford Road Brattleboro VT   802-254-2610 (888-409-7579)
In addition to offering a rich cultural history, this forested park offers 217 acres for recreational use. Dogs of all sizes are allowed for no additional pet fee, and they must be declared at the time of reservation. All dogs must have proof of rabies inoculation, be on no more than a 10 foot leash or crated, and cleaned up after at all times. Dogs must be quiet, well behaved, and never left unattended. Dogs are not allowed in picnic areas or playgrounds; they are allowed on the trails and camping areas.

Outdoor Restaurants

Top of the Hill Grill 632 Putney Road Brattleboro VT   802-258-9178
http://www.topofthehillgrill.com/home/
This tasty barbecue eatery offers outdoor picnic style seating and some really great scenery. Dogs are allowed at the outer tables. Dogs must be under owner's control, leashed, and cleaned up after at all times.

Burlington

Accommodations

Sheraton Burlington Hotel & Conference Center 870 Williston Road Burlington VT   802-865-6600 (888-625-5144)
Dogs of all sizes are allowed. There are no additional pet fees. Dogs are not allowed to be left alone in the room.
Hampton Inn 42 Lower Mountain View Drive Colchester VT   802-655-6177
Dogs of all sizes are allowed. There are no additional pet fees. Dogs are not allowed to be left alone in the room.
Motel 6 - Burlington - Colchester 74 South Park Drive Colchester VT   802-654-6860 (800-466-8356)
One well-behaved family pet per room. Guest must notify front desk upon arrival. Guest is liable for any damages. In consideration of all guests, pets must never be left unattended in the guest rooms.
The Inn at Essex 94 Poker Hill Road Essex VT   802-878-1100 (800-727-4295)
http://www.VTCulinaryResort.com
A luxury hotel featuring the acclaimed New England Culinary Institute. There is a $25 per night pet fee. There is a $300 fully refundable pet-damage deposit required.

Inn at Buckhollow Farm 2150 Buckhollow Farm Fairfax VT   802-849-2400
Dogs of all sizes are allowed. There is a $10 one time fee per room for one night, and a $15 one time fee per room for 2 or more nights. Shots for pets must be up to date.
Holiday Inn 1068 Williston Rd S. Burlington VT   802-863-6363 (877-270-6405)
Dogs of all sizes are allowed for an additional one time pet fee of $20.
Best Western Windjammer Inn & Conference Center 1076 Williston Road South Burlington VT   802-863-1125 (800-780-7234)
Dogs are allowed for an additional fee of $10 per night per pet.
Residence Inn by Marriott 35 Hurricane Lane Williston VT   802-878-2001
Dogs of all sizes are allowed. There is a $75 one time fee and a pet policy to sign at check in.
TownePlace Suites Burlington Williston 66 Zephyr Road Williston VT   802-872-5900
Dogs of all sizes are allowed. There is a $75 one time pet fee per visit.

Campgrounds and RV Parks

Mount Philo State Park 5425 Mt Philo Road Charlotte VT   802-425-2390 (888-409-7579)
This scenic park offers some great hiking areas and is the state's oldest state park. Because of the steep road, trailers are not recommended. Dogs of all sizes are allowed for no additional pet fee, and they must be declared at the time of reservation. All dogs must have proof of rabies inoculation, be on no more than a 10 foot leash or crated, and cleaned up after at all times. Dogs must be quiet, well behaved, and never left unattended. Dogs are not allowed in picnic areas or playgrounds; they are allowed on the trails and camping areas. The camp area has a total of 10 sites (including 3 lean-tos) with great views of the lake and valley, flush toilets, and showers ($). This RV park is closed during the off-season. The camping and tent areas also allow dogs. There is a dog walk area at the campground. There are no electric or water hookups at the campgrounds.
Lone Pine Campsites 52 Sunset View Road Colchester VT   802-878-5447
http://www.lonepinecampsites.com
One dog of any size is allowed. There are no additional pet fees. Dogs may not be left unattended, must be leashed, and cleaned up after. There are some breed restrictions. This RV park is closed during the off-season. The camping and tent areas also allow dogs. There is a dog walk area at the campground.
Homestead Campgrounds 864 Ethan Allen H Milton VT   802-524-2356
http://www.homesteadcampgrounds.net
Dogs of all sizes are allowed. There are no additional pet fees. Dogs must be well behaved, be on a leash, and cleaned up after. This RV park is closed during the off-season. The camping and tent areas also allow dogs. There is a dog walk area at the campground.
Shelburne Camping Area 4385 Shelburne Road Shelburne VT   802-985-2540
http://www.shelburnecamping.com
Dogs of all sizes are allowed. There are no additional pet fees. Dogs may not be left unattended, must be leashed at all times, and cleaned up after. The camping and tent areas also allow dogs. There is a dog walk area at the campground.

Attractions

Ethan Allen Homestead Park Area 1 Ethan Allen Homestead, Suite 1 Burlington VT   802-865-4556
Dogs are not allowed in the actual homestead or the museum, but they are allowed in the park surrounding the site. Dogs must be friendly, well behaved, and leashed. The Winooski Valley Park District is also a contact for the park at 802-863-5744. The homestead is open year round.
TOP 200 PLACE Lake Champlain Ferries King Street Dock Burlington VT   802-864-9804
http://www.ferries.com/
Leashed dogs of all sizes are allowed on the Lake Champlain Ferry crossing that travels between New York and Vermont. Ferry schedules changes constantly so please confirm the time of your voyage.

Shopping Centers

Church Street Marketplace 2 Church Street Burlington VT   802-863-1648
http://www.churchstmarketplace.com/
This historic, award winning shopping area was revitalized by a collaboration of the community, businesses, and government working together, and there are now over 100 shops at this popular 4 block long pedestrian mall with several special events happening here throughout the year. Dogs are allowed on leash. They must be under owner's control and cleaned up after at all times. It is up to individual stores whether dogs are allowed inside.
Essex Shoppes and Cinema 21 Essex Way Essex VT   802-657-2777
http://www.essexshoppes.com/
This nicely landscaped, shopping, dining, and entertainment Mecca is a destination for all ages. Your friendly, well behaved dog is welcome to walk the grounds. It is up to the individual stores whether they are allowed inside. Dogs must be under owner's control, leashed, and cleaned up after at all times.

Stores

Outdoor Gear Exchange Store 152 Cherry Street Burlington VT   802-860-0190
This store is open year round, and they will allow your dog on leash.
Petco Pet Store 861 Williston Rd Burlington VT   802-651-5228
Your licensed and well-behaved leashed dog is allowed in the store.
The Dog and Cat 4 Carmichael Street Essex Junction VT   802-872-8900
http://www.thedogandcatvt.com/
This pet bakery specializes in providing natural dog food, gourmet treats, and supplies that will satisfy even the
most discerning pet. Dogs must be leashed and under owner's control/care at all times.
PetSmart Pet Store 21 Trader Lane Williston VT   802-872-1819
Your licensed and well-behaved leashed dog is allowed in the store.

Parks

TOP 200 PLACE **Burlington Bike Path** Lake Champlain Shoreline Burlington VT 802-864-0123
Dogs on leash are allowed to accompany you as you walk or jog this 7.6 mile bike path on the shore of beautiful
Lake Champlain. It stretches from Oakledge Park in the south to the Winooski River in the north. Please clean
up after your dog.
Mount Philo State Park 5425 Mt Philo Road Charlotte VT   802-425-2390 (888-409-7579)
This scenic park offers some great hiking areas and is the state's oldest state park. Because of the steep road,
trailers are not recommended. Dogs of all sizes are allowed for no additional pet fee, and they must be declared
at the time of reservation. All dogs must have proof of rabies inoculation, be on no more than a 10 foot leash or
crated, and cleaned up after at all times. Dogs must be quiet, well behaved, and never left unattended. Dogs are
not allowed in picnic areas or playgrounds; they are allowed on the trails and camping areas.

Off-Leash Dog Parks

Starr Farm Dog Park Starr Farm Rd Burlington VT   802-864-0123
http://www.burlingtondogpark.org/
This off-leash dog park is fenced and offers separate large and small dogs sections. It is located west of the bike
path and adjacent to the Starr Farm Community Garden. Parking is available. The dog park is open 8am to 8pm
in April through October and 8am to 6pm in November through March. To get there from I-89, take exit #14w
towards Burlington(west). The road becomes Main Street. Turn right on Route 127 and go about a half of a mile.
Turn left on Sherman Street. Sherman St. becomes North Avenue. Go about 3 miles and turn left on Starr Farm
Road. The park is located off Starr Farm Road, near Lake Champlain and adjacent to the community garden.
Waterfront Dog Park near Moran Building Burlington VT   802-865-7247
This off-leash dog park is fenced and provides access to the lake. It is located about 1,000 feet north of the
Moran Building (the old electric generating station). It is a walk-in area with parking at the north end of Waterfront
Park or at North Beach. The park is open daily with no hour restrictions. To get there from I-89, take exit #14w
towards Burlington(west). The road becomes Main Street. Main Street turns to the right (north) and becomes
Lake Street. Park at the north end of Waterfront Park or at North Beach.

Outdoor Restaurants

Greenstreet's 30 Main Street Burlington VT   802-862-4930
Dogs are allowed at the outdoor tables. The restaurant has outdoor tables only in the Summer.
Healthy Living 4 Market Street Burlington VT   802-863-2569
Dogs are allowed at the outdoor tables. The restaurant has outdoor tables only in the Summer.
Lake Champlain Chocolates 750 Pine Street Burlington VT   802-864-1807
This chocolate store allows well behaved dogs at the outdoor tables.
Quiznos Sub 92 Church Street Burlington VT   802-864-4000
Dogs are allowed at the outdoor tables. The restaurant has outdoor tables only in the Summer.
Sweetwaters 120 Church Street Burlington VT   802-864-9800
Dogs are allowed at the outdoor tables. The restaurant has outdoor tables only in the Summer.
Vermont Pub & Brewery 144 College Street Burlington VT   802-865-0500
Well behaved dogs are allowed at the outdoor tables. The restaurant has outdoor tables only in the Summer.
Quiznos Sub 1335 Shelburne Road S Burlington VT   802-864-0800
Dogs are allowed at the outdoor tables. The restaurant has outdoor tables only in the Summer.

Craftsbury Common

Accommodations

TOP 200 PLACE **Craftsburg Outdoor Center** 535 Lost Nation Road Craftsbury Common VT   802-586-7767
http://www.craftsbury.com
This 320 acre four season resort is located beside a secluded lake. They allow dogs in a couple of their non-smoking cabins. There is a $50 one time pet fee. Well-behaved dogs of all sizes are welcome and there is limit of 2 pets per cabin. Summer activities include hiking and mountain biking. Winter activities include dog-friendly cross-country skiing on 7 kilometers of groomed trails.
Inn on the Common 1162 N Craftsbury Road Craftsbury Common VT   802-586-9619
Dogs of all sizes are allowed. There is a $25 per night per pet fee and a pet policy to sign at check in.

Cross Country Ski Resorts
Craftsburg Outdoor Center 535 Lost Nation Road Craftsbury Common VT   802-586-7767
http://www.craftsbury.com
This resort allows dogs on two lake trails which are both about 7km long. These groomed trails are called Big Osmore and Little Osmore. The trails make a nice loop around the lake. Dogs can be off-leash but need to be under direct voice control. The resort rents both skis and snowshoes. If you are looking for a place to stay, they have a couple of non-smoking cabins that allow pets.

East Burke

Accommodations
Inn at Mountain View Farm 3383 Darling Hill Road East Burke VT   802-626-9924 (800-572-4509)
http://www.innmtnview.com/
This 440-acre historic farm estate presents visitors with breathtaking views, pastoral settings, and they are home to the Mountain View Farm Animal Sanctuary on the same property, and miles and miles of multi-use, all season trails nationally known as the Kingdom Trails. Dogs of all sizes are allowed for an additional fee of $25 per night per pet. Dogs must be quiet, well mannered, leashed, cleaned up after, and crated when left alone in the room.

Enosburg Falls

Accommodations
Phineas Swann Inn 195 Main Street Montgomery Center VT   802-326-4306
http://www.phineasswann.com/
In an area bustling with activity and recreational opportunities, this Victorian home offers guests year round lodging, beautiful grounds, and fresh baked goodies available all day. It is evident that there is a love of dogs here as the owner has been collecting just about everything "Dog" for over 30 years; there are hundreds of dog figurines from the 1880's to the 1950's, advertising items, tins, furniture, and signs. Some of the collection is at the inn and most of the rest is at their antique store a short distance away. Since most items are for sale, they say "just ask", and your well mannered pooch is welcome inside the antique store as well. There are no additional pet fees. Dogs must be under owner's care/control at all times.

Campgrounds and RV Parks
Lake Carmi State Park 460 Marsh Farm Rd Enosburg Falls VT   802-933-8383
http://www.vtstateparks.com
Dogs of all sizes are allowed. There are no additional pet fees. Dogs may not be left unattended at any time, they must be on no more than a 10 foot leash, and be cleaned up after. Dogs are not allowed in any day use areas, including parking lots, picnic areas, beach and swim areas, playgrounds, or buildings. Dogs must be at least 6 months old and have a current rabies certificate and shot records. Dogs on lead are allowed on the trails. The camping and tent areas also allow dogs. There is a dog walk area at the campground. Dogs are allowed in the camping cabins. There are no electric or water hookups at the campground.

Parks
Hazen's Notch Hazen's Notch Road/H 58 (Welcome Center) Montgomery Center VT   802-326-4799
http://www.hazensnotch.org/Hiking.htm
More than 15 miles of trails winding through a variety of wildlife habitats, fields of wildflowers, ponds, and wooded areas are maintained by the Hazen Notch Association for public use in Summer and Fall. Trails are closed to all

hikers during Winter and Spring mud season from December 15th to May 19th. Trail information can be obtained at the Bear Paw Pond and High Ponds Farm parking areas, or at the Welcome Center (partially staffed in Summer/Fall) where maps and nature brochures are available outside if no one is on site. Dogs must be under owner's control; kept on a short leash at all times (no retractables), and be cleaned up after.

Fairlee

Accommodations
Silver Maple Lodge 520H 5 S Fairlee VT   802-333-4326 (800-666-1946)
http://www.silvermaplelodge.com/
In addition to being the state's oldest continually running inn, they are also central to an array of year round local attractions and activities. Dogs of all sizes are welcome for no additional fee in the cottages but not in the lodge. Dogs must be very well behaved, under owner's control at all times, and leashed and cleaned up after.

Green Mountain National Forest

Accommodations
The Mount Tabor Inn 217 Troll Hill Road Mount Tabor VT 802-293-5907
Well behaved and housebroken dogs of all sizes are allowed. There is a $10 per night per room fee and a pet policy to sign at check in. They also request you feed your dog in the bathroom as the floor is easier to clean.
Snow Goose Inn 259 H 100, Box 366 West Dover VT 802-464-3984
Dogs of all sizes are allowed. There is a $25 per night per pet additional fee. Dogs must be leashed while on site. There are only 2 pet friendly rooms.

Campgrounds and RV Parks
Camping on the Battenkill Route 7A-Camping on the Battenkill Arlington VT   802-375-6663
Dogs of all sizes are allowed. There are no additional pet fees. Dogs must have a current rabies certificate, be on leash and cleaned up after. This RV park is closed during the off-season. There is a dog walk area at the campground.
Dorset RV Park 1567 H 30 Dorset VT 802-867-5754
http://www.dorsetrv.com
Dogs of all sizes are allowed. There are no additional pet fees. Dogs may not be left unattended, must be leashed, and cleaned up after. This RV park is closed during the off-season. The camping and tent areas also allow dogs. There is a dog walk area at the campground.
Emerald Lakes State Park 75 Emerald Lake Lane East Dorset VT   802-254-2610
http://www.vtstateparks.com
Dogs of all sizes are allowed. There are no additional pet fees. Dogs may not be left unattended at any time, they must be on no more than a 10 foot leash, and be cleaned up after. Dogs are not allowed in any day use areas, including parking lots, picnic areas, playgrounds, beaches, or buildings. Dogs must be at least 6 months old and have a current rabies certificate and shot records. Dogs on leash are allowed on the trails. The camping and tent areas also allow dogs. There is a dog walk area at the campground. There are no electric or water hookups at the campground.
Jamaica State Park 285 Salmon Hole Lane Jamaica VT   802-874-4600
http://www.vtstateparks.com
Dogs of all sizes are allowed. There are no additional pet fees. Dogs may not be left unattended at any time, they must be on no more than a 10 foot leash, and be cleaned up after. Dogs are not allowed in any day use areas, including parking lots, picnic areas, beach and swim areas, playgrounds, or buildings. Dogs must be at least 6 months old and have a current rabies certificate and shot records. Dogs on leash are allowed on all the trails, except the children's nature trail. The camping and tent areas also allow dogs. There is a dog walk area at the campground. There are no electric or water hookups at the campground.
Green Mountain National Forest On H 7N Rutland VT   802-747-6700
http://www.vtstateparks.com
Dogs of all sizes are allowed. There are no additional pet fees. Dogs may not be left unattended, and they must be well behaved, leashed, and cleaned up after. Dogs are not allowed in the picnic or pond areas. Dogs on lead are allowed on all the trails. There are 7 campgrounds in this national forest, 2 remain open all year. The camping and tent areas also allow dogs. There is a dog walk area at the campground. There are no electric or water hookups at the campground.
Molly Stark State Park 705 Route 9 East Wilmington VT   802-464-5460 (888-409-7579)

This park offers wide open lawn areas, woods, picnic areas, amazing Fall foliage, and a hiking trail that leads to an old fire tower and some fantastic views. Dogs of all sizes are allowed for no additional pet fee, and they must be declared at the time of reservation. All dogs must have proof of rabies inoculation, be on no more than a 10 foot leash or crated, and cleaned up after at all times. Dogs must be quiet, well behaved, and never left unattended. Dogs are not allowed at the picnic areas or playgrounds; they are allowed on the trails and camping areas. The camping loops have 23 sites and 11 lean-tos, restrooms, showers, and a playground. This RV park is closed during the off-season. The camping and tent areas also allow dogs. There is a dog walk area at the campground. There are no electric or water hookups at the campgrounds.

Attractions
Green Mountain Flagship Company 389 H 9 West Wilmington VT   802-464-2975
http://www.greenmountainflagship.com/
Although dogs are not allowed on passenger cruises, they are allowed on watercraft rentals. There is no additional pet fee. Dogs must be well mannered, leashed when not on the boat, and cleaned up after at all times.

Parks
Emerald Lake State Park 65 Emerald Lake Lane East Dorset VT   802-362-1655 (888-409-7579)
Once of importance for its marble quarry, it is now a 430 acre lakeside park with a variety of recreational opportunities. Dogs of all sizes are allowed for no additional pet fee, and they must be declared at the time of reservation. All dogs must have proof of rabies inoculation, be on no more than a 10 foot leash or crated, and cleaned up after at all times. Dogs must be quiet, well behaved, and never left unattended. Dogs are not allowed at the beaches, picnic areas, or playgrounds; they are allowed on the trails and camping areas.
Green Mountain National Forest H 7N Rutland VT   802-747-6700
Located in southwestern and west-central Vermont and covering almost 400,000 acres, this "recovered" forest now offers abundant habitats for all forms of wildlife and a wide variety of recreational opportunities. Dogs are allowed throughout the park, campground, and on the trails; they are not allowed in picnic or pond areas. Dogs may not be left unattended, and they must be well behaved, leashed, and cleaned up after at all times.
Molly Stark State Park 705 Route 9 East Wilmington VT   802-464-5460 (888-409-7579)
This park offers wide open lawn areas, woods, picnic areas, amazing Fall foliage, and a hiking trail that leads to an old fire tower and some fantastic views. Dogs of all sizes are allowed for no additional pet fee, and they must be declared at the time of reservation. All dogs must have proof of rabies inoculation, be on no more than a 10 foot leash or crated, and cleaned up after at all times. Dogs must be quiet, well behaved, and never left unattended. Dogs are not allowed at the picnic areas or playgrounds; they are allowed on the trails and camping areas.

Groton

Campgrounds and RV Parks
Big Deer State Park 303 Boulder Beach Road Groton VT   802-372-4300
http://www.vtstateparks.com
Dogs of all sizes are allowed. There are no additional pet fees. Dogs may not be left unattended, and they must be on no more than a 10 foot leash, and be cleaned up after. Dogs are not allowed at the swim beach, however dogs are allowed to swim at the beach by the boat docks. Dogs must have current rabies shot records. There are a series of trails nearby, and dogs on lead are allowed. This campground is closed during the off-season. The camping and tent areas also allow dogs. There is a dog walk area at the campground. There are no electric or water hookups at the campground.
Stillwatere State Park 44 Stillwater Road Groton VT   802-584-3822
http://www.vtstateparks.com
Dogs of all sizes are allowed. There are no additional pet fees. Dogs may not be left unattended, they must be on no more than a 10 foot leash, and be cleaned up after. Dogs are not allowed at the swim beach, however dogs are allowed to swim at the beach by the boat docks. Dogs must have current rabies shot records. There are a series of trails nearby, and dogs on lead are allowed. This campground is closed during the off-season. The camping and tent areas also allow dogs. There is a dog walk area at the campground. There are no electric or water hookups at the campground.

Hero Islands

Accommodations

Paradise Bay 50 Light House Road South Hero VT 802-372-5393
This scenic inn sits by the lake, and dogs of all sizes are welcome for no additional pet fees. They request that if your pooch goes swimming to make sure they are dried off before entering the rooms. Dogs must be friendly to humans and other animals, and be quiet and well behaved. Dogs must be leashed and cleaned up after.

Campgrounds and RV Parks
Alburg RV Resort 1 Blue Rock Road Alburg VT 802-796-3733
Dogs of all sizes are allowed. There are no additional pet fees. Dogs are not allowed at the pool or lake, must be leashed at all times, and cleaned up after. This RV park is closed during the off-season. There is a dog walk area at the campground.
Grand Isle State Park 36 East Shore South Grand Isle VT 802-372-4300 (888-409-7579)
Located on the largest island on the lake, this 226 acre park is a commemorative to the early settlers who lived here that served in the American Revolution and offers a variety of land and water recreation. Dogs of all sizes are allowed for no additional pet fee, and they must be declared at the time of reservation. All dogs must have proof of rabies inoculation, be on no more than a 10 foot leash or crated, and cleaned up after at all times. Dogs must be quiet, well behaved, and never left unattended. Dogs are not allowed at the cabins, beaches, picnic areas, or playgrounds; they are allowed on the trails and camping areas. This is the state's 2nd largest state campground, and they have running water, hot showers, a dump station, gaming areas, and sites large enough to take self-contained RVs. This RV park is closed during the off-season. The camping and tent areas also allow dogs. There is a dog walk area at the campground. There are no electric or water hookups at the campgrounds.
North Hero State Park 3803 Lakeview Drive North Hero VT 802-372-8727
http://www.vtstateparks.com
Dogs of all sizes are allowed. There are no additional pet fees. Dogs may not be left unattended at any time, they must be on no more than a 10 foot leash, and be cleaned up after. Dogs are not allowed in any day use areas, including parking lots, picnic areas, pools, beaches, playgrounds, or buildings. Dogs must be at least 6 months old and have a current rabies certificate and shot records. Dogs on leash are allowed on the trails. The camping and tent areas also allow dogs. There is a dog walk area at the campground. There are no electric or water hookups at the campground.
Apple Island Resort Box 183 H 2 South Hero VT 802-372-5398
http://www.appleislandresort.com
Dogs of all sizes are allowed. There are no additional pet fees. Dogs may not be left unattended, must be leashed, and cleaned up after. This RV park is closed during the off-season. The camping and tent areas also allow dogs. There is a dog walk area at the campground. Dogs are allowed in the camping cabins.
Apple Island Resort 71 H 2W South Hero VT 802-372-3800
http://www.appleislandresort.com/
Some of the perks at this 188 acre resort are their marina, a 9-hole executive golf course, lots of special events, many planned fun activities, and a full service campground with all the extras including a heated pool and hot tub. Dogs of all sizes are allowed for no additional pet fee; however, they must be current on tags and shots. Dogs must be well behaved, leashed, cleaned up after at all times, and may never be left unattended. Dogs are allowed throughout the park, on the trails, and they are also allowed on watercraft rentals. This RV park is closed during the off-season. The camping and tent areas also allow dogs. There is a dog walk area at the campground.

Attractions
Allenholm Farm 150 South Street South Hero VT 802-372-5566
http://www.allenholm.com/index.html
Whether shopping at the farm store, trying their mouthwatering pies and other foods, picking your own fruits, or visiting the farm animals, there is a little bit of something for everyone here. Dogs are allowed around the grounds; they are not allowed in the store. Dogs must be under owner's control, leashed, and cleaned up after at all times.
TOP 200 PLACE **Apple Island Marina** H 2 South Hero VT 802-372-3922
http://www.appleislandresort.com/
In addition to be a full service marina, they also offer canoe and kayak rentals. Dogs are allowed on the watercraft rentals for no additional fee. Dogs must be well behaved, leashed when not on the boat, and cleaned up after at all times.

Parks
Grand Isle State Park 36 East Shore South Grand Isle VT 802-372-4300 (888-409-7579)
Located on the largest island on the lake, this 226 acre park is a commemorative to the early settlers who lived here that served in the American Revolution and offers a variety of land and water recreation. Dogs of all sizes are allowed for no additional pet fee, and they must be declared at the time of reservation. All dogs must have proof of rabies inoculation, be on no more than a 10 foot leash or crated, and cleaned up after at all times. Dogs must be quiet, well behaved, and never left unattended. Dogs are not allowed at the cabins, beaches, picnic

areas, or playgrounds; they are allowed on the trails and camping areas.

Island Pond

Campgrounds and RV Parks
Brighton State Park 102 State Park Road Island Pond VT   802-723-4360
http://www.vtstateparks.com
Dogs of all sizes are allowed. There are no additional pet fees. Dogs may not be left unattended at any time, and they must be quiet, well behaved, leashed and cleaned up after. Dogs are not allowed on the beach, the trails, the day use areas, or the buildings. Dogs must have up to date rabies shot records and a current license. This campground is closed during the off-season. The camping and tent areas also allow dogs. There is a dog walk area at the campground. There are no electric or water hookups at the campground.

Killington

Accommodations
The Cascades Lodge Killington Village, 58 Old Mill Rd Killington VT   802-422-3731 (800-345-0113)
http://www.cascadeslodge.com/contact/
This mountain ski resort offers 45 guest rooms, an indoor pool, eateries and a lounge, and year round recreation. Dogs of all sizes are allowed for an additional pet fee of $50 per night per pet with advance notice only and a credit card on file. Dogs must be current on all vaccinations, and be flee and tic free. Dogs must be leashed and cleaned up after at all times; there are waste bags in the room and more at the front desk if needed. Dogs may not be left alone in the room at any time.
The Cortina Inn and Resort Route 4 Killington VT   800-451-6108 (800-451-6108)
http://www.cortinainn.com
This inn caters to pets. They have pet treats on arrival and make your pet feel welcome. There is a $10 per day additional pet fee.
TOP 200 PLACE **The Paw House** 1376 Clarendon Avenue Killington VT   802-438-2738 (866-PAW-HOUSE)
http://www.pawhouseinn.com
The Paw House Inn is a popular B&B that caters exclusively to dog owners and their pets. Dog care is available on site. Before staying here with your dog you will be required to submit an application in advance.

Vacation Home Rentals
Wise Vacations P. O. Box 231 Killington VT   802-422-3139 (800-639-4680)
http://www.wisevacations.com/
This vacation rental company offers pet friendly accommodations in the Killington area; there are 3 tri-level homes listed-Telefon Trail, The Meadows, and Dream Maker. The pet policy may vary some as well as the fee and number of pets allowed, but there would be no higher than a $250 one time pet fee. Dogs must be well behaved, cleaned up after inside and out, and depending on the location of the property, dogs may not have to be leashed if they are under voice control.

Stores
Base Camp Outfitters 2363 H 4 Killington VT   802-775-0166
http://www.basecampvt.com/
This outdoor outfitting store will allow your well behaved, house-trained pet to join you in the store. Dogs must be under owner's control/care and leashed at all times.

Parks
Killington Ski Resort Killington Road Killington VT   802-422-6200
http://www.killington.com/
Although dogs are not allowed on the mountain during the Winter months, this scenic park has plenty to see and do the rest of the year with some great hiking trails and a variety of recreational opportunities. Dogs are allowed on the trails and throughout the park. Dogs must be under owner's control, leashed, and cleaned up after.

Ludlow

Accommodations
Best Western Ludlow Colonial - Ludlow, VT 93 Main Street Ludlow VT   802-228-8188 (800-780-7234)
http://www.bestwesternludlow.com
This pet-friendly hotel is located in the heart of the Green Mountains.
The Combs Family Inn 953 E Lake Road Ludlow VT   802-228-8799 (802-822-8799)
http://www.combesfamilyinn.com/
Located in the state's lush lake and mountain region on 50 acres of meadows and woods, this inn offers all the comforts of a cozy home, and a great location to numerous year round local activities and events. Dogs of all sizes are welcome for no additional pet fee. Dogs must be quiet, well behaved, leashed, and cleaned up after.

Campgrounds and RV Parks
Canton Place Campground 2419 East Road Cavendish VT   802-226-7767
Dogs of all sizes are allowed. There are no additional pet fees. Dogs must be leashed and cleaned up after. This RV park is closed during the off-season. The camping and tent areas also allow dogs. There is a dog walk area at the campground.
Crown Point Camping 131 Bishop Camp Road Perkinsville VT   802-263-5555
http://www.crownpointcamping.com
Dogs of all sizes are allowed. There are no additional pet fees. Dogs must be well behaved and leashed and cleaned up after. The camping and tent areas also allow dogs. There is a dog walk area at the campground.

Manchester Center

Stores
The Mountain Goat 4886 Historic Main Street Manchester Center VT   802-362-5159
http://www.mountaingoat.com/
This outdoor outfitting store will allow your well behaved, house-trained pet to join you in the store. Dogs must be under owner's control/care and leashed at all times.

Montpelier

Campgrounds and RV Parks
New Discovery State Park 4239 H 232 Marshfield VT   802-426-3042
http://www.vtstateparks.com
Dogs of all sizes are allowed. There are no additional pet fees. Dogs may not be left unattended at any time, they must be on no more than a 10 foot leash, and be cleaned up after. Dogs are not allowed in any day use areas, including parking lots, picnic areas, playgrounds, or buildings. Dogs must be at least 6 months old and have a current rabies certificate and shot records. Dogs on leash are allowed on the trails. The camping and tent areas also allow dogs. There is a dog walk area at the campground. There are no electric or water hookups at the campground.
Green Valley Campground 1368 H 2 Montpelier VT   802-223-6217
http://www.greenvalleyrvpark.com
Dogs of all sizes are allowed. There are no additional pet fees. Dogs may not be left unattended, must be leashed, and cleaned up after. This RV park is closed during the off-season. The camping and tent areas also allow dogs. There is a dog walk area at the campground.
Limehurst Lake Campground 4104 H 14 Williamstown VT   802-433-6662
http://www.limehurstlake.com
Dogs of all sizes are allowed. There are no additional pet fees. Dogs must be quiet, well behaved, and leashed and cleaned up after. There are some breed restrictions. This RV park is closed during the off-season. The camping and tent areas also allow dogs. There is a dog walk area at the campground. Dogs are allowed in the camping cabins.

Newport

Accommodations
Lady Pearl's Inn and Lodging 1724 E Main Street Newport VT   802-334-6748
Dogs of all sizes are allowed in the motel or cabins, but not the inn. There are no additional pet fees, but a credit card must be on file.

Plymouth

Campgrounds and RV Parks
Coolidge State Park 855 Coolidge State Park Road Plymouth VT   802-672-3612
http://www.vtstateparks.com
Dogs of all sizes are allowed. There are no additional pet fees. Dogs may not be left unattended, and they must be leashed and cleaned up after. Dogs must have current rabies shot records. Dog on lead are allowed on the trails. This campground is closed during the off-season. The camping and tent areas also allow dogs. There is a dog walk area at the campground. There are no electric or water hookups at the campground.

Randolph Center

Campgrounds and RV Parks
Lake Champagne Campground 53 Lake Champagne Drive Randolph Center VT   802-728-5293
http://www.lakechampagne.com
Dogs of all sizes are allowed. There are no additional pet fees. Dogs must be leashed and cleaned up after; they are not allowed on the beach or the picnic areas. This RV park is closed during the off-season. The camping and tent areas also allow dogs. There is a dog walk area at the campground.

Rutland

Accommodations
Mountain Top Inn and Resort 196 Mountain Top Road Chittenden VT   802-483-2311 (800.445.2100)
http://www.mountaintopinn.com/
This year round resort sits on 350 acres above a beautiful mountain lake and a vast national forest. Dogs of all sizes are allowed in the cabins and chalets for an additional pet fee of $25 per night per pet plus a $200 security deposit. They are not allowed in the lodge area. Your pooch will feel pampered here with a doggy bed, food and water bowls, and a treat upon arrival. Dogs must be leashed, cleaned up after, and crated when left alone in the room. Pet sitters are available with a 3 day advance notice. Pets are allowed on select cross country ski trails and on all the hiking trails.
Red Clover Inn 7 Woodward Road Mendon VT   802-775-2290 (800-752-0571)
http://www.redcloverinn.com/
This scenic 1840's farmhouse estate is located on 13 country acres, offers a warm and cozy atmosphere, an intimate pub, a restaurant, and it also serves as a great starting point for a wide variety of year round activities and recreation. Dogs of all sizes are allowed in certain rooms in the Carriage House for an additional fee of $20 per night per pet. Dogs must be leashed and cleaned up after at all times, and crated when left alone in the room. Dogs are not allowed in the main inn building.
Holiday Inn 476 US Route 7 South Rutland VT   802-775-1911 (877-270-6405)
Dogs of all sizes are allowed for an additional fee of $25 per night per pet.
Red Roof Inn - Rutland - Killington 401 US Route 7 South Rutland VT   802-775-4303 (800-RED-ROOF)
One well-behaved family pet per room. Guest must notify front desk upon arrival. Guest is liable for any damages. In consideration of all guests, pets must never be left unattended in the guest rooms.

Campgrounds and RV Parks
Bomoseen State Park 22 Cedar Mountain Rd, Fair Haven VT   802-265-4242
http://www.vtstateparks.com
Dogs of all sizes are allowed. There are no additional pet fees. Dogs may not be left unattended at any time, they must be on no more than a 10 foot leash, and be cleaned up after. Dogs are not allowed in any day use areas,

including parking lots, picnic areas, beach and swim areas, playgrounds, or buildings. Dogs must be at least 6 months old and have a current rabies certificate and shot records. Dogs on leash are allowed on the trails. The camping and tent areas also allow dogs. There is a dog walk area at the campground. There are no electric or water hookups at the campground.

Lake Bomoseen Campground 18 Campground Drive Hubbardton VT   802-273-2061
http://www.lakebomoseen.com
Dogs of all sizes are allowed. There is a $1 per night per pet additional fee. Dogs may not be left unattended, must be leashed, and cleaned up after. Dogs must have shot records. There are some breed restrictions. This RV park is closed during the off-season. The camping and tent areas also allow dogs. There is a dog walk area at the campground.

Lake St Catherine State Park 3034 H 30S Poultney VT   802-287-9158
http://www.vtstateparks.com
Dogs of all sizes are allowed. There are no additional pet fees. Dogs may not be left unattended at any time, they must be on no more than a 10 foot leash, and be cleaned up after. Dogs are not allowed in any day use areas, including parking lots, picnic areas, pools, beaches, playgrounds, or buildings. Dogs must be quiet during quiet hours. Dogs must be at least 6 months old and have a current rabies certificate and shot records. Dogs on leash are allowed on the trails. The camping and tent areas also allow dogs. There is a dog walk area at the campground. There are no electric or water hookups at the campground.

Cross Country Ski Resorts

TOP 200 PLACE The Nordic Ski Touring Center 195 Mountian Top Road Chittenden VT   802-483-2311
http://www.mountaintopinn.com/
This Nordic center sits amid thousands of acres of forest and mountain lakes, with miles and miles of year round, multi-use trails offering visitors a variety of land and water recreation. Dogs are allowed on select cross country ski trails and on all the hiking trails. There are no additional pet fees. Dogs must be under owner's control, leashed, and cleaned up after. There are some trails where dogs may be off-lead if they are under good voice control, and pet friendly lodging is available on site.

Springfield

Accommodations
Holiday Inn Express Springfield 818 Charlestown Road Springfield VT   802-885-4516 (877-270-6405)
A quiet dog is allowed for an additional pet fee of $25 (plus tax) per night.

St Albans

Campgrounds and RV Parks
Burton Island State Park Burton Island St Albans VT   802-524-6353 (800-449-2580)
This 253 acre island park is accessible only by boat; ferry service is available from Kill Kare State Park. There is a 100 slip full-service marina, boat moorings, a nature center/museum, and plenty of hiking trails. Dogs of all sizes are allowed for no additional pet fee, and they must be declared at the time of reservation. All dogs must have proof of rabies inoculation, be on no more than a 10 foot leash or crated, and cleaned up after at all times. Dogs must be quiet, well behaved, and never left unattended. Dogs are not allowed at pools, beaches, picnic areas, or playgrounds; they are allowed on the trails and camping area. The camp area offers 17 tent sites, 26 lean-to sites, picnic areas, restrooms with hot showers, a park store, and food service. This RV park is closed during the off-season. The camping and tent areas also allow dogs. There is a dog walk area at the campground. There are no electric or water hookups at the campgrounds.

Parks
Burton Island State Park Burton Island St Albans VT   802-524-6353 (800-449-2580)
This 253 acre island park is accessible only by boat; ferry service is available from Kill Kare State Park. There is a 100 slip full-service marina, boat moorings, a nature center/museum, and plenty of hiking trails. Dogs of all sizes are allowed for no additional pet fee, and they must be declared at the time of reservation. All dogs must have proof of rabies inoculation, be on no more than a 10 foot leash or crated, and cleaned up after at all times. Dogs must be quiet, well behaved, and never left unattended. Dogs are not allowed at pools, beaches, picnic areas, or playgrounds; they are allowed on the trails and camping area.

St Johnsbury

Accommodations
Inn at Maplemont 2742 H 5S Barnet VT   802-633-4880
Dogs of all sizes are allowed. There is a pet policy to sign at check in and there are no additional pet fees.
Aime's Motel RR 1, Box 332 St Johnsbury VT   802-748-3194
Dogs of all sizes are allowed.
Fairbanks Inn 401 Western Avenue St Johnsbury VT   802-748-5666
http://www.stjay.com
There is a $5 per day pet fee.

Campgrounds and RV Parks
Sugar Ridge RV Village 24 Old Stage Coach Road Danville VT   802-684-2550
http://www.sugarridgervpark.com
Dogs of all sizes are allowed. There are no additional pet fees. Dogs must current rabies certificate, and be leashed and cleaned up after. Dogs are not allowed in the rentals. This RV park is closed during the off-season. There is a dog walk area at the campground.
Moose River Campground 2870 Portland Street St Johnsbury VT   002-748-4334
http://www.mooserivercampground.com
Dogs of all sizes are allowed. There are no additional pet fees. Dogs must be quiet and may not be left unattended. Dogs must be leashed and cleaned up after. Pets are not allowed in any of the rentals. This RV park is closed during the off-season. The camping and tent areas also allow dogs. There is a dog walk area at the campground.

Attractions
TOP 200 PLACE Stephen Huneck Gallery at Dog Mountain 143 Parks Road St Johnsbury VT   800-449-2580
http://www.dogmt.com/
This amazing dog friendly estate is the home and showcase of the dog lover,artist and author Stephen Huneck. There is a variety of doggy art, books, gifts, and clothing available, lots of green lawns, a pond, and a Dog Chapel where all denominations are welcome to commune with their pet. Also on site is a Dog Agility Course providing fun romps for the pooch, and the gallery is home to special doggy events through the year. Dogs must be friendly, under owner's control, leashed (unless under good voice control), and cleaned up after at all times.

Events
Stephen Huneck Gallery Summer Party and Fall Dog Fest 143 Parks Road St Johnsbury VT   800-449-2580

http://www.dogmt.com/parties.php
This amazing dog friendly estate is the home and showcase of the doggy lover/artist/author Stephen Huneck, and there are a variety of doggy art, books, gifts, and clothing available here, as well as lots of green lawns, a pond, a Dog Chapel, and a Dog Agility Course. There are 2 annual events that draw pooches and their owners here from hundreds of miles; the Summer Party usually at the beginning of August and the Fall Dog Fest usually held at the beginning of October. There is barbecue for pooches and their owners, contests, and more. Dogs must be friendly (other dogs in residence), under owner's control, leashed (unless under good voice control), and cleaned up after at all times.

Stowe

Accommodations
Andersen Lodge - An Austrian Inn 3430 Mountain Road Stowe VT   802-253-7336
The lodge is open from May 30 to October 25 each year. There are no additional pet fees.
Commodores Inn 823 South Main St Stowe VT   802-253-7131
There are no additional pet fees.
LJ's Lodge 2526 Waterbury Rd Stowe VT   802-253-7768 (800-989-7768)
http://www.ljslodge.com
Dogs are allowed in this lodge with mountain views of the Vermont mountains. There is a fenced in dog play

area. There is a one time $5 pet fee and there are dog beds and bowls for your room.
Stowe Motel and Snowdrift 2043 Mountain Road Stowe VT   802-253-7629 (800-829-7629)
http://www.stowemotel.com/
This scenic mountain resort sits on 16 meticulously landscaped grounds with great mountain views, an alpine
stream, year round activities and recreation, a central location to a variety shops and restaurants, and it is near
the award-winning Stowe Recreation Path. Dogs of all sizes are allowed for an additional fee of $10 per night per
pet. Dogs must be leashed, cleaned up after, and crated if left alone in the room.
Ten Acres Lodge 14 Barrows Rd Stowe VT   802-253-7638
http://tenacres.newnetwork.com/
Dogs are welcome in the cottages. There are no additional pet fees.
The Mountain Road Resort 1007 Mountain Rd Stowe VT   802-253-4566
There is a $15 one time pet fee. Maximum of 1 pet per room.
The Riverside Inn 1965 Mountain Road Stowe VT   802-253-4217 (800-966-4217)
http://www.rivinn.com
This early 1800's converted farmhouse gives visitors a comfy stay while offering a great location to several
activities, shops, and eateries. They also back right up to the river and Stowe's well-known recreation path. Dogs
of all sizes are allowed for an additional fee of $5 per night per pet. Dogs must be quiet, well behaved, leashed,
and cleaned up after. Dogs may only be left alone in the room if the owner is confident in the pet's behavior.
Topnotch at Stowe Resort and Spa 4000 Mountain Road Stowe VT   802-253-8585 (800-451-8686)
http://www.topnotchresort.com
This 120-acre resort is nestled into a Vermont mountainside. There are no additional pet fees.

Campgrounds and RV Parks
Elmore State Park 856 H 12 Lake Elmore VT   802-888-2982
http://www.vtstateparks.com
Dogs of all sizes are allowed. There are no additional pet fees. Dogs may not be left unattended, and they must
be leashed and cleaned up after. Dogs are not allowed on the beach, the picnic areas, or in day use areas. Dogs
on lead are allowed on the trails. Dogs must have current rabies shot records. This campground is closed during
the off-season. The camping and tent areas also allow dogs. There is a dog walk area at the campground. There
are no electric or water hookups at the campground.
Smugglers Notch State Park 6443 Mountain Road/H 108 Stowe VT   802-253-4014 (888-409-7579)
This corridor park provides easy access for some great picnicking along this scenic byway, and it is also a
trailhead for some of the state's most popular hiking trails. Dogs of all sizes are allowed for no additional pet fee,
and they must be declared at the time of reservation. All dogs must have proof of rabies inoculation, be on no
more than a 10 foot leash or crated, and cleaned up after at all times. Dogs must be quiet, well behaved, and
never left unattended. Dogs are not allowed in picnic areas or playgrounds; they are allowed on the trails and
camping areas. The campground offers great views, water, hot showers, restrooms, and a dump station. This
RV park is closed during the off-season. The camping and tent areas also allow dogs. There is a dog walk area
at the campground. There are no electric or water hookups at the campgrounds.

Cross Country Ski Resorts
Top Notch Resort - Nordic Barn 4000 Mountain Road Stowe VT   802-253-8585
http://www.topnotchresort.com
This pet-friendly resort offers cross-country skiing trails right across the street. While pets are allowed on the
trails, they do ask that since the trails are groomed that you have your dog walk next to you but off of the ski
tracks. There are 15 kilometers of trails. Pets need to be leashed on the trail. Please pick up after your dog. Ski
rentals are located at the Nordic Barn which is across the street from the resort.

Parks
Smugglers Notch State Park 6443 Mountain Road/H 108 Stowe VT   802-253-4014 (888-409-7579)
This corridor park provides easy access for some great picnicking along this scenic byway, and it is also a
trailhead for some of the state's most popular hiking trails. Dogs of all sizes are allowed for no additional pet fee,
and they must be declared at the time of reservation. All dogs must have proof of rabies inoculation, be on no
more than a 10 foot leash or crated, and cleaned up after at all times. Dogs must be quiet, well behaved, and
never left unattended. Dogs are not allowed in picnic areas or playgrounds; they are allowed on the trails and
camping areas.

Swanton

Parks

Missisquoi National Wildlife Refuge 29 Tabor Road Swanton VT 802-868-4781
Over 6,500 acres of quiet waters, wetlands, open meadows, and forest draw thousands of migratory birds here in addition to providing habitat for a wide variety of resident and other wildlife. Dogs are allowed on site. They must be under owner's control, leashed, and cleaned up after at all times.

Thetford

Campgrounds and RV Parks
Rest N Nest Campground 300 Latham East Thetford VT 802-785-2997
http://www.restnnest.com
Dogs of all sizes are allowed. There are no additional pet fees. Dogs may not be left unattended, must be leashed, and cleaned up after. This RV park is closed during the off-season. The camping and tent areas also allow dogs. There is a dog walk area at the campground.
Thetford Hill State Park 622 Academy Road Thetford Center VT 802-785-2266
http://www.vtstateparks.com
Dogs of all sizes are allowed. There are no additional pet fees. Dogs may not be left unattended at any time, they must be on no more than a 10 foot leash, and be cleaned up after. Dogs are not allowed in any day use areas, including parking lots, picnic areas, beach and swim areas, playgrounds, or buildings. Dogs must be at least 6 months old and have a current rabies certificate and shot records. Dogs on leash are allowed on the trails. The camping and tent areas also allow dogs. There is a dog walk area at the campground. There are no electric or water hookups at the campground.

Townshend

Accommodations
Four Colulms Inn 21 West Street Newfane VT 802-365-7713 (800-787-6633)
http://www.fourcolumnsinn.com/
This Federal style inn sits on a 150 acre private mountain with wooded nature trails, manicured lawns, a fine dining restaurant that is open for diner, and they are central to numerous activities and recreation. Dogs of all sizes are allowed for an additional fee of $35 per night per pet. There may be up to 2 small to medium or 1 large dog per room. Dogs must be leashed and cleaned up after at all times.

Campgrounds and RV Parks
Bald Mountain Campground 1760 State Forest Road Townshend VT 802-365-7510
Dogs of all sizes are allowed. There are no additional pet fees. Dogs may not be left unattended, and must be leashed and cleaned up after. This RV park is closed during the off-season. The camping and tent areas also allow dogs. There is a dog walk area at the campground.
Townshend State Park 2755 State Forest Road Townshend VT 802-365-7500 (888-409-7579)
This park is located at the foot of the mountain on a bend in the river with a 1,100 foot, vertical, geologically interesting trail that leads to the top of the mountain and panoramic views. Dogs of all sizes are allowed for no additional pet fee, and they must be declared at the time of reservation. All dogs must have proof of rabies inoculation, be on no more than a 10 foot leash or crated, and cleaned up after at all times. Dogs must be quiet, well behaved, and never left unattended. Dogs are not allowed on beaches, at picnic areas, or playgrounds; they are allowed on the trails and camping areas. The wooded camp area has 30 sites and 4 lean-tos, restrooms, and showers ($). This RV park is closed during the off-season. The camping and tent areas also allow dogs. There is a dog walk area at the campground. There are no electric or water hookups at the campgrounds.

Parks
Townshend State Park 2755 State Forest Road Townshend VT 802-365-7500 (888-409-7579)
This park is located at the foot of the mountain on a bend in the river with a 1,100 foot, vertical, geologically interesting trail that leads to the top of the mountain and panoramic views. Dogs of all sizes are allowed for no additional pet fee, and they must be declared at the time of reservation. All dogs must have proof of rabies inoculation, be on no more than a 10 foot leash or crated, and cleaned up after at all times. Dogs must be quiet, well behaved, and never left unattended. Dogs are not allowed on beaches, at picnic areas, or playgrounds; they are allowed on the trails and camping areas.

Vergennes

Accommodations

Whitford House Inn 912 Grandey Road Addison VT   802-758-2704 (800-746-2704)
This restored 1790's New England inn, sitting amid rich farm land on 37 acres of beautifully kept grounds, offers bicycles and canoes for guests, a bottomless cookie jar, and a path that leads to a wildlife preserve. One gentle dog of any size is allowed in the guest house only. The dog must be very friendly and well behaved towards other animals as there are sheep, a cat, and dogs on site. Dogs may not be left alone at any time, and they must be leashed and cleaned up after.

Basin Harbor Club 4800 Basin Harbor Road Vergennes VT   802-475-2311 (800-622-4000)
Lush and sitting on the shores of beautiful Lake Champlain, this 700+ acre resort offers a complete vacation experience with a variety of accommodations, land and water recreation for all age levels, miles of hiking trails, various eateries, splendid gardens, a golf course, and much more. Dogs of all sizes are allowed in the cottages only for an additional fee of $10 per night per pet; they are not allowed in any of the 4 guesthouses. Dogs must be leashed and cleaned up after at all times, and they are not allowed in the pool or waterfront areas.

Campgrounds and RV Parks

Button Bay State Park 5 Button Bay State Park Road Vergennes VT   802-475-2377 (888-409-7579)
Sitting high on the bluff, this 253 acre treed park features large grassy fields overlooking the lake, picnic areas, a playground, and plenty of land and water recreation. Dogs of all sizes are allowed for no additional pet fee, and they must be declared at the time of reservation. All dogs must have proof of rabies inoculation, be on no more than a 10 foot leash or crated, and cleaned up after at all times. Dogs must be quiet, well behaved, and never left unattended. Dogs are not allowed at the pool, beaches, picnic areas, or playgrounds; they are allowed on the trails and camping areas. The camp area offers 73 sites and 13 lean-tos, flush toilets, showers, and a dump station. This RV park is closed during the off-season. The camping and tent areas also allow dogs. There is a dog walk area at the campground. There are no electric or water hookups at the campgrounds.

Parks

Button Bay State Park 5 Button Bay State Park Road Vergennes VT   802-475-2377 (888-409-7579)
Sitting high on the bluff, this 253 acre treed park features large grassy fields overlooking the lake, picnic areas, a playground, and plenty of land and water recreation. Dogs of all sizes are allowed for no additional pet fee, and they must be declared at the time of reservation. All dogs must have proof of rabies inoculation, be on no more than a 10 foot leash or crated, and cleaned up after at all times. Dogs must be quiet, well behaved, and never left unattended. Dogs are not allowed at the pool, beaches, picnic areas, or playgrounds; they are allowed on the trails and camping areas.

Warren

Cross Country Ski Resorts

TOP 200 PLACE **Blueberry Lake Ski Area** 424 Robinson Road Warren VT   802-496-6687
Called the "Snow Bowl of Sugarbush" this cross-country ski area offers almost 20 miles of groomed trails with some of the trails lit for night skiing. Dogs are allowed on the trails and they may be off leash if they are under good voice control. Dogs must be cleaned up after at all times.

Waterbury

Accommodations

The Black Bear Inn 4010 Bolton Access Road Bolton Valley VT   802-434-2126 (800-395-6335)
http://www.blackbearinn.travel/
There are miles and miles of trails to explore and enjoy at this retreat sitting on 6000 private acres, as well as tennis courts, an outdoor heated pool, a gift shop, a bar, and dinning for breakfast and dinner. They have a couple of standard rooms that are pet friendly, and there is an additional fee of $20 per night per pet. Dogs must be quiet, well mannered, and leashed and cleaned up after at all times. This inn also features the "Bone and Biscuit Inn"; a seasonal kennel with 3 private indoor/outdoor combination runs for an additional fee of $10 per

day per pet.
Grunberg Haus 94 Pine Street/3 miles S of Waterbury on H 100 Waterbury VT   802-244-7726
Dogs of all sizes are allowed in the cabins. There can be one large dog or 2 small dogs per cabin. There is a $5 per night per room additional pet fee. They are open from May to late October.

Woodstock

Accommodations
The Pond House Inn PO Box #234-423 Shattuck Hill Road Brownsville VT   802-484-0011
http://www.pondhouseinn.com
Nestled in the mountains just south of Woodstock, this inn features a stone walled herb garden and patio, a spring-fed pond with a jumping board for the pooch, and being close to 3 major ski resorts, there are plenty of year round recreational opportunities. Sociable, friendly dogs of all sizes are allowed for an additional fee of $10 per night per pet. There can be 1 large or 2 small dogs per room, and they are to be leashed in and around the house and around other guests. Dogs are not allowed on the furniture or in the dining areas, and they must be cleaned up after at all times. They also allow horses.
Quality Inn at Quechee Gorge 5817 Woodstock Road Quechee VT   802-295-7600 (877-424-6423)
Dogs are allowed for an additional one time pet fee of $10 per room.
The Parker House Inn and Restaurant 1792 Main Street Quechee VT   802-295-6077
http://www.theparkerhouseinn.com
This B&B allows pets with the prior permission of management. They reserve the right to limit the size of a dog to sixty pounds, but may allow larger dogs. There is horse and other large animal boarding at the owners nearby farm. There is a $30 pet fee per night, per pet.
Bailey's Mills Bed and Breakfast 1347 Baileys Mills Road Reading VT   802-484-7809 (800-639-3437)
http://www.baileysmills.com
This B&B on 48 acres with trails welcomes dogs "up to the size of a golden retriever". Dogs should not be left alone in the rooms.
Kedron Valley Inn 10671 South Road South Woodstock VT   802-457-1473 (800-836-1193)
http://www.kedronvalleyinn.com/
This 175 year old guest house is still offering guests a variety of services and modern amenities with plenty to explore, like the spring-fed pond with 2 white sandy beaches or the many trails, and although every season brings its own beauty and activities here, it is especially convenient for a variety of Winter recreation. Dogs of all sizes are allowed in the Lodge or Tavern buildings for an additional one time fee of $15 per pet. Dogs must be leashed, cleaned up after, and they may only be left alone in the room if owners are confident that the dog will be quiet and well behaved. Dogs are not allowed in the main house.
Comfort Inn 56 Ralph Lehman Drive White River Junction VT   802-295-3051 (877-424-6423)
Dogs are allowed for no additional pet fee. Dogs may not be left alone in the room.
Super 8 White River Junction Route 5 S White River Junction VT   802-295-7577 (800-800-8000)
Dogs of all sizes are allowed. There are no additional pet fees. Dogs are not allowed to be left alone in the room. Smoking and non-smoking rooms are available for pet rooms.

Campgrounds and RV Parks
Pine Valley RV Resort 3700 Woodstock Road White River Junction VT   802-296-6711
http://www.pinevalleyrv.com
Dogs of all sizes are allowed. There are no additional pet fees. Dogs must be well behaved, not left unattended, and must be leashed and cleaned up after. There are some breed restrictions. This RV park is closed during the off-season. There is a dog walk area at the campground.
Quechee Gorge State Park 764 Dewey Mills Road White River Junction VT   802-295-2990
http://www.vtstateparks.com
Dogs of all sizes are allowed. There are no additional pet fees. Dogs may not be left unattended at any time, they must be on no more than a 10 foot leash, and be cleaned up after. Dogs are not allowed in any day use areas, including parking lots, picnic areas, beach and swim areas, playgrounds, or buildings. Dogs must be at least 6 months old and have a current rabies certificate and shot records. Dogs on leash are allowed on the trails. The camping and tent areas also allow dogs. There is a dog walk area at the campground. There are no electric or water hookups at the campground.

Attractions
Sugarbush Farm 591 Sugarbush Farm Road Woodstock VT   802-457-1757
http://www.sugarbushfarm.com/
This family run farm is known for their Pure Vermont Maple Syrup, their variety of fine waxed cheeses, and their

beautiful lawns/grounds and woods. Dogs are welcome throughout the farm; they are not allowed in buildings, in the tasting area, or on tours. Dogs must be under owner's control, leashed, and cleaned up after at all times.

Parks

Marsh-Billings-Rockefeller National Historical Park 54 Elm Street/H 12 Woodstock VT   802-457-3368
http://www.okemo.com/okemosummer/
Miles and miles of scenic trails and carriage roads crisscross through one of the oldest sustainable managed woodlands in the US at this park. When you need a rest, try a bench at the 14 acre pond near the top of the mountain summit that offers great views of the valley below. Dogs are welcome throughout the park; they are not allowed on the formal grounds or the mansion tour. Dogs must be under owner's control, leashed, and cleaned up after at all times.

Chapter 5

Massachusetts
Dog Travel Guide

Barre

Campgrounds and RV Parks
Coldbrook Resort and Campground 864 Old Coldbrook Road Barre MA   978-355-2090
http://www.coldbrookcountry.com/
Dogs of all sizes are allowed. There is a $5 per night per pet additional fee. Dogs may not be left unattended, and they must be leashed and cleaned up after. This RV park is closed during the off-season. The camping and tent areas also allow dogs. There is a dog walk area at the campground.

Berkshires

Accommodations
Sally's Place 160 Orchard Street Lee MA   413-243-1982
This one bedroom apartment sleeps up to four people and is only a few minutes from the lake. Dogs of all sizes are welcome for no additional fee, but they must be very friendly with children. Dogs must be well mannered, leashed, and cleaned up after at all times.
Birchwood Inn-Fireflies and Firesides 7 Hubbard Street Lenox MA   413-637-2600 (800-524-1646)
www.birchwood-inn.com
Located on the National Register of Historic Places, this 1767 mansion offers a colonial setting, and is located only a short distance to Lenox Village. There is a service dog on site and they ask that other pets do not disturb him while he is "working". Dogs of all sizes are welcome for an additional fee of $25 per night per pet and a pet policy to sign at check in. Dogs must be quiet, well trained, leashed and cleaned up after at all times, and crated when left alone in the room. Dogs are not allowed on the bed or any of the furnishings, and they must be walked off the property.
Cranwell Resort, Spa & Golf Club 55 Lee Road Lenox MA   413-637-1364 (800-272-6935)
http://www.cranwell.com/
This sprawling hilltop mansion is a premier year round resort that sits on 380 groomed acres and is home to the Golf Digest School, an 18 hole championship golf course, and a glass enclosed indoor heated pool. Dogs up to 35 pounds are allowed for an additional one time fee of $100 per pet. Dogs must be leashed, cleaned up after, and crated when in the room alone.
Seven Hills Inn 40 Plunkett Street Lenox MA   413-637-0060 (800-869-6518)
http://www.sevenhillsinn.com
The Seven Hills Inn offers pet-friendly accommodations in the Terrace House. Thanks to one of our readers who writes: "They are on 27 beautifully groomed acres with lots of room for pets to roam." There is a $40 per visit pet fee.
Walker House 64 Walker Street Lenox MA   413-637-1271 (800-235-3098)
http://www.walkerhouse.com/
This 1804 house features 8 themed rooms and they have a cinema house where plays, films, and other notable events are shown on a large 12 foot screen. Dogs of all sizes are welcome for an additional pet fee of $10 per day. Dogs must be quiet, leashed, cleaned up after at all times, and cat-friendly. Dogs may only be left alone in the room if assured they will be well behaved.
The Porches Inn 231 River Street North Adams MA   413-664-0400
http://www.porches.com/
This inn features get-away packages, a nice long porch with rockers, and a year-round outdoor lap pool with heated deck. Dogs of all sizes are allowed for an additional $50 one time pet fee per room. One large dog or 2 small to medium dogs are allowed per room. Dogs must be well mannered, leashed and cleaned up after at all times.
Birch Hill Bed and Breakfast 254 S Undermountain Road/H 41 Sheffield MA   413-229-2143 (800-359-3969)
http://www.birchhillbb.com/
This grand 1780 bed and breakfast filled with period antique furnishings, sits on 20 acres at the foot of Mt Everett, and offer a good variety of activities and recreation. Dogs of all sizes are allowed for no additional fee. Dogs may not be left alone in the room at any time; they are not allowed on the bed or furniture, and they must be walked away from the lawn, flowers, and pool areas. Dogs must be leashed and cleaned up after at all times.
Staveleigh House 59 Main Street Sheffield MA   413-229-2129 (800-980-2129)
http://www.staveleigh.com/
This 1817 colonial home provides comfort and a convenient location to several attractions and activities. One dog of any size is welcome for a one time pet fee of $20. Dogs must be well mannered, leashed, and cleaned up

after at all times.
The Red Lion Inn 30 Main Street Stockbridge MA 413-298-5545
http://www.redlioninn.com/home.html
The surroundings and décor of this historic inn offer visitors a look into the past, but they have also provided many modern niceties, including an outdoor heated pool and hot tub surrounded by a heated stone patio. Dogs up to 80 pounds are allowed for an additional fee of $40 per night per pet, and they must be declared at the time of reservations. Pooches also get a special treat upon arrival. Dogs must be quiet, well trained, leashed, cleaned up after, and crated when left alone in the room.
Cozy Corner Motel 284 Sand Springs Rd Williamstown MA 413-458-8006
There is a $10 per day additional pet fee.

Campgrounds and RV Parks
Walker Island Family Camping Resort 27 Route 20 Chester MA 413-354-2295
http://www.walkerisland.com
Dogs of all sizes are allowed. There are no additional pet fees. Dogs may not be left unattended, and they must be quiet, friendly, leashed, and cleaned up after. Dogs must have proof of current shots. Dogs are not allowed in the pool area, or in buildings. This RV park is closed during the off season. The camping and tent areas also allow dogs. There is a dog walk area at the campground.
Clarksburg State Park 1199 Middle Road Clarksburg MA 413-664-8345
Dogs of all sizes are allowed. There are no additional pet fees. Dogs may not be left unattended, and they must have a current rabies certificate and shot records. Dogs must be quiet during quiet hours, leashed, and cleaned up after. Dogs are allowed on the trails, but not on the beach or in the swim area. Although the campground is seasonal, the park is open year round. This campground is closed during the off-season. There is a dog walk area at the campground. Dogs are allowed in the camping and tent areas. There are no electric or water hookups at the campground.
Hidden Valley Campground 15 Scott Road (Box700) Lanesborough MA 413-447-9419
Only one dog is allowed for the local residents, however, out of town travelers with 2 dogs are allowed if they are both small. They are allowed in the RV area only, not the campsites. Dogs must be quiet, be on a 6 foot max leash, cleaned up after, and not left unattended at any time. There are some breed restrictions.
Mount Greylock State Reservation Rockwell Road, P.O. Box 138 Lanesborough MA 413-499-4262 (877-I-CAMP-MA (877-422-6762))
The camping and tent areas allow dogs. There is a dog walk area at the campground. There are no electric or water hookups at the campgrounds.
October Mountain State Forest 317 Woodland Road Lee MA 413-243-1778
Dogs of all sizes are allowed. There are no additional pet fees. Dogs may not be left unattended, they must have current rabies certificate and shot records, be on no more than a 10 foot leash, and be cleaned up after. Dogs are allowed on all the trails, but they are not allowed in any buildings. This campground is closed during the off-season. The camping and tent areas also allow dogs. There is a dog walk area at the campground. There are no electric or water hookups at the campground.
Pittsfield State Forest 1041 Cascade Street Pittsfield MA 413-442-8992
Dogs of all sizes are allowed. There are no additional pet fees. Dogs may not be left unattended, they must have a current rabies certificate and shot records, be on no more than a 10 foot leash, and be cleaned up after. Dogs are allowed on all of the trails, but not at the swimming area. This campground is closed during the off-season. The camping and tent areas also allow dogs. There is a dog walk area at the campground. There are no electric or water hookups at the campground.
Savoy Mountain State Forest Central Shaft Road Savoy MA 413-663-8469
http://www.mass.gov/dcr/listing.htm
Dogs of all sizes are allowed. There are no additional pet fees. Dogs may not be left unattended, and they must have a current rabies certificate and shot records. Dogs must be quiet during quiet hours, be leashed, and cleaned up after. This campground is closed during the off-season. The camping and tent areas also allow dogs. There is a dog walk area at the campground. There are no electric or water hookups at the campground.
Summit Hill Campground 34 Old Middlefield Washington MA 413-623-5761
http://www.summithillcampground.com
Dogs of all sizes are allowed. There are no additional pet fees, and rabies shots and licenses must be up to date. There is a dog walk area at the campground.

Attractions
Windy Knoll Farm 40 Stringer Avenue Lee MA 413-243-0989
For over an hour, this horse drawn wagon will take visitors through the natural settings of backcountry roads. Dogs are welcome for no additional fee. Dogs must be under owner's control/care, leashed, and cleaned up after at all times.
The Mohawk Trail P. O. Box 1044 North Adams MA 413-743-8127
http://www.mohawktrail.com/

This was New England's first scenic road, and it is now considered "The" 4 season vacation highway with a hundred miles of historic beauty and activities to explore. There are 5 driving tours mapped out in the Mohawk Trails region which are available through the Trail Association or it can be downloaded from the web. The trail webpage is http://www.mohawktrail.com/. Dogs must be leashed and cleaned up after when out of the vehicle.

Stores
Petco Pet Store 690 Merrill Rd Pittsfield MA 413-448-2707
Your licensed and well-behaved leashed dog is allowed in the store.

Parks
Mount Greylock State Reservation Rockwell Road, P.O. Box 138 Lanesborough MA 413-499-4262 (877-I-CAMP-MA (877-422-6762))
PLEASE NOTE: Roads are closed at this park for the 2007/8 seasons for updates and repairs so many places are not available by car; the visitor center and trails will remain open.
Ashuwillticook Rail Trail Lanesborough, Cheshire, Adams MA 413-442-8928
This former railroad now provides a 10 foot wide, 11+ mile, accessible, easy recreation path from the Berkshire Mall off Hwy 8 in Lanesborough to the center of Adams, and offers some beautiful scenery following along the river and wetlands. Picnic areas, parking, and restrooms are available along the way. Dogs are allowed with current proof of rabies inoculation. Dogs must be on no more than a 10 foot leash and be cleaned up after.
TOP 200 PLACE **Natural Bridge State Park** Mc Cauley Road North Adams MA 413-663-6392
This 48 acre seasonal park offers many unique geological features, an old marble quarry, a short walkway through a chasm, walking trails, picnic areas, and scenic overlooks. Dogs are allowed throughout the park and on the trails. Dogs must be under owner's control at all times, be on no more than a 10 foot leash, cleaned up after, and have proof of current rabies inoculation.

Off-Leash Dog Parks
French Park Dog Park Baldwin Hill Road Egremont MA 413-528-0182
This fenced, off-leash dog park is located in French Park. It is open during daylight hours.

Boston

Accommodations
Best Western Roundhouse Suites 891 Massachusetts Avenue Boston MA 617-989-1000 (800-780-7234)
Dogs are allowed for an additional fee of $20 (plus tax) per night per pet.
Boston Harbor Hotel 70 Rowes Wharf Boston MA 617-439-7000
http://www.bhh.com/
There are no additional pet fees. Pet owners must sign a pet waiver.
Comfort Inn 900 Morrissey Blvd Boston MA 617-287-9200 (877-424-6423)
One dog is allowed for no additional fee. Dogs must be crated when left alone in the room.
Doubletree 400 Soldiers Field Road Boston MA 617-783-0090
Dogs of all sizes are allowed. There is a $250 refundable deposit per room. You must use the service elevators when you are with your dog.
Hilton 85 Terminal Road Boston MA 617-568-6700
Dogs are allowed for no additional pet fee.
Hyatt Regency Boston One Ave de Lafayette Boston MA 617-451-2600
Pet owners must sign a pet waiver. You need to specifically request a non-smoking pet room if you want one. Dogs need to stay in the first through fourth floors only. Pets may not be left alone in the rooms. The hotel can recommend pet sitters if needed.
TOP 200 PLACE **Nine Zero Hotel** 90 Tremont Street Boston MA 617-772-5800 (866-906-9090)
This boutique hotel located in downtown Boston has all the amenities for the business and leisure traveler and is located across the street from Boston Common, a pet-friendly 50 acre public park. Dogs of all sizes are welcome for no additional pet fee. They offer a pet bed, bowls, and a special treat for all their canine guests. Dogs may only be left alone in the room if assured they will be quiet, well behaved, and the "Dog in Room" sign is put on the door. Dogs must be leashed and cleaned up after at all times.
Onyx Hotel 155 Portland Street Boston MA 617-557-9955 (866-660-6699)
http://www.onyxhotel.com
This Kimpton boutique hotel allows dogs of all sizes. There are no additional pet fees. Pet sitting is available for $20 per hour.
Residence Inn by Marriott 34-44 Charles River Avenue Boston MA 617-242-5554

Dogs of all sizes are allowed. There is a $75 one time fee per pet and a pet policy to sign at check in.
Seaport Hotel 1 Seaport Ln Boston MA 617-385-4000
http://www.seaporthotel.com/
Dogs up to 50 pounds allowed.
Sheraton Boston Hotel 39 Dalton St. Boston MA 617-236-2000 (888-625-5144)
Dogs up to 50 pounds are allowed for no additional pet fee. Dogs may not be left alone in the room.
Taj Boston 15 Arlington Street Boston MA 617-536-5700 (800-223-6800)
This landmark luxury hotel is only a short walk from the financial and theater districts, and sits along side
Boston's grand public garden. Dogs of all sizes are allowed for an additional one time pet fee of $125 per room.
Dogs may not be left alone in the room, and they must be leashed and cleaned up after at all times.
The Eliot Suite Hotel 370 Commonwealth Ave Boston MA 617-267-1607
There are no additional pet fees. Pets may not be left alone in the rooms.
The Ritz-Carlton, Boston Common 10 Avery Street Boston MA 617-574-7100 (800-241-3333)
This hotel of contemporary luxury and design with 193 guestrooms offers dramatic city views, in-house gourmet
dining, and is conveniently located between the financial and theater districts. Dogs of all sizes are welcome for
an additional $125 one time fee per room, and there is a pet policy to sign at check in. Dogs may not be left
alone in the room, and they must be leashed and cleaned up after at all times.
Holiday Inn Boston - Brookline 1200 Beacon St. Brookline MA 617-277-1200 (877-270-6405)
http://www.basshotels.com/holiday-inn
Dogs of all sizes are allowed for an additional pet fee of $15 per night per room.
Best Western Hotel Tria 220 Alewife Brook Pkwy Cambridge MA 617-491-8000 (800-780-7234)
Dogs are allowed for an additional fee of $25 per night per pet.
Hotel Marlowe 25 Edwin H. Land Blvd. Cambridge MA 617-868-8000
Dogs of all kinds and sizes are welcome at this pet-friendly and family-friendly hotel. The luxury boutique hotel
offers both rooms and suites. Hotel amenities include a fitness room and 24 hour room service. There are no pet
fees, just sign a pet waiver.
Residence Inn by Marriott 6 Cambridge Center Cambridge MA 617-349-0700
Dogs of all sizes are allowed. There is a $150 one time fee and a pet policy to sign at check in. They ask you
make arrangemets for housekeeping.
Sheraton Commander Hotel 16 Garden St. Cambridge MA 617-547-4800 (888-625-5144)
Dogs up to 75 pounds are allowed for no additional pet fee. Dogs may not be left alone in the room.
The Charles Hotel in Harvard Square 1 Bennett St Cambridge MA 617-864-1200
There is a $50 one time pet fee. Pets may not be left alone in the rooms, and pet owners must sign a pet
agreement.
Comfort Inn and Suites Logan International Airport 85 American Legion H Revere MA 781-485-3600 (877-
424-6423)
Dogs are allowed for an additional fee of $10 per night per pet.
La Quinta Inn & Suites Boston Somerville 23 Cummings Street Somerville MA 617-625-5300 (800-531-
5900)
One dog of any size is allowed. There are no additional pet fees. Dogs must be leashed, cleaned up after, and
crated if left alone in the room.
The Inn at Crystal Cove 600 Shirley Street Winthrop MA 617-846-9217
http://www.inncrystalcove.com
Great view and dog-friendly people. The inn is located on Boston Harbor. The inn is a comfortable, colonial-style
hotel located in a residential neighborhood of Winthrop, just minutes from downtown Boston. Their swimming
pool and Jacuzzi make comfortable lodging at a reasonable rate.

Transportation Systems

TOP 200 PLACE Boston T   Boston MA 617-222-3200
http://www.mbta.com/
Both small and large dogs are allowed on the Boston T (subway) and the commuter trains run by the T from
Boston. Small dogs may be transported in a carrier. Larger dogs may be taken on the T during off-peak hours
and must be leashed and controlled at all times. At no time should a pet compromise safety, get in a passenger's
way or occupy a seat.
Salem Ferry New England Aquarium Dock Boston MA 978-741-0220
http://www.salemferry.com/
This high speed catamaran offers 45 minute service between downtown Boston and Salem. Dogs on leash are
allowed. The service is open seasonally from late May through October. There is a snack bar on the boat and the
ride offers excellent views of downtown Boston, the Harbor, Airport, and the north coast.

The Boston T

Attractions

Bay State Cruise Company The Pier at the World Trade Center Boston MA   617-748-1428
http://www.baystatecruises.com
These ferry rides are about 1 to 1 1/2 hours long. Dogs are allowed, but they must be leashed and cleaned up after, so bring doggy bags. The ferry goes from Boston to Provincetown on Cape Cod.
Black Heritage Trail 46 Joy Street Boston MA   617-725-0022
http://www.afroammuseum.org/trail.htm
This walking tour examines the heritage and culture of Boston's 19th century African American community. Well behaved dogs are welcome on the guided tours (Memorial Day weekend through Labor Day), or self guided tour maps are also available. Dogs must be under owner's control, leashed, and cleaned up after at all times.
Boston African American National Historic Site 14 Beacon Street Ste 503 Boston MA   617-742-5415
http://www.nps.gov/boaf/
Dogs must be on leash and must be cleaned up after in the park area. They are not allowed in buildings. The park features a museum, park, and walking tours. This site includes 15 pre-Civil War structures relating to the history of Boston's 19th century African-American community.
Faneuil Hall Marketplace North St and Merchants Row Boston MA
http://www.faneuilhallmarketplace.com/
A large and usually crowded outdoor shopping and eating area. If your dog isn't used to crowds, this is not the place to be. In the evenings, horse and carriage rides leave from here.
TOP 200 PLACE Freedom Trail Tremont and Temple Boston MA
This 2.5 mile historical tour marked by a red line on the sidewalk takes you by many famous sites including the Boston Common, Faneuil Hall and the Old North Church. Your dog may join you on the self-guided tour but may not go inside buildings.
Horse and Carriage (Bridal Carriage) Faneuil Hall Marketplace Boston MA   781-871-9224
Well behaved dogs are allowed on the carriages that depart from Faneuil Hall Marketplace in the evenings if the weather is appropriate.
Secret Tour of Boston's North End Four Battery Street Boston MA   617-720-2283
This touring company welcomes friendly, quiet dogs to come alone and learn the many secrets, and not so secrets, of this interesting historic area with their owners. The 2 hour tours begin at Old North Square across from the house of Paul Revere, and there are only 4 churches that dogs are not allowed to go inside. Dogs must be under owner's control, leashed, and cleaned up after at all times.

Freedom Trail

The Cheers Building-Outside View 84 Beacon St Boston MA
You and your dog can walk by on the sidewalk and view the outside of the building that was used for the outside pictures of the bar in the popular TV series 'Cheers'. Dogs are not allowed inside the building.
John F Kennedy National Historic Site 83 Beals Street Brookline MA   617-566-7937
http://www.nps.gov/jofi/
Dogs must be on leash and must be cleaned up after in front of the house or on the sidewalk. They are not allowed in the house. There is no property to tour.
Harvard University Campus 1350 Massachusetts Avenue/Harvard Square Cambridge MA   617-495-1000
http://www.harvard.edu/
Rich in its history, this beautiful campus will allow guests to bring their pooch to enjoy the trees, wide sweeping lawns, and even the occasional special events. Dogs must be under owner's control at all times, leashed, and cleaned up after.
Longfellow National Historic Site 105 Brattle Street Cambridge MA   617-876-4491
http://www.nps.gov/long/
Dogs must be on leash and must be cleaned up after on the grounds of this site. They are not allowed in the house or buildings.
Boston College Campus 140 Commonwealth Avenue Chestnut Hill MA   617-552-8000
http://www.bc.edu/
Being one of the oldest Jesuit, Catholic universities in the U.S., it is rich in history and culture. Your well mannered pet is welcome to explore this beautiful campus too, with its trees, wide sweeping lawns, historic buildings (from the outside only), and even the occasional special events with their owners. Dogs must be under owner's control at all times, leashed, and cleaned up after.

Shopping Centers
Downtown Crossing Shopping Center 59 Temple Place Boston MA   617-482-2139
This historic area is more than a pedestrian mall, it is a vibrant hub of city life with places to sit and just enjoy the ambiance, go shopping, dining, attended special events, go to the theater, or partake in the nightlife as almost everything you need is within walking distance. Your pooch is welcome to explore this area too. Dogs must be under owner's control/care at all times, and be leashed and cleaned up after.
Harvard Square Shopping Center JFK Street at Massachusetts Avenue Cambridge MA   617-491-3434
http://www.harvardsquare.com/#
From a 1630's colonial village to a lively shopping, dining, and cultural hub of activity with hundreds of businesses Harvard Square has something for everyone. There are often kiosks, street performers and other

outdoor acts. Friendly dogs are welcome throughout the square, but it is up to individual stores as to whether they may go inside. Dogs must be leashed and cleaned up after at all times.

Stores

Petco Pet Store 304 Western Avenue Brighton MA   617-254-8800
Your licensed and well-behaved leashed dog is allowed in the store.
Cause to Paws 1386A Beacon Street Brookline MA   617-738-PAWS (7297)
http://www.causetopaws.com/
You'll have "Cause to Paws" at this fun pet boutique. Bring in your dog to pick out their favorite items. Dogs must be leashed, cleaned up after, and under the owner's control at all times.
Petco Pet Store 119 First St Cambridge MA 617-868-3474
Your licensed and well-behaved leashed dog is allowed in the store.
PetSmart Pet Store 5 Mystic View Rd Everett MA   617-387-2568
Your licensed and well-behaved leashed dog is allowed in the store.
Petco Pet Store 169 Parkingway Quincy MA   617-471-5973
Your licensed and well-behaved leashed dog is allowed in the store.
Polka Dog Bakery 256 Shawmut Ave Roxbury MA   617-338-5155
This dog bakery has cookies and other snacks for your dog.

Beaches

Carson Beach I-93 and William Day Blvd Boston MA   617-727-5114
Dogs are only allowed on the beach during the off-season. Pets are not allowed from Memorial Day weekend through Labor Day weekend. Dogs must be leashed and people are required to clean up after their pets.

Parks

Arnold Arboretum 125 Arborway Boston MA   617-524-1718
http://www.arboretum.harvard.edu/
Dogs must be on leash and must be cleaned up after at all times. The arboretum has a collection of trees, shrubs, and vines on 265 acres.
Back Bay Fens The Fenway and Park Drive Boston MA
Leashed dogs are allowed at this Back Bay park.

Boston Common Park

TOP 200 PLACE **Boston Common Park** Beacon Street/H 2 Boston MA   617-635-4505

At 350 years old, this is the country's oldest park and it boasts an interesting cultural and natural history. The Freedom Trail Visitor Center is on site, and the park is a hub for the Emerald Necklace system that links several parks and areas of the city. The 50 acre park is also home to many large, public events, a children's play area, a public garden, several memorials, the Frog Pond (skating in Winter and a spray pool for Summer), and the entrance to the oldest subway in America is here as well. Dogs are welcome here, on the trails, and may be present during public events. Dogs must be well behaved, be on no more than an 8 foot leash, and be cleaned up after. Dogs are not allowed in the community garden. There are off-leash hours in certain areas of the park in the early mornings and evenings.

Boston Harbor Islands 408 Atlantic Avenue Ste 228 Boston MA   617-223-8666
http://www.nps.gov/boha/
Dogs must be on leash and must be cleaned up after on the ferry ride. Dogs are only allowed on the more developed islands of Deer and Nut. They are not allowed on other islands in the park. The park is accessed only by ferry or private boat.

Boston National Historical Park Charleston Navy Yard Boston MA   617-242-5642
http://www.nps.gov/bost/
Dogs must be on leash and must be cleaned up after in the park. They are not allowed in any buildings. The park features the revolutionary generation of Bostonians who blazed a trail from colonialism to independence.

Fort Independence William J. Day Blvd Boston MA
This park and a historical fort can be viewed by your dog.

Sudbury, Assabet, and Concord Wild and Scenic Rivers 15 State Street Boston MA   617-223-525
http://www.nps.gov/suas/
Dogs must be on leash and must be cleaned up after in most park areas. You must follow local and state park rules. The park features camping, hiking, fishing, boating, and more.

Frederick Law Olmsted National Historic Site 99 Warren Street Brookline MA   617-566-1689
http://www.nps.gov/frla/
Dogs must be on leash and must be cleaned up after on the property. They are not allowed in buildings. The park features nature walks at Frederick Law Olmsted's former home, who is recognized as the founder of American landscape architecture and the nation's foremost parkmaker.

Larz Anderson Park Goddard St and Newton St Brookline MA
Dogs are allowed on-leash only.

Fresh Pond Reservation Fresh Pond Parkway Cambridge MA   617-349-4800
Dogs are allowed off-leash in this park. They need to be under direct voice control and need to be cleaned up after. The park is located in Northwest Cambridge and is bounded by Fresh Pond Parkway, Blanchard Avenue, Concord Avenue, Grove Street and Huron Avenue.

Belle Isle Reservation Bennington Street East Boston MA   617-727-5350
Dogs must be leashed in the park.

Off-Leash Dog Parks

Boston Common Off-Leash Dog Hours Beacon Street/H 2 Boston MA   617-635-4505
Well-behaved dogs under solid verbal control are allowed off-leash in the Boston Common between the hours of 6 am to 9 am and 4 pm - 8 pm. Please observe any signs with areas where dogs are not allowed or must be on leash.

Peters Park Dog Run E. Berkeley and Washington St. Boston MA
http://www.peterspark.org/
This off-leash dog park is located in South Boston on East Berkeley Street between Shawmut and Washington Streets.

Cambridge Dog Park Mt. Auburn and Hawthorne Cambridge MA   617-349-4800
This dog park is located at Mount Auburn and Hawthorne Streets. Dogs need to be under voice control. Please remember to clean up after your dog.

Danehy Park 99 Sherman Street Cambridge MA   617-349-4800
This park is a 50 acre recreational facility that was built on a former city landfill. There is a unfenced leash free area located with this park. The park is located in North Cambridge, on Sherman Street, adjacent to Garden and New Streets.

Fort Washington Park Waverly Street Cambridge MA
This park offers an off-leash dog run. Dogs need to be under voice control. The park is located on Waverly Street between Erie Street and Putnam Avenue. Please remember to clean up after your dog.

Nunziato Field 22 Vinal Avenue Somerville MA   617-947-1191
This neighborhood doggy play area offers a stone dust even surface, trees, and benches. Dogs must be sociable, current on all vaccinations, licensed, and under owner's control/care at all times. Dogs must be leashed when not in designated off-lead areas.

Outdoor Restaurants

Baja Fresh 1 Faneuil Hall Market Place Boston MA   617-557-5111

This restaurant serves Mexican food. Dogs are allowed at the outdoor tables.
Hamersley's Bistro 553 Tremont St Boston MA   617-423-2700
This restaurant serves American cuisine. Dogs are allowed at the outdoor tables.
Joe's American Bar and Grill 279 Dartmouth St Boston MA   617-536-4200
This restaurant and bar serves American. Dogs are allowed at the outdoor tables.
Kinsale Irish Pub 2 Center Plz Boston MA   617-742-5577
Dogs are allowed at the outdoor tables.
Salty Dog Seafood Grille 206 Faneuil Hall Market P1 Boston MA   617-742-2094
Dogs are allowed at the outdoor tables.
Sel De La Terre 255 State St Boston MA   617-720-1300
This restaurant serves Mexican food. Dogs are allowed at the outdoor tables on the edge of the sidewalk.
Tremont 647 647 Tremont Street Boston MA   617-266-4600
http://www.tremont647.com/
This restaurant offers "adventurous" American cuisine. Well-behaved leashed dogs are allowed at the outdoor
tables.
Whole Foods Market 15 Westland Avenue Boston MA   617-375-1010
This restaurant serves deli-type food. Dogs are allowed at the outdoor tables.
Wisteria House Chinese 264 Newbury St Boston MA   617-536-8866
Dogs are allowed at the outdoor tables.
Taberna de Haro 999 Beacon Street Brookline MA   617-277-8272
http://tabernadeharo.boston.swbd.net/
This restaurant serves Spanish cuisine. Well-behaved leashed dogs are allowed at the outdoor tables as long as
they sit or lay quietly under the table.
Au Bon Pain 1360 Massachusetts Avenue, Harvard Square Cambridge MA   617-497-9797
http://www.aubonpain.com
This chain restaurant offers both baked goodies as well as a variety of sandwiches. Well-behaved leashed dogs
are allowed at the outdoor tables.
Cafe Paradiso 1 Harvard Square Cambridge MA   617-868-3240
This restaurant serves Italian cuisine. Well-behaved leashed dogs are allowed at the outdoor tables.
Cambridge Brewing Company One Kendall Square Cambridge MA   617-494-1994
http://www.cambrew.com/
In addition to the wide selection of beer on tap, this brewery also offers burgers, pizzas and fresh seafood. They
are open for lunch and dinner. Well-behaved leashed dogs are welcome at the outdoor tables.
Henrietta's Table 1 Bennett Street Cambridge MA   617-661-5005
This restaurant serves homestyle American cuisine. Well-behaved leashed dogs are allowed at the outdoor
tables.
Pizzeria Uno 22 JFK Street Cambridge MA   617-497-1530
This restaurant serves Italian food. Dogs are allowed at the outdoor tables and brought water.
Einsteins Bagels 1010 Morressy Boulevard Dorchester MA   617-822-8996
This restaurant serves deli-type. Dogs are allowed at the outdoor tables.

Boston Area

Accommodations
Holiday Inn 242 Adams Place Boxborough MA   978-263-8701 (877-270-6405)
Dogs up to 75 pounds are allowed for an additional one time pet fee of $75 per room.
Candlewood Suites 235 Wood Rd Braintree MA   781-849-7450 (877-270-6405)
Dogs of all sizes are allowed for an additional pet fee per room of $75 for 1 to 7 days, and $150 for 8 days or
more.
Hampton Inn 215 Wood Road Braintree MA   781-380-3300
Dogs of all sizes are allowed. There are no additional pet fees.
Holiday Inn Express 190 Wood Rd Braintree MA   781-848-1260 (877-270-6405)
Dogs up to 50 pounds are allowed for an additional one time fee of $10 per pet.
Motel 6 - Boston South - Braintree 125 Union Street Braintree MA   781-848-7890 (800-466-8356)
One well-behaved family pet per room. Guest must notify front desk upon arrival. Guest is liable for any
damages. In consideration of all guests, pets must never be left unattended in the guest rooms.
Sheraton Braintree Hotel 37 Forbes Rd. Braintree MA   781-848-0600 (888-625-5144)
Dogs up to 60 pounds are allowed for no additional pet fee. Dogs may not be left alone in the room.
Residence Inn by Marriott 124 Liberty Street Brockton MA   508-583-3600
Dogs of all sizes are allowed. There is a $75 one time fee and a pet policy to sign at check in.
Staybridge Suites 11 Old Concord Road Burlington MA   781-221-2233 (877-270-6405)
Dogs of all sizes are allowed. There is a $12 per night per room additional pet fee.

Best Western Historic Concord 740 Elm St Concord MA   978-369-6100 (800-780-7234)
Dogs are allowed for an additional fee of $10 per night per pet.
Motel 6 - Boston - Danvers 65 Newbury Street/US Route 1 North Danvers MA   978-774-8045 (800-466-8356)
One well-behaved family pet per room. Guest must notify front desk upon arrival. Guest is liable for any damages. In consideration of all guests, pets must never be left unattended in the guest rooms.
Residence Inn by Marriott 51 Newbury Street Danvers MA   978-777-7171
Dogs of all sizes are allowed. There is a $75 one time fee and a pet policy to sign at check in.
TownePlace Suites Boston North Shore/Danvers 238 Andover Street Danvers MA   978-777-6222
Dogs of all sizes are allowed. There is a $75 one time pet fee per visit.
Residence Inn by Marriott 259 Elm Street Dedham MA   781-407-0999
Dogs of all sizes are allowed. There is a $75 one time fee and a pet policy to sign at check in.
Residence Inn by Marriott 250 Foxborough Blvd Foxborough MA   508-698-2800
Dogs of all sizes are allowed. There is a $75 one time fee and a pet policy to sign at check in.
Motel 6 - Boston West - Framingham 1668 Worcester Road Framingham MA   508-620-0500 (800-466-8356)
One well-behaved family pet per room. Guest must notify front desk upon arrival. Guest is liable for any damages. In consideration of all guests, pets must never be left unattended in the guest rooms.
Red Roof Inn - Boston Framingham 650 Cochituate Road Framingham MA   508-872-4499 (800-RED-ROOF)
One well-behaved family pet per room. Guest must notify front desk upon arrival. Guest is liable for any damages. In consideration of all guests, pets must never be left unattended in the guest rooms.
Residence Inn by Marriott 400 Staples Drive Framingham MA   508-370-0001
Dogs of all sizes are allowed. There is a $75 one time fee and a pet policy to sign at check in.
Sheraton Framingham Hotel 1657 Worcester Rd. Framingham MA   508-879-7200 (888-625-5144)
Dogs up to 80 pounds are allowed for no additional pet fee. Dogs may not be left alone in the room.
Residence Inn by Marriott 4 Forge Parkway Franklin MA   508-541-8188
Dogs of all sizes are allowed. There is a $75 one time fee and a pet policy to sign at check in.
Cape Ann Motor Inn 33 Rockport Road Gloucester MA   978-281-2900
Well behaved and quiet dogs of all sizes are allowed. There are no additional pet fees.
Hampton Inn 224 Winthrop Ave Lawrence MA   978-975-4050
Dogs of all sizes are allowed. There is a $15 per night per pet fee and a pet policy to sign at check in. Dogs are not allowed to be left alone in the room.
Quality Inn and Suites 440 Bedford Street Lexington MA   781-861-0850 (877-424-6423)
Dogs are allowed for an additional one time fee of $25 per pet.
Holiday Inn Mansfield-Foxboro Area 31 Hampshire Street Mansfield MA   508-339-2200 (877-270-6405)
Dogs up to 50 pounds are allowed for an additional one time fee of $10 per pet.
Red Roof Inn - Mansfield/Foxboro 60 Forbes Boulevard Mansfield MA   508-339-2323 (800-RED-ROOF)
One well-behaved family pet per room. Guest must notify front desk upon arrival. Guest is liable for any damages. In consideration of all guests, pets must never be left unattended in the guest rooms.
Holiday Inn Express 50 Fortune Blvd Milford MA   508-634-1054 (877-270-6405)
Dogs of all sizes are allowed for an additional one time fee of $25 per pet.
La Quinta Inn Milford 24 Beaver Street Milford MA   508-478-8243 (800-531-5900)
Dogs of all sizes are allowed. There are no additional pet fees. Dogs must be leashed and cleaned up after, and they are not allowed in the breakfast area.
Crowne Plaza 1360 Worcester Road Natick MA   508-653-8800 (877-270-6405)
Dogs up to 50 pounds are allowed for no additional fee.
Sheraton Needham Hotel 100 Cabot St. Needham MA   781-444-1110 (888-625-5144)
Dogs of all sizes are allowed. There are no additional pet fees. Dogs are not allowed to be left alone in the room.
Holiday Inn Hotel & Suites Boston-Peabody Us 1 North & Us 128 North Peabody MA   978-535-4600 (877-270-6405)
Dogs of all sizes are allowed for an additional one time fee of $25 per pet, and they may not be left alone in the room.
Best Western Rockland 909 Hingham Street Rockland MA   781-871-5660 (800-780-7234)
Dogs are allowed for an additional pet fee of $25 per night per room. Dogs may not be left alone in the room
Sandy Bay Motor Inn 173 Main St Rockport MA   978-546-7155
There is a $10 per day pet charge. The hotel has two non-smoking rooms in their pet building.

Hawthorne Hotel

TOP 200 PLACE Hawthorne Hotel 18 Washington Square Salem MA   978-744-4080 (800-729-7829)
http://www.hawthornehotel.com/
Keeping in character with its New England charm, this historic hotel has tastefully appointed the rooms with 18th style reproduction furniture. The Salem hotel is within walking distance of several other pet-friendly attractions. Dogs of all sizes are welcome for an additional fee of $10 per night per pet plus a $100 refundable deposit. Dogs must be leashed, cleaned up after, and a contact number left at the desk if they are in the room alone.

Stephen Daniels House 1 Daniels Street Salem MA   978-744-5709
This 300 year old house, furnished with antiques, offers canopy beds and fireplaces in every room, and a quaint English garden. Dogs of all sizes are welcome for no additional fee. Dogs must be quiet, well behaved, leashed, and cleaned up after.

Red Roof Inn - Boston Saugus 920 Broadway Saugus MA   781-941-1400 (800-RED-ROOF)
One well-behaved family pet per room. Guest must notify front desk upon arrival. Guest is liable for any damages. In consideration of all guests, pets must never be left unattended in the guest rooms.

Red Roof Inn - Boston Southborough 367 Turnpike Road Southborough MA   508-481-3904 (800-RED-ROOF)
One well-behaved family pet per room. Guest must notify front desk upon arrival. Guest is liable for any damages. In consideration of all guests, pets must never be left unattended in the guest rooms.

Clarion Carriage House Inn 738 Boston Post Road Sudbury MA   978-443-2223 (877-424-6423)
Dogs are allowed for an additional fee of $10 per night per pet. There is a pet agreement to sign at check in.

Holiday Inn 4 Highwood Drive Tewksbury MA   978-640-9000 (877-270-6405)
Dogs of all sizes are allowed for an additional one time pet fee of $50 per room.

Motel 6 - Tewksbury 95 Main Street Tewksbury MA   978-851-8677 (800-466-8356)
One well-behaved family pet per room. Guest must notify front desk upon arrival. Guest is liable for any damages. In consideration of all guests, pets must never be left unattended in the guest rooms.

Residence Inn by Marriott 1775 Andover Street Tewksbury MA   978-640-1003
Dogs of all sizes are allowed, however there can only be 2 small or 1 large dog per room. There is $75 one time fee and a pet policy to sign at check in.

TownePlace Suites Boston Tewksbury/Andover 20 International Place Tewksbury MA   978-863-9800
Dogs of all sizes are allowed. There is a $75 one time pet fee per visit.

TOP 200 PLACE Sheraton Colonial Hotel & Golf Club Boston North One Audubon Rd. Wakefield MA   781-245-9300 (888-625-5144)
Dogs up to 80 pounds are allowed. There are no additional pet fees. Dogs are not allowed to be left alone in the room.

Holiday Inn Express 385 Winter St Waltham MA   781-890-2800 (877-270-6405)

Dogs of all sizes are allowed for an additional one time pet fee of $50 per room.
Homestead Village 52 Fourth Ave Waltham MA   781-890-1333
$75 one time fee. This is a long term stay hotel.
The Westin-Waltham Boston 70 Third Ave. Waltham MA   781-290-5600 (888-625-5144)
Dogs up to 50 pounds are allowed for no additional pet fee. Dogs may not be left alone in the room.
Best Western New Englander 1 Rainin Road Woburn MA   781-935-8160 (800-780-7234)
Dogs are allowed for an additional fee of $10 per night per pet or $25 per pet for 3 days.
Holiday Inn Select Boston-Woburn 15 Middlesex Canal Park Road Woburn MA   781-935-8760 (877-270-6405)
Dogs of all sizes are allowed for an additional one time pet fee of $50 per room.
Red Roof Inn - Boston Woburn 19 Commerce Way Woburn MA   781-935-7110 (800-RED-ROOF)
One well-behaved family pet per room. Guest must notify front desk upon arrival. Guest is liable for any damages. In consideration of all guests, pets must never be left unattended in the guest rooms.
Residence Inn by Marriott 300 Presidential Way Woburn MA   781-376-4000
Dogs of all sizes are allowed. There is a $75 one time fee and a pet policy to sign at check in.

Campgrounds and RV Parks
Circle Farm 131 Main Street Bellingham MA 508-966-1136
http://hometown.aol.com/cgfrmcamp
Well behaved dogs of all sizes are allowed. There are no additional pet fees. Dogs must be quiet, leashed, and cleaned up after.
TOP 200 PLACE Normandy Farms 72 West Street Foxboro MA   508-543-7600
http://normandyfarms.com
This large, full-service RV campground has it all, including an indoor and outdoor pool, restaurant with outdoor seating and a clubhouse. It's kind of like a hotel for your RV. There is also a new off-leash dog park. Well behaved dogs of all sizes are allowed. There are no additional pet fees. Dogs must be quiet, leashed, cleaned up after, and not left unattended at any time.
Wompatuck State Park Union Street Hingham MA   781-749-7160
Dogs of all sizes are allowed. There are no additional pet fees. Dogs may not be left unattended, they must have current rabies certificate and shot records, be leashed, and cleaned up after. Dogs are allowed on all the trails. This campground is closed during the off-season. The camping and tent areas also allow dogs. There is a dog walk area at the campground. There are no water hookups at the campground.
Boston Minuteman Campground 264 Ayer Road Littleton MA   877-677-0042
http://minutemancampground.com
Well behaved dogs of all sizes are allowed. There are no additional pet fees. Dogs must be quiet, leashed, and cleaned up after. There is a dog walk area at the campground.
KOA 438 Plymouth Street Middleboro MA   508-947-6435 (800-562-3046)
http://www.bostonsouthkoa.net
Dogs of all sizes are allowed. There are no additional pet fees. Dogs may not be left unattended, must be quiet at night, be leashed, and cleaned up after. This RV park is closed during the off-season. The camping and tent areas also allow dogs. There is a dog walk area at the campground.
Winter Island Park 50 Winter Island Road Salem MA   978-745-9430
http://www.mass.gov/dcr/listing.htm
This is a marine recreational park, and dogs of all sizes are allowed to camp in your RV but not in a tent. There are no additional pet fees. Dogs may not be left unattended outside, and may only be left inside your unit if it will not cause a danger to the animal. They must have a current rabies certificate and shot records. Dogs must be quiet during quiet hours, leashed, and cleaned up after. Dogs are allowed on the trails, but not on the beach or in the buildings. Although the campground is seasonal, the park is open year round from 7 am to 10 pm. This campground is closed during the off-season. There is a dog walk area at the campground. There are no electric or water hookups at the campground.
Rusnik Campground 115 Lafayette Road Salisbury MA 978-462-9551
http://rusnik.com
Well behaved dogs of all sizes are allowed. There are no additional pet fees. Dogs must be quiet, leashed, and cleaned up after.

Transportation Systems

Salem Ferry

Salem Ferry Derby Street at Blaney Street Salem MA   978-741-0220
http://www.salemferry.com/
This high speed catamaran offers 45 minute service between downtown Boston and Salem. Dogs on leash are allowed. The service is open seasonally from late May through October.

Attractions
Concord Guides & Press Walking Tours P.O. Box 1335 Concord MA   978-287-0897
http://www.concordguides.com/
From the front porch of the Colonial Inn in Monument Square you will step back in time to experience the "Revolution, Renaissance and Renewal" tour and learn about the unique heritage of this area. Your well behaved dog is welcome to come along. Dogs must be under owner's control, leashed, and cleaned up after at all times.
Minute Man National Historical Park Rt 2A and I-95 Concord MA
http://www.nps.gov/mima/
This park is a very popular tourist destination. Dogs are allowed on all the paths and to all the markers here. The Battle Road path goes all the way through the park, with a few interruptions.
Cape Ann Whale Watch 415 Main Street Gloucester MA   978-283-5110
http://www.seethewhales.com/
This whale watch touring company will allow dogs to come aboard when the boat is not fully loaded. They request that visitors with pets try the morning tours as they are less crowded, but an afternoon tour would be OK if they are not full. Dogs must be friendly, well behaved, under owner's control at all times, and leashed and cleaned up after.

TOP 200 PLACE **Dogtown Common** Dogtown Road at Cherry Gloucester MA
Dogtown Common hosts the remains of an old abandoned town. It is named Dogtown because while the town was decaying only dogs remained. There are boulders with messages written on them throughout the park. Guides to the park are available at the Glouster Tourist Center at Stage Fort Park. Dogtown Common is 3000 acres with trails and historic sites. Dogs on and off-leash under voice control are allowed. To get to Dogtown Commons exit Rt 128 to Washington Street North. Turn right on Reynard, left on Cherry and right on Dogtown Road.
Charles River Canoe Center 2401 Common Wealth Avenue Newton MA   617-965-5110
http://www.paddleboston.com
A well behaved dog on lead and under control is allowed.
Haunted Foot Steps Ghost Tour 8 Central Street Salem MA   978-645-0666
Well behaved dogs on lead are allowed to join the tour. The tours run from May through October. Dogs can visit any month except October because that is their busiest month.

Salem Trolley 2 New Liberty Street Salem MA   978-744-5469
http://www.salemtrolley.com
Dogs on lead are allowed on the trolley if the other passengers are not afraid of the dog or object. Smaller dogs are usually better for this tour. Dogs are not allowed on the weekends as this is their busiest time.

On the Salem Walking Tour

Salem Walking Tour   Salem MA
A red line on the sidewalk shows you the way for a two mile walking tour of Salem and all of the "Witch City" attractions.

TOP 200 PLACE **Salem Willows Amusement Park** 171-185 Fort Avenue Salem MA   978 745-0251
http://www.salemwillowspark.com/
A park since 1858, this scenic wooded and hilly peninsula is the place for great outings with shaded seaside grounds, a public pier, grand ocean views, numerous eateries, activity/gaming areas, an historic 1866 carousel, kiddie rides, a bandstand and seating area for outdoor concerts, and more. Dogs are welcome throughout the park and the water areas; they are not allowed in buildings. Dogs must be friendly, under owner's control at all times, and leashed and cleaned up after.

Stores

Petco Pet Store 20 Stockwell Drive Avon MA   508-580-4055
Your licensed and well-behaved leashed dog is allowed in the store.
PetSmart Pet Store 213 Hartford Ave Bellingham MA   508-966-0048
Your licensed and well-behaved leashed dog is allowed in the store.
The Dog Spa Inc 45 Enon Street Beverly MA   978-922-9227
http://www.dogspa.net/
The Dog Spa is located at the Commodore Plaza and features a great selection of hard to find items for dogs, including hundreds of leashes, handmade bowls, an extraordinary selection of apparel, one of a kind gift items, grooming supplies, nutritional supplements, holistic diets and even a bakery with fresh, natural treats.
PetSmart Pet Store 250 Grossman Dr Braintree MA   781-356-5980
Your licensed and well-behaved leashed dog is allowed in the store.
PetSmart Pet Store 607 Belmont St Brockton MA   508-580-1196
Your licensed and well-behaved leashed dog is allowed in the store.
Petco Pet Store 51 Middlesex Turnpike Burlington MA   781-221-7160
Your licensed and well-behaved leashed dog is allowed in the store.
PetSmart Pet Store 104 Andover St Danvers MA   978-774-3694
Your licensed and well-behaved leashed dog is allowed in the store.

Petco Pet Store 1324-1334 Worcester Rd Natick MA   508-651-1441
Your licensed and well-behaved leashed dog is allowed in the store.
Petco Pet Store 163 Highland Avenue Needham MA   781-444-8100
Your licensed and well-behaved leashed dog is allowed in the store.
Petco Pet Store 1210 Providence Highway Norwood MA   781-762-9000
Your licensed and well-behaved leashed dog is allowed in the store.
Petco Pet Store 10 Sylvan St Peabody MA   978-531-7387
Your licensed and well-behaved leashed dog is allowed in the store.
PetSmart Pet Store 10 Traders Way Salem MA   978-745-2112
Your licensed and well-behaved leashed dog is allowed in the store.
Petco Pet Store 682 Broadway #1 Saugus MA   781-231-2088
Your licensed and well-behaved leashed dog is allowed in the store.
Petco Pet Store 75 Linden St Waltham MA   781-736-0200
Your licensed and well-behaved leashed dog is allowed in the store.
Petco Pet Store 103 Commerce Way Woburn MA   781-933-2193
Your licensed and well-behaved leashed dog is allowed in the store.

Beaches
Singing Beach Beach Street Manchester MA   978-526-2040
Dogs under excellent voice control are allowed off-leash from October 1 through May 1 on the pristine Singing Beach. Dogs are not allowed on the beach during the other months. From Manchester, take Beach Street to the water. Parking can be difficult in this area.

Parks
Whitney and Thayer Woods Park Rte 3A Cohasset MA   617-821-2977
Dogs on leash are allowed.
Callahan State Park Millwood Street Framingham MA   508-653-9641
Dogs are allowed on leash or in some areas, off-leash but under strict voice control. This 820 acre day use park offers 7 miles of hiking and walking trails, and a pond where dogs can swim. The park is located west of Boston. Take Route 9 to Edgell Road in Framingham, turn left on Belknap and then right onto Millwood St.
Wompatuck State Park Union St Hingham MA   781-749-7160
Dogs on leash are allowed this park.
World's End Park Martin's Lane Hingham MA   781-821-2977
Dogs are allowed on leash. There is a $4 fee per person to enter. This park offers over 240 acres and about 5 miles of shoreline.
Lexington Battle Green Massachusetts Ave and Bedford St Lexington MA
Dogs on leash are allowed in the park.
Minuteman Commuter Bikeway Massachusetts Ave and Waltham Lexington MA
This 10 mile trail extends from Arlington, thru Lexington, and to Bedford. Dogs must be leashed in this park.
Lynn Woods Reservation Great Woods Road Lynn MA   781-593-7773
Dogs must be leashed in this park.
Blue Hills Reservation 1904 Canton Ave Milton MA   617-698-1802
Leashed dogs are allowed in this park which offers over 125 of trails.
Halibut Point State Park Gott Avenue Rockport MA   978-546-2997
Rich in cultural and natural history, this day-use coastal park offers sweeping views, trails and tide pools, meadows of wildflowers, a visitor center in an historic 60 foot tall building that gives views up to the coast of Maine, and Summer interpretive programs. Dogs must be under owner's control, be on no more than a 10 foot leash, cleaned up after, and have proof of current rabies inoculation.
Essex National Heritage Area 140 Washington Street Salem MA   978-740-0444
http://www.nps.gov/esse/
Dogs must be on leash and must be cleaned up after in most of the park areas. You must follow local and state park rules and pet policies for trails and camping. The area starts 10 miles north of Boston and extends for 40 miles along the scenic coast of Massachusetts. It features auto touring, boating, camping, hiking, swimming, and more.
Salem Common Washington Square Salem MA
Leashed dogs are allowed. This park is the second largest municipal park in the United States and offers over 30 miles of trails.
Salem Maritime National Historic Site 174 Derby Street Salem MA   978-740-1650
http://www.nps.gov/sama/
Dogs must be on leash and must be cleaned up after in the park and walking areas. Dogs are not allowed in any buildings. Open daily 9am-5pm. The park features walking tours, fishing, boating, and more. This is the first National Historic site in the National Park System, was established to preserve and interpret the maritime history of New England and the US.

Winter Island Maritime Park 50 Winter Island Road Salem MA   978-745-9430
Dogs on leash are allowed throughout the park except that dogs are not permitted at all on the beaches.

Off-Leash Dog Parks
Stoddard's Neck Dog Run Route 3A Hingham MA
Stoddard's Neck is an unfenced, large off-leash park where dogs can run off-leash. It is surrounded on three sides by water and there is only one entrance from land. You can hike while your dog runs off-leash on the approximately one mile round trip path.There are swimming areas for your pup in the harbor. The park is located on the west side of Hingham on Route 3A. There is a gate at the entrance to the peninsula.
Henry Garnsey Canine Recreation Park Cottage Street and Village Street Medway MA
http://www.medwaydogpark.com
This fenced off-leash dog park allows your dog to stretch his legs off-leash.
Sharon Dog Park East Foxboro Street Sharon MA
http://www.sharondogpark.org
This dog park is fenced, and is about one acre in size. It is free to use and has water, benches and a few trees. The dog park is located on East Foxboro Street about 1/4 mile from Sharon Center near the skateboard park. Park near the skateboard park and follow the walking trail to the dog park.

Outdoor Restaurants
Tapas Corner 284 Cabot Street (Route 62) Beverly MA   978-927-9983
This restaurant serves American food. Dogs are allowed at the outdoor tables.
Country Kitchen 181 Sudbury Road Concord MA   978-371-0181
This sandwich shop offers indoor and outdoor dining. Well behaved dogs are allowed at the outer tables. Dogs must be under owner's control/care at all times, and be leashed and cleaned up after.
Virgilios Italian Bakery 29 Main Street Gloucester MA   978-283-5295
This popular bakery and sub shop is solely a takeout eatery, but the waterfront with benches are less than 2 blocks away. Dogs must be under owner's control/care at all times, and be leashed and cleaned up after.
Dabin Restaurant 10 Muzzey St #1 Lexington MA   781-860-0171
This Japanese and Korean restaurant is in historic Lexington, near the Green.
Khushboo Restaurant 1709 Massachusetts Avenue Lexington MA   781-863-2900
http://www.khushboorestaurant.com/
This eatery specializes in East Indian cuisine and offer indoor and outdoor patio dining. Well behaved dogs are allowed at the outer tables. Dogs must be under owner's control/care at all times, and be leashed and cleaned up after.
Helmut's Strudel Shop 69 Bearskin Neck Rockport MA   978-546-2824
This pastry and coffee shop offers takeout, outdoor dining, and ocean views. Well behaved dogs are allowed at the outer tables. Dogs must be under owner's control/care at all times, and be leashed and cleaned up after.
Roy Moore Lobster Company 39 Bearskin Neck Rockport MA   978-546-6696
Specializing in lobster and other seafood dishes, this restaurant offers indoor and outdoor dining on the back dock. Well behaved dogs are allowed at the outer tables. Dogs must be under owner's control/care at all times, and be leashed and cleaned up after.
Coffee Merchant 196 Essex St Salem MA   978-744-1729
Dogs are allowed at the outdoor tables.
Baja Fresh 113 Main St Stoneham MA   781-438-0277
This restaurant and bar serves Mexican. Dogs are allowed at the outdoor tables.
Red Rock Bistro and Bar 141 Humphrey Street Swampscott MA   781-595-1414
This restaurant and bar serves seafood and gourmet food. Dogs are allowed at the outdoor tables.

Day Kennels
PetsHotel by PetsMart Day Kennel 1 Worcester Rd. Framingham MA   508.370.9612
http://www.petsmart.com/PETsHOTEL/
This PetSmart pet store offers day care, day camp and overnight care. You may drop off and pick up your dog during the hours the store is open seven days a week. Dogs must have proof of current rabies, DPP and Bordatella vaccinations.

Cape Cod

Accommodations
Greylin House 2311 Main St Brewster MA   508-896-0004 (800-233-6662)
http://capecodtravel.com/greylin/

One non-smoking room for pets. Dog must be able to get along with the owners 2 dogs.
Bay Motor Inn 223 Main St Buzzards Bay MA 508-759-3989
http://capecodtravel.com/baymotorinn/
There is a $10 per day pet fee. The motel has no designated smoking or non-smoking rooms. Pets must be attended at all times.
Centerville Corners Inn 1338 Craigville Beach Rd Centerville MA 508-775-7223
There is a $10 per day pet fee.
Foley Real Estate 703 Main Street/H28 Falmouth MA 508-548-3415
This rental company offers several pet friendly vacation houses in the Falmouth area and pet policy and/or fees may vary per rental. Aggressive breeds are not allowed, and dogs must be under owner's control/care at all times.
Cape Cod Harbor House Inn 119 Ocean St Hyannis MA 508-771-1880
This inn has 19 non-smoking mini-suites located near the center of Hyannis. Pets are welcome, please mention your pet when making reservations.
Comfort Inn - Hyannis/Cape Cod 1470 Route 132 Hyannis MA 508-771-4804 (877-424-6423)
http://www.comfortinn-hyannis.com
This hotel allows pets in a number of pet-friendly rooms for an additional $5 per night.
TOP 200 PLACE **Simmons Homestead Inn** 288 Scudder Ave. Hyannis Port MA 800-637-1649
http://www.SimmonsHomesteadInn.com
The B & B is at an 1800 Sea Captain's estate in Hyannis Port in the center of Cape Cod. There are 14 rooms in two buildings. They offer a wine hour, beach stuff, billiards and a bunch more. A chance to see the collection of over 50 classic red sports cars behind the Inn at Toad Hall is probably worth the trip by itself.
Outer Reach Resort 535 H 6 North Truro MA 508-487-9500 (800-942-5388)
http://www.outerreachresort.com
Sitting on 12 acres of the highest bluff on the Lower Cape affords great views of the ocean and Pilgrim Lake, and in addition to a pool and gaming courts, there are great trails to walk with your pet down to the beach. They open for the season in mid-May. Dogs of all sizes are welcome for an additional $15 per night per pet. Dogs must be leashed and cleaned up after.
BayShore on the Water 493 Commercial Street Provincetown MA 508-487-9133
http://www.bayshorechandler.com
This five house complex has been converted to studios, one bedroom and two bedroom units. There are a few non-smoking units and the rest are not designated as smoking or non-smoking. There is a $15 per day pet fee for 1 dog, or a $20 per day pet fee for 2 dogs.
Cape Inn Resorts 698 Commercial Street Provincetown MA 508-487-1711 (800-422-4224)
http://www.capeinn.com
Cape Inn is located at the east end of Provincetown about one mile from the town center. Pets of all sizes are welcome, but may not be left alone in the rooms.
Four Gables Cottages 15 Race Road Provincetown MA 508-487-2427 (866-487-2427)
http://www.fourgables.com
These Provincetown cottages and apartments welcome your pets to visit with you. Properties have decks and porches.
Keep Inn 698 Commercial St Provincetown MA 508-487-1711
There are no additional pet fees. Pets must be attended at all times.
White Sands Motel 1001 Commercial St. Provincetown MA 508-487-0244
http://www.provincetownlodging.com
This beachfront hotel in Provincetown allows pets in select rooms. Pets require approval at the time of reservation and there is a $20 per night pet fee. The hotel is within two miles of the Cape Cod National Seashore.
White Wind Inn 174 Commercial St Provincetown MA 508-487-1526

Sandwich Lodge and Resort 54 Route 6A Sandwich MA 508-888-2275
There is a $10.00 per night pet fee per pet. Pets are allowed in standard rooms only.
The Earl of Sandwich Motor Manor 378 Rt 6A Sandwich MA 508-888-1415
There are no additional pet fees.
Quality Inn 1314 H 28 South Yarmouth MA 508-394-4000 (877-424-6423)
Dogs are allowed for an additional fee of $15 per night per pet.
Colonial House Old Kings Hwy Yarmouth Port MA 508-362-4348 (800-999-3416)
http://www.colonialhousecapecod.com/
There is a $5.00 per day pet charge.

Campgrounds and RV Parks
Bay View Campgrounds 260 McArthur Blvd Bourne MA 508-759-7610
http://bayviewcampgrounds.com
Dogs of all sizes are allowed. There are no additional pet fees. Dogs must be quiet, leashed, cleaned up after,

and not left unattended at any time. There is a dog walk area at the campground.
Bourne Scenic Park Campground 370 Scenic Highway Bourne MA   508-759-7873
http://bournescenicpark.com
Dogs of all sizes are allowed. There are no additional pet fees. Dogs must be quiet, leashed, and cleaned up after.
Nickerson State Park Campgrounds Route 6A Brewster MA   508-896-3491
This state park has 1900 acres of land and offers over 400 campsites. Your dog is welcome at the campgrounds, but they ask that your dog never be left unattended. Dogs are also allowed on the hiking trails, and paved trails. Dogs are not allowed in the pond or on public beaches. However, you can take your dog to an uncrowded beach, where there are not many other people. Dogs must be leashed and you must have proof of your dog's rabies vaccination.
Cape Cod Camp Resort 176 Thomas Landers Road East Falmouth MA   508-548-1458
http://www.resortcamplands.com
Dogs of all sizes are allowed. There is a $4 per night per pet additional fee and there must be proof of shots; either tags or paperwork. Dogs must be cleaned up after, leashed, and not left unattended at any time. There are some breed restrictions.
Peter's Pond Park 185 Cotuit Road Sandwich MA   508-477-1775
http://www.peterspond.com
Dogs of all sizes are allowed in the RV section only. There is one street where they park all the RVs. There are no additional pet fees. Dogs must be leashed and cleaned up after. There is a dog walk area at the campground.
Shawme-Crowell State Forest 42 Main Street Sandwich MA   508-888-0351
Dogs of all sizes are allowed. There are no additional pet fees. Dogs may not be left unattended, they must have current rabies certificate and shot records, be leashed, and cleaned up after. Dogs are allowed on all of the trails. The forest is open from 8am to 8pm daily. The camping and tent areas also allow dogs. There is a dog walk area at the campground. There are no electric or water hookups at the campground.
Waquoit Bay National Estuarine Research Reserve 149 Waquoit H/H 28 Waquoit MA   508-457-0495 (877-422-6762)
http://www.waquoitbayreserve.org/
Located on the south shore of Cape Cod and accessible by boat only, this 330 acre park and research reserve is one of the last undeveloped coastal properties on the cape with barrier beaches, an oak and pine forest, coastal salt ponds, marshlands, and uplands. Dogs of all sizes are allowed for no additional fee. Dogs must be leashed, cleaned up after, and have proof of current rabies inoculation. Dogs are not allowed on the beaches at any time because of endangered birds. Primitive camping is allowed with prior camping permits and reservations through Reserve America. The camp area has composting toilets during the Summer, and potable water is not available. The camping and tent areas also allow dogs. There is a dog walk area at the campground. There are no electric or water hookups at the campgrounds.

Vacation Home Rentals
The Sandpiper Beach House 165 Commercial Street Provincetown MA   508-487-1928 (800-354-8628)
http://www.sandpiperbeachhouse.com
There is a $25 per visit pet fee.

Transportation Systems
Island Queen Ferry Falmouth Heights Road Falmouth MA   508-548-4800
http://www.islandqueen.com/
This ferry carries passengers, bicycles and leashed dogs. It does not transport vehicles. The ferry runs between Falmouth in Cape Cod and Oak Bluffs in Martha's Vineyard (about 35 to 45 minutes).
Hy-Line Cruises Ferry Service Ocean Street Dock Hyannis MA   508-778-2600
http://www.hy-linecruises.com/
This ferry service runs from Cape Cod to Nantucket Island (1 hour on the high speed ferry) or Martha's Vineyard (1.5 hours). They also offer the only Inter-Island Ferry between Nantucket and Martha's Vineyard (2.25 hours). Pets are allowed on the ferries, but not in the first class lounge. Pets need to be leashed. This ferry company provides year-round service to Nantucket and seasonal service to Martha's Vineyard. The Inter-Island Ferry is also seasonal. No vehicles are transported on these ferries. Call ahead to make reservations.
Nantucket Airlines 660 Barnstable Road/North Ramp Hyannis MA   508-790-0300 (800-635-8787)
http://www.nantucketairlines.com
This airline offers daily flights between Hyannis and Nantucket (20 minute flight). Dogs are allowed in the cabin with you on this airline! Dogs under 35 pounds can be carried on your lap and no kennel is required. For dogs over 35 pounds, there is a "shelf" which is just a few inches off the floor, in the back of the plane where your dog can sit or lay. While you cannot sit next to your dog, you can try to get the seat directly in front of him or her. There is no reserved seating, so you'll need to arrive early to try and make special arrangements to sit in front of your pooch. Large dogs must be properly restrained with a leash, harness or similar device. No kennel is required. You will need to reserve a space for your pet in advance as the airline usually only allows one dog per

flight. Their sister airline, Cape Air also allows dogs in the cabin, but most flights require your dog to be in a kennel, and they have a size limit for dogs.

Steamship Authority Ferry Service South Street Dock Hyannis MA 508-477-8600
http://www.steamshipauthority.com
This ferry services runs from Cape Cod to Nantucket Island (2.25 hours) or Martha's Vineyard (1.5 hours). Pets are allowed on all ferries except for the M/V Flying Cloud fast ferry. Pets must be leashed or in a crate at all times. Pets are not allowed on the seats, tables, or in the concession areas. The ferries transport both passengers and cars. They provide year-round service to Nantucket and Martha's Vineyard. Call ahead to make reservations.

Attractions

Green Briar Nature Center 6 Discovery Hill East Sandwich MA 508-888-6870
The famous author Thorton Burgess grew up in Sandwich and wrote over 170 books and 15,000 stories about Peter Rabbit and his animal friends. As a child, he used to go for walks in what is now the conservation area next to the Nature Center. The Nature Center offers interpretive nature trails and a special wild flower garden. Leashed dogs are allowed on the nature trails and throughout the trails in the flower garden. Pets are not allowed inside the buildings. The adjacent 166 acre Briar Patch Conservation Area also allows dogs on their trails. Pets must be on leash, except during the months of September through March when dogs are allowed off-leash, but must be under voice control. The conservation area is the home of Peter Rabbit and other Burgess animal characters. The Nature Center offers trail guides for the conservation area. Green Briar is located off Route 6A.

Hy-Line Harbor Cruises Ocean Street Docks Hyannis MA 508-790-0696
The harbor cruises are about 1 hour, and a well behaved dog on leash is allowed.

Hyannisport Harbor Cruises Ocean Street Dock Hyannis MA 508-778-2600
http://www.hy-linecruises.com/
Enjoy a one hour leisurely cruise on Lewis Bay and Hyannis Harbor. You will see vistas of historic interest, scenic islands and beaches, a few presidential Summer homes, and more. Tours are held rain or shine. Dogs are allowed, but need to be leashed.

TOP 200 PLACE **Cape Cod Canal Cruise** Town Pier Onset MA 508-295-3883
http://www.hy-linecruises.com/
This 2 or 3 hour boat cruise starts at the pier in the Victorian village of Onset. The cruise will take you through the Cape Cod Canal to the Sandwich Yacht Basin. You will be able to enjoy live commentary about the history and sights. Some points of interest include Taylor Point, Massachusetts Maritime Academy Training Ship, Vertical Lift Railroad Bridge, Sagamore Bridge and more. Well-behaved, leashed dogs are allowed.

Goose Hummock Outdoor Center 13 Old County Road Orleans MA 508-255-2620
This company rents canoes, and at the end of each season they sell their canoes and buy new ones for the next season. A well behaved dog on leash is allowed to canoe with you.

Bay State Cruise Company

TOP 200 PLACE **Bay State Cruise Company** MacMillan Pier Provincetown MA   617-748-1428
http://www.baystatecruises.com
These ferry rides are about 1 to 1 1/2 hours long and go between Provincetown and Boston. Dogs are allowed,
but they must be leashed and cleaned up after, so bring doggy bags.
Dolphin Fleet of Provincetown Whale Watch 307 Commercial Street Provincetown MA   508-349-1900 (800-
826-9300)
http://www.whalewatch.com/
This whale watching tour company offers you and your well-behaved dog the opportunity to view a variety of
whales including Baleen, Toothed, Humpback, Fin and Right Whales. Each tour is about 3 to 4 hours long.
Small dogs are allowed on all of the boat tours. Large dogs are also allowed, but there are a few requirements.
The smaller tour boats are recommended for large dogs, because these boats are less crowded and offer more
space. They also recommend that you call first to make sure that there is space available. All dogs need to be
leashed.
Flyer's Boat Rentals 131 Commercial Street Provincetown MA   508-487-0898
In addition to offering parties and cruises, this company has a large fleet of boats for rent and they will allow well
behaved pets to come aboard on rentals for no additional fee. Dogs must be under owner's control/care at all
times, and be leashed and cleaned up after.
TOP 200 PLACE **Wellfleet Drive-in Movie Theater** 51 H 6 Wellfleet MA   508-349-7176
http://www.wellfleetcinemas.com/
This drive-in theater will allow well behaved, quiet dogs to come to the movies too. Dogs must be leashed and
cleaned up after at all times. Dogs are not allowed here during flea market hours unless they belong to one of
the vendors.

Stores
Petco Pet Store 7 Davis Straits Falmouth MA   508-540-2842
Your licensed and well-behaved leashed dog is allowed in the store.
PetSmart Pet Store 1070 Iyannough Rd Hyannis MA   508-778-1601
Your licensed and well-behaved leashed dog is allowed in the store.
Wag This Way Store and Training Center 58C Corporation Road Hyannis MA   508-771-9247
http://www.wagthisway.com
In addition to a full array of pet supplies, toys, and food, they also have a frequent buyer program, workshops for
owners and their pets, and a training center that offers a variety of classes and seminars. Well mannered dogs
are welcome to explore the store and sniff out their favorites. Dogs must be under owner's control/care, leashed,
and cleaned up after at all times.
Hot Diggity 24 North Street Mashpee MA   508-477-BONE (2663)
Designer dog products, unique dog toys, designer and holiday themed collars and leashes, classic dog t-shirts
and dresses for the lady dogs, Halloween costumes, organic dog food and gourmet dog treats, are just a few of
the items to be found here. Your pet is welcome to explore the store with you on leash, and there will probably be
a bowl of water at the front door in case your pooch is thirsty.
Hot Diggity 891 Main Street Osterville MA   508-428-3647
http://www.hotdiggityonline.com/
Designer dog products, unique dog toys, designer and holiday themed collars and leashes, classic dog t-shirts
and dresses for the lady dogs, Halloween costumes, organic dog food and gourmet dog treats, are just a few of
the items to be found here. They are open 10 am to 4 pm Tuesday through Saturday, and from 11 am to 4 pm on
Sunday. Your pet is welcome to explore the store with you, and there will probably be a bowl of water at the front
door in case your pooch is thirsty.
Paws and Whiskers Dog Bakery and Pawticulars 259 Commercial Street Provincetown MA   508-487-3441
http://www.pawsnwhiskers.com/
Your pet will have fun browsing through a large number of gifts, apparel, toys, and yummy treats at this pet
boutique. Dogs must be well mannered, leashed, and under owner's care at all times.

Beaches
Barnstable Town Beaches off Route 6A Barnstable MA   508-790-6345
Dogs are allowed only during the off-season, from September 15 to May 15. Dogs must be on leash or under
voice control. People need to clean up after their pets. The town of Barnstable oversees Hyannis beaches and
the following beaches: Craigville, Kalmus, and Sandy Neck. Before you go, always verify the seasonal dates and
times when dogs are allowed on the beach.
Chatham Town Beaches off Route 28 Chatham MA   508-945-5100
Dogs are allowed only during the off-season, from mid September to end the end of May. Dogs must be leashed
and people need to clean up after their pets. The town of Chatham oversees the following beaches: Hardings,
Light, and Ridgevale. Before you go, always verify the seasonal dates and times when dogs are allowed on the
beach.
Dennis Town Beaches Route 6A Dennis MA   508-394-8300

Dogs are allowed only during the off-season, from after Labor Day up to Memorial Day. There is one exception. Dogs are allowed year-round on the four wheel drive area of Chapin Beach. Dogs must be leashed on all town beaches, and people need to clean up after their pets. The town of Dennis oversees the following beaches: Chapin, Mayflower, Howes Street and Sea Street. Before you go, always verify the seasonal dates and times when dogs are allowed on the beach.

Falmouth Town Beaches off Route 28 Falmouth MA   508-457-2567
Dogs are not allowed during the Summer from May 1 through October 1. During the off-season, dogs are allowed all day. Dogs must be leashed and people need to clean up after their pets. The town of Falmouth oversees the following beaches: Menauhant, Surf Drive, and Old Silver. Before you go, always verify the seasonal dates and times when dogs are allowed on the beach.

Harwich Town Beach off Route 28 Harwich MA   508-430-7514
Dogs are allowed only during the off-season, from October to mid-May. Dogs must be on leash or under voice control. People need to clean up after their pets. The town of Harwich oversees Red River Beach. Before you go, always verify the seasonal dates and times when dogs are allowed on the beach.

Orleans Town Beaches off Route 28 Orleans MA   508-240-3775
Dogs are allowed only during the off-season, from after Columbus Day to the Friday before Memorial Day. Dogs are allowed off leash, but must be under voice control. People need to clean up after their pets. The town of Orleans oversees Nauset and Skaket beaches. Before you go, always verify the seasonal dates and times when dogs are allowed on the beach.

Provincetown Town Beaches off Route 6 Provincetown MA   508-487-7000
Dogs on leash are allowed year-round. During the Summer, from 6am to 9am, dogs are allowed off-leash. The town of Provincetown oversees the following beaches: Herring Cove and Race Point. Before you go, always verify the seasonal dates and times when dogs are allowed on the beach.

Sandwich Town Beaches off Route 6A Sandwich MA   508-888-4361
Dogs are allowed only during the off-season, from October through March. Dogs must be leashed and people need to clean up after their pets. The town of Sandwich oversees the following beaches: East Sandwich and Town Neck. Before you go, always verify the seasonal dates and times when dogs are allowed on the beach.

Truro Town Beaches off Route 6 Truro MA   508-487-2702
Dogs are allowed during the Summer, only before 9am and after 6pm. This policy is in effect from about the third weekend in June through Labor Day. During the off-season, dogs are allowed all day. Dogs must be leashed and people need to clean up after their pets. The town of Truro oversees the following beaches: Ballston, Corn Hill, Fisher, Great Hollow, Head of the Meadow, Longnook and Ryder. Before you go, always verify the seasonal dates and times when dogs are allowed on the beach.

Cape Cod National Seashore Route 6 Wellfleet MA   508-349-3785
http://www.nps.gov/caco
The park offers a 40 mile stretch of pristine sandy beaches. Dogs on leash are allowed year-round on all of the seashore beaches, except for seasonally posted nesting or lifeguarded beaches. Leashed pets are also allowed on fire roads, and the Head of the Meadow bicycle trail in Truro. Check with the visitor center or rangers for details about fire road locations. To get there from Boston, take Route 3 south to the Sagamore Bridge. Take Route 6 east towards Eastham.

Wellfleet Town Beaches off Route 6 Wellfleet MA   508-349-9818
Dogs are allowed during the Summer, only before 9am and after 6pm. During the off-season, from after Labor Day to the end of June, dogs are allowed all day. Dogs must be leashed and people need to clean up after their pets. The town of Wellfleet oversees the following beaches: Marconi, Cahoon Hollow, and White Crest. Before you go, always verify the seasonal dates and times when dogs are allowed on the beach.

Sandy Neck Beach 425 Sandy Neck Road West Barnstable MA   508-362-8300
In addition to being a haven for endangered bird and wildlife, this 6 mile long coastal barrier beach also shares a unique ecology and rich cultural history. There is an off-road beach, a public beach and miles of trails here. Dogs are allowed on the trails and on the Off-Road beach area anytime (but stay on water side) throughout the year, but they are not allowed on the public beach from May 15 to September 15. Dogs are not allowed in the primitive camp area. Visitors and their pets must remain on designated trails, off the dunes, and off the few areas of private property. Please consult trail maps. Dogs must be leashed and cleaned up after at all times.

Parks

Nickerson State Park Route 6A Brewster MA   508-896-3491
This state park has 1900 acres of land and miles of trails. Dogs are allowed on the hiking trails, and paved trails. Dogs are not allowed in the pond or on public beaches. However, you can take your dog to an uncrowded beach, where there are not many other people. Dogs must be leashed and you must have proof of your dog's rabies vaccination. Your dog is also welcome at the campgrounds, but they ask that your dog never be left unattended.

Cape Cod Rail Trail   Dennis - Wellfleet MA   508 896-3491
A former railroad right-of-way, this 22 mile rail trail offers visitors a paved surface with few hills, scenic viewing areas, occasional restrooms, good markings, and year round recreation. You will find several free parking areas along the trail. Due to some construction on the trail, please check ahead for closed areas. Dogs are welcome; they must be under owner's control, leashed, and cleaned up after at all times.

Waquoit Bay National Estuarine Research Reserve 149 Waquoit H/H 28 Waquoit MA 508-457-0495 (877-422-6762)
http://www.waquoitbayreserve.org/
Located on the south shore of Cape Cod and accessible by boat only, this 330 acre park and research reserve is one of the last undeveloped coastal properties on the cape with barrier beaches, an oak and pine forest, coastal salt ponds, marshlands, and uplands. Dogs of all sizes are allowed for no additional fee. Dogs must be leashed, cleaned up after, and have proof of current rabies inoculation. Dogs are not allowed on the beaches at any time because of endangered birds.

TOP 200 PLACE **Cape Cod National Seashore** 99 Marconi Station Site Road Wellfleet MA 508-349-3785
The Seashore is a forty-mile long stretch of pristine sandy beach. Dogs of all sizes are allowed. There are no additional pet fees, but they request that guests pick up a pet brochure at the visitor's center when they arrive. Dogs may not be left unattended, and they must be leashed and cleaned up after. Dogs are not allowed on the self guided nature trails, at the fresh water ponds, nor in the the picket fenced areas. Parking lots are open 6 A.M. to midnight, daily, year-round. The Salt Pond Visitor Center is open from 9 A.M. to 4:30 P.M. daily, year-round, with extended hours during the Summer months. The Province Lands Visitor Center is open from 9 A.M. to 5 P.M. daily, early-May through late-October.

Cape Cod Rail Trail off Route 6 Wellfleet MA 508-896-3491
This paved trail extends 25 miles through the towns of Dennis, Harwich, Brewster, Orleans, Eastham and Wellfleet. The paved trail is for bicycles, and there is a wide unpaved shoulder for walkers, runners, and horseback riders. Dogs on leash are allowed. There are multiple parking areas along the trail. One is located off Route 6 at LeCount Hollow Road in Wellfleet. Another is located in Nickerson State Park, off Route 6A.

Off-Leash Dog Parks

Pilgrim Bark Park Corner of Shank Painter Road and H 6 Provincetown MA 508-487-1325
http://www.provincetowndogpark.org/
Located next to the Cumberland Farms, this off leash park offers almost an acre of play area with 2 sections; one being for dogs less than 25 pounds. Dogs must be sociable, current on all vaccinations and license, and under owner's control/care at all times. Dogs must be leashed when not in designated off-lead areas.

Outdoor Restaurants

Cobie's Outdoor restaurant 3260 Main St Brewster MA 508-896-7021
This clam shack offers fried clams, seafood rolls, burgers, smoothies and more. They are open from about the end of May to mid September. Well-behaved, leashed dogs are allowed at the outdoor tables.

Schoolhouse Ice Cream and Yogurt 749 Route 28 Harwich Port MA 508-432-7355
This popular ice cream shop offers over 30 flavors, including sherbet, low-fat yogurt and fruit ices. Well-behaved, leashed dogs are allowed at the outdoor tables. Outdoor seating is seasonal. They are located on Route 28, just past Saquatucket Harbor and Brax Landing Restaurant heading towards Chatham.

Starbuck's Coffee House 38 Nanthan Ellis Hwy Mashpee MA 508-477-5806
http://www.starbucks.com
Well-behaved, leashed dogs are allowed at the outdoor tables. Outdoor seating is seasonal.

The Tea Shoppe 13 Steeple Street Mashpee MA 508-477-7261
Anyone who would like to eat outside at this restaurant, needs to get food in a to go container, because they cannot serve their porcelain outside. Well-behaved, leashed dogs are welcome to join you at the outdoor sidewalk tables. Outdoor seating is seasonal.

The Cheese Corner and Deli 56 Main Street Orleans MA 508-255-1699
http://www.thecheesecornerdeli.com
This Cape Cod deli offers homemade soups and a variety of sandwiches on bread baked daily. Sandwiches include all of the classic deli favorites and many specialties such as the "Dirty Bird," "Whydah" and "Mad Russian." They carry a vast selection of traditional Scandinavian foods and baked goods, a great selection of imported cheeses, yummy breakfast goodies and sweet treats. Open daily - call for hours in the off-season. Well-behaved, leashed dogs are allowed at the outdoor tables. Outdoor seating is seasonal.

Frappo66 214 Commercial Street Provincetown MA 508-487-9066
http://www.frappo66.com/
Think "fine-dining" fast food to take in or to have on site. Outside seating is available; dogs are allowed at the outer tables. They must be leashed and under owner's control/care at all times.

P.J.'s Family Restaurant H 6 and School Street Wellfleet MA 508-349-2126
Thirty plus years and still popular, especially for their seafood dishes, this eatery offers takeout, indoor dining, or an outside ordering window for those eating at the picnic tables. Well behaved dogs are allowed at the outer tables. Dogs must be under owner's control/care at all times, and be leashed and cleaned up after.

Fall River

Accommodations
Holiday Inn Express 110 Middle St. Fairhaven MA   508-997-1281 (877-270-6405)
Dogs of all sizes are allowed for an additional one time fee of $10 per pet; there can be 1 large dog or 2 small to medium dogs per room.
Captain Haskell's Octagon House 347 Union Street New Bedford MA   508-999-3933
Dogs of all sizes are allowed. There is a pet policy to sign at check in and there are no additional pet fees. They also provide you with a map of dog friendly places in the local area.
Comfort Inn 171 Faunce Corner Road North Dartmouth MA   508-996-0800 (877-424-6423)
Dogs are allowed for an additional one time pet fee of $50 per room.
Residence Inn by Marriott 181 Faunce Corner Road North Dartmouth MA   508-984-5858
Dogs of all sizes are allowed. There is a $75 one time fee and a pet policy to sign at check in.
Quality Inn 1878 Wilbur Avenue Somerset MA   508-678-4545 (877-424-6423)
Dogs are allowed for no additional fee; there may be 1 average sized dog or 2 small dogs per room.

Campgrounds and RV Parks
Horseneck Beach State Reservations On H 88 Westport Point MA   508-636-8817
http://www.mass.gov/dcr/listing.htm
This park is popular because of it's almost 2 miles of beaches and it's salt marsh. Dogs of all sizes are allowed. There are no additional pet fees. Dogs may not be left unattended, and they must have a current rabies certificate and shot records. Dogs must be quiet during quiet hours, be leashed, and cleaned up after. Dogs are allowed on the trails, but not on the beach, in the buildings, or at the sand dunes. This campground is closed during the off-season. The camping and tent areas also allow dogs. There is a dog walk area at the campground. There are no water hookups at the campground.

Stores
Doggie Boutique 812 Kempton Street New Bedford MA   508-997-2490
This boutique specializes in pet products and services and welcomes your pet to come inside and check out the variety of supplies and treats. Dogs must be well mannered, leashed, and under owner's care at all times.

Parks
New Bedford Whaling National Historical Park 33 William Street New Bedford MA   508-996-4095
http://www.nps.gov/nebe/
Dogs must be on leash and must be cleaned up after in the park area. They are not allowed in any buildings. Open daily 9am-5pm. The park commemorates the heritage of the world's preeminent whaling port during the 19th century.

Outdoor Restaurants
Candleworks Restaurant 72 N Water Street New Bedford MA   508-997-1294
Serving fine Italian cuisine and seafood, this eatery also features live piano music 7 days a week, and in the Summer they offer outside dining. Well behaved dogs are allowed at the outer tables. Dogs must be under owner's control/care at all times, and be leashed and cleaned up after.

Fitchburg

Accommodations
Best Western Royal Plaza Hotel & Conf. Center 150 Royal Plaza Drive Fitchburg MA   978-342-7100 (800-780-7234)
Pets are allowed at the hotel.
Super 8 Gardner 22 N Pearson Blvd Gardner MA   978-630-2888 (800-800-8000)
Dogs up to 60 pounds are allowed. There is a $10 per night pet fee per pet. Reservations are recommended due to limited rooms for pets. Smoking and non-smoking rooms are available for pet rooms.
Motel 6 - Leominster 48 Commercial Street Leominster MA   978-537-8161 (800-466-8356)
One well-behaved family pet per room. Guest must notify front desk upon arrival. Guest is liable for any damages. In consideration of all guests, pets must never be left unattended in the guest rooms.

Campgrounds and RV Parks

Otter River State Forest 86 Winchendon Road Baldwinville MA   978-939-8962
Dogs of all sizes are allowed. There are no additional pet fees. Dogs may not be left unattended, and they must be leashed and cleaned up after. Dogs are allowed on all of the trails, but they are not allowed in the water. This campground is closed during the off-season. The camping and tent areas also allow dogs. There is a dog walk area at the campground. There are no electric or water hookups at the campground.

Stores

Petco Pet Store 48 Water Tower Plaza Leominster MA   978-840-5810
Your licensed and well-behaved leashed dog is allowed in the store.

Parks

Wachusett Mountain State Reservation 345 Mountain Road Princeton MA   978 464-2987
This day-use park offers 3000 acres of year round recreational opportunities, a historic site, 17+miles of trails, a visitor center, an interesting bog area, and a variety of habitats and wildlife. Dogs must be on no more than a 10 foot leash, be cleaned up after, and have proof of current rabies inoculation.

Franklin County - Mohawk Trail

Accommodations

Red Roof Inn - South Deerfield 9 Greenfield Road South Deerfield MA   413-665-7161 (800-RED-ROOF)
One well-behaved family pet per room. Guest must notify front desk upon arrival. Guest is liable for any damages. In consideration of all guests, pets must never be left unattended in the guest rooms.

Campgrounds and RV Parks

Mohawk Trail State Forest On H 2 Charlemont MA   413-339-5504
Dogs of all sizes are allowed. There are no additional pet fees. Dogs may not be left unattended, they must have current rabies certificate and shot records, be leashed, and cleaned up after. Dogs are allowed on all the trails. This campground is closed during the off-season. The camping and tent areas also allow dogs. There is a dog walk area at the campground. Dogs are allowed in the camping cabins. There are no electric or water hookups at the campground.
Erving State Forest Laurel Lake Road Erving MA   978-544-3939
Dogs of all sizes are allowed. There are no additional pet fees. Dogs may not be left unattended, they must have current rabies certificate and shot records, be leashed, and cleaned up after. Dogs are allowed on all of the trails, but not on the beach. This campground is closed during the off-season. The camping and tent areas also allow dogs. There is a dog walk area at the campground. There are no electric or water hookups at the campground.
Peppermint Park Camping Resort 169 Grant Street Plainfield MA   413-634-5385
http://www.peppermintpark.net
Dogs of all sizes are allowed. There is a $10 per night per pet additional fee and dogs must have proof of up to date shots. Dogs must be leashed, cleaned up after, and can not be left unattended. The camping and tent areas also allow dogs. There is a dog walk area at the campground.
Country Aire Campground 1753 Mohaw Trail Shelburne Falls MA   413-625-2996
http://countryairecampground.com
Well behaved dogs of all sizes are allowed. There are no additional pet fees. Dogs must be quiet, leashed, cleaned up after, and not left unattended.
White Birch Campground 214 North Street Whately MA   800-244-4941
Dogs of all sizes are allowed. There are no additional pet fees. Dogs must be quiet, leashed, and cleaned up after.

Attractions

TOP 200 PLACE Historic Deerfield Village Old Main Street Deerfield MA   413-775-7214
http://www.historic-deerfield.org/
Dogs are welcome to stroll the streets of this authentic New England Village with their owners. They are not allowed in any of the buildings. Dogs must be leashed and cleaned up after at all times.
Bridge of Flowers 16-22 Water Street Shelburne Falls MA   413-625-2526
A wonderful balm to all the senses, this 400 foot 1908 trolley bridge is now home to more than 500 varieties of flowers, vines, and shrubs with continual blooming from April to October. This garden is attended to by the Shelburne Falls Women's Club. Dogs are welcome to come and smell the flowers as well. Dogs must be under owner's control, leashed, and cleaned up after at all times.

Parks

Poets Seat Tower Mountain Road and Maple Street Greenfield MA   413-773-5463
Views from the historic tower area are wide and reaching across Greenfield and its green, fertile valley to the mountains on the other side. In addition to the incredible views, there are miles of woodland trails, wildlife, and bird/eagle viewing. Dogs are welcome for no additional fees. Dogs must be leashed and cleaned up after.
Tully Mountain Wildlife Management Area and Trail Tully Road Orange MA   508-835-3607
A very diverse area with at least 13 habitat types from a variety of forests, rich wetlands, to open slabs of bedrock, this 1200 acre wildlife area supports numerous species, and offers a 22 mile trail that winds through several sections of the park. Dogs are allowed for no additional fee. Dogs may only be off lead if they are under good voice control, and they will not chase wildlife. Dogs must be leashed in public areas, and cleaned up after at all times.

Lawrence

Accommodations

Comfort Suites 4 Riverside Drive Andover MA   978-475-6000 (877-424-6423)
Well behaved dogs are allowed for an additional one time pet fee of $75 per room.
La Quinta Inn & Suites Andover 131 River Road Andover MA   978-685-6200 (800-531-5900)
Dogs of all sizes are allowed. There are no additional pet fees. There is a pet waiver to sign at check in. Dogs must be leashed and cleaned up after.
Residence Inn by Marriott 500 Minuteman Road Andover MA   978-683-0382
Dogs of all sizes are allowed. There is a $75 one time fee per pet and a pet policy to sign at check in.
Staybridge Suites 4 Tech Drive Andover MA   978-686-2000 (877-270-6405)
Dogs of all sizes are allowed for an additional one time pet fee per room.
Best Western Merrimack Valley 401 Lowell Avenue Haverhill MA   978-373-1511 (800-780-7234)
Dogs up to 70 pounds are allowed for an additional pet fee of $20 per night per room.

Campgrounds and RV Parks

Harold Parker State Forest 305 Middleton Road North Andover MA   978-686-3391
Dogs of all sizes are allowed. There are no additional pet fees. Dogs may not be left unattended, they must have current rabies certificate and shot records, be quiet, leashed, and cleaned up after. Dogs are allowed on all the trails. This campground is closed during the off-season. The camping and tent areas also allow dogs. There is a dog walk area at the campground. There are no electric or water hookups at the campground.

Lowell

Accommodations

Residence Inn by Marriott 7 LAN Drive Westford MA   978-392-1407
Dogs of all sizes are allowed. There is a $75 one time fee and a pet policy to sign at check in.

Campgrounds and RV Parks

Wyman's Beach Family Camping 48 Wyman's Beach Road Westford MA   978-692-6287
http://www.wymanscamping.com
Well behaved dogs of all sizes are allowed. There are no additional pet fees. Dogs must remain in one's own site and be leashed at all times. There is a dog walk area close by that you can drive to. Dogs are allowed in the camping cabins.

Stores

Fido and Fifi's Pet Boutique 1794 Bridge Street Dracut MA   978-458-1101
This pet boutique welcomes your pet to come inside and check out the variety of supplies and treats. Dogs must be well mannered, leashed, and under owner's care at all times.

Parks

Lowell National Historical Park 67 Kirk Street Lowell MA   978-970-5000
http://www.nps.gov/lowe/

Dogs must be on leash and must be cleaned up after in the park area. They are not allowed in any buildings. The park shows the history of America's Industrial Revolution in Lowell, Massachusetts.

Marthas Vineyard

Accommodations

Colonial Inn 38 North Water Street Edgartown MA 508-627-4711
http://www.colonialinnmvy.com/
This family friendly inn offers two pet-friendly suites for travelers with dogs. You can enjoy the daily complimentary continental breakfast outside in the Garden Courtyard with your pooch. There is a $30 per day pet fee. The entire inn is non-smoking.
Shiverick Inn 5 Pease Point Way Edgartown MA 508-627-3797
http://www.shiverickinn.com/
Pets up to about 75 pounds are allowed in the three bedroom suite which is located just off the library. Dogs are not allowed in the indoor common areas, just inside your room and outside. There is a $50 pet deposit. Pets cannot be left alone in the room. The entire inn is non-smoking.
Martha's Vineyard Surfside Hotel 7 Oak Bluffs Avenue Oak Bluffs MA 508-693-2500 (800-537-3007)
http://www.mvsurfside.com
Overlooking Nantucket Sound, the Surfside offers a premier location in Oak Bluffs, with Oak Bluffs Harbor and the ocean in your backyard and shopping, fine restaurants and historic sites in your frontyard. A year round hotel with 39 rooms and suites just footsteps from the Oak Bluffs Ferry Dock, Inkwell Beach and the historic Flying Horses Carousel. They have no weight restrictions on dogs and offer a "doggie package" of treats and pet scooper. There is an additional $10 pet charge which may be refunded on checkout.

Vacation Home Rentals

Martha's Vineyard Vacation Homes Call to Arrange. Edgartown MA 203-374-8624
http://www.vineyardvacationhomes.com/
Some of the vacation homes are pet-friendly. There is a $100 weekly pet fee, and a $150 security deposit for pet damage or additional cleaning.
Martha's Vineyard Rental Houses Call to Arrange. Vineyard Haven MA 508-693-6222
Select from a variety of pet-friendly rental homes. Pet fees may vary per property.

Transportation Systems

Hy-Line Cruises Ferry Service Ocean Street Dock Hyannis MA 508-778-2600
http://www.hy-linecruises.com/
This ferry service runs from Cape Cod to Nantucket Island (1 hour on the high speed ferry) or Martha's Vineyard (1.5 hours). They also offer the only Inter-Island Ferry between Nantucket and Martha's Vineyard (2.25 hours). Pets are allowed on the ferries, but not in the first class lounge. Pets need to be leashed. This ferry company provides year-round service to Nantucket and seasonal service to Martha's Vineyard. The Inter-Island Ferry is also seasonal. No vehicles are transported on these ferries. Call ahead to make reservations.
Steamship Authority Ferry Service South Street Dock Hyannis MA 508-477-8600
http://www.steamshipauthority.com
This ferry services runs from Cape Cod to Nantucket Island (2.25 hours) or Martha's Vineyard (1.5 hours). Pets are allowed on all ferries except for the M/V Flying Cloud fast ferry. Pets must be leashed or in a crate at all times. Pets are not allowed on the seats, tables, or in the concession areas. The ferries transport both passengers and cars. They provide year-round service to Nantucket and Martha's Vineyard. Call ahead to make reservations.
Viking Fleet 462 W Lake Drive Montauk MA 631-668-5700
This ferry features a triple decker, 120 foot vessel with comfort amenities on board, and service is provided between Montauk Long Island and Block Island RI, New London CT, and Martha's Vineyard, MA. Well behaved dogs are allowed on board for no additional fee. Dogs must be under owner's control/care and leashed at all times.

Attractions

West Tisbury Farmer's Markets State Road West Tisbury MA 508-693-0085
The farmer's market is a great place to buy local, fresh fruits and vegetables. The market is usually held from mid-June to mid-August on Saturdays, from 9am to 12pm. Well-behaved dogs are allowed, but they must be held on a tight leash and you will need to watch them closely and avoid letting them play with other dogs. You will also need to make sure that your pooch does not go the bathroom in the market area, or on a vendors booth or produce. Please let your dog relieve himself or herself before you get there. The farmer's market is located

between the Grange Hall and the playground.

Stores
Edgartown Book Store 44 Main Street Edgartown MA   508-627-8463
A well behaved dog on leash is allowed in the bookstore.

Beaches
Joseph Sylvia State Beach Beach Road Edgartown MA   508-696-3840
Dogs are allowed during the Summer, only before 9am and after 5pm. You will need to keep your dog away from any bird nesting areas, which should have signs posted. During the off-season, from mid-September to mid-April, dogs are allowed all day. This beach is about 2 miles long. Dogs must be leashed and people need to clean up after their pets. Before you go, always verify the seasonal dates and times when dogs are allowed on the beach.
Norton Point Beach end of Katama Road Edgartown MA   508-696-3840
Dogs are allowed during the Summer, only before 9am and after 5pm. You will need to keep your dog away from any bird nesting areas, which should have signs posted. During the off-season, from mid-September to mid-April, dogs are allowed all day. This beach is about 2.5 miles long. Dogs must be leashed and people need to clean up after their pets. Before you go, always verify the seasonal dates and times when dogs are allowed on the beach.
South Beach State Park Katama Road Edgartown MA   508-693-0085
Dogs are allowed during the Summer, only after 5pm. During the off-season, from mid-September to mid-April, dogs are allowed all day. This 3 mile beach is located on the South Shore. Dogs must be leashed and people need to clean up after their pets. Before you go, always verify the seasonal dates and times when dogs are allowed on the beach.
Eastville Point Beach At bridge near Vineyard Haven Oak Bluffs MA   508-696-3840
Dogs are allowed during the Summer, only before 9am and after 5pm. You will need to keep your dog away from any bird nesting areas, which should have signs posted. During the off-season, from mid-September to mid-April, dogs are allowed all day. Dogs must be leashed and people need to clean up after their pets. Before you go, always verify the seasonal dates and times when dogs are allowed on the beach.

Parks
Manuel F. Correllus State Forest Barnes Road Marthas Vineyard MA   508-693-2540
Originally set aside as a Heath Hen Reserve in the early 1900's, this park covers 5,100+ acres in the heart of Martha's Vineyard, and is now the focal point of one of the largest environmental restorations projects in the continental US. Dogs are allowed throughout the park and on the trails. Dogs must be under owner's control, be on no more than a 10 foot leash, cleaned up after, and have proof of current rabies inoculation.
Cedar Tree Neck Sanctuary/Bruce Irons Trail Obed Dagget Road West Tisbury MA   508-693-5207
This is one of the areas managed by the Sheriff's Meadow Foundation who are dedicated to educating about and preserving the natural character of all the natural habitats and wildlife here on Martha's Vineyard. Dogs are welcome to walk this area; they must be leashed and cleaned up after at all times. Dogs, nor their owners, are allowed on the dunes.

Outdoor Restaurants
Carousel Ice Cream Factory 15 Circuit Avenue Oak Bluffs MA   508-693-7582
They do not have tables outside, but you and your pooch can enjoy the ice cream at the outdoor benches.
Coop de Ville Restaurant Dockside Marketplace Oak Bluffs MA   508-693-3420
http://www.coop.vineyard.net/index.html
This restaurant offers a variety of food including wings, soup, veggies, seafood, chicken, hamburgers and even veggie burgers. Well-behaved, leashed dogs are allowed at the outdoor tables.
Nancy's Snack Bar and Harborview Restaurant 29 Lake Avenue Oak Bluffs MA
Well-behaved, leashed dogs are allowed at the downstairs tables only, not upstairs.
Daily Grind 79 Beach Road Vineyard Haven MA   508-693-5200
There is one outdoor table in the back, near the water. Well-behaved, leashed dogs are allowed at the outdoor table. The cafe is open for breakfast and lunch.
John's Fish Market State Road Vineyard Haven MA   508-693-1220
They are open for lunch and dinner. Well-behaved, leashed dogs are allowed at the outdoor picnic tables. Tables are seasonal.
Louis' Tisbury Cafe 350 State Road Vineyard Haven MA   508-693-3255
http://www.mvol.com/louis/
This cafe serves Italian favorites, pizza, ribs, chicken, lasagna, eggplant parmesan and more. Well-behaved, leashed dogs are allowed at the outdoor picnic tables.

Nantucket

Accommodations

Brass Lantern Inn 11 North Water Street Nantucket MA   508-228-4064
http://www.brasslanternnantucket.com/
Dogs up to about 65 pounds are allowed. Call to inquire if you have a larger dog. There is a $30 per day pet fee.
All rooms are non-smoking.
Safe Harbor Guest House 2 Harbor View Way Nantucket MA   508-228-3222
http://www.beesknees.net/safeharbor/
Dogs are allowed at this guest house. All rooms have private bathrooms. If your dog will be on the bed, please
bring a sheet with you to place over the bedspread. There is no pet fee, they just request that you give the
housekeeper a tip for extra cleaning, if necessary.
TOP 200 PLACE **The Cottages at the Boat Basin (Woof Cottages)** New Whale Street P.O. Box
1139 Nantucket MA   508-325-1499 (866-838-9253)
http://www.thecottagesnantucket.com
Dogs and cats are welcome in "The Woof Cottages." These cottages are one and two bedroom cottages which
include special pet amenities like a welcome basket of pet treats and play toys, a pet bed, food and water bowls,
and a Nantucket bandana. When you make a reservation, let them know what size your pet is, so they can have
the appropriate size pet bed and bowls in the room. All cottages are non-smoking. There is a $25 one time per
stay pet fee.
The Grey Lady P.O. Box 1292 Nantucket MA   508-228-9552
Pets and children are welcome at this guest house. While there is no pet fee, they have certain pet rooms which
cost more per night than a standard room. All rooms are non-smoking. There may be a two or three night
minimum stay during the Summer. They also offer weekly cottage rentals at the Boat House.
Woof Hotel at Harbor House Village South Beach Street Nantucket MA   508-228-1500 (866-325-9300)
http://www.harborhousevillage.com
This 12 room dog centric and friendly hotel has a fenced in yard for dogs to play, a pet concierge, welcome
basket for canine visitors and a "Yappie Hour" on Fridays in the Summer.

Vacation Home Rentals

Quidnuck Vacation Rental Call to Arrange. Nantucket MA   202-663-8439
http://www.ifb.com/quidnuck/
One dog is allowed at this vacation rental home. They ask that you do not bring a puppy and to never leave your
dog alone in the house. There is a $75 one time per stay pet fee which will be used towards spraying the house
for fleas. Ask for Jack when calling.

Transportation Systems

Hy-Line Cruises Ferry Service Ocean Street Dock Hyannis MA   508-778-2600
http://www.hy-linecruises.com/
This ferry service runs from Cape Cod to Nantucket Island (1 hour on the high speed ferry) or Martha's Vineyard
(1.5 hours). They also offer the only Inter-Island Ferry between Nantucket and Martha's Vineyard (2.25 hours).
Pets are allowed on the ferries, but not in the first class lounge. Pets need to be leashed. This ferry company
provides year-round service to Nantucket and seasonal service to Martha's Vineyard. The Inter-Island Ferry is
also seasonal. No vehicles are transported on these ferries. Call ahead to make reservations.
TOP 200 PLACE **Nantucket Airlines** 660 Barnstable Road/North Ramp Hyannis MA   508-790-0300 (800-
635-8787)
http://www.nantucketairlines.com
This airline offers daily flights between Hyannis and Nantucket (20 minute flight). Dogs are allowed in the cabin
with you on this airline! Dogs under 35 pounds can be carried on your lap and no kennel is required. For dogs
over 35 pounds, there is a "shelf" which is just a few inches off the floor, in the back of the plane where your dog
can sit or lay. While you cannot sit next to your dog, you can try to get the seat directly in front of him or her.
There is no reserved seating, so you'll need to arrive early to try and make special arrangements to sit in front of
your pooch. Large dogs must be properly restrained with a leash, harness or similar device. No kennel is
required. You will need to reserve a space for your pet in advance as the airline usually only allows one dog per
flight. Their sister airline, Cape Air also allows dogs in the cabin, but most flights require your dog to be in a
kennel, and they have a size limit for dogs.
Steamship Authority Ferry Service South Street Dock Hyannis MA   508-477-8600
http://www.steamshipauthority.com
This ferry services runs from Cape Cod to Nantucket Island (2.25 hours) or Martha's Vineyard (1.5 hours). Pets

are allowed on all ferries except for the M/V Flying Cloud fast ferry. Pets must be leashed or in a crate at all times. Pets are not allowed on the seats, tables, or in the concession areas. The ferries transport both passengers and cars. They provide year-round service to Nantucket and Martha's Vineyard. Call ahead to make reservations.

Attractions
Nantucket Adventures 34 Washington St #77 Nantucket MA   508-228-6365
http://www.nantucketadventures.com
Dogs on leash are allowed on the boat tours. The boats leave from the Nantucket Town Pier. Boat tours land at the islands of Tuckernuck and Musketget for exploration.
Nantucket Regional Transit Authority (NRTA) 22 Federal Street Nantucket MA   508-228-7025
http://www.shuttlenantucket.com/
Well-behaved dogs of all sizes are allowed on Nantucket shuttle buses. Pets must be leashed or caged, well-behaved, clean and dry, and pets cannot sit on the seats. While you can still take a car onto Nantucket Island, the transit authority encourages everyone to leave their cars on the mainland.

Stores
Cold Noses Pet Boutique Straight Wharf and Courtyard Nantucket MA   508-228-KISS (5477)
http://www.coldnoses.net/
There is a good selection of items for pet owners in addition to all the pet accessories, food/treats, and toys at this boutique. Dogs must be well mannered, leashed, and under owner's care at all times.
Geronimo's of Nantucket 119 Pleasant Street Nantucket MA   508-228-3731
http://www.geronimos.com/nantucket.htm
Dogs can accompany you to this pet store which offers treats, unique pet accessories and gifts.

Beaches
Nantucket Island Beaches various locations Nantucket MA   508-228-1700
Dogs are allowed during the Summer on beaches with lifeguards only before 9am and after 5pm. On beaches that have no lifeguards, or during the Winter months, dogs are allowed all day on the beach. Dogs must always be leashed. Before you go, always verify the seasonal dates and times when dogs are allowed on the beach.

Outdoor Restaurants
Espresso To Go 1 Toombs Court Nantucket MA   508-228-6930
In addition to the variety of specialty coffees, this cafe also serves pizza, sandwiches, salads, pasta, muffins and baked goods. Leashed dogs are welcome to join you at the tables in the outside garden.
Henry's Sandwich Shop 2 Broad Street Nantucket MA   508-228-0123
They are open for breakfast, lunch and dinner. Well-behaved, leashed dogs are welcome at the outdoor tables.
Something Natural 50 Cliff Road Nantucket MA   508-228-0504
This restaurant serves health food. Dogs are allowed at the outdoor tables.

Northampton Area

Accommodations
Quality Inn 237 Russell Street/H 9 Hadley MA   413-584-9816 (877-424-6423)
Well behaved dogs are allowed for an additional one time fee of $25 per pet.

Campgrounds and RV Parks
Daughters of the American Revolution (DAR) State Forest 78 Cape Street Goshen MA   413 268-7098
With an original donation of 1,020 acres by the Daughters of the American Revolution, this park has now grown to almost 1,800 acres and has become a popular year round recreational destination with such features as the Upper and Lower Highland Lakes, miles and miles of scenic multi-use trails, and a fire tower that gives clear day views into 5 states. Dogs of all sizes are allowed for no additional fee. Dogs must be on no more than a 10 foot leash, be cleaned up after, and have proof of current rabies inoculation. Dogs are not allowed on the sandy beach area. The camp area is available with reservations from mid-May through mid-October, and on a first-come/first-served basis during the off-season. The 51 site campground sits above a scenic wetland where wildlife sighting is common, and accessible restrooms, water, and a dump station are available. The camping and tent areas also allow dogs. There is a dog walk area at the campground.

Stores

Tail Waggers Boutique 123 Hawley Street #5 Northampton MA 413-586-7226
This pet boutique specializes in animal care products, Natural dry and frozen pet foods, and grooming. Dogs must be well mannered, leashed, and under owner's care at all times.

Parks

Mount Holyoke Range State Park H 116 Amherst MA 413-586-0350
This day use park of over 3000 acres provides several diverse habitats for a variety of wildlife, and there are more than 30 miles of multi-use marked trails for year round activities. Dogs are allowed for no additional fee. Dogs must be under owner's control, leashed, and cleaned up after at all times.
Frank Newhall Look Memorial Park 300 N Main Street Florence MA 413-584-5457
http://www.lookpark.org/
Gifted to the city by Mrs. Fannie B. Look, this 150 acre park features a variety of activities, attractions, recreation, a picnic store, and a visitor center. Dogs are allowed for no additional fee. Dogs must be under owner's control, leashed, and cleaned up after at all times. Dogs are allowed on the walking path and throughout the park; they are not allowed on the rides or at the zoo.
Daughters of the American Revolution (DAR) State Forest 78 Cape Street Goshen MA 413 268-7098
With an original donation of 1,020 acres by the Daughters of the American Revolution, this park has now grown to almost 1,800 acres and has become a popular year round recreational destination with such features as the Upper and Lower Highland Lakes, miles and miles of scenic multi-use trails, and a fire tower that gives clear day views into 5 states. Dogs of all sizes are allowed for no additional fee. Dogs must be on no more than a 10 foot leash, be cleaned up after, and have proof of current rabies inoculation. Dogs are not allowed on the sandy beach area.
J.A. Skinner State Park H 47 Hadley MA 413-586-0350
Scenic views, year round hiking trails, 20 picnic sites with grills, a historical site, various habitats and wildlife, and a variety of recreational opportunities are all to be found at this 390 acre park. Dogs must be under owner's control, be on no more than a 10 foot leash, cleaned up after, and have proof of current rabies inoculation.
Norwottuck Rail Trail Damon Road Northampton MA 413 586-8706 ext. 12
Because of the path's level landscape, this 8.5 mile walking path is an easy, safe passage for all ages and abilities. There is parking at both ends of the trail, and restrooms are available at the Elwell parking area. Dogs are welcome to walk this path also. They must be under owner's control, leashed, and cleaned up after at all times.

Outdoor Restaurants

Rao's Coffee Roasting Company 17 Kellogg Avenue Amherst MA 413-253-9441
http://www.raoscoffee.com/
This coffeehouse offers some of the finest coffees available, and indoor and outside seating. Well behaved dogs are welcome to sit with their owner's at the outer tables. Dogs must be under owner's control/care and leashed at all times.

Oakham

Campgrounds and RV Parks

Pine Acres Family Camping Resort 203 Bechan Road Oakham MA 508-882-9509
http://www.pineacresresort.com
Dogs of all sizes are allowed. There is a $2 per night per pet additional fee. Dogs must be leashed and cleaned up after. The camping and tent areas also allow dogs. There is a dog walk area at the campground.

Plymouth

Campgrounds and RV Parks

Ellis Haven Family Campground 531 Furnace Road Plymouth MA 508-746-0803
http://www.ellishaven.com
Dogs of all sizes are allowed. There is a $2 per night additional fee for a dog. Dogs may not be left unattended outside, and they must be leashed and cleaned up after. This RV park is closed during the off-season. Only one dog is allowed per campsite. The camping and tent areas also allow dogs. There is a dog walk area at the campground.

Myles Standish State Forest 1941 Cranberry Road South Carver MA   508-866-2526
http://www.mass.gov/dcr/listing.htm
Dogs of all sizes are allowed. There are no additional pet fees. Dogs may not be left unattended, and they must have a current rabies certificate and shot records. Dogs must be quiet during quiet hours, be leashed, and cleaned up after. Dogs are allowed on the trails, but not on the beach or swim areas, and not in the buildings. This campground is closed during the off-season. The camping and tent areas also allow dogs. There is a dog walk area at the campground. There are no electric or water hookups at the campground.

Stores
PetSmart Pet Store 64 Long Pond Rd Plymouth MA   508-746-2077
Your licensed and well-behaved leashed dog is allowed in the store.
Petco Pet Store 216 Colony Place Plymouth MA   508-747-4132
Your licensed and well-behaved leashed dog is allowed in the store.

Beaches
Plymouth City Beach Route 3A Plymouth MA   508-747-1620
The beach in Plymouth allows dogs year round on the beach and in the water. Dogs must be leashed and cleaned up after.

Parks

Pilgrim Memorial State Park

Pilgrim Memorial State Park Water Street Plymouth MA   508 866-2580
Although the smallest park in the state, it draws a large number here to see where the passengers of the Mayflower 1st disembarked on this continent and turned an unassuming glacial boulder that sat on the shore into a famous symbol for the pioneering spirit. Dogs must be under owner's control/care at all times, be on no more than a 10 foot leash, cleaned up after, and have proof of current rabies inoculation.
Myles Standish State Forest 194 Cranberry Road South Carver MA   508-866-2526 (877-422-6762)
Although a beautiful natural area, kept well maintained in common areas, this is an unusual forest in that vegetation is quite different from what is found elsewhere in the state, and there are a number of multi-use trails for exploring this scenic park. Dogs of all sizes are allowed for no additional fees; however owners must provide proof of rabies inoculation for camping. Dogs must be well behaved, leashed, and cleaned up after at all times. Dogs are not allowed on the beach or at the picnic shelters.

Outdoor Restaurants

Lobster Hut 25 Town Wharf Plymouth MA   508-746-2270
After ordering and picking up your order at the inside counter you have an option of indoor dining or dining on the large back deck that overlooks the bay. Well behaved dogs are allowed at the outer tables. Dogs must be under owner's control/care at all times, and be leashed and cleaned up after.

Providence Area

Accommodations

Motel 6 - Providence - Seekonk 821 Fall River Avenue Seekonk MA   508-336-7800 (800-466-8356)
One well-behaved family pet per room. Guest must notify front desk upon arrival. Guest is liable for any damages. In consideration of all guests, pets must never be left unattended in the guest rooms.

Stores

PetSmart Pet Store 1385 S Washington St North Attleboro MA   508-695-2300
Your licensed and well-behaved leashed dog is allowed in the store.
Petco Pet Store 75 Highland Avenue #6 Seekonk MA   508-336-0700
Your licensed and well-behaved leashed dog is allowed in the store.
Petco Pet Store 287 Washington St South Attleboro MA   508-761-8900
Your licensed and well-behaved leashed dog is allowed in the store.

Raynham

Accommodations

Days Inn Taunton 164 New State Hwy Raynham MA   508-824-8647 (800-329-7466)
Dogs of all sizes are allowed. There is a $10 per night pet fee per pet.

Springfield

Accommodations

Motel 6 - Springfield - Chicopee 36 Johnny Cake Hollow Rd. Chicopee MA   413-592-5141 (800-466-8356)
One well-behaved family pet per room. Guest must notify front desk upon arrival. Guest is liable for any damages. In consideration of all guests, pets must never be left unattended in the guest rooms.
Park Inn 450 Memorial Drive Chicopee MA   413-739-7311
Dogs of all sizes are allowed. There is a $35 additional pet fee for the first night and $5 for each additional night.
Quality Inn 463 Memorial Drive Chicopee MA   413-592-6171 (877-424-6423)
Dogs are allowed for an additional one time pet fee of $15 per room. Dogs may not be left alone in the room for more than an hour unless crated.
Holiday Inn 711 Dwight St Springfield MA   413-781-0900 (877-270-6405)
Dogs of all sizes are allowed for an additional one time pet fee of $35 per room.
Sheraton Springfield Monarch Place Hotel One Monarch Place Springfield MA   413-781-1010 (888-625-5144)
One dog of any size is allowed for an additional one time pet fee of $50 per room. Dogs may not be left alone in the room.
Candlewood Suites West Springfield 572 Riverdale St. West Springfield MA   413-739-1122 (877-270-6405)
Dogs of all sizes are allowed for an additional pet fee per room of $25 per night.
Hampton Inn 1011 Riverdale Street West Springfield MA   413-732-1300
Dogs of all sizes are allowed. There is a $75 one time fee and a pet policy to sign at check in.
Quality Inn 1150 Riverdale Street West Springfield MA   413-739-7261 (877-424-6423)
Dogs are allowed for an additional one time fee of $35 per pet for large dogs; the fee is $25 for small dogs.
Red Roof Inn - West Springfield 1254 Riverdale Street West Springfield MA   413-731-1010 (800-RED-ROOF)
One well-behaved family pet per room. Guest must notify front desk upon arrival. Guest is liable for any damages. In consideration of all guests, pets must never be left unattended in the guest rooms.
Residence Inn by Marriott 64 Border Way West Springfield MA   413-732-9543

Dogs of all sizes are allowed. There is a $75 one time fee and a pet policy to sign at check in.

Campgrounds and RV Parks
Prospect Mountain Campground 1349 Main Road (H 57) Granville MA 888-550-4PMC (762)
http://www.prospectmtncampground.com/
Dogs of all sizes are allowed. There are no additional pet fees. Dogs may not be left unattended outside, and left inside only for short periods. There is a day kennel close by for your pet when you will be gone longer. Dogs must be leashed and cleaned up after. This RV park is closed during the off-season. The camping and tent areas also allow dogs. There is a dog walk area at the campground.
Sunset View Farms 57 Town Farm Road Monson MA 413-267-9269
http://www.sunsetview.com
Dogs of all sizes are allowed. There are no additional pet fees. Dogs must have current rabies shots, be leashed, and cleaned up after. Dogs may not be left unattended.

Stores
Petco Pet Store 45 Holyoke St Holyoke MA 413-539-9197
Your licensed and well-behaved leashed dog is allowed in the store.
Petco Pet Store 1694 Boston Rd Springfield MA 413-543-2085
Your licensed and well-behaved leashed dog is allowed in the store.

Parks
Dinosaur Footprints Park H 5 Holyoke MA 413-684-0148
This small, narrow park by the railroad tracks is home to 134 of some of our biggest land animals that frequented the area 190 million years ago, and were uncovered during the construction of Route 5. Crossing the tracks for river access is not allowed here. Dogs are allowed for no additional fee. Dogs must be under owner's control, leashed, and cleaned up after at all times.
Forest Park Sumner Avenue and Main Greeting Road Springfield MA 413-787-6440
This city park features plenty of gaming and picnic areas, a pool, spray structure and water fountain, and accessible restrooms. Dogs are welcome and they must be under owner's control at all times, leashed, and cleaned up after.
Springfield Armory National Historic Site One Armory Square Ste 2 Springfield MA 413-734-8551
http://www.nps.gov/spar/
Dogs must be on leash and must be cleaned up after on the grounds. Dogs are not allowed in any buildings. This is the first National Armory that began manufacturing muskets in 1794. Within decades Springfield Armory had perfected pioneering manufacturing methods that were critical to American industrialization.

Sturbridge

Accommodations
Vienna Restaurant and Historic Inn 14 South Street Southbridge MA 508-764-0700 (866-2-VIENNA (284-3662))
Rich in European ambiance, this 1812 inn is on the National Historic Register, and they offer spacious accommodations, fine dining, music, a venue for special events, a veranda, and a lovely patio. One dog is allowed per room for an additional one time pet fee of $25. Dogs must be quiet, well behaved, non-shedding, and friendly to people and other pets. They are not allowed on the furniture or beds. Dogs are allowed at the outer tables of the restaurant; they must be leashed and under owner's control/care at all times.
Comfort Inn and Suites Colonial 215 Charlton Road Sturbridge MA 508-347-3306 (877-424-6423)
Dogs are allowed for an additional fee of $15 per night per pet.
Days Inn Sturbridge 66-68 Haynes St Sturbridge MA 508-347-3391 (800-329-7466)
Dogs of all sizes are allowed. There is a $7 per night pet fee per pet.
Publick House Historic Inn On the Common, Route 131 Sturbridge MA 508-347-3313 (800-PUBLICK)
http://www.publickhouse.com/
There is a $5 per day additional pet fee.
Sturbridge Host Hotel 366 Main Street Sturbridge MA 508-347-7393
Dogs of all sizes are allowed. There is a $15 fee for the first night; if more than one night, it is a $25 one time fee per room. There is a pet policy to sign at check in.
Super 8 Sturbridge 358 Main Street Sturbridge MA 508-347-9000 (800-800-8000)
Dogs of all sizes are allowed. There is a $10 per night pet fee per pet. Smoking and non-smoking rooms are available for pet rooms.

Campgrounds and RV Parks
Jellystone Park 30 River Road Sturbridge MA   508-347-9570
http://www.jellystonessturbridge.com
Dogs of all sizes are allowed. There are no additional pet fees. The camping and tent areas also allow dogs.
There is a dog walk area at the campground.
Wells State Park 159 Walker Pond Road Sturbridge MA   508-347-9257
Dogs of all sizes are allowed. There are no additional pet fees. Dogs may not be left unattended, they must have
a current rabies certificate and shot records, be leashed at all times, and cleaned up after. Dogs are allowed on
all the trails, but not on the beach. This campground is closed during the off-season. The camping and tent areas
also allow dogs. There is a dog walk area at the campground. There are no electric or water hookups at the
campground.
Oak Haven Family Campground 22 Main Street Wales MA   413-245-7148
http://www.oakhavencampground.com
Dogs of all sizes are allowed. There are no additional pet fees. Dogs must have current rabies records, be
leashed, and cleaned up after.
The Old Sawmill Campground Box 377 Longhill Road West Brookfield MA   508-867-2427
http://oldsawmillcampground.com
Dogs of all sizes are allowed. There are no additional pet fees. Dogs must be leashed and cleaned up after.

Outdoor Restaurants
Pioneer Brewing Company 195 Arnold Road Fiskdale MA   508-347-7500
http://www.hylandbrew.com/
This brewery will allowed friendly, house-trained dogs to come inside here except when very crowed during
events. Dogs must be under owner's control/care, leashed, and cleaned up at all times.
Vienna Restaurant (and Historic Inn) 14 South Street Southbridge MA   508-764-0700
http://www.thevienna.com/restaurant.html
Rich in European ambiance, this inn offers fine dining, music, a venue for special events, and a lovely patio.
Dogs are allowed at the outer tables; they must be leashed and under owner's control/care at all times. One dog
per room is also allowed in the inn.

Taunton

Campgrounds and RV Parks
Massasoit State Park 1361 Middleboro E Taunton MA   508-822-7405
Dogs of all sizes are allowed. There are no additional pet fees. Dogs may not be left unattended, they must have
current rabies certificate and shot records, be quiet, well behaved, leashed, and cleaned up after. Dogs are
allowed on the trails. This campground is closed during the off-season. The camping and tent areas also allow
dogs. There is a dog walk area at the campground. There are no water hookups at the campground.

Stores
Petco Pet Store 65a Taunton Depot Drive Taunton MA   508-823-8084
Your licensed and well-behaved leashed dog is allowed in the store.

Topsfield

Stores
Petco Pet Store 239 Newburyport Turnpike Topsfield MA   978-887-7387
Your licensed and well-behaved leashed dog is allowed in the store.

Worcester

Accommodations
Comfort Inn 426 Southbridge Street Auburn MA   508-832-8300 (877-424-6423)
Dogs are allowed for an additional one time pet fee of $20 per room.

La Quinta Inn Auburn/Worcester 446 Southbridge Street Auburn MA   508-832-7000 (800-531-5900)
Dogs of all sizes are allowed. There are no additional fees. There is a pet waiver to sign at check in. Dogs may not be left unattended, except for short periods. Dogs must be leashed and cleaned up after.
Comfort Inn 399 Turnpike Road Westborough MA   508-366-0202 (877-424-6423)
Dogs are allowed for an additional fee of $10 per night per pet.
Residence Inn by Marriott 25 Connector Road Westborough MA   508-366-7700
Dogs up to 100 pounds are allowed. There is a $75 one time fee and a pet policy to sign at check in.
Crowne Plaza 10 Lincoln Square Worcester MA   508-791-1600 (877-270-6405)
A dog up to 50 pounds is allowed for an additional pet fee of $25 per night, and pets must be crated when left alone in the room.

Campgrounds and RV Parks
KOA-Webster/Sturbridge 106 Douglas Road Webster MA   508-943-1895 (800-562-1895)
http://www.webstercamp.com
Dogs of all sizes are allowed. There are no additional pet fees. Dogs must be leashed and cleaned up after. There are some breed restrictions. This RV park is closed during the off-season. The camping and tent areas also allow dogs. There is a dog walk area at the campground.

Attractions
Blackstone River Bikeway Worcester Square Worcester MA   401-762-0250
http://www.blackstoneriverbikeway.com/
Eventually this bikeway will cover 48 miles from Providence, RI to Worcester, MA, and will pass through the historic John H. Chafee Blackstone River Valley National Heritage Corridor as well as many other significant natural and historic components. Currently there are 2 ½ miles available in MA, and 10 miles of trail in RI. Dogs are welcome on the trail. They must be under owner's control/care, leashed, and cleaned up after at all times.

Stores
Petco Pet Store 438 Southbridge St Auburn MA   508-721-2241
Your licensed and well-behaved leashed dog is allowed in the store.
PetSmart Pet Store 70 Worcester Providence Turnpike Millbury MA   508-865-4241
Your licensed and well-behaved leashed dog is allowed in the store.
Petco Pet Store 87 Boston Turnpike #9 Shrewsbury MA   508-831-1116
Your licensed and well-behaved leashed dog is allowed in the store.

Parks
Tufts University School of Veterinary Medicine 200 Westboro Rd/H 30 North Grafton MA   508-839-5302
The campus of this veterinary school is located among rolling hills with several great walking trails, and although private property, they welcome hikers with their canine companions. If you are eastbound on Highway 30, there is a parking area off to the left as you are just passing the university. Dogs may be off lead only if they are friendly and well behaved with people as well as other animals, and they respond to voice control. Please clean up after your pet when on the trails and you will need to bring your own supplies.

Outdoor Restaurants
Java Hut 1073 - A Main Street/H 9 Worcester MA   508-752-1678
http://www.javahutma.com/
This coffeehouse offers outside seating, and well behaved dogs are welcome to sit with their owner's at the outer tables. Dogs must be under owner's control/care and leashed at all times.

Chapter 6

Rhode Island
Dog Travel Guide

Barrington

Off-Leash Dog Parks
Haines Park Dog Park Rt 103 Barrington RI   401-253-7482
http://www.riparks.com/haines.htm
This fenced dog park is located on the west side of the 100 acre Haines Memorial State Park in Barrington. Dogs must be on leash when outside of the off-leash area. The park is open during daylight hours. From East Providence exit I-195 at Route 103 and head south to the park.

Block Island

Accommodations
TOP 200 PLACE The Blue Dory Inn Dodge Street Block Island RI   401-466-2254 (800-992-7290)
http://www.blockislandinns.com/
This historic 1862 mansion sits at the head of Crescent Beach only a mile from the Atlantic Ocean on 5 rolling acres, and every afternoon guests can meet in the parlor for wine, hors d'oevres and their specialty-Blue Dory cookies. Dogs of all sizes are welcome for an additional $25 one time fee per pet. Dogs must be leashed and cleaned up after.
The Island Home Beach Avenue Block Island RI   401-466-5944
One large dog up to about 50 pounds or 2 dogs at about 10 pounds each are allowed. There is a pet policy to sign at check in and there are no additional pet fees.

Vacation Home Rentals
Vacation Rentals by Owner Calico Hill Block Island RI   401-497-0631
http://www.vrbo.com/90721
Set upon rolling hills with views of the harbor and the town only a few minutes away, this 1871 farmhouse offers all the modern amenities, and a great starting point for a wide variety of activities, and land and water recreation. Dogs of all sizes are allowed for no additional pet fees. Dogs must be house trained, well behaved, and leashed and cleaned up after at all times inside and outside.

Transportation Systems
Block Island Ferry two location-see comments Block Island RI   401-783-4613
This ferry line provides passenger and vehicle service from Point Judith to Block Island (one hour trip) and from Fort Adams in Newport to Block Island (two hour trip). Pets on a leash or in a carrier are allowed on the ferry. One way fares start at just under $10 per person and about $5 per child. Vehicles are transported on the ferry that leaves from Point Judith. Rates for vehicles range from about $40 to $95 or more depending on the size and type of vehicle. Call ahead to make reservations for vehicles. Only cash or travelers checks are accepted at the Newport location. At Point Judith, credit cards are also accepted. Rates are subject to change. Parking for the Point Judith ferry is located across the street from the ferry. Prices range from $5 to $10 per day. Parking for the Newport ferry is located at Fort Adams State Park at no charge.
Viking Fleet 462 W Lake Drive Montauk RI   631-668-5700
This ferry features a triple decker, 120 foot vessel with comfort amenities on board, and service is provided between Montauk Long Island and Block Island RI, New London CT, and Martha's Vineyard, MA. Well behaved dogs are allowed on board for no additional fee. Dogs must be under owner's control/care and leashed at all times. The ferry docks on Block Island at Champlin's Marina.

Beaches
TOP 200 PLACE Block Island Beaches Corn Neck Road Block Island RI   401-466-2982
Dogs are allowed year-round on the island beaches, but they must be leashed and people are required to clean up after their pets. To get to the beaches, take a right out of town and follow Corn Neck Road. To get to the island, you will need to take the Block Island Ferry which allows leashed dogs. The ferry from Port Judith, RI to Block Island operates daily. If you are taking the ferry from Newport, RI or New London, CT to the island, please note these ferries only operate during the Summer. If you are bringing a vehicle on the ferry, reservations are required. Call the Block Island Ferry at 401-783-4613 for auto reservations.

Outdoor Restaurants

Old Post Office Bagel Shop Corner of Corn Neck Road & Ocean Avenue Block Island RI 401-466-5959
This bagel shop offers indoor and outdoor dining. Dogs are permitted at the outdoor tables. Dogs must be well behaved, under owner's control, and leashed and cleaned up after at all times.

Chepachet

Campgrounds and RV Parks

George Washington Management Area 2185 Putnam Park Chepachet RI 401-568-2248
http://www.riparks.com
Dogs of all sizes are allowed. There are no additional pet fees. Dogs may not be left unattended, they must have current rabies certificate and shot records, be leashed, and cleaned up after. Dogs are allowed on the trails, but not on the beach. This campground is closed during the off-season. The camping and tent areas also allow dogs. There is a dog walk area at the campground. There are no electric or water hookups at the campground.

Foster

Campgrounds and RV Parks

Ginny-B Campground 7 Harrington Road Foster RI 401-397-9477
http://www.ginny-b.com
Dogs of all sizes are allowed. There are no additional pet fees. Dogs must be well behaved, leashed, and cleaned up after. The camping and tent areas also allow dogs.

Glocester

Campgrounds and RV Parks

George Washington Memorial Camping Area Putnam Pike Glocester RI 401-568-2013
There are a variety of plant, bird, and wildlife habitats to explore here, as well as historic sites, many trails with varying difficulties, and various land and water recreation. Dogs are allowed for no additional fee; they must have a valid license tag, and owners must carry proof of current rabies inoculation. Dogs must be quiet, well behaved, leashed (6 foot), and properly cleaned up after at all times. They may not be left unattended; with exception for hunting season or dog trials at which time dogs may be left alone in a vehicle. Dogs are not allowed at bathing beaches, or to be washed in any natural body of water. Dogs must be registered with the state prior to camping (not needed for day use), and the form can be obtained at http://www.riparks.com/pdfs/Pet%20Certification%20Form.pdf. Campsites are available on a first come, first served basis, drinking water is available, there are gaming areas, waterfront sites, and they have either outhouses or pit toilets. This RV park is closed during the off-season. The camping and tent areas also allow dogs. There is a dog walk area at the campground. There are no electric or water hookups at the campgrounds.

Parks

George Washington Memorial Camping Area Putnam Pike Glocester RI 401-568-2013
There are a variety of plant, bird, and wildlife habitats to explore here, as well as historic sites, many trails with varying difficulties, and various land and water recreation. Dogs are allowed for no additional fee; they must have a valid license tag, and owners must carry proof of current rabies inoculation. Dogs must be quiet, well behaved, leashed (6 foot), and properly cleaned up after at all times. They may not be left unattended; with exception for hunting season or dog trials at which time dogs may be left alone in a vehicle. Dogs are not allowed at bathing beaches, or to be washed in any natural body of water. Dogs must be registered with the state prior to camping (not needed for day use), and the form can be obtained at http://www.riparks.com/pdfs/Pet%20Certification%20Form.pdf.

N Kingston

Stores

Shaggy Chic Pet Boutique 3 Main Street N Kingston RI   401-667-7273
www.shaggychicpets.com
Your pooch will need some time to see the wide variety of pet products at this boutique, from their tastiest treats to couture evening wear and everything in between. Dogs must be well behaved, under owner's control/care, and leashed.

Newport

Accommodations

Howard Johnson Inn 351 West Main Rd. Middletown RI   401-849-2000 (800-446-4656)
Dogs of all sizes are welcome. There is a $10 per day pet fee. Pets may not be left unattended in the room.
Almy Cottage 141 Coggeshall Ave Newport RI   401-864-0686
This vacation cottage is close to many of the attractions that draw people here such as Mansion Row on Bellevue Avenue or the exhilarating Cliff Walk, and it is only a short walk to a small private beach. Dogs of all sizes are welcome for no additional pet fee. They are allowed in the garden cottage only, and they must be leashed and cleaned up after at all times. Dogs may only be left alone in the cottage if they are comfortable being alone and will be quiet and well behaved.
Chestnut Inn 99 3rd Street Newport RI   401-847-6949
http://members.aol.com/chstnut99/
This year round family or couples destination feature 2 oversized Victorian bedrooms, a continental breakfast, and a great location to several other attractions and recreational pursuits. Dog of all sizes are allowed for no additional fee. There can only be one dog if only 1 room is rented; however, up to 2 dogs are allowed if both rooms are taken. Dogs must be well mannered, leashed, and cleaned up after.
Hotel Viking One Bellview Avenue Newport RI   401-847-3300 (800-556-7126)
Although a small boutique hotel of former days and registered with Historic Hotels of America, this wonderfully updated spa hotel has numerous amenities and services for the business or leisure traveler, a convenient location to a number of sites of interest, fine dining, and more. Dogs of all sizes are allowed for an additional fee of $75 per pet per stay. Complimentary organic doggy biscuits await their canine guests, and Canine room service is only a call away. Dogs must be quiet, well behaved, leashed, cleaned up after, and crated when left alone in the room.
Motel 6 - Newport 249 JT Connell Highway Newport RI   401-848-0600 (800-466-8356)
One well-behaved family pet per room. Guest must notify front desk upon arrival. Guest is liable for any damages. In consideration of all guests, pets must never be left unattended in the guest rooms.
Murray House 1 Murray Place Newport RI   401-846-3337
http://www.murrayhouse.com/
Located in the famed Newport Mansion District, this guest house features a nice beach a short walk away, private entrance to each of the rooms, a gourmet breakfast brought to your room or served on your private patio area, an in-ground pool and hot-tub, and flower gardens. Dogs of all sizes are allowed for an additional fee of $10 per night per pet for small dogs and $35 per night per pet for medium-large to large dogs. There can be 1 large dog or 2 small to medium dogs per room. Dogs must be leashed and cleaned up after at all times.
The Beech Tree Inn 34 Rhode Island Avenue Newport RI   401-847-9794 (800-748-6565)
http://www.beechtreeinn.com/
This modernized 1880's Victorian home features bright, spacious rooms, a garden, and rooftop decks. Dogs of all sizes are welcome for an additional fee of $25 per night per pet. There can be 1 large dog or 2 small to medium dogs per room. Dogs may only be left alone in the room if they are comfortable being alone and will be quiet and well behaved. Dogs must be leashed, cleaned up after, and crated with a contact number left at the front desk if they are in the room alone.
The Poplar House 19 Poplar Avenue Newport RI   401-846-0976
Well behaved, clean, friendly dogs of all sizes are allowed. There is a $10 per night per room additional pet fee. Dogs are not allowed to be left alone in the room.

Vacation Home Rentals

Dun Rovin 7 Florence Ave. Newport RI   401-846-2294
3 bedroom 2 bath house in the southern part of Newport. All pets are welcome. The home is near the Ocean Drive, Gooseberry Beach, Bellevue Ave. mansions,Ft. Adams, New York yacht club and Salve Regina University. All linens, dishes etc. are provided as well as cable TV, DVD, garden patio, W/D,local phone. There is a separate apt. on the premise which is occupied from time to time. There is no smoking allowed.

Transportation Systems

Interstate Navigation/Block Island Ferry 304 Grey Island Road Narragansett RI   401-783-4613
http://www.blockislandferry.com
The ferry rides are about 1 hour, and they are open all year. Ther ferries leave from Newport at Fort Adams State Park and Point Judith (Galilee) just south of Narragansett. The ferries sail from Old Harbor on Block Island. Dogs are allowed, but they must be friendly, well behaved, and leashed. They request to have dogs relieve themselves before boarding, and doggie bags are required.

Attractions
Newport Historical Society 82 Touro Street Newport RI   401-846-0813
This is about a 1 hour historical tour, and a well behaved dog on a leash is allowed.
Touro Synagogue National Historic Site 85 Touro Street Newport RI   401-847-4794
http://www.nps.gov/tosy/index.htm
Dogs must be on leash and must be cleaned up after on the grounds. Dogs are not allowed in buildings. Touro Synagogue, dedicated in 1762, is the oldest synagogue in the United States and the only one that survives from the colonial era.

Stores
Petco Pet Store 1309 West Main Rd Middletown RI   401-846-8105
Your licensed and well-behaved leashed dog is allowed in the store.

Beaches
Easton's Beach Memorial Blvd. Newport RI   401-847-6875
Dogs are only allowed on the beach during the off-season. They are not allowed on the beach from Memorial Day weekend through Labor Day weekend. Pets must be on leash and people need to clean up after their pets. The beach is located off Route 138A (Memorial Blvd.). There is a parking fee.

Parks
Beavertail State Park Beavertail Road Jamestown RI   401-884-2010
http://www.riparks.com/beaverta1.htm
Displaying some of the most beautiful New England coastline, this park can be enjoyed by car to the 4 overlooks or by foot through various hiking trails. Dogs are allowed for no additional fee; they must have a valid license tag, and owners must carry proof of current rabies inoculation. Dogs must be quiet, well behaved, leashed (6 foot), and properly cleaned up after at all times. They may not be left unattended; with exception for hunting season or dog trials at which time dogs may be left alone in a vehicle. Dogs are not allowed at bathing beaches, or to be washed in any natural body of water.
Brenton Point State Park Ocean Drive Newport RI   401-849-4562
http://www.riparks.com/BRENTON.HTM
This park is located on the grounds of a grand old estate that offer gardens, scenic hiking trails, about 20 picnic tables on a 1st served basis, and outstanding views of where the ocean meets the rocky headlands here. Dogs (2) of all sizes are allowed for no additional fee; they must have a valid license tag, and owners must carry proof of current rabies inoculation. Dogs must be quiet, well behaved, leashed (6 foot), and properly cleaned up after at all times. They may not be left unattended at any time; with exception for hunting season or dog trials at which time dogs may be left alone in a vehicle. Dogs are not allowed at bathing beaches, and they may not be washed in any natural body of water.
TOP 200 PLACE **Fort Adams State Park** Harrison Avenue Newport RI   401-847-2400
http://www.riparks.com/fortadams.htm
In addition to sitting prominently on Newport Harbor with spectacular panoramic views and year round recreation, this historic park is also host to various festivals and concerts. Dogs are allowed for no additional fee; they must have a valid license tag, and owners must carry proof of current rabies inoculation. Dogs must be quiet, well behaved, leashed (6 foot), and properly cleaned up after at all times. They may not be left unattended; with exception for hunting season or dog trials at which time dogs may be left alone in a vehicle. Dogs are not allowed at bathing beaches, or to be washed in any natural body of water.

Off-Leash Dog Parks
Newport Dog Park Connell Highway Newport RI   401-845-5800
This dog park is located on Connell Highway in Newport. It is a fenced dog park and is open from 6 am to 9 pm.

Outdoor Restaurants
Tricias 14 Narragansett Ave Jamestown RI   401-423-1490
Specializing in tropical grill, this café also offers a full bar, a romantic ambiance, and outdoor dining. Dogs are

allowed at the outer tables; they must be leashed and under owner's control/care at all times.

Canfield House Restaurant and Pub 5 Memorial Blvd Newport RI   401-847-0167
Located downstairs from the historic Canfield House, this New York-style bar and grille is a favorite spot with dog owners for their Monday night K-9 Cocktails. You can sit at the outside bar to enjoy the ambiance of this 1860's Victorian home with your pup, and enjoy drinks and the doggy biscuits given out by the owner, Maggie. It was once a world renowned gambling casino at the turn of the century and has been completely restored to it's original luster. K-9 Cocktails is on Monday nights only, and they open at 5 pm. All dogs are welcome, but happy dogs and owners are preferred. Dogs must be leashed and cleaned up after.

Loca 109 Long Wharf Newport RI   401-843-8300
Innovative Mexican cuisine, a fun atmosphere, extreme cocktails, and seasonal alfresco dining have made this a popular destination. Dogs are allowed at the outer tables, they must be leashed and under owner's control/care at all times.

Nikolas Pizza Newport 38 Memorial Blvd W Newport RI   401-849-6611
This traditional pizza, sandwich, and beer eatery offers outdoor dining during the warm season. Dogs are allowed to join you at the outdoor tables; just go in and place your order. Dogs must be well behaved, under owner's control at all times, and leashed.

O'Brien's Pub 501 Thames Street Newport RI   401-849-6623
http://www.theobrienspub.com/
This pub and restaurant features an outdoor garden patio, and during the Summer months they offer live outdoor entertainment as well. Dogs are permitted at the outdoor tables. Dogs must be well behaved, under owner's control, and leashed and cleaned up after at all times.

Salvation Army Cafe 140 Broadway Newport RI   401-847-2620
http://www.salvationcafe.com/
Serving brunch through dinner, this eatery features fresh innovative cuisine with a seasonally influenced menu, and also offers indoor and outdoor dining options. Dogs are permitted at the outdoor tables, and they are known to bring water for your pup as well. Dogs must be well behaved, under owner's control, and leashed and cleaned up after at all times.

Sardella's Restaurant 30 Memorial Blvd Newport RI   401-849-6312
http://www.sardellas.com/
This restaurant offers Italian cuisine, and a selection of wines and champagnes. Outdoor dining service in a beautiful garden setting is also available for those with canine companions. Dogs must be well behaved, attended to at all times, and leashed. They ask that you phone ahead so they can reserve a table that is out of the main line of foot traffic.

The Canfield House Restaurant 5 Memorial Blvd Newport RI   401-847-0416
The Canfield House, listed on the National Registry of Historic Places, has been restored to its 1860's Victorian elegance, and now features fine American cuisine. Only on Monday nights during the Summer months (from about May until too cold) they allow your pooch to join you on the patio. Dogs must be well behaved, leashed, and under owner's control at all times.

Providence

Accommodations

Providence Marriott Downtown One Orms Street Providence RI   401-272-2400 (800-228-9290)
One dog up to 50 pounds is allowed. There is a $50 one time additional pet fee. Dogs may not be left alone in the room, and they must be leashed and cleaned up after.

The Cady House 127 Power Street Providence RI   401-273-5398
http://www.cadyhouse.com/
Built in 1838, the Cady house offers rooms individually decorated with period antiques and items from around the world, a garden patio where guests can dine in good weather, and a convenient location to an array of local activities, universities, shops, and eateries. Dogs of all sizes are welcome for no additional pet fee. Dogs are allowed in the garden apartment only, and they must be well behaved and friendly towards the other pets in residence. Dogs must be leashed and cleaned up after, and they may only be left alone in the room if they will be calm and comfortable.

Crowne Plaza 801 Greenwich Ave Warwick RI   401-732-6000 (877-270-6405)
Dogs of all sizes are allowed for no additional fee; dogs must be crated when left alone in the room.

Hampton Inn 2100 Post Road Warwick RI   401-739-8888
Dogs of all sizes are allowed. There are no additional pet fees.

Holiday Inn Express & Suites 901 Jefferson Blvd Warwick RI   401-736-5000 (877-270-6405)
Dogs of all sizes are allowed for a $50 refundable pet deposit per room.

Motel 6 - Providence - Warwick 20 Jefferson Boulevard Warwick RI   401-467-9800 (800-466-8356)
One well-behaved family pet per room. Guest must notify front desk upon arrival. Guest is liable for any damages. In consideration of all guests, pets must never be left unattended in the guest rooms.

Residence Inn by Marriott 500 Kilvert Street Warwick RI   401-737-7100
Dogs of all sizes are allowed, however only two pets can be in the studio or double rooms, and up to three pets in the Penthouse suite. There is also a pet policy to sign at check in.
Sheraton Providence Airport Hotel 1850 Post Road Warwick RI   401-738-4000 (888-625-5144)
Dogs up to 80 pounds are allowed for no additional pet fee. Dogs may not be left alone in the room.

Campgrounds and RV Parks

Bowdish Lake 40 Safari Road Glocester RI   401-568-8890
http://www.bowdishlake.com
Dogs of all sizes are allowed, but some breeds are not. There is a $10 per night per pet additional fee. Dogs must be well behaved, leashed, and cleaned up after. The camping and tent areas also allow dogs. There is a dog walk area at the campground.
Holiday Acres Camping Resort 591 Snakehill Road N Scituate RI   401-934-0780
http://www.holidayacrescampground.com
Dogs of all sizes are allowed, however some breeds are not. There are no additional pet fees. Dogs must be well behaved and they are not allowed on other sites or the beach. They must be leashed and cleaned up after. The camping and tent areas also allow dogs. There is a dog walk area at the campground.

Attractions

New England Fast Ferry 8 Point Street Providence RI   617-748-1428
http://www.baystatecruises.com
This ferry covers the area from Providence, RI to Newport, RI and back. Rides are between an hour and an hour and a half. Well behaved dogs are allowed at no additional fee. Dogs must be leashed and cleaned up after, so bring doggy bags.

Walk along the river with Downtown Providence in the distance

Providence Preservation Society Walking Tours 21 Meeting Street Providence RI   401-831-7440
Here is a walking/driving tour that you and your pooch can both enjoy. Tour books are available on the web or at the Preservation Society. There is a $3 fee for booklets of individual neighborhoods, or a 320-page guide featuring 12 different self-guided tours for a total cost of $26.95. Both will give visitors an inside look at the unique architecture and historical heritage of this area. Dogs must be on lead and cleaned up after at all times.

Rhode Island - Please always call ahead to make sure that an establishment is still dog-friendly

Roger Williams National Memorial

Roger Williams National Memorial 282 North Main Street Providence RI   401-521-7266
http://www.nps.gov/rowi/index.htm
Dogs must be on leash and must be cleaned up after on the grounds of the site. Dogs are not allowed in
buildings. The site features nature walks and a museum. The memorial commemorates the life of the founder of
Rhode Island and a champion of the ideal of religious freedom.
Walking Tours of Providence 52 Power Street Providence RI   401-331-8575
http://www.rihs.org
This is a narrated historical walking tour that begins at the John Brown House on Power Street and lasts about
an hour. A quiet, well behaved, leashed dog is allowed on the tour.
Blackstone River Valley National Heritage Corridor One Depot Square Woonsocket RI   401-762-0250
http://www.nps.gov/blac/
Dogs on leash are allowed on the property site. They are not allowed in any buildings. The park features
camping, hiking, boating, auto touring, and more. You must follow rules of local state parks and cities within the
corridor.

Stores

Petco Pet Store 585 N Main St Providence RI   401-454-4956
Your licensed and well-behaved leashed dog is allowed in the store.
PetSmart Pet Store 1276 Bald Hill Rd Warwick RI   401-828-0500
Your licensed and well-behaved leashed dog is allowed in the store.
Petco Pet Store 1400 Bald Hill Rd Warwick RI   401-826-7387
Your licensed and well-behaved leashed dog is allowed in the store.

Parks

Snake Den State Park 2321 Hartford Avenue Johnston RI   401-222-2632
http://www.riparks.com/snakeden.htm
This 1000 acre park features self-guided walking trails through floral and forested areas. There is a small parking
lot on Brown Avenue, and they are open year round from sunrise to sunset. There are no facilities of any kind.
Dogs are allowed on the grounds and the trails; they are not allowed in the working farm area. Dogs must be
under owner's control/care at all times, and be leashed and cleaned up after.
Roger Williams Park 1000 Elmwood Avenue Providence RI   401-785-3510
Nationally declared as one of America's premier historic urban parks, it is multi-recreational/educational and
offers the public more than just a "Jewel" of a park with miles of trails, grassy or shady picnic areas, and various

year round events. Dogs of all sizes are allowed in the park; they are not allowed in the zoo. Dogs must be under owner's control, leashed, and cleaned up after at all times.

Off-Leash Dog Parks
Gano Street Dog Park Gano Street and Power Providence RI   401-785-9450
This fenced, off-leash dog park opened on June 14, 2006. It is Providence's first official off-leash area for dogs. The park is maintained by the Providence Dog Park Association which is looking to make some improvements to the park. To get to the dog park you can enter Gano Street Park at Gano and Power. Pass the Fox Point Community Garden and turn right. The dog park is behind the basketball courts.
Warwick Dog Park 40 Asylum Road Warwick RI   401-734-3690
This is a 33,000 square foot fenced dog park with grass, shade and benches. The dog park is open during daylight hours and is located in Warwick City Park at the end of Asylum Road.

Outdoor Restaurants
Amy's Place 214 Wickenden Street Providence RI   401-274-9966
http://www.thechubbins.com/
Open for breakfast and lunch, this eatery offers indoor and outdoor dining. Dogs are permitted at the outdoor tables; however they request quests with pets dine during the non-busy hours. Dogs must be well behaved, under owner's control, and leashed and cleaned up after at all times.
Cable Car Cinema 204 S Main Providence RI   401-272-3970
http://www.cablecarcinema.com/
This café offers indoor and outdoor dining and movies. Dogs are permitted at the outdoor tables. Dogs must be well behaved, under owner's control, and leashed and cleaned up after at all times.
Hemenway's 121 S Main Street Providence RI   401-351-8570
http://www.hemenwaysrestaurant.com
This seafood grill and oyster bar is open for lunch and dinner and offer indoor and outdoor dining. Dogs are permitted at the outdoor tables. Dogs must be well behaved, under owner's control, and leashed and cleaned up after at all times.

Southern Rhode Island

Accommodations
The Kings' Rose 1747 Mooresfield Road South Kingston RI   401-783-5222
This colonial style home, listed on the National Register of Historic Places, features 16 guest rooms, over 2 acres of gardens, and a convenient location to several other attractions and activities. Dogs of all sizes are welcome for no additional pet fees. Dogs must be leashed, cleaned up after, and crated when left alone in the room.

Campgrounds and RV Parks
Burlingame State Campground Route 1 Charlestown RI   401-322-7337
http://www.riparks.com/burlgmcamp.htm
Featuring 3,100 acres of rocky woodland, an almost 600 acre lake, extensive picnic facilities, and a swimming beach with a bathhouse have made this a popular recreational destination. Dogs are allowed for no additional fee; they must have a valid license tag, and owners must carry proof of current rabies inoculation. Dogs must be quiet, well behaved, leashed (6 foot), and properly cleaned up after at all times. They may not be left unattended; with exception for hunting season or dog trials at which time dogs may be left alone in a vehicle. Dogs are not allowed at bathing beaches, or to be washed in any natural body of water. Dogs must be registered with the state prior to camping (not needed for day use), and the form can be obtained at http://www.riparks.com/pdfs/Pet% 20Certification%20Form.pdf. Dogs are not allowed at the Burlingame picnic area from April 1st through September 30th. The camp area offers several hundred sites on a first come first served basis. There is a camp store, restrooms with showers as well as porta-potties, and dumping stations. This RV park is closed during the off-season. The camping and tent areas also allow dogs. There is a dog walk area at the campground. There are no electric or water hookups at the campgrounds.
Whispering Pines 41 Sawmill Road Hope Valley RI   401-539-7011
http://whisperingpinescamping.com
Well behaved dogs of all sizes are allowed. There are no additional pet fees. No aggressive dogs are allowed, and they must be kept leashed and cleaned up after. There are some breed restrictions.
Fishermen's State Park and Campground 1011 Point Judith Road Narragansett RI   401-789-8374
http://www.riparks.com/fisherma.htm
With landscaped grounds and tree-lined paths, this 90 acre park can feel more like a seaside village, and they

offer a good variety of land and water recreational opportunities. Dogs are allowed for no additional fee; they must have a valid license tag, and owners must carry proof of current rabies inoculation. Dogs must be quiet, well behaved, leashed (6 foot), and properly cleaned up after at all times. They may not be left unattended; with exception for hunting season or dog trials at which time dogs may be left alone in a vehicle. Dogs are not allowed at bathing beaches, or to be washed in any natural body of water. Dogs must be registered with the state prior to camping (not needed for day use), and the form can be obtained at http://www.riparks.com/pdfs/Pet%20Certification%20Form.pdf. The camp area offers picnic tables, a playground, restrooms, coin operated showers, and a dump station. This RV park is closed during the off-season. The camping and tent areas also allow dogs. There is a dog walk area at the campground.

Wordon Pond Family Campground 416 A Worden Pond Road Wakefield RI   401-789-9113
http://www.wordenpondcampground.com/
Dogs of all sizes are allowed. There are no additional pet fees. Dogs must be leashed and cleaned up after. This RV park is closed during the off-season. The camping and tent areas also allow dogs. There is a dog walk area at the campground.

Wawaloam Campground 510 Gardner Road West Kingston RI   401-294-3039
http://www.wawaloam.com
Dogs of all sizes are allowed. There is a $3 per night per pet additional fee. Dogs must be leashed and cleaned up after. The camping and tent areas also allow dogs. There is a dog walk area at the campground.

Transportation Systems

Interstate Navigation/Block Island Ferry 304 Grey Island Road Narragansett RI   401-783-4613
http://www.blockislandferry.com
The ferry rides are about 1 hour, and they are open all year. Ther ferries leave from Newport at Fort Adams State Park and Point Judith (Galilee) just south of Narragansett. The ferries sail from Old Harbor on Block Island. Dogs are allowed, but they must be friendly, well behaved, and leashed. They request to have dogs relieve themselves before boarding, and doggie bags are required.

Beaches

East Beach State Beach East Beach Road Charlestown RI   401-322-0450
http://www.riparks.com/misquamicut.htm
Dogs are only allowed on the beach during the off-season, from October 1 through March 31. Pets must be on leash and people are required to clean up after their pets. However, according to a representative at the Rhode Island State Parks Department, in a conversation with them July 2004, the rules may change in the future to have no dogs on the beach year round. To get there, take I-95 to Route 4 South. Then take Route 1 South to East Beach exit in Charlestown.

Salty Brine State Beach 254 Great Road Narragansett RI   401-789-3563
http://www.riparks.com/saltybrine.htm
Dogs are only allowed on the beach during the off-season, from October 1 through March 31. Pets must be on leash and people are required to clean up after their pets. However, according to a representative at the Rhode Island State Parks Department, in a conversation with them July 2004, the rules may change in the future to have no dogs on the beach year round. To get there, take I-95 to Route 4 South. Then take Route 1 South to Route 108 South to Point Judith. If you are there during the Summer, take the dog-friendly ferry at Pt. Judith to Block Island where leashed dogs are allowed year-round on the island beaches.

East Matunuck State Beach 950 Succotash Road South Kingston RI   401-789-8585
http://www.riparks.com/eastmatunuck.htm
Dogs are only allowed on the beach during the off-season, from October 1 through March 31. Pets must be on leash and people are required to clean up after their pets. However, according to a representative at the Rhode Island State Parks Department, in a conversation with them July 2004, the rules may change in the future to have no dogs on the beach year round. To get there, take I-95 to Route 4 South. Then take Route 1 South to East Matunuck Exit and follow the signs to the state beach.

Misquamicut State Beach 257 Atlantic Avenue Westerly RI   401-596-9097
http://www.riparks.com/misquamicut.htm
Dogs are only allowed on the beach during the off-season, from October 1 through March 31. Pets must be on leash and people are required to clean up after their pets. However, according to a representative at the Rhode Island State Parks Department, in a conversation with them July 2004, the rules may change in the future to have no dogs on the beach year round. To get there, take I-95 to Route 4 South. Then take Route 1 South to Westerly. Follow the signs to the state beach.

Parks

Burlingame State Campground Route 1 Charlestown RI   401-322-7337
http://www.riparks.com/burlgmcamp.htm
Featuring 3,100 acres of rocky woodland, an almost 600 acre lake, extensive picnic facilities, and a swimming beach with a bathhouse have made this a popular recreational destination. Dogs are allowed for no additional

fee; they must have a valid license tag, and owners must carry proof of current rabies inoculation. Dogs must be quiet, well behaved, leashed (6 foot), and properly cleaned up after at all times. They may not be left unattended; with exception for hunting season or dog trials at which time dogs may be left alone in a vehicle. Dogs are not allowed at bathing beaches, or to be washed in any natural body of water. Dogs must be registered with the state prior to camping (not needed for day use), and the form can be obtained at http://www.riparks.com/pdfs/Pet% 20Certification%20Form.pdf. Dogs are not allowed at the Burlingame picnic area from April 1st through September 30th.

Fishermen's State Park and Campground 1011 Point Judith Road Narragansett RI   401-789-8374
http://www.riparks.com/fisherma.htm
With landscaped grounds and tree-lined paths, this 90 acre park can feel more like a seaside village, and they offer a good variety of land and water recreational opportunities. Dogs are allowed for no additional fee; they must have a valid license tag, and owners must carry proof of current rabies inoculation. Dogs must be quiet, well behaved, leashed (6 foot), and properly cleaned up after at all times. They may not be left unattended; with exception for hunting season or dog trials at which time dogs may be left alone in a vehicle. Dogs are not allowed at bathing beaches, or to be washed in any natural body of water. Dogs must be registered with the state prior to camping (not needed for day use), and the form can be obtained at http://www.riparks.com/pdfs/Pet% 20Certification%20Form.pdf.

Watch Hill Lighthouse 14 Lighthouse Road Watch Hill RI   401-596-7761
http://lighthouse.cc/watchhill/
Although the lighthouse is not open to the public, it is a nice 15 minute walk from town to this scenic area, and in addition to the lighthouse there is an 1856 keeper's house, a 1909 fog signal building, garage, and oil house. There is no parking close to the lighthouse. Your pooch is welcome here but they must be leashed and cleaned up after at all times.

Tiverton

Outdoor Restaurants

Gray's Ice Cream 16 East Street Tiverton RI   401-624-45000
http://www.graysicecream.com/
This ice creamery allows well mannered dogs at their outdoor tables. Dogs must be under owner's control, and leashed and cleaned up after at all times.

Chapter 7

Connecticut
Dog Travel Guide

Berkshire Region

Accommodations

TOP 200 PLACE **Interlaken Inn** 74 Interlaken Road Lakeville CT   860-435-9878
http://www.interlakeninn.com/
This is a charming resort with lakes to swim in, trails to walk and a PUPS amenity package. It's located in the heart of the Berkshires. The hotel offers 30 open acres with a lake shore and is a great property to frolic on. There are off-leash play areas too. There are miles of pet-friendly walking and hiking trails nearby. There is a $15 per day pet fee.
Litchfield Hills B&B 548 Bantam Road/H 202 Litchfield CT   860-567-2057
http://www.litchfieldhillsbnb.com/
This 1735 colonial inn is surrounded by untouched woodlands, beautiful gardens, stone patios and pathways, and they are located within a short distance to many other attractions, activities, and recreation. Dogs of all sizes are allowed for no additional pet fee. Dogs must be quiet, well behaved, leashed, and cleaned up after.

Campgrounds and RV Parks

American Legion and Peoples State Forests West River Road Barkhamsted CT   860-379-2469
This forest park is a year round land and water recreational destination that feature cultural and historic sites, more than 11 miles of hiking trails, a seasonal museum, a lighthouse, and they are also participants in the state forest Letterboxing. Dogs are permitted for no additional pet fee. Dogs are allowed at the picnic areas and on the hiking trails; they are not allowed in park buildings. Dogs must be under owner's control at all times, and be leashed and cleaned up after. Only one dog is allowed per campsite. The camp area offers 30 wooded sites with picnic tables, showers, restrooms, a dump station, and reservations are accepted from April 20th through Columbus Day. The phone number for the campground office (May-September) is 860-379-0922. This RV park is closed during the off-season. The camping and tent areas also allow dogs. There is a dog walk area at the campground. There are no electric or water hookups at the campgrounds.
Lone Oak Campsites 360 Norfolk E Canaan CT   860-824-7051
http://loneoakcampsites.com
Dogs of all sizes are allowed. There are no additional pet fees. Dogs must be leashed, cleaned up after, and have proof of rabies shots. There is a dog walk area at the campground.
Hemlock Hill Camp Resort 118 Hemlock Hill Road Litchfield CT   860-567-2267
http://www.hemlockhillcamp.com
One dog of any size per site is the usual allowance, however two dogs are allowed if they are both under 25 pounds. Pit Bulls, Rottweilers, and some other breeds are not allowed. Dogs must have proof of rabies shots. The camping and tent areas also allow dogs. There is a dog walk area at the campground.
American Legion/Peoples State Forests West River Road, P.O. Box 1 Pleasant Valley CT 860-379-2469
This state forest is home to a variety of multi-use trails, year round water and land recreation, seasonal interpretive programs, and the park also partakes in Letterboxing. Dogs are allowed throughout the park and the campground for no additional fee. Dogs must be under owner's control, be well behaved, leashed, and cleaned up after at all times. The camp area offer 30 wooded sites on a first come first served basis, and only one dog is allowed per campsite. The camp areas provide water, fireplaces, bathrooms, and showers. This RV park is closed during the off-season. The camping and tent areas also allow dogs. There is a dog walk area at the campground. There are no electric or water hookups at the campgrounds.

Attractions

Norfolk Chamber Music Festival Routes 44 and 272 Norfolk CT   203-432-1966
http://www.yale.edu/norfolk/
All performances are at the Ellen Battell Stoeckel 1906 Estate in the Music Shed amid meticulously landscaped grounds. Although dogs are not allowed in any of the buildings, the stunning acoustics allow the music to be enjoyed by those outside the music hall. Well mannered, leashed dogs are allowed around the grounds whether there is a concert occurring or not, and they must be cleaned up after.
Sharon Audubon Center 325 Cornwall Bridge/H 4 Sharon CT   860-364-0520
http://www.sharon.audubon.org/
With over 1,100 acres of meadows, wetlands, steams, ponds, forests, and more than 11 miles of scenic hiking trails, this nature research center offers visitors an interesting and educational "one with nature" experience. Well behaved dogs on lead are welcome. Dogs must be under owner's control and cleaned up after at all times. Dogs are not allowed in park buildings; they are allowed throughout the park and on most of the trails. A trail map can be obtained at the visitor center.

Clarke Outdoors Canoe Rental 163 H 7 West Cornwall CT 860-672-6365
http://www.clarkeoutdoors.com/
This outdoor recreation company rents canoes and rafts and your dog can join you on a 6 or 10 mile journey along a section of the Housatonic River. They do not provide shuttle service for visitors with pets, and there is no additional fee for the pet. Dogs must be under owner's control/care at all times.

Stores
Petco Pet Store 980 Torringford St Torrington CT 860-489-6853
Your licensed and well-behaved leashed dog is allowed in the store.

Parks
American Legion and Peoples State Forests West River Road Barkhamsted CT 860-379-2469
This forest park is a year round land and water recreational destination that feature cultural and historic sites, more than 11 miles of hiking trails, a seasonal museum, a lighthouse, and they are also participants in the state forest Letterboxing. Dogs are permitted for no additional pet fee. Dogs are allowed at the picnic areas and on the hiking trails; they are not allowed in park buildings. Dogs must be under owner's control at all times, and be leashed and cleaned up after.
Kent Falls State Park 462 Kent Cornwall Road Kent CT 860-927-3238
Lush greenery, scenic hiking trails and picnic areas, and falls that take a series of drops and cascades 250 feet down on its way to the Housatonic River, are some of the features of this park. This park is a member of the Impressionist Art Trail with reproductions of art painted in the 19th century exhibited at this park and at other host sites. Dogs are permitted for no additional pet fees. Dogs are allowed at the picnic areas and on the hiking trails; they are not allowed in park buildings or in swimming areas. Dogs must be under owner's control at all times, and be leashed and cleaned up after.
Topsmead State Forest Buell Road Litchfield CT 860-567-5694
Originally a Summer estate, this beautiful 1925 English Tudor home and landscaped grounds have been kept much as they were upon the owner's passing upon her request. They offer free seasonal guided tours, and guests may informally picnic on the grounds or residence lawns (no fires/grills), or walk the numerous trails and a 7/10 mile interpretive walk. Dogs are permitted for no additional pet fees. Dogs are allowed on the grounds and on the hiking trails; they are not allowed in park buildings. Dogs must be under owner's control at all times, and be leashed and cleaned up after.
Haystack Mountain State Park H 272 Norfolk CT 860-482-1817
Lush greenery, scenic (sometimes tree canopied) hiking trails, an overlook, picnic areas, and a 34 foot stone tower at the top of the summit offers views from the Long Island Sound to the peaks of New York. Dogs are permitted for no additional pet fees. Dogs are allowed at the picnic areas and on the hiking trails. Dogs must be under owner's control at all times, and be leashed and cleaned up after.
American Legion/Peoples State Forests West River Road, P.O. Box 1 Pleasant Valley CT 860-379-2469
This state forest is home to a variety of multi-use trails, year round water and land recreation, seasonal interpretive programs, and the park also partakes in Letterboxing. Dogs are allowed throughout the park and the campground for no additional fee. Dogs must be under owner's control, be well behaved, leashed, and cleaned up after at all times.
Housatonic Meadows H 7 Sharon CT 860-672-6772
Located along the scenic Housatonic River in a nature's paradise setting, this park has a variety of land and water recreation opportunities. Dogs are permitted for no additional pet fees. Dogs are allowed at the picnic areas and on the hiking trails; they are not allowed in the campground, in park buildings, or in swimming areas. Dogs must be under owner's control at all times, and be leashed and cleaned up after.
Burr Pond State Park Mountain Road Torrington CT 860-482-1817
This historic park shows evidence of its colonial beginnings, the businesses that evolved from the convergence of the several mountain streams, and it has the distinction of being the place where evaporated milk was born. Dogs are permitted for no additional pet fee in the picnic areas and on the miles of hiking trails; they are not allowed on the beach. Dogs must be under owner's control at all times, and be leashed and cleaned up after.

Bridgeport

Accommodations
Holiday Inn 1070 Main Street Bridgeport CT 203-334-1234 (877-270-6405)
Dogs up to 80 pounds are allowed for an additional fee of $10 per night per pet plus a $50 refundable deposit per room.
Best Western Black Rock Inn 100 Kings Highway Cutoff Fairfield CT 203-659-2200 (800-780-7234)
Dogs are allowed for an additional fee of $20 per night per pet.

Red Roof Inn - Milford 10 Rowe Avenue Milford CT   203-877-6060 (800-RED-ROOF)
One well-behaved family pet per room. Guest must notify front desk upon arrival. Guest is liable for any damages. In consideration of all guests, pets must never be left unattended in the guest rooms.
Residence Inn by Marriott 62 Rowe Ave Milford CT   203-283-2100
Dogs of all sizes are allowed. There is a $75 one time fee and a pet policy to sign

Stores
Perfectly Spoiled Pet Boutique 125 N Broad Street/H 62 Milford CT   860-292-6446
http://www.perfectlyspoiled.com/
Your pooch is welcomed at this boutique that specializes in a large variety of high-end luxury pet products. Dogs must be well behaved, under owner's control/care, and leashed.

Beaches
Town of Fairfield Beaches off Highway 1 Fairfield CT   203-256-3010
Dogs are only allowed on the town beaches during the off-season. Pets are not allowed on the beaches from April 1 through October 1. Dogs must be on leash and people need to clean up after their pets.

Parks
Sherwood Island State Park Sherwood Island Connector Road Green Farms CT   203-226-6983
Covering 235 acres with miles of waterfront, this scenic park offers several picnic sites, a variety of recreation, concessionaires, and an observation platform for viewing marsh life. Dogs are not allowed at this park from April 15th through September 30th. From October 1st through April 14th dogs are allowed on leash only. Dogs are not allowed on the beach at any time, in park buildings, swimming areas, or park campgrounds. Dogs must be under owner's control/care and cleaned up after at all times.
Silver Sands State Park Silver Sands Parkway Milford CT   203-735-4311
This park has an island that holds a mystery; in 1699 did Captain Kidd really bury his treasure on the island that is reached from the park by a sand/gravel bar that is exposed at high tide? Dogs are permitted for no additional pet fees, and they are allowed throughout the park except on the beach. Dogs must be under owner's control at all times, and be leashed and cleaned up after.

Off-Leash Dog Parks
Eisenhower Park Dog Run North Street Milford CT   203-783-3280
There is an off-leash dog run in Eisenhower Park.

Danbury

Accommodations
Microtel Inn and Suites 80 Benedict Road Bethel CT   203-748-8318
Dogs of all sizes are allowed. There is a $100 refundable deposit plus $10 per night per pet and a pet policy to sign at check in.
Twin Tree Inn 1030 Federal Rd Brookfield CT   203-775-0220
There is a $10.00 one time pet fee.
Holiday Inn 80 Newtown Rd Danbury CT   203-792-4000 (877-270-6405)
Dogs of all sizes are allowed for an additional fee of $15 per night per pet.
Quality Inn and Suites 78 Federal Road Danbury CT   203-743-6701 (877-424-6423)
Dogs are allowed for an additional fee of $20 per night per pet.
Residence Inn by Marriott 22 Segar Street Danbury CT   203-797-1256
Dogs of all sizes are allowed. There is a $75 one time fee and a pet policy to sign at check in. They also request to please not leave your pet unattended.
Sheraton Danbury Hotel 18 Old Ridgebury Road Danbury CT   203-794-0600 (888-625-5144)
Dogs up to 80 pounds are allowed. There are no additional pet fees. Dogs are not allowed to be left alone in the room.

Stores
Petco Pet Store 169 Federal Rd Brookfield CT   203-775-3337
Your licensed and well-behaved leashed dog is allowed in the store.

Off-Leash Dog Parks
Bark Park Governor Street Ridgefield CT
There are two fenced parks, one for large dogs and one for small dogs. There is water at the park. From Route 35 take Main Street. Turn right on Governor Street and proceed to the end of Governor Street. The park is on the right.

Outdoor Restaurants
Molten Java 102 Greenwood Ave Bethel CT   203-739-0313
This coffee shop allows pets at the outdoor tables. Water is provided.

East Haddam

Parks
Devil's Hopyard State Park 366 Hopyard Road East Haddam CT   860-873-8566
Born through glacial activity, this park has many interesting geological features, scenic hiking trails, viewing vistas, and the Chapman Falls which has more than a 60 foot drop over a series of rocky steps. Dogs are permitted for no additional pet fees. Dogs are allowed at the picnic areas and on the hiking trails; they are not allowed in the campground, in park buildings, or in swimming areas. Dogs must be owner's control at all times, and be leashed and cleaned up after.
Gillette Castle State Park 67 River Road East Haddam CT   860-526-2336
The focal point of this 184 acre park located along the Connecticut River is the 24 room medieval fortress, but the grounds are as interesting with stone-arch bridges, a vegetable cellar, a RR station, ponds, and a variety of trails that run through tunnels, over trestles, and along a 3 mile stretch of a former railroad. Dogs are permitted for no additional pet fees. Dogs are allowed at the picnic areas and on the hiking trails; they are not allowed in park buildings, or on decks, terraces or walkways leading to the castle. Dogs must be under owner's control at all times, and be leashed and cleaned up after.

Hartford

Accommodations
Residence Inn by Marriott 55 Simsbury Road Avon CT   800-331-3131
Dogs of all sizes are allowed. There is a $25 per day fee up to a total of $250 for the month and a pet policy to sign at check in.
Holiday Inn 363 Roberts St East Hartford CT   860-528-9611 (877-270-6405)
Dogs of all sizes are allowed for an additional one time pet fee of $35 per room.
Sheraton Hartford Hotel 100 East River Drive East Hartford CT   860-528-9703 (888-625-5144)
Dogs of all sizes are allowed. There are no additional pet fees. Dogs are not allowed to be left alone in the room.
Motel 6 – Hartord - Enfield 11 Hazard Avenue Enfield CT   860-741-3685 (800-466-8356)
One well-behaved family pet per room. Guest must notify front desk upon arrival. Guest is liable for any damages. In consideration of all guests, pets must never be left unattended in the guest rooms.
Red Roof Inn - Enfield, CT 5 Hazard Avenue Enfield CT   860-741-2571 (800-RED-ROOF)
One well-behaved family pet per room. Guest must notify front desk upon arrival. Guest is liable for any damages. In consideration of all guests, pets must never be left unattended in the guest rooms.
Days Inn Hartford Dwtn 207 Brainard Rd Hartford CT   860-247-3297 (800-329-7466)
Dogs of all sizes are allowed. There is a $5 per night pet fee per pet.
Holiday Inn Express Hartford - Downtown 440 Asylum Street Hartford CT   860-246-9900 (877-270-6405)
Dogs of all sizes are allowed for an additional one time pet fee of $50 per room.
Motel 6 - Hartford Downtown 100 Weston Street Hartford CT   860-724-0222 (800-466-8356)
One well-behaved family pet per room. Guest must notify front desk upon arrival. Guest is liable for any damages. In consideration of all guests, pets must never be left unattended in the guest rooms.
Residence Inn by Marriott 942 Main Street Hartford CT   860-524-5550
Dogs of all sizes are welcome. There is a $75 one time fee and a pet policy to sign at check in.
Clarion Suites Inn 191 Spencer Street Manchester CT   860-643-5811 (877-424-6423)
Dogs are allowed for an additional fee of $20 per night per pet.
Residence Inn by Marriott 201 Hale Road Manchester CT   860-432-4242
Well behaved dogs of all sizes are welcome. There is a $75 one time fee and a pet policy to sign at check in.
Candlewood Suites 1511 East Main Street Meriden CT   203-379-5048 (877-270-6405)

One dog up to 80 pounds is allowed for an additional pet fee of $75 for 1 to 6 days, and $150 for 7+ days per room.
Residence Inn by Marriott 390 Bee Street Meriden CT   203-634-7770
Dogs of all sizes are allowed. There is a $75 one time fee and a pet policy to sign at check in.
Iron Horse Inn 969 Hopmeadow St Simsbury CT   860-658-2216 (800245-9938)

Howard Johnson Express Inn 451 Hartford Turnpike Vernon CT   860-875-0781 (800-446-4656)
Dogs of all sizes are welcome. There is a $10 per day pet fee per pet.
Quality Inn Conference Center 51 Hartford Turnpike/H 83 Vernon CT   860-646-5700 (877-424-6423)
Dogs are allowed for an additional fee of $25 per night per pet.
Motel 6 - HARTFORD - WETHERSFIELD 1341 Silas Deane Highway Wethersfield CT   860-563-5900 (800-466-8356)
One well-behaved family pet per room. Guest must notify front desk upon arrival. Guest is liable for any damages. In consideration of all guests, pets must never be left unattended in the guest rooms.
Residence Inn by Marriott 100 Dunfey Lane Windsor CT   860-688-7474
Dogs of all sizes are allowed. There is a $75 one time fee and a pet policy to sign at check in.
Candlewood Suites Windsor Locks 149 Ella Grasso Turnpike Windsor Locks CT   860-623-2000 (877-270-6405)
Dogs of all sizes are allowed for an additional pet fee of $75 for 1 to 6 nights, and $150 for 7+ nights per room.
Homewood Suites 65 Ella Grasso Turnpike Windsor Locks CT   860-627-8463
There is a $150 one time pet charge and guests need to sign a pet policy.
Motel 6 - HARTFORD - WINDSOR LOCKS 3 National Drive Windsor Locks CT   860-292-6200 (800-466-8356)
One well-behaved family pet per room. Guest must notify front desk upon arrival. Guest is liable for any damages. In consideration of all guests, pets must never be left unattended in the guest rooms.
Sheraton Bradley Airport Hotel 1 Bradley International Airport Windsor Locks CT   860-627-5311 (888-625-5144)
Dogs of all sizes are allowed. There are no additional pet fees. Dogs are not allowed to be left alone in the room.

Campgrounds and RV Parks
Del-Aire Campground 704 Shenipsit Road Tolland CT   860-875-8325
Dogs of all sizes are allowed. There are no additional pet fees. Dogs must be well behaved, quiet, leashed, and cleaned up after. Dogs may not be left on site unattended. The camping and tent areas also allow dogs. There is a dog walk area at the campground.

Attractions
State Historic Preservation Museum 59 S Prospect Street Hartford CT   860-566-3005
http://www.ctfreedomtrail.com/
This statewide "museum" is a tribute to the participants in America's quest for freedom for all peoples and it tells of the cultures of and from that time, the Underground Railroad, the laws of freedom that were enacted, what event prompted the laws' beginning, and more. Brochures are available statewide or at the website. This part driving, part walking tour can be taken with your canine companions. Dogs just may not go on private properties or in any buildings, and they must be leashed and cleaned up after.

Stores
Petco Pet Store 9 West Avon Rd Avon CT   860-404-8880
Your licensed and well-behaved leashed dog is allowed in the store.
Precious Pets Grooming Boutique 259 S Main Street/H 5 East Windsor CT   860-292-6446
Bring your pooch in for a make-over at this boutique. Dogs must be well behaved, under owner's control/care, and leashed.
Petco Pet Store 25 Hazard Avenue Enfield CT   860-745-7671
Your licensed and well-behaved leashed dog is allowed in the store.
Petco Pet Store 1600 SE Rd Farmington CT   860-674-9599
Your licensed and well-behaved leashed dog is allowed in the store.
PetSmart Pet Store 1520 Pleasant Valley Rd Manchester CT   860-644-2366
Your licensed and well-behaved leashed dog is allowed in the store.
Petco Pet Store 432a Buckland Hills Drive Manchester CT   860-648-2990
Your licensed and well-behaved leashed dog is allowed in the store.
Petco Pet Store 188 Kitts Lane Newington CT   860-667-9621
Your licensed and well-behaved leashed dog is allowed in the store.
Petco Pet Store 335 N Main St West Hartford CT   860-523-0601
Your licensed and well-behaved leashed dog is allowed in the store.

Three Dog Bakery 967 A Farmington Avenue West Hartford CT   860-232-6299
http://www.threedog.com
Three Dog Bakery provides cookies and snacks for your dog as well as some boutique items. You well-behaved, leashed dog is welcome.

Parks
Talcott Mountain State Park H 185 Bloomfield CT   860-424-3200
Built as a Summer retreat in 1914, there are some great scenic walking trails here, including part of the Metacomet Trail and the 1¼ mile hike to the Tower where a 1,000 promontory offers outstanding views of over 12,000 square miles. Dogs are permitted for no additional pet fees. Dogs are allowed at the picnic areas and on the hiking trails; they are not allowed in park buildings. Dogs must be under owner's control at all times, and be leashed and cleaned up after.
Metacomet-Monadnock Trail Rising Corner Road (beginning) West Suffield CT   617-523-0655
http://www.amcberkshire.org/mm-trail
This long distance, maintained hiking footpath covers almost 114 miles from the Metacomet Trail at the Connecticut state line to Mt. Monadnock in NH., and passes through some of the most beautiful landscapes in the state. It is maintained by the Appalachian Mountain Club. The trails are marked, but they suggest buying a trail guidebook (can be ordered from website) to use in addition to the excerpts of information on the web. Dogs are allowed on this trail. They must be under owner's control at all times, leashed, and cleaned up after.

Off-Leash Dog Parks
Granby D.O.G.G.S. Park 215 Salmon Brook Street/H 202 Granby CT   860-653-0173
http://www.granbydogpark.com
D.O.G.G.S. (Dog Owners of Granby Getting Social) is a community volunteer organization that established this fenced-in off-leash recreation area within Salmon Brook Park. Dogs of all sizes are allowed, and there can be up to 3 dogs per person. All dogs must have current license and shot tags on their collar/harness; be accompanied and in sight of their owners/custodians at all times, and under voice control. Choke, prong, or spiked collars are not allowed inside the off-leash area. Owners/custodians must carry a leash at all times, and dogs must be leashed entering and exiting the dog park. If you have a small, older, infirmed, or a shy dog, use the small dog area. You must clean up after your pet immediately, dispose of their waste properly, and fill in any holes they may dig. Females in heat; unaltered males, sick, or aggressive dogs are prohibited in the park and for the safety of all, immediately leash your dog if it exhibits aggressive behavior and leave the dog park area. The picnic tables are for the dogs to play on, but feel free to have a seat; however, food or drink for humans is not allowed within the fenced area.
Mill Woods Park Dog Park 154 Prospect St Wethersfield CT   860-721-2890
http://www.wethersfielddogpark.org
The one acre fenced dog park is located in Mill Woods Park. In all Connecticut parks dogs must display their license tags on their collars at all times.

Outdoor Restaurants
Hot Tomato's Restaurant 1 Union Place Hartford CT   860-249-5100
Fresh fish, steaks, unique pasta dishes, an extensive wine list, and their signature garlic bread have made this a popular eatery. Dogs are welcome at their outer tables. Dogs must be well behaved, under owner's control, leashed, and cleaned up after at all times.

Jewett City

Accommodations
Homespun Farm Bed and Breakfast 306 Preston Road/H 164 Griswold CT   860-376-5178 (888-889-6673)
http://www.homespunfarm.com/
This colonial farmhouse inn is listed on the National Register of Historic Places as well as being a certified National Wildlife Federation Backyard Wildlife Habitat. Dogs of all sizes are allowed for an additional pet fee of $15 per night per room, and they only allow one guest with a pet to stay at a time. Dogs must be leashed, cleaned up after, and securely crated and the front desk informed when they are alone in the room. Please use a mat under their water/food dishes or feed pets outside, wipe dogs off before entering if they are wet (towel provided), and place your own throw on any furniture pets may want to be on. Dogs must be declared at the time of registration, and be quiet and friendly as there are other pets in residence.

Campgrounds and RV Parks

Ross Hill Park 170 Ross Hill Road Lisbon CT   860-376-9606 (800-308-1089)
http://www.rosshillpark.com/
Pets of all sizes are allowed. There are no additional pet fees. Dogs allowed on leash only, and fecal matter must be cleaned up immediately. Failure to pick up after your pet will result in eviction. Pets are not allowed in the swimming area. This RV park is closed during the off-season. The camping and tent areas also allow dogs. There is a dog walk area at the campground.

Lebanon

Campgrounds and RV Parks
Water's Edge Family Campground 271 Leonard Bridge Road Lebanon CT   860-642-7470
http://www.watersedgecampground.com
Dogs of all sizes are allowed. There are no additional pet fees. Dogs must be leashed and cleaned up after. Dogs are allowed in the camping cabins.

New Haven

Accommodations
Motel 6 - NEW HAVEN - BRANFORD 320 E Main Street Branford CT   203-483-5828 (800-466-8356)
One well-behaved family pet per room. Guest must notify front desk upon arrival. Guest is liable for any damages. In consideration of all guests, pets must never be left unattended in the guest rooms.
Premiere Hotel and Suites 3 Long Wharf Drive New Haven CT   203-777-5337
http://www.newhavensuites.com
Pets of all sizes are allowed. There is a $75 one time fee and a pet policy to sign at check in.
Residence Inn by Marriott 1001 Bridgeport Avenue Shelton CT   203-926-9000
Pets of all sizes are allowed. There is a $75 one time fee per pet and a pet policy to sign at check in.

Transportation Systems
TOP 200 PLACE **Thimble Islands Cruise & Charters** P.O. Box 3138 Stony Creek CT   203-488-8905
http://www.thimbleislandcruise.com/
Well behaved pooches are welcome aboard the ferry for transport to the islands for no additional fee; they are not allowed on tours. Dogs must be crated or leashed, cleaned up after, and under owner's control at all times.

Stores
Petco Pet Store 2100 Dixwell Avenue Hamden CT   203-230-1888
Your licensed and well-behaved leashed dog is allowed in the store.
Petco Pet Store 420 Universal Drive North Haven CT   203-234-8112
Your licensed and well-behaved leashed dog is allowed in the store.
Petco Pet Store 955 Ferry Blvd Stratford CT   203-378-9004
Your licensed and well-behaved leashed dog is allowed in the store.
Petco Pet Store 848 Colony Rd Wallingford CT   203-294-0039
Your licensed and well-behaved leashed dog is allowed in the store.

Parks
TOP 200 PLACE **Sleeping Giant State Park** 200 Mount Carmel Avenue Hamden CT   203-789-7498
Offering scenic vistas from a stone observation tower, nature trails, stream fishing (a designated trout stocked park), and some great hiking trails, this park is also known for the 2 miles of the mountaintop that resemble a large "sleeping giant". Dogs are permitted for no additional pet fees. Dogs are allowed at the picnic areas and on the hiking trails; they are not allowed in park buildings. Dogs must be under owner's control at all times, and be leashed and cleaned up after.
New Haven Green Temple Street New Haven CT   203-946-8019
http://www.newhavenparks.org
Sitting serenely amid a hub of activity, this park is bordered by College, Chapel, Church and Elm streets in the heart of the city, and is the site of numerous concerts, events, and community gatherings. This park was originally the town square and created in 1638. Well mannered dogs are allowed. Dogs must be on leash and cleaned up after at all times.

Off-Leash Dog Parks

The Hamden Dog Park at Bassett On Waite Street at Ridge Road Hamden CT
http://www.hamdenrdog.org
The Hamden Dog Park is completely fenced with a brick path and patio, a separate small dog area with separate entrance, benches and picnic tables (mostly for the dogs to play on or under), and a compressed gravel trail. It is wheelchair accessible. Dogs of all sizes are allowed, but owners/custodians must carry their leashes on them at all times. All dogs must have current license and shot tags on their collar/harness; be accompanied and in sight of their owners/custodians at all times, and under voice control. If you have a small, older, infirmed, or a shy dog, use the small dog area. You must clean up after your pet immediately, dispose of their waste properly, and fill in any holes they may dig. Female dogs in heat, and aggressive dogs are prohibited in the park and for the safety of all, immediately leash your dog if it exhibits aggressive behavior and leave the dog park area. Dogs younger than four months should not be brought to the park.

Outdoor Restaurants

The Place 901 Boston Post Road Guilford CT   203-453-9276
This restaurant serves steaks and seafood. It's an outdoor type restaurant. Pets are allowed. Only open in the evenings.

New London - Mystic

Accommodations

Abbey's Lantern Hill Inn 780 Lantern Hill Road Ledyard CT   860-572-0483
http://www.abbeyslanternhill.com/
Nestled among the trees and rolling countryside, this contemporary inn features fireplaces, Jacuzzis, 6 outer decks, and it is also close to other activities, recreation, and a couple of casinos. Dogs of all sizes are allowed in the private bungalow. There is no fee for one dog. There is an additional $15 one time fee for a second dog. Dogs must be leashed, cleaned up after, and may only be left alone in the room if they will be quiet and well behaved.
Econo Lodge 251 Greenmanville Avenue Mystic CT   860-536-9666 (877-424-6423)
http://www.choicehotels.com/
Only 5 miles from the airport and central to many other attractions, this hotel, formally the Old Mystic Motor Lodge, welcomes dogs of all sizes for an additional fee of $10 per night per pet. Dogs must be leashed and cleaned up after at all times.
Harbour Inne & Cottage 15 Edgemont Street Mystic CT   860-572-9253
http://www.harbourinne-cottage.com/
The Harbour Inne & Cottage B&B is an easy walk to all the shops, restaurants and sights of downtown Mystic. The inne has a social area with a fireplace and piano. The four bedrooms each have a private bath, kitchen privileges, cable television and are air conditioned. Pets are welcome for $10 per night.
Residence Inn by Marriott 40 Whitehall Avenue Mystic CT   860-536-5150
Dogs of all sizes are allowed. There is a $75 one time fee and a pet policy to sign at check in.
Red Roof Inn - New London 707 Colman Street New London CT   860-444-0001 (800-RED-ROOF)
One well-behaved family pet per room. Guest must notify front desk upon arrival. Guest is liable for any damages. In consideration of all guests, pets must never be left unattended in the guest rooms.
Motel 6 - NEW LONDON - NIANTIC 269 Flanders Road Niantic CT   860-739-6991 (800-466-8356)
One well-behaved family pet per room. Guest must notify front desk upon arrival. Guest is liable for any damages. In consideration of all guests, pets must never be left unattended in the guest rooms.

Campgrounds and RV Parks

Aces High RV Park 301 Chesterfield Road East Lyme CT 860-739-8858
http://www.aceshighrvpark.com
Well behaved dogs of all sizes are allowed. There are no additional pet fees. Dogs are not allowed in other people's sites and they also have a separate swim area for them. Dogs must be quiet, leashed and cleaned up after. There is a dog walk area at the campground.
Seaport Campground Old Campground Road Old Mystic CT   860-536-4044
http://www.seaportcampground.com/
This scenic family camp area features spacious sites, free internet, a store, laundry, pool-but beaches are close by too, a fishing pond, mini-golf, planned activities, and live entertainment. There is no additional pet fee for 1 dog; it is $5 per day extra if there is a 2nd dog. One dog is allowed in tents with permission from the management, and they may not be left alone in a tent at any time. Dogs may not be left outside alone, and they

must be leashed and cleaned up after at all times. Guests must have proof of current rabies inoculation for their pet. This RV park is closed during the off-season. The camping and tent areas also allow dogs. There is a dog walk area at the campground.

Transportation Systems

Viking Fleet 462 W Lake Drive Montauk CT   631-668-5700
This ferry features a triple decker, 120 foot vessel with comfort amenities on board, and service is provided between Montauk Long Island and Block Island RI, New London CT, and Martha's Vineyard, MA. Well behaved dogs are allowed on board for no additional fee. Dogs must be under owner's control/care and leashed at all times. The ferries leave from the Cross Sound Ferry Dock.

Cross Sound Ferry Services 2 Ferry Street, PO Box 33 New London CT   860-443-5281
This auto ferry service provides transportation between New London, CT and Orient Point on Long Island, NY. Dogs are allowed on the car ferry in dog designated areas only for no additional fee. Dogs must be well behaved, leashed or in an approved pet carrier, and cleaned up after at all times.

Fishers Island Ferry 5 Waterfront Park New London CT   860-442-0165
http://www.fiferry.com/
This is the connector ferry between New London, Connecticut and Fisher's Island, New York. Dogs of all sizes are allowed for no addition fee. Dogs must be well behaved, leashed, and cleaned up after at all times.

Attractions

Downtown Mystic (Greater Mystic Chamber of Commerce) 14 Holmes Street Mystic CT   866-572-9578
http://www.downtownmystic.com
Dogs on leash are allowed in the downtown area and some outdoor seating. Many stores do allow dogs inside (there are signs and water bowls on the most dog friendly stores). There are designated areas for your dog's use and cleanup stations. Overall, this is a very dog friendly town.

Mystic Seaport - The Museum of America and the Sea

TOP 200 PLACE Mystic Seaport - The Museum of America and the Sea 75 Greenmanville Ave Mystic CT   860-572-0711
http://www.mysticseaport.org
Referred to as the Museum of America and the Sea, it is considered to be one of the nation's leading maritime museums, and there is plenty to see with an authentic 19th century village with about 40 buildings complete with storytellers, a waterfront of tall ships and other historic vessels, a preservation shipyard where visitors can watch restoration of antique vessels, several exhibits and galleries, and a lot more. Dogs are allowed throughout the

port; they are not allowed in any of the buildings or on the ship. Dogs must be under owner's care, leashed, and cleaned up after at all times.

Shopping Centers

Olde Mistic Village Shopping Center

TOP 200 PLACE Olde Mistic Village 27 Coogan Blvd Mystic CT   860-536-4941
http://www.oldmysticvillage.com/
More than 40 unique shops are nestled in this shopping center that is reminiscent of a 1720's era New England village with lots of foliage, flowers, waterscapes, and trees creating wonderful little places to take repose. Your well behaved pooch is welcome to explore this area as long as they are on leash and picked up after. It is up to the individual stores as to whether pets are allowed inside. There is a pet boutique store here.

Stores

Bank Square Books 53 W Main Street Mystic CT   860-536-3795
Well behaved dogs on lead are allowed in the store.
Petco Pet Store 825 Hartford Rd Waterford CT   860-437-0712
Your licensed and well-behaved leashed dog is allowed in the store.

Parks

Bluff Point State Park Depot Road Groton CT   860-444-7591
This is the last remaining significant piece of undeveloped land along the state's coast, and because of being designated a Coastal Reserve, access to the bluff is only allowed by foot or non-motorized vehicles to this unique and beautiful area. Dogs are permitted for no additional pet fee. Dogs are allowed throughout the park. Dogs must be under owner's control at all times, and be leashed and cleaned up after.
Fort Griswold Battlefield State Park 57 Fort Street Groton CT   860-444-7591
This seasonal monument park is an historic Revolutionary War site where the infamous Benedict Arnold led a 1781 massacre. Dogs are permitted throughout the park; they must be leashed and cleaned up after at all times.
Fort Trumbull State Park 90 Walbach Street New London CT 860-444-7591
This area along Thames River, that has been an active military site since early colonial days, now shares its rich history and unusual fort with visitors, and informative markers and displays are throughout the park. Dogs are permitted around the park for no additional pet fees; they are not allowed in park buildings (including the fort) or on the fishing pier. Dogs must be under owner's control at all times, and be leashed and cleaned up after.

Outdoor Restaurants

Seamen's Inn Restaurant and Pub 105 Greenmanville Ave Mystic CT 860-572-5305
This restaurant and bar serves seafood. Dogs are allowed at the outdoor tables.

New Milford

Attractions

The Silo at Hunt Hill Farm 44 Upland Road New Milford CT 860-355-0300
This combination cooking school, gourmet kitchenware/food store, and art gallery has been at the Hunt Hill Farm since 1972; the farm has the Silo, a museum, 10 historic out-buildings, woodlands, and a land preserve on its 40 scenic acres and it is also a popular location for special events. Pets are allowed throughout the property. Dogs must be friendly, well behaved, leashed, and cleaned up after at all times.

Northeast Connecticut

Accommodations

Holiday Inn Express & Suites Killingly 16 Tracy Road Dayville CT 860-779-3200 (877-270-6405)
Dogs of all sizes are allowed for an additional $10 per night per pet.
King's Inn 5 Heritage Rd Putnam CT 860-928-7961
Dogs are allowed at the hotel.
Elias Child House 50 Perrin Road Woodstock CT 860-974-9836 (877-974-9836)
http://www.eliaschildhouse.com/
Rich in colonial craftsmanship, this inn sits on 47 acres of woodlands and pastures with an in-ground pool, walking trails, great shopping opportunities close by, and they even offer hearth cooking demonstrations; there are 2 walk-in cooking hearths. Dogs of all sizes are allowed for an additional fee of $20 per night per pet. Dogs must go with the owners when they leave the premises, but can be crated in the room if they are on the property. Dogs must be well mannered, leashed, cleaned up after, and be friendly to other animals as there is another dog there who likes to greet the canine visitors.

Campgrounds and RV Parks

Brialee RV and Tent Park 174 Laurel Lane Ashford CT 860-429-8359 (800-303-2267)
http://www.brialee.com
Dogs of all sizes are allowed. There are no additional pet fees. Dogs must be leashed and under your control at all times and must be cleaned up after. The camping and tent areas also allow dogs. There is a dog walk area at the campground.
Stateline Camp Resort 1639 Hartford Pike Killingly CT 860-774-3016
http://www.resortcamplands.com
Dogs of all sizes are allowed, however some breeds are not. There is a $3 per night per pet additional fee. Dogs must be well behaved, quiet, leashed, and cleaned up after. Dogs are not to be left unattended. The camping and tent areas also allow dogs. There is a dog walk area at the campground.
Beaver Pines Campground 1728 H 198 Woodstock CT 860-974-0110
http://www.beaverpinescampground.com/
Dogs of all sizes are allowed at no additional fee. Dogs may not be left unattended, and they must have current rabies and shot records. Dogs must be leashed and cleaned up after. There are some breed restrictions. This RV park is closed during the off-season. The camping and tent areas also allow dogs. There is a dog walk area at the campground.

Attractions

Connecticut Audubon Center 189 Pomfret Street Pomfret Center CT 860-928-4948
A new environmental educational center sits at the beginning of this 700 acre "back to nature" wonderland with streams, fertile grassland habitats, forests, and open meadows giving home to a variety of plant, bird, and wildlife. Your well behaved dog is welcome to join you on the grounds and trails; they are not allowed in park buildings. Dogs must be under owner's control, leashed, and cleaned up after at all times.

Parks

Mashamoquet Brook State Park 147 Wolf Den Drive Pomfret Center CT 860-928-6121

Actually 3 parks, each rich in folklore, and natural and cultural history, combined to what is now a 900 acre park with miles of hiking trails and a variety of recreational opportunities. Dogs are permitted for no additional pet fees. Dogs are allowed at the picnic areas and on the hiking trails; they are not allowed in the campground, on the beach, or at the picnic shelter. Dogs must be under owner's control at all times, and be leashed and cleaned up after.

Quinebaug and Shetucket Rivers Valley National Heritage Center 107 Providence Street Putnam CT 860-963-7226
http://www.nps.gov/qush/index.htm
Dogs must be on leash and must be cleaned up after on most of trails around the river areas. You must follow local and state park rules and pet policies. The park features auto touring, hiking and boating.

Norwalk

Stores
PetSmart Pet Store 525 Connecticut Ave Norwalk CT 203-854-1772
Your licensed and well-behaved leashed dog is allowed in the store.
Petco Pet Store 431 Westport Avenue #1 Norwalk CT 203-840-0331
Your licensed and well-behaved leashed dog is allowed in the store.

Parks
Weir Farm National Historic Site 735 Nod Hill Road Wilton CT 203-834-1896
http://www.nps.gov/wefa/index.htm
Dogs must be on leash and must be cleaned up after in the park. Dogs are not allowed in buildings. The park features hiking, nature walks, and more.

Norwich

Campgrounds and RV Parks
Acron Acres Campground 135 Lake Road Bozrah CT 860-859-1020
http://www.acornacrescampsites.com
Dogs of all sizes are allowed. There are no additional pet fees. Dogs must be quiet, well behaved, leashed and cleaned up after. There are some breed restrictions. The camping and tent areas also allow dogs. There is a dog walk area at the campground.
Odetah Campground 38 Bozrah Street Extension Bozrah CT 860-889-4144
http://www.odetah.com
Dogs of all sizes are allowed to stay in the campground but are not allowed to leave your camp site. There are no additional pet fees. Dogs must be well behaved, quiet, and kept leashed. There is a dog walk area at the campground.
Strawberry Park Resort Campground 42 Pierce Road Preston CT 860-886-1944
http://www.strawberrypark.net
Dogs of all sizes are allowed, but some breeds are not. There are no additional pet fees. Dogs must remain on your site and are not to be walked or carried around the campground. The camping and tent areas also allow dogs.
Salem Farms Campground 39 Alexander Road Salem CT 860-859-2320
http://www.salemfarmscampground.com
Dogs of all sizes are allowed. There are no additional pet fees. Dogs must be leashed, are not allowed to be on the grass areas, and must be cleaned up after. The camping and tent areas also allow dogs. There is a dog walk area at the campground.
Witch Meadow Lake Campground 139 Witch Meadow Road Salem CT 860-859-1542
http://www.witchmeadowcampground.com/
Dogs of all sizes are allowed. There are no additional pet fees. Dogs may not be left unattended, and they must be leashed and cleaned up after. Dogs must be kept on the campsite or walked on the dog walk trail at the back of the campground. There are some breed restrictions. This RV park is closed during the off-season. The camping and tent areas also allow dogs. There is a dog walk area at the campground.

Off-Leash Dog Parks
Pawsitive Park Dog Park, Estelle Cohn Memorial Dog Park 261 Asylum Street Norwich CT 860-367-7271
http://www.pawsitivepark.com/

Dogs of all sizes are allowed at this beautiful off leash dog-park. There can be up to 3 dogs per person. All dogs must have current license and shot tags on their collar/harness; be accompanied and in sight of their owners/custodians at all times, and under voice control. If you have a small, older, infirmed, or a shy dog, use the small dog area. Choke, prong, or spiked collars are not allowed inside the off-leash area. Water is available for dogs to drink and for filling up the wading pools in both dog play areas. You must clean up after your pet immediately and dispose of their waste properly. Poop bags and pooper scoopers are always available for people who have forgotten to bring theirs. Females in heat; unaltered males and aggressive dogs are prohibited in the park and for the safety of all, immediately leash your dog if it exhibits aggressive behavior and leave the dog park area. There is also a dog-free zone that is a fenced in area for small children or for people who just want to come, sit, and watch the dogs in the park. There are also landscaped trails around the entire park that you can walk with your dog on lead.

Old Lyme - Connecticut River

Accommodations
Copper Beach Inn 46 Main Street Ivoryton CT 860-767-0330 (888-809-2056)
http://www.copperbeechinn.com/
This 1890 inn rests in a beautiful garden setting, has been the recipient of several awards for the inn itself, for their 4-diamond restaurant, and for their 5,000+ bottle wine cellar. Dogs of all sizes are welcome on the 1st floor of the Carriage House for an additional fee of $35 per night for 1 dog, and there is an additional fee of $10 per night if there is a 2nd dog. Dogs must be leashed, cleaned up after, and may only be left alone in the room if they are crated and will be quiet and well behaved.
Old Lyme Inn 85 Lyme Street Old Lyme CT 860-434-2600 (800-434-5352)
http://www.oldlymeinn.com/
This small, but elegant inn is just minutes from the beach and two large outlet malls. Dogs of all sizes are allowed for a $50 refundable deposit per stay. Dogs may not be left alone in the room, and they must be leashed and cleaned up after at all times.
Beach Plum Inn 1935 Boston Post Rd Westbrook CT 860-399-9345
There are no additional pet fees. Dogs are allowed in the cabins.

Transportation Systems
The Chester - Hadlyme Ferry Ferry Landing Chester CT 860-526-2743
This ferry runs between April 1st and November 30th providing a convenient link across the Connecticut River between Chester and Hadlyme. Well behaved dogs on leash are allowed on the ferry for no additional fee.

Attractions
Florence Griswold Museum 96 Lyme Street Old Lyme CT 860-434-5542
http://www.flogris.org/
Although it began as a boarding house, artists were drawn to the beauty of this country retreat and it wasn't long before it became the center of Impressionism Art in America. Pets are not allowed in the house, but they are allowed to explore the gardens and grounds. Dogs must be well behaved, leashed, and cleaned up after at all times.

Stores
Essex Saybrook Antiques Village 345 Middlesex Turnpike Old Saybrook CT 860-388-0689
This 3-story antiques barn features more than 75 dealers all under one roof. Well behaved, trained dogs are welcome to join their caretakers exploring the grounds and the antiques barn. Dogs must be under owner's control, leashed, and cleaned up after at all times.

Stamford

Accommodations
Delmar Greenwich Harbor Hotel 500 Steamboat Road Greenwich CT 203-661-9800 (866-335-2627)
http://www.thedelamar.com/index2.html
This luxury waterfront inn has mooring on its own private dock (yachts up to 160'), sits near a cornucopia of eateries and shops, offers indoor or outdoor dining, and most of the room have spacious balconies that overlook the harbor. Dogs up to 45 pounds are allowed for an additional fee of $25 per night per pet. Dogs get their own

special welcome package; some items included are a cushy doggie bed, personalized ID tag, a bottle of Figi water, and a food and water bowl. Dogs must be quiet, well mannered, leashed, and cleaned up after.
Sheraton Stamford Hotel 2701 Summer Street Stamford CT   203-359-1300 (888-625-5144)
Dogs up to 50 pounds are allowed. There are no additional pet fees. Dogs are not allowed to be left alone in the room.
Stamford Marriott Hotel and Spa Two Stamford Forum Stamford CT   203-357-9555 (800-732-9689)
Dogs of all sizes are allowed. There is a $20 per night per room additional pet fee. Dogs must be quiet, leashed, cleaned up after, and the Dog in Room sign put on the door and a contact number left with the front desk if they are in the room alone.

Stonington

Accommodations
High Acres 222 NW Corner Road North Stonington CT   860-887-4355 (888-680-7829 (STAY))
http://www.highacresbb.com/
This 150 acre, groomed hilltop 18th century estate is a delight of green meadows, wildflowers, gardens, woodlands, and country charm, with horses in the fields, numerous hiking trails, and many other activities and recreation only a few minutes away. They have 1 pet friendly room, and dogs of all sizes are allowed for no additional fee. Dogs must be quiet, well behaved, cleaned up after, and they must have their own bedding as they are not allowed on the furnishings. Dogs may be off lead on the estate only if they are under firm voice control.

Campgrounds and RV Parks
Pachaug State Forest Chapman Area H 49/ P. O. Box 5 Voluntown CT   860-376-4075 (866-287-2757)
This state forest is home to miles and miles of multi-use year round trails, a beautiful walk through a rare Rhododendron Sanctuary (blooms early July), a scenic overlook, a stocked fishing pond, and the park also partakes in Letterboxing. Dogs are allowed throughout the park and the campground for no additional fee. Dogs must be under owner's control, be well behaved, leashed, and cleaned up after at all times. Two camping areas offer 40 wooded sites on a first come first served basis, and only one dog is allowed per campsite. The camp areas provide water, fireplaces and pit toilets. This RV park is closed during the off-season. The camping and tent areas also allow dogs. There is a dog walk area at the campground. There are no electric or water hookups at the campgrounds.

Parks
Pachaug State Forest Chapman Area H 49/ P. O. Box 5 Voluntown CT   860-376-4075 (866-287-2757)
This state forest is home to miles and miles of multi-use year round trails, a beautiful walk through a rare Rhododendron Sanctuary (blooms early July), a scenic overlook, a stocked fishing pond, and the park also partakes in Letterboxing. Dogs are allowed throughout the park and the campground for no additional fee. Dogs must be under owner's control, be well behaved, leashed, and cleaned up after at all times.

Outdoor Restaurants
Nonis Deli 142 Water Street Stonington CT   860-535-0797
This deli offers outdoor seating. Dogs are permitted at the outdoor tables (seasonal). Dogs must be well behaved, under owner's control, and leashed and cleaned up after at all times

Waterbury

Accommodations
Days Inn Hartford 1845 Meridian Waterbury Turnpike Milldale CT   860-621-9181 (800-329-7466)
Dogs of all sizes are allowed. There is a $10 per night pet fee per pet. Reservations are recommended due to limited rooms for pets.
Howard Johnson Express Inn 462 Queen Street Southington CT   860-621-0181 (800-446-4656)
Dogs of all sizes are welcome. There is a $10 per day pet fee.
Motel 6 - HARTFORD - SOUTHINGTON 625 Queen Street Southington CT   860-621-7351 (800-466-8356)
One well-behaved family pet per room. Guest must notify front desk upon arrival. Guest is liable for any damages. In consideration of all guests, pets must never be left unattended in the guest rooms.
Residence Inn by Marriott 778 West Street Southington CT   860-621-4440

Pets of all sizes are allowed. There is a $75 one time fee per pet for a minimum of 5 nights stay and a pet policy to sign at check in.

Attractions
The Glebe House Museum and Gertrude Jekyll Garden 49 Hollow Road Woodbury CT   203-263-2855
http://www.theglebehouse.org/index.jsp
A seasonal museum, they research, preserve and educate the public about the heritage of this unique historical landmark considered to be the birthplace of the Episcopal Church in the New World. Dogs are allowed to explore the grounds and the beautiful garden; they are not allowed in any of the buildings. Dogs must be under owner's control, leashed, and cleaned up after at all times.

Stores
PetSmart Pet Store 278 New Britain Ave Plainville CT   860-747-9399
Your licensed and well-behaved leashed dog is allowed in the store.
Petco Pet Store 760 Queen St Southington CT   860-620-6667
Your licensed and well-behaved leashed dog is allowed in the store.
PetSmart Pet Store 475 Bank St Waterbury CT   203-596-9997
Your licensed and well-behaved leashed dog is allowed in the store.
Petco Pet Store 983 Wolcott Rd Waterbury CT   203-754-3880
Your licensed and well-behaved leashed dog is allowed in the store.

Parks
Southford Falls State Park 175 Quaker Farms Road Southbury CT   203-264-5169
Born of glacial activity, this park features a lot of exposed geology with ever changing scenery, waterfalls, a fire tower that gives some nice views of the valley below, year round recreation, and is a designated Trout Park. Dogs are permitted for no additional pet fee. Dogs are allowed at the picnic areas and on hiking trails; they are not allowed in park buildings or in swimming areas. Dogs must be under owner's control at all times, and be leashed and cleaned up after.

Off-Leash Dog Parks
Bark Park Main Street N Southbury CT   860-274-0802
http://www.roar-ridgefield.org/park.html
This off lead area is fenced on 3 sides, and open to the river on the other side. Doggy play toys, table and chairs, and benches are on site. Dogs must be sociable, current on all vaccinations, licensed, and under owner's control/care at all times. Dogs must be leashed when not in designated off-lead areas

Weathersfield

Attractions
Webb-Deane-Stevens Museum 211 Main Street Weathersfield CT   860-529-0612
http://www.webb-deane-stevens.org/
This museum is a collection of historic houses amid lush trees and lawns, a barn, museum shop, and a Colonial Revival Garden. Many events and celebrations are hosted here. Well behaved dogs are welcome to explore the grounds, but they are not allowed inside the houses or any park buildings. Dogs must be leashed and cleaned up after at all times.

Chapter 8

New York
Dog Travel Guide

Adirondacks

Accommodations

The Trout House Village Resort 9117 Lakeshore Drive Hague NY 518-543-6088 (800-368-6088)
http://www.trouthouse.com/
This resort, on the shores of Lake George, offers beautiful views of the lake and surrounding Adirondack Mountains, and provides a wide array of activities and recreation, a 9-hole putting green, and rentals for bikes and watercraft. Although dogs are not allowed during the Summer months between June 15th and September 15th, the beauty and activities here are year round. One dog is allowed per unit for an additional pet fee of $25 per night. Dogs are not allowed on the bed or the furniture, they must be leashed and cleaned up after, and they may not be left alone in the room. Dogs must be quiet and well mannered.

Fourpeaks Stonehouse Road Jay NY 518-524-6726
http://www.4peaks.com/home.htm
Fourpeaks sits secluded in a hidden valley at the end of a dirt road, and they offer a variety of accommodations, year round land and water recreation, numerous hiking trails (4 with major destinations), and cabins with full kitchens. The resident pooch here welcomes all friendly canine guests to play, go hiking, running, swimming, or just kick back at this scenic 700-acre wilderness playground of private forest land, and if they are under voice control and well behaved-no leashes are required. There are no additional pet fees. Dogs must be under owner's control/care at all times.

Jay Lodge 13112 NY State H 9N Jay NY 518-946-7467
Dogs of all sizes are allowed. There are no additional pet fees, and dogs must be on a leash when out. Dogs are not allowed to be left alone in the room.

Trails End Inn 62 Trails End Way Keene Valley NY 518-576-9860 (800-281-9860)
http://www.trailsendinn.com/
Secluded, but easily accessible, this 1902 mountain lodge offers a large front yard and porches, a barbecue and picnic area, whirlpool tubs, and it is in a great location for numerous year round recreational pursuits. Dogs of all sizes are allowed for an additional $20 per night per pet, and owners are responsible for any pet-incurred damages. There can be 1 large dog or 2 small dogs per room, and please keep them off the furniture and beds. Dogs may only be left alone in the room if assured they will be quiet and they must be crated. Dogs are not allowed in the common areas like the front porch or through the interior halls of the inn; use outer doors or stairs. Outside the inn dogs can be off lead if they are under good voice control, and "doggy towels" are provided for muddy paws. Dogs must be picked up after at all times.

Lake George Gardens Motel 2107 H 9N Lake George NY 518-668-2232
Dogs of all sizes are allowed. There is a $25 refundable deposit per stay and there is a 2 night minimum stay. There are weekly rates available. Dogs may not be left unattended for very long at a time and must be on a leash when out.

Luzerne Court 508 Lake Ave Lake Luzerne NY 518-696-2734
http://www.saratoga.org/luzernecourt/
There are no additional pet fees. Dogs must not be left alone in the rooms.

Art Devline's Olympic 350 Main St Lake Placid NY 518-523-3700
http://artdevlins.com/
There are no additional pet fees.

Comfort Inn 2125 Saranac Avenue/H 86 Lake Placid NY 518-523-9555 (877-424-6423)
Dogs are allowed for no additional pet fee. Dogs may not be left alone in the room.

Crowne Plaza Resort & Golf Club 101 Olympic Drive Lake Placid NY 518-523-2556 (877-270-6405)
Dogs of all sizes are allowed for an additional fee of $10 per night per pet. Dogs may not be left alone in the room at any time.

Edge of the Lake Motel 56 Saranac Ave Lake Placid NY 518-523-9430
There is a $10.00 per night charge per dog. Dogs are permitted up to 75 pounds. There are no designated smoking or non-smoking rooms.

Hilton One Mirror Lake Drive Lake Placid NY 518-523-4411
Dogs are allowed for an additional one time fee of $25 per pet, and there is a pet agreement to sign at check in. Dogs must be declared at the time of registration, and they may only be left alone in the room for short periods.

Lake Placid Lodge Whiteface Inn Rd. Lake Placid NY 518-523-2700
http://www.lakeplacidlodge.com
There is a $50 one time pet fee. Pets are allowed in the cabins.

Best Western The Inn at Smithfield 446 Route 3 Plattsburgh NY 518-561-7750 (800-780-7234)
Dogs are allowed for an additional one time pet fee of $10 per room.

La Quinta Inn Plattsburgh 16 Plaza Boulevard Plattsburgh NY 518-562-4000 (800-531-5900)
Dogs of all sizes are allowed. There are no additional fees. There is a pet waiver to sign at check in. Dogs must

be attended or removed for housekeeping. Dogs must be leashed and cleaned up after.

Super 8 Plattsburgh 7129 Route 9 North Plattsburgh NY 518-562-8888 (800-800-8000)
Dogs of all sizes are allowed. There is a $10 per night pet fee per pet. Reservations are recommended due to limited rooms for pets. Smoking and non-smoking rooms are available for pet rooms.

Super 8 Queensbury/Glen Falls Area 191 Corinth Rd Queensbury NY 518-761-9780 (800-800-8000)
Dogs up to 50 pounds are allowed. There is a $30 pet fee per pet for the first night and $10 per night pet fee per pet. Reservations are required with notification about the pet.

Lake Flower Inn 15 Lake Flower Ave Saranac Lake NY 518-891-2310
Management requests that dogs are not left alone in the rooms and that guests clean up after their pets. Dogs are not allowed on the beds.

Lake Side 27 Lake Flower Ave Saranac Lake NY 518-891-4333
There are a limited number of pets allowed in the hotel at a time. There are no additional pet fees.

Blue Ridge Motel Route 9 Schroon Lake NY 518-532-7521
Dogs are allowed in some of the rooms.

Starry Night Cabins 37 Fowler Avenue Schroon Lake NY 518-532-7907
Dogs of all sizes are allowed. There is a $5 per night per pet fee for a short haired dog, and there is a $10 per night per pet fee for long haired dogs. Dogs are not allowed to be left alone in the room.

Circle Court 440 Montcalm St Ticonderoga NY 518-585-7660
Dogs are allowed in some of the rooms.

The Wawbeek on Upper Saranac Lake 553 Hawk Ridge Tupper Lake NY 518-359-2656 (800-953-2656)
http://www.wawbeek.com/
This mountain inn sits on 40 scenic acres along the shores of the Upper Saranac Lake giving guests a true Adirondack experience and great views, hiking and cross-country opportunities, use of their boats, and Lake Placid's Olympic Village is only a short distance away. Dogs of all sizes are allowed for an additional fee of $25 per night per pet. Dogs must be leashed, cleaned up after, and may be crated when left alone in the room if they will be quiet and comfortable.

Willkommen Hof 5367 H 86 Whiteface NY 518-946-SNOW (7669) (800-541-9119)
http://www.willkommenhof.com/
This comfort-minded mountain inn features an outdoor spa and indoor sauna, and its location allows for numerable outdoor year round activities. Dogs of all sizes are allowed for an additional $10 per night per pet plus a $50 refundable security deposit. They must be kenneled when left in the room alone, or they may be put in the inn's outdoor run; kennels can be provided if needed. Dogs are not allowed on the beds or furniture. Dogs must be friendly, well behaved, leashed, and cleaned up after at all times.

Hungry Trout (on Route 86) Wilmington NY 518-946-2217 (800-766-9137)
http://www.hungrytrout.com/
There is an additional $5 per day charge for a pet.

Campgrounds and RV Parks

Alpine Lake RV Resort 78 Heath Road Corinth NY 518-654-6260
http://www.alpinelakervresort.com
Dogs of all sizes are allowed, however some breeds are not. There are no additional pet fees. Dogs must have proof of rabies shots, be leashed, and cleaned up after. The camping and tent areas also allow dogs. There is a dog walk area at the campground.

Schroon River Resort 969 E Schroon River Road Diamond Point NY 518-623-3954
Dogs of all sizes are allowed. There are no additional pet fees. Current shot records and proof of insurance is required for some breeds. Dogs must be leashed and cleaned up after. The camping and tent areas also allow dogs. There is a dog walk area at the campground.

Lake George RV Park 74 State H 149 Lake George NY 518-792-3775
http://lakegeorgervpark.com
Dogs of all sizes are allowed. There are no additional pet fees. Dogs must be leashed, cleaned up after, and not left unattended. The camping and tent areas also allow dogs. There is a dog walk area at the campground.

KOA Lake George/Saratoga 564 Lake Avenue Lake Luzerne NY 518-696-2615 (800-562-2618)
http://www.lakegeorgekoa.com
Dogs of all sizes are allowed. There are no additional pet fees. Dogs must be leashed and cleaned up after. There are some breed restrictions. This RV park is closed during the off-season. The camping and tent areas also allow dogs. There is a dog walk area at the campground.

Plattsburgh RV Park 7182 H 9N Plattsburgh NY 518-563-3915
http://www.plattsburghrvpark.com
Dogs of all sizes are allowed. There are no additional pet fees. Dogs must be well behaved and under control of owner. Dogs must be leashed and cleaned up after. The camping and tent areas also allow dogs. There is a dog walk area at the campground. Dogs are allowed in the camping cabins.

Saranac Lake Islands 58 Bayside Drive Saranac Lake NY 518-897-1309 (800-456-CAMP (2267))
This park provides many miles of boating recreation with direct access to other lakes through a set of locks that raise and lower vessels through to the next water level. Dogs are welcome for no additional fee, but they must

have proof of current rabies inoculation. Dogs may not be left unattended anywhere, and they must be quiet, well mannered, leashed (no more than 6 foot), and cleaned up after at all times. Dogs are not permitted on Lake George Islands, the beach, picnic areas, or in park buildings. The camping area offers 87 primitive sites with fireplaces, picnic tables, and restrooms.

Glen Hudson Campsite 564 River Road Thurman NY 518-623-9871
Nestled along the banks of the Hudson River, this RV park offers a camping store, laundry, showers, rec hall, and a variety of land and water recreation. Dogs of all sizes are allowed for no additional fees. Dogs must be well behaved, leashed, and cleaned up after at all times. This RV park is closed during the off-season. There is a dog walk area at the campground.

TOP 200 PLACE **Daggett Lake Campsites & Cabins** 660 Glen Athol Rd Warrensburg NY 518-623-2198
http://www.daggettlake.com
Well behaved, leashed pets are welcome in the RV Park and the cabins. There is no additional charge for pets in the campground and a $50 cleaning fee for cabins. Proof of rabies shots are required in the campground and flea control in the cabins. This campground is home of the "DOG BEACH" where dogs can go off leash if they are under voice control. There are 400 acres with hiking and mountain biking trails, canoe, kayak, and rowboat rentals, and a sandy swim beach for people.

Schroon River Campsites 74 State H 149 Warrensburg NY 518-623-2171
http://www.lakegeorgervpark
Dogs of all sizes are allowed. There are no additional pet fees. Dogs must be well behaved, cleaned up after, and not left unattended. The camping and tent areas also allow dogs. There is a dog walk area at the campground.

KOA Lake Placid/Whiteface Mountain 77 Foxfarm Road Wilmington NY 518-946-7878 (800-562-0368)
http://www.koacampground.com
Dogs of all sizes are allowed in the camp and RV sites, but only one dog up to 40 pounds is allowed in the cabin. There are no additional pet fees. Dogs may not be left unattended and must have a valid rabies certificate. They must be leashed and cleaned up after. There are some breed restrictions. This RV park is closed during the off-season. The camping and tent areas also allow dogs. There is a dog walk area at the campground. Dogs are allowed in the camping cabins.

Transportation Systems

Lake Champlain Ferries 838-842 Cumberland Head Road Plattsburgh NY 802-864-9804
http://www.ferries.com/
Leashed dogs of all sizes are allowed on the Lake Champlain Ferry crossing that travels between New York and Vermont. Ferry schedules changes constantly so please confirm the time of your voyage.

Attractions

Lake George Kayak Company 3 Boathouse Ln Bolton Landing NY 518-644-9366
This kayak rental company will allow a dog to accompany their owner on rentals for no additional fee. Dogs must be under owner's control/care at all times, be leashed, and cleaned up after.

Mountainman Outdoor Supply Company 221 H 28 Inlet NY 315-357-6672
http://www.mountainmanoutdoors.com/
This outfitters supply company has two locations for watercraft rentals; the one listed and on Hwy 28 in Old Forge. Dogs are welcome to join their owners on rentals for no additional fee. Dogs must be friendly to other dogs (there is one on site at Inlet) and people, be under the owner's control, leashed, and cleaned up after at all times. Dogs are not allowed during the annual Paddle Fest, usually held mid-May, or on their shuttle.

Water Safari Enchanted Forest 3138 H 28 Old Forge NY 315-369-6145
http://www.watersafari.com/
There are more than 50 rides and attractions, and special events throughout the year, plus a whole lot more at what is the state's largest water theme park. Dogs are allowed for no additional fee. They must be friendly, well mannered, under owner's control, leashed, and cleaned up after at all times. Dogs may not be left unattended at any time or left in vehicles. Dogs are not allowed in the water ride areas or most buildings; they are allowed throughout the rest of the park unless otherwise noted.

Adirondack Lakes and Trails Outfitters 541 Lake Flower AvenueH 86 Saranac NY 518-891-7450
http://www.adirondackoutfitters.com/
This outfitters supply company offers canoe and kayak rentals, and dogs may accompany their owner on rentals for no additional fee. Dogs must be under owner's control/care at all times, be leashed, and cleaned up after.

TOP 200 PLACE **St Regis Canoe Outfitters** 73 Dorsey Street Saranac Lake NY 518-891-1838
http://www.canoeoutfitters.com/
This outfitters supply company offers canoe and kayak rentals and dogs may accompany their owners on rentals, with no additional fee if there is no additional cleaning is needed. If dogs need to be shuttled between sites the fee is the same as an adult ticket and starts at about $10. Dogs must be under owner's control/care at all times, be leashed, and cleaned up after.

TOP 200 PLACE Whiteface Mountain Veterans Memorial Highway 5021 RT 86 Wilmington NY 518-523-1655
http://www.whiteface.com/
Grab your leash and hit the trails of Whiteface Mountains Veterans Memorial Highway. Beautiful views are just one of the things you will remember after your trip. Dogs are not allowed inside the buildings or the elevators but are welcome anywhere else on the mountain. The Veterans Highway is closed during the Winter.
Westport Marina 20 Washington Street Westport NY 800-626-0342
http://www.westportmarina.com/
This company provides watercraft rentals for exploring the Lake Champlain area, and dogs may accompany their owner for no additional fee if there is no additional clean-up. Dogs must be under owner's control/care at all times, be leashed, and cleaned up after.

Cross Country Ski Resorts

TOP 200 PLACE Crowne Plaza Resort & Golf Club 101 Olympic Drive Lake Placid NY 518-523-2556 (877-270-6405)
http://www.lakeplacidcp.com
The cross-country ski rental center at this resort is only open on the weekends. They have over 25km of groomed cross-country and snowshoeing trails. Dogs are allowed on the lower cross-country ski trails which are located south of route 86. They just ask that dogs walk alongside but not directly on the groomed trails. It is a short walk from the Golf Course Shop where you rent the skis to the trailhead. This trail system connects up to the 50km Jackrabbit Trail. Dogs need to be leashed at the resort and on the trails. Pets are welcome to stay with you at this resort for an extra pet fee.

Shopping Centers

Lake George Plaza Factory Outlets Center H 9 Lake George NY 518-798-7234
Your pooch is welcome to explore this area as long as they are on leash and picked up after. It is up to the individual stores as to whether pets are allowed inside.

Stores

Adirondack Craft Center 2114 Saranac Avenue/H 86 Lake Placid NY 518-523-2062
http://www.adirondackcraftcenter.com/
Originally created as an outlet for handcrafted products by regional artists, this center of over 4000 square feet now offers unique furnishings and giftware from more than 300 sources. Your well behaved pooch is welcome to join you in the store. Dogs must be under owner's control/care at all times.
PetSmart Pet Store 67 Consumer Square Plattsburgh NY 518-562-8600
Your licensed and well-behaved leashed dog is allowed in the store.
Petco Pet Store 28 Centre Drive Plattsburgh NY 518-561-9325
Your licensed and well-behaved leashed dog is allowed in the store.
Benson's Pet Center 118 Quaker Road Queensbury NY 518 793-6655
http://www.bensonspet.com/
In addition to offering a full line of supplies for all pets, this store also carries a good selection of high quality dog foods. Well behaved, leashed dogs are welcome in the store.

Parks

Lake George Battle Field Park Fort George Rd Lake George NY 518-668-3352
Bring your leashed dog for a tour of historic Lake George Battle Field Park. Tour the monuments that mark the first and second engagements of the battle. Park hours are dawn until dusk.
Saranac Lake Islands 58 Bayside Drive Saranac Lake NY 518-897-1309 (800-456-CAMP (2267))
This park provides many miles of boating recreation with direct access to other lakes through a set of locks that raises and lowers vessels through to the next water level. Dogs are welcome for no additional fee, but they must have proof of current rabies inoculation. Dogs may not be left unattended anywhere, and they must be quiet, well mannered, leashed (no more than 6 foot), and cleaned up after at all times. Dogs are not permitted on Lake George Islands, the beach, picnic areas, or in park buildings.

Outdoor Restaurants

Davidson Brothers Restaurant and Brewery 184 Glen St/H 9 Glens Falls NY 518-743-9026
http://www.davidsonbrothers.com/
Called a "world-class brewpub" this tavern offers a full lunch and dinner menu (plus a kid's menu too) with many of their own specialties including ale-simmered chili, weekly entertainment, and outside dining. Dogs are allowed at the outside tables; they must be leashed and under owner's control/care at all times.

Christie's on the Lake 6 Christie Lane Lake George NY   518-668-2515
This restaurant and bar serves American. Dogs are allowed at the outdoor tables.
Frank's Pizzeria 1483 State Rt 9 Lake George NY   518-793-7909
This restaurant serves pizza. Dogs are allowed at the outdoor tables. There are no servers outside but you can order at the window.
Guiseppe's Food and Drink Emporium 365 Canada Street Lake George NY   518-668-2981
This restaurant and bar serves Italian and seafood. Dogs are allowed at the outdoor tables along the sidewalk.
King Neptune's Pub and Night Club 4 Kurosaka Lane Lake George NY 518-668-2017
This restaurant and bar serves deli-type food. Dogs are allowed at the outdoor tables.
Lake George Barnsider Restaurant Route 9 South Lake George Lake George NY 518-668-5268
http://www.barnsider.com
This restaurant serves barbecue and American food. Dogs are allowed at the outdoor tables.
Log Jam Restaurant 1484 State Route 9 Site 1 Lake George NY   518-798-1155
This restaurant serves American food. Dogs are allowed at the outdoor tables.
Sicilian Spaghetti House 371 Canada Street Lake George NY 518-668-2582
This restaurant serves Italian food. Dogs are allowed at the outdoor tables on sidewalk edge.
Simple Simon's 3 Lower Montcalm Street Lake George NY   518-668-4988
This restaurant serves American food. Dogs are allowed at the outdoor tables.
Subway 275 Canada Street Lake George NY 518-668-3051
This restaurant serves deli-type food. Dogs are allowed at the outdoor tables.
Waterhouse Restaurant Route 9 North Lake Luzerne NY 518-696-3115
This restaurant serves American food. Dogs are allowed at the outdoor tables.
Bazzi's Pizza 138 Main St Lake Placid NY   518-523-9056
This restaurant serves Italian food. Dogs are allowed at the outdoor tables.
The Downhill Grill 434 Main Street Lake Placid NY   518-523-9510
This restaurant and bar serves American. Dogs are allowed at the outdoor tables.
The Grill at Martha's 1133 State Route 9 Queensbury NY 518-798-3021
This restaurant and bar serves American. Dogs are allowed at the outdoor tables.
Jake's Round- Up 23 Main Street South Glens Falls NY 518-761-0015
This restaurant and bar serves American. Dogs are allowed at the outdoor tables.

Albany

Accommodations
Best Western Sovereign Hotel - Albany 1228 Western Avenue Albany NY   518-489-2981 (800-780-7234)
Dogs are allowed with advance reservations for an additional fee of $15 per night per pet. Dogs may not be left alone in the room.
Comfort Inn and Suites 1606 Central Avenue Albany NY   518-869-5327 (877-424-6423)
Dogs are allowed for an additional pet fee of $15 per night per room.
Cresthill Suites Hotel 1415 Washington Avenue Albany NY   518-454-0007 (888-723-1655)
http://www.cresthillsuites.com
In addition to offering a great starting location to many other local attractions, this hotel also has an outdoor courtyard pool with a patio and barbecues, and lots of extras. Dogs of all sizes are allowed for an additional $75 one time fee per pet. They request that dogs be removed or crated for housekeeping. Dogs must be leashed, cleaned up after, and may only be left alone in the room if they will be quiet and well behaved.
Holiday Inn Albany On Wolf Road 205 Wolf Rd. Albany NY 518-458-7250 (877-270-6405)
Dogs of all sizes are allowed for an additional pet fee per room of $35 (plus tax) for 1 to 3 nights; the fee is $100 for 4 or more nights.
Motel 6 - ALBANY, NY 100 Watervliet Avenue Albany NY 518-438-7447 (800-466-8356)
One well-behaved family pet per room. Guest must notify front desk upon arrival. Guest is liable for any damages. In consideration of all guests, pets must never be left unattended in the guest rooms.
Red Roof Inn - Albany 188 Wolf Road Albany NY 518-459-1971 (800-RED-ROOF)
One well-behaved family pet per room. Guest must notify front desk upon arrival. Guest is liable for any damages. In consideration of all guests, pets must never be left unattended in the guest rooms.
TownePlace Suites Albany SUNY 1379 Washington Avenue Albany NY 518-435-1900
Dogs of all sizes are allowed. There is a $75 one time pet fee per visit.
Century House Inn 997 New Loudon Road Latham NY 518-785-0931
http://www.centuryhouse.inter.net/
There is a $15 one time pet fee.
Holiday Inn Express 946 New Loudon Road US 9 Latham NY 518-783-6161 (877-270-6405)
Dogs of all sizes are allowed for an additional fee of $20 per night per pet.
Microtel 7 Rensselaer Ave Latham NY 518-782-9161

There are no additional pet fees.
Quality Inn 611 Troy-Schenectady RoadH 7 Latham NY   518-785-5891 (877-424-6423)
Dogs are allowed for an additional one time pet fee of $35 per room.
Residence Inn by Marriott 1 Residence Inn Drive Latham NY   518-783-0600
Dogs of all sizes are allowed. There is a $75 one time fee and a pet policy to sign at check in.
The Century House Hotel 997 New Loudon Road Latham NY   518-785-0931 (888-674-6873)
http://www.thecenturyhouse.com/
In additional to a complimentary country-style breakfast buffet, this hotel also offers a full service restaurant and bar, an outdoor pool and tennis courts, and an historic nature trail to walk your four legged companion. Dogs of all sizes are allowed for an additional fee of $15 per night per pet. Dogs may only be left alone in the room if they will be quiet, well behaved, and a contact number is left with the front desk. Dogs must be leashed and cleaned up after.

Attractions

Hudson River Way Pedestrian Bridge Broadway Albany NY   518-434-2032
This 650 foot bridge spans across the I-787 connecting the City of Albany to its historic riverfront and the Corning Preserve Park. The walkway is known for its more than 30 historic paintings and murals that depict the region from pre-historic times to the present. Dogs are allowed on the bridge. Dogs must be leashed and cleaned up after at all times.
Howe Caverns 255 Discovery Drive Howes Cave NY   518-296-8900
http://www.howecaverns.com/
Whether taking a regular tour or a specialty tour, the 156 foot drop to this prehistoric world for a boat ride on an underground lake is one of geological amazement. Leashed dogs are allowed in all of the above ground cave areas as well as any of the walking tours. The tour takes about 80 minutes. Because of movement restrictions, pets are not allowed in the caves; however they do provide a locked kennel for no additional fee. Dogs must be kept on lead when not in the kennel and be cleaned up after.

Shopping Centers

Stuyvesant Plaza 1475 Western Avenue Albany NY   518-482-8986
http://www.stuyvesantplaza.com/
There are 60 shops (many one of a kind) for browsing and dining here in addition to being a pleasing place to explore. Dogs are welcome to explore this outdoor mall; it is up to individual stores whether a pet is allowed inside. Dogs must be under owner's control, leashed, and cleaned up after at all times.

Stores

PetSmart Pet Store 161 Washington Ave Extension Albany NY   518-452-5683
Your licensed and well-behaved leashed dog is allowed in the store.
Benson's Pet Center 12 Fire Road Clifton Park NY   518-373-1007
http://www.bensonspet.com/
In addition to offering a full line of supplies for all pets, this store also carries a good selection of high quality dog foods. Well behaved, leashed dogs are welcome in the store.
Petco Pet Store 6 Halfmoon Crossing Clifton Park NY   518-373-8007
Your licensed and well-behaved leashed dog is allowed in the store.
Benson's Pet Center 197 Wolf Rd Colonie NY   518 435-1738
http://www.bensonspet.com/
In addition to offering a full line of supplies for all pets, this store also carries a good selection of high quality dog foods. Well behaved, leashed dogs are welcome in the store.
Petco Pet Store 1440 Central Avenue Colonie NY   518-453-9025
Your licensed and well-behaved leashed dog is allowed in the store.
PetSmart Pet Store 609 Troy Schenectady Rd Latham NY   518-785-4621
Your licensed and well-behaved leashed dog is allowed in the store.

Parks

Albany Riverfront Park at the Corning Preserve 25 Quackenbush Square Albany NY   518-434-2032
This riverfront preserve park offers a boat launch, a bike trail, an amphitheater, visitor center, comfort stations, and beautiful places to walk. The park is also connected to the city and all it has to offer via the Hudson River Way Pedestrian Bridge. Dogs are allowed throughout the park and there is no fee. This park is host to several events through the year and dogs are not allowed at the park during events. Dogs must be under owner's control, leashed, and cleaned up after at all times.
Vischer Ferry Nature Preserve Riverview Rd. Clifton Park NY
The nature preserve, popular with local dog walkers, follows the Mohawk River and the Erie Canal for a number of miles. You will see a number of historical sites such as locks on the canal and other various historical

markers. The area is also a wetland habitat for birds and plants. Dogs must be on leash at all times and must be cleaned up after. Take Cresent Road (Hwy 92) west from I-87 2.5 miles and turn left onto Van Vranken Rd. Turn right at Riverview Rd and the preserve will be on your left.

Erie Canalway National Heritage Corridor PO Box 219 Waterford NY   518-237-8643
http://www.nps.gov/erie/index.htm
Dogs must be on leash and must be cleaned up after in most of the park area. You must follow local and state park rules for pets. Some auto touring is involved with stops for fishing, hiking, boating, and more.

Off-Leash Dog Parks
Department of General Services Off Lead Area Erie Blvd Albany NY   518-434-CITY (2489)
This off lead area sit just north of the I 90 bridge overpass. Dogs must be sociable, current on all vaccinations, and under owner's control/care at all times. Dogs must be leashed when not in designated off-lead areas.
Hartman Road Dog Park Hartman Road Albany NY   518-434-CITY (2489)
Only a ½ mile past the Thruway Bridge, this off lead area sits adjacent to the Community Garden. Dogs must be sociable, current on all vaccinations, and under owner's control/care at all times. Dogs must be leashed when not in designated off-lead areas.
Normanskill Farm Dog Park Mill Road/Delaware Avenue Albany NY   518-434-CITY (2489)
Off the beaten track a bit makes for a nice setting for an off leash area. Dogs must be sociable, current on all vaccinations, and under owner's control/care at all times. Dogs must be leashed when not in designated off-lead areas.
Westland Hills Dog Park Anthony Street Albany NY   518-434-CITY (2489)
This off lead area is located in Westland Hills Park. Dogs must be sociable, current on all vaccinations, and under owner's control/care at all times. Dogs must be leashed when not in designated off-lead areas.

Outdoor Restaurants
Londonberry Cafe 1475 Western Avenue, Suite 30 Albany NY   518-489-4288
This Stuyvesant Plaza bistro allows a guest to have their dog at the outer tables. Dogs must be well mannered, under owner's control, leashed, and cleaned up after at all times.
Nicole's Bistro 25 Quackenbush Square Albany NY   518-467-1111
http://www.nicolesbistro.com/
Located in the historic Quackenbush House, this popular bistro features traditional French cuisine with an international flair. Dogs are permitted at the outdoor tables (seasonal). Dogs must be well behaved, under owner's control, leashed, and cleaned up after at all times.

Alexandria

Campgrounds and RV Parks
Keywaydin State Park 45165 H 12 Alexandria NY   315-482-3331
http://www.nysparks.state.ny.us/
Dogs of all sizes are allowed. There are no additional pet fees. Dogs may not be left unattended, they must have a current rabies certificate and shot records, be well behaved, on no more than a 6 foot leash, and be cleaned up after. Dogs are allowed on the trails, but not in the picnic or bathroom areas. This campground is closed during the off-season. The camping and tent areas also allow dogs. There is a dog walk area at the campground. There are no water hookups at the campground.

Alexandria Bay

Attractions
TOP 200 PLACE Uncle Sam Boat Tours 47 James Street Alexandria Bay NY   315-482-2611
http://www.usboattours.com/
A variety of cruises are featured by this company that cruise the 1000 Islands area daily through the end of October. Your well behaved pooch is welcome to join you on several of the cruises; they are not allowed on lunch or dinner cruises. Dogs must be under owner's control, leashed, and cleaned up after at all times.

Apalachin

New York - Please always call ahead to make sure that an establishment is still dog-friendly

Accommodations
Quality Inn Binghamton West 7666 Route 434 Apalachin NY   607-625-4441 (877-424-6423)
Dogs are allowed for an additional fee of $10 per night per pet.

Averill Park

Campgrounds and RV Parks
Alps Family Campground 1928 State H 43 Averill Park NY   518-674-5565
Dogs of all sizes are allowed. There are no additional pet fees. Dogs must have proof of rabies shots, be leashed, cleaned up after, and not left unattended. The camping and tent areas also allow dogs. There is a dog walk area at the campground.

Barryville

Attractions
Indian Head Canoes 3883 H 97 Barryville NY   800-874-2628
http://www.indianheadcanoes.com/
This watercraft rental company will allow dogs for no additional fee. Owners are responsible for any damage caused by their pet. Aggressive dogs are not allowed. Dogs must be under owner's control, leashed (except when on the water), and cleaned up after at all times.

Batavia

Accommodations
Comfort Inn 4371 Federal Drive Batavia NY   585-344-9999 (877-424-6423)
Dogs are allowed for an additional one time fee of $10 per pet.
Days Inn Batavia 200 Oak St Batavia NY   585-343-6000 (800-329-7466)
Dogs of all sizes are allowed. There is a $10 per night pet fee per pet.
Quality Inn and Suites 8200 Park Road Batavia NY   585-344-7000 (877-424-6423)
Dogs are allowed for an additional fee of $10 per night per pet.

Berkshire Region

Accommodations
The Inn at The Shaker Mill Farm 40 Cherry Lane Canaan NY   518-794-9345
http://www.shakermillfarminn.com/
This converted 1824 Shaker mill, complete with a brook and waterfall, features 20 uniquely different rooms with private baths, and woodland trails to explore. Dogs of all sizes are allowed for no additional fee. Dogs must be very well behaved, quiet, leashed, and cleaned up after.
Mountain House 150 Berkshire Way Stephentown NY   800-497-0176
http://www.berkshirebb.com/
A spring-fed pond, 50 rolling acres of meadows and woods, walking trails, and a spacious house on the hill with great views of all, make this a popular retreat. Dogs of all sizes are welcome for no additional fees. Dogs must be friendly with other dogs and well mannered. Dogs must be under owner's control and cleaned up after at all times.

Campgrounds and RV Parks
Woodland Hills Campground 386 Foghill Road Austerlitz NY   518-392-3557
http://www.whcg.net
Dogs of all sizes are allowed. There are no additional pet fees. Dogs must be quiet, leashed, and cleaned up

after. The camping and tent areas also allow dogs. There is a dog walk area at the campground.

Attractions
Old Chatham Sheepherding Company 155 Shaker Museum Road Old Chatham NY   888-SHEEP-60 (743-3760)
http://www.blacksheepcheese.com/
You don't want to miss this farm of more than a thousand East Friesain pure and crossbred sheep where they produce many award wining cheeses and yogurts on what is the US's largest sheep farm. Your pet is welcome to explore the grounds. Dogs must be under owner's control, leashed, and cleaned up after at all times.

Binghamton

Accommodations
Clarion Collection: The Grand Royal Hotel 80 State Street Binghamton NY   607-722-0000 (877-424-6423)
Dogs are allowed for an additional fee of $10 per night per pet.
Motel 6 - Binghamton 1012 Front Street Binghamton NY   607-771-0400 (800-466-8356)
One well-behaved family pet per room. Guest must notify front desk upon arrival. Guest is liable for any damages. In consideration of all guests, pets must never be left unattended in the guest rooms.
Quality Inn and Suites 1156 Front Street Binghamton NY   607-722-5353 (877-424-6423)
Dogs are allowed for an additional one time pet fee of $15 per room.
Super 8 Binghamton/Front Street 650 Old Front St Binghamton NY   607-773-8111 (800-800-8000)
Dogs of all sizes are allowed. There is a $35 returnable deposit required per room. Reservations are recommended due to limited rooms for pets. Smoking and non-smoking rooms are available for pet rooms.
La Quinta Inn Johnson City 581 Harry L. Drive Johnson City NY   607-770-9333 (800-531-5900)
A dog of any size is allowed. There are no additional pet fees. There is a pet waiver to sign at check in. Dogs are not allowed to be left alone in the rooms, but if you have to go for a short time, a contact number must be left with the front desk.
Red Roof Inn - Binghamton 590 Fairview Street Johnson City NY   607-729-8940 (800-RED-ROOF)
One well-behaved family pet per room. Guest must notify front desk upon arrival. Guest is liable for any damages. In consideration of all guests, pets must never be left unattended in the guest rooms.
Residence Inn by Marriott 4610 Vestal Parkway E Vestal NY   607-770-8500
Dogs of all sizes are allowed. There is a $75 one time fee and a pet policy to sign at check in.
Holiday Inn 4105 Vestal Parkway Vestal Parkway NY   607-729-6371 (877-270-6405)
Quiet dogs of all sizes are allowed for an additional one time pet fee of $25 per room.

Campgrounds and RV Parks
Chenango Valley State Park 153 State Park Road Chenango Forks NY   607-648-5251
http://www.nysparks.state.ny.us
Dogs of all sizes are allowed. There are no additional pet fees. Dogs may not be left unattended, they must have a current rabies certificate and shot records. Dogs must be quiet, leashed, and cleaned up after. Dogs are allowed on the trails, but not on the beach or in the water. Although the campground is seasonal, the park is open year-round. This campground is closed during the off-season. The camping and tent areas also allow dogs. There is a dog walk area at the campground. Dogs are allowed in the camping cabins.
Kellystone Park 51 Hawkins Road Nineveh NY   607-639-1090
http://www.kellystonepark.com
Dogs of all sizes are allowed, however some breeds are not. There are no additional pet fees. Dogs must be quiet, well behaved, leashed, and cleaned up after. The camping and tent areas also allow dogs. There is a dog walk area at the campground.

Brockport

Accommodations
Holiday Inn Express 4908 South Lake Rd Brockport NY   585-395-1000 (877-270-6405)
Dogs of all sizes are allowed for an additional one time fee of $15 per pet.

Stores
PetSmart Pet Store 1901 Transit Way Brockport NY   585-637-7508

Your licensed and well-behaved leashed dog is allowed in the store.

Brocton

Campgrounds and RV Parks

Lake Erie State Park 5905 Lake Road Brocton NY 716-792-9214 (800-456-CAMP (2267))
With ¾ of a mile of beach and great lake views, this family camp area also offers hiking and biking trails with cross-country ski trails in Winter, a nature trail, playground, concessionaire, picnic pavilions, and a variety of land and water recreation. Dogs of all sizes are allowed for no additional fee. Dogs must be crated or on a leash not more than 10 feet, and they are not allowed in swim areas, public buildings, or on cross-country ski trails. Dogs must be cleaned up after. The camp area has 97 campsites with tables, fire pits, showers, restrooms, and dump stations. This RV park is closed during the off-season. The camping and tent areas also allow dogs. There is a dog walk area at the campground. Dogs are allowed in the camping cabins. There are no water hookups at the campgrounds.

Parks

Lake Erie State Park 5905 Lake Road Brocton NY 716-792-9214 (800-456-CAMP (2267))
With ¾ of a mile of beach and great lake views, this family camp area also offers hiking and biking trails with cross-country ski trails in Winter, a nature trail, playground, concessionaire, picnic pavilions, and a variety of land and water recreation. Dogs of all sizes are allowed for no additional fee. Dogs must be crated or on a leash not more than 10 feet, and they are not allowed in swim areas, public buildings, or on cross-country ski trails. Dogs must be cleaned up after.

Buffalo

Accommodations

Comfort Inn University 1 Flint Road Amherst NY 716-688-0811 (877-424-6423)
Dogs are allowed for an additional fee of $20 per night per pet.
Lord Amherst 5000 Main St Amherst NY 716-839-2200 (800-544-2200)
There are no additional pet fees.
Motel 6 - Buffalo - Amherst 4400 Maple Road Amherst NY 716-834-2231 (800-466-8356)
One well-behaved family pet per room. Guest must notify front desk upon arrival. Guest is liable for any damages. In consideration of all guests, pets must never be left unattended in the guest rooms.
Red Roof Inn - Buffalo Amherst 42 Flint Road Amherst NY 716-689-7474 (800-RED-ROOF)
One well-behaved family pet per room. Guest must notify front desk upon arrival. Guest is liable for any damages. In consideration of all guests, pets must never be left unattended in the guest rooms.
Clarion Hotel S-3950 McKinley Parkway Blasdell NY 716-648-5700 (877-424-6423)
One dog is allowed for an additional pet fee of $10 per night.
Red Roof Inn - Buffalo Airport 146 Maple Drive Bowmansville NY 716-633-1100 (800-RED-ROOF)
One well-behaved family pet per room. Guest must notify front desk upon arrival. Guest is liable for any damages. In consideration of all guests, pets must never be left unattended in the guest rooms.
Holiday Inn 620 Delaware Avenue Buffalo NY 716-886-2121 (877-270-6405)
Dogs of all sizes are allowed for an additional one time pet fee of $30 per room; dogs must be crated when alone in the room.
Residence Inn by Marriott 107 Anderson Road Buffalo NY 716-892-5410
Dogs of all sizes are allowed. There is a $75 one time fee and a pet policy to sign at check in.
Holiday Inn Buffalo-Intl Airport 4600 Genesee Street Cheektowaga NY 716-634-6969 (877-270-6405)
Dogs of all sizes are allowed for an additional one time pet fee of $25 per room.
Holiday Inn Express Hotel and Suites 131 Buell Avenue Cheektowaga NY 716-631-8700 (877-270-6405)
One dog of any size is allowed for an additional one time pet fee of $30.
Asa Ransom House 10529 Main Street Clarence NY 716-759-2315
Dog only are allowed and of all sizes. There is a $100 refundable deposit and a pet policy to sign at check in.
Comfort Inn and Suites 3615 Commerce Place Hamburg NY 716-648-2922 (877-424-6423)
Dogs are allowed for an additional fee of $10 per night per pet.
Holiday Inn 5440 Camp Road (NY 75) Hamburg NY 716-649-0500 (877-270-6405)
Dogs of all sizes are allowed for an additional fee of $15 per night per pet.
Red Roof Inn - Buffalo Hamburg 5370 Camp Road Hamburg NY 716-648-7222 (800-RED-ROOF)
One well-behaved family pet per room. Guest must notify front desk upon arrival. Guest is liable for any

damages. In consideration of all guests, pets must never be left unattended in the guest rooms.
Super 8 Kenmore/Buffalo/Niagara Falls Area 1288 Sheridan Drive Kenmore NY 716-876-4020 (800-800-8000)
Dogs of all sizes are allowed. There are no additional pet fees. Pet must be kept in kennel when left alone and not for long periods of time. Smoking and non-smoking rooms are available for pet rooms.
Microtel 1 Hospitality Centre Way Tonawanda NY 716-693-8100 (800-227-6346)
There is a $10 per day additional pet fee.
Residence Inn by Marriott 100 Maple Road Williamsville NY 716-623-6622
Dogs of all sizes are allowed. There is a $75 one time fee and a pet policy to sign at check in.

Campgrounds and RV Parks
Jellystone Park 5204 Youngers Road North Java NY 585-457-9644 (800-232-4039)
http://www.wnyjellystone.com
Dogs of all sizes are allowed. There are no additional pet fees unless staying in the pet friendly Boo Boo Chalets. Then there would be an additional $25 per unit. Dogs must be quiet, well behaved, leashed and cleaned up after. Dogs may not be left unattended. This RV park is closed during the off-season. The camping and tent areas also allow dogs. There is a dog walk area at the campground. Dogs are allowed in the camping cabins.

Attractions
Theodore Roosevelt Inaugural National Historic Site 641 Delaware Avenue Buffalo NY 716-884-0095
http://www.nps.gov/thri/index.htm
Dogs must be on leash and must be cleaned up after on walking tours of the historical neighborhoods. Dogs are not allowed in the house or gardens.
The Canine Rehabilitation Center of Western New York 6551 Main St. Williamsville Williamsville NY 716-634-0000
http://www.swimyourdog.com/index.php
In addition to offering a wide range of physical therapy services and products in conjunction with the pets' primary veterinarian, they also offer recreational swim services for healthy dogs; no referral needed. They will also host private events and doggy birthday parties. Recreational swim fees are $21 per half hour with package discounts available. Dogs must be well behaved, clean, and current on all vaccinations.

Stores
PetSmart Pet Store 1579 Niagara Falls Blvd Amherst NY 716-834-9264
Your licensed and well-behaved leashed dog is allowed in the store.
Petco Pet Store 1459 Niagara Falls Blvd Amherst NY 716-832-2373
Your licensed and well-behaved leashed dog is allowed in the store.
PetSmart Pet Store 4405 Milestrip Rd Blasdell NY 716-821-0723
Your licensed and well-behaved leashed dog is allowed in the store.
PetSmart Pet Store 5061 Transit Rd Buffalo NY 716-565-2398
Your licensed and well-behaved leashed dog is allowed in the store.
PetSmart Pet Store 1734 Walden Ave Cheektowaga NY 716-893-2398
Your licensed and well-behaved leashed dog is allowed in the store.
Petco Pet Store 330 Orchard Park Rd West Seneca NY 716-826-1500
Your licensed and well-behaved leashed dog is allowed in the store.

Outdoor Restaurants
Spot Coffee 227 Delaware Avenue Buffalo NY 716-332-2299
http://www.spotcoffee.com/
The holder of numerous "best of" awards, this coffee shop makes their own rich flavor blends and roast their beans in small batches for their unique flavor. Dogs are welcome at the outer tables. Dogs must be well behaved, under owner's control, leashed, and cleaned up after at all times.
The Saigon Cafe 1098 Elmwood Avenue Buffalo NY 716-883-1252
http://www.thesaigoncafe.com/
Specializing in fine Vietnamese and Thai cuisine, this restaurant also offers indoor and outdoor dining. Dogs are welcome at the outer tables. Dogs must be well behaved, under owner's control, leashed, and cleaned up after at all times.

Cambridge

Campgrounds and RV Parks
Lake Lauderdale Campground 744 Country Route 61 Cambridge NY   518-677-8855
http://www.lakelauderdalecampground.com
Dogs of all sizes are allowed. There are no additional pet fees. Dogs must be well behaved, leashed, and cleaned up after. Dogs are not to be left unattended. The camping and tent areas also allow dogs. There is a dog walk area at the campground.

Camden

Accommodations
Blue Harbor House 67 Elm Street Camden NY   207-236-3196 (800-248-3196)
http://www.blueharborhouse.com/
This 1810 harbor house features a nice blending of old and new worlds, and is about a 4 minute walk to the harbor and a quaint costal village. They offer one suite for guests with pets, complete with a whirlpool tub and it's own outside entrance. One dog of any size is allowed for an additional fee of $25 per night. Dogs must be leashed and cleaned up after.

Canastota

Accommodations
Days Inn Syracuse/Canastota 377 N Petersboro St Canastota NY   315-697-3309 (800-329-7466)
Dogs of all sizes are allowed. There are no additional pet fees.

Catskills

Accommodations
Cedar Terrace Resort 665 Main Street Cairo NY   518-622-9313
Nestled in the scenic Northern Catskill Mountains, this picturesque resort offers a relaxing atmosphere in addition to well-manicured grounds and gardens, great views, and comfortable rooms. Some of their features include gaming courts, a 9-hole miniature golf course, a multi-use sports field with bleachers, big swings, a pool, table tennis, catering for groups, and wonderful wooded hiking paths. Dogs of all sizes are allowed. There is a $10 per night per pet additional fee. Dogs may not be left alone in the room at any time, and they must be leashed and cleaned up after.
Mountain View Log Home Hunter Mountain Catskills NY 212-381-2375
This fully-loaded, ready to enjoy tri-level log cabin sits on 10 elevated hilly, wooded acres and offers a sauna, a pool/gaming room, many extras-including great views of Hunter Mountain, and they are just minutes from an abundance of activities and recreation. Dogs of all sizes are welcome for no additional pet fee. They ask that dogs are kept off the furniture and the bed. Dogs must be leashed and cleaned up after.
River Run 882 Main Street Fleischmanns NY 845-254-4884
http://www.riverrunbedandbreakfast.com/
This large custom built Victorian house sits elevated on 10 acres, features a fun "Retro Suite" (50/60's era), is just a short walk to the village park and a stream, and is central to an array of activities and recreational pursuits. Dogs over a year old of all sizes are welcome during the Spring, Summer, and Fall seasons only, and they must be declared at the time of reservations. Dogs must be friendly, quiet, well behaved, flea free, clean, and current on all vaccinations. There is a $10 per night per pet additional fee, and they ask that you register before bringing in your pet. Feeding mats are provided, but please bring their own food, bedding, comfort toys, etc. They have poop-n-scoop bags, and ask that dogs be cleaned up after and leashed at all times. Dogs may not be left alone in the room, except while in the inn, and then they must be crated.
Inn at Lake Joseph 400 Saint Joseph Road Forestburgh NY 845-791-9506
http://www.lakejoseph.com
The inn is a romantic 135-year-old Victorian Country Estate on a 250-acre private lake, surrounded by thousands of acres of hardwood forest and wildlife preserve. The Inn provides a variety of Summer and Winter recreational facilities including the use of their nearby full service health and fitness club. Breakfast is served on the screened-in Veranda allowing you to enjoy the sounds and feel of the lush green forest. When glassed in during Winter, you can experience the beauty of a surrounding snowscape. Dogs are welcomed in their Carriage House

and Cottage. The inn is located in Forestburgh at Lake Joseph.
Hunter Inn 7344 Main Street Hunter NY 518-263-3777 (800-270-3992)
http://www.hunterinn.com/
In addition to having beautiful vistas of the Catskill Mountains and hundreds of hiking trails, this inn offers a cocktail lounge, a family game room, and an outdoor hot tub. Dogs of all sizes are allowed during the months of May through October only; there is an additional $20 per night per pet fee plus a $50 refundable deposit. Dogs must be well behaved, leashed, and cleaned up after.
The Guest House 408 Debruce Road Livingston Manor NY 845-439-4000
Dogs of all sizes are allowed. There is a $10 per night per room additional pet fee.
Howard Johnson Hotel 551 Rt. 211 East Middletown NY 845-342-5822 (800-446-4656)
Dogs of all sizes are welcome. There are no additional pet fees.
Emerson Resort and Spa 5340 H 28 Mount Tremper NY 845-688-2828 (877-688-2828)
http://www.emersonplace.com/
Lovingly restored, sitting among tall pines and manicured grounds alongside a stream with Mt. Tremper in the background, this resort has become a premier vacation destination for a variety of reasons. A visitor favorite is the 64 foot silo they have turned into the world's largest Kaleidoscope. Dogs are allowed for an additional fee of $25 per night per pet, and advance notification. Dogs may not be left alone in the room, and they need to be removed for housekeeping. Dogs must be quiet, well behaved, under owner's control, leashed, and cleaned up after at all times. Dogs are not allowed in the pool or food areas, or the General Store.
Point Lookout Mountain Inn 7604 H 23 Windham NY 518-734-3381
http://www.pointlookoutinn.com/
This mountain inn is known for quality lodging, dining (inside or out), as a "special occasion" place, and as the inn with the spectacular 5 state view. There is also a wide variety of activities and recreation available here. They have 2 pet friendly rooms available, and dogs must have their own bedding. Dogs may only be left alone in the room if guests are in-house, such as in the lounge or restaurant; dogs must go with owners when they leave the property. There is an additional $25 pet fee per night. Dogs must be well mannered, leashed, and cleaned up after.

Campgrounds and RV Parks

Catskill State Park On Highways 28, 23 and 23A Catskill Area NY 845-256-3000 (800-456-CAMP (2267))
Covering 700,000 acres of some of the most complex natural areas anywhere in the East, this park offers good multi-use trails, numerous plant, animal, and bird habitats, a fish hatchery, and year-round land and water recreation. Dogs are allowed for no additional fee. Dogs may be off lead in open forested land if they are under very good voice control, but they must be leashed on trails and in common or camp areas. Dogs are not allowed in park buildings. There are several campgrounds available here, including the popular Bear Spring Mountain Campground. Camp areas include picnic tables, grills, and restrooms. This RV park is closed during the off-season. The camping and tent areas also allow dogs. There is a dog walk area at the campground.
Nickerson Park Campground 378 Stryker Road Gilboa NY 607-588-7327
http://www.nickersonparkcampground.com/
Dogs of all sizes are allowed. There are no additional pet fees. Dogs must be quiet, well behaved, leashed, and cleaned up after. This establishment also shares the New York trail system. The camping and tent areas also allow dogs. There is a dog walk area at the campground.
Skyway Camping Resort 99 Mountain Dale Road Greenfield Park NY 845-647-5747
http://www.skywaycamping.com
Dogs of all sizes are allowed, however some breeds are not. There are no additional pet fees. Dogs must be leashed and cleaned up after. The camping and tent areas also allow dogs. There is a dog walk area at the campground.
Catskill Forest Preserve/North South Lake County H 18 Haines Falls NY 518-357-2234
This park offers a variety of seasonal nature programs, land and water recreation, historic sites, stunning vistas, and the highest waterfall in the state, the double-tiered Kaaterskill Falls. Dogs with valid rabies inoculation papers are welcome. Dogs may not be left unattended anywhere, and they must be quiet, well mannered, leashed (no more than 6 foot), and cleaned up after at all times. Dogs are not permitted on Lake George Islands, the beach, picnic areas, or park buildings. The campground features 7 camping loops with 219 sites, gaming areas, modern restrooms, hot showers, a boat launch for non-motorized craft, 2 picnic areas with tables and grills, and a dump station. The phone number for the campground is 518-589-5058. This RV park is closed during the off-season. The camping and tent areas also allow dogs. There is a dog walk area at the campground. There are no electric or water hookups at the campgrounds.
Whip-O-Will Family Campsite 644 H 31 Roundtop NY 518-622-3277
http://www.whip-o-willcampsites.com
Dogs of all sizes are allowed. There are no additional pet fees. Dogs must be kept under control, on a leash, and cleaned up after. The camping and tent areas also allow dogs. There is a dog walk area at the campground.
Swan Lake Camplands 106 Fulton Road Swan Lake NY 845-292-4781
http://www.swanlakecamplands.com
Dogs of all sizes are allowed. There are no additional pet fees. Dogs must be leased and cleaned up after. The

camping and tent areas also allow dogs. There is a dog walk area at the campground. Dogs are allowed in the camping cabins.
Jellystone Park at Birchwood Acres 85 Martinfeld Road, Box 482 Woodridge NY 845-434-4743 (800-552-4724)
http://www.nyjellystone.com
One dog of any size is allowed, except in the rentals or lodge. Dogs may not be left unattended, must be leashed, and cleaned up after. There are some breed restrictions. This RV park is closed during the off-season. The camping and tent areas also allow dogs. There is a dog walk area at the campground.

Vacation Home Rentals
Fall Foliage Ski Vacation Rental Call to Arrange Woodstock NY 845-246-6666
http://www.waterfallrental.com
This vacation rental is pet-friendly and sleeps 2 to 6 people. There are two bedrooms with separate bathrooms. The house is available for weekends, weeks or monthly.

Attractions
Pratt Rock Park H 23 Prattsville NY 518-299-3395
The climb to this "ode to the town's founder's life" is a steep one (but with graded inclines) to the painted carvings 500 feet above the road; however, there are some interesting chairs and benches carved from rocks along the way, and the view from the top would make a good picnic site. Dogs are welcome on the trails and throughout the park; they are not allowed in the museum. Dogs must be leashed and cleaned up after.
Catskill Scenic Trial Railroad Avenue and South Street Stamford NY 607-652-2821
http://catskillscenictrail.org/
One of the popular features of the multi-use, 19 mile Rails to Trails' path is its gentle grade with only a 400 foot altitude change over the entire trail and the beautiful every changing scenery. Dogs are allowed on leash, and they must be cleaned up after.
The Mountain Top Arboretum H 23C and Maude Adams Road Tannersville NY 518-589-3903
http://www.mtarbor.org/
Educational, recreational, and beautiful describes this unique living history museum of trees and shrubs that sits at about 2500 feet in the Catskill Mountains. Your pooch is welcome to hike the trails and smell the flowers too. They must be under owner's control, and be leashed and cleaned up after at all times.
TOP 200 PLACE **Woodstock Byrdcliffe** Upper Byrdcliffe Road Woodstock NY 845-679-2079
http://www.woodstockguild.org/
Thirty buildings, 300 acres on the slope of a mountain, and listed on the National Register of Historic Places, this scenic art and craft colony offers plenty to see and places to hike, and it is also home to an Artist-in-Residence program hosting various exhibitions and performances for guests. Dogs are allowed to walk through the village and on the trails up the mountain; they are not allowed in buildings. Dogs must be well mannered, leashed, and cleaned up after at all times.

Stores
PetSmart Pet Store 88-25 Dunning Rd Middletown NY 845-342-1261
Your licensed and well-behaved leashed dog is allowed in the store.
Petco Pet Store 600 North Galleria Drive Middletown NY 845-692-6691
Your licensed and well-behaved leashed dog is allowed in the store.

Parks
Catskill State Park On Highways 28, 23 and 23A Catskill Area NY 845-256-3000 (800-456-CAMP (2267))
Covering 700,000 acres of some of the most complex natural areas anywhere in the East, this park offers good multi-use trails, numerous plant, animal, and bird habitats, a fish hatchery, and year-round land and water recreation. Dogs are allowed for no additional fee. Dogs may be off lead in open forested land if they are under very good voice control, but they must be leashed on trails and in common or camp areas. Dogs are not allowed in park buildings.
TOP 200 PLACE **Ice Caves of the Shawangunks** 400 Sams Point Road Cragsmoor NY 518-272-0195
Born of glacial activity, this park features an unusual landscape with miles of hiking trails and impressive geological features, but the ice caves (some rare) are the exciting draw here. A few of the caves may not be pet-friendly, so they suggest using some caution, bring an electric torch light, and dress warm. Dogs are allowed throughout the park and on the trails. Dogs must be under owner's care at all times, be leashed, and cleaned up after.
Catskill Forest Preserve/North South Lake County H 18 Haines Falls NY 518-357-2234
This park offers a variety of seasonal nature programs, land and water recreation, historic sites, stunning vistas, and the highest waterfall in the state, the double-tiered Kaaterskill Falls. Dogs with valid rabies inoculation

papers are welcome. Dogs may not be left unattended anywhere, and they must be quiet, well mannered, leashed (no more than 6 foot), and cleaned up after at all times. Dogs are not permitted on Lake George Islands, the beach, picnic areas, or park buildings.

Minnewaska State Park Preserve 5281 H 44/55 Kerhonkson NY 845-255-0752
Covering about 16,000 square miles with almost 60 miles of hiking and biking trails and carriage roads, this beautiful park also features several waterfalls, 2 lakes, and a variety of recreational pursuits. Dogs of all sizes are allowed for no additional fee. Dogs must be on no more than a 6 foot leash at all times, and they are not allowed in park buildings, the Summer camp area, on ski trails in the Winter, or the picnic or swimming areas. Dogs must be cleaned up after in common areas and on the trails.

Outdoor Restaurants
Matthews on Main 19 Lower Main Street Callicoon NY 845-887-5636
This eatery offers free WiFi and outside dining options. Dogs are allowed at the outer tables. Dogs must be under owner's control/care and leashed at all times.

Chateaugay

Campgrounds and RV Parks
High Falls Park Campground 34 Cemetery Road Chateaugay NY 518-497-3156
http://www.highfallspark.com
Dogs of all sizes are allowed. There are no additional pet fees. Dogs must be kept leashed and cleaned up after. The camping and tent areas also allow dogs. There is a dog walk area at the campground.

Clayton

Campgrounds and RV Parks
Cedar Point State Park 36661 Cedar Point State Park Drive Clayton NY 315-654-2522 (800-456-CAMP (2256))
Not to be confused with Cedar Point County Park on Long Island, this park is one of the state's oldest parks and is a popular spot for a variety of water and land recreational activities. It sits on a jut of land on the St Lawrence River, and there are also great views of ocean-going vessels from the overlook area. Dogs must have proof of rabies inoculation and there are no additional pet fees. Dogs must be crated or leashed (6 foot) and cleaned up after. They are not allowed in buildings, picnic, or swim areas. Dogs are allowed throughout the rest of the park and on trails. The large scale camping area features 175 sites with restrooms, hot showers, picnic tables, fire pits, gaming fields, and a dump station. This RV park is closed during the off-season. The camping and tent areas also allow dogs. There is a dog walk area at the campground.

Grass Point State Park 36661 Cedar Point State Park Drive Clayton NY 315-686-4472
http://www.nysparks.state.ny.us/
Dogs of all sizes are allowed. There are no additional pet fees. Dogs may not be left unattended, they must have a current rabies certificate and shot records, be well behaved, on no more than a 6 foot leash, and be cleaned up after. Dogs are allowed on the trails, but not in the picnic or bathroom areas. This campground is closed during the off-season. The camping and tent areas also allow dogs. There is a dog walk area at the campground. There are no water hookups at the campground.

Merry Knoll 1000 Islands Campground 38115 H 12E Clayton NY 315-686-3055
http://www.merryknollcampground.com
Dogs of all sizes are allowed. There are no additional pet fees. Dogs must be quiet, leashed, and cleaned up after. The camping and tent areas also allow dogs. There is a dog walk area at the campground.

Parks
Cedar Point State Park 36661 Cedar Point State Park Drive Clayton NY 315-654-2522 (800-456-CAMP (2256))
Not to be confused with Cedar Point County Park on Long Island, this park is one of the state's oldest parks and is a popular spot for a variety of water and land recreational activities. It sits on a jut of land on the St Lawrence River, and there are also great views of ocean-going vessels from the overlook area. Dogs must have proof of rabies inoculation and there are no additional pet fees. Dogs must be crated or leashed (6 foot) and cleaned up after. They are not allowed in buildings, picnic, or swim areas. Dogs are allowed throughout the rest of the park and on trails.

Cobleskill

Accommodations
Best Western Inn of Cobleskill 121 Burgin Dr Cobleskill NY   518-234-4321 (800-780-7234)
Dogs are allowed for an additional pet fee of $15 per night per room.
Super 8 Cobleskill/Howe Caverns 955 E Main St Cobleskill NY   518-234-4888 (800-800-8000)
Dogs of all sizes are allowed. There is a $10 one time per pet fee per visit. Reservations are recommended due to limited rooms for pets. Smoking and non-smoking rooms are available for pet rooms.

Cooperstown

Accommodations
Herkimer Motel 100 Marginal Rd Herkimer NY   315-866-0490
There are no additional pet fees. Dogs must not be left alone in the rooms.
TOP 200 PLACE **Glen Highland Farm** 217 Pegg Road Morris NY   607-263-5415
http://glenhighlandfarm.com/
This "Canine County Getaway" sits on 175 picturesque acres complete with ponds, a stream, trails, open meadows and forests, and dogs may explore anywhere on the farm off-leash. The farm is home to several dogs but it is also a Border Collier rescue sanctuary that functions as a training/recovery and placement center, and their complete obstacle course is also available to guests and their dogs. There are several mini-activity camps and programs available to help strengthen the bond between dogs and their companions such as the "Canine Discovery" camp to learn about how smart your dog really is and the "Inner Dog" camp for a greater understanding of your dog. There is even a trainer on staff available to work one on one with guests. The getaway lodging for guests and their canine companions include cottages, cabins, rentable RVs, a few RV spaces, and a camping shelter that has all the amenities on hand for meal prep plus private showers and flush toilets are only a few feet away. There are no additional pet fees. Dogs may not be left alone, they just have to be friendly and have a great time.
Holiday Inn 5206 State Highway 23 Oneonta NY   607-433-2250 (877-270-6405)
Dogs up to 60 pounds are allowed for an additional one time pet fee of $25 (plus tax) per room.
Super 8 Oneonta 4973 State Hwy 23 Southside Oneonta NY   607-432-9505 (800-800-8000)
Dogs of all sizes are allowed. There are no additional pet fees. Dogs are not allowed to be left alone in the room. Smoking and non-smoking rooms are available for pet rooms.

Campgrounds and RV Parks
Glimmerglass State Park 1527 H 31 Cooperstown NY   607-547-8662 (800-456-CAMP (2267))
Sitting alongside Otsego Lake, this scenic woodland park is home to a variety of plant, bird, and wildlife and offers a variety of year-round recreation, multi-use trails, a Beaver Pond Nature Trail, a covered bridge, food concessions, and a mansion. Dogs are allowed throughout the park and on the trails except on the beach or in park buildings. Dogs may not be left alone at any time, they must be on no more than a 6 foot leash, and be cleaned up after at all times. There must be currant proof of rabies inoculation for camping. The camp area offers 37 well-maintained sites with modern restrooms, showers, tables, fire pits, charcoal grills, and a playground. This RV park is closed during the off-season. The camping and tent areas also allow dogs. There is a dog walk area at the campground. There are no electric or water hookups at the campgrounds.
KOA Cooperstown 565 Ostrander Road Cooperstown NY   315-858-0236 (800-562-3402)
http://www.koa.com
Dogs of all sizes are allowed. There are no additional pet fees. Dogs are allowed at the cabins but must be kept off the beds. There is a large field where dogs can run off leash if they will come to your command. Otherwise dogs must be leashed and cleaned up after. Dogs may not be left unattended except for short periods, and only if the dog is well behaved and comfortable with a short absence. This RV park is closed during the off-season. The camping and tent areas also allow dogs. There is a dog walk area at the campground. Dogs are allowed in the camping cabins.
Shadowbrook Campground 2149 County H 31 Cooperstown NY   607-264-8431
http://www.cooperstowncamping.com
Dogs of all sizes are allowed, however some breeds are not. There are no additional pet fees. Dogs must be leashed and cleaned up after. The camping and tent areas also allow dogs. There is a dog walk area at the campground.
Yogi Bear Jellystone Park at Crystal Lake 111 East Turtle Lake Road Garrattsville NY   607-965-8265 (800-231-1907)

182

http://www.cooperstownjellystone.com
Dogs of all sizes are allowed, except in the rentals. There is no fee if there are only 2 dogs; if there are more, it is $1.50 per night per pet additional fee. Dogs must have a current rabies certificate, be leashed, and cleaned up after. Dogs are not allowed at the pool, pavillion, playground, the rentals, or in the buildings. This RV park is closed during the off-season. The camping and tent areas also allow dogs. There is a dog walk area at the campground.
Meadow-Vale Campsites 505 Gilbert Lake Road Mount Vision NY   607-293-8802 (800-701-8802)
http://www.meadow-vale.com
Dogs of all sizes are allowed, however some breeds are not. There are no additional pet fees. Dogs must be leashed and cleaned up after. The camping and tent areas also allow dogs. There is a dog walk area at the campground.

Attractions
Fly Creek Cider Mill and Orchard 288 Goose Street Fly Creek NY   607-547-9692
http://www.flycreekcidermill.com/
For over 150 years this cider mill has been providing delicious cider to visitors, and now they have grown adding a wide variety of hand-crafted foods, beverages, and treats. Well behaved dogs are welcome to explore the grounds, but they are not allowed inside buildings. Dogs must be leashed and cleaned up after at all times.

Parks
Glimmerglass State Park 1527 H 31 Cooperstown NY   607-547-8662 (800-456-CAMP (2267))
Sitting alongside Otsego Lake, this scenic woodland park is home to a variety of plant, bird, and wildlife and offers a variety of year-round recreation, multi-use trails, a Beaver Pond Nature Trail, a covered bridge, food concessions, and a mansion. Dogs are allowed throughout the park and on the trails except on the beach or in park buildings. Dogs may not be left alone at any time, they must be on no more than a 6 foot leash, and be cleaned up after at all times. There must be currant proof of rabies inoculation for camping.

Cortland

Accommodations
Holiday Inn Cortland 2 River Street Cortland NY   607-756-4431 (877-270-6405)
Dogs up to 50 pounds are allowed for an additional fee of $15 per night per pet.
Quality Inn 188 Clinton Avenue Cortland NY   607-756-5622 (877-424-6423)
Dogs are allowed for an additional one time pet fee of $20 per room.

Dansville

Accommodations
Days Inn Danville 1 Commerce Dr Dansville NY   585-335-6023 (800-329-7466)
Dogs of all sizes are allowed. There are no additional pet fees.

Campgrounds and RV Parks
Sugar Creek Glen Campground 11288 Poagf Hole Road Dansville NY   585-335-6294
http://www.sugarcreekglencampground.com
Dogs of all sizes are allowed. There is a pet policy to sign at check in and there are no additional pet fees. Dogs must not be left unattended for very long periods, and only if they are quiet and well behaved. Dogs must be leashed and cleaned up after. The camping and tent areas also allow dogs. There is a dog walk area at the campground. Dogs are allowed in the camping cabins.

Dunkirk

Accommodations
Best Western Dunkirk and Fredonia 3912 Vineyard Dr Dunkirk NY   716-366-7100 (800-780-7234)
Dogs are allowed for an additional pet fee per pet of $10 for the 1st night and $5 for each additional night.

Comfort Inn 3925 Vineyard Drive Dunkirk NY   716-672-4450 (877-424-6423)
Dogs up to 50 pounds are allowed for an additional fee of $10 per night per pet.

Ellicottville

Accommodations
The Jefferson Inn 3 Jefferson Street Ellicottville NY   716-699-5869 (800-577-8451)
http://www.thejeffersoninn.com/
A central location to numerous recreational activities, a wide wraparound porch, relaxed ambiance, and a village park a short distance away make this a nice destination for pets and their owners. Dogs of all sizes are allowed in the efficiency units for an additional fee of $10 per night per pet. Dogs must be leashed and cleaned up after, and they may only be left alone in the room if assured they will be quiet, relaxed, and well mannered.

Elmira

Attractions
Walking Tour of Elmira 353 Davis Street Elmira NY   607-733-4924
http://www.nwnainc.com/
Nestled away in the beautiful Finger Lakes Region upstate is what is considered the largest concentration of turn-of-the-century Victorian architecture in the state, and there is an association dedicated to restoring and maintaining these wonderful buildings. A self-guided walking map is available at the Chamber of Commerce. Dogs are allowed to take the tour too. Dogs must be leashed and cleaned up after at all times. Dogs are not allowed in any of the buildings.

TOP 200 PLACE Woodlawn Cemetery - Mark Twain's Burial Site 1200 Walnut Street Elmira NY   607-732-0151
There are several notables buried at this cemetery, but probably the most famous person buried here is Mark Twain. Your pooch is welcome to visit with you. Dogs must be leashed and cleaned up after at all times.

Stores
Petco Pet Store 831 County Rd 64 Elmira NY   607-739-2977
Your licensed and well-behaved leashed dog is allowed in the store.

Fair Haven

Campgrounds and RV Parks
Fair Haven Beach State Park 14985 Park Road Fair Haven NY 315-947-5205
http://www.nysparks.state.ny.us
Dogs of all sizes are allowed. There are no additional pet fees. Dogs may not be left unattended, they must have a current rabies certificate and shot records, be on no more than a 6 foot leash, and be cleaned up after. Dogs are allowed on the trails, but they are not allowed on any sandy areas, at the beach, or in the water. Although the campground is seasonal, some cabins remain open all year. This campground is closed during the off-season. The camping and tent areas also allow dogs. There is a dog walk area at the campground. Dogs are allowed in the camping cabins. There are no water hookups at the campground.

Farmington

Campgrounds and RV Parks
KOA Canandaigua/Rochester 5374 FarmingtonTownline Road Farmington NY   585-398-3582 (800-562-0533)
http://www.koa.com
Dogs of all sizes are allowed. There is no additional pet fee for RV or tent sites, however there is a $25 refundable pet deposit when renting the cabins. Dogs may not be left unattended; they must be quiet, well

behaved, leashed, and cleaned up after. There are some breed restrictions. This RV park is closed during the off-season. The camping and tent areas also allow dogs. There is a dog walk area at the campground. Dogs are allowed in the camping cabins.

Finger Lakes

Accommodations

TOP 200 PLACE Caboose Motel 8620 State Route 415 Avoca NY 607-566-2216
http://www.caboosemotel.net
Small to large dogs are allowed in the 5 cabooses that serve as guestrooms at this unique hotel.
Days Inn Bath 330 W Morris St Bath NY 607-776-7644 (800-329-7466)
Dogs of all sizes are allowed. There are no additional pet fees.
Econo Lodge 170 Eastern Blvd Canandaigua NY 716-394-9000 (800-797-1222)
There are no additional pet fees.
Inn On The Lake 777 S. Main St Canandaigua NY 716-394-7800 (800-228-2801)
http://www.theinnonthelake.com
There is a $25 per day additional pet fee.
Staybridge Suites 201 Townley Avenue Corning NY 607-936-7800 (877-270-6405)
Dogs up to 60 pounds are allowed for an additional one time pet fee of $75 per room.
Stiles Motel 9239 Victory Highway Corning NY 607-962-5221
There is a $3 per day pet charge.
Motel 6 - Geneva 485 Hamilton Street Geneva NY 315-789-4050 (800-466-8356)
One well-behaved family pet per room. Guest must notify front desk upon arrival. Guest is liable for any damages. In consideration of all guests, pets must never be left unattended in the guest rooms.
Ramada Geneva Lakefront 41 Lakefront Drive Geneva NY 315-789-0400
This lakefront hotel offers a long list of amenities and services. Dogs of all sizes are allowed for an additional fee of $10 per night per pet. Dog may not be left alone in the room at any time, and they must be leashed and cleaned up after. Dogs are not allowed in common areas; they may come through the lobby to the elevators and in the corridors going to the room.
Best Western Marshall Manor 3527 Watkins Rd Horseheads NY 607-739-3891 (800-780-7234)
Dogs are allowed for an additional fee of $10 per night for 1 pet, and $5 for each additional pet.
Motel 6 - Elmira - Horseheads 4133 Route 17 Horseheads NY 607-739-2525 (800-466-8356)
One well-behaved family pet per room. Guest must notify front desk upon arrival. Guest is liable for any damages. In consideration of all guests, pets must never be left unattended in the guest rooms.
Clarion University Hotel and Conference Center 1 Sheraton Drive Ithaca NY 607-257-2000 (877-424-6423)
Dogs are allowed for an additional one time pet fee of $20 per room.
Comfort Inn 356 Elmira Road Ithaca NY 607-272-0100 (877-424-6423)
Dogs of all sizes are allowed. There is a $25 per stay per room fee and a pet policy to sign at check in.
Econo Lodge Cayuga Mall Ithaca NY 607-257-1400
There is a $10 per day pet charge.
Hampton Inn 337 Elmira Road Ithaca NY 607-277-5500
Dogs up to 60 pounds are allowed. There is a pet policy to sign at check in and there are no addition pet fees.
Holiday Inn 222 South Cayuga Street Ithaca NY 607-272-1000 (877-270-6405)
Dogs of all sizes are allowed for an additional one time pet fee of $15 per room. Dogs may not be left alone in the room at any time.
Log Country Inn South Danby and La Rue Roads Ithaca NY 607-589-4771 (800-274-4771)
http://www.logtv.com/inn/hispeed.html
Sitting at the edge of a vast state forest in a scenic country setting on 100 wooded acres, this spacious log home features custom made country furniture and rooms with "around the world" themes (there are even "themed" hiking trails), and they are close to wide variety of activities, recreation, and the Ithaca Falls. Dogs of all sizes are welcome for no additional pet fee. Dogs must be well behaved, leashed, and cleaned up after. Puppies must always be crated when left alone in the room, and if the owner's are confident in their dogs behavior (must be quiet), older dogs do not have to be crated.
The William Henry Miller Inn 303 N Aurora Street Ithaca NY 607-256-4553 (877-25-MILLER (256-4553))
http://www.millerinn.com/
Originally built in 1880 by Cornell University's first student of architecture, the house is rich in detail with stained glass windows and woodwork, and it is located near the Ithaca Commons area that is abundant with eateries, shops, theaters, and recreation. There is 1 pet friendly suite in the Carriage House, and dogs of all sizes are welcome for no additional pet fee. They will provide water and food dishes, but they ask that you bring your own pets bedding. Dogs must be leashed, cleaned up after, and they may not be left alone in the room at any time.
The Vagabond Inn 3300 Sliter Road Naples NY 585-554-6271

http://www.thevagabondinn.com/
Secluded on a mountain, this 7000 square foot inn offers great views, but they are also home to an American craft gallery, a seasonal outdoor pool, a Japanese garden, lush lawns and grounds, and many other pluses. They offer 2 pet friendly rooms, and dogs of all sizes are welcome for no additional pet fee. Dogs must be well trained, friendly, leashed, and cleaned up after. They may only be left alone in the room for a short time if they will be quiet and owners are confident in their behavior.

Quality Inn Finger Lakes Region 125 N Main Street Newark NY 315-331-9500 (877-424-6423)
Dogs are allowed for no additional pet fee with a credit card on file; there is a $25 refundable deposit if paying cash.

Tillinghast Manor 7246 S Main Street Ovid NY 716-869-3584
This historical 1873 Victorian home is located in the heart of the Finger Lakes area, and offers a central location to several other activities and recreational pursuits. Dogs of all sizes are welcome for no additional pet fee. Dogs must be quiet, well mannered, leashed, and cleaned up after. Dogs may only be left alone in the room if the owner is confident in their behavior.

Microtel Inn 1966 Routes 5 an 20 Seneca Falls NY 318-539-8438 (888-771-7171)
http://www.senecafallsmicrotelinn.com/
This inn provides clean comfortable lodging and a central location to several attractions and activities in the Finger Lakes areas. Dogs up to 80 pounds are allowed for an additional pet fee of $15 per night per room. Dogs must be quiet, well mannered, leashed, and cleaned up after at all times. Dogs may only be left alone in the room for a short time, and a contact number must be left with the front desk.

Hampton Inn 7637 New York St Route 96 Victor NY 585-924-4400
Dogs of all sizes are allowed. There are no additional pet fees. Dogs are not allowed to be left alone in the room except for short periods.

Holiday Inn 2468 Nys Rt 414 Mound Road Waterloo NY 315-539-5011 (877-270-6405)
Dogs of all sizes are allowed for an additional fee of $10 per night per pet.

Campgrounds and RV Parks

Hickory Hill Farm Camping Resort 7531 H 13/Mitchellsville Road Bath NY 607-776-4345 (800-760-0947)
http://www.hickoryhillcampresort.com/
This full service family camping resort has all the extras for family fun including 2 pools, playing courts/fields, an 18 hole mini-golf course, internet access, hiking trails, a store, and lots more. Dogs are allowed for no additional fee for tent or RV camping. In a rental unit, the fees are $20 per unit per stay, and please have proof of current vaccinations. Dogs may not be left alone at any time at a campsite or in a rental, and they must be leashed and cleaned up after at all times. This RV park is closed during the off-season. The camping and tent areas also allow dogs. There is a dog walk area at the campground. Dogs are allowed in the camping cabins.

Letchworth State Park 1 Letchworth State Park Castile NY 585-493-3600 (800-456-2267)
This multi-faceted park provides opportunities for a wide range of year-round activities and recreation, and is considered the "Grand Canyon of the East" with 3 major waterfalls, 600 foot high cliffs along the river flanked by lush forests, 70 miles of incredible hiking trails, plenty of food options, and a museum/visitor center that provides the history of the area. Dogs must have proof of rabies inoculation and there are no additional pet fees. Dogs must be crated or leashed (6 foot) and cleaned up after. They are not allowed in buildings, cabins or cabin areas, or swim areas. Dogs are allowed throughout the rest of the park and on the trails. The campground area has a camp store, playground, pool, showers, restrooms, laundry, recreation hall, playing fields, and a dump station. There is also a primitive camp area in the lower falls area. This RV park is closed during the off-season. The camping and tent areas also allow dogs. There is a dog walk area at the campground. There are no water hookups at the campgrounds.

Spruce Row Campground and RV Resort 2271 Kraft Road Ithaca NY 607-387-9225 (800-456-CAMP (2267))
http://www.sprucerow.com/
This resort hosts several events throughout the year, and offer guests camp sites on a first come first served basis, a huge pool, recreation room, camp store, picnic areas, playing fields, restrooms and showers. Dogs of all sizes are allowed for no additional fee, and proof of current rabies inoculation is required. Dogs must be quiet, crated or leashed, and cleaned up after at all times. Dogs are not allowed at the pool, playground, or in the store. This RV park is closed during the off-season. The camping and tent areas also allow dogs. There is a dog walk area at the campground.

Cayuga Lake State Park 2678 Lower Lake Road Seneca Falls NY 315-568-5163 (800-456-CAMP(2267))
Nestled among trees with a large lawn area in front facing an expansive view of the lake, this park offers a long list of amenities and year-round land and water recreation. Dogs of all sizes are allowed for no additional fee, and owners must have proof of rabies inoculation if camping. Dogs may not be left unattended in cabins or campsites, and they must be leashed (6 foot) and cleaned up after. They are not allowed in swim areas or the playground. Dogs are allowed throughout the rest of the park and on the trails. The camp area offers 50 sites with fireplaces, children's and adult recreation areas, a nature trail, ice machines, restrooms with showers, and laundry facilities. This RV park is closed during the off-season. The camping and tent areas also allow dogs. There is a dog walk area at the campground. Dogs are allowed in the camping cabins. There are no water

hookups at the campgrounds.

Taughannock Falls State Park 2221 Taughannock Park Road Trumansburg NY 607-387-6739 (800-456-2267)
Taller than Niagara Falls by 33 feet, the namesake waterfall of this park plunges 215 feet over craggy cliffs towering nearly 400 feet above the gorge providing spectacular views from lookout points or along the multi-use trails, and there are planned activities like tours and concerts during the Summer season. Dogs must have proof of rabies inoculation and there are no additional pet fees. Dogs may not be left unattended in cabins, and they must be leashed (6 foot) and cleaned up after. They are not allowed in buildings or swim areas. Dogs are allowed throughout the rest of the park and on the trails. Camp areas have picnic areas with tables and fireplaces, hot showers, flush toilets, a playground, concession stand, and a dump station. This RV park is closed during the off-season. The camping and tent areas also allow dogs. There is a dog walk area at the campground. Dogs are allowed in the camping cabins. There are no water hookups at the campgrounds.

KOA Watkins Glen/Corning 1710 H 414 Watkins Glen NY 607-535-7404 (800-562-7430)
http://www.watkinsglenkoa.com
Dogs of all sizes are allowed. There are no additional pet fees. Dogs may not be left unattended, and must be leashed and cleaned up after. This RV park is closed during the off-season. The camping and tent areas also allow dogs. There is a dog walk area at the campground.

Watkins Glen State Park South end of Seneca Lake Watkins Glen NY 607-535-4511 (800-456-2267)
This park is famous for an amazing gorge stone path that descends 400 feet past 200 foot cliffs and winds under and through waterfalls, lush greenery, and sculptured rocks created by its 19 cascading waterfalls. Although dogs are not allowed on the Gorge Trail, there are several other scenic trails here, and a variety of land and water recreation year-round. Dogs of all sizes are allowed for no additional fee; however there must be written proof of rabies inoculation. Dogs must be well behaved, crated or on no more than a 6 foot leash, and cleaned up after at all times. The camp area offers an Olympic-size pool, gaming fields, picnic areas, food, restrooms, showers, a gift shop, playground, and a dump station. This RV park is closed during the off-season. The camping and tent areas also allow dogs. There is a dog walk area at the campground. There are no water hookups at the campgrounds.

Attractions

Roy's Marina 4398 Clark's Point/H 14 Geneva NY 315-789-3094
http://www.roysmarina.net/
This 50 year old company offers several other services and supplies in addition to watercraft rentals. Your well behaved dog is welcome to cruise with you. Dogs must be under owner's control/care at all times.

North Country Kayak and Canoe Rentals 16878 West Lake Road/H 54A Hammondsport NY 607-868-7456
You can both pick up and put in your watercraft rental at their livery or this company will deliver and pick up at your cottage. Your pooch is welcome to ride too for no additional fees.

TOP 200 PLACE **Cornell Plantations** 1 Plantations Road Ithaca NY 607-255-3020
Cornell Plantations is a museum of plants including the arboretum and botanical garden of Cornell University. See the crop garden portraying how technology and other cultures have influenced American gardens. Additionally, plants native to New York grow in the wildflower garden and a number of trails allow for hiking and nature study. The grounds are open free of charge from sunrise to sunset daily. Dogs are allowed on a short lead.

TOP 200 PLACE **Tiohero Tours Boat Cruises** 435 Old Taughannock Blvd Ithaca NY 866-846-4376
http://www.tioherotours.com/
This company offers daily, historically narrated tours on beautiful Cayuga Lake from two locations; the one above and also at Steamboat Landing. Guests are welcome to bring a dog aboard for no additional fee, and they prefer that only 1 hour tours be taken with pets. Guests with dogs are seated in front of the pilot house where they are not under the canopy. Dogs must be under owner's control, leashed or crated, and cleaned up after at all times.

Montezuma National Wildlife Refuge 3395 Route 5 and 20 East Seneca Falls NY 315-568-5987
http://www.fws.gov/r5mnwr/
This wildlife preserve offers a variety of avenues for observing the habitats, and bird and wildlife here; there is a 3.5 mile wildlife drive; observation towers, an informative visitor center, and a variety of walking areas. Dogs are welcome on leash, and they must be cleaned up after at all times. Dogs must be under owner's control and not be a threat to any wildlife; they are not allowed in park buildings.

Ganondagan State Historic Site 1488 H 444 Victor NY 585-742-1690
http://www.ganondagan.org/
The 3 trails here; The Trail of Peace-depicting history and oral teachings; The Earth is Our Mother Trail-identifying plants and their usage, and the Granary Trail-where visitors can experience a day in the history of what befell this area, have illustrated the history of this once flourishing Native American community and how it impacted our country's Constitution, woman's rights, and natural foods and medicines. The historic site is seasonal, but the trails are open year-round. Your well behaved pooch is welcome to explore the grounds and trails; they are not allowed in buildings. Dogs must be leashed and cleaned up after at all times.

Shopping Centers

Waterloo Premium Outlets 655 H 318 Waterloo NY   315-539-1100
This open air mall features more than 100 stores. Well mannered dogs are welcome to stroll the avenues, but it is up to individual stores whether they may enter. Dogs must be under owner's control/care, leashed, and cleaned up after at all times.

Stores

MacKenzie-Childs 3260 H 90 Aurora NY   315-364-7123
http://www.mackenzie-childs.com/
This home and garden store will allow well behaved pooches to explore the store with their two legged companions. Dogs must be leashed or in a carrier and under owner's control/care at all times.
PetSmart Pet Store 742 S Meadow St Ithaca NY   607-277-3391
Your licensed and well-behaved leashed dog is allowed in the store.

Parks

Kershaw Park-Canandaigua Lake Lakeshore Dr Canandaigua NY   585-396-5080
Dogs on leash are allowed in this park. The only restriction is that they are not allowed on the beach. There are walking paths, boat launch area, picnic areas, and a snack bar. Open 7 days a week from 6am-11pm.
TOP 200 PLACE Letchworth State Park 1 Letchworth State Park Castile NY   585-493-3600 (800-456-2267)
This multi-faceted park provides opportunities for a wide range of year-round activities and recreation, and is considered the "Grand Canyon of the East" with 3 major waterfalls, 600 foot high cliffs along the river flanked by lush forests, 70 miles of incredible hiking trails, plenty of food options, and a museum/visitor center that provides the history of the area. Dogs must have proof of rabies inoculation and there are no additional pet fees. Dogs must be crated or leashed (6 foot) and cleaned up after. They are not allowed in buildings, cabins or cabin areas, or swim areas. Dogs are allowed throughout the rest of the park and on the trails.
Finger Lakes National Forest 5218 H 414 Hector NY   607-546-4470
Dogs are allowed on the trails. Dogs must be on a leash.
Sampson State Park 6096 Route 96A Romulus NY   315-585-6392
http://nysparks.state.ny.us
Dogs on a 6 foot leash are allowed in this park. Proof of Rabies vaccination is required at all times. Dogs are not allowed in the bathing areas. This state park features electric and non-electric camping, a playground, swimming, hiking, fishing, and more. Open year-round.
Cayuga Lake State Park 2678 Lower Lake Road Seneca Falls NY   315-568-5163 (800-456-CAMP(2267))
Nestled among trees with a large lawn area in front facing an expansive view of the lake, this park offers a long list of amenities and year-round land and water recreation. Dogs of all sizes are allowed for no additional fee, and owners must have proof of rabies inoculation if camping. Dogs may not be left unattended in cabins or campsites, and they must be leashed (6 foot) and cleaned up after. They are not allowed in swim areas or the playground. Dogs are allowed throughout the rest of the park and on the trails.
Dean's Cove 2678 Lower Lake Rd Seneca Falls NY   315-568-5163
http://nysparks.state.ny.us
Dean's Cove is open year-round. Dogs on leash are allowed in this park. Fishing, boating, hiking, picnic tables and more are available. Dogs are not allowed on the public beaches.
Women's Rights National Historical Park 136 Fall Street Seneca Falls NY   315-568-2991
http://www.nps.gov/wori/index.htm
Dogs must be on leash and must be cleaned up after on grounds. Dogs are not allowed in any buildings.
TOP 200 PLACE Taughannock Falls State Park 2221 Taughannock Park Road Trumansburg NY   607-387-6739 (800-456-2267)
Taller than Niagara Falls by 33 feet, the namesake waterfall of this park plunges 215 feet over craggy cliffs towering nearly 400 feet above the gorge providing spectacular views from lookout points or along the multi-use trails, and there are planned activities like tours and concerts during the Summer season. Dogs must have proof of rabies inoculation and there are no additional pet fees. Dogs may not be left unattended in cabins, and they must be leashed (6 foot) and cleaned up after. They are not allowed in buildings or swim areas. Dogs are allowed throughout the rest of the park and on the trails.
Watkins Glen State Park South end of Seneca Lake Watkins Glen NY   607-535-4511 (800-456-2267)
This park is famous for an amazing gorge stone path that descends 400 feet past 200 foot cliffs and winds under and through waterfalls, lush greenery, and sculptured rocks created by its 19 cascading waterfalls. Although dogs are not allowed on the Gorge Trail, there are several other scenic trails here, and a variety of land and water recreation year-round. Dogs of all sizes are allowed for no additional fee; however there must be written proof of rabies inoculation. Dogs must be well behaved, crated or on no more than a 6 foot leash, and cleaned up after at all times.

Outdoor Restaurants

Blue Stone Bar and Grill 110 N Aurora Street Ithaca NY 607-272-2371
http://www.bluestoneithaca.com/
Offering contemporary American cuisine and a full bar with Mojitos their specialty, they also offer indoor and outdoor dining. Dogs are welcome at the outer tables. Dogs must be well behaved, under owner's control, leashed, and cleaned up after at all times.

Madeline's Restaurant 215 East State Street, The Commons Ithaca NY 607-277-2253
Specializing in French and Asian cuisine, this restaurant and bar also offers indoor and outdoor dining. Dogs are welcome at the outer tables; however they request that guests with pets come during non-peak hours or on evenings when they are slow. Dogs must be well behaved, under owner's control, leashed, and cleaned up after at all times.

Downtown Deli 53 Falls Street/H 5 Seneca Falls NY 315-568-9943
Specializing in New York style sandwiches, salads, and soups, this deli features a deck facing the canal. Dogs are welcome at the outer tables. Dogs must be well behaved, under owner's control, leashed, and cleaned up after at all times.

Florida

Campgrounds and RV Parks

Black Bear Campground 197 Wheeler Road Florida NY 845-651-7717
http://www.blackbearcampground.com
Dogs of all sizes are allowed, however some breeds are not. There are no additional pet fees. Dogs must be well behaved, leashed, and cleaned up after. The camping and tent areas also allow dogs. There is a dog walk area at the campground. Dogs are allowed in the camping cabins.

Franklin

Campgrounds and RV Parks

KOA Unadilla/Oneonta 242 Union Church Road Franklin NY 607-369-9030 (800-562-9032)
http://www.koaunadilla.com
Dogs of all sizes are allowed. There are no additional pet fees. Dogs may not be left unattended, and must be leashed and cleaned up after. This RV park is closed during the off-season. The camping and tent areas also allow dogs. There is a dog walk area at the campground.

Fredonia

Accommodations

Brookside Manor 3728 Route 83 Fredonia NY 716-672-7721 (800-929-7599)
http://www.bbonline.com/ny/brookside/
Built in 1875 with over 6,000 square feet of living space, this Victorian manor sits on 5.5 partially wooded acres with its own spring-fed brook, manicured lawns and gardens, and there is beauty and activities here year-round. Dogs of all sizes are welcome for no additional fee with advance registration; when doing so on line they request that you make note in the "special needs" comments that pets will be coming. Dogs must be well mannered, leashed, and cleaned up after.

Henderson Harbor

Campgrounds and RV Parks

Association Island RV Resort & Marina Snowshoe Road Henderson Harbor NY 315-938-5655
http://www.associationislandresort.com
Dogs of all sizes are allowed, however some breeds are not. There are no additional pet fees. Dogs must be leashed, cleaned up after, and have proof of rabies shots. The camping and tent areas also allow dogs. There is

a dog walk area at the campground.

Herkimer

Campgrounds and RV Parks
KOA Herkimer 800 Mohawk Street Herkimer NY   315-891-7355 (800-562-0897)
http://www.koa.com/where/ny/32224/
Dogs of all sizes are allowed. There are no additional pet fees. Dog must be leashed and cleaned up after. This RV park is closed during the off-season. The camping and tent areas also allow dogs. There is a dog walk area at the campground.

Hornell

Accommodations
Days Inn Hornell Route 36 & Webb Xing Hornell NY   607-324-6222 (800-329-7466)
Dogs of all sizes are allowed. There is a $10 per night pet fee per pet.

Hudson Valley

Accommodations
Quality Inn and Conference Center 704 H 23 Catskill NY   518-943-5800 (877-424-6423)
Dogs are allowed for an additional fee of $20 (plus tax) per night per pet.
Residence Inn by Marriott 14 Schuyler Blvd Fishkill NY   854-896-5210
Dogs of all sizes are allowed. There is a $75 one time fee and a pet policy to sign at check in.
Holiday Inn 503 Washington Ave Kingston NY   845-338-0400 (877-270-6405)
Dogs of all sizes are allowed for an additional fee of $10 per night per pet.
Buttermilk Inn and Spa 220 North Road Milton NY   845-795-1310 (877-7-INN-SPA (877-746-6772))
http://www.buttermilkfallsinn.com/
This inn, set on 70 acres of meticulously landscaped acres (affording exceptional hiking), offers lush garden and river views, an extended breakfast buffet, and a number of amenities/services for business or leisure travelers and special events. Dogs of all sizes are allowed in the carriage house only for an additional one time pet fee of $25 plus a $190 refundable deposit. Pets are not allowed in the main house. Dogs must be leashed and cleaned up after, and they may only be left alone for short time periods.
Super 8 Montgomery/Maybrook Area 207 Montgomery Rd Montgomery NY   845-457-3143 (800-800-8000)
Dogs of all sizes are allowed. There is a $10 one time per pet fee per visit. Reservations are recommended due to limited rooms for pets. Smoking and non-smoking rooms are available for pet rooms.
LeFevre House 14 Southside Avenue New Paltz NY   845-255-4747
http://www.lefevrehouse.com/
In addition to offering a spa, and tailor-made services and dining requests for one or many, this 1870's Victorian home also features an International art gallery (many items for sale), and gives access to a variety of scenic trails. Dogs of all sizes are allowed for an additional $75 one time pet fee per pet, and there is a pet waiver to sign at check in. Dogs are not allowed on the furniture and they must be crated when left alone in the room. Dogs must be leashed and cleaned up after at all times.
Super 8 Newburgh 1287 Route 300 Newburgh NY   845-564-5700 (800-800-8000)
Dogs of all sizes are allowed. There is a $10 per night pet fee per pet. Smoking and non-smoking rooms are available for pet rooms.
Best Western Inn & Conference Center 2170 South Road Poughkeepsie NY   845-462-4600 (800-780-7234)
Dogs are allowed for no additional pet fee with a credit card on file. There is a $50 refundable deposit if paying cash. Dogs may not be left alone in the room.
Residence Inn by Marriott 2525 South Road Poughkeepsie NY   845-463-4343
Dogs of all sizes are welcome. There is a $75 one time fee and a pet policy to sign at check in.
WhistleWood Farm 52 Pells Road Rhinebeck NY   845-876-6838
http://www.whistlewood.com/
Guests can explore the wooded trails and wildflower gardens, sit out on large decks enjoying the views, take in the afternoon desert fare, and more at this retreat. Housebroken dogs of all sizes are allowed for an additional pet fee of $20 per night per pet. Dogs must be quiet, well behaved, leashed and cleaned up after, and crated

when left alone in the room.

Inn at Stone Ridge Route 209 Stone Ridge NY 845-687-0736
http://www.innatstoneridge.com/
Whether it's by the entire inn as a guest house or by individual rooms, this 18th century Dutch Colonial mansion has a lot to offer, including 150 acres of well manicured lawns and gardens, unspoiled woods, and an apple orchard. Dogs of all sizes are welcome for no additional pet fee. Dogs must be friendly, well trained, leashed and cleaned up after. Dogs may not be left alone unless owners are confident in their behavior.

TOP 200 PLACE Audrey's Farmhouse 2188 Brunswyck Road Wallkill NY 845-895-3440 (800-501-3872)
http://www.audreysfarmhouse.com/
Sweeping manicured lawns, stately trees, an outdoor pool, Jacuzzi, sundeck and a central location to an array of other activities make this 1740's dog-friendly country inn an attractive destination for both people and their dogs. Pets also like the many hiking trails in the area. Dogs of all sizes are allowed for no additional pet fee. Dogs must be well mannered, leashed, and cleaned up after.

Best Western New Baltimore Inn 12600 Route 9 W West Coxsackie NY 518-731-8100 (800-780-7234)
Dogs are allowed for an additional fee of $10 per night per pet.

Campgrounds and RV Parks

Clarence Fahnestock State Park 1498 H 301 Carmel NY 845-225-7207 (800-456-2267)
There are plenty of land and water recreational opportunities, camping, and many scenic hiking trails at this 14,000+ acre recreational destination, including a piece of the Appalachian Trail. Dogs are allowed in designated camp areas and on the trails; there are no additional pet fees. Dogs must be on no more than a 10 foot leash and be cleaned up after. Dogs are not allowed on the beach or picnic areas. The campground has 80 campsites, each with a picnic table and fire ring, and restrooms and showers are nearby. They also show movies for the campers on Saturday evenings. Dogs are allowed in campsites 70 through 81. This RV park is closed during the off-season. The camping and tent areas also allow dogs. There is a dog walk area at the campground. There are no electric or water hookups at the campgrounds.

Jellystone Park 50 Bevier Road Gardiner NY 845-255-5193
http://www.lazyriverny.com
Dogs of all sizes are allowed. There are no additional pet fees. Dogs must be quiet at night, be leashed, and cleaned up after. This RV park is closed during the off-season. There is a dog walk area at the campground.

KOA Newburgh/NYC North 119 Freetown Highway Plattekill NY 845-564-2836 (800-562-7220)
http://www.newburghkoa.com
Dogs of all sizes are allowed. There are no additional pet fees. Dogs must be leashed and cleaned up after. This RV park is closed during the off-season. The camping and tent areas also allow dogs. There is a dog walk area at the campground. Dogs are allowed in the camping cabins.

KOA Saugerties/Woodstock 882 H212 Saugerties NY 845-246-4089 (800-562-4081)
http://www.koa.com
Dogs of all sizes are allowed. There are no additional fees for site rentals, however there is a $4 per night per pet additional fee for the cabins. Dogs must be leashed and cleaned up after. There are some breed restrictions. This RV park is closed during the off-season. The camping and tent areas also allow dogs. There is a dog walk area at the campground. Dogs are allowed in the camping cabins.

Attractions

Fort Montgomery State Historical Site 690 H 9W Fort Montgomery NY 845-446-2134 (Summer)
Located at the union of Popolopen Creek and the Hudson River on a cliff rising 100 feet above the river, this historic site is considered to be one of America's first major strategic construction projects. Dogs are allowed for no additional fee. Dogs must be leashed and cleaned up after, and they are not allowed in park buildings.

Wright's Apple Farm 699 H 208 Gardiner NY 845-255-5300
http://www.eatapples.com/
Located in the beautiful Hudson Valley you will find the largest fruit stand in the valley where you can do your own flower picking in Spring, fruit picking throughout the seasons, picnicking, and shopping for a wide variety of tasty treats. This huge farm of about 500 acres also welcomes your four legged friend to join you on the farm, and they can be around the stand or the bakery shop. Dogs must be well behaved, leashed, and cleaned up after at all times.

Clermont State Historic Site One Clermont Avenue Germantown NY 518-537-4240
http://www.friendsofclermont.org/
Looking much like it did before the Great Depression this historic estate was home to 7 generations before being gifted to the state, and sits on 500 scenic acres along the Hudson River. There are several outbuildings, gardens, beautiful picnic areas, carriage and hiking trails, a museum store, and they host a variety of activities and events throughout the year. Dogs are allowed to explore the grounds, but they are not allowed in any of the buildings. Dogs must be well mannered, under owner's control, and leashed and cleaned up after at all times.

TOP 200 PLACE Vanderbilt Mansion - FDR Homesite 4079 Albany Post Road Hyde Park NY 800-337-8474

http://www.nps.gov/vama/
Located in Hyde Park along with 2 other National Historic Sites; F. D. Roosevelt's home and Mrs. Roosevelt's country cottage, Val-Kill, the Vanderbilt Mansion and surrounding property is a significant historic reflection of American industrialization after the Civil War. Although dogs are not allowed in the mansion or any other estate buildings, they are allowed to explore the meticulously kept grounds (open daily from 7 am to sunset), hike along old carriage trails or to the Hudson River, or picnic at the Overlook. Dogs must be leashed and cleaned up after at all times.

Martin Van Buren National Historic Site 1013 Old Post Road Kinderhook NY 518-758-9589
http://www.nps.gov/mava
This historic estate is open 7 days a week from May until the end of October for tours, but the grounds are open year-round from 7 am to dusk at no charge. Although dogs are not allowed in any of the estate buildings, but they are allowed on the old carriage trails which also have interpretive exhibits along the way, and around the grounds. Dogs must be well mannered, leashed and cleaned up after at all times, and they may not be left unattended in vehicles.

Hudson River Maritime Museum 50 Rondout Landing Kingston NY 845-338-0071
http://www.hrmm.org/
This is the only museum in the state for the preservation and education of the Hudson River's maritime history, its tributaries, and the industries it inspired; they are also host to a variety of special events, offer indoor and outdoor exhibits, and a gift shop. Dogs are permitted on the grounds and along the riverfront; they are not allowed in the buildings. Dogs must be well behaved, leashed, and cleaned up after at all times.

Old Rhinebeck Aerodrome 42 Old Stone Church Road Rhinebeck NY 845-752-3200
http://www.oldrhinebeck.org/
This museum of antique airplanes, aircraft engines, and automobiles welcomes the public from about Father's Day weekend through October offering shows on the weekends, weather permitting. Your well behaved dog is welcome to join you. Dogs must be under owner's control at all times, leashed, and cleaned up after.

Sleepy Hollow Cemetery 540 N Broadway Sleepy Hollow NY 914-631-0081
http://www.sleepyhollowcemetery.org/
Rich in folk lore and unprecedented beauty, this cemetery began in the early 1600's by the Dutch colonists and has grown to cover almost 100 acres. This is the sight of the Headless Horseman legends. Dogs are allowed at the cemetery, and they must be leashed and cleaned up after at all times.

Shopping Centers

Woodbury Common Premium Outlets 498 Red Apple Court Central Valley NY 845-928-4000
There are 220 stores at this premium outlet shopping center, and your well behaved dog is welcome to join you exploring the area. It is up to individual stores whether they permit pets inside. Dogs must be under owner's control, be leashed, and cleaned up after at all times.

Stores

PetSmart Pet Store 501 N Frank Sottile Blvd Kingston NY 845-336-0485
Your licensed and well-behaved leashed dog is allowed in the store.

PetSmart Pet Store 3131 E Main St Mohegan Lake NY 914-528-4478
Your licensed and well-behaved leashed dog is allowed in the store.

Parks

Hudson Highlands State Park H 9D Beacon NY
Consisting of nearly 6,000 acres of undeveloped preserve, this day-use park is a perfect place for a number of outdoor activities, and the extensive trails system goes from easy to challenging with some outstanding views. Dogs are allowed throughout the park on no more than a 10 foot lead and they must be cleaned up after. They suggest not bringing dogs on a hot day, and to always bring extra water for them when hiking upland.

Clarence Fahnestock State Park 1498 H 301 Carmel NY 845-225-7207 (800-456-2267)
There are plenty of land and water recreational opportunities, camping, and many scenic hiking trails at this 14,000+ acre recreational destination, including a piece of the Appalachian Trail. Dogs are allowed in designated camp areas and on the trails; there are no additional pet fees. Dogs must be on no more than a 10 foot leash and be cleaned up after. Dogs are not allowed on the beach or picnic areas.

Mohonk Preserve Nature 3197 H 44/55 Gardiner NY 845-255-0919
http://www.mohonkpreserve.org/
Open year-round, this mountain refuge provides over 6,500 acres of forests, fields, lakes, ponds, streams, and cliffs, has more than 100 miles of multi-use trails, and it is also one of the best premier rock climbing/scrambling areas in the Northeast. Dogs of all sizes are allowed for no additional fee from Spring through Fall; they are not allowed in the park in the Winter or after snowfall. Dogs must be kept close to owners, preferably on a 4 foot to a 6 foot leash, depending on the dog due to snakes in the area. Dogs are not allowed on the Mountain House property; maps are available at the visitor center. Please clean up after your pet on the trails and common areas.

Eleanor Roosevelt National Historic Site 4097 Albany Post Road Hyde Park NY 845-229-9115

http://www.nps.gov/elro/index.htm
Dogs must be on leash and must be cleaned up after on the grounds and trails. Dogs are not allowed in any buildings. This is the only National Historic Site dedicated to a First Lady.

Off-Leash Dog Parks

Kennedy Dells Dog Park 355 North Main Street New City NY 845-364-2670
There is a fenced, off-leash area in the nearly 200 acre Kennedy Dells Park. Dogs must be leashed when outside of the dog park area. In addition to the dog park there is also a parcourse fitness trail, ball fields and hiking trails.
Kingsland Point Park Dog Park Palmer Ave at Munroe Ave Sleepy Hollow NY 914-366-5104
This dog park is located in Kingland Point Park which is located on the Hudson River just west of Route 9. Dogs must be licensed, vaccinated against rabies and must get a pass to use the park.The annual pass is $25 and you can call 914-366-5104 to get a pass, which also includes parking fees.

Outdoor Restaurants

The Piggy Bank Restaurant 448 Main Street Beacon NY 845-838-0028
http://www.piggybankrestaurant.com/
This Southern barbecue eatery offers indoor and outdoor dining options. Dogs are permitted at the outdoor tables in the back at any time and at the outer front tables when no one else is there. Dogs must be well behaved, under owner's control, and leashed and cleaned up after at all times.
DePuy Canal House Restaurant 1315 H 213 High Falls NY 845-687-7700
http://www.depuycanalhouse.net/
In addition to offering fine dining, being registered as a National Historic Property, and providing an active "event" calendar, this eatery at the Inn at Canal House (no pets at inn) also offers indoor and outdoor dining options. Dogs are permitted at the outdoor tables. Dogs must be well behaved, under owner's control, and leashed and cleaned up after at all times.
The Bakery 13-A North Front Street New Paltz NY 845-255-8840
This restaurant serves American food. Dogs are allowed at the outdoor tables.
Cena 2000 Restorante and Bar 50 Front Street Newburgh NY 845-561-7676
Specializing in Northern Italian food with a full service bar, they offer indoor and outdoor dining that affords visitors a great view of the Hudson River and the Highlands. Dogs are permitted at the outdoor tables (seasonal). Dogs must be well behaved, under owner's control, and leashed and cleaned up after at all times.

Jamestown

Accommodations

Best Western Downtown Jamestown 200 W 3rd Street Jamestown NY 716-484-8400 (800-780-7234)
Dogs are allowed for an additional one time fee of $25 per pet.
Comfort Inn 2800 N Main Street Jamestown NY 716-664-5920 (877-424-6423)
Dogs are allowed for an additional one time fee of $15 per pet.
Red Roof Inn - Jamestown-Falconer 1980 East Main Street Jamestown NY 716-665-3670 (800-RED-ROOF)
One well-behaved family pet per room. Guest must notify front desk upon arrival. Guest is liable for any damages. In consideration of all guests, pets must never be left unattended in the guest rooms.

Johnstown

Accommodations

Holiday Inn 308 N. Comrie Ave Johnstown NY 518-762-4686 (877-270-6405)
Dogs of all sizes are allowed for no additional fee.

Little Falls

Accommodations

Best Western Little Falls Motor Inn 20 Albany St Little Falls NY 315-823-4954 (800-780-7234)

Dogs are allowed for a $10 refundable pet deposit per room, and a credit card must be on file.

Long Island - Nassau

Accommodations
Residence Inn by Marriott 9 Gerhard Road Plainview NY   516-433-6200
Dogs of all sizes are allowed. There is a $75 one time fee per pet and a pet policy to sign at check in.
Best Western Mill River Manor 173 Sunrise Highway Rockville Centre NY   516-678-1300 (800-780-7234)
Dogs are allowed for an additional fee of $15 per night per pet.
Red Roof Inn - Long Island 699 Dibblee Drive Westbury NY   516-794-2555 (800-RED-ROOF)
One well-behaved family pet per room. Guest must notify front desk upon arrival. Guest is liable for any damages. In consideration of all guests, pets must never be left unattended in the guest rooms.

Campgrounds and RV Parks
Nickerson Beach Campground 880 Lido Blvd Lido Beach NY   516-571-7700
This campground has been newly renovated and offer gaming courts, a 'Fun Zone' kids center, skating park, beach showers and cabanas, an enclosed dog run, 2 pools, a kiddie pool, modern restrooms, and new benches and grills. For more information on the campgrounds, call 516-571-7701 through March 30th, and during camping season call the number listed above. Dogs of all sizes are allowed for no additional fee. Dogs may be in the campground area, parking lot, or at the dog run. Dogs are not allowed on the beach or trails. Dogs may not be left unattended at any time, and they must be leashed (except in dog run) and cleaned up after. The camping and tent areas also allow dogs. There is a dog walk area at the campground.
Battle Row Campground Claremont Road Old Bethpage NY   516-572-8690
This camp area is located at the Old Bethpage County Park with large grassy lawns, surrounded by woods, and is the only park in the county that allows tent camping. Camping begins the first Friday in April and ends the last Sunday in November. Dogs are allowed throughout the park; there is no additional pet fee. Dogs must be well mannered, leashed, and cleaned up after at all times. This RV park is closed during the off-season. The camping and tent areas also allow dogs. There is a dog walk area at the campground.

Transportation Systems
Long Island Railroad and Buses Regional Long Island NY   718-330-1234
http://www.mta.nyc.ny.us
Small dogs in carriers are allowed on the Long Island Railroad, Long Island Bus and New York City Transit buses and subways. Small dogs in carriers or on a secure leash are allowed on the Metro-North Railroad. The pet carrier should be able to fit on your lap and should not occupy a seat. Dogs should not bother other passengers.

Attractions
TOP 200 PLACE **Sagamore Hill Estate** 20 Sagamore Hill Road Oyster Bay NY   516-922-4447
http://www.nps.gov/sahi
Home to Theodore Roosevelt, our 26th President, for 34 years, this beautiful estate welcomes guests to tour the mansion, explore the grounds, or hike down a nature trail to the harbor. Dogs are not allowed in the buildings, but they are allowed on the grounds and on the trails. Dogs must be on no more than a 6 foot leash and be cleaned up after at all times.

Shopping Centers
Americana Manhasset 2060 Northern Boulevard at Searingtown Road Manhasset NY   516-627-2277
http://www.americanamanhasset.com/
Dogs are allowed to walk along this strip mall with their owners as long as they are leashed, cleaned up after, and under owner's control at all times. It is up to the individual stores whether they permit pets inside.

Stores
Petco Pet Store 806 Sunrise Highway Baldwin NY   516-868-7120
Your licensed and well-behaved leashed dog is allowed in the store.
Petco Pet Store 189 Old Country Rd Carle Place NY   516-746-9623
Your licensed and well-behaved leashed dog is allowed in the store.
Huntington Antique Center 129 Main Street/H 25A Cold Spring Harbor NY   631-549-0105
Your well behaved dog up to about 55 pounds is welcome in this antique store. Dogs must be leashed, and

under owner's care/control at all times. They are open 10:30 am to 5 pm Tuesday through Friday, and from noon to 5 pm on Sunday; closed Tuesday.
Petco Pet Store 2300 Jericho Turnpike Garden City NY   516-739-0031
Your licensed and well-behaved leashed dog is allowed in the store.
Petco Pet Store 345 Rockaway Turnpike Lawrence NY   516-371-4510
Your licensed and well-behaved leashed dog is allowed in the store.
PetSmart Pet Store 3545 Hempstead Tpke Levittown NY   516-731-2592
Your licensed and well-behaved leashed dog is allowed in the store.
Petco Pet Store 5500 Sunrise Highway Massapequa NY   516-797-5727
Your licensed and well-behaved leashed dog is allowed in the store.
Petco Pet Store 565 Jericho Turnpike Syosset NY   516-921-0722
Your licensed and well-behaved leashed dog is allowed in the store.
Petco Pet Store 366 West Sunrise Highway Valley Stream NY   516-561-7088
Your licensed and well-behaved leashed dog is allowed in the store.

Off-Leash Dog Parks

Nickerson Beach Park Dog Run Merrick Road at Wantagh Avenue Lido Beach NY   516-571-7700
There is a fenced dog run in Nickerson Beach Park across the parking lot from the "Fun Zone" playground area. There are two areas, a larger area for large dogs and a smaller area for smaller dogs. During beach season there may be fees to park at the dog park. To get to the park take Meadowbrook Pkwy South and look for signs to Lido and Nickerson State Park.
Christopher Morley Park Dog Run Searingtown Road Roslyn NY   516-571-8113
There is a fenced dog run in Wantagh Park near the maintenance building. Dogs must be leashed while walking from your car to the dog run.
Cedar Creek Dog Run Merrick Road at Wantagh Avenue Seaford NY   516-571-7470
There is a fenced dog run in Cedar Creek Park. Dogs are only allowed in the dog run area. They are not allowed to use the rest of the park.
Wantagh Park Dog Run Kings Road at Canal Place Wantagh NY   516-571-7460
There is a fenced dog run in Wantagh Park near the maintenance building. Dogs must be leashed while walking from your car to the dog run.

Outdoor Restaurants

Baja Fresh 1468 Union Turnpike New Hyde Park NY   516-354-2252
This restaurant serves Mexican food. Dogs are allowed at the outdoor tables.
Quiznos 1161 Old Country Road Plainview NY   516-942-5188
Dogs are allowed at the outdoor tables. The restaurant has outdoor tables only in the Summer.
Green Cactus Grill 215 Mineola Ave Roslyn Heights NY   516-626-3100
This restaurant and bar serves Mexican. Dogs are allowed at the outdoor tables.

Long Island - Suffolk

Accommodations

Gansett Green Manor 273 Main Street Amagansett NY   631-267-3133
Well behaved dogs of all sizes are allowed. There can be up to 3 small dogs or 2 big dogs per room. The fee is $20 for the 1st 4 days then $5 for each day thereafter per pet. Dogs must be healthy and free of tics and fleas.
TOP 200 PLACE Bend In the Road Guest House 58 Spring Close H East Hampton NY   631-324-4592
http://www.bendintheroadguesthouse.com/
With a convenient location to the beaches, eateries, and shops, this inn (that also functions as a pottery studio) sits on 22 acres of farmland featuring a driving range for golfers, a private jogging path great for running your pooch, a large lawn area, and a secluded garden with a large swimming pool. Dogs of all sizes are welcome for no additional pet fee. Dogs may not be left alone in the room at any time, and they must be leashed and cleaned up after in common areas.
The Bassett House Inn 128 Montauk H East Hampton NY   631-324-6127
http://www.bassetthouseinn.com/
This spacious, country 1830's inn offers 12 individually adorned guest rooms, garden-style grounds, a central location to the village, walking trails, and beaches. Dogs of all sizes are welcome (with prior notice) for an additional $15 per night per pet. Dogs must be well behaved, and leashed and cleaned up after. They may only be left alone in the room for a short time if they will be quiet and the owner is confident in their behavior.
The Mill House Inn 31 N Main Street East Hampton NY   631-324-9766
http://www.millhouseinn.com

This inn has been recently renovated to allow guests to have a true Long Island lodging experience with great ocean views, gas fireplaces, whirlpool baths, private decks, and the dog friendly suites have heated stone floors. Dogs of all sizes are allowed for an additional $50 per night per pet. Dogs may only be left alone in the suite if they will be quiet and owners are confident in their behavior. Dogs must be under owner's care/control at all times, and please clean up after your pet.

Bowen's by the Bays 177 West Montauk Highway Hampton Bays NY 631-728-1158 (800-533-3139) http://www.gobowens.com

This lovely resort, located in the heart of the Hamptons, is very pet friendly. It offers individually decorated guest rooms and guest cottages, swimming pool, tennis court, small pond with waterfall and beautiful gardens. Pets are welcome in the guest cottages. Pet fees are $20 per pet/per day and guests are required to abide by the posted pet regulations, i.e. pets must be on leash, owners must clean up after pet, etc. Bowen's is situated on four landscaped acres, and is close to restaurants, shopping, and the North Fork, as well as the charming towns of the Hamptons.

Residence Inn by Marriott 850 Veterans Memorial Highway Hauppauge NY 631-724-4188

Dogs of all sizes are allowed. There is a $75 one time fee and a pet policy to sign at check in.

Sheraton Long Island 110 Motor Parkway Hauppauge NY 631-231-1100 (888-625-5144)

Dogs up to 80 pounds are allowed. There are no additional pet fees. Dogs are not allowed to be left alone in the room.

Residence Inn by Marriott 25 Middle Avenue Holtsville NY 631-475-9500

Dogs of all sizes are allowed. There is a $75 one time fee and a pet policy to sign at check in.

Villa Rosa B&B Inn 121 Highland Street Kings Park NY 631-724-4872

http://www.thevillarosainn.com/

Built in 1920, this bed and breakfast inn is surrounded by spacious landscaped grounds. Some of the inn's rooms have private baths. This dog-friendly inn offers a fenced dog park area. Guests are welcome to bring their well-behaved dog, but pets must be leashed when in shared areas. There is a $20 per day pet charge. Weekly and monthly rates are available. They also have parking for larger vehicles like motorhomes and trailers.

Hither House Cottages 10 Lincoln Road Montauk NY 631-668-2714

http://www.hitherhouse.com/

This well-kept, scenic retreat offers various sized cottages, is only a mile from the ocean, and they are just minutes from numerous activities, recreation, and eateries. From Memorial Day to October 1st dogs are not allowed on the beaches between the hours of 10 am and 6 pm, but off season pooches are welcome to run off lead if they are under voice control. Dogs of all sizes are allowed for an additional fee of $15 per night, and there is a pet policy to sign at check in. Dogs are welcome in the garden and on the lawn, but it is requested that they be walked off the premises to do their business. They are not allowed on the furniture and with tiled floors they suggest bringing the pets bedding. Dogs must be well behaved, leashed, cleaned up after, and they may be left alone in the cottage only if they will be quiet and the owner is confident in their behavior.

Holiday Inn Express Hotel & Suites East End 1707 Old Country Rd. Riverhead NY 631-548-1000 (877-270-6405)

Dogs up to 60 pounds are allowed for an additional one time fee of $50 per pet.

The Atlantic 1655 County Road 39 Southampton NY 631-283-6100

http://www.hrhresorts.com/atlantic.htm

This boutique motel sits on 5 groomed acres 3 miles from the ocean, is a premier vacation, special occasion, and event destination, and they offer a variety of land and water recreation on site. Dogs up to 40 pounds are allowed for an additional fee of $40 per night per pet; larger dogs may be allowed at an increased fee. Pets must have current vaccinations for rabies, distemper, and bordetella, and owners must provide documentation if needed. Dogs must be leashed and cleaned up after at all times, and plastic bags are available at the front desk if needed. Please walk your pets on the acres surrounding the property. Dogs may not be left alone in the room at any time.

The Bentley 161 Hill Station Road Southampton NY 631-283-6100

http://www.hrhresorts.com/bentley.htm

This retreat offers 39 large suites (750 sq. ft.), groomed grounds, an outdoor pool, can accommodate special events, and is only 3 miles from the ocean. Dogs up to 40 pounds are allowed for an additional fee of $40 per night per pet; larger dogs may be allowed at an increased fee. Pets must have current vaccinations for rabies, distemper, and bordetella, and be able to provide documentation if needed. Dogs must be leashed and cleaned up after at all times, and plastic bags are available at the front desk if needed. Please walk your pets on the acres surrounding the property. Dogs may not be left alone in the room at any time.

Campgrounds and RV Parks

Cedar Point County Park Stephen Hands Path East Hampton NY 631-852-7620

There are 607 recreational acres here with great views of the bay, an historic lighthouse, nature trails, outer beach access with permit, and a general store and snack bar. One dog of any size is allowed for no additional fee, but they must have current proof of rabies inoculation, leashed (maximum-6 foot), and cleaned up after at all times. Dogs may not be left unattended at any time, and they must be current in license from their home state. The camp areas offer picnic tables, fire rings, a children's playground, restrooms, and free use of recreational equipment. This RV park is closed during the off-season. The camping and tent areas also allow dogs. There is a dog walk area at the campground. There are no electric or water hookups at the campgrounds.

Watch Hill Campground by Otis Pike High Dunes Fire Island NY 631-567-6664
This tent camping area offers 26 family sites and 1 group site, and permits are needed if camping in the back country that is accessible from here. Dogs are not allowed in the back country during plover nesting season. The camp area has a 188 slip marina, interpretive programs, a store, restaurant, restrooms and showers, and a self-guided nature tour. Dogs may not be left unattended at any time, and they must be leashed (6 foot) and cleaned up after at all times. This RV park is closed during the off-season. The camping and tent areas also allow dogs. There is a dog walk area at the campground. There are no electric or water hookups at the campgrounds.

Eastern Long Island Kampgrounds On Queen Street Greenport NY 631-477-0022
http://www.greenport.com/kampground
Dogs of all sizes are allowed, however some breeds are not. There are no additional pet fees. Dogs must have proof of rabies shots. Dogs must be leashed, cleaned up after, and not left unattended. The camping and tent areas also allow dogs. There is a dog walk area at the campground.

Fire Island National Seashore 120 Laurel Street Patchogue NY 631-661-4876
http://www.nps.gov/fiis/
Land taxi service isn't available on this 30 mile long, ½ mile wide barrier island. It is home to the tallest lighthouse in the U.S.; 80% of it's over 19,500 acres is undeveloped public park land, and it has a special environment nurturing a diverse selection of plants, animals, birds, marine life, and even people. Land and water recreation, dining, an active nightlife, and shopping opportunities abound here. The best way to arrive on the island is by watercraft; however parking is available in parking lot # 5 at the end of the Causeway. Although dogs are not allowed in the lighthouse or other park buildings, they are allowed to enjoy the miles of boardwalks, trails, beaches, and self-guided nature walks. Dogs may not be in life-guarded areas of the beach, picnic or wildlife habitat areas, and they must be on no more than a 6 foot leash in the park area and cleaned up after at all times. Dogs must be well behaved and not left unattended at any time or tied to any park facilities. The campground (seasonal) has 26 sand sites, and is only a short walk to the visitor center, beach, and marina. Amenities here include a Summer lifeguard, general store, showers and restrooms, water, grills, a snack bar, and a Tiki Bar. Wilderness camping is year-round, and a permit is required. (Certain areas are restricted to dogs during the Summer. Check for updates prior to arrival.) The camping and tent areas also allow dogs. There is a dog walk area at the campground. There are no electric or water hookups at the campgrounds.

Blydenburgh County Park New Mill Road Smithtown NY 631-854-3713
In addition to providing a long list of land and water recreational pursuits and some nice hiking areas, this 627 acre park holds some historic interests, and they are home to an off leash dog area located in the south area of the park. Dogs are allowed throughout the park and at the camp area for no additional fee; they must be registered at the time of entry, and may not be left unattended at the campsite. Dogs must be sociable, current on all vaccinations-proof required, and under owner's control/care at all times. Dogs must be leashed on no more than a 6 foot leash when not in the designated off-lead area, and they are not allowed in picnic areas, designated swim areas, or comfort stations. From about mid-October to mid-May the camp area is open Thursday to Sunday, and from mid-May to early October they are open 7 days a week. During the off-season only self-contained campers are allowed; there is no water services, and tents are not allowed. The camping and tent areas also allow dogs. There is a dog walk area at the campground.

Vacation Home Rentals

Fire Island Real Estate Fire Island Pines P. O. Box 219 Sayville NY 631-597-7575
http://www.pinesharbor.com/
This realty offers vacation homes in the Fire Island Pines area (a premiere gay community), and about 90% of the rentals allow dogs. Special conditions for the pets or deposits and fees, and the location of the rental in question are disclosed at the time of reservations. Dogs must be housetrained, well mannered, leashed, and cleaned up after.

Transportation Systems

Fire Island Ferry 99 Maple Avenue Bay Shore NY 631-665-3600
http://www.fireislandferries.com/
After 4th avenue becomes Maple Avenue, the main terminal for Ocean Beach is on the left, and the Seaview/Ocean Bay Park terminal is on the right. Dogs may not go on the trips to Ocean Beach as dogs are not allowed there. Well behaved dogs are allowed on the ferry to Seaview/Ocean Bay for an additional fee of $4 each way. Dogs must be well mannered, and leashed and cleaned up after at all times.

Long Island Railroad and Buses Regional Long Island NY 718-330-1234
http://www.mta.nyc.ny.us
Small dogs in carriers are allowed on the Long Island Railroad, Long Island Bus and New York City Transit buses and subways. Small dogs in carriers or on a secure leash are allowed on the Metro-North Railroad. The pet carrier should be able to fit on your lap and should not occupy a seat. Dogs should not bother other passengers.

Viking Fleet 462 W Lake Drive Montauk NY   631-668-5700
This ferry features a triple decker, 120 foot vessel with comfort amenities on board, and service is provided between Montauk Long Island and Block Island RI, New London CT, and Martha's Vineyard, MA. Well behaved dogs are allowed on board for no additional fee. Dogs must be under owner's control/care and leashed at all times. The ferry docks at Montauk at the Viking Dock at 462 Westlake Drive.

Cross Sound Ferry Services 2 Ferry Street, PO Box 33 New London NY   860-443-5281
This auto ferry service provides transportation between New London, CT and Orient Point on Long Island, NY. Dogs are allowed on the car ferry in dog designated areas only for no additional fee. Dogs must be well behaved, leashed or in an approved pet carrier, and cleaned up after at all times.

Sayville Ferry Service 41 River Road Sayville NY   631-589-0810
http://www.sayvilleferry.com/
This ferry service offers daily schedules to a variety of stops in the South Bay area, and dogs are allowed for an additional $4 per round trip. Dogs must be under owner's control/care at all times, and they must be leashed and cleaned up after.

North Ferry Company 12 Summerfield Place Shelter Island Heights NY   631-749-0139
http://www.northferry.com/
This ferry provides transportation service between Long Island and Shelter Island. Dogs of all sizes are allowed for no additional fee. Dogs must be under owner's control, leashed, and cleaned up after at all times.

Attractions

Eagle's Neck Paddling Company 49295 Main Road/ H25 Southold NY   631-765-3502
http://www.eaglesneck.com/
This company offers gear and watercraft for all skill levels to explore the natural beauty of this area with miles of coastline, creeks, marshes, numerous inlets, and where bird and wildlife are plentiful. They will allow a dog to accompany owners on rentals for no additional fee. Dogs must be under owner's control/care at all times, be leashed, and cleaned up after.

Shopping Centers

Outlets at Bellport Farber Drive Bellport NY   631-286-3872
Well mannered dogs of all sizes are welcome to explore the area. Dogs must be leashed and cleaned up after at all times. It is up to the individual stores as to whether they permit a dog to come inside.

Tanger Outlet Center 1770 W Main Street Riverhead NY   631-369-2732
Your well behaved pooch is welcome to explore this area as long as they are on leash and picked up after. It is up to the individual stores as to whether pets are allowed inside.

Stores

Petco Pet Store 1851 Sunrise Highway Bay Shore NY   631-206-1047
Your licensed and well-behaved leashed dog is allowed in the store.

Petco Pet Store 30 Veterans Memorial Highway Commack NY   631-462-1643
Your licensed and well-behaved leashed dog is allowed in the store.

Ralph Lauren Polo Country Store 31-33 Main Street East Hampton NY   631-324-1222
This high end store welcomes well behaved dogs to accompany their owners here. Dogs must be quiet, under owner's control/care at all times, and leashed.

Petco Pet Store 227 Forest Avenue Glen Cove NY   516-676-8030
Your licensed and well-behaved leashed dog is allowed in the store.

PetSmart Pet Store 350 Walt Whitman Rd Unit 9 Huntington Station NY   631-425-0913
Your licensed and well-behaved leashed dog is allowed in the store.

Petco Pet Store 31 Middle Country Rd Lake Grove NY   631-580-9343
Your licensed and well-behaved leashed dog is allowed in the store.

Petco Pet Store 401 Sunrise Highway Patchogue NY   631-289-7240
Your licensed and well-behaved leashed dog is allowed in the store.

Petco Pet Store 1524 Old Country Rd Riverhead NY   631-727-8545
Your licensed and well-behaved leashed dog is allowed in the store.

Petco Pet Store 1100 Middle Country Rd Selden NY   631-451-8021
Your licensed and well-behaved leashed dog is allowed in the store.

Saks Fifth Avenue 1 Hampton Road Southampton NY   631-283-3500
http://www.saksfifthavenue.com/Entry.jsp
This high end store welcomes well behaved dogs to accompany their owners here. Dogs must be quiet, under owner's control/care at all times, and leashed or crated.

Petco Pet Store 655 West Montauk Highway West Babylon NY   631-669-8413
Your licensed and well-behaved leashed dog is allowed in the store.

Beaches

Camp Hero State Park 50 South Fairview Avenue Montauk NY 631-668-3781
http://www.nysparks.com/maps/
The park boasts some of the best surf fishing spots in the world. Dogs on a 6 foot or less leash are allowed on the beach year-round, but not in the picnic areas. To get to the park, take Route 27 (Sunrise Highway) east to the end. The park is about 130 miles from New York City.
Hither Hills State Park 50 South Fairview Avenue Montauk NY 631-668-2554
http://www.nysparks.com/maps/
This park offers visitors a sandy ocean beach. Dogs are allowed with certain restrictions. During the off-season, dogs are allowed on the beach. During the Summer, dogs are not allowed on the beach, except for the undeveloped area on the other side of the freeway. Dogs must be on a 6 foot or less leash and people need to clean up after their pets. Dogs are not allowed in buildings or on walkways and they are not allowed in the camping, bathing and picnic areas.
Montauk Point State Park 50 South Fairview Avenue Montauk NY 631-668-3781
http://www.nysparks.com/maps/
This park is located on the eastern tip of Long Island. Dogs are allowed on the beach, but not near the food area. Dogs must be on a 6 foot or less leash and people need to clean up after their pets. Dogs are not allowed in buildings or on walkways and they are not allowed in the camping, bathing and picnic areas. Please note that dogs are not allowed in the adjacent Montauk Downs State Park. The park is located 132 miles from Manhattan, off Sunrise Highway (Route 27).

Parks

Cedar Point County Park Stephen Hands Path East Hampton NY 631-852-7620
There are 607 recreational acres here with great views of the bay, an historic lighthouse, nature trails, outer beach access with permit, and a general store and snack bar. One dog of any size is allowed for no additional fee, but they must have current proof of rabies inoculation, leashed (maximum-6 foot), and cleaned up after at all times. Dogs may not be left unattended at any time, and they must be current in license from their home state.
West Hills County Park Sweet Hollow Rd Huntington NY 631-854-4423
This is an over 700 acre park with nature trails and hiking including the Whitman Trail to the 400 foot Jayne's Hill which is Long Island's highest point. There is also a horseback riding facility and bridle paths in the park. Dogs must be on leash in the park outside of the small off-leash enclosed dog run in the park.
Montauk Point Lighthouse and Museum 2000 Montauk H Montauk NY 631-668-2544
This lighthouse is the oldest one in the state and 4th oldest active lighthouse in the U.S., and the beauty of the area leads to a number of special events taking place here. Although dogs are not allowed in the lighthouse or in the museum, they are allowed for day use, on the beach, and the area offers a number of areas to hike and explore. Dogs must be leashed, cleaned up after, and under owner's control at all times.
Fire Island National Seashore 120 Laurel Street Patchogue NY 631-661-4876
http://www.nps.gov/fiis/
Land taxi service isn't available on this 30 mile long, ½ mile wide barrier island. It is home to the tallest lighthouse in the U.S.; 80% of it's over 19,500 acres is undeveloped public park land, and it has a special environment nurturing a diverse selection of plants, animals, birds, marine life, and even people. Land and water recreation, dining, an active nightlife, and shopping opportunities abound here. The best way to arrive on the island is by watercraft; however parking is available in parking lot # 5 at the end of the Causeway. Although dogs are not allowed in the lighthouse or other park buildings, they are allowed to enjoy the miles of boardwalks, trails, beaches, and self-guided nature walks. Dogs may not be in life-guarded areas of the beach, picnic or wildlife habitat areas, and they must be on no more than a 6 foot leash in the park area and cleaned up after at all times. Dogs must be well behaved and not left unattended at any time or tied to any park facilities.
Blydenburgh County Park New Mill Road Smithtown NY 631-854-3713
In addition to providing a long list of land and water recreational pursuits and some nice hiking areas, this 627 acre park holds some historic interests, and they are home to an off leash dog area located in the south area of the park. Dogs are allowed throughout the park and at the camp area for no additional fee; they must be registered at the time of entry, and may not be left unattended at the campsite. Dogs must be sociable, current on all vaccinations-proof required, and under owner's control/care at all times. Dogs must be leashed on no more than a 6 foot leash when not in the designated off-lead area, and they are not allowed in picnic areas, designated swim areas, or comfort stations.

Off-Leash Dog Parks

West Hills County Park Dog Run Sweet Hollow Rd at Old Country Road Huntington NY 631-854-4423
http://www.lidog.org/li_dogparks.htm
There is a small fenced dog run in West Hills County Park. This is an over 700 acre park with nature trails and hiking. Dogs must be on leash in the park outside of the dog run.
Blydenburgh County Park Dog Park Veterans Memorial Highway Smithtown NY 631-854-4949
Located in the south area of the 627 acre Blydenburgh County Park, this 1.8 acre doggy play area offers open

fields, woods, a separate large and small dog section, benches, waste bag dispensers, and water fountains for pooches and humans. Dogs must be sociable, current on all vaccinations, and under owner's control/care at all times. Dogs must be leashed on no more than a 6 foot leash when not in designated off-lead areas.

Outdoor Restaurants
Rowdy Hall 10 Main Street East Hampton NY   631-324-8555
http://www.rowdyhall.com/
Offering indoor or outdoor dining options, this eatery features English Pub/French Bistro cuisine. Dogs are permitted at the outdoor tables. Dogs must be well behaved, under owner's control, and leashed and cleaned up after at all times.
Harbourfront Deli 48 Front Street Greenport NY   631-477-1878
This full service deli serves breakfast, lunch and dinner daily, and also offers a good variety of pastries, bagels, coffees, and deli items. Dogs are permitted at the outdoor tables (seasonal). Dogs must be well behaved, under owner's control, and leashed and cleaned up after at all times

Events
Hampton Classic Horse Show 240 Snake Hollow Road Bridgehampton NY   631-537-3177
Thousands of spectators attend this event; the country's largest hunter/jumper horse show where there is more than 1,300 horses and a $500,000 purse at stake. There are 60 acres of showgrounds located along beautiful ocean fronts, several shops and restaurants, demonstrations, educational programs, and it is considered one of the most extravagant social events of the Summer. Well mannered dogs of all sizes are welcome. They must be under owner's control, leashed, and cleaned up after at all times. Dogs are not allowed in the shopping or food areas.

Day Kennels
PetsHotel by PetsMart Day Kennel 350 Walt Whitman Rd Huntington NY   631-425-0184
http://www.petsmart.com/PETsHOTEL/
This PetSmart pet store offers day care, day camp and overnight care. You may drop off and pick up your dog during the hours the store is open seven days a week. Dogs must have proof of current rabies, DPP and Bordatella vaccinations.

Mexico

Campgrounds and RV Parks
Jellystone Park 601 County Road 16 Mexico NY   315-963-7096 (800-248-7096)
http://www.jellystoneny.com
One dog of any size is allowed, some breeds are not. There are no additional pet fees. Dogs must be walked in the pet walk area only, not around the park. Dogs may not be left unattended and must be leashed and cleaned up after. This RV park is closed during the off-season. The camping and tent areas also allow dogs. There is a dog walk area at the campground.

NYC Boroughs

Accommodations
Holiday Inn Express New York-Brooklyn 625 Union St. Brooklyn NY   718-797-1133 (877-270-6405)
Dogs of all sizes are allowed for an additional one time fee of $50 per pet.
Sheraton La Guardia East Hotel 135-20 39th Ave. Flushing NY   718-460-6666 (888-625-5144)
Dogs up to 60 pounds are allowed. There are no additional pet fees. Dogs are not allowed to be left alone in the room.

Attractions
New York City Boardwalks Various Brooklyn NY   212-NEW-YORK
Leashed dogs are allowed year-round on the boardwalks and promenade at Coney Island, Brighton, Midland, South and Manhattan Beaches. Leashed dogs are allowed on the sand at certain NYC beaches only between October 1 and April 30. These beaches are Rockaway Beach, Coney Island, Brighton Beach, Manhattan Beach, Midland Beach and South Beach. Dogs are not allowed on the sand at any New York City beaches from May 1

through September 30. Please check the website at http://www.nycgovparks.org for updated information and changes.

Stores
Petco Pet Store 15720 Cross Bay Blvd Howard Beach NY   718-845-3331
Your licensed and well-behaved leashed dog is allowed in the store.
Crazy for Animals 8016 Cooper Avenue Queens NY   718-366-3310
http://www.crazyforanimals.com
Located at a 12 acre shopping and entertainment mecca, this pet boutique is the city's first "Green" pet store providing 1,000 square feet of doggy fun with an indoor dog run, specialty treats from the Pawtsserie, quality foods, fashions for pets and owners, and a wide variety of eco-friendly products. The 1,000 square foot shop was built with eco-friendly construction, and even the sales personnel wear corn-fiber clothing. Dogs are welcome; they must be leashed and under owner's control/care at all times.
PetSmart Pet Store 1520 Forest Ave Staten Island NY   718-273-3874
Your licensed and well-behaved leashed dog is allowed in the store.

Beaches
New York City Beaches and Boardwalks Various Brooklyn NY   212-NEW-YORK
From October 1 through April 30 each year, leashed dogs are allowed on the sand and the boardwalk at certain beaches. Currently, these beaches are Rockaway Beach, Coney Island, Brighton Beach, Manhattan Beach, Midland Beach and South Beach. Dogs are not allowed on the sand at any New York City beaches between May 1 and September 30. Leashed dogs are allowed year-round on the boardwalks and promenade at Coney Island, Brighton, Midland, South and Manhattan Beaches. Please check the website at http://www.nycgovparks.org for updated information and changes.

Parks
Flushing Meadows Corona Park Grand Central Parkway Flushing NY   718-760-6565
One of New York City's flagship parks, this 1,255 acre major recreational destination also holds environmental and historical importance. The park is home to Shea Stadium, a tennis center, the New York Hall of Science, the Queens Museum of Art, a wildlife center, Meadow Lake, children's playgrounds, and much more. There are several entrance points depending on the activity. Dogs are allowed throughout the park; they are not allowed in buildings or at the playgrounds. Dogs must be well behaved, under owner's control, leashed, and cleaned up after at all times.
Gateway National Recreation Area 210 New York Avenue Staten Island NY   718-354-4606
http://www.nps.gov/gate/index.htm
Dogs must be on leash and must be cleaned up after in the park. The park features auto touring, boating, fishing, and more. You must follow any local or state park rules and pet policies.

Off-Leash Dog Parks
Ewen Park Dog Run Riverdale to Johnson Aves., South of West 232nd St. Bronx NY   212-NEW-YORK
This is an official off-leash dog run. All New York City Off-leash Dog Parks are run by the New York City Parks Department. They can be reached at 212-NEW-YORK or by calling 311 from a phone in the city of New York.
Frank S. Hackett Park Dog Run Riverdale Ave. and W. 254th Street Bronx NY   212-NEW-YORK
This is an official off-leash dog run. All New York City Off-leash Dog Parks are run by the New York City Parks Department. They can be reached at 212-NEW-YORK or by calling 311 from a phone in the city of New York.
Pelham Bay Park Dog Run Middletown Rd. & Stadium Ave., Northwest of Parking Lot Bronx NY   212-NEW-YORK
This is an official off-leash dog run. All New York City Off-leash Dog Parks are run by the New York City Parks Department. They can be reached at 212-NEW-YORK or by calling 311 from a phone in the city of New York.
Seton Park Dog Run West 232nd St. & Independence Ave. Bronx NY   212-NEW-YORK
This is an official off-leash dog run. All New York City Off-leash Dog Parks are run by the New York City Parks Department. They can be reached at 212-NEW-YORK or by calling 311 from a phone in the city of New York.
Van Cortlandt Park Dog Run West 251st Street & Broadway Bronx NY   212-NEW-YORK
This is an official off-leash dog run. All New York City Off-leash Dog Parks are run by the New York City Parks Department. They can be reached at 212-NEW-YORK or by calling 311 from a phone in the city of New York.
Williamsbridge Oval Dog Run 3225 Reservoir Oval East Bronx NY   212-NEW-YORK
This is an official off-leash dog run. All New York City Off-leash Dog Parks are run by the New York City Parks Department. They can be reached at 212-NEW-YORK or by calling 311 from a phone in the city of New York.
Brooklyn Bridge Park Dog Run Adams Street and N/S Plymouth St Brooklyn NY   212-NEW-YORK
This is an official off-leash dog run. All New York City Off-leash Dog Parks are run by the New York City Parks Department. They can be reached at 212-NEW-YORK or by calling 311 from a phone in the city of New York.
Cooper Park Dog Run Olive St at Maspeth Ave Brooklyn NY   212-NEW-YORK

This is an official off-leash dog run. All New York City Off-leash Dog Parks are run by the New York City Parks Department. They can be reached at 212-NEW-YORK or by calling 311 from a phone in the city of New York.
DiMattina Park Dog Run Hicks, Coles and Woodhull Streets Brooklyn NY   212-NEW-YORK
There are two official off-leash dog runs in DiMattina Park. All New York City Off-leash Dog Parks are run by the New York City Parks Department. They can be reached at 212-NEW-YORK or by calling 311 from a phone in the city of New York.
Dyker Beach Park Dog Run 86th Street from 7th Ave to 14th Ave Brooklyn NY   212-NEW-YORK
This is an official off-leash dog run. All New York City Off-leash Dog Parks are run by the New York City Parks Department. They can be reached at 212-NEW-YORK or by calling 311 from a phone in the city of New York.
Hillside Park Dog Run Columbia Heights & Vine Street Brooklyn NY   212-NEW-YORK
http://www.hillsidedogs.org
This is an official off-leash dog run. All New York City Off-leash Dog Parks are run by the New York City Parks Department. They can be reached at 212-NEW-YORK or by calling 311 from a phone in the city of New York.
J J Byrne Memorial Park Dog Run 3rd to 4th Streets between 4th and 5th Ave Brooklyn NY   212-NEW-YORK
This is an official off-leash dog run. All New York City Off-leash Dog Parks are run by the New York City Parks Department. They can be reached at 212-NEW-YORK or by calling 311 from a phone in the city of New York.
Manhattan Beach Dog Run East of Ocean Avenue, North Shore Rockaway inlet Brooklyn NY   212-NEW-YORK
This is an official off-leash dog run. All New York City Off-leash Dog Parks are run by the New York City Parks Department. They can be reached at 212-NEW-YORK or by calling 311 from a phone in the city of New York.
McCarren Park Dog Run Nassau Ave, Bayard, Leonard & N. 12th Sts Brooklyn NY   212-NEW-YORK
This is an official off-leash dog run. All New York City Off-leash Dog Parks are run by the New York City Parks Department. They can be reached at 212-NEW-YORK or by calling 311 from a phone in the city of New York.
McGolrick Park Dog Run North Henry Street at Driggs Ave Brooklyn NY   212-NEW-YORK
This is an official off-leash dog run. All New York City Off-leash Dog Parks are run by the New York City Parks Department. They can be reached at 212-NEW-YORK or by calling 311 from a phone in the city of New York.
Owls Head Park Dog Run Shore Pkwy, Shore Rd, Colonial Rd, 68th Street Brooklyn NY   212-NEW-YORK
This is an official off-leash dog run. All New York City Off-leash Dog Parks are run by the New York City Parks Department. They can be reached at 212-NEW-YORK or by calling 311 from a phone in the city of New York.
Palmetto Playground Dog Run Atlantic Ave, Furman, Columbia, State Streets Brooklyn NY   212-NEW-YORK
This is an official off-leash dog run. All New York City Off-leash Dog Parks are run by the New York City Parks Department. They can be reached at 212-NEW-YORK or by calling 311 from a phone in the city of New York.
Prospect Park   Brooklyn NY   212-NEW-YORK
Prospect Park, in Brooklyn, allows dogs in much of the park on leash has a number of large off-leash areas during specified hours. Dogs are allowed off-leash before 9 am and after 9 pm in the Summer and after 5 pm in the Winter in the Long Meadow, Nethermead and the Peninsula Meadow areas of the park. Dogs are not allowed in the children's playground or on the Bridle paths. Owners must clean up after their dogs. There's even a man made dog beach in the park.
Seth Low Playground Dog Run Avenue P, Bay Parkway, W. 12th Street Brooklyn NY   212-NEW-YORK
This is an official off-leash dog area. All New York City Off-leash Dog Parks are run by the New York City Parks Department. They can be reached at 212-NEW-YORK or by calling 311 from a phone in the city of New York.
Forest Park Dog Run Park Lane South & 85th Street Forest Park NY   212-NEW-YORK
This is an official off-leash dog area. Its hours are 8 am to 8 pm seven days a week. All New York City Off-leash Dog Parks are run by the New York City Parks Department. They can be reached at 212-NEW-YORK or by calling 311 from a phone in the city of New York.
Other New York City Off-Leash Areas   New York NY   212-NEW-YORK
In addition to the off-leash dog runs listed, New York City allows dogs to be off-leash in designated areas of certain parks between the hours of 9 pm and 9 am during hours when the parks are open. There are many park areas that are designated this way in all boroughs. To find these designated parks, see the website http://www.nycgovparks.org/sub_things_to_do/facilities/af_dog_runs.html. Please check this website for updates to the off-leash policies in New York. New York City Off-leash Dog Parks are run by the New York City Parks Department. They can be reached at 212-NEW-YORK or by calling 311 from a phone in the city of New York.
Alley Pond Park Dog Run Alley Picnic Field Number 12 Queens NY   212-NEW-YORK
This is an official off-leash dog area. All New York City Off-leash Dog Parks are run by the New York City Parks Department. They can be reached at 212-NEW-YORK or by calling 311 from a phone in the city of New York.
Cunningham Park Dog Run 193rd Street between Aberdeen Road and Radnor Road Queens NY   212-NEW-YORK
This is an official off-leash dog run. All New York City Off-leash Dog Parks are run by the New York City Parks Department. They can be reached at 212-NEW-YORK or by calling 311 from a phone in the city of New York.
K-9 Dog Run in Forest Park Park Lane South at 85th Street Queens NY   212-NEW-YORK
This is an official off-leash dog run open from 8 am to 8 pm seven days a week. All New York City Off-leash Dog Parks are run by the New York City Parks Department. They can be reached at 212-NEW-YORK or by calling 311 from a phone in the city of New York.

Little Bay Dog Run Cross Island Parkway between Clearview Expwy and Utopia Parkway Queens NY 212-NEW-YORK
This is an official off-leash dog run. All New York City Off-leash Dog Parks are run by the New York City Parks Department. They can be reached at 212-NEW-YORK or by calling 311 from a phone in the city of New York.
Murray Playground Dog Run 21st Street & 45th Road on the SE side of park Queens NY 212-NEW-YORK
This is an official off-leash dog run. All New York City Off-leash Dog Parks are run by the New York City Parks Department. They can be reached at 212-NEW-YORK or by calling 311 from a phone in the city of New York.
Sherry Park Dog Run Queens Boulevard, 65 Place and the BQE Queens NY 212-NEW-YORK
This is an official off-leash dog run. All New York City Off-leash Dog Parks are run by the New York City Parks Department. They can be reached at 212-NEW-YORK or by calling 311 from a phone in the city of New York.
Underbridge Playground Dog Run 64th Ave and 64th Road on Grand Central Parkway service road Queens NY 212-NEW-YORK
This is an official off-leash dog run. All New York City Off-leash Dog Parks are run by the New York City Parks Department. They can be reached at 212-NEW-YORK or by calling 311 from a phone in the city of New York.
Veteran's Grove Dog Run Judge & Whitney on the south side of the park Queens NY 212-NEW-YORK
This is an official off-leash dog run. All New York City Off-leash Dog Parks are run by the New York City Parks Department. They can be reached at 212-NEW-YORK or by calling 311 from a phone in the city of New York.
Windmuller Park Dog Run Woodside Ave., 54-56 Sts. Queens NY 212-NEW-YORK
This is an official off-leash dog run. All New York City Off-leash Dog Parks are run by the New York City Parks Department. They can be reached at 212-NEW-YORK or by calling 311 from a phone in the city of New York.
Silver Lake Park Dog Run Victory Blvd just within Silver Lake Park Staten Island NY 212-NEW-YORK
This is an fenced off-leash dog run. All New York City Off-leash Dog Parks are run by the New York City Parks Department. They can be reached at 212-NEW-YORK or by calling 311 from a phone in the city of New York.
Wolfe's Pond Park Dog Run End of Huguenot & Chester Avenues Staten Island NY 212-NEW-YORK
This is an official off-leash dog run. All New York City Off-leash Dog Parks are run by the New York City Parks Department. They can be reached at 212-NEW-YORK or by calling 311 from a phone in the city of New York.

Outdoor Restaurants

El Greco Diner 1821 Emmons Avenue Brooklyn NY 718-934-1288
A 24 hour diner, this eatery specializes in typical Greek foods, and they also offer outside dining. Dogs are allowed at the outside tables; they must be leashed and under owner's control/care at all times.
Maria's Mexican Bistro 669 Union St Brooklyn NY 718-638-2344
This restaurant serves Mexican food. Dogs are allowed at the outdoor tables.
The Gate 321 5th Avenue Brooklyn NY 718-768-4329
This neighborhood tavern offers many brews on tap and an outside patio area. Well behaved dogs are allowed at the outside tables; they must be leashed and under owner's control/care at all times.
Green Cactus Grill 10718 70th Rd Forest Hills NY 718-268-1427
This restaurant and bar serves Mexican. Dogs are allowed at the outdoor tables.
Baja Fresh 1093 Jackson Ave Long Island City NY 718-706-8783
This restaurant serves Mexican food. Dogs are allowed at the outdoor tables.

Events

TOP 200 PLACE New York Mets Dog Day at Shea Shea Stadium Flushing NY
http://newyork.mets.mlb.com
The New York Mets Baseball team holds an annual Dog Day Event at the baseball game. The event helps to support the North Shore Animal League which is the world's largest no-kill animal rescue. There is a dog parade on the field before the game and the dogs get to watch the game with you. Check with the Mets for the dates scheduled for these events.

New York

Accommodations

70 Park Avenue Hotel 70 Park Ave New York NY 212-973-2400 (877-707-2752)
http://www.70parkave.com
This Kimpton boutique hotel is located at Park Avenue and 38th Street. Dogs of all sizes are allowed. There are no additional pet fees.
Embassy Suites Hotel New York 102 North End Avenue New York NY 212-945-0100
Dogs of all sizes are allowed. There is a $75 one time pet fee per visit. Dogs are not allowed to be left alone in the room.
Holiday Inn Express New York City Fifth Avenue 15 West 45th Street New York City NY 212-302-

9088 (877-270-6405)
One dog of any size is allowed for no additional fee; there is a pet agreement to sign at check in.
Holiday Inn Express NYC Manhattan Chelsea Area 232 West 29th Street New York City NY 212-695-7200 (877-270-6405)
Quiet dogs of all sizes are allowed for an additional one time fee of $25 per pet.
Hotel Wales 1295 Madison Avenue New York NY 212-876-6000 (866-WALES-HOTEL)
http://www.waleshotel.com
This recently renovated Upper East Side hotel close to Central Park offers 88 guestrooms, including 42 suites. There is a $75 per stay pet fee and dogs up to 100 pounds are allowed.
Le Parker Meridien New York 118 West 57th St. New York NY 212-245-5000
Dogs of all sizes are allowed. There are no additional pet fees. Dogs are not allowed to be left alone in the room.
Novotel - New York 226 West 52nd Street New York NY 212-315-0100
Novotel Hotels welcome a maximum of 2 animals (cats and dogs) per room and never require a fee. Each guest checking in with a pet will be given a Royal Canine/Novotel Pet Welcome Kit.
Regency Hotel 540 Park Avenue New York NY 212-759-4100
All well-behaved dogs of any size are welcome. This upscale hotel offers their "Loews Loves Pets" program which includes special pet treats, local dog walking routes, and a list of nearby pet-friendly places to visit. There are no pet fees.
Renaissance New York Hotel 714 7th Avenue New York NY 212-765-7676
http://www.renaissancehotel.com/NYCRT/
They allow dogs up to about 70 pounds.This hotel is located in Times Square. It is located at the intersection of Broadway and Seventh Avenue. Amenities include room service, an in-room refreshment center, and an exercise/weight room. The hotel lobby is located on the third floor. There is a $65 one time charge for pets.
Ritz-Carlton Central Park 50 Central Park S New York NY 212-308-9100
Dogs up to 60 pounds are allowed. There is a $125 one time pet fee per visit. Pet sitting, emergency veterinarian and dog walking services are available.
Sofitel Hotel 45 West 44th Street New York NY 212-354-8844
http://www.tribecagrand.com
This French hotel overlooks 5th Ave. Amenities include a fitness room. There are no additional pet fees.
Soho Grand Hotel 310 West Broadway New York NY 212-965-3000
http://www.sohogrand.com/
This hotel is VERY pet-friendly and there are no size restrictions at all for dogs. They are owned by the Hartz Mountain Company which manufactures the 2 in 1 pet products. The hotel is located in the artistic heart of New York's cultural capital SoHo (South of Houston Street), and within an easy walking distance to the surrounding neighborhoods of Tribeca, Greenwich Village, Little Italy and Chinatown. The hotel is also just steps from Wall Street, and only minutes from Midtown Manhattan. Amenities include 24 room service and a fitness center. One of our readers has this to say about the hotel: "This is the most incredibly dog friendly hotel. Bellboys carry dog treats, there is a dog room service menu, doggie day care is provided. It's also one of New York's super chic hotels." There are no pet fees.
Swissotel NY -The Drake 440 Park Avenue New York NY 212-421-0900
http://www.swissotel.com/brochure/nyc/
Located in Midtown Manhattan, The Drake is just a couple of blocks from several dog-friendly stores and only 5 blocks from Central Park. Amenities include 24 hour room service and a fitness center/spa. No extra pet charge, just sign a pet waiver. Dogs up to about eighty pounds are allowed.
TOP 200 PLACE The Muse 130 West 46th Street New York NY 212-485-2400 (877-NYC-MUSE)
http://www.themusehotel.com
There are no additional pet fees at this pet-friendly Kimpton boutique hotel. They offer a pampered pooch package for an additional fee.
Tribeca Grand Hotel 2 Avenue of the Americas New York NY 212-519-6600
http://www.tribecagrand.com
This dog-friendly hotel is located just 2 blocks from it's sister hotel, the dog-friendly Soho Grand Hotel. This hotel is located within walking distance of Little Italy, Chinatown, Greenwich Village, and many department stores. Room rates begin at $399 and up. There are no pet fees.
W New York - Union Square 201 Park Avenue South New York NY 212-253-9119
Dogs up to 50 pounds are allowed. There is a $100 one time pet fee per visit and a $25 per night additional pet fee. Dogs are not allowed to be left alone in the room.

Campgrounds and RV Parks
Liberty Harbor RV Park 11 Marin Blvd Jersey City NY 201-387-7500
http://www.libertyharborrv.com/
This campground is located in New Jersey near Liberty State Park and just across the Holland Tunnel from New York. Dogs of all sizes are allowed. There are no additional pet fees. Dogs must be leashed, cleaned up after, and not be left unattended. There is a dog walk area at the campground.

Accommodations - Only Small Dogs
Trump International Hotel & Tower 1 Central Park West New York NY 888-448-7867
http://www.trumpintl.com/
This luxury hotel allows small dogs only up to 15 pounds are allowed. There is a $250 per visit pet fee.

Transportation Systems
MTA Regional New York NY 718-330-1234
http://www.mta.nyc.ny.us
Small dogs in carriers are allowed on the Long Island Railroad, Long Island Bus and New York City Transit buses and subways. Small dogs in carriers or on a secure leash are allowed on the Metro-North Railroad. The pet carrier should be able to fit on your lap and should not occupy a seat. Dogs should not bother other passengers.
Madison Avenue Limousine Inc. 348 East 15th Street, Suite 16 New York NY 212-674-0060
http://www.madisonavenuelimo.com/
This Limousine company will pick you and your pup up at your front door, and there is no additional pet fee if there is no extra cleaning. They suggest bringing a large sheet or cover depending on how large or hairy the dog is. There is a 2 hour rental minimum and they suggest calling 48-72 hours in advance. Dogs must be under owner's care/control at all times.
Metro-North Railroad 42nd Street and Park Avenue New York NY 212-532-4900
http://www.mta.info/mnr/index.html
Dogs up to 65 pounds are allowed on the train for no additional pet fee. Dogs are not allowed on the train when it is crowed or during peak hours and they may not take up a seat. Dogs must be well behaved, under owner's control/care at all times, and they must be securely leashed or in a carrier and cleaned up after at all times.
Pet Chauffeur New York NY 718-752-1767 (866-PETRIDE)
http://petride.com
This pet transportation service will take you and your pet (or your pet alone) just about anywhere you need or want to go. They recommend calling well in advance but you can try last minute bookings.
Pet Taxi 227 E 56th St New York NY 212-755-1757
When want to get around town without driving, there are numerous taxi cabs. A typical New York yellow taxi cab is supposed to pick up people with pets, however, they don't always stop if you have a pooch. Don't feel too bad, many NY cabs don't stop even for people without pets! However, with a little advance planning, you can reserve the Pet Taxi. The Pet Taxi makes runs to the vet, groomer and other pet related stuff. But they are also rented to transport you and your pooch to a park, outdoor restaurant, across town, etc. For example, if you are at a hotel near Central Park but would like to go to Little Italy and Chinatown for half a day, they will take you to your destination and then several hours later, they will pick you up and take you back to your hotel. Just be sure to reserve the Pet Taxi at least one day in advance during the weekdays. If you need the taxi on Saturday or Sunday, book your reservation by Thursday or Friday. They are open from 8am-7pm during the weekday and by reservation on the weekends. They can be reserved for $35 per hour or $25 each way for a pick up or drop off. Pet Taxi serves the Manhattan area.

Seastreak Ferry Rides

TOP 200 PLACE Seastreak Ferry Rides various (see below) New York NY 800-BOAT-RIDE

http://www.seastreakusa.com
Want to enjoy the sights of New York City from the water, including the Manhattan Skyline and the Statue of Liberty? Or maybe you want to stay at a hotel in New Jersey and visit New York City during the day. Well, the nice folks at Seastreak allow dogs onboard their commuter ferries. Here are the rules: Dogs of all sizes must stay on the outside portion of the ferry and they need to be on a short leash. Dogs are not allowed on the inside area regardless of the weather unless you have a small dog and he or she is in a carrier. The ferries operate between Manhattan and New Jersey on a daily basis with up to 11 ferry rides during the weekday and about 4 ferry rides on the weekend. The ride lasts about 45 minutes each way and costs approximately $20 per round trip, half price for children and free for dogs! The ferries depart from Pier 11 (Wall Street) and East 34th Street in Manhattan and Atlantic Highlands and Highlands in New Jersey. Please visit their website for current ferry schedules, times and fares.
Staten Island Ferry Whitehall Street New York NY   718-876-8441
http://www.siferry.com/
Small dogs in a cage or carrier are allowed on these ferries. The ferry service provides passenger transportation between St. George, Staten Island and Whitehall Street in Manhattan. The 25 minute ride provides a great view of New York Harbor, the Statue of Liberty and Ellis Island.

Attractions
Brooklyn Bridge Self-Guided Walk Park Row New York NY
Enjoy the sights and skyline of New York City from the Brooklyn Bridge! You and your pooch can stroll along the bridge on the wooden walkway which is elevated over the traffic. The Brooklyn Bridge, designed by architect John Roebling between 1867 and 1883, is the world's first steel suspension bridge. It was constructed to link Brooklyn and Manhattan. This popular walk takes about 20-40 minutes each way, depending on your pace. If you need a break along the way, benches located on the walkway. The footpath begins at a street called Park Row (across from the City Hall Park).
Federal Hall National Memorial 26 Wall Street New York NY   212-825-6888
http://www.nps.gov/feha/index.htm
Dogs are not allowed in the building and there are no grounds to tour. You can walk around the building that served as New York City's first city hall and the meeting place for the Continental Congress.
General Grant National Monument Riverside Drive and 122nd St New York NY   212-666-1640
http://www.nps.gov/gegr/index.htm
Dogs must be on leash and must be cleaned up after on the grounds of memorial. Dogs are not allowed in buildings. Burial site of Ulysses S Grant and his wife, Julia Dent Grant.
TOP 200 PLACE **Horse & Carriage Rides** 59th Street and Fifth Avenue New York NY
You and your pooch are welcome to hop on the horse and carriage rides for a tour of Central Park and NYC. The carriage driver will also supply a blanket for humans (and possibly your pooch!) if it is a little chilly outside. Carriages are available seven days a week after 10am, weather permitting. The carriages are located at the south end of Central Park, at 59th Street and Fifth Avenue (up to 6th Avenue).
NYC Dog Walking Tour various (see below) New York NY   914-633-7397
The Zuckerman Family offers "dog-friendly" walking tours of New York City. The tours last from 3-5 hours. Each tour will include many historical facts about the most incredible city in the world. Some highlights of the tour are visits to the following neighborhoods : Greenwich Village, Soho, Lower East Side, Little Italy, Central Park and any other area in Manhattan that you wish to visit. A special highlight is a walk across the Brooklyn Bridge at dusk. Call for tour rates or to arrange a guided tour.
New York City Boardwalks Various New York NY   212-NEW-YORK
Leashed dogs are allowed year-round on the boardwalks and promenade at Coney Island, Brighton, Midland, South and Manhattan Beaches. Leashed dogs are allowed on the sand at certain NYC beaches only between October 1 and April 30. These beaches are Rockaway Beach, Coney Island, Brighton Beach, Manhattan Beach, Midland Beach and South Beach. Dogs are not allowed on the sand at any New York City beaches from May 1 through September 30. Please check the website at http://www.nycgovparks.org for updated information and changes.
South Street Seaport South Street New York NY   212-732-8257
http://www.southstreetseaport.com
South Street Seaport, located on Lower Manhattan's historic waterfront, is a community with a maritime museum, great views, shops, cafes and restaurants. This seaport area was a world popular port town between 1815 and 1860. While dogs are not allowed inside the museum, you and your leashed pooch can walk around and explore the seaport, and enjoy the views. Pets are allowed at some of the outdoor restaurants like Il Porto and Heartland Brewery & Beer Hall. If you are coming from New Jersey, you can drive, or take the dog-friendly Seastreak Ferry which allows leashed dogs of all sizes. Dogs need to stay on the outside portion of the ferry, not inside. Or to reach the seaport by car from the West Side, George Washington Bridge, Lincoln and Holland Tunnels, take West Street south. Follow the signs to FDR Drive. Take the underpass and keep right. Take Exit 1 a tthe end of the underpass. Turn right on South Street and go six blocks. For the East Side, take FDR Drive south to exit 3 onto South Street. Go for about a mile on South Street. There are over 3,000 parking spaces in paid lots within a six block radius. For details about parking or for rates, call Edison Parking at 212-732-2670.

Statue of Liberty National Monument Liberty Island New York NY   212-363-3200
http://www.nps.gov/stli/index.htm
Pets are not allowed on ferry or Liberty Island. To get a view of the Statue of Liberty with your dog you can go to lower Manhattan

TV Broadcasts various (see below) New York NY
Ever watch the NBC or CBS morning shows and see people standing outside holding signs or just wanting to get captured on national TV? Well, the filming locations are right here in the Big Apple. Located just outside the NBC and CBS broadcast studio buildings are designated areas for the public to line up for a chance at 15 minutes of fame. The live cameras film the crowds between 8am and 9am every day. If you want to get in the front of the line, you must arrive around 6am during nice weather and around 7am during bad weather. There is usually a larger crowd on sunny days. Please note that your pooch may not like crowds, especially if you are in the front. People may be pushing to get to the front, so your pooch may prefer to watch from the back. While you are waiting, you can also watch the live morning broadcast and the well-known anchor people from the outside through the large windows at the studios. The NBC studio is located in Rockefeller Center near 49th Street and the CBS studio is located on Fifth Avenue between 58th and 59th Streets.

Theodore Roosevelt Birthplace National Historic Site 28 East 20th Street New York NY   212-260-1616
http://www.nps.gov/thrb/index.htm
Dogs on leash are allowed on the sidewalk outside of house. Dogs are not allowed in the house.

Times Square Walking Tour 1560 Broadway New York NY 212-768-1560
The Times Square BID (Business Improvement District) holds free guided walking tours every Friday at Noon for a behind-the-scenes look at Times Square. Visit historic theaters and the best of the neighborhood during this walking tour. Your pooch is welcome on the outdoor part of the tour. Sometimes the tour will enter a few Theaters and unless you can convince the Theaters to allow your pup, you will need to wait outside. However, the majority of the tour should be outside. The tour leaves, rain or shine, every Friday, from the new Times Square Visitors Center, 1560 Broadway between 46th and 47th Streets.

TOP 200 PLACE **William Secord Gallery** 52 East 76th Street New York NY 212-249-0075
http://www.dogpainting.com/
The William Secord Gallery, located in Manhattan's Upper East Side, specializes in nineteenth century dog paintings, bronzes and works on paper. The only gallery of its kind in North America, it was established by William Secord in 1990. Since then, it has become a popular destination for those interested in dog art and collectibles. In addition to creating the gallery, William Secord was the founding director of The Dog Museum of America and is the author of Dog Painting, 1840-1940, a Social history of the Dog in Art, as well as European Dog Painting, both books available at the gallery. And of course, your well-behaved dog is welcome inside! If you ask, they will serve your pooch cookies and water. If you want a portrait of your own pooch, this gallery can direct you to several painters like Christine Merrill and Barrie Barnett. Samples of their work are located at the gallery. Merrill has painted several pet portraits for celebrities like Oprah Winfrey and Bob Schieffer. Prices for consignment portraits start at $7,000 and up. The gallery is open Monday - Saturday 10a.m. to 5:00p.m. and by appointment. It is located on the third floor, so when you enter from the street, press the "William Secord" button. One of the staff members will then buzz the door open. Once inside, you can either take the small elevator or use the stairs. The toll free number is 1-877-249-DOGS.

Shopping Centers
TOP 200 PLACE **Time Warner Center** 10 Columbus Circle New York NY   212-823-6000
http://www.shopsatcolumbuscircle.com
Time Warner Center is an upscale, indoor shopping mall located on Columbus Circle on the Southwest corner of Central Park. Dogs on leash, if very well behaved, are allowed in the mall. It is up to the stores if dogs are allowed inside the stores. We have seen many dogs here after walks in the park during our previous visits.

Stores
Banana Republic 130 East 59th Street New York NY   212-751-5570
http://www.bananarepublic.com/
Dogs are allowed in many of the Banana Republic stores in the area.

Bed Bath and Beyond 410 East 61st Street New York NY   646-215-4702
Dogs are allowed at this variety department store. Dogs must be leashed and under owner's control/care at all times.

Bloomingdale's 1000 Third Avenue New York NY   212-705-2000
http://www.bloomingdales.com/
Well behaved dogs are allowed at this famous department store; they are not allowed in the restaurant. Dogs must be leashed and under owner's control/care at all times.

Bloomingdale's 59th Street and Lexington Avenue New York NY   212-705-2000
http://www.bloomingdales.com/
Thanks to one of our viewers who writes: "during one of our visits, Captain (my Dane) was invited to be apart of a photo shoot. He was then invited back for a fashion show."

Time Warner Center

Doggy Style Gift Shop 100 Thompson Street New York NY   212-431-9200
This gift shop carries a variety of pet supplies, toy, clothing, collars, leashes, and more. They are open from Noon to 7 pm Monday through Saturday, and from Noon to 6 pm on Sunday. Your well behaved, leashed, pet is allowed to explore the shop with you.
Downtown Doghouse 259 West 18th Street New York NY   212-924-5300
http://downtowndoghouse.com/
This dog boutique has natural cookies, dog clothes, and bowls for your four legged companion. Bring your dog with you when you visit.
For Pets Only Pet Boutique 87 Mercer Street New York NY   212-925-5264
This pet boutique offers a variety of clothing and accessories for your canine companion. Your well behaved dog is welcome to explore the store with you.
Petco Pet Store 860 Broadway New York NY   212-358-0692
Your licensed and well-behaved leashed dog is allowed in the store.
Petco Pet Store 147-149 E 86th St New York NY   212-831-8001
Your licensed and well-behaved leashed dog is allowed in the store.
Petco Pet Store 560 Second Avenue New York NY   212-779-4550
Your licensed and well-behaved leashed dog is allowed in the store.
Petco Pet Store 2475 Broadway New York NY   212-877-1270
Your licensed and well-behaved leashed dog is allowed in the store.
Polo Ralph Lauren 72nd & Madison New York NY
Thanks to one of our viewers who writes: "they will bring your dog cookies and water on a silver tray. Very lovely."
Restoration Hardware 935 Broadway New York NY   212-260-9479
http://www.restorationhardware.com/
They love having dogs in the store!
Saks Fifth Avenue 611 Fifth Avenue New York NY   212-753-4000
Well-behaved leashed dogs are allowed inside the store. Thanks to one of our readers for recommending this store.
The Gap 59th Street and Lexington Avenue New York NY   212-751-1543
Dogs are allowed in many of the Gap stores in the area.
Tiffany's Fifth Avenue at 57th Street New York NY   212-755-8000
http://www.tiffany.com/

Tourneau 12 East 57th Street New York NY   212-758-7300
http://www.tourneau.com/

Dogs are allowed in many of the Tourneau stores in the area.

Beaches

New York City Beaches and Boardwalks Various New York NY 212-NEW-YORK
From October 1 through April 30 each year, leashed dogs are allowed on the sand and the boardwalk at certain beaches. These beaches are Rockaway Beach, Coney Island, Brighton Beach, Manhattan Beach, Midland Beach and South Beach. Dogs are not allowed on the sand at any New York City beaches between May 1 and September 30. Leashed dogs are allowed year-round on the boardwalks and promenade at Coney Island, Brighton, Midland, South and Manhattan Beaches. Please check the website at http://www.nycgovparks.org for updated information and changes.
Prospect Park Dog Beach Prospect Park - Brooklyn New York NY 212-NEW-YORK
This man made, concrete beach was designed for our canine friends. It is located in Prospect Park in Brooklyn, off 9th Street on the path leading down from the Tennis House. Dogs may only be off-leash before 9 am and after 9 pm in the Summer and after 5 pm in the Winter. People are not permitted to swim in the dog pool. There is a fence to keep the dogs in so you don't have to chase them across the pond.

Parks

Battery Park State Street New York NY
http://www.ci.nyc.ny.us/html/dpr/
From this 23 acre city park, you can view the Statue of Liberty and Ellis Island in the distance. There are numerous picnic tables and several sidewalk vendors in the park. This park also contains several sculptures and the Clinton Castle Monument, a sandstone fort built in 1811. Your leashed dog is allowed in the park, but much of the grass area is fenced off.
Canine Court Henry Hudson Parkway New York NY
http://www.ci.nyc.ny.us/html/dpr/
In April of 1998, New York City's first public dog playground (agility course) opened in Van Cortlandt Park. Canine Court was also the first public dog agility course/playground in the country. Canines now have a fenced-in play area that totals 14,000 square feet - one half as a dog run and the other half as a dog agility course. The agility equipment consists of several chutes or tunnels for pooches to run through, a teeter-totter and a pair of hurdles. Canine Court was made possible by $3,000 from the Friends of Van Cortlandt Park and $1,000 from the City Parks Foundation (CPF). The NYC event called PawsWalk, held every April/May helped to fund some of the equipment, fencing and benches. The doggie playground is located in Van Cortlandt Park in the Bronx. From the Henry Hudson Parkway, follow signs to Van Cortlandt Park. Canine Court is located across the Parkway from the horse barn/stable. It is located between a running track/soccer field area and the Parkway. You cannot really see it from the road, so you will need to park and then walk along the running path, towards the Parkway.

Central Park

TOP 200 PLACE **Central Park** Central Park W & Fifth Ave. New York NY
http://www.centralpark.org/
Central Park, located the heart of Manhattan, is the world's most famous park. This 843 acre park is so nice and refreshing that you'll find it hard to believe it is in the middle of the country's largest city. When we visited Central Park, it seemed very clean and safe, however there are two rules of thumb to follow. Only walk in the park during daylight hours and stay on the main paths. It is best to go on main paths where other people are walking. The park is 6 miles long and has an inner path which is a 4 mile loop. Also inside the park is a popular running track which is a 1.58 mile loop (between 86th and 96th Streets). When inside the park, be sure to stop by the Shakespeare Garden - leashed pooches are welcome on the paths. And don't miss Balto - a bronze sculpture of Balto, the sled dog. Balto is located between the Shakespeare Garden and Fifth Street (around 67th Street). If 66th Street were to go through the Park, the statue of Balto would be on 66th Street. Another popular area for dog fanatics is "Dog Hill". On a nice day, you will find dogs of all shapes, sizes and breeds socializing here. It is located near Central Park West and 79th Street (north of 79th Street.) Sections of Central Park now have off-leash hours. Be sure to follow the signs for the correct areas and hours for off-leash activity.
Manhattan Sites National Park Service 26 Wall Street New York NY   212-825-6888
http://www.nps.gov/masi/index.htm
Dogs must be on leash and must be cleaned up after on the pathways in this city park on Wall Street. There are six separate sites representing the 1600's to the present.
Riverside Park Riverside Drive New York NY
http://www.ci.nyc.ny.us/html/dpr/
This waterfront park has a path which stretches for 4 miles alongside the Hudson River. Your leashed pooch is welcome.

Off-Leash Dog Parks
Carl Schurz Park Dog Run East End Ave.between 84th and 89th Street New York NY   212-NEW-YORK
This is an official off-leash dog run. All New York City Off-leash Dog Parks are run by the New York City Parks Department. They can be reached at 212-NEW-YORK or by calling 311 from a phone in the city of New York.
Central Park Off-Leash Hours and Areas   New York NY   212-NEW-YORK
Central Park is a designated off-leash area for the hours of 9 pm until 9 am daily. Dogs are allowed off-leash in most of Central Park during these hours. They are never allowed at all in playgrounds, display fountains, ballfields, Elm Islands, Sheep Meadow, East Green and Strawberry Fields. They must always be leashed in the the woodlands, Conservatory Garden, Shakespeare Garden, Bridle Trail, Cedar Hill, Kerbs Boathouse Plaza and whereever signs are posted. Between 9 am and 9 pm and in areas where off-leash is not allowed dog owners will be fined if their dogs are off-leash. New York City Off-leash Dog Parks are run by the New York City Parks Department. They can be reached at 212-NEW-YORK or by calling 311 from a phone in the city of New York.
Chelsea Waterside Park Dog Run 22nd St and 11th Avenue New York NY   212-627-2020
This fenced dog park is located in the Hudson River Park on land owned by the Hudson River Park Trust which is a partnership between New York State and the city. The dog run is open from 6 am to 1 am. Dogs are required to be on leash outside of the dog run areas and are not allowed on many of the lawns in the park.
Coleman Oval Park Dog Run Pike St at Monroe St New York NY   212-NEW-YORK
This is an official off-leash dog run. All New York City Off-leash Dog Parks are run by the New York City Parks Department. They can be reached at 212-NEW-YORK or by calling 311 from a phone in the city of New York.
DeWitt Clinton Park Dog Run Between 10th and 11th Ave at 52nd and 54th New York NY   212-NEW-YORK
This is an official off-leash dog run. All New York City Off-leash Dog Parks are run by the New York City Parks Department. They can be reached at 212-NEW-YORK or by calling 311 from a phone in the city of New York.
East River Esplanade Dog Run East River at East 60th Street New York NY   212-NEW-YORK
This is an official off-leash dog run. All New York City Off-leash Dog Parks are run by the New York City Parks Department. They can be reached at 212-NEW-YORK or by calling 311 from a phone in the city of New York.
Fish Bridge Park Dog Run Dover St., between Pearl & Water St. New York NY   212-NEW-YORK
This is an official off-leash dog run. All New York City Off-leash Dog Parks are run by the New York City Parks Department. They can be reached at 212-NEW-YORK or by calling 311 from a phone in the city of New York.
Fort Tryon Park Dog Run Margaret Corbin Drive, Washington Heights New York NY   212-NEW-YORK
This is an official off-leash dog run. All New York City Off-leash Dog Parks are run by the New York City Parks Department. They can be reached at 212-NEW-YORK or by calling 311 from a phone in the city of New York.
Highbridge Park Dog Run Amsterdam at Fort George Avenue New York NY   212-NEW-YORK
This is an official off-leash dog run. All New York City Off-leash Dog Parks are run by the New York City Parks Department. They can be reached at 212-NEW-YORK or by calling 311 from a phone in the city of New York.
Hudson River Park - Greenwich Village Dog Run Leroy Street at Pier 40 New York NY   212-NEW-YORK
This is an official off-leash dog run. All New York City Off-leash Dog Parks are run by the New York City Parks Department. They can be reached at 212-NEW-YORK or by calling 311 from a phone in the city of New York.
Hudson River Park - North Chelsea Dog Run W 44th Street at Pier 84 New York NY   212-NEW-YORK
This is an official off-leash dog run. All New York City Off-leash Dog Parks are run by the New York City Parks

Department. They can be reached at 212-NEW-YORK or by calling 311 from a phone in the city of New York.
Inwood Hill Park Dog Run Dyckman St and Payson Ave New York NY 212-NEW-YORK
This is an official off-leash dog run. All New York City Off-leash Dog Parks are run by the New York City Parks
Department. They can be reached at 212-NEW-YORK or by calling 311 from a phone in the city of New York.
J. Hood Wright Dog Run Fort Washington & Haven Aves., West 173rd St. New York NY 212-NEW-YORK
This is an official off-leash dog run. All New York City Off-leash Dog Parks are run by the New York City Parks
Department. They can be reached at 212-NEW-YORK or by calling 311 from a phone in the city of New York.
Madison Square Park Dog Run Madison Ave. To 5th Ave. between East 23rd St. & East 26th St. New
York NY 212-NEW-YORK
This is an official off-leash dog run. All New York City Off-leash Dog Parks are run by the New York City Parks
Department. They can be reached at 212-NEW-YORK or by calling 311 from a phone in the city of New York.
Marcus Garvey Park Dog Run Madison Ave at East 120th Street New York NY 212-NEW-YORK
This is an official off-leash dog run. All New York City Off-leash Dog Parks are run by the New York City Parks
Department. They can be reached at 212-NEW-YORK or by calling 311 from a phone in the city of New York.
Morningside Park Dog Run Morningside Avenue between 114th and 119th Streets New York NY 212-NEW-
YORK
This is an official off-leash dog run. All New York City Off-leash Dog Parks are run by the New York City Parks
Department. They can be reached at 212-NEW-YORK or by calling 311 from a phone in the city of New York.
Other New York City Off-Leash Areas   New York NY 212-NEW-YORK
In addition to the off-leash dog runs listed, New York City allows dogs to be off-leash in designated areas of
certain parks between the hours of 9 pm and 9 am during hours when the parks are open. There are many park
areas that are designated this way in all boroughs. To find these designated parks, see the website
http://www.nycgovparks.org/sub_things_to_do/facilities/af_dog_runs.html. Please check this website for updates
to the off-leash policies in New York. New York City Off-leash Dog Parks are run by the New York City Parks
Department. They can be reached at 212-NEW-YORK or by calling 311 from a phone in the city of New York.
Peter Detmold Park Dog Run West Side of FDR Drive between 49th and 51st New York NY 212-NEW-
YORK
This is an official off-leash dog run. All New York City Off-leash Dog Parks are run by the New York City Parks
Department. They can be reached at 212-NEW-YORK or by calling 311 from a phone in the city of New York.
Riverside Park Dog Runs Riverside Dr at W 72nd,87th, and 105th New York NY 212-NEW-YORK
There are three official off-leash dog areas in Riverside Park. All New York City Off-leash Dog Parks are run by
the New York City Parks Department. They can be reached at 212-NEW-YORK or by calling 311 from a phone
in the city of New York.
Robert Moses Park Dog Run 41st Street and 1st Ave. New York NY 212-NEW-YORK
This is an official off-leash dog run. All New York City Off-leash Dog Parks are run by the New York City Parks
Department. They can be reached at 212-NEW-YORK or by calling 311 from a phone in the city of New York.
Sirius Dog Run Liberty St and South End Avenue New York NY
On September 8, 2005 this dog park was named for Sirius, a Police Labrador Retriever killed on September 11
in the World Trade Center. It is in the Kowsky Plaza and is run by the Port Authority of New York and New
Jersey, not the park department.
St Nicholas Park Dog Run St Nicholas Ave at 135th Street New York NY 212-NEW-YORK
This is an official off-leash dog area. It is located in the center of St Nicholas Park in Harlem between 135th and
137th Streets. All New York City Off-leash Dog Parks are run by the New York City Parks Department. They can
be reached at 212-NEW-YORK or by calling 311 from a phone in the city of New York.
Theodore Roosevelt Park Dog Run Central Park West and W 81st St. New York NY 212-NEW-YORK
This is an official off-leash dog run. All New York City Off-leash Dog Parks are run by the New York City Parks
Department. They can be reached at 212-NEW-YORK or by calling 311 from a phone in the city of New York.
Thomas Jefferson Park Dog Run East 112th Street at FDR Drive New York NY 212-NEW-YORK
This is an official off-leash dog run. All New York City Off-leash Dog Parks are run by the New York City Parks
Department. They can be reached at 212-NEW-YORK or by calling 311 from a phone in the city of New York.
Tompkins Square Park Dog Run 1st Ave and Ave B between 7th and 10th New York NY 212-NEW-YORK
This is an official off-leash dog run. All New York City Off-leash Dog Parks are run by the New York City Parks
Department. They can be reached at 212-NEW-YORK or by calling 311 from a phone in the city of New York.
Union Square Dog Run Union Square New York NY 212-NEW-YORK
This is an official off-leash dog area located on 15th Street at Union Square. All New York City Off-leash Dog
Parks are run by the New York City Parks Department. They can be reached at 212-NEW-YORK or by calling
311 from a phone in the city of New York.
Washington Sq. Park Dog Run Washington Sq. South New York NY
http://www.ci.nyc.ny.us/html/dpr/
This dog run is located in Washington Square Park in Greenwich Village. The run is located in the south side of
the park near Thompson Street.

Outdoor Restaurants
79th Street Boat Basin West 79th Street New York NY 212-496-5542

This restaurant serves American food. Dogs are allowed at the outdoor tables. Water and treats are provided for your pet.
Allegria 1350 Ave of the Americas New York NY 212-956-7755
This restaurant serves Italian cuisine. Dogs are allowed at the outdoor tables. Water is provided for your pet.
Amaranth Restaurant 21 East 62nd St. New York NY 212-980-6700
This Italian restaurant welcomes dogs at their outdoor tables.

Amish Market

Amish Market 17 Battery Place New York NY 212-871-6300
Dogs are allowed at the outdoor tables. You will have to go inside and get your food without your dog.
Barking Dog Luncheonette 1453 York Ave New York NY 212-861-3600
This restaurant serves American food. Dogs are allowed at the outdoor tables.
Blind Tiger Ale House 518 Hudson St New York NY 212-675-3848
This bar allows pets inside.
Cascina 281 Bleecker St New York NY 212-633-2941
This Italian restaurant allows dogs at the outdoor tables.
Da Rosina Ristorante 342 W 46th St New York NY 212-977-7373
This Italian restaurant allows dogs at the outdoor tables.
Dolci on Park Caffe 66 Mercer St New York NY 212-686-4331
This restaurant serves Italian food. Dogs are allowed at the outdoor tables.
F &B Gudt Food Restaurant 150 East 52nd St New York NY 212-421-8600
This restaurant serves European style food. Dogs are allowed at the outdoor tables.
F &B Gudt Food Restaurant 269 W 23rd St New York NY 917-662-1846
This restaurant serves European style food. Dogs are allowed at the outdoor tables.
Fetch 1649 Third Avenue New York NY 212-289-2700
http://www.fetchbarandgrill.com/
Visitors can enjoy contemporized American cuisine at this canine themed bar and grill; there is even an Adopt-A-Dog wall, and adoption applications are available on site. Outdoor dining is available - weather permitting. Dogs are allowed at the outside tables; they must be leashed and under owner's control/care at all times.
Firehouse 522 Columbus Avenue New York NY 212-787-FIRE (3473)
http://firehousetavern.com/
A popular gathering spot, this café and tavern also offers seasonal outdoor seating. Dogs are allowed at the outer tables; they must be leashed and under owner's control/care at all times.
Fratelli Ristorante 115 Mulberry St New York NY 212-226-5555
Dogs are allowed at the outdoor tables at this Italian restaurant.
Gavroche 212 West 14th Street New York NY 212-647-8553

http://www.gavroche-ny.com/
This French country café offers a down-to-earth ambiance, traditional recipes, and a beautiful outdoor garden dining area. Dogs are allowed at the outside tables; they must be leashed and under owner's control/care at all times.
Grey Dog's Cafe 33 Carmine St New York NY 212-462-0041
This restaurant serves American food. Dogs are allowed at the outdoor tables and inside with permission.
Heartland Brewery & Beer Hall 93 South Street at Fulton New York NY 646-572-2337
http://www.heartlandbrewery.com/
This American restaurant handcrafted beers, homemade sodas and entrees like beef, chicken and salmon. Well-behaved leashed dogs are allowed at the outdoor seats. The restaurant is located in the South Street Seaport area.
Il Porto 11 Fulton Street New York NY 212-791-2181
This restaurant offers Mediterranean and Italian cuisine. It is located in the historic Fulton Market Building in the South Street Seaport area. Well-behaved leashed dogs are allowed at the outdoor seats.
Kaijou 21 S End Ave New York NY 212-786-9888
http://www.kaijounewyork.com/
In addition to presenting an array of traditional and modern Japanese cuisine, guests are afforded wonderful views of Battery Park and the Statue of Liberty at this waterside restaurant. During the Summer there is outside dining. Dogs are allowed at the outer tables; they must be under owner's control/care at all times.
New Leaf Cafe 1 Margaret Corbin Drive New York NY 212-568-5323
This restaurant serves American food. Dogs are allowed at the outdoor tables. Reservations are required.
P J Clarke's on the Hudson 250 Vesey Street New York NY 212-285-1500
Located in the city's financial district, this restaurant offer guests a cold oyster bar, the "ultimate" in burgers, and seasonal alfresco dining. Dogs are allowed at the outer tables; they must be under owner's control/care at all times.
Phillip Marie Restaurant 569 Hudson New York NY 212-242-6200
This restaurant serves American cuisine. Dogs are allowed at the outdoor tables. Water is provided for your pet.
San Martin Restaurant 143 E 49th Street New York NY 212-832-0888
This Italian restaurant has delicious food and allows dogs at the outdoor tables. There are only 3 tables and they are pretty close together, but even a large pooch can lay beside you (assuming there is no one sitting at the table next to you).
Sidewalks 94 Avenue A New York NY 212-473-7373
Dogs are allowed at the outdoor tables. The restaurant has outdoor tables only in the Summer.
Sorrento Restaurant 132 Mulberry St New York NY 212-219-8634
Dogs are allowed at the end outdoor tables at this Italian Restaurant. There is not much space in the outdoor seating area, so a large dog may need to lay under the table.
The Old Homestead Steakhouse 56 9th Avenue New York NY 212-242-9040
A New York landmark for over 137 years, this upscale steakhouse also makes a good venue for special occasions. Outside dining is available when weather permits. Dogs are allowed at the outside tables; they must be leashed and under owner's control/care at all times.
Zocalo 174 E 82nd Street New York NY 212-717-7772
This restaurant serves Mexican food. Dogs are allowed at the outdoor tables. Water and treats are provided for your pet.

Events

New York Mets Dog Day at Shea Shea Stadium Flushing NY
http://newyork.mets.mlb.com
The New York Mets Baseball team holds an annual Dog Day Event at the baseball game. The event helps to support the North Shore Animal League which is the world's largest no-kill animal rescue. There is a dog parade on the field before the game and the dogs get to watch the game with you. Tickets for the last event were $26 for people and $5 for dogs. Check with the Mets for the dates scheduled for these events.

Pet Sitters

Petaholics 320 E. 54th Street New York NY 866-910-5430
http://www.petaholics.com
This pet sitting and dog walking service serves the midtown hotels for travelers with dogs.

New York Area North

Accommodations

Wellesley Inn Armonk 94 Business Park Drive Armonk NY   914-273-9090 (800-531-5900)
Dogs of all sizes are allowed. There are no additional pet fees. Dogs may only be left alone in the room if they will be quiet and well behaved, and they must be leashed and cleaned up after.
Holiday Inn 1 Holiday Inn Dr Mount Kisco NY   914-241-2600 (877-270-6405)
Dogs of all sizes are allowed for an additional one time pet fee of $49 per room.
Candlewood Suites 20 Overlook Blvd Nanuet NY   845-371-4445 (877-270-6405)
Dogs up to 70 pounds is allowed for an additional one time pet fee of $75 per room.
Days Inn Nanuet 367 Rte 59 Nanuet NY   845-623-4567 (800-329-7466)
Dogs of all sizes are allowed. There is a $10 per night pet fee per pet.
Residence Inn by Marriott 35 Le Count Place New Rochelle NY   914-636-7888
Dogs of all sizes are allowed. There is a $75 one time fee and a pet policy to sign at check in.
Super 8 Norwich 6067 St Route 12 Norwich NY   607-336-8880 (800-800-8000)
Dogs of all sizes are allowed. There are no additional pet fees. Smoking and non-smoking rooms are available for pet rooms.
Holiday Inn Suffern #3 Executive Blvd Suffern NY   845-357-4800 (877-270-6405)
A dog up to 50 pounds is allowed for an additional one time pet fee of $50.
Wellesley Inn Suffern 17 North Airmont Road Suffern NY   845-368-1900 (800-531-5900)
Dogs of all sizes are allowed. There is a $10 one time additional pet fee per room. Dogs may only be left alone in the room if they will be quiet and well behaved. Dogs must be leashed and cleaned up after.
Residence Inn by Marriott 5 Barker Avenue White Plains NY   914-761-7700
Dogs of all sizes are allowed. There is a $75 one time fee and a pet policy to sign at check in.
Summerfield Suites 101 Corporate Park Drive White Plains NY   914-251-9700
Dogs of all sizes are allowed. There is a $150 one time fee per room and a pet policy to sign at check in.

Attractions

The De Wint House, George Washington Historical Site 20 Livingston Street Tappan NY   845-359-1359
http://www.dewinthouse.com/
Rich in colonial and cultural history, the De Wint house sits on 6 landscaped acres and host various events throughout the year. This was once President Washington's temporary headquarters, and it is also considered an historic Masonic site. Dogs are welcome to explore the area, but they may not be in any of the park buildings. Dogs must be under owner's control, leashed, and cleaned up after at all times.

Stores

Petco Pet Store 324 North Central Avenue South Hartsdale NY   914-421-0900
Your licensed and well-behaved leashed dog is allowed in the store.
Petco Pet Store 500 East Sandford Blvd, Ste 570 Mount Vernon NY   914-699-3270
Your licensed and well-behaved leashed dog is allowed in the store.
PetSmart Pet Store 155 E Route 59 Nanuet NY 845-620-1301
Your licensed and well-behaved leashed dog is allowed in the store.
Petco Pet Store 164 Rockland Plaza Nanuet NY 845-624-5741
Your licensed and well-behaved leashed dog is allowed in the store.
Petco Pet Store 2350 Central Park Avenue Yonkers NY 914-961-8287
Your licensed and well-behaved leashed dog is allowed in the store.

Parks

Bear Mountain State Park 7 Lakes Drive Bear Mountain NY 845-786-2701
Dogs of all sizes are allowed at no additional fee. Dogs must be on no more than a 6 foot leash and be cleaned up after. Dogs are not allowed in the zoo, in any of the buildings, or at the picnic areas. The park is open from dawn to dusk year-round.

Off-Leash Dog Parks

Elmsford Dog Park North Everts at Winthrop Avenue Elmsford NY
This 5000 square foot fenced dog-park has two separate areas for small dogs and larger dogs. The surface is grass and dirt. Violent dogs are not allowed and dogs must have their vaccinations.
Kakiat Park Dog Park 668 Haverstraw Road Montebello NY 845-364-2670
The fenced, off-leash dog park area is located near the parking lot. In addition to the dog park area, there is significant hiking in the 370 acre park. The trails from the park also lead into the Harriman State Park. There is a log cabin from 1922 and a footbridge across the Mahwah River.
Ward Acres Park Broadfield Rd at Quaker Ridge Road New Rochelle NY
http://www.animal-link.org/parks.shtml
This non-fenced 62 acre park was formerly the estate of the Ward Family. Effective April, 2007 dogs will be allowed off-leash in the mornings until 10 am daily. From November 15 to March 31 dogs may also run

unleashed from 4 pm on on weekdays. During the rest of the year dogs can run unleashed starting again at 5 pm. Dogs may not run off-leash in the afternoons or evenings on weekends and holidays. In order to use the park a permit must be purchased. The cost of the permit is $50 for city residents and $250 for others. Dogs will need to have proof of rabies vaccinations. The park is maintained by the Friends of Ward Acres Park.

Cedar Lane Dog Park 235 Cedar Lane Ossining NY   914-941-3189
http://www.ossiningdogpark.com/
This free, fenced dog park has lights for night use and is open 24 hours. It was the first fenced off-leash park in Westchester County when it opened in 2003. The park has benches and tables and there is parking available. The There are various toys around for the dogs. The dog park is maintained by the Friends of Ossining Dog Park.

White Plains Bark Park Brockway Place at South Kensico Road White Plains NY   914-422-1336
This 14,000 square foot fenced dog park has two areas; one for large dogs and one for small dogs. Its surface is gravel.

Outdoor Restaurants

Lanterna Tuscan Bistro 3 S Broadway Nyack NY   845-353-8361
http://www.lanternausa.com/
This Italian bistro offers a couple of small sidewalk tables out front when the weather permits where guests may sit with their dog. Dogs are allowed at the outer tables only, and they must be under owner's control at all times, well behaved, leashed and cleaned up after.

Horsefeathers 94 N Broadway/H 9 Tarrytown NY   914-631-6606
http://www.horsefeatherstarrytown.com/
Known for their tasty and large menu, this lunch and dinner diner also provides brews, wines, and outside dining. Dogs are allowed at the outside tables; they must be leashed and under owner's control/care at all times.

Niagara Falls

Accommodations

Chateau Motor Lodge 1810 Grand Island Blvd Grand Island NY   716-773-2868
There is an $9 per day pet fee.

Holiday Inn 100 Whitehaven Rd Grand Island NY   716-773-1111 (877-270-6405)
Dogs of all sizes are allowed for an additional one time fee of $25 per room.

Comfort Inn 551 S Transit Road Lockport NY   716-434-4411 (877-424-6423)
Dogs up to 50 pounds are allowed for an additional fee of $10 per night per pet.

Holiday Inn Lockport 515 South Transit Rd Lockport NY   716-434-6151 (877-270-6405)
Dogs of all sizes are allowed for an additional pet fee of $10 per night per room, and there is a pet agreement to sign at check in.

Best Western Summit Inn 9500 Niagara Falls Boulevard Niagara Falls NY   716-297-5050 (800-780-7234)
Dogs are allowed for an additional fee of $8 per night per pet.

Howard Johnson Hotel 454 Main St. Niagara Falls NY   716-285-5261 (800-446-4656)
Dogs of all sizes are welcome. There is a $10 per day pet fee. Dogs are allowed in all rooms.

Quality Hotel and Suites 240 Rainbow Blvd Niagara Falls NY   716-282-1212
Dogs are allowed for an additional fee of $20 per night per pet.

Campgrounds and RV Parks

KOA Niagara Falls 2570 Grand Island Blvd Grand Island NY   716-773-7583 (800-562-0787)
http://www.koaniagarafalls.com
Dogs of all sizes are allowed. There are no additional pet fees. Dogs must be friendly, well behaved, leashed, and cleaned up after. This RV park is closed during the off-season. The camping and tent areas also allow dogs. There is a dog walk area at the campground.

KOA Niagara Falls N/Lewiston 1250 Pletcher Road Youngstown NY   716-754-8013 (800-562-8715)
http://www.niagarafallsnorthkoa.com/
Dogs of all sizes are allowed. There are no additional pet fees. Dogs may not be left unattended, and must be leashed and cleaned up after. There are some breed restrictions. This RV park is closed during the off-season. The camping and tent areas also allow dogs. There is a dog walk area at the campground. Dogs are allowed in the camping cabins.

Attractions

Lockport Cave & Underground Boat Ride 2 Pine Street Lockport NY   716-438-0174
http://www.lockportcave.com/

In addition to exploring artifacts and construction of the historic Erie Canal Locks 67-71, walking through tunnels blasted out of solid rock, and learning the history of this early industrial age, you also get to be awestruck by a unique boat ride on America's longest underground river ride. This is a seasonal attraction and takes about 70 minutes. Your well behaved pooch is welcome to come along on this journey for no additional fee. They must not be too nervous about being underground and on a boat, and they must be under owner's control, leashed, and cleaned up after at all times.

Niagara Falls State Park

TOP 200 PLACE Niagara Falls State Park Robert Moses Parkway Niagara Falls NY 716-278-1796
This park surrounds Niagara Falls and is the oldest state park in the United States. It offers beautiful views of the falls and you can expect to get wet with some of the mist from the water if you walk up to the railings at the falls. Dogs on a six foot or less leash are allowed on the hiking and walking trails, but are not allowed on the trolley, inside buildings or on the attractions like the boat rides. Pets must be cleaned up after. From the park you can walk along the water and view Niagara Falls and the gorge. There are miles of trails at the park and some have steep stairs and rocks to climb over. Remember to stay away from the river as it has very strong currents. If all the hiking makes you work up an appetite, the park service has several outdoor snack stands in the park. Stop at the visitor's center for trail details. The center is open daily from 8am to 10pm in the Summer and daily from 8am to 6pm in the Winter and closed Christmas and New Years Day. The park is open year-round. To get there, take the Robert Moses Parkway into Niagara Falls.
Old Fort Niagara Robert Moses Parkway North Youngstown NY 716-745-7611
http://www.oldfortniagara.org
Dogs on leash are allowed in this historical fort about 10 miles north of Niagara Falls. This is a great place for a picnic.

Parks
Earl W. Bydges Artpark 450 S 4th Street Louiston NY 716-754-9000
http://www.artpark.net
This park was created for the the education, entertainment, and interative enjoyment of the arts. Dogs are allowed on leash, and they must be cleaned up after.

Outdoor Restaurants
Papa Leo's Pizzeria 2265 Niagara Falls Blvd. Niagara Falls NY 716-731-5911
http://www.papaleos.com/
This restaurant serves pizza, subs, sandwiches, tacos, and salads. They have a couple of picnic tables outside.

Well-behaved leashed dogs are allowed at the outdoor tables. The restaurant is located at 6 Corners by Bell Aerospace.

Ogdensburg

Accommodations
Quality Inn 6765 H 37 Ogdensburg NY   315-393-4550 (877-424-6423)
Dogs are allowed for an additional fee of $10 per night per pet.

Orangeburg

Accommodations
Holiday Inn Orangeburg-Rockland/Bergen Co 329 Route 303 Orangeburg NY   845-359-7000 (877-270-6405)
Dogs up to 70 pounds are allowed for no additional fee.

Oswego

Outdoor Restaurants
Rudy's Lakeside Washington Blvd Oswego NY   315-343-2671
http://www.rudyshot.com/
Located on the shores of Lake Ontario, this seasonal, family owned restaurant is the place for Fish & Chips, and they have their own specialty Texas Hot Sauce too. Dogs are welcome at the outer tables. Dogs must be well behaved, under owner's control, leashed, and cleaned up after at all times.

Oxford

Campgrounds and RV Parks
Bowman Lake State Park 745 Bilven Sherman Road Oxford NY   607-334-2718
Dogs of all sizes are allowed. There are no additional pet fees. Dogs may not be left unattended and they must have a current rabies certificate and shot record. Dogs must be quiet, well behaved, on no more than a 6 foot leash, and be cleaned up after. Dogs are allowed on the trails, but not on the beach or in any of the buildings. The camping and tent areas also allow dogs. There is a dog walk area at the campground. There are no electric or water hookups at the campground.

Painted Post

Accommodations
Best Western Lodge on the Green 3171 Canada Rd Painted Post NY   607-962-2456 (800-780-7234)
Dogs are allowed for no additional pet fee.

Pine City

Accommodations
Rufus Tanner House 60 Sagetown Road Pine City NY   607-732-0213 (800-360-9259)
http://www.rufustanner.com/
Built in 1864 in Greek revival style and renovated for privacy and relaxation, this 2.5 acre farmhouse features a

garden hideaway, large porches and decks, an outdoor hot tub, and is only minutes from several other activities, eateries, and plenty of recreation. Dogs of all sizes are allowed for no additional pet fees. Dogs must be leashed, cleaned up after, and crated when left alone in the room.

Pulaski

Campgrounds and RV Parks

Brennan Beach RV Resort 80 Brennan's Beach Road Pulaski NY   315-298-2242
http://www.brennanbeach.com
Dogs of all sizes are allowed. There are no additional pet fees. Dogs must be leased and cleaned up after. The camping and tent areas also allow dogs. There is a dog walk area at the campground.
Selkirk Sores State Park 7101 H 3 Pulaski NY   315-298-5737
http://www.nysparks.state.ny.us
Dogs of all sizes are allowed. There are no additional pet fees. Dogs may not be left unattended, and they must have a current rabies certificate and shot record, be on no more than a 6 foot leash, and be cleaned up after. Dogs are allowed on the trails and at the beach. This campground is closed during the off-season. The camping and tent areas also allow dogs. There is a dog walk area at the campground. Dogs are allowed in the camping cabins. There are no water hookups at the campground.

Randolph

Campgrounds and RV Parks

Pope Haven Campgrounds 11948 Pope Road Randolph NY   716-358-4900
http://www.popehaven.com
Dogs of all sizes are allowed. There are no additional pet fees. Dogs must have proof of rabies shots, and be leashed and cleaned up after. They must also be quiet and well behaved. The camping and tent areas also allow dogs. There is a dog walk area at the campground.

Rochester

Accommodations

Red Roof Inn - Rochester Henrietta 4820 West Henrietta Road Henrietta NY   585-359-1100 (800-RED-ROOF)
One well-behaved family pet per room. Guest must notify front desk upon arrival. Guest is liable for any damages. In consideration of all guests, pets must never be left unattended in the guest rooms.
Clarion Hotel Riverside 120 Main Street E Rochester NY   585-546-6400 (877-424-6423)
Dogs are allowed for a $50 refundable pet deposit.
Comfort Inn West 1501 W Ridge Road Rochester NY   585-621-5700 (877-424-6423)
Dogs are allowed for an additional pet fee of $10 per night per room.
Comfort Suites 2085 Hylan Drive Rochester NY   585-334-6620 (877-424-6423)
Dogs up to 50 pounds are allowed for an additional one time pet fee of $75 per room.
Hampton Inn 500 Center Place Drive Rochester NY   585-663-6070
Dogs of all sizes are allowed, however there can only be 1 large or 2 medium/small pets per room. There is a pet policy to sign at check in, and there are no addtional pet fees.
Holiday Inn Express 2200 Goodman St N Rochester NY   585-342-0430 (877-270-6405)
Dogs of all sizes are allowed for an additional one time pet fee of $75 per room
Residence Inn by Marriott 1300 Jefferson Road Rochester NY   585-272-8850
Dogs of all sizes are allowed. There is a $75 one time fee and a pet policy to sign at check in.
Residence Inn by Marriott 500 Paddy Creek Circle Rochester NY   585-865-2090
Dogs of all sizes are welcome. There is a $75 one time fee and a pet policy to sign at check in.

Campgrounds and RV Parks

Genesee Country Campgrounds 40 Flinthill Road Caledonia NY   585-538-4200
http://www.geneseecountrycampgrounds.com
Dogs of all sizes are allowed. There are no additional pet fees. Dogs must be leashed and cleaned up after. The

camping and tent areas also allow dogs. There is a dog walk area at the campground. Dogs are allowed in the camping cabins.

Attractions
VRA Imperial Limousine, Inc.   Rochester NY   800-303-6100
http://www.implimo.com/
Servicing the Rochester and Finger Lakes area, this limousine service has a variety of vehicles available for just about any occasion. This is a great way to do wine tasting in the region without having to be concerned about driving. They will transport a dog for no additional fee. Owners must bring a cover for the seat and a doggy seat belt. Dogs must be under owner's control/care at all times. Dogs are not allowed on tours.

Stores
PetSmart Pet Store 3042 West Ridge Rd Greece NY 585-227-6700
Your licensed and well-behaved leashed dog is allowed in the store.
Petco Pet Store 2373 Ridge Rd West Greece NY   585-227-2180
Your licensed and well-behaved leashed dog is allowed in the store.
Petco Pet Store 300 Hylan Drive Henrietta NY 585-273-0150
Your licensed and well-behaved leashed dog is allowed in the store.
Petco Pet Store 2255 East Ridge Rd Irondequoit NY 585-467-0310
Your licensed and well-behaved leashed dog is allowed in the store.
PetSmart Pet Store 420 Jefferson Rd Rochester NY 585-427-7160
Your licensed and well-behaved leashed dog is allowed in the store.
Petco Pet Store 3200 Monroe Avenue Rochester NY 585-385-6850
Your licensed and well-behaved leashed dog is allowed in the store.
PetSmart Pet Store 917 Holt Rd Webster NY 585-872-0850
Your licensed and well-behaved leashed dog is allowed in the store.

Outdoor Restaurants
Open Face 651 South Avenue Rochester NY 585-232-3050
This restaurant serves American food. Dogs are allowed at the outdoor tables.

Rome

Campgrounds and RV Parks
Delta Lake State Park 8797 H 46 Rome NY   315-337-04670 (800-456-CAMP (2267))
Located on a fairly flat peninsula on the Delta Reservoir, this scenic park offers hiking and nature trails, and a variety of year-round activities and recreation. Dogs are allowed (for no fee) throughout the park and on the trails except not in swim areas. Dogs may not be left alone at any time, they must be crated or on no more than a 6 foot leash, and be cleaned up after at all times. Currant proof of rabies inoculation is required. The camp area offers about 100 sites, many on the lake front, and there is a picnic table and fire ring at each site with restrooms, showers, and recreation areas nearby. There is also a dump station and boat launch. This RV park is closed during the off-season. The camping and tent areas also allow dogs. There is a dog walk area at the campground. There are no electric or water hookups at the campgrounds.
Verona Beach State Park 6541 Lakeshore Road S Verona Beach NY   315-762-4463 (800-456-2267)
Open for year-round activities and recreation, this lake-shore park is also home to one of the most diverse aquatic habitats in the region with a great nature walk through the "Woods and Wetlands" trail. Dogs are allowed (for no fee) throughout the park and on the trails except not in swim areas or in park buildings. Dogs may not be left alone at any time, they must be on no more than a 6 foot leash, and be cleaned up after at all times. Currant proof of rabies inoculation is required. There is a 1000 acre area across from the park where dogs may be off lead if they are under very good voice control and will not chase other wildlife. The shaded camp area offers 45 sites with a view of the lake, picnic areas, restrooms, showers, a playground, recreation room, and a concession stand. This RV park is closed during the off-season. The camping and tent areas also allow dogs. There is a dog walk area at the campground. There are no electric or water hookups at the campgrounds.

Attractions
TOP 200 PLACE Erie Canal Village 5789 New London Road /H 46 & 49 Rome NY   315-337-3999
http://www.eriecanalvillage.net/
This reconstructed 19th century settlement is an outdoor living history museum on the site where the building of the canal began, and there are 3 museums; The Erie Canal Museum, The Harden Museum, and the Museum of

Cheese in addition to several other typical structures of the era. Well behaved dogs are allowed to explore the grounds, but they are not allowed in the buildings. Dogs must be friendly toward other dogs and people, under owner's control, leashed, and cleaned up after at all times.
Fort Stanwix National Monument 112 E Park Street Rome NY 315-338-7730
http://www.nps.gov/fost
This historical fort, secured by a deep trench with only a drawbridge for access, is also a living museum of the peoples involved in achieving one of our country's most significant victories, offering a variety of educational and recreational activities for learning about America's Revolutionary history. Dogs are allowed throughout the park; they are not allowed in the visitor center or in most of the buildings. Dogs must be under owner's control, leashed, and cleaned up after at all times.

Parks
Delta Lake State Park 8797 H 46 Rome NY 315-337-04670 (800-456-CAMP (2267))
Located on a fairly flat peninsula on the Delta Reservoir, this scenic park offers hiking and nature trails, and a variety of year-round activities and recreation. Dogs are allowed (for no fee) throughout the park and on the trails except not in swim areas. Dogs may not be left alone at any time, they must be crated or on no more than a 6 foot leash, and be cleaned up after at all times. Currant proof of rabies inoculation is required.
Verona Beach State Park 6541 Lakeshore Road S Verona Beach NY 315-762-4463 (800-456-2267)
Open for year-round activities and recreation, this lake-shore park is also home to one of the most diverse aquatic habitats in the region with a great nature walk through the "Woods and Wetlands" trail. Dogs are allowed (for no fee) throughout the park and on the trails except not in swim areas or in park buildings. Dogs may not be left alone at any time, they must be on no more than a 6 foot leash, and be cleaned up after at all times. Currant proof of rabies inoculation is required. There is a 1000 acre area across from the park where dogs may be off lead if they are under very good voice control and will not chase other wildlife.

Off-Leash Dog Parks
Bark Park 500 Chestnut Street Rome NY 315-339-7656
There is a two acre fenced dog park that opened in 2006. The park also features an agility course. In order to use the dog park, owners must fill out an application for each dog. To get a permit to use the dog park the dog is required to have a rabies shot and an DHLPPV vaccine. There is a $25 fee for the first year and a $15 renewal fee annually.

Salamanca

Accommodations
Holiday Inn Express Hotel and Suites 779 Broad Street Salamanca NY 716-945-7600 (877-270-6405)
Dogs up to 50 pounds are allowed for an additional one time pet fee of $25 per room. There can be 1 medium/large dog or 2 small dogs per room.

Campgrounds and RV Parks
Allegany State Park 2373 ASP, Route 1, Suite 3 Salamanca NY 716-354-9121 (800-456-2267)
The state's largest park, it is a popular year-round recreational destination with more than 65,000 acres of forests, over 70 miles of hiking trails, a nature trail, scenic drives with roadside wildlife viewing, and a museum/visitor center. Dogs must have proof of rabies inoculation and there are no additional pet fees. Dogs must be crated or leashed (6 foot) and cleaned up after. They are not allowed in buildings, cabins, bathing areas, or cross country ski areas. Dogs are allowed throughout the rest of the park and on the trails. The campground area has a camp store, playground, pool, showers, restrooms, laundry, playing fields, boat launch, a dump station, and more. This RV park is closed during the off-season. The camping and tent areas also allow dogs. There is a dog walk area at the campground. There are no water hookups at the campgrounds.

Parks
Allegany State Park 2373 ASP, Route 1, Suite 3 Salamanca NY 716-354-9121 (800-456-2267)
The state's largest park, it is a popular year-round recreational destination with more than 65,000 acres of forests, over 70 miles of hiking trails, a nature trail, scenic drives with roadside wildlife viewing, and a museum/visitor center. Dogs must have proof of rabies inoculation and there are no additional pet fees. Dogs must be crated or leashed (6 foot) and cleaned up after. They are not allowed in buildings, cabins, bathing areas, or cross country ski areas. Dogs are allowed throughout the rest of the park and on the trails.

Saratoga

Accommodations
Best Western Park Inn 3291 S Broadway Saratoga Springs NY   518-584-2350 (800-780-7234)
Dogs under 50 pounds are allowed for an additional fee of $15 per night per pet; the fee is $20 for dogs over 50 pounds.
Holiday Inn 232 Broadway Rt 9 Saratoga Springs NY   518-584-4550 (877-270-6405)
Dogs of all sizes are allowed for no additional fee. A contact number must be left with the front desk if a pet is left alone in the room.
Super 8 Saratoga Springs 17 Old Gick Rd Saratoga Springs NY   518-587-6244 (800-800-8000)
Dogs of all sizes are allowed. There are no additional pet fees. Smoking and non-smoking rooms are available for pet rooms.
Union Gables 55 Union Avenue Saratoga Springs NY   518-584-1558 (800-398-1558)
http://www.uniongables.com/
This stately Queen Anne-style 100 year old plus residence complete with a large lawn area and big verandas, sits central to several attractions, recreation, eateries and shops. Dogs of all sizes are allowed for a $25 one time additional pet fee per room. Dogs must be quiet, well behaved, leashed, and cleaned up after.

Campgrounds and RV Parks
Lake George Resort 427 Fortsville Road Gansevoort NY   518-792-3519 (800-340-6867)
Dogs of all sizes are allowed. There are no additional pet fees. Proof of up to date shots and insurance papers for some breeds is required. Dogs must be leashed and cleaned up after. The camping and tent areas also allow dogs. There is a dog walk area at the campground.
Sarasota Springs Resort 265 Brigham Road Greenfield Center NY   518-893-0537
Dogs of all sizes are allowed. There are no additional pet fees. Dogs must have proof of shots, be leashed, and cleaned up after. The camping and tent areas also allow dogs. There is a dog walk area at the campground.
Whispering Pines Campsites and RV Park 550 Sand Hill Road Greenfield Center NY   518-893-0416
This full service family camping resort sits on 75 acres with towering pines, 2 stream-fed ponds and a trout brook, an in-ground pool, store, playgrounds, rec hall and game room/courts, laundry, hot showers, hi-speed internet access, and a full activity calendar. Dogs of all sizes are allowed for $1 per pet and proof of rabies inoculation. Dogs must be well mannered, leashed, and cleaned up after at all times. Dogs are not allowed in swim areas or in park buildings. This RV park is closed during the off-season. The camping and tent areas also allow dogs. There is a dog walk area at the campground.

Attractions
Bliss Glad Farm 129 Hop City Road Ballston Spa NY   518-885-9314
There is a half acre of flowers growing here offering whiffs of fragrance throughout the area, and although they specialize in gladiolus bulbs there is also seasonal produce, and cut and potted flowers. The farm stand is open from July through September. Friendly dogs are welcome to explore the property with their owners, but they are not allowed in the buildings. Dogs must be crated or leashed, and cleaned up after at all times.
Point Breeze Marina 1459 H 9P Saratoga Springs NY   518-587-3397
This company provides a large selection of watercraft rentals for exploring the Saratoga Lake. Well mannered dogs are welcome for no additional fee. Dogs must be under owner's control/care at all times, and be crated or leashed.
Saratoga Boatworks 549 Union Avenue Saratoga Springs NY   518-584-2628
This company offers boat rentals in addition to other watercraft services. Well behaved dogs are welcome on the rentals for no additional fee. Dogs must be under owner's control/care at all times, and they must be leashed or crated.
Saratoga Horse and Carriage P. O. Box 5184 Saratoga Springs NY   518-584-8820
http://www.saratogahorseandcarriage.com/
Beautifully restored Victorian carriages drawn by regal black Percheron horses will take you on a number of tours or they are available for special occasions. Public rides begin in front of the Wine Bar on Broadway. Your well behaved dog is welcome to join in on the ride for no additional fee; they must be horse and people friendly. Dogs must be well behaved, under owner's control, and leashed and cleaned up after at all times
TOP 200 PLACE **Yaddo Gardens** H 9P/P. O. Box 395 Saratoga Springs NY   518-584-0746
http://www.yaddo.org
A gift of love, the gardens here are breathtaking as you wind by pools with fountains, statuary, a castle, wide sweeping lawns, tree lined paths bordered by lush greenery, and a rose and rock garden. Only the gardens are open to the public; the rest of the estate is private. Dogs are welcome for no fee. Dogs must be friendly, leashed, and cleaned up after at all times.

Saratoga Apple, Inc. 1174 H 29 Schuylerville NY   518-695-3131
Pick your apples here in season or just enjoy the market off season. In September and October there is live music and activities on the weekends. Dogs are welcome to accompany their owners for apple picking and for exploring the areas; they are not allowed in the market or other buildings. Dogs must be under owner's control, leashed, and cleaned up after at all times.

Stores
Paw Lickers Bakery and Boutique 2528 H 9 Greenfield Center NY   518-893-2112
http://www.pawlickers.com/
This pet bakery and boutique all started with a cookie; and the rest is history. Dogs are welcome to come in and sniff out their favorite treats, and for owners to find those hard-to-find or unique items. Dogs must be well behaved and under owner's control/care at all times.
Benson's Pet Shop 3073 H 50 Saratoga Springs NY   518-584-7777
http://www.bensonspet.com
In addition to offering a full line of supplies for all pets, this store also carries a good selection of high quality dog foods. Well behaved, leashed dogs are welcome in the store.
PetSmart Pet Store 3033 Route 50 Saratoga Springs NY   518-580-9374
Your licensed and well-behaved leashed dog is allowed in the store.
Sloppy Kisses 493 Broadway/H 50 Saratoga Springs NY   518-587-2207
http://www.sloppykissesofsaratoga.com/
This pet bakery and boutique offers a wide variety of specialty and healthy items for pets. Dogs are welcome to come in and sniff out their favorite treats or a fun outfit. Dogs must be well behaved and under owner's control/care at all times.

Parks
Congress Park Broadway and Congress Saratoga Springs NY   518-587-3550
This beautiful city park has natural mineral water springs, large grassy lawns, flowers throughout, ponds, and historic statues. Well behaved dogs are welcome here. They must be on leash and cleaned up after at all times.
Sarasota Springs State Park 19 Roosevelt Drive Saratoga Springs NY   518-584-2535
http://www.saratogaspastatepark.org/
In addition to eateries, theater, mineral baths, automobile and dance museums, golf courses, picnic areas with comfort stations, and more, this year-round recreation and entertainment destination offers a wide variety of year-round, multi-use trails. Well behaved dogs on leash are allowed for no additional fee, and they must have current proof of rabies inoculation. Dogs must be under owner's control at all times and be cleaned up after. Dogs are allowed throughout the park and on the trails; they are not allowed in any of the buildings, food, or swim areas.
Saratoga National Historical Park 648 H 32 Stillwater NY   518-664-9821
http://www.nps.gov/sara
Home to a crucial American Victory, there are 3 main historical sites at this 3400 acre scenic park; 1st and largest being the battlefield, 2nd is the Schuyler House, and 3rd is the Saratoga Monument. Dogs are welcome for no additional fees. Dogs must be attended to, leashed, and cleaned up after at all times. Dogs are allowed throughout the park and on the trails; they are not allowed in any of the buildings.

Off-Leash Dog Parks
Kelly Park Dog Run Ralph Street Ballston Spa NY   518-885-9220
There is a fenced dog run in Kelly Park. Kelly Park is located where Ralph Street intersects with Malta Avenue (Route 63).

Outdoor Restaurants
Sperry's Restaurant 30 1/2 Caroline Street Saratoga Springs NY   518-584-9618
http://www.saratoga.org/sperrys/
Best known for their grilled seafood, steaks, eclectic cuisine, and their 30's style art deco atmosphere, they also offer indoor or outdoor patio dining options. Your well behaved dog is welcome at the outdoor tables; however they request that guests with pets come during non-busy hours. Dogs must be well behaved, under owner's control, and leashed and cleaned up after at all times.

Events
The Inn at Saratoga Dog Days of Summer 231 Broadway Saratoga Springs NY   518-583-1890
Every Thursday throughout the summers, this restaurant hosts a canine and human "Yappy Hour" from 5 pm - 8 pm. There will be cocktails, human food and a special canine menu.

Schenectady

Accommodations

Days Inn Albany/Schenectady 167 Nott Terrace Schenectady NY 518-370-3297 (800-329-7466)
Dogs of all sizes are allowed. There is a $10 per night pet fee per pet.
Super 8 Schenectady/Albany Area 3083 Carman Rd Schenectady NY 518-355-2190 (800-800-8000)
Dogs of all sizes are allowed. There is a $10 per night pet fee per pet. Reservations are recommended due to limited rooms for pets. Smoking and non-smoking rooms are available for pet rooms.

Stores

PetSmart Pet Store 406 Balltown Rd Schenectady NY 518-372-0300
Your licensed and well-behaved leashed dog is allowed in the store.

Schoharie

Accommodations

Holiday Inn Express Hotel and Suites 160 Holiday Way Schoharie NY 518-295-6088 (877-270-6405)
One dog of any size is allowed for an additional pet fee of $17 per night per room.

Sidney

Accommodations

Super 8 Sidney 4 Mang Drive Sidney NY 607-563-8880 (800-800-8000)
Dogs of all sizes are allowed. There is a $10 per night pet fee per pet. Smoking and non-smoking rooms are available for pet rooms.

Sodus Point

Campgrounds and RV Parks

South Shore RV Park 7867 Lake Road Sodus Point NY 315-483-8679
http://www.southshorervpark.com
Dogs of all sizes are allowed. There are no additional pet fees. Dogs must be quiet, leashed, and cleaned up after. Dogs must not be left unattended at any time, especially in the cabins. The camping and tent areas also allow dogs. There is a dog walk area at the campground. Dogs are allowed in the camping cabins.

Stow

Campgrounds and RV Parks

Camp Chautauqua Camping Resort 3900 Westlake Road Stow NY 716-789-3435
http://www.campchautauqua.com
Dogs of all sizes are allowed. There are no additional pet fees. Shot records must be up to date, and dogs must be kept under owner's control and be quiet during the night. The camping and tent areas also allow dogs. There is a dog walk area at the campground.

Syracuse

Accommodations

Days Inn Auburn 37 William Street Auburn NY 315-252-7567 (800-329-7466)
Dogs of all sizes are allowed. There is a $5 per night pet fee per pet.
Super 8 Auburn/Finger Lakes Area 19 McMaster St Auburn NY 315-253-8886 (800-800-8000)
Dogs of all sizes are allowed. There is a $10 per night pet fee per pet. Smoking and non-smoking rooms are available for pet rooms.
Lincklaen House 79 Albany St Cazenovia NY 315-655-3461
http://www.cazenovia.com/lincklaen/
A landmark since 1836, this hotel was built as a luxurious stopover for colonial travelers. All rooms are non-smoking. There are no additional pet fees.
Holiday Inn 6555 Old Collamer Rd South East Syracuse NY 315-437-2761 (877-270-6405)
Two dogs up to 50 pounds, or 1 dog 50 pounds or over, are allowed per room for a one time pet fee of $25 per room.
Motel 6 - Syracuse 6577 Baptist Way East Syracuse NY 315-433-1300 (800-466-8356)
One well-behaved family pet per room. Guest must notify front desk upon arrival. Guest is liable for any damages. In consideration of all guests, pets must never be left unattended in the guest rooms.
BN on 7th North 400 7th North St Liverpool NY 315-451-1511
Dogs of all sizes are allowed. There is a $10 per night pet fee per pet.
Knights Inn 430 Electronics Pkwy Liverpool NY 315-453-6330 (800-843-5644)
There is a $8 per day pet charge.
Doubletree 6701 Buckley Road N Syracuse NY 315-457-4000 (800-572-1602)
Dogs up to 60 pounds are allowed. There are no additional pet fees.
Bird's Nest 1601 E Genesee St Skaneateles NY 315-685-5641
There is a $150.00 refundable pet deposit.
Skaneateles Suites 4114 W Genesee Street Skaneateles NY 315-685-7568
Dogs of all sizes are allowed. There is a $35 one time fee per pet and a pet policy to sign at check in.
Candlewood Suites 6550 Baptist Way Syracuse NY 315-432-1684 (877-270-6405)
Dogs of all sizes are allowed for an additional one time fee of $25 per pet.
Candlewood Suites 5414 South Bay Road Syracuse NY 315-454-8999 (877-270-6405)
Dogs up to 75 pounds are allowed for an additional one time pet fee of $25 per room.
Comfort Inn 6491 Thompson Road Syracuse NY 315-437-0222 (877-424-6423)
Dogs up to 50 pounds are allowed for an additional one time pet fee of $30 per room.
Comfort Inn Fairgrounds 7010 Interstate Island Road Syracuse NY 315-453-0045 (877-424-6423)
Dogs are allowed for an additional one time pet fee of $20 per room.
Holiday Inn 100 Farrell Rd Syracuse NY 315-457-8700 (877-270-6405)
Dogs of all sizes are allowed for an additional one time pet fee of $25 per room.
Red Roof Inn - Syracuse 6614 North Thompson Road Syracuse NY 315-437-3309 (800-RED-ROOF)
One well-behaved family pet per room. Guest must notify front desk upon arrival. Guest is liable for any damages. In consideration of all guests, pets must never be left unattended in the guest rooms.
Residence Inn by Marriott 6420 Yorktown Circle Syracuse NY 315-432-4488
Dogs of all sizes are allowed. There is a $75 one time fee and a pet policy to sign at check in.
Sheraton Syracuse University Hotel & Conference Center 801 University Ave. Syracuse NY 315-475-3000 (888-625-5144)
Dogs up to 80 pounds are allowed. There are no additional pet fees. Dogs are not allowed to be left alone in the room.

Attractions

TOP 200 PLACE **Skaneateles Historical Walking Tour** The Creamery, 28 Hannum Street Skaneateles NY 315-685-1360
http://www.skaneateles.com/
This lakeside scenic town is home to several carefully restored buildings, some dating back to 1796, and a brochure of the walking tour can be obtained at the above listed address or at the Chamber of Commerce at 22 Jordon Street. Visitors are allowed to bring their dogs on this tour. Dogs must be under owner's control, leashed, and cleaned up after at all times.

Stores

Petco Pet Store 3150 Erie Blvd East, Ste 500 De Witt NY 315-449-0084
Your licensed and well-behaved leashed dog is allowed in the store.
PetSmart Pet Store 3865 State Route 31 Liverpool NY 315-652-1627
Your licensed and well-behaved leashed dog is allowed in the store.
Petco Pet Store 310 Northern Lights (Route 11) North Syracuse NY 315-454-3949
Your licensed and well-behaved leashed dog is allowed in the store.

The Sailboat Shop 1322 E Genesee Street/H 20 Skaneateles NY   315-685-7558
http://www.thesailboatshop.com/
This watercraft rental and sales company has boats they will allow your pooch to join you on. There is no additional pet fee as long as there is no additional cleaning needed. Dogs must be under owner's control/care, leashed (when not on board), and cleaned up after at all times.
PetSmart Pet Store 3401 Erie Blvd E Syracuse NY   315-446-6320
Your licensed and well-behaved leashed dog is allowed in the store.

Off-Leash Dog Parks
Jamesville Beach Park Off-Leash Area South Street at Coye Rd Jamesville NY
There is a fenced off-leash dog park in Jamesville Beach Park which accesses the Jamesville Reservoir. Proof of a current rabies vaccine may be required on site. Dogs on leash are allowed in the rest of the park except that they are not allowed in the beach areas during the Summer beach season. During the Winter dogs may use the beach areas on leash. There is a disc golf course in the park. Dogs must always be cleaned up after throughout the park. To get to the park from I-81 take Route 173 east to Jamesville, then head south on South Stree to the park.
Wegmans Good Dog Park Route 370 Liverpool NY
The first dog park in central New York state is located in Onondaga Lake Park. You should use the Cold Springs entrance to the park. The dog park is 40,000 square feet in size and has a separate area for small dogs. Proof of a current rabies vaccine may be required on site.

Outdoor Restaurants
Dinosaur Barbeque 246 W Willow Street Syracuse NY   315-476-4937
This barbecue eatery has stepped it up a notch with a full bar, seasonal outdoor dining, live music, and they also produce and market their own popular brand of specialty barbecue sauces. Dogs are welcome at the outer tables. Dogs must be well behaved, under owner's control, leashed, and cleaned up after at all times.
Pastabilities 311 S Franklin Street Syracuse NY   315-474-1153
http://www.pastabilities.com/
Specializing in pasta entrees, fresh salads, and artisan breads, this eatery features cafeteria style lunches, full service dining and bar in the evenings, and outdoor dining. Dogs are welcome at the outer tables. Dogs must be well behaved, under owner's control, leashed, and cleaned up after at all times.

Utica

Accommodations
Best Western Gateway Adirondack Inn 175 N Genesee St Utica NY   315-732-4121 (800-780-7234)
Dogs are allowed for an additional one time fee of $25 per pet.
Motel 6 - Utica 150 N Genesee Street Utica NY   315-797-8743 (800-466-8356)
One well-behaved family pet per room. Guest must notify front desk upon arrival. Guest is liable for any damages. In consideration of all guests, pets must never be left unattended in the guest rooms.
Red Roof Inn - Utica 20 Weaver Street Utica NY   315-724-7128 (800-RED-ROOF)
One well-behaved family pet per room. Guest must notify front desk upon arrival. Guest is liable for any damages. In consideration of all guests, pets must never be left unattended in the guest rooms.
Super 8 Utica 309 N Genesee St Utica NY   315-797-0964 (800-800-8000)
Dogs of all sizes are allowed. There is a $5 per night pet fee per pet. Smoking and non-smoking rooms are available for pet rooms.

Campgrounds and RV Parks
Turning Stone RV Park 5065 State H 365 Verona NY   315-361-7275
http://www.turningstone.com
Dogs of all sizes are allowed. There are no additional pet fees. Dogs must be leased and cleaned up after. If your dog will remain next to you and not chase other dogs or people, it can be off leash on your own site. There is a dog walk area at the campground.

Stores
PetSmart Pet Store 4731 Commercial Dr New Hartford NY   315-768-2335
Your licensed and well-behaved leashed dog is allowed in the store.

Warwick

Accommodations
MeadowLark Farm 180 Union Corners Road Warwick NY   845-651-4286
http://www.meadowlarkfarm.com/
Every season gets its full due at this scenic 1800's English style farm house and there is also a variety of local year-round activities and recreational opportunities available. Dogs of all sizes are allowed for an additional fee of $10 per night per pet, but they must be friendly towards other animals as well as humans as there are other pets that live on site. Dogs may not be left alone in the room, and they must be house trained, leashed, and cleaned up after.

Waterport

Campgrounds and RV Parks
Lakeside Beach State Park Lakeside, H 18 Waterport NY   585-682-4888
http://www.nysparks.state.ny.us/
Dogs of all sizes are allowed. There are no additional pet fees. Dogs may not be left unattended, they must have a current rabies certificate and shot records, be on no more than a 6 foot leash, and be cleaned up after. Dogs are allowed on the trails, but when in the campground they must stay in the camping loops that are designated for pets. This campground is closed during the off-season. The camping and tent areas also allow dogs. There are no water hookups at the campground.

Watertown

Accommodations
Best Western Carriage House Inn and Conf Cntr 300 Washington St Watertown NY   315-782-8000 (800-780-7234)
Dogs are allowed for an additional fee of $15 per night per pet.

Campgrounds and RV Parks
Black River Bay Campground 16129 Foster Park Road (Box541) Dexter NY   315-639-3735
http://www.blackriverbaycamp.com
Dogs of all sizes are allowed, however only 2 dogs are allowed per site or 3 dogs are ok if they are all small. There are no additional pet fees. Dogs must be leashed and cleaned up after. The camping and tent areas also allow dogs. There is a dog walk area at the campground.
KOA Natural Bridge/Watertown 6081 State H 3 Natural Bridge NY   315-644-4880 (800562-4780)
http://www.aticamping.com
Dogs of all sizes are allowed. There are no additional pet fees. Dogs must be leashed and cleaned up after. This RV park is closed during the off-season. The camping and tent areas also allow dogs. There is a dog walk area at the campground.
Long Point State Park-Thousand Islands 7495 State Park Road Three Mile Bay NY   315-649-5258 (800-456-CAMP (2267))
This peaceful park, located on a grassy, semi-wooded peninsula on Lake Ontario, provides a sheltered harbor for boats and a variety of land and water recreational activities. Dogs must have proof of rabies inoculation and there are no additional pet fees. Dogs must be crated or leashed (6 foot) and cleaned up after. They are not allowed in picnic areas. Dogs are allowed throughout the rest of the park and on trails. The camp area offers picnic tables, a children's playground, restrooms, and showers. This RV park is closed during the off-season. The camping and tent areas also allow dogs. There is a dog walk area at the campground.

Parks
Long Point State Park-Thousand Islands 7495 State Park Road Three Mile Bay NY   315-649-5258 (800-456-CAMP (2267))
This peaceful park, located on a grassy, semi-wooded peninsula on Lake Ontario, provides a sheltered harbor for boats and a variety of land and water recreational activities. Dogs must have proof of rabies inoculation and

there are no additional pet fees. Dogs must be crated or leashed (6 foot) and cleaned up after. They are not allowed in picnic areas. Dogs are allowed throughout the rest of the park and on trails.

Westfield

Campgrounds and RV Parks

KOA Westfield/Lake Erie 8001 H 5 Westfield NY   716-326-3573 (800-562-3973)
http://www.koa.com
Dogs of all sizes are allowed. There are no additional pet fees. Dogs may not be left unattended, and must be leashed and cleaned up after. This RV park is closed during the off-season. The camping and tent areas also allow dogs. There is a dog walk area at the campground. Dogs are allowed in the camping cabins.

Chapter 9

New Jersey
Dog Travel Guide

Atlantic City

Accommodations

TOP 200 PLACE Sheraton Atlantic City Convention Center Hotel Two Miss America Parkway Atlantic City NJ 609-344-3535 (888-625-5144)
Dogs up to 80 pounds are allowed at this resort hotel in Atlantic City. There are no additional pet fees. Dogs are not allowed to be left alone in the room.
Residence Inn by Marriott 900 Mays Landing Road Somers Point NJ 609-927-6400
Dogs of all sizes are allowed. There is a $75 one time fee and a pet policy to sign at check in.

Campgrounds and RV Parks

Shady Pines Camping Resort 443 S 6th Avenue Absecon Highlands NJ 609-652-1516
One dog of any size is allowed. There are no additional pet fees. Dogs must be leashed and cleaned up after. The camping and tent areas also allow dogs. There is a dog walk area at the campground.
Buena Vista Camping Park 775 Harding Highway Buena NJ 856-697-5555
http://www.bvcp.com
Dogs of all sizes are allowed, however some breeds are not. There are no additional pet fees. Dogs must be well behaved, quiet, leashed, and cleaned up after. The camping and tent areas also allow dogs. There is a dog walk area at the campground.
Holly Acres RV Park 218 S Frankfurt Avenue Egg Harbor NJ 609-965-3387 (888-2RV-CAMP)
Dogs of all sizes are allowed. There are no additional pet fees. Dogs may not be left unattended outside, and they must be quiet, well behaved, leashed and cleaned up after. There are some breed restrictions. This RV park is closed during the off-season. There is a dog walk area at the campground.
Whipporwill Campground 810 S Shore Road Marmora NJ 609-390-3458
http://www.campwhippoorwill.com
Dogs of all sizes are allowed. There are no additional pet fees. Dogs must be quiet and well behaved. They are allowed to be off lead on your site if they will stay regardless of what goes by. Dogs must otherwise be leashed and cleaned up after. The camping and tent areas also allow dogs. There is a dog walk area at the campground.
Winding River Campground 6752 Weymouth Road Mays Landing NJ 609-625-3191
http://www.windingrivercamping.com
Dogs of all sizes are allowed. There are no additional pet fees. Dogs must be quiet, leashed, cleaned up after, and have current shot records. The camping and tent areas also allow dogs. There is a dog walk area at the campground.
Yogi Bear's Jellystone Park 1079 12th Avenue Mays Landing NJ 609-476-2811 (800-355-0264)
http://www.atlanticcityjellystone.com
Dogs of all sizes are allowed. There are no additional pet fees. Dogs must have a valid rabies certificate, be well behaved, leashed, and cleaned up after. The camping and tent areas also allow dogs. There is a dog walk area at the campground.
Timberline Lake 345 H 679 New Gretna NJ 609-296-7900
http://www.timberlinelake.com
Well behaved dogs of all sizes are allowed. There are no additional pet fees. Dogs must be friendly, leashed, and cleaned up after. All dogs must have recent shot records. The camping and tent areas also allow dogs. There is a dog walk area at the campground.
Blueberry Hill RV Park 283 Clarks Landing Road/H624 Port Republic NJ 609-652-1644
http://www.blueberryhillrvpark.com/
This family shore-side RV park offers shaded or sunny, well-maintained groomed sites, various events throughout the year, gaming courts, modern restrooms, an ice cream and coffee shop, a store, laundry, and more. Dogs are allowed for no additional fee. Dogs must be well behaved, leashed, and cleaned up after. Dogs are not allowed at the playground. This RV park is closed during the off-season. The camping and tent areas also allow dogs. There is a dog walk area at the campground.

Attractions

The Civil Rights Garden Martin Luther King Blvd. Atlantic City NJ 609-347-0500
This is a public, sculpture garden of quiet, powerful symbolism. It is one of the largest civil rights memorials in the US and gives reflection to Freedom through the inscriptions, the 11 Africa, black granite columns, reflecting pool, gardens, and the bronze bell at its center that chimes throughout the day. Dogs are allowed throughout the park. Dogs must be under owner's control, leashed, and cleaned up after at all times.
Bay Cats 316 Bay Avenue Ocean City NJ 609-391-7960

http://www.baycats.com/
This watercraft rental company will allow your well behaved dog to come aboard rentals and cruise the bay.
There is no additional pet fee. They do suggest that dogs already be acclimated to water travel before cruising
the bay area. Dogs must be under owner's control, leashed, and cleaned up after at all times. Neither people nor
pets are allowed on the islands as they are nature sanctuaries.

Stores
PetSmart Pet Store 420 Consumer Square Mays Landing NJ   609-677-1620
Your licensed and well-behaved leashed dog is allowed in the store.

Parks
Historic Gardner's Basin 800 New Hampshire Avenue Atlantic City NJ   609-348-2880
http://oceanlifecenter.com/hours.html
This is an 8 acre sea-oriented park where visitors can view working fishermen, shop the local artists "cabins",
picnic, or just hike around with your pet. Dogs are allowed; they must be well mannered, under owner's control,
leashed, and cleaned up after at all times. Dogs are not allowed in the restaurants or in the aquarium.
Penn State Forest PO Box 118 New Gretna NJ 609-296-1114
Dogs on leash are allowed in the State Park. They are not allowed in the campground area. The park features
hiking, fishing, canoeing, and picnicking.
Corson's Inlet State Park Ocean Drive and Bay Avenue Ocean City NJ   609-861-2404
This 350 acre oceanfront park is home to a rich diversity of natural habitats and wildlife, exceptional scenery,
hiking trails, and it is also a popular area for saltwater fishing and crabbing. Dogs are allowed throughout the
park with the exception that they are not allowed on the beach from April 1st through to September 15th. Dogs
must be under owner's control, leashed, and cleaned up after at all times.
Edwin B. Forsythe National Wildlife Refuge 800 Great Creek Road Oceanville NJ   609-652-1665
http://www.fws.gov/northeast/forsythe/
This 46,000 acre refuge is open 7 days a week with a few exceptions for wildlife management, so they suggest
calling ahead or checking the website. There is excellent wildlife viewing at the Brigantine Division of the park
where there are also accessible facilities, the start of several walking trails, and an 8 mile auto tour. Dogs are
allowed for no additional fee. Dogs must be kept on a short lead, be under owner's control at all times, leashed,
and cleaned up after. Dogs are not allowed at the Holgate's dune area.

Off-Leash Dog Parks
Cape May County Dog Park 45th Street and Haven Avenue Ocean City NJ
http://www.oceancitydogpark.org/
This off lead area is by membership; yearly or weekly Summer passes are available. Paw Passes can be
obtained at the City Hall at 9th Street and Asbury Avenue or on-line. The park has 3 sections on about an acre,
with benches, a shaded pavilion, drinking fountains for hounds and humans, and agility equipment. Dogs must
be sociable, have proof of vaccinations, be licensed, and cleaned up after at all times. Dogs must be leashed
when not in designated off-lead areas.

Outdoor Restaurants
Bashful Banana Cafe and Bakery 944 Ocean City Boardwalk Ocean City NJ   609-398-9677
This restaurant serves gourmet sandwiches. Dogs are allowed at the outdoor tables.

Blairstown

Attractions
Double D Guest Ranch 81 Mount Hermon Road Blairstown NJ   908-459-9044
http://www.doubledguestranch.com/
This ranch offers a variety of riding experiences for all experience levels and they can also provide a venue for
your special events. They are host to their own events throughout the year as well. Dogs are welcome to come
along for the 1 hour rides and get a taste of the "old west". They must be under owner's control, leashed, and
cleaned up after at all times.

Camden Area

Accommodations

Howard Johnson Express Inn 832 North Black Horse Pike Blackwood NJ   856-228-4040 (800-446-4656)
Dogs of all sizes are welcome. There is a $10 per day pet fee.
Clarion Hotel and Conference Center H 70 and I 295 Cherry Hill NJ   856-428-2300 (877-424-6423)
Dogs up to 50 pounds are allowed for an additional one time fee of $50 per pet.
Holiday Inn Route 70 and Sayer Avenue Cherry Hill NJ   856-663-5300 (877-270-6405)
Dogs of all sizes are allowed for an additional $75 refundable pet deposit per room.
Residence Inn by Marriott 1821 Old Cuthbert Road Cherry Hill NJ   856-429-6111
Dogs of all sizes are allowed. There is a $75 one time fee and a pet policy to sign at check in.
Residence Inn by Marriott 1154 Hurffville Road Deptford NJ   856-686-9188
Dogs of all sizes are allowed. There is a $75 one time fee and a pet policy to sign at check in.
Motel 6 - Philadelphia - Mt Laurel 2798 Route 73 North Maple Shade NJ   856-235-3550 (800-466-8356)
One well-behaved family pet per room. Guest must notify front desk upon arrival. Guest is liable for any damages. In consideration of all guests, pets must never be left unattended in the guest rooms.
Best Western Burlington Inn 2020 Rt 541, RD 1 Mount Holly NJ   609-261-3800 (800-780-7234)
Dogs are allowed for an additional fee of $5 per night per pet.
Candlewood Suites 4000 Crawford Place Mount Laurel NJ   856-642-7567 (877-270-6405)
Dogs up to 80 pounds are allowed for an additional one time fee of $75 per pet.
Radisson Hotel Mount Laurel 915 Route 73 Mount Laurel NJ   856-234-7300
Dogs of all sizes are allowed. There is a $50 one time additional pet fee.
Red Roof Inn - Mt. Laurel 603 Fellowship Road Mount Laurel NJ   856-234-5589 (800-RED-ROOF)
One well-behaved family pet per room. Guest must notify front desk upon arrival. Guest is liable for any damages. In consideration of all guests, pets must never be left unattended in the guest rooms.
Staybridge Suites Philadelphia-Mt. Laurel 4115 Church Road Mount Laurel NJ   856-722-1900 (877-270-6405)
Dogs up to 60 pounds are allowed for an additional one time fee of $75 per pet. Dogs may not be left alone in the room.
TownePlace Suites Mt Laurel 450 Century Parkway Mount Laurel NJ   856-778-8221
Dogs of all sizes are allowed. There is a $75 one time pet fee per visit.

Campgrounds and RV Parks

Timberlane Campground 117 Timberlane Road Clarksboro NJ   856-423-6677
http://www.timberlanecampground.com
Dogs of all sizes are allowed. There are no additional pet fees. Dogs may not be left unattended, and they must be quiet, leashed, and cleaned up after. The camping and tent areas also allow dogs. There is a dog walk area at the campground.

Attractions

Amalthea Cellars 209 Vineyard Road Atco NJ   856-768-8585
http://www.amaltheacellars.com
Dogs on leash are allowed at the outdoor tables. There is plenty of shade to cool off on the premises.
Lewis W Barton Arboretum at Medford Leas One Medford Leas Way Medford NJ   609-654-3000
http://www.medfordleas.org/
This beautiful 168 acre site offers visitors recreational areas, landscaped grounds, patio and courtyard gardens, and areas of wildflowers and woods. Dogs are welcome to explore the grounds and trails. Dogs must be leashed and cleaned up after at all times.

Shopping Centers

Rancocas Woods Village of Shops 114 Creek Road Mount Laurel NJ   856-235-0758
http://www.rancocaswoods.net/index.html
This "old time" shopping center features a variety of quaint shops full of unique treasures, plus there are several special events, and antique and craft shows to enjoy throughout the year. Well behaved dogs are welcome around the property and on the paths. It is up to the individual stores whether they may go inside. Dogs must be under owner's control, leashed, and cleaned up after at all times.

Stores

PetSmart Pet Store 2135 Route 38 Ste B Cherry Hill NJ   856-910-1400
Your licensed and well-behaved leashed dog is allowed in the store.
Petco Pet Store 2230 Marlton Pike West Ste 3 Cherry Hill NJ   856-488-0643
Your licensed and well-behaved leashed dog is allowed in the store.
Petco Pet Store 2501 Route 130 South Cinnaminson NJ   856-303-0944

Your licensed and well-behaved leashed dog is allowed in the store.
PetSmart Pet Store 4004 Route 130 Delran NJ 856-461-0353
Your licensed and well-behaved leashed dog is allowed in the store.
Petco Pet Store 1730 Clements Bridge Rd Deptford NJ 856-384-9609
Your licensed and well-behaved leashed dog is allowed in the store.
PetSmart Pet Store 1331 Nixon Dr Moorestown NJ 856-439-9899
Your licensed and well-behaved leashed dog is allowed in the store.
PetSmart Pet Store 62 Centerton Rd Mount Laurel NJ 856-802-9949
Your licensed and well-behaved leashed dog is allowed in the store.
PetSmart Pet Store 215 Route 73 N West Berlin NJ 856-753-9130
Your licensed and well-behaved leashed dog is allowed in the store.
Petco Pet Store 4318 Route 130 North Willingboro NJ 609-877-9711
Your licensed and well-behaved leashed dog is allowed in the store.
PetSmart Pet Store 1800 Clements Bridge Rd 1 Woodbury NJ 856-853-0042
Your licensed and well-behaved leashed dog is allowed in the store.

Parks
Dr. Ulysses S. Wiggins Waterfront Park Between the Delaware River and Mickle Blvd Camden NJ 856-795-7275
This park was developed for recreational boating, but the beauty of the area also makes it a nice walking and relaxing area. Dogs are allowed throughout the park and on the walkways. Dogs must be leashed at all times on land and on the boats, and they must be cleaned up after at all times.

Off-Leash Dog Parks
Cooper River Dog Park North Park Drive at Cuthbert Blvd Cherry Hill NJ 856-795-PARK
This dog park has separate areas for large dogs and small dogs. The dog park has benches and lighting. To get to the park take the Cuthbert Blvd South Jughandle and turn onto North Park Drive. The dog park is at the east end of North Park Drive.
Pooch Park (Cooper River Park) North Park Drive Cherry Hill NJ 856-225-5431
http://www.camdencounty.com
The Pooch Park portion of the park allows dogs to be unleashed in the fenced in area. The dog park offers water and cleanup stations, tables, and lighting. Open 6am-10pm with no fee.
Freedom Park Dog Park Union Street at Main Street Medford NJ 609-654-2512
This dog park is located in Medford's Freedom Park. It has benches, water and shade trees.

Outdoor Restaurants
Olde World Bakery 1000 Smithville Road Mount Holly NJ 609-265-1270
This restaurant serves deli-type food. Dogs are allowed at the outdoor tables.
Robin's Nest Restaurant and the Crow Bar 2 Washington Street Mount Holly NJ 609-261-6149
http://www.robinsnestmountholly.com/
Specializing in creating unique, French American cuisine, they also offer a full-service bar and al fresco waterside dining. Dogs are allowed at the outer tables. Dogs must be under owner's control/care and leashed at all times.
Baja Fresh 1120 White Horse Road, Suite 138 Voorhees NJ 856-784-5955
This restaurant serves Mexican food. Dogs are allowed at the outdoor tables.

Day Kennels
PetsHotel by PetsMart Day Kennel 310 White Horse Pike North Lawnside NJ 856-310-5215
http://www.petsmart.com/PETsHOTEL/
This PetSmart pet store offers day care, day camp and overnight care. You may drop off and pick up your dog during the hours the store is open seven days a week. Dogs must have proof of current rabies, DPP and Bordatella vaccinations.

Cape May

Accommodations
Billmae Cottage 1015 Washington Street Cape May NJ 609-898-8558
http://www.billmae.com
Billmae Cottage offers 1 and 2 bedroom suites each with a living room, bath, and kitchen. They have occasional

"Yappie Hours" on the porch. Well behaved dogs of all sizes are welcome.

Marquis de Lafayette Hotel 501 Beach Avenue North Cape May NJ   609-884-3500 (800-257-0432)
http://www.marquiscapemay.com/
This beach front inn affords wonderful ocean views and breezes and the inn is central to a wide variety of recreational pursuits, shops, eateries, and nightlife. Dogs of all sizes are allowed for an additional fee of $20 per night per pet, plus a $100 cash deposit (credit card not applicable), refundable upon inspection of the room. Dogs must be leashed and cleaned up after.

Surf 16 Motel 1600 Surf Avenue North Wildwood NJ   609-522-1010
http://members.aol.com/surf16motl/
This motel near the beach is open during the Summer only. Dogs of all sizes are accepted. They are open from May 1st through mid-October. Dogs are allowed on the beach before May 15 and after September 15. The hotel has a fenced in dog run. There is a $10 per day pet charge.

The Highland House 131 N Broadway West Cape May NJ   609-898-1198
Dogs of all sizes are allowed. There are no additional pet fees.

Campgrounds and RV Parks

Pomona Campground Oak Drive Cape May NJ   609-965-2123
Dogs of all sizes are allowed. There are no additional pet fees. Dogs must be well behaved, quiet, leashed, and cleaned up after. The camping and tent areas also allow dogs. There is a dog walk area at the campground.

Seashore Campsites 720 Seashore Road Cape May NJ   609-884-4010
http://www.seashorecampsites.com
Dogs of all sizes are allowed. There are no additional pet fees. Dogs must be leashed, cleaned up after, and not left unattended. The camping and tent areas also allow dogs. There is a dog walk area at the campground.

Big Timber Lake Camping Resort 116 Swainton-Goshen Road Cape May Courthouse NJ   609-465-4456
http://www.bigtimberlake.com
Dogs of all sizes are allowed. There are no additional pet fees. Dogs may not be left unattended, and they must be leashed and cleaned up after. This RV park is closed during the off-season. The camping and tent areas also allow dogs. There is a dog walk area at the campground.

Ocean View Resort 2555 H 9 Ocean View NJ   609-624-1675
http://www.ovresort.com
Dogs of all sizes are allowed. There are no additional pet fees. Dogs must be leashed and cleaned up after. There is a dog walk area at the campground.

Pine Haven Camping Resort 2339 H 9 Ocean View NJ   609-624-3437
http://www.rvinthesun.com
Dogs of all sizes are allowed. There are no additional pet fees. Dogs must be leashed and cleaned up after. The camping and tent areas also allow dogs.

Transportation Systems

Cape May-Lewes Ferry

TOP 200 PLACE **Cape May-Lewes Ferry** Sandman Blvd. & Lincoln Drive North Cape May NJ   609-889-

7200
http://www.capemaylewesferry.com/
This ferry service provides transportation for vehicles and passengers between Cape May, New Jersey and Lewes, Delaware. The ferry cuts miles off of driving along the Atlantic coast. Pets are welcome but the following rules apply. For the M.V. Cape May, M.V. Delaware and M.V. Twin Cape ferries, pets are welcome on the ferry on exterior decks and any lounge areas where food is not being made, served or eaten. Pets are not allowed in the lounge area whenever there is a private party being hosted. For the M.V. Cape Henlopen and M.V. New Jersey ferries, pets are not allowed in any interior space but are allowed on all exterior decks. For all ferries, dogs of all sizes are allowed but need to be kept under control at all times and leashed or in a carrier. People need to clean up after their pets. Pets are not allowed in the shuttles. Rates start at $20 to $25 for a vehicle and driver. For a foot passenger with no car, rates start at $6 to $8 per person. Larger vehicles can be accommodated but there is an extra charge. The Cape May Terminal is located at Sandman Blvd. and Lincoln Drive in North Cape May, New Jersey. The Lewes Terminal is located at 43 Henlopen Drive in Lewes, Delaware. Rates are subject to change. For reservations or to check rates, call the ferry line toll free at 1-800-643-3779.

Attractions

TOP 200 PLACE **Cape May Whale Watcher** 2nd Avenue & Wilson Drive Cape May NJ   609-884-5445
http://www.capemaywhalewatcher.com/
Dogs are welcome aboard the 110 foot Cape May Whale Watcher for the whale and dolphin tours for no additional fee. Dogs must be well behaved, and under owner's control/care at all times.

TOP 200 PLACE **Historic Cold Spring Village** 720 H 9S Cape May NJ   609-898-2300
http://www.hcsv.org/
This open-air living history museum depicting 18th century life, offers a variety of entertainment, recreation, activities, and a trail that meanders through the 22 acres where visitors may take pleasure in the gardens or observe the heritage crops. Dogs are welcome to explore the park. Dogs must be on no more than a 4 foot leash, under owner's control, and cleaned up after at all times. Dogs are not allowed in any of the buildings.

Miss Chris Marina 1218 Wilson Drive Cape May NJ   609-884-3351
http://www.misschrismarina.com/
Although dogs are not allowed on the touring boats, they are allowed on watercraft rentals for no additional fee. Dogs must be under owner's control, leashed, and cleaned up after at all times.

The Wetlands Institute 1075 Stone Harbor Blvd Stone Harbor NJ   609-368-1211
http://www.wetlandsinstitute.org/
Dedicated to the conservation, preservation, and education of coastal ecosystems, they offer a variety of entertainment, activities, and events to make this a fun learning experience. There are beautiful gardens and picnic areas to enjoy as well. Dogs are welcome for no additional fee. Dogs must be under owner's control, leashed, and cleaned up after at all times. Dogs are not allowed in any of the buildings.

Stores

Woodland Pet Boutique 1943 N H 9 Cape May NJ   609-624-3322
This store is open from 10 am to 5 pm 7 days a week and welcomes well behaved dogs to come in and explore. Dogs must be under owner's control/care at all times and leashed.

Beaches

Higbee Beach Wildlife Management Area County Road 641 Cape May NJ   609-628-2103
This park offers a 1 1/2 mile stretch of beach. The beach is managed specifically to provide habitat for migratory wildlife. Dogs on leash and under control are allowed at the beach from September through April. To get there, take SR 109 west to US9. Turn left onto US9 and go to the first traffic light. Turn left onto County Road 162 (Seashore Rd.). Then turn right onto Country Road 641 (New England Rd.). Take CR641 for 2 miles to the end and the beach access parking area. Parking areas near the beach may be closed during the Summer. The park is open daily from dawn to dusk.

Cape May Point State Park Lighthouse Avenue Cape May Point NJ   609-884-2159
Dogs are only allowed on the beach during the off-season. Pets are not allowed from April 15 through September 15. Pets must be on a 6 foot or less leash and people need to clean up after their pets. The park is located off the southern end of the Garden State Parkway. Go over the Cape May Bridge to Lafayette Street. At the intersection, go right onto Route 606 (Sunset Blvd.), then turn left onto Lighthouse Ave.

Parks

Cape May Point State Park PO Box 107 Cape May Point NJ   609-884-2159
Dogs on leash are allowed on the state park grounds. They are only allowed on the beach after September 15th due to bird nesting. The park features picnicking, trails, lighthouse, and WWII bunkers located on the beach.

Outdoor Restaurants

Jackson Mountain Cafe 400 Washington Street Cape May NJ   609-884-5648
This cafe serves up American favorites and offers indoor and outdoor dining. Dogs are allowed at the outer tables. Dogs must be under owner's control, leashed, and cleaned up after.
Sunset Beach Grill Foot of Sunset Blvd Cape May Point NJ   609-898-9677
This restaurant serves American food. Dogs are allowed at the outdoor tables.
Mike's Seafood and Raw Bar 4222 Park Road Sea Isle City NJ   609-263-1136
http://www.mikesseafood.com/
This seaside seafood restaurant offers indoor and outdoor "dock" dining. Dogs are allowed at the outer tables. Dogs must be under owner's control, leashed, and cleaned up after at all times.

Central Shore

Accommodations

Engleside Inn 30 Engleside Avenue Beach Haven NJ   609-492-1251 (800-762-2214)
http://engleside.com/Engleside/index.htm
This is a nice place to go with your pet in the off season. They are right on the beach, have 3 in-house restaurants, and are only minutes from many attractions, activities, and recreation. Dogs of all sizes are allowed from September 10th to May 4th only (their off-season) for an additional fee of $10 per night per pet. Dogs must be leashed, cleaned up after, and they may only be left alone in the room for short periods if they will be quiet, comfortable, and well behaved.
The Sea Shell Motel, Restaurant & Beach Club 10 S. Atlantic Ave. Beach Haven NJ   609-492-4611
http://www.seashellclub.com/
This ocean front retreat offers 2 eateries, a pool, and live entertainment as they are home to 2 party hotspots; the Beach Club and Tiki Bar. This resort opens about the 1st of April and dogs are allowed up until June 21st, and then they are not allowed again until after Labor Day. Dogs of all sizes are allowed for an additional fee of $10 per night per pet. Dogs must be leashed and cleaned up after.

Campgrounds and RV Parks

Atlantic City North Family Campground Stage Road Tuckerton NJ   609-296-9163
Dogs of all sizes are allowed. There are no additional pet fees. Dogs may not be left unattended outside or in the cabins, and they must be leashed and cleaned up after. This RV park is closed during the off-season. The camping and tent areas also allow dogs. There is a dog walk area at the campground. Dogs are allowed in the camping cabins.
Sea Pirate Campground Bay side of H 9, Box 271 West Creek NJ   609-296-7400 (800-822-CAMP (2267))
http://www.sea-pirate.com/
Up to two dogs of any size are allowed at the tent and RV sites at no additional fee. Basic Cabins and 2 Room Basic Cabins allow one pet at $5 per night with a $200 security deposit. Dogs may not be left unattended, and they must be leashed and cleaned up after. This RV park is closed during the off-season. The camping and tent areas also allow dogs. There is a dog walk area at the campground. Dogs are allowed in the camping cabins.

Attractions

Blackbeards Cave Entertainment Center 136 H 9 Bayville NJ   732-286-4414
http://www.blackbeardscave.com/
This family entertainment center offers an impressive list of activities and gaming areas for all ages and interests. Dogs are welcome for no additional fee. Dogs must be under owner's control, leashed, and cleaned up after at all times.

Stores

PetSmart Pet Store 1900 Route 70 Lakewood NJ   732-262-1606
Your licensed and well-behaved leashed dog is allowed in the store.
PetSmart Pet Store 1232 Hooper Ave Toms River NJ   732-240-1540
Your licensed and well-behaved leashed dog is allowed in the store.
Petco Pet Store 1331 Hooper Avenue Toms River NJ   732-473-9818
Your licensed and well-behaved leashed dog is allowed in the store.

Beaches

Barnegat Lighthouse State Park Beaches At Broadway and the Bay Barnegat Light NJ   609-494-2016

Although dogs are not allowed in the lighthouse or on the beaches from April 15th to August 15, and never on the trails here, they are allowed in the park and picnic areas which provide visitors with great views of the ocean and waterway activities. Dogs are allowed on the park beaches from August 16 through April 14 each year. Dogs are welcome for no additional fee. Dogs must be under owner's control, leashed, and cleaned up after at all times.

Island Beach State Park off Route 35 Seaside Park NJ 732-793-0506

One of the states last significant remnants of a barrier island ecosystem, it is home to diverse wildlife and maritime plant life, and with a variety of land and water activities and 8 interesting trails. During the Winter months, dogs are allowed on all of the beaches, but must be on a 6 foot or less leash. People are required to clean up after their pets. To get to the park, take Route 37 east. Then take Route 35 south to the park entrance. Dogs are not allowed on the beaches during the Summer.

Parks

Double Trouble State Park PO Box 175 Bayville NJ 732-341-6662

Dogs on leash are allowed on the state park grounds. The park features fishing, hiking trails, Cedar swamps, cranberry, bogs, picnicking, and more. This an old cranberry farm with a historical village for touring.

Off-Leash Dog Parks

Ocean County Park Dog Park Route 88 Lakewood NJ 732-506-9090

http://www.ocean.nj.us/parks/Dogpark.pdf

There is a clean, fenced off-leash dog park in Ocean County Park. There are separate areas for large and small dogs. Children under 8 are not allowed in the dog park. Dogs must receive an Ocean County annual permit to use the dog parks in the county. The fee is $20 for the first dog and $10 for each additional dog. Dogs must have a valid dog license to be registered and male dogs must be neutered. See the website at http://www.ocean.nj.us/parks/Dogpark.pdf or call the parks department at 732-506-9090 for locations to register.

Chatsworth

Attractions

Mick's Canoe and Kayak Rental 3107 H 563 Chatsworth NJ 609-726-1380

http://www.mickscanoerental.com/

This watercraft rental company provides access for cruising the waterways of Wharton State Forest, and they will allow your well behaved dog to come aboard rentals. There is no additional pet fee. Dogs must be leashed and cleaned up after at all times.

Pine Barrens Canoe Rental 3260 H 563 Chatsworth NJ 609-726-1515

http://www.pinebarrenscanoe.com/

This watercraft rental company will allow a dog aboard the rental canoes for day trips for no additional fee; they are not allowed on the overnight rentals. Dogs must be under owner's control at all times, leashed, and cleaned up after.

Delaware Bridge Area

Accommodations

Holiday Inn Express Hotel and Suites 506 Pennsville-Auburn Rd Carneys Point NJ 856-351-9222 (877-270-6405)

Dogs of all sizes are allowed for no additional fee with a credit card on file.

Wellesley Inn & Suites Carneys Point 517 S. Pennsville-Auburn Road Penns Grove NJ 856-299-3800 (800-531-5900)

Dogs of all sizes are allowed. There is a $10 per night per pet additional fee. Dogs may not be left unattended, and they must be leashed and cleaned up after.

Campgrounds and RV Parks

Four Seasons Family Campground 158 Woodstown Road Pilesgrove NJ 856-769-3635 (888-372- CAMP (2267))

http://www.fourseasonscamping.com/

Dogs of all sizes are allowed. There are no additional pet fees. Dogs may not be left unattended outside, and they must be leashed and cleaned up after. Dogs are not allowed on the beach or at the playground, and they are not allowed in or around the cabin areas. Dogs must be licensed and have current shot records. The camping and tent areas also allow dogs. There is a dog walk area at the campground.

Parks

Fort Mott State Park 454 Fort Mott Road Pennsville NJ   856-935-3218
Once used as a coastal defense system, this park now features interpretive signs with in-depth descriptions throughout the fort, and there are nice places along the Delaware River for walking and picnicking. Dogs are allowed throughout the park and on the trails. They are not allowed in any buildings. Dogs must be well mannered, leashed, and cleaned up after at all times.

Hammonton

Parks

Wharton State Park 4110 Nesco Rd Hammonton NJ   609-561-0024
Dogs on leash are allowed in the park grounds, except for the campground. The park features hiking, picnicking, and Batsto Village, which is an historical village.

High Bridge

Outdoor Restaurants

Circa Restaurant 37 Main Street High Bridge NJ   908-638-5560
http://www.circa-restaurant.com/
Specializing in innovative (and some French inspired) cuisine with a focus on using seasonal products and produce from local suppliers, this restaurant also offers a full bar, catering, and outside dining. Dogs are allowed at the outside tables; they must be leashed and under owner's control/care at all times.

Hunterdon County

Accommodations

The Widow McCrea House 53 Kingwood Avenue Frenchtown NJ   908-996-4999
http://www.widowmccrea.com/
This attractive 1878 Italian Victorian Inn is only a 2 minute walk from all the town has to offer and the Delaware River, and they offer a cottage with an oversized Jacuzzi and a fireplace for guests with pets. Dogs of all sizes are allowed for an additional fee of $35 per night per pet with a credit card on file, and there is a pet agreement to sign at check in. Dogs must be well behaved, leashed, cleaned up after, and crated when left alone in the room.
Woolverton Inn 6 Woolverton Road Stockton NJ   609-397-0802 (888-264-6648)
http://www.woolvertoninn.com/
Set on 300 lush, scenic acres of rolling hills and woodlands, this 1792 stone manor luxury inn offers guests indoor or outdoor garden dining, and a favorite pastime here is a walk to the Delaware River to catch the amazing sunsets over the water. Dogs of all sizes are allowed in the Garden Cottage for no additional pet fee. Dogs must be housebroken, quiet, leashed, and cleaned up after. Dogs may only be left alone in the room if owners are confident in their behavior.

Shopping Centers

TOP 200 PLACE Liberty Village Premium Outlets One Church Street Flemington NJ   908-782-8550
Enjoy the neatly landscaped and red cobblestones streets of this shopping area that offer 60 stores to explore. Well mannered dogs are welcome. Dogs must be leashed and cleaned up after at all times. It is up to individual stores whether dogs are allowed inside.

Stores

Decoys and Wildlife Gallery 55 Bridge Street Frenchtown NJ   908-996-6501
http://www.decoyswildlife.com/
This duck decoy and wildlife gallery features an impressive stock of carved items, artwork, bronzes, and many

more displays of the bird world. Well mannered dogs are welcome. Dogs must be under owner's control, leashed, and they must be house trained.

Off-Leash Dog Parks

The Hunterdon County Off-Leash Dog Area 1020 State Route 31 Flemington NJ 908-782-1158
This off lead dog area offers 1.75 fenced acres with a scattering of trees for shade. There is no water available here, so water for pets is highly recommended. Dogs must be leashed going into and out of the off-lead area, and cleaned up after at all times. Dogs must be spayed or neutered, and puppies under 6 months old are prohibited.

Outdoor Restaurants

Buck's Ice Cream and Espresso Bar, 52 Bridge Street Frenchtown NJ 908-996-7258
Your well behaved pooch is welcome to come and get an ice cream too. They offer outside seating. Dogs are allowed at the outer tables. Dogs must be well behaved, under owner's control, leashed, and cleaned up after at all times.
The Frenchtown Inn 7 Bridge Street Frenchtown NJ 908-996-3300
http://www.frenchtowninn.com/
This fine dining restaurant offers a variety of menus with indoor and outdoor dining options. Dogs are allowed at the outer tables. Dogs must be well behaved, under owner's control, leashed, and cleaned up after at all times.
De Anna's Restaurant 54 N Franklin Street Lambertville NJ 609-397-8957
http://www.deannasrestaurant.com/
Specializing in homemade pasta and great wine-pairing with a wide range of Italian fare, this eatery also offers indoor and outdoor dining. Dogs are allowed at the outer tables. Dogs must be well behaved, under owner's control, leashed, and cleaned up after at all times.
Hamilton's Grill Room at the Porkyard 8 Coryell Street Lambertville NJ 609-397-4343
This eatery features contemporary Mediterranean cooking, open grill cooking, and a European style courtyard. Dogs are allowed at the outer tables. Dogs must be well behaved, under owner's control, leashed, and cleaned up after at all times.
Cravings 10 Risler Street Stockton NJ 609-397-2911
This is the place for all the good American favorites, and they offer indoor and outdoor dining. Dogs are allowed at the outer tables. Dogs must be well behaved, under owner's control, leashed, and cleaned up after at all times.
Stockton Inn Restaurant and Tavern 1 Main Street Stockton NJ 609-397-1250
http://www.stocktoninn.com/
This historic inn offers a fine dining steak and seafood restaurant with seasonal outside dining, and a tavern that was established in 1832. Dogs are allowed at the outer tables on the porch where the bartender will be happy to serve you. Dogs are not allowed on the back patio. Dogs must be under owner's control/care and leashed at all times.

I-78 Corridor

Stores

Petco Pet Store 1209 New Brunswick Avenue Phillipsburg NJ 908-454-6381
Your licensed and well-behaved leashed dog is allowed in the store.

Parks

Spruce Run Recreation Area 68 Van Syckel's Road Clinton NJ 908-782-8572
Home to the 3rd largest reservoir in the state, this year-round park offers a wide variety of land and water recreation. Dogs are allowed for no additional fee. Dogs must be under owner's control at all times, be on no more than a 6 foot leash, and cleaned up after. Dogs are allowed throughout the park and on the trails; they are not allowed in the campgrounds or on the beach.
Voorhees State Park 251 County Road Route 513 Glen Gardner NJ 908-638-6969
Dogs on leash are allowed in the state park for day use only. They are not allowed in the campground area. The park features hiking, fishing, picnicking, and more. This park was once a Civilian Conservation Corps used to help young men get back to work during the Depression. It was in use between 1933-1941 after being established by President Franklin Roosevelt.
Round Valley Rec Area 1220 Lebanon-Stanton Road Lebanon NJ 908-236-6355
There is a good variety of water recreation with a 2,000+ acre reservoir at this 3,684 acre park in addition to some great hiking trails, and scenic picnic areas with tables, grills, restrooms, and playgrounds. Dogs are allowed throughout the park and on the trails. Dogs must be leashed and cleaned up after at all times. Dogs are

not allowed in the campground or on the beach. There are places where they may go in the water, but they must still be on lead.

I-80 Corridor

Accommodations
The Inn at Millrace Pond 313 Johnsonburg Road/H 519N Hope NJ   908-459-4884 (800-746-6467)
http://innatmillracepond.com/
Historic buildings, individually decorated rooms in period reproductions, and an active restaurant and tavern highlight this retreat. They offer a couple of pet-friendly rooms, and dogs of all sizes are allowed for no additional pet fee. Dogs must be leashed, cleaned up after, and they are not allowed on the beds. They request dogs be crated when left alone in the room unless the owner is confident the pet will be quiet and well mannered.
Days Inn Lake Hopatcong 1691 Route 46 Ledgewood NJ   973-347-5100 (800-329-7466)
Dogs of all sizes are allowed. There are no additional pet fees.

Attractions
Dow's Boat Rental 145 Nolan's Point Rd Lake Hopatcong NJ   973-663-3826
This boat rental establishment allows dogs. It is located on Lake Hopatcong for fishing and relaxation.
Lakes End Marina 91 Mount Arlington Blvd Landing NJ   973-398-5707
This establishment rents boats for a day out on the lake with your dog.

Stores
Hopatcong Boathouse 156 H 181 Lake Hopatcong NJ   973-962-6999
Your furry companion can also check out the boats at this watercraft store. Dogs must be under owner's control, leashed, and cleaned up after at all times.

Parks
Allamuchy Mountain State Park 800 Willow Grove St Hackettstown NJ   908-852-3790
Dogs on leash are allowed in the state park. They are not allowed in the camping area. The park features hiking, fishing, picnicking, boating, and more. Also featured is the Waterloo Village, a 400 year old Lenape Indian Village that later became a port for the Morris Canal.
Jenny Jump State Park 330 State Park Road Hope NJ   908-459-4366
This recreation destination offers a variety of activities, panoramic views and green rolling hills, a shaded picnic area with tables and grills, hiking trails, and is it home to the Greenwood Observatory. Dogs are allowed; they must be under owner's control, leashed, and cleaned up after at all times. Dogs are allowed throughout the park and on the trails; they are not allowed at the observatory.
Bass River State Forest 762 Stage Rd New Green NJ   609-296-1114
Dogs on leash are allowed in the state park. They are not allowed in the campground area or public beaches. The park features hiking, fishing, picnicking, boating, and more.

Jackson

Campgrounds and RV Parks
Butterfly Camping Resort 360 Butterfly Road Jackson NJ   732-928-2107
http://www.butterflycamp.com
Dogs of all sizes are allowed, some breeds are not. There are no additional pet fees. Dogs must be leashed and cleaned up after. The camping and tent areas also allow dogs. There is a dog walk area at the campground.
Tip Tam Camping Resort 301 Brewer's Bridge Road Jackson NJ   877-TIP-TAM1
http://www.tiptam.com
Dogs of all sizes are allowed, however some breeds are not. There are no additional pet fees. Dogs must remain on your own site, be leashed, and cleaned up after. The camping and tent areas also allow dogs.

Attractions
Rova Farm Resort 120 Cassville Road Jackson NJ   732-928-0928
Historically noted as a meeting area for Russian Americans, it is now home to 2 Russian churches, a Russian restaurant, and there is a flea market open on Tuesdays. Friendly, well mannered dogs are allowed at the flea

market and around the grounds. They are not allowed in buildings. Dogs must be under owner's control, leashed, and cleaned up after at all times.

Monmouth Battlefield State Park 347 Freehold Road Manalapan NJ   732-462-9616
http://www.monmouthbattlefield.com/
With the distinction of being the site of the longest battle of the American Revolution, it is now preserved as an 18th century rural setting with wooded areas, fields, orchards, and wetlands with miles and miles of trails, picnic areas and a restored farmhouse. They are also host to various activities and events throughout the year, as well as an annual reenactment of the famous battle. Dogs are allowed throughout the park and on the trails. Dogs must be under owner's control, leashed, and cleaned up after at all times. They are not allowed in the buildings.

Shopping Centers

Jackson Premium Outlets 537 Monmouth Road Jackson NJ   732-833-0503
There are 70 outlets at this shopping mecca. Dogs are welcome to explore the grounds; it is up to the individual stores as to whether they may go inside. Dogs must be under owner's control, leashed, and cleaned up after at all times.

Stores

PetSmart Pet Store 7 Route 9 Manalapan NJ   732-683-1119
Your licensed and well-behaved leashed dog is allowed in the store.

Northwest Mountains

Campgrounds and RV Parks

Panther Lake Camping Resort 6 Panther Lake Road/H 206 Andover NJ   973-347-4440 (800-543-2056)
One hundred and sixty acres, a variety of land and water recreation, hiking trails, a 45-acre lake, and only 50 miles from New York City, make this a popular get-a-way. Dogs of all sizes are allowed for no additional fee, and they must be leashed and cleaned up after at all times. Dogs are allowed throughout the park, but they are not allowed in the rental units. This RV park is closed during the off-season. The camping and tent areas also allow dogs. There is a dog walk area at the campground.

Beaver Hill Campground 120 Big Springs Road Hamburg NJ   973-827-0670
Dogs of all sizes are allowed. There is a $1 per night per pet additional fee. Dogs must be leashed, cleaned up after, and not left unattended. The camping and tent areas also allow dogs. There is a dog walk area at the campground.

Cedar Ridge Campground 205 River Road Montague NJ   973-293-3512
http://www.cedarridgecampground.com/
One dog of any size is allowed. There are no additional pet fees. Dogs may not be left unattended at any time, and they must be leashed and cleaned up after. Dogs must be licensed and have up to date shot records. There are some breed restrictions. This RV park is closed during the off-season. The camping and tent areas also allow dogs. There is a dog walk area at the campground.

Pleasant Acres Farm Campground 61 DeWitt Road Sussex NJ   973-875-4166 (800-722-4166)
http://www.pleasantacres.com/
From a working 300 acre farm to a modern, award-winning campground (sorry, no tent sites), this recreation destination gives visitors a back-to-nature, rural farm experience with many common (and uncommon) amenities included in the rates. Dogs of all sizes are allowed for no additional fee. Dogs must be quiet, well behaved, leashed, and cleaned up after (except in the fenced dog exercise area). Dogs may not be left unattended at any time. There is a dog walk area at the campground.

Attractions

Sterling Hill Mining Museum 30 Plant Street Ogdensburg NJ   973-209-7212
http://www.sterlinghill.org/
This museum is dedicated to the research, education, and preservation of this unique mining area. Although dogs are not allowed on tours of the mines they may explore the grounds where there are outdoor exhibits of mining equipment. Dogs must be under owner's control, leashed, and cleaned up after at all times. Dogs are not allowed in any of the buildings.

Shopping Centers

Olde LaFayette Village Shopping Center 75 H 15q Lafayette NJ   973-383-8323
http://www.lafayettevillageshops.com/
Enjoy the country atmosphere as you stroll the well landscaped paths lined with a variety of unique shops,

benches, and old fashioned light posts. Well mannered dogs are welcome. Dogs must be leashed and cleaned up after at all times. It is up to individual stores whether dogs are allowed inside.

Parks

Kittatinny Valley State Park PO Box 621 Andover NJ   973-786-6445
Dogs on leash are allowed in the state park. They are not allowed in the campground areas. The park features hiking, fishing, picnicking, boating, and more.
Stokes State Forest 1 Coursen Road Branchville NJ   973-948-3820
Dogs on a 6 ft leash are allowed in the state park. They are not allowed in the campground areas. Features hiking, swimming, fishing, boating, and more. Located in Sunrise Mountain along the Appalachian Trail.
High Point State Park 1480 H 23 Sussex NJ   973-875-4800
There are more than 15,000 scenic acres at this park that offers numerous trails (including a piece of the Appalachian Trail), panoramic views of 3 states from its high point, a spring-fed lake, year-round interpretive and educational programs, and much more. Dogs of all sizes are allowed at this park for no additional fee. Dogs must be well behaved, leashed, cleaned up after, and owners are responsible for them at all times. Dogs may not be left unattended at any time. Dogs are not allowed in the campground area.
Swartswood State Park PO Box 123 Swartswood NJ   973-383-5230
Dogs on leash are allowed in the state park. They are not allowed in the campground areas. The park features hiking, fishing, picnicking, boating, and swimming. This was the first established state park in NJ.

New Brunswick

Accommodations

Somerset Hills Hotel 200 Liberty Corner Road Bridgewater NJ   908-647-6700 (800-688-0700)
http://www.shh.com
This premier boutique hotel is reminiscent of the hotels of Europe, and they feature indoor and outdoor dining areas, room service, an outdoor pool, live entertainment on the weekends, and much more. Dogs of all sizes are allowed for an additional fee of $25 per night per pet. Dogs may not be left unattended in the room at any time, and they must be leashed and cleaned up after.
Motel 6 - East Brunswick 244 Route 18 East Brunswick NJ   732-390-4545 (800-466-8356)
One well-behaved family pet per room. Guest must notify front desk upon arrival. Guest is liable for any damages. In consideration of all guests, pets must never be left unattended in the guest rooms.
Studio 6 - East Brunswick 246 Rt 18 East Brunswick NJ   732-238-3330 (800-466-8356)
One well-behaved family pet per room. Guest must notify front desk upon arrival. Guest is liable for any damages. In consideration of all guests, pets must never be left unattended in the guest rooms.
Red Roof Inn - Edison 860 New Durham Road Edison NJ   732-248-9300 (800-RED-ROOF)
One well-behaved family pet per room. Guest must notify front desk upon arrival. Guest is liable for any damages. In consideration of all guests, pets must never be left unattended in the guest rooms.
Sheraton Edison Hotel Raritan Center 125 Raritan Center Parkway Edison NJ   732-225-8300 (888-625-5144)
Dogs up to 50 pounds are allowed. There are no additional pet fees but there is a $50 refundable deposit. Dogs are not allowed to be left alone in the room.
Sheraton Woodbridge Place Hotel 515 US Highway 1S Iselin NJ   732-634-3600 (888-625-5144)
Dogs up to 50 pounds are allowed. There are no additional pet fees. Dogs are not allowed to be left alone in the room.
Embassy Suites Hotel Piscataway - Somerset 121Centennial Avenue Piscataway NJ   732-980-0500
Dogs up to 50 pounds are allowed. There are no additional pet fees. Dogs are not allowed to be left alone in the room.
Motel 6 - Piscataway 1012 Stelton Road Piscataway NJ   732-981-9200 (800-466-8356)
One well-behaved family pet per room. Guest must notify front desk upon arrival. Guest is liable for any damages. In consideration of all guests, pets must never be left unattended in the guest rooms.
Candlewood Suites Somerset 41 Worlds Fair Drive Somerset NJ   732-748-1400 (877-270-6405)
Dogs of all sizes are allowed for an additional one time fee of $75 per pet.
Holiday Inn 195 Davidson Ave Somerset NJ   732-356-1700 (877-270-6405)
Dogs of all sizes are allowed for an additional fee of $15 per night per pet.
Qualilty Inn 1850 Easton Avenue Somerset NJ   732-469-5050
One dog is allowed for an additional pet fee of $20 per night.
Residence Inn by Marriott 37 Worlds Fair Drive Somerset NJ   732-627-0881
Dogs of all sizes are allowed. There is a $75 one time fee and a pet policy to sign at check in.
Staybridge Suites 260 Davidson Ave Somerset NJ   732-356-8000 (877-270-6405)
A dog up to 50 pounds is allowed for an additional one time pet fee of $150.

Attractions

Sayen House and Gardens 155 Hughes Drive Hamilton NJ   609-890-3543
http://www.sayengardens.org/
Thirty acres of lush, elaborate gardens greet visitors here, and in addition to rare flora gathered and brought here from around the world, there are also gazebos, ponds, historic sites, scenic walking trails, and special events. Dogs are allowed throughout the park and on the trails. They are not allowed in any buildings. Dogs must be well mannered, leashed, and cleaned up after at all times.
The Rutgers Gardens at Rutgers University 112 Ryders Lane New Brunswick NJ   732-932-8451
Showcasing a diverse list of horticultural collections arranged in garden settings, this 50 acre plant education garden allows visitors to see and learn about various plants and plant growing techniques for year-round enjoyment. Well behaved dogs are welcome throughout the park and on the trails; they are not allowed in any of the buildings or in any of the gardens. Dogs must be under owner's control, leashed, and cleaned up after at all times.
TOP 200 PLACE East Jersey Olde Towne Village 1050 River Road Piscataway NJ   732-745-3030
Dedicated to the historical education of the people who founded the area of Raritan Valley, this replicated 18th/19th century village offers a wide variety of activities, educational programs, and entertaining stories of their traditions, folk art, and craftsmanship. Well behaved dogs are welcome throughout the park and on the trails; they are not allowed in any of the buildings. Dogs must be under owner's control, leashed, and cleaned up after at all times.

Stores

PetSmart Pet Store 145 Promenade Blvd Bridgewater NJ   732-748-7266
Your licensed and well-behaved leashed dog is allowed in the store.
PetSmart Pet Store 269 US Hwy 18 S East Brunswick NJ   732-651-0700
Your licensed and well-behaved leashed dog is allowed in the store.
Petco Pet Store 1029 US Route 1 South Edison NJ   732-516-0330
Your licensed and well-behaved leashed dog is allowed in the store.
PetSmart Pet Store 170 Marketplace Blvd Hamilton NJ   609-585-4418
Your licensed and well-behaved leashed dog is allowed in the store.
Petco Pet Store 300 Ryders Lane Milltown NJ   732-651-0260
Your licensed and well-behaved leashed dog is allowed in the store.
Petco Pet Store 1060 US Hwy 9 Parlin NJ   732-721-9610
Your licensed and well-behaved leashed dog is allowed in the store.
Petco Pet Store 1333 Centennial Avenue Piscataway NJ   732-981-8189
Your licensed and well-behaved leashed dog is allowed in the store.
Petco Pet Store 300 US Highway 202 Raritan NJ   908-203-8840
Your licensed and well-behaved leashed dog is allowed in the store.
PetSmart Pet Store 863 St George Ave Woodbridge NJ   732-750-1090
Your licensed and well-behaved leashed dog is allowed in the store.

Off-Leash Dog Parks

Veteran's Park Dog Park Kuser Road Hamilton NJ
This fenced dog park is located in Veterans Park. Use the park entrance on Kuser Rd and go 1500 feet into the park to the dogpark on the right. There are separate areas for big dogs and little dogs.
Colonial Park Leash-Free Area Mettlers Road Somerset NJ   732-873-2695
This is a three acre fenced off-leash dog run area. The park is located off Mettlers Road and is on the same driveway as the Spooky Brook Golf Maintenance Area.

New Lisbon

Parks

Batona Trail H 72 New Lisbon NJ   609-561-3262
Located in the Brendan T. Byrne State Forest, this 50 mile hiking trail winds over 50 miles through the New Jersey Pinelands, and it is also used for cross-country skiing and snow shoeing in the Winter months. Dogs are allowed on the trail throughout the year. Dogs must be under owner's control, leashed, and cleaned up after at all times.
Brendan T Byrne State Forest PO Box 215 New Lisbon NJ   609-726-1191
Dogs on leash are allowed in the state park. They are not allowed in the campground area. The park features

hiking, fishing, picnicking, and more. The park also includes the deserted Whitesbog Village and some cranberry farms.

Pinelands Natural Area 15 Springfield Road New Lisbon NJ 609-894-7300
http://www.nj.gov/pinelands/reserve/
This 1.1 million acre ecologically important region is the largest open space area on the Mid-Atlantic seaboard, is home to some of the purest water available, is part of the US Biosphere Reserve of Man and the Biosphere Program, and it also holds the distinction of being the country's first National Reserve area. Dogs are allowed throughout the park and on the trails; they are not allowed in wildlife sensitive areas or in park buildings.

Rancocas PO Box 215 New Lisbon NJ 609-726-1191
Dogs on leash are allowed in the State Park. They are not allowed in the campground areas. The park features hiking, picnicking, and a replica of the Powhatan Indian Village of the 1600s.

Newark - NYC Area

Accommodations

Wellesley Inn Clifton 265 Route 3 East Clifton NJ 973-778-6500 (800-531-5900)
Dogs of all sizes are allowed. There is a $10 per night per pet additional fee. Dogs may not be left unattended, and they must be leashed and cleaned up after.

Sheraton Meadowlands Hotel & Conference Center 2 Meadowlands Plaza East Rutherford NJ 201-896-0500 (888-625-5144)
Dogs up to 50 pounds are allowed. There is a $50 one time additional pet fee. Dogs are not allowed to be left alone in the room.

Hilton 1170 Spring Street Elizabeth NJ 908-351-3900
Dogs are allowed for no additional pet fee.

Residence Inn by Marriott 83 Glimcher Realty Way Elizabeth NJ 908-352-4300
Dogs of all sizes are allowed. There is a $75 one time fee and a pet policy to sign at check in.

Radisson Hotel Englewood 401 South Van Brunt Street Englewood NJ 201-871-2020
Dogs of all sizes are allowed. There is a $50 one time additional pet fee. Dogs may not be left alone in the rooms unless they are in a crate.

Candlewood Suites Jersey City 21 Second Street Jersey City NJ 201-659-2500 (877-270-6405)
One dog of any size is allowed for an additional pet fee of $75 for 1 to 6 nights, and $150 for 7 nights or more.

Sheraton Newark Airport Hotel 128 Frontage Road Newark NJ 973-690-5500 (888-625-5144)
Dogs up to 65 pounds are allowed. There are no additional pet fees. Dogs are not allowed to be left alone in the room.

La Quinta Inn Paramus 393 North State Route 17 Paramus NJ 201-265-4200 (800-531-5900)
Dogs of all sizes are allowed. There are no additional pet fees. There is a pet waiver to sign at check in. Dogs must be leashed, cleaned up after, and crated when left alone in the room.

Holiday Inn Harmon Meadow Secaucus 300 Plaza Dr Secaucus NJ 201-348-2000 (877-270-6405)
Dogs of all sizes are allowed for an additional one time pet fee of $50 per room. Dogs may not be left alone in the room.

Red Roof Inn - Secaucus Meadowlands N.Y.C. 15 Meadowlands Parkway Secaucus NJ 201-319-1000 (800-RED-ROOF)
One well-behaved family pet per room. Guest must notify front desk upon arrival. Guest is liable for any damages. In consideration of all guests, pets must never be left unattended in the guest rooms.

Sheraton Suites on the Hudson 500 Harbor Blvd. Weehawken NJ 201-617-5600 (888-625-5144)
Dogs of all sizes are allowed. There is a $75 one time pet fee per visit.

Residence Inn by Marriott 107 Prospect Avenue West Orange NJ 973-669-4700
Dogs of all sizes are allowed. There is a $75 one time cleaning fee plus $15 per night per pet and a pet policy to sign at check in.

Campgrounds and RV Parks

Liberty Harbor RV Park 11 Marin Blvd Jersey City NJ 201-387-7500
http://www.libertyharborrv.com/
Dogs of all sizes are allowed. There are no additional pet fees. Dogs must be leashed, cleaned up after, and not be left unattended. There is a dog walk area at the campground.

Transportation Systems

NJ Transit Regional Hoboken NJ 973-762-5100
http://www.njtransit.com
Small dogs in carriers are allowed on the trains.

Attractions

Edison National Historic Site Main Street and Lakeside Avenue West Orange NJ   973-736-0551
http://www.nps.gov/edis/index.htm
Dogs on leash are allowed outside of the house. They are not allowed in the house.

Stores

Petco Pet Store 780 Route 3 West Clifton NJ   973-472-3344
Your licensed and well-behaved leashed dog is allowed in the store.
PetSmart Pet Store 60 N State Route 17 Paramus NJ   201-843-0540
Your licensed and well-behaved leashed dog is allowed in the store.
Petco Pet Store 450 North State Route 17 Paramus NJ   201-261-6306
Your licensed and well-behaved leashed dog is allowed in the store.
PetSmart Pet Store 300 Mill Creek Dr Secaucus NJ   201-583-0861
Your licensed and well-behaved leashed dog is allowed in the store.
PetSmart Pet Store 2438 Route 22 E Union NJ   908-686-9333
Your licensed and well-behaved leashed dog is allowed in the store.
Petco Pet Store 201 Prospect Avenue West Orange NJ   973-325-5040
Your licensed and well-behaved leashed dog is allowed in the store.

Parks

Palisades Interstate Park Palisades Interstate Parkway Alpine NJ   201-768-1360
http://www.njpalisades.org/
Designated a National Historic Landmark, this park features more than 30 miles of hiking trails with great views of the Palisades, the Hudson River, and the New York skyline, a scenic riverside drive, riverfront picnic areas, historic sites, and more. Dogs are welcome to explore the park and all the trails. Dogs must be under owner's control, leashed, and cleaned up after at all times. Dogs are not allowed in the Greenbrook Sanctuary.
Elysian Park 10th and Hudson Street Hoboken NJ   201-420-229
This neighborhood park has a long cultural history and is known for being the place that hosted the first officially recorded, organized baseball game on June 19, 1846. There are gaming courts/fields, lots of shade, and a fenced in dog run area. Well behaved dogs are allowed throughout the park on leash and they must be cleaned up after at all times; the exception being when they are in the fenced dog run area.
Hoboken Riverfront Walkway Waterfront in Hoboken Hoboken NJ
Dogs on leash are permitted on the Waterfront Walkway along the Hudson River. Dogs are not permitted on the grass areas or other interior walkways. Dogs are not permitted in the Shipyard Park.
TOP 200 PLACE Liberty State Park Morris Pesin Drive Jersey City NJ   201-915-3440
http://www.libertystatepark.org/
Once the heart of an extensive transportation network for industry, this area served an even bigger role as the passage point for thousands and thousands of immigrants in the 19th and early 20th century, and now it provides over 300 developed acres for public recreation less than 2,000 feet from the Statue of Liberty. This is the closest view from land that your dog can get of the Statue of Liberty. Dogs are allowed throughout the park, on the trails, and at the picnic areas. Dogs must be leashed and cleaned up after at all times.
Branch Brook Park Park Avenue and Lake Street Newark NJ   973-263-3500
America's oldest county park is a major recreation destination with one of the largest recreational open green spaces to be found in the county, a large lake, playgrounds, gaming fields/courts, a four mile scenic drive, trails and pedestrian bridges. There are also 2,000 cherry trees that bloom every April, and more, plus there are various special events and festivals held here throughout the year. Dogs are allowed throughout the park and on the trails; they are not allowed in buildings. Dogs must be well mannered, leashed, and cleaned up after.

Off-Leash Dog Parks

Bayonne Dog Park 1st Street at Kennedy Blvd Bayonne NJ   201-858-7181
This small dog park located next to Kill Van Kull Park in Bayonne is fully fenced and has shade and benches. The dog park is located behind the baseball park. The dog park is open during daylight hours.
Church Square Dog Run 4th and 5th, between Garden and Willow Hoboken NJ
There are two dog runs in Church Square Park. One is for larger dogs and another for small dogs only.
Elysian Park Dog Run Hudson between 10th and 11th Hoboken NJ
There is an off-leash dog run in the park.
Stevens Park Dog Run Hudson between 4th and 5th Hoboken NJ
There is an off-leash dog run in the park.
Van Vorst Dog Park Jersrey Avenue and Montgomery Street Jersey City NJ   201-433-5127
http://www.stevenfulop.com/dogrun.htm

This nicely landscaped neighborhood dog park offers separate sections for large and small dogs, water spouts, and benches. Dogs must be sociable, current on all vaccinations, licensed, and cleaned up after at all times. Dogs must be leashed when not in designated off-lead areas.

Overpeck County Park Dog Run Fort Lee Road Leonia NJ   201-336-7275
There is an official Bergen County off-leash dog run area in Overpeck County Park.

Riverside County Park Dog Run Riverside Ave Lyndhurst NJ   201-336-7275
There is an official Bergen County off-leash dog run area in Riverside County Park.

Essex County South Mountain Dog Park Crest Drive Millburn NJ   973-268-3500
In addition to an honorary memorial to lost rescue dogs of 9-11, this 2 acre, 2 sectioned doggy park offers agility equipment, benches, drinking fountains for hounds and humans, a washing station, walking paths, and waste dispenser stations. Dogs must be sociable, current on all vaccinations, licensed, and cleaned up after at all times. Dogs must be leashed when not in designated off-lead areas.

Hudson County Park Dog Park Bergenline Ave at 81st North Bergen NJ   201-915-1386
http://www.hudsoncountynj.org
This fenced dog park is lit for evening use and has trees and benches. Dogs must be on leash outside of the dog run area in the rest of the 170 acre park. The dog park is behind the North Bergen High School stadium.

Outdoor Restaurants

Panera Bread 51 State Route 17 East Rutherford NJ   201-531-1480
This restaurant serves deli-type food and more. Dogs are allowed at the outdoor tables.

Baja Fresh 417 H 17S Hackensack NJ   201-441-9096
This restaurant serves Mexican food. Dogs are allowed at the outdoor tables. The restaurant has outdoor tables only in the Summer.

Margherita's Pizza and Cafe 740 Washington St Hoboken NJ   201-222-2400
This restaurant serves Italian and pizza. Dogs are allowed at the outdoor tables.

Panera Bread 308 Washington St Hoboken NJ   201-876-3233
This restaurant serves deli-type food and more. Dogs are allowed at the outdoor tables.

Quiznos 100 Hudson Street Hoboken NJ   201-656-2280
Dogs are allowed at the outdoor tables. The restaurant has outdoor tables only in the Summer.

Sinatra Park Cafe 525 Sinatra Drive Hoboken NJ   201-420-9900
This restaurant serves American food. Dogs are allowed at the outdoor tables.

Texas-Arizona's 76 River Street Hoboken NJ   201-420-0304
This restaurant serves American food. Dogs are allowed at the outdoor tables.

Tutta Pasta Restaurant 200 Washington St Hoboken NJ   201-792-9102
This restaurant serves Italian food. Dogs are allowed at the outdoor tables.

Bertucci's Brick Oven Pizzeria 560 Washington Blvd Jersey City NJ   201-222-8160
This restaurant serves Italian food. Dogs are allowed at the outdoor tables.

Café Angelique 1 Piermont Road Tenafly NJ   201-541-1010
Located in the city's fashion district, this is considered a "gem" by the locals for its affordable French cuisine, coffees, deserts, and nice patio dining area. Dogs are allowed at the outside tables; they must be leashed and under owner's control/care at all times.

Day Kennels

PetsHotel by PetsMart Day Kennel 400 Mill Creek Blvd. Secaucus NJ   201-583-1015
http://www.petsmart.com/PETsHOTEL/
This PetSmart pet store offers day care, day camp and overnight care. You may drop off and pick up your dog during the hours the store is open seven days a week. Dogs must have proof of current rabies, DPP and Bordatella vaccinations.

Newark - NYC Suburbs

Accommodations

Inn at Somerset Hills 80 Allen Road Basking Ridge NJ   908-580-1300 (800-688-0700)
http://www.shh.com
Dogs of all sizes are allowed for an additional pet fee of $25 per night per room. Dogs must be leashed, cleaned up after, and crated when left alone in the room.

Ramada Inn 130 H 10 W East Hanover NJ   973-386-5622
Dogs of all sizes are allowed. There is a pet policy to sign at check in and there are no additional pet fees.

Sheraton Mahwah Hotel 1 International Blvd., Route 17 North Mahwah NJ   201-529-1660 (888-625-5144)
Dogs of all sizes are allowed. There are no additional pet fees. Dogs are not allowed to be left alone in the room.

Candlewood Suites 100 Candlewood Drive Morris Plains NJ   973-984-9960 (877-270-6405)
One dog up to 75 pounds is allowed for an additional pet fee of $75 for 1 to 6 nights, and $150 for 7 nights or more.
Red Roof Inn - Parsippany N.Y.C. 855 U.S. 46 Parsippany NJ   973-334-3737 (800-RED-ROOF)
One well-behaved family pet per room. Guest must notify front desk upon arrival. Guest is liable for any damages. In consideration of all guests, pets must never be left unattended in the guest rooms.
Residence Inn by Marriott 3 Gatehall Drive Parsippany NJ   973-984-3313
Dogs of all sizes are allowed. There is a $75 one time fee and a pet policy to sign at check in.
Sheraton Parsippany Hotel 199 Smith Road Parsippany NJ   973-515-2000 (888-625-5144)
Dogs up to 80 pounds are allowed. There are no additional pet fees. Dogs are not allowed to be left alone in the room.
Staybridge Suites Parsippany 61 Interpace Pkwy Parsippany NJ   973-334-2907 (877-270-6405)
Dogs up to 70 pounds are allowed for an additional fee of $150 per pet.
The Pillars of Plainfield 922 Central Avenue Plainfield NJ   908-753-0922 (888 PILLARS (745-5277))
http://www.pillars2.com/
This beautifully restored Victorian mansion is surrounded by lush greenery, gardens, and comfort, and they are central to numerous other activities, places of interest, and recreation. Dogs up to 50 pounds are allowed for no additional pet fee. Dogs are allowed on the 2nd floor only, they must be leashed and cleaned up after, and they must be crated when left alone in the room.
Best Western The Inn at Ramsey 1315 Route 17 South Ramsey NJ   201-327-6700 (800-780-7234)
Dogs are allowed for an additional fee of $10 per night per pet.
Best Western The Inn at Rockaway 14 Green Pond Rd Rockaway NJ   973-625-1200 (800-780-7234)
Dogs are allowed for an additional fee of $25 per night per pet.
Residence Inn by Marriott 7 Boroline Road Saddle River NJ   201-934-4144
Dogs of all sizes are allowed. There is a $75 one time fee and a pet policy to sign at check in.
Holiday Inn 304 Rt 22 W Springfield NJ   973-376-9400 (877-270-6405)
Dogs are allowed for no additional fee. Dogs may not be left alone in the room.

Attractions
Alstede Farms 84 H 513 (Old Route 24), Chester NJ   908-879-7189
Offering fresh produce, event space, a greenhouse, a country store, farm animal feeding, self picking fields, and tours, this farm also offers plenty of relaxation. Dogs are welcome on the grounds. Dogs must be under owner's control, leashed, and cleaned up after at all times.

TOP 200 PLACE Long Pond Ironworks Historic District 1304 Sloatsburg Road, c/o Ringwood State Park Ringwood NJ   973-962-7031
Located within the Ringwood State Park, this 175 acre district is rich in historical and natural beauty and stands as an example of pre-independence ironworks plantations. Leashed dogs may also explore this area. Dogs must be under owner's control and cleaned up after at all times.

Stores
Petco Pet Store 150 State Route 10 East Hanover NJ   973-515-9500
Your licensed and well-behaved leashed dog is allowed in the store.
PetSmart Pet Store 50 International Dr South Flanders NJ   973-448-7601
Your licensed and well-behaved leashed dog is allowed in the store.
Petco Pet Store 9 Interstate Shopping Center Ramsey NJ   201-327-5080
Your licensed and well-behaved leashed dog is allowed in the store.
PetSmart Pet Store 367 Mount Hope Ave Rockaway NJ   973-361-7970
Your licensed and well-behaved leashed dog is allowed in the store.
Petco Pet Store One Route 46 West Totowa NJ   973-256-9175
Your licensed and well-behaved leashed dog is allowed in the store.
Petco Pet Store 339 Pompton Avenue Verona NJ   973-571-9800
Your licensed and well-behaved leashed dog is allowed in the store.
PetSmart Pet Store 1515 US Highway 22 Watchung NJ   908-769-1250
Your licensed and well-behaved leashed dog is allowed in the store.
Petco Pet Store 1701 US Route 22 West Watchung NJ   908-322-2844
Your licensed and well-behaved leashed dog is allowed in the store.
PetSmart Pet Store 57 Route 23 Wayne NJ   973-785-4479
Your licensed and well-behaved leashed dog is allowed in the store.

Parks
Fairwiew Farm Wildlife Preserve 2121 Larger Cross Road Bedminster NJ   908-234-1852
http://www.urwa.org/land/bedminster.html

A bit unusual for a "park" as there are no picnic tables, trash cans, or play areas, this park is about preserving, educating, protecting, and providing a quality nature experience for all the wildlife inhabitants who call it home and its visitors. Dogs are welcome here; they must be leashed and cleaned up after at all times. Dogs are allowed throughout the park and on the trails, they are not allowed in the ponds.

Wawayanda State Park 885 Warwick Tunpike Hewitt NJ 973-853-4462
Covering more than 34,000 acres, this park features a natural 2,167 acre swamp area, more than 60 miles of well marked trails (including a piece of the Appalachian Trail), a beautiful lake surrounded by forested hills, and a variety of land and water recreation. Dogs of all sizes are allowed at this park for no additional fee. Dogs must be well behaved, leashed, cleaned up after, and owners are responsible for them at all times. Dogs may not be left unattended at any time.

Silas Condict County Park William Lewis Arthur Drive Kennelon Boroughs NJ 973-326-7600
Featuring 1,000 acres of activities and recreation for every age, this year-round park also offers event and private meeting space. Dogs of all sizes are allowed. They must be under owner's control, leashed, and cleaned up after.

Hacklebarney State Park 119 Hacklebarney Rd Long Valley NJ 908-638-6969
A long stone staircase brings visitors into this 978 acre glacial valley with gorges carved from the Black River, steep ravines covered in hard-wood forests, rare plants and animals, miles of trails, and a variety of land and water recreation. Dogs are allowed throughout the park and on the trails. Dogs must be leashed and cleaned up after at all times.

Morristown National Historical Park Tempe Wick Road Morristown NJ 973-539-2016
http://www.nps.gov/morr
There are over 27 miles of foot and horse trails, the beginning of a 2 mile auto loop tour, and a visitor center at the Jockey Hollow area of this park that marks the Winter-quarters for the Continental Army during a rather harsh weather period. Dogs are allowed on the grounds and on the trails. Dogs must be on no more than a 6 foot leash and cleaned up after at all times.

Watchung Reservation/Trailside Nature & Science Center 452 New Providence Road Mountainside NJ 908-789-3670
http://www.ucnj.org/trailside/index.html
Rich in folk-lore and cultural history, this 1,900+ acre park is popular for the many hiking and riding trails; and there is a playground, picnic areas, stables, a trailside nature center, and a visitor center as well. It is suggested that a trail map be picked up at the science center, adjacent to the parking lot, prior to hiking in any unfamiliar area as there may be trail closures in effect at different times. Dogs are allowed throughout the park and on the trails. They are not allowed in any park buildings. Dogs must be under owner's control, leashed, and cleaned up after at all times.

TOP 200 PLACE Great Falls of the Passaic River McBride Avenue Paterson NJ 973-279-9587
This 89 acre National Historic Site Park boasts a long, rich cultural and industrial history, trails, and a 77+ foot waterfall. Well behaved dogs are welcome. Dogs must be under owner's control, leashed, and cleaned up after at all times. Dogs are not allowed in buildings.

Shakespeare Garden/Cedar Brook Park Pemberton and Park Avenues Plainfield NJ 908-753-3000
This county park is home to a 1920's garden containing a bust of Shakespeare along with plants that were cited in his works. Dogs are allowed throughout the park and on the trails. Dogs must be leashed and cleaned up after at all times.

Hasenclever Iron Trail 1304 Sloatsburg Road, c/o Ringwood State Park Ringwood NJ 973-962-7031
From deep woodlands to rocky vistas this trail connects Ringwood and Skylands State Parks. Dogs are allowed on the trail. They must be on no more than a 6 foot leash and cleaned up after at all times.

Long Pond Ironworks State Park 1304 Sloatsburg Rd Ringwood NJ 973-962-7031
Dogs on leash are allowed in the state park. The park features hiking, fishing, and boating. It is the historical site of Long Pond Ironworks of 1766 ironwork building and a reconstructed waterwheel. There is no swimming for people but pets can wade in the water while leashed.

Ramapo Mountain State Forest 1304 Sloatsburg Rd Ringwood NJ 973-962-7031
Dogs on leash are allowed in the state park. The park features hiking, fishing, and canoeing. People are not allowed to swim but pets are allowed to wade in the water while on leash.

Ringwood State Park 1304 Sloatsburg Road Ringwood NJ 973-962-7031
Home to such attractions as a 74 acre lake, 2 mansions, 96 acres of gardens, and numerous blazed trails, this 4000+ acre park also provides a wide variety of year-round land and water recreation. Dogs are allowed throughout the park and on the trails; they are not allowed in any of the buildings or in public swim areas. They must be under owner's control, leashed, and cleaned up after at all times.

Off-Leash Dog Parks

Bedminster Dog Park River Road at Rt 206 Bedminster NJ 908-212-7014
http://www.bedminster.us
This fenced dog park located in Bedminster's River Road Park. The dog park is open during daylight hours.

Echo Lake Dog Park Rt 22 Westfield NJ 908-527-4900
This 3 acre, fenced off-leash dog park is open during daylight hours. The park is located just off Rt 22 East on

the Mountainside/Westfield border. The park is managed by the Union County Department of Parks.
Wood Dale County Park Dog Run Prospect Avenue Woodcliff Lake NJ 201-336-7275
There is an official Bergen County off-leash dog run area in Wood Dale County Park.

Outdoor Restaurants
Baja Fresh 136 H 10 East Hanover NJ 973-952-0080
This restaurant serves Mexican food. Dogs are allowed at the outdoor tables. Dogs are allowed at the outdoor tables.
Camille's Sidewalk Cafe 161 South Street Morristown NJ 973-540-9727
http://www.camillescafe.com/
This sidewalk café offers al fresco dining with an eclectic variety of menu items and beverages. Dogs are allowed at the outer tables. Dogs must be under owner's control/care and leashed at all times.
Cathay 22 124 Route 22 West Springfield NJ 973-467-8688
This restaurant and bar serves Chinese. Dogs are allowed at the outdoor tables.
Baja Fresh 1600 H 23N Wayne NJ 973-872-2555
This restaurant serves Mexican food. Dogs are allowed at the outdoor tables. The restaurant has outdoor tables only in the Summer.

North Shore

Accommodations
Avon Manor Inn 109 Sylvania Avenue Avon-by-the-Sea NJ 732-776-7770
http://www.avonmanor.com
Completely remodeled and updated, this inn features indoor or outdoor dining, many extras around the property, is only 2 miles from Spring Lake, and sits only 1 block from the beach and boardwalk. Dogs of all sizes are allowed in the cottages for no additional fee. Dogs must be quiet, well behaved, leashed, cleaned up after, and may be left alone in the room only if the owner is confident in the dogs behavior.
Staybridge Suites Eatontown-Tinton Falls 4 Industrial Way East Eatontown NJ 732-380-9300 (877-270-6405)
Dogs of all sizes are allowed for an additional pet fee per room of $100 for 1 to 14 nights; the fee is $150 for 15 to 29 nights.
Holiday Inn Hazlet 2870 Highway 35 Hazlet NJ 732-888-2000 (877-270-6405)
Dogs of all sizes are allowed for an additional one time pet fee of $25 per room.
Ocean Place Resort and Spa One Ocean Blvd Long Branch NJ 732-571-4000 (800-411-6493)
http://oceanplaceresort.com/
This premier ocean front resort sits amid lush greenery and white sandy beaches, and serves as a great home base for a wide variety of activities and recreation. Dogs of all sizes are allowed for an additional one time fee of $150 per pet. Dogs must be well mannered, leashed, and cleaned up after.
Comfort Inn Middletown 750 Route 35 S Middletown NJ 732-671-3400 (877-424-6423)
Dogs are allowed for an additional pet fee of $25 per night per room.
Red Roof Inn - Princeton North 208 New Road Monmouth Jct NJ 732-821-8800 (800-RED-ROOF)
One well-behaved family pet per room. Guest must notify front desk upon arrival. Guest is liable for any damages. In consideration of all guests, pets must never be left unattended in the guest rooms.
Days Inn Neptune 3310 Hwy 33 East Neptune NJ 732-643-8888 (800-329-7466)
Dogs of all sizes are allowed. There is a $10 per night pet fee per pet.
Red Roof Inn - Tinton Falls 11 Centre Plaza Tinton Falls NJ 732-389-4646 (800-RED-ROOF)
One well-behaved family pet per room. Guest must notify front desk upon arrival. Guest is liable for any damages. In consideration of all guests, pets must never be left unattended in the guest rooms.
Residence Inn by Marriott 90 Park Road Tinton Falls NJ 732-389-8100
Dogs of all sizes are allowed. There is a $75 one time fee and a pet policy to sign at check in.

Campgrounds and RV Parks
Turkey Pond Swamp Campground 200 Georgia Road Freehold NJ 732-842-4000
Dogs of all sizes are allowed. There are no additional pet fees. Dogs may not be left unattended except for short periods, and they must be quiet, leashed, and cleaned up after. The camping and tent areas also allow dogs. There is a dog walk area at the campground.
Pine Cone Resort 340 Georgia Road Pine Cone NJ 732-462-2230
http://pineconenj.com
Dogs up to about 75 pounds are allowed; some breeds are not. There are no additional pet fees. Dogs must be leashed, cleaned up after, and not left unattended. Only one dog is allowed per campsite. The camping and tent

areas also allow dogs. There is a dog walk area at the campground.

Attractions

Salt Water Safari-Treasure Island 201 Union Lane Brielle NJ 732-528-9248
http://www.manasquanwatertaxi.com
Dogs on leash are allowed on the ferry ride and Treasure Island. You must cleanup after your dog. Treasure Island features swimming and hiking. The island sits in the middle of Manasquan River. There are no concession stands, so bring plenty of food and water for you and your pet. Reservations are required for the ferry ride.
Bliss Price Arboretum and Wildlife Sanctuary North side of Wykcoff Road/H 537 Eatontown NJ 732-389-7621
From dawn to dusk visitors can enjoy the variety of trees, trails, and wildlife this scenic area has to offer. Dogs must be under owner's control, leashed, and cleaned up after at all times.

TOP 200 PLACE **Allaire Village** 4265 Atlantic Avenue Farmingdale NJ 732-919-3500
http://www.allairevillage.org/
This living history museum offers more than just a step back in time with beautifully manicured lawns, lots of shaded areas and trails, various special events such as the Spring Planting Festival, flea and craft markets, master craftsmen demonstrations, and a bakery featuring daily, fresh flat cakes. Dogs are welcome here for no additional fee. Dogs must be under owner's control, leashed, and cleaned up after at all times. Dogs are not allowed in any of the buildings.

A. Casola Farms

A. Casola Farms 178 Hwy 34 Holmdel NJ 732-332-1533
http://www.casolafarms.com
This farm has a number of attractions such as picking pumpkins, a corn maze, Halloween events, tractor rides, pony rides and more. Well-behaved, leashed dogs are allowed in the outdoor areas of the farm. The farm is located at Hwy 34 near Schanck Rd.

Stores

Petco Pet Store 4345 US Route 9 Freehold NJ 732-866-0517
Your licensed and well-behaved leashed dog is allowed in the store.
PetSmart Pet Store 2101 US Hwy 35 Ste 201 Holmdel NJ 732-615-9770
Your licensed and well-behaved leashed dog is allowed in the store.
Petco Pet Store 4755 US Highway 9 Howell NJ 732-942-7364
Your licensed and well-behaved leashed dog is allowed in the store.

Paw Palace 19 W Front Street/H 10 Red Bank NJ   877-747-9744
http://www.pawpalaceonline.com/
A comprehensive luxury pet boutique, this shop allows for pure pup pampering-and then some. Dogs must be current on vaccines, be leashed, and under owner's control/care at all times
PetSmart Pet Store 310 State Hwy 36 West Long Branch NJ   732-544-8970
Your licensed and well-behaved leashed dog is allowed in the store.

Beaches
Fisherman's Cove Conservation Area 391 Third Avenue Manasquan NJ   732-922-4080
This is a 52 acre tract on the Manasquan Inlet. It is used for fishing, walking on the beach and sunbathing. Dogs must be on-leash everywhere in the park. To get to the beach take exit 98 from the Garden State Parkway and head south on Rt 34 which becomes Rt 35. Turn right on Higgins Avenue, then left onto Union Avenue (Rt 71), right on Fisk Avenue and right onto 3rd Ave.

Parks
Henry Hudson Aberdeen to Atlantic Highlands Atlantic Highlands NJ   732-787-3033
Dogs on a six foot leash are allowed on this fifteen mile paved trail along an old railroad right of way. The trail may be extended in the future to Freehold Borough.
Dorbrook Recreation Area 209 Route 537 Colts Neck NJ   732-542-1642
Dogs on a six foot leash are allowed on the trails at this 535 acre park. There are 2 1/2 miles of paved trails in the park.
Turkey Swamp Park 200 Georgia Road Freehold Twp NJ   732-462-7286
There are 4 miles of trails and rowboat rentals available on the 17 acre lake. Dogs on a six foot leash are allowed on the trails and in the rowboats.
Gateway National Rec Area/Sandy Hook Unit 128 S Hartshorne Drive Highlands NJ   732-872-5970
This park has a long history as a defense lookout point for America, its home to the country's oldest operating lighthouse, and it is a year-round recreational destination. Dogs are allowed on the ocean beaches except during the Piping Plover nesting season from March 15 through September 15. Dogs are not allowed at any time in the Jamaica Bay Wildlife Refuge area. There is a dog beach area on the bay side of the park. Dogs must be under owner's control, leashed, and cleaned up after at all times.
Holmdel Park 44 Longstreet Road Holmdel NJ   732-946-3758
www.monmouthcountyparks.com
One of the county's most popular and beautiful parks for nature enjoyment and a variety of recreation, this 564 acre park offers 10 miles of trails, a playground, gaming courts, and on 9 acres they have re-created a living history farm. Well behaved dogs are welcome throughout the park and on the trails; they are not allowed in any of the buildings or at the farm. Dogs must be under owner's control, leashed, and cleaned up after at all times.
Manasquan Reservoir 311 Windeler Road Howell NJ   732-919-0996
Dogs on a six foot leash are allowed on the five mile perimeter trail that circles the Manasquan Reservoir. They are also allowed to accompany you in a rowboat on the water. Rowboats may be rented at the park.
Huber Woods Park 25 Brown's Dock Road Locust NJ   732-872-2670
Dogs on a six foot leash are allowed on the approximately seven miles of trails. Also enjoy the views of the Navesink River flowing by.
Cheesequake State Park 300 Gordon Road Matawan NJ   732-566-2161
This is a unique park as it sits between 2 different ecosystems of saltwater and freshwater marches, Pine Barrens and hardwood forest, and there are 5 blazed trails of varying difficulty to explore the unusual geology of the area. Well behaved dogs are welcome throughout the park and on the trails; they are not allowed in any of the buildings, at the campground, or on the swimming beach. Dogs must be under owner's control, leashed, and cleaned up after at all times.
Hartshorne Woods Park Navesink Avenue Middletown NJ   732-872-0336
Dogs on a six foot leash are allowed on the trails at this 741 acre park with 15 miles of dirt trails and 3 miles of roads closed to vehicles. The park is used by hikers, bicycles and equestrians.
Tatum Park 251 Red Hill Road Middletown NJ   732-671-6050
Dogs on a six foot leash are allowed on the four miles of trails.
Clayton Park Emley's Hill Road Upper Freehold NJ   609-259-5794
Dogs on a six foot leash are allowed on the trails at this 421 acre park. The park is used by hikers, bicycles and equestrians.
Assunpink Wildlife Management Area Monmouth County Upper Freehold Township NJ   609-259-2132
This 6,000+ acre park has a 225 acre lake making for a variety of land and water recreation, and especially popular for fishing and hiking. Dogs are allowed throughout the park on leash from September 1st through April 31st, and from May 1st through August 31 they are allowed in the dog training area only. They may be off lead in the training area if they are under good voice control. Dogs must be cleaned up after at all times.
Shark River Park 1101 Schoolhouse Road Wall NJ   732-922-4080
Dogs on a six foot leash are allowed on the trails at this 588 acre park. The park is used by hikers, bicycles and

equestrians.

Off-Leash Dog Parks

RJ Miller Airpark Dog Park Route 530 Berkeley Township NJ   732-506-9090
http://www.ocean.nj.us/parks/Dogpark.pdf
There is a fenced off-leash dog park in RJ Miller Airpark. There are separate areas for large and small dogs. Children under 8 are not allowed in the dog park. Dogs must receive an Ocean County annual permit to use the dog parks in the county. The fee is $20 for the first dog and $10 for each additional dog. Dogs must have a valid dog license to be registered and male dogs must be neutered. See the website at http://www.ocean.nj.us/parks/Dogpark.pdf or call the parks department at 732-506-9090 for locations to register.
Thompson Park Dog Park 805 Newman Springs Road Lincroft NJ   732-842-4000x4256
This fenced off-leash dog park is located in Thompson Park adjacent to the Craft Center. Access the area using the park maintenance entrance which is west of the park gate and follow the road to the end and turn right.

Outdoor Restaurants

Bistro Ole 230 Main st Asbury Park NJ   732-897-0048
This restaurant serves Spanish food. Dogs are allowed at the outdoor tables.
Circus Drive-In State Hwy 35 North Belmar NJ   732-449-2650
This restaurant serves American food. Dogs are allowed at the outdoor tables.
Federico's Pizza and Restaurant 700 Main St Belmar NJ   732-774-8448
This restaurant serves Italian food. Dogs are allowed at the outdoor tables.
La Tuscany Italia LLC 705 Main St Belmar NJ   732-681-6611
This restaurant serves Italian food. Dogs are allowed at the outdoor tables.
Windmill Hot Dogs 1201 River Road Belmar NJ   732-870-6098
http://www.windmillhotdogs.com/
Specialty hot dogs, barbecue, and many more favorites are offered at this eatery, and they offer indoor and outdoor dining options. Dogs are allowed at the outer tables. Dogs must be under owner's control, leashed, and cleaned up after at all times.
Bagel International 48 Main St Bradley Beach NJ   732-775-7447
This restaurant serves deli-type food. Dogs are allowed at the outdoor tables.
Giamano's Restaurant 301 Main St Bradley Beach NJ   732-775-4275
This restaurant serves Italian food. Dogs are allowed at the outdoor tables.
Piancone's Deli and Bakery 804 Main St Bradley Beach NJ   732-775-0846
http://www.piancone.com
This restaurant serves deli-type food. Dogs are allowed at the outdoor tables.
Vic's Italian Restaurant 60 Main St Bradley Beach NJ   732-774-8225
This restaurant serves Italian food. Dogs are allowed at the outdoor tables.
Baja Fresh 550 H 35S Middletown NJ   732-758-0058
This restaurant serves Mexican food. Dogs are allowed at the outdoor tables. The restaurant has outdoor tables only in the Summer.
Labrador Lounge 3581 H 35 N Normandy Beach NJ   732-830-5770
http://www.kitschens.com/
Noted for its futuristic menu with several "best of" notations, this beach area tavern also offers a venue for special events and outside dining. Dogs are allowed at the outside tables; they must be leashed and under owner's control/care at all times.
Windmill Hot Dogs 200 Ocean Avenue North Long Branch NJ   732-870-6098
http://www.windmillhotdogs.com/
Specialty hot dogs, barbecue, and many more favorites are offered at this eatery, and they offer indoor and outdoor dining options. Dogs are allowed at the outer tables. Dogs must be under owner's control, leashed, and cleaned up after at all times.
Zebu Forno 2 Inc 2150 State Route 35 Oakhurst NJ   732-974-7128
This restaurant serves Italian and American food. Dogs are allowed at the outdoor tables.
Starbucks Coffee 4 White St Red Bank NJ   732-530-3667
This coffee shop will allow dogs on leash at the outdoor tables.
Zebu Forno Inc 20 Broad St Red Bank NJ   732-449-2650
This restaurant serves Italian and American food. Dogs are allowed at the outdoor tables.
Cypress Cafe 555 Shrewsbury Ave Shrewsbury NJ   732-219-8646
This restaurant serves American food. Dogs are allowed at the outdoor tables.
Pasta Fresca Cafe and Market 637 Broad St Shrewsbury NJ   732-747-5616
This restaurant serves Italian and deli-type food. Dogs are allowed at the outdoor tables.
Susan Murphy's Ice Cream 601 Warren Avenue Spring Lake Heights NJ   732-449-1130
http://www.icecreamhomemade.com/
Made fresh daily with the best available ingredients have made this a popular ice creamery. They offer a bench

outside for visitors who may want to bring their pooch in for a cone too. Dogs must be under owner's control, leashed, and cleaned up after at all times.

Princeton

Accommodations
Staybridge Suites 1272 South River Road Cranbury NJ   609-409-7181 (877-270-6405)
Dogs of all sizes are allowed for an additional one time fee of $75 per pet.
Clarion Hotel Palmer Inn 3499 Route 1 S Princeton NJ   609-452-2500 (877-424-6423)
Dogs are allowed for an additional pet fee of $20 per night per room. There may be 1 dog up to 50 pounds or 2 dogs up to 20 pounds each per room.
Residence Inn by Marriott 4225 US Route 1 Princeton NJ   732-329-9600
Dogs of all sizes are allowed. There is a $100 one time fee and a pet policy to sign at check in.

Attractions
Morven Museum and Gardens 55 Stockton Street Princeton NJ   609-683-4495
http://www.historicmorven.org/
The Morven museum is located in the former Governor's mansion and displays the cultural history of the state, and although dogs are not allowed inside the mansion, they are allowed to walk through the beautifully manicured lawns and gardens. Dogs must be under owner's control, leashed, and cleaned up after at all times.
Princeton Canoe and Kayak Rental 483 Alexander Street Princeton NJ   609-452-2403
http://www.canoenj.com/prince1.htm
This watercraft rental company provides access to several local waterways, and they will allow your well behaved dog to come aboard rentals. There is no additional pet fee. Dogs must be leashed and cleaned up after at all times.
Princeton University Campus Nassau Street Princeton NJ   609-258-1766
http://www.princeton.edu/main/
Located in the heart of town, the Princeton campus is a hub of the town and tours are offered daily from the First Campus Welcome Center. Your friendly pooch is welcome to explore the area with you. Dogs must be under owner's control at all times, leashed, and cleaned up after.

Stores
PetSmart Pet Store 111 Nassau Park Blvd Princeton NJ   609-520-9200
Your licensed and well-behaved leashed dog is allowed in the store.

Off-Leash Dog Parks
Rocky Top Private Dog Park 4106 Route 27 Princeton NJ   732-297-6527
http://www.rockytopdogpark.com
This private dog park is located on 2 acres in Princeton. They offer weekly, monthly and yearly plans and also options for single visits. For non-members there is usually afternoon hours on weekends to visit the park. For details please check with the website at rockytopdogpark.com or call.
Mercer County Park Old Trenton Road at Robbinsville Rd West Windsor NJ   609-448-1947
The dog park, located within the 2500 acre Mercer County Park, has separate areas for large and small dogs. It is open during daylight hours. Dogs must be on leash outside of the fenced dog park. The Trenton Kennel Dog Show is held in the park annually.

Trenton

Accommodations
Howard Johnson Inn 2995 Rt. 1 South Lawrenceville NJ   609-896-1100 (800-446-4656)
Dogs of all sizes are welcome. There is a $10 per day pet fee.
Red Roof Inn - Princeton 3203 Brunswick Pike Lawrenceville NJ   609-896-3388 (800-RED-ROOF)
One well-behaved family pet per room. Guest must notify front desk upon arrival. Guest is liable for any damages. In consideration of all guests, pets must never be left unattended in the guest rooms.

Attractions

TOP 200 PLACE **Trenton Battle Monument** N Broad Street/H 206 Trenton NJ 609-737-0623
This monument stands as a testament to an important American victory which occurred here the day after Christmas 1776. Dogs are allowed throughout the park and on the trails. Dogs must be on no more than a 6 foot leash, cleaned up after, and under owner's control at all times. Dogs are not allowed in the buildings.

Parks

Washington Crossing State Park 355 Washington Crossing-Pennington Road Titusville NJ 609-737-0623
This was the historic site where General George Washington and his army landed after crossing the Delaware, and the park is now home to a wide variety of plant, animal, and birdlife, with year-round recreation, and more than 15 miles of trails for exploring. Well behaved dogs are welcome throughout the park and on the trails; they are not allowed in any of the buildings or in the campground. However, you will be able to see a good portion of the park from outside. Dogs must be under owner's control, be on no more than a 6 foot leash, and cleaned up after at all times.

New Jersey State House West State Street Trenton NJ 609-633-2709
Home to the State Assembly and other state offices, this beautiful building and landscaped area is open to the public and your well mannered dog is welcome to join you on the grounds. Dogs are not allowed inside the building. Dogs must be under owner's control, leashed, and cleaned up after at all times.

Vineland

Accommodations

Best Western Millville 1701 N 2nd Street Millville NJ 856-327-3300 (800-780-7234)
Dogs are allowed for an additional fee of $10 per night per pet.

Campgrounds and RV Parks

Yogi Bear Tall Pines 49 Beal Road Elmer NJ 800-252-2890
http://www.tallpines.com
Dogs of all sizes are allowed, some breeds are not. There are no additional pet fees. Dogs must be leashed, cleaned up after, and not left unattended. This RV park is closed during the off-season. The camping and tent areas also allow dogs. There is a dog walk area at the campground. Dogs are allowed in the camping cabins.

Attractions

Bisconte Farms 350 Morton Avenue Rosenhayn NJ 856-455-3405
This seasonal farm specializes in strawberries where you can pick your own, and it is always a good idea to call ahead for harvest dates. Dogs are allowed on the farm. They must be under owner's control at all times, and be leashed and cleaned up after.

Shopping Centers

Dutch Neck Village 97 Trench Road Bridgeton NJ 856-451-2188
This colonially designed shopping area features landscaped grounds with hundreds of types of plants, shaded picnic areas, an arboretum, and a good variety of uncommon shops offering a wide line of unique gifts. Dogs are welcome around the grounds; they are not allowed in any of the buildings. Dogs must be well behaved, under owner's control at all times, leashed, and cleaned up after.

TOP 200 PLACE **Glasstown Arts District** 22 N High Street Millville NJ 800-887-4957
http://www.glasstownartsdistrict.com/
You and your pooch can both enjoy exploring this unique artesian district with its rich architecture, unique shops, eateries, and a 700 foot river walk with a riverfront park. Dogs are welcome along the streets, trails, and at the park. It is up to the individual store whether they are allowed inside. A couple of the eateries have seasonal outdoor seating and allow pets at the outer tables. Dogs must be under owner's control, leashed, and cleaned up after at all times.

Parks

Bridgeton City Park Mayor Aitken Drive Bridgeton NJ 609-455-3230 ext. 280
This city park provides 1100 recreational acres for a wide range of land and water activities, and they are also home to historic sites, an amphitheater, and a zoo. Well behaved dogs are welcome throughout the park and on the trails; they are not allowed at the zoo or on the ball fields. Dogs must be under owner's control, leashed, and cleaned up after at all times.

New Jersey Coastal Heritage Trail Route National Park 389 Fortescue Road Newport NJ 856-447-0103

http://www.nps.gov/neje/index.htm
Dogs must be on leash and must be cleaned up after on most trails and stops on the route. You must follow local and state parks rules and pet policies along the route. Mainly auto touring, but also features hiking, boating, swimming, and more.

Parvin State Park 701 Almond Road Pittsgrove NJ   856-358-8616
Dogs on leash are allowed in the state park. They are not allowed in the campground area or beach. The park features canoeing, picnicking, hiking, swimming, fishing, and more. The park also has historic information of the American Indians, Civilian Conservation Corps in 1933-1941, Summer camp for children of displaced Japanese Americans in 1943, POW camp for German prisoners in 1944, and temporary housing for the Kalmychs of Eastern Europe in 1952.

Chapter 10

Pennsylvania
Dog Travel Guide

Altoona

Accommodations

Econo Lodge 2906 Pleasant Valley Blvd/H 220 Altoona PA 814-944-3555 (877-424-6423)
Central to a wealth of historic sites and recreation, this inn also has an Oriental restaurant on site. Dogs are allowed for no additional fee. Dogs must be quiet, well behaved, leashed, and cleaned up after.
Motel 6 - Altoona 1500 Sterling Street Altoona PA 814-946-7601 (800-466-8356)
One well-behaved family pet per room. Guest must notify front desk upon arrival. Guest is liable for any damages. In consideration of all guests, pets must never be left unattended in the guest rooms.
Ramada Inn 1 Sheraton Drive Altoona PA 814-946-1631 (800-311-5192)
Dogs of all sizes are allowed for an additional $20 one time cleaning fee per room. Dogs must be well behaved, leashed, and cleaned up after at all times.
Super 8 Altoona 3535 Fairway Dr Altoona PA 814-942-5350 (800-800-8000)
Dogs of all sizes are allowed. There is a $6 per night pet fee per pet. Smoking and non-smoking rooms are available for pet rooms.
Comfort Inn 111 Cook Road Ebensburg PA 814-472-6100 (877-424-6423)
Dogs are allowed for an additional fee of $15 (plus tax) per night per pet with a credit card on file. There is an extra refundable deposit of $25 if paying by cash.

Parks

Canoe Creek State Park William Penn H Hollidaysburg PA 814-695-6807
This 958 acre day use area has a 155 acre lake allowing for a variety of land and water recreational opportunities. Dogs are allowed; they must be well behaved, on no more than a 6 foot leash or crated, and cleaned up after at all times. Dogs must be licensed with proof of vaccinations. Aggressive dogs are not allowed. Dogs may not be left unattended outside at any time and if in a vehicle only for very short times. Dogs must stay on selected pet routes/trails and areas. They are not allowed in swim or campground areas, or in park buildings.

Barnesville`

Parks

Locust Lake State Park Burma Road/H 1006 Barnesville` PA 570-467-2404
A mountain lake surrounded by beautiful forests with plenty of recreation, easy to difficult hiking trails, and a lot more are all offered at this 1,089 acre park. Dogs are allowed at the park for day use from mid-October to the beginning of April only. They are not allowed when the campground is open from early April to mid-October. Dogs must be well behaved, under owner's control, on no more than a 6 foot leash or crated, and cleaned up after at all times. Dogs must be licensed with proof of vaccinations. Aggressive dogs are not allowed. Dogs may not be left unattended outside at any time and if in a vehicle only for very short times. Dogs must stay on selected pet routes/trails and areas; they may not be in designated swim areas, park buildings, or in the campground area.

Bedford Area

Accommodations

Best Western Bedford Inn 4517 Business 220 Exit 146 PA Tpk Bedford PA 814-623-9006 (800-780-7234)
Dogs are allowed for an additional pet fee of $10 per night per room.
Quality Inn Bedford 4407 BH 220 Bedford PA 814-623-5188 (877-424-6423)
Dogs up to 50 pounds are allowed for an additional fee of $15 per night per pet.
Super 8 Bedford 4498 Business 220 Bedford PA 814-623-5880 (800-800-8000)
Dogs of all sizes are allowed. There is a $5 per night pet fee per pet. Smoking and non-smoking rooms are available for pet rooms.
Best Western Plaza Motor Lodge 16407 Lincoln Highway Breezewood PA 814-735-4352 (800-780-7234)
Dogs are allowed for an additional fee of $10 per night per pet.
Penn-Aire Motel 16359 Lincoln Way Breezewood PA 814-735-4351

Dogs of all sizes are allowed. There are no additional pet fees.

Campgrounds and RV Parks

Hidden Springs Campground 815 Beans Cove Road Clearville PA 814-767-9676
Dogs of all sizes are allowed. There are no additional pet fees. Dogs must be quiet, leashed, and cleaned up after. This RV park is closed during the off-season. The camping and tent areas also allow dogs. There is a dog walk area at the campground.

Blue Knob State Park 124 Park Road Imler PA   814-276-3576 (888-727-2757)
Popular for wildlife viewing through all seasons and for its feel of wilderness, this 6,100+ acre park is the 2nd highest place in the state and offers great views in addition to a wealth of recreational activities. Dogs are allowed for an additional $2 per pet per stay when camping, and no charge for day use. They must be well behaved, under owner's control, on no more than a 6 foot leash or crated, and cleaned up after at all times. Dogs must be licensed with proof of vaccinations. Aggressive dogs are not allowed. Dogs may not be left unattended outside at any time and if in a vehicle only for very short times. Dogs must stay on selected pet routes/trails and areas. They are not allowed in swim areas or in park buildings. The campsites have tables, fire rings, water, playground equipment, modern restrooms, showers, laundry tubs, and a dump station. This RV park is closed during the off-season. The camping and tent areas also allow dogs. There is a dog walk area at the campground. There are no water hookups at the campgrounds.

Shawnee Sleepy Hollow Campground 147 Sleepy Hollow Road Schellsburg PA   814-733-4380
Dogs up to about 65 pounds are allowed. There is a $1 per night per pet additional fee. Dogs must be quiet, well behaved, leashed and cleaned up after. There are some breed restrictions. This RV park is closed during the off-season. The camping and tent areas also allow dogs. There is a dog walk area at the campground.

Shawnee State Park 132 State Park Road Schellsburg PA 814-733-4218
http://www.dcnr.state.pa.us/stateparks
Dogs of all sizes are allowed. There is a $2 per night per pet additional fee. Pets are to be walked in designated walking areas of the campground and on designated pet walkways when accessing other areas of the park from the campground. Dogs must be leashed and under physical control at all times, and pet waste must be disposed of quickly and properly. Pet food must remain inside the camping unit, and dogs must have current rabies certificate and shot records, be quiet and well behaved. Dogs are allowed on the trails and day use areas, but they are not allowed on any sand areas, at the beach shoreline, or in any of the buildings. Dogs may not be left unattended except for very short periods; then they must be left inside your unit, weather permitting. There are some breed restrictions. This campground is closed during the off-season. The camping and tent areas also allow dogs. There is a dog walk area at the campground. There are no water hookups at the campground.

Attractions

TOP 200 PLACE **Old Bedford Village** 220 Sawblade Road Bedford PA   800-238-4347
This living history village offers a rich variety of educational and entertainment activities, including a diverse assortment of military and civilian reenactments, exhibits, festivals, an antique car show, classes to learn the old west way of doing things, holiday themed specials, and a lot more. They are open daily from Memorial Day through Labor Day from 9 am to 5 pm (closed on Wednesday); from Labor Day through October 27 they are open Thursday through Sunday from 9 am to 5 pm, and then open a few days on the holidays. Dogs of all sizes are allowed throughout the village; they are not allowed in the buildings or in any food service areas. Dogs must be leashed and cleaned up after at all times.

Parks

Blue Knob State Park 124 Park Road Imler PA   814-276-3576 (888-727-2757)
Popular for wildlife viewing through all seasons and for its feel of wilderness, this 6,100+ acre park is the 2nd highest place in the state and offers great views in addition to a wealth of recreational activities. Dogs are allowed for an additional $2 per pet per stay when camping, and no charge for day use. They must be well behaved, under owner's control, on no more than a 6 foot leash or crated, and cleaned up after at all times. Dogs must be licensed with proof of vaccinations. Aggressive dogs are not allowed. Dogs may not be left unattended outside at any time and if in a vehicle only for very short times. Dogs must stay on selected pet routes/trails and areas. They are not allowed in swim areas or in park buildings.

Bloomsburg

Accommodations

Quality Inn & Suites 15 Valley West Road Danville PA   570-275-5100 (877-424-6423)
Dogs up to 50 pounds are allowed for an additional one time fee of $25 per pet.

Red Roof Inn - Danville 300 Red Roof Road Danville PA   570-275-7600 (800-RED-ROOF)
One well-behaved family pet per room. Guest must notify front desk upon arrival. Guest is liable for any damages. In consideration of all guests, pets must never be left unattended in the guest rooms.
Super 8 Mifflinville 450 WEST 3RD STREET Mifflinville PA   570-759-6778 (800-800-8000)
Dogs of all sizes are allowed. There is a $10 one time per pet fee per visit. Smoking and non-smoking rooms are available for pet rooms.

Campgrounds and RV Parks

Lackawanan State Park N Abington Road/H 407 Benton PA   570-945-3239 (888-PA-PARKS (727-2757))
This 1,411 acre park with a 198 acre lake offers modern facilities, year-round land and water recreation, environmental education, and trails that wander through a variety of scenic landscapes. Dogs of all sizes are allowed for an additional $2 per pet per stay. Dogs must be well behaved, under owner's control, leashed or crated, and cleaned up after at all times (exceptions during hunting season). Dogs must be licensed and have proof of all vaccinations. Aggressive dogs are not allowed. Dogs may not be left unattended outside at any time and may only be left alone in a vehicle for very short periods. Dogs must stay on selected pet routes/trails and areas; they may not be in designated swim areas or in park buildings. The campground has modern sites, wash houses with hot showers, children's play areas, and some small fishing ponds close by. There is also a dump station available. The camping and tent areas also allow dogs. There is a dog walk area at the campground. There are no water hookups at the campgrounds.
Knoebel's Campground Route 487 Elysburg PA   800-ITS-4FUN
This campground is located next to the Knoebel's Amusement Park which is the largest free admission amusement park in the country. Dogs are allowed at your RV or tent site. Pets are not allowed in the cabins.

Attractions

TOP 200 PLACE **Ashland Coal Mine and Steam Train** 19th and Oak Streets Ashland PA   570-325-3850
http://www.pioneertunnel.com/home.shtml
There are 2 tours offered here; Pioneer Tunnel takes visitors deep into the mountain for a lesson in "hard coal" coal mining, and the Henry Clay is a gauge steam train (once used to haul coal cars), that now take visitors 3,000 feet along side the mountain. Your pooch is welcome on both tours if they are well behaved and comfortable with being in the mine cars or on the train. Dogs must be under owner's control at all times, and be leashed and cleaned up after. Tours last about 30 to 35 minutes.
TOP 200 PLACE **Knoebel's Amusement Park** Route 487 Elysburg PA   800-ITS-4FUN
http://www.knoebels.com
This amusement park is the largest free admission amusement park in the country. From roller coasters to kiddie rides this park has it all. Dogs on leash are allowed in the amusement park and in the camping area. Dogs are not allowed in any of the buildings, on the rides, or in the pool.

Parks

Lackawanan State Park N Abington Road/H 407 Benton PA   570-945-3239 (888-PA-PARKS (727-2757))
This 1,411 acre park with a 198 acre lake offers modern facilities, year-round land and water recreation, environmental education, and trails that wander through a variety of scenic landscapes. Dogs of all sizes are allowed for an additional $2 per pet per stay. Dogs must be well behaved, under owner's control, leashed or crated, and cleaned up after at all times (exceptions during hunting season). Dogs must be licensed and have proof of all vaccinations. Aggressive dogs are not allowed. Dogs may not be left unattended outside at any time and may only be left alone in a vehicle for very short periods. Dogs must stay on selected pet routes/trails and areas; they may not be in designated swim areas or in park buildings.
Ricketts Glen State Park 695 State Route 487 Benton PA   570-477-5675
The main attraction at this 13,000+ acre park is the Glens Natural Area, a registered National Natural Landmark, where visitors will find 21 waterfalls along its Falls Trail. Dogs must be well behaved, under owner's control, leashed or crated, and cleaned up after at all times (exceptions during hunting season). Dogs must be licensed and have proof of all vaccinations. Aggressive dogs are not allowed. Dogs may not be left unattended outside at any time and may only be left alone in a vehicle for very short periods. Dogs must stay on selected pet routes/trails and areas; they may not be in designated swim areas or in park buildings.
World's End State Park H 154 Forks PA   570-924-3287
Nestled in a narrow valley with a swift moving stream, this park offers incredible scenery (especially the Fall foliage), interpretive programs, and over 20 miles of moderate to difficult trails. Dogs are allowed at the park for day use. Dogs must be well behaved, under owner's control, on no more than a 6 foot leash or crated, and cleaned up after at all times. Dogs must be licensed with proof of vaccinations. Aggressive dogs are not allowed. Dogs may not be left unattended outside at any time and in a vehicle for very short times. Dogs must stay on selected pet routes/trails and areas; they may not be in designated swim areas, park buildings, or in the campground area.

Bradford

Accommodations
Best Western Bradford Inn 100 Davis St Bradford PA   814-362-4501 (800-780-7234)
Dogs are allowed for an additional fee of $10 per night per pet.
Comfort Inn 76 Elm Street Bradford PA   814-368-6772 (877-424-6423)
Dogs are allowed for an additional fee of $10 per night per pet.

Campgrounds and RV Parks
Kinzua East KOA Klondike Road, Kinzua Heights Bradford PA   814-368-3662 (800-562-3682)
http://www.kinzuacamping.com
One dog of any size is allowed. There are no additional pet fees. Dogs may not be left unattended, must be leashed, and cleaned up after. There are some breed restrictions. This RV park is closed during the off-season. The camping and tent areas also allow dogs. There is a dog walk area at the campground.

Brookville

Accommodations
Days Inn Brookville 230 Allegheny Blvd Brookville PA   814-849-8001 (800-329-7466)
Dogs of all sizes are allowed. There is a $10 per night pet fee per pet. Reservations are recommended due to limited rooms for pets.
Holiday Inn Express 235 Allegheny Blvd Brookville PA   814-849-8381 (877-270-6405)
Dogs of all sizes are allowed for an additional one time fee of $15 per pet.

Butler

Accommodations
Comfort Inn 1 Comfort Lane Butler PA   724-287-7177 (877-424-6423)
Dogs are allowed for an additional fee of $20 per night per pet.
Days inn Butler 139 Pittsburgh Rd Butler PA   724-287-6761 (800-DAYS-INN)
Dogs of all sizes are allowed. There is a $30 per night pet fee per pet.

Chambersburg

Accommodations
Best Western Chambersburg 211 Walker Rd Chambersburg PA   717-262-4994 (800-780-7234)
Dogs are allowed for an additional fee of $9 per night per pet.
Comfort Inn 3301 Black Gap Road Chambersburg PA   717-263-6655 (877-424-6423)
Dogs are allowed for an additional fee of $10 per night per pet.
Days Inn Chambersburg 30 Falling Spring Rd Chambersburg PA   717-263-1288 (800-329-7466)
Dogs of all sizes are allowed. There is a $10.90 per night pet fee per pet.
Comfort Inn 50 Pine Drive Greencastle PA   717-597-8164 (877-424-6423)
Dogs are allowed for an additional fee of $10 per night per pet.
Best Western Shippensburg Hotel 125 Walnut Bottom Road Shippensburg PA   717-532-5200 (800-780-7234)
Dogs are allowed for an additional fee of $10 per night per pet.

Campgrounds and RV Parks
Twin Bridge Meadow Campground 1345 Twin Bridges Road Chambersburg PA   717-369-2216
Dogs of all sizes are allowed. There are no additional pet fees. Dogs may not be left unattended, must be leashed, and cleaned up after. There are some breed restrictions. This RV park is closed during the off-season.

The camping and tent areas also allow dogs. There is a dog walk area at the campground.

Parks

Buchanan's Birthplace State Park H 16 Cove Gap PA   717-485-3948
Birthplace to one of our most renowned Presidents, this park shares the history of his and his youngest daughter's very important contributions to the country, and offers a variety of recreational pursuits and an environmental education program as well. Dogs are allowed; they must be well behaved, on no more than a 6 foot leash or crated, and cleaned up after at all times. Dogs must be licensed with proof of vaccinations. Aggressive dogs are not allowed. Dogs may not be left unattended outside at any time and if in a vehicle only for very short times. Dogs must stay on selected pet routes/trails and areas. They are not allowed in swim areas or in park buildings.

Clarion

Accommodations

Holiday Inn I-80 Rt 68 Clarion PA   814-226-8850 (877-270-6405)
Dogs of all sizes are allowed for an additional pet fee of $10 per night per room.
Quality Inn and Suites 24 United Drive Clarion PA   814-226-8682 (877-424-6423)
Dogs are allowed for no additional pet fee.
Super 8 Clarion 135 Hotel Road Clarion PA   814-226-4550 (800-800-8000)
Dogs of all sizes are allowed. There are no additional pet fees. Smoking and non-smoking rooms are available for pet rooms.

Clearfield

Accommodations

Comfort Inn 1821 Industrial Park Road Clearfield PA   814-768-6400 (877-424-6423)
Dogs are allowed for an additional pet fee of $15 per night per room.
Days Inn Clearfield 14451 Clearfield Shawville Hwy Clearfield PA   814-765-5381 (800-329-7466)
Dogs of all sizes are allowed. There is a $10 per night pet fee per pet.
Super 8 Clearfield 14597 Clearfield/Shawville Hwy Clearfield PA   814-768-7580 (800-800-8000)
Dogs of all sizes are allowed. There is a $5 per night pet fee per pet. Smoking and non-smoking rooms are available for pet rooms.
Victorian Loft 216 S Front Street Clearfield PA   814-765-4805 (800-798-0456)
http://www.victorianloft.com/
This beautiful 1894 Victorian home sits along the river just a short walk from the town and a variety of activities, eateries, and recreation. Dogs of all sizes are allowed for an additional pet fee of $10 per night for one dog, and if there are 2 dogs, the second dog is an additional $5 per night. Dogs may not be left alone in the room at any time, and they must be leashed and cleaned up after.

Cooksburg

Campgrounds and RV Parks

Cook Forest State Park River Road Cooksburg PA   814-744-8407 (888-PA-PARKS (727-2757))
Famous for its "Forest Cathedral" of virgin white pine and hemlock stands that resulted in it being listed as a National Natural Landmark, this 7,000+ acre park offers an array of land and water recreation and 27 blazed trails. Dogs must be quiet, well behaved, under owner's control, leashed or crated, and cleaned up after at all times. Dogs must be licensed and have proof of all vaccinations. Aggressive dogs are not allowed. Dogs may not be left unattended outside at any time and may only be left alone in a vehicle for very short times. Dogs must stay on selected pet routes/trails and areas; they may not be in designated swim areas or in park buildings, and pet food may not be left outside. The camp areas have picnic tables, fire rings, restrooms, showers, laundry facilities, and a dump station. Dogs are allowed in the Ridge Campground only. This RV park is closed during the off-season. The camping and tent areas also allow dogs. There is a dog walk area at the campground. There are no electric or water hookups at the campgrounds.

Parks

Cook Forest State Park River Road Cooksburg PA   814-744-8407 (888-PA-PARKS (727-2757))
Famous for its "Forest Cathedral" of virgin white pine and hemlock stands that resulted in it being listed as a
National Natural Landmark, this 7,000+ acre park offers an array of land and water recreation and 27 blazed
trails. Dogs must be quiet, well behaved, under owner's control, leashed or crated, and cleaned up after at all
times. Dogs must be licensed and have proof of all vaccinations. Aggressive dogs are not allowed. Dogs may
not be left unattended outside at any time and may only be left alone in a vehicle for very short times. Dogs must
stay on selected pet routes/trails and areas; they may not be in designated swim areas or in park buildings, and
pet food may not be left outside.

Coudersport

Parks

Cherry Springs State Park 4639 Cherry Springs Road Coudersport PA   814-435-5010
This park offers a variety of events (mostly stargazing), year-round environmental interpretive programs, and the
Susquehanna Trail passes nearby for miles of hiking. Dogs are allowed at the park for day use. Dogs must be
well behaved, under owner's control, on no more than a 6 foot leash or crated, and cleaned up after at all times.
Dogs must be licensed with proof of vaccinations. Aggressive dogs are not allowed. Dogs may not be left
unattended outside at any time and in a vehicle for very short times. Dogs must stay on selected pet routes/trails
and areas; they may not be in park buildings, or in the campground area.
Susquehannock State Forest H 6 Coudersport PA   814-274-3600
This state forest is home to numerous diverse ecosystems that support a large variety of plants, fish, mammals,
bird species, and year-round recreation. There are several multi-use trails; the main trail is an 85 mile loop
through some magnificent scenery, especially in the Fall, and there are also 16 vistas points for greater viewing.
Primitive camping is allowed. Dogs must be under owner's control/care, leashed, and cleaned up after at all
times.

Delaware Water Gap

Accommodations

The New Muir House 102 H 2001 Milford PA   570-722-3526
http://www.muirhouse.com/
This inn and restaurant allows dogs at the inn for no additional pet fee, and they are also welcome to sit with their
owner's at the outside dining tables. Dogs must be quiet, under owner's control, leashed or crated, and cleaned
up after at all times.

Campgrounds and RV Parks

Tri-State RV Park 200 Shay Lane Matamoras PA   800-562-2663
http://www.tsrvpark.com
Dogs of all sizes are allowed. There are no additional pet fees. Dogs must have current shot records, be
leashed, and cleaned up after. There is a dog walk area at the campground.

Attractions

Kittatinny Canoes 2130 H 739 Dingmans Ferry PA   800-356-2852
http://www.kittatinny.com/
This adventure company will allow dogs on watercraft rentals for no additional fee, but owners are responsible
for any damage caused by their pet. Dogs must be under owner's control, leashed (except when on the water),
and cleaned up after at all times. Dogs going on rafts must have their nails recently clipped.

Parks

TOP 200 PLACE **Bushkill Falls** P.O. Box 151 Bushkill PA   888-628-7454
http://www.visitbushkillfalls.com
This park features a series of eight waterfalls and natural beauty. Dogs on leash are allowed in the park. Dogs
are allowed on most of the trails throughout the park. Dogs are not allowed in the buildings and must be cleaned
up after.
Delaware National Scenic River Park HQ River Rd off Rt 209 Bushkill PA   570-588-2452

http://www.nps.gov/dela/index.htm
Dogs on leash are allowed in most park areas. They are not allowed at Smithfield Beach and McDade Trail during certain seasons. Call the park for more details. Dogs are not allowed in any of the campsites in New Jersey.
Delaware Water Gap National Recreation Area In the Gap Road Delaware Water Gap PA 570-426-2435
http://www.nps.gov/dewa
Visitors can enjoy a variety of recreational pursuits here, walk the trails that have been used for hundreds of years, or enjoy all the benefits the Middle Delaware River has to offer. Dogs of all sizes are allowed at this park for no additional fee. Dogs must be well behaved, leashed, cleaned up after, and owners are responsible for them at all times. Dogs may not be left unattended at any time. Dogs are allowed on the trails unless otherwise marked, and they are not allowed on beaches.

Outdoor Restaurants
Muir House Inn and Restaurant 102 H 2001 Milford PA 570-296-6373
http://www.muirhouse.com/
This inn and restaurant allows dogs at the inn for no additional pet fee, and they are also welcome to sit with their owner's at the outside dining tables. Dogs must be quiet, under owner's control, leashed or crated, and cleaned up after at all times.

Delmont

Accommodations
Super 8 Delmont 180 Sheffield Dr Delmont PA 724-468-4888 (800-800-8000)
Dogs of all sizes are allowed. There is a $5 per night pet fee per pet. Dogs are not allowed to be left alone in the room. Smoking and non-smoking rooms are available for pet rooms.

Derry

Campgrounds and RV Parks
Keystone State Park 1150 Keystone Park Road Derry PA 724-668-2939
Dogs of all sizes are allowed. There is a $2 per night per pet additional fee. Pets are to be walked in designated walking areas of the campground and on designated pet walkways when accessing other areas of the park from the campground. Dogs must be leashed, under physical control at all times, and cleaned up after. Pet food must remain inside the camping unit, and dogs must have current shot records and a rabies certificate, be quiet, and well behaved. Dogs are allowed on the trails and day use areas, but they are not allowed on the beach, in any swim areas, or in any of the buildings. Dogs may not be left unattended except for very short periods; then they must be left inside your unit, weather permitting. Dogs are allowed on the trails. This campground is closed during the off-season. The camping and tent areas also allow dogs. There is a dog walk area at the campground. There are no water hookups at the campground.

Downingtown

Stores
PetSmart Pet Store 1010 E Lancaster Ave Downingtown PA 610-518-0250
Your licensed and well-behaved leashed dog is allowed in the store.

DuBois

Accommodations
Best Western Inn & Conference Center 82 N Park Place DuBois PA 814-371-6200 (800-780-7234)
Dogs are allowed for an additional fee of $10 per night per pet.

Dutch Country

Accommodations

Adamstown Inn 62 W Main Street Adamstown PA   717-484-0800 (800-594-4808)
http://www.adamstown.com/
Located in a premier antiques and recreational destination, and only 10 minutes from an outlet shopping mecca, this garden inn offers 1 Victorian and 2 English style pet friendly cottages. Dogs of all sizes are allowed for an additional one time pet fee of $50. Dogs must be well behaved, housebroken, and leashed and cleaned up after. Dogs may not be left alone in the cottage at any time.

Black Forest Inn 500 Lancaster Ave Adamstown PA   717-484-4801
There is a $10 per day additional pet fee.

The Barnyard Inn 2145 Old Lancaster Pike Adamstown PA   717-484-1111 (888-738-6624)
http://www.barnyardinn.com/
Although quite an elegant inn, there really is a barnyard of farm animals and llamas here at this 150 year old restored German schoolhouse that sits on 2½ wooded acres in the heart of a busy antiquing area, and close to the Pennsylvania Dutch attractions. Dogs of all sizes are allowed in the Carriage House and the Chicken Coop (a cute new addition) for an additional one time pet fee of $20 per room. Dogs must be friendly to humans and the other animals on site, leashed, and cleaned up after.

The Boxwood 1320 Diamond Street Akron PA   717-859-3466 (800-238-3466)
http://www.theboxwoodinn.net/
Surrounded by wooded and well kept grounds, this renovated colonial stone farmhouse sits on over 3 acres, and is a graceful setting for the casual or business traveler, and for special events. Dogs of all sizes are allowed in the carriage house for an additional one time pet fee of $15 (not neutered is $15 per night per pet). Dogs must be well behaved, leashed, and cleaned up after.

Comfort Inn 2017 N Reading Road Denver PA   717-336-4649 (877-424-6423)
Dogs up to 50 pounds are allowed for an additional one time pet fee of $20 per room.

Holiday Inn 1 Denver Road Denver PA   717-336-7541 (877-270-6405)
Dogs of all sizes are allowed for an additional fee of $10 per night per pet.

Motel 6 - Gordonville 2959 Lincoln Hwy East Gordonville PA   717-687-3880 (800-466-8356)
One well-behaved family pet per room. Guest must notify front desk upon arrival. Guest is liable for any damages. In consideration of all guests, pets must never be left unattended in the guest rooms.

Super 8 Lancaster 2129 Lincoln Hwy East Lancaster PA   717-393-8888 (800-800-8000)
Dogs of all sizes are allowed. There is a $10 per night pet fee per pet. Smoking and non-smoking rooms are available for pet rooms.

Travel Lodge 2101 Columbia Avenue Lancaster PA   717-397-4201
Dogs of all sizes are allowed. There is a $10 per night per pet additional fee.

General Sutter Inn 14 E Main St Lititz PA   717-626-2115
http://www.generalsutterinn.com
Dogs up to 75 pounds are permitted.

B. F. Hiestand House 722 E Market Street Marietta PA   717-426-8415 (877-560-8415)
http://www.bfhiestandhouse.com/
This Queen Anne style 1887 Victorian treasure sits along Susquehanna River and offers a convenient location to numerous attractions, recreational pursuits, shops, and eateries. Dogs of all sizes are allowed for an additional fee of $10 per night per pet. Dogs must be leashed at all times when out of guests' room, cleaned up after, and they may be left crated in the room alone for short time periods only. There are other pets on site.

The Olde Square Inn 127 E Main Street Mount Joy PA   717-653-4525 (800-742-3533)
http://www.oldesquareinn.com/
Located near the heart of Amish country, and numerous other attractions/activities, and year-round recreation, this lovely inn, surrounded by lawns and gardens, offers a full breakfast buffet with indoor or outdoor dining, and a seasonal outdoor pool. Dogs of all sizes are welcome for an additional one time pet fee of $10 per room, and are asked to come in and meet the innkeeper; there are also other dogs on site. Dogs must be leashed at all times when out of the room and be cleaned up after inside and out. Please use a mat under the pet's food and water, and a cover for the bed and/or furniture if the pet is on them. Dogs must be crated when left alone in the room and they suggest leaving on the radio or TV and having a comfort item for the pup.

MainStay Suites 314 Primrose Lane Mountville PA   717-285-2500
Dogs are allowed for an additional fee of $10 per night per pet.

The Hollander Motel 320 E Main St New Holland PA   717-354-4377
There is a $5.00 per day pet charge.

Campgrounds and RV Parks
Sun Valley Campground 451 Maple Grove Road Bowmansville PA   717-445-6262

http://www.sunvalleycamping.com
Dogs of all sizes are allowed. There are no additional pet fees. Dogs must be leashed and cleaned up after. This RV park is closed during the off-season. The camping and tent areas also allow dogs. There is a dog walk area at the campground.
Hickory Run Camping Resort 285 Greenville Road Denver PA 717-336-5564
http://www.hickoryruncampingresort.com
Dogs of all sizes are allowed. There are no additional pet fees. Dogs must be leashed and cleaned up after. They can be left in your unit if they are well behaved, and there is sufficient cooling. This RV park is closed during the off-season. The camping and tent areas also allow dogs. There is a dog walk area at the campground.
Pinch Pond Family Campground 2649 Camp Road Manheim PA 717-665-7120
http://www.gretnaoaks.com
Dogs of all sizes are allowed. There are no additional pet fees. Dogs must be leashed and cleaned up after. This RV park is closed during the off-season. The camping and tent areas also allow dogs. There is a dog walk area at the campground.
Spring Gulch 475 Lynch Road New Holland PA 866-864-8524
http://www.rvonthego.com
Dogs of all sizes are allowed. There are no additional pet fees. Dogs must be well behaved, leashed, and cleaned up after. Dogs are not allowed in the rentals This RV park is closed during the off-season. The camping and tent areas also allow dogs. There is a dog walk area at the campground.
Jellystone Park 340 Blackburn Road Quarryville PA 717-786-3458
http://www.jellystonepa.com
Dogs of all sizes are allowed. There are no additional pet fees. Dogs must be quiet and well behaved. Dogs may not be left unattended, must be leashed, and cleaned up after. This RV park is closed during the off-season. The camping and tent areas also allow dogs. There is a dog walk area at the campground.

Attractions

Aaron and Jessica's Buggy Rides

Aaron and Jessica's Buggy Rides 3121A Old Philadelphia Pike/H 340 Bird-in-hand PA 717-768-8828 (barn phone)
http://www.amishbuggyrides.com/
Guests will experience real Amish life on this narrated tour and will be able to meet several groups of Amish peoples, see their shops, farm stands, schools, and more. Well behaved dogs are allowed on the tour. Dogs must be under owner's control/care, and leashed and cleaned up after at all times.
TOP 200 PLACE **Abe's Buggy Rides** 2596 Old Philadelphia Pike Bird-in-hand PA 717-392-1794
http://www.800padutch.com/abes.html
Take a ride in an Amish Horse Drawn Buggy. Well-behaved dogs are allowed to accompany you on these buggy

rides through Amish Country.
Carriage Rides at Kitchen Kettle Village Route 340 Intercourse PA   717-768-8261
http://www.kitchenkettle.com/
Well behaved dogs can accompany their people on the rides.
The Amish Farm and House 2395 Covered Bridge Drive (for GPS: 2395 Lincoln H E) Lancaster PA   717-394-6185
http://www.amishfarmandhouse.com/
Some of the points of interest to be found on this tour include an 1805 home, a unique Penn-Dutch 1803 barn and lime kiln, a 1775 operational bake oven, and a lot more. In addition, visitors get a true account of historical and contemporary Amish culture. Dogs are allowed on the grounds and on the tour for no additional fee. Dogs must be under owner's control, leashed or crated, and cleaned up after at all times.
Wheatland - The Estate of President James Buchanan 1120 Marietta Avenue Lancaster PA   717-392-8721

http://www.wheatland.org/
This beautiful 4+ acre, park-like estate features the home of James Buchanan, who was the state's only citizen to become President. In addition to educating and preserving its history, they offer numerous educational opportunities, period landscaped grounds and gardens, and an arena for several special events/occasions throughout the year. Well behaved dogs are allowed on the grounds; they are not allowed in buildings. Dogs must be under owner's control, leashed or crated, and cleaned up after.
Allimax Farms Horse-Drawn Carriage Tours 377 Shreiner Rd Leola PA   717-669-2042
http://www.carriagevacations.com/
Tours give visitors entertaining and educational insight to the unique lifestyle of one of the last exclusively Amish communities in the county. Well behaved dogs are welcome to come along. Dogs must be under owner's control, leashed, and cleaned up after.

Shopping Centers

Kitchen Kettle Village

Kitchen Kettle Village 3529 Old Philadelphia Pike Intercourse PA   717-768-8261
http://www.kitchenkettle.com/
This open air shopping village features a canning kitchen, a variety of unique shops, various festivals, and more. Dogs are allowed throughout the village grounds. It is up to individual stores whether they are allowed inside or not. There are horse and carriage rides at the village during certain hours and your dog may be able to accompany you on the carriage rides. Dogs are not allowed in the lodging area. Dogs must be well behaved, leashed, and cleaned up after.
Tanger Outlet 311 Stanley K. Tanger Blvd Lancaster PA   717-392-7260

http://www.tangeroutlet.com/center/LAN
This factory outlet shopping area offers over 60 shops and services. Dogs are allowed throughout the village; they are not allowed in stores. Dogs must be under owner's control, leashed or crated, and cleaned up after at all times. Dogs may not be left unattended at any time, including in vehicles.

Stores
PetSmart Pet Store 1700 Fruitville Pike K Lancaster PA 717-481-9902
Your licensed and well-behaved leashed dog is allowed in the store.
PetSmart Pet Store 2405 Covered Bridge Dr Ste 145 Lancaster PA 717-393-0820
Your licensed and well-behaved leashed dog is allowed in the store.

Off-Leash Dog Parks
Buchanon Park Dog Park Buchanan Avenue and Race Avenue Lancaster PA
http://www.fandm.edu/x2050.xml
This fenced off-leash dog park is in the 22 acre Buchanon Park. This city owned park is run by Franklin & Marshall University. The park is located at the F& M campus.

Outdoor Restaurants
Kettle House Cafe Route 340 Intercourse PA 717-768-8261
http://www.kitchenkettle.com/
Dogs are allowed at the outdoor tables.
Lapp Valley Farm Ice Cream Route 340 Intercourse PA
http://www.kitchenkettle.com/
Dogs are allowed at the outdoor tables.
Isaac's Restaurant and Deli 25 N Queen Street/H 72 Lancaster PA 717-394-5544
http://www.isaacsdeli.com/
Famous for their Pretzel Roll sandwiches as well as a number of other dishes, they also feature a fun kid's menu, and indoor or outdoor dining options. Dogs are allowed at the outer tables. Dogs must be well mannered, under owner's control/care, and leashed at all times.
Dienner's Country Restaurant 2855 Lincoln H E/H 30 Ronks PA 717-687-9571
http://www.dienners.com/
This eatery features a long list of American favorites and indoor or outdoor dining options. Dogs are allowed at the outer tables. Dogs must be well mannered, under owner's control/care, and leashed at all times.

Erie

Accommodations
Best Western Erie Inn and Suites 7820 Perry Highway Erie PA 814-864-1812 (800-780-7234)
Dogs are allowed for an additional one time fee of $10 per pet. Dogs must be quiet and well behaved.
Country Inns & Suites by Carlson 8040 Oliver Road Erie PA 814-864-5810
Dogs up to 75 pounds are allowed. There is a $25 one time additional pet fee.
Days Inn Erie 7415 Schultz Rd Erie PA 814-868-8521 (800-329-7466)
Dogs of all sizes are allowed. There is a $5 per night pet fee per pet.
Motel 6 - Erie 7875 Peach Street Erie PA 814-864-4811 (800-466-8356)
One well-behaved family pet per room. Guest must notify front desk upon arrival. Guest is liable for any damages. In consideration of all guests, pets must never be left unattended in the guest rooms.
Red Roof Inn - Erie 7865 Perry Highway Erie PA 814-868-5246 (800-RED-ROOF)
One well-behaved family pet per room. Guest must notify front desk upon arrival. Guest is liable for any damages. In consideration of all guests, pets must never be left unattended in the guest rooms.
Residence Inn by Marriott 8061 Peach Street Erie PA 814-864-2500
Dogs of all sizes are allowed. There is a $75 one time fee and a pet policy to sign at check in.
Super 8 Erie/I-90 8040 Perry Hwy Erie PA 814-864-9200 (800-800-8000)
Dogs of all sizes are allowed. There is a $5 per night pet fee per pet. Smoking and non-smoking rooms are available for pet rooms.

Campgrounds and RV Parks
Erie KOA 6645 West Road McKean PA 814-476-7706 (800-562-7610)

http://www.eriekoa.com
Dogs of all sizes are allowed. There are no additional pet fees. Dogs may not be left unattended, must be leashed, and cleaned up after. This RV park is closed during the off-season. The camping and tent areas also allow dogs. There is a dog walk area at the campground. Dogs are allowed in the camping cabins.

Stores
PetSmart Pet Store 7451 Peach St Erie PA 814-866-6821
Your licensed and well-behaved leashed dog is allowed in the store.
Petco Pet Store 1960 Edinboro Rd Erie PA 814-864-9256
Your licensed and well-behaved leashed dog is allowed in the store.

Beaches
TOP 200 PLACE Presque Isle State Park Beach PA Route 832 Erie PA 814-833-7424
This state park offers beaches and almost 11 miles of hiking trails. Popular activities at the park include surfing, swimming, boating, hiking, in-line skating and bicycling. Dogs are allowed on a 6 foot or less leash at the park including on the hiking trails and only on beaches that are not guarded by lifeguard staff. Dogs can go into the water, still on leash, but people can only wade in up to their knees since there are no lifeguards in those areas. The unguarded beaches are located throughout the park, but if you want to know exact locations, please stop at the park office for details. The park is located four miles west of downtown Erie, off Route 832.

Parks
Presque Isle 301 Peninsula Drive Erie PA 814-833-7424
This 3,200 acre sandy peninsula park on Lake Erie allows for the state's only "seashore", and in addition to its historical significance, it is a geological and biological diverse area with many endangered species. There is an educational center on site with interactive exhibits and a 75 foot observation tower. Dogs must be well behaved, under owner's control, be on no more than a 6 foot leash or crated, and cleaned up after at all times. Dogs must be licensed and have proof of all vaccinations. Aggressive dogs are not allowed. Dogs may not be left unattended outside at any time and may only be left alone in a vehicle for very short times. Dogs must stay on selected pet routes/trails and areas; they may not be in designated swim areas or in park buildings.

Franklin

Accommodations
Super 8 Franklin 847 Allegheny Blvd Franklin PA 814-432-2101 (800-800-8000)
Dogs of all sizes are allowed. There is a $10 per night pet fee per pet. Dogs are not allowed to be left alone in the room. Smoking and non-smoking rooms are available for pet rooms.

Galeton

Campgrounds and RV Parks
Lyman Run State Park 454 Lyman Run Road Galeton PA 814-435-5010
Dogs of all sizes are allowed. There is a $2 per night per pet additional fee. Pets are to be walked in designated walking areas of the campground and on designated pet walkways when accessing other areas of the park from the campground. Dogs must be leashed, under physical control at all times, and cleaned up after. Pet food must remain inside the camping unit, and dogs must have current shot records and a rabies certificate, be quiet, and well behaved. Dogs are allowed on the trails and day use areas, but they are not allowed on the beach, in any swim areas, or in any of the buildings. Dogs may not be left unattended except for very short periods; then they must be left inside your unit, weather permitting. Dogs are allowed on the trails. This campground is closed during the off-season. The camping and tent areas also allow dogs. There is a dog walk area at the campground. There are no water hookups at the campground.

Gallitzin

Attractions

Allegheny Portage Railroad National Heritage Site 110 Federal Park Road/H 22 Gallitzin PA   814-886-6150

http://www.nps.gov/alpo/
A variety of trails, including a nature trail, special planned events, and interpretive programs are offered at this historic railroad site that was once the fastest way to get through the rough terrain of the state. Dogs are allowed on the grounds; they are not allowed in buildings. Dogs must be leashed and cleaned up after, and they may not be left unattended.

Gettysburg

Accommodations
America Best Inn 301 Steinwehr Avenue Gettysburg PA   717-334-1188
Friendly dogs of all sizes are allowed. They say they perfer to take only 2 dogs per room, but if well behaved, will take up to 4 dogs. There are no additional pet fees.
Comfort Inn 871 York Road Gettysburg PA   717-337-2400 (877-424-6423)
Dogs are allowed for an additional fee of $10 per night per pet.
Gettysburg Travelodge 64 Steinwehr Ave Gettysburg PA   717-334-9281
There are no pet fees.
Holiday Inn 516 Baltimore St Gettysburg PA   717-334-6211 (877-270-6405)
Dogs of all sizes are allowed for an additional one time pet fee of $10 per room.

Campgrounds and RV Parks
Mountain Creek Campground 349 Pine Grove Road Gardners PA   717-486-7681
http://www.mtncreekcg.com
Dogs of all sizes are allowed. There are no additional pet fees. Dogs must be quiet, well behaved, leashed, and cleaned up after. This RV park is closed during the off-season. The camping and tent areas also allow dogs. There is a dog walk area at the campground.
Artillery Ridge Camping Resort 610 Taneytown Road Gettysburg PA   717-334-1288 (866-932-2674)
http://www.artilleryridge.com/
There is a long list of amenities, activities, attractions, and events here to enjoy, but a highlight is the largest Battlefield diorama in the US with over 800 feet of display of Gettysburg and of the battle fought there. Dogs are allowed throughout the resort; there is no additional fee. Dogs must be leashed and cleaned up after. This RV park is closed during the off-season. The camping and tent areas also allow dogs. There is a dog walk area at the campground.
Drummer Boy Camping Resort 1300 Hanover Road Gettysburg PA   800-293-2808
http://www.drummerboycamping.com
Dogs of all sizes are allowed. There are no additional pet fees. Dogs may not be left unattended, must be leashed, and cleaned up after. They are also not allowed to be tied up outside alone or be in any of the buildings. This RV park is closed during the off-season. The camping and tent areas also allow dogs. There is a dog walk area at the campground.
Gettysburg Campground 2030 Fairfield Road/H 116 Gettysburg PA   717-334-3304 (888 879-2241)
http://www.gettysburgcampground.com/
This full service family campground offers a long list of amenities, activities, attractions, and events at this recreational destination, plus they have an ice cream parlor on site. Dogs are allowed throughout the resort; there is no additional fee. Dogs must be leashed and cleaned up after at all times. This RV park is closed during the off-season. The camping and tent areas also allow dogs. There is a dog walk area at the campground.
Gettysburg/Battlefield KOA 20 Knox Road Gettysburg PA   717-642-5713 (800-562-1869)
http://www.gettysburgkoa.com
Dogs of all sizes are allowed, and there are no additional pet fees for tent or RV sites. There is a $10 one time pet fee for cabin rentals. Dogs may not be left unattended at any time, must be leashed, and cleaned up after. This RV park is closed during the off-season. The camping and tent areas also allow dogs. There is a dog walk area at the campground. Dogs are allowed in the camping cabins.
Round Top Campground 180 Night Road Gettysburg PA   717-334-9565
http://www.roundtopcamp.com
Dogs of all sizes are allowed. There are no additional pet fees. Dogs may not be left unattended, must be leashed, and cleaned up after. Dogs are not allowed in the rentals. The camping and tent areas also allow dogs. There is a dog walk area at the campground.

Attractions
Eisenhower National Historic Site 97 Taneytown Road Gettysburg PA   717-338-9114

Pennsylvania - Please always call ahead to make sure that an establishment is still dog-friendly

http://www.nps.gov/eise/index.htm
Dogs must be on leash and must be cleaned up after on property. Dogs are not allowed in the house or buildings. Open daily 9am-4pm.

Gettysburg National Military Park

Hiking in the Gettysburg Battlefields

TOP 200 PLACE **Gettysburg National Military Park** Gettysburg PA 717-334-1124

http://www.nps.gov/gett/
Probably the most famous American battlefield, Gettysburg marked the turning point in the Civil War. Later, President Lincoln gave his famous Gettysburg Address here. Dogs are allowed to visit the outside portions of the battlefield on leash. They are not allowed into buildings or the cemetery. The battlefield consists of auto touring, walking and you can get tapes or CDs to guide you on your tour.

TOP 200 PLACE **Jenny Wade House Ghost Tours** 528 Baltimore St Gettysburg PA   717-334-4100
Your dog may accompany you on the Candlelit Ghost Tour that leaves from the Jenny Wade House Gift Shop regularly during the Summer. The tour walks around and explores the ghostly history of Gettysburg and includes entry into the Jenny Wade House.

Shopping Centers
Gettysburg Village 1863 Gettsyburg Village Drive Gettysburg PA   717-337-9705
http://www.gettysburgvillage.com/
This factory outlet village offers a collection of stores, specialty shops, and services, in addition to hosting a variety of special events, including SPCA Day (an event usually held the last weekend in June). Dogs are allowed throughout the village; they are not allowed in the food court. It is up to the individual stores whether they are allowed inside or not. Dogs must be under owner's control, leashed or crated, and cleaned up after at all times.

Outdoor Restaurants
Hunt's Fresh Cut Fries 61 Steinwehr Avenue Gettysburg PA   717-334-4787
This restaurant serves American food. Dogs are allowed at the outdoor tables.
O'Rorkes 44 Steinwehr Ave Gettysburg PA   717-334-2333
http://www.ororkes.com/
Dogs are allowed at the outdoor tables.

Greensburg

Accommodations
Four Points by Sheraton Greensburg 100 Sheraton Dr., Route 30 East Greensburg PA   724-836-6060 (888-625-5144)
Dogs of all sizes are allowed. There is a $10 per stay pet fee per pet. Dogs are not allowed to be left alone in the room.

Attractions
Bushy Run Battlefield 151 Bushy Field Road Jeannette PA   724-527-5584
http://www.bushyrunbattlefield.com
Rich in colonial and Native American history, this 213 acre park has strong historical significance, and they are dedicated to sharing this history through a variety of interpretive exhibits, guided/self-guided tours, special events, and reenactments. Dogs must be on no more than a 6 foot leash or crated, cleaned up after at all times, and licensed with proof of vaccinations. Aggressive dogs are not allowed. Dogs may not be left unattended outside at any time and if in a vehicle only for very short times. Dogs must stay on selected pet routes/trails and areas. They are not allowed in park buildings.

Stores
PetSmart Pet Store RR 6 Box 214 Hempfield Square Greensburg PA   724-850-7780
Your licensed and well-behaved leashed dog is allowed in the store.
Petco Pet Store 1810 Greengate Centre Circle Greensburg PA   724-838-1570
Your licensed and well-behaved leashed dog is allowed in the store.

Greentown

Campgrounds and RV Parks
Promised Land State Park Park Avenue Greentown PA   570-676-3428 (888-PA-PARKS (727-2757))
This scenic 3,000 acre park includes natural areas, forests, 2 lakes, several small streams, waterfalls, and about

50 miles of hiking trails in the park and the surrounding state forest. Dogs of all sizes are allowed for an additional $2 per pet per stay. Dogs must be well behaved, under owner's control, leashed or crated, and cleaned up after at all times (exceptions during hunting season). Dogs must be licensed and have proof of all vaccinations. Aggressive dogs are not allowed. Dogs may not be left unattended outside at any time and may only be left alone in a vehicle for very short periods. Dogs must stay on selected pet routes/trails and areas; they may not be in designated swim areas or in park buildings. There are 4 modern to rustic campgrounds with picnic tables, fire pits, restrooms, and hot showers. This RV park is closed during the off-season. The camping and tent areas also allow dogs. There is a dog walk area at the campground. There are no water hookups at the campgrounds.

Parks
Promised Land State Park Park Avenue Greentown PA   570-676-3428 (888-PA-PARKS (727-2757))
This scenic 3,000 acre park includes natural areas, forests, 2 lakes, several small streams, waterfalls, and about 50 miles of hiking trails in the park and the surrounding state forest. Dogs of all sizes are allowed for an additional $2 per pet per stay. Dogs must be well behaved, under owner's control, leashed or crated, and cleaned up after at all times (exceptions during hunting season). Dogs must be licensed and have proof of all vaccinations. Aggressive dogs are not allowed. Dogs may not be left unattended outside at any time and may only be left alone in a vehicle for very short periods. Dogs must stay on selected pet routes/trails and areas; they may not be in designated swim areas or in park buildings.

Hanover

Accommodations
Howard Johnson Inn 1080 Carlisle Street Hanover PA   717-646-1000 (800-446-4656)
Well-behaved dogs of all sizes are allowed. There is a $10 per day additional pet fee.

Campgrounds and RV Parks
Codorus State Park 1066 Blooming Grove Rd Hanover PA   717-637-2418
http://www.dcnr.state.pa.us/stateparks
Dogs of all sizes are allowed. There is a $2 per night per pet additional fee. Dogs are to be leashed and under physical control at all times. Pet food must remain inside the camping unit, and pet waste must be disposed of quickly and properly. Pets are to be walked in designated walking areas of the campground and on designated pet walkways when accessing other areas of the park from the campground. Dogs are not permitted in swimming areas or inside buildings, they must have current rabies certificate and shot records, be quiet, and well behaved. Dogs may not be left unattended except for very short periods, and then they must be inside, weather permitting. Dogs on lead are allowed on the trails. There are some breed restrictions. This campground is closed during the off-season. The camping and tent areas also allow dogs. There is a dog walk area at the campground. There are no water hookups at the campground.

Stores
Petco Pet Store 416 Eisenhower Drive Hanover PA   717-646-9157
Your licensed and well-behaved leashed dog is allowed in the store.

Harrisburg - Hershey

Accommodations
Comfort Suites 10 S Hanover Street Carlisle PA   717-960-1000 (877-424-6423)
Dogs are allowed for an additional fee of $10 per night per pet.
Days Inn Carlisle 101 Alexander Spring Rd Carlisle PA   717-258-4147 (800-329-7466)
Dogs of all sizes are allowed. There is a $6 per night pet fee per pet. There is a $10 fee per night for smoking rooms.
Hampton Inn 1164 Harrisburg Pike Carlisle PA   717-240-0200
Well behaved dogs of all sizes are allowed. There are no additional pet fees, and a cell number needs to be left with the front desk if your pet is left in the room.
Holiday Inn 1450 Harrisburg Pike Carlisle PA   717-245-2400 (877-270-6405)
Dogs of all sizes are allowed for an additional fee of $10 per night per pet.
Motel 6 - Harrisburg - Carlisle 1153 Harrisburg Pike Carlisle PA   717-249-7622 (800-466-8356)

One well-behaved family pet per room. Guest must notify front desk upon arrival. Guest is liable for any damages. In consideration of all guests, pets must never be left unattended in the guest rooms.
Pheasant Field 150 Hickorytown Road Carlisle PA   717-258-0717 (877-258-0717)
http://www.pheasantfield.com/
Pastoral fields, wooded and nature walks, a labyrinth, gardens, and a pond are all compliment to this 200 year old restored brick farmhouse, and they are also in an area famous for collector car shows. Dogs of all sizes are welcome in the Pet-sylvania Room for an additional pet fee of $10 per night per room. Dogs must be well behaved, leashed, cleaned up after, and crated when left alone in the room. Arrangements need to be made for housekeeping, and if the owner is confident in their pets behavior and housekeeping is done, pets may be in the room without being crated, just inform the front desk they are there.
Quality Inn 1255 Harrisburg Pike Carlisle PA   717-243-6000 (877-424-6423)
Dogs are allowed for an additional fee of $10 per night per pet.
Super 8 Carlisle/South 100 Alexander Spring Rd Carlisle PA   717-245-9898 (800-800-8000)
Dogs of all sizes are allowed. There is a $6 per night pet fee per pet. Smoking and non-smoking rooms are available for pet rooms.
Holiday Inn Hershey Exit 28 I-81 Grantville PA   717-469-0661 (877-270-6405)
Dogs of all sizes are allowed for no additional fee with a credit card on file; there is a $70 refundable deposit if paying by cash. After 1-1-08 there may be an additional daily fee.
Best Western Capital Plaza 150 Nationwide Drive Harrisburg PA   717-545-9089 (800-780-7234)
Dogs are allowed for no additional pet fee.
Best Western Harrisburg/Hershey Hotel & Suites 300 N Mountain Road Harrisburg PA   717-652-7180 (800-780-7234)
Dogs are allowed in the standard rooms for an additional pet fee of $10 per night per room; the fee is $25 for suites.
Comfort Inn 7744 Linglestown Road Harrisburg PA   717-540-8400 (877-424-6423)
Dogs are allowed for an additional fee of $10 per night per pet in the Winter months (November to February), and $25 per night per pet during the other months.
Comfort Inn East 4021 Union Deposit Road Harrisburg PA   717-561-8100 (877-424-6423)
Dogs are allowed for an additional fee of $10 per night per pet.
Comfort Inn Riverfront 525 S Front Street Harrisburg PA   717-233-1611 (877-424-6423)
Dogs up to 50 pounds are allowed for an additional fee of $25 per night per pet.
Crowne Plaza Hotel Harrisburg-Hershey 23 S Second St Harrisburg PA   717-234-5021 (877-270-6405)
Dogs up to 50 pounds are allowed for an additional one time pet fee of $50 per room.
Daystop Harrisburg 7848 Linglestown Rd Harrisburg PA   717-652-9578 (800-DAYS-INN)
Dogs of all sizes are allowed. There is a $6 per night pet fee per pet.
Holiday Inn 4751 Lindle Rd Harrisburg PA   717-939-7841 (877-270-6405)
Dogs up to 50 pounds are allowed for a $75 refundable deposit.
Holiday Inn Express Hotel and Suites 5680 Allentown Blvd Harrisburg PA   717-657-2200 (877-270-6405)
Dogs of all sizes are allowed for an additional fee of $25 per night per pet. There may be no more than 5 beings per room.
Howard Johnson 7930 Linglestown Rd. Harrisburg PA   717-540-9100 (800-446-4656)
Well-behaved dogs of all sizes are allowed. There is a $10 per day additional pet fee.
La Quinta Inn Harrisburg Airport/Hershey 990 Eisenhower Boulevard Harrisburg PA   717-939-8000 (800-531-5900)
Dogs of all sizes are allowed. There are no additional fees. Dogs must be leashed and cleaned up after. Dogs must be crated if left unattended in the room, and removed or crated for housekeeping.
Red Roof Inn - Harrisburg North 400 Corporate Circle Harrisburg PA   717-657-1445 (800-RED-ROOF)
One well-behaved family pet per room. Guest must notify front desk upon arrival. Guest is liable for any damages. In consideration of all guests, pets must never be left unattended in the guest rooms.
Red Roof Inn - Harrisburg South 950 Eisenhower Boulevard Harrisburg PA   717-939-1331 (800-RED-ROOF)
One well-behaved family pet per room. Guest must notify front desk upon arrival. Guest is liable for any damages. In consideration of all guests, pets must never be left unattended in the guest rooms.
Residence Inn by Marriott 4480 Lewis Road Harrisburg PA   717-561-1900
Dogs up to 80 pounds are allowed. There is a $100 one time fee and a pet policy to sign at check in.
Best Western Inn Hershey Route 422 & Sipe Avenue Hershey PA   717-533-5665 (800-780-7234)
Dogs are allowed for an additional one time pet fee of $25 per room.
Comfort Inn at the Park 1200 Mae Street Hummelstown PA   717-566-2050 (877-424-6423)
Dogs of all sizes are allowed. There is a $35 one time fee per room and a pet policy to sign at check in.
Comfort Inn Capital City 1012 Wesley Drive Mechanicsburg PA   717-766-3700 (877-424-6423)
Dogs are allowed for an additional fee of $25 per night per pet.
Days Inn Harrisburg South 353 Lewisburg Rd New Cumberland PA   717-774-4156 (800-329-7466)
Dogs of all sizes are allowed. There is a $15 per night pet fee per pet.
Motel 6 - Harrisburg 200 Commerce Drive New Cumberland PA   717-774-8910 (800-466-8356)
One well-behaved family pet per room. Guest must notify front desk upon arrival. Guest is liable for any

damages. In consideration of all guests, pets must never be left unattended in the guest rooms.

Campgrounds and RV Parks

Union Canal Campground and the Swatara Creek Water Trail 1929 Blacks Bridge Road Annville PA 717-838-9580
This recreation destination offers canoe rentals (dogs allowed), a trail that follows the river, an 18-hole chip and putt golf course, and camping. Dogs are allowed in the camp area for no additional pet fee. Dogs must be quiet, well behaved, leashed, and cleaned up after at all times. This RV park is closed during the off-season. The camping and tent areas also allow dogs. There is a dog walk area at the campground.
Western Village RV Park 200 Greenview Drive Carlisle PA 717-243-1179
http://www.westernvillagervpark.com
Dogs of all sizes are allowed. There are no additional pet fees. Dogs may not be left unattended, must be leashed, and cleaned up after. Dogs are not allowed on other guests' sites. There is a dog walk area at the campground.
Hershey Conewago Campground 1590 Hershey Road Elizabethtown PA 717-367-1179
http://www.hersheyconewago.com
Dogs of all sizes are allowed. There are no additional pet fees. Dogs may not be left unattended at any time, must be leashed, and cleaned up after. This RV park is closed during the off-season. The camping and tent areas also allow dogs. There is a dog walk area at the campground.
Hershey Highmeadow Campground 1200 Matlock Road Hummelstown PA 717-534-8999
http://www.hersheycamping.com
Dogs of all sizes are allowed. There are no additional pet fees. Dogs must be leashed and cleaned up after. There is a dog walk area at the campground.

Attractions

Union Canal Canoe Rental 1929 Blacks Bridge Road Annville PA 717-838-9580
This watercraft rental company will allow dogs on rentals for no additional fee. Dogs must be well trained, under owner's control/care at all times, and leashed. There is a campground on site that also allows pets.
Pennsylvania State Capitol Complex N 3rd and State Streets Harrisburg PA 717-787-6810
http://www.legis.state.pa.us/
In addition to indoor tours of this elaborate complex, there are also acres of landscaped grounds and a beautiful central fountain. Dogs are allowed on the grounds; they are not allowed in any of the buildings. Dogs must be well behaved, leashed, and cleaned up after at all times.
Hersheypark Amusement Park Kennels 100 W Hershey Park Drive Hershey PA 800-HERSHEY
http://www.hersheypa.com/
This park is a major family recreation and entertainment destination, and although dogs are not allowed in the amusement park, they can relax in the air conditioned, staffed day kennel located in the Barking Lot near the entrance. The fee is $10 per day per pet, and they provide water and security. Pet owners are responsible for the exercising and feeding of their pet. Dogs must be under owner's control/care and leashed (when not in the kennel).

Shopping Centers

The Outlets at Hershey 150 Hershey Park Drive Hershey PA 717-520-1236
http://www.theoutletsathershey.com/
This outlet village features 60 name brand stores. Dogs are allowed throughout the village; they are not allowed in the stores and they may not be left unattended or alone in any vehicle. Dogs must be under owner's control, leashed or crated, and cleaned up after at all times. They must be friendly and well behaved.

Stores

PetSmart Pet Store 248 Westminster Dr Carlisle PA 717-218-0107
Your licensed and well-behaved leashed dog is allowed in the store.
PetSmart Pet Store 4200 Derry St Harrisburg PA 717-558-7642
Your licensed and well-behaved leashed dog is allowed in the store.
PetSmart Pet Store 5900 Carlisle Pike Mechanicsburg PA 717-795-2449
Your licensed and well-behaved leashed dog is allowed in the store.

Parks

Stony Valley Railroad Grade Trail 2001 Elmerton Avenue Harrisburg PA 717-787-9612
This former RR corridor now offers 22 miles of multi-use trail and is quite popular because of its location and beauty. Well mannered dogs are allowed on the trail. Dogs must be under owner's control, leashed, and cleaned up after at all times.

Hazleton

Accommodations

Best Western Genetti Lodge Route 309, RR2 Hazleton PA   570-454-2494 (800-780-7234)
Dogs are allowed for an additional fee of $10 per night per pet.
Hazelton Motor Inn 615 E Broad Street Hazleton PA   570-459-1451
http://www.hazletonmotorinn.com/
This motor inn sits central to a variety of activities and recreational opportunities. Dogs of all sizes are allowed for an additional fee of $5 per night per pet. Dogs must be leashed, cleaned up after, and they may only be left for a short time in the room if they will be quiet and well behaved. Guests with one dog may request a non-smoking room; guests with two or more dogs are placed in a smoking room.
Comfort Inn 58 H 93 West Hazleton PA   570-455-9300 (877-424-6423)
Dogs are allowed for an additional fee of $10 per night per pet.

Campgrounds and RV Parks

Locust Lake State Park Burma Road/H 1006 Barnesville PA   570-467-2404
A mountain lake surrounded by beautiful forests with plenty of recreation, easy to difficult hiking trails, and a lot more are all offered at this 1,089 acre park. Dogs of all sizes are allowed for an additional $2 per pet per stay. Visitors are not allowed to bring dogs for day use when the campground is open from early April to mid-October; they are allowed in the park from mid-October to the beginning of April. Dogs must be well behaved, under owner's control, leashed or crated, and cleaned up after at all times (exceptions during hunting season). Dogs must be licensed with proof of vaccinations. Aggressive dogs are not allowed. Dogs may not be left unattended outside at any time and if in a vehicle only for very short times. Dogs must stay on selected pet routes/trails and areas; they may not be in designated swim areas, park buildings, or in the campground area. Trail maps allowing dogs can be obtained at the park office. The camp area has nice wooded sites with a parking pad, fire rings, picnic tables, and modern restrooms, showers, playgrounds, and a dump station are nearby. This RV park is closed during the off-season. The camping and tent areas also allow dogs. There is a dog walk area at the campground. There are no water hookups at the campgrounds.

Parks

Locust Lake State Park Burma Road/H 1006 Barnesville PA   570-467-2404
A mountain lake surrounded by beautiful forests with plenty of recreation, easy to difficult hiking trails, and a lot more are all offered at this 1,089 acre park. Dogs of all sizes are allowed for an additional $2 per pet per stay. Visitors are not allowed to bring dogs for day use when the campground is open from early April to mid-October; they are allowed in the park from mid-October to the beginning of April. Dogs must be well behaved, under owner's control, leashed or crated, and cleaned up after at all times (exceptions during hunting season). Dogs must be licensed with proof of vaccinations. Aggressive dogs are not allowed. Dogs may not be left unattended outside at any time and if in a vehicle only for very short times. Dogs must stay on selected pet routes/trails and areas; they may not be in designated swim areas, park buildings, or in the campground area. Trail maps allowing dogs can be obtained at the park office.

Hermitage

Attractions

Avenue of the Flags, Hillcrest Memorial Park 2619 East State Street Hermitage PA   724-346-3818
http://www.avenueofflags.com/
Begun to represent the safe return of the Iranian hostages, an American flag was erected each day until their release - a total of 444 days and 444 flags. There is also the eternal flame at this picturesque 71-acre memorial park which stands as a symbol of hope and freedom, and also pays homage to the 8 who gave their lives in an attempt to rescue the hostages. Dogs must be well mannered, leashed, and cleaned up after at all times.

Hookstown

Campgrounds and RV Parks

Raccoon Creek State Park 3000 State Route 18 Hookstown PA 724-899-2200
Dogs of all sizes are allowed. There is a $2 per night per pet additional fee. Pets are to be walked in designated walking areas of the campground and on designated pet walkways when accessing other areas of the park from the campground. Dogs must be leashed, under physical control at all times, and cleaned up after. Pet food must remain inside the camping unit, and dogs must have current shot records and a rabies certificate, be quiet, and well behaved. Dogs are allowed on the trails and day use areas, but they are not allowed on the beach, in any swim areas, or in any of the buildings. Dogs may not be left unattended except for very short periods; then they must be left inside your unit, weather permitting. Dogs are allowed on all the trails. This campground is closed during the off-season. The camping and tent areas also allow dogs. There is a dog walk area at the campground. There are no water hookups at the campground.

Huntingdon

Campgrounds and RV Parks
Penn Roosevelt Stone Creek Road Huntingdon PA 814-667-1800
Dogs of all sizes are allowed. There is a $2 per night per pet additional fee. Pets are to be walked in designated walking areas of the campground and on designated pet walkways when accessing other areas of the park from the campground. Dogs must be leashed, under physical control at all times, and cleaned up after. Pet food must remain inside the camping unit, and dogs must have current shot records and a rabies certificate, be quiet, and well behaved. Dogs are allowed on the trails and day use areas, but they are not allowed on the beach, in any swim areas, or in any of the buildings. Dogs may not be left unattended except for very short periods. Dogs are allowed on the trails. The camping and tent areas also allow dogs. There is a dog walk area at the campground. There are no electric or water hookups at the campground.

Hyner

Parks
Hyner Run State Park 86 Hyner Park Road Hyner PA 570-923-6000
Nestled in a small valley amid steep mountains, this park offers a cozy getaway for picnicking, hiking (they are the eastern trailhead for the 50-mile Donut Hole Trail system), and a variety of other recreation. Dogs are allowed; they must be well behaved, under owner's control, on no more than a 6 foot leash or crated, and cleaned up after at all times. Dogs must be licensed with proof of vaccinations. Aggressive dogs are not allowed. Dogs may not be left unattended outside at any time and if in a vehicle only for very short times. Dogs must stay on selected pet routes/trails and areas. They are not allowed in swim or campground areas, or in park buildings.
Hyner View State Park Hyner Mountain Rd Hyner PA 570-923-6000
The central attraction at this state park is the overlook wall giving visitors breathtaking views of the Susquehanna River and the nearby mountains. It is also a favorite spot for hang gliding. Dogs are allowed; they must be well behaved, under owner's control, on no more than a 6 foot leash or crated, and cleaned up after at all times. Dogs must be licensed with proof of vaccinations. Aggressive dogs are not allowed. Dogs may not be left unattended outside at any time and if in a vehicle only for very short times. Dogs must stay on selected pet routes/trails and areas.

Jim Thorpe

Attractions
The Switch Back Trail Railroad Station Jim Thorpe PA 570-325-8255
Passing through landscape once called the Switzerland of America, the Switch Back Trail is an 18 mile round trip "Rails to Trails" trail between Summit Hill and Jim Thorpe that also educates visitors on the historic Switch Back Gravity Railroad. Trail maps are available at the train station and at other sites along the way. Dogs are welcome on the trail; they must be leashed and cleaned up after.
TOP 200 PLACE Eckleys Miners Village 2 Eckley Main Street Weatherly PA 570-636-2070
http://www.eckleyminers.org/about.html
This historic village is a museum dedicated to the everyday lives of the "hard coal" miners and their families. Well behaved dogs are allowed on the grounds; they are not allowed in buildings. Dogs must be under owner's control, leashed or crated, and cleaned up after.

Parks

Lehigh Gorge State Park Lehigh Gorge Drive Jim Thorpe PA 570-443-0400
This 4,548 acre park follows about 30 miles along the Lehigh River with some 26 miles of abandoned railroad grade creating a number of year-round land and water recreational opportunities, and some great sightseeing areas. Dogs must be well behaved, under owner's control, leashed or crated, and cleaned up after at all times (exceptions during hunting season). Dogs must be licensed and have proof of all vaccinations. Aggressive dogs are not allowed. Dogs may not be left unattended outside at any time and may only be left alone in a vehicle for very short periods. Dogs are not allowed in designated swim areas or in park buildings.

Johnstown

Accommodations

Best Western University Inn 1545 Wayne Ave Indiana PA 724-349-9620 (800-780-7234)
Dogs are allowed for an additional fee of $10 per night per pet. Dogs may not be left alone in the room.
Comfort Inn and Suites 455 Theatre Drive Johnstown PA 814-266-3678 (877-424-6423)
Dogs are allowed for an additional fee of $15 per night per pet.
Holiday Inn 250 Market St Johnstown PA 814-535-7777 (877-270-6405)
Dogs of all sizes are allowed for an additional one time pet fee of $10 per room
Holiday Inn Express 1440 Scalp Ave Johnstown PA 814-266-8789 (877-270-6405)
Dogs of all sizes are allowed for an additional one time fee of $25 per pet. Dogs may not be left alone in the room.
Sleep Inn 453 Theatre Drive Johnstown PA 814-262-9292 (877-424-6423)
Dogs are allowed for an additional fee of $15 per night per pet.
Super 8 Johnstown 627 Soloman Run Rd Johnstown PA 814-535-5600 (800-800-8000)
Dogs of all sizes are allowed. There are no additional pet fees. Smoking and non-smoking rooms are available for pet rooms.
Knights Inn 585 Ramada Rd Somerset PA 814-445-8933 (800-843-5644)
There are no additional pet fees.

Stores

Petco Pet Store 410 Town Centre Drive Johnstown PA 814-266-0820
Your licensed and well-behaved leashed dog is allowed in the store.

Parks

Johnstown Flood National Memorial 733 Lake Road South Fork PA 814-495-4643
http://www.nps.gov/jofl/index.htm
Dogs must be on leash and must be cleaned up after on the grounds. Dogs are not allowed in buildings. Hiking and picnicking areas are available. The Johnstown Flood Museum and site is the story of a wealthy resort, the destruction of a working class city, and an inspiring relief effort. Occurring in 1889, over 2000 people died and more were injured when the dam gave in, making it one of the worst disasters in our Nation's history.

Jonestown

Accommodations

Days Inn Lebanon 3 Everest Lane Jonestown PA 717-865-4064 (800-329-7466)
Dogs of all sizes are allowed. There is a $10 per night pet fee per pet.

Campgrounds and RV Parks

Jonestown/I-81,78 KOA 145 Old Route 22 Jonestown PA 717-865-2526 (800-562-1501)
http://www.koa.com
Dogs of all sizes are allowed, but there can only be 1 large dog or 2 small dogs per site. There are no additional pet fees. Dogs may not be left unattended, and they must be leashed and cleaned up after. There are some breed restrictions. This RV park is closed during the off-season. The camping and tent areas also allow dogs. There is a dog walk area at the campground.

Kittanning

Accommodations
Comfort Inn 13 Hilltop Plaza Kittanning PA   724-543-5200 (877-424-6423)
Well behaved dogs up to 30 pounds are allowed for an additional one time fee of $15 per pet.
Quality Inn Royle 405 Butler Road Kittanning PA   724-543-1159 (877-424-6423)
Dogs are allowed for an additional fee of $5 per night per pet.

Knox

Campgrounds and RV Parks
Wolf's Camping Resort 308 Timberwolf Run Knox PA   814-797-1103
http://www.wolfscampingresort.com
Dogs of all sizes are allowed. There are no additional pet fees. Dogs must be quiet, well behaved, not left
unattended, and leashed and cleaned up after. There is limited Winter camping. The camping and tent areas
also allow dogs. There is a dog walk area at the campground.

Lamar

Accommodations
Comfort Inn 31 Comfort Inn Lane Lamar PA   570-726-4901 (877-424-6423)
Dogs are allowed for an additional pet fee of $10 per night per room.

Lebanon

Accommodations
Quality Inn Lebanon Valley 625 Quentin Road Lebanon PA   717-273-6771 (877-424-6423)
Dogs are allowed for an additional fee of $10 per night per pet.
The Berry Patch 115 Moore Road Lebanon PA   717-865-7219
http://www.berrypatchbnb.com
Set amid lush lawns and towering trees on 20 acres, this newly built log home features large verandas with a
view, the Strawberry Rose Garden, is close to hiking/biking trails, and are central to many other activities and
attractions. Dogs of all sizes are allowed for an additional fee of $10 per night per pet. Dogs must be well
behaved, leashed and cleaned up after, and crated when left alone in the room.

Lehigh Valley

Accommodations
Allenwood Motel 1058 Hausman Rd Allentown PA   610-395-3707
There is a $15 per day pet fee.
Comfort Inn 7625 Imperial Way Allentown PA   610-391-0344 (877-424-6423)
Dogs are allowed for an additional one time fee of $25 per pet.
Crowne Plaza Hotel Allentown 904 West Hamilton St Allentown PA   610-433-2221 (877-270-6405)
Dogs of all sizes are allowed for an additional one time fee of $30 per pet.
Days Inn Allentown Conference Cntr 1151 Bulldog Drive Allentown PA   610-395-3731 (800-329-7466)
Dogs of all sizes are allowed. There is a $15 per night pet fee per pet. Pet must be kept in kennel when left
alone.
Four Points Sheraton Hotel & Suites Allentown Jetport 3400 Airport Road, Road #4 Allentown PA   610-
266-1000 (888-625-5144)
Dogs of all sizes are allowed. There is a $49 per stay additional pet fee per pet. This includes a pet care kit with

a bed, treats and toys. Pets are restricted to 1st floor rooms only. Dogs are not allowed to be left alone in the room.
Holiday Inn 7736 Adrienne Drive Allentown PA   610-391-1000 (877-270-6405)
Dogs of all sizes are allowed for an additional one time fee of $49 per pet.
Red Roof Inn - Allentown Bethlehem 1846 Catasauqua Road Allentown PA   610-264-5404 (800-RED-ROOF)
One well-behaved family pet per room. Guest must notify front desk upon arrival. Guest is liable for any damages. In consideration of all guests, pets must never be left unattended in the guest rooms.
Sleep Inn 327 Star Road Allentown PA   610-395-6603 (877-424-6423)
Dogs are allowed for an additional fee of $15 per night per pet.
Staybridge Suites 1787 A. Airport Road Allentown PA   610-443-5000 (877-270-6405)
Dogs of all sizes are allowed for an additional one time pet fee per room of $50 for 1 to 14 days, and $100 for 15 days or more.
Staybridge Suites Allentown West 327c Star Road Allentown PA   610-841-5100 (877-270-6405)
Dogs of all sizes are allowed for an additional one time pet fee of $100 per room.
Super 8 Allentown 1715 Plaza Lane Allentown PA   610-435-7880 (800-800-8000)
Dogs up to 80 pounds are allowed. There is a $10 per night pet fee per pet. Smoking and non-smoking rooms are available for pet rooms.
Best Western Lehigh Valley Hotel & Conference Center 300 Gateway Drive Bethlehem PA   610-866-5800 (800-780-7234)
Dogs are allowed for an additional fee of $10 per night per pet.
Comfort Inn H 22 and H 191 Bethlehem PA   610-865-6300 (877-424-6423)
Dogs are allowed for an additional fee of $10 (plus tax) per night per pet.
Residence Inn by Marriott 2180 Motel Drive Bethlehem PA   610-317-2662
Dogs of all sizes are allowed. There is a $100 one time cleaning fee plus $6 per night and a pet policy to sign at check in.
Comfort Inn H 22 at 25th Street Easton PA   610-253-0546 (877-424-6423)
Dogs up to 65 pounds are allowed for an additional fee of $20 per night per pet.
The Lafayette Inn 525 W Monroe Street Easton PA   610-253-4500 (800-509-6990)
www.lafayetteinn.com
This inn has a big wrap around porch, is surrounded by trees and gardens with a fountain, and serves as a great home base to a variety of activities, recreation, and historical sites. Dogs of all sizes are allowed for an additional fee of $20 per night per pet; they provide treats, mat, a towel, and clean-up bags. Dogs must be leashed and cleaned up after at all times, and crated when left alone in the room.
Hampton Inn 1915 John Fries H Quakertown PA   215-536-7779
A dog up to 50 pounds is allowed. There is a $10 per night additional pet fee.

Campgrounds and RV Parks
Allentown KOA 6750 KOA Drive New Tripoli PA   610-298-2160 (800-562-2138)
http://www.koa.com
Dogs of all sizes are allowed. There are no additional pet fees. Dogs must be leashed and cleaned up after. There are some breed restrictions. This RV park is closed during the off-season. The camping and tent areas also allow dogs. There is a dog walk area at the campground.

Attractions
Burnside Plantation 1461 Schoenersville Road Bethlehem PA   610-868-5044
This colonial farm depicts early American agricultural life with a variety of exhibits, buildings (restored), and tools from the 18th century. Dogs are allowed throughout the property; they are not allowed in any of the buildings. Dogs must be well behaved, leashed, and cleaned up after at all times.

TOP 200 PLACE Colonial Industrial Quarter 459 Old York Road Bethlehem PA   610-691-6055
http://www.historicbethlehem.org/
It's easy to feel like you have been transported back in time as one walks the historic streets of this colonial town and the surrounding points of interest. The welcome center is a good place to stop first for beginner's information. Dogs are allowed throughout the town; they are not allowed in any of the buildings. Dogs must be well behaved, leashed, and cleaned up after at all times.

TOP 200 PLACE Moyer Aviation 3800 Sullivan Trail Easton PA   610-258-0473
http://www.moyeraviation.com/
This aviation company offers a variety of services, including 10 to 40 minute tours with advance reservations (2 person minimum). A dog up to about 50 pounds is allowed for no additional fee. Dogs must be under owner's control/care, and leashed or crated at all times.
Dutch Hex Tour Old Route 22 Kutztown PA   800-HEX-TOUR (439-8687)
http://www.hexsigns.org/

The Hex barns are a reflection of the influence of 18th/19th century Swiss and German immigrants (aka-Pennsylvania Dutch), and are beautiful representations of their folk art. In addition to viewing the artistic barns, there are several covered bridges and great scenery to pass through. There are numerous places to stop along the way, and your pet is welcome to get out and stretch its legs too. Dogs must be under owner's control, leashed, and cleaned up after at all times. Brochures are available at the Crystal Cave Gift Shop on Crystal Cove Road off Old H 22.

Stores
Petco Pet Store 3300 Lehigh St Allentown PA   610-797-4656
Your licensed and well-behaved leashed dog is allowed in the store.
Petco Pet Store 2429 Nazareth Rd Easton PA   610-330-0740
Your licensed and well-behaved leashed dog is allowed in the store.

Parks
Delaware and Lehigh National Heritage Corridor 1 South Third Street 8th Floor Easton PA   610-923-3548
http://www.nps.gov/dele/index.htm
Dogs must be on leash and must be cleaned up after in most of the corridor. You must follow local and state park rules and pet policies. The corridor features auto touring, boating, hiking, and more.
Pool Wildlife Sanctuary, Wildlands Conservancy 3701 Orchid Place Emmaus PA   610-965-4397
This 72 acre wildlife area sits alongside Little Lehigh Creek, and in addition to the beautifully kept grounds, there are a variety of informative and interactive exhibits to explore. Dogs are allowed on the grounds, but they are not allowed on the nature trails or in buildings. Dogs must be under owner's control, leashed, and cleaned up after at all times.
Nockamixon State Park 1542 Mountain View Drive Quakertown PA   215-529-7300
This 5,283 acre state park has a 1,450 acre lake for a wide variety of land and water recreational opportunities. Dogs are allowed throughout the park and on the trails; they are not allowed at the cabins or in the pool area. Dogs must be well behaved, leashed, and cleaned up after at all times.

Off-Leash Dog Parks
Op Barks Farm 2590 Schukraft Rd Quakertown PA   888-672-2757
http://www.opbarks.com/bark/index.cfm
In addition to providing training and behavior services, there are opportunities for lots of fun with 5 acres with nature trails, a creek, wooded areas, and a dog and people friendly pool. There are also special events, an indoor training space, and a full agility course.

Outdoor Restaurants
The Brew Works 569 Main Street Bethlehem PA   610-882-1300
http://www.thebrewworks.com/
This brewery has a line of popular signature beers, seasonal taps, and an eatery that features many items that have incorporated their handcrafted beers. Dogs are allowed at the outer tables. Dogs must be well behaved, under owner's control/care, and leashed or crated at all times. Please keep dogs out of pathways.

Lenhartsville

Campgrounds and RV Parks
Blue Rocks Family Campground 341 Sousley Road Lenhartsville PA   610-756-6366
http://www.bluerockscampground.com
Dogs of all sizes are allowed. There are no additional pet fees. Dogs must have current shot records and be quiet and well behaved. Dogs must be leashed and cleaned up after. This RV park is closed during the off-season. The camping and tent areas also allow dogs. There is a dog walk area at the campground.
Robin Hill Camping Resort 149 Robin Hill Road Lenhartsville PA   610-756-6117
http://www.robinhillrvresort.com
Dogs of all sizes are allowed. There are no additional pet fees. Dogs must be well behaved, not left unattended, and be leashed and cleaned up after. This RV park is closed during the off-season. The camping and tent areas also allow dogs. There is a dog walk area at the campground.

Lock Haven

Accommodations
Best Western Lake Haven 101 East Walnut St Lock Haven PA 570-748-3297 (800-780-7234)
Dogs are allowed for an additional fee of $10 per night per pet.

Mansfield

Accommodations
Comfort Inn 300 Gateway Drive Mansfield PA 570-662-3000 (877-424-6423)
Dogs are allowed for an additional fee of $10 per night per pet. Dogs must be crated when left alone in the room.

Meadville

Accommodations
Days Inn Meadville 18360 Conneaut Lake Rd Meadville PA 814-337-4264 (800-329-7466)
Dogs of all sizes are allowed. There is a $10 per night pet fee per pet.
Motel 6 - Meadville 11237 Shaw Avenue Meadville PA 814-724-6366 (800-466-8356)
One well-behaved family pet per room. Guest must notify front desk upon arrival. Guest is liable for any damages. In consideration of all guests, pets must never be left unattended in the guest rooms.

Campgrounds and RV Parks
Camperland at Conneaut Lake Park 12382 Center Street Conneaut Lake PA 814-382-7750
This full service family campground offers a long list of amenities, activities, attractions, and events at this recreational destination, plus they have an ice cream parlor on site. Dogs are allowed throughout the resort; there is no additional fee. Dogs may not be left unattended, and they must be leashed and cleaned up after at all times. There are some breed restrictions. This RV park is closed during the off-season. There is a dog walk area at the campground.
Pymatuning State Park 2660 Williamsfield Road Jamestown PA 724-932-3141 (888-PA-PARKS (727-2757))
This is the state's largest park at 21,122 acres; it has the largest lake, unique protected natural areas, environmental interpretive programs, miles of hiking trails, and a wide range of land and water recreation. The camp area has modern restrooms with showers, a playground, amphitheater, a dump station, camp store, and more. There are some breed restrictions. This RV park is closed during the off-season. The camping and tent areas also allow dogs. There is a dog walk area at the campground. There are no water hookups at the campgrounds.
Brookdale Family Campground 25164 H 27 Meadville PA 814-789-3251
http://www.brookdalecampground.com
Dogs of all sizes are allowed. There are no additional pet fees. Dogs must be quiet, be leashed at all times, and be cleaned up after. Dogs may not be tied up outside alone. They can be left in the camper or RV if they are well behaved and have cool air. This RV park is closed during the off-season. The camping and tent areas also allow dogs. There is a dog walk area at the campground.

Parks
Pymatuning State Park 2660 Williamsfield Road Jamestown PA 724-932-3141 (888-PA-PARKS (727-2757))
This is the state's largest park at 21,122 acres; it has the largest lake, unique protected natural areas, environmental interpretive programs, miles of hiking trails, and a wide range of land and water recreation.

Middletown

Accommodations
Days Inn Harrisburg East 800 South Eisenhower Blvd Middletown PA 717-939-4147 (800-329-7466)
Dogs of all sizes are allowed. There is a $10 per night pet fee per pet.

New Castle Area

Accommodations
Comfort Inn 137 Gibb Road Barkeyville PA   814-786-7901 (877-424-6423)
Dogs are allowed for an additional fee of $10 per night per pet.
Old Arbor Rose 114 W Main Street Grove City PA   724-458-6425 (877 596-6767)
http://www.oldarborrosebnb.com/
This 1912 rambling house offers a hint of the sea in the décor, a full gourmet breakfast, a hot tub on a private deck, and they are central to a wide variety of activities, recreation, shops, and eateries. Dogs of all sizes are allowed for an additional fee of $10 per night per pet. Dogs must be well behaved, leashed, and cleaned up after.
Super 8 Harrisville/Barkeyville Area 1010 Dholu Road Harrisville PA 814-786-8375 (800-800-8000)
Dogs of all sizes are allowed. There is a $5 per night pet fee per pet. Smoking and non-smoking rooms are available for pet rooms.
Howard Johnson Inn 835 Perry Hwy. Mercer PA   724-748-3030 (800-446-4656)
Dogs of all sizes are allowed. There are no additional pet fees.

Campgrounds and RV Parks
Mercer/Grove City KOA 1337 Butler Pike Mercer PA   724-748-3160 (800-562-2802)
http://www.mercerkoa.com
Dogs of all sizes are allowed. There are no additional pet fees. Dogs must be well behaved, leashed, and cleaned up after. This RV park is closed during the off-season. The camping and tent areas also allow dogs. There is a dog walk area at the campground. Dogs are allowed in the camping cabins.
Rose Point Campground 314 Rose Point Road New Castle PA   724-924-2415 (800-459-1561)
http://rosepointpark.com/
Some of the amenities at this full service campground included a 4-star recreation program, landscaped grounds, several play/gaming areas, free WiFi, a camp store, and miles of hiking trails. Well behaved dogs of all sizes are allowed for no additional pet fee. Dogs must be under owner's control, leashed, and cleaned up after at all times. There are some breed restrictions. The camping and tent areas also allow dogs. There is a dog walk area at the campground.
Cooper's Lake Campground 205 Currie Road Slippery Rock PA 724-368-8710
http://www.cooperslake.com
Friendly dogs of all sizes are allowed. There are no additional pet fees. Dogs must be quiet, not left unattended, leashed and cleaned up after. The camp closes for the month of August every year. The camping and tent areas also allow dogs. There is a dog walk area at the campground.

Attractions
Harlansburg Station Transportation Museum 424 Old Route 19 New Castle PA   724-652-9002
http://harlansburgstation.com/
A labor of love for over 30 years resulted in this transportation museum with numerous displays of various types of transport. Well behaved dogs are welcome throughout the grounds; they are not allowed in some of the buildings. Dogs must be leashed and cleaned up after at all times.

Shopping Centers
Prime Outlets at Grove City 1911 Leesburg Grove City Road/H 208 Grove City PA   724-748-4770
This outlet village offers 114 stores, specialty shops, services, and a variety of special events throughout the year. Dogs are allowed throughout the village; they are not allowed in the food court. It is up to the individual stores whether they are allowed inside or not. Dogs must be under owner's control, leashed or crated, and cleaned up after at all times. Dogs may not be left unattended at any time, including in vehicles. There are designated pet walking areas, waste stations at the Center, and doggy treats at Guest Services..

New Hope - Washington Crossing

Accommodations
Golden Pheasant Inn 763 River Road/H 32S Erwinna PA 610-294-9595 (800-830-4474)
http://www.goldenpheasant.com/
This inn, sitting along the Delaware Canal, specializes in French cuisine, and in the Spring they offer cooking classes. There is a gated cottage suite with a porch overlooking the canal for guests with pets, and dogs up to 55

pounds are allowed for an additional pet fee of $25 per night per pet. Dogs must be well mannered, leashed, and cleaned up after.

Barley Sheaf Farm 5281 York Road/H 202/263 Holicong PA   215-794-5104
http://www.barleysheaf.com/
Set in the heart of a cultural and historic region, this 100+ acre luxury estate contains woodlands, pastures, gardens, 2 ponds, picturesque walking paths, a junior Olympic swimming pool, and more. One dog of any size is allowed in the "Beggar on Horseback" room for an additional fee of $50 per night with advanced reservations, and there is a pet policy to sign at check in. Dogs must be well behaved, leashed and cleaned up after at all times, and crated when left alone in the room.

1833 Umpleby House 111 W Bridge Street New Hope PA   215-862-3936
Sitting on 2 park-like acres, this 1833 Classic Revival manor house is on the National Registry of Historic Places, is only minutes from the village center and the Delaware River, and registered guests are welcome at the inn's private mountaintop pool and tennis club. One well traveled and well behaved dog is allowed per room for an additional $20 per night. Dogs must be flea and tick free, have their own bedding, and they may not be left alone in the room. Dogs must be quiet, well mannered, leashed, and cleaned up after at all times.

Wedgwood Inn 111 W Bridge Street New Hope PA   215-862-2570
http://www.wedgwoodinn.com/index.htm
This historic 1870 Wedgwood-blue Victorian home features 2 acres of lush lawns and gardens, home baked goodies available all day, and is only a short walk to the eclectic, vibrant village of New Hope, and to the walking bridge to New Jersey. Dogs of all sizes are allowed for an additional fee of $20 per night per pet. Dogs may be left alone only for short periods and only if they will be quiet, well behaved, and a contact number is left with the front desk. Dogs must be leashed and cleaned up after at all times.

Campgrounds and RV Parks

Colonial Woods Family Camping Resort 545 Lonely Cottage Drive Upper Black Eddy PA   610-847-5808
http://www.colonialwoods.com
Dogs of all sizes are allowed. There are no additional pet fees. Dogs must be quiet, well behaved, leashed, and cleaned up after. This RV park is closed during the off-season. The camping and tent areas also allow dogs. There is a dog walk area at the campground.

Attractions

Washington Crossing Historical Park

TOP 200 PLACE **Washington Crossing Historical Park** 1112 River Road Washington Crossing PA   215-

493-4076
This historic park commemorates where General Washington and his men crossed the Delaware in the dead of Winter to win a major victory towards America's independence. Dogs are allowed throughout the grounds; they must be leashed and cleaned up after at all times. Dogs must be under owner's control and well behaved, and they may not be left unattended anywhere-including vehicles. Dogs are not allowed in the visitor center or in any of the historic structures, including Bowman's Hill Tower.
Carousel Village at Indian Walk 591 Durham Road/H 413 Wrightstown PA   215-598-0707
The main store here is in an 1800's barn filled with all kinds of unique, bargain, and collectible items. Dogs are allowed throughout the property. Dogs must be well behaved, under owner's control, leashed or crated, and cleaned up after at all times.

Shopping Centers
Peddler's Village 81 Peddler Village Road Lahaska PA   215-794-4000
This beautifully landscaped shopping village offers 70 specialty shops and a lot more. Dogs are allowed throughout the village grounds; they are not allowed in stores, restaurants, or in the Golden Plough Inn. Dogs must be under owner's control, leashed or crated, and cleaned up after at all times.
Penn's Purchase Factory Outlet Village H 202 Lahaska PA   215-794-2232
http://www.pennspurchase.com/
This small factory outlet shopping area offers a variety of shops and services. Dogs are allowed throughout the village. It is up to the individual stores whether they are allowed inside or not. Dogs must be under owner's control, leashed or crated, and cleaned up after at all times. Dogs may not be left unattended at any time, including in vehicles.

Parks
Peace Valley Park Peace Valley Park Creek Road Doylestown PA   215-345-1097
Dogs on leash are allowed in the park and lake. The park features hiking, fishing, camping, and more.
New Hope Towpath 3620 Windy Rd New Hope PA
This towpath dirt walking trail begins in the center of New Hope. There are a number of dog-friendly restaurants in New Hope.

Outdoor Restaurants
Main Squeeze 95 S Main Street New Hope PA   215-862-6330
Dogs are allowed at the outdoor tables. The restaurant has outdoor tables only in the Summer.
Triumph Brewing Company 400 Union Square New Hope PA   215-862-8300
http://www.triumphbrewing.com
For feasting, enjoying a handcrafted brew, gathering with friends, or listening to live music, this brewery offers it all plus indoor and outdoor dining options. Dogs are allowed at the outer tables. Dogs must be under owner's control/care and leashed or crated at all times.
Wildflowers Garden Cafe 8 W Mechanic Street New Hope PA   215-862-2241
http://www.wildflowersnewhope.com/
Sitting creekside in a lush garden setting, this eatery specializes in American home cooking, authentic Thai and Mexican dishes, and specialty beverages. Dogs are allowed at the outer tables. Dogs must be under owner's control/care, leashed at all times, and out of pathways.

New Stanton

Accommodations
Howard Johnson Inn 112 W. Byers Ave. New Stanton PA   724-925-3511 (800-446-4656)
Well-behaved dogs of all sizes are allowed. There is a $7 per day additional pet fee.
Quality Inn 110 N Main New Stanton PA   724-925-6755 (877-424-6423)
Dogs are allowed for an additional fee of $10 per night per pet.

Northumberland

Accommodations
Comfort Inn 330 Commerce Park New Columbia PA   570-568-8000 (877-424-6423)
Dogs are allowed for no additional pet fee; there is a pet agreement to sign at check in.

Holiday Inn Express 160 Commerce Park Drive New Columbia PA 570-568-1100 (877-270-6405)
Dogs of all sizes are allowed for an additional one time pet fee of $25 per room.
Hampton Inn 3 Stettler Avenue Selinsgrove PA 570-743-2223
Well behaved dogs of all sizes are allowed. There is a $25 per pet per stay fee.
Quality Inn and Suites 2 Susquehanna Trail Shamokin Dam PA 570-743-1111 (877-424-6423)
Dogs of all sizes are allowed. There is a $10 per night per pet additional fee.
River View Inn 103 Chestnut Street Sunbury PA 570-286-4800 (866-592-4800)
http://www.riverview-inn.com/
This 1870's elegant Victorian inn sits along the Susquehanna River and across from the Merle Phillips Park, and is updated with all the modern comforts. They have one pet friendly room and one dog of any size is allowed for an additional pet fee of $25 per night. Dogs must be very quiet and well behaved, leashed and cleaned up after inside and out, and shots up to date. Dogs may not be left alone in the room.

Campgrounds and RV Parks
Hidden Valley Campgrounds 162 Hidden Valley Lane Mifflinburg PA 570-966-1330
http://www.hiddenvalleycamping.com
Dogs of all sizes are allowed. There are no additional pet fees. Dogs must be quiet, well behaved, leashed, and cleaned up after. This RV park is closed during the off-season. The camping and tent areas also allow dogs. There is a dog walk area at the campground.
Nittany Mountain Campground 2751 Miller's Bottom Road New Columbia PA 570-568-5541
http://www.fun-camping.com
One dog of any size is allowed in the rentals. Dogs of all sizes are allowed in the camping and RV area. There is a $1 per night per pet additional fee. Dogs must be leashed and cleaned up after. This RV park is closed during the off-season. The camping and tent areas also allow dogs. There is a dog walk area at the campground. Dogs are allowed in the camping cabins.
Yogi-on-the-River 213 Yogi Blvd Northumberland PA 570-473-8021 (800-243-1056)
http://www.riverandfun.com
Dogs of all sizes are allowed. There are no additional pet fees. Dogs may not be left unattended, must be leashed, and cleaned up after. Dogs are allowed to go to the river, but you may not access the river across others'sites. This RV park is closed during the off-season. The camping and tent areas also allow dogs. There is a dog walk area at the campground.

Attractions
Reptiland 18628 H 15 Allenwood PA 570-538-1869
http://www.reptiland.com
In addition to offering a variety of entertaining, environmental educational programs to introduce visitors to the reptilian animal kingdom, this park also offers picnic areas, a gift shop, and special events. Quiet, very well behaved dogs are allowed. They must be under owner's control, firmly short leashed, and cleaned up after at all times.

Patton

Campgrounds and RV Parks
Prince Gallitzin State Park 966 Marina Road Patton PA 814-674-1000
Dogs of all sizes are allowed. There is a $2 per night per pet additional fee. Pets are to be walked in designated walking areas of the campground and on designated pet walkways when accessing other areas of the park from the campground. Dogs must be leashed, under physical control at all times, and pet waste must be disposed of quickly and properly. Pet food must remain inside the camping unit, and dogs must have a current rabies certificate and shot records, be quiet and well behaved. Dogs are allowed on the trails and day use areas, but they are not allowed in the swim areas or in any of the buildings. Dogs can be at the boat launch area and on the trails. Dogs may not be left unattended except for very short periods; then they must be left inside your unit, weather permitting. This campground is closed during the off-season. The camping and tent areas also allow dogs. There is a dog walk area at the campground. There are no water hookups at the campground.

Perkasie

Accommodations

TOP 200 PLACE **Our Farm Under the Mimosa Tree** 1487 Blue School Road Perkasie PA 215-249-9420
http://www.mimosatreebnb.com/
This scenic 20 acre, 200 year old farmhouse surrounded by mimosa trees, has numerous farm animals, peacocks, 2 ponds, a Japanese garden complete with a koi pond, hiking trails, and many places for picnicking and exploring. Dogs of all sizes are allowed for no additional pet fee. Puppies are not allowed, and dogs must be friendly toward humans and the farm animals. Dogs must be well behaved, leashed, cleaned up after, and they are not allowed on the furnishings.

Philadelphia

Accommodations
Four Points by Sheraton at Philadelphia Airport 4010 A Island Ave. Philadelphia PA 215-492-0400 (888-625-5144)
Dogs up to 80 pounds are allowed. There are no additional pet fees. Dogs are not allowed to be left alone in the room.

Loews Philadelphia Hotel

TOP 200 PLACE **Loews Philadelphia Hotel** 1200 Market Street Philadelphia PA 215-627-1200
All well-behaved dogs of any size are welcome. This upscale hotel offers their "Loews Loves Pets" program which includes special pet treats, local dog walking routes, and a list of nearby pet-friendly places to visit. There are no pet fees.
Residence Inn by Marriott One East Penn Square Philadelphia PA 215-557-0005
Dogs of all sizes are allowed. There is a $150 one time fee and a pet policy to sign at check in.
Sheraton Philadelphia City Center Hotel 17th & Race St. Philadelphia PA 215-448-2000 (888-625-5144)
Dogs up to 50 pounds are allowed. There are no additional pet fees. Dogs are not allowed to be left alone in the room.
Sheraton Society Hill Hotel One Dock Street Philadelphia PA 215-238-6000 (888-625-5144)
Dogs up to 75 pounds are allowed. There are no additional pet fees. Dogs are not allowed to be left alone in the room.
Sheraton Suite Philadelphia 4101 B Island Ave. Philadelphia PA 215-365-6600 (888-625-5144)
Dogs up to 80 pounds are allowed. There are no additional pet fees. Dogs are not allowed to be left alone in the room.
Sheraton University City Hotel 36th and Chestnut Streets Philadelphia PA 215-387-8000 (888-625-5144)

Dogs up to 80 pounds are allowed. There are no additional pet fees. Dogs are not allowed to be left alone in the room.
The Conwell Inn 1331 W Berks Street Philadelphia PA   215-235-6200 (888-379-9737)
http://www.conwellinn.com/
This historic, landmark hotel is located in the middle of Temple University, and is close to downtown and numerous sites of interest. Dogs of all sizes are allowed for an additional fee of $20 per night per room. Dogs must be quiet, leashed, cleaned up after, and crated if left alone in the room.
The Rittenhouse 210 W Rittenhouse Square Philadelphia PA   215-546-9000
http://www.rittenhousehotel.com/
There are no additional pet fees.

Attractions

Ben Franklin Bridge

Ben Franklin Bridge 5th St and Vine St Philadelphia PA
You and your dog can walk across the Ben Franklin bridge from 5th St and Vine St. You can walk part of the way for a nice view of downtown. The bridge connects Philadelphia with New Jersey.
Ben Franklin's Grave 5th St and Arch St Philadelphia PA
Dogs are not allowed in the burial grounds at the church. However, Ben Franklin's grave is accessible and viewable from the street sidewalk at 5th and Arch.
Edgar Allan Poe National Historic Site 532 N Seventh Street Philadelphia PA   215-597-8780
http://www.nps.gov/edal/index.htm
Pets are not allowed in the house. They are only allowed on the sidewalk outside of the house. However, you may view the house from the outside.
Gloria Dei Church National Historic Site Columbus Blvd and Christian Street Philadelphia PA   215-389-1513
http://www.nps.gov/glde/index.htm
Pets are not allowed in the church or on the grounds. They are allowed in front of the church on the sidewalks and paved areas.

Ben Franklin's Grave

Horse and Carriage Rides at Independence Mall

TOP 200 PLACE **Horse and Carriage Rides at Independence Mall** At the Liberty Bell
Pavilion Philadelphia PA
The horse and carriage rides leave from next to Independence Hall on Independence Mall. The tours are from 20

minutes up and will take you around the Center City and the historical area of Philadelphia. Most drivers will allow well behaved dogs.

Independence National Historic Park

TOP 200 PLACE **Independence National Historic Park** Market St and 5th St Philadelphia PA
http://www.nps.gov/inde
Walk your dog through history. You can view all of the historic buildings from the Congress of 1776. You can see the Liberty Bell through the shaded glass windows if you stay outside with your dog. If you would like to see the Liberty Bell from the inside then someone would have to stay outside with the dog. Dogs are also allowed through the security gate to the area behind Independence Hall but are not allowed in any of the historic buildings.
South Street District South St and 2nd Ave Philadelphia PA
There are a number of dog-friendly eateries and stores in this colorful district.
Thaddeus Kosciuszko National Memorial 301 Pine Street Philadelphia PA   215-597-9618
http://www.nps.gov/thko/index.htm
Pets are not allowed in the house or museum. They are only allowed on a leash on the sidewalk in front of house.

Stores
Anthropologie 1801 Walnut Street Philadelphia PA   215-568-2114
http://www.anthropologie.com
This clothing, accessory and home decor store allows well-behaved leashed dogs inside.
Commerce Bank 201 S 18th Street Philadelphia PA   215-546-1655
http://bank.commerceonline.com/
This multi-service bank also services their canine visitors at all their branches; they are known to keep water at the entrance and plenty of doggie treats on hand. Dogs must be well mannered, leashed and under owner's control/care at all times.
In the Doghouse 706 N 24th Street Philadelphia PA   267-514-1949
http://www.inthedoghouseinc.com/
Specializing in providing products and supplies that will satisfy even the most discerning dog, this pet boutique welcomes your well mannered pet to come inside and look around too. Dogs must be under owner's control/care at all times.
PetSmart Pet Store 7501 Horrocks St Philadelphia PA   215-728-7166
Your licensed and well-behaved leashed dog is allowed in the store.
PetSmart Pet Store 4640-60 E Roosevelt Blvd Philadelphia PA   215-743-9602

Your licensed and well-behaved leashed dog is allowed in the store.
PetSmart Pet Store 11000 Roosevelt Blvd Philadelphia PA 215-698-8320
Your licensed and well-behaved leashed dog is allowed in the store.
PetSmart Pet Store 2360 W Oregon Ave Philadelphia PA 215-462-2080
Your licensed and well-behaved leashed dog is allowed in the store.
Petco Pet Store 3300 Aramingo Avenue Philadelphia PA 215-423-4414
Your licensed and well-behaved leashed dog is allowed in the store.
Petco Pet Store 9717 Roosevelt Blvd Philadelphia PA 215-671-9601
Your licensed and well-behaved leashed dog is allowed in the store.
Urban Outfitters 1627 Walnut Street Philadelphia PA 215-569-3131
http://www.urbanoutfitters.com/
This men and women's clothing store allows well-behaved dogs on leash or carried.

Parks
Ben Franklin Parkway Ben Franklin Pkwy and 19th St. Philadelphia PA
Ben Franklin Parkway is a large avenue surrounded by Grass and Trees. It is scenic and a good area to walk a dog in downtown Philadelphia.
Deshler-Morris House National Park 5442 Germantown Avenue Philadelphia PA 215-596-1748
http://www.nps.gov/demo/index.htm
Dogs must be on leash and must be cleaned up after in the park. Dogs are not allowed in the house.
Fairmount Park 4231 N. Concourse Dr Philadelphia PA 215-685-0000
This address is the Park commission headquarters in the park. The park is very big and stretches from the Center of Philadelphia to the northwest. Leashed dogs are allowed.
Manuyunk Towpath and Canal Main Street Philadelphia PA
This is a two mile path in the Manayunk area of Philadelphia. There are a lot of dog-friendly eating places in the area, also.
Pennypack Park Algon Ave and Bustleton Ave Philadelphia PA
http://balford.com/fopp/
Leashed dogs are allowed at this large 1600 acre city park.
Rittenhouse Square Park Walnut St and 18th St Philadelphia PA
Located in downtown Philadelphia, this park is a gathering spot for people who wish to sit and rest on a bench or on the lawn. Leashed dogs are allowed.
Washington Square Park Walnut St and 6th St Philadelphia PA
Leashed dogs are allowed at this city park.

Off-Leash Dog Parks
Chester Avenue Dog Park Chester Ave and 48th Philadelphia PA 215-748-3440
This nearly one acre park is a privately run dog park. Membership is required to use the park and runs $50 per year. For membership information, please contact Linda Amsterdam at 215-748-3440.
Eastern State Dog Pen Corinthian Ave & Brown St Philadelphia PA
http://www.fairmountdog.org/
This is a fenced dog park. Barking in the park is prohibited between 9 pm and 9 am.
Orianna Hill Dog Park North Orianna St, between Poplar and Wildey Philadelphia PA 215-423-4516
http://www.oriannahill.org
This is a privately owned fenced dog run. Dues are required and are $20 per year. To join, please call 215-423-4516.
Pretzel Park Dog Run Cresson St Philadelphia PA
This is a fenced in dog park in the dog-friendly Manayunk region of Philadelphia.
Schuylkill River Park Dog Run 25th St between Pine and Locust Philadelphia PA
http://www.phillyfido.net
This fenced dog park is located near the Centre City across the Schuylkill River from the 30th Street Train Station.
Segar Dog Park 11th Street between Lombard and South St. Philadelphia PA
http://www.segerdogrunonline.org
Located in Segar Park, this is a fenced dog park with separate areas for small dogs and large dogs.

Outdoor Restaurants
Adobe Cafe 4550 Mitchell Street Philadelphia PA 215-483-3947
This is a popular place for some off-beat Tex-Mex fare with a variety of specialty frozen drinks, and indoor or outdoor dining options. Dogs are allowed at the outer tables. Dogs must be under owner's control/care and leashed at all times.
Astral Plane Restaurant 1708 Lombard Street Philadelphia PA 215-546-6230

This restaurant serves American cuisine. Dogs are allowed at the outdoor tables.
Azure Restaurant 931 N Second Street Philadelphia PA   215-629-0500
http://www.azurerestaurant.net
All well behaved dogs on lead are welcome here at their outdoor cafe. Please clean up after your pet.
Brasserie Perrier 1619 Walnut St Philadelphia PA   215-568-3000
Well-behaved dogs are welcome here.
Bucks County Coffee Co. 4311 Main Street Philadelphia PA   215-487-3927
http://www.buckscountycoffee.com/
There are a few tables and a bench outside. Leashed dogs are welcome outside and there is usually a dog bowl
of water.
Cafe Zesty 4382 Main St Philadelphia PA   215-483-6226
Dogs are allowed at the outdoor tables.
Caribou Cafe 1126 Walnut St Philadelphia PA   215-625-9535
Dogs are allowed at the outdoor tables.
Cebu Restaurant and Bar 123 Chestnut Street Philadelphia PA   215-629-1100
http://www.cebuphiladelphia.com/
Specializing in authentic Philippine fare with a Spanish influence and a fairly long Tapas menu, this eatery also
offers indoor or outdoor dining options. Dogs are allowed at the outer tables. Dogs must be under owner's
control/care and leashed at all times.
Crescent City Restaruant 600-602 S 9th Street Philadelphia PA   215-627-6780
http://www.crescentcityphilly.com/
Specializing in American cooking, the slow Southern way, this eatery also offers a good wine list, live music
every Monday and Friday night, and indoor and outdoor dining options. Dogs are allowed at the outer tables.
Dogs must be under owner's control/care and leashed at all times.
Devon's Seafood 225 18th St F1 1 Philadelphia PA   215-546-5940
Dogs are allowed at the outdoor tables.
Fork Restaurant 306 Market Street Philadelphia PA   215-625-9425
http://www.forkrestaurant.com/
This New American bistro offers menu items like the Summer Fruit Salad with Lavender Syrup, House-Smoked
Trout Salad Sandwich, Grilled Hanger Steak, Vegetarian Stir-Fry with Rice Noodles, Braised "Free-Range"
Chicken and Pan-Seared Hazelnut-Cilantro Crusted Salmon. Well-behaved leashed dogs are welcome at the
outdoor tables. The restaurant is open for lunch for lunch Monday through Friday, brunch on Sunday and dinner
daily. Reservations are recommended. Dress is casual.
Garden Gate Cafe 8139 Germantown Ave Philadelphia PA   215-247-8487
Dogs are allowed at the outdoor tables.
Le Bus 4266 Main St Philadelphia PA   215-487-2663
Well-behaved dogs are welcome here at the outdoor tables.

Pat's King of Steaks

TOP 200 PLACE **Pat's King of Steaks** 1237 E Passyunk Ave Philadelphia PA   215-468-1546
http://www.patskingofsteaks.com
While in Philadelphia you need to try one of the original Cheesesteaks places. At Pat's you order food outside at a window and can eat on the tables here or take out.
Peacock on the Parkway 1700 Benjamin Franklin Parkway Philadelphia PA   215-569-8888
http://www.peacockontheparkway.com/
This restaurant serves sandwiches, soup, salad, pasta and entrees like Chicken Curry Over Rice, Shish Kabobs, Grilled Salmon Fillet, Lobster Ravioli and Homemade Meatloaf. Well-behaved leashed dogs are allowed at the outdoor tables.
Philadelphia Fish & Co. 207 Chestnut Street Philadelphia PA   215-625-8605
http://www.philadelphiafish.com/
This seafood restaurant offers a variety of food including fish chowder, salmon, crabcakes, trout, chicken, steak and veggie side dishes. Well-behaved leashed dogs are allowed at the outdoor tables. The restaurant is open for lunch Monday through Saturday and for dinner daily.
Philadelphia Java Company 518 4th St Philadelphia PA   215-928-1811
Dogs are allowed at the outdoor tables.
Potchen 227 South 18th St Philadelphia PA   215-546-9400
This restaurant serves American food.
Society Hill Hotel Rest. 301 Chestnut St Philadelphia PA   215-925-1919
Dogs are allowed in the outdoor eating area. However, dogs are not allowed to stay at the hotel.
Standard Tap 901 N 2nd St Philadelphia PA   215-238-0630
This restaurant and bar serves barbecue. Dogs are allowed at the outdoor tables.
Tavern 17 220 S 17th Street; Rittenhouse Square Philadelphia PA   215-790-1799
http://www.tavern17restaurant.com/
Featuring 3 dining areas and a 1,200 bottle wine cellar, this classic tavern presents a modern menu update offering such specials as "Flights"-the pairing of beverages with menu items or "Bites"-miniature drink and food samplings, and they offer al fresco dining (weather permitting) for guests with pets. They have a canine menu to treat your pooch with such favorites as Hot Diggity Dog (sliced beef hot dog), Gobble Up (lean turkey patty) or even a Veggie Pup (fried green tomato), but all the food is dog friendly if you want to share. Dogs must be well behaved, under owner's control/care, and leashed at all times. They ask that dogs are tied to the chair - not the table, and kept out of the path of pedestrian traffic.
The Abbaye 637 N 3rd Street Philadelphia PA   215-627-6711
This bar does not serve food but will allow your dog at the outdoor tables.
The Continental 134 Market Street Philadelphia PA   215-923-6069
This New American - Asian restaurant allows well-behaved leashed dogs at their outdoor tables. The restaurant is located near Second Street.
Valley Green Inn Springfield Ave and Wissahickon Philadelphia PA   215-247-1730
This restaurant serves American food. Dogs are allowed at the outdoor tables.

White Dog Cafe

White Dog Cafe 3420 Sansom St Philadelphia PA   215-386-9224

http://www.whitedogcafe.com
Located near Penn, this organic and natural food restaurant has a nice outdoor patio with good service. Your well-behaved leashed dog may join you at the outdoor patio.

Philadelphia Area

Accommodations
Holiday Inn 3499 Street Rd Bensalem PA 215-638-1500 (877-270-6405)
Dogs up to 50 pounds are allowed for an additional one time pet fee of $30 per room.
Residence Inn by Marriott 600 W Swedesford Road Berwyn PA 610-640-0330
Dogs of all sizes are allowed. There is a $150 one time fee and a pet policy to sign at check in.
Residence Inn by Marriott 191 Washington Street Conshohocken PA 610-828-8800
Dogs of all sizes are allowed. There is a $75 one time fee and a pet policy to sign at check in. They also request a cell number if you leave your pet in the room.
Holiday Inn 45 Industrial hwy Essington PA 610-521-2400 (877-270-6405)
Dogs of all sizes are allowed for an additional one time pet fee of $50 per room.
Motel 6 - Philadelphia Airport - Essington 43 Industrial Highway Essington PA 610-521-6650 (800-466-8356)
One well-behaved family pet per room. Guest must notify front desk upon arrival. Guest is liable for any damages. In consideration of all guests, pets must never be left unattended in the guest rooms.
Red Roof Inn - Philadelphia Airport 49 Industrial Highway Essington PA 610-521-5090 (800-RED-ROOF)
One well-behaved family pet per room. Guest must notify front desk upon arrival. Guest is liable for any damages. In consideration of all guests, pets must never be left unattended in the guest rooms.
Sheraton Great Valley Hotel 707 East Lancaster Ave, Route 202 & 30 Frazer PA 610-524-5500 (888-625-5144)
Dogs up to 85 pounds are allowed. There are no additional pet fees. Dogs are not allowed to be left alone in the room
Candlewood Suites 250 Business Center Drive Horsham PA 215-328-9119 (877-270-6405)
Dogs of all sizes are allowed for an additional one time fee of $75 per pet.
Days Inn Philadelphia/Horsham 245 Easton Rd Horsham PA 215-674-2500 (800-329-7466)
Dogs of all sizes are allowed. There is a $10 per night pet fee per pet.
Residence Inn by Marriott 3 Walnut Grove Drive Horsham PA 215-443-7330
Dogs of all sizes are allowed. There is a $150 one time fee plus $6 per night per room and a pet policy to sign at check in.
TownePlace Suites Philadelphia Horsham 198 Precision Drive Horsham PA 215-323-9900
Dogs up to 75 pounds are allowed. There is a $75 one time pet fee per visit.
Motel 6 - Philadelphia - King of Prussia 815 West Dekalb Pike King of Prussia PA 610-265-7200 (800-466-8356)
One well-behaved family pet per room. Guest must notify front desk upon arrival. Guest is liable for any damages. In consideration of all guests, pets must never be left unattended in the guest rooms.
Red Roof Inn - Philadelphia Oxford Valley 3100 Cabot Boulevard West Langhorne PA 215-750-6200 (800-RED-ROOF)
One well-behaved family pet per room. Guest must notify front desk upon arrival. Guest is liable for any damages. In consideration of all guests, pets must never be left unattended in the guest rooms.
Sheraton Bucks County Hotel 400 Oxford Valley Road. Langhorne PA 215-547-4100 (888-625-5144)
Dogs up to 70 pounds are allowed. There are no additional pet fees. Dogs are not allowed to be left alone in the room.
Homewood Suites 12 E Swedesford Rd Malvern PA 610-296-3500
For those people who are staying 1 - 6 nights there is a $25 non-refundable pet fee. The one-time fee is $50 for 7 - 29 nights and the fee is $100 for 30 or more nights.
Staybridge Suites 20 Morehall Road Malvern PA 610-296-4343 (877-270-6405)
Dogs of all sizes are allowed for an additional fee of $10 per night per pet. Dogs must be crated when left alone in the room.
Residence Inn by Marriott 1110 Bethlehem Pike North Wales PA 267-468-0111
Dogs of all sizes are allowed. There is a $75 one time fee and a pet policy to sign at check in.
Radisson Hotel Philadelphia NE 2400 Old Lincoln Highway Trevose PA 215-638-8300 (800-333-3333)
Pets must stay on the first floor. Dogs up to 75 pounds are allowed. People with Pets must book the 'pet-friendly rate' when making reservations.
Red Roof Inn - Philadelphia Trevose 3100 Lincoln Highway Trevose PA 215-244-9422 (800-RED-ROOF)
One well-behaved family pet per room. Guest must notify front desk upon arrival. Guest is liable for any damages. In consideration of all guests, pets must never be left unattended in the guest rooms.

Campgrounds and RV Parks

Timberland Campground 117 Timber Lane Clarksboro PA   856-423-6677
http://www.timberlanecampground.com
Dogs of all sizes are allowed. There are no additional pet fees. Dogs must be quiet and well behaved. Dogs may not be left unattended, must be leashed, and cleaned up after. The camping and tent areas also allow dogs. There is a dog walk area at the campground.

Attractions

Valley Forge National Historical Park

TOP 200 PLACE **Valley Forge National Historical Park** 1400 North Outer Line Drive King of Prussia PA
610-783-1077
http://www.nps.gov/vafo/
Dedicated to the education and preservation of the Revolutionary War generation and of the common citizens who overcame great hardships and adversity in the name of freedom, this park offers a variety of ongoing informative programs and special events. Dogs are allowed throughout the park and on the trails; they are not allowed in any of the buildings. This is a large park so you will probably want to take an auto tour and walk to see the attractions from the nearest parking areas. Dogs must be well behaved, leashed, and cleaned up after at all times.

Stores

Petco Pet Store 2353-2355 St Rd Bensalem PA   215-245-7133
Your licensed and well-behaved leashed dog is allowed in the store.
PetSmart Pet Store 2940 Springfield Rd Broomall PA   610-353-4446
Your licensed and well-behaved leashed dog is allowed in the store.
Petco Pet Store 520 West Baltimore Pike Clifton Heights PA   610-259-2448
Your licensed and well-behaved leashed dog is allowed in the store.
PetSmart Pet Store 176 Swedesford Rd Devon PA   610-644-3676
Your licensed and well-behaved leashed dog is allowed in the store.
PetSmart Pet Store 220 Commerce Blvd Fairless Hills PA   215-949-9602
Your licensed and well-behaved leashed dog is allowed in the store.
Petco Pet Store 97 E St Rd Feasterville PA   215-354-0820
Your licensed and well-behaved leashed dog is allowed in the store.
PetSmart Pet Store 901 Old York Rd Jenkintown PA   215-885-3635

Your licensed and well-behaved leashed dog is allowed in the store.
Petco Pet Store 145 West Dekalb Pike King of Prussia PA 610-337-4484
Your licensed and well-behaved leashed dog is allowed in the store.
Canine Creature Comforts 81 Lancaster Avenue Malvern PA 610-590-2192
http://www.caninecreaturecomforts.com/
This doggy day care center offers more than recreation and socialization; they also offer grooming, training, special days like "Indoor Dog Park Saturdays", weekly swim trips, and they host a number of special events throughout the year. Dogs must be well behaved, healthy, and current on all vaccines.
Petco Pet Store 181 Lancaster Avenue Malvern PA 610-644-9959
Your licensed and well-behaved leashed dog is allowed in the store.
Petco Pet Store 753 Route 309 Montgomeryville PA 215-393-5760
Your licensed and well-behaved leashed dog is allowed in the store.
PetSmart Pet Store 145 Witchwood Dr North Wales PA 215-699-9366
Your licensed and well-behaved leashed dog is allowed in the store.
PetSmart Pet Store 2100 Chemical Rd Plymouth Meeting PA 610-567-2933
Your licensed and well-behaved leashed dog is allowed in the store.
PetSmart Pet Store 934 West St Rd Warminster PA 215-773-9016
Your licensed and well-behaved leashed dog is allowed in the store.
Petco Pet Store 624 York Rd Warminster PA 215-443-5225
Your licensed and well-behaved leashed dog is allowed in the store.
Petco Pet Store 41 North York Rd Willow Grove PA 215-659-9916
Your licensed and well-behaved leashed dog is allowed in the store.

Parks
Evansburg State Park US Route 422 Evansburg PA
Pets must be leashed. This park is over 1000 acres.
Fort Washington State Park Bethlehem Pike Fort Washington PA
Dogs must be leashed. This park offers over 3.5 miles of hiking trails.

Off-Leash Dog Parks
Mondaug Bark Park 1130 Camphill Road Fort Washington PA
This park opened in July, 2005. It is a one acre fenced off-leash dog park. There is a separate dog park for small dogs and there is a double entry fence around the dog park. There are also trails around the dog park where you can walk your leashed dog. There is a stream where your leashed dog can play.

Outdoor Restaurants
Baja Fresh 1437 Old York Road Abington PA 215-885-4296
This restaurant serves Mexican food. Dogs are allowed at the outdoor tables. The restaurant has outdoor tables only in the Summer.
Spring Mill Cafe 164 Barren Hill Road Conshohocken PA 610-828-2550
This restaurant serves French cuisine. Dogs are allowed at the outdoor tables.
Baja Fresh 340 W DeKalb Pike King of Prussia PA 610-337-2050
This restaurant serves Mexican food. Dogs are allowed at the outdoor tables. The restaurant has outdoor tables only in the Summer.
Starbucks 140 West DeKalb Pike King of Prussia PA 610-768-5130
http://www.starbucks.com
Enjoy coffee or a pastry at Starbucks. Well-behaved leashed dogs are welcome at the outdoor tables.

Philipsburg

Campgrounds and RV Parks
Black Moshannon State Park 4216 Beaver Road Philipsburg PA 814-342-5960 (888-727-2757)
Rich in environmental education and recreation, this park covers almost 4,000 acres with a 250 acre spring fed lake, plus there are a network of boardwalks and trails for exploring this unique, natural park. Dogs are allowed for an additional $2 per pet per stay when camping, and no charge for day use. They must be well behaved, under owner's control, on no more than a 6 foot leash or crated, and cleaned up after at all times. Dogs must be licensed with proof of vaccinations. Aggressive dogs are not allowed. Dogs may not be left unattended outside at any time and if in a vehicle only for very short times. Dogs must stay on selected pet routes/trails and areas. They are not allowed in swim areas or in park buildings. The campsites have tables, fire rings, modern restrooms, showers, laundry tubs, and a dump station. This RV park is closed during the off-season. The

camping and tent areas also allow dogs. There is a dog walk area at the campground. There are no water hookups at the campgrounds.

Parks

Black Moshannon State Park 4216 Beaver Road Philipsburg PA 814-342-5960 (888-727-2757)
Rich in environmental education and recreation, this park covers almost 4,000 acres with a 250 acre spring fed lake, plus there are a network of boardwalks and trails for exploring this unique, natural park. Dogs are allowed for an additional $2 per pet per stay when camping, and no charge for day use. They must be well behaved, under owner's control, on no more than a 6 foot leash or crated, and cleaned up after at all times. Dogs must be licensed with proof of vaccinations. Aggressive dogs are not allowed. Dogs may not be left unattended outside at any time and if in a vehicle only for very short times. Dogs must stay on selected pet routes/trails and areas. They are not allowed in swim areas or in park buildings.

Pine Grove

Accommodations

Comfort Inn H 443 and I 81 Pine Grove PA   570-345-8031 (877-424-6423)
Dogs are allowed for an additional pet fee of $10 per night per room.

Campgrounds and RV Parks

Pine Grove KOA 1445 Suedburg Road Pine Grove PA   717-865-4602 (800-562-5471)
http://www.twingrovecampground.koa.com
Dogs of all sizes are allowed. There are no additional pet fees. Dogs must be quiet, leashed, and cleaned up after. There are some breed restrictions. The camping and tent areas also allow dogs. There is a dog walk area at the campground. Dogs are allowed in the camping cabins.

Pittsburgh

Accommodations

Candlewood Suites 100 Chauvet Drive Pittsburgh PA   412-787-7770 (877-270-6405)
A dog up to 80 pounds is allowed for an additional fee of $75 for 1 to 6 days; the fee is $150 for 7 or more days.
Comfort Inn Conference Center 699 Rodi Road Pittsburgh PA   412-244-1600 (877-424-6423)
Quiet dogs are allowed for an additional fee of $10 per night per pet.
Comfort Inn and Suites 2898 Banksville Road Pittsburgh PA   412-343-3000 (877-424-6423)
Dogs are allowed for a $100 refundable deposit plus an additional fee of $15 per night per pet.
Days Inn Pittsburgh/Harmarville 6 Landings Drive Pittsburgh PA 412-828-5400 (800-329-7466)
Dogs of all sizes are allowed. There is a $10 one time per pet fee per visit.
Embassy Suites Hotel Pittsburgh - International Airport 550 Cherrington Parkway Pittsburgh PA   412-269-9070
Dogs of all sizes are allowed. There is a $50 one time pet fee per visit. Dogs are not allowed to be left alone in the room.
Hampton Inn 555 Trumbull Drive Pittsburgh PA   412-922-0100
Dogs of all sizes are allowed. There is a pet policy to sign at check in and there are no additional pet fees. They request you kennel your pet for housekeeping and dogs are not allowed in food areas.
Holiday Inn 401 Holiday Dr Pittsburgh PA   412-922-8100 (877-270-6405)
Dogs of all sizes are allowed for no additional pet fee.
Holiday Inn Express Hotel & Suites Pittsburgh Airport 5311 Campbells Run Road Pittsburgh PA   412-788-8400 (877-270-6405)
Dogs of all sizes are allowed for an additional one time pet fee of $15 per room.
Holiday Inn Hotel and Suites 180 Gamma Dr Pittsburgh PA   412-963-0600 (877-270-6405)
A dog up to 50 pounds is allowed for no additional fee with a credit card on file; a $50 refundable deposit is required if paying by cash.
MainStay Suites 1000 Park Lane Drive Pittsburgh PA   412-490-7343
Dogs up to 50 pounds are allowed for a fee per pet of $25 for 1 to 4 nights; $50 for 5 to 10 nights; $75 for 11 to 28 nights, and $100 for 29+ nights.
Morning Glory Inn 2119 Sarah Street Pittsburgh PA   412-431-1707
http:www.morningglorybedandbreakfast.com

A perfect blend of sophistication and casual comfort, this 1862 Italian style Victorian brick inn features lush greenery, a beautiful garden patio, and they are central to a host of other activities and an active nightlife. Dogs of all sizes are allowed in one suite for no additional fee. Dogs must be well mannered, they are not allowed on the furnishings, and they must be leashed and cleaned up after.
Motel 6 - Pittsburgh - Crafton 211 Beecham Drive Pittsburgh PA   412-922-9400 (800-466-8356)
One well-behaved family pet per room. Guest must notify front desk upon arrival. Guest is liable for any damages. In consideration of all guests, pets must never be left unattended in the guest rooms.
Radisson Hotel Pittsburgh Green Tree 101 Radisson Drive Pittsburgh PA   412-922-8400
Dogs of all sizes are allowed. There are no additional pet fees. Pet owners need to sign a pet waiver.
Red Roof Inn - Pittsburgh South Airport 6404 Steubenville Pike Pittsburgh PA   412-787-7870 (800-RED-ROOF)
One well-behaved family pet per room. Guest must notify front desk upon arrival. Guest is liable for any damages. In consideration of all guests, pets must never be left unattended in the guest rooms.
Residence Inn by Marriott 1500 Park Lane Drive Pittsburgh PA   412-787-3300
Dogs of all sizes are allowed. There is a $75 one time fee and a pet policy to sign at check in.
Super 8 Pittsburgh/Monroeville Area 1807 RT 286 Pittsburgh PA   724-733-8008 (800-800-8000)
Dogs of all sizes are allowed. There is a $5 per night pet fee per pet. Smoking and non-smoking rooms are available for pet rooms.

Transportation Systems
Port Authority of Allegheny County 534 Smithfield Street Pittsburgh PA   412-442-2000
http://www.ridegold.com
A small dog in an enclosed carrier is allowed on both light rail and the buses at no additional fee.

Shopping Centers
Station Square 100 W Station Square Drive Pittsburgh PA   412-261-2811
This is an entertainment, sightseeing, shopping, and dining center. Dogs are allowed around the Station grounds and at outdoor areas; they are not allowed in any of the buildings. Dogs must be well behaved, leashed, and cleaned up after at all times.

Stores
PetSmart Pet Store 420 Home Dr Pittsburgh PA   412-490-0191
Your licensed and well-behaved leashed dog is allowed in the store.
PetSmart Pet Store 1134 Northway Mall Pittsburgh PA   412-364-2720
Your licensed and well-behaved leashed dog is allowed in the store.
Petco Pet Store 4801 McKnight Rd Pittsburgh PA   412-366-1866
Your licensed and well-behaved leashed dog is allowed in the store.
Petco Pet Store 251 Clairton Blvd Pittsburgh PA   412-650-0175
Your licensed and well-behaved leashed dog is allowed in the store.
Petco Pet Store 976 Freeport Rd Room A2 Pittsburgh PA   412-781-6040
Your licensed and well-behaved leashed dog is allowed in the store.
Petco Pet Store 6512 Steubenville Pike Pittsburgh PA   412-787-4390
Your licensed and well-behaved leashed dog is allowed in the store.

Parks
TOP 200 PLACE Hartwood County Park and Amphitheater 215 Saxonburg Blvd Pittsburgh PA   412-767-9200
This 629 acre park allows dogs on leash in most of the park and off-leash in an unfenced specified off-leash dog exercise area. Of special interest in the park is the outdoor amphitheater and its Summer Concert Series and other musical events. Your leashed dog is allowed to accompany you to listen to the concerts. There is an off-leash area in the park behind the amphitheater
Highland Park The Hill Road Pittsburgh PA   412-682-7275
This park is home to the Pittsburgh Zoo and the PPG Aquarium, but other popular features include a hilltop walking trail that overlooks a large reservoir and the city's only long-course swimming pool. Dogs are allowed throughout the park with exception of the zoo, playgrounds and gaming courts. Dogs must be under owner's control, leashed, and cleaned up after at all times in all areas of the park.
Point State Park 101 Commonwealth Place Pittsburgh PA   412-471-0235
A majestic 150 foot tall water fountain, a paved river promenade, dramatic city views, 23 commemorative historic markers, trails that connect the area to several points in the city, and more are offered at this 36 acre park that sits at the tip of the city's "Golden Triangle". Dogs are allowed throughout the grounds; they must be leashed and cleaned up after.

Schenley Park 3898 Boulevard of the Allies Pittsburgh PA 412-682-7275
http://www.pittsburghparks.org/_76.php
This beautifully landscaped 456 acre park offers reprieve amongst a bustling university and business district with a long list of recreational opportunities, special events/programs, a pool, easy to difficult hiking trails, and a Plaza area. The Plaza, a public green space, offers food, restrooms, lawns and gardens, and free WiFi. Dogs are allowed throughout the park with exception to playgrounds and gaming courts. Dogs are allowed at the Plaza on paved areas only, and they must be under owner's control, leashed, and cleaned up after at all times in all areas of the park.

TOP 200 PLACE The **Duquesne Incline** 1220 Grandview Avenue Pittsburgh PA 412-381-1665
http://incline.pghfree.net/
The Duquesne Incline is actually a working museum with 2 original 1877 cable cars that connects the upper and lower levels of the city, and not only does this tram save miles and gives outstanding views of the city, but your pooch can ride too. There is free parking at the bottom, but not at the top. Dogs must be well behaved, under owner's control, leashed, and cleaned up after at all times.

Off-Leash Dog Parks
Frick Park 6750 Forbes Avenue Pittsburgh PA 412-255-2539
This off leash dog area is located in the city's largest park which is a popular area for its extensive trails, its historical and educational opportunities, and for the variety of recreation available. The off leash dog area is about a ½ mile past the Blue Slide Playground on Riverview Trail. Dogs must be kept leashed until in the fenced area, and they must be under owner's control and cleaned up after at all times.
Hartwood Acres Off-Leash Park Middle Road Pittsburgh PA 412-767-9200
This fenced, off leash dog area is located on a beautifully landscaped 629 acre historic country estate with more than 30 miles of hiking trails. Dogs are allowed throughout the park; they are not allowed in buildings. The off-leash dog area is off Middle Road behind the amphitheater. Dogs must remain on lead when not in this area, and they must be cleaned up after at all times.
Upper Frick Dog Park Beechwood and Nicholson Pittsburgh PA
This fenced dog park has pickup bags. It is about one acre in size.

Outdoor Restaurants
Baja Fresh 3615 Forbes Ave Pittsburgh PA 412-687-7700
This restaurant serves Mexican food. Dogs are allowed at the outdoor tables.
Baja Fresh 310 Mcholme Dr Pittsburgh PA 412-788-0370
This restaurant serves Mexican food. Dogs are allowed at the outdoor tables.
Cafe Zinho 238 Spahr St Pittsburgh PA 412-363-1500
This restaurant serves American and European cuisine. Dogs are allowed at the outdoor tables. Cafe Zinho does not serve alcohol, but you can bring your own.
Crazy Mocha Café 420 Fort Duquesne Pittsburgh PA 412-281-7940
http://www.crazymocha.com/
This coffee shop also offers a variety of bakery items and outside seating. Dogs are allowed at the outside tables; they must be leashed and under owner's control/care at all times.
Del's Bar and Ristorante 4428 Liberty Ave Pittsburgh PA 412-683-1448
http://www.delrest.com
This restaurant serves Italian and seafood. Dogs are allowed at the outdoor tables.
Lot 17 Bar and Grill 4617 Liberty Ave Pittsburgh PA 412-687-8117
This restaurant and bar serves American. Dogs are allowed at the outdoor tables.
Panera Bread 942 Freeport Road #114 Pittsburgh PA 412-799-0210
http://www.panera.com
This restaurant serves deli-type cuisine. Dogs are allowed at the outdoor tables.
Pepperoni's 28 Donati Rd Pittsburgh PA 412-854-7400
This restaurant serves Italian food. Dogs are allowed at the outdoor tables.
Roland's Seafood Grill 1904 Penn Ave Pittsburgh PA 412-261-3401
This restaurant and bar serves American and seafood. Dogs are allowed at the outdoor tables.
Whole Foods Market 5880 Centre Ave Pittsburgh PA 412-441-3040
This restaurant serves deli-type food. Dogs are allowed at the outdoor tables.

Pittsburgh Area

Accommodations
Holiday Inn 7195 Eastwood Rd Beaver Falls PA 724-846-3700 (877-270-6405)

Dogs of all sizes are allowed for an additional one time pet fee of $35 per room.
Crowne Plaza Hotel Pittsburgh-Intl Airport 1160 Thorn Run Road Coraopolis PA   412-262-2400 (877-270-6405)
Dogs of all sizes are allowed for no additional pet fee; there is a pet agreement to sign at check in.
Motel 6 - Pittsburgh Airport 1170 Thorn Run Road Coraopolis PA   412-269-0990 (800-466-8356)
One well-behaved family pet per room. Guest must notify front desk upon arrival. Guest is liable for any damages. In consideration of all guests, pets must never be left unattended in the guest rooms.
Pittsburgh Airport Marriott 777 Aten Road Coraopolis PA   412-788-8800 (800-328-9297)
Dogs of all sizes are allowed. There is a $50 one time additional pet fee per pet. Dogs must be leashed, cleaned up after, and the Pet in Room sign put on the door when they are in the room alone.
Holiday Inn Express 20003 Rt 19 Cranberry Township PA   724-772-1000 (877-270-6405)
Dogs of all sizes are allowed for an additional fee of $10 per night per room.
Red Roof Inn - Pittsburgh North Cranberry TWP 20009 U.S.19 & Marguerite Road Cranberry Township PA 724-776-5670 (800-RED-ROOF)
One well-behaved family pet per room. Guest must notify front desk upon arrival. Guest is liable for any damages. In consideration of all guests, pets must never be left unattended in the guest rooms.
Residence Inn by Marriott 1308 Freedom Road Cranberry Township PA   724-779-1000
Dogs of all sizes are allowed. There is a $75 one time fee and a pet policy to sign at check in.
Comfort Inn North 5137 H 8 Gibsonia PA   724-444-8700 (877-424-6423)
Dogs up to 50 pounds are allowed for an additional fee of $10 per night per pet.
Comfort Inn Cranberry Twp. 924 Sheraton Drive Mars PA   724-772-2700 (877-424-6423)
Dogs up to 100 pounds are allowed for an additional one time fee of $10 per pet.
Motel 6 - Pittsburgh - Cranberry 19025 Perry Highway Mars PA   724-776-4333 (800-466-8356)
One well-behaved family pet per room. Guest must notify front desk upon arrival. Guest is liable for any damages. In consideration of all guests, pets must never be left unattended in the guest rooms.
Holiday Inn Express Hotel and Suites 105 Stone Quarry Rd Monaca PA   724-728-5121 (877-270-6405)
Dogs of all sizes are allowed for an additional fee of $10 per night per pet.
Days Inn Pittsburgh/Monroeville 2727 Mosside Blvd Monroeville PA   412-856-1610 (800-329-7466)
Dogs of all sizes are allowed. There is a $25 per night pet fee per pet.
Red Roof Inn - Pittsburgh East - Monroeville 2729 Mosside Boulevard Monroeville PA   412-856-4738 (800-RED-ROOF)
One well-behaved family pet per room. Guest must notify front desk upon arrival. Guest is liable for any damages. In consideration of all guests, pets must never be left unattended in the guest rooms.
Holiday Inn - Airport 8256 University Blvd. Moon Township PA   412-262-3600 (877-270-6405)
Dogs of all sizes are allowed for an additional one time pet fee of $50 per room.
La Quinta Inn Pittsburgh Airport 8507 University Boulevard Moon Township PA   412-269-0400 (800-531-5900)
Dogs of all sizes are allowed. There are no additional pet fees. Dogs must be quiet, well behaved, leashed and cleaned up after.
Clarion Hotel 300 Tarentum Bridge Road New Kensington PA   724-335-9171 (877-424-6423)
Dogs are allowed for no additional pet fee. There is a pet agreement to sign at check in, and dogs may not be left alone in the room.
Residence Inn by Marriott 3896 Bigelow Blvd Oakland PA   412-621-2200
Dogs of all sizes are allowed. There is a fee of $10 per night per room up to 30 days. If the stay is 30 days or more then it is a $100 one time fee. There is also a pet policy to sign at check in.
Indian Rock Inn 155 Keen Lake Waymart PA   610-982-9600
Well behaved dogs up to 75 pounds are allowed. There is a $15 one time additional pet fee per room.
Keen Lake Camping and Cottage Resort 155 Keen Lake Waymart PA   570-488-5522
Dogs of all sizes are allowed. There is a $50 one time pet fee for cottages and there is no additional pet fee for the camp sites. Dogs are not to be left alone at any time.
Holiday Inn Express Hotel and Suites 3122 Lebanon Church Rd West Mifflin PA   412-469-1900 (877-270-6405)
Dogs of all sizes are allowed for an additional fee of $10 per night per pet.

Campgrounds and RV Parks

Bear Run Campground 184 Badger Hill Road Portersville PA   888-737-2605
http://www.bearruncampground.com
Dogs of all sizes are allowed. There are no additional pet fees. Dogs must be leashed and cleaned up after. Dogs are not allowed in the buildings or rentals. There are some breed restrictions. This RV park is closed during the off-season. The camping and tent areas also allow dogs. There is a dog walk area at the campground.
Madison/Pittsburgh SE KOA 764 Waltz Mill Road Ruffs Dale PA   724-722-4444 (800-562-4034)
http://www.pittsburghkoa.com
Dogs of all sizes are allowed. There are no additional pet fees. Dogs must be leashed and cleaned up after. There are some breed restrictions. This RV park is closed during the off-season. The camping and tent areas

also allow dogs. There is a dog walk area at the campground. Dogs are allowed in the camping cabins.
Keen Lake Camping and Cottage Resort 155 Keen Lake Road Waymart PA 570-488-5522
http://www.keenlake.com
Dogs of all sizes are allowed, and there are no additional pet fees for RV or tent sites. There is a $50 one time additional pet fee for a cottage rental plus a $250 refundable pet deposit. Dogs must be quiet, may not be left unattended, and must be leashed and cleaned up after. This RV park is closed during the off-season. The camping and tent areas also allow dogs. There is a dog walk area at the campground. Dogs are allowed in the camping cabins.

Attractions

TOP 200 PLACE **Air Heritage Museum** 35 Piper Street Beaver Falls PA 724-843-2820
http://airheritage.org/
Dedicated to the education and preservation of America's history of flight, this museum will take guests through the challenges and victories leading to today's flight technology. Well behaved dogs are welcome to accompany their owners. Dogs must be leashed and cleaned up after at all times.

Stores

Petco Pet Store 59 Fort Couch Rd Bethel Park PA 412-835-6008
Your licensed and well-behaved leashed dog is allowed in the store.
Petco Pet Store 20111 Route 19 Unit 201c Cranberry Township PA 724-779-9003
Your licensed and well-behaved leashed dog is allowed in the store.
PetSmart Pet Store 1717 Route 228 Cranberry Turnpike PA 724-779-9570
Your licensed and well-behaved leashed dog is allowed in the store.
Petco Pet Store 590 East Waterfront Drive Homestead PA 412-461-1229
Your licensed and well-behaved leashed dog is allowed in the store.
PetSmart Pet Store 115 Wagner Rd Monaca PA 724-770-0505
Your licensed and well-behaved leashed dog is allowed in the store.
PetSmart Pet Store 3739 William Penn Hwy Monroeville PA 412-372-8424
Your licensed and well-behaved leashed dog is allowed in the store.
Petco Pet Store 2723 Stroschein Rd Monroeville PA 412-856-9920
Your licensed and well-behaved leashed dog is allowed in the store.
PetSmart Pet Store 3500 Mountain View Dr West Mifflin PA 412-653-7071
Your licensed and well-behaved leashed dog is allowed in the store.

Parks

McConnells Mill State Park McConnells Mills Road Portersville PA 724-368-8091
Rich in environmental and geological education and recreation, this 2,546 acre glacially carved park features an 1800's gristmill, a steep scenic gorge, waterfalls, and river rafting/hiking trails of varying difficulty. Dogs are allowed throughout the park. Dogs may not be left unattended at any time, and they must be leashed and cleaned up after at all times.
Sewickley Heights Park Fern Hollow Rd Sewickley Heights PA
This park west of Pittsburgh has about 12 miles of trails. Dogs under voice control are allowed off leash throughout the park. There are streams, hills and meadows in the park.

Off-Leash Dog Parks

South Park Dog Park Corrigan Drive at South Park Library PA 412-350-7275
This fenced dog park has drinking water, pickup bags and benches. Dogs on leash are allowed in most of the rest of this 2000 acre park.
White Oak Dog Park Route 48 McKeesport PA 412-350-7275
This fenced dog park in White Oak Park has water, pickup bags and benches. It is about 2 acres in size. The dog park can be accessed from Route 48. Take the White Oak Park entrance. Dogs are allowed on leash in most of the rest of this 810 acre park.
Heritage Park Dog Park 2364 Saunders Station Road Monroeville PA 412-350-7275
http://www.monroeville.pa.us/dogpark/
This fenced dog park has shade, water, and pickup bags. The park is open from sunrise to sunset.

Outdoor Restaurants

Panera Bread 5243 Library Road Bethel Park PA 412-854-2007
http://www.panera.com
This restaurant serves deli-type cuisine. Dogs are allowed at the outdoor tables.
The Hartwood Restaurant 3400 Harts Run Road Glenshaw PA 412-767-3500

This restaurant and bar serves Hawaiian Fusion cuisine and British food. Dogs are allowed at the outdoor tables.
Baja Fresh 4145 William Penn H, Suite 1 Monroeville PA 412-374-8100
This restaurant serves Mexican food. Dogs are allowed at the outdoor tables. The restaurant has outdoor tables only in the Summer.
Il Pizzaiolo 703 Washington Rd Mount Lebanon PA 412-344-4123
This restaurant serves Italian food. Dogs are allowed at the outdoor tables.

Day Kennels
PetsHotel by PetsMart Day Kennel 3739 William Penn Hwy Monroeville PA 412-372-8431
http://www.petsmart.com/PETsHOTEL/
This PetSmart pet store offers day care, day camp and overnight care. You may drop off and pick up your dog during the hours the store is open seven days a week. Dogs must have proof of current rabies, DPP and Bordatella vaccinations.

Poconos - Scranton Area

Accommodations
Comfort Inn 811 Northern Blvd Clarks Summit PA 570-586-9100 (877-424-6423)
Dogs are allowed for an additional pet fee of $10 per night per room.
Residence Inn by Marriott 947 Viewmont Drive Dickson City PA 570-343-5121
Dogs of all sizes are allowed. There is a $75 one time fee and a pet policy to sign at check in.
Days Inn Scranton/Dunmore 1226 O'Neill Hwy Dunmore PA 570-348-6101 (800-329-7466)
Dogs of all sizes are allowed. There is a $5 per night pet fee per pet.
Holiday Inn 200 Tigue St Dunmore PA 570-343-4771 (877-270-6405)
Dogs of all sizes are allowed for an additional fee of $10 per night per pet.
Sleep Inn and Suites 102 Monahan Avenue Dunmore PA 570-961-1116 (877-424-6423)
Dogs are allowed for an additional fee of $10 per night per pet.
Super 8 Dunmore/Scranton Area 1027 Oneill Hwy Dunmore PA 570-346-8782 (800-800-8000)
Dogs of all sizes are allowed. There is a $10 per night pet fee per pet. Smoking and non-smoking rooms are available for pet rooms.
Falls Port Inn 330 Main Ave Hawley PA 570-226-2600
Large dogs are allowed in the larger rooms. There is a $20 one time pet fee.
Comfort Inn 117 Twin Rocks Road Lake Ariel PA 570-689-4148 (877-424-6423)
Dogs are allowed for an additional fee of $15 per night per pet. Dogs may not be left alone in the room.
Clarion Hotel 300 Meadow Avenue Scranton PA 570-344-9811 (877-424-6423)
Dogs are allowed for an additional pet fee of $25 per night per room.
Days Inn Scranton 1946 Scranton-Carbondale hwy Scranton PA 570-383-9979 (800-329-7466)
Dogs of all sizes are allowed. There is a $5 per night pet fee per small pet or $20 per large pet.
Howard Johnson Express Inn 320 Franklin Ave. Scranton PA 570-346-7061 (800-446-4656)
Dogs of all sizes are welcome. There is a $10 per day pet fee.
Best Western Genetti Hotel & Conference Center 77 E Market Street Wilkes-Barre PA 570-823-6152 (800-780-7234)
Dogs are allowed for an additional pet fee of $10 per night per room.
Holiday Inn 880 Kidder St, Rt 115 & 309 Wilkes-Barre PA 570-824-8901 (877-270-6405)
Dogs of all sizes are allowed for an additional one time pet fee of $15 per room.
Red Roof Inn - Wilkes-Barre 1035 Highway 315 Wilkes-Barre PA 570-829-6422 (800-RED-ROOF)
One well-behaved family pet per room. Guest must notify front desk upon arrival. Guest is liable for any damages. In consideration of all guests, pets must never be left unattended in the guest rooms.

Campgrounds and RV Parks
Frances Slocum State Park 565 Mount Olivet Road Wyoming PA 570-696-3525 (888-PA-PARKS (727-2757))
Offering a good variety of land and water recreation, this 1,000+ acre park has a beautiful horseshoe shaped 165 acre lake, and 9 miles of blazed trails, including an interpretive trail that starts at the environmental center. Dogs of all sizes are allowed for no additional fee. Dogs must be well behaved, under owner's control, leashed or crated, and cleaned up after at all times (exceptions during hunting season). Dogs must be licensed and have proof vaccinations. Aggressive dogs are not allowed. Dogs may not be left unattended outside at any time and may only be left alone in a vehicle for very short periods. Dogs must stay on selected pet routes/trails and areas; they may not be in designated swim areas or in park buildings. Reservations are highly recommended as pet camp sites are limited. The camp area has 100 sites available, each with a picnic table and fire ring, and modern

restrooms, showers, potable water, and a dump station are close by. This RV park is closed during the off-season. The camping and tent areas also allow dogs. There is a dog walk area at the campground. There are no water hookups at the campgrounds.

Attractions
Steamtown National Historic Site 150 South Washington Avenue Scranton PA   570-340-5206
http://www.nps.gov/stea/index.htm
Dogs must be on leash and must be cleaned up after on grounds and parking area. Dogs are not allowed in the museum. Open year-round 9am-5pm.

Stores
PetSmart Pet Store 650 Commerce Blvd Dickson City PA   570-347-1006
Your licensed and well-behaved leashed dog is allowed in the store.
Petco Pet Store 529 Scranton Carbondale Highway Dickson City PA   570-343-3117
Your licensed and well-behaved leashed dog is allowed in the store.
PetSmart Pet Store 427 Arena Hub Plaza Wilkes-Barre PA 570-825-8425
Your licensed and well-behaved leashed dog is allowed in the store.
Petco Pet Store 3480 Wilkes-Barre Township Commons Wilkes-Barre PA   570-820-5973
Your licensed and well-behaved leashed dog is allowed in the store.

Parks
Upper Delaware Scenic and Recreational River 274 River Road Beach Lake PA   570-685-4871
http://www.nps.gov/upde/index.htm
Dogs must be on leash and must be cleaned up after in most of the federal park areas. You must follow state and local park rules in other areas. The park features auto touring, camping, boating, fishing, and more.
Keen Lake Route 6 Carbondale PA 570-488-6161
http://www.keenlake.com
Dogs on leash are allowed in the park and camping areas. They are not allowed in the pool, buildings, or public beaches. The park features boating, swimming, picnicking and camping. Located in Poconos Mountains.
Archbald Pothole State Park Scranton Carbondale H/H 6 Scranton PA   570-945-3239
Named for a glacially created geological feature that formed about 15,000 years, this 150 acre park offers a variety of educational and recreational opportunities. Dogs of all sizes are allowed for no additional fee. Dogs must be under owner's control, leashed, and cleaned up after at all times.
Frances Slocum State Park 565 Mount Olivet Road Wyoming PA   570-696-3525 (888-PA-PARKS (727-2757))
Offering a good variety of land and water recreation, this 1,000+ acre park has a beautiful horseshoe shaped 165 acre lake, and 9 miles of blazed trails, including an interpretive trail that starts at the environmental center. Dogs of all sizes are allowed for no additional fee. Dogs must be well behaved, under owner's control, leashed or crated, and cleaned up after at all times (exceptions during hunting season). Dogs must be licensed and have proof vaccinations. Aggressive dogs are not allowed. Dogs may not be left unattended outside at any time and may only be left alone in a vehicle for very short periods. Dogs must stay on selected pet routes/trails and areas; they may not be in designated swim areas or in park buildings. Reservations are highly recommended as pet camp sites are limited.

Outdoor Restaurants
State Street Grill 114 S State Street/H 6/11 Clarks Summit PA   570-585-5590
http://www.statestreetofmind.com/
Whether looking for fine dining, a brew, or just light fare, this eatery can accommodate, and they also offer outdoor dining. Dogs are allowed at the outer tables. Dogs must be under owner's control/care and leashed at all times.

Poconos - Stroudsburg Area

Accommodations
Red Rose Inn 243 Meckesville Road Albrightsville PA   570-722-3526
http://www.theredroseinn.com/
Secluded, yet central to numerous recreational activities, this B&B sits surrounded by flourishing greenery, tall trees, and some beautiful walking paths. One dog is allowed for no additional pet fee. Dogs must be quiet, leased or crated, and cleaned up after.

Best Western Inn at Blakeslee-Pocono Route 115 Blakeslee PA   570-646-6000 (800-780-7234)
Dogs are allowed for a $50 refundable deposit.
The Merry Inn H 390 Canadensis PA   570-595-2011 (800-858-4182)
http://www.themerryinn.com/
Nestled amongst lush greenery and towering trees, this mountain inn offers an outdoor hot tub on an upper deck
facing the woods, and they sit central to a host of other activities and year-round recreational pursuits. Dogs of all
sizes are allowed for a one time additional pet fee of $22 per room. Dogs must be quiet, leashed, cleaned up
after, and they may be left alone in the room only if the owner is confident in the pet's behavior.
Budget Inn and Suites 340 Greentree Drive East Stroudsburg PA   570-424-5451 (888-233-8144)
http://www.poconobudgetinn.com/
Dogs of all sizes are allowed for no additional pet fees. A credit card must be on file and there is a pet waiver to
sign at check in. Dogs must be quiet, leashed or crated, cleaned up after, and crated when left alone in the room.

Campgrounds and RV Parks
Delaware Water Gap KOA 233 Hollow Road E Stroudsburg PA   570-223-8000 (800-562-0375)
http://www.koa.com
Dogs of all sizes are allowed. There are no additional pet fees. Dogs must be leased and cleaned up after. There
are some breed restrictions. This RV park is closed during the off-season. The camping and tent areas also
allow dogs. There is a dog walk area at the campground.
Mountain Vista Campground 50 Taylor Drive E Stroudsburg PA   570-223-0111
http://www.mountainvistacampground.com
Dogs of all sizes are allowed. There are no additional pet fees. Dogs must be well behaved, leashed, and
cleaned up after. This RV park is closed during the off-season. The camping and tent areas also allow dogs.
There is a dog walk area at the campground.
Otter Lake Camp Resort 4805 Marshall's Creek Road E Stroudsburg PA   570-223-0123
http://www.otterlake.com
Dogs of all sizes are allowed. There are no additional pet fees. Dogs may not be left unattended, must be
leashed, and cleaned up after. The camping and tent areas also allow dogs. There is a dog walk area at the
campground.
Tobyhanna State Park On H 423 Tobyhanna PA   570-894-8336 (888-PA-PARKS 727-2757)
Dogs of all sizes are allowed. There is a $2 per night per pet additional fee. Pets are to be walked in designated
walking areas of the campground and on designated pet walkways when accessing other areas of the park from
the campground. Dogs must be leashed, under physical control at all times, and cleaned up after. Pet food must
remain inside the camping unit, and dogs must have current shot records and a rabies certificate, be quiet, and
well behaved. Dogs are allowed on the trails and day use areas, but they are not allowed on the beach, in any
swim areas, or in any of the buildings. Dogs may not be left unattended except for very short periods; then they
must be left inside your unit, weather permitting. Dogs are allowed on the trails. This campground is closed
during the off-season. The camping and tent areas also allow dogs. There is a dog walk area at the campground.
There are no electric or water hookups at the campground.
Hickory Run State Park H 534 White Haven PA   570-443-0400 (888-PA-PARKS (727-2757))
Three natural areas, more than 40 miles of scenic, blazed hiking trails rich in history, miles of trout streams, and
a National Natural Landmark - the Boulder Field, are on site, and there are a variety of year-round land and water
recreational and educational opportunities available. Dogs of all sizes are allowed for an additional $2 per pet per
stay. Dogs must be well behaved, under owner's control, leashed or crated, and cleaned up after at all times
(exceptions during hunting season). Dogs must be licensed and have proof of vaccinations. Aggressive dogs are
not allowed. Dogs may not be left unattended outside at any time and may only be left alone in a vehicle for very
short periods. Dogs must stay on selected pet routes/trails and areas; they may not be in designated swim areas
or in park buildings. The camp area offers forested or open sites with modern restrooms, a dump station, and a
general store. This RV park is closed during the off-season. The camping and tent areas also allow dogs. There
is a dog walk area at the campground. There are no water hookups at the campgrounds.

Shopping Centers
The Crossing Premium Outlets 1000 H 611 Tannersville PA   570-629-4650
This factory outlet shopping area offers more than 100 shops and services. Dogs are allowed throughout the
village; they are not allowed in stores or the food court. Dogs must be under owner's control, leashed or crated,
and cleaned up after at all times. Dogs may not be left unattended at any time, including in vehicles.

Parks
Mountain Vista Campground 50 Taylor Dr East Stroudsburg PA   570-223-0111
http://www.mtnvistacampground.com
Dogs on leash are allowed in the park and camping areas. The park features camping, hiking, swimming, and
more.
Driftstone on the Delaware 2731 River Rd Mount Bethel PA   888-355-6859

http://www.driftstone.com
Dogs on leash are allowed in the park and camping areas. The park features swimming, hiking, boating, camping, and more.
Hickory Run State Park H 534 White Haven PA   570-443-0400 (888-PA-PARKS (727-2757))
Three natural areas, more than 40 miles of scenic, blazed hiking trails rich in history, miles of trout streams, and a National Natural Landmark - the Boulder Field, are on site, and there are a variety of year-round land and water recreational and educational opportunities available. Dogs of all sizes are allowed for an additional $2 per pet per stay. Dogs must be well behaved, under owner's control, leashed or crated, and cleaned up after at all times (exceptions during hunting season). Dogs must be licensed and have proof of vaccinations. Aggressive dogs are not allowed. Dogs may not be left unattended outside at any time and may only be left alone in a vehicle for very short periods. Dogs must stay on selected pet routes/trails and areas; they may not be in designated swim areas or in park buildings.

Outdoor Restaurants
Everybody's Cafe 905 Main Street Stroudsburg PA   570-424-0896
Dogs are allowed at the outdoor tables. The restaurant has outdoor tables only in the Summer.

Pottstown

Accommodations
Comfort Inn 99 Robinson Street Pottstown PA   610-326-5000 (877-424-6423)
Dogs are allowed for an additional pet fee of $10 per night per room.
Days Inn Pottstown 29 High St Pottstown PA   610-970-1101 (800-329-7466)
Dogs of all sizes are allowed. There is a $10 per night pet fee per pet.
Motel 6 - Pottstown 78 Robinson Street Pottstown PA   610-819-1288 (800-466-8356)
One well-behaved family pet per room. Guest must notify front desk upon arrival. Guest is liable for any damages. In consideration of all guests, pets must never be left unattended in the guest rooms.

Stores
PetSmart Pet Store 1112 Town Square Rd Pottstown PA   610-705-9922
Your licensed and well-behaved leashed dog is allowed in the store.
Petco Pet Store 130 West Main St Trappe PA   610-489-9830
Your licensed and well-behaved leashed dog is allowed in the store.

Reading

Accommodations
Holiday Inn 6170 Morgantown Rd Morgantown PA   610-286-3000 (877-270-6405)
Dogs of all sizes are allowed for an additional fee of $20 per night per pet.
Sheraton Reading Hotel 1741 Papermill Road Reading PA   610-376-3811 (888-625-5144)
Dogs of all sizes are allowed. There is a $10 per night pet fee per pet. Dogs are not allowed to be left alone in the room.

Campgrounds and RV Parks
French Creek State Park 843 Park Road Elverson PA   610-582-9680 (888-PA-PARKS (727-2757))
With 2 beautiful lakes and almost 40 miles of well-marked trails, this beautifully forested 7,339 acre park offers a wide variety of educational and recreational opportunities. Dogs of all sizes are allowed for an additional $2 per pet per stay. Dogs must be well behaved, under owner's control, leashed or crated, and cleaned up after at all times (exceptions during hunting season). Dogs must be licensed and have proof of all vaccinations. Aggressive dogs are not allowed. Dogs may not be left unattended outside at any time and may only be left alone in a vehicle for very short periods. Dogs must stay on selected pet routes/trails and areas; they may not be in designated swim areas or in park buildings. Trail maps allowing dogs can be obtained at the park office. The campground offers 201 modern, wooded sites with flush toilet facilities and showers close by. The camping and tent areas also allow dogs. There is a dog walk area at the campground. There are no water hookups at the campgrounds.

Attractions
Daniel Boone Homestead 400 Daniel Boone Road Birdsboro PA 610-582-4900
http://www.danielboonehomestead.org/
This 579+ acre state historic site offers educational and interpretive programs in addition to a variety of hiking areas, special events, demonstrations, and workshops throughout the year. Well behaved dogs are allowed on the grounds; they are not allowed in buildings. Dogs must be under owner's control, leashed or crated, and cleaned up after at all times.
Hopewell Furnace National Historic Site 2 Mark Bird Lane Elverson PA 610-582-8773
http://www.nps.gov/hofu/index.htm
Dogs must be on leash and must be cleaned up after on site. Dogs are not allowed in buildings. The site features hiking, nature walks, and site touring. Hopewell Furnace was founded in 1771 by Ironmaster Mark Bird. The furnace operated until 1883.

Shopping Centers
VF Outlets Village 801 Hill Avenue Wyomissing PA 610-378-0408
http://www.vfovillage.com/
This factory outlet shopping area offers over 60 shops and services. Dogs are allowed throughout the village; they are not allowed in stores. Dogs must be under owner's control, leashed or crated, and cleaned up after at all times. Dogs may not be left unattended at any time, including in vehicles.

Stores
Petco Pet Store 2765 Papermill Rd Unit G-1 Reading PA 610-376-3203
Your licensed and well-behaved leashed dog is allowed in the store.
PetSmart Pet Store 1183 Berkshire Blvd Wyomissing PA 610-396-3660
Your licensed and well-behaved leashed dog is allowed in the store.

Parks
French Creek State Park 843 Park Road Elverson PA 610-582-9680 (888-PA-PARKS (727-2757))
With 2 beautiful lakes and almost 40 miles of well-marked trails, this beautifully forested 7,339 acre park offers a wide variety of educational and recreational opportunities. Dogs of all sizes are allowed for an additional $2 per pet per stay. Dogs must be well behaved, under owner's control, leashed or crated, and cleaned up after at all times (exceptions during hunting season). Dogs must be licensed and have proof of all vaccinations. Aggressive dogs are not allowed. Dogs may not be left unattended outside at any time and may only be left alone in a vehicle for very short periods. Dogs must stay on selected pet routes/trails and areas; they may not be in designated swim areas or in park buildings. Trail maps allowing dogs can be obtained at the park office.

Saint Marys

Accommodations
Comfort Inn 195 Comfort Lane Saint Marys PA 814-834-2030 (877-424-6423)
Dogs are allowed for an additional fee of $15 (plus tax) per night per pet.

Sayre

Accommodations
Best Western Grand Victorian Inn 255 Spring Street Sayre PA 570-888-7711 (800-780-7234)
Dogs are allowed for an additional fee of $10 per night per pet. Dogs must be quiet and well mannered.

Sellinsgrove

Accommodations
Comfort Inn 710 H 11/15 Sellinsgrove PA 570-374-8880 (877-424-6423)
Quiet dogs are allowed for an additional one time fee of $10 per pet. Dogs must be crated when left alone in the

room.

Shartlesville

Campgrounds and RV Parks
Appalachian Campsites 60 Motel Drive Shartlesville PA   610-488-6319
http://www.appalachianrvresort.com
Dogs of all sizes are allowed. There are no additional pet fees. Dogs must be leashed and cleaned up after. The camping and tent areas also allow dogs. There is a dog walk area at the campground.

Sheffield

Campgrounds and RV Parks
Whispering Winds Campground 277 Tollgate Road Sheffield PA   814-968-4377
http://www.WhisperingWindsPA.com
This family campground has full camping facilities, a laundry, playground and a pool. Pets are welcome with no additional fee. They must be kept on a leash or in a crate or a pen and under control. There is a pet walk area.

Somerset

Accommodations
Best Western Executive Inn of Somerset 165 Waterworks Rd Somerset PA   814-445-3996 (800-780-7234)
Dogs are allowed for an additional fee of $7 per night per pet.
Days Inn Somerset 220 Waterworks Rd Somerset PA   814-445-9200 (800-329-7466)
Dogs of all sizes are allowed. There is a $6 per night pet fee per pet.
Holiday Inn 202 Harmon St Somerset PA   814-445-9611 (877-270-6405)
Dogs of all sizes are allowed for an additional one time pet fee of $35 per room.
Quality Inn 215 Ramada Road Somerset PA   814-443-4646 (877-424-6423)
Dogs are allowed for an additional fee of $10 per night per pet.
Super 8 Somerset 125 Lewis Dr Somerset PA   814-445-8788 (800-800-8000)
Dogs of all sizes are allowed. There is a $7 per night pet fee per pet. Smoking and non-smoking rooms are available for pet rooms.

Campgrounds and RV Parks
Kooser State Park 934 Glades Pike Somerset PA   814-445-7725
Dogs of all sizes are allowed. There is a $2 per night per pet additional fee. Pets are to be walked in designated walking areas of the campground and on designated pet walkways when accessing other areas of the park from the campground. Dogs must be leashed, under physical control at all times, and cleaned up after. Pet food must remain inside the camping unit, and dogs must have current shot records and a rabies certificate, be quiet, and well behaved. Dogs are allowed on the trails and day use areas, but they are not allowed on the beach, in any swim areas, or in any of the buildings. Dogs may not be left unattended except for very short periods; then they must be left inside your unit, weather permitting. Dogs are allowed on the trails. The camping and tent areas also allow dogs. There is a dog walk area at the campground. There are no water hookups at the campground.

Shopping Centers
Georgian Place 317 Georgian Place Somerset PA   814-443-3818
http://www.georgianplace.net/
This premier shopping and office village offers a wide variety of shops and services and beautifully landscaped grounds with lots of green areas. Dogs are allowed throughout the property and possibly in a few of the stores, especially at the Pet Boutique. Dogs must be well mannered, leashed, and cleaned up after at all times.

Parks
Flight 93 National Memorial Park 109 West Main Street Ste 104 Somerset PA   814-443-4557
http://www.nps.gov/flni/index.htm

Dogs on leash are allowed roadside to view the memorial for the passengers and crew of flight 93 that gave their lives on 9/11. Dogs are not allowed past the site to respect private property owners.

Springfield

Outdoor Restaurants
Baja Fresh 1138 Baltimore Pike Springfield PA   610-690-1064
Dogs are allowed at the outdoor tables. The restaurant has outdoor tables only in the Summer.

Starlight

Accommodations
The Inn at Starlight Lake 2890 Starlight Lake Road Starlight PA   570-798-2519 (800-248-2519)
http://www.innatstarlightlake.com/
Set among lush greenery on the lakefront, this family getaway features a game room, sunroom, restaurant and bar, and they are central to a wide variety of land and water year-round recreation. Dogs of all sizes are allowed in the cottages only for no additional pet fee. Dogs must be at least one year old, they are not allowed in the main house, and they may not be left unattended in the room for more than 2 hours. Dogs must be leashed and cleaned up after at all times.

State College

Accommodations
Holiday Inn I-80 & US 150 N Milesburg PA   814-355-7521 (877-270-6405)
Dogs of all sizes are allowed for no additional pet fee.
Comfort Suites 132 Village Drive State College PA   814-235-1900 (877-424-6423)
Dogs are allowed for a $50 refundable deposit plus an additional fee of $20 per night per pet.
Days Inn Penn State 240 S Pugh St State College PA   814-238-8454 (800-329-7466)
Dogs of all sizes are allowed. There is a $10 per night pet fee per pet.
Motel 6 - STATE COLLEGE - PENN STATE UNIVERSITY 1274 North Atherton Street State College PA   814-234-1600 (800-466-8356)
One well-behaved family pet per room. Guest must notify front desk upon arrival. Guest is liable for any damages. In consideration of all guests, pets must never be left unattended in the guest rooms.
Residence Inn by Marriott 1555 University Drive State College PA   814-285-6960
Dogs of all sizes are allowed. There is a $175 one time fee and a pet policy to sign at check in.

Campgrounds and RV Parks
Bellefonte/State College KOA 2481 Jacksonville Road Bellefonte PA   814-355-7912 (814-355-7912)
http://www.koa.com
Dogs of all sizes are allowed. There are no additional pet fees. Dogs must be leashed and cleaned up after. This RV park is closed during the off-season. The camping and tent areas also allow dogs. There is a dog walk area at the campground. Dogs are allowed in the camping cabins.

Outdoor Restaurants
Berkey Creamery at PSU 119 Food Science Building University Park PA   814-865-7535
http://www.creamery.psu.edu/
This is the largest university creamery in the US, and they also produce about half their products from a university owned 200+ cow herd. There are outer tables and benches, and your pooch may join you there for a tasty treat. Dogs must be well behaved, leashed, and cleaned up after.

Transportation Systems
the Centre Area Transportation Authority 2081 W. Whitehall Road (Main Office) State College PA   888-738-CATA
http://www.catabus.com/acoffice.htm

This city bus line will allow pooches to ride with their human companions for no additional fee. They may not be allowed if they are very large or aggressive. Dogs must be in a secure pet carrier, or leashed and muzzled, and they must be under owner's control/care at all times.

Stores
Petco Pet Store 40 Colonnade Way State College PA   814-235-9890
Your licensed and well-behaved leashed dog is allowed in the store.

Titusville

Accommodations
Arlington Hotel 1 Seneca St Oil City PA   814-677-1221
There is a $10 per day additional pet fee.

Attractions

TOP 200 PLACE Oil Creek and Titusville Railroad 409 S Perry Street Titusville PA   814-676-1733
http://www.octrr.org/
Various amenities and activities are offered at this 1892 freight station including picnic areas, water and comfort stations, a river, trails (one is a bypass to the Appalachian Trail), the only railroad post office in the US, and guided tours in open-air rail cars describing the people and places where the US oil history began. Visitors can also get on and off the train at different stops. Dogs are allowed throughout the grounds and on the touring train for no additional fee. Dogs must be under owner's control at all times, and be leashed and cleaned up after. Guests with pets will need to sign a pet responsibility form.

Parks
Oil Creek State Park 305 State Park Road Oil City PA   814-676-5915
Historical interpretive displays/programs, including full-scale building tableaus (movie-set style) depicting the eras of Oil Creek, an excursion train that takes visitors on a 26 mile guided tour of the area, and more are offered at this park. Dogs are allowed throughout the park and on the train for no additional fee (guests with pets must sign a pet waiver for the train rides). Dogs must be on no more than a 6 foot leash or crated, and cleaned up after at all times, and licensed with proof of vaccinations. Aggressive dogs are not allowed. Dogs may not be left unattended outside at any time and if in a vehicle only for very short times. Dogs must stay on selected pet routes/trails and areas. They are not allowed in swim areas or in park buildings.

Uniontown

Campgrounds and RV Parks
Jelllystone Park 839 Mill Run Road Mill Run PA   724-455-2929 (800-HEY-YOGI (439-9644))
http://www.jellystonemillrun.com
Dogs of all sizes are allowed. There is a $2 per night per pet additional fee. Dogs must be leashed and cleaned up after. Dogs are not allowed in the rentals. The camping and tent areas also allow dogs. There is a dog walk area at the campground.

Attractions
Fort Necessity National Battlefield 1 Washington Parkway Farmington PA   724-329-5805
http://www.nps.gov/fone/
This park was the "opening action" site of the French and Indian War, resulting in the removal of the French power here and setting the stage for the American Revolution. Also, part of the National Road Heritage Corridor (noted as the road that built this nation) runs through the park. Dogs must be on no more than a 6 foot leash or crated, cleaned up after at all times, and licensed with proof of vaccinations. Aggressive dogs are not allowed. Dogs may not be left unattended outside at any time and if in a vehicle only for very short times. Dogs must stay on selected pet routes/trails and areas. They are not allowed in park buildings.
Friendship Hill National Historic Site 223 New Geneva Road Point Marion PA   724-725-9190
http://www.nps.gov/frhi/index.htm
Dogs must be on leash and must be cleaned up after on the site. Dogs are not allowed in any buildings. The site features touring, hiking, fishing, and more. This site preserves the country estate of Albert Gallatin, a Swiss

emigrant who served his adopted nation during the early years of the republic.

Parks

Fort Necessity National Battlefield One Washington Parkway Farmington PA 724-329-5512
http://www.nps.gov/fone/index.htm
Dogs must be on leash and must be cleaned up after in the site. Open daily 9am-5pm. This is the site of the opening battle of the French and Indian War that began a seven year struggle between England and France for control of North America. The site features hiking and picnicking.

TOP 200 PLACE **Ohiopyle State Park** 171 Dinner Bell Road Ohiopyle PA   724-329-8591
Offering over 19,000 recreational acres, this park's several trails take visitors by waterfalls, unique geological formations, overlook platforms offering stunning views, and more than 14 miles of the Youghiogheny River Gorge running through the heart of the park. Dogs are allowed at the park for day use for no additional fee. Dogs must be quiet, well behaved, under owner's control, leashed or crated, and cleaned up after at all times. Dogs must be licensed and have proof of all vaccinations. Aggressive dogs are not allowed. Dogs may not be left unattended outside at any time and may only be left alone in a vehicle for very short times. Dogs must stay on selected pet routes/trails and areas; they may not be in designated swim areas or in park buildings, and pet food may not be left outside.

Warfordsburg

Accommodations

Days Inn Breezewood 9648 Old 126 Warfordsburg PA 814-735-3860 (800-329-7466)
Dogs of all sizes are allowed. There is a $10 per night pet fee per pet.

Warren

Campgrounds and RV Parks

Allegheny National Forest 222 Liberty Street Warren PA   814-723-5150
This park is located in northwestern Pennsylvania and covers over 24,000 acres. Dogs of all sizes are allowed. There are no additional pet fees. Dogs may not be left unattended, and they must have a current rabies certificate and shot records. Dogs must be quiet during quiet hours, be leashed, and cleaned up after. Dogs are allowed on the trails, but not on the beach or in the buildings. This campground is closed during the off-season. The camping and tent areas also allow dogs. There is a dog walk area at the campground. There are no water hookups at the campground.

Washington

Accommodations

Motel 6 - Washington, PA 1283 Motel 6 Drive Washington PA   724-223-8040 (800-466-8356)
One well-behaved family pet per room. Guest must notify front desk upon arrival. Guest is liable for any damages. In consideration of all guests, pets must never be left unattended in the guest rooms.
Red Roof Inn - Washington 1399 West Chestnut Street Washington PA   724-228-5750 (800-RED-ROOF)
One well-behaved family pet per room. Guest must notify front desk upon arrival. Guest is liable for any damages. In consideration of all guests, pets must never be left unattended in the guest rooms.

Campgrounds and RV Parks

Washington KOA 7 KOA Road Washington PA   724-225-7590 (800-562-0254)
http://www.koa.com
Dogs of all sizes are allowed. There are no additional pet fees. In the cabins there can only be one large dog or two small dogs. There are a couple of more dogs allowed on tent and rv sites. Dogs must be leashed and cleaned up after. The camping and tent areas also allow dogs. There is a dog walk area at the campground. Dogs are allowed in the camping cabins.

Stores

PetSmart Pet Store 327 Washington Rd Washington PA   724-223-1227
Your licensed and well-behaved leashed dog is allowed in the store.
Petco Pet Store 70 Trinity Point Drive Washington PA   724-229-9142
Your licensed and well-behaved leashed dog is allowed in the store.

Wellsboro

Accommodations
Kaltenbachs Inn 743 Stoney Fork Road Wellsboro PA   570-724-4954 (800-722-4954)
http://www.kaltenbachsinn.com/
This sprawling country inn is on a 72 acre ranch with farm animals, plenty of wildlife, views, pastures and forests, picnicking areas with barbecues, and they are also only a short biking/driving distance from the newly opened 62 mile Pine Creek Rail Trail. Dogs of all sizes are allowed for an additional fee of $5 per night per pet. Dogs must be very well behaved, quiet, leashed, cleaned up after, and crated when left alone in the room.

Attractions
Pine Creek Outfitters and Rentals 5142 H 6 Wellsboro PA   570-724-3003
http://www.pinecrk.com/
This outfitting store also offers watercraft rentals. Dogs are allowed on the rentals if they are well trained and are already accustomed to being on the water. They are also allowed to enter the store. Dogs must be under owner's control, leashed, and cleaned up after at all times.

Parks
Colton Point State Park Forest Road Wellsboro PA   570-724-3061
This park offers several areas with stunning views of the 800 foot deep, glacially carved canyon (the Grand Canyon of PA), educational and recreational activities, and miles of hiking trails, including the Turkey Path Trail featuring a 70 foot waterfall about a ½ mile down the trail. Dogs are allowed at the park for day use for no additional fee. Dogs must be well behaved, under owner's control, on no more than a 6 foot leash or crated, and cleaned up after at all times. Dogs must be licensed with proof of vaccinations. Aggressive dogs are not allowed. Dogs may not be left unattended outside at any time and in a vehicle for very short times. Dogs must stay on selected pet routes/trails and areas; they may not be in designated swim areas, park buildings, or in the campground area.
Leonard Harrison State Park 4797 H 660 Wellsboro PA   570-724-3061
This 585 acre park offers a variety of educational programs, recreational opportunities, trails (medium to difficult), and an overlook at the visitor center that offers stunning views. Dogs are allowed at the park for day use for no additional fee. Dogs must be well behaved, under owner's control, on no more than a 6 foot leash or crated, and cleaned up after at all times. Dogs must be licensed and have proof of all vaccinations. Aggressive dogs are not allowed. Dogs may not be left unattended outside at any time and may only be left alone in a vehicle for very short times. Dogs must stay on selected pet routes/trails and areas; they may not be in designated swim areas, in park buildings, or in the campground area.

West Chester

Accommodations
The Pennsbury Inn 883 Baltimore Pike/H1 Chadds Ford PA   610-388-1435
http://www.pennsburyinn.com/
Rich in colonial heritage and country charm, and listed on the National Register of Historic Places, this inn, surrounded by lush greenery and award winning gardens, serves also for a good starting point to several other activities and historic sites. Dogs of all sizes are allowed for an additional fee of $15 to $20 per pet, depending on size/hair. Dogs must be quiet, very well mannered, leashed and cleaned up after, and crated when left alone in the room.
Hamanassett B&B and Carriage House Indian Springs Drive Chester Heights PA   610-459-3000 (877-836-8212)
www.hamanassett.com
Blending old world charm and elegance with modern-day comforts, this 1856 English country-style home and estate offers guests exceptional dining, landscaped grounds complete with forested areas, green pastures, and koi ponds, and a convenient location to several other local attractions. Dogs of all sizes are welcome for an additional fee of $25 per night per pet. One dog is allowed per room in the house area, and up to 3 dogs are

allowed in the carriage house, which also has a yard. Dogs must be well mannered, leashed, and cleaned up after at all times.
Hampton Inn 4 N Pottstown Pike Exton PA 610-363-5555
Dogs of all sizes are allowed. There are no additional pet fees.
Residence Inn by Marriott 10 N Pottstown Pike Exton PA 610-594-9705
Well behaved dogs of all sizes are allowed. There is a $75 one time fee and a pet policy to sign at check in.
Sweetwater Inn 50 Sweetwater Road Glen Mills PA 610-459-4711 (800-SWEETWATER (793-3892))
http://www.sweetwaterfarmbb.com/
This wooded 50 acre estate of lush greenery has some great hiking trails, features a golf green, Jacuzzi and pool, indoor and outdoor dining (when weather permits), a large patio and porch, and also serves as a good starting point to explore the attractions of Brandywine Valley. Dogs of all sizes are allowed in the cottages only for an additional fee of $35 per night per pet. Dogs must be well mannered, leashed, and cleaned up after.

Campgrounds and RV Parks
Philadelphia/West Chester KOA 1659 Embreeville Road Coatsville PA 610-486-0447 (800-562-1726)
http://www.koa.com
Well behaved and friendly dogs of all sizes are allowed. There are no additional pet fees. Dogs may not be left unattended, must be leashed, and cleaned up after. This RV park is closed during the off-season. The camping and tent areas also allow dogs. There is a dog walk area at the campground.

Attractions
TOP 200 PLACE **Brandywine Battlefield Historic Site** H 1 Chadds Ford PA 610-459-3342
This historic site depicts the largest encounter of the Revolutionary War (9-11-1777) with permanent and altering interpretive exhibits, special events, a visitor center with a museum and gift shop, and 3 different self-guided driving tours of significant sites. Dogs are allowed throughout the park and on the trails. Dogs must be under owner's control, leashed, and cleaned up after at all times.
Newlin Grist Mill 219 S Cheyney Road Glen Mills PA 610-459-2359
http://www.newlingristmill.org/
This 150 acre preserve puts a focus on education and environmental appreciation, shares the history of the 1704 water-powered mill, and offers a variety of recreational pursuits. A special treat is the Water Walk with its green trails, streams, and historic buildings. Dogs are allowed throughout the park and on the trails; they are not allowed in any of the buildings. Dogs must be well behaved, leashed, and cleaned up after at all times.
Northbrook Canoe Company 1810 Beagle Road West Chester PA 610-793-2279
This watercraft rental and touring company will allowed well behaved dogs aboard to explore the Brandywine River area for no additional fee. Dogs must be under owner's control, leashed or crated, and cleaned up after at all times. Reservations are required.

Shopping Centers
Glen Eagle Square H 202 at Springhill Road Chadds Ford PA 610-558-8000
This factory outlet village offers a unique collection of stores, specialty shops, and services, in addition to occasional hostings of special events. Dogs are allowed throughout the village; it is up to the individual stores whether they are allowed inside or not. Dogs must be under owner's control, leashed or crated, and cleaned up after at all times.

Stores
Petco Pet Store 125 West Lincoln Highway Exton PA 610-524-6460
Your licensed and well-behaved leashed dog is allowed in the store.
Baldwin's Book Barn 865 Lenape Road/H 52 West Chester PA 610-696-0816
http://www.bookbarn.com/contact.htm
Even your pup will mostly likely enjoy the ambiance of this bookstore located in an 1822 5-story building full of nooks, crannies, stone walls, friendly ambiance, and a vast variety of books (common to the rare), maps, and prints. Dogs must be very friendly as there are cats on site. Dogs must be under owner's control/care and leashed at all times.

Outdoor Restaurants
Kennett Square Inn 201 E State Street Kennett Square PA 610-444-5687
http://www.kennettinn.com/
Nestled away in a small Victorian town is this1835 renovated house turned eatery offering fine lunch and dinners, a full service bar, and when the weather permits - dining on the veranda. Dogs are allowed at the outer tables. Dogs must be under owner control/care and leashed at all times.

Whitehall

Stores
PetSmart Pet Store 2180 MacArthur Rd Whitehall PA   610-437-7197
Your licensed and well-behaved leashed dog is allowed in the store.
Petco Pet Store 2621 Macarthur Rd Whitehall PA   610-266-4212
Your licensed and well-behaved leashed dog is allowed in the store.

Williamsport

Accommodations
Best Western Williamsport Inn 1840 E 3rd Street Williamsport PA   570-326-1981 (800-780-7234)
Dogs are allowed for an additional one time pet fee of $15 per room.
Candlewood Suites Williamsport 1836 East Third St. Williamsport PA   570-601-9100 (877-270-6405)
Dogs of all sizes are allowed for additional one time fees ranging from $35 to $150 per room, depending on the length of stay and size of dog.
Quality Inn & Conference Center 234 H 15 Williamsport PA   570-323-9801 (877-424-6423)
One dog is allowed for an additional one time pet fee of $25.

Parks
Loyalsock Trail H 87 Loyalsockville PA   570-745-3375
http://www.lycoming.org/alpine/Index.htm
Lush forest, spectacular views, waterfalls, unique rock formations, and miles of blazed trails to explore it all, are offered on this almost 60 mile linear trail. It begins in Wyoming County, PA and ends on Meade Road 2 miles from Hwy 220 near Laporte. Dogs are allowed on the trail, and they may be off lead if they are under very good voice control, although caution is needed for dogs off lead as the area has porcupines. Dogs must be under owner's control and cleaned up after, especially on the trail.

Wynnewood

Stores
Petco Pet Store 270 East Lancaster Avenue Wynnewood PA   610-658-9710
Your licensed and well-behaved leashed dog is allowed in the store.

Wysox

Accommodations
Comfort Inn RR 6 Box 6167A Wysox PA   570-265-5691 (877-424-6423)
Dogs are allowed for an additional one time pet fee of $15 (plus tax) per room, and there is a pet agreement to sign at check in.

York

Accommodations
Jackson House 6 E Main Street Railroad PA 717-227-2022 (877-782-4672)
http://www.jacksonhousebandb.com/
This scenic inn features terraced gardens offering great views from the top and a relaxing waterfall. They are the only state inn to sit right on the multi-use Heritage Rail Trail, a 21 mile trail that also connects to the 20 mile long Northern Central Rail Trail. They offer one pet friendly room with a private entrance, and there is an additional

one time fee of $20 per pet. Dogs are not allowed in the common areas of the house, and they must be crated when left alone in the room. Dogs must be well behaved, leashed, and cleaned up after at all times.
Holiday Inn 2000 Loucks Rd York PA   717-846-9500 (877-270-6405)
Dogs of all sizes are allowed for an additional fee of $10 per night per room.
Motel 6 - York 125 Arsenal Road York PA   717-846-6260 (800-466-8356)
One well-behaved family pet per room. Guest must notify front desk upon arrival. Guest is liable for any damages. In consideration of all guests, pets must never be left unattended in the guest rooms.
Quality Inn and Suites 2600 E Market Street York PA   717-755-1966 (877-424-6423)
Dogs are allowed for an additional fee of $10 per night per pet. There may be 1 large or 2 small dogs per room.
Red Roof Inn - York 323 Arsenal Road York PA   717-843-8181 (800-RED-ROOF)
One well-behaved family pet per room. Guest must notify front desk upon arrival. Guest is liable for any damages. In consideration of all guests, pets must never be left unattended in the guest rooms.

Stores
PetSmart Pet Store 351 Loucks Rd York PA   717-854-5624
Your licensed and well-behaved leashed dog is allowed in the store.
Petco Pet Store 905 Loucks Rd York PA   717-699-2825
Your licensed and well-behaved leashed dog is allowed in the store.

Parks
Heritage Rail Trail County Park Pershing Avenue York PA   717-840-7440
This Rail Trail covers 176 acres over 21 miles, starts in York behind the county Colonial Courthouse and runs to the Maryland state line sharing great scenery, historic sites, a tunnel, and 2 train stations along the way. Dogs are allowed on the trail. They must be leashed, under owner's control at all times, and kept off the tracks as the railway is operational. Pets must be cleaned up after.

Chapter 11

Delaware
Dog Travel Guide

Bethany Beach

Accommodations

Bethany Beach House Off Central Avenue Bethany Beach DE   443-621-6649
http://www.quietresortbeachhouse.com/
This spacious home puts visitors within minutes of over a dozen golf courses, the beach, the boardwalk, and a number of eateries, attractions, and recreation. Dogs of all sizes are welcome for a refundable deposit of $75 per pet, and there is also a large fenced yard for them to enjoy. A visit to their website shows a number of pets who have enjoyed their visits here. The city enforces a leash and pooper-scooper law, and dogs are not allowed on the beach or boardwalk from May 15th to September 30th. At all other times dogs must be leashed and cleaned up after.

Lagoon Front/#125307 217 Belle Road Bethany Beach DE   954-782-8277
This vacation house sits facing the lagoon for great crabbing right off the deck, is just 3 blocks from the beach, is large enough to accommodate family reunions and group retreats, and is also close to many other interests and activities. Dogs of all sizes are allowed for no additional pet fee, and they must be housetrained and cleaned up after at all times. Dogs are allowed on the lower level of the house and on the fenced-in back deck only. Dogs are allowed on the beach on no more than a 6 foot leash, and are not to be walked where people are sunbathing.

Waterfront Retreat/#125305 104 Petherton Drive Bethany Beach DE   954-782-8277
Facing the canal just one block from the beach, this retreat is large enough to accommodate family reunions and group retreats, and it is quite close to innumerable shops, restaurants, activities, and recreational pursuits. Dogs of all sizes are allowed for no additional pet fee, and they must be housetrained and cleaned up after at all times. Dogs are allowed on the lower level of the house and on the fenced-in back deck only. Dogs are allowed on the beach on no more than a 6 foot leash, and are not to be walked where people are sunbathing.

Beaches

Bethany Beach off Route 1 Bethany Beach DE   302-539-8011
From May 15 to September 30, pets are not allowed on the beach or boardwalk at any time. But during the off-season, dogs are allowed but need to be leashed and cleaned up after.

South Bethany Beach off Route 1 South Bethany DE   302-539-3653
http://www.southbethany.org/
From May 15 to October 15, dogs are not allowed on the beach at any time. The rest of the year, during the off-season, dogs are allowed on the beach. Pets must be leashed and cleaned up after. The beach is located of Route 1, south of Dewey Beach.

Parks

Assawoman Wildlife Area Mulberry Landing Road Bayard DE   302-539-3160
Divided into 3 sections, and managed for migrating, wintering, and resident bird and plant/wildlife, this unique and interesting park offers an auto tour marked by wooden stakes along the road with a corresponding brochure to guide you along. The trail can also be hiked, and be sure to check ahead during times of inclement weather in case of road closures. Entrance is free for both pets and their owners. Dogs must be licensed, under owner's control at all times, and cleaned up after.

Fenwick Island State Park H 1 Bethany Beach DE   302-539-1055 (May/October)
Open daily from 8 am to sunset year-round, this 344 acre park is a 3 mile long barrier island with plenty of surf and turf recreational opportunities. Concessionaires and modern conveniences are available. Dogs are allowed throughout the park and on the surf fishing beaches; they are not allowed on swim beaches. Dogs must be well behaved, leashed, and cleaned up after at all times.

Claymont

Accommodations

Holiday Inn Select 630 Naamans Rd Claymont DE   302-792-2700 (877-270-6405)
Dogs of all sizes are allowed for an additional one time pet fee of $50 per pet.

Dover

Accommodations

Comfort Inn 222 S DuPont H Dover DE   302-674-3300 (877-424-6423)
Dogs are allowed for an additional one time pet fee of $35 per room.
Red Roof Inn - Dover, DE 652 N DuPont Hwy Dover DE   302-730-8009 (800-RED-ROOF)
One well-behaved family pet per room. Guest must notify front desk upon arrival. Guest is liable for any damages. In consideration of all guests, pets must never be left unattended in the guest rooms.
Sheraton Dover Hotel 1570 North DuPont Highway Dover DE   302-678-8500 (888-625-5144)
Dogs of all sizes are allowed. There is a $50 one time nonrefundable pet fee per visit. Dogs are not allowed to be left alone in the room.

Campgrounds and RV Parks

Killens Pond State Park 5025 Killens Pond Road Felton DE   302-284-3412 (877-987-2757)
This resort type park features an all new water park, a variety of hiking trails, nature study, and land and water recreation. Dogs of all sizes are allowed at no additional fee. Dogs may not be left unattended, and they must be on no more than a 6 foot leash, and be cleaned up after. Dogs are not allowed in the buildings, but they are allowed on the trails. The camping and tent areas also allow dogs. There is a dog walk area at the campground.

Attractions

Air Mobility Command Museum 1301 Heritage Road Dover DE   302-677-5938
http://www.amcmuseum.org/
Open Tuesday through Sunday from 9am to 4pm, this aircraft museum also offers a commemorative park, gift shop, and a variety of fun and educational programs. When a volunteer is available visitors can attempt to fly any of the museum aircraft (+ more) via a flight simulator with an experienced pilot to guide you from the take-off to landing. Dogs are allowed around the grounds but not in some of the buildings. Dogs must be under owner's control, leashed, and cleaned up after at all times.

Stores

PetSmart Pet Store 1380 N DuPont Hwy Dover DE   302-736-5260
Your licensed and well-behaved leashed dog is allowed in the store.

Parks

Silver Lake Park Washington Street and Kings H Dover DE   302-736-7050
This 183 acre park offers open spaces, forested areas, picnic areas, an exercise court, playing courts/fields, various trails, and much more. Dogs are allowed throughout the park and on the trails. Dogs must be under owner's control, leashed, and cleaned up after at all times.

Fenwick Island

Beaches

Fenwick Island Beach off Route 1 Fenwick Island DE   302-539-2000
http://www.fenwickisland.org
From May 1 to September 30, dogs are not allowed on the beach at any time. The rest of the year, pets are allowed on the beach but must be leashed and cleaned up after. The beach is located of Route 1, south of Dewey Beach.

Georgetown

Accommodations

Comfort Inn and Suites 507 N Dupont H Georgetown DE   302-854-9400 (877-424-6423)
Dogs are allowed for an additional one time pet fee of $15 per room.

Laurel

Campgrounds and RV Parks

Trap Pond State Park 33587 Bald Cypress Lane Laurel DE   302-875-2392 (877-987-2757)
Trap Pond State Park offers an opportunity to explore a wetland forest and its inhabitants on both land and water and a variety of recreational activities and pursuits. Dogs of all sizes are allowed at no additional fee. Dogs may not be left unattended, and they must be leashed and cleaned up after. Dogs are not allowed in buildings. This campground is closed during the off-season. The camping and tent areas also allow dogs. There is a dog walk area at the campground.

Lewes

Accommodations

TOP 200 PLACE **Lazy L at Willow Creek - A B&B Resort** 16061 Willow Creek Road Lewes DE   302-644-7220
http://www.lazyl.net
Located on 8 secluded acres overlooking a marsh and creek, the Lazy L offers creature comforts for pets and pet owners. They offer 5 large rooms with Queen sized beds, a swimming pool, hot tub, pool table, guest kitchen and a barbecue. The dogs have a fenced in one acre run area, are allowed to sleep in the guest rooms and stay by themselves while you shop or go to dinner.
Sleep Inn 1595 H One Lewes DE   302-645-6464 (877-424-6423)
One dog is allowed for an additional pet fee of $25 per night.

Campgrounds and RV Parks

G and R Campground 4075 Gun and Rod Club Road Houston DE   302-398-8108
http://www.gnrcampground.com
Dogs of all sizes are allowed, and there are no additional pet fees for the tent or RV sites. There is a $15 per night per pet additional fee for the cabin rentals, and there are only 2 pets per cabin allowed. Dogs must be quiet and well behaved. Dogs may not be left unattended, must be leashed, and cleaned up after. There are some breed restrictions. The camping and tent areas also allow dogs. There is a dog walk area at the campground. Dogs are allowed in the camping cabins.
Cape Henlopen State Park 42 Cape Henlopen Drive Lewes DE   302-645-8983 (1-877-98 PARKS (72757))
A main year-round land and water recreation destination with a variety of activities, concerts, and special events, this 129-acre barrier island park also has various scenic seaside trails, or nature trails through the pines to an observation tower, and an 18 hold disc golf course. Dogs of all sizes are allowed for no additional pet fee. Dogs must be quiet, well behaved, under owner's control, leashed, and cleaned up after at all times. Dogs must have proof of currents shots, and they may not be left unattended at any times. Dogs are allowed throughout the park, on the trails, and on the surf-fishing beaches; they are not allowed on swim beaches. The camp area offers 150 spacious sites, drinking water, restrooms, showers, a laundry, playing fields, and a dump station. This RV park is closed during the off-season. The camping and tent areas also allow dogs. There is a dog walk area at the campground. There are no electric hookups at the campgrounds.
Tall Pines Camping Resort 29551 Persimmon Road Lewes DE   302-684-0300
http://www.tallpines-del.com
Dogs of all sizes are allowed. There are no additional pet fees. Dogs must be quiet, well behaved, and are not to be left unattended. They must be leashed and cleaned up after. The camping and tent areas also allow dogs. There is a dog walk area at the campground.

Transportation Systems

Cape May-Lewes Ferry Sandman Blvd. & Lincoln Drive N Cape May DE   609-889-7200
http://www.capemaylewesferry.com/
This ferry service provides transportation for vehicles and passengers between Cape May, New Jersey and Lewes, Delaware. The ferry cuts miles off of driving along the Atlantic coast. Pets are welcome but the following rules apply. For the M.V. Cape May, M.V. Delaware and M.V. Twin Cape ferries, pets are welcome on the ferry on exterior decks and any lounge areas where food is not being made, served or eaten. Pets are not allowed in the lounge area whenever there is a private party being hosted. For the M.V. Cape Henlopen and M.V. New Jersey ferries, pets are not allowed in any interior space but are allowed on all exterior decks. For all ferries, dogs of all sizes are allowed but need to be kept under control at all times and leashed or in a carrier. People need to clean up after their pets. Pets are not allowed in the shuttles. Rates start at $20 to $25 for a vehicle and driver. For a foot passenger with no car, rates start at $6 to $8 per person. Larger vehicles can be accommodated but there is an extra charge. The Cape May Terminal is located at Sandman Blvd. and Lincoln

Drive in North Cape May, New Jersey. The Lewes Terminal is located at 43 Henlopen Drive in Lewes, Delaware. Rates are subject to change. For reservations or to check rates, call the ferry line toll free at 1-800-643-3779.

Attractions
Fisherman's Wharf by the Drawbridge Anglers Road Lewes DE   302-645-8862
http://www.fishlewes.com/index.html
Overlooking the historical Lewes Rehoboth Canal, this wharf area makes for a nice seaside walk. Dogs are allowed on the wharf but they are not allowed on the charters or at the outer tables of the restaurant. Dogs must be well mannered, leashed, and cleaned up after at all times.
Lil Angler Charters Angler Road Lewes DE   302-645-8688
http://www.beach-net.com/lilangler/
This seafaring charter company offers a variety of cruising options, and will allow a well mannered dog to come aboard for no additional fee. Dogs must be under owner's control/care and leashed at all times. (Pit Bulls are not allowed.)

Beaches
Cape Henlopen State Park 42 Cape Henlopen Drive Lewes DE   302-645-8983
This park draws thousands of visitors who enjoy sunbathing and ocean swimming. Dogs on a 6 foot or less leash are allowed on the beach, with some exceptions. Dogs are not allowed on the two swimming beaches during the Summer, but they are allowed on surfing and fishing beaches, bike paths and some of the trails. Pets are not allowed on the fishing pier. During the off-season, dogs are allowed on any of the beaches, but still need to be leashed. People are required to clean up after their pets. The park is located one mile east of Lewes, 1/2 mile past the Cape May-Lewes Ferry Terminal.

Parks
Cape Henlopen State Park 42 Cape Henlopen Drive Lewes DE   302-645-8983 (1-877-98 PARKS (72757))
A main year-round land and water recreation destination with a variety of activities, concerts, and special events, this 129-acre barrier island park also has various scenic seaside trails, or nature trails through the pines to an observation tower, and an 18 hold disc golf course. Dogs of all sizes are allowed for no additional pet fee. Dogs must be quiet, well behaved, under owner's control, leashed, and cleaned up after at all times. Dogs must have proof of currents shots, and they may not be left unattended at any times. Dogs are allowed throughout the park, on the trails, and on the surf-fishing beaches; they are not allowed on swim beaches.
Prime Hook National Wildlife Refuge 11978 Turkle Pond Road Milton DE   302-684-8419
http://www.fws.gov/northeast/primehook/
This 10,000 acre refuge has quite a diverse ecology with one of the largest freshwater impoundments on the East Coast, and offers a home or a migration area for a wide variety of bird and wildlife. Dogs are allowed throughout the park on the trails. Dogs must be under owner's control, leashed, and cleaned up after at all times.

Outdoor Restaurants
Gilligan's Waterfront Restaurant and Bar 134 Market Street Lewes DE   302-644-7230
This fresh seafood eatery sits over 90 feet of water frontage for a great outdoor dining experience during their Summer season. Your well behaved pooch is allowed at the outer tables. Dogs must be under owner's control, leashed, and cleaned up after at all times.

Millsboro

Campgrounds and RV Parks
Holly Lake Campsites 32087 Hollly Lake Road Millsboro DE   302-945-3410
http://www.hollylakecampsites.com/
Dogs of all sizes are allowed. There are no additional pet fees. Dogs may not be left unattended outside and they must be quiet, well behaved, leashed and cleaned up after. Dogs are allowed on the trails. This RV park is closed during the off-season. The camping and tent areas also allow dogs. There is a dog walk area at the campground.

Newark

Accommodations

Days Inn Newark 900 Churchmans Rd Newark DE   302-368-2400 (800-329-7466)
Dogs of all sizes are allowed. There is a $10 per night pet fee per pet.
Howard Johnson Inn 1119 South College Avenue Newark DE   302-368-8521 (800-446-4656)
Dogs of all sizes are welcome. There is a $10 per day pet fee.
Quality Inn University 1120 S College Avenue Newark DE   302-368-8715 (877-424-6423)
Dogs are allowed for an additional fee of $10 per night per pet.
Red Roof Inn - Wilmington, DE 415 Stanton Christiana Road Newark DE   302-292-2870 (800-RED-ROOF)
One well-behaved family pet per room. Guest must notify front desk upon arrival. Guest is liable for any
damages. In consideration of all guests, pets must never be left unattended in the guest rooms.
Residence Inn by Marriott 240 Chapman Road Newark DE   302-453-9200
Pets of all sizes are allowed. There is a $50 per day fee up to a total of $200 per room and a pet policy to sign at
check in.
Staybridge Suites Wilmington-Newark 270 Chapman Road Newark DE   302-366-8097 (877-270-6405)
Dogs of all sizes are allowed for an additional $10 per night per pet.

Campgrounds and RV Parks

Lums Pond State Park 1068 Howell School Road Bear DE   302-368-6989 (877-987-2757)
This park of over 1,700 acres with a 200 surface acre lake, offers sports facilities, and a variety of land and water
recreation. Dogs of all sizes are allowed at no additional fee. Dogs may not be left unattended, and they must be
quiet, be on no more than a 6 foot leash, and be cleaned up after. Dogs are not allowed in buildings, in picnic
areas, or on the trails. However, just past this park on Buck's Jersey Road, there is an off leash training area for
dogs. This campground is closed during the off-season. The camping and tent areas also allow dogs. There is a
dog walk area at the campground. There are no water hookups at the campground.

Stores

Petco Pet Store 200 Center Blvd Christiana DE   302-894-0290
Your licensed and well-behaved leashed dog is allowed in the store.
PetSmart Pet Store 1291 Churchmans Rd Newark DE   302-266-6170
Your licensed and well-behaved leashed dog is allowed in the store.

Off-Leash Dog Parks

Lums Pond Dog Area   Bear DE   302-368-698
This area is part of Lums Pond State Park. This is a place where you can take your dog to swim in Lums Pond. It
does not have much area for running or play. To get to the off-leash area take Howell School Rd to Buck Jersey
Road. At the end of Buck Jersey Road the parking lot will be on the left.

Rehoboth - Dewey Beach

Accommodations

Atlantic Oceanside Hotel 1700 Coastal H Dewey Beach DE   302-227-8811 (800-422-0481)
http://www.atlanticoceanside.com/
Dogs of all sizes are allowed for an additional fee of $5 per night per pet, and a credit card must be on file. Dogs
are not allowed in the motel rooms from Memorial Day through Labor Day; however, they are allowed at their
Suites property year-round. Pets may only be left alone in rooms for a short time if they will be quiet and well
behaved. Dogs must be leashed, cleaned up after, and removed for housekeeping.
Sea-Esta Motel I 2306 Hwy 1 Dewey Beach DE   302-227-7666
http://www.seaesta.com/
There is a $6.00 charge per pet per night. There are no designated smoking or non-smoking rooms.
American Hotel 329 Z Airport Road Rehoboth DE   302-226-0700
Dogs of all sizes are allowed. There is a $20 per night per pet fee and a pet policy to sign at check in.
Sea Esta Motel III 1409 DE 1 Rehoboth Beach DE   302-227-4343 (800-436-6591)
http://www.seaesta.com/
There is a $6 per day additional pet fee.
The Homestead at Rehoboth 35060 Warrington Road Rehoboth Beach DE   302-226-7625
http://www.homesteadatrehoboth.com/
This charming country inn sits on 2 acres by the ocean and is only a short walk to the beach and the boardwalk;
they are also a short distance from tax-free shopping. Dogs of all sizes are welcome, but if they are over 80
pounds, prior arrangements must be made. There is an additional fee of $15 per night per pet. Dogs must be

cleaned up after inside and out; clean-up bags and a towel (if wet or sandy from the beach) are provided. They ask that you cover the bed if your pet will be on it, and they may only be left for short periods alone in the room. Dogs may be off lead if they respond well to voice command.

Campgrounds and RV Parks
Big Oaks Family Campground 35567 Big Oaks Lane Rehoboth Beach DE   302-645-6838
http://www.bigoakscamping.com
Dogs of all sizes are allowed in the campground area but not in the rentals. There are no additional pet fees. Dogs must be on a 6 foot or shorter leash and cleaned up after. The camping and tent areas also allow dogs. There is a dog walk area at the campground.
Delaware Seashore State Park 130 Coastal H Rehoboth Beach DE   302-539-7202 (877-987-2757)
This park, being on the coast, offers a wide variety of water related activities. Dogs of all sizes are allowed at no additional fee. Dogs may not be left unattended, and they must be on no more than a 6 foot leash, and be cleaned up after. Dogs are not allowed in public swim areas or buildings. Dogs are allowed on the beach at the North end, at T-Box Road, Conquest Road, and the 3 Rs. The camping and tent areas also allow dogs. There is a dog walk area at the campground.

Vacation Home Rentals
Ocean Block #47227 given at time of reservations Dewey Beach DE   302-542-3570
http://www.vrbo.com/47227
This duplex vacation rental is only a few steps from the Atlantic Ocean and great bay views, sleeps up to 12 people, is only a short distance from town, and offers a fenced in dog run. Dogs of all sizes are allowed for a one time additional pet fee of $200. Dogs must be housebroken, leashed, and cleaned up after.

Shopping Centers
Tanger Outlets 36470 Seaside Outlet Drive Rehoboth Beach DE   302-226-9223
http://www.tangeroutlet.com/center/REH
Offering 130 brand name outlets at 3 locations along Highway 1, this shopping Mecca also allows dogs to explore the grounds. It is up to individual stores whether they are allowed inside or not. Dogs must be well mannered, leashed, and cleaned up after at all times.

Beaches
TOP 200 PLACE **Dewey Beach** Coastal Highway/Route 1 Dewey Beach DE   302-227-1110
Dogs are allowed on the beach year-round only with a special license and with certain hour restrictions during the Summer season. A special license is required for your dog to go on the beach. You do not have to be a resident of Dewey Beach to get the license. You can obtain one from the Town of Dewey Beach during regular business hours at 105 Rodney Avenue in Dewey Beach. The cost is $5 per dog and is good for the lifetime of your dog. During the Summer, from May 15 to September 15, dogs are only allowed before 9:30am and after 5:30pm. During the off-season there are no hourly restrictions. Year-round, dogs can be off-leash but need to be under your control at all times and cleaned up after.
Delaware Seashore State Park Inlet 850 Rehoboth Beach DE   302-227-2800
This park offers six miles of ocean and bay shoreline. Dogs on a 6 foot or less leash are allowed on the beach, with a couple of exceptions. Dogs are not allowed at the lifeguarded swimming areas. However, there are plenty of non-guarded beaches where people with dogs can walk or sunbathe. During the off-season, dogs are allowed on any of the beaches, but still need to be leashed. People are required to clean up after their pets. The park is located south of Dewey Beach, along Route 1.
Rehoboth Beach off Route 1 Rehoboth Beach DE   302-227-6181
http://www.cityofrehoboth.com/
From April 1 to October 31, pets are not allowed on the beach or boardwalk at any time. However, during the off-season, dogs are allowed but need to be leashed and cleaned up after. The beach is located off Route 1, north of Dewey Beach.

Outdoor Restaurants
Sharky's Grill Hwy 1 and Read Street Dewey Beach DE   302-226-3116
This restaurant serves Cajun American/Seafood. Dogs are allowed at the outdoor tables.

Events
TOP 200 PLACE **Greyhounds Reach the Beach** The beach Dewey Beach DE   617-527-8843
http://www.adopt-a-greyhound.org/dewey/
For more than 120 years thousands of greyhounds and their owners have gathered to participate in this event

held annually on Columbus Day weekend. There are a variety of activities, contests, educational and rescue programs, and plenty of doggy and human shopping available. The town's dog license requirement is covered under a special events license that covers all the dogs registered. Dogs must be leashed and cleaned up after at all times; please bring clean up supplies. Dogs are allowed on Dewey Beach after October 1st; however, Rehoboth Beach has implemented a 4-day permit for the event as they usually do not allow dogs on the beach until after October 31st. Dogs must be attended to at all times. The contact phone number for the organization is 617-527-8843 at 295 Tremont Street, Newton MA.

Smyrna

Attractions
Bombay Hook National Wildlife Refuge 2591 Whitehall Neck Road Smyrna DE   302) 653-6872
http://www.fws.gov/northeast/bombayhook/
At almost 16,000 acres, this park plays an important part as a link in a chain of refuges dedicated to the preservation and education of hundreds of species of wildlife in their natural settings. This park also has one of the largest tidal salt marshes in the mid-Atlantic area. Dogs are allowed throughout the park and on the trails. Dogs must be well behaved, under owner's control, leashed, and cleaned up after at all times.

Wilmington

Accommodations
Motel 6 - Wilmington 1200 West Avenue/South Highway 9 New Castle DE   302-571-1200 (800-466-8356)
One well-behaved family pet per room. Guest must notify front desk upon arrival. Guest is liable for any damages. In consideration of all guests, pets must never be left unattended in the guest rooms.
Quality Inn Skyways 147 N Dupont H New Castle DE   302-328-6666 (877-424-6423)
Dogs are allowed for an additional fee of $10 per night per pet.
Rodeway Inn 111 S Dupont Hwy New Castle DE   302-328-6246
There is a $10 per day pet fee.
Best Western Brandywine Valley Inn 1807 Concord Pike Wilmington DE   302-656-9436 (800-780-7234)
Dogs are allowed for an additional one time pet fee of $25 per room.
Days Inn Wilmington 5209 Concord Pike Wilmington DE   302-478-0300 (800-329-7466)
Dogs of all sizes are allowed. There is a $10 per night pet fee per pet.
Sheraton Suites Wilmington 422 Delaware Ave. Wilmington DE   302-654-8300 (888-625-5144)
Dogs up to 80 pounds are allowed. There are no additional pet fees. Dogs are not allowed to be left alone in the room.

Campgrounds and RV Parks
Delaware Motel and RV Park 235 S. Dupont Highway New Castle DE   302-328-3114
Dogs of all sizes are allowed. There are no additional pet fees. Dogs must be well behaved and not left unattended at any time. There is a dog walk area at the campground.

Attractions
Christina River Boat Company Inc. 201 A Street Wilmington DE   302-530-5069
Offering public and private tours of the historical Brandywine and Christina Rivers, this charter company will allow pets on private charters only. Private Charters are $250 per hour with a 4 person preference for comfort, plus a pet. Dogs must be well mannered, and under owner's control/care at all times.
Rockwood Museum Washington Street Extension Wilmington DE   302-761-4340
Located in Rockwood Park and reminiscent of an English country estate with its Gothic revival architecture, this mid-1800's renovated estate now houses a museum, a Victorian style cafe, more than 2 miles of lighted walking trails leading to the Northern Delaware Greenway, and meticulously landscaped grounds and gardens. Dogs are allowed throughout the park; they are not allowed in the museum or anywhere in the mansion. Dogs must be under owner's control, leashed, and cleaned up after at all times.

Shopping Centers
The Shipyard Shops 900 South Madison Street Wilmington DE   302-425-5000
http://www.shipyardshopsoutlets.com/
Located along the waterfront, this shopping Mecca offers tax-free shopping and outlet prices. Dogs are allowed

in the common areas of the mall; they are not allowed in stores. Dogs must be under owner's control, leashed, and cleaned up after at all times.

TOP 200 PLACE **Trolley Square Shopping Center** 21A Trolley Square Wilmington DE   302-428-1040
Trolley Square sits amid a lovely Victorian neighborhood and is considered a premium tax-free shopping area with dozens of shops, eateries, galleries, and numerous services. There are a couple of doggy boutiques, and some of the restaurants with outside seating will allow well mannered pooches. Dogs must be friendly, under owner's control, leashed, and cleaned up after at all times.

Stores

PetSmart Pet Store 3010 Brandywine Pkwy Wilmington DE   302-475-0618
Your licensed and well-behaved leashed dog is allowed in the store.

Parks

Bellevue State Park 800 Carr Road Wilmington DE   302-761-6963
This 328 acre park offers a number of features and activities such as a Summer concert series, a 1+ mile fitness track, a catch and release fishing pond, paved and unpaved trails, gaming courts/fields, an arts center, and much more. Dogs are allowed throughout the park and on the trails. Dogs must be under owner's control, leashed, and cleaned up after at all times.

Tubman-Garrett Riverfront Park End of Market Street Wilmington DE   302-425-4890
This park offers scenic repose sitting along the river at the edge of the city and it is also a popular area for holding special events. There is an amphitheater in the park. Dogs are welcome throughout the park. They must be under owner's control at all times, leashed, and cleaned up after.

Off-Leash Dog Parks

Brandywine Dog Park North Park Drive at North Adams Wilmington DE   302-577-7020
This is an unfenced dog area. It is located in Brandywine Park along the Brandywine River in Wilmington and near the Wilimington Zoo.

Carousel Park Off-Leash Area 3700 Limestone Rd Wilmington DE   302-995-7670
This nearly 50 acre unfenced off-leash area for dogs includes a lake for swimming and lots of area for running. The park is often quite busy with dogs on weekends. Throughout the rest of Carousel Park dogs must be leashed. The park closes at dark.

Rockford Dog Park Rockford Rd at Tower Road Wilmington DE   302-577-7020
This unfenced dog park is over ten acres in size. It has recently been officially recognized as an off-leash area after serving as an unofficial off-leash area for years. There are cleanup bags available. The park is open during daylight hours.

Talley Day Bark Park 1300 Foulk Road Wilmington DE   302-395-5654
This was the first fenced dog park in the state of Delaware. There is a separate area for large dogs and small dogs. It is located off Foulk Rd at the back of the Talley-Day grounds behind the Brandywine Hundred Library. The address given to the park is that of the library.

Outdoor Restaurants

Catherine Rooney's 1616 Delaware Avenue, Trolley Square Wilmington DE   302-654-9700
http://www.catherinerooneys.com/
This Irish pub features food from land and sea, hosts special events, and offer indoor and outdoor dining options. Dogs are allowed at the outer tables. Dogs must be under owner control/care and leashed at all times.

Chapter 12

Maryland
Dog Travel Guide

Aberdeen - Havre de Grace

Accommodations

Four Points Hotels by Sheraton 980 Hospitality Way Aberdeen MD   410-273-6300 (888-625-5144)
http://www.fourpointsaberdeen.com/
There are no additional pet fees.
Red Roof Inn - Aberdeen 988 Hospitality Way Aberdeen MD   410-273-7800 (800-RED-ROOF)
One well-behaved family pet per room. Guest must notify front desk upon arrival. Guest is liable for any
damages. In consideration of all guests, pets must never be left unattended in the guest rooms.
Best Western Invitation Inn 1709 Edgewood Rd Edgewood MD   410-679-9700 (800-780-7234)
Dogs are allowed for an additional one time pet fee of $15 per room.
Super 8 Havre de Grace 929 Pulaski Hwy Havre De Grace MD   410-939-1880 (800-800-8000)
Dogs of all sizes are allowed. There is a $10 per night pet fee per pet. Reservations are recommended due to
limited rooms for pets. Smoking and non-smoking rooms are available for pet rooms.

Campgrounds and RV Parks

Susquehanna State Park 4122 Wilkinson Road Havre de Grace MD   410-557-7994 (888-432-2267)
Rich in historical significance and recreational opportunities, this forested, river valley park offers a variety of
trails to explore, a working grist mill, and an archery range. Dogs of all sizes are allowed throughout the park for
no additional fee. Dogs must be leashed and cleaned up after at all times. Dogs are not allowed in picnic or
historic areas or at the cabins. The campground offers 69 sites with picnic tables, grills, comfort stations, hot
showers, a playground, and an amphitheater. This RV park is closed during the off-season. The camping and
tent areas also allow dogs. There is a dog walk area at the campground. There are no water hookups at the
campgrounds.

Attractions

TOP 200 PLACE **The Skipjack Martha Lewis** South end of Union Avenue/Tidings Park Havre de
Grace MD   410-939-4078
http://www.skipjackmarthalewis.org/
This 2-sail bateau (skipjack) is one of the few working oyster dredge boats left in the bay, and in addition to being
an onboard classroom, it is also a venue for special events or just cruising. Well mannered dogs are allowed on
board for no additional fee. They must be under owner's firm control/care at all times, and must remain leashed.
Since there is no cover on the sailboat to speak of, they suggest bringing a non-glass water dish for your pet and
any protective covering deemed necessary.

Stores

Burlane Cat and Dog Boutique 108 N Tollgate Road Bel Air MD   410-879-1459
http://www.burlanecat-dog.com/
This is a 42 year established grooming business that grew to add a small storefront of cat and dog gifts, treats,
and specialty care products. They are open Tuesday to Saturday from 8 am to 5 pm, and your pet is welcome to
come in and explore. Dogs must be leashed.
PetSmart Pet Store 602 Boulton St Bel Air MD   410-638-0330
Your licensed and well-behaved leashed dog is allowed in the store.
Petco Pet Store 615 Belair Rd, Ste P Bel Air MD   410-420-6754
Your licensed and well-behaved leashed dog is allowed in the store.

Parks

Frank Hutchins Memorial Park Congress Street at the Susquehanna River Havre de Grace MD   410-939-
6724
This 2-acre waterfront park is located on the bank of the Susquehanna River with a nice pier for fishing. Dogs
are allowed in the park and on the pier. Dogs must be under owner's control, leashed, and cleaned up after at all
times.
Susquehanna State Park 4122 Wilkinson Road Havre de Grace MD   410-557-7994 (888-432-2267)
Rich in historical significance and recreational opportunities, this forested, river valley park offers a variety of
trails to explore, a working grist mill, and an archery range. Dogs of all sizes are allowed throughout the park for
no additional fee. Dogs must be leashed and cleaned up after at all times. Dogs are not allowed in picnic or
historic areas or at the cabins.

Annapolis

Accommodations
Homestead Hotel 120 Admiral Chochrane Drive Annapolis MD   410-571-6600
This extended stay hotel suggests one pet is allowed per room; however they may allow additional pets. There is an additional pet fee of $25 per day to a maximum of $75. Dogs must be quiet, well mannered, leashed, and cleaned up after at all times.
Loews Annapolis Hotel 126 West Street Annapolis MD   410-263-7777
All well-behaved dogs of any size are welcome. This upscale hotel offers their "Loews Loves Pets" program which includes special pet treats, local dog walking routes, and a list of nearby pet-friendly places to visit. There are no pet fees.
Sheraton Annapolis Hotel 173 Jennifer Rd. Annapolis MD   410-266-3131 (888-625-5144)
Dogs up to 80 pounds are allowed. There are no additional pet fees. Dogs are not allowed to be left alone in the room.
TownePlace Suites Bowie Town Center 3700 Town Center Blvd Bowie MD   301-292-8045
Dogs of all sizes are allowed. There is a $75 one time pet fee per visit.

Campgrounds and RV Parks
Washington DC - NE KOA 768 Cecil Avenue N Millersville MD   410-923-2771 (800-562-0248)
http://www.koa.com
Dogs of all sizes are allowed. There are no additional pet fees. Dogs may not be left unattended, must be leashed, and cleaned up after. Dogs are not allowed at the lodge. This RV park is closed during the off-season. The camping and tent areas also allow dogs. There is a dog walk area at the campground. Dogs are allowed in the camping cabins.

Attractions
Annapolis Digital Walking Tours 99 Main Street Annapolis MD   410-267665
http://reservations.annapolis.org/
The local historic foundation offer self-guided tours of this revolutionary city using digital audio players; the digital player is rented by the day. Dogs are allowed on the tours; they are not allowed in buildings. Dogs must be under owner's control/care, leashed, and cleaned up after at all times.
Annapolis Maritime Museum 723 2nd Street Annapolis MD   410-295-0104
http://www.annapolismaritimemuseum.org/
This maritime museum's objective is to preserve, maintain, and educate the public about the maritime heritage of the city and the neighboring waters of the Chesapeake Bay; the Eastport Walking Tour here consists of 14 quality wayside information panels. Well mannered dogs are welcome to explore too. Dogs must be under owner's control/care, leashed, and cleaned up after at all times.
Annapolis Small Boat Rentals 808 Boucher Avenue Annapolis MD   410-268-2628
http://asmallboatrental.com/
This watercraft rental company will help visitors to have a great day on the water with tips and maps. Dogs are allowed on board for no additional fee; they must be well behaved, under owner's control/care, and cleaned up after at all times.
Annapolis Trolley Tours 99 Main Street Annapolis MD   410-626-6000
The city offers public tours by trolley for some fun sightseeing to several major points of interest and there are 2 different locations to choose from to start your tour; at the above address or at the visitor center at Northwest and Calvert Streets. Dogs are welcome, but they must ask at the beginning of the tour if there is anyone who objects for health reasons (allergies, etc), but they say rarely does anyone object. Dogs must be well mannered, under owner's control, leashed, and cleaned up after at all times.
TOP 200 PLACE **Watermark Cruises** 1 Dock Street Annapolis MD   800-569-9622
Well behaved dogs are allowed on the 40 minute boat tours for no extra charge. The size and/or number of dogs allowed will depend on how full the tour is. It is a narrated tour and covers the area's history from the 17th century to the present. The tours explore the residential areas of Old Annapolis, the headwaters of Spa Creek, along the banks of the US Navel Academy, and/or the Severn River where you can catch a glimpse of the Bay Bridge. Beer, non-alcoholic beverages, and snacks are available. Tour times may sometimes vary depending on weather, but they usually run every hour on the hour. Dogs must be leashed, and please bring clean up bags just in case.

Shopping Centers
Annapolis Harbor Center 2472 Solomon's Island Road/H2 Annapolis MD   410-266-5857

http://www.annapolisharbourcenter.com/
This scenic seaside village-style shopping center also features a variety of events and concerts throughout the year. Your well mannered dog is welcome to explore they area and the waterfront; they are not allowed inside the stores. Dogs must be under owner's control, leashed, and cleaned up after at all times.

Stores
Paws Pet Boutique 64 State Circle Annapolis MD   410-263-8683
http://www.pawspetboutique.com/
This store is known for their extensive pet collar collection and unique gifts for those hard-to-buy-for pet loving people. They also have toys, treats, treat jars, bowls, beds, spa products and more. They are open from 10 am to 6 pm Monday through Saturday, and from Noon to 6 pm on Sunday. Your friendly, leashed pet is welcome to come in and explore the store with you.
PetSmart Pet Store 2601 Housley Rd Annapolis MD   410-571-8646
Your licensed and well-behaved leashed dog is allowed in the store.
Petco Pet Store 2319-D Forest Drive Annapolis MD   410-224-8323
Your licensed and well-behaved leashed dog is allowed in the store.
PetSmart Pet Store 4500 Mitchellville Rd Bowie MD   301-352-7286
Your licensed and well-behaved leashed dog is allowed in the store.
Petco Pet Store 15461 Excelsior Drive Bowie MD   301-805-4447
Your licensed and well-behaved leashed dog is allowed in the store.

Beaches
TOP 200 PLACE Quiet Waters Park Dog Beach 600 Quiet Waters Park Road Annapolis MD   410-222-1777
http://friendsofquietwaterspark.org
This park is located on Chesapeake Bay. Dogs are welcome to run off-leash at this dog beach and dog park. The dog park is closed every Tuesday. Leashed dogs are also allowed at Quiet Waters Park. The park offers over 6 miles of scenic paved trails, and a large multi-level children's playground. People need to clean up after their pets. To get there, take Route 665 until it ends and merges with Forrest Drive. Take Forrest Drive for 2 miles and then turn right onto Hillsmere Drive. The park entrance is about 100 yards on the right. The dog beach is located to the left of the South River overlook. Park in Lot N.

Parks
Back Creek Nature Center Edgewood Road Annapolis MD   410-263-1183
In addition to being developed as an environmental educational resource area with several important eco-related projects completed or in progress, there are scenic trails, nature areas, a fishing pier, picnic areas, and restrooms. Dogs must be well mannered, under owner's control, leashed, and cleaned up after at all times.

Off-Leash Dog Parks
Quiet Waters Dog Park 600 Quiet Waters Park Rd Annapolis MD   410-222-1777
http://friendsofquietwaterspark.org
This fenced off-leash dog park is located between the South River and Harness Creek in Quiet Waters Park. There is a separate fenced dog park for small and older dogs. The dog park is next to the dog beach (see separate listing).
Bowie Dog Park Northview Drive and Enfield Drive Bowie MD
This one acre fenced dog park has two areas, one for larger dogs and one for small or shy dogs.

Outdoor Restaurants
Buddy's Crabs and Ribs 100 Main Street Annapolis MD   410-626-1100
http://www.buddysonline.com/
In addition to their specialty ribs/crab dishes and a full menu, they also offer an "all you can eat" seafood buffet and raw bar on the weekends, and outside dining during the Summer. Dogs are allowed at the outside tables; they must be leashed and under owner's control/care at all times.
Grump's Cafe Bay Ridge Plaza 117 Hillsmere Drive Annapolis MD   410-267-0229
http://www.grumpscafe.com/
This waterside eatery touts to have the best burger and crab cakes around, and in addition to dine in or carry-out, they also offer alfresco dining. Dogs are allowed at the outer tables; they must be under owner's control/care and leashed at all times.
Rams Head Tavern 33 West Street Annapolis MD   410-268-4545
This tavern specializes in daily, freshly prepared steak and seafood with a wide variety of accompaniments, a full bar with over 100 bottled beers and 30 draught selections, and indoor or outdoor dining options. Dogs are

allowed at the outer tables in the front of the eatery or in the back patio. Dogs must be under owner's control/care, leashed, and cleaned up after at all times.

Sly Fox Pub 7 Church Circle Annapolis MD   443-482-9000
This restaurant and bar serves American. Dogs are allowed at the outdoor tables.

Stan and Joe's Saloon 37 West Street/H 450 Annapolis MD   410-263-1993
http://www.stanandjoes.com/
There are always "specials" going on of some kind at this tavern, as well as various music venues, and a back outdoor patio for dining and other activities. Dogs are allowed at the outside tables; they must be leashed and under owner's control/care at all times.

Events

Animal Tales Walking Tour 64 State Circle Annapolis MD   410-263-0033
Watermark Tours and Paws Pet Boutique presents an annual 60 minute walking tour every March for animal lovers that are filled with fun and entertaining animal stories. Tours leave from the boutique on State Street, and if the first tour is booked, another tour will immediately follow. Dogs must be well mannered, under owner's control, leashed, and cleaned up after at all times.

Assateague Island

Campgrounds and RV Parks

TOP 200 PLACE **Assateague Island National Seashore** 7206 National Seashore Lane Assateague Island MD   410-641-1441 (877-444-6777)
http://www.nps.gov/asis/
This undeveloped barrier island park allows visitors educational as well as numerous land, water, and seaside recreational opportunities. Dogs are allowed in the Maryland portion of the National Seashore for day and overnight use for no additional fee. Dogs are allowed on the many unguarded beaches on the Maryland portion of the National Seashore. They are not allowed in the Maryland State Park, on the Virginia part of the island-(even in a vehicle), or north of the State Park to the Ocean City inlet. They may not be on life-guarded beaches or on nature trails. Dogs may not be left unattended, and they must be on no more than a 6 foot leash and cleaned up after at all times. The camp area includes chemical toilets, cold-water showers, picnic tables, grills, and water. The camping and tent areas also allow dogs. There is a dog walk area at the campground. There are no electric or water hookups at the campgrounds.

Beaches

Assateague Island National Seashore Route 611 Assateague Island MD   410-641-1441
http://www.nps.gov/asis/
Dogs on leash are allowed on beaches, except for any lifeguarded swimming beaches (will be marked off with flags). There are plenty of beaches to enjoy at this park that are not lifeguarded swimming beaches. Dogs are not allowed on trails in the park. The park is located eight miles south of Ocean City, at the end of Route 611.

Parks

Assateague Island National Seashore 7206 National Seashore Lane Assateague Island MD   410-641-1441 (877-444-6777)
http://www.nps.gov/asis/
This undeveloped barrier island park allows visitors educational as well as numerous land, water, and seaside recreational opportunities. Dogs are allowed in the Maryland portion of the National Seashore for day and overnight use for no additional fee. They are not allowed in the Maryland State Park, on the Virginia part of the island-(even in a vehicle), or north of the State Park to the Ocean City inlet. They may not be on life-guarded beaches or on nature trails. Dogs may not be left unattended, and they must be on no more than a 6 foot leash and cleaned up after at all times.

BWI Airport Area

Accommodations

TownePlace Suites Baltimore Fort Meade 120 National Business Pkwy Annapolis Junction MD   301-498-7477

Dogs of all sizes are allowed. There is a $75 one time pet fee per visit.
Red Roof Inn - Washington, DC - BW Parkway 7306 Parkway Drive South Hanover MD   410-712-4070 (800-RED-ROOF)
One well-behaved family pet per room. Guest must notify front desk upon arrival. Guest is liable for any damages. In consideration of all guests, pets must never be left unattended in the guest rooms.
Residence Inn by Marriott 7035 Arundel Mills Circle Hanover MD   410-799-7332
Dogs of all sizes are allowed but they must be able to fit into a kennel when out of room. There is a $75 one time fee and a pet policy to sign at check in.
Red Roof Inn - Washington, DC Columbia - Jessup 8000 Washington Boulevard Jessup MD   410-796-0380 (800-RED-ROOF)
One well-behaved family pet per room. Guest must notify front desk upon arrival. Guest is liable for any damages. In consideration of all guests, pets must never be left unattended in the guest rooms.
Candlewood Suites Baltimore-Linthicum 1247 Winterson Rd. Linthicum MD   410-850-9214 (877-270-6405)
Dogs of all sizes are allowed for an additional one time fee of $75 per pet.
Holiday Inn 890 Elkridge Landing Road Linthicum MD   410-859-8400 (877-270-6405)
Dogs of all sizes are allowed for an additional one time pet fee of $50 per room, and they must be crated when left alone in the room.
Residence Inn by Marriott 1160 Winterson Road Linthicum MD   410-691-0255
Dogs of all sizes are allowed. There is a $75 one time fee and a pet policy to sign at check in.
Staybridge Suites Baltimore Bwi Airport 1301 Winterson Road Linthicum MD   410-850-5666 (877-270-6405)
Dogs up to 50 pounds are allowed for an additional one time fee of $100 per pet.
Comfort Suites BWI Airport 815 Elkridge Landing Road Linthicum Heights MD   410-691-1000 (877-424-6423)
Dogs are allowed for an additional one time pet fee of $25 per room.
Homestead Hotel - BWI 939 International Drive Linthicum Heights MD   410-691-2500
All studio suite rooms offer a fully equipped kitchen. There is a $75 one time per stay pet fee.
Homewood Suites Hotel BWI 1181 Winterson Rd Linthicum Heights MD   410-684-6100
There is a $200.00 one time pet fee.
Motel 6 - Baltimore - BWI Airport 5179 Raynor Avenue Linthicum Heights MD   410-636-9070 (800-466-8356)
One well-behaved family pet per room. Guest must notify front desk upon arrival. Guest is liable for any damages. In consideration of all guests, pets must never be left unattended in the guest rooms.
Red Roof Inn - Washington, DC - BWI Airport 827 Elkridge Landing Road Linthicum Heights MD   410-850-7600 (800-RED-ROOF)
One well-behaved family pet per room. Guest must notify front desk upon arrival. Guest is liable for any damages. In consideration of all guests, pets must never be left unattended in the guest rooms.

Stores
PetSmart Pet Store 7663 Arundel Mills Circle Hanover MD   443-755-9936
Your licensed and well-behaved leashed dog is allowed in the store.

Parks
BWI Bike Trail Dorsey Road BWI Airport MD
This trail is a nice paved trail at the airport, near a number of the dog-friendly hotels.

Baltimore

Accommodations
Brookshire Suites 120 E. Lombard Street Baltimore MD   410-625-1300
All well-behaved dogs are welcome at this suites hotel. There are no pet fees.
Four Points by Sheraton BWI Airport 7032 Elm Rd. Baltimore MD   410-859-3300 (888-625-5144)
Dogs of all sizes are allowed. There is a $25 per night pet fee per pet. Dogs are not allowed to be left alone in the room.
Motel 6 - Baltimore West 1654 Whitehead Court Baltimore MD   410-265-7660 (800-466-8356)
One well-behaved family pet per room. Guest must notify front desk upon arrival. Guest is liable for any damages. In consideration of all guests, pets must never be left unattended in the guest rooms.
Pier 5 Hotel 711 Eastern Avenue Baltimore MD   410-539-2000
The entire hotel offers a smoke free environment. All well-behaved dogs are welcome and there are no pet fees.
Residence Inn by Marriott 4980 Mercantile Road Baltimore MD   410-933-9554
Dogs of all sizes are allowed. There is a $75 one time fee and a pet policy to sign at check in.
Residence Inn by Marriott 7335 Wisconsin Avenue Baltimore MD   301-718-0200

Dogs of all sizes are allowed. There is a $200 non-refundable cleaning fee plus $10 per night per pet and a pet policy to sign at check in.

Sheraton Baltimore City Center Hotel (formally Wyndham) 101 W Fayette Street Baltimore MD   410-752-1100 (888-625-5144)
Dogs up to 80 pounds are allowed for no additional fee. There is a pet waiver to sign at check in. Dogs must be well mannered, leashed or crated, and cleaned up after.

Sheraton Baltimore North Hotel 903 Dulaney Valley Blvd. Baltimore MD   410-321-7400 (888-625-5144)
Dogs of all sizes are allowed. There are no additional pet fees. Dogs are not allowed to be left alone in the room.

Sheraton Inner Harbor Hotel 300 South Charles St. Baltimore MD   410-962-8300 (888-625-5144)
Dogs up to 50 pounds are allowed. There are no additional pet fees. Dogs are not allowed to be left alone in the room.

The Admiral Fell Inn

TOP 200 PLACE The Admiral Fell Inn 888 South Broadway Baltimore MD   410-522-7377
http://www.harbormagic.com
The Admiral Fell Inn is a historic inn in the waterfront village of Fell's Point. All well-behaved dogs are welcome and there no additional pet fees.

Tremont Park Hotel 8 East Pleasant Street Baltimore MD   410-576-1200 (800-TREMONT)
Dogs may stay in four of the one bedroom suites in this hotel. They'll provide bowls for food and water, a treat and a Pampered Pet Placement. There is a $10 pet service fee that will be donated to the American Humane Society if there is no damage.

Chase Suite Hotel by Woodfin 10710 Beaver Dam Road Cockeysville MD   410-584-7370
All well-behaved dogs are welcome. All rooms are suites with a full kitchen. Hotel amenities include a complimentary breakfast buffet. There is a $5 per day pet fee.

Days Inn Glen Burnie 6600 Ritchie Hwy Glen Burnie MD   410-761-8300 (800-329-7466)
Dogs of all sizes are allowed. There is a $20 per night pet fee per pet.

Red Roof Inn - Baltimore North - Timonium 111 West Timonium Road Timonium MD   410-666-0380 (800-RED-ROOF)
One well-behaved family pet per room. Guest must notify front desk upon arrival. Guest is liable for any damages. In consideration of all guests, pets must never be left unattended in the guest rooms.

Holiday Inn 1100 Cromwell Bridge Rd Towson MD   410-823-4410 (877-270-6405)
Dogs of all sizes are allowed for an additional one time pet fee of $40.

Attractions

Baltimore Adventures 1001 Fell Street Baltimore MD   410-342-2004
http://www.fishbaltimore.com/
There are a variety of cruise and fishing options, as well as rentals available at this charter company. Well behaved dogs are welcome aboard. Dogs must be under owner's control/care at all times.

Cylburn Arboretum

Cylburn Arboretum 4915 Greenspring Avenue Baltimore MD   410-367-2217
http://www.cylburnassociation.org
This city nature preserve park offers 207 acres of beautifully landscaped grounds with trails winding through rare trees, gardens, and native vegetation, plus they have various educational opportunities, numerous events, and mansion tours. Dogs are allowed throughout the grounds; they are not allowed in buildings. Dogs must be under owner's control, leashed, and cleaned up after at all times.

Henderson's Wharf Marina 1001 Fell Street Baltimore MD   410-342-2004
http://www.fishbaltimore.com/
Offering a variety of cruise options for the Chesapeake Bay and Baltimore Inner Harbor, this seafaring company will also allow pooches to come aboard for no additional fee. They only request that pet owners try not to schedule on weekends during the busy Summer months. Dogs must be well behaved, under owner's control/care and leashed or crated at all times.

Heritage Walk Self-Guided Walking Tour 401 Light Street/H2 Baltimore MD   877-BALTIMORE(225-8466)
http://www.heritagewalk.org/
This self-guided tour booklet tells of the city's past and guides visitors by all 20 of the walk's star attractions. Tour booklets can be obtained at many of the sites along the way, by mail order, or at Baltimore's Inner Harbor Visitor Center. Dogs are allowed on the self-guided tours. Dogs must be leashed and cleaned up after at all times. Dogs are not allowed in any of the buildings.

Horse and Carriage Rides Inner Harbor Baltimore MD
Well-behaved dogs are allowed on the carriage rides. Carriage rides leave during good weather from the area in front of the Inner Harbor.

Maryland Sled Dog Adventures LLC   Baltimore MD   443-562-5736
http://www.marylanddogsledding.com/
All tours and programs are by reservation only at this unique recreational/educational activity. Most tours take place along the scenic Northern Central Rail Trail, and activities include running or giving lessons to visiting dogs, dog sled tours (snow or no snow), bikejoring, skijoring, special events, and a lot more. Dogs must have a current license, be healthy, and have proof of inoculations.

TOP 200 PLACE The Original Fell's Point Ghost Walk Tour P. O. Box 38140 Baltimore MD   410-522-7400
http://www.fellspointghost.com/
This outdoor tour weaves the history and lore of a city rich with mystery. It was the birthplace of the dangerous Baltimore Clipper ships, was the privateer capital during the War of 1812, and a bohemian enclave during the 60's. They tell fun and spooky stories about this shipbuilding town, the founder of the city, about bars, rough pirates, ladies of the night, typhoid outbreaks, Edgar Allen Poe, and the War of 1812. The tours are one hour long and less then a mile. Tours depart from Max's Darthouse on Broadway, at 731 S. Broadway near the Fell's Point Square in Baltimore, Maryland. The tours run rain or shine (unless dangerous weather), and leave promptly at 7 pm. Since tours sometimes sell out, usually in the Fall - October especially, advance ticket purchases are recommended. Also, parking can be difficult on evenings and weekends, so they suggest the parking garage on Caroline Street as it is very close to the departure point. Well behaved, dogs on leash are allowed to join you on this walking tour, and please be prepared to clean up after your pet.

Westminster Cemetery 509 W. Fayette Street Baltimore MD   410-706-2072
Famous for being the final resting place of Edgar Allen Poe and being the town's oldest cemetery, there are also other colonial dignitaries buried here. Dogs are allowed throughout the grounds; they must be leashed and cleaned up after at all times.
Benjamin Banneker Historical Park and Museum 300 Oella Avenue Catonsville MD   410-887-1081
Although dogs are not allowed inside the museum that conveys the history of Mr. Banneker and of some of America's colonial history, they are allowed on the grounds. Dogs must be leashed and cleaned up after at all times.

Stores

PetSmart Pet Store 9921 Pulaski Hwy Baltimore MD   410-687-6101
Your licensed and well-behaved leashed dog is allowed in the store.
Petco Pet Store 8640 Pulaski Highway, Ste 104 Baltimore MD   410-686-4037
Your licensed and well-behaved leashed dog is allowed in the store.
Pretentious Pooch 1017 Cathedral Street Baltimore MD   443-524-7777
http://www.pretentiouspooch.com/
This boutique offers a long line of pet products and treats, plus they have several events and offer a number of specialty services/items. Dogs are welcome in the store; they must be under owners strict and direct control at all times. Dogs must be properly socialized with people and animals, be friendly, healthy, up to date on shots, and licensed.
PetSmart Pet Store 6501 C Baltimore Nat Pike Catonsville MD   410-747-8570
Your licensed and well-behaved leashed dog is allowed in the store.
PetSmart Pet Store 1559 Merritt Blvd Dundalk MD   410-285-6302
Your licensed and well-behaved leashed dog is allowed in the store.
PetSmart Pet Store 597-C E Ordnance Rd Glen Burnie MD   410-582-9444
Your licensed and well-behaved leashed dog is allowed in the store.
PetSmart Pet Store 24 Mountain Rd Glen Burnie MD   410-766-7190
Your licensed and well-behaved leashed dog is allowed in the store.
PetSmart Pet Store 57 W Aylesbury Rd Lutherville MD   410-308-1140
Your licensed and well-behaved leashed dog is allowed in the store.
Petco Pet Store 1719 York Rd Lutherville MD   410-453-9131
Your licensed and well-behaved leashed dog is allowed in the store.
Petco Pet Store 10383 Reisterstown Rd Owings Mills MD   410-581-9888
Your licensed and well-behaved leashed dog is allowed in the store.
PetSmart Pet Store 1238 Putty Hill Ave Towson MD   410-823-4593
Your licensed and well-behaved leashed dog is allowed in the store.
PetSmart Pet Store 625 Baltimore Blvd Westminster MD   410-751-9380
Your licensed and well-behaved leashed dog is allowed in the store.

Beaches

Downs Park Dog Beach 8311 John Downs Loop Pasadena MD   410-222-6230
This dog beach is located on Chesapeake Bay. People are not permitted to go swimming, but dogs can run off-leash at this beach. The dog beach is closed every Tuesday. Dogs on leash are also allowed in Downs Park. People need to clean up after their pets. Take Route 100 until it merges with Moutain Road (Rt. 177 East). Follow Mt. Road for about 3.5 miles and the park entrance will be on your right. The dog beach is located in the northeast corner of the park.

Parks

BWI Bike Trail Dorsey Road BWI Airport MD
This trail is a nice paved trail at the airport, near a number of the dog-friendly hotels.
Cromwell Valley Park 2175 Cromwell Bridge Rd Baltimore MD   410-887-2503
Dogs on leash are welcome.
Cylburn Arboretum 4915 Greenspring Ave Baltimore MD   410-396-0180
Well behaved dogs on leash are welcome at this over 20 acre nature preserve and city park.
Druid Hill Park Druid Park Lake Drive Baltimore MD
Druid Hill Park is a large city park in the center of Baltimore. Dogs on leash are allowed in the park.

Maryland   - Please always call ahead to make sure that an establishment is still dog-friendly

Federal Hill

Federal Hill Key Hwy and Light St Baltimore MD
http://www.baltimoremd.com/federalhill/
This nice park with a nice view of the Inner Harbor is also easy walking distance from the Inner Harbor. Most of the park is up on a hill overlooking downtown. Dogs on leash are welcome.
Fort McHenry 2400 E Fort Avenue Baltimore MD   410-962-4290
http://www.nps.gov/fomc/
Rich in colonial history, this star-shaped 18th century fort was the birthplace of the country's National Anthem. Dogs are allowed around the outer (landscaped) grounds, down by the river, and at the picnic areas; they are not allowed inside gated areas. Dogs must be leashed and cleaned up after at all times.
Gwynns Fall Trail and Park Franklintown Rd and Holly Ave Baltimore MD
This is a city park with a paved bike trail. Dogs on leash are welcome.
Robert E Lee Park Falls Road and Lake Ave Baltimore MD
Dogs must be on leash at all times in the park.
Oregon Ridge Park Beaver Dam Road Cockeysville MD   410-887-1818
Dogs on leash are allowed. This is a very large park with lots of trails.
Fort Howard Park North Point Blvd Edgemere MD   410-887-7529
Dogs must be leashed in this park.
North Point State Park Old North Point Rd Edgemere MD   410-592-2897
Dogs must be leashed in this park.
Baltimore & Annapolis Bike Trail   Glen Burnie MD
This is a 13 mile paved trail from Baltimore to Annapolis. Leashed dogs are allowed.
Gunpowder Falls State Park   Hereford MD 410-592-2897
This is a huge park with over 100 miles of trails. It follows the Gunpowder Falls River and extends as far as Pennsylvania. Dogs on leash are allowed.

Hampton Historical Site

Hampton Historical Site 535 Hampton Lane Towson MD   410-823-1309
http://www.nps.gov/hamp/
Dogs on leash are allowed in the outdoor areas. There is an admission fee to the park, which is an 1800's plantation.

Off-Leash Dog Parks
Canton Dog Park Clinton & Toone Streets Baltimore MD   410-396-7900
This fenced dog park has two areas. One is for small dogs and one is for larger dogs. Water is provided and the dog park is open during daylight hours. To get to the park, take the I-95 Boston Street Exit, then west to Clinton Street. Turn right on Clinton Street.

Outdoor Restaurants
Bonjour 6070 Falls Rd Baltimore MD   410-372-0238
Dogs are allowed at the outdoor tables.
Dangerously Delicious Pies 1036 Light Street Baltimore MD   410-522-PIES (7437)
http://www.dangerouspies.com/
Famous for their homemade pies, they also offer outside dining for guests with pets. Dogs must be under owner's control/care and leashed at all times.
Ethel and Ramone's 1615 Sulgrave Ave Baltimore MD   410-664-2971
This restaurant is in the Mt Washington district. Dogs are allowed at the outdoor tables.
Germano's Trattoria 300 S High Street Baltimore MD   410-752-4515
http://www.germanostrattoria.com/
This restaurant specializes in organic pastas, and Tuscan and regional Italian dishes. They offer outdoor dining options; dogs are allowed at the outer tables. Dogs must be under owner's control/care and leashed at all times.
Glas Z Cafe 6080 Falls Rd Baltimore MD   410-377-9060
Dogs are allowed at the outdoor tables.
Greene Turtle 722 S Broadway Baltimore MD   410-342-4222
Dogs are allowed at the outdoor tables.
Kiss Cafe 2400 Boston St Baltimore MD   410-327-9889
This restaurant serves American food. Dogs are allowed at the outdoor tables.
LuLu's off Broadway 1703 Aliceanna Street Baltimore MD   410-537-5858
This bar allows dogs at their outdoor tables.
Metropolitan 904 S Charles St Baltimore MD   410-234-0235
Dogs are allowed at the outdoor tables.
Patterson Perk 2501 Eastern Avenue Baltimore MD   410-534-1286
This coffee shop serves pastries. Dogs are allowed at the outdoor tables. Treats are provided for your pet.
Shuckers 1629 Thames Street Baltimore MD   410-522-6300
http://www.shuckersoffellspoint.com/
This waterfront restaurant specializes in fresh seafood and all American favorites, plus they offer a sports bar

with multiple large TVs, a venue for special events, and outside dining options. Dogs are allowed at the outside tables; they must be leashed and under owner's control/care at all times.
Taste Restaurant 510 E Belvedere Ave Baltimore MD   443-278-9001
http://www.tasterestaurant.biz/
Specializing in a Tex-Mex, Carolina, Pacific Rim, French-inspired menu, with good wine and company, this eatery also offers al fresco dining. Dogs are allowed at the outer tables. Dogs must be under owner's control/care and leashed at all times.
Checkers 1915 E Joppa Rd Parkville MD   410-663-5798
Dogs are allowed at the outdoor tables.

Cambridge

Accommodations
Hyatt Regency Chesapeake Bay Golf Resort, Spa and Marina. 100 Heron Blvd Cambridge MD   410-901-1234 (888) 591 1234)
This beautiful bay shore hotel has many features and amenities for the business or leisure traveler with a full service business center, a championship golf course and a 150 slip marina. Dogs up to 70 pounds are welcome for an additional fee of $50 per night per pet, and reservations must be made at least 7 days in advance or more as there are only 9 pet-friendly rooms available. Current shot records must be provided upon arrival, and dogs must be under owner's control, leashed, and cleaned up after at all times.

Campgrounds and RV Parks
Taylors Island Family Campground 4362 Bay Shore Road Taylors Island MD   410-397-3275
Dogs of all sizes are allowed. There are no additional pet fees. Dogs may not be left unattended except for short periods, and they must be quiet, well behaved, leashed, and cleaned up after. The camping and tent areas also allow dogs. There is a dog walk area at the campground.

Attractions
Dorchester Arts Center Walking Tours 120 High Street Cambridge MD   410-228-7782
http://www.dorchesterartscenter.org/
Each Fall the arts center presents guided historic and ghost tours drawn from real life stories. Your pooch is welcome on the walking tours if they are well behaved and will be quiet; they are not allowed on the trolley or bus tours. Dogs must be under owner's control, leashed, and cleaned up after at all times.

Outdoor Restaurants
Snappers Waterfront Cafe 112 Commerce Street Cambridge MD   410-228-0112
http://www.snapperswaterfrontcafe.com/
This waterfront café and Tiki Bar offers a couple of outdoor dining options. Although dogs are not allowed at the outer deck tables, they are allowed at the picnic tables on the patio area. Dogs must be well behaved, under owner's control/care and leashed at all times.

Chestertown

Accommodations
Brampton Inn 25227 Chestertown Road Chestertown MD   410-778-1860 (866-305-1860)
http://www.bramptoninn.com/
Stately and romantic, this historical estate sits on 20 wooded and landscaped acres just a short distance from the river. Dogs of all sizes are allowed in one of the cottages for an additional $30 per night. Dogs must be leashed and cleaned up after.

Attractions
Virginia Gent Decker Arboretum 300 Washington Avenue/H 213 Chestertown MD   800-422-1782 ext/7726
http://www.arboretum.washcoll.edu/
Located on the 104 acre Washington College campus, this arboretum features over 90 species with more than 700 labeled trees, and they are dedicated to ongoing research, collection, education, and to providing a venue where the community may enjoy passive recreation. Dogs are welcome on the campus and throughout the

arboretum; they are not allowed in buildings. Dogs must be under owner's control, leashed, and cleaned up after at all times.

Clarksburg

Campgrounds and RV Parks
Little Bennet Regional Park 23701 Frederick Road Clarksburg MD 301-972-9222
This scenic park of 3,600 acres and 20 miles of trails offers a variety of activities and recreational pursuits. Dogs of all sizes are allowed at no additional fee. Dogs may not be left unattended, and they must be on no more than a 6 foot leash, and be cleaned up after. This campground is closed during the off-season. The camping and tent areas also allow dogs. There is a dog walk area at the campground. There are no water hookups at the campground.

Columbia

Accommodations
Sheraton Columbia Hotel 10207 Wincopin Circle Columbia MD   410-730-3900 (888-625-5144)
Dogs up to 50 pounds are allowed. There are no additional pet fees. Dogs are not allowed to be left alone in the room.
Staybridge Suites 8844 Columbia 100 Pkwy Columbia MD   410-964-9494 (877-270-6405)
Dogs of all sizes are allowed for an additional one time pet fee of $75 per room.

Stores
PetSmart Pet Store 9041 Snowden Sq River Rd Columbia MD   410-312-0950
Your licensed and well-behaved leashed dog is allowed in the store.
Petco Pet Store 6181 Old Dobbin Lane, Ste 800 Columbia MD   410-290-1313
Your licensed and well-behaved leashed dog is allowed in the store.

Day Kennels
PetsHotel by PetsMart Day Kennel 9041 Snowden Sq. River Rd. Columbia MD   410-312-4890
http://www.petsmart.com/PETsHOTEL/
This PetSmart pet store offers day care, day camp and overnight care. You may drop off and pick up your dog during the hours the store is open seven days a week. Dogs must have proof of current rabies, DPP and Bordatella vaccinations.

Crisfield

Attractions
Tangier Island Cruises 1001 West Main Street/H 413 Crisfield MD   410-968-2338
http://www.tangierislandcruises.com/
Offering cruises and water taxi service to Tangier Island, this company will also allow your pooch to come aboard for no additional fee. Dogs must be under owner's control/care at all times, and be leashed and cleaned up after.

Outdoor Restaurants
The Waterman Inn 901 W Main Street/H 413 Crisfield MD   410-968-1565
http://crisfield.com/watermens/
Specializing in Chesapeake Crab soups and chowders, this eatery offers meals from breakfast through dinner, a seasonal menu, cocktails and wine, and outdoor dining options. Dogs are allowed at the outer tables. They must be well behaved, under owner's control/care at all times, and leashed.

Crofton

Stores
Crunchy's Natural Pet Foods 2421 Crofton Lane, Suite 11 Crofton MD   410-721-5432
http://www.crunchies.com/
This pet food store specializes in natural, holistic products, and carries some of the best quality brands available. Your pooch is welcome to come into the store to sniff out their favorites. Dogs must be under owner's control/care and leashed at all times.

Cumberland

Accommodations
Holiday Inn 100 S. George St Cumberland MD   301-724-8800 (877-270-6405)
Dogs of all sizes are allowed for an additional one time pet fee of $10 per room.

Campgrounds and RV Parks
Greenridge State Forest 28700 Headquarters Drive NE Flintstone MD   301-478-3124
The second largest forest in the state, this 44,000-acre oak-hickory forest offers a variety of trails, various land and water recreation, and some spectacular lookout points. Dogs of all sizes are allowed at no additional fee. Dogs may not be left unattended, they must be leashed, and cleaned up after in camp areas. Dogs are allowed on the trails. This campground is closed during the off-season. The camping and tent areas also allow dogs. There is a dog walk area at the campground. There are no electric or water hookups at the campground.
Rocky Gap State Park 12500 Pleasant Valley Road NE Flintstone MD   301-722-1480 (888-432-CAMP (2267))
A popular recreation destination, this 3,000+ acre park has a 243 acre lake surrounded by rugged, forested mountains, offers breathtaking views, and a variety of land and water activities. There are interpretive programs, areas for special events, and easy to challenging trails including a 4 ½ mile trail that encircles the lake and a mile-long gorge trail. Dogs are allowed on the trails, throughout the park, and in designated camp areas; they are not allowed on the beach. Dogs must be leashed and cleaned up after at all times. There are 278 campsites with restrooms, showers, a game room, laundry, camp store, fire rings, and a dump station is close by. This RV park is closed during the off-season. The camping and tent areas also allow dogs. There is a dog walk area at the campground. There are no water hookups at the campgrounds.

Attractions
George Washington's Headquarters Greene Street Cumberland MD   301-777-5132
Built in 1754-55, this is the only structure still standing from what was Ft Cumberland, and it was used by the "President to be" while he was an aide to General Braddock. Viewing is from the outside only, and your pet is welcome to take a peek also. Dogs must be leashed and cleaned up after.

Parks
C and O Canal Historical Park Cumberland Visitor Center/13 Canal Street Cumberland MD   301-739-4200
http://www.nps.gov/choh/
Dedicating to preserving and educating the public about the canal era and America's transportation history, several visitor centers can be found along this 184½ mile long canal trail as well as various recreation opportunities. The trail goes from Georgetown in the District of Columbia to Cumberland, Maryland, and the park is also home to the 3,118 foot Paw Paw Tunnel that took more than 6 million bricks and 12 years to build. Dogs are allowed throughout the park and on the canal trail. Dogs must be under owner's control, leashed, and cleaned up after at all times.
Rocky Gap State Park 12500 Pleasant Valley Road NE Flintstone MD   301-722-1480 (888-432-CAMP (2267))
A popular recreation destination, this 3,000+ acre park has a 243 acre lake surrounded by rugged, forested mountains, offers breathtaking views, and a variety of land and water activities. There are interpretive programs, areas for special events, and easy to challenging trails including a 4 ½ mile trail that encircles the lake and a mile-long gorge trail. Dogs are allowed on the trails, throughout the park, and in designated camp areas; they are not allowed on the beach. Dogs must be leashed and cleaned up after at all times.

Outdoor Restaurants
City Lights 59 Baltimore St Cumberland MD   301-722-9800
This restaurant serves American food. Dogs are allowed at the outdoor tables.

Deep Creek Lake

Accommodations

Yough Valley Motel   138 Walnut St Friendsville MD   301-746-5700
Dogs of all sizes are allowed. There is a $10 per dog per night additional pet fee.
The Savage River Lodge 1600 Mount Aetna Rd Frostburg MD   301-689-3200
http://www.savageriverlodge.com/dogs.htm
This extremely pet friendly lodge has a special page on its website for visitors with pets. While there you may be greeted by Bodhi, the Lodge Dog. Visitors stay in individual non-smoking cabins. There is a $25 per night per pet fee. You must make advanced reservations with a pet. The lodge is about 30 minutes from Deep Creek Lake.
WISP Resort & Conference Center 296 Marsh Hill Road McHenry MD   301-387-4911 (800-462-9477)
http://www.wispresort.com
Dogs up to 50 pounds are allowed in this resort lodge right at WISP ski resort. There is a $50 per stay additional pet fee. The entire property is non-smoking.
Alpine Village Inn 19638 Garrett Highway Oakland MD   301-387-5534 (800-745-1174)
http://www.alpinevillageinn.com
Dogs of all sizes are allowed in a few pet rooms. There is a $20 per night per pet additional pet fee.
Swallow Falls Inn 1691 Swallow Falls Rd Oakland MD   301-387-9348

Campgrounds and RV Parks

Garrett State Forest 222 Herrington Lane Oakland MD   301-334-2038
This forest displays a wide variety of trees, abundant wildlife, glimpses of beaver ponds and cranberry bogs and provides various land and water recreation. Dogs of all sizes are allowed at no additional fee. Dogs may not be left unattended, and they may be off lead if they are well behaved and under voice control. Dogs are allowed on the trails. The camping and tent areas also allow dogs. There is a dog walk area at the campground. There are no electric or water hookups at the campground.
Potomac State Forest 1431 Potomac Camp Road Oakland MD   301-334-2038
Mountains and valleys, forests and streams, overlooks displaying great views, primitive camping, and a variety of land and water recreational opportunities (including a 3-D archery range) are all available at this 11,535 acre forest, which also has the highest point of any other state forest at 3,220 feet. Dogs are allowed throughout the park, on the trails, and for overnight camping. Dogs must be under strict voice control or leashed, and cleaned up after at all times. Primitive camping is allowed at pre-existing campsites; new forging of campsites is prohibited. The camping and tent areas also allow dogs. There is a dog walk area at the campground. There are no electric or water hookups at the campgrounds.
Swallow Falls State Park 222 Harrington Lane Oakland MD   301-387-6938 (888-432-CAMP (2267))
Hike through old growth forest at this mountain park that is home to Maryland's highest waterfall, and some of the states most breathtaking scenery. Dogs are not allowed in the day use area or on the trails between the Saturday before Memorial Day and Labor Day. Dogs may not be left unattended outside, and they must be leashed and cleaned up after. This campground is closed during the off-season. The camping and tent areas also allow dogs. There is a dog walk area at the campground.
Deep Creek Lake State Park 898 State Park Road Swanton MD   301-387-5563 (888-432-CAMP (2267))
This year-round park offers an educational/interpretive center with hands on exhibits, trails varying from moderate to difficult, and a variety of land and water recreation. Dogs of all sizes are allowed at no additional fee. Dogs may not be left unattended, and they must be leashed and cleaned up after. Dogs are not allowed in picnic, swim areas, or in buildings. Dogs are allowed on the trails. This campground is closed during the off-season. The camping and tent areas also allow dogs. There is a dog walk area at the campground. There are no water hookups at the campground.

Vacation Home Rentals

Railey Mountain Lake Vacations 5 Vacation Way Deep Creek Lake MD   301-387-2124 (800-846-RENT (7368))
http://www.deepcreek.com/
Offering a variety of property options and amenities in numerous recreational areas, this agency has about 125 pet friendly vacation rentals available in the Deep Creek Lake area. Dogs of all sizes are allowed for an additional fee of $45 for the 1st two days and $12 each night after, or $84 for the weekly rate per pet (the standard fee for any rental). Pets are not allowed in non-pet homes, and they must be pre-registered and paid for prior to arrival. Pets must be under owner's control/care at all times.
Deep Creek Lake Resort Vacation Rentals 23789 Garrett Highway, Suite 3 McHenry MD   301-387-5832 (800-336-7303)
http://www.deepcreekresort.com/
Every season here brings its own beauty, pleasures, and recreational pursuits, and this agency offers a variety of property options and amenities in the Deep Creek Lake area. Dogs of all sizes are allowed for an additional $65

per pet per stay. Dogs must be well trained, and under owner's control/care at all times.

Attractions
Bill's Marine Service Boat Rentals 20721 Garrett H/H 219 Oakland MD   301-387-5536
This watercraft rental company rents a variety of lake-faring craft for exploring Deep Creek Lake. Dogs are
allowed on the rentals for no additional fee. Dogs must be under owner's control/care and leashed at all times.

Shopping Centers
Red House School Country Mall 3039 Garrett Highway/H 219 Red House MD   301-334-2800
This former elementary school turned country mall features more than 12,000 square feet of Amish goods/crafts,
antiques, and collectibles. Your well mannered pooch is welcome to join you inside; just please keep them close
by. Owners accept 100% responsibility for their pets, and dogs must be under owner's control/care and leashed
at all times.

Stores
Schoolhouse Earth 1224 Friendsville Road Friendsville MD   301-746-8603
This eclectic shop invites guests to enjoy a "magical" experience exploring the unique gifts, jewelry, music,
gourmet goods, and homespun items in the store, or learning how to create your own gardens, or to refresh a bit
in the garden room or water garden. Your well mannered pooch is welcome to join you inside; just please keep
them close by. Owners accept 100% responsibility for their pets, and dogs must be under owner's control/care
and leashed at all times.

Parks
Potomac State Forest 1431 Potomac Camp Road Oakland MD   301-334-2038
Mountains and valleys, forests and streams, overlooks displaying great views, primitive camping, and a variety of
land and water recreational opportunities (including a 3-D archery range) are all available at this 11,535 acre
forest, which also has the highest point in any Maryland State Forest at 3,220 feet. Dogs are allowed throughout
the park, on the trails, and for overnight camping. Dogs must be under strict voice control or leashed, and
cleaned up after at all times.
Deep Creek Lake State Park 898 State Park Road Swanton MD   301-387-5563 (888-432-CAMP (2267))
Interpretive programs, plenty of land and water recreation, numerous habitats and wildlife, and lots of great
camping sites along the state's largest man-made lake can all be enjoyed at this park. Dogs are allowed on the
hiking trails and in the campground; there is no additional pet fee. Dogs may not be left unattended at any time,
and they must be leashed and cleaned up after. Dogs are not allowed at the waterfront or day use areas.

Outdoor Restaurants
Lakeside Creamery 20282 Garrett H/H 219 Deep Creek Lake MD   301-387-2580
In addition to homemade, hand-dipped ice cream, this old-fashioned creamery also offers a variety of
sandwiches and other fare with outdoor dining options. Dogs are allowed at the outer tables, and they must be
under owner's control/care and leashed at all times.
Canoe on the Run 2622 Deep Creek Drive McHenry MD   301-387-5933
This upscale café offers various coffees, lunch fare, and outdoor seating. Dogs are allowed at the outer tables,
and they must be under owner's control/care and leashed at all times.

Easton

Accommodations
Days Inn Easton 7018 Ocean Eastyway Easton MD   410-822-4600 (800-329-7466)
Dogs of all sizes are allowed. There is a $13.08 per night pet fee per pet.
Tidewater Inn 101 E Dover Street/H 331 Easton MD   410-822-1300 (800-237-8775)
http://www.tidewaterinn.com/
This historic inn is as rich in old world charm as it is in modern amenities and services, and it is only a short
distance from Washington D.C. and Baltimore. Dogs are allowed for an additional one time fee of $25 per pet,
and there is a pet agreement to sign at check in. They request that guests bring their own pet covers for the bed
and furniture. A contact number must be left with the front desk when there is a pet alone in the room. Dogs
must be leashed and under owner's control/care at all times.

Attractions

Historical Society of Talbot County 25 S Washington Street Easton MD   410-822-0773
http://www.hstc.org/
In dedication to the education, preservation, and celebration of Talbot County's rich past, the Historical Society provides numerous activities, special events, shops, a comprehensive museum, and a beautiful, prized Federal Garden. Dogs are allowed along the streets and through the garden area; they are not allowed in buildings. Dogs must be leashed and cleaned up after at all times.

Stores
Jake's Pet Boutique 21 Goldsborough Street Easton MD   410-822-2660
http://www.jakespetboutique.com/
This boutique offers a long line of pet products, treats, clothing, bedding, and unique specialty items. Dogs are welcome in the store; they must be leashed and under owner's direct control at all times. Dogs must be healthy and properly socialized with people and pets.

Ellicott City

Accommodations
Residence Inn by Marriott 4950 Beaver Run Ellicott City MD   410-997-7200
Dogs of all sizes are allowed. There is a $75 one time fee and a pet policy to sign at check in.
TOP 200 PLACE Turf Valley Resort 2700 Turf Valley Road Ellicott City MD   410-465-1500 (888-833-8873)
http://www.turfvalleyresort.com
Turf Valley Resort has over 1000 acres of land with golf, spas, meeting rooms, a children's playground, a driving range and more. Pets are allowed for a $150 one time additional pet fee.

Campgrounds and RV Parks
Patapsco Valley State Park 8020 Baltimore National Pike Ellicott City MD   410-461-5005 (888-432-CAMP (2267))
This scenic park of 14,000 acres runs along 32 miles of shoreline, and features the world's longest multiple-arched stone railroad bridge, a 300 foot suspension bridge, a variety of trails, and various land and water recreation. Dogs of all sizes are allowed at no additional fee. Dogs may not be left unattended outside, and they must be leashed and cleaned up after. Dogs are not allowed to use the trails at the main entrance of the park or to be in developed areas. They are allowed only on marked trails, on the road, or just outside the park. This campground is closed during the off-season. The camping and tent areas also allow dogs. There is a dog walk area at the campground.

Attractions
Ghost Tours 8267 Main Street Ellicott City MD   410-313-8141
There "appears" to be enough lingering ghosts still roaming the original cobblestone streets and underground tunnels and structures for many a story based on factual events of the town's history. Dogs must be well behaved, leashed, and cleaned up after at all times.

Stores
Petco Pet Store 10060 US Highway 40 Ellicott City MD   410-465-7714
Your licensed and well-behaved leashed dog is allowed in the store.

Off-Leash Dog Parks
Worthington Park 8170 Hillsborough Road Ellicott City MD   410-313-PARK (7275)
This 2.7 acre off-lead dog area has a separate section for smaller or older dogs. All users of the park must have a permit; daily permits can be obtained on site. Dogs must have current vaccine and license tags. Sanitary stations are available, and they suggest bringing a non-glass water bowl for your pet (water available on site 4-15/11-01). Dogs must be under owner's control and cleaned up after at all times. Dogs must be on leash when out of the off-lead area. The inclement weather line is 410-313-4455.

Frederick

Accommodations

Comfort Inn 7300 Executive Way Frederick MD   301-668-7272 (877-424-6423)
Dogs are allowed for an additional one time pet fee of $10 per room.
Holiday Inn - Frederick 999 W Patrick St Frederick MD   301-662-5141 (877-270-6405)
Dogs of all sizes are allowed for no additional fee.
Holiday Inn - Holidome 5400 Holiday Dr Frederick MD   301-694-7500 (877-270-6405)
Dogs of all sizes are allowed for an additional pet fee of $10 per night per room.
Holiday Inn Express 5579 Spectrum Dr Frederick MD   301-695-2881 (877-270-6405)
Dogs of all sizes are allowed for an additional pet fee of $10 per night per room.
Mainstay Suites 7310 Executive Way Frederick MD   301-668-4600
Dogs are allowed for an additional fee of $10 per night per pet.
Residence Inn by Marriott 5230 Westview Drive Frederick MD   301-360-0010
Dogs of all sizes are allowed. There is a $75 one time fee and a pet policy to sign at check in. They request you kennel your pet if you leave it in the room.
Travelodge 200 E Walser Drive Frederick MD   301-663-0500
Dogs of all sizes are allowed. There is a $25 refundable deposit and a pet policy to sign at check in.

Attractions

The Monocacy National Battlefield 5201 Urbana Pike/H 355 Frederick MD   301-662-3515
http://www.nps.gov/mono/
Battles at various historic sites at this park were instrumental in securing the safety of Washington DC in the Summer of 1864, and a self-guided auto tour plus 5 walking trails introduce the historic and natural features of this area that has remained fairly unchanged since the 19th century. Dogs are allowed throughout the park and on the trails; they are not allowed in park buildings. Dogs must be under owner control, leashed, and cleaned up after at all times.
River and Trail Outfitters 604 Valley Road Knoxville MD   301-695-5177
http://www.rivertrail.com/
Many activities are available in the scenic Harpers Ferry area, and this outfitters offer guided and instructional recreation in addition to offering a variety of watercraft rentals. Dogs are allowed on the rentals for no additional fee. If shuttle service is needed for drop-off and pick-up, dogs are allowed on the shuttle, but they must be dried off prior to boarding, very well behaved because at times the shuttle is full, and quiet. Dogs must be under owner's control, leashed, and cleaned up after at all times. Reservations are necessary.

Stores

PetSmart Pet Store 5401 Urbana Pike Frederick MD   301-662-2033
Your licensed and well-behaved leashed dog is allowed in the store.

Outdoor Restaurants

La Paz 51 South Market Street Frederick MD   301-694-8980
http://www.lapazmex.com/
Specializing in Mexican favorites with new surprise menu selections, specialty margaritas, and homemade sangria, this eatery also offers creekside dining on a spacious patio. Dogs are allowed at the outer tables. Dogs must be under owner's control/care and leashed at all times.

Freeland

Campgrounds and RV Parks

Morris Meadows 1523 Freeland Road Freeland MD   410-329-6636
http://www.morrismeadows.us
Dogs of all sizes are allowed. There are no additional pet fees. Dogs must have current shot records, may not be left unattend, and must be on no more than a 6 foot leash and cleaned up after. There are some breed restrictions. The camping and tent areas also allow dogs. There is a dog walk area at the campground.

Grantsville

Accommodations

Comfort Inn 2541 Chestnut Ridge Road Grantsville MD   301-895-5993 (877-424-6423)
Dogs are allowed for an additional fee of $10 per night per pet.

Campgrounds and RV Parks
Big Run State Park 349 Headquarters Lane Grantsville MD   301-895-5453 (888-432-CAMP (2267))
This park of about 300 acres offers land and water recreation, but since it is surrounded by the Savage River
State Forest, visitors are offered an even wider variety of options. Dogs of all sizes are allowed at no additional
fee. Dogs may not be left unattended, and they must be leashed and cleaned up after. Dogs are allowed on the
trails. The camping and tent areas also allow dogs. There is a dog walk area at the campground. There are no
electric or water hookups at the campground.
Savage River State Forest 127 Headquarters Lane Grantsville MD 301-895-5759
Over 12,000 acres of this 54,000 acre forest has been designated wildlands. It is the largest facility in the state
forest system, it preserves an important watershed area, and there are a variety of trails (maps available at the
office) and recreational opportunities. Dogs of all sizes are allowed throughout the park, in the camp area, and
on the trails. There is no additional pet fee. Dogs must be leashed and cleaned up after at all times. Fifty-two
primitive, self-registering roadside campsites with fire rings and picnic tables are available on a 1st come 1st
served basis. The camping and tent areas also allow dogs. There is a dog walk area at the campground. There
are no water hookups at the campgrounds.

Attractions

TOP 200 PLACE Spruce Forest Artisan Village 177 Casselman Road Grantsville MD   301-895-3332
http://spruceforest.org/
Dedicated to the education, preservation, and promotion to the uncommon beauty of the Appalachian culture
and their craftspeople, this agency offers a living craft village where visitors can view artisan's studios and their
craft up close or purchase handcrafted items. There are also several special events, activities, workshops, music
jams, and their "Christmas in the Village" for visitors to enjoy. Your well mannered pooch is welcome in the
village. Owners accept 100% responsibility for their pets, and dogs must be under owner's control/care, leashed,
and cleaned up after at all times.

Parks
Savage River State Forest 127 Headquarters Lane Grantsville MD   301-895-5759
Over 12,000 acres of this 54,000 acre forest has been designated wildlands. It is the largest facility in the state
forest system, it preserves an important watershed area, and there are a variety of trails (maps available at the
office) and recreational opportunities. Dogs of all sizes are allowed throughout the park, in the camp area, and
on the trails. There is no additional pet fee. Dogs must be leashed and cleaned up after at all times.

Grasonville

Accommodations
Best Western Kent Narrows Inn 3101 Main Street Grasonville MD   410-827-6767 (800-780-7234)
Dogs are allowed for an additional fee of $10 per night per pet.

Hagerstown

Accommodations
Econo Lodge 18221 Mason Dixon Rd Hagerstown MD   301-791-3560
There is a $3 per day pet fee.
Motel 6 - Hagerstown 11321 Massey Boulevard Hagerstown MD   301-582-4445 (800-466-8356)
One well-behaved family pet per room. Guest must notify front desk upon arrival. Guest is liable for any
damages. In consideration of all guests, pets must never be left unattended in the guest rooms.
Quality Inn 1101 Dual H Hagerstown MD   301-733-2700 (877-424-6423)
Dogs are allowed for an additional fee of $10 per night per pet.
Sleep Inn and Suites 18216 Colonel H K Douglas Drive Hagerstown MD   301-766-9449 (877-424-6423)
Dogs are allowed for an additional fee of $10 per night per pet.
Super 8 Halfway/Hagerstown Area 16805 Blake Rd Hagerstown MD   301-582-1992 (800-800-8000)
Dogs of all sizes are allowed. There is a $15 returnable deposit required per room. There is a $11.10 one time

per pet fee per visit. Only non-smoking rooms are used for pets. Reservations are recommended due to limited rooms for pets.

Red Roof Inn - Hagerstown - Williamsport 310 East Potomac Street Williamsport MD   301-582-3500 (800-RED-ROOF)
One well-behaved family pet per room. Guest must notify front desk upon arrival. Guest is liable for any damages. In consideration of all guests, pets must never be left unattended in the guest rooms.

Campgrounds and RV Parks

Fort Frederick State Park 11100 Fort Frederick Road Big Pool MD 301-842-2155 (888-432-CAMP(2267))
Restored to its original 1758 appearance, this site was the State's frontier defense during the French and Indian War. There are interpretive activities depicting the historical significance of this site, a number of water and land recreational pursuits, and the Western Maryland Rail Trail is only a 1/2 mile from the fort. Dogs are allowed in the park for no additional fee; they are not allowed inside the fort, park buildings, or the picnic areas. Dogs are allowed on the trails, in other areas of the park, and at the campground. They must be leashed and cleaned up after at all times. The camp area offers a camp store and 29 primitive 1st come 1st served sites with fire rings, tables, and portable toilets. The camping and tent areas also allow dogs. There is a dog walk area at the campground. There are no electric or water hookups at the campgrounds.

KOA Hagerstown/Snug Harbor 11759 Snug Harbor Lane Williamsport MD 301-223-7571
http://www.hagerstownkoa.com
Dogs of all sizes are allowed. There are no additional pet fees. Dogs must be quiet, be on no more than a 6 foot leash, and be cleaned up after. This RV park is closed during the off-season. The camping and tent areas also allow dogs. There is a dog walk area at the campground. Dogs are allowed in the camping cabins.

Yogi Bear Jellystone Park 16519 Lappans Road Williamsport MD 800-421-7116
http://www.jellystonemaryland.com
Dogs of all sizes are allowed. There are no additional pet fees. Dogs must be leashed and cleaned up after. Dogs are not allowed at the cabins. The camping and tent areas also allow dogs. There is a dog walk area at the campground.

Attractions

Antietam National Battlefield 5831 Dunker Church Road Sharpesburg MD 301-432-5124
http://www.nps.gov/anti/
The battle here led to a chain of significant historic events and they offer interpretive exhibits/programs that share its history as well as various trails for exploring the area. Dogs are allowed throughout the park, on the trails, and day use areas; they are not allowed in the National Cemetery or in park buildings. Dogs must be under owner's control, leashed, and cleaned up after at all times.

Stores

PetSmart Pet Store 17740 Garland Groh Blvd Hagerstown MD 301-665-2820
Your licensed and well-behaved leashed dog is allowed in the store.

Parks

Fort Frederick State Park 11100 Fort Frederick Road Big Pool MD 301-842-2155 (888-432-CAMP(2267))
Restored to its original 1758 appearance, this site was the states frontier defense during the French and Indian War. There are interpretive activities depicting the historical significance of this site, a number of water and land recreational pursuits, and the Western Maryland Rail Trail is only a 1/2 mile from the fort. Dogs are allowed in the park for no additional fee; they are not allowed inside the fort, park buildings, or the picnic areas. Dogs are allowed on the trails, in other areas of the park, and at the campground. They must be leashed and cleaned up after at all times.

Hancock

Accommodations

Super 8 Hancock 118 Limestone Rd Hancock MD 301-678-6101 (800-800-8000)
Dogs of all sizes are allowed. There is a $10 one time per pet fee per visit. Smoking and non-smoking rooms are available for pet rooms.

Jarrettsville

Campgrounds and RV Parks
Susquehanna State Park 3318 Rocks Chrome Hill Road Jarrettsville MD   410-557-7994 (888-432-CAMP (2267))
A variety of land and water recreation and a wide range of trails varying in length and difficulty greet visitors at this park. Dogs of all sizes are allowed at no additional fee. Dogs may not be left unattended, and they must be on no more than a 10 foot leash, and be cleaned up after. Dogs are not allowed in picnic areas or buildings. Dogs are allowed on the trails. This campground is closed during the off-season. The camping and tent areas also allow dogs. There is a dog walk area at the campground. There are no water hookups at the campground.

Parks
Rocks State Park 3318 Rocks Chrome Hill Road Jarrettsville MD   410-557-7994
Dense with forest and large boulders, this 855 acre park sitting above Deer Creek is popular for fishing and tubing and there are also many secluded areas along the creek and hiking trails that connect different areas of the park. Dogs of all sizes are allowed throughout the park for no additional fee; they must be leashed and cleaned up after at all times. Dogs are not allowed in picnic or historic areas or at the cabins.

Lexington Park

Accommodations
Days Inn Lexington Park 21847 Three Notch Road Lexington Park MD   240-725-0100 (800-329-7466)
Dogs of all sizes are allowed for an additional $8 per night per pet. Dogs must be leashed and cleaned up after.

Nanticoke

Campgrounds and RV Parks
Roaring Point 2360 Nanticoke Wharf Road Nanticoke MD   410-873-2553
http://www.roaringpoint.com
Dogs of all sizes are allowed. There are no additional pet fees. Dogs must be well behaved, not left unattended, be leashed, and cleaned up after. This RV park is closed during the off-season. The camping and tent areas also allow dogs. There is a dog walk area at the campground.

North East

Accommodations
Knights Inn 262 Belle Hill Rd Elkton MD   410-392-6680
There is a $10 per day pet fee.
Motel 6 - Elkton 223 Belle Hill Road Elkton MD   410-392-5020 (800-466-8356)
One well-behaved family pet per room. Guest must notify front desk upon arrival. Guest is liable for any damages. In consideration of all guests, pets must never be left unattended in the guest rooms.

Campgrounds and RV Parks
Elk Neck State Park 4395 Turkey Point Road North East MD   410-287-5333 (888-432-CAMP (2267))
This peninsula park is home to the Turkey Point Lighthouse and offers a diversified topography for a variety of activities and recreation. Dogs of all sizes are allowed at no additional fee. Dogs may not be left unattended outside, and they must be leashed and cleaned up after. Dogs are not allowed on the beach, in buildings, or in day use areas. Dogs are allowed in the NE loop, at the "Y" pet area, and on the trails. The camping and tent areas also allow dogs. There is a dog walk area at the campground.

Outdoor Restaurants
Bayard House 11 Bohemia Avenue Chesapeake City MD   410-885-5040
http://www.bayardhouse.com/

Located along the waterfront, this eatery features traditional Eastern Shore cuisine with a touch of European influence and al fresco dining. Dogs are allowed at the outer tables, and they must be under owner's control/care and leashed at all times.

Ocean City

Accommodations

Clarion Resort Fontainebleau Hotel 10100 Coastal H Ocean City MD   410-524-3535 (877-424-6423)
Dogs are allowed for an additional fee of $38.15 per night per pet.
Serene Hotel and Suites 12004 Coastal H Ocean City MD   410-250-4000
Dogs of all sizes are allowed. There is a pet policy to sign at check in and there are no additional pet fees.

Campgrounds and RV Parks

Frontier Town 8428 Stephen Decatur H Berlin MD   410-641-0880
http://www.frontiertown.com
Friendly dogs of all sizes are allowed. There are no additional pet fees. Dogs may not be left unattended, must be leashed, and cleaned up after. Dogs are not allowed in the rentals. There are some breed restrictions. This RV park is closed during the off-season. The camping and tent areas also allow dogs. There is a dog walk area at the campground.
Ocean City Campground 105 70th Street Ocean City MD   410-524-7601
http://www.occamping.com
Dogs of all sizes are allowed. There are no additional pet fees. Pets must be on a leash and exercised outside of the campground property. Dogs must be leashed and cleaned up after. Pets cannot be left unattended inside or outside of camper at any time. No pets in tents or RV's without air conditioning. The camping and tent areas also allow dogs.
Fort Whaley 11224 Dale Road Whaleysville MD   410-641-9785
http://www.fortwhaley.com
Dogs of all sizes are allowed. There are no additional pet fees. Dogs must be well behaved, leashed, and cleaned up after. Dogs may only be left inside of your unit if there is air conditioning on and if they will be quiet. The camping and tent areas also allow dogs. There is a dog walk area at the campground.

Beaches

Ocean City Beaches Route 528 Ocean City MD   1-800-OC-OCEAN
Dogs are only allowed during certain times of the year on this city beach. Pets are not allowed on the beach or boardwalk at any time from May 1 through September 30. The rest of the year, dogs are allowed on the beach and boardwalk, but must be on leash and people must clean up after them.

Outdoor Restaurants

Macky's Bayside Bar and Grill 54th Street on the Bay Ocean City MD   410-723-5565
http://www.mackys.com/
Located on the waterfront, this steak and seafood bar and grill offers seating on their private beach with tables and chairs set to the water's edge. Dogs are welcome at the outer tables on the sand. Dogs must be under owner's control/care and be leashed at all times.

Events

Victorian Christmas Main Street/H 818 Berlin MD   410-641-1554
http://www.berlinmdcc.org/main.asp
From a Victorian Fashion show-set with teas, a parade, carriage rides, animated story window displays, to breakfast with Santa, and everything else you can imagine from an old-fashioned Victorian Christmas can probably be experienced or found at this yearly event. Also, for some "cool" pre-Christmas shopping, they have a "Christmas in July" party that is usually held annually mid-July. Your well mannered pooch is welcome to join you at the festivities. Dogs must be under owner's control/care, leashed, and cleaned up after at all times. Dogs are not allowed in the buildings.

Oxford

Accommodations
Combsberry 4837 Evergreen Road Oxford MD   410-226-5353
http://www.combsberry.net/
Sitting lakeside at the end of a private dirt road is this beautiful historic brick mansion surrounded by magnolias, willows, and formal gardens. Dogs of all sizes are allowed for no additional fee. Dogs must be well behaved, leashed, and cleaned up after at all times.

Pocomoke

Accommodations
Days Inn Pocomoke 1540 Ocean Hwy on US 13 Pocomoke MD   410-957-3000 (800-329-7466)
Dogs of all sizes are allowed. There is a $10 per night pet fee per pet.
Quality Inn 825 Ocean H Pocomoke MD   410-957-1300 (877-424-6423)
Dogs are allowed for no additional pet fee.

Princess Anne

Accommodations
Waterloo Country Inn 28822 Mt. Vernon Road Princess Anne MD   410-651-0883
Dogs of all sizes are allowed. There are no additional pet fees. They request you keep large dogs off the beds and furniture, and there is only 1 pet friendly room available.

Queen Anne

Campgrounds and RV Parks
Tuckahoe State Park 13070 Crouse Mill Road Queen Anne MD   410-820-1668 (888-432-CAMP (2267))
This park offers a 60 acre lake, 20 miles of scenic multi-use trails, and an arboretum that encompasses 500 acres of park land with almost three miles of surfaced walkways featuring tagged native species of trees and shrubs. Dogs of all sizes are allowed at no additional fee. Dogs must be on leash, and when in camp, cleaned up after. Dogs are allowed on the trails, but not in the lake area. This campground is closed during the off-season. The camping and tent areas also allow dogs. There is a dog walk area at the campground. There are no water hookups at the campground.

Rock Hall

Accommodations
Huntingfield Manor Bed & Breakfast 4928 Eastern Neck Rd Rock Hall MD   410-639-7779
http://travelassist.com/reg/md104s.html
This B&B is located on a 70 acre working farm. Pets are allowed in the cottage which is not designated as smoking or non-smoking. There are no additional pet fees.

Parks
Eastern Neck National Wildlife Refuge 1730 Eastern Neck Road Rock Hall MD   410-639-7056
Observation towers, boardwalks, and various trails allow visitors to truly explore and enjoy this wildlife refuge. They suggest visitors pick up a map at the entrance. Dogs are allowed throughout the park and on the trails. Dogs must be under owner's control, leashed, and cleaned up after at all times.

Outdoor Restaurants
Miss Virginia's Crabcakes 5793 Kent Avenue Rock Hall MD   410-639-7871
http://www.rockhallmd.com/crabcakes/
This is a popular "to go" only establishment for the one of a kind Miss Virginia's Crabcakes, and you can get

them already prepared, or frozen to take home.

Salisbury

Accommodations
Best Western Salisbury Plaza 1735 N Salisbury Blvd Salisbury MD   410-546-1300 (800-780-7234)
Dogs are allowed for an additional fee of $10 per night per pet.
Comfort Inn 2701 N Salisbury Blvd Salisbury MD   410-543-4666 (877-424-6423)
Dogs are allowed for no additional pet fee.

Stores
PetSmart Pet Store 105 E Northpoint Blvd Salisbury MD   410-546-4822
Your licensed and well-behaved leashed dog is allowed in the store.

Snow Hill

Accommodations
River House Inn Bed and Breakfast 201 E Market St Snow Hill MD   410-632-2722
http://www.riverhouseinn.com/
This B&B is a National Register Victorian home located on the Pocomoke River on Maryland's Eastern Shore.

Campgrounds and RV Parks
Pocomoke River State Forest and Park 3461 Worcester Highway/H113 Snow Hill MD   401-632-2566
888-432-CAMP (2267)
There is a long list of water and land recreational opportunities here in addition to being an ecology school-room
with its stand of loblolly pine, the cypress swamps that border the Pocomoke River and the wide variety of plant,
animal, bird life that make their home here. Dogs of all sizes are allowed for no additional fee at Milburn Landing;
they are not allowed at Shad Landing. Only registered campers are to have pets in the park; day use only is not
allowed. Dogs must be leashed and cleaned up after. The camp areas all have picnic tables and fire rings with
hot water showers, flush toilets, a laundry tub, playground, and a dump station close by. The camping and tent
areas also allow dogs. There is a dog walk area at the campground. There are no water hookups at the
campgrounds.

St Marys Peninsula

Campgrounds and RV Parks
Point Lookout State Park 11175 Point Lookout Road Scotland MD   301-872-5688 (888-432-CAMP(2267))
Rich in folk lore, historical significance, recreation, and educational opportunities, this beautiful peninsula park
has much to offer. Dogs are allowed throughout the park and at certain designated areas for no additional fee.
Although dogs are not allowed on the public swim beach, they are allowed on the "Pet Beach". Dogs are
permitted in Malone Circle, Tulip Loop, Hoffman's Loop, Green's Point Loop, on the pavement part of the
causeway, and on the beach (north of causeway) to the entrance of Tanner's Creek. Dogs are not allowed at
picnic areas, day use areas, or on other trails. Dogs must be leashed and cleaned up after at all times. The
campground offers a variety of camp sites, grills, picnic tables, a camp store, and a dump station. The camping
and tent areas also allow dogs. There is a dog walk area at the campground.

Attractions
Bunky's Charter Boats 14448 Solomons Island Road S Solomons MD   410-326-3241
Although dogs are not allowed on the public cruises, they are allowed on the boat rentals for no additional fee.
They offer 16 foot skiffs for exploring the Patuxent River. Dogs must be firmly under owner's control/care at all
times, and be leashed. Dogs must be well mannered.

Beaches

Elm's Beach Park Bay Forest Road Hermanville MD   301-475-4572
The park is located on Chesapeake Bay, not on the ocean. Enjoy great views of the bay or swim at the beach. Dogs on leash are allowed at the beach. People need to clean up after their pets. Take Route 235 to Bay Forest Road and then go 3 miles. The park will be on the left.

Parks
Point Lookout State Park 11175 Point Lookout Road Scotland MD   301-872-5688 (888-432-CAMP(2267))
Rich in folk lore, historical significance, recreation, and educational opportunities, this beautiful peninsula park has much to offer. Dogs are allowed throughout the park and at certain designated areas for no additional fee. Although dogs are not allowed on the public swim beach, they are allowed on the "Pet Beach". Dogs are permitted in Malone Circle, Tulip Loop, Hoffman's Loop, Green's Point Loop, on the pavement part of the causeway, and on the beach (north of causeway) to the entrance of Tanner's Creek. Dogs are not allowed at picnic areas, day use areas, or on other trails. Dogs must be leashed and cleaned up after at all times.
Jefferson Patterson Park and Museum 10515 Mackall Road St Leonard MD   410-586-8500
http://www.jefpat.org/
This state history and archaeology museum is dedicated to educating and preserving the history and cultures of the past 12,000 years of the Chesapeake Bay region. Dogs are allowed throughout the park, along the riverfront, and on the trails; they are not allowed in the museum or other park buildings. Dogs must be well behaved, leashed, and cleaned up after at all times.

St Michaels

Accommodations
Five Gables Inn and Spa 209 North Talbot Street St Michaels MD   410-745-0100 (877-466-0100)
http://www.fivegables.com/
This inn offers 19th century ambiance, an indoor pool and spa, numerous amenities, and there is also an upscale pet boutique among the shops. One dog up to 75 pounds is allowed for an additional $35 one time fee. Dogs must be leashed or crated and cleaned up after.
The Inn at Perry Cabin 308 Watkins Lane St Michaels MD   410-745-2200 (866-278-9601)
Rich in colonial history, this grand manor house resort now features numerous amenities, a horizon-edged swimming pool, a spa, docking facilities, and a lot more. Dogs up to 75 pounds are allowed with advance notification for an additional fee of $75 per pet per stay. Dogs must be well mannered, leashed, and cleaned up after.

Attractions
St. Michaels Harbor Shuttle 101 N Harbor Road St Michaels MD   410-924-2198
This seasonal watercraft service will allow dogs on board for the 25 minute sightseeing tours or for water taxi service for no additional fee. Dogs must be under owner's control/care and leashed at all times.

Stores
Flying Freds Gifts for Pets 202 N Talbot Street St Michaels MD   410-745-9601
http://www.flyingfreds.com/
In addition to a variety of pet products, gifts, and supplies, they also host various events such as Yappy Hour on the first Friday of each month, the Jack Russell races, pooch porch parties, and more. Dogs must be under owner's control, leashed, and cleaned up after all times.

Outdoor Restaurants
St Michaels Crab House 305 Mulberry Street St Michaels MD   410-745-3737
http://www.stmichaelscrabhouse.com/
This historic building now house a "made to order" crab eatery with outdoor dining options. Dogs are allowed at the outer tables. Dogs must be under owner's control/care and leashed at all times.

Thurmont

Campgrounds and RV Parks
Catoctin Mountain Park 6602 Foxville Road Thurmont MD   301-663-9388

http://www.nps.gov/cato/
This 5,810-acre hardwood forest park comes complete with rushing streams, scenic vistas, and a variety of recreational pursuits. Dogs of all sizes are allowed at no additional fee. Dogs may not be left unattended, and they must be quiet, be on no more than a 6 foot leash, and be cleaned up after. Dogs are allowed at Owens Creek Campground and on the trails. They are not allowed in camps 1, 2 and 4, the youth camp, or in the Adirondack backcountry shelters. Dogs are also not allowed at the waterfall in the adjoining state park, or left in the car at that location. This campground is closed during the off-season. The camping and tent areas also allow dogs. There is a dog walk area at the campground. There are no electric or water hookups at the campground.
Grambrill State Park 14039 Catoctin Hollow Road Thurmont MD   301-271-7574 (888-432-CAMP (2267))
Some points of interests at this park of over 1,100 acres include 3 native stone scenic overlooks, a good variety of trails, interpretive programs, and a nature center. Dogs of all sizes are allowed at no additional fee. Dogs may not be left unattended, and they must be leashed and cleaned up after. Dogs are allowed on the trails and throughout the park, unless otherwise posted. This campground is closed during the off-season. The camping and tent areas also allow dogs. There is a dog walk area at the campground. There are no water hookups at the campground.

Tilghman Island

Accommodations
The Tilghman Island Inn 21384 Coopertown Road Tilghman Island MD   401-886-2141 (800-866-2141)
In addition to providing a scenic setting, this waterside inn hosts several special events through the season, and also provides a venue for special occasions. Dogs are allowed for an additional $15 per night per pet in the first floor rooms. Dogs must be well behaved, leashed, and cleaned up after.

Attractions
Dockside Express Cruises Phillips Wharf Tilghman MD   888-312-7847
This charter company shares the rich and colorful history of the state's Eastern Shore, and they will allow your pooch to come aboard on the private charters (prices start around $300 per hour). They are not allowed on any of the public tours. Dogs must be very well mannered and friendly. Dogs must be under owner's control/care at all times.
Tilghman Island Marina 6140 Mariners Court Tilghman Island MD   410-886-2500
http://www.tilghmanmarina.com/
This marina offers a park-like setting overlooking the bay, and in addition to a wide variety of watercraft rentals and charters, they are also host to numerous special events/parties/feasts. Dogs are allowed at the marina and on the watercraft rentals for no additional fee. They usually prefer that larger dogs use the pontoon boats, however if a quilt is brought to protect the seats, they may be allowed on the other watercraft. Dogs must be well mannered, under owner's control, leashed, and cleaned up after at all times.

Washington Suburbs

Accommodations
Sheraton College Park Hotel 4095 Powder Mill Rd. Beltsville MD   301-937-4422 (888-625-5144)
Dogs of all sizes are allowed. There are no additional pet fees. Dogs are not allowed to be left alone in the room.
Days Inn Camp Springs/Andrews AFB 5001 Mercedes Blvd Camp Springs MD   301-423-2323 (800-329-7466)
Dogs of all sizes are allowed. There is a $10 per night pet fee per pet.
Motel 6 - Washington, DC SE - Camp Springs 5701 Allentown Road Camp Springs MD   301-702-1061 (800-466-8356)
One well-behaved family pet per room. Guest must notify front desk upon arrival. Guest is liable for any damages. In consideration of all guests, pets must never be left unattended in the guest rooms.
Motel 6 - Washington, DC - Capitol Heights 75 Hampton Park Boulevard Capitol Heights MD   301-499-0800 (800-466-8356)
One well-behaved family pet per room. Guest must notify front desk upon arrival. Guest is liable for any damages. In consideration of all guests, pets must never be left unattended in the guest rooms.
Comfort Inn at Shady Grove 16216 Frederick Road Gaithersburg MD   301-330-0023 (877-424-6423)
Dogs are allowed for an additional fee of $15 per night per pet.
Motel 6 - Washington, DC - Gaithersburg 497 Quince Orchard Road Gaithersburg MD   301-977-3311 (800-466-8356)

One well-behaved family pet per room. Guest must notify front desk upon arrival. Guest is liable for any damages. In consideration of all guests, pets must never be left unattended in the guest rooms.
Residence Inn by Marriott 9721 Washington Blvd Gaithersburg MD 301-590-3003
Dogs of all sizes are allowed. There is a $75 one time fee and a pet policy to sign at check in.
TownePlace Suites Gaithersburg 212 Perry Parkway Gaithersburg MD 301-590-2300
Dogs of all sizes are allowed. There is a $75 one time pet fee per visit and a $5 per night additional pet fee.
Residence Inn by Marriott 6320 Golden Triangle Drive Greenbelt MD 301-982-1600
Dogs of all sizes are allowed. There is a $75 one time fee and a pet policy to sign at check in.
Red Roof Inn - Washington, DC - Lanham 9050 Lanham Severn Road Lanham MD 301-731-8830 (800-RED-ROOF)
One well-behaved family pet per room. Guest must notify front desk upon arrival. Guest is liable for any damages. In consideration of all guests, pets must never be left unattended in the guest rooms.
Motel 6 - Washington, DC NE - Laurel 3510 Old Annapolis Road Laurel MD 301-497-1544 (800-466-8356)
One well-behaved family pet per room. Guest must notify front desk upon arrival. Guest is liable for any damages. In consideration of all guests, pets must never be left unattended in the guest rooms.
Red Roof Inn - Washington, DC - Laurel 12525 Laurel Bowie Road Laurel MD 301-498-8811 (800-RED-ROOF)
One well-behaved family pet per room. Guest must notify front desk upon arrival. Guest is liable for any damages. In consideration of all guests, pets must never be left unattended in the guest rooms.
Best Western Washington Gateway Hotel 1251 W Montgomery Ave Rockville MD 301-424-4940 (800-780-7234)
Dogs are allowed for an additional fee of $10 per night per pet. Pit Bulls are not allowed.
Red Roof Inn - Washington, DC - Rockville 16001 Shady Grove Road Rockville MD 301-987-0965 (800-RED-ROOF)
One well-behaved family pet per room. Guest must notify front desk upon arrival. Guest is liable for any damages. In consideration of all guests, pets must never be left unattended in the guest rooms.
Woodfin Suite Hotel 1380 Piccard Drive Rockville MD 301-590-9880
All well-behaved dogs are welcome. Every room is a suite with either a wet bar or full kitchen. Hotel amenities includes a pool, free video movies and a complimentary hot breakfast buffet. There is a $5 per day pet fee per pet. If you are staying for one month, the pet fee is $50 for the month.
Days Inn Waldorf 11370 Days Court Waldorf MD 301-932-9200 (800-329-7466)
Dogs of all sizes are allowed. There is a $15 per night pet fee per pet.

Campgrounds and RV Parks
Cherry Hill Park 9800 Cherry Hill Road College Park MD 800-801-6449
http://www.cherryhillpark.com
Dogs of all sizes are allowed. There are no additional pet fees. Dogs must be well behaved, not be left unattended, be leashed, and cleaned up after. The camping and tent areas also allow dogs. There is a dog walk area at the campground.
Duncan's Family Campground 5381 Sands Beach Road Lothian MD 410-741-9558
http://www.duncansfamilycampground.com
Dogs of all sizes are allowed. There are no additional pet fees. Dogs must be quiet, leashed, and cleaned up after. Dogs may not be left tied up at the site. The camping and tent areas also allow dogs. There is a dog walk area at the campground.

Stores
Petco Pet Store 10464 Baltimore Avenue Beltsville MD 301-937-1222
Your licensed and well-behaved leashed dog is allowed in the store.
PetSmart Pet Store 6800 Wisconsin Ave Bethesda MD 240-497-1350
Your licensed and well-behaved leashed dog is allowed in the store.
The Posh Pooch 8009 Norfolk Avenue Bethesda MD 301-652-1199
www.theposhpooch.com
This comprehensive pet store offers more than just pet treats, necessities, or the "newest" such as the new crash tested doggy car-seat harnesses; there are also numerous events, holiday themed gifts, decorative items for inside and out of the home, and even hand blown glass ornaments in 106 breeds. Dogs are welcome inside the store; they must be well behaved, leashed, and cleaned up after.
Petco Pet Store 3034 Donnell Drive Forestville MD 301-420-0875
Your licensed and well-behaved leashed dog is allowed in the store.
PetSmart Pet Store 220 Kentlands Blvd Gaithersburg MD 301-977-9677
Your licensed and well-behaved leashed dog is allowed in the store.
Petco Pet Store 275 Muddy Branch Rd Gaithersburg MD 301-975-9888
Your licensed and well-behaved leashed dog is allowed in the store.
PetSmart Pet Store 20924 Frederick Rd Germantown MD 301-916-2029

Your licensed and well-behaved leashed dog is allowed in the store.
Petco Pet Store 12960 Middlebrook Rd #520A Germantown MD   301-515-8153
Your licensed and well-behaved leashed dog is allowed in the store.
PetSmart Pet Store 7475 Greenbelt Rd Greenbelt MD   301-220-1295
Your licensed and well-behaved leashed dog is allowed in the store.
PetSmart Pet Store 5154 Nicholson Lane Kensington MD   301-770-1343
Your licensed and well-behaved leashed dog is allowed in the store.
PetSmart Pet Store 10464 Campus Way S Way Largo MD   301-350-4099
Your licensed and well-behaved leashed dog is allowed in the store.
PetSmart Pet Store 13600 Baltimore Ave, Ste 160 Laurel MD   301-497-3253
Your licensed and well-behaved leashed dog is allowed in the store.
Petco Pet Store 915 Washington Blvd #83 Laurel MD   301-490-7452
Your licensed and well-behaved leashed dog is allowed in the store.
PetSmart Pet Store 6005 Oxon Hill Rd Oxon Hill MD   301-839-4900
Your licensed and well-behaved leashed dog is allowed in the store.
Petco Pet Store 1507 Rockville Pike Rockville MD   301-984-9733
Your licensed and well-behaved leashed dog is allowed in the store.
PetSmart Pet Store 12020 Cherry Hill Rd Silver Spring MD   301-586-8262
Your licensed and well-behaved leashed dog is allowed in the store.
PetSmart Pet Store 3045 Festival Way Waldorf MD   301-705-5308
Your licensed and well-behaved leashed dog is allowed in the store.
Petco Pet Store 3077 Waldorf Market Place Waldorf MD   301-374-2297
Your licensed and well-behaved leashed dog is allowed in the store.

Parks

Glen Echo Park 7300 MacArthur Blvd Glen Echo MD   301-492-6229
http://www.nps.gov/glec
Some of the highlights at this park include a carousel, a Spanish ballroom, weekend "night" programs, and year-around events and educational activities. Dogs are allowed throughout the grounds and at the events. Dogs must be friendly to both people and other animals, under owner's control, leashed, and cleaned up after at all times.
Greenbelt Park 6565 Greenbelt Rd Greenbelt MD   301-344-3944
http://www.nps.gov/gree/
Dogs must be leashed in this park.
TOP 200 PLACE **Chesapeake and Ohio Canal National Historical Park** 11710 MacArthur Blvd, Great Falls
Tavern Visitor Center Potomac MD   301-767-3714
http://www.nps.gov/choh
Dedicated to preserving and educating the public about the canal era and America's transportation history, several visitor centers can be found along this 184 mile long canal trail. Dogs are allowed throughout the park and on the canal trail. Dogs must be under owner's control, leashed, and cleaned up after at all times.
Wheaton Regional Park 2000 Shorefield Rd Wheaton MD
http://www.our-kids.com/wheaton.htm
An excellent park for kids and dogs. There are a number of annual dog events here and trails to jog or walk on. Dogs must be leashed in the park except within the fenced off-leash dog area.

Off-Leash Dog Parks

Black Hills Regional Park Dog Park 20930 Lake Ridge Rd Boyds MD   301-972-9396
http://www.mc-dog.org/black_hill.html
This fenced dog park is located in the Black Hills Regional Park. The park also has over ten miles of trails to hike with your leashed dog.
Green Run Dog Park Bickerstaff Rd and I-370 Gaithersburg MD
This dog park is run by the city of Gaithersburg and charges a $25 fee for non-residents to use the park.
Ridge Road Recreational Dog Park 21155 Frederick Road Germantown MD   301-972-9396
http://www.mc-dog.org/ridge_rd.html
This is a fenced off-leash dog park.
Laurel Dog Park Brock Bridge Road Laurel MD   410-222-7317
This fenced dog park has two areas, one for larger dogs and one for small or shy dogs.
Wheaton Regional Park Dog Exercise Area 11717 Orebaugh Ave Silver Spring MD   301-680-3803
http://www.mc-dog.org/wheaton_main.html
This fenced off-leash dog park is located in Wheaton Regional Park. Use the Orebaugh Ave entrance to the park.

Outdoor Restaurants
Wok Inn Restaurant 4924 Saint Elmo Ave Bethesda MD   301-986-8590
Dogs are allowed at the outdoor tables.
Pepino's Trattoria Italiano 15721 Columbia Pike Burtonsville MD   301-384-1655
This restaurant serves Italian food. Dogs are allowed at the outdoor tables and served water.
Chicken Out Rotisserie 1560 Rockville Pike Rockville MD   301-230-2020
Dogs are allowed at the outdoor tables.
Red Dog Cafe 8301 Grubb Road Silver Spring MD   301-588-6300
http://www.reddogcafe.com/
Located at the Rock Creek Shopping Center, this full service restaurant also offers outdoor seating and catering.
Dogs are allowed at the outside tables; they must be leashed and under owner's control/care at all times.
Savory Cafe 7071 Carroll Avenue Takoma Park MD   301-270-2233
Well-behaved leashed dogs are allowed at the outdoor tables. Thanks to one of our readersfor recommending
this dog-friendly cafe.

Day Kennels
PetsHotel by PetsMart Day Kennel 6800 Wisconsin Ave. Bethesda MD   240-497-1980
http://www.petsmart.com/PETsHOTEL/
This PetSmart pet store offers day care, day camp and overnight care. You may drop off and pick up your dog
during the hours the store is open seven days a week. Dogs must have proof of current rabies, DPP and
Bordatella vaccinations.

Woodbine

Campgrounds and RV Parks
Ramblin Pines Campground 801 Hoods Mill Road Woodbine MD   410-795-5161 (800-550-8733)
http://www.ramblinpines.com
Dogs of all sizes are allowed. There are no additional pet fees. Dogs may not be left unattended, and they must
be leashed and cleaned up after. There is a fenced in dog run area where pets may be off lead. There are some
breed restrictions. The camping and tent areas also allow dogs. There is a dog walk area at the campground.

Chapter 13

Washington D.C.
Dog Travel Guide

Washington

Accommodations

Crowne Plaza 14th and K Street NW Washington DC   202-682-0111 (877-270-6405)
One dog up to 50 pounds or 2 dogs totaling no more than a combined weight of 50 pounds is allowed for a $250 refundable pet deposit per room.
Hilton 1919 Connecticut Avenue NW Washington DC   202-483-3000
Dogs are allowed for no additional pet fee.
Hotel George 15 E Street, NW Washington DC   202-347-4200
http://www.hotelgeorge.com
This Kimpton boutique hotel allows dogs of all sizes. There are no additional pet fees.
Hotel Harrington 436 11th Street NW Washington DC   202-628-8140
Dogs of all sizes are allowed. There are no additional pet fees. Dogs are not allowed to be left unattended.
Hotel Helix 1430 Rhode Island Ave Washington DC   202-462-9001
http://www.hotelhelix.com/
Well-behaved dogs of all sizes are welcome at this hotel. The boutique hotel offers both rooms and suites. Amenities include room service, and a 24 hour on-site exercise room. There are no pet fees.
Hotel Madera 1310 New Hampshire Ave Washington DC   202-296-7600
http://www.hotelmadera.com/
Well-behaved dogs of all sizes are welcome at this boutique hotel. Amenities include an evening wine hour, and room service. There are no pet fees.
Hotel Monaco 700 F Street NW Washington DC   202-628-7177
http://www.monaco-dc.com/
Well-behaved dogs of all sizes are welcome. There is no pet fee.
Hotel Palomar 2121 P Street NW Washington DC   202-448-1800 (877-866-3070)
http://www.hotelpalomar-dc.com
This Kimpton boutique hotel allows dogs of all sizes. There are no additional pet fees.
Hotel Rouge 1315 16th Street NW Washington DC   202-232-8000
http://www.rougehotel.com/
Well-behaved dogs of all sizes are welcome at this luxury boutique hotel. Amenities include complimentary high speed Internet access in the rooms, 24 hour room service, and a 24 hour on-site fitness room. There are no pet fees.
Hotel Washington 515 15th St NW Washington DC   202-638-5900
http://www.hotelwashington.com/
There are no additional pet fees.
L'Enfant Plaza Hotel 480 L'Enfant Plaza, SW Washington DC   202-484-1000
This centrally located hotel in Washington, DC is near the Smithsonian, the National Mall and all of the major attractions. Rooms and suites are available. Pets are welcome to accompany guests at the hotel.
Marriott Wardman Park Hotel 2660 Woodley Road NW Washington DC   202-328-2000 (800-228-9290)
Dogs up to 50 pounds are allowed. There is a $50 one time additional pet fee. Dogs must be well behaved, leashed, cleaned up after, and the Do Not Disturb sign put on the door and the front desk notified if they are in the room alone.
Motel 6 - Washington 6711 Georgia Avenue Washington DC   202-722-1600 (800-466-8356)
One well-behaved family pet per room. Guest must notify front desk upon arrival. Guest is liable for any damages. In consideration of all guests, pets must never be left unattended in the guest rooms.
Park Hyatt Washington 1201 24th St NW Washington DC   202-789-1234
There are no additional pet fees.
Red Roof Inn - Washington, DC - Downtown 500 H Street Northwest Washington DC   202-289-5959 (800-RED-ROOF)
One well-behaved family pet per room. Guest must notify front desk upon arrival. Guest is liable for any damages. In consideration of all guests, pets must never be left unattended in the guest rooms.
Residence Inn by Marriott 333 E Street SW Washington DC   282-484-8280
Dogs of all sizes are allowed. There is a $200 one time fee plus $10 per night per room and a pet policy to sign at check in.
Residence Inn by Marriott 2120 P Street NW Washington DC   202-466-6800
Dogs of all sizes are allowed. There is a $75 one time fee and a pet policy to sign at check in.
Residence Inn by Marriott 1199 Vermont Avenue NW Washington DC   202-898-1100
Dogs of all sizes are allowed. There is a $150 one time fee plus $8 per night per room and a pet policy to sign at check in.
Sofitel Lafayette Square 806 15th Street N.W. Washington DC   202-730-8441

http://www.sofitel.com
There are no additional pet fees.
The Fairmont, Washington DC 2401 M Street NW Washington DC   202-429-2400 (800-257-7544)
http://www.fairmont.com/washington/
This elegant hotel surrounds visitors inside and out with the luxurious colors of nature, and the 415 spacious, beautifully appointed guestrooms offer features for the business or leisure traveler. They offer 'Gold Floor' accommodations, a garden courtyard, gift shop, restaurants and lounge, in room dining, an indoor pool and spa, and numerous in room amenities. Dogs of all sizes are welcome for no additional fee; there is a pet policy to sign at check in. Dogs may not be left alone in the room at any time, and they must be cleaned up after. They also feature the 'Very Important Dog' program where your pet is greeted with healthy treats, water, and a placemat. Guests with pets also receive 5% of their room rate donated to the Animal Rescue League, walking maps, a list of pet-friendly restaurants, cafes and stores, and a special 'Paw' sign for the room.
The Jefferson Hotel 1200 16th St. NW Washington DC   202-347-2200
Well-behaved dogs of any size are welcome. There is a $25 per day additional pet fee.
The Madison, A Loews Hotel 1177 Fifteenth St. NW Washington DC   202-862-1600
All well-behaved dogs of any size are welcome. This upscale hotel offers their "Loews Loves Pets" program which includes special pet treats, local dog walking routes, and a list of nearby pet-friendly places to visit. There are no pet fees.
The Williard - Washington 1401 Pennsylvania Avenue NW Washington DC   202-628-9100
One dog up to 40 pounds is allowed for an additional one time pet fee of $100.
Topaz Hotel 1733 N Street NW Washington DC   202-393-3000 (800-775-1202)
http://www.topazhotel.com
This Kimpton boutique hotel allows dogs of all sizes. There are no additional pet fees.

Transportation Systems
WMATA Regional Washington DC   202-962-1234
http://www.wmata.com
Small dogs in carriers are allowed on the buses and trains. Pets must remain in the carrier, with no possibility that the pet can get out.

Attractions
Capitol River Cruises 31st and K St, NW Washington DC   301-460-7447
http://www.capitolrivercruises.com/
Dogs are allowed on these water tours of Washington on the Potomac River. The 1 hour tour passes most of the major attractions downtown.

FDR Memorial

FDR Memorial National Mall Washington DC

http://www.nps.gov/fdrm/index.htm
Leashed dogs are allowed in the FDR Memorial, which is entirely outdoors. There is a statue of FDR's dog for your dog to pose with. There are audio tours of the memorial available as well.

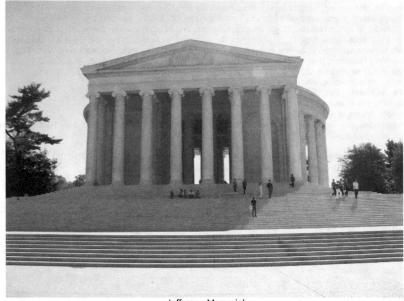
Jefferson Memorial

National Mall

Fletcher's Boat House 4940 Canal Rd NW Washington DC 202-244-0461
http://www.fletchersboathouse.com/
Rent a canoe or a boat on the C & O Canal or the Potomac River.
Jefferson Memorial National Mall Washington DC
http://www.nps.gov/thje/index.htm
According to the National Park Service, well behaved dogs are allowed on leash except in the area underneath the dome.
Lincoln Memorial National Mall Washington DC
http://www.nps.gov/linc/index.htm
According to the National Park Service, well behaved, leashed dogs are allowed at the memorial except underneath the dome. This allows a pretty close view of the statue for your pup.
TOP 200 PLACE **National Mall** Independence Ave and 14th St. Washington DC
http://www.nps.gov/nama
Dogs are permitted on the National Mall on leash. According to the National Park Service, they are permitted up to the monuments except in indoor or covered areas. The mall is two miles long and is an excellent place for dog walking downtown. You may get up-close views of the Capital, White House and most of the Monuments. Dogs are not permitted on the walkways at the Vietnam or Korean War Memorials or inside the Washington Monument.

Stores

Metro Pet Shop 4220 Fessenden Street NW Washington DC 202-966-7387
This dog boutique features a good variety of treats, dining ware, toys, apparel, accessories, bedding, carriers, cages, hygiene/health items, and gifts. They are open from 10 am to 7 pm Monday through Friday; from 10 am to 6 pm on Saturday, and from Noon to 5 pm on Sunday. Your well mannered, leashed, dog is allowed to explore the shop with you. Please clean up after your pet.
Petco Pet Store 3505 Connecticut Avenue Washington DC 202-686-0901
Your licensed and well-behaved leashed dog is allowed in the store.

Parks

C & O Canal Towpath

C & O Canal Towpath M Street Washington DC 301-739-4200
http://www.fred.net/kathy/canal.html
The 184 mile towpath extends all the way from Georgetown, in Washington, DC to Cumberland, MD. It is a dirt

trail and can be accessed at many points along the way. Dogs must be leashed on the towpath.
Capital Crescent Trail Water Street, NW Washington DC
This paved bike trail starts in Georgetown and heads to the Maryland Suburbs. Dogs must be leashed on the trail.
TOP 200 PLACE **National Arboretum** 3501 New York Ave NE Washington DC   202-245-2726
http://www.ars-grin.gov/na/
The National Arboretum allows dogs on leash. There are miles of walking trails here through the many beautiful gardens.
Rock Creek Park   Washington DC   202-426-6828
http://www.nps.gov/rocr/
Rock Creek Park is a large city park run by the National Park Service. Dogs on leash are allowed in the park. There is a paved trail and lots of picnic areas, trails and activities. The park extends from near downtown Washington to Maryland.

Outdoor Restaurants
Bangkok Bistro 3251 Prospect Street NW Washington DC   202-337-2424
This restaurant serves Asian cuisine. Dogs are allowed at the outdoor tables. Water is provided for your pet.
Dupont Italian Kitchen and Bar 1637 17th Street NW Washington DC   202-328-3222
This restaurant and bar serves Italian. Dogs are allowed at the outdoor tables.
Furin's of Georgetown 2805 M St NW Washington DC 202-965-1000
Dogs are allowed at the outdoor tables.
Guapos Mexican Cuisine and Cantina 4515 Wisconsin Ave NW Washington DC   202-686-3588
http://www.guaporestaurant.com
This restaurant and bar serves Mexican. Dogs are allowed at the outdoor tables.
Paper Moon 1073 31st St NW Washington DC   202-965-6666
Dogs are allowed at the outdoor tables.
Park Place Gourmet 1634 I St NW Washington DC   202-783-4496
Dogs are allowed at the outdoor tables.
Pasha Bistro 1523 17th St NW Washington DC   202-588-7477
http://www.pashabistro.com/
This eatery offers Mediterranean cuisine and during the Summer there is outside dining. Dogs are allowed at the outer tables; they must be under owner's control/care at all times.
Sweetlicks 1704 R Street NW Washington DC   202-797-2736
This ice cream shop allows pets at their outdoor seating.

Chapter 14

Virginia
Dog Travel Guide

Ashland

Accommodations
Days Inn Ashland 806 England St Ashland VA   804-798-4262 (800-329-7466)
Dogs of all sizes are allowed. There is a $10 per night pet fee per pet.
Quality Inn and Suites 810 England Street Ashland VA   804-798-4231 (877-424-6423)
Dogs are allowed for an additional fee of $15 per night per pet.
Days Inn Carmel Church 24320 Rogers Clark Blvd Carmel Church VA   804-448-2011 (800-329-7466)
Dogs of all sizes are allowed. There is a $10 per night pet fee per pet.
Best Western Kings Quarters 16102 Theme Park Way Doswell VA   804-876-3321 (800-780-7234)
Dogs are allowed for a $25 refundable deposit per room.
Howard Johnson Express Inn 23786 Rogers Clark Blvd. Ruther Glen VA   804-448-2499 (800-446-4656)
Dogs of all sizes are welcome. There is a $5 per day pet fee. Please place a Do Not Disturb Sign on the door so that housekeepers do not open the door while the pet is in the room.
Red Roof Inn - Ruther Glen - Carmel Church 23500 Welcome Way Drive Ruther Glen VA   804-448-2828 (800-RED-ROOF)
One well-behaved family pet per room. Guest must notify front desk upon arrival. Guest is liable for any damages. In consideration of all guests, pets must never be left unattended in the guest rooms.

Attractions
Kings Dominion Amusement Park Kennels 16000 Theme Park Way Doswell VA   804-876-5400
This amusement and water park has recreation for all ages. Although dogs are not allowed inside the park, there are secured, individual kennels available. The fee is $5 per day and they will provide water. Pet owners are expected to provide food and walks.

Berryville

Accommodations
The Lost Dog 211 S Church Street Berryville VA   540-955-1181
Well behaved pets of all sizes are allowed. There is a town leash law to obey. There are no additional pet fees, but prior approval of your dogs are required. Dogs are not allowed to be left alone in the room. There are 3 pet friendly rooms.

Blacksburg

Accommodations
Clay Corner Inn B&B 401 Clay Street SW Blacksburg VA   540-953-2604
http://www.claycorner.com
There is a $15 per day pet fee.
Comfort Inn 3705 S Main Street Blacksburg VA   540-951-1500 (877-424-6423)
Dogs are allowed for no additional pet fee. There is a pet agreement to sign at check in and a contact number must be left with the front desk if there is a pet alone in the room.

Parks
Virginia Tech Campus Southgate Drive and Duckpond Drive Blacksburg VA   540-231-6000
http://www.vt.edu/
This beautifully landscaped 2,600 acre campus was founded in 1872 and has bloomed into a comprehensive, innovated research university with the state's largest full-time student population, and it has more than 100 buildings, an airport, and more. Dogs are allowed on the grounds but not in any of the buildings. Dogs must be well behaved, under owner's control, leashed, and cleaned up after at all times.

Blue Ridge Parkway

Accommodations

Doe Run Lodging Milepost 189 Blue Ridge Parkway Fancy Gap VA   276-398-4099 (866-398-4099)
http://doerunlodging.com/rentals/
Lush green hills against a backdrop of wooded areas, spectacular valley views from the 3000 feet altitude, and a variety of rental options make this an attractive mountain getaway. Dogs of all sizes are allowed for an additional fee of $25 per pet per stay. Dogs must be housebroken, well mannered, leashed, and cleaned up after.
Grasssy Creek Cabooses 278 Caboose Lane Fancy Gap VA 276-398-1100
http://www.grassycreekcabooses.com/
Sitting on grassy knolls on 33 acres along Grassy Creek, these refurbished cabooses with modern amenities (including an inside Jacuzzi) make for a unique getaway. One dog is welcome; they must be quiet, of a friendly nature, and well mannered. Dogs must be leashed and cleaned up after, and they are not allowed on the furniture.
Miracle Farm Spa and Resort 179 Ida Rose Lane Floyd VA   540-789-2214
http://www.miraclefarmbnb.com/
In addition to providing guests as healthy an environment and cuisine as possible, this inn also helps to support a non-profit animal sanctuary for injured and abandoned animals. Vegetarian food (with meat substitutes) is the fare and there are several maintained hiking paths. Guests wanting to learn about eco-friendly living are encouraged to observe operations or to participate. Dogs of all sizes are allowed for an additional fee of $25 per stay for one dog, and $10 per stay for each subsequent dog. Dogs must be under owner's control, leashed, and cleaned up after at all times. Pet sitting may be available if notified in advance.
Best Western Four Seasons South 57 Airport Road Hillsville VA   276-728-4136 (800-780-7234)
Dogs are allowed for an additional one time pet fee of $10 per room.

Campgrounds and RV Parks

Otter Creek Campground Blue Ridge Parkway M.P. 60.8 Big Island VA   434-299 5941
http://www.blueridgeparkway.org/
There are 45 tent and 24 RV sites available on a first come first served basis with many by the river, and campfire circles, drinking water, restrooms, dump stations, concessionaires, and interpretive services are available here. Four beautiful trails can be accessed, one being the James River Canal Trail leading to the restored 1845-51 canal locks that went from Richmond to Buchanan, Virginia. Dogs are allowed throughout the park and on the trails for no additional pet fee. Dogs must be well behaved, under owner's control, on no more than a 6 foot leash, and cleaned up after at all times. This RV park is closed during the off-season. The camping and tent areas also allow dogs. There is a dog walk area at the campground. There are no electric or water hookups at the campgrounds.
Rocky Knob Campground Blue Ridge Parkway, Milepost 167-169 Meadows of Dan VA   540-745-9662
http://www.blueridgeparkway.org/
This camp area with 100+ sites offers a campfire circle that can accommodate up to 150 campers, picnic areas, restrooms, Mabry Mill's eatery and gift shop, and one of the hikes here takes visitors to Rockcastle Gorge, a 124 acre wooded gorge displaying 2 waterfalls. Dogs are allowed throughout the park and on the trails. Dogs must be well behaved, under owner's control, on no more than a 6 foot leash, and cleaned up after at all times. This RV park is closed during the off-season. The camping and tent areas also allow dogs. There is a dog walk area at the campground. There are no electric or water hookups at the campgrounds.
Roanoke Mountain Campground Blue Ridge Parkway M.P. 120.4 Vinton VA   540-745-9660
http://www.blueridgeparkway.org/
This camp area offers easy access to Explore Park, an 1,100 acre living history museum depicting life from the first settlers to the present with several special events throughout the year, and the Roanoke River giving a variety of land and water recreational opportunities. There is hiking along the river, the ridge, through mountains, and up the Roanoke Mountain Summit Trail. Dogs are allowed throughout the park and on the trails. Dogs must be well behaved, under owner's control, on no more than a 6 foot leash, and cleaned up after at all times. This RV park is closed during the off-season. The camping and tent areas also allow dogs. There is a dog walk area at the campground. There are no electric or water hookups at the campgrounds.

Bristol

Accommodations

Days Inn Abingdon 887 Empire Drive Abingdon VA   276-628-7131 (800-329-7466)

Dogs of all sizes are allowed. There is a $8 per night pet fee per pet.
Holiday Inn Express Abingdon 940 E. Main St Abingdon VA   276-676-2829 (877-270-6405)
Dogs up to 50 pounds are allowed for an additional one time pet fee of $25 per room.
Super 8 Abingdon 298 Town Centre Dr Abingdon VA   276-676-3329 (800-800-8000)
Dogs of all sizes are allowed. There are no additional pet fees. Smoking and non-smoking rooms are available for pet rooms.
Motel 6 - Bristol 21561 Clear Creek Road Bristol VA   276-466-6060 (800-466-8356)
One well-behaved family pet per room. Guest must notify front desk upon arrival. Guest is liable for any damages. In consideration of all guests, pets must never be left unattended in the guest rooms.
Super 8 Bristol 2139 Lee Hwy Bristol VA   276-466-8800 (800-800-8000)
Dogs up to 60 pounds are allowed. There is a $10 one time per pet fee per visit. Smoking and non-smoking rooms are available for pet rooms.

Attractions

Historic Main Street Main Street Abingdon VA   276-676-2282
http://www.abingdon.com/
Having the distinction of being the oldest English speaking settlement west of the Blue Ridge, this historic town has a long, rich and interesting cultural history, a 20 block long historic Main Street, one of the oldest professional residence theaters in the US, and it is also host to the popular Virginia Highlands Festival. Dogs are allowed to explore the town too; they must be leashed and cleaned up after at all times, and they are not allowed in any of the buildings.
The Cave House 279 E Main Street/H 11 Abingdon VA   276-628-7721 (store)
Sitting behind this craft co-op (dogs are not allowed inside the store) on Plum Alley, is a cave made famous by a wolf attack on Daniel Boone's dogs. The entrance is gated, but visitors can view the inside. Dogs must be leashed and cleaned up after.
White's Mill White's Mill Road Abingdon VA   276-628-2960
http://www.whitesmill.org/home.html
Listed on the National Register of Historic Places, this mill sits in a scenic, verdant valley and has been under-going renovation since 2001 with new improvements on the way, but there is plenty to see and do at present with a gift shop featuring more than 100 local artisans, and they are also host to a variety of community events. Dogs are allowed on the grounds; they are not allowed in any buildings. Dogs must be leashed and cleaned up after at all times.

Parks

Virginia Creeper Trail P.O. Box 2382 Abingdon VA
http://www.vacreepertrail.org/
This multi-use trail covers about 34 miles through some of the state's most breathtaking mountain scenery from Abingdon through Damascus to the North Carolina state line traversing 47 trestles, passing 3 seasonal visitor centers, historic sites, several small communities, and more. They also feature special events including a Dog Sled event. Dogs are allowed on the trail, and they must be kept on no more than a 6 foot leash and cleaned up after at all times. Primitive camping is allowed off trail on non-private property away from waterways.

Burkeville

Campgrounds and RV Parks

Twin Lakes State Park 788 Twin Lakes Road Green Bay VA   434-392-3435 (800-933-PARKS (7275))
This secluded park also provides a conference center in addition to a variety of lakefront activities, recreation, and interpretive programs. Dogs of all sizes are allowed for an additional $3 per night per pet for camping, and for $5 per night per pet for cabins. Cabins are available year round. Dogs may not be left unattended, and they must be leashed and cleaned up after. Dogs are not allowed on the beach or in the lake, but they are allowed on the trails. This campground is closed during the off-season. The camping and tent areas also allow dogs. There is a dog walk area at the campground. Dogs are allowed in the camping cabins.

Cape Charles

Accommodations

Kiptopeke Inn 29106 Lankford hwy Cape Charles VA   757-331-1000
Dogs of all sizes are allowed. There is a $10 per night pet fee per pet.

Charles City

Attractions
Berkeley Plantation 12602 Harrison Landing Road Charles City VA   804-829-6018
http://www.berkeleyplantation.com/
This historic plantation is the site of the first Thanksgiving, and the birthplaces of Benjamin Harrison (a signer on the Declaration of Independence), and of President Harrison. Dogs are allowed throughout the beautifully landscaped gardens and grounds; they are not allowed in buildings. Dogs must be well mannered, leashed, and cleaned up after at all times.

Charlottesville

Accommodations
Comfort Inn 1807 Emmet Street Charlottesville VA   434-293-6188 (877-424-6423)
Dogs are allowed for an additional fee of $10 per night per pet.
Days Inn Charlottesville/University Area 1600 Emmet St Charlottesville VA   434-293-9111 (800-329-7466)
Dogs of all sizes are allowed. There is a $10 per night pet fee per pet.
Holiday Inn 1200 5th Street Charlottesville VA   434-977-5100 (877-270-6405)
Dogs of all sizes are allowed for an additional fee of $15 per night per pet.
Quality Inn 1600 Emmet Street Charlottesville VA   434-971-3746 (877-424-6423)
Dogs are allowed for an additional fee of $10 per night per pet.
Red Roof Inn - Charlottesville 1309 West Main Street Charlottesville VA   434-295-4333 (800-RED-ROOF)
One well-behaved family pet per room. Guest must notify front desk upon arrival. Guest is liable for any damages. In consideration of all guests, pets must never be left unattended in the guest rooms.
Residence Inn by Marriott 1111 Millmont Street Charlottesville VA   434-923-0300
Dogs of all sizes are allowed. There is a fee of $75 for 1 to 3 nights; 4 to 5 nights is $100, and continues up to a maximum total of $200 per stay. There is also a pet policy to sign at check in.
Sleep Inn and Suites Monticello 1185 5th Street SW Charlottesville VA   434-244-9969 (877-424-6423)
Dogs are allowed for an additional fee of $15 per night per pet.
TOP 200 PLACE **Montfair Resort Farm** 2500 Bezaleel Drive Crozet VA   434-823-5202
http://www.montfairresortfarm.com
These pet-friendly cottages and country retreat allows dogs. It is located just 15 miles from Charlottesville. There is a $24.00 additional one time pet fee for your first pet plus $5 for any additional pets. Montfair's rustic lodge is available for a variety of pet-friendly events such as weddings, retreats or reunions.

Campgrounds and RV Parks
Charlottesville KOA 3825 Red Hill Lane Charlottesville VA   434-296-9881 (800-562-1743)
http://www.charlottesvillekoa.com
Dogs of all sizes are allowed. There are no additional pet fees. Dogs must be leashed and cleaned up after. This RV park is closed during the off-season. The camping and tent areas also allow dogs. There is a dog walk area at the campground.
Misty Mountain Campground 56 Misty Mountain Road Crozet VA   888-647-8900
http://www.mistycamp.com/
This scenic 50 acre park has a creek that runs through the property, and they offer secluded treed sites, a pond for some fishing, several playground/game areas, a general store, recreation room, live music and dances, and special events throughout the year. Dogs of all sizes are allowed for an additional pet fee of $2 per night per pet. Dogs must be well behaved, leashed or crated, and cleaned up after at all times. There are some breed restrictions. The camping and tent areas also allow dogs. There is a dog walk area at the campground.

Attractions
Red Hill - The Patrick Henry National Memorial 1250 Red Hill Road Brookneal VA   434-376-2044
http://www.redhill.org/rh/redhill.htm
This historic estate stands as a testament to the values of liberty that Patrick Henry felt so strongly about, and it gives visitors a sense of life during that time as the fields and forests have changed very little since the 18th century. There is an expanding system of scenic interpretive trails, and dogs are allowed on the trails and throughout the estate; they are not allowed in any of the buildings. Dogs must be well behaved, leashed, and cleaned up after.

TOP 200 PLACE **Thomas Jefferson's Monticello Estate** 931 Thomas Jefferson Parkway Charlottesville VA   434-984-9822
http://www.monticello.org/
This historically significant estate was designed and built by Thomas Jefferson, who also had a love of nature and planted flower, fruit, vegetable, International gardens, and a wide variety of trees. Guided tours are offered of its vibrant history. Dogs are allowed on the grounds; they are not allowed in buildings. Dogs must be under owner's control, leashed, and cleaned up after at all times.
Thomas Jefferson's Poplar Forest Estate 1008 Poplar Forest Drive Forest VA   434-525-1806
http://www.poplarforest.org/
A personal masterpiece for Thomas Jefferson (considered America's first architect), this octagonal home and the surrounding landscape served as a peaceful retreat as well as a working plantation, and guided tours and a museum now pass on its history. Dogs are allowed on the grounds; they are not allowed in buildings. Dogs must be under owner's control, leashed, and cleaned up after at all times.
Booker T. Washington National Monument 12130 Booker T. Washington H Hardy VA   540-721-2094
http://www.nps.gov/bowa
This historic site stands as testament to the amazing story of a slave who came to be known as the most influential African American of his time. This working farm also affords visitors a glimpse of what life was like then. Dogs are welcome on the grounds and on the trails; they are not allowed in the buildings. Dogs must be leashed and cleaned up after.

Shopping Centers
Charlottesville Historic Downtown Mall Downtown Charlottesville Charlottesville VA   434-977-1783
http://charlottesvilletourism.org
Dogs on leash are allowed in the mall area. They are allowed to sit at many of the outdoor seating areas. Water bowls sit out at many shop entrances.

Stores
PetSmart Pet Store 101 Community St Charlottesville VA   434-964-9213
Your licensed and well-behaved leashed dog is allowed in the store.

Parks
Pen Park Pen Park Road Charlottesville VA   434-970-3589
At 280 acres, it is the city's largest park and it provides a myriad of recreational facilities and gaming/play areas for all ages, including a physical fitness course, a mile and a half nature trail along the river, and an 18-hole golf course. Dogs are allowed throughout the park and on the trials. Dogs must be well mannered, under owner's control, leashed, and cleaned up after at all times. The park usually has a stock of plastic bags available at the start of the Fitness Trail.
Rivanna River Greenbelt Trail end of Chesapeake Street Charlottesville VA   434-970-3333
This beautifully treed and paved pedestrian trail encircles the city, offers fishing spots along the way, and common wildlife sightings. Dogs are allowed off leash on designated portions of the Rivanna Trail on Tuesdays, Wednesdays, and Thursdays only. At all other times dogs must be leashed. Dogs must be under owner's control and cleaned up after at all times.

Off-Leash Dog Parks
Darden Towe Park 1445 Darden Towe Park Road Charlottesville VA   434-296-5844
This 110 acre park is open from 7 am to dark year round offering gaming fields/courts, trails, picnic areas with grills, and a 1 acre fenced-in off leash dog area. Dogs are allowed throughout the rest of the park and on the trails as long as they are on leash and cleaned up after at all times. Dogs must be under good voice control when not on lead.
Rivanna River Greenbelt Trail end of Chesapeake Street Charlottesville VA   434-970-3333
This beautifully treed and paved pedestrian trail encircles the city, marks off the ¼ mile, offers fishing spots along the way, and common wildlife sightings. Dogs are allowed off leash on designated portions of the Rivanna Trail on Tuesdays, Wednesdays, and Thursdays only. At all other times dogs must be leashed. Dogs must be under owner's control and cleaned up after at all times.

Outdoor Restaurants
Baja Bean Company 1327 W Main Street Charlottesville VA   434-293-4507
http://www.bajabean.com/
Specializing in fresh, healthy Southern California style Mexican foods, this eatery also has a full bar, ongoing special events, and indoor or outdoor dining options. Dogs are allowed at the outer tables. Dogs must be well behaved, under owner's control/care, and leashed or crated at all times.

Bang! 213 Second Street SW Charlottesville VA   434-984-2264
Specializing in Asian Tapas and designer Martinis, this eatery also offers seasonal patio dining. Dogs are allowed at the outer tables. Dogs must be well behaved, under owner's control/care, and leashed or crated at all times.
Blue Light Grill and Raw Bar 120 E Main Street Charlottesville VA   434-295-1223
http://www.bluelightgrill.com/
Offering upscale dining of traditional seafood and Asian dishes with notable international flavors, they also feature an active bar scene, and indoor or seasonal outdoor dining options. Dogs are allowed at the outer tables. Dogs must be well behaved, under owner's control/care, and leashed or crated at all times.
Downtown Grille 201 W Main Street Charlottesville VA   434-817-7080
http://www.downtowngrille.com/index.html
This steak and seafood eatery is located in the town's historic mall, offers an extensive wine list, and indoor or seasonal outdoor dining options. Dogs are allowed at the outer tables. Dogs must be well behaved, under owner's control/care, and leashed or crated at all times.
Oxo Restaurant 215 W Water Street Charlottesville VA   434-977-8111
http://www.oxorestaurant.com/
Reservations are suggested at this fine dining eatery that specializes in classical French cooking with a modern touch. They also offer a full bar and indoor or outdoor dining. Dogs are allowed at the outer tables. Dogs must be well behaved, under owner's control/care, and leashed or crated at all times.
The Biltmore Grill 16 Elliewood Avenue Charlottesville VA   434-293-6700
Located near Virginia State University, this eatery is also a prime nightspot with indoor and outdoor seating options. Dogs are allowed at the outer tables. Dogs must be well behaved, under owner's control/care, and leashed or crated at all times.
The Mudhouse 213 W Main Street Charlottesville VA   434-984-6833
http://www.mudhouse.com/
This coffee house and espresso bar offers Wi-Fi, art exhibits, a variety of ongoing entertainments, and indoor or outdoor seating. Just order and pick up inside. Dogs are allowed at the outer tables. Dogs must be well behaved, under owner's control/care, and leashed or crated at all times.
Zocalo Restaurant 201 E Main Street Charlottesville VA   434-977-4944
http://www.zocalo-restaurant.com/
This fine dining restaurant is centrally located with indoor and seasonal outdoor seating. Dogs are allowed at the outer tables. Dogs must be well behaved, under owner's control/care, and leashed or crated at all times.

Chincoteague Island

Accommodations
Channel Bass Inn 6228 Church Street Chincoteague VA   757-336-6148 (800-249-0818)
http://www.channelbassinn.com/
This beautiful 1892, 6,800 square foot home sits surrounded by Japanese and perennial gardens with a pond and provide a good central location for exploring the island; they also have complimentary bikes for guests. One dog of any size is welcome for an additional $10 per night, and they must be people and pet friendly as there are resident cats. Dogs must be well behaved, leashed, and cleaned up after.
Chincoteague Island 6378 Church Street Chincoteague Island VA   757-336-3100 (800-668-7836)
Offering a variety of property options and amenities in various locations around the island, this agency has more than 20 pet friendly vacation rentals available. Dogs of all sizes (depending on the rental) are allowed for an additional fee of $75 per pet per stay. Dogs must be housebroken, well behaved, leashed, and cleaned up after in and out of the unit. Dogs may not be left unattended, and they are not allowed in a "no pet" house. Dogs are not allowed anywhere on the refuge, even if they are in a car.
VIP Island Vacation Rentals 6353 Maddox Blvd Chincoteague Island VA   757-336-7288
This company offers several properties with various amenities at a variety of sites on this small island that is accessed from the mainland by a 4 mile long bypass. Dogs of all sizes are allowed for an additional fee of $75 per pet per stay. Dogs must be well behaved, leashed, and cleaned up after.
Garden and Sea Inn 4188 Nelson Road New Church VA   800-824-0672
http://www.gardenandseainn.com/
With an emphasis on privacy and relaxation, this historic 1804 inn sits on 4 gorgeous landscaped acres with gardens, ponds, a seasonal pool, and they also offer gourmet dining and a convenient location to several other activities. Dogs of all sizes are allowed for no additional fee. Dogs must be quiet, leashed, and cleaned up after at all times.

Attractions
TOP 200 PLACE **Barnacle Bill's Boat Tours** 3691 Main Street Chincoteague Island VA   757-336-5920

This water touring company will allow dogs on board for no additional fee. They also have a bait and tackle shop at this location. There is a 2 person minimum per trip. Dogs must be well behaved, under owner's control/care at all times, and leashed.

Stores
Captain Cody's Chincoteague Pet Boutique 4067 Main Street/H 175 Chincoteague Island VA   757-336-5544

http://captaincodys.com/
Specializing in unique gifts for pets and their owners, this boutique also offers a line of gourmet doggy treats. Well behaved dogs are allowed in the store. Dogs must be under owner's control/care and be leashed at all times.

Christiansburg

Accommodations
Days Inn Christiansburg 2635 Roanoke St Christiansburg VA   540-382-0261 (800-329-7466)
Dogs of all sizes are allowed. There is a $5 per night pet fee per small pet and $10 for large pet.
Howard Johnson Express Inn 100 Bristol Drive Christiansburg VA   540-381-0150 (800-446-4656)
Dogs of all sizes are welcome. There is a $7 per day pet fee for small pets and a $10 per day pet fee for a larger pet.
Quality Inn 50 Hampton Blvd Christiansburg VA   540-382-2055 (877-424-6423)
Dogs are allowed for an additional pet fee of $10 per night per room.
Super 8 Christiansburg/Blacksburg Area 55 Laurel Street NE Christiansburg VA   540-382-5813 (800-800-8000)
Dogs of all sizes are allowed. There is a $20 one time per pet fee per visit. Smoking and non-smoking rooms are available for pet rooms.
Super 8 Christiansburg/East 2780 Roanoke St Christiansburg VA   540-382-7421 (800-800-8000)
Dogs of all sizes are allowed. There is a $10 per night pet fee per pet. Smoking and non-smoking rooms are available for pet rooms.

Collinsville

Accommodations
Quality Inn Dutch Inn 2360 Virginia Avenue Collinsville VA   276-647-3721 (877-424-6423)
Dogs are allowed for an additional fee of $10 per night per pet.

Covington

Accommodations
Best Value Inn 908 Valley Ridge Drive Covington VA   540-962-7600 (800-843-5644)
There is a $10 one time pet charge.
Best Western Mountain View 820 E Madison Street Covington VA   540-962-4951 (800-780-7234)
Dogs are allowed for an additional one time pet fee of $12 per room.

Campgrounds and RV Parks
Douthat State Park Rt 1, Box 212 Clifton Forge VA   540-862-8100 (800-933-PARK (7275))
This park, a Nationally Registered Historic District, offers interpretive programs, more than 40 miles of hiking trails, and a variety of land and water events and recreation. Dogs of all sizes are allowed for $3 per night per pet for the camp area, and at $5 per night per pet for the cabins. Dogs may not be left unattended, and they must be leashed and cleaned up after. Dogs are not allowed at the lodge or on the beach, but they are allowed on the trails. This campground is closed during the off-season. The camping and tent areas also allow dogs. There is a dog walk area at the campground. Dogs are allowed in the camping cabins.

Culpeper

Accommodations
Comfort Inn 890 Willis Lane Culpeper VA   540-825-4900 (877-424-6423)
Dogs are allowed for an additional fee of $15 per night per pet.
Inn at Meander Plantation 2333 N James Madison H Lotus Dale VA   540-672-4912 (800-385-4936)
http://www.meander.net/
This country inn offers visitors everything they need to have a fun, relaxing visit with gaming areas, trails through woods and fields with plenty of bird and wildlife, landscaped grounds and gardens, and good food. Dogs of all sizes are allowed for an additional fee of $25 per night per pet. Dogs must be leashed and cleaned up after at all times. Please take pets to the back yard; scoopers are available. They request that the "dog sheet" they provide be used if pets are accustomed to being on the bed or furniture. Dogs are not allowed in the main house, and they may be only left alone in the room for short times and they must be crated. Dogs must be quiet, well behaved, and friendly to both people and other animals on site.

Cumberland

Campgrounds and RV Parks
Bear Creek State Park 929 Oak Hill Road Cumberland VA   804-492-4410 (800-933-PARK (7275))
This park of 326 acres has a lake of 40 acres, and offers fishing, hiking, nature study, and a variety of land and water recreation. Dogs of all sizes are allowed for an additional fee of $3 per night per pet. Dogs may not be left unattended, and they must be on no more than a 6 foot leash, and be cleaned up after. Dogs are not allowed on the beach or in the water. Dogs are allowed on the trails. This campground is closed during the off-season. The camping and tent areas also allow dogs. There is a dog walk area at the campground.

Danville

Accommodations
Comfort Inn and Suites 100 Tower Drive Danville VA   434-793-2000 (877-424-6423)
Dogs are allowed for an additional pet fee of $10 per night per room.
Days Inn Danville 1390 Piney Forest Rd Danville VA   434-836-6745 (800-329-7466)
Dogs of all sizes are allowed. There is a $5 per night pet fee per pet.
Holiday Inn Express Danville 2121 Riverside Dr Danville VA   434-793-4000 (877-270-6405)
Dogs of all sizes are allowed for an additional fee of $10 per night per pet.
Super 8 Danville 2385 Riverside Dr Danville VA   434-799-5845 (800-800-8000)
Dogs of all sizes are allowed. There is a $20 one time per pet fee per visit. Smoking and non-smoking rooms are available for pet rooms.

Duffield

Campgrounds and RV Parks
Natural Tunnel State Park Rt 3, Box 250 Duffield VA   276-940-2674 (800-933-PARK (7275))
This park offers a visitor center, an amphitheater, interpretive programs, a wide variety of recreational pursuits, and more, but it's amazing natural tunnel is the real attraction. Dogs of all sizes are allowed for an additional fee of $3 per night per pet. Dogs may not be left unattended, they must be leashed at all times, and cleaned up after. Dogs are allowed on the trails. This campground is closed during the off-season. The camping and tent areas also allow dogs. There is a dog walk area at the campground.

Emporia

Accommodations
Best Western Emporia 1100 West Atlantic ST Emporia VA   434-634-3200 (800-780-7234)
Dogs are allowed for an additional fee of $10 per night per pet.
Comfort Inn 1411 Skippers Road Emporia VA   434-348-3282 (877-424-6423)
Dogs are allowed for an additional fee of $5 per night per pet.
Hampton Inn 1207 W Atlantic Street Emporia VA   434-634-9200
Dogs of all sizes are allowed. There are no additional pet fees.

Campgrounds and RV Parks
Jellystone Park 2940 Sussex Drive Emporia VA   434-634-3115
http://www.campingbear.com
Dogs of all sizes are allowed. There are no additional pet fees. Dogs must be well behaved, may not be left
unattended, and be leashed and cleaned up after. Dogs are not allowed in the buildings or at the playground.
The camping and tent areas also allow dogs. There is a dog walk area at the campground.

Franklin

Accommodations
Days Inn Franklin 1660 Armory Dr Franklin VA   757-562-2225 (800-329-7466)
Dogs of all sizes are allowed. There is a $5 per night pet fee per pet.

Fredericksburg

Accommodations
Best Western Fredericksburg 2205 William St Fredericksburg VA   540-371-5050 (800-780-7234)
Dogs are allowed for an additional fee of $10 per night per pet.
Country Inn and Suites Fredericksburg South 5327 Jefferson Davis Highway Fredericksburg VA   540-898-
1800 (800-456-4000)
Dogs of all sizes are allowed for a pet fee of $20 per visit.
Days Inn Fredericksburg North 14 Simpson Rd Fredericksburg VA   540-373-5340 (800-329-7466)
Dogs of all sizes are allowed. There is a $5 per night pet fee per pet.
Days Inn Fredericksburg South 5316 Jefferson Davis Hwy Fredericksburg VA   540-898-6800 (800-329-
7466)
Dogs of all sizes are allowed. There is a $5 per night pet fee per pet.
Holiday Inn 564 Warrenton Rd Fredericksburg VA   540-371-5550 (877-270-6405)
Dogs of all sizes is allowed for no additional pet fee.
Motel 6 - Fredericksburg 401 Warrenton Road Fredericksburg VA   540-371-5443 (800-466-8356)
One well-behaved family pet per room. Guest must notify front desk upon arrival. Guest is liable for any
damages. In consideration of all guests, pets must never be left unattended in the guest rooms.
Quality Inn 543 Warrenton Road Fredericksburg VA   540-373-0000 (877-424-6423)
Dogs are allowed for an additional fee of $10 per night per pet.
TownePlace Suites Fredericksburg 4700 Market Street Fredericksburg VA   540-891-0775
Dogs of all sizes are allowed. There is a $75 one time pet fee per visit.
Holiday Inn Express 28 Greenspring Drive Stafford VA   540-657-5566 (877-270-6405)
Dogs of all sizes are allowed: Dogs 15 pounds or under is an additional $10 per night; the fee is 20 per night for
dogs over 15 pounds.
Quality Inn 6409 Danbell Lane Thornburg VA   540-582-1097 (877-424-6423)
Dogs are allowed for an additional fee of $10 per night per pet.

Campgrounds and RV Parks
Fredericksburg/Washington DC S KOA 7400 Brookside Lane Fredericksburg VA   540-898-7252 (800-562-
1889)
http://www.fredericksburgkoa.com
Dogs of all sizes are allowed. There are no additional pet fees, for tent or RV sites. There is a $5 per night per
pet addtional fee for cabins. Dogs must be quiet, well behaved, leashed, and cleaned up after. The camping and
tent areas also allow dogs. There is a dog walk area at the campground. Dogs are allowed in the camping
cabins.

Prince William Forest Park 18100 Park Headquarters Road Triangle VA   703-221-7181 (800-933-PARK (7275))
http://www.nps.gov/prwi/
With over 19,000 acres, this park offers a variety of nature study, land and water recreation. Dogs of all sizes are allowed at no additional fee. Dogs may not be left unattended, and they must be on no more than a 6 foot leash, and be cleaned up after. Dogs are not allowed in the Chopawamsic backcountry, Turkey Run Ridge Group Campground, or in the buildings. Dogs are allowed on the trails. The camping and tent areas also allow dogs. There is a dog walk area at the campground. There are no electric or water hookups at the campground.

Attractions
Chancellorsville Battlefield 9001 Plank Road Fredericksburg VA   540-786-2880
Home to many historic events, this park preserves, protects, and educates the public to the significance of the activities that took place here with exhibits, interpretive programs/tours, 5 walking trails and a 7 mile auto loop driving tour. Dogs are allowed throughout the park and on the trails. Dogs must be under owner's control, leashed, and cleaned up after at all times.
TOP 200 PLACE **Fredericksburg Battlefield Park** 1013 Lafayette Blvd Fredericksburg VA   540-373-6122
http://www.nps.gov/frsp
The battle here was purportedly one of General Lee's easiest victories of all the battles of the Civil War that occurred in this region. It features exhibits, interpretive programs, and a five mile driving tour that connects this section to the other battlefront areas. Dogs are allowed at all the sites along the way. Dogs must be under owner's control, leashed, and cleaned up after at all times.
Gari Melchers Home and Studio Belmont, 224 Washington Street Fredericksburg VA   540-654-1015
http://www.umw.edu/gari_melchers/
This artist is known for his ability to replicate the true character of a place or people; this museum is home to his largest collection of work, and it is now also the official Stafford County Visitor Center. Dogs are allowed throughout the grounds; they are not allowed in buildings. Dogs must be under owner's control, leashed, and cleaned up after at all times.
George Washington's Ferry Farm 268 Kings Hwy/H 3 Fredericksburg VA   540-373-3381
This idyllic farm setting was the boyhood home of George Washington, and its historic secrets are shared with visitors through a variety of interpretive programs, tours, special events, and more. Dogs are allowed throughout the park; they are not allowed in buildings. Dogs must be under owner's control, leashed, and cleaned up after at all times.
Kenmore Plantation and Gardens 1201 Washington Ave Fredericksburg VA   540-373-3381
The curators of this beautiful 1770's Georgian mansion (accurately restored) offer numerous educational opportunities for visitors to learn of plantation life in colonial Virginia with interpretive programs, demonstration gardens, and a Wilderness Walk containing 18th century native American plants. Dogs are allowed throughout the grounds; they are not allowed in buildings. Dogs must be under owner's control, leashed, and cleaned up after at all times.
Stonewall Jackson Shrine 12019 Stonewall Jackson Road/H 606 Woodford VA   804-633-6076
http://www.nps.gov/archive/frsp/js.htm
This shrine to "Stonewall" Jackson sits in a rural area where little has changed since the general passed away here, and it is the only structure that still remains of the plantation. Dogs are allowed on the grounds; they must be leashed and cleaned up after at all times, and they are not allowed in the building.

Stores
PetSmart Pet Store 1421 Carl D Silver Pky Fredericksburg VA   540-785-9851
Your licensed and well-behaved leashed dog is allowed in the store.
PetSmart Pet Store 1160 Stafford Market Place Stafford VA   540-658-9272
Your licensed and well-behaved leashed dog is allowed in the store.
Petco Pet Store 309 Worth Avenue, Ste 123 Stafford VA   540-657-7491
Your licensed and well-behaved leashed dog is allowed in the store.

Outdoor Restaurants
Baja Fresh 1500 Central Park Blvd Fredericksburg VA   540-785-3833
This restaurant serves Mexican food. Dogs are allowed at the outdoor tables.

Gladstone

Campgrounds and RV Parks

James River State Park Rt 1, Box 787 Gladstone VA 434-933-4355 (800-933-PARK (7275))
A fairly new park offers 20 miles of multiple use trails, three fishing ponds, and various activities and recreation. Dogs of all sizes are allowed for an additional $3 per night per pet for camping, and for $5 per night per pet for cabins. Cabins are available year round. Dogs may not be left unattended, and they must be leashed in camp areas, and cleaned up after. Dogs are allowed on the trails. The camping and tent areas also allow dogs. There is a dog walk area at the campground. Dogs are allowed in the camping cabins. There are no electric or water hookups at the campground.

Grundy

Campgrounds and RV Parks
Breaks Interstate Park 769 H 80 Breaks VA   276-865-4413
This year round 4,600 acre park has often been called the "Little Grand Canyon", and in addition to panoramic views, there are a wide variety of land and water activities. Dogs are allowed at no additional fee for camping; there is a $7 per night per pet additional fee for the lodge. Dogs may not be left unattended in rooms, but they may be tethered in the camp area if they will be well behaved, quiet, and checked in on. Dogs are allowed on the trails. This campground is closed during the off-season. The camping and tent areas also allow dogs. There is a dog walk area at the campground. Dogs are allowed in the camping cabins.

Harrisonburg

Accommodations
Candlewood Suites Harrisonburg 1560 Country Club Road Harrisonburg VA 540-437-1400 (877-270-6405)
Dogs up to 50 pounds are allowed for an additional one time pet fee of $50 per room.
Comfort Inn 1440 E Market Street Harrisonburg VA   540-433-6066 (877-424-6423)
Dogs are allowed for an additional fee of $10 per night per pet.
Days Inn Harrisonburg 1131 Forest Hill Rd Harrisonburg VA   540-433-9353 (800-329-7466)
Dogs of all sizes are allowed. There is a $10 per night pet fee per pet.
Motel 6 - Harrisonburg 10 Linda Lane Harrisonburg VA   540-433-6939 (800-466-8356)
One well-behaved family pet per room. Guest must notify front desk upon arrival. Guest is liable for any damages. In consideration of all guests, pets must never be left unattended in the guest rooms.
Super 8 Harrisonburg 3330 S Main Harrisonburg VA   540-433-8888 (800-800-8000)
Dogs of all sizes are allowed. There is a $10 per night pet fee per pet. Smoking and non-smoking rooms are available for pet rooms.

Campgrounds and RV Parks
Harrisonburg/New Market 12480 Mountain Valley Road Broadway VA   540-896-8929 (800-562-5406)
http://www.koa.com
Up to 2 dogs are allowed per RV or tent site, at no additional fee. There is a $20 per stay fee for one dog only in the cabins. Dogs may not be left unattended, must be leashed, and cleaned up after. The camping and tent areas also allow dogs. There is a dog walk area at the campground. Dogs are allowed in the camping cabins.

Stores
Petco Pet Store 253 Burgess Rd Harrisonburg VA 540-432-3830
Your licensed and well-behaved leashed dog is allowed in the store.

Irvington

Accommodations
Hope and Glory Inn 65 Tavern Road Irvington VA   804-438-6053 (800-497-8228)
Wooded areas, wide open fields, manicured lawns, and English gardens all add to the ambiance of this beautiful 1890's waterfront inn that sits central to a wide range of land and water recreational opportunities. Dogs of all sizes are allowed in 2 of the cottages for an additional fee of $40 per night per pet. Dogs must be well groomed (no heavy shedders), well mannered, leashed and cleaned up after. Dogs are not allowed on the bed or any of the furniture. There is a great lawn across from the inn where dogs may want to take in a good run.

Outdoor Restaurants

The Local 4337 Irvington Road/H 200 Irvington VA 804-438-9356
This sandwich bar offers outside dining. Dogs are allowed at the outer tables; they must be under owner's control/care and leashed at all times.
Trick Dog Cafe 4357 Irvington Road/H 200 Irvington VA 804-438-1055
http://www.trickdogcafe.com/about.htm
Named from a bit of folklore, this popular eatery offers casual, fine dining fare and alfresco dining. Dogs are allowed at the outer tables; they must be under owner's control/care and leashed at all times.

Lake Area

Accommodations

Needmoor Inn Bed and Breakfast 801 Virginia Avenue Clarksville VA 434-374-2866
http://www.kerrlake.com/needmoor
This Bed and Breakfast Inn is a Virginia landmark that has welcomed guests for over a century. This wonderfully restored farmhouse style B&B can be your destination for recreation and relaxation, or your place of rest on a longer journey. The inn has an area for dogs to play, and many parks nearby. The owners have a dog that loves company. Room rates are approximately $75.
Holiday Inn Express 1074 Bill Tuck Highway South Boston VA 434-575-4000 (877-270-6405)
Dogs of all sizes are allowed for an additional fee of $20 per night per pet.
Quality Inn 2001 Seymour Drive South Boston VA 434-572-4311 (877-424-6423)
Dogs of all sizes are allowed. There is a $10 per night per room additional pet fee.
Comfort Inn 918 E Atlantic Street South Hill VA 434-447-2600 (877-424-6423)
Dogs are allowed for an additional fee of $10 per night per pet.

Campgrounds and RV Parks

Occoneechee State Park 1192 Occoneechee Park Road Clarksville VA 434-374-2210 (800-933-PARK (7275))
This historical park is located on Virgina's largest lake and offers a variety of land and water recreation, however, swimming is not allowed. Dogs of all sizes are allowed at $3 per dog per day for the camp area. Dogs may not be left unattended unless very well behaved, and they must have current rabies and shot records. Dogs must be on no more than a 6 foot leash, and be cleaned up after. This campground is closed during the off-season. The camping and tent areas also allow dogs. There is a dog walk area at the campground.
Staunton River State Park 1170 Staunton Trail Scottsburg VA 434-572-4623 (800-933-PARK (7275))
This year round park covers almost 1,600 acres, is home to the largest lake in Virginia, offers interpretive programs, and a variety of land and water recreation. Dogs of all sizes are allowed for an additional $3 per night per pet for camping, and for $5 per night per pet for cabins. Cabins are available year round. Dogs may not be left unattended outside or in a tent, and they must be leashed and cleaned up after. Dogs are not allowed in the pool area, but they are allowed on the trails. This campground is closed during the off-season. The camping and tent areas also allow dogs. There is a dog walk area at the campground. Dogs are allowed in the camping cabins.

Leesburg

Accommodations

Days Inn Leesburg Dwtn 721 E Market St Leesburg VA 703-777-6622 (800-329-7466)
Dogs of all sizes are allowed. There is a $6 per night pet fee per pet.

Attractions

Waterford Village Main Street Waterford VA 540-882-3018
http://www.waterfordva.org/
The town of Waterford, listed on the National Register of Historic Landmarks, offers visitors recreational and educational opportunities, a concert and lecture series, interactive programs, special events, and more. Dogs are welcome through the village; it is up to individual shops whether a pet is allowed inside. Dogs are not allowed at all during Fair Time, usually held the beginning of October. Dogs must be friendly, leashed, and cleaned up after.

Shopping Centers

Leesburg Corner Premium Outlets 241 Fort Evans Road NE Leesburg VA   703-737-3071
This attractive open air mall has nice seating areas amid foliage in addition to the 110 outlet stores. Dogs are allowed throughout the mall; they are not allowed in the food court. Dogs must be well behaved, leashed, and cleaned up after at all times.

Stores

Dog Day Afternoon 305 E Market Street #B Leesburg VA   703-779-1333
http://www.thedogdayafternoon.com/
This pet store offers a wonderful assortment of unique, quality pet products and gifts, and they are always on the lookout for something new. They carry a full line of pet accessories, lots of toys, puppy supplies, and all the basics, including quality pet foods. This is also a full service pet care facility. They are open from 7 am to 7 pm Monday through Friday; from 11 am to 3 pm on Saturday, and closed on Sunday. Your well behaved pet is welcome to explore the store with you.
PetSmart Pet Store 510 D East Market St Leesburg VA   703-669-5056
Your licensed and well-behaved leashed dog is allowed in the store.
Petco Pet Store 200-250 Fort Evans Rd NE Leesburg VA   703-669-3517
Your licensed and well-behaved leashed dog is allowed in the store.

Parks

Washington and Old Dominion Trail 21293 Smiths Switch Road (office) Ashburn VA   703-729-0596
http://www.wodfriends.org/
A Regional Park and designated a National Recreation Trail, this is one of the skinniest parks at about 100 feet across, but it is also one of the longest with a 45 mile long multi-use trail. There are several historic sites and many points of interest along the way, and the website lists a number of points of entry. Dogs are allowed throughout the park; they must be under owner's control, leashed, and cleaned up after at all times.
Ball's Bluff Regional Park 17500 Balls Bluff Road NE Leesburg VA   703-737-7800
Home to one of the smallest national cemeteries with only 25 headstones, this historic 168 acre wooded park saw the largest Civil War battle in the county and offers trails, interpretive exhibits, scenic views of the Potomac River, and day use areas. Dogs are welcome throughout the park and on the trails. Dogs must be leashed and cleaned up after.
Morven Park 17263 S Planter Lane Leesburg VA   703-777-2414
http://www.morvenpark.org/
Reenactments, living history programs, the Winmill Carriage Collection, formal gardens and grounds, an equestrian center, numerous special events throughout the year, and a mansion are some of the highlights of this multi-recreational 1,200 acre park. (An extensive restoration project may limit access to some areas.) Dogs of all sizes are allowed throughout the park, at the picnic areas, and on the trails; they are not allowed in any of the buildings or on any of the tours. Dogs must be under owner's control, leashed, and cleaned up after at all times. They ask that visitors, and their pets, stay in designated areas only.

Outdoor Restaurants

Eiffel Tower Cafe 107 Loudoun Street SE Leesburg VA   703-777-5142
http://www.eiffeltowercafe.com/
Visitors can experience a touch of the "south of France" at this authentic French restaurant tucked away in the town's historic district. There is outdoor dining when the weather permits. Dogs are allowed at the outer tables; they must be leashed and under owner's control/care at all times.
South Street Under 203 Harrison St SE Leesburg VA   703-771-9610
http://www.southstreetunder.com/
This bakery, fresh soup and sandwich bar offers alfresco dining; just order and pay inside and they will bring out the order. Dogs are allowed at the outer tables; they must be under owner's control/care and leashed at all times.

Lexington

Accommodations

1780 Stone House, rental #1350 218 S Main Street/H 11 Lexington VA   540-463-2521
http://www.vrbo.com/1350
This 200 year old, restored stone home has 2 foot thick walls, guaranteeing quiet times after exploring the areas many sites of interests. Dogs of all sizes are allowed for no additional fee. Dogs must be well behaved, leashed, and cleaned up after inside and out.

Applewood Inn 242 Tarn Beck Lane Lexington VA 540-463-1962 (800-463-1902)
http://www.applewoodbb.com/
Although there are a variety of activities and sites of interest guests can explore here and in the vicinity, this place also makes a good "back to nature" getaway with plenty of wildlife, scenic views, nature trails, seasonal gardens, and a lot more. Dogs are allowed for an additional fee. One dog is $20 for the first night and each night after is $10 per night. A second dog is an additional $10 per night. Dogs must be well mannered, leashed, and cleaned up after.
Best Western Inn at Hunt Ridge 25 Willow Springs Rd Lexington VA 540-464-1500 (800-780-7234)
Dogs are allowed for an additional one time pet fee of $25 per room.
Best Western Lexington Inn 850 N Lee Highway Lexington VA 540-458-3020 (800-780-7234)
Dogs are allowed for an additional one time pet fee of $25 per room.
Days Inn Lexington 325 West Midland Trail Lexington VA 540-463-2143 (800-329-7466)
Dogs of all sizes are allowed. There is a $10 per night pet fee per pet. Reservations are recommended due to limited rooms for pets.
Howard Johnson Inn 2836 N. Lee Hwy. Lexington VA 540-463-9181 (800-446-4656)
Dogs of all sizes are welcome. There is a $5 per day pet fee.
Super 8 Lexington 1139 North Lee Hwy Lexington VA 540-463-7858 (800-800-8000)
Dogs of all sizes are allowed. There are no additional pet fees. Smoking and non-smoking rooms are available for pet rooms.
Fox Hill Bed & Breakfast & Cottage Suites 4383 Borden Grant Trail Lexington/Fairfield VA 540-377-9922 (800-369-8005)
http://www.foxhillbb.com
This 38 acre B&B in the Virginia countryside allows dogs of all sizes. There is a $12 per dog pet fee per night. Dogs may be left alone in the room if crated and if a cell phone number is left.

Attractions
TOP 200 PLACE **Hull's Drive-In** Rr 5 Lexington VA 540-463-2621
http://www.hullsdrivein.com
This pet friendly drive-in theater allows well behaved pets of all sizes to come to the movies for no additional fee. Dogs must be quiet, and leashed and cleaned up after at all times. The gates open at 7:00pm, and the movie starts at 9:00 - 9:15pm Monday through Saturday. The movie starts sooner on Sundays.
Lexington Carriage Company 106 E Washington Street Lexington VA 540-463-5647
http://www.lexcarriage.com/
This carriage company is available for festivals and special occasions in addition to being a fun and unique way to explore this 19th century college town. Their season runs from April 1 to October 31, and tours are usually about 1 hour. Friendly dogs are welcome on the tours for no additional fee. Dogs must be well mannered, under owner's control/care, and leashed at all times.

Shopping Centers
Lexington Antique and Craft Mall 1495 N Lee Hwy/H 11 Lexington VA 540-463-9511
There are about 250 antique and quality craft dealers at this 40,000 square foot store. Well behaved dogs are allowed in the store. Dogs must be under owner's control/care, and short leashed at all times.

Stores
Artists in Cahoots 1 W Washington Street Lexington VA 540-44-1147
http://www.artistsincahoots.com/
A member run gallery, it was begun as an outlet for local artisans, and since a lot of the arts and craft work here depicts much of the area's beauty and historical sites, it can also be a good souvenir stop. Dogs are allowed in the store. Dogs must be under owner's immediate control/care and short leashed at all times.

Outdoor Restaurants
Joyful Spirit Cafe 26 Main Street/H 11 Lexington VA 540-463-4191
This breakfast and lunch café offers outdoor seating. Dogs are allowed at the outer tables. Dogs must be under owner's control/care and leashed at all times.

Louisa

Accommodations
Ginger Hill 47 Holly Springs Drive Louisa VA 540-967-3260

Dogs of all sizes are allowed. There are no additional pet fees. Dogs are placed in a covered outdoor kennel with a dog house that are just outside of the guest rooms.

Lynchburg - Appomattox

Accommodations

Comfort Suites 1558 Main Street Altavista VA   434-369-4000 (877-424-6423)
Dogs are allowed for an additional fee of $6 per night per pet. Dogs may not be left alone in the room.
Days Inn Bedford 921 Blue Ridge Ave Bedford VA   540-586-8286 (800-329-7466)
Dogs of all sizes are allowed. There is a $10 per night pet fee per pet.
Holiday Inn Select 601 Main Street Lynchburg VA   434-528-2500 (877-270-6405)
Dogs of all sizes are allowed for an additional one time pet fee of $25 per room.
Quality Inn 3125 Albert Lankford Drive Lynchburg VA   434-847-9041 (877-424-6423)
Dogs are allowed for an additional one time pet fee of $25 per room.

Campgrounds and RV Parks

Holiday Lake State Park Rt 2, Box 622; State Park Road 692 Appomattox VA   434-248-6308 (800-933-PARK (7275))
A paradise for the outdoor enthusiast, this park offers a variety of land and water activities, and recreational pursuits. Dogs of all sizes are allowed for $3 per night per dog. Dogs must be leashed and cleaned up after. Dogs may be left tethered on site if they will be quiet, well behaved, are shaded, and have food and water. Dogs are allowed on the trails, but they are not allowed in the lake. The camping and tent areas also allow dogs. There is a dog walk area at the campground.
Peaks of Otter Lodge and Campground Mile Post 86 Blue Ridge Parkway Bedford VA   540-586-7321
http://www.blueridgeparkway.org/
Although dogs are not allowed at the lodge here, they are allowed at the campground for no additional fee. A 24 acre lake with a 1-mile loop trail, a visitor center, amphitheater, and gift shop are some of the features here. Campsites are on a first come first served basis, and provide drinking water, restrooms, and a dump station. There are several hiking trails, including the Sharp Top Trail which marked the most northern land of the Cherokee Nation. Dogs are allowed throughout the park and on the trails. Dogs must be well behaved, under owner's control, on no more than a 6 foot leash, and cleaned up after at all times. This RV park is closed during the off-season. The camping and tent areas also allow dogs. There is a dog walk area at the campground. There are no electric or water hookups at the campgrounds.
Smith Mountain State Park 1235 State Park Road Huddleston VA   540-297-6066 (800-933-PARK (7275))
Hardwood and pine forests, secluded coves and picturesque vistas are the backdrop for a variety of trails, land,water activities, and recreation at this year round park. Dogs of all sizes are allowed for an additional $3 per night per pet for camping, and for $5 per night per pet for cabins. Cabins are available year round. Dogs may not be tied to trees, and they must be leashed and cleaned up after. Dogs may only be left unattended if they will be quiet and well behaved in owners' absence. Dogs are allowed on the trails. This campground is closed during the off-season. The camping and tent areas also allow dogs. There is a dog walk area at the campground. Dogs are allowed in the camping cabins.

Attractions

TOP 200 PLACE **Appomattox Court House NHP** Hwy 24, PO Box 218 Appomattox VA   434-352-8987
http://www.nps.gov/apco/
Steeped in a rich cultural and revolutionary history; In April 1865 this was the site where the agreements were made to end the Civil War and the 13th, 14th, and 15th amendments to the Constitution were enacted as a result. Dogs are allowed throughout the property and on the trails. They must be under owner's control, leashed, and cleaned up after at all times. Dogs may never be tied up and left unattended, and they are not allowed in any of the buildings.

Stores

PetSmart Pet Store 4026-B Wards Rd Lynchburg VA   434-237-0036
Your licensed and well-behaved leashed dog is allowed in the store.

Marion

Campgrounds and RV Parks
Hungry Mother State Park 2854 Park Blvd Marion VA   276-781-7400 (800-933-PARK (7275))
This park is rich in folklore and history, and offers interpretive programs, a variety of land and water activities, and recreation. Dogs of all sizes are allowed for an additional $3 per night per pet for camping, and for $5 per night per pet for cabins. Cabins are available year round. Dogs may not be left unattended, and they must be leashed and cleaned up after. Dogs are not allowed on the beaches or in buildings, but they are allowed on the trails. This campground is closed during the off-season. The camping and tent areas also allow dogs. There is a dog walk area at the campground. Dogs are allowed in the camping cabins.
Mount Rogers National Rec Area 3714 H 16 Marion VA   540-265-5100 (877-444-6777)
http://www.fs.fed.us/r8/gwj/mr/
Home to a vast variety of plant, bird, and wildlife, this diverse recreation area offers plenty of land and water recreation, including over 400 miles of designated trails, scenic drives, wilderness and wildlife areas, and more. Dogs are allowed throughout the park and at the camp areas. Dogs must be leashed and cleaned up after, and they are not allowed in swimming areas or park buildings. There are 7 campgrounds with varying amenities and environments. This RV park is closed during the off-season. The camping and tent areas also allow dogs. There is a dog walk area at the campground.

Parks
Mount Rogers National Rec Area 3714 H 16 Marion VA   540-265-5100 (877-444-6777)
http://www.fs.fed.us/r8/gwj/mr/
Home to a vast variety of plant, bird, and wildlife, this diverse recreation area offers plenty of land and water recreation, including over 400 miles of designated trails, scenic drives, wilderness and wildlife areas, and more. Dogs are allowed throughout the park and at the camp areas. Dogs must be leashed and cleaned up after, and they are not allowed in swimming areas or park buildings.

Martinsville

Accommodations
Best Western Martinsville 1755 Virginia Ave Martinsville VA   276-632-5611 (800-780-7234)
Dogs are allowed for an additional pet fee of $10 per night per room.
Holiday Inn Express 1895 Virginia Ave Martinsville VA   276-666-6835 (877-270-6405)
Dogs of all sizes are allowed for an additional one time pet fee of $25 per room.

Monterey

Accommodations
Highland Inn 68 West Main Street/H 250 Monterey VA 540-468-2143 (888-466-4682)
http://www.highland-inn.com/
Beautiful in any season, this 1904 3-story inn is a great starting point to a number of other activities, historic sites, and recreation. Dogs are allowed for an additional $20 per night per room. Dogs must be quiet, well behaved, leashed, and cleaned up after at all times.

Montross

Campgrounds and RV Parks
Westmoreland State Park 1650 State Park Road Montross VA 804-493-8821 (800-933-PARK (7275))
At almost 1,300 acres, this park features about a mile and a half of Potomac riverfront with great views, seasonal historical and ecological programs, and self-guided interpretive, nature trails. Dogs of all sizes are allowed for an additional fee of $3 per night per pet for the campground and $5 per night per pet for camping cabins; there is no fee for day use. Dogs must be kept on a leash no longer than 6 feet when outside and they must be brought in at night. Camp areas have fire rings, grills, a camp store, a boat launch for overnight guests, restrooms with showers, laundry facilities at campground A, and concessionaires. This RV park is closed during the off-season. The camping and tent areas also allow dogs. There is a dog walk area at the campground. Dogs are allowed in the camping cabins.

Parks

Westmoreland State Park 1650 State Park Road Montross VA   804-493-8821 (800-933-PARK (7275))
At almost 1,300 acres, this park features about a mile and a half of Potomac riverfront with great views, seasonal historical and ecological programs, and self-guided interpretive, nature trails. Dogs of all sizes are allowed for an additional fee of $3 per night per pet for the campground and $5 per night per pet for camping cabins; there is no fee for day use. Dogs must be kept on a leash no longer than 6 feet when outside and they must be brought in at night.

Mount Jackson

Accommodations

The Widow Kip's Country Inn 355 Orchard Drive Mount Jackson VA   540-477-2400 (800-478-8714)
http://www.widowkips.com/
This 1830 restored Victorian homestead features 7 rural acres overlooking the Shenandoah River with 3½ acres of landscaped grounds and a fenced 5 acre field for plenty of safe pet exercise. Dogs of all sizes are allowed in the cottages for an additional fee of $15 per night per pet. Dogs must be well behaved, leashed (except in field) and cleaned up after at all times.

Mouth of Wilson

Accommodations

Rugby Creek Cabins and Equestrian Resort 1228 Rugby Road Mouth of Wilson VA   276-579-4215
www.rugbycreek.com
Nestled high in the Blue Ridge Mountains, this 63 acre private farm is a place you can vacation with both your horse and your pooch (or just your pooch). Dogs of all sizes are allowed in the Overlook Cabin with prior approval for an additional fee of $10 per night per pet, and they provide doggy beds, bowls, toys, and a fenced yard for their canine guests. Dogs must be leashed and cleaned up after.

Campgrounds and RV Parks

Grayson Highlands State Park 829 Grayson Highlands Lane Mouth of Wilson VA   276-579-7092 (800-933-PARK (7275))
Nestled away in the Jefferson National Forest, this 4,800+ acre state park offers stunning views, 9 hiking trails, nature/history programs, event venues, festivals, workshops, and much more. Dogs are allowed throughout the park and in the campground for an additional fee of $3 per night per pet; there is no charge for day use only. Dogs must be well behaved, leashed, and cleaned up after. Dogs are not allowed in any buildings. Camp areas have mostly wooded sites, fire rings/grills, restrooms, and showers. This RV park is closed during the off-season. The camping and tent areas also allow dogs. There is a dog walk area at the campground.

Parks

Grayson Highlands State Park 829 Grayson Highlands Lane Mouth of Wilson VA   276-579-7092 (800-933-PARK (7275))
Nestled away in the Jefferson National Forest, this 4,800+ acre state park offers stunning views, 9 hiking trails, nature/history programs, event venues, festivals, workshops, and much more. Dogs are allowed throughout the park and in the campground for an additional fee of $3 per night per pet; there is no charge for day use only. Dogs must be well behaved, leashed, and cleaned up after. Dogs are not allowed in any buildings.

Natural Bridge

Accommodations

1926 Caboose Vacation Rental 218 S Main Street/H 11 Natural Bridge VA   540-463-2521
http://www.guestcaboose.com/
This interesting 1926 Caboose vacation getaway is one of two of their rentals that allow pets. Dogs of all sizes are allowed for no additional fee. Dogs must be well trained, leashed, and cleaned up after inside and outside of the units.

Natural Bridge Hotel 15 Appledore Lane Natural Bridge VA   540-291-2121 (800-533-1410)
This unique getaway has been serving travelers since the late 1700's, and there are a variety of attractions here such as the Natural Bridge and the Drama of Creation seasonal, nightly shows, Foamhenge, a Styrofoam replica of Stonehenge, and much more. Dogs are allowed in the cottages for no additional pet fee. Dogs must be leashed and cleaned up after at all times. Dogs are not allowed in buildings, the museums, or the caverns; they are allowed on the trails and at Natural Bridge Park.

Campgrounds and RV Parks
Natural Bridge/Lexington KOA 214 Killdeer Lane Natural Bridge VA   540-291-2770 (800-562-8514)
http://www.naturalbridgekoa.com
Dogs of all sizes are allowed, and there can be more than two dogs. There are no additional pet fees for tent or RV sites. There is a $5 per stay per pet additional fee for cabins, and there can be 2 dogs. Dogs must be well behaved, leashed, and cleaned up after. The camping and tent areas also allow dogs. There is a dog walk area at the campground. Dogs are allowed in the camping cabins.
Yogi Bear at Natural Bridge 16 Recreation Lane Natural Bridge Station VA   540-291-2727 (800-258-9532)
http://www.campnbr.com/index2.html
This scenic park, located along the James River, offers a variety of land and water activities and recreational pursuits. Dogs of all sizes are allowed at no additional fee. Dogs may not be left unattended, and they must be leashed and cleaned up after. Dogs are not allowed on the beach, the game area, food areas, or in buildings. Dogs are allowed on the trails. This campground is closed during the off-season. The camping and tent areas also allow dogs. There is a dog walk area at the campground. Dogs are allowed in the camping cabins.

Attractions
Natural Bridge 15 Appledore Lane Natural Bridge VA   540-291-2121
On the National Register of Historic Places, this "7th Natural Wonder of the World" has been amazing visitors for hundreds of years, and it took on a spectacular transformation when night illumination was added with musical accompaniment in 1927 and the "Drama of Creation" shows were born. There is also abundant wildlife, a 1500 year old Arbor Vitae tree, and a wonderful nature trail here leading to Lace Falls. Dogs are allowed in the park and on the trails; they are not allowed in buildings, the museum, caverns, or at the living history village. Dogs must be leashed and cleaned up after at all times.

New Market

Accommodations
Days Inn New Market 9360 George Collins Pkwy New Market VA   540-740-4100 (800-329-7466)
Dogs of all sizes are allowed. There is a $5 per night pet fee per pet.
Quality Inn Shenandoah Valley 162 W Old Cross Road New Market VA   540-740-3141 (877-424-6423)
Dogs are allowed for an additional one time pet fee of $10.50 per room.

Newport News - Hampton

Accommodations
Arrow Inn 3361 Commander Shepard Boulevard Hampton VA   757-865-0300 (800-833-2520)
http://www.arrowinn.com/
This inn offers fully equipped efficiencies and kitchenettes, and a great central location to several other points of interest and recreational opportunities. Dogs are allowed for $5 per night per pet or $30 by the month. Dogs must be well mannered, leashed, and cleaned up after at all times.
Candlewood Suites 401 Butler Farm Road Hampton VA   757-766-8976 (877-270-6405)
Dogs up to 80 pounds are allowed for an additional one time pet fee per room of $75 for 1 to 6 nights; $150 for 7 or more nights, and there is a pet agreement to sign at check in.
Holiday Inn 1815 W. Mercury Blvd. Hampton VA   757-838-0200 (877-270-6405)
Dogs up to 80 pounds are allowed for an additional one time pet fee per room of $75 for 1 to 6 nights; $150 for 7 or more nights, and there is a pet agreement to sign at check in.
Red Roof Inn - Hampton, VA 1925 Coliseum Drive Hampton VA   757-838-1870 (800-RED-ROOF)
One well-behaved family pet per room. Guest must notify front desk upon arrival. Guest is liable for any damages. In consideration of all guests, pets must never be left unattended in the guest rooms.
Comfort Inn 12330 Jefferson Avenue Newport News VA   757-249-0200 (877-424-6423)
Dogs are allowed for an additional fee of $50 per night per pet.

Days Inn Newport News 14747 Warwick Blvd Newport News VA   757-874-0201 (800-329-7466)
Dogs of all sizes are allowed. There is a $10 per night pet fee per pet.
Days Inn Newport News/Oyster Point 11829 Fishing Pt Dr Newport News VA   757-873-6700 (800-329-7466)
Dogs of all sizes are allowed. There is a $15 per night pet fee per pet.
Motel 6 - Newport News 797 J Clyde Morris Boulevard Newport News VA   757-595-6336 (800-466-8356)
One well-behaved family pet per room. Guest must notify front desk upon arrival. Guest is liable for any damages. In consideration of all guests, pets must never be left unattended in the guest rooms.

Attractions
Endview Plantation 362 Yorktown Road Newport News VA   757-887-1862
http://www.endview.org/
This 1769 colonial plantation is dedicated to honoring, preserving, and educating the public through a number of programs, activities, reenactments, and special events of the significance it played in shaping America's culture and history. Dogs are allowed throughout the park; they are not allowed in buildings. Dogs must be under owner's control, leashed, and cleaned up after at all times.

TOP 200 PLACE **Mariner's Museum** 100 Museum Drive Newport News VA   757-596-2222
http://www.mariner.org/
Located on 550 wooded acres on the shores of Lake Maury, this is one of the world's largest international maritime history museums. Here visitors can also see a full-scale replica of the Civil War ironclad USS Monitor and they have an annual 5-week concert series each Summer. Dogs are allowed throughout the park and on the trails; they are not allowed in buildings. Dogs must be under owner's control, leashed, and cleaned up after at all times.

Stores
PetSmart Pet Store 12142 Jefferson Ave Newport News VA   757-249-2007
Your licensed and well-behaved leashed dog is allowed in the store.

Parks
Grandview Nature Preserve 22 Lincoln Street Hampton VA   757-850-5134
A beautiful nature trail leads to a 2½ mile long sandy beach at this 500 acre preserve, and it serves as a great place for bird and wildlife viewing. Dogs are allowed throughout the park and on the beach from September 16th through May 14th; they are not allowed during the Summer on ANY Hampton public beach. Dogs must be leashed and cleaned up after at all times.
Sandy Bottom Nature Park and Off Leash Dog Park 1255 Big Bethel Road Hampton VA   757-825-4657
http://www.hampton.gov/sandybottom/
This 456 acre environmental education and wildlife management facility offers a variety of programs, events, activities, recreational opportunities, and an off leash dog park. The dog park requires pre-registration which can be obtained at the front office for a fee of $10. Dogs must be licensed and have proof of current vaccinations and rabies shots. Dogs are allowed throughout the park; they are not allowed in buildings. Dogs must be leashed (except in designated areas) and cleaned up after at all times.

Northern Virginia

Accommodations
Holiday Inn Hotel and Suites 625 First Street Alexandria VA   703-548-6300 (877-270-6405)
Dogs of all sizes are allowed for an additional fee of $25 per night per pet.
Morrison House Hotel 116 S Alfred St Alexandria VA   703-838-8000
http://www.morrisonhouse.com
This Kimpton boutique hotel allows dogs of all sizes. There are no additional pet fees.
Red Roof Inn - Washington, DC - Alexandria 5975 Richmond Highway Alexandria VA   703-960-5200 (800-RED-ROOF)
One well-behaved family pet per room. Guest must notify front desk upon arrival. Guest is liable for any damages. In consideration of all guests, pets must never be left unattended in the guest rooms.
Sheraton Suites Old Town Alexandria 801 North Saint Asaph St. Alexandria VA   703-836-4700 (888-625-5144)
Dogs up to 70 pounds are allowed. There are no additional pet fees. Dogs are not allowed to be left alone in the room.
Washington Suites 100 South Reynolds Street Alexandria VA   703-370-9600
Once an apartment building, this hotel offers the largest suites in the area from 500 to 1,600 square feet and is

only 9 miles from Washington DC. Dogs of all sizes are allowed for an additional $20 per night per pet. Dogs must be quiet, leashed, and cleaned up after.
Quality Inn Courthouse Plaza 1200N Courthouse Road Arlington VA   703-524-4000 (877-424-6423)
Dogs of all sizes are allowed. There is a $35 fee for the first night then it is $10 per night per pet.
Residence Inn by Marriott 550 Army Navy Drive Arlington VA   703-413-6630
Dogs of all sizes are allowed, however there can only be 1 large pet or 2 medium to small pets per room. There is a $200 one time cleaning fee plus $8 per night per pet and a pet policy to sign at check in.
Sheraton Crystal City Hotel 1800 Jefferson Davis Highway Arlington VA   703-486-1111 (888-625-5144)
Dogs of all sizes are allowed. There are no additional pet fees. Dogs are not allowed to be left alone in the room.
TownePlace Suites Chantilly 14036 Thunderbolt Place Chantilly VA   703-709-0453
Dogs of all sizes are allowed. There is a $75 one time pet fee per visit.
Candlewood Suites 11400 Random Hills Road Fairfax VA   703-359-4490 (877-270-6405)
Dogs of all sizes are allowed for an additional one time pet fee of $75 per room.
Comfort Inn University Center 11180 Fairfax Blvd Fairfax VA   703-591-5900 (877-424-6423)
Dogs are allowed: 1 dog is an additional one time pet fee of $25 per room; a 2nd dog is an additional one time fee of $10.
Residence Inn by Marriott 12815 Fair Lakes Parkway Fairfax VA   703-266-4900
Dogs of all sizes are allowed. There is a $150 one time fee and a pet policy to sign at check in.
Residence Inn by Marriott 8125 Gatehouse Road Falls Church VA   703-573-5200
Dogs of all sizes are allowed. There is a $150 one time fee and a pet policy to sign at check in.
TownePlace Suites Falls Church 205 Hillwood Avenue Falls Church VA   703-237-6172
Dogs of all sizes are allowed. There is a $75 one time pet fee per visit.
Candlewood Suites 13845 Sunrise Valley Drive Herndon VA   703-793-7100 (877-270-6405)
Dogs of all sizes are allowed for an additional one time fee per pet of $75 for 1 to 15 days, and $150 for 16 or more days.
Residence Inn by Marriott 315 Elden Street Herndon VA   703-435-0044
Dogs of all sizes are allowed. There is a $75 one time fee and a pet policy to sign at check in.
Staybridge Suites - Dulles 13700 Coppermine Rd Herndon VA   703-713-6800 (877-270-6405)
Dogs up to 50 pounds are allowed for an additional one time pet fee of $150 for a 1 bedroom suite, and $250 for a 2 bedroom suite.
Comfort Inn Gunston Corner 8180 Silverbrook Road Lorton VA   703-643-3100 (877-424-6423)
Dogs are allowed for an additional one time pet fee of $25 per room.
Best Western Battlefield Inn 10820 Balls Ford Road Manassas VA   703-361-8000 (800-780-7234)
Dogs are allowed for an additional fee of $10 per night per pet. Extra large dogs can not be accommodated.
Red Roof Inn - Washington, DC - Manassas 10610 Automotive Drive Manassas VA   703-335-9333 (800-RED-ROOF)
One well-behaved family pet per room. Guest must notify front desk upon arrival. Guest is liable for any damages. In consideration of all guests, pets must never be left unattended in the guest rooms.
Best Western Tysons Westpark 8401 Westpark Drive McLean VA   703-734-2800 (800-780-7234)
Dogs are allowed for no additional pet fee.
Staybridge Suites 6845 Old Dominion Dr McLean VA   703-448-5400 (877-270-6405)
Dogs of all sizes are allowed for an additional one time pet fee of $75 per room.
Sheraton Reston Hotel 11810 Sunrise Valley Dr. Reston VA   703-620-9000 (888-625-5144)
Dogs up to 80 pounds are allowed. Dogs are not allowed to be left alone in the room.
Comfort Inn 6560 Loisdale Court Springfield VA   703-922-9000 (877-424-6423)
Dogs up to 50 pounds are allowed for no additional pet fee. Dogs must be crated when left alone in the room and a contact number left with the front desk.
Hampton Inn 6550 Loisdale Court Springfield VA   703-924-9444
Well behaved dogs of all sizes are allowed. There are no additional pet fees.
Red Roof Inn - Washington, DC Southwest - Springfield 6868 Springfield Boulevard Springfield VA   703-644-5311 (800-RED-ROOF)
One well-behaved family pet per room. Guest must notify front desk upon arrival. Guest is liable for any damages. In consideration of all guests, pets must never be left unattended in the guest rooms.
TownePlace Suites Springfield 6245 Brandon Avenue Springfield VA   703-569-8060
Dogs of all sizes are allowed. There is a $75 one time pet fee per visit.
Candlewood Suites 45520 East Severn Way Sterling VA   703-674-2288 (877-270-6405)
Dogs of all sizes are allowed for an additional one time pet fee of $75 per room.
Hampton Inn 46331 McClellan Way Sterling VA   703-450-9595
Well behaved dogs of all sizes are allowed. There is an additional $25 per room for the first night, and each night thereafter the fee is $10 per room. There is a pet policy to sign at check in.
Hampton Inn 45440 Holiday Drive Sterling VA   703-471-8300
Dogs of all sizes are allowed. There is a $25 per pet per stay fee and a pet policy to sign at check in.
Holiday Inn Washington-Dulles Intl Airport 1000 Sully Rd Sterling VA   703-471-7411 (877-270-6405)
Dogs up to 50 pounds are allowed for an additional one time pet fee of $50 per room.

TownePlace Suites Sterling 21123 Whitfield Place Sterling VA   703-421-1090
Dogs of all sizes are allowed. There is a $75 one time pet fee per visit.
TownePlace Suites Washington Dulles Airport 22744 Holiday Park Dr Sterling VA   703-707-2017
Dogs of all sizes are allowed. There is a $75 one time pet fee per visit.
Homestead Tyson's Corner 8201 Old Courthouse Road Vienna VA   703-356-6300
Dogs of all sizes are allowed. There is a $75 one time fee per pet.
Residence Inn by Marriott 8616 Westwood Center Drive Vienna VA   703-893-0120
One dog of any size is allowed. There is a $75 one time fee and a pet policy to sign at check in.
Residence Inn by Marriott 8400 Old Courthouse Road Vienna VA   703-917-0800
Dogs of all sizes are allowed. There is a $75 one time fee and a pet policy to sign at check in.
Quality Inn 1109 Hormer Road Woodbridge VA   703-494-0300 (877-424-6423)
Dogs are allowed for an additional fee of $20 (plus tax) per night per pet.
Residence Inn by Marriott 14301 Crossing Place Woodbridge VA   703-490-4020
Dogs of all sizes are allowed. There is a $75 one time fee and a pet policy to sign at check in.

Campgrounds and RV Parks
Bull Run Regional Park 7700 Bull Run Drive Centreville VA   703-631-0550
http://www.nvrpa.org/bullruncamp.html
This scenic park offers year round recreation and is close to Washington DC and other area attractions. Dogs of all sizes are allowed at no additional fee. Dogs may not be left unattended, and they must be leashed and cleaned up after. Dogs are not allowed in the pool area, but they are allowed on the trails. The camping and tent areas also allow dogs. There is a dog walk area at the campground. There are no water hookups at the campground.
Pohick Bay Park 6501 Pohick Bay Drive Lorton VA   703-352-5900
This water oriented 1,000 acre park has one of only 3 access points to the Potomac River in northern Virginia, and many other features make this a popular recreation area. It also features a "treehouse" playground area, mini-golf, an outdoor freeform pool, plenty of bird and wildlife, and hiking trails. Dogs are allowed throughout the park and the campground for no additional fee. Dogs may not be left unattended in the campground, and they must be under owner's control, leashed, and cleaned up after at all times. Campsites have grills, fire rings, picnic tables, and a camp store, restrooms, hot showers, a laundry, and a dump station are close by. The camping and tent areas also allow dogs. There is a dog walk area at the campground.
Lake Fairfax Park 1400 Lake Fairfax Drive Reston VA   703-471-5415
This park of 476 acres, with an 18 acre lake, offers fishing, hiking, nature study, and a variety of land and water recreation. Dogs of all sizes are allowed at no additional fee. Dogs may not be left unattended outside, and they must be leashed and cleaned up after. Dogs are not allowed on the athletic fields, but they are allowed on the trails. The camping and tent areas also allow dogs. There is a dog walk area at the campground. There are no water hookups at the campground.

Attractions
Alexandria's Footsteps to the Past Walking Tours 221 King Street Alexandria VA   703-683-3451
http://footstepstothepast.com/
Generations of knowledge are shared with visitors on historic Alexandria, the hometown of George Washington and Robert E. Lee. History and ghost walking tours are offered day or night with varying times and lengths, and your well behaved pooch is welcome to join in the fun for no additional fee. Dogs must be under owner's control/care and leashed at all times.

TOP 200 PLACE **Doggie Happy Hour** 480 King Street Alexandria VA   703-549-6080
http://www.doggiehappyhour.com
Dogs on leash are allowed at the outdoor tables in the courtyard. Open to dogs of all sizes between April-October 31st on Tuesdays and Thursdays. All they ask is to stay away from bar area and to keep paws off the tables and chairs. Water and gourmet biscuits are served to your pets.
Fort Ward Museum and Historic Site 4301 W Braddock Road Alexandria VA   703-838-4848
http://www.fortward.org/
A historic fort, living history events, Summer camps, tours, interpretive and educational programs, a museum, and more are offered at this 45 acre site that also preserves and elucidates to the fort's important significance during the American Civil War. Dogs are allowed throughout the park; they are not allowed in buildings. Dogs must be leashed and cleaned up after.
George Washington's Grist Mill and Distillery Mt Vernon Memorial H/H 235 Alexandria VA   703-780-2000
Located 3 miles south of Mt Vernon, this reconstructed gristmill and distillery sits on the original site of George Washington's first mill. Dogs are allowed around the grounds; they are not allowed in the buildings or on the tours. Dogs must be leashed and cleaned up after at all times.
Old Town Horse and Carriage Duke St Alexandria VA   703-765-8976
http://ci.alexandria.va.us/
Take a horse and carriage ride with your pup or just roam around the Old Town Alexandria area. Pick up the

horse and carriage ride in Old Town.

TOP 200 PLACE **Potomac Riverboat Co. Canine Cruises** Cameron and Union Streets Alexandria VA 703-548-9000
Every second Thursday in May through September, Potomac Riverboat hosts a Canine Cruise. This is a 40 minute Cruise in the Potomac River that invites you to bring your dog along. Dogs must be on a 6 foot leash. Canine Cruises leave from the Alexandria City Marina. The price for a tour is $11 per person and the dog rides free. The boats depart at 6:00, 7:00, 8:00 and 9:00pm. Only one dog per person is allowed.

Woodlawn Plantation 9000 Richmond H/H 1 Alexandria VA   703-780-4000
http://www.woodlawn1805.org/
George Washington provisioned the land to his nephew where this beautiful mansion was built, and this park's main objective is to preserve and share its multi-leveled history. Dogs are allowed on the grounds; they are not allowed in any of the buildings. Dogs must be leashed and cleaned up after at all times.

Arlington National Cemetery Memorial Drive Arlington VA
http://www.arlingtoncemetery.org/
Well behaved, leashed dogs are allowed in Arlington Cemetery. Please respect the grounds here. Your well behaved dog can accompany you to the Kennedy grave and other outdoor sites at the cemetery.

Iwo Jima Memorial   Arlington VA
http://www.nps.gov/gwmp/usmc.htm
Leashed dogs can accompany you to the Iwo Jima, or the Marine Corp War Memorial as it is formally called.

Sully Historic Site 3601 Sully Road Chantilly VA   703-437-1794
Dedicated to preserving and sharing the history of the Lee family and of Fairfax County from the early 19th century to the present, this park features original outbuildings, gardens, a representative slave area, exhibits, and interpretive programs. Dogs are allowed throughout the grounds. They are not allowed in any of the buildings. This is a seasonal attraction, and they are closed on Tuesday.

Manassas National Battlefield 6511 Sudley Road Manassas VA   703-361-1339
http://www.nps.gov/mana
Visitors can explore 2 major battles of the Civil War that was fought here through interpretive programs, hiking the area, or checking out the museum. Dogs are allowed throughout the park; they are not allowed in buildings. Dogs must be under owner's control, leashed, and cleaned up after at all times.

Mount Vernon

TOP 200 PLACE **Mount Vernon** George Washington Pkwy Mount Vernon VA 703-780-2000
http://www.mountvernon.org/
Your dog is welcome to explore the vast estate that George Washington called home. Your leashed, well behaved dog can accompany you to all outdoor areas of Mount Vernon. If you would like to take the mansion

tour then someone will need to watch the dog. Otherwise, most of the site is outdoors.

Shopping Centers

Reston Town Center

Reston Town Center 11900 Market Street Reston VA   703-689-4699
http://www.restontowncenter.com/
Year round shopping and dining are only a part of what's available here; there are free Summer concerts, an annual dog event usually in May, a seasonal ice-skating rink, a busy open air event pavilion, and more. Dogs are allowed at the plaza; it is up to the individual stores as to whether dogs are allowed inside. Dogs must be under owner's control, leashed, and cleaned up after at all times.

Stores

Fetch Dog and Cat Bakery Boutique 101 A S St. Asaph Street Alexandria VA   703-518-5188
http://www.fetch-bakery.com/
No matter the size of your pup or how discerning their taste, this bakery aims to please their palates with a wide assortment of natural homemade treats; they also have a good assortment of pet (and people) necessities and gifts. Dogs must be friendly, under owner's control/care, and leashed at all times.
Madeleine's Dogs Couture 1222 King Street Alexandria VA   703-836-9046
http://www.madeleinesdogs.com/
This upscale dog boutique offers yummy treats plus a wide inventory of unique gifts. Dogs are welcome in the store; they must be leashed and under owner's control/care at all times.
PetSmart Pet Store 3351 Jefferson Davis Hwy Unit 10 Alexandria VA   703-739-4844
Your licensed and well-behaved dog is allowed in the store.
PetSmart Pet Store 7690 Richmond Hwy Alexandria VA   703-721-0650
Your licensed and well-behaved leashed dog is allowed in the store.
Petco Pet Store 6612 Richmond Highway Alexandria VA   703-660-1300
Your licensed and well-behaved leashed dog is allowed in the store.
Sugar House Day Spa 111 North Alfred Street Alexandria VA   703-549-9940
http://www.sugarhousedayspa.com/home.asp
This salon will allow your well behaved pooch to stay with you inside the salon area; they are not allowed upstairs in the day spa. Dogs must be under owner's control/care at all times.
Petco Pet Store 3200 North Washington Blvd Arlington VA   703-276-7387
Your licensed and well-behaved leashed dog is allowed in the store.
Petco Pet Store 5825 Leesburg Pike Bailey's Crossroads VA   703-845-2780

Your licensed and well-behaved leashed dog is allowed in the store.
Petco Pet Store 9230-B Old Keene Mill Rd Burke VA   703-455-2007
Your licensed and well-behaved leashed dog is allowed in the store.
Petco Pet Store 4167 Cheshire Station Plaza Dale City VA   703-590-8823
Your licensed and well-behaved leashed dog is allowed in the store.
PetSmart Pet Store 12971 Fair Lakes Cntr Fairfax VA   703-802-1027
Your licensed and well-behaved leashed dog is allowed in the store.
Petco Pet Store 10708 Lee Highway Fairfax VA   703-352-3300
Your licensed and well-behaved leashed dog is allowed in the store.
Petco Pet Store 13053 Lee Jackson Memorial Highway Fairfax VA   703-817-9444
Your licensed and well-behaved leashed dog is allowed in the store.
PetSmart Pet Store 6100 Arlington Blvd Falls Church VA   703-536-2708
Your licensed and well-behaved leashed dog is allowed in the store.
Petco Pet Store 2441-F Centreville Rd Herndon VA   703-713-1552
Your licensed and well-behaved leashed dog is allowed in the store.
PetSmart Pet Store 10834 Sudley Manor Dr Manassas VA   703-335-1755
Your licensed and well-behaved leashed dog is allowed in the store.
Petco Pet Store 10800 Promenade Lane Manassas VA   703-257-6373
Your licensed and well-behaved leashed dog is allowed in the store.
PetSmart Pet Store 6536 Frontier Dr Springfield VA   703-922-4990
Your licensed and well-behaved leashed dog is allowed in the store.
PetSmart Pet Store 46220 Potomac Run Plaza Sterling VA   703-444-6500
Your licensed and well-behaved leashed dog is allowed in the store.
Happy Tails Dog Spa 8528-F Tyco Road Tyson's Corner VA   703-821-0700
This store features a wide variety of unique items as well as grooming supplies, food, treats, toys, a large canine selection of sweaters, collars, leashes and bandanas, gift certificates, and they are a full service animal care center. They are open from 7 am to 7 pm Monday through Friday; from 10 am to 5 pm on Saturday, and from 11 am to 2 pm on Sunday. Your well behaved, leashed, pet may explore the store with you.
Petco Pet Store 1929 Old Gallows Rd Vienna VA   703-448-3401
Your licensed and well-behaved leashed dog is allowed in the store.
PetSmart Pet Store 13337 Worth Ave Woodbridge VA   703-490-8676
Your licensed and well-behaved leashed dog is allowed in the store.

Parks

Holmes Run Park Holmes Run Pkwy and S Jordon St Alexandria VA
This park has a bike trail, creek, and picnic areas. Dogs are allowed on leash. There is also an off leash dog park at the Duke St intersection with the park.
Huntley Meadows Park 3701 Lockheed Blvd Alexandria VA   703-768-2525
http://users.erols.com/huntleymeadows/
Dogs on leash are allowed in most of the park. However, they are not allowed on the wooden boardwalk.
Mount Vernon Trail George Washington Parkway Alexandria VA   703-285-2601
This bike trail is very scenic and connects Mt Vernon with Washington. Dogs on leash are allowed.
Gravelly Point Park George Washington Pkwy Arlington VA
You and your dog can watch the airline traffic at National Airport. It can get noisy. You need to access the park from the northbound direction on the George Washington Parkway. Dogs must be leashed in this park.
TOP 200 PLACE **Theodore Roosevelt Island Park and Memorial** George Washington Parkway Arlington VA   703-289-2500
http://www.nps.gov/this/
Theodore Roosevelt Island park has nice dirt trails and an impressive memorial to Theodore Roosevelt. Your dog will probably like this memorial the most in Washington as it has many acres of trails and nature. Dogs may accompany you on leash in the park. Parking is on the George Washington Parkway on the north-bound side and you walk to the island over a bridge.
Pohick Bay Park 6501 Pohick Bay Drive Lorton VA   703-352-5900
This water oriented 1,000 acre park has one of only 3 access points to the Potomac River in northern Virginia, and many other features make this a popular recreation area. It also features a "treehouse" playground area, mini-golf, an outdoor freeform pool, plenty of bird and wildlife, and hiking trails. Dogs are allowed throughout the park and the campground for no additional fee.
Wolf Trap National Park for the Performing Arts 1551 Trap Road Vienna VA   703-255-1800
http://www.nps.gov/wotr/
This park is the first national park for the performing arts, and it offers a wealth of natural and cultural resources, interpretive programs, and "Theater in the Woods". The park is open daily from dawn to dusk, however there are some exceptions; during park festivals and Filene Center performances. Dogs are allowed throughout the park, except they are not allowed in the concert area during performances. Dogs of all sizes are allowed at no additional fee. Dogs may not be left unattended, and they must be leashed and cleaned up after.

Off-Leash Dog Parks

Ben Brenman Dog Park at Backlick Creek Alexandria VA 703-838-4343
This is an official off-leash dog area. The park is completely fenced. These parks are controlled by the Alexandria Department of Recreation, Parks and Cultural Activities.

Braddock Road Dog Run Area SE Corner of Braddock Rd and Commonwealth Alexandria VA 703-838-4343
This is an unfenced official off-leash dog area. Alexandria Off-leash dog parks are controlled by the Alexandria Department of Recreation, Parks and Cultural Activities.

Chambliss Street Dog Run Area Chambliss St Alexandria VA 703-838-4343
This is an unfenced official off-leash dog area. It is located south of the tennis courts. Alexandria Off-leash dog parks are controlled by the Alexandria Department of Recreation, Parks and Cultural Activities.

Chinquapin Park Dog Run Area Chinquapin Park East of Loop Alexandria VA 703-838-4343
This is an unfenced official off-leash dog area. Alexandria Off-leash dog parks are controlled by the Alexandria Department of Recreation, Parks and Cultural Activities.

Duke Street Dog Park 5000 block of Duke Street Alexandria VA 703-838-4343
This is an official off-leash dog area. The park is completely fenced. The park is located east of the Beatley Library. These parks are controlled by the Alexandria Department of Recreation, Parks and Cultural Activities.

Fort Ward Park Offleash Dog Run East of Park Road Alexandria VA 703-838-4343
This is an unfenced official off-leash dog area. Alexandria Off-leash dog parks are controlled by the Alexandria Department of Recreation, Parks and Cultural Activities.

Fort Williams Dog Run Area Between Ft Wiliams and Ft Williams Parkway Alexandria VA 703-838-4343
This is an unfenced official off-leash dog area. Alexandria Off-leash dog parks are controlled by the Alexandria Department of Recreation, Parks and Cultural Activities.

Founders Park Dog Run Area Oronoco St and Union St Alexandria VA 703-838-4343
This is an unfenced official off-leash dog area. Alexandria Off-leash dog parks are controlled by the Alexandria Department of Recreation, Parks and Cultural Activities.

Hooff's Run Dog Run Area Commonwealth between Oak and Chapman St Alexandria VA 703-838-4343
This is an unfenced official off-leash dog area. Alexandria Off-leash dog parks are controlled by the Alexandria Department of Recreation, Parks and Cultural Activities.

Montgomery Park Dog Park Fairfax and 1st Streets Alexandria VA 703-838-4343
This is an official off-leash dog area. The park is completely fenced. These parks are controlled by the Alexandria Department of Recreation, Parks and Cultural Activities.

Monticello Park Dog Run Area Monticello Park Alexandria VA 703-838-4343
This is an unfenced official off-leash dog area. Alexandria Off-leash dog parks are controlled by the Alexandria Department of Recreation, Parks and Cultural Activities.

Simpson Stadium Dog Park Monroe Avenue Alexandria VA 703-838-4343
This is an official off-leash dog area. The park is completely fenced. These parks are controlled by the Alexandria Department of Recreation, Parks and Cultural Activities.

Tarleton Park Dog Run Area Old Mill Run west of Gordon St Alexandria VA 703-838-4343
This is an unfenced official off-leash dog area. Alexandria Off-leash dog parks are controlled by the Alexandria Department of Recreation, Parks and Cultural Activities.

W&OD Railroad Dog Run Area Raymond Avenue Alexandria VA 703-838-4343
This is an unfenced official off-leash dog area. Alexandria Off-leash dog parks are controlled by the Alexandria Department of Recreation, Parks and Cultural Activities.

Windmill Hill Park Dog Run Area Gibbon and Union Streets Alexandria VA 703-838-4343
This is an unfenced official off-leash dog area. Alexandria Off-leash dog parks are controlled by the Alexandria Department of Recreation, Parks and Cultural Activities.

Mason District 6621 Columbia Pike Annandale VA
This fenced dog park is open from dawn to dusk. The park is controlled by the Fairfax County Park Authority and sponsored by the Mason District Dog Opportunity Group.

Benjamin Banneker Park Dog Run 1600 Block North Sycamore Arlington VA
This partially off-leash dog park is open during daylight hours. It is over eleven acres. This dog park is maintained by Banneker Dogs.

Fort Barnard Dog Run Corner of South Pollard St and South Walter Reed Drive Arlington VA
This dog run is open from dawn to dusk. It is sponsored by Douglas Dogs.

Glencarlyn Park Dog Run 301 South Harrison St Arlington VA
This is an unfenced dog run area in Glencarlyn Park. The area is located near a creek. It is open during daylight hours.

Madison Community Center Dog Park 3829 North Stafford St Arlington VA
This 15 acre fully fenced dog park is located at the Madison Community Center. Please note that dogs are not allowed on the adjacent soccer field and that you need to park in the Community Center front lot and not the back lot.

Shirlington Park Dog Run 2601 South Arlington Mill Drive Arlington VA

This unfenced dog park is located along the bicycle path between Shirlington Rd and South Walter Reed Dr. It is open during daylight hours.

Towers Park Dog Park 801 South Scott St Arlington VA
This fenced dog park is located in Towers Park behind the tennis courts. There is a separate fenced small dog off-leash area.

Chandon Dog Park 900 Palmer Drive Herndon VA
This fenced dog park is open from dawn to dusk. The park is controlled by the Fairfax County Park Authority and sponsored by Herndon Dogs, Inc.

Blake Lane Dog Park 10033 Blake Lane Oakton VA
This fenced dog park is open from dawn to dusk. The park is controlled by the Fairfax County Park Authority and sponsored by OaktonDogs, Inc.

Baron Cameron Dog Park 11300 Baron Cameron Avenue Reston VA
This fenced dog park is open from dawn to dusk. The park is controlled by the Fairfax County Park Authority and sponsored by RestonDogs, Inc. This dog park has a separate area for small dogs and water for your dog.

South Run Dog Park 7550 Reservation Drive Springfield VA
This fenced dog park is open from dawn to dusk. The park is controlled by the Fairfax County Park Authority and sponsored by Lorton Dogs, Inc.

Outdoor Restaurants

Baja Fresh 3231 Duke Street Alexandria VA   703-823-2888
This restaurant serves Mexican food. Dogs are allowed at the outdoor tables. The restaurant has outdoor tables only in the Summer.

Caboose Cafe & Bakery 2419 Mount Vernon Avenue Alexandria VA   703-566-1283
Dogs are allowed at the outdoor tables. This restaurant has food and water bowls for dogs.

Fish Market 105 King Street Alexandria VA   703-836-5676
Dogs are allowed at the outdoor tables.

Five Guys Burgers and Fries 107 N Fayette Street Alexandria VA   703-549-7991
http://www.fiveguys.com/
This eatery is a popular stop for a "great burger" and all that goes with them. Dogs are allowed at the outer tables; they must be under owner's control/care and leashed at all times.

Gadsby's Tavern 138 N Royal Street Alexandria VA   703-548-1288
http://www.gadsbystavernrestaurant.com/
In operation since the 1770's, this tavern offers a great colonial dining experience with authentic décor and indoor or patio dining options. Dogs are allowed at the outer tables. Dogs must be under owner's control/care and be leashed at all times.

Joe Theismann's Restaurant 1800 Diagonal Road Alexandria VA   703-739-0777
Dogs are allowed at the outdoor tables. This restaurant is owned by the former Redskin quarterback.

TOP 200 PLACE **Pat Troy's Irish Pub** 111 N Pitt Street Alexandria VA 703-549-4535
http://www.pattroysirishpub.com
This restaurant serves traditional Irish and American cuisine as well as providing an active entertainment calendar of fun events. They also offer a dog friendly patio and a doggylicious menu. The menu for dogs include chopped chicken, chopped burger, beef stew, and lamb stew.

Quiznos 1640 King Street Alexandria VA   703-838-8425
Dogs are allowed at the outdoor tables.

Taqueria Poblano 2400-B Mount Vernon Ave Alexandria VA   703-548-8226
This restaurant serves Mexican food. Dogs are allowed at the outdoor tables. Water is provided for your pet.

Aegan Taverna 2950 Clarendon Blvd Arlington VA   703-841-9494
This restaurant serves Mediterranean and Greek food. Dogs are allowed at the outdoor tables. The restaurant has outdoor tables only in the Summer.

Bertucci 2700-2800 Clarendon Blvd, WR 930 Arlington VA   703-528-9177
http://www.bertucci.com
Dogs are allowed at the outdoor tables. The restaurant has outdoor tables only in the Summer.

Faccia Luna 2909 Wilson Blvd Arlington VA   703-276-3099
This restaurant serves Italian pasta and pizza. Dogs are allowed at the outdoor tables. The restaurant has outdoor tables only in the Summer.

Il Raddiccio 1801 Clarendon Blvd Arlington VA   703-276-2627
This restaurant serves Italian pasta and pizza. Dogs are allowed at the outdoor tables. The restaurant has outdoor tables only in the Summer.

Lazy Sundae 2925 Wilson Blvd Arlington VA   703-525-4960
There are benches out front where you can sit with your dog, and they also have Doggy Ice Creams.

Mexicali Blues 2933 Wilson Blvd Arlington VA   703-812-9352
This restaurant serves Mexican and Hispanic foods. Dogs are allowed at the outdoor tables. The restaurant has outdoor tables only in the Summer. They will also bring water out to your dog.

Quiznos 2201 Wilson Blvd Arlington VA   703-248-8888

Dogs are allowed at the outdoor tables. The restaurant has outdoor tables only in the Summer.
Quiznos 1555 Wilson Blvd Arlington VA   703-248-9585
Dogs are allowed at the outdoor tables. The restaurant has outdoor tables only in the Summer.
The Boulevard Wood Grille 2901 Wilson Blvd Arlington VA   703-875-9663
Dogs are allowed at the outdoor tables. The restaurant has outdoor tables only in the Summer.
Withlows 2854 Wilson Blvd Arlington VA   703-276-9693
http://www.whitlows.com/
Dogs are allowed at the outdoor tables. The restaurant has outdoor tables only in the Summer. They will also
bring a bowl of water for the dog.
Baja Fresh 13940 Lee-Jackson Memorial Highway Chantilly VA   703-378-3804
This restaurant serves Mexican food. Dogs are allowed at the outdoor tables. The restaurant has outdoor tables
only in the Summer.
Quiznos 13661 Lee Jackson Memorial H Chantilly VA   703-817-1244
Dogs are allowed at the outdoor tables. The restaurant has outdoor tables only in the Summer.
Baja Fresh 2815 Clarendon Blvd Clarendon VA   703-528-7010
This restaurant serves Mexican food. Dogs are allowed at the outdoor tables. The restaurant has outdoor tables
only in the Summer.
Hard Times Cafe 3028 Wilson Blvd Clarendon VA   703-528-2233
Dogs are allowed at the outdoor tables. The restaurant has outdoor tables only in the Summer.
Baja Fresh 12150 Fairfax Town Center Fairfax VA   703-352-1792
This restaurant serves Mexican food. Dogs are allowed at the outdoor tables. The restaurant has outdoor tables
only in the Summer.
Coyote Grill Cantina 10266 Main Street/H 236 Fairfax VA   703-591-0006
http://coyote.squarespace.com/
Specializing in Southwestern cuisine, this eatery also offers special event menus and venues, Sunday brunches,
signature cocktails, catering, and alfresco dining. Dogs are allowed at the outer tables; they must be under
owner's control/care and leashed at all times.
Bagel Cafe 300 Elder St Herndon VA   703-318-7555
This restaurant serves American deli-type food. Dogs are allowed at the outdoor tables. Only open for breakfast
and lunch.
Baja Fresh 2405 Centerville Road Herndon VA   703-793-0878
This restaurant serves Mexican food. Dogs are allowed at the outdoor tables.
Baja Fresh 8099 Sudley Road Manassas VA   703-365-2077
This restaurant serves Mexican food. Dogs are allowed at the outdoor tables.
Chili's Grill and Bar 10600 Sudley Manor Dr Manassas VA   703-330-0208
This restaurant and bar serves American food. Dogs are allowed at the outdoor tables.
Baja Fresh 11690 Plaza America Drive Reston VA   703-689-0993
This restaurant serves Mexican food. Dogs are allowed at the outdoor tables.
Clyde's of Reston 11905 Market Street Reston VA   703-787-6601
Specializing in using fresh, local foods, this eatery offers a seasonally changing menu, wines and brews, and
alfresco dining. Dogs are allowed at the outer tables; they must be leashed and under owner's control/care at all
times.

Pet Sitters
Peggie's Pet Services, Pet-sitting & Dog Walking Ashby Street Alexandria VA   703-863-4209
http://www.peggiespets.com
These folks offer dog walking and pet-sitting in your hotel, or other pet-friendly accommodation in Northern
Virginia.

Day Kennels
PetsHotel by PetsMart Day Kennel 3351 Jefferson Davis Hwy Alexandria VA   703-739-8940
http://www.petsmart.com/PETsHOTEL/
This PetSmart pet store offers day care, day camp and overnight care. You may drop off and pick up your dog
during the hours the store is open seven days a week. Dogs must have proof of current rabies, DPP and
Bordatella vaccinations.
PetsHotel by PetsMart Day Kennel 12971 Fair Lake Pkwy Fairfax VA   703-802-9616
http://www.petsmart.com/PETsHOTEL/
This PetSmart pet store offers day care, day camp and overnight care. You may drop off and pick up your dog
during the hours the store is open seven days a week. Dogs must have proof of current rabies, DPP and
Bordatella vaccinations.
PetsHotel by PetsMart Day Kennel 6536 Frontier Dr Springfield VA   703-922-4990
http://www.petsmart.com/PETsHOTEL/
This PetSmart pet store offers doggy day care only. You may drop off and pick up your dog during the hours the

store is open seven days a week. Dogs must have proof of current rabies, DPP and Bordatella vaccinations.

Orange

Accommodations
Holladay House 155 W Main Street Orange VA   540-672-4893 (800-358-4422)
http://www.holladayhousebandb.com/
Historically significant, this 1830's home features a rich Federal architecture, an extensive civil war and classical novel library, a variety of refreshments throughout the day, and close proximity to a number of area attractions and activities. Dogs are allowed in the Garden or Ivy rooms for an additional fee of $25 per night per pet. Dogs must be quiet, well mannered, leashed, and cleaned up after at all times.

Petersburg

Accommodations
Days Inn Petersburg/Walthall 2310 Indian Hill Rd Colonial Heights VA   804-520-1010 (800-329-7466)
Dogs of all sizes are allowed. There is a $6 per night pet fee per pet.
Candlewood Suites 5113 Plaza Drive Hopewell VA   804-541-0200 (877-270-6405)
Dogs up to 80 pounds are allowed for an additional pet fee per room of $75 for 1 to 14 nights, and $150 for 15 or more nights.
Days Inn Petersburg/Fort Lee South 12208 S Crater Rd Petersburg VA   804-733-4400 (800-329-7466)
Dogs up to 60 pounds are allowed. There is a $10 per night pet fee per pet.
Quality Inn 11974 S Crater Road Petersburg VA   804-732-2900 (877-424-6423)
Dogs are allowed for an additional fee of $5 per night per pet.
Hampton Inn 10476 Blue Star H Stony Creek VA   434-246-5500
Dogs up to 50 pounds are allowed. There is a $10 one time cleaning fee.
Sleep Inn 11019 Blue Star H Stony Creek VA   434-246-5100 (877-424-6423)
Dogs up to 60 pounds are allowed for an additional fee of $15 per pet for the first night, and $10 per pet for each additional night.

Campgrounds and RV Parks
Petersburg KOA 2809 Cortland Road Petersburg VA   804-732-8345 (800-562-8545)
http://www.koa.com
Dogs of all sizes are allowed. There are no additional pet fees. Dogs must be quiet, leashed, and cleaned up after. The camping and tent areas also allow dogs. There is a dog walk area at the campground. Dogs are allowed in the camping cabins.

Attractions
Petersburg National Battlefield 1539 Hickory Hill Drive Petersburg VA 804-732-3531
http://www.nps.gov/pete
Dedicated to honoring, preserving, and educating the public of our historic beginnings, this park tells of the 292 day siege which led to the fall of the Confederacy. Dogs are allowed throughout the park and on the trails; they are not allowed in buildings. Dogs must be leashed and cleaned up after at all times.

Stores
PetSmart Pet Store 42 Southgate Square Colonial Heights VA 804-520-0801
Your licensed and well-behaved leashed dog is allowed in the store.

Pocahontas

Attractions
Pocahontas Exhibition Coal Mine and Museum Centre Street Pocahontas VA 276-945-9522
The history of coal, its importance, and how production of coal has changed through the years are explained in the tour of the mine, and the walking tour (with or without a guide) of the historic town gives visitors a glimpse of

the past. Some of the other highlights at this National Historic Landmark are a 7 acre park with pavilions and a playground, and several 1800's era buildings. Dogs are allowed on the mine tours as well as the historic walking tour; they must be leashed, and under owner's control/care at all times.

Potomac River Mouth

Accommodations
Fleeton Fields 2783 Fleeton Road Reedville VA   804-453-7016 (800-497-8215)
http://www.fleetonfields.com/
Set in a gorgeous park-like setting with garden benches, manicured lawns, a tidal pond, and herb and flower gardens, this beautiful colonial style, Victorian inspired retreat also offers guests complimentary bicycles, kayaks, and canoes. Dogs of all sizes are allowed for no additional fee. Dogs must be well behaved, leashed, and cleaned up after at all times.
Days Inn Tappahannock Dwtn 1414 Tappahannock Blvd Tappahannock VA   804-443-9200 (800-329-7466)
Dogs of all sizes are allowed. There is a $10 per night pet fee per pet.

Campgrounds and RV Parks
Belle Isle State Park Belle Isle State Park Lancaster VA   804-462-5030 (800-933-PARK (7275))
This 733 acre park also has 7 miles of waterfront footage on the north shore of the Rappahannock with Deep and Mulberry creeks along its boarder creating a variety of diverse wetland areas and wildlife. Dogs of all sizes are allowed for an additional fee of $3 per night per pet. Dogs must be kept on a leash no longer than 6 feet when outside and they must be brought in at night. Campsites have fire rings, grills, a picnic table, lantern hanger, modern restroom with showers, a laundry, a free boat launch for overnight guests, a camp store, and dump station. This RV park is closed during the off-season. The camping and tent areas also allow dogs. There is a dog walk area at the campground.
Chesapeake Bay Camp Resort 382 Campground Road Reedville VA   804-453-3430
A popular recreation destination, this 20 acre park sits out on the point where the Potomac meets the Chesapeake Bay offering great views plus a good variety of land and water activities. A KOA for many years, there are a number of amenities and extras here such as a crabbing pier and a marina. Dogs of all sizes are allowed, and there is no fee for one medium or large, or 2 small dogs per site in the camp area. There is a $7 per night per pet fee for the cabins, and "doggy visitors" are not allowed at any cabin unless they are registered there. Dogs must be leashed and cleaned up after at all times. Dogs are not allowed in the buildings or in the pool area. This RV park is closed during the off-season. The camping and tent areas also allow dogs. There is a dog walk area at the campground. Dogs are allowed in the camping cabins.

Parks
Caledon Natural Area 11617 Caledon Road/H 218 King George VA   540-663-3861
This natural area allots visitors the rare opportunity to learn about and view bald eagles, and there are 5 scenic hiking trails through mature forests that are open year round. One of the trails (Boyd's Hole Trail) is only open from October 1st to March 1st. Dogs of all sizes are allowed. Dogs must be under owner's control, on no more than a 6 foot leash, and cleaned up after.
Belle Isle State Park Belle Isle State Park Lancaster VA   804-462-5030 (800-933-PARK (7275))
This 733 acre park also has 7 miles of waterfront footage on the north shore of the Rappahannock with Deep and Mulberry creeks along its boarder creating a variety of diverse wetland areas and wildlife. Dogs of all sizes are allowed for an additional fee of $3 per night per pet. Dogs must be kept on a leash no longer than 6 feet when outside and they must be brought in at night.

Pounding Mill

Accommodations
Holiday Inn Express Hotel & Suites Claypool Hill (Richlands Area) 180 Clay Dr. Pounding Mill VA   276-596-9880 (877-270-6405)
Dogs up to 60 pounds are allowed for an additional fee of $25 per night per pet.

Pulaski

Accommodations

Comfort Inn 4424 Cleburne Blvd Dublin VA   540-674-1100 (877-424-6423)
Dogs are allowed for an additional fee of $10 per night per pet.
Days Inn Pulaski 3063 Old Rt 100 Rd Pulaski VA   540-980-2230 (800-329-7466)
Dogs of all sizes are allowed. There is a $10 per night pet fee per pet.
Best Western Radford Inn 1501 Tyler Avenue Radford VA   540-639-3000 (800-780-7234)
Dogs are allowed for an additional fee of $10 per night per pet.
Super 8 Radford 1600 Tyler Ave Radford VA   540-731-9355 (800-800-8000)
Dogs of all sizes are allowed. There is a $15.75 one time per pet fee per visit. Smoking and non-smoking rooms are available for pet rooms.

Campgrounds and RV Parks

Bluecat on the New Camping 2800 Wysor H (100) Draper VA   276-766-3729
http://www.bluecatonthenew.com/
This campground of over 4 acres with 1,200 feet of riverfront has tipis for rent or one of 6 campsites for tent camping only. Dogs of all sizes are allowed in the tipis and in the camp area for no additional fee. Dogs must be under owner's control, leashed, and cleaned up after at all times. This RV park is closed during the off-season. The camping and tent areas also allow dogs. There is a dog walk area at the campground. There are no electric or water hookups at the campgrounds.
New River Trail State Park 176 Orphanage Drive Foster Falls VA   276-699-6778 (800-933-PARK (7275))
This 57 mile long, converted "Rails to Trails" state park parallels 39 miles of one of the world's oldest rivers, passes through 2 tunnels, crosses about 30 smaller bridges and trestles, and offers access to many other recreational activities along the way. Dogs are allowed in the day use areas of the park for no additional fee; there is an additional fee of $3 per night per pet for camping. Dogs must be leashed and cleaned up after at all times. There are 5 campgrounds with various site options, fire rings, a lantern post, picnic table, non-flush toilets, and drinking water. The camping and tent areas also allow dogs. There is a dog walk area at the campground. There are no electric or water hookups at the campgrounds.

Parks

New River Trail State Park 176 Orphanage Drive Foster Falls VA   276-699-6778 (800-933-PARK (7275))
This 57 mile long, converted "Rails to Trails" state park parallels 39 miles of one of the world's oldest rivers, passes through 2 tunnels, crosses about 30 smaller bridges and trestles, and offers access to many other recreational activities along the way. Dogs are allowed in the day use areas of the park for no additional fee; there is an additional fee of $3 per night per pet for camping. Dogs must be leashed and cleaned up after at all times.

Raphine

Accommodations

Days Inn Raphine 584 Oakland Cr Raphine VA   540-377-2604 (800-329-7466)
Dogs of all sizes are allowed. There is a $5 per night pet fee per pet.

Richmond

Accommodations

Days Inn Chester 2410 W Hundred Rd Chester VA   804-748-5871 (800-329-7466)
Dogs of all sizes are allowed. There is a $6 per night pet fee per pet.
Candlewood Suites 4120 Brookriver Drive Glen Allen VA   804-364-2000 (877-270-6405)
Dogs of all sizes are allowed for an additional one time fee of $75 per pet.
TownePlace Suites Richmond 4231 Park Place Court Glen Allen VA   804-747-5253
Dogs of all sizes are allowed. There is a $75 one time pet fee per visit.
Candlewood Suites 4301 Commerce Road Richmond VA   804-271-0016 (877-270-6405)
Dogs up to 80 pounds are allowed for an additional one time fee of $50 per pet.
Days Inn Richmond 6910 Midlothian Turnpike Richmond VA   804-745-7100 (800-329-7466)
Dogs of all sizes are allowed. There is a $20 one time per pet fee per visit.

Jefferson Hotel 101 West Franklin Street Richmond VA   804-788-8000
Noted for its outstanding public spaces and accommodations, this hotel is centrally located in the downtown historic district. Dogs of all sizes are allowed for an additional $40 per night per pet. Dogs may not be left alone in the room, and they must be leashed and cleaned up after at all times. There is a dog sitting and/or walking service for an additional fee of $7.50 per hour.
Motel 6 - Richmond Chippenham 100 Greshamwood Place Richmond VA   804-745-0600 (800-466-8356)
One well-behaved family pet per room. Guest must notify front desk upon arrival. Guest is liable for any damages. In consideration of all guests, pets must never be left unattended in the guest rooms.
Quality Inn West End 8008 W Broad Street Richmond VA   804-346-0000 (877-424-6423)
One dog is allowed for an additional one time fee of $35.
Red Roof Inn - Richmond South, VA 4350 Commerce Road Richmond VA   804-271-7240 (800-RED-ROOF)
One well-behaved family pet per room. Guest must notify front desk upon arrival. Guest is liable for any damages. In consideration of all guests, pets must never be left unattended in the guest rooms.
Residence Inn by Marriott 3940 Westerre Parkway Richmond VA   804-762-9852
Dogs of all sizes are allowed. There is a $75 one time fee and a pet policy to sign at check in.
Residence Inn by Marriott 2121Dickens Road Richmond VA   804-285-8200
Dogs of all sizes are allowed. There is a $75 one time fee and a pet policy to sign at check in.
Sheraton Park South Hotel 9901 Midlothian Turnpike Richmond VA   804-323-1144 (888-625-5144)
Dogs up to 80 pounds are allowed. There are no additional pet fees. Dogs are not allowed to be left alone in the room.
Sheraton Richmond West Hotel 6624 West Broad St. Richmond VA   804-285-2000 (888-625-5144)
Dogs up to 50 pounds are allowed. There are no additional pet fees. Dogs are not allowed to be left alone in the room.
Super 8 Richmond/Midlothian Tnpk 8260 Midlothian Turnpike Richmond VA   804-320-2823 (800-800-8000)
Dogs of all sizes are allowed. There is a $25 per night pet fee per pet. Smoking and non-smoking rooms are available for pet rooms.
Days Inn Richmond Airport 5500 Williamsburg Rd Sandston VA   804-222-2041 (800-329-7466)
Dogs of all sizes are allowed. There is no charge for small pet and a $20 fee per large pet per night.
Motel 6 - Richmond Airport 5704 Williamsburg Road (US Route 60) Sandston VA   804-222-7600 (800-466-8356)
One well-behaved family pet per room. Guest must notify front desk upon arrival. Guest is liable for any damages. In consideration of all guests, pets must never be left unattended in the guest rooms.

Campgrounds and RV Parks
Pocohontas State Park 10301 State Park Road Chesterfield VA   804-796-4255 (800-933-PARK (7275))
Popular, educational, multi-functional, and recreational, all describe this year round park. Dogs of all sizes are allowed for an additional $3 per night per pet. Dogs may not be left unattended outside or in a tent, and they must be leashed and cleaned up after. Dogs are not allowed in food areas or at the pool. Dogs are allowed on the trails. This campground is closed during the off-season. The camping and tent areas also allow dogs. There is a dog walk area at the campground.

Transportation Systems
GRTC Regional Richmond VA   804-358-GRTC
http://www.ridegrtc.com
Small dogs in carriers are allowed on the buses.

Attractions
James River Cellars 11008 Washington Highway Glen Allen VA   804-550-7516
http://www.jamesrivercellars.com
Dogs on leash are allowed at the outdoor tables. Open Tuesday-Saturday 10am-5pm and Sunday and Monday 11am-5pm. Some light fare are available for picnics. It is located 10 miles from Richmond.
Hollywood Cemetery 412 S Cherry Street Richmond VA   804-648-8501
http://www.hollywoodcemetery.org/
Although dogs are not usually allowed at this historic and serene graveyard, about 4 times a year "History Hounds" have an event where pooches may join their owners on a guided tour here to explore and sniff out various sites of interest. Dogs must be very friendly with other dogs and people, be current with their shots, and be leashed and cleaned up after at all times. The fee is $10 and they suggest bringing water for pets.
Richmond National Battlefield 470 Tredegar Street Richmond VA   804-226-1981
http://www.nps.gov/rich
An 80 mile driving tour takes in 4 visitor centers, numerous sites displaying original fortifications, battlefields, the Confederates largest hospital and more, plus this park commemorates major events of the Civil War with interpretive programs/exhibits, (podcast) tours, special events, and reenactments. Dogs are allowed at all the sites and on the trails, but they must be kept off the earthworks and they are not allowed in park buildings. Dogs

must be under owner's control, leashed, and cleaned up after at all times.
Riverfront District and Canal Walk N 14th and E Cary Street Richmond VA   804-788-6466
Central to just about everything for local residents as well as visitors, the River District has an eclectic
combination of fare, fun, food, and shops with a great 1 mile walk along the river against a beautiful city
backdrop. Dogs are welcome throughout the district and on the canal walk. Dogs must be leashed and cleaned
up after at all times. Dogs are not allowed at large events in the plaza area, but they are allowed on the canal
trail any time.
Virginia State Capitol Bank Street Richmond VA   804-698-1788
http://legis.state.va.us/
Although dogs are not allowed in any of the buildings, there are 12 acres of beautifully landscaped grounds here
surrounded by an impressive 1818 cast iron fence for sniffing out and exploring. Dogs may not be left alone at
any time and they must be leashed and cleaned up after at all times.

Shopping Centers

Stony Point Fashion Park

TOP 200 PLACE **Stony Point Fashion Park** 9200 Stony Point Parkway Richmond VA   804-560-SHOP
http://www.shopstonypoint.com/
This open air mall is home to such stores as Nordstroms, Sharper Image and The Banana Republic, and they
have recently opened a Three Dog Bakery providing freshly baked treats and foods for dogs. You will find "pit
stop" areas for your pet where there are waterbowls and clean up supplies throughout the mall. Many stores
allow your pet inside; just look for the large dog sticker in the window. Dogs of all sizes are allowed, and dogs
must be friendly, leashed at all times (or in a carrier), and please clean up after your pet. They are open from 10
am to 9 pm Monday through Saturday, and from noon to 6 pm on Sunday.

Stores

PetSmart Pet Store 9870 Brook Rd Glen Allen VA   804-266-1476
Your licensed and well-behaved leashed dog is allowed in the store.
PetSmart Pet Store 7225 Bell Creek Rd Ste 228 Mechanicsville VA   804-730-7545
Your licensed and well-behaved leashed dog is allowed in the store.
PetSmart Pet Store 12264 Chattanooga Plaza Midlothian VA   804-763-6058
Your licensed and well-behaved leashed dog is allowed in the store.
For the Love of Pete 322 Libbie Avenue Richmond VA   804-288-3674
http://www.theloveofpete.com/

Offering a variety of chic and hip clothing items, this pet boutique also carries a wide range of items to pamper your pet, plus they have a beautiful garden for your pooch to enjoy. Dogs must be under owner's control/care.
PetSmart Pet Store 1276 Car Mia Way Richmond VA   804-897-9490
Your licensed and well-behaved leashed dog is allowed in the store.
PetSmart Pet Store 7504 W Broad St Richmond VA   804-672-0137
Your licensed and well-behaved leashed dog is allowed in the store.
PetSmart Pet Store 5515 W Broad St Richmond VA   804-282-6455
Your licensed and well-behaved leashed dog is allowed in the store.
PetSmart Pet Store 11740 W Broad St Ste A Richmond VA   804-364-2570
Your licensed and well-behaved leashed dog is allowed in the store.
Three Dog Bakery 9200 Stony Point Parkway #152A Richmond VA   804-330-3536
http://www.threedog.com
Three Dog Bakery provides cookies and snacks for your dog as well as some boutique items. You well-behaved, leashed dog is welcome.

Parks
Brown's Island N 7th and Tredegar Streets Richmond VA   804-788-6466
http://www.brownsisland.com/
When not being used for concerts and special events, this island park offers a variety of outdoor recreational activities. Dogs are allowed throughout the island, except during events. Dogs must be leashed and cleaned up after at all times.

Outdoor Restaurants
Ellwood Thompson's Natural Food Market 11400 W. Huguenot Rd Midlothian VA   804-897-5300
Dogs are allowed at the outdoor tables. You will have to go inside and get your food without your dog.
McAlister's Deli 11400 West Huguenot Road Midlothian VA   804-897-9686
http://www.mcalistersdeli.com/
Much more than a deli, there are more than 100 selections of food, drinks, deserts, and their specialty-super stuffed spuds available at this eating place. Outside seating is available when weather permits. Dogs are allowed at the outer tables; they must be leashed and under owner's control/care at all times.
Acacia Restaurant 3325 E Cary Street/H 147 Richmond VA   804-354-6060
http://www.acaciarestaurant.com/
Specializing in seasonally inspired signature dishes, this eatery also offers alfresco dining. Dogs are allowed at the outer tables. Dogs must be under owner control/care and leashed at all times.
Chipotle Mexican Grill 9200 Stony Point Parkway Richmond VA   804-272-6322
http://www.chipotle.com/#
This fresh-mex eatery offers outside dining. Dogs are allowed at the outer tables. Dogs must be under owner control/care and leashed at all times.
Copeland's Cheesecake Bistro 9200 Stony Point Parkway, Suite 101 Richmond VA   804-323-1133
This eatery is popular for their large menu and an eclectic array of fine food; they also offer outside dining. Dogs are allowed at the outer tables. Dogs must be under owner control/care and leashed at all times.
Millies Diner 2603 E Main Street/H 5 Richmond VA   804-643-5512
http://www.milliesdiner.com/
This unpretentious diner offers a few surprises in food, décor, and ambiance. There is outdoor dining available for lunch or just drinks when weather permits; dinner is served indoors only. Dogs are allowed at the outer tables; they must be leashed and under owner's control/care at all times.
Panera Bread 9200 Stony Point Parkway, Suite 158D Richmond VA   804-560-9700
http://www.panerabread.com/
This bakery/café offers outside dining. Just place and pick up order inside. Dogs are allowed at the outer tables. Dogs must be under owner control/care and leashed at all times.
Poe's Pub 2706 E Main Street/H 60/5 Richmond VA   804-648-2120
http://www.poespub.com/
Specializing in good fun and good food, this restaurant also features live music of all kinds and alfresco dining. Dogs are allowed at the outer tables. Dogs must be under owner control/care and leashed at all times.
Quiznos 8906B W Broad Street Richmond VA   804-346-3766
Dogs are allowed at the outdoor tables.

Roanoke

Accommodations

Best Western Inn at Valley View 5050 Valley View Boulevard NW Roanoke VA   540-362-2400 (800-780-7234)
Dogs are allowed for an additional one time pet fee of $20 per room.
Comfort Inn Airport 5070 Valley View Road Roanoke VA   540-527-2020 (877-424-6423)
Dogs are allowed for an additional one time fee of $25 per pet.
Days Inn Roanoke Airport 8118 Plantation Rd Roanoke VA   540-366-0341 (800-329-7466)
Dogs of all sizes are allowed. There is a $15 one time per pet fee per visit.
Days Inn Roanoke Civic Center/Dwtn 535 Orange AVe Roanoke VA   540-342-4551 (800-329-7466)
Dogs of all sizes are allowed. There is a $5 per night pet fee per small pet and $10 for large pet.
Motel 6 - Roanoke 3695 Thirlane Road Roanoke VA   540-563-0229 (800-466-8356)
One well-behaved family pet per room. Guest must notify front desk upon arrival. Guest is liable for any damages. In consideration of all guests, pets must never be left unattended in the guest rooms.
Quality Inn Roanoke Airport 6626 Thirlane Road Roanoke VA   540-366-8861 (877-424-6423)
Dogs are allowed for an additional one time pet fee of $15 per pet.
Super 8 Roanoke 6616 Thirlane Rd Roanoke VA   540-563-8888 (800-800-8000)
Dogs of all sizes are allowed. There is a $10 returnable deposit required per room. Smoking and non-smoking rooms are available for pet rooms.
Comfort Inn 2545 Lee H Troutville VA   540-992-5600 (877-424-6423)
Dogs are allowed for an additional one time pet fee of $20 per room.
Red Roof Inn - Roanoke - Troutville 3231 Lee Highway South Troutville VA   540-992-5055 (800-RED-ROOF)
One well-behaved family pet per room. Guest must notify front desk upon arrival. Guest is liable for any damages. In consideration of all guests, pets must never be left unattended in the guest rooms.

Campgrounds and RV Parks

George Washington and Jefferson National Forests 5162 Valleypointe Parkway/S area Forest
HQ Roanoke VA   540-265-5100 (877-444-6777)
http://www.fs.fed.us/r8/gwj/index.shtml
A headquarters plus 8 ranger districts take care of the almost 1.8 million acres of this forest that spreads over 3 states, making it one of the largest public land areas in the eastern US. There are a wide variety of landscapes and habitats providing for innumerable bird, plant, and wildlife, year round activities and recreational pursuits, and many educational opportunities as well. Dogs are allowed throughout the forest, in the campgrounds, and on the trails. Dogs must be leashed and cleaned up after in developed recreational sites, and they are not allowed in swimming areas. Developed and primitive camping is available at several different locations throughout the forest. Reservations are suggested for favored areas. Most of the developed sites offer tables, grills, drinking water, toilet facilities, and are closer to recreational areas. Primitive camping requires campers to "Leave No Trace" and offers no services. This RV park is closed during the off-season. The camping and tent areas also allow dogs. There is a dog walk area at the campground. There are no water hookups at the campgrounds.

Stores

PetSmart Pet Store 4749 Valley View Blvd NW Roanoke VA 540-362-2994
Your licensed and well-behaved leashed dog is allowed in the store.

Parks

Explore Park Milepost 115 Blue Ridge Parkway Roanoke VA   540-427-1800
http://www.explorepark.org/
This major land and water recreation destination is an 1,100 acre park on the Blue Ridge Parkway astride the Roanoke River that also features an outdoor living history museum, a film center, special event venues, miles of trails, historic areas, and stunning views of its beautiful diversity. Dogs are welcome throughout the park with the exception of the Historic Park area or in buildings. For visitors with pets who would like to visit the historic areas, there are free locked kennels; just pick up keys and a water bowl at the admissions office. Dogs must be leashed and cleaned up after at all times.
George Washington and Jefferson National Forests 5162 Valleypointe Parkway/S area Forest
HQ Roanoke VA   540-265-5100 (877-444-6777)
http://www.fs.fed.us/r8/gwj/index.shtml
A headquarters plus 8 ranger districts take care of the almost 1.8 million acres of this forest that spreads over 3 states, making it one of the largest public land areas in the eastern US. There are a wide variety of landscapes and habitats providing for innumerable bird, plant, and wildlife, year round activities and recreational pursuits, and many educational opportunities as well. Dogs are allowed throughout the forest, in the campgrounds, and on the trails. Dogs must be leashed and cleaned up after in developed recreational sites, and they are not allowed in swimming areas.

Outdoor Restaurants

Awful Arthur's 2229 Colonial Avenue SW Roanoke VA   540-344-2997
http://www.awfularthurs.com/
This lunch and dinner eatery specializes in seafood, featurea a raw bar, and offer alfresco dining. Dogs are allowed at the outer tables. Dogs must be under owner's control/care and leashed at all times.

Rocky Mount

Accommodations
Comfort Inn Smith Mt Lake 1730 N Main Street Rocky Mount VA   540-489-4000 (877-424-6423)
Dogs are allowed for an additional one time pet fee of $25 per room.
Holiday Inn Express Hotel & Suites Rocky Mount/Smith Mtn Lake 395 Old Franklin Trnpk. Rocky Mount VA   540-489-5001 (877-270-6405)
Dogs of all sizes are allowed for an additional one time pet fee of $25 per room.

Shenandoah National Park

Accommodations
Bluemont Inn 1525 N. Shenandoah Ave. Front Royal VA   540-635-9447
They have several pet rooms. There are no additional pet fees.
Hot Tub Heaven Off I 66 (address given with reservation) Front Royal VA   540-636-1522
Dogs only are allowed and of all sizes. There is a $20 first night fee for up to 2 dogs, thereafter it is an additional $10 per dog per night. There is a pet policy to sign at check in and one of the rooms has a tall fenced in back yard.
Quality Inn Skyline Drive 10 Commerce Avenue Front Royal VA   540-635-3161 (877-424-6423)
Dogs up to 50 pounds are allowed for an additional fee of $15 per night per pet.
Super 8 Front Royal 111 South St Front Royal VA   540-636-4888 (800-800-8000)
Dogs of all sizes are allowed. There is a $6 per night pet fee per pet. Smoking and non-smoking rooms are available for pet rooms.
Accokeek Farm 170 Kibler Drive Luray VA   540-743-2305
http://www.shentel.net/accokeek/
Nestled at the base of a mountain along the river, this inn offers guests lodging in an historic restored 19th century, 4 story bank barn, several recreation areas, canoes, and a great starting location for exploring several other sites of interest. Dogs of all sizes are allowed for an additional fee of $50 per pet per stay. Dogs must be well mannered, leashed, and cleaned up after at all times.
Adventures Await Luray VA   540-743-5766 (800-433-6077)
http://www.adventuresawait.com/
This company offers several properties with various amenities in the Shenandoah River valley and mountain region around Luray. Dogs of all sizes are allowed for no additional fee. Dogs must be well behaved, leashed, and cleaned up after at all times.
Allstar Lodging 21 Wallace Avenue Luray VA   540-843-0606 (866-780-STAR (7827))
http://www.allstarlodging.com/
This realty offers several vacation rentals with various amenities in and around Luray in the scenic Shenandoah Valley. Dogs are allowed in their cabins for an additional fee of $10 per night per pet. Dogs must be under owner's control/care, leashed, and cleaned up after.
Days Inn Luray 138 Whispering Hill Rd Luray VA   540-743-4521 (800-329-7466)
Dogs of all sizes are allowed. There is a $10 per night pet fee per pet.
Hopkins Ordinary 47 Main Street Sperryville VA   540-987-3383
http://www.hopkinsordinary.com/
Listed on the National Register of Historic Places and built around 1820 as a roadside inn and tavern, it once served the needs of the "ordinary" traveler, and now provides visitors extra-ordinary accommodations and fare, and close proximity to a number of area attractions and activities. Dogs are allowed in the garden cottage for an additional fee of $25 per night per pet (adjustable for multiple days). Dogs must be friendly (other animals on site), well mannered, leashed or crated when out of the cottage, and cleaned up after at all times.
Days Inn Waynesboro 2060 Rosser Ave Waynesboro VA   540-943-1101 (800-329-7466)
Dogs of all sizes are allowed. There is a $10 per night pet fee per pet.
Quality Inn 640 W Broad Street Waynesboro VA   540-942-1171 (877-424-6423)
Dogs are allowed for an additional pet fee of $10 per night per room.
Super 8 Waynesboro 2045 Rosser Ave Waynesboro VA   540-943-3888 (800-800-8000)
Dogs of all sizes are allowed. There is a $5 per night pet fee per pet. Smoking and non-smoking rooms are

available for pet rooms.

Campgrounds and RV Parks

Big Meadows Campground Skyline Drive, Milepost 51.2 Luray VA   540-999-3500 (877-444-6777)
http://www.nps.gov/shen/
Although secluded, this camp area is close to major amenities and popular trails, and offers wide sweeping
meadows (many times with wildlife), and 3 nearby waterfalls. There are restrooms, hot showers, a laundry,
water, and a dump station as well. Dogs of all sizes are allowed for no additional fee. Dogs must be under
owner's control, on no more than a 6 foot leash or securely crated, and cleaned up after at all times. Dogs are
not to be left unattended. Dogs are not allowed on about 14 miles of the trails; please ask the attendant at the
gate for a list of the trails. Dogs are not allowed in buildings. This RV park is closed during the off-season. The
camping and tent areas also allow dogs. There is a dog walk area at the campground. There are no electric or
water hookups at the campgrounds.

Jellystone Park 2250 H 211E Luray VA   540-743-4002 (800-420-6679)
http://www.campluray.com
Dogs of all sizes are allowed. There are no additional pet fees. Dogs must be well behaved, leashed, and
cleaned up after. Dogs are not allowed to be left staked outside your unit. They may be left inside your RV if they
will be quiet. This RV park is closed during the off-season. The camping and tent areas also allow dogs. There is
a dog walk area at the campground. Dogs are not allowed in the camping cabins.

Lewis Mountain Campground Skyline Drive, Milepost 57.5 Luray VA   540-743-3500
http://www.nps.gov/shen/
This is the smallest campground in the park and offers a quiet rustic setting. The 32 sites are on a first-come
first-served basis, and flush toilets, coin showers, a laundry, and campstore are on site. Since the Appalachian
Trail runs through this campground, hikers pitching a tent for the night are a common sight. Dogs of all sizes are
allowed for no additional fee. Dogs must be under owner's control, on no more than a 6 foot leash or securely
crated, and cleaned up after at all times. Dogs are not to be left unattended. Dogs are not allowed on about 14
miles of the trails; please ask the attendant at the gate for a list of the trails. Dogs are not allowed in buildings.
This RV park is closed during the off-season. The camping and tent areas also allow dogs. There is a dog walk
area at the campground. There are no electric or water hookups at the campgrounds.

Loft Mountain, Shenandoah National Park Skyline Blvd, Milepost 79.5 Luray VA   540-999-3500 (877-444-
6777)
http://www.nps.gov/shen/
This is the park's largest and southern-most camp area, and sitting atop a mountain at 3,400 feet it offers great
panoramic views. There are 219 fairly secluded sites available on a first come first served basis and by
reservation, and the camp area provides restrooms, showers, a laundry, picnic tables, fire grates, amphitheater,
a camp store, dump station, and close by is a restaurant and gas station. Dogs of all sizes are allowed for no
additional fee. Dogs must be under owner's control, on no more than a 6 foot leash or securely crated, and
cleaned up after at all times. Dogs are not to be left unattended. Dogs are not allowed on about 14 miles of the
trails; please ask the attendant at the gate for a list of the trails. Dogs are not allowed in buildings. This RV park
is closed during the off-season. The camping and tent areas also allow dogs. There is a dog walk area at the
campground. There are no electric or water hookups at the campgrounds.

Mathews Arm Campground Skyline Drive, Milepost 22.1 Luray VA   540-999-3500 (877-444-6777)
http://www.nps.gov/shen/
This is the closest camp area entering from the north, and it offers a nature trail, a hiking trail to the tallest
waterfall in the park, and a seasonal wayside with a cafeteria, camp store, snack bar, and gift shop. There is also
potable water and a dump station. Dogs of all sizes are allowed for no additional fee. Dogs must be under
owner's control, on no more than a 6 foot leash or securely crated, and cleaned up after at all times. Dogs are
not to be left unattended outside, or for more than an hour inside an RV. Dogs are not allowed on about 14 miles
of the trails; please ask the attendant at the gate for a list of the trails. Dogs are not allowed in buildings. This RV
park is closed during the off-season. The camping and tent areas also allow dogs. There is a dog walk area at
the campground. There are no electric or water hookups at the campgrounds.

Attractions

Downriver Canoe Company 884 Indian Hollow Road Bentonville VA   540-635-5526
http://www.downriver.com/downriver/
Set along the South Fork of the Shenandoah River at one of the leading canoeing areas in the east, this
watercraft rental company will also allow your pooch on the canoes. Dogs should have some prior experience on
the water. Dogs must be well behaved, under owner's control/care, and leashed when not on the canoe.

Blue Ridge Parkway Auto Tour Blue Ridge Parkway, Milepost 0 Waynesboro VA   828-271-4779
http://www.blueridgeparkway.org/
More than 50 years in the making and setting standards in engineering and design along the way, there are
thousands of recreational acres and exceptional scenery to explore as this rural parkway connects the
Shenandoah NP with the Great Smoky Mountains NP (max speed limit is 45 MPH). Its natural and cultural

history reveals itself as visitors drive through the 469 miles of the country's first (and longest) rural parkway, or by hiking its many diverse trails. Visitors will also pass over the Linn Cove Viaduct, considered to be one of the most complicated concrete bridges ever built at milepost 304.6. From May through October ranger programs are offered, and there are a number of campgrounds, trails, eateries, viewing areas, and historic/interpretive sites along the way. Dogs are allowed at all the camp areas and on all the trails. Dogs must be very well behaved, under owner's control, on no more than a 6 foot leash or securely crated, and cleaned up after at all times.

Parks

TOP 200 PLACE **Shenandoah National Park** 3655 U.S. Highway 211 East Luray VA   540-999-3500
http://www.nps.gov/shen/
Covering 300 mostly forested square miles of the Blue Ridge Mountains the park provides many diverse habitats for thousands of birds and wildlife. The park also provides a wide range of recreational opportunities. There are more than 500 miles of trails, including 101 miles of the Appalachian Trail, Summer and Fall festivals/reenactments, a rich cultural history to share, interpretive programs, and breathtaking natural beauty. There are several highlights along the 105 mile long, 35 MPH, Skyline Drive (the only public road through the park), such as 75 scenic overlooks and Mary's Rock Tunnel at milepost 32. The 610 foot-long tunnel was considered an engineering feat in 1932; just note that the clearance for the tunnel is 12'8". Dogs of all sizes are allowed for no additional fee. Dogs must be under owner's control, on no more than a 6 foot leash or securely crated, cleaned up after at all times, and are not to be left unattended. Dogs are not allowed in buildings or on about 14 miles of the trails; please ask the attendant at the gate for a list of the trails.

Staunton

Accommodations
Best Western Staunton Inn 92 Rowe Rd Staunton VA   540-885-1112 (800-780-7234)
Dogs are allowed for no additional pet fee.
Comfort Inn 1302 Richmond Avenue Staunton VA   540-886-5000 (877-424-6423)
Dogs up to 50 pounds are allowed for an additional fee of $10 per night per pet.
Days Inn Staunton 273 D Bells Lane Staunton VA   540-248-0888 (800-329-7466)
Dogs of all sizes are allowed. There is a $10 per night pet fee per pet.
Days Inn Staunton/Blue Ridge Mountains 372 White Hill Rd Staunton VA   540-337-3031 (800-329-7466)
Dogs of all sizes are allowed. There is a $8 per night pet fee per pet.
Holiday Inn 152 Fairway Lane Staunton VA   540-248-6020 (877-270-6405)
Dogs of all sizes are allowed: Non-priority guests pay an additional one time pet fee per room of $15 for 1 pet and $5 for a 2nd pet; priority club members pay a $10 one time fee and $5 for a 2nd pet.
Quality Inn 96 Baker Lane Staunton VA   540-248-5111 (877-424-6423)
Dogs are allowed for an additional fee of $10 per night per pet.
Sleep Inn 222 Jefferson H Staunton VA   540-887-6500 (877-424-6423)
Dogs are allowed for no additional pet fee. Dogs may not be left alone in the room.
Super 8 Staunton 1015 Richmond Rd Staunton VA   540-886-2888 (800-800-8000)
Dogs of all sizes are allowed. There is a $10 per night pet fee per pet. Smoking and non-smoking rooms are available for pet rooms.
Twelfth Night Inn 402 E Beverly Staunton VA   540-885-1733
Dogs of all sizes are allowed. There is a $15 per night fee for one pet and it is $20 per night for two.

Campgrounds and RV Parks
Staunton/Verona KOA 296 Riner Lane Verona VA   540-248-2746 (800-562-9949)
http://www.koa.com
Dogs of all sizes are allowed, and there are no additional pet fees for tent or RV sites. There is a $10 per night per pet additional fee for cabins. Dogs must be leashed and cleaned up after. This RV park is closed during the off-season. The camping and tent areas also allow dogs. There is a dog walk area at the campground. Dogs are allowed in the camping cabins.

Attractions
Historic Staunton Guided and Self-Guided Walking Tours 35 S New Street/H 250 Staunton VA   540-332-3971
http://www.staunton.va.us/
The city offers free guided tours, or maps are available (here and at several other places around town) for self-guided walking tours of Staunton's five National Historic Districts. Dogs are allowed on the tours. For the guided

tours dogs will not be allowed to go in any of the buildings, but most of the tour is outside. Dogs must be under owner's control, leashed, and cleaned up after at all times.

Woodrow Wilson Library and Birthplace 18-24 N Coalter Street Staunton VA   540-885-0897
Although dogs are not allowed in the buildings, there are beautifully landscaped grounds and Victorian-style terraced gardens to check out while their owners take turns exploring the birthplace, museum and library of President Wilson. Dogs must be well behaved, leashed, and cleaned up after at all times.

Outdoor Restaurants
Wright's Dairy-Rite 346 Greenville AvenueH 250 Staunton VA   540-886-0435
http://www.dairy-rite.com/
An original drive-in restaurant, they offer an "All America favorites" menu with burgers, hot dogs, ice cream, and more. Dogs are allowed at the outer tables, and they must be under owner's control, leashed, and cleaned up after at all times.

Stuart

Campgrounds and RV Parks
Fairy Stone State Park 967 Fairystone Lake Drive Stuart VA   276-930-2424 (800-933-PARK (7275))
Rich in folklore, this park of 4,868 acres with a 168 acre lake provides a variety of land and water recreation, but the Fairy Stones (naturally formed crosses in small rocks) are the real attraction in this park. Dogs of all sizes are allowed for an additional $3 per night per pet for camping, and for $5 per night per pet for cabins. Cabins are available year round. Dogs must be leashed and cleaned up after in camp areas. Dogs are not allowed on the beach, in the water, or at the conference center. Dogs are allowed on the trails. This campground is closed during the off-season. The camping and tent areas also allow dogs. There is a dog walk area at the campground. Dogs are allowed in the camping cabins.

Suffolk

Accommodations
Days Inn Suffolk 1526 Holland Road Suffolk VA   757-539-5111 (800-329-7466)
Dogs of all sizes are allowed. There is a $7 per night pet fee per pet.

Tangier Island

Attractions
Tangier Island Buggy Tours Tangier Pier Tangier Island VA
Getting to the island is a picturesque delight and since it has changed little since the 1700's, there are plenty of natural, undisturbed sites to explore on this 1 by 3 mile isle. There are a number of buggy tour guides that meet the boats when they come in and some of them will allow a dog to come along on the tour. Visitors just need to ask the individual drivers. Dogs must be well behaved, under owner's control, leashed, and cleaned up after at all times.

Virginia Beach Area

Accommodations
Red Roof Inn - Chesapeake 724 Woodlake Drive Chesapeake VA   757-523-0123 (800-RED-ROOF)
One well-behaved family pet per room. Guest must notify front desk upon arrival. Guest is liable for any damages. In consideration of all guests, pets must never be left unattended in the guest rooms.
TownePlace Suites Chesapeake 2000 Old Greenbrier Road Chesapeake VA   757-523-5004
Dogs of all sizes are allowed. There is a $75 one time pet fee per visit.
Days Inn Norfolk Marina/Beachfront 1631 Bayville St Norfolk VA   757-583-4521 (800-329-7466)
Dogs of all sizes are allowed. There is a $15 per night pet fee per pet. Reservations are recommended due to

limited rooms for pets.

Econo Lodge 9601 4th View St Norfolk VA 757-480-9611
There is a $5 per day pet fee.

Motel 6 - Norfolk 853 North Military Highway Norfolk VA 757-461-2380 (800-466-8356)
One well-behaved family pet per room. Guest must notify front desk upon arrival. Guest is liable for any damages. In consideration of all guests, pets must never be left unattended in the guest rooms.

Page House Inn 323 Fairfax Avenue Norfolk VA 757-625-5033 (800-599-7659)
http://www.pagehouseinn.com/
This stately historic mansion gives guests a glimpse of past luxury, as well as a good central location to a variety of recreation, shopping, and dining. Dogs of all sizes are allowed for an additional fee of $25 per night per pet. Dogs must be quiet, well behaved, leashed, and cleaned up after. Dogs must be crated if left alone for more than a few minutes and a cell number left at the front desk.

Quality Suites Lake Wright 6280 Northampton Blvd Norfolk VA 757-461-6251
Dogs are allowed for an additional one time fee of $25 per pet for the standard rooms; the fee is $35 per pet for suites.

Residence Inn by Marriott 1590 N Military Highway Norfolk VA 757-333-3000
Dogs of all sizes are allowed. There is a $75 one time fee and a pet policy to sign at check in.

Sheraton Norfolk Waterside Hotel 777 Waterside Drive Norfolk VA 757-622-6664 (888-625-5144)
Dogs up to 60 pounds are allowed. There are no additional pet fees. Dogs are not allowed to be left alone in the room.

Sleep Inn Lake Wright 6280 Northampton Blvd Norfolk VA 757-461-1133 (877-424-6423)
Dogs are allowed for an additional one time fee of $25 per pet for the standard rooms; the fee is $35 per pet for suites.

Holiday Inn 8 Crawford Pkwy Portsmouth VA 757-393-2573 (877-270-6405)
Dogs of all sizes are allowed for an additional pet fee of $10 per night per pet.

Candlewood Suites Virginia Beach/Norfolk 4437 Bonney Road Virginia Beach VA 757-213-1500 (877-270-6405)
Dogs of all sizes are allowed for an additional pet fee per room of $75 for 1 to 6 nights, and $150 for 7 nights or more.

Days Inn Virginia Beach Oceanfront 3107 Atlantic Ave Virginia Beach VA 757-428-7233 (800-329-7466)
Dogs of all sizes are allowed. There is a $25 per night pet fee per pet.

Doubletree 1900 Pavilion Drive Virginia Beach VA 757-422-8900
Two dogs with no more than a combined weight of 90 pounds are allowed. There is a $25 per week per room fee and a pet policy to sign at check in.

Holiday Inn Hotel & Suites Va Beach-Surfside (26Th St) 2607 Atlantic Ave Virginia Beach VA 757-491-6900 (877-270-6405)
Dogs of all sizes are allowed for an additional one time pet fee of $40 per room.

La Quinta Inn Norfolk Virginia Beach 192 Newtown Rd. Virginia Beach VA 757-497-6620 (800-531-5900)
Dogs of all sizes are allowed. There are no additional pet fees. Dogs must be leashed, cleaned up after, and crated if left unattended in the room.

Red Roof Inn - Virginia Beach 196 Ballard Court Virginia Beach VA 757-490-0225 (800-RED-ROOF)
One well-behaved family pet per room. Guest must notify front desk upon arrival. Guest is liable for any damages. In consideration of all guests, pets must never be left unattended in the guest rooms.

Red Roof Inn - Virginia Beach - Norfolk Airport 5745 Northampton Boulevard Virginia Beach VA 757-460-3414 (800-RED-ROOF)
One well-behaved family pet per room. Guest must notify front desk upon arrival. Guest is liable for any damages. In consideration of all guests, pets must never be left unattended in the guest rooms.

Sandbridge Realty 581 Sandbridge Road Virginia Beach VA 757-426-6262 (800-933-4800)
http://www.sandbridge.com/
This realty offers a variety of vacation rentals with various amenities in the Sandbridge Beach area. Dogs of all sizes are allowed in the house rentals (not the condos) for an additional fee of $115 per pet per stay. Dogs must be licensed, and leashed and cleaned up after at all times. Dogs are not allowed on the beach, the boardwalk, or the grassy area west of the boardwalk between Rudee Inlet and 42nd Street from the Friday before Memorial Day to Labor Day unless they are in an escape-proof container.

Sheraton Oceanfront Hotel 3501 Atlantic Ave. Virginia Beach VA 757-425-9000 (888-625-5144)
Dogs up to 60 pounds are allowed. Pets are restricted to first and third floor rooms only. Dogs are not allowed to be left alone in the room.

TownePlace Suites Virginia Beach 5757 Cleveland St Virginia Beach VA 757-490-9367
Dogs up to 75 pounds are allowed. There is a $75 one time pet fee per visit.

Campgrounds and RV Parks

False Cape State Park 4001 Sandpiper Road Virginia Beach VA 757-426-3657 (800-933-PARK (7275))
As one of the last undeveloped spaces along the east coast, this park offers a true "back to nature" experience with constant efforts to protect the very diverse environment and its inhabitants, an active education center,

history programs, special events, and more. There is no vehicular access, and boat, foot, bike, beach transporter, or tram allow the only accesses and services vary depending on the season. Dogs are allowed in the park; they are not allowed through/in the refuge, except during October. Pets can be brought in by boat or the beach trail only from November 1st to March 31st, and from April to September they can only come to the park by boat. Dogs must be under owner's control, leashed, and cleaned up after at all times. There are 12 primitive campsites available with drinking water and pit toilets nearby. Reservations are required (no exceptions) and can be made on the same day or in advance. This is a carry in/carry out camp area. The camping and tent areas also allow dogs. There is a dog walk area at the campground. There are no electric or water hookups at the campgrounds.

First Landing State Park 2500 Shore DriveH 60 Virginia Beach VA   757-412-2320 (800-933-PARK (2725))
This 2,888 acre historic park has over a mile of beach, 9 walking trails covering almost 19 miles, interpretive programs, an authentic Indian village, and a variety of land and water recreational opportunities. Dogs of all sizes are allowed for no additional fee for day use, and $3 per night per pet for overnight campers. They are allowed throughout the park and on the beach here. Dogs must be under owner's control, on no more than a 6 foot leash, and cleaned up after at all times. Owners must carry proof of rabies vaccination as it is a requirement for dogs in Virginia Beach. The camp sites each have a picnic table and fire grill, and there are restrooms, hot showers, and laundry facilities close by. The camping and tent areas also allow dogs. There is a dog walk area at the campground.

Virginia Beach KOA 1240 General Booth Blvd Virginia Beach VA   757-428-1444 (800-562-4150)
http://www.koa.com
Dogs of all sizes are allowed. There are no additional pet fees. Dogs must be leashed and cleaned up after. Dogs are not allowed to be in an outside pen unattended. There is a dog walk area at the campground.

Transportation Systems

Elizabeth River Ferry 6 Crawford Parkway Portsmouth VA   757-393-5111
Famous for being the oldest continually operating public transport in America, this ferry system can be boarded at #1 High Street or at the Parkway address, and it connects pedestrians from Olde Towne Portsmouth to Norfolk's Waterside Festival Marketplace. Dogs are allowed on board for no additional fee. Dogs must be well behaved, under owner's control/care, and leashed at all times.

Attractions

Kayak Adventure Rentals 110 W Randall Avenue Norfolk VA   757-480-1999
http://www.kayaknaturetours.net/main.php
This watercraft rental company will allow dogs on the kayak rentals. They prefer that dogs have had prior experience on the water. Dogs must be well behaved, under owner's control, leashed, and cleaned up after. Prior reservations are required, and they are not located on a water access.

Portsmouth Olde Towne Walking Tour 6 Crawford Parkway Portsmouth VA   757-393-5111
Walking tour brochures are available at the visitor center for the various locations of the self-guided walking tours of the Old Towne Historic District of Portsmouth. Dogs are allowed on the walk; they are not allowed in buildings. Dogs must be leashed and cleaned up after.

Stores

PetSmart Pet Store 1236 Greenbriar Pkwy Chesapeake VA   757-436-7559
Your licensed and well-behaved leashed dog is allowed in the store.

PetSmart Pet Store 4300 Portsmouth Blvd Ste A Chesapeake VA   757-405-3143
Your licensed and well-behaved leashed dog is allowed in the store.

Maggie Wags Dog Boutique 503 Botetourt Street Norfolk VA   757-640-0199
http://www.maggiewags.com/
This upscale doggy boutique provides a variety of fashion items, carriers, beds, fine art, and gourmet treats, and your well mannered pooch is welcome in the store. Dogs must be under owner's control/care and leashed at all times.

Skipjack Nautical Wares 629 High Street Portsmouth VA   757-399-5012
http://www.skipjacknauticalwares.com/
This nautical wares and marine gallery offer antiques, a wide array of art work, supplies, and just about everything with an ocean motif. Well behaved dogs are allowed in the store. They must be under owner's control/care and on a short leash at all times.

Canino's Pet Bakery and Boutique 4216 Virginia Beach Blvd/H 58 Virginia Beach VA   757-747-2275
http://www.caninos.biz/
A pooch boutique with an Italian flair, this store offers a variety of fashions, accessories, and yummy all natural treats. Dogs are allowed in store; they must be well behaved, under owner's control/care, and leashed at all times.

PetSmart Pet Store 3413 Virginia Beach Blvd Virginia Beach VA   757-486-1233
Your licensed and well-behaved leashed dog is allowed in the store.

PetSmart Pet Store 4421 Virginia Beach Blvd Virginia Beach VA   757-497-1279
Your licensed and well-behaved leashed dog is allowed in the store.

Beaches
Back Bay National Wildlife Refuge Sandpiper Road Virginia Beach VA   757-721-2412
http://backbay.fws.gov/
Dogs are only allowed on the beach during the off-season. Dogs are allowed on the beach from October 1
through March 31. Pets must be leashed (on leashes up to 10 feet long) and people need to clean up after their
pets. This park is located approximately 15 miles south of Viriginia Beach. From I-64, exit to I-264 East (towards
the oceanfront). Then take Birdneck Road Exit (Exit 22), turn right onto Birdneck Road. Go about 3-4 miles and
then turn right on General Booth Blvd. Go about 5 miles. After crossing the Nimmo Parkway, pay attention to
road signs. Get into the left lane so you can turn left at the next traffic light. Turn left onto Princess Anne Rd. The
road turns into Sandbridge Rd. Keep driving and then turn right onto Sandpiper Road just past the fire station.
Follow Sandpiper Road for about 4 miles to the end of the road.
First Landing State Park 2500 Shore Drive Virginia Beach VA   757-412-2300
Dogs on a 6 foot or less leash are allowed year-round on the beach. People need to clean up after their pet. All
pets must have a rabies tag on their collar or proof of a rabies vaccine. To get there, take I-64. Then take the
Northampton Blvd/US 13 North (Exit 282). You will pass eight lights and then turn right at the Shore Drive/US 60
exit. Turn right onto Shore Drive and go about 4.5 miles to the park entrance.
Virginia Beach Public Beaches off Highway 60 Virginia Beach VA   757-437-4919
Dogs are only allowed during off-season on Virginia Beach public beaches. From the Friday before Memorial
Day through Labor Day weekend, pets are not allowed on public sand beaches, the boardwalk or the grassy area
west of the boardwalk, from Rudee Inlet to 42nd Street. People are required to clean up after their pets and dogs
must be leashed.

Parks
Dismal Swam Canal Trail Dominion Blvd and H 17 Chesapeake VA   757-382-6411
Running 8½ miles along the Dismal Swam Canal on the eastern side of the refuge, this former highway multi-
use trail features some of the most significant historical and ecological habits in the US, and offers plenty of land
and water recreation along the way. Dogs are welcome; they must be well behaved, leashed at all times, and
cleaned up after.
Back Bay National Wildlife Refuge 4005 Sandpiper Road Virginia Beach VA   757-721-2412
http://www.fws.gov/backbay/
Located on a barrier island, this 9000 acre park is home to wildlife, migrating birds, and other habitats. They also
offer various educational opportunities. Dogs are not allowed here in the Summer at all; they are allowed from
November 1st to March 31st in areas open to the public only. Dogs must be leashed, or under strict voice control
when not crowded, and cleaned up after at all times.
False Cape State Park 4001 Sandpiper Road Virginia Beach VA   757-426-3657 (800-933-PARK (7275))
As one of the last undeveloped spaces along the east coast, this park offers a true "back to nature" experience
with constant efforts to protect the very diverse environment and its inhabitants, an active education center,
history programs, special events, and more. There is no vehicular access, and boat, foot, bike, beach
transporter, or tram allow the only accesses and services vary depending on the season. Dogs are allowed in the
park; they are not allowed through/in the refuge, except during October. Pets can be brought in by boat or the
beach trail only from November 1 to March 31, and from April to September they can only come to the park by
boat. Dogs must be under owner's control, leashed, and cleaned up after at all times.
First Landing State Park 2500 Shore DriveH 60 Virginia Beach VA   757-412-2320 (800-933-PARK (2725))
This 2,888 acre historic park has over a mile of beach, 9 walking trails covering almost 19 miles, interpretive
programs, an authentic Indian village, and a variety of land and water recreational opportunities. Dogs of all sizes
are allowed for no additional fee for day use, and $3 per night per pet for overnight campers. They are allowed
throughout the park and on the beach here (not so at other park beaches). Dogs must be under owner's control,
on no more than a 6 foot leash, and cleaned up after at all times. Owners must carry proof of rabies vaccination
as it is a requirement for dogs in Virginia Beach.

Off-Leash Dog Parks
Brambleton Dog Park Booth Street and Malloy Ave Norfolk VA   757-441-2400
This off-leash dog park is not fenced. You must control your dog at all times.
Cambridge Dog Park Cambridge Place and Cambridge Place Norfolk VA   757-441-2400
This off-leash dog park is not fenced. You must control your dog at all times.
Dune Street Dog Park Dune St & Meadow Brook Lane Norfolk VA   757-441-2400
This off-leash dog park is not fenced. You must control your dog at all times.
Red Wing Park Dog Park 1398 General Booth Blvd. Virginia Beach VA   757-563-1100
This is a one acre fenced dog park. The park is open from 7:30 am until sunset. There is a $5 annual fee. Dogs
must also show proof of license and vaccination. You may get the annual pass at the Maintenance Office at the

dog park.
Woodstock Park Dog Park 5709 Providence Rd. Virginia Beach VA   757-563-1100
This is a one acre fenced dog park. The park is open from 7:30 am until sunset. There is a $5 annual fee. Dogs must also show proof of license and vaccination. You may get the annual pass at the Maintenance Office at the dog park.

Outdoor Restaurants
Carrot Tree 411 Reed Street Norfolk VA   757-246-9559
This bakery/restaurant offers outside dining. Dogs are allowed at the outer tables. Dogs must be under owner's control/care at all times.
Kincaid's Fish, Chop, and Steak House 300 Monticello Avenue, Suite 147 (MacArthur Center) Norfolk VA 757-622-8000
Time honored favorites are featured here and patio dining is available. Dogs are allowed at the outer tables. Dogs must be under owner's control/care and leashed at all times.
Abby Road Restaurant and Pub 203 22nd Street Virginia Beach VA   757-425-6330
http://www.abbeyroadpub.com/
Fun, entertainment, an interesting eclectic menu, WiFi, and outdoor dining options are all offered at this upbeat eatery. Dogs are allowed at the outer tables. Dogs must be under owner's control/care and leashed at all times.

Day Kennels
PetsHotel by PetsMart Day Kennel 3413 Virginia Beach Blvd. Virginia Beach VA   757-486-5294
http://www.petsmart.com/PETsHOTEL/
This PetSmart pet store offers day care, day camp and overnight care. You may drop off and pick up your dog during the hours the store is open seven days a week. Dogs must have proof of current rabies, DPP and Bordatella vaccinations.

Warrenton

Accommodations
Comfort Inn 7379 Comfort Inn Drive Warrenton VA   540-349-8900 (877-424-6423)
Dogs are allowed for an additional fee of $10 per night per pet.
Hampton Inn 501 Blackwell Road Warrenton VA   540-349-4200
Dogs of all sizes are allowed. There are no additional pet fees.
Howard Johnson Inn 6 Broadview Ave. Warrenton VA   540-347-4141 (800-446-4656)
Dogs up to 85 pounds are allowed. There is a $10 per day pet fee.

Stores
PetSmart Pet Store 13241 Gateway Center Dr Bldg P Gainesville VA   571-248-4300
Your licensed and well-behaved leashed dog is allowed in the store.

Williamsburg

Accommodations
Quarterpath Inn 620 York Street East Williamsburg VA   757-220-0960 (800-446-9222)
http://www.quarterpathinn.com/
This inn is located only a short walk to the historical restored town of Colonial Williamsburg. Dogs of all sizes are allowed for no additional fee. Dogs must be quiet, well behaved, leashed, cleaned up after at all times, and the Do Not Disturb sign put on the door when alone in the room.
Days Inn Williamsburg/Colonial Dwtn 902 Richmond Rd Williamsburg VA   757-229-5060 (800-329-7466)
Dogs of all sizes are allowed. There is a $10 per night pet fee per small pet and $15 per large pet.
Four Points by Sheraton Williamsburg Historic District 351 York St. Williamsburg VA   757-229-4100 (888-625-5144)
Dogs of all sizes are allowed. There is a $25 per night pet fee per pet. After 3 nights the nightly fee per pet is higher. Dogs are not allowed to be left alone in the room.
Motel 6 - Williamsburg 3030 Richmond Road Williamsburg VA   757-565-3433 (800-466-8356)
One well-behaved family pet per room. Guest must notify front desk upon arrival. Guest is liable for any damages. In consideration of all guests, pets must never be left unattended in the guest rooms.

Red Roof Inn - Williamsburg 824 Capitol Landing Rd Williamsburg VA 757-259-1948 (800-RED-ROOF)
One well-behaved family pet per room. Guest must notify front desk upon arrival. Guest is liable for any damages. In consideration of all guests, pets must never be left unattended in the guest rooms.
Residence Inn by Marriott 1648 Richmond Road Williamsburg VA 757-941-2000
Dogs of all sizes are allowed. There is a $75 one time fee and a pet policy to sign at check in.
Woodlands Cascades Motel 105 Visitor Center Drive Williamsburg VA 757-229-1000
This contemporary Motor Inn, surrounded by landscaped grounds, is adjacent to Colonial Williamsburg and an abundance of activities. Dogs up to a combined weight of 60 pounds are allowed for no additional fee. Dogs must be well behaved, leashed, and cleaned up after.
Candlewood Suites 329 Commonwealth Drive Yorktown VA 757-952-1120 (877-270-6405)
Dogs up to 80 pounds are allowed for an additional one time fee of $75 per pet per.
Marl Inn 220 Church Street Yorktown VA 757-898-3859 (800-799-6207)
http://www.marlinnbandb.com/
This colonial styled inn sits only a short distance from a number of activities, the river, historical sites, and an eclectic array of eateries and shops. Dogs of all sizes are allowed for no additional fee. Dogs must be housebroken, well behaved, leashed, cleaned up after, and friendly to the other pets on site.
TownePlace Suites Newport News/Yorktown 200 Cybernetics Way Yorktown VA 757-874-8884
Dogs of all sizes are allowed. There is a $75 one time pet fee per visit.

Campgrounds and RV Parks
Chippokes Plantation 695 Chippokes Park Road Surry VA 757-294-3625 (800-933-PARK (7275))
As one of the oldest working farms in the US, Chippokes is a living historical exhibit, and among the cultivated gardens and woodlands, all the traditional recreation is offered. Dogs of all sizes are allowed for an additional $3 per night per pet. Dogs may not be left unattended, and they must be on no more than a 6 foot leash, and be cleaned up after. Dogs are not allowed in the buildings, but they are allowed on the trails unless otherwise marked. This campground is closed during the off-season. The camping and tent areas also allow dogs. There is a dog walk area at the campground.
Pottery Campground Lightfoot Road/H 646 Williamsburg VA 757-565-2101 (800-892-0320)
Only minutes from Williamsburg Pottery where purchases can earn free camping nights, this 550 site campground offers wooded sites, comfort stations, a playground, and a large swimming pool. Dogs of all sizes are allowed for no additional fee. Dogs must be well behaved, leashed, and cleaned up after at all times. The camping and tent areas also allow dogs. There is a dog walk area at the campground.
Williamsburg KOA 5210 Newman Road Williamsburg VA 757-565-2907 (800-562-1733)
http://www.williamsburgkoa.com
Dogs of all sizes are allowed. There are no additional pet fees. Dogs must be leashed and cleaned up after. This RV park is closed during the off-season. The camping and tent areas also allow dogs. There is a dog walk area at the campground.
Williamsburg/Colonial KOA 4000 Newman Road Williamsburg VA 757-565-2734 (800-562-7609)
http://www.koa.com
Dogs of all sizes are allowed. There are no additional pet fees. Dogs must be leashed and cleaned up after. This RV park is closed during the off-season. The camping and tent areas also allow dogs. There is a dog walk area at the campground.

Attractions
Historic Jamestown Colonial Parkway Jamestown VA 757-898-2410
http://www.nps.gov/jame/index.htm
Home to the first successful English colonization of North America and part of the Colonial National Historical Park, Jamestown's is rich history is shared through a number of programs, activities, reenactments, and special events. Dogs are allowed throughout the park. Dogs must be leashed and cleaned up after at all times. Dogs are not allowed in buildings.
Busch Gardens Kennels 1 Busch Garden Blvd Williamsburg VA 800-343-7946
Numerous thrill rides (including the world's tallest/floorless roller coaster), a large water-park, entertainment, a generous variety of foods and shops, and plenty of opportunities to experience the history of Europe and America are offered at this world class adventure park, and more. Although dogs are not allowed inside the park, they do provide 50 large and small, secured kennels on a first come first served basis for $6 per day. They are large open-air, individual stalls and water is provided. Owners must supply food and exercise, and they suggest bringing a comfort toy/item. When entering the park, mention at the toll booth that there is a pet so they can direct you to the proper area.

Colonial Williamsburg

TOP 200 PLACE Colonial Williamsburg   Williamsburg VA
http://www.history.org
Colonial Williamsburg is a preservation of life in Virginia before the Declaration of Independence. The main park area is about three square miles and there are many historical buildings. Colonial Williamsburg allows dogs in all outdoor areas. If you want to go inside the buildings, then someone will need to stay outside with the dog. Tour materials are available such as tapes, CDs and guide books. There are also horse and carriage tours which may take your dog as it is up to the driver. You can easily spend a full day or even two here with your dog.
Mini-Golf America 1901 Richmond Rd Williamsburg VA 757-229-7200
Play mini-golf while your leashed dog joins you.
The College of William and Mary Grigsby Drive Williamsburg VA 757-221-4000
http://www.wm.edu/
This historic school is America's 2nd oldest college, and in addition to many notable achievements through the years, they also have a beautiful campus to explore. Dogs are welcome on leash. They must be under owner's control and cleaned up after at all times. Dogs are not allowed in buildings.
Historic Yorktown Historical Tour Drive Yorktown VA 757-898-2410
http://www.nps.gov/york/index.htm
Noted as the site where independence for the new America was secured, this park is dedicated to honoring, preserving, and educating the public through a number of programs, activities, reenactments, and special events. Dogs are allowed throughout the park; they are not allowed in buildings. Dogs must be leashed and cleaned up after at all times.
Yorktown Riverwalk Landing Water Street Yorktown VA 757-890-3300
A thriving seaport since colonial times, this updated waterfront offers all the modern conveniences, beautiful scenery, and an eclectic array of eateries, shops, and activity areas. Dogs are allowed on the riverwalk and through the retail areas. It is up to the individual stores/restaurant as to whether a dog is allowed inside or at the outer tables. Dogs must be under owner's control, leashed, and cleaned up after at all times.

Shopping Centers
Prime Outlets 5715-62A Richmond Road Williamsburg VA 757-565-0702
Featuring more than 90 outlet stores with more on the way, this shopping Mecca is also pet friendly. Guest Services have free doggy treats, and if pooch wants more, there are also gourmet treats that can be bought at D.O.G. Street Treats. The following stores allow pets: Ann Taylor (if held), BCBG Max Azria, BOSE Factory Store, Brown Shoe Closet, Designer Fragrances & Cosmetics Company, Dana Buchman, Ecco, Johnston & Murphy, Kitchen Collection (if held), Little Me, Saucony, Ultra Diamond, and the Waterford Wedgwood. Dogs must be well mannered, under owner's control at all times, leashed, and cleaned up after. Doggie clean-up bags

are available near Bass.

Stores
The Williamsburg Pottery Factory 6692 Richmond Road Lightfood VA   757-564-3326
http://www.williamsburgoutletmall.com/
Drawing millions of customers worldwide, this pottery store carries an immense inventory of pottery from more than 20 countries, and offer other services in the "how to" department as well. Pottery Campground, a short distance away, allows dogs and free nights can be earned from purchases at the pottery store. Dogs on leash are welcome. Dogs must be under owner's control/care at all times.
Paws Applause 4680 Monticello Avenue/H 321 Williamsburg VA   757-565-7970
http://www.pawsapplauseltd.com/
For holistic grooming and a doggie day spa, this is the spot, but they also offer a store full of doggy supplies, foods, treats, and gifts. Well behaved dogs are welcome in the store. Dogs must be under owner's control/care and leashed at all times.
PetSmart Pet Store 4900 Monticello Ave Williamsburg VA   757-259-1630
Your licensed and well-behaved leashed dog is allowed in the store.

Parks
Quarterpath Park Quarterpath Road and Rt 60 East Williamsburg VA   757-220-6170
This is a small city park with a ballfield and playground. Dogs on leash are allowed. Please clean up after your dog.
Waller Mill Park Airport Road Williamsburg VA   757-220-6178
This park has a number of trails and hiking areas. It is a little out of town.

Outdoor Restaurants

Aroma's

Aroma's 431 Prince George St Williamsburg VA   757-221-6676
This is a very dog-friendly restaurant at its outdoor patio. And the food is good too.
Ben and Jerry's Ice Cream 7097 Pocahontas Trail Williamsburg VA   757-253-0180
Dogs are allowed at the outdoor tables.
Blue Talon Bistro 420 Prince George Street Williamsburg VA   757-476-BLUE (2583)
In addition to offering time-honored favorites, this eatery offers original "comfort food" dishes, wines, an appealing ambiance, and alfresco dining. Dogs are allowed at the outer tables; they must be leashed and under

owner's control/care at all times.
Pierce's Bar-B-Que 447 Rochambeau Dr Williamsburg VA   757-565-2955
Dogs are allowed at the outdoor tables.
Season's Cafe 110 S Henry St Williamsburg VA   757-220-9775
This restaurant serves American food. Dogs are allowed at the outdoor tables.
The College Delly and Pizza Restaurant 336 Richmond Rd Williamsburg VA   757-229-6627
This restaurant serves pizza, burgers, and deli-type food. Dogs are allowed at the outdoor tables.

Winchester

Accommodations
Super 8 Middletown/Winchester Area 2120 Reliance Rd Middletown VA   540-868-1800 (800-800-8000)
Dogs of all sizes are allowed. There is a $10 per night pet fee per pet. Smoking and non-smoking rooms are available for pet rooms.
Comfort Inn 167 Town Run Lane Stephens City VA   540-869-6500 (877-424-6423)
Dogs are allowed for an additional pet fee of $15 per night per room.
Best Value Inn 2649 Valley Avenue Winchester VA   540-662-2521 (888-315-2378)
This inn offers a number of amenities plus 4 meticulously landscaped acres to explore with your pooch. Dogs are allowed for an additional fee of $5 per pet per night. Dogs must be quiet, well behaved, leashed, and cleaned up after.
Best Western Lee-Jackson Motor Inn 711 Millwood Ave Winchester VA   540-662-4154 (800-780-7234)
Dogs are allowed for an additional fee of $5 per night per pet.
Candlewood Suites Winchester 1135 Millwood Pike Winchester VA   540-667-8323 (877-270-6405)
Dogs up to 80 pounds are allowed for an additional fee of $12 per night per pet.
Days Inn Winchester 2951 Valley Ave Winchester VA   540-667-1200 (800-329-7466)
Dogs of all sizes are allowed. There is a $5 per night pet fee per pet.
Holiday Inn 1017 Millwood Pike Winchester VA   540-667-3300 (877-270-6405)
Dogs up to 60 pounds are allowed for no additional pet fee.
Red Roof Inn - Winchester 991 Millwood Pike Winchester VA   540-667-5000 (800-RED-ROOF)
One well-behaved family pet per room. Guest must notify front desk upon arrival. Guest is liable for any damages. In consideration of all guests, pets must never be left unattended in the guest rooms.
Super 8 Winchester 1077 Millwood Pike Winchester VA   540-665-4450 (800-800-8000)
Dogs of all sizes are allowed. There is a $7 per night pet fee per pet. Smoking and non-smoking rooms are available for pet rooms.

Attractions
African-American Heritage Driving Tour 1360 S Pleasant Valley Road Winchester VA   540-542-1326
One of the driving tours offered by the city of Winchester is the African-American Heritage tour that takes visitors through 200 years of interesting facts and dates of famous locals. Self-driven tour information can be obtained at the Visitor Center at the listed address.
Battle of Third Winchester Driving Tour 1360 S Pleasant Valley Road Winchester VA   540-542-1326
This driving tour takes visitors to the site of the largest battle of the Civil War that occurred in the valley. Self-driven tour information can be obtained at the Visitor Center at the listed address.
Deer Meadow Wines 199 Vintage Lane Winchester VA   800-653-6632
http://www.dmeadow.com
Dogs on leash are allowed at the outdoor tables. Some light fare is available for picnics. Open March-December from 11am-5pm on Wednesday-Sunday.
Follow the Apple Trail Auto Tour 1360 S Pleasant Valley Road Winchester VA   540-542-1326
This auto tour takes visitors through historic sites and the rolling hills of farming communities where many family-owned farms and markets still carry on the apple industry. Self-driven tour information can be obtained at the Visitor Center at the listed address. Dogs may be allowed at some of the farms.
TOP 200 PLACE **Pirates of the Shenandoah Treasure Hunt** 1360 S Pleasant Valley Road Winchester VA   877-871-1326
Your pup can go with you on this treasure hunting expedition. Dogs are not allowed in the cemetery, so they will need to skip this one spot. Visitors can pick up maps for this interactive family game at the visitor center, and then after the hunt and solving the puzzle, check on the county's web site or at the visitor center to see if the mission was accomplished. Dogs must be leashed and cleaned up after at all times, and they are not allowed in any buildings.
Stonewall Jackson's Headquarters Museum 415 N Braddock Street/H 522/11 Winchester VA   540-667-3242
Once the headquarters of Stonewall Jackson, this museum now shares this historic spot with visitors daily from

April 1st through October 31st, and there are occasional special events and exhibits here also. Dogs are allowed on the grounds; they are not allowed in the museum. Dogs must be well behaved, leashed, and cleaned up after while on the grounds.

Washington's Office Museum 32 W Cork Street Winchester VA   540-662-4412
Once the office of President Washington, this museum now shares this historic spot with visitors daily from April 1st through October 31st, and there are occasional special events and exhibits here also. Dogs are allowed on the grounds; they are not allowed in the museum. Dogs must be well behaved, leashed, and cleaned up after while on the grounds.

Shopping Centers
Old Town Mall Loudoun Street Winchester VA   877-871-1326
Visitors will find an eclectic combination of shops, services, eateries (some alfresco), and galleries in this historic Old Town area where streets are lined with 18th and 19th century buildings and there activities and special events throughout the year. Dogs are allowed throughout the shopping district; it is up to individual shops whether pets are allowed inside. Dogs must be under owner's control, leashed, and cleaned up after at all times.

Stores
PetSmart Pet Store 2310 Legge Blvd Winchester VA   540-662-5544
Your licensed and well-behaved leashed dog is allowed in the store.

Woodstock

Accommodations
Comfort Inn 1011 Motel Drive Woodstock VA   540-459-7600 (877-424-6423)
Dogs are allowed for an additional fee of $10 per night per pet.

Wytheville

Accommodations
Super 8 Ft Chiswell/Max Meadows Area 194 Ft Chiswell Rd Max Meadows VA   276-637-4141 (800-800-8000)
Dogs of all sizes are allowed. There is a $10.50 per night pet fee per pet. Smoking and non-smoking rooms are available for pet rooms.
Best Western Wytheville Inn 355 Nye Rd Wytheville VA   276-228-7300 (800-780-7234)
Dogs are allowed for an additional pet fee of $6.66 per night per room.
Comfort Inn 2594 East Lee H Wytheville VA   276-637-4281 (877-424-6423)
Dogs are allowed for an additional fee of $10 per night per pet.
Days Inn Wytheville 150 Malin Dr Wytheville VA   276-228-5500 (800-329-7466)
Dogs of all sizes are allowed. There is a $5 per night pet fee per pet.
Motel 6 - Wytheville 220 Lithia Road Wytheville VA   276-228-7988 (800-466-8356)
One well-behaved family pet per room. Guest must notify front desk upon arrival. Guest is liable for any damages. In consideration of all guests, pets must never be left unattended in the guest rooms.
Super 8 Wytheville 130 Nye Circle Wytheville VA   276-228-6620 (800-800-8000)
Dogs of all sizes are allowed. There is a $10 one time per pet fee per visit. Smoking and non-smoking rooms are available for pet rooms.

Campgrounds and RV Parks
Whtheville KOA 231 KOA Road Wytheville VA   276-228-2601 (800-562-3380)
http://www.wythevillekoa.com
Dogs of all sizes are allowed. There are no additional pet fees. Dogs must be leashed and cleaned up after. There are some breed restrictions. The camping and tent areas also allow dogs. There is a dog walk area at the campground. Dogs are allowed in the camping cabins.

Shopping Centers
Fort Chiswell Outlets Factory Outlet Drive Max Meadows VA   276-637-6214
http://www.ftchiswelloutlets.com/

Virginia   - Please always call ahead to make sure that an establishment is still dog-friendly

This outlet mall offers 11 stores and easy access from Interstates 77 and 81. Dogs are allowed in the courtyard areas; it is up to the individual stores whether a pet is permitted inside. Dogs must be well mannered, leashed, and cleaned up after at all times.

Chapter 15

West Virginia
Dog Travel Guide

Beckley

Accommodations

Best Western Four Seasons Inn 1939 Harper Road Beckley WV   304-252-0671 (800-780-7234)
Dogs are allowed for an additional fee of $5.60 per night per pet.
Comfort Inn 1909 Harper Road Beckley WV   304-255-2161 (877-424-6423)
Dogs are allowed for no additional pet fee.
Super 8 Beckley 2014 Harper Rd Beckley WV   304-253-0802 (800-800-8000)
Dogs up to 70 pounds are allowed. There is a $10 one time per pet fee per visit. Smoking and non-smoking rooms are available for pet rooms.
Quality Inn New River Gorge 103 Elliotts Way Fayetteville WV   304-574-3443 (877-424-6423)
Dogs are allowed for an additional fee of $5 per night per pet.

Campgrounds and RV Parks

Babcock State Park HC 35, Box 150 Clifftop WV   304-438-3004 (800-CALL WVA (225-5982))
http://www.babcocksp.com/
Offering over 4,000 scenic, diverse acres with an abundance of land and water recreation, this park also has a recreated working Grist Mill where visitors may purchase milled products. Healthy dogs are allowed in camp areas for no charge, and the cabins/cottages for a $50 refundable deposit, plus $40 for the first night and $5 for each additional night per pet. A credit card must be on file, and there is a pet agreement to sign at check in. Pets must be securely crated when left alone in the cabins or cottages, they are not allowed to be tied/chained on the porch or yard, and their food may not be kept outside. Dogs must have certified proof of inoculations from a veterinarian, be on no more than a 10 foot leash, and picked up after. The 52 site campground is open from mid-April to mid-October and offer picnic tables, grills, restrooms, showers, a laundry, drinking water, and 2 dump stations. This RV park is closed during the off-season. The camping and tent areas also allow dogs. There is a dog walk area at the campground. Dogs are allowed in the camping cabins. There are no water hookups at the campgrounds.
New River Gorge National River 104 Main Street Glen Jean WV   304-465-0508
http://www.nps.gov/neri/
In addition to a number of recreational activities, this dramatically scenic and diverse 70,000 acre park offers a rich natural cultural history as well as educational opportunities. Also, once a year the New River Gorge Bridge is opened for parachute BASE jumpers, and Amtrak is available at 3 stops in the park. Dogs are allowed for no additional fee; they must be leashed and under owner's control/care at all times. There are 4 primitive, riverside camp areas with limited restroom facilities and no drinking water. They are Stone Cliff Beach off H 25 near Thurmond; Army Camp off H 41 near Prince; Grandview Sandbar on Glade Creek Road, and Glade Creek at the end of Glade Creek Road. The camping and tent areas also allow dogs. There is a dog walk area at the campground. There are no electric or water hookups at the campgrounds.
The Gauley River National Recreation Area H 129/ P. O. Box 246 Glen Jean WV   304-465-0508
http://www.nps.gov/gari/
Although home to one of the most adventurous white water rafting corridors in the east, this recreation area offers hiking trails, scenic gorges, a variety of natural habitats, and historic sites. Dogs are allowed for no additional pet fees. Dogs must be under owner's control/care at all times. Primitive camping is allowed at the Summersville Dam tail-waters area. The camping and tent areas also allow dogs. There is a dog walk area at the campground. There are no electric or water hookups at the campgrounds.
Bluestone State Park HC 78 Box 3/H 20 Hinton WV   304-466-2805 (800-CALL WVA (225-5982))
http://www.bluestonesp.com/
Offering historical as well as recreational interests, this 2,100 forested, mountain park sits adjacent to the State's 3rd largest body of water. Healthy dogs are allowed in camp areas for no charge and the cabins/cottages for a $50 refundable deposit, plus $40 for the first night and $5 for each additional night per pet. A credit card must be on file, and there is a pet agreement to sign at check in. Pets may not be left unattended outside, they must be securely crated when left alone in the cabins or cottages, they are not allowed to be tied/chained on the porch or yard, and their food may not be kept outside. Dogs must have certified proof of inoculations from a veterinarian, be on no more than a 10 foot leash, and picked up after. Campsites consist of 32 sites with central restrooms, showers, and a dump station; a 44 rustic site camp area with restrooms and cold showers, and a 39 site area that is accessible only by boat. This RV park is closed during the off-season. The camping and tent areas also allow dogs. There is a dog walk area at the campground. Dogs are allowed in the camping cabins. There are no water hookups at the campgrounds.
Twin Falls Resort State Park Route 97, Box 667 Mullens WV   304-294-4000 (800-CALL WVA (225-5982))
http://www.twinfallsresort.com/

This mountain recreation getaway offers 12 hiking trails, an amphitheater, an 18-hole golf course, an 1830's living history farm, and much more. Healthy dogs are allowed in camp areas for no charge and the cabins/cottages for a $50 refundable deposit, plus $40 for the first night and $5 for each additional night per pet. A credit card must be on file, and there is a pet agreement to sign at check in. Pets may not be left unattended outside, they must be securely crated when left alone in the cabins or cottages, they are not allowed to be tied/chained on the porch or yard, and their food may not be kept outside. Dogs must have certified proof of inoculations from a veterinarian, be on no more than a 10 foot leash, and picked up after. The campground has 50 sites-25 can be reserved, and there is a small convenience store, a laundry, 2 bathhouses, picnic tables and grills, and a dump station. The camping and tent areas also allow dogs. There is a dog walk area at the campground. Dogs are allowed in the camping cabins. There are no water hookups at the campgrounds.

Plum Orchard Lake Wildlife Management Area Plum Orchard Lake Road Scarbro WV   304-469-9905 (800-CALL WVA (225-5982))
http://www.plumorchardlakewma.com/
There are 3,201 recreational acres at this forested park with a 202 acre, 6 ½ mile shoreline lake that's quite popular for fishing. Healthy dogs are allowed for no additional fee. A credit card must be on file, and there is a pet agreement to sign at check in. Pets may not be left unattended outside, and their food must be kept inside. Dogs must have certified proof of inoculations from a veterinarian, be on no more than a 10 foot leash, and picked up after. The park has 21 primitive sites at Beech Bottom, and 17 primitive sites above the dam, each with a tent pad, picnic table, and grill. Restrooms and drinking water is nearby. The camping and tent areas also allow dogs. There is a dog walk area at the campground. There are no electric or water hookups at the campgrounds.

Lake Stephens Park 1400 Lake Stephens Road/H 3 Surveyor WV   304-256-1747
http://www.lakestephenswv.com/
There is a wide variety of activities and recreation at this 2,300 acre county park that also has a 300 acre clear mountain lake. Dogs are allowed for no additional pet fees; they must be on no more than a 10 foot leash, and cleaned up after at all times. The campground has 100 RV and 28 tent sites with an additional overflow area. The sites have picnic tables, and restrooms and showers are located at the campground store/office. Also in the camp area is a laundry, recreation area, and gaming courts. This RV park is closed during the off-season. The camping and tent areas also allow dogs. There is a dog walk area at the campground.

Parks

Fitzpatrick Park 896 Fitzpatrick Road/H 20 Beckley WV   304-934-5323
This 12 acre park offers a fishing pond, playground, picnic shelter, and 4 ball fields. Dogs on leash are allowed.

Babcock State Park HC 35, Box 150 Clifftop WV   304-438-3004 (800-CALL WVA (225-5982))
http://www.babcocksp.com/
Offering over 4,000 scenic, diverse acres with an abundance of land and water recreation, this park also has a recreated working Grist Mill where visitors may purchase milled products. Healthy dogs are allowed in camp areas for no charge, and the cabins/cottages for a $50 refundable deposit, plus $40 for the first night and $5 for each additional night per pet. A credit card must be on file, and there is a pet agreement to sign at check in. Pets must be securely crated when left alone in the cabins or cottages, they are not allowed to be tied/chained on the porch or yard, and their food may not be kept outside. Dogs must have certified proof of inoculations from a veterinarian, be on no more than a 10 foot leash, and picked up after.

Bluestone National Scenic River P. O. Box 246 Glen Jean WV   304-465-0508
http://www.nps.gov/blue/
Unspoiled natural landscapes, a variety of habitats and wildlife, a warm water fishing spot, and the beautiful 10½ mile Turnpike Trail all combine to make this a popular relaxing or recreational destination. Dogs are allowed throughout the park and on the trails on leash.

New River Gorge National River 104 Main Street Glen Jean WV   304-465-0508
http://www.nps.gov/neri/
In addition to a number of recreational activities, this dramatically scenic and diverse 70,000 acre park offers a rich natural cultural history as well as educational opportunities. Also, once a year the New River Gorge Bridge is opened for parachute BASE jumpers, and Amtrak is available at 3 stops in the park. Dogs are allowed for no additional fee; they must be leashed and under owner's control/care at all times.

The Gauley River National Recreation Area H 129/ P. O. Box 246 Glen Jean WV   304-465-0508
http://www.nps.gov/gari/
Although home to one of the most adventurous white water rafting corridors in the east, this recreation area offers hiking trails, scenic gorges, a variety of natural habitats, and historic sites. Dogs are allowed for no additional pet fees. Dogs must be under owner's control/care at all times.

Bluestone State Park HC 78 Box 3/H 20 Hinton WV   304-466-2805 (800-CALL WVA (225-5982))
http://www.bluestonesp.com/
Offering historical as well as recreational interests, this 2,100 forested, mountain park sits adjacent to the State's 3rd largest body of water. Healthy dogs are allowed in camp areas for no charge and the cabins/cottages for a $50 refundable deposit, plus $40 for the first night and $5 for each additional night per pet. A credit card must be on file, and there is a pet agreement to sign at check in. Pets may not be left unattended outside, they must be

securely crated when left alone in the cabins or cottages, they are not allowed to be tied/chained on the porch or yard, and their food may not be kept outside. Dogs must have certified proof of inoculations from a veterinarian, be on no more than a 10 foot leash, and picked up after.

Twin Falls Resort State Park Route 97, Box 667 Mullens WV   304-294-4000 (800-CALL WVA (225-5982))
http://www.twinfallsresort.com/
This mountain recreation getaway offers 12 hiking trails, an amphitheater, an 18-hole golf course, an 1830's living history farm, and much more. Healthy dogs are allowed in camp areas for no charge and the cabins/cottages for a $50 refundable deposit, plus $40 for the first night and $5 for each additional night per pet. A credit card must be on file, and there is a pet agreement to sign at check in. Pets may not be left unattended outside, they must be securely crated when left alone in the cabins or cottages, they are not allowed to be tied/chained on the porch or yard, and their food may not be kept outside. Dogs must have certified proof of inoculations from a veterinarian, be on no more than a 10 foot leash, and picked up after.

Plum Orchard Lake Wildlife Management Area Plum Orchard Lake Road Scarbro WV   304-469-9905 (800-CALL WVA (225-5982))
http://www.plumorchardlakewma.com/
There are 3,201 recreational acres at this forested park with a 202 acre, 6 ½ mile shoreline lake that's quite popular for fishing. Healthy dogs are allowed for no additional fee. A credit card must be on file, and there is a pet agreement to sign at check in. Pets may not be left unattended outside, and their food must be kept inside. Dogs must have certified proof of inoculations from a veterinarian, be on no more than a 10 foot leash, and picked up after.

Lake Stephens Park 1400 Lake Stephens Road/H 3 Surveyor WV   304-256-1747
http://www.lakestephenswv.com/
There is a wide variety of activities and recreation at this 2,300 acre county park that also has a 300 acre clear mountain lake. Dogs are allowed for no additional pet fees; they must be on no more than a 10 foot leash, and cleaned up after at all times.

Outdoor Restaurants

Pasquale Mira Restaurant 224 Harper Park Drive Beckley WV   304-255-5253
http://beckleyitalian.com/
This Italian restaurant offers casual, intimate formal or outdoor patio dining options. Dogs are allowed at the outer tables; they must be under owner's control/care at all times.

Dirty Ernie's Rib Pit 310 Keller Avenue Fayetteville WV   304-574-4822
http://www.dirtyernies.com/index.html
This seasonal eatery serves up a variety of foods including barbecue items, pastas, soups, and sandwiches, plus they also offer outside dining. Dogs are allowed at the outer tables; they must be under owner's control/care at all times.

Events

New River Gorge National River Bridge Day H 19 (Box 202) Fayetteville WV   800-927-0263
http://www.officialbridgeday.com/
Bridge day, the 3rd weekend in October, is a major yearly event with thousands of visitors, and the largest gathering of BASE jumpers for the biggest extreme sports event in the world. There are hundreds of vendors, tours, and more at this annual festival. Dogs are only allowed on the bridge this one day. They must be leashed and under owner's control/care at all times.

Berkeley Springs

Accommodations

Berkeley Springs Motel 468 Wilkes Street Berkeley Springs WV   304-258-1776
http://www.berkeleyspringsmotel.net/
Dogs are allowed for no additional pet fee.

Hannah's House 867 Libby's Ridge Road Berkeley Springs WV   304-258-1718 (800-526-0807)
This antique farm home offers seclusion and convenience to a number of local activities and recreation. Well behaved dogs are allowed for an additional fee of $25 per pet for weekends, and $50 per pet by the week. Dogs are not allowed on the furniture, and they must be crated when left alone in the room.

Sleepy Creek Tree Farm 37 Shades Lane Berkeley Springs WV   304-258-4324 (866-275-8303)
Located on 8 scenic acres of a Christmas tree farm, this is a nature lover's get-a-way. One dog is allowed for no additional pet fee. Dogs must be able to climb stairs (or be carried); they must be friendly to cats and other dogs, and they may not be left unattended at any time.

Sunset Mountain Farm Stickey Kline Road Berkeley Springs WV   304-258-4239

http://www.sunsetmountainfarm.com/
Great views, 40 private acres, convenience to a number of local activities and recreation, and more are offered at this get-away. Dogs are allowed for an additional one time fee of $25 per pet. Dogs must be well behaved, quiet, and the furniture/beds must be covered if pets are used to being on furnishings.

Attractions
TOP 200 PLACE Berkeley Springs Walking Tour 127 Fairfax Street Berkeley Springs WV   800-447-8797
Home to the country's first spa and believed to have curative powers, this resort town is rich in its history and architecture, and compact enough to make a nice stroll through the streets, as there has been little change to this historic town. Brochures for the walking tour are available at the visitor center or at several of the shops in town. Dogs on leash are allowed throughout the town; they are not allowed in most buildings, and they must be picked up after.
Washington Heritage Trail 127 Fairfax Street (Visitor Center) Berkeley Springs WV   800-447-8797
Five 18th century towns each offering their own story of early America are to be found on this 127 mile auto tour that highlights a spa town, sites of industry, Civil War sites, railroad landmarks, and of George Washington's time spent here. It is approved as a National and West Virginia Scenic Byway.

Stores
Berkeley Springs Antique Mall 7 Fairfax Street Berkeley Springs WV   304-258-5676
Well mannered and trained dogs are welcome in the store; they must be leashed and under owner's control/care at all times.
Old Factory Antique Mall 282 Williams Street Berkeley Springs WV   304-258-1788
Well mannered and trained dogs are welcome in the store; they must be leashed and under owner's control/care at all times.

Parks
Berkeley Springs State Park #2 S Washington Street Berkeley Springs WV   304-258-2711
Berkeley Springs State Park
This park has drawn visitors since pre-colonial times for the warm spring mineral waters believed to have curative powers. Dogs are allowed on the grounds, but they are not allowed in the back of the park where the mineral spas are. Dogs must be leashed and under owner's control/care at all times.
Cacapon Resort State Park 818 Cacapon Lodge Drive Berkeley Springs WV   304-258-1022 (800-CALL WVA (225-5982))
http://www.cacaponresort.com/
There is a wide number of land and water recreation options, nature education programs, 20 miles of hiking trails, and much more are available at this 6,000 acre mountain resort. Healthy dogs are allowed in cabins/cottages for a $50 refundable deposit, plus $40 for the first night and $5 for each additional night per pet. A credit card must be on file, and there is a pet agreement to sign at check in. Pets may not be left unattended outside, they must be securely crated when left alone in the cabins or cottages, they are not allowed to be tied/chained on the porch or yard, and their food may not be kept outside. Dogs must have certified proof of inoculations from a veterinarian, be on no more than a 10 foot leash, and picked up after.

Outdoor Restaurants
Maria's Garden and Inn 42 Independence Street Berkeley Springs WV   304-258-2021
http://www.mariasgarden.com/
Located at the town's first Bed and Breakfast, this Italian eatery offers a warm ambience and outdoor dining when weather permits. Dogs are allowed at the outer tables; they must be under owner's control/care at all times. (Dogs are not allowed at the Inn)

Bluefield

Accommodations
Econo Lodge 3400 Cumberland Rd. Bluefield WV   304-327-8171
There is a $10 per day pet charge.
Holiday Inn US 460 Bluefield WV   304-325-6170 (877-270-6405)
Dogs of all sizes are allowed for an additional fee of $10 per night per pet.
Holiday Inn Express Princeton/I-77 805 Oakvale Rd. Princeton WV   304-425-8156 (877-270-6405)
Dogs up to 50 pounds are allowed for an additional fee of $20 per night per pet.
Sleep Inn and Suites 1015 Oakvale Road Princeton WV   304-431-2800 (877-424-6423)

Dogs are allowed for no additional pet fee.

Campgrounds and RV Parks

Camp Creek State Park 2390 Camp Creek Road Camp Creek WV   304-425-9481 (800-CALLWVA (225-5982))
http://www.campcreekstatepark.com/
This scenic mountain park offers a variety of trails, land and water recreation, and it is also adjacent to the Camp Creek State Forest. Dogs of all sizes are allowed at no additional fee. Dogs may not be left unattended, and they must be leashed and cleaned up after. Dogs are allowed on the trails. This campground is closed during the off-season. The camping and tent areas also allow dogs. There is a dog walk area at the campground. There are no water hookups at the campground.

Bluestone Wildlife Management Area HC 65/91 Indian Mills Road Indian Mills WV   304-466-3398 (800-CALL WVA (225-5982))
http://www.bluestonewma.com/
With well over 17,000 acres adjacent to the State's 2nd largest lake, this park offers a wide variety of outdoor recreational pursuits. Healthy dogs are allowed for no additional fee. A credit card must be on file, and there is a pet agreement to sign at check in. Pets may not be left unattended outside, and their food may not be kept outside. Dogs must have certified proof of inoculations from a veterinarian, be on no more than a 10 foot leash, and picked up after. There are more than 330 primitive campsites available in a variety of settings. The camping and tent areas also allow dogs. There is a dog walk area at the campground. There are no electric or water hookups at the campgrounds.

TOP 200 PLACE **Pipestem Resort State Park** H 20 N/ Pipestem WV   304-466-1800 (800-CALL WVA (225-5982))
http://www.pipestemresort.com/
Two golf courses, a Nature Center, an eatery, recreation center with a pool, an amphitheater, a 3600 foot aerial tramway, and 20 different hiking trails are just some of the amenities found at this popular park. Healthy dogs are allowed in camp areas for no charge and the cabins/cottages for a $50 refundable deposit, plus $40 for the first night and $5 for each additional night per pet. A credit card must be on file, and there is a pet agreement to sign at check in. Pets may not be left unattended outside, they must be securely crated when left alone in the cabins or cottages, they are not allowed to be tied/chained on the porch or yard, and their food may not be kept outside. Dogs must have certified proof of inoculations from a veterinarian, be on no more than a 10 foot leash, and picked up after. Dogs are allowed on the aerial tram. The campground offers 82 sites with a heated bathroom, a camp store, laundry, a playground, and other gaming areas. The camping and tent areas also allow dogs. There is a dog walk area at the campground. Dogs are allowed in the camping cabins.

Berwind Lake Wildlife Management Area Rt. 16 Box 38 Warriormine WV   304-875-2577 (800-CALL WVA (225-5982))
http://www.berwindlake.com/
One of the largest wildlife management areas in the state with 18,000 mountainous acres, it also has hiking trails, an overlook, a 20 acre lake with a foot trail around it, and an accessible fishing pier. Healthy dogs are allowed for no additional fee. A credit card must be on file, and there is a pet agreement to sign at check in. Pets may not be left unattended outside, and their food must be kept inside. Dogs must have certified proof of inoculations from a veterinarian, be on no more than a 10 foot leash, and picked up after. There are 8 campsites, each with a picnic table, lantern post, and grill. The camping and tent areas also allow dogs. There is a dog walk area at the campground.

Parks

Bluestone Wildlife Management Area HC 65/91 Indian Mills Road Indian Mills WV   304-466-3398 (800-CALL WVA (225-5982))
http://www.bluestonewma.com/
With well over 17,000 acres adjacent to the State's 2nd largest lake, this park offers a wide variety of outdoor recreational pursuits. Healthy dogs are allowed for no additional fee. A credit card must be on file, and there is a pet agreement to sign at check in. Pets may not be left unattended outside, and their food may not be kept outside. Dogs must have certified proof of inoculations from a veterinarian, be on no more than a 10 foot leash, and picked up after.

Pipestem Resort State Park H 20 N/ Pipestem WV   304-466-1800 (800-CALL WVA (225-5982))
http://www.pipestemresort.com/
Two golf courses, a Nature Center, an eatery, recreation center with a pool, an amphitheater, a 3600 foot aerial tramway, and 20 different hiking trails are just some of the amenities found at this popular park. Healthy dogs are allowed in camp areas for no charge and the cabins/cottages for a $50 refundable deposit, plus $40 for the first night and $5 for each additional night per pet. A credit card must be on file, and there is a pet agreement to sign at check in. Pets may not be left unattended outside, they must be securely crated when left alone in the cabins or cottages, they are not allowed to be tied/chained on the porch or yard, and their food may not be kept outside. Dogs must have certified proof of inoculations from a veterinarian, be on no more than a 10 foot leash, and

picked up after. Dogs are allowed on the aerial tram.

Berwind Lake Wildlife Management Area Rt. 16 Box 38 Warriormine WV   304-875-2577 (800-CALL WVA (225-5982))

http://www.berwindlake.com/

One of the largest wildlife management areas in the state with 18,000 mountainous acres; It also has hiking trails, an overlook, a 20 acre lake with a foot trail around it, and an accessible fishing pier. Healthy dogs are allowed for no additional fee. A credit card must be on file, and there is a pet agreement to sign at check in. Pets may not be left unattended outside, and their food must be kept inside. Dogs must have certified proof of inoculations from a veterinarian, be on no more than a 10 foot leash, and picked up after.

Buckhannon

Accommodations

Centennial Motel 22 N Locust St Buckhannon WV   304-472-4100
There are no additional pet fees.

Campgrounds and RV Parks

Audra State Park Rt. 4 Box 564 Buckhannon WV   304-457-1162 (800-CALL WVA)

http://www.audrastatepark.com/

A highlight of this wooded park along the Middle Fork River is the stunning view from the boardwalk that follows along the cave's overhanging ledge. Healthy dogs are allowed for no additional pet fee. Dogs must be restrained on no more than a 10 foot leash, be picked up after, and have certified proof of inoculations from a veterinarian. Open from mid-April to mid-October on a first come, first served basis, this camp area offers 2 modern bathhouses, a laundry, playground, and a dump station. The sites each have a picnic table and grill. This RV park is closed during the off-season. The camping and tent areas also allow dogs. There is a dog walk area at the campground. There are no electric or water hookups at the campgrounds.

Parks

TOP 200 PLACE **Audra State Park** Rt. 4 Box 564 Buckhannon WV   304-457-1162 (800-CALL WVA)

http://www.audrastatepark.com/

The highlight of this wooded park along the Middle Fork River is the stunning view from the boardwalk that follows along the cave's overhanging ledge. Healthy dogs are allowed for no additional pet fee. Dogs must be restrained on no more than a 10 foot leash, be picked up after, and have certified proof of inoculations from a veterinarian.

Cabins

Accommodations

North Fork Mountain Inn Smoke Hole Road Cabins WV   304-257-1108

http://www.northforkmtninn.com/

Located in a lush mountain setting, this retreat is open year round offering the best of all the seasons. Dogs are allowed at the Hideaway Cabin here but not in the inn. There is a fee of $15 per night per pet.

Canaan Valley

Accommodations

A Room with A View Black Bear Woods Resort-Northside Cortland Rd Canaan Valley WV   301-767-6853
This is Unit 132 in the Black Bear Woods Resort. It is a single room suite without a kitchen with a view of Canaan Valley. There are two Queen beds and a large bathroom with a Jacuzzi. Well-behaved dogs are welcome for a $30 cleaning fee per stay.

Campgrounds and RV Parks

Kumbrabow State Forest Kumbrabow Forest Road/H 219 Huttonsville WV   304-335-2219 (800-CALL WVA (225-5982))

http://www.kumbrabow.com/
There is an emphasis on outdoor recreation and entertainment at this 9,474 multi-colored, thriving forest (the state's tallest); they offer seasonal Story Tellers and a variety of live shows. Healthy dogs are allowed in camp areas for no charge and the cabins/cottages for a $50 refundable deposit, plus $40 for the first night and $5 for each additional night per pet. A credit card must be on file, and there is a pet agreement to sign at check in. Pets may not be left unattended outside, they must be securely crated when left alone in the cabins or cottages, they are not allowed to be tied/chained on the porch or yard, and their food may not be kept outside. Dogs must have certified proof of inoculations from a veterinarian, be on no more than a 10 foot leash, and picked up after. Along a stream where flowers bloom in abundance, there are 13 campsites with picnic tables, fireplaces, drinking water, and pit toilets. Showers, a laundry, firewood and ice are available at the forest headquarters. This RV park is closed during the off-season. The camping and tent areas also allow dogs. Dogs are allowed in the camping cabins. There are no electric or water hookups at the campgrounds.

Cross Country Ski Resorts

White Grass Touring Center Freeland Rd off Route 32 Canaan Valley WV   304-866-4114
http://www.whitegrass.com
This rental center allows dogs on one trail. The Timberline Trail is about one mile long and is sometimes groomed. The trail goes into Forest Service Road 80. Dogs can be off-leash but need to be under direct voice control.

Parks

Kumbrabow State Forest Kumbrabow Forest Road/H 219 Huttonsville WV   304-335-2219 (800-CALL WVA (225-5982))
http://www.kumbrabow.com/
There is an emphasis on outdoor recreation and entertainment at this 9,474 multi-colored, thriving forest (the state's tallest); They offer seasonal Story Tellers and a variety of live shows. Healthy dogs are allowed in camp areas for no charge and the cabins/cottages for a $50 refundable deposit, plus $40 for the first night and $5 for each additional night per pet. A credit card must be on file, and there is a pet agreement to sign at check in. Pets may not be left unattended outside, they must be securely crated when left alone in the cabins or cottages, they are not allowed to be tied/chained on the porch or yard, and their food may not be kept outside. Dogs must have certified proof of inoculations from a veterinarian, be on no more than a 10 foot leash, and picked up after.

Cass

Campgrounds and RV Parks

Seneca State Forest Rt. 1 Box 140/H 28 Dunmore WV   304-799-6213 (800-CALL WVA (225-5982))
http://www.senecastateforest.com/
As the state's oldest forest with 11,684 acres, there is an abundance of land and water recreation available. Healthy dogs are allowed in camp areas for no charge and the cabins/cottages for a $50 refundable deposit, plus $40 for the first night and $5 for each additional night per pet. A credit card must be on file, and there is a pet agreement to sign at check in. Pets may not be left unattended outside, they must be securely crated when left alone in the cabins or cottages, they are not allowed to be tied/chained on the porch or yard, and their food may not be kept outside. Dogs must have certified proof of inoculations from a veterinarian, be on no more than a 10 foot leash, and picked up after. The rustic camp area offers large, secluded sites on a first come, first served basis with picnic tables, fireplaces, drinking water, and vault toilets. Firewood, showers, and a laundry are available for a small fee. This RV park is closed during the off-season. The camping and tent areas also allow dogs. There is a dog walk area at the campground. Dogs are allowed in the camping cabins. There are no electric or water hookups at the campgrounds.

Parks

Cass Scenic Railroad State Park Snowshoe-Cass-Greenback Road Cass WV   304-456-4300 (800-CALL WVA (225-5982))
http://www.cassrailroad.com/
The highlight of this park is the early 1900's stream-driving locomotives that take visitors for a ride back in time, the recreated logging camp, and the restored railroad town of Cass. Dogs are not allowed on the train, but an attendant will walk/water/feed pets that have kennels. Healthy dogs are for a $50 refundable deposit, plus $40 for the first night and $5 for each additional night per pet. A credit card must be on file, and there is a pet agreement to sign at check in. Pets may not be left unattended outside, they must be securely crated when left alone in the cabins or cottages, they are not allowed to be tied/chained on the porch or yard, and their food may not be kept outside. Dogs must have certified proof of inoculations from a veterinarian, be on no more than a 10 foot leash,

and picked up after. There are a limited number of cabins that are pet friendly, and no RV/tent camping.
Seneca State Forest Rt. 1 Box 140/H 28 Dunmore WV   304-799-6213 (800-CALL WVA (225-5982))
http://www.senecastateforest.com/
As the state's oldest forest with 11,684 acres, there is an abundance of land and water recreation available.
Healthy dogs are allowed in camp areas for no charge and the cabins/cottages for a $50 refundable deposit, plus
$40 for the first night and $5 for each additional night per pet. A credit card must be on file, and there is a pet
agreement to sign at check in. Pets may not be left unattended outside, they must be securely crated when left
alone in the cabins or cottages, they are not allowed to be tied/chained on the porch or yard, and their food may
not be kept outside. Dogs must have certified proof of inoculations from a veterinarian, be on no more than a 10
foot leash, and picked up after.

Charleston

Accommodations
Charleston Marriott Town Center 200 Lee Street E Charleston WV   304-345-6500 (800-228-9290)
Dogs of all sizes are allowed. There is a $75 one time additional pet fee per room. Dogs must be quiet, leashed,
cleaned up after, and the Do Not Disturb sign put on the door and a contact number left with the front desk if they
are in the room alone.
Comfort Suites 107 Alex Lane Charleston WV   304-925-1171 (877-424-6423)
Dogs up to 50 pounds are allowed for an additional one time fee of $25 per pet.
Country Inns & Suites by Carlson 105 Alex Lane Charleston WV   304-925-4300
There are no room discounts if bringing a pet and there is a $5 per day pet fee per pet if you are bringing more
than one dog.
Motel 6 - Charleston East 6311 MacCorkle Ave SE Charleston WV   304-925-0471 (800-466-8356)
One well-behaved family pet per room. Guest must notify front desk upon arrival. Guest is liable for any
damages. In consideration of all guests, pets must never be left unattended in the guest rooms.
Residence Inn by Marriott 200 Hotel Circle Northgate Business Park Charleston WV   304-345-4200
Dogs of all sizes are allowed. There is a $100 one time cleaning fee plus $5 per night per pet and a pet policy to
sign at check in.
Comfort Inn West 102 Racer Drive Cross Lanes WV   800-798-7886 (877-424-6423)
Dogs up to 100 pounds are allowed for an additional pet fee of $15 per night per room. Dogs are not allowed in
the lobby, and they may not be left alone in the room.
Motel 6 - Charleston West-Cross Lanes 330 Goff Mountain Rd Cross Lanes WV   304-776-5911 (800-466-
8356)
One well-behaved family pet per room. Guest must notify front desk upon arrival. Guest is liable for any
damages. In consideration of all guests, pets must never be left unattended in the guest rooms.
Red Roof Inn - Charleston West - Hurricane, WV 500 Putnam Village Drive Hurricane WV   304-757-
6392 (800-RED-ROOF)
One well-behaved family pet per room. Guest must notify front desk upon arrival. Guest is liable for any
damages. In consideration of all guests, pets must never be left unattended in the guest rooms.
Super 8 Hurricane 419 Hurricane Creek Rd Hurricane WV   304-562-3346 (800-800-8000)
Dogs of all sizes are allowed. There is a $10 per night pet fee per pet. Smoking and non-smoking rooms are
available for pet rooms.
Red Roof Inn - Charleston - Kanawha City, WV 6305 MacCorkle Avenue SE Kanawha City WV   304-925-
6953 (800-RED-ROOF)
One well-behaved family pet per room. Guest must notify front desk upon arrival. Guest is liable for any
damages. In consideration of all guests, pets must never be left unattended in the guest rooms.

Campgrounds and RV Parks
Kanawha State Forest Rt. 2 Box 285 Charleston WV   304-558-3500 (800-CALL WVA (225-5982))
http://www.kanawhastateforest.com/
Featuring diverse habitats with an abundance of birds and wildlife, this lush 9,300 acre forest provides a number
of recreational pursuits, great hiking trails, and a variety of special events during the season. Dogs are allowed
throughout the park and in the camp area for no additional fee. Dogs must be leashed and under owner's
control/care at all times. The campground offers 46 sites, each with picnic tables and fireplaces, and
bathhouses, a laundry facility, and a dump station are nearby. There is also a children's playground, and
firewood and ice is available on site. This RV park is closed during the off-season. The camping and tent areas
also allow dogs. There is a dog walk area at the campground.

Stores

PetSmart Pet Store 39 RHL Blvd Charleston WV   304-746-6275
Your licensed and well-behaved leashed dog is allowed in the store.

Parks

Cato Park Edgewood Drive Charleston WV   304-348-6860
This is the city's largest municipal park and it offers such features as an Olympic-sized pool, scenic picnic areas, a par 3 golf course and pro shop, picnic areas, and gaming fields/courts. Dogs are allowed at the park; they are not allowed on the golf course. Dogs must be leashed and under owner's control/care at all times
Coonskin Park 2000 Coonskin Drive Charleston WV   304-341-8000
This popular city park offers a variety of land and water recreational opportunities, a home team Soccer field, an amphitheater, fishing lake, swimming pool, putt-putt golf, an 18-hole golf course, picnic areas, and nature trails. Dogs are allowed at the park. They are not allowed on the golf course, Soccer field, or swim areas. Dogs must be leashed and under owner's control/care at all times.
Kanawha State Forest Rt. 2 Box 285 Charleston WV   304-558-3500 (800-CALL WVA (225-5982))
http://www.kanawhastateforest.com/
Featuring diverse habitats with an abundance of birds and wildlife, this lush 9,300 acre forest provides a number of recreational pursuits, great hiking trails, and a variety of special events during the season. Dogs are allowed throughout the park and in the camp area for no additional fee. Dogs must be leashed and under owner's control/care at all times.

Outdoor Restaurants

Cozumel Mexican Restaurant 1120 Fledderjohn Road Charleston WV   304-342-0113
This Mexican eatery offers outside dining, weather permitting. Dogs are allowed at the outer tables; they must be under owner's control/care at all times.

Clarksburg

Accommodations

Holiday Inn 100 Lodgeville Rd Bridgeport WV   304-842-5411 (877-270-6405)
One dog of any size is allowed for an additional pet fee of $5 per night.
Knights Inn 1235 West Main Street Bridgeport WV   304-842-7115 (800-843-5644)
There are no additional pet fees.
Sleep Inn 115 Tolley Road Bridgeport WV   304-842-1919 (877-424-6423)
Dogs are allowed for no additional pet fee.
Super 8 Bridgeport/Clarksburg Area 168 Barnett Run Rd Bridgeport WV   304-842-7381 (800-800-8000)
Dogs of all sizes are allowed. There are no additional pet fees. Smoking and non-smoking rooms are available for pet rooms.

Campgrounds and RV Parks

Tygart Lake State Park Rt. 1 Box 260 Grafton WV   304-265-6144 (800-CALL WVA (225-5982))
http://www.tygartlake.com/
Located among rolling hills next to a 10 mile long, 1,750 acre lake, this park has plenty of land and water recreation and free guided nature programs and special events/performers through the Summer. Healthy dogs are allowed in camp areas for no charge and the cabins/cottages for a $50 refundable deposit, plus $40 for the first night and $5 for each additional night per pet. A credit card must be on file, and there is a pet agreement to sign at check in. Pets may not be left unattended outside, they must be securely crated when left alone in the cabins or cottages, they are not allowed to be tied/chained on the porch or yard, and their food may not be kept outside. Dogs must have certified proof of inoculations from a veterinarian, be on no more than a 10 foot leash, and picked up after. The camp area offers a total of 40 sites, each with a fire ring and picnic table. There is also drinking water, restrooms with showers on site, and ice and firewood for sale. This RV park is closed during the off-season. The camping and tent areas also allow dogs. There is a dog walk area at the campground. Dogs are allowed in the camping cabins. There are no water hookups at the campgrounds.

Parks

Tygart Lake State Park Rt. 1 Box 260 Grafton WV   304-265-6144 (800-CALL WVA (225-5982))
http://www.tygartlake.com/
Located among rolling hills next to a 10 mile long, 1,750 acre lake, this park has plenty of land and water recreation and free guided nature programs and special events/performers through the Summer. Healthy dogs are allowed in camp areas for no charge and the cabins/cottages for a $50 refundable deposit, plus $40 for the

first night and $5 for each additional night per pet. A credit card must be on file, and there is a pet agreement to sign at check in. Pets may not be left unattended outside, they must be securely crated when left alone in the cabins or cottages, they are not allowed to be tied/chained on the porch or yard, and their food may not be kept outside. Dogs must have certified proof of inoculations from a veterinarian, be on no more than a 10 foot leash, and picked up after.

Daniels

Accommodations
The Resort at Glade Springs 255 Resort Drive Daniels WV   866-562-8054 (800-634-5233)
http://www.gladesprings.com/
This resort offers year round recreational activities with a complete Leisure Center that offers a 10-lane bowling alley, an indoor poor, a small movie theater, arcade, gaming courts, and more. Dogs up to 50 pounds are welcome with advance registration for a fee per pet of $70 for the first night and $20 for each additional night. Dogs may not be left alone in the room at any time, and the front desk will also provide sanitary bags for pets.

Davis

Campgrounds and RV Parks
Blackwater Falls State Park Blackwater Falls Road Davis WV   304-259-5216 (800-CALL WVA (225-5982))
http://www.blackwaterfalls.com/
Named for the amber colored waters and the beautiful falls (a popular photography site), this park also offers a wide variety of land and water recreation, and many special fun events throughout the season. Healthy dogs are allowed in camp areas for no charge and the cabins/cottages for a $50 refundable deposit, plus $40 for the first night and $5 for each additional night per pet. A credit card must be on file, and there is a pet agreement to sign at check in. Pets may not be left unattended outside, they must be securely crated when left alone in the cabins or cottages, they are not allowed to be tied/chained on the porch or yard, and their food may not be kept outside. Dogs must have certified proof of inoculations from a veterinarian, be on no more than a 10 foot leash, and picked up after. The 65 unit camp area has modern restrooms, showers, a laundry, and a dump station. This RV park is closed during the off-season. The camping and tent areas also allow dogs. There is a dog walk area at the campground. Dogs are allowed in the camping cabins.
Canaan Valley Resort HC70, Box 330 Davis WV   304-866-4121 (800-622-4121)
http://www.canaanresort.com/
Surrounded by a million acres of forest at 3,300 feet, this scenic resort offers all the year round recreational opportunities, plus numerous special events, and casual or fine dining. Healthy dogs are allowed in camp areas for no charge and the cabins/cottages for a $50 refundable deposit, plus $40 for the first night and $5 for each additional night per pet. A credit card must be on file, and there is a pet agreement to sign at check in. Pets may not be left unattended outside, they must be securely crated when left alone in the cabins or cottages, they are not allowed to be tied/chained on the porch or yard, and their food may not be kept outside. Dogs must have certified proof of inoculations from a veterinarian, be on no more than a 10 foot leash, and picked up after. The camp area has 34 paved, wooded sites with restrooms, showers, and a laundry, plus a playground and gaming; a dump station is nearby. The camping and tent areas also allow dogs. There is a dog walk area at the campground. Dogs are allowed in the camping cabins.

Cross Country Ski Resorts
Canaan Valley Resort and Conference Center 32 Canaan Valley Davis WV   304-866-4121
The 3.5 miles of cross-country ski trails at this resort are ungroomed. The center rents both skis and snowshoes. Dogs are allowed on the trails but they ask you to walk your dog to the side of the trail and not directly on the main trail. Pets must be on a ten foot leash at all times.

Parks
Blackwater Falls State Park Blackwater Falls Road Davis WV   304-259-5216 (800-CALL WVA (225-5982))
http://www.blackwaterfalls.com/
Named for the amber colored waters and the beautiful falls (a popular photography site), this park also offers a wide variety of land and water recreation, and many special fun events throughout the season. Healthy dogs are allowed in camp areas for no charge and the cabins/cottages for a $50 refundable deposit, plus $40 for the first night and $5 for each additional night per pet. A credit card must be on file, and there is a pet agreement to sign at check in. Pets may not be left unattended outside, they must be securely crated when left alone in the cabins

or cottages, they are not allowed to be tied/chained on the porch or yard, and their food may not be kept outside. Dogs must have certified proof of inoculations from a veterinarian, be on no more than a 10 foot leash, and picked up after.
Canaan Valley State Park 32 Canaan Valley Davis WV   304-866-4121
http://www.canaanresort.com
This state park is home to the Canaan Valley Resort. The park offers 18 miles of hiking and mountain biking trails with adjacent Monongahela National Forest trails. During the Winter the resort rents cross-country skis and snowshoes. Pets are allowed on the trails and on the ski trails but need to be on a 10 foot or less leash at all times. The resort also allows leashed pets in their RV park and campground.

Dunlow

Campgrounds and RV Parks
Cabwaylingo State Forest Rt. 1 Box 85/H 41 Dunlow WV   304-385-4255 (800-CALL WVA (225-5982))
http://www.cabwaylingo.com/
This 8,123 acre state forest offers visitors outstanding scenery full of wildlife, plenty of hiking trails, picnic areas, a fire tower, and a wide range of recreation. Healthy dogs are allowed in camp areas for no charge and the cabins/cottages for a $50 refundable deposit, plus $40 for the first night and $5 for each additional night per pet. A credit card must be on file, and there is a pet agreement to sign at check in. Pets may not be left unattended outside, they must be securely crated when left alone in the cabins or cottages, they are not allowed to be tied/chained on the porch or yard, and their food may not be kept outside. Dogs must have certified proof of inoculations from a veterinarian, be on no more than a 10 foot leash, and picked up after. There are 2 campsite areas: 1 modern and 1 rustic. All sites have tables, fireplaces, firewood, and drinking water; restrooms and showers are nearby. This RV park is closed during the off-season. The camping and tent areas also allow dogs. There is a dog walk area at the campground. Dogs are allowed in the camping cabins.

Parks
Cabwaylingo State Forest Rt. 1 Box 85/H 41 Dunlow WV   304-385-4255 (800-CALL WVA (225-5982))
http://www.cabwaylingo.com/
This 8,123 acre state forest offers visitors outstanding scenery full of wildlife, plenty of hiking trails, picnic areas, a fire tower, and a wide range of recreation. Healthy dogs are allowed in camp areas for no charge and the cabins/cottages for a $50 refundable deposit, plus $40 for the first night and $5 for each additional night per pet. A credit card must be on file, and there is a pet agreement to sign at check in. Pets may not be left unattended outside, they must be securely crated when left alone in the cabins or cottages, they are not allowed to be tied/chained on the porch or yard, and their food may not be kept outside. Dogs must have certified proof of inoculations from a veterinarian, be on no more than a 10 foot leash, and picked up after.

Elkins

Accommodations
Cheat River Lodge Route 1, Box 115 Elkins WV   304-636-2301
http://www.cheatriverlodge.com/
Dogs are allowed in the lodge and the cabins at this riverside getaway. The fee is $10 per night per pet for the lodge, and $20 per night per pet for the cabins. Dogs may be left for short periods if they are crated when left alone in the room.
Days Inn Elkins 1200 Harrison Ave Elkins WV   304-637-4667 (800-329-7466)
Dogs of all sizes are allowed. There is a $5 per night pet fee per pet.
Econo Lodge U.S. 33 East Elkins WV   304-636-5311 (800-553-2666)
There is a $5 per day pet charge.

Campgrounds and RV Parks
Jellystone Park Route 33 E Faulkner Road Elkins WV   304-637-8898 (866-988-5267)
http://www.jellystonewestvirginia.com
Dogs of all sizes are allowed. There are no additional pet fees. Dogs must be quiet, leashed, and cleaned up after. This RV park is closed during the off-season. The camping and tent areas also allow dogs. There is a dog walk area at the campground. Dogs are allowed in the camping cabins.
Monongahela National Forest 200 Sycamore Street Elkins WV   304-636-1800 (800-CALLWVA (225-5982))
http://www.fs.fed.us/r9/mnf/index.shtml

This forest has 6 ranger districts, almost a million acres, and diverse ecosystems that support a large variety of plants, animals, and recreation. Dogs are allowed at no additional fee. Dogs may not be left unattended, and they must be leashed and cleaned up after in the camp areas. Dogs are allowed on the trails. The camping and tent areas also allow dogs. There is a dog walk area at the campground. There are no water hookups at the campground.

Revelle's River Resort 9 Faulkner Road Elkins WV 877-988-2267
http://www.revelles.com
Dogs of all sizes are allowed, and there are no additional pet fees for tent or RV sites. There is a $5 per night per pet additional fee plus a cash security deposit of $50 for the regular cabins, and the same daily fee plus a $100 deposit for the upscale cabins. Dogs must be leashed and cleaned up after. The camping and tent areas also allow dogs. There is a dog walk area at the campground. Dogs are allowed in the camping cabins.

Gap Mills

Campgrounds and RV Parks
Moncove Lake State Park HC 83, Box 73A Gap Mills WV 304-772-3450 (800-CALLWVA (225-5982))
http://www.moncovelakestatepark.com/
This park of 250 acres has an adjoining 500 acre wildlife management area and a 144 acre lake in addition to a variety of land and water recreational pursuits. Dogs of all sizes are allowed at no additional fee. Dogs may not be left unattended, and they must be quiet, well behaved, leashed and cleaned up after. This campground is closed during the off-season. The camping and tent areas also allow dogs. There is a dog walk area at the campground. There are no water hookups at the campground.

Glenville

Campgrounds and RV Parks
Cedar Creek State Park 2947 Cedar Creek Road Glenville WV 304-462-7158 (800-CALLWVA (225-5982))
http://www.cedarcreeksp.com/
This park offers 2,483 lush acres of rolling hills, wide valleys, and a variety of recreational pursuits. Dogs of all sizes are allowed at no additional fee. Dogs may not be left unattended, and they must be quiet, well behaved, leashed and cleaned up after. Dogs are not allowed in buildings or at the pool, but they are allowed on the trails. This campground is closed during the off-season. The camping and tent areas also allow dogs. There is a dog walk area at the campground.

Hacker Valley

Campgrounds and RV Parks
Holly River State Park 680 State Park Road Hacker Valley WV 304-493-6353 (800-CALL WVA (225-5982))
http://www.hollyriver.com/
Nestled in a narrow valley bordered by dense forest, lies this scenic, secluded 8,101 acre park that offers a number of recreation and activities. Healthy dogs are allowed in camp areas for no charge and the cabins/cottages for a $50 refundable deposit, plus $40 for the first night and $5 for each additional night per pet. A credit card must be on file, and there is a pet agreement to sign at check in. Pets may not be left unattended outside, they must be securely crated when left alone in the cabins or cottages, they are not allowed to be tied/chained on the porch or yard, and their food may not be kept outside. Dogs must have certified proof of inoculations from a veterinarian, be on no more than a 10 foot leash, and picked up after. They are also allowed at the outer tables of their seasonal restaurant. There are 88 camps sites with picnic tables and grills at each site, and restrooms, hot showers, a laundry, and a dump station are nearby. Firewood is also available for a small fee. This RV park is closed during the off-season. The camping and tent areas also allow dogs. There is a dog walk area at the campground. Dogs are allowed in the camping cabins. There are no water hookups at the campgrounds.

Parks
Holly River State Park 680 State Park Road Hacker Valley WV 304-493-6353 (800-CALL WVA (225-5982))
http://www.hollyriver.com/

Nestled in a narrow valley bordered by dense forest, lies this scenic, secluded 8,101 acre park that offers a number of recreation and activities. Healthy dogs are allowed in camp areas for no charge and the cabins/cottages for a $50 refundable deposit, plus $40 for the first night and $5 for each additional night per pet. A credit card must be on file, and there is a pet agreement to sign at check in. Pets may not be left unattended outside, they must be securely crated when left alone in the cabins or cottages, they are not allowed to be tied/chained on the porch or yard, and their food may not be kept outside. Dogs must have certified proof of inoculations from a veterinarian, be on no more than a 10 foot leash, and picked up after. They are also allowed at the outer tables of their seasonal restaurant.

Harpers Ferry

Campgrounds and RV Parks
Harpers Ferry/Washington DC NW KOA 343 Campground Road Harpers Ferry WV   304-535-6895 (800-562-9497)
http://www.harpersferrykoa.com
Dogs of all sizes are allowed. There is a $3 per pet per stay additional fee. Dogs must be leashed and cleaned up after. There are some breed restrictions. The camping and tent areas also allow dogs. There is a dog walk area at the campground. Dogs are allowed in the camping cabins.

Attractions
Appalachian National Scenic Trail Harpers Ferry Center Harpers Ferry WV   304-535-6278
Dogs must be on leash and must be cleaned up after on most of the trail. Dogs are not allowed in the Great Smoky Mountain National Park and Baxter State Park in the Maine portion of Trail. You must follow the general rules and pet policies of state parks and locations along the trail. Most sites have hiking, camping, fishing, and more.
Appalachian Trail in West Virginia Off Sandy Hook Road Harpers Ferry WV   304-535-6331
The historic Appalachian Trail enters the state at Harpers Ferry by footbridge over the Potomac River and travels 4 miles in the state, and then after crossing the Shenandoah River, it follows along the State's border for several miles. The elevation goes from 265 to 1,200 through this corridor, and the best hiking is between mid-April to mid-June, and September through October because of the Summer heat/humidity. Dogs on leash are allowed on the trail; they must be under owner's control/care at all times.
TOP 200 PLACE **Ghost Tours of Harpers Ferry** 173 Potomac Street Harpers Ferry WV   304-725-8019
http://www.harpersferryghost.20m.com
Dogs are allowed to go on the ghostly tours to assist you in your search for ghosts from Harpers Ferry's past. The tours are given on Saturdays in April and May and Fridays and Saturdays from Memorial Day to November 8th. Reservations are required for October and November. The tour starts at the Old Towne Cafe.
TOP 200 PLACE **Harpers Ferry National Historical Park** P.O. Box 65 Harpers Ferry WV   304-535-6029
http://www.nps.gov/hafe
According to the National Park Service (NPS), Harpers Ferry was made into a national historical site because of a number of different events. The NPS states "Harpers Ferry witnessed the first successful application of interchangeable manufacture, the arrival of the first successful American railroad, John Brown's attack on slavery, the largest surrender of Federal troops during the Civil War, and the education of former slaves in one of the earliest integrated schools in the United States." Dogs are allowed on leash at all outdoor areas of the park. However, dogs are not allowed on the shuttle buses from the visitors center to the historic area. There is limited parking at the historic area next to the train station for you to park with your dog. Otherwise, you will need someone to stay with your dog while someone parks the car and takes the shuttle bus back. Once at the historical town, you can walk around town, on trails and a pedestrian bridge over the river.

Parks
Potomac Heritage National Scenic Trail PO Box B Harpers Ferry WV   202-619-7222
http://www.nps.gov/pohe/index.htm
Dogs must be on leash and must be cleaned up after on the trail sites and park areas. You must follow all rules of the state parks. The park features in most areas camping, boating, hiking, swimming, and more. The trail is a partnership to develop and sustain a system of trails for recreation, transportation, health, and education between the mouth of the Potomac River and the Allegheny Highlands.

Harpers Ferry National Historical Park

Outdoor Restaurants
Mountain House Cafe 179 High St Harpers Ferry WV   304-535-2339
This restaurant and bar serves deli-type food. Dogs are allowed at the outdoor tables.
Old Towne Cafe 173 Potomac Street Harpers Ferry WV
Dogs on leash are allowed at the outdoor tables.
The Coffee Mill 101 Potomac Ter Harpers Ferry WV   304-535-1257
This coffee shop serves gourmet sandwiches. Dogs are allowed at the outdoor tables.
The Iron Horse Cafe 201 Potomac St Harpers Ferry WV   304-535-2168
This restaurant serves American food. Dogs are allowed at the outdoor tables.
The Swiss Miss 102 Potomac Ter Harpers Ferry WV   304-535-1250
This restaurant and bar serves American. Dogs are allowed at the outdoor tables.

Huntington

Accommodations
Comfort Inn 249 Mall Road Barboursville WV   304-733-2122 (877-424-6423)
Dogs are allowed for an additional one time pet fee of $20 per room.
Econo Lodge 3325 US 60 E. Huntington WV   304-529-1331 (800-55-ECONO)
There is a $10 per day pet charge.
Red Roof Inn - Huntington, WV 5190 US Route 60 E Huntington WV   304-733-3737 (800-RED-ROOF)
One well-behaved family pet per room. Guest must notify front desk upon arrival. Guest is liable for any
damages. In consideration of all guests, pets must never be left unattended in the guest rooms.
Stone Lodge 5600 U.S. Route 60 East Huntington WV   304-736-3451
There are no additional pet fees.

Campgrounds and RV Parks
Beech Fork State Park 5601 Long Branch Road Barboursville WV   304-528-5794 (800-CALL WVA (225-
5982))
http://www.beechforksp.com/

Offering an abundance of flora and fauna, this 3,144 acre lakeside park also offers a variety of land and water recreation. Healthy dogs are allowed in camp areas for no charge and the cabins/cottages for a $50 refundable deposit, plus $40 for the first night and $5 for each additional night per pet. A credit card must be on file, and there is a pet agreement to sign at check in. Pets may not be left unattended outside, they must be securely crated when left alone in the cabins or cottages, they are not allowed to be tied/chained on the porch or yard, and their food may not be kept outside. Dogs must have certified proof of inoculations from a veterinarian, be on no more than a 10 foot leash, and picked up after. The campground offers 275 sites in various settings and each site has a picnic table and grill, with restrooms, showers, a laundry, and playground nearby. The camping and tent areas also allow dogs. There is a dog walk area at the campground. Dogs are allowed in the camping cabins.

Fox Fire Resort Route 2, Box 655 Milton WV   304-743-5622
http://www.foxfirewv.com/
Dogs of all sizes are allowed. There are no additional pet fees. Dogs must be leashed and cleaned up after. This RV park is closed during the off-season. There are some breed restrictions.

Parks

Beech Fork State Park 5601 Long Branch Road Barboursville WV   304-528-5794 (800-CALL WVA (225-5982))
http://www.beechforksp.com/
Offering an abundance of flora and fauna, this 3,144 acre lakeside park also offers a variety of land and water recreation. Healthy dogs are allowed in camp areas for no charge and the cabins/cottages for a $50 refundable deposit, plus $40 for the first night and $5 for each additional night per pet. A credit card must be on file, and there is a pet agreement to sign at check in. Pets may not be left unattended outside, they must be securely crated when left alone in the cabins or cottages, they are not allowed to be tied/chained on the porch or yard, and their food may not be kept outside. Dogs must have certified proof of inoculations from a veterinarian, be on no more than a 10 foot leash, and picked up after.

Lewisburg

Campgrounds and RV Parks

Greenbrier State Forest HC 30 Box 154/Harts Run Road Caldwell WV   304-536-1944 (800-CALL WVA (225-5982))
http://www.greenbriersf.com/
Amid more than 5,100 acres of forested mountain sits this major family recreation destination that offers gaming courts/fields, shooting ranges, picnicking areas, a pool, and a variety of special events. Healthy dogs are allowed in camp areas for no charge and the cabins/cottages for a $50 refundable deposit, plus $40 for the first night and $5 for each additional night per pet. A credit card must be on file, and there is a pet agreement to sign at check in. Pets may not be left unattended outside, they must be securely crated when left alone in the cabins or cottages, they are not allowed to be tied/chained on the porch or yard, and their food may not be kept outside. Dogs must have certified proof of inoculations from a veterinarian, be on no more than a 10 foot leash, and picked up after. The 16 site campground offers restrooms with hot showers, drinking water, and each site has a table and stone fireplace grill. This RV park is closed during the off-season. The camping and tent areas also allow dogs. There is a dog walk area at the campground. Dogs are allowed in the camping cabins. There are no water hookups at the campgrounds.

Attractions

Historic Downtown Lewisburg 209 W Washington Street Lewisburg WV   304-645-4333
http://www.lewisburg-wv.com/
This historic pre-Civil War town offers visitors a restored main street with quite an active and diverse arts scene, sidewalk cafes, specialty boutiques, casual or elegant eateries, and occasional special events. Dogs are allowed on leash, and they must be under owner's control/care at all times.

Parks

Greenbrier State Forest HC 30 Box 154/Harts Run Road Caldwell WV   304-536-1944 (800-CALL WVA (225-5982))
http://www.greenbriersf.com/
Amid more than 5,100 acres of forested mountain sits this major family recreation destination that offers gaming courts/fields, shooting ranges, picnicking areas, a pool, and a variety of special events. Healthy dogs are allowed in camp areas for no charge and the cabins/cottages for a $50 refundable deposit, plus $40 for the first night and $5 for each additional night per pet. A credit card must be on file, and there is a pet agreement to sign at check

in. Pets may not be left unattended outside, they must be securely crated when left alone in the cabins or cottages, they are not allowed to be tied/chained on the porch or yard, and their food may not be kept outside. Dogs must have certified proof of inoculations from a veterinarian, be on no more than a 10 foot leash, and picked up after.

Logan

Accommodations
Holiday Inn Express Hotel and Suites 101 George Costas Drive Logan WV   304-752-6495 (877-270-6405)
Dogs up to 30 pounds are allowed for an additional fee of $25 per night per pet. Dogs may not be left alone in the room.

Campgrounds and RV Parks
Chief Logan State Park General Delivery Logan WV   304-792-7125 (800-CALLWVA (225-5982))
http://www.chiefloganstatepark.com/
This 4,000 acre park offers a modern restaurant, an outdoor amphitheater, a wildlife center, miles of trails, and a variety of recreational pursuits. Dogs of all sizes are allowed at no additional fee. Dogs must be well behaved, leashed, and cleaned up after. Dogs are not allowed at the wildlife exhibit or at the pool, but they are allowed on the trails. This campground is closed during the off-season. The camping and tent areas also allow dogs. There is a dog walk area at the campground.

Marlington

Accommodations
Old Clark Inn 302 Third Avenue Marlington WV   304-799-6377
Dogs of all sizes are allowed, however the number and size of pets is determined by the room that is rented. There is a $5 per day per pet fee and a pet policy to sign at check in. There is a day kennel with a 4 foot high fence that also has a dog house. This is for small dogs and there is a $5 per day fee for guests only to use.

Marlinton

Campgrounds and RV Parks
Watoga State Park HC 82, Box 252 Marlinton WV   304-799-4087 (800-CALL WVA (225-5982))
http://www.watoga.com/
There are over 10,000 recreational acres at this mountain park that also provides a park commissary, restaurant (no outside seating for pets), naturalist programs, a seasonal pool, and gaming fields/courts. Healthy dogs are allowed in camp areas for no charge and the cabins/cottages for a $50 refundable deposit, plus $40 for the first night and $5 for each additional night per pet. A credit card must be on file, and there is a pet agreement to sign at check in. Pets may not be left unattended outside, they must be securely crated when left alone in the cabins or cottages, they are not allowed to be tied/chained on the porch or yard, and their food may not be kept outside. Dogs must have certified proof of inoculations from a veterinarian, be on no more than a 10 foot leash, and picked up after. Two separate campgrounds offer a total of 88 sites; each site has tables and grills, and bathhouses, restrooms, a laundry, and dishwashing stations are nearby. This RV park is closed during the off-season. The camping and tent areas also allow dogs. There is a dog walk area at the campground. Dogs are allowed in the camping cabins. There are no water hookups at the campgrounds.

Parks
Watoga State Park HC 82, Box 252 Marlinton WV   304-799-4087 (800-CALL WVA (225-5982))
http://www.watoga.com/
There are over 10,000 recreational acres at this mountain park that also provides a park commissary, restaurant (no outside seating for pets), naturalist programs, a seasonal pool, and gaming fields/courts. Healthy dogs are allowed in camp areas for no charge and the cabins/cottages for a $50 refundable deposit, plus $40 for the first night and $5 for each additional night per pet. A credit card must be on file, and there is a pet agreement to sign at check in. Pets may not be left unattended outside, they must be securely crated when left alone in the cabins or cottages, they are not allowed to be tied/chained on the porch or yard, and their food may not be kept outside.

Dogs must have certified proof of inoculations from a veterinarian, be on no more than a 10 foot leash, and picked up after.

Martinsburg

Accommodations
Holiday Inn Express North 1220 TJ Jackson Drive Falling Waters WV   304-274-6100 (877-270-6405)
Dogs of all sizes are allowed for an additional fee of $10 per night per pet. Dogs may not be left alone in the room at any time.
Days Inn Martinsburg 209 Viking Way Martinsburg WV   304-263-1800 (800-329-7466)
Dogs of all sizes are allowed. There are no additional pet fees.
Holiday Inn 301 Foxcroft Avenue Martinsburg WV   304-267-5500 (877-270-6405)
Quiet dogs of all sizes are allowed for an additional one time pet fee of $15 per room.
Knights Inn 1599 Edwin Miller Blvd Martinsburg WV   304-267-2211 (800-843-5644)
There is a $5 per day additional pet fee.

Morgantown

Accommodations
Days Inn Fairmont 228 Middletown Road Fairmont WV   304-366-5995 (800-329-7466)
Dogs of all sizes are allowed. There is a $10 per night pet fee per pet.
Red Roof Inn - Fairmont, WV 50 Middletown Road Fairmont WV   304-366-6800 (800-RED-ROOF)
One well-behaved family pet per room. Guest must notify front desk upon arrival. Guest is liable for any damages. In consideration of all guests, pets must never be left unattended in the guest rooms.
Super 8 Fairmont 2208 Pleasant Valley Rd Fairmont WV   304-363-1488 (800-800-8000)
Dogs up to 60 pounds are allowed. There are no additional pet fees. Smoking and non-smoking rooms are available for pet rooms.
Alpine Lake 700 West Alpine Drive Morgantown WV   304-789-2481 (800-752-7179)
http://www.alpinelake.com/
In addition to its beautiful location and numerous amenities, this resort is also a year round recreational destination. Dogs are allowed for an additional $10 per night per pet.
Comfort Inn 225 Comfort Inn Drive Morgantown WV   304-296-9364 (877-424-6423)
Dogs are allowed for a $25 refundable pet deposit per room. Dogs are not allowed in the lobby, and they may not be left alone in the room.
Econo Lodge Coliseum 3506 Monongahela Blvd. Morgantown WV   304-599-8181 (800-55-ECONO)
There are no additional pet fees.

Campgrounds and RV Parks
Big Bear Lake Campground Hazelton Big Bear Lake Road Bruceton Mills WV   304-379-4382
http://www.bigbearwv.com
Dogs of all sizes are allowed. There are no additional pet fees. Dogs may not be left unattended, and they must be leashed and cleaned up after. This RV park is closed during the off-season. The camping and tent areas also allow dogs. There is a dog walk area at the campground. Dogs are allowed in the camping cabins. There are no water hookups at the campgrounds.

Attractions
Arthurdale Heritage H 92 Arthurdale WV 304-864-3959
http://www.arthurdaleheritage.org/
This museum encompasses several buildings in Arthurdale, now listed on the National Register of Historic Places, and they still have 160 of the original 165 homes from America's first New Deal Homestead in the 1930's. They are also host to a number of special events. Although dogs are not allowed inside any of the buildings, they are allowed throughout the town. Dogs must be leashed and under owner's control/care at all times.

Stores
Petco Pet Store 4101 University Town Center Drive Morgantown WV   304-599-0670
Your licensed and well-behaved leashed dog is allowed in the store.

Parkersburg

Accommodations
Blennerhassett Hotel Fourth and Market Streets Parkersburg WV   304-422-3131 (800-678-8946)
This 1889 hotel is listed on the National Register of Historic Hotels. There is a $50 one time pet charge.
Expressway Motor Inn 6333 Emerson Ave Parkersburg WV 304-485-1851
There is a $5 per day pet charge.
Motel 6 - Parkersburg 3604 1/2 East 7th Street Parkersburg WV   304-424-5100 (800-466-8356)
One well-behaved family pet per room. Guest must notify front desk upon arrival. Guest is liable for any
damages. In consideration of all guests, pets must never be left unattended in the guest rooms.
Red Roof Inn - Parkersburg 3714 East 7th Street Parkersburg WV   304-485-1741 (800-RED-ROOF)
One well-behaved family pet per room. Guest must notify front desk upon arrival. Guest is liable for any
damages. In consideration of all guests, pets must never be left unattended in the guest rooms.

Ripley

Accommodations
Best Western McCoys Inn & Conference Center 701 Main Street W Ripley WV   304-372-9122 (800-780-
7234)
Dogs are allowed for no additional pet fee. Dogs may not be left alone in the room.
Holiday Inn Express One Hospitality Drive Ripley WV   304-372-5000 (877-270-6405)
Dogs of all sizes are allowed for no additional pet fee.

Roanoke

Campgrounds and RV Parks
Stonewall Resort 940 Resort Drive Roanoke WV   304-269-7400 (888-278-8150)
http://www.stonewallresort.com/
In addition to the numerous amenities at this full service 2,000 acre lake resort with 82 miles of shoreline, they
also provide a 374-slip marina, a golf course, driving range, fitness facilities, pools, and much more. Although
dogs are not allowed at the resort, they are allowed in the campground for no additional pet fee. Campers are
welcome to use the amenities at the resort. Dogs must be leashed and cleaned up after at all times. The
campsites are located lakeside and offer tables, fire pits, a playground, mooring posts, and comfort stations. The
camping and tent areas also allow dogs. There is a dog walk area at the campground.

Seneca Rocks

Campgrounds and RV Parks
Yokum's Vacationland HC 59, Box 3 Seneca Rocks WV   800-772-8343
http://www.yokums.com
Dogs of all sizes are allowed, and there are no additional pet fees for tent or RV sites. There is a $10 per night
per pet additional fee for the motel. Dogs must be leashed and cleaned up after. The camping and tent areas
also allow dogs. There is a dog walk area at the campground. Dogs are allowed in the camping cabins.

Snowshoe

Accommodations
Morning Glory Inn H 219 Snowshoe WV   304-572-5000 (866-572-5700)
http://www.morninggloryinn.com/
Guests can relax and enjoy the views from their 90 foot front porch or explore a myriad of local activities and

recreation from this retreat. One dog is allowed for no additional pet fee. Dogs must be quiet and well mannered.

Springfield

Campgrounds and RV Parks
Milleson's Walnut Grove Campground 28/5 Milleson's Road Springfield WV   304-822-5284
http://www.millesonscampground.com
Dogs of all sizes are allowed for no additional fee. Dogs may not be left unattended outside, and they must have current rabies vaccine records. Dogs must be leashed and cleaned up after. There are some breed restrictions. This RV park is closed during the off-season. The camping and tent areas also allow dogs. There is a dog walk area at the campground.

Triadelphia

Accommodations
Comfort Inn Dallas Pike Triadelphia WV   304-547-0610 (877-424-6423)
Dogs are allowed for an additional fee of $10 per night per pet.
Holiday Inn Express I-70 Exit 11 Dallas Pike Triadelphia WV   304-547-1380 (877-270-6405)
Dogs of all sizes are allowed for an additional fee of $25 per night per pet.

Campgrounds and RV Parks
Wheelings Dallas Pike Campground Road 1, Box 231 Triadelphia WV   304-547-0940
http://www.dallaspikecampgrounds.com
Dogs of all sizes are allowed. There are no additional pet fees. Dogs must be leashed and cleaned up after. There are some breed restrictions. The camping and tent areas also allow dogs. There is a dog walk area at the campground.

Weirton

Accommodations
Holiday Inn 350 Three Springs Drive Weirton WV   304-723-5522 (877-270-6405)
Dogs of all sizes are allowed for an additional one time fee per room of $25 for dogs under 25 pounds, and $50 for dogs over 25 pounds.

Weston

Accommodations
Comfort Inn 2906 H 33E Weston WV   304-269-7000 (877-424-6423)
Dogs up to 50 pounds are allowed for an additional pet fee of $10 per night per room.

Wheeling

Accommodations
Oglebay's Wilson Lodge Route 88 North Wheeling WV   304-243-4000 (800-624-6988)
http://www.oglebay-resort.com/lodge.htm
Dogs are not allowed in the lodge, but are welcome in the cottages. There are no designated smoking or non-smoking cottages. There are no additional pet fees.

Chapter 16

North Carolina
Dog Travel Guide

Albemarle

Accommodations
Best Western Executive Inn null Albemarle NC   704-983-6990 (800-780-7234)
Dogs under 40 pounds are allowed for an additional one time fee of $40 per pet; the fee is $100 for dogs over 40 pounds.

Campgrounds and RV Parks
Morrow Mountain State Park 49104 Morrow Mountain Road Albemarle NC   704-982-4402
Rich in natural and cultural history, this park offers an exhibit hall and a historic site, an amphitheater, 15 miles of blazed hiking trails, and a wide variety of land and water activities and recreation. Dogs of all sizes are allowed at no additional fee. Dogs may not be left unattended, and they must be on no more than a 6 foot leash, and be cleaned up after. Dogs are not allowed in buildings, however they are allowed on the trails. The camping and tent areas also allow dogs. There is a dog walk area at the campground. There are no electric or water hookups at the campground.

Asheville

Accommodations
Comfort Inn Asheville Airport 15 Rockwell Road Arden NC   828-687-9199 (877-424-6423)
Dogs up to 50 pounds are allowed for an additional pet fee of $15 per night per room.
Best Western of Asheville Biltmore East 501 Tunnel Road Asheville NC   828-298-5562 (800-780-7234)
Dogs are allowed for an additional fee of $10 per night per pet.
Comfort Suites Biltmore Square Mall 890 Brevard Road Asheville NC   828-665-4000 (877-424-6423)
Dogs are allowed for an additional pet fee of $20 per night per room.
Days Inn Asheville Biltmore East 1435 Tunnel Road Asheville NC   828-298-4000 (800-329-7466)
Dogs of all sizes are allowed. There is a $15 per first night pet fee per pet and $5 for each additional night.
Days Inn Asheville Mall 201 Tunnel Rd Asheville NC   828-252-4000 (800-329-7466)
Dogs up to 60 pounds are allowed. There is a $15 per first night pet fee per pet and $5 for each additional nights.
Days Inn Asheville Patton Ave 120 Patton Ave Asheville NC   828-254-9661 (800-329-7466)
Dogs of all sizes are allowed. There is a $15 per first night pet fee per pet and $5 for each additional night.
Engadine Cabins 2630 Smoky Park Highway Asheville NC   828-665-8325 (800-665-8868)
http://www.engadinecabins.com
The Cabins At Engadine are situated on a hilltop overlooking the Inn. The cabins are only 20 minutes from one of the best known ski resorts in North Carolina, Cataloochee Ski Resort. Also nearby are whitewater rafting, tubing, horse back riding, and hot air ballooning. The cabins are 15 minutes to downtown Asheville. Both Cabins offer privacy and are self-contained with bedroom, kitchen, living area, bathroom with Hot Tub, and porches with a panoramic view of the Blue Ridge Mountains. The Reese Cabin is a single-bedroom unit and the Alex Andrea is a two-bedroom unit. Children and Pets of any size are welcome. The cabins are both non-smoking.
Holiday Inn - Blue Ridge Parkway 1450 Tunnel Rd Asheville NC   828-298-5611 (877-270-6405)
http://www.ashevilleholidayinn.com
The Holiday Inn is nestled in the Blue Ridge Mountains and near the area's most popular attractions. There are mountain views and a heated outdoor pool. They have a number of pet friendly rooms for a pet fee of $20 per night. They provide pet walking areas and complimentary treats for dogs.
Holiday Inn Sunspree Resorts One Holiday Inn Drive Asheville NC   828-254-3211 (877-270-6405)
Dogs of all sizes are allowed for an additional one time pet fee of $20 per room.
Log Cabin Motor Court 330 Weaverville Highway Asheville NC   828-645-6546 (800-295-3392)
http://www.cabinlodging.com
There are 18 one or two bedroom log cabins available. There is a $15 per night additional pet fee. Dogs must be crated if left alone in the cabin. Up to 2 dogs are allowed in each cabin.
Motel 6 - Asheville 1415 Tunnel Road Asheville NC   828-299-3040 (800-466-8356)
One well-behaved family pet per room. Guest must notify front desk upon arrival. Guest is liable for any damages. In consideration of all guests, pets must never be left unattended in the guest rooms.
Red Roof Inn - Asheville West 16 Crowell Road Asheville NC   828-667-9803 (800-RED-ROOF)
One well-behaved family pet per room. Guest must notify front desk upon arrival. Guest is liable for any damages. In consideration of all guests, pets must never be left unattended in the guest rooms.

Residence Inn by Marriott 701 Biltmore Avenue Asheville NC 828-281-3361
Dogs of all sizes are allowed. There is a $75 one time fee and a pet policy to sign at check in.
Sleep Inn West 1918 Old Haywood Road Asheville NC 828-670-7600 (877-424-6423)
Dogs are allowed for an additional pet fee of $25 per night per room.
Super 8 Asheville/Biltmore Square Area 9 Wedgefield Rd Asheville NC 828-670-8800 (800-800-8000)
Dogs of all sizes are allowed. There is a $15 per night pet fee per pet. Smoking and non-smoking rooms are available for pet rooms.
Super 8 Asheville/East 1329 Tunnel Rd Asheville NC 828-298-7952 (800-800-8000)
Dogs of all sizes are allowed. There is a $15 one time per pet fee per visit. Smoking and non-smoking rooms are available for pet rooms.
Super 8 Black Mountain 101 Flat Creek Rd Black Mountain NC 828-669-8076 (800-800-8000)
Dogs of all sizes are allowed. There is a $5 per night pet fee per pet. Smoking and non-smoking rooms are available for pet rooms.
Apple Blossom Cottage 46 Drawspring Road Candler NC 828-255-0704
Dogs of all sizes are allowed. There is a $100 refundable pet deposit and pets must be flea protected.
Days Inn Asheville West 2551 Smoky Park Hwy Candler NC 828-667-9321 (800-329-7466)
Dogs of all sizes are allowed. There is a $5 per night pet fee per pet.
Suzanne's Farm and Gardens 31 Toms Road Candler NC 828-670-5248
Well behaved dogs of all sizes are allowed. There are no additional pet fees. Dogs are not allowed on the beds.
Days Inn Asheville Airport 183 Underwood Rd Fletcher NC 828-684-2281 (800-329-7466)
Dogs of all sizes are allowed. There is a $25 one time per pet fee per visit.
Holiday Inn 550 Airport Road Fletcher NC 828-684-1213 (877-270-6405)
Dogs of all sizes are allowed for an additional one time pet fee of $50 per room.

Campgrounds and RV Parks
Bear Creek RV Park 81 S Bear Creek Road Asheville NC 828-253-0798
http://www.ashevillevearcreek.com
Dogs of all sizes are allowed. There are no additional pet fees for the first two dogs. For more than 2 dogs, there is a $5 per night per pet additional fee. Dogs must be leashed and cleaned up after. The camping and tent areas also allow dogs. There is a dog walk area at the campground.
Pisgah National Forest 1001 Pisgah H (H276) Asheville NC 828-877-3350
http://www.cs.unca.edu/nfsnc/
This forest's diverse ecosystems support a large variety of trails, plants, fish, mammals, bird species, recreation, and are also home to the Looking Glass Falls. Dogs of all sizes are allowed at no additional fee. Dogs may not be left unattended, and they must be leashed and cleaned up after. Dogs are not allowed in buildings, however, they are allowed on the trails. Dogs are not allowed on the trails in the Great Smokey Mountains National Forest that adjoins the park. The camping and tent areas also allow dogs. There is a dog walk area at the campground. There are no electric or water hookups at the campground.
Creekside Mountain Camping 24 Chimney View Road Bat Cave NC 800-248-8118
http://www.creeksidecamping.com
Dogs of all sizes are allowed. There are no additional pet fees. Dogs may not be left unattended, and they must be quiet, leashed, and cleaned up after. The camping and tent areas also allow dogs. There is a dog walk area at the campground.
Asheville West KOA 309 Wiggins Road Candler NC 828-665-7015 (800-562-9015)
http://www.koa.com
Dogs of all sizes are allowed. There are no additional pet fees. Dogs must be leashed and cleaned up after. There are some breed restrictions. The camping and tent areas also allow dogs. There is a dog walk area at the campground. Dogs are allowed in the camping cabins.
Rutledge Lake RV Park 170 Rutledge Road Fletcher NC 828-654-7873
http://www.koa.com
Dogs up to about 70 pounds are allowed. There are no additional pet fees. Dogs may not be left unattended outside, and they must be inside at night. Dogs must be well behaved, leashed and cleaned up after. There are some breed restrictions. The camping and tent areas also allow dogs. There is a dog walk area at the campground.

Vacation Home Rentals
Carolina Mornings/Asheville Cabins Call to Arrange Asheville NC 800-770-9055
http://www.asheville-cabins.com
This vacation rental company centered in Asheville offers cabins in town and out in the country. They manage over 95 vacation properties that are pet-friendly.
Hummingbird Pond Call to Arrange Asheville NC 828-712-3504
http://www.hummingbirdpond.com
This dog-friendly vacation rental in the mountains is fifteen minutes from downtown Asheville. It has five

bedrooms and 3 baths. There is also a private pond and high speed Internet.
Spring Pond Cabin 640 E US Hwy 176 Saluda NC   828-749-9824
http://www.saluda.com/springpond
This cozy cabin in the woods is available for rent to you and your pets. There is a covered porch with fenced in area as well as a half mile hiking loop on the property which is wooded and has two spring fed ponds. The cabin is fully equipped and sleeps five. They ask that you bring your own linens if your dog sleeps on the bed.

Attractions

TOP 200 PLACE Asheville Historic Trolley Tour 151 Haywood Street/Asheville Visitor Center Asheville NC   888-667-3600
http://www.ashevilletrolleytours.com/
Hop aboard this state-of-the-art Touring Trolley for a funny and historically narrated cruise to see the best that Asheville has to offer. Tickets are available at several locations around town including the one listed. Well mannered dogs are allowed on the trolley for no additional fee. Dogs must be under owner's control/care and short leashed at all times.

Asheville Urban Trail 2 South Pack Square (Pack Place) Asheville NC   828-258-0710
This unique outdoor art museum celebrates 5 periods of the city's social history marked by pink granite makers in the sidewalk and 30 "stations" of sculptures and plaques that define the 1.7 mile long trail. There are also several eateries, shops, and public gathering areas along the way. Audiocassettes are available for self-guided tours at Pack Place. Dogs are welcome on the trail. They must be under owner's control at all times and be leashed and cleaned up after.

TOP 200 PLACE Biltmore Estate 1 Approach Road Asheville NC   800-624-1575
http://www.biltmore.com/
This opulent estate of George Vanderbilt is America's largest home covering 4 acres with 250 rooms on 8000 acres. The variety of sites and activities include an interpretive 1890's working farm, an award winning winery, extraordinary formal gardens, a one-of-a-kind shopping center, several eateries, and a variety of festivals and special events throughout the year. Dogs of all sizes are allowed throughout the grounds; they are not allowed in buildings. It is up to individual stores whether a dog is permitted inside. Dogs must be under owner's control, leashed, and cleaned up after at all times.

Craggy Gardens Milepost 364 Blue Ridge Parkway Asheville NC   828-298-0398
Offering some of the most dramatic scenery of the Parkway, this lookout area and trails also become ablaze with an abundance of wildflowers during the Spring. Dogs are allowed, but they must be leashed and under owner's control/care at all times.

North Carolina Arboretum 100 Fredrick Asheville NC   828-665-2492
http://www.ncarboretum.org/
The 434 acres of this arboretum is considered to be one of the most beautiful natural garden settings in America with easy to difficult trails through a variety of scenic landscapes. There are garden demonstrations, educational programs, and development and research activities, with focus on conservation and preservation. Dogs are allowed throughout the park and on the trails. They are not allowed in any buildings or in the Bonsai garden. Dogs must be under owner's control, leashed, and cleaned up after.

Old Pressley Sapphire Mine 240 Pressley Mine Road Canton NC   828-648-6320
http://www.oldpressleymine.com/
Featured in the Guinness Book of World Records, and home to the finding of the world's largest sapphire-at 1,445 carats, this mine is one of the oldest operating mines in the state. Dogs are allowed on the grounds. Dogs must be well behaved, under owner's control at all times, leashed, and cleaned up after at all times.

Vance Birthplace 911 Reems Creek Rd. Weaverville NC   828-645-6706
This reconstructed, 5-room log house, the out buildings, and furnishings portrays life in the early 1800's and tells the story of Zebulon Vance and family and of their outstanding contributions to the state. Dogs of all sizes are allowed for no additional fee. Small dogs that may be carried are allowed to go in buildings (when not crowed), but larger dogs may not. Dogs are allowed throughout the grounds, and they must be well behaved, leashed, and cleaned up after at all times.

Shopping Centers

Biltmore Village Biltmore Plaza Asheville NC   888-561-5437
www.biltmorevillage.com
This 1890's village sits at the entrance to the Biltmore Estate. Its unique with its shops in original early 1900's houses along tree-lined bricked sidewalks, offering quality, unusual, and one-of-a-kind merchandise. There are a variety of retailers, eateries, galleries, salons, and more to explore. Dogs of all sizes are allowed throughout the grounds; they are not allowed in buildings. It is up to individual stores whether a dog is permitted inside. Dogs must be under owner's control, leashed, and cleaned up after at all times.

Grove Arcade Public Market 1 Page Avenue Asheville NC   828-252-7799, ext.302
http://www.grovearcade.com/
Grove Arcade shares a collection of shops, restaurants, offices, over 40 luxury apartments, and more. A

movement by the local people brought this public market back making it quite a popular destination. Although dogs are not allowed in the building, they are allowed throughout the market area and some of the eateries will allow pets at the outer tables. Dogs must be under owner's control at all times, leashed or crated, and cleaned up after at all times. Dogs may not be left alone at any time.

Stores

PetSmart Pet Store 3 McKenna Rd Arden NC   828-681-5343
Your licensed and well-behaved leashed dog is allowed in the store.
Blaze N Skyy Pet Boutique 62 Wall Street Asheville NC   828-253-2850
http://www.blazenskyy.com/
This diversified boutique offers a full line of pet clothing, accessories, carriers, special occasion items, treats, and pet foods, in addition to having special events and festivals, and adoption opportunities. Your well mannered dog is welcome in the store to explore all the goodies. Dogs must be well behaved, under owner's control/care at all times, and leashed or crated.
PetSmart Pet Store 437 Swannanoa River Rd Asheville NC   828-298-5670
Your licensed and well-behaved leashed dog is allowed in the store.
Three Dog Bakery 21 Battery Park, Suite 103 Asheville NC   828-252-1818
http://www.threedog.com
Three Dog Bakery provides cookies and snacks for your dog as well as some boutique items. You well-behaved, leashed dog is welcome.

Parks

Chimney Rock Park H 64/74A Chimney Rock NC   800-277-9611
http://www.chimneyrockpark.com/
This park offers the best of the mountains in one place, from unique geological formations to sweeping views. Enjoy spectacular 75-mile plus views from the top of the Skyline Trail (Exclamation Point) or Inspiration Point, explore a 404-foot waterfall from the top or bottom, check out a variety of interesting trails, or try the 185 stair walk that threads between a narrow passage, and is called the "eye of the needle". You'll also find a variety of special events, a nature center, a native plant nursery, guided tours, and much more. Dogs are allowed throughout the park and on the stairs, but they are not allowed on the elevator or in the Skylight Cafe. Dogs must be well behaved, on leash, and cleaned up after at all times.

Outdoor Restaurants

Asheville Pizza and Brewing Company 675 Merrimon Avenue Asheville NC   828-254-1281
http://www.ashevillepizza.com/
For pizza, brews, and entertainment, this is the place, and they offer indoor and outdoor dining options. Dogs are allowed at the outer tables. They must be under owner's control/care, and leashed or crated at all times.
Carmel's Restaurant and Bar Corner of Page Avenue and Battery Park Asheville NC   828-252-8730
http://www.carmelsofasheville.com/
This restaurant offers a fine dining atmosphere, contemporary American Cuisine, and indoor or outdoor dining options. Dogs are allowed at the outer tables. Dogs must be well mannered, under owner's control at all times, leashed or crated, and cleaned up after at all times.
Cats and Dawgs 1 Page Avenue, Suite 132 Asheville NC   828-281-8100
Specializing in all beef hot dogs and catfish sandwiches, this eatery also offers indoor or outdoor dining options. Dogs are allowed at the outer tables. Dogs must be well behaved, under owner's control/care, and leashed or crated at all times.
Dog Day Cafe 204 Weaverville Hwy Asheville NC   828-658-3917
This ice cream shop also serves coffee and grilled hotdogs. Dogs are allowed at the outdoor tables and they also have a runner.
Earth Fare Natural Food Market 66 Westgate Parkway Asheville NC   828-253-7656
http://www.earthfare.com/
This store offers more than 45,000 organic all natural items, a deli and hot bar, and they also host various special events. There are outside dining tables and dogs are allowed at the outer tables. They must be under owner's control/care, and leashed or crated at all times.
KAMM'S Frozen Custard Shop 111 O'Henry Avenue Asheville NC   828-225-7200
Located at the Grove Arcade, this creamery offers a variety of daily homemade ice creams and for those who like to build their own flavor there is "Flavor by Request". Dogs are allowed to have their share at the outer tables only. Dogs must be well behaved, under owner's control at all times, leashed or crated, and cleaned up after at all times.
Little Venice 800 Fairview Road, Suite 9 Asheville NC   828-299-8911
http://www.littlevenice.biz/
In addition to their New York style Pizza, they offer a variety of Italian and some Greek favorites, and year-around outdoor dining (weather permitting). Dogs are allowed at the outer tables located by the railing, with exception

being during musical events. They must be under owner's control/care, and leashed or crated at all times.
Sunny Point Cafe and Bakery 626 Haywood Road Asheville NC   828-252-0055
http://www.sunnypointcafe.com/
This eatery and bakery specializes in using local, organic ingredients with dinner and daily specials, and indoor and outdoor dining options. Dogs are allowed at the outer tables. Dogs must be under owner's control/care, and leashed and cleaned up after at all times.
The Laughing Seed Cafe 40 Wall Street Asheville NC   828-252-3445
This vegetarian restaurant incorporates global influences with fresh, locally grown organic ingredients, offers a full exotic bar, and seasonal outdoor dining. Dogs are allowed at the outer tables. They must be under owner's control/care, and leashed or crated at all times.
Urban Burrito 640 Merrimon Avenue Asheville NC   828-251-1921
http://www.urbanburrito.com/
Dogs are allowed at the outer tables of this eatery; just go inside to order and pick-up. Dogs must be under owner's control/care, and leashed or crated at all times.

Bath

Transportation Systems
North Carolina Ferry-Bayview 229 H 306N Bath NC   800-BY FERRY (293-3779)
These vehicle and passenger transport ferries are run by the state and provide service every day of the year on all routes; however weather conditions can influence travel. Dogs are allowed on all ferries for no additional fee; they must be kept in the vehicle or leashed when out of the vehicle. Dogs must be under owner's control/care at all times.

Benson

Accommodations
Days Inn Benson 202 N Honeycutt St Benson NC   919-894-2031 (800-329-7466)
Dogs of all sizes are allowed. There is a $7 per night pet fee per pet.

Biscoe

Accommodations
Days Inn Biscoe 531 East Main St Biscoe NC   910-428-2525 (800-329-7466)
Dogs of all sizes are allowed. There is a $5 per night pet fee per pet.

Blue Ridge Parkway

Accommodations
Best Western Mountain Lodge at Banner Elk 1615 Tynecastle Highway - Highway 184 Banner Elk NC   828-898-4571 (800-780-7234)
http://www.bestwesternbannerelk.com
The Best Western is located in the "Heart of the High Country" in a mountain setting. The hotel offers a full service restaurant and lounge, conference facilities, picnic areas, guest laundry, game room, and a large outdoor heated pool that is open year round. They have dog treats and a large dog walking area.
Holiday Inn Express Hotel and Suites 1570 Asheville Hwy Brevard NC   828-862-8900 (877-270-6405)
Dogs of all sizes are allowed for an additional one time pet fee of $50 per room.
Blue Ridge Motel 204 West Blvd Burnsville NC   828-682-9100
Dogs of all sizes are allowed. There is a $5 per day per room or $25 per week additional pet fee.
Mountain View Motel H 19E Burnsville NC   828-682-2115
Dogs of all sizes are allowed. There is a $5 per night per pet fee for small dogs and a $10 per night per pet fee for large dogs.
Mountain View Lodge & Cabins Blue Ridge Parkway Mile Post 256 Glendale Springs NC   336-982-2233

(800-903-6811)
http://www.mtnviewlodge.com
Vacation with your pet at this retreat on the Blue Ridge Parkway in the northern mountains of North Carolina. Trails, grassy lawn for romping, nearby pond for swimming. 1-2 bedroom cabins with kitchenettes, full bathrooms and porches. There is no size limit for dogs.
Valle Crucis Log Cabin Rentals P.O. Box 554 Valle Crucis NC 828-963-7774
This company has many properties and one large dog or 2 small dogs are allowed. There is a $50 one time fee per pet additional fee. They ask you bring a blanket to cover the bed or furniture if your pet is inclined to get on them.
Carolina Mountain Resort 8 N Jefferson Avenue West Jefferson NC 336-246-3010
Dogs of all sizes are allowed. There is a $50 one time fee and a pet policy to sign at check in.
Dog House Resort 134 John H. Pierce Sr. Lane West Jefferson NC 336-977-3482
http://www.dog-house-resort.com
Dog House Resort is a Bed & Breakfast for people vacationing with their dogs on three acres overlooking the Blue Ridge Mountains. Dogs of all sizes are welcome. There is a fenced-in dog park and pet-sitting is available.

Campgrounds and RV Parks
Julian Price Memorial Park Blue Ridge Parkway Milepost 297 Blowing Rock NC 828-295-7591 (877-444-6777)
http://www.blueridgeparkway.org/
This is the largest of the camp areas along the parkway and they offer numerous recreational opportunities and hiking trails of varying length and difficulty, picnic grounds, interpretive programs, an amphitheater, and it sits adjacent to Price Lake. Although most campsites are on a first come first served basis, some sites are available for reservations. Dogs are allowed throughout the park and on the trails. Dogs must be well behaved, under owner's control, on no more than a 6 foot leash, and cleaned up after at all times. This RV park is closed during the off-season. The camping and tent areas also allow dogs. There is a dog walk area at the campground. There are no electric or water hookups at the campgrounds.
Boone KOA 123 Harmony Mountain Lane Boone NC 828-264-7250 (800-562-2806)
http://www.koa.com
Dogs of all sizes are allowed. There are no additional pet fees. Dogs may not be left unattended, and they must be leashed and cleaned up after. This RV park is closed during the off-season. The camping and tent areas also allow dogs. There is a dog walk area at the campground. Dogs are allowed in the camping cabins.
Mount Mitchell State Park 2388 H 128 Burnsville NC 828-675-4611
In addition to being the highest point east of the Mississippi with its outstanding views, this 1,855 acre park also offers a number of scenic trails, an observation tower, an interpretive center, concessionaires, and picnic areas with tables and grills. There is also a 9 site, tents only camping area on a first come first served basis. Dogs are allowed throughout the park and on the trails; they are not allowed in park buildings. Dogs must be leashed and cleaned up after at all times. This RV park is closed during the off-season. The camping and tent areas also allow dogs. There is a dog walk area at the campground. There are no electric or water hookups at the campgrounds. There are special amenities given to dogs at this campground.
Linville Falls Campground Blue Ridge Parkway mile 316.4 Linville Falls NC 828-765-7818 (877-444-6777)
http://www.blueridgeparkway.org/
Although the smallest campground along the parkway, it is one of the most popular with sites all along the waterfront and it is home to one of the most famous waterfalls in the Blue Ridge. The falls offer a spectacular view as they cascade into a deep lush gorge, and trails lead to views of both the upper and lower falls. Dogs are allowed throughout the park and on the trails. Dogs must be well behaved, under owner's control, on no more than a 6 foot leash, and cleaned up after at all times. This RV park is closed during the off-season. The camping and tent areas also allow dogs. There is a dog walk area at the campground. There are no electric or water hookups at the campgrounds.
Crabtree Meadows Campground Blue Ridge Parkway, Milepost 339.5 Little Switzerland NC 828-765-6082
http://www.blueridgeparkway.org/
This 250 acre recreation area has a restaurant, gift shop, large picnic area, nature walks, and a campground with 71 tent and 22 RV sites on a first come first served basis. One of the best viewing times here is in early Summer when wildflowers blaze vast lawns of color, and there is a 70 foot falls for those that can do the 2.5 mile (round trip) strenuous hike. Dogs are allowed throughout the park and on the trails. Dogs must be well behaved, under owner's control, on no more than a 6 foot leash, and cleaned up after at all times. This RV park is closed during the off-season. The camping and tent areas also allow dogs. There is a dog walk area at the campground. There are no electric or water hookups at the campgrounds.
Rivercamp USA 2221 Kings Creek Road Piney Creek NC 336-359-2267
http://www.rivercampusa.com
Dogs of all sizes are allowed. There are no additional pet fees. Dogs may not be left unattended outside, and they must be quiet, leashed, and cleaned up after. This RV park is closed during the off-season. The camping and tent areas also allow dogs. There is a dog walk area at the campground.
Doughton Park Campground Blue Ridge Parkway Milepost 239.2 Sparta NC 336-372-8568

http://www.blueridgeparkway.org/
Located at one of the Parkway's largest developed areas, this camp area offers 110 tent and 25 RV first come first served sites, a picnicking and concession area, service station, an information center, and a short stroll to the Wildcat Rocks Overlook and kiosk. There are also more than 30 miles of trails of varying difficulty and a variety of recreation available. Dogs are allowed throughout the park and on the trails. Dogs must be well behaved, under owner's control, on no more than a 6 foot leash, and cleaned up after at all times. This RV park is closed during the off-season. The camping and tent areas also allow dogs. There is a dog walk area at the campground. There are no electric or water hookups at the campgrounds.

Vacation Home Rentals
Weddens Way, Too 231 Legra Rd Piney Creek NC   336-372-2985
http://www.sparta-nc.com/weddensway/
Fully furnished cabin overlooking the New River. Sleeps up to 7, rate for two is $80 plus tax per night. Pets are welcome for a $50 fee for the entire stay. Fish, canoe or enjoy the view.

Attractions
TOP 200 PLACE **Blowing Rock** H 321 S Blowing Rock NC   828-295-7111
http://www.theblowingrock.com/
Known as the state's oldest travel destination, this 4000 foot cliff overhanging the Johns River Gorge is rich in Native American folklore. There is an unusual atmospheric condition that occurs here that made Ripley's Believe-it-or-Not comment that it is "the only place in the world where snow falls upside down". Dogs are allowed and they must be leashed and under owner's control/care at all times.
Tweetsie Railroad 300 Tweetsie Railroad Lane Blowing Rock NC   828-264-9061
http://www.tweetsie.com/
This seasonal "Old Wild West", family-oriented theme park offers some special features such as the last surviving narrow-gauge, coal-fired, steam locomotive (#12-known as Tweetsie) of the original line, live action entertainment, and various special events. Although dogs are not allowed in buildings or on the train, there is plenty for them to enjoy. Dogs must be under owner's control/care at all times.
Wahoo's Adventures H 321S Boone NC   828-262-5774
http://www.wahoosadventures.com/
From gentle to extreme, guided or self-guided, this water adventure company offers a variety of activities and convenient locations. Dogs are allowed on some of the tours and on rentals; they are not allowed on white water rafting excursions. Dogs must be acclimated to water activities, and under owner's control/care at all times.

Grandfather Mountain

TOP 200 PLACE **Grandfather Mountain** near Blue Ridge Parkway Linville NC   828-733-4337
http://www.grandfather.com
This rugged mountain is full of hiking trails and natural beauty. At the top there is a swinging bridge to walk out on as it is usually quite windy. The bridge is quite a spectacle. Dogs are allowed on leash throughout. There is calmer hiking lower on the mountain.
Emerald Village Mining Museum 331 McKinney Mine Road Little Switzerland NC   828-ROK-MINE (765-6463)
http://emeraldvillage.com/

In addition to mining history, memorabilia, and a miniature mining town, this seasonal mining area will also give visitors hands-on experience looking for their own gems. Dogs are allowed throughout the property; they must be well mannered, and under owner's control/care at all times.

TOP 200 PLACE **Blue Ridge Parkway Auto Tour** Blue Ridge Parkway, Milepost 0 Waynesboro NC   828-271-4779

http://www.blueridgeparkway.org/

Taking more than 50 years to build and setting standards in engineering and design along the way, the Blue Ridge Parkway offers thousands of recreational acres and exceptional scenery to explore as it connects the Shenandoah National Park with the Great Smoky Mountains National Park. The maximum speed limit is 45 MPH on the parkway so this is not the fastest route to take. Its natural and cultural history reveals itself as visitors drive through the 469 miles of the country's first and longest rural parkway, or by hiking its many diverse trails. Visitors will also pass over the Linn Cove Viaduct, considered to be one of the most complicated concrete bridges ever built at Milepost 304.6. From May through October ranger programs are offered, and there are a number of campgrounds, trails, eateries, viewing areas, and historic/interpretive sites along the way. Dogs are allowed at all the camp areas and on all the trails. Dogs must be very well behaved, under owner's control, on no more than a 6 foot leash or securely crated, and cleaned up after at all times.

Shopping Centers
Tanger Shoppes on the Parkway H 321 Blowing Rock NC   828-295-4444

http://www.tangeroutlet.com/center/BLR

There are more than 30 brand name outlets and services at this center. Dogs are allowed in the common areas; they must be well behaved, leashed, and cleaned up after at all times.

Parks
Pisgah National Forest various Asheville NC   828-257-4200

http://www.cs.unca.edu/nfsnc/

The forest offers miles of dog-friendly hiking trails. It is located about 2 hours from the Great Smoky Mountains National Park.

Moses H. Cone Memorial Park MM 295 Blue Ridge Parkway Blowing Rock NC   828-271 4779

Located in the Grandfather Mountain corridor, this scenic 3,600 acre park's centerpiece is the turn-of-the-century Cone Manor-now a visitor and craft center. There are picnic areas, numerous trails, and waterways. Dogs are allowed on the grounds; they are not allowed in buildings. Dogs must be leashed and under owner's control/care at all times.

Whitewater Falls Off H 281 Cashiers NC   828-257-4200

At 411 feet, this is the highest waterfall east of the Rocky Mountains, and its lush environment gives way to an abundance of flora and fauna and some great sightseeing trails and lookouts. Restrooms and picnic tables are on site. Dogs are allowed, but they must be kept leashed and picked up after at all times. This falls continue into South Carolina and there is another 400 foot waterfall.

Outdoor Restaurants
Tijuana Fats 1182 Main St Blowing Rock NC   828-295-9683

Dogs are allowed at the outdoor tables.

Burlington

Accommodations
Days Inn Burlington 978 Plantation Dr Burlington NC   336-227-3681 (800-329-7466)

Dogs of all sizes are allowed. There is a $10 per night pet fee per pet.

La Quinta Inn Burlington 2444 Maple Ave. Burlington NC   336-229-5203 (800-531-5900)

Dogs of all sizes are allowed. There are no additional pet fees. Dogs must be leashed, cleaned up after, and crated or removed for housekeeping.

Motel 6 - Burlington 2155 Hanford Road Burlington NC   336-226-1325 (800-466-8356)

One well-behaved family pet per room. Guest must notify front desk upon arrival. Guest is liable for any damages. In consideration of all guests, pets must never be left unattended in the guest rooms.

Red Roof Inn - Burlington, NC 2133 West Hanford Road Burlington NC   336-227-1270 (800-RED-ROOF)

One well-behaved family pet per room. Guest must notify front desk upon arrival. Guest is liable for any damages. In consideration of all guests, pets must never be left unattended in the guest rooms.

Shopping Centers

Burlington Outlet Village 2839 Corporation Parkway Burlington NC   336-227-2872
There are more than 42 brand name outlets and services at this center. Dogs are allowed in the common areas; it is up to individual stores whether they are allowed inside. Dogs must be well behaved, leashed, and cleaned up after at all times.

Stores
PetSmart Pet Store 1459 University Dr F Burlington NC   336-524-0229
Your licensed and well-behaved leashed dog is allowed in the store.

Cape Fear Beaches

Campgrounds and RV Parks
Carolina Beach State Park 1010 State Park Road Carolina Beach NC   910-458-8206
http://www.ncparks.gov/Visit/main.php
This 761 acre park was started to preserve and educate the public of its unique intra-coastal waterway and to provide recreation; there are miles of trails through a variety of habitats with some unusual inhabitants-including the Venus flytrap, and various events and interpretive programs. Dogs are allowed for no additional fee; they must have proof of currant rabies inoculation. Dogs may not be left unattended and are to be confined to vehicles or tents during quiet hours. They must be well behaved, on no more than a 6 foot leash, and cleaned up after at all times. Dogs are not allowed in any park buildings or swimming areas. The campground offers 83 first come first served sites in a wooded setting with picnic tables and grills at each site; restrooms, showers, water, and a dump station are nearby. The camping and tent areas also allow dogs. There is a dog walk area at the campground. There are no electric or water hookups at the campgrounds.
Long Beach Campground 5011 E Oak Island Drive Oak Island NC   910-278-5737
Dogs of all sizes are allowed. There are no additional pet fees. Dogs must be leashed and cleaned up after. Dogs are allowed at the beach. The camping and tent areas also allow dogs. There is a dog walk area at the campground.

Vacation Home Rentals
United Beach Vacations 1001 North Lake Park Blvd. Carolina Beach NC   800-334-5806
http://www.pleasureislandholiday.com
This vacation rental company has many pet-friendly vacation rentals in the Carolina Beach area. Rentals range in size from 2 to 5 bedrooms.
Oak Island Accommodations, Inc 8901 East Oak Island Drive Oak Island NC   910-278-6011 (800-243-8132)
http://www.rentalsatthebeach.com
This rental agency offers over 600+ resort rentals from Oceanfront to Soundside. Pets allowed in designated homes. Dogs 60 pounds and under allowed with a non-refundable $100 + tax pet fee for Cleaning and Extermination.

Transportation Systems
Fort Fisher Ferry Fort Fisher Blvd S Fort Fisher NC   800-BY FERRY (293-3779)
http://www.ncdot.org/transit/ferry/
This water taxi provides services between the outer islands and the mainland. Dogs are allowed on board for no additional fee; they must be leashed, crated, or in a vehicle for the duration of the trip. Dogs must be under owner's control/care at all times.
North Carolina Ferry-Fort Fisher Fort Fisher Road S/H 421 Fort Fisher NC   800-BY FERRY (293-3779)
These vehicle and passenger transport ferries are run by the state and provide service every day of the year on all routes; however weather conditions can influence travel. Dogs are allowed on all ferries for no additional fee; they must be kept in the vehicle or leashed when out of the vehicle. Dogs must be under owner's control/care at all times.
North Carolina Ferry-Southport Southport Ferry Road Southport NC   800-BY FERRY (293-3779)
These vehicle and passenger transport ferries are run by the state and provide service every day of the year on all routes; however weather conditions can influence travel. Dogs are allowed on all ferries for no additional fee; they must be kept in the vehicle or leashed when out of the vehicle. Dogs must be under owner's control/care at all times.

Attractions
Orton Plantation Gardens 9149 Orton Road SE Winnabow NC   910-371-6851

http://www.ortongardens.com/
At already almost a hundred years old, these stunning formal gardens give visitors 20 acres of self-guided walking paths, specialty gardens, ponds, a river, pine forest, 60 total aces of lush plant-life, and more; it is also a premier bird-watching location. The house is not open to the public. Dogs are allowed throughout the park; they are not allowed at the chapel or in park buildings. Dogs must be leashed and cleaned up after at all times.

Stores
Cool Dogs and Crazy Cats 310 N Howe Street Southport NC   910-457-0115
http://www.cooldogscrazycats.com/
In addition to a providing a line of all natural, human grade treats, this pet boutique also carries a line of accessories for pets and unique art and gifts for pet owners. Dogs are welcome in the store; they must be well behaved, under owner's control/care, and leashed at all times.

Beaches
Ft. Fisher State Recreation Area Highway 421 Kure Beach NC   910-458-5798
Enjoy miles of beachcombing, sunbathing or hunting for shells at this beach. Dogs on leash are allowed everywhere on the beach, except for swimming areas that have lifeguards on duty. People need to clean up after their pets. The park is located on the southern tip of Pleasure Island, near Wilmington.
Oak Island Beaches Beach Drive Oak Island NC   910-278-5011
http://www.oakislandnc.com/
Dogs are allowed on city beaches year round, but from mid November to about the 1st of April dogs may be off lead if they are under strict voice control. Dogs must be under owner's control, leashed April to November, and cleaned up after at all times.

Parks
Carolina Beach Lake Park 400 S Lake Park Blvd/H 421 Carolina Beach NC   910-458-7416
Once listed in the Guinness Book of World Records as the closest freshwater lake to salt water, this park offers a range of water and land recreation, a sheltered picnic area, playground, restrooms, and gazebos. Leashed dogs are allowed in the park year round and on the beach from November 1st to February 28th. Pet owners must carry clean-up supplies and pick-up after their pets at all times.
Carolina Beach State Park 1010 State Park Road Carolina Beach NC   910-458-8206
http://www.ncparks.gov/Visit/main.php
This 761 acre park was started to preserve and educate the public of its unique intra-coastal waterway and to provide recreation; there are miles of trails through a variety of habitats with some unusual inhabitants-including the Venus flytrap, and various events and interpretive programs. Dogs are allowed for no additional fee; they must have proof of currant rabies inoculation. Dogs may not be left unattended and are to be confined to vehicles or tents during quiet hours. They must be well behaved, on no more than a 6 foot leash, and cleaned up after at all times. Dogs are not allowed in any park buildings or swimming areas.
Freeman Park Recreation Area 1204 N Lake Park BlvdH 421 Carolina Beach NC   910-458-4716
This popular park offers a wide range of land and sea recreation, bird, marine, and wildlife, and scenic sand dunes blended against sea grasses and sea. Permits for the park are available at the entrance and several other places in town. Dogs are allowed at the park; from April 1st to September 30th dogs must be on leash, and from October 1st to March 31st dogs may be off lead only if they are under good voice control. Dogs must be under owner's control and cleaned up after at all times.
Fort Fisher State Historic Park 1610 Fort Fisher Blvd S/H 421 Kure Beach NC   910-458-5538
Rich in colonial history, this park affords visitors educational as well as recreational avenues with exhibits, interpretive programs, and special events. Dogs are allowed throughout the park; they are not allowed in buildings or on the beach. Dogs must be on no more than a 6 foot leash and cleaned up after at all times.
Brunswick Town State Historic Site 8884 St Phillips Road SE Winnabow NC   910-371-6613
Displays inside the visitor center and on the grounds, monuments, self-guided trails with signage, living history 18th century colonial and 19th century Civil War events, and more tell of the rich colonial and military history of this historic area. Dogs are allowed throughout the park and on the trails; they are not allowed in buildings. Dogs must be leashed and cleaned up after at all times.

Outdoor Restaurants
Trolley Stop 111A S Howe Street/H 211 Southport NC   910-457-7017
This sandwich shop will allow your pooch at the outer tables; dogs must be under owner's control/care and leashed at all times.

Cape Hatteras

Campgrounds and RV Parks

Frisco Woods Campground 53124 H 12 Frisco NC   800-948-3942
http://www.outer-banks.com/friscowoods
Dogs of all sizes are allowed. There is an additional $5 one time fee per pet. Dogs may not be left unattended, and they must be leashed and cleaned up after. This RV park is closed during the off-season. The camping and tent areas also allow dogs. There is a dog walk area at the campground. Dogs are allowed in the camping cabins.

Hatteras Sands 57316 Eagle Pass Road Hatteras Village NC   252-986-2422
http://www.hatterassands.com
Dogs of all sizes are allowed. There is a $2 per night per pet additional fee. Dogs may not be left unattended, and they must be leashed and cleaned up after. This RV park is closed during the off-season. The camping and tent areas also allow dogs. There is a dog walk area at the campground. Dogs are allowed in the camping cabins.

TOP 200 PLACE Cape Hatteras National Seashore 1401 National Park Drive Manteo NC   252-473-2111
http://www.nps.gov/caha/
This National Park offers a captivating combination of natural and cultural resources. The park is rich in maritime history, is stretched over 70 miles of barrier islands and offers a variety of recreational pursuits. Dogs of all sizes are allowed at no additional fee. Dogs may not be left unattended, and they must be on no more than a 6 foot leash or crated, and cleaned up after. Dogs are not allowed in public swim areas, however, they are allowed on the trails. The camping and tent areas also allow dogs. There is a dog walk area at the campground. There are no electric or water hookups at the campground.

Camp Hatteras Campground 24798 H 12 Rodanthe NC   252-987-2777
http://www.camphatteras.com
Dogs of all sizes are allowed. There is a $2 per night additional pet fee for up to 3 dogs. Dogs are not allowed in the clubhouse, and they may not be tied to cars, porches, or tables. Dogs may not be left unattended outside, and they must be leashed and cleaned up after. The camping and tent areas also allow dogs. There is a dog walk area at the campground.

Cape Hatteras KOA 25099 H 12 Rodanthe NC   252-987-2307 (800-562-5268)
http://www.capehatteraskoa.com
Dogs of all sizes are allowed, and there are no additional pet fees for tent or RV sites. There is a $5 one time pet fee for the cabins. Dogs may not be left unattended, and must be leashed and cleaned up after. This RV park is closed during the off-season. The camping and tent areas also allow dogs. There is a dog walk area at the campground. Dogs are allowed in the camping cabins.

Transportation Systems

North Carolina Ferry-Ocracoke #1 H 12 N end of Island (to Hatteras) Ocracoke NC   800-BY FERRY (293-3779)
These vehicle and passenger transport ferries are run by the state and provide service every day of the year on all routes; however weather conditions can influence travel. Dogs are allowed on all ferries for no additional fee; they must be kept in the vehicle or leashed when out of the vehicle. Dogs must be under owner's control/care at all times.

North Carolina Ferry-Ocracoke #2 H 12 S end of Island (to Cedar Island and Swan Quarter) Ocracoke NC   800-BY FERRY (293-3779)
These vehicle and passenger transport ferries are run by the state and provide service every day of the year on all routes; however weather conditions can influence travel. Dogs are allowed on all ferries for no additional fee; they must be kept in the vehicle or leashed when out of the vehicle. Dogs must be under owner's control/care at all times.

Attractions

Manteo Beaches N Virginia Dare Trail/H 12 Manteo NC   252-441-5508
http://www.townofmanteo.com/
Dogs are allowed on the waterfront year round; they must be licensed, have current rabies tags, be under owner's control, on no more than a 6 foot leash, and cleaned up after at all times.

Wright Brothers National Memorial 1401 National Park Drive Manteo NC   252-441-7430
http://www.nps.gov/wrbr
Home to the first successful airplane flight, there are exhibits, full-scale reproductions of the 1902 glider and the 1903 flying machine, a commemorative boulder, educational programs, and much more to mark this historic event. Dogs are allowed on the grounds and on the trails; they are not allowed in buildings. They also caution to keep to the trails because of cactus. Dogs must be leashed and cleaned up after at all times.

Ocracoke Sports Fishing Charters PO Box 429 Ocracoke NC   252-928-4841
Offshore, near-shore, and inshore charters covering such areas as Ocracoke and Portsmouth Island, and the

Pamlico Sound are offered by this seafaring company. Up to 6 people are allowed per charter and they suggest bringing food and drinks for self and pooch, sunscreen, your lucky fishing charm, and a camera. Well behaved dogs are allowed on board; they must be under owner's control/care and leashed.

The Anchorage Inn Marina 180 Irvin Garrish H/H 12 Ocracoke Village NC 252-928-6661
Sitting along the shores of Silver Lake Harbor, this full service marina will allow your pooch to explore the docks too. Dogs are allowed on the rentals; they are not allowed on tours. Dogs must be well behaved, under owner's control, leashed and cleaned up after at all times. Their inn (The Anchorage Inn) also allows pets for an additional fee of $20 per night per pet.

Stores
Manteo Booksellers Sir Walter Raleigh Street/H 400 Manteo NC 252-473-1221
http://www.manteobooksellers.com/
Specializing in the culture, history, sites of interest, nature books, and folklore of the Outer Banks, this bookstore also carries a wide range of topics, and they host various authors during the year. Your pooch is welcome to browse the store also, but they must be very people, and dog and cat friendly as there are resident animals. Dogs must be very well behaved, under owner's control/care, and leashed at all times.
Village Diva 285 Irvin Garrish Highway/H 12 Ocracoke Village NC 252-928-2828
This natural fabric clothing store also offers a line of clothing and home accessories, bath and yard products, and also a few things for the pets. Dogs are allowed in the store; they must be under owner's control/care and leashed at all times.

Beaches
Cape Hatteras National Seashore Highway 12 Manteo NC 252-473-2111
http://www.nps.gov/caha/
This park offers long stretches of pristine beach. Dogs on a 6 foot or less leash are allowed year-round, except on any designated swimming beaches. Most of the beaches are non-designated swim beaches. People are required to clean up after their pets.

Parks
Ocracoke Island P. O. Box 456 Ocracoke NC 252-928-6711
http://www.ocracoke-nc.com/
Walking maps are available at the Association for exploring this beautiful island. Dogs are allowed throughout the area and on the beaches; they must be leashed and cleaned up after at all times.

Outdoor Restaurants
Pelican Restaurant and Patio Bar H 12 Ocracoke NC 252-928-7431
Nestled among the trees, this eatery serves all meals daily, plus in the Summer they have outdoor seating with entertainment 5 nights a week. Dogs are allowed at the outer tables; they must be under owner's control/care and leashed at all times.

Cape Lookout

Accommodations
Atlantis Lodge 123 Salter Path Road Atlantic Beach NC 252-726-5168 (800-682-7057)
http://www.atlantislodge.com
The Atlantis has 42 units on the ocean, most with efficiency kitchens, dining, living and sleeping areas. All have patios or decks facing the surf. Use of beach chairs, lounges and umbrellas is complimentary. The outdoor pool is not the normal concrete hole, but an environment created within the woods. Great for reading, lounging or floating. They accept dogs for a minimal fee, no matter the size as long as they are well behaved.
Carteret Country Home 299 H 101 Beaufort NC 252-728-4611
One large dog or 2 small dogs are allowed per room. There is a $15 per night per pet additional fee.
Holiday Inn Express Hotel and Suites 5063 Executive Dr Morehead City NC 252-247-5001 (877-270-6405)
Dogs of all sizes are allowed for an additional one time pet fee of $25 (plus tax) per room.

Campgrounds and RV Parks
Holiday Trav-L-Park Resort 9102 Coast Guard Road Emerald Isle NC 252-354-2250
http://www.htpresort.com
Dogs of all sizes are allowed. There is a $5 per night per pet additional fee. Dogs must be leashed and cleaned

up after. This RV park is closed during the off-season. There is a dog walk area at the campground.
Cape Lookout National Seashore 131 Charles Street Harkers Island NC   252-728-2250
http://www.nps.gov/calo/
Although isolated, the natural and historic features provide an incentive to visit Cape Lookout. It offers interpretive programs, a lighthouse complex, and a variety of land and water activities and recreation. This park is either reached by private boat or by ferry. One of three ferries runs all year, the Local Yocal Ferry. Dogs may ride the ferry for an additional $6 fee per pet and dogs must be leashed at all times. Dogs of all sizes are allowed at no additional fee. Dogs may not be left unattended, and they must be on no more than a 6 foot leash, and cleaned up after. The camping and tent areas also allow dogs. There is a dog walk area at the campground. There are no electric or water hookups at the campground.
Goose Creek Resort 350 Red Barn Road Newport NC   866-839-2628
http://www.goosecreekcamping.com
Dogs of all sizes are allowed. There are no additional pet fees. Dogs must be leashed and cleaned up after. There are some breed restrictions. There is a dog walk area at the campground.

Vacation Home Rentals
Tea House on Goose Bay 862 Crow Hill Rd. Beaufort NC   252-728-7806
http://www.teahouseongoosebay.com
This vacation rental cabin allows dogs for a $50 one time additional pet fee.
Bluewater GMAC Real Estate 200 Mangrove Emerald Isle NC   888-258-9287
http://www.petfriendlyncbeaches.com
This vacation rental company has over 170 dog-friendly vacation homes in the Southern Outer Banks.

Attractions
Beaufort Historic Site 130 Turner Street Beaufort NC   252-728-5225
http://www.beauforthistoricsite.org/
Visitors can experience the coastal heritage of this beautiful historic site through their living history programs, exhibits, authentically restored buildings, and guided tours, plus they offers several special events and activities throughout the year. Dogs are allowed throughout the park; they are not allowed in buildings (unless they can be carried) or on any of the tours. Dogs must be under owner's control, leashed, and cleaned up after at all times.

Beaches
Fort Macon State Park Highway 58 Atlantic Beach NC   252-726-3775
This park offers beach access. Dogs on a 6 foot leash or less are allowed on the beach, but not inside the Civil War fort located in the park. People need to clean up after their pets. The park is located on the eastern end of Bogue Banks, south of Morehead City.

Parks
Fort Macon State Park 2300 E Fort Macon Road/H 58 Atlantic Beach NC   252-726-3775
This historic site is located on a barrier island peninsula, which creates a lively coastal ecosystem and plenty of recreational activities, plus it shares a rich colonial history with a Civil War fort and regularly held educational and interpretive programs. Dogs are allowed on the beach, grounds and trails; they are not allowed in the fort or park buildings. Dogs must be under owner's control, on no more than a 6 foot leash, and cleaned up after at all times.
Cape Lookout National Seashore Harkers Island Road Harkers Island NC   252-728-2250
www.nps.gov/calo
Accessible by boat or ferry only, this park consists of 56 miles of beaches covering 4 barrier islands, and dogs are allowed on the beaches here. They must be leashed and cleaned up after at all times. They suggest bringing fresh water for pets as there is little shade on the island and dogs are not allowed in buildings. Dogs may not be left alone at any time.

Cedar Island

Transportation Systems
North Carolina Ferry-Cedar Island H 12 Cedar Island NC   800-BY FERRY (293-3779)
These vehicle and passenger transport ferries are run by the state and provide service every day of the year on all routes; however weather conditions can influence travel. Dogs are allowed on all ferries for no additional fee; they must be kept in the vehicle or leashed when out of the vehicle. Dogs must be under owner's control/care at all times.

Cedar Mountain

Campgrounds and RV Parks
Black Forest Family Camping Resort 100 Summer Road Cedar Mountain NC   828-884-2267
http://www.blackforestcampground.com
Dogs of all sizes are allowed. There are no additional pet fees. Dogs must be leashed and cleaned up after. This RV park is closed during the off-season. The camping and tent areas also allow dogs. There is a dog walk area at the campground.

Chapel Hill

Accommodations
Holiday Inn 1301 N Fordham Blvd Chapel Hill NC   919-929-2171 (877-270-6405)
Dogs of all sizes are allowed for an additional one time pet fee of $35 per room.

Attractions
Historic Chapel Hill 610 E Rosemary Street Chapel Hill NC   919-942-7818
http://www.chapelhillpreservation.com
The Preservation Society of Chapel Hill was founded in 1972 to protect the atmosphere of Chapel Hill by preserving its historic, natural and man-made landmarks. Dogs are not allowed on the guided tours to homes, but there is a short self guided walking tour around the Horace Williams house, and on Franklin Street to downtown. Dogs must be on leash. Get a brochure at the address above before you begin the walk.
The North Carolina Botanical Garden Old Mason Farm Road Chapel Hill NC   919-962-0522
http://www.ncbg.unc.edu/
A branch of the University of North Carolina at Chapel Hill, this botanical garden offers nature trails, natural areas, display gardens, and an information center. Friendly dogs are welcome on the trails and in several other areas; they are not allowed inside fenced garden areas. A pail of water and a pet tie-up post is provided for those wanting to enter these areas. Dogs must be leashed and under owner's control/care.

Outdoor Restaurants
Patio Loco Mexican Grill 407 West Franklin St Chapel Hill NC   919-967-9060
This restaurant serves Mexican food. Dogs are allowed at the outdoor tables.
The Cave 452 1/2 Franklin Street Chapel Hill NC   919-968-9308
http://www.caverntavern.com
Dogs on leash are allowed in this bar and music club. Open 7 days 2:30pm-2:am. Serves beer only. Check website for music events.

Charlotte

Accommodations
Candlewood Suites 5840 Westpark Drive Charlotte NC   704-529-7500 (877-270-6405)
Dogs up to 60 pounds are allowed for an additional one time fee of $75 per pet.
Candlewood Suites 8812 University East Drive Charlotte NC   704-598-9863 (877-270-6405)
Dogs of all sizes are allowed for an additional one time fee of $75 per pet.
Comfort Inn Executive Park 5822 Westpark Drive Charlotte NC   704-525-2626 (877-424-6423)
Dogs are allowed for an additional one time fee of $25 per pet.
Comfort Inn UNCC 5111 Equipment Drive Charlotte NC   704-598-0007 (877-424-6423)
Well groomed dogs are allowed for an additional fee of $20 (plus tax) per night per pet.
Comfort Suites 7735 University City Blvd Charlotte NC   704-547-0049 (877-424-6423)
Dogs are allowed for an additional one time pet fee of $25 per room.
Crowne Plaza Hotel Crowne Plaza Charlotte 201 South Mcdowell St. Charlotte NC   704-372-7550 (877-270-6405)
Dogs of all sizes are allowed for an additional one time pet fee of $50 per room.
Days Inn Charlotte Central 601 N Tryon Charlotte NC   704-333-4733 (800-329-7466)

Dogs of all sizes are allowed. There is a $10 per night pet fee per pet. Reservations are recommended due to limited rooms for pets.
Days Inn Charlotte North 1408 W Sugar Creek Rd Charlotte NC   704-597-8110 (800-329-7466)
Dogs of all sizes are allowed. There is a $5.38 per night pet fee per pet.
Drury Inn & Suites 415 West W.T. Harris Blvd. Charlotte NC   704-593-0700 (800-378-7946)
Dogs of all sizes are permitted. Pets are not allowed in the breakfast area of the hotel. Pets are not to be left unattended, and each guest must assume liability for damage of property or other guest complaints. There is a limit of one pet per room.
Holiday Inn 321 W Woodlawn Road Charlotte NC   704-523-1400 (877-270-6405)
Dogs of all sizes are allowed for an additional one time pet fee of $35 per room.
La Quinta Inn & Suites Charlotte Airport South 4900 S. Tryon Street Charlotte NC   704-523-5599 (800-531-5900)
Dogs of all sizes are allowed. There are no additional pet fees. Dogs must be leashed and cleaned up after. Dogs may not be left unattended unless they will be quiet, well behaved, and a contact number left with the front desk.
La Quinta Inn Charlotte Airport 3100 Queen City Drive Charlotte NC   704-393-5306 (800-531-5900)
Dogs of all sizes are allowed. There are no additional pet fees. Dogs must be leashed, cleaned up after, and the Do Not Disturb sign left on the door if there is a pet alone in the room.
Motel 6 - Charlotte Coliseum 131 Red Roof Drive Charlotte NC   704-529-1020 (800-466-8356)
One well-behaved family pet per room. Guest must notify front desk upon arrival. Guest is liable for any damages. In consideration of all guests, pets must never be left unattended in the guest rooms.
Motel 6 - Charlotte East University 5116 North I-85 Charlotte NC   704-596-8222 (800-466-8356)
One well-behaved family pet per room. Guest must notify front desk upon arrival. Guest is liable for any damages. In consideration of all guests, pets must never be left unattended in the guest rooms.
Quality Inn 440 Griffith Road Charlotte NC   704-525-0747 (877-424-6423)
Dogs are allowed for an additional one time pet fee of $35 per room.
Red Roof Inn - Charlotte - Huntersville 13830 Statesville Road Charlotte NC   704-875-7880 (800-RED-ROOF)
One well-behaved family pet per room. Guest must notify front desk upon arrival. Guest is liable for any damages. In consideration of all guests, pets must never be left unattended in the guest rooms.
Red Roof Inn - Charlotte Airport (West) 3300 Queen City Drive Charlotte NC   704-392-2316 (800-RED-ROOF)
One well-behaved family pet per room. Guest must notify front desk upon arrival. Guest is liable for any damages. In consideration of all guests, pets must never be left unattended in the guest rooms.
Residence Inn by Marriott 5115 Piper Station Drive Charlotte NC   704-319-3900
One dog up to 85 pounds is allowed. There is a $75 one time fee and a pet policy to sign at check in. Per city ordinance, no Rottweilers or Pit Bulls are allowed.
Residence Inn by Marriott 6030 J.A. Jones Drive Charlotte NC   704-554-7001
Dogs of all sizes are allowed. There is a $75 one time fee and a pet policy to sign at check in.
Residence Inn by Marriott 8503 N Tryon Street Charlotte NC   704-547-1122
Dogs of all sizes are allowed. There is a $75 one time fee and a pet policy to sign at check in.
Residence Inn by Marriott 404 S Mint Street Charlotte NC   704-340-4000
Dogs of all sizes are allowed. There is a $75 one time fee and a pet policy to sign at check in.
Sheraton Charlotte Airport Hotel 3315 Scott Futkell Dr. Charlotte NC   704-392-1200 (888-625-5144)
Dogs of all sizes are allowed. There are no additional pet fees.
Staybridge Suites 15735 John J Delaney Drive Charlotte NC   704-248-5000 (877-270-6405)
Dogs of all sizes are allowed for an additional one time pet fee per room of $100 for 1 or 2 nights; 3 or more nights is $200.
Staybridge Suites 7924 Forest Pine Drive Charlotte NC   704-527-6767 (877-270-6405)
Dogs of all sizes are allowed for an additional one time pet fee of $100 per room.
Studio 6 - Charlotte Airport 3420 Queen City Drive Charlotte NC   704-394-4993 (800-466-8356)
One well-behaved family pet per room. Guest must notify front desk upon arrival. Guest is liable for any damages. In consideration of all guests, pets must never be left unattended in the guest rooms.
Summerfield Suites 4920 S Tryon Street Charlotte NC   704-525-2600
Dogs of all sizes are allowed. There is a $75 one time per room additional pet fee. Pet rooms are located on the first floor.
Super 8 Charlotte/Sunset Road 4930 Sunset Road Charlotte NC   704-598-7710 (800-800-8000)
Dogs of all sizes are allowed. There is a $10 per night pet fee per pet. Smoking and non-smoking rooms are available for pet rooms.
The Westin Charlotte 601 South College St. Charlotte NC   704-375-2600 (888-625-5144)
Dogs up to 50 pounds are allowed for no additional pet fee. A contact number must be left with the front desk if a pet is in the room alone.
TownePlace Suites Charlotte Arrowood 7805 Forest Point Blvd Charlotte NC   704-227-2000
Dogs of all sizes are allowed. There is a $75 one time pet fee per visit.
TownePlace Suites Charlotte University Research Park 8710 Research Drive Charlotte NC   704-548-0388

Dogs of all sizes are allowed. There is a $75 one time pet fee per visit.
Days Inn Concord 5125 Davidson Hwy Concord NC   704-786-9121 (800-329-7466)
Dogs of all sizes are allowed. There is a $10 per night pet fee per pet.
Super 8 Concord 1601 US 29 North Concord NC   704-786-5181 (800-800-8000)
Dogs of all sizes are allowed. There is a $1 per pound fee per pet. Smoking and non-smoking rooms are available for pet rooms.
Holiday Inn Express Gastonia 1911 Broadcast Drive Gastonia NC   704-884-3300 (877-270-6405)
Dogs of all sizes are allowed for an additional fee of $10 per night per pet. Dogs may not be left alone in the room at any time.
Motel 6 - Gastonia 1721 Broadcast Street Gastonia NC   704-868-4900 (800-466-8356)
One well-behaved family pet per room. Guest must notify front desk upon arrival. Guest is liable for any damages. In consideration of all guests, pets must never be left unattended in the guest rooms.
Country Inns & Suites by Carlson 2001 Mount Harmony Church Rd Matthews NC   704-846-8000
Dogs of all sizes are allowed. There is a $5 per day additional pet fee.
Holiday Inn Express Monroe 608 E. West Roosevelt Blvd Monroe NC   704-289-1555 (877-270-6405)
Dogs of all sizes are allowed for an additional fee of $10 per night per pet.
Motel 6 - Monroe 350 Venus Street Monroe NC   704-289-9111 (800-466-8356)
One well-behaved family pet per room. Guest must notify front desk upon arrival. Guest is liable for any damages. In consideration of all guests, pets must never be left unattended in the guest rooms.

Campgrounds and RV Parks

Carowinds Camp Wilderness Resort 14523 Carowinds Blvd Charlotte NC   704-588-2600 (800-888-4386)
In addition to being located at a major amusement park, this campground offers a number of amenities including WiFi, a pool, gaming areas, a laundry, free shuttle to the park, and more. Dogs are allowed for no additional pet fee. Dogs are allowed in tents and there is a dog walk area.
McDowell Nature Preserve Campground 15222 York Road Charlotte NC   704-583-1284
In addition to providing a number of exhibits and environment/educational programs about this 108 acre preserve, they also offer a variety of land and water recreation, a gift shop, gardens, hiking trails, and more. Dogs are allowed for no additional fee. Dogs may not be left unattended outside at any time, and they must be kept leashed and cleaned up after. The camp area offers picnic areas and restrooms. The camping and tent areas also allow dogs. There is a dog walk area at the campground.
Fleetwood RV Racing Camping Resort 6600 Speedway Blvd Concord NC   704-455-4445
http://www.rvingusa.com
Dogs of all sizes are allowed. There are no additional pet fees. Dogs may not be left unattended outside, and they must be leashed and cleaned up after. There is a dog walk area at the campground.
Charlotte/Fort Mill KOA 940 Gold Hill Road Fort Mill NC   803-548-1148 (888-562-4430)
http://www.charlottekoa.com
Dogs of all sizes are allowed. There are no additional pet fees. Dogs may not be left unattended, and they must be leashed and cleaned up after. The camping and tent areas also allow dogs. There is a dog walk area at the campground.

Attractions

Carolinas Aviation Museum Carolinas Aviation Museum Charlotte NC   704-359-8442
http://www.carolinasaviation.org/
Dedicated to obtaining, preserving, and educating visitors about the aviation history of the Carolinas, this museum has amassed an impressive collection of aircraft, aviation artifacts, and one of the nations largest aviation libraries. Dogs are allowed on site and in the hangers; they are not allowed in the main museum. Dogs must be leashed and under owner's control/care.
Carowinds Theme Park Kennels 14523 Carowinds Park Road Charlotte NC   803-548-5300
http://carowinds.com/#actions
This 112 acre amusement park has the scope on recreation with thrill rides, a 20 acre water park, ongoing entertainment, over 30 eateries, a Nickelodeon play area, and a lot more. Although dogs are not allowed in the park, they do provide secured dog kennels on a first come first served basis for $10 per day per pet. Dogs must be current on license and shots, be well mannered, and leashed when not kenneled. Owners should bring food and water, dishes, and any other comfort supplies. There is also a campground on site where pets are allowed for no additional pet fee.
Charlotte Knights-Dog Day Game Gold Hill Road (Exit 88 off I-77) Fort Mill SC   704-357-8071
Once a year, the Charlotte Knights minor league baseball team invites four-legged fans to attend their Dog Day Game. This dog-friendly game is usually in August. Dogs are welcome to sit with their owners at any seat throughout the ballpark. If your pooch is itching to walk around, dogs are also welcome on the concourse. Just remember to clean up after your pooch!
Reed Gold Mine State Historic Site 9621 Reed Mine Road Midland NC   704-721-4653
Home to the first documented find of gold in America, this reconstructed 1890's stamp mill and refurbished gold

mine offer visitors on-hands experience and a glimpse into the history and progression of their gold mining history. Leashed dogs are allowed on the grounds; they are not allowed in any buildings or in the mine.
Hanging Rock River Trips 3466 Moores Spring Road Westfield NC 336-593-8283
http://www.hroconline.com/index.html
This company offers full and half day river adventures in canoes or kayaks. Your kids and dogs are welcome to join you. Be sure to bring a leash. They are open Wednesday through Sunday in early March to late November. It is about a one hour drive from Charlotte, NC.

Stores
Barbara's Canine Cafe and Catering 1447 S Tryon Street Charlotte NC 704-LUV-DOGS (588-3647)
http://www.k9treat.com/
This dog boutique features a good variety of fresh, daily baked treats that include such items as a puppy pizza, or specialty items like birthday cakes, or even a Muttgaritta. They also carry an assortment of toys, diningware, apparel, accessories, bedding, hygiene/health items, and gift baskets. Your well mannered, leashed, dog is allowed to explore the shop with you, or you can bring your own lunch and sit out front on the patio while your pet enjoys their treats. They are open Monday through Friday from 11 am to 6pm; Saturday from 10 am to 5 pm, and Sunday from 1 to 5 pm. Please clean up after your pet.
PetSmart Pet Store 5401 S Blvd Ste 14 Charlotte NC 704-523-0132
Your licensed and well-behaved leashed dog is allowed in the store.
PetSmart Pet Store 8116 University City Blvd Charlotte NC 704-599-3989
Your licensed and well-behaved leashed dog is allowed in the store.
Petco Pet Store 9515 South Blvd Charlotte NC 704-552-0515
Your licensed and well-behaved leashed dog is allowed in the store.
Petco Pet Store 8070 Concord Mills Blvd Concord NC 704-979-1952
Your licensed and well-behaved leashed dog is allowed in the store.
PetSmart Pet Store 3698 E Franklin Gastonia NC 704-824-5010
Your licensed and well-behaved leashed dog is allowed in the store.
PetSmart Pet Store 1815 Windsor Square Dr Matthews NC 704-845-5844
Your licensed and well-behaved leashed dog is allowed in the store.
PetSmart Pet Store 2875 West Highway 74 Monroe NC 704-225-9447
Your licensed and well-behaved leashed dog is allowed in the store.
PetSmart Pet Store 10200 Centrum Pkwy Pineville NC 704-543-1307
Your licensed and well-behaved leashed dog is allowed in the store.

Parks
Freedom Park 1900 East Boulevard Charlotte NC 704-336-2884
http://www.parkandrec.com
This is a popular park complete with athletic fields, tennis and basketball courts, playgrounds, a 7 acre lake, picnic shelters, concessions, and paved trails. Pets must be leashed and under your control at all times. From this park, you can begin the Lower Little Sugar Creek Trail (1.3 mile trail).
Lower Little Sugar Creek Trail 1900 East Boulevard Charlotte NC 704-336-3854
http://www.parkandrec.com
Take your pooch out for some exercise on this 1.3 mile paved trail. Pets must be leashed and under your control at all times. Use the parking lot at Freedom Park and begin your walk.
Mallard and Clark's Creek Greenway 9801 Mallard Creek Road Charlotte NC 704-336-8866
http://www.parkandrec.com
Go for a walk or jog with your dog on this 3.6 mile paved trail. Pets must be leashed and under your control at all times. Parking is available at the Mallard Creek Elementary School, off Mallard Creek Road.
McAlpine Creek Greenway 8711 Monroe Road Charlotte NC 704-568-4044
http://www.parkandrec.com
You can go for a nice long walk with your dog at this trail system which offers over 8 miles of paved and gravel trails. Pets must be leashed and under your control at all times. There are many starting points, but you can park at either the McAlpine Creek Park (has a 5K championship cross country course) located at 8711 Monroe Road or the James Boyce Park located at 300 Boyce Road.
McDowell Nature Preserve Campground 15222 York Road Charlotte NC 704-583-1284
In addition to providing a number of exhibits and environment/educational programs about this 108 acre preserve, they also offer a variety of land and water recreation, a gift shop, gardens, hiking trails, and more. Dogs are allowed for no additional fee. Dogs may not be left unattended outside at any time, and they must be kept leashed and cleaned up after.
Upper Little Sugar Creek Trail 2100 North Davidson Street Charlotte NC 704-336-3367
http://www.parkandrec.com
Go for a walk on this 1.1 mile trail which joins Cordelia Park and Alexander Park. Pets must be leashed and under your control at all times. You can begin your walk at the parking lot in Cordelia Park.

McMullen Creek Greenway Pineville-Matthews Road Pineville NC   704-643-3405
http://www.parkandrec.com
Enjoy a stroll with your pooch on this 1.5 mile paved and gravel trail. Pets must be leashed and under your control at all times. The parking lot as well as a picnic area is located off Pineville-Matthews Road (across from the McMullen Creek Marketplace.)

Off-Leash Dog Parks
Barkingham Park Dog Park - Reedy Creek 2900 Rocky River Rd. Charlotte NC   704-336-3854
http://www.fidocarolina.org/
Reedy Creek Dog Park opened in the Summer of 2003. It consists of 4 acres. The park has an off-leash dog park. Charlotte Dog Parks require a annual pooch pass which you can get by signing a liability form. Currently the fee is $35 per year for a pooch pass. More information is available from FidoCarolina at http://www.fidocarolina.org.
Fetching Meadows Dog Park McAlpine Park Charlotte NC   704-336-3854
http://www.fidocarolina.org/
Fetching Meadows Dog Park opened in late 2002. Charlotte Dog Parks require a annual pooch pass which you can get by signing a liability form. Currently the fee is $35 per year for a pooch pass. More information is available from FidoCarolina at http://www.fidocarolina.org.

Outdoor Restaurants
Burgers & Bagels 4327 Park Road Bldg 25 Charlotte NC   704-525-5295
Dogs on leash are allowed at the outdoor tables.
Burgers on East Blvd 1531 East Blvd Charlotte NC   704-332-5991
Dogs on leash are allowed at the outdoor tables. The restaurant has outdoor tables only in the Summer.
TOP 200 PLACE Dog Bar NoDa 3307 N Davidson Street Charlotte NC   704-370-3595
http://www.dogbarnoda.com/
Dogs of all shapes and sizes are welcome at this unique, beer, wine, and liquor bar. In addition to being able to hang out at the bar with your pet, they offer special events for dog lovers, free doggy biscuits, and in the warmer months they rent out the Dog Bar for social events, and dog birthday or adoption parties. In the Summer they are closed Mon. and Tue., and open Wed. and Thurs. from 4pm - 11pm, Fri. 4pm - 2am, Sat. 3pm - 2am, and Sun 3pm - 10pm. In the Winter the bar is open on Wed. and Thurs. 7 - 11 pm, Fri and Sat 7 - 2 am, and Sunday from 1 - 10. Dogs must be well behaved, friendly, and have a current rabies certificate (either tags or show papers to staff). Dogs may be leashed or off-leash. They must be cleaned up after; they provide a scooper on the side of the building. While on the Dog Bar premises, owners are solely responsible for their pet.
Fuel Pizza 214 N Tryon Charlotte NC   704-350-1680
Dogs are allowed at the outdoor tables. The restaurant has outdoor tables only in the Summer.
Fuel Pizza 1501 Central Avenue Charlotte NC   704-376-3835
Dogs on leash are allowed at the outdoor tables.
Fuel on the Green 500 S College Street Charlotte NC   704-370-2755
Dogs are allowed at the outdoor tables. The restaurant has outdoor tables only in the Summer.
Jackalope Jack's 1936 E 7th Street Charlotte NC   704-347-1918
This restaurant and bar serves American food. Dogs are allowed at the outdoor tables.
Moe's Southwest Grill 1500 East Blvd. Charlotte NC   704-377-6344
http://www.moessouthwestgrill.com/
Food here is fresh and made from scratch. Burritos, quesadillas, fajitas, margaritas and more are all on the menu. Well-behaved dogs are allowed at the outdoor tables.
Rudino's Pizza and Grinders 2000 South Blvd Charlotte NC   704-333-3124
http://www.rudinospizza.com/
This family pizzeria offers a pizza buffet, calzones, salads, a fresh baked bread sandwich full of meats and cheeses called a Grinder, and more; they also have a nice patio dining area. Dogs are allowed at the outside tables; they must be leashed and under owner's control/care at all times.
Smelly Cat Coffee House 514 E 36th Street Charlotte NC   704-374-9656
http://www.smellycatcoffee.com/
This coffee bar offers outside seating; dogs are allowed at the outer tables. They must be under owner's control/care at all times.
Starbucks 1401 East Blvd Charlotte NC   704-338-9911
Dogs on leash are allowed at the outdoor tables.
Thomas Street Tavern 1218 Thomas Ave. Charlotte NC   704-376-1622
Your dog is welcome to join you at the tables on the front patio.
Wing Stop 7629 Pineville-Matthews Rd Charlotte NC   704-540-8311
This restaurant serves bbq. Dogs are allowed at the outdoor tables. Water is provided for your pet.
Wolfman Pizza 8418 Park Rd Charlotte NC   704-552-4979
This restaurant serves Pizza and more. Dogs are allowed at the outdoor tables.

Cherokee - Smoky Mountain NP

Accommodations
Mountain Vista Log Cabins 300 Fernwood Drive Bryson City NC   828-508-4391 (888-508-4838)
Dogs of all sizes are allowed. There is a $45 one time additional pet fee per cabin.
Days Inn Franklin 1320 East Main St Franklin NC   828-524-6491 (800-329-7466)
Dogs of all sizes are allowed. There is a $15 per three nights pet fee per pet.
Maggie Mountain 60 Twin Hickory Maggie Valley NC   828-926-4258
Dogs of all sizes are allowed. There is a $10 per night fee for one pet and $5 per night for each additional pet.

Campgrounds and RV Parks
Moonshine Creek Campground 27 Moonshine Creek Trail Balsam NC   828-586-6666
http://www.moonshinecreekcampground.com
Dogs of all sizes are allowed. There are no additional pet fees. Dogs must be leashed and cleaned up after. This
RV park is closed during the off-season. The camping and tent areas also allow dogs. There is a dog walk area
at the campground.
Cherokee/Great Smokies KOA 92 KOA Campground Road Cherokee NC   828-497-9711 (800-562-7784)
http://www.cherokeekoa.com
Dogs of all sizes are allowed. There are no additional pet fees. Dogs may not be left unattended, and they must
be leashed and cleaned up after. The camping and tent areas also allow dogs. There is a dog walk area at the
campground. Dogs are allowed in the camping cabins.
Yogi in the Smokies 317 Galamore Bridge Road Cherokee NC   828-497-9151 (877-716-6711)
http://www.jellystone-cherokee.com
Dogs of all sizes are allowed. There are no additional pet fees. Dogs may not be left unattended, must be quiet,
leashed, and cleaned up after. This RV park is closed during the off-season. The camping and tent areas also
allow dogs. There is a dog walk area at the campground.
Mount Pisgah Campground Blue Ride Parkway Milepost 408.6 Waynesville NC   828-648-2644 (877-444-6777)
http://www.blueridgeparkway.org/
Once part of the Vanderbilt estate, this camp area offers seclusion, the highest and coolest location on the
Parkway, an interesting example of a southern Appalachian bog and its ecosystems, an extensive trail system,
and outstanding views. Dogs are allowed throughout the park and on the trails. Dogs must be well behaved,
under owner's control, on no more than a 6 foot leash, and cleaned up after at all times. This RV park is closed
during the off-season. The camping and tent areas also allow dogs. There is a dog walk area at the campground.
There are no electric or water hookups at the campgrounds.

Attractions
TOP 200 PLACE **Oconaluftee Cherokee Indian Village** 498 Tsali Blvd. Cherokee NC   828-497-2315
http://www.cherokee-nc.com/index.php?page=17
This original 1750's Indian village and grounds are dedicated to living and passing on of the Cherokee's
ancestral ways. This region is home to the world's oldest mountains, rich with lush greenery, colorful each Spring
with explosion of wildflowers, and numerous waterways, Dogs are allowed on the grounds; they are not allowed
in buildings, and they must be under owner's control/care at all times.
Smoky Mountain Gold and Ruby Mine H 441 North Cherokee NC   828-497-6574
http://www.smgrm.com/contact.asp
Open from March to November, this mining area allows free admission, equipment, and identification of any
gemstones found such as rubies, garnets, sapphires, emeralds, amethysts, and more; they will also polish and
mount treasures found for a fee. Dogs are allowed throughout the property; they must be well mannered, and
under owner's control/care at all times.
Gold City Gem Mine 9410 Sylva Road Franklin NC   828-369-3905
At this popular mine guests can mine for both native and enriched gemstones, and then have them identified on
site for free. They also provide professional cutting and setting services and sell gems. Dogs are allowed on the
grounds. Dogs must be well behaved, under owner's control at all times, leashed, and cleaned up after at all
times.

Parks
Nantahala National Forest various Asheville NC   828-257-4200
http://www.cs.unca.edu/nfsnc/
The forest offers miles of dog-friendly hiking trails. It is located about 2 hours from the Great Smoky Mountains

National Park.

Creswell

Campgrounds and RV Parks
Pettigrew State Park 2252 Lake Shore Road Creswell NC   252-797-4475
There are over 1,200 land acres with 16,000 acres of water at this scenic park that offers a rich natural history, a wide variety of recreational and educational activities, and several great hiking trails. Dogs are welcome for no additional fee throughout the park, on the trails, and in the camp area. Campsite are first come first served, and each site has a picnic table and grill with seasonally provided restrooms, showers, and water. The camping and tent areas also allow dogs. There is a dog walk area at the campground. There are no electric or water hookups at the campgrounds.

Parks
Pettigrew State Park 2252 Lake Shore Road Creswell NC   252-797-4475
There are over 1,200 land acres with 16,000 acres of water at this scenic park that offers a rich natural history, a wide variety of recreational and educational activities, and several great hiking trails. Dogs are welcome for no additional fee throughout the park, on the trails, and in the camp area.

Currie

Attractions
Moores Creek Bridge 40 Patriots Hall Drive Currie NC   910-283-5591
http://www.nps.gov/mocr
The battle at this historic bridge site resulted in a 1776 victory for freedom from English rule. The park offers exhibits, reenactments, special events, educational interpretations, a .3 mile colonial forest trail, and a picnic ground. Dogs are allowed throughout the park and on the bridge. Dogs must be leashed and cleaned up after at all times.

Dunn

Accommodations
The Ramada Inn 1011 E Cumberland Street Dunn NC   910-892-8010
Dogs of all sizes are allowed. There is a $15 per night per pet additional fee and they state this amount is flexible depending on how long and type of dog.

Durham

Accommodations
Best Western Skyland Inn 5400 US Hwy 70 West Durham NC   919-383-2508 (800-780-7234)
Dogs are allowed for an additional fee of $10 per night per pet.
Candlewood Suites 1818 E Highway 54 Durham NC   919-484-9922 (877-270-6405)
One dog of any size is allowed for an additional pet fee of $75 for 1 to 14 days, and 15 or more days is $125.
Comfort Inn University 3508 Moriah Road Durham NC   919-490-4949 (877-424-6423)
Dogs up to 60 pounds are allowed for no additional pet fee unless a pet amenity kit is requested for $49 per pet.
Holiday Inn Express Durham 2516 Guess Road Durham NC   919-313-3244 (877-270-6405)
Dogs up to 50 pounds are allowed for an additional fee of $10 per night per pet.
Holiday Inn Express Hotel & Suites Research Triangle Park 4912 South Miami Blvd Durham NC   919-474-9800 (877-270-6405)
Dogs up to 50 pounds are allowed for an additional fee of $25 per night per pet.
La Quinta Inn & Suites Durham Chapel Hill 4414 Durham Chapel Hill Blvd. Durham NC   919-401-9660 (800-531-5900)

Dogs of all sizes are allowed. There are no additional pet fees. Dogs must be leashed and cleaned up after. Dogs may not be left unattended, and they are not allowed in the lobby or the pool area.
Red Roof Inn - Chapel Hill 5623 Durham-Chapel Hill Boulevard Durham NC   919-489-9421 (800-RED-ROOF)
One well-behaved family pet per room. Guest must notify front desk upon arrival. Guest is liable for any damages. In consideration of all guests, pets must never be left unattended in the guest rooms.
Red Roof Inn - Durham - Duke University Medical Center 1915 North Pointe Drive Durham NC   919-471-9882 (800-RED-ROOF)
One well-behaved family pet per room. Guest must notify front desk upon arrival. Guest is liable for any damages. In consideration of all guests, pets must never be left unattended in the guest rooms.
Red Roof Inn - Durham Triangle Park 4405 APEX Highway 55 East Durham NC   919-361-1950 (800-RED-ROOF)
One well-behaved family pet per room. Guest must notify front desk upon arrival. Guest is liable for any damages. In consideration of all guests, pets must never be left unattended in the guest rooms.
Residence Inn by Marriott 201Residence Inn Blvd Durham NC   919-361-1266
Dogs of all sizes are welcome. There is a $75 one time fee and a pet policy to sign at check in.
Sleep Inn 5208 New Page Road Durham NC   919-993-3393 (877-424-6423)
A dog up to 60 pounds is allowed for no additional pet fee.
Super 8 Durham/University Area 2337 Guess Rd Durham NC   919-286-7746 (800-800-8000)
Dogs of all sizes are allowed. There is a $6 per night pet fee per pet. Smoking and non-smoking rooms are available for pet rooms.

Attractions
Duke Homestead 2828 Duke Homestead Road Durham NC   919-477-5498
The Duke Homestead is a museum of the tobacco industry. They are open Tuesday through Saturday from 10:00 a.m. to 4:00 p.m. Dogs are allowed anywhere on the grounds and on the guided outdoor tours, but they are not allowed in any of the buildings.
Duke University Duke University Road Durham NC   919-684-3701
http://www.duke.edu/
Among the lush greenery and gardens of the beautiful campus visitors will find many attractions, educational and recreational events, walking paths, historical sites, and more. Dogs are allowed on campus; they must be well behaved, under owner's control, leashed, and cleaned up after at all times.
Durham Downtown Walking Tour 101 East Morgan Street Durham NC   919-687-0288
http://www.durham-nc.com/
In addition to being the state's first commercial district (now listed on the National Register of Historic Places) this area is home to a number of historic and noteworthy sites. Self guided tour maps can be obtained at the visitor center or at several of the local hotels. Dogs are not allowed in buildings, and they must be leashed and cleaned up after at all times.

Stores
Petco Pet Store 8200 Renaissance Pkwy Durham NC   919-572-9638
Your licensed and well-behaved leashed dog is allowed in the store.
Petco Pet Store 4011 Durham Chapel Hill Blvd Durham NC   919-401-2464
Your licensed and well-behaved leashed dog is allowed in the store.
PetSmart Pet Store 3615 Witherspoon Blvd Durham NC   919-403-6902
Your licensed and well-behaved leashed dog is allowed in the store.
PetSmart Pet Store 1720 N Pointe Dr North Durham NC   919-471-6474
Your licensed and well-behaved leashed dog is allowed in the store.

Parks
Duke University Forest W Main Street/H 70 Durham NC   919-613-8013
http://www.env.duke.edu/forest/
Dedicated to the management, resources, ecological and environmental sciences, the 7,000+ acre Duke University Forest is unequaled by any other university as an outdoor forest laboratory, and there are a number of recreational pursuits allowed here as well. There are six sections to the forest with 45 separate entrances. Dogs are allowed in the forest and on all the trails; they must be well behaved, under owner's control, leashed, and cleaned up after at all times.
Sarah P. Duke Gardens 426 Anderson Street Durham NC   919-684-3698
http://www.hr.duke.edu/dukegardens/
Recognized as one of the country's premier public gardens, this 55 acre site, located on Duke's University West campus, is world renowned for its design, diversity, quality, and for its stunning and inspiring beauty. Dogs are allowed on campus and in the garden; they must be well behaved, under owner's control, leashed, and cleaned up after at all times.

Outdoor Restaurants

Panzanella 200 Greensboro Street Carrboro NC   919-929-6626
http://www.panzanella.com/
This Italian eatery offers all the extras plus outside dining, weather permitting. Dogs are allowed at the outer tables; they must be under owner control/care at all times.
The Cafe at Weaver Street Market 101 E Weaver Street Carrboro NC   919-929-0010
Well behaved pooches and their owners are welcome at the outer tables of this eatery, weather permitting. Dogs must be under owner's control/care at all times.
Cosmic Cantina 1920 Perry Street Durham NC   919-286-1875
This eatery offers Mexican food favorites, vegetarian options, a lounge, and outside seating-weather permitting. Dogs are allowed at the outer tables; they must be under owner's control/care at all times.
Grayson's Cafe 2300 Chapel Hill Road Durham NC   919-403-9220
http://www.graysonscafe.com/index.html
Serving breakfast and lunch favorites, this eatery also specializes in catering and Take-out and offer alfresco dining. Dogs are allowed at the outer tables; they must be under owner's control/care and leashed at all times.
Oh! Brians 4818 H 55 Durham NC   919-484-1742
http://www.ohbrians.com/
Burgers, ribs, steaks and seafood are some of the specialties at the lunch and dinner eatery. Dogs are allowed at the outer tables (weather permitting). They must be under owner's control/care at all times.
The Original Q Shack 2510 University Drive Durham NC   919-402-4227
http://www.theqshackoriginal.com/
Offering their special in-house smoked meats with a tasty list of accompaniments, this barbecue shack also has take out and offer "Tailgate Specials" to go, plus catering, and a patio with picnic tables/benches. Well behaved dogs are allowed at the outside tables; they must be leashed and under owner's control/care at all times.

Elizabeth City

Accommodations

Quality Inn 522 S Hughes Blvd Elizabeth City NC   252-338-3951 (877-424-6423)
Dogs are allowed for an additional one time pet fee of $25 per room for the first night, and $10 for each additional night.

Elizabethtown

Campgrounds and RV Parks

Jones Lake State Park 4117 H 242N Elizabethtown NC   910-588-4550
This 2,208-acre park is a nature lover's delight, and offers educational and interpretive programs as well as a variety of trails and recreational pursuits. Dogs of all sizes are allowed at no additional fee. Dogs may not be left unattended, and they must be on no more than a 6 foot leash, and cleaned up after. Dogs are not allowed in swim areas, however they are allowed on the trails. There is only one site that has an electric hook-ups. The camping and tent areas also allow dogs. There is a dog walk area at the campground. With the exception of one site there are no electric or water hookups at the campground.

Enfield

Campgrounds and RV Parks

Enfield/Rocky Mount KOA 101 Bell Acres Enfield NC   252-445-5925 (800-562-5894)
http://www.koa.com
Dogs of all sizes are allowed, and there are no additional pet fees for tent or RV sites. There is a $2 per night per pet additional fee for the cabins. Dogs may not be left unattended in the cabins or outside, and they must be leashed and cleaned up after. There are some breed restrictions. The camping and tent areas also allow dogs. There is a dog walk area at the campground. Dogs are allowed in the camping cabins.

Fayetteville

Accommodations
Best Western Fayetteville-Ft Bragg 2910 Sigman St Fayetteville NC   910-485-0520 (800-780-7234)
Dogs are allowed for an additional fee of $15 per pet for each 1 to 3 nights stay.
Comfort Inn 1957 Cedar Creek Road Fayetteville NC   910-323-8333 (877-424-6423)
Dogs are allowed for an additional fee of $10 per night per pet.
Comfort Inn Cross Creek 1922 Skibo Road Fayetteville NC   910-867-1777 (877-424-6423)
Dogs up to 50 pounds are allowed for an additional one time pet fee of $49 per room.
Days Inn Fayetteville East of Ft Bragg 333 Person St Fayetteville NC   910-483-0431 (800-329-7466)
Dogs of all sizes are allowed. There is a $15 per night pet fee per pet.
Holiday Inn 1944 Cedar Creek Rd Fayetteville NC   910-323-1600 (877-270-6405)
Dogs of all sizes are allowed for an additional one time pet fee of $25 per room.
Motel 6 - Fayetteville 2076 Cedar Creek Road Fayetteville NC   910-485-8122 (800-466-8356)
One well-behaved family pet per room. Guest must notify front desk upon arrival. Guest is liable for any damages. In consideration of all guests, pets must never be left unattended in the guest rooms.
Red Roof Inn - Fayetteville, NC 1569 Jim Johnson Road Fayetteville NC   910-321-1460 (800-RED-ROOF)
One well-behaved family pet per room. Guest must notify front desk upon arrival. Guest is liable for any damages. In consideration of all guests, pets must never be left unattended in the guest rooms.
Days Inn Raeford 115 Fayetteville Rd/115 US 401 Byp Raeford NC   910-904-1050 (800-329-7466)
Dogs of all sizes are allowed. There is a $7 per night pet fee per pet. Reservations are recommended due to limited rooms for pets.
Holiday Inn Express Hotel and Suites 103 Brook Lane Spring Lake NC   910-436-1900 (877-270-6405)
Dogs of all sizes are allowed; 1 dogs is a $65 one time additional fee; a 2nd dog would be an additional one time fee of $15.
Days Inn Fayetteville North 3945 Goldsboro Hwy Wade NC   910-323-1255 (800-329-7466)
Dogs of all sizes are allowed. There is a $6 per night pet fee per pet.

Campgrounds and RV Parks
Fayetteville/Wade KOA 6250 Wade Stedman Road Wade NC   910-484-5500 (800-562-5350)
http://www.koa.com
Dogs of all sizes are allowed, and there are no additional pet fees for tent or RV sites. There is a $4 nightly pet fee for the cabins and pets are only allowed in one cabin, so be sure and call ahead. Leashed pets are allowed to be walked throughout the campground which also has a fenced off-leash area. Dogs may not be left unattended, and must be quiet, leashed, and cleaned up after. The camping and tent areas also allow dogs.

Stores
PetSmart Pet Store 2061 Skibo Rd Fayetteville NC   910-867-2300
Your licensed and well-behaved leashed dog is allowed in the store.

Ferry Dock Road

Transportation Systems
North Carolina Ferry-Knotts Island S end of H 615 (on the island) Ferry Dock Road NC   800-BY FERRY (293-3779)
These vehicle and passenger transport ferries are run by the state and provide service every day of the year on all routes; however weather conditions can influence travel. Dogs are allowed on all ferries for no additional fee; they must be kept in the vehicle or leashed when out of the vehicle. Dogs must be under owner's control/care at all times.

Flat Rock

Campgrounds and RV Parks
Lakewood RV Resort 915 Ballenger Road Flat Rock NC   888-819-4200

http://www.lakewoodrvresort.com
Dogs of all sizes are allowed. There are no additional pet fees. Dogs are not allowed at any of the rentals, the clubhouse, or in any of the buildings. Dogs may not be left unattended, and they must be leashed and cleaned up after. There is a dog walk area at the campground.

Attractions

Carl Sandburg Historical Park 81 Carl Sandburg Lane Flat Rock NC   828-693-4178
http://www.nps.gov/carl/
This historic site is managed by the National Park Service, and the landscape consists of the Sandburg residence, a dairy goat farm, several outbuildings, rolling pastures, mountainside woods, 5 miles of hiking trails, several ponds and 2 small lakes. There are also flower and vegetable gardens, an apple orchard, guided tours, and from June to mid-August, they offer live performances of Sandburg's Rootabaga Stories and excerpts from the Broadway play, "The World of Carl Sandburg", at the park's amphitheater. The office is open and tours are offered from 9 am to 5 pm daily (except Christmas). The grounds are open for visitors from dawn to dusk. Dogs must be on no more than a 6 foot leash and cleaned up after at all times. Dogs are allowed on the trails and throughout the park, but they are not allowed in buildings or the barn area.
Carl Sandburg Home 81 Carl Sandburg Lane Flat Rock NC   828-693-4178
http://www.nps.gov/carl
This estate home is a historic remembrance of an American who through his reflections of what it meant to be a true American earned him 2 Pulitzer prizes, and he left as his legacy numerous poetry, songs, and writings. Dogs are allowed throughout the grounds and on the more than 5 miles of trails; they are not allowed in buildings. Dogs must be under owner's control, leashed, and cleaned up after at all times.

Gatesville

Campgrounds and RV Parks

Merchants Millpond State Park 71 H 158E/Millpond Road Gatesville NC   252-357-1191
A rare ecological setting of coastal pond and southern swamp forest gives this park the look of an enchanted forest and it provides a wide variety of habitats for wildlife, an abundance of land and water recreation, educational opportunities, and more. Dogs are allowed throughout the park and on the trails; they are also allowed on the canoe rentals. Dogs may not be left alone at any time, and they must be well mannered, on no more than a 6 foot leash, and cleaned up after at all times. The camp sites are first come first served and each have picnic tables and grills with seasonally supplied water, restroom, and showers. The camping and tent areas also allow dogs. There is a dog walk area at the campground. There are no electric or water hookups at the campgrounds.

Parks

Merchants Millpond State Park 71 H 158E/Millpond Road Gatesville NC   252-357-1191
A rare ecological setting of coastal pond and southern swamp forest gives this park the look of an enchanted forest and it provides a wide variety of habitats for wildlife, an abundance of land and water recreation, educational opportunities, and more. Dogs are allowed throughout the park and on the trails; they are also allowed on the canoe rentals. Dogs may not be left alone at any time, and they must be well mannered, on no more than a 6 foot leash, and cleaned up after at all times.

Goldsboro

Accommodations

Best Western Goldsboro Inn 801 Hwy 70 Bypass E Goldsboro NC   919-735-7911 (800-780-7234)
Dogs are allowed for an additional pet fee of $10 per night per room.
Days Inn Goldsboro 2000 Wayne Memorial Dr Goldsboro NC   919-734-9471 (800-329-7466)
Dogs of all sizes are allowed. There is a $5 per night pet fee per pet.
Holiday Inn Express 909 N Spence Ave Goldsboro NC   919-751-1999 (877-270-6405)
Dogs of all sizes are allowed for an additional one time pet fee of $20 per room.

Campgrounds and RV Parks

Cliffs of the Neuse State Park 345A Park Entrance Road Seven Springs NC   919-778-6234
Rich in geological and biological history, this park offers a museum, educational and interpretive programs, and

a variety of recreational pursuits. Dogs of all sizes are allowed at no additional fee. Dogs may not be left unattended, and they must be on no more than a 6 foot leash, and cleaned up after. Dogs are not allowed in the swim areas or in buildings, however, they are allowed on the trails. The camping and tent areas also allow dogs. There is a dog walk area at the campground. There are no electric or water hookups at the campground.

Greensboro

Accommodations
Candlewood Suites 7623 Thorndike Rd Greensboro NC 336-454-0078 (877-270-6405)
Dogs of all sizes are allowed for an additional one time fee of $75 per pet.
Clarion Hotel Greensboro Airport 415 Swing Road Greensboro NC 336-299-7650 (877-424-6423)
Dogs are allowed for an additional one time pet fee of $50 per room.
Days Inn Greensboro Airport 501 S Regional Rd Greensboro NC 336-668-0476 (800-329-7466)
Dogs of all sizes are allowed. There is a $25 one time per pet fee per visit.
Drury Inn & Suites 3220 High Point Road Greensboro NC 336-856-9696 (800-378-7946)
Dogs of all sizes are permitted. Pets are not allowed in the breakfast area of the hotel. Pets are not to be left unattended, and each guest must assume liability for damage of property or other guest complaints. There is a limit of one pet per room.
Extended StayAmerica Greensboro - Wendover Ave. 4317 Big Tree Way Greensboro NC 336-299-0200
There is a one time pet fee of $25.00 for one night stays, $50.00 for two night stays, and $75.00 for any stay of three nights or longer.
Holiday Inn Express Greensboro-(I-40 @ Wendover) 4305 Big Tree Way Greensboro NC 336-854-0090 (877-270-6405)
Dogs up to 20 pounds are allowed for an additional pet fee of $10 per night per room.
La Quinta Inn & Suites Greensboro 1201 Lanada Road Greensboro NC 336-316-0100 (800-531-5900)
Dogs of all sizes are allowed. There are no additional pet fees. Dogs may not be left unattended, and they must be leashed and cleaned up after.
Motel 6 - Greensboro Airport 605 South Regional Road Greensboro NC 336-668-2085 (800-466-8356)
One well-behaved family pet per room. Guest must notify front desk upon arrival. Guest is liable for any damages. In consideration of all guests, pets must never be left unattended in the guest rooms.
Motel 6 - Greensboro South 831 Greenhaven Drive Greensboro NC 336-854-0993 (800-466-8356)
One well-behaved family pet per room. Guest must notify front desk upon arrival. Guest is liable for any damages. In consideration of all guests, pets must never be left unattended in the guest rooms.
Red Roof Inn - Greensboro Airport 615 Regional Road South Greensboro NC 336-271-2636 (800-RED-ROOF)
One well-behaved family pet per room. Guest must notify front desk upon arrival. Guest is liable for any damages. In consideration of all guests, pets must never be left unattended in the guest rooms.
Red Roof Inn - Greensboro Coliseum 2101 West Meadowview Road Greensboro NC 336-852-6560 (800-RED-ROOF)
One well-behaved family pet per room. Guest must notify front desk upon arrival. Guest is liable for any damages. In consideration of all guests, pets must never be left unattended in the guest rooms.
Residence Inn by Marriott 2000 Veasley Street Greensboro NC 336-294-8600
Dogs of all sizes are allowed. There is a $75 one time fee and a pet policy to sign at check in.
Radisson Hotel High Point 135 South Main Street High Point NC 336-889-8888
Dogs of all sizes are allowed. There is a $50 one time additional pet fee.

Attractions
Piedmont Environmental Center 1220 Penny Road High Point NC 336-883-8531
http://piedmontenvironmental.com/
Dedicated to providing a number of fun environmental educational opportunities, this 376 acre nature preserve also offers 11 miles of hiking trails and a variety of recreation. Leashed dogs are allowed, and they must be picked up after.
Mendenhall Plantation 603 W Main Street Jamestown NC 33-454-3819
http://www.mendenhallplantation.org/
Listed on the National Register of Historic Places, this early 1800's plantation features a main house and several outbuildings, and tells the story of those who lived here and their struggles for freedoms and daily life. Dogs are allowed on the grounds; they are not allowed in any of the buildings.

Stores
PetSmart Pet Store 1206 Bridford Pkwy Greensboro NC 336-218-8188

Your licensed and well-behaved leashed dog is allowed in the store.
PetSmart Pet Store 2641 Lawndale Dr Greensboro NC   336-545-6225
Your licensed and well-behaved leashed dog is allowed in the store.
Petco Pet Store 4217 West Wendover Avenue, Ste G Greensboro NC   336-294-2681
Your licensed and well-behaved leashed dog is allowed in the store.
PetSmart Pet Store 265 Eastchester Dr 130 High Point NC   336-887-0525
Your licensed and well-behaved leashed dog is allowed in the store.

TOP 200 PLACE **Replacements, Ltd.** 1089 Knox Road Mcleansville NC   800-REPLACE (737-5223)
http://www.replacements.com/
Well behaved, leashed dogs are welcome to explore this amazing store of almost a half a million square feet that
is home to the world's largest selection of replacement and new dinnerware. Their showroom is stocked with new
and used china, crystal, silver and collectibles. Dogs must be under owner's control and care at all times.

Bring your dog to work

More and more companies are allowing employees to bring their dogs with them
to the office. They find that this improves morale and allows employees be more
productive. Replacements, Ltd is one of the pioneers in this regard and has had
upwards of 70 dogs in the building on some days. With hundreds of employees
this is one of the largest dog-friendly employers out there. And their customers
may also bring their dogs to their large showroom of new and used china, crystal,
silver and collectibles. More information about taking your dog with you to work
can be found at www.DogFriendly.com.

Parks
Guilford Courthouse National Military Park 2332 New Garden Road Greensboro NC   336-288-1776
http://www.nps.gov/guco/
As well as having a comprehensive visitor center/book store regarding the events of the significant battle that
was fought here and other Revolutionary War actions, they also feature almost 30 honorary monuments
throughout the park and a walking trail. Visitors must be sure to have cars parked outside the gates before 5 PM
when they lock them for the night. Dogs must be leashed and under owner's care at all times.
Tannenbaum Historic Park 2200 New Garden Road Greensboro NC   336-545-5315
This park preserves and educates the public of the historic significance of this area during America's colonial
times as well as being a venue for various events throughout the year. Dogs are welcome, but they must be
leashed and cleaned up after.

Off-Leash Dog Parks
Bark Park 3905 Nathaneal Greene Drive Greensboro NC   336-545-5343
http://www.gsobarkpark.org/
Located in the Country Park, there are 3 separate fenced, off leash areas to choose from-each with their own
features; Lot B is often used for fund raising events. The park is closed to vehicles on weekends and holidays,
but there is a place to park and paths. Dogs must be sociable, current on all vaccinations and license, and under
owner's control/care at all times. Dogs must be leashed when not in designated off-lead areas.

Outdoor Restaurants
Baja Fresh 1410 Westover Terrace, Suite 100C Greensboro NC   336-378-0700
This restaurant serves Mexican food. Dogs are allowed at the outdoor tables.

Greenville

Accommodations
Motel 6 - Greenville 301 Southeast Greenville Boulevard Greenville NC   252-756-2792 (800-466-8356)
One well-behaved family pet per room. Guest must notify front desk upon arrival. Guest is liable for any
damages. In consideration of all guests, pets must never be left unattended in the guest rooms.

Stores

PetSmart Pet Store 600 Greenville Blvd SE Greenville NC   252-756-7706
Your licensed and well-behaved leashed dog is allowed in the store.

Hatteras

Transportation Systems

North Carolina Ferry-Hatteras H 12 Hatteras NC   800-BY FERRY (293-3779)
These vehicle and passenger transport ferries are run by the state and provide service every day of the year on all routes; however weather conditions can influence travel. Dogs are allowed on all ferries for no additional fee; they must be kept in the vehicle or leashed when out of the vehicle. Dogs must be under owner's control/care at all times.

Havelock

Transportation Systems

North Carolina Ferry-Cherry Branch Ferry Road Havelock NC   800-BY FERRY (293-3779)
These vehicle and passenger transport ferries are run by the state and provide service every day of the year on all routes; however weather conditions can influence travel. Dogs are allowed on all ferries for no additional fee; they must be kept in the vehicle or leashed when out of the vehicle. Dogs must be under owner's control/care at all times.

Henderson

Campgrounds and RV Parks

Kerr Lake State Rec Area 6254 Satterwhite Point Road Henderson NC   252-438-7791
This park touts a 50,000-acre man-made lake with many miles of wooded shoreline and provides a variety of land and water recreation areas, woodlands, trails, and wildlife habitats. Dogs of all sizes are allowed at no additional fee. Dogs may not be left unattended, and they must be on no more than a 6 foot leash at all times, and cleaned up after. Dogs are not allowed in buildings, but they are allowed on the trails. The camping and tent areas also allow dogs. There is a dog walk area at the campground.

Hendersonville

Accommodations

Comfort Inn 206 Mitchell Drive Hendersonville NC   828-693-8800 (877-424-6423)
Dogs are allowed for an additional pet fee of $10 per night per room.
Red Roof Inn - Hendersonville, NC 240 Mitchelle Drive Hendersonville NC   828-697-1223 (800-RED-ROOF)
One well-behaved family pet per room. Guest must notify front desk upon arrival. Guest is liable for any damages. In consideration of all guests, pets must never be left unattended in the guest rooms.

Attractions

TOP 200 PLACE **Historic Johnson Farm** 3346 Hayward Road Hendersonville NC   828-891-6585
Listed on the National Register of Historic Places, this late 19th/early 20th century farm offers mountain farming "hands-on" experiences, a number of historic buildings, and nature trails. Dogs are allowed on the trails and at the farm; they are not allowed in buildings. Dogs must be leashed and cleaned up after.

Parks

Holmes Educational State Forest 1299 Crab Creek Road Hendersonville NC   828-692-0100
http://www.ncesf.org/HESF/home.htm
Scenic views, brilliant seasonal flora, and well marked trails with displays and exhibits, offer visitors an

educational experience as well as a recreational one. Leashed dogs are allowed.

Hickory

Accommodations
Holiday Inn Express 2250 Highway 70 SE Hickory NC   828-328-2081 (877-270-6405)
Dogs up to 70 pounds are allowed for an additional one time pet fee of $35 per room.
Red Roof Inn - Hickory 1184 Lenoir Rhyne Boulevard Hickory NC   828-323-1500 (800-RED-ROOF)
One well-behaved family pet per room. Guest must notify front desk upon arrival. Guest is liable for any damages. In consideration of all guests, pets must never be left unattended in the guest rooms.

Stores
PetSmart Pet Store 1610 8th St Dr SE Hickory NC   828-322-1202
Your licensed and well-behaved leashed dog is allowed in the store.

Highlands

Campgrounds and RV Parks
Nantahala National Forest 2010 Flat Mountain Road Highlands NC   828-526-3765
This forest, the largest in the state with over half a million acres, provides over 600 miles of hiking trails, diverse ecosystems that support a large variety of plants, fish, mammals, bird species, and various recreational pursuits. Dogs of all sizes are allowed at no additional fee. Dogs may not be left unattended, and they must be leashed and cleaned up after. Dogs are not allowed in buildings, however, they are allowed on the trails. Dogs are not allowed on the trails in the Great Smokey Mountains National Forest that adjoin the park. The camping and tent areas also allow dogs. There is a dog walk area at the campground. There are no electric or water hookups at the campground.

Attractions
Highlands Botanical Garden 930 Horse Cove Road Highlands NC   828-526-2602
http://www.wcu.edu/hbs/Garden.htm
Open year round and free to the public, this living flora museum preserves and educates the public about native plant species. Leashed dogs are allowed.

Hollister

Campgrounds and RV Parks
Medoc Mountain State Park 1541 Medoc State Park Road/ H 1322 Hollister NC   252-586-6588
This park is home to a large variety of plant and animal life and offers educational and interpretive programs, seven different trails, and various recreational pursuits. Dogs of all sizes are allowed at no additional fee. Dogs may not be left unattended except for short periods, and they must be on no more than a 6 foot leash, and cleaned up after. Dogs are not allowed in buildings, but they are allowed on the trails. The camping and tent areas also allow dogs. There is a dog walk area at the campground.

Jacksonville

Accommodations
Hampton Inn 474 Western Blvd Jacksonville NC   910-347-6500
Dogs of all sizes are allowed. There are no additional pet fees. Kennel dog for housekeeping.
Super 8 Motel - Jacksonville 2149 N. Marine Blvd. Jacksonville NC   910-455-6888 (800-800-8000)
http://www.innworks.com/jacksonville
There is a $10 per stay pet fee for up to 3 dogs in each room.

Stores
PetSmart Pet Store 1335 Western Blvd Jacksonville NC 910-938-2410
Your licensed and well-behaved leashed dog is allowed in the store.

Jonesville

Accommodations
Comfort Inn 1633 Winston Road Jonesville NC 336-835-9400 (877-424-6423)
Dogs are allowed for an additional fee of $10 per night per pet.
Holiday Inn Express I-77 and US 67 Exit 82 Jonesville NC 336-835-6000 (877-270-6405)
Dogs of all sizes are allowed for an additional fee of $10 per night per pet.

Kenly

Accommodations
Days Inn Kenly 1139 Johnston Pkwy Kenly NC 919-284-3400 (800-329-7466)
Dogs of all sizes are allowed. There is a $10 per night pet fee per pet.

Lake Norman Area

Accommodations
MainStay Suites 3200 Cloverleaf Parkway Kannapolis NC 704-788-2140
Dogs are allowed for an additional one time pet fee of $35 per room.
Best Western Statesville Inn 1121 Morland Dr Statesville NC 704-881-0111 (800-780-7234)
Dogs are allowed for an additional pet fee of $15 per night per room.
Motel 6 - Statesville 1137 Morland Drive Statesville NC 704-871-1115
One well-behaved family pet per room. Guest must notify front desk upon arrival. Guest is liable for any
damages. In consideration of all guests, pets must never be left unattended in the guest rooms.
Red Roof Inn - Statesville 1508 East Broad Street Statesville NC 704-878-2051 (800-RED-ROOF)
One well-behaved family pet per room. Guest must notify front desk upon arrival. Guest is liable for any
damages. In consideration of all guests, pets must never be left unattended in the guest rooms.
Super 8 Statesville 1125 Greenland Dr Statesville NC 704-878-9888 (800-800-8000)
Dogs of all sizes are allowed. There is a $6 per night pet fee per pet. Smoking and non-smoking rooms are
available for pet rooms.

Campgrounds and RV Parks
Wildlife Woods Campground 4582 Beaver Blvd Sherrills Ford NC 704-483-5611
Dogs of all sizes are allowed. There are no additional pet fees. Dogs may not be left unattended, and they must
be leashed and cleaned up after. There are some breed restrictions. The camping and tent areas also allow
dogs. There is a dog walk area at the campground.
Statesville KOA 162 KOA Lane Statesville NC 704-873-5560 (800-562-5705)
http://www.koa.com
Dogs of all sizes are allowed. There are no additional pet fees. Dogs may not be left unattended, and they must
be quiet, leashed, and cleaned up after. There are some breed restrictions. The camping and tent areas also
allow dogs. There is a dog walk area at the campground.
Lake Norman State Park 159 Inland Sea Lane Troutman NC 704-528-6350
Located along the state's largest manmade lake, this park supports a wide variety of plant and animal life,
provides educational and interpretive programs, and various land and water activities. Dogs of all sizes are
allowed at no additional fee. Dogs may not be left unattended, and they must be on no more than a 6 foot leash,
and cleaned up after. Dogs are not allowed in public swim areas or buildings, and they must be in your unit at
night. Dogs are allowed on the trails. This campground is closed during the off-season. The camping and tent
areas also allow dogs. There is a dog walk area at the campground. There are no electric or water hookups at
the campground.

Attractions
Dale Earnhardt Plaza and Statue Dale Earnhardt Blvd/H 3 Kannapolis NC   704-938-3200
Set among beautifully landscaped tree-lined streets, this memorial plaza holds a 9 foot, 900 pound bronze statue of the racing star dedicated by his hometown friends and family, plus a granite monument that was bequeathed by his fans. The Visitor Center (200 West Street) also has an on-going exhibit highlighting Earnhardt's career. Dogs are allowed throughout the town and at the plaza. Dogs must be well mannered, under owner's control, leashed, and cleaned up after at all times.

Shopping Centers
Cannon Village 200 West Avenue (Visitor Center) Kannapolis NC   704-938-3200
http://www.cannonvillage.com/
This downtown area is reminiscent of a Southern Colonial landscape, and it will soon become another part of the North Carolina Research Campus with research focused on nutrition and health. Dogs are allowed throughout the town, and it is up to individual stores whether they are allowed inside. Dogs must be well mannered, under owner's control, leashed, and cleaned up after at all times.

Stores
PetSmart Pet Store 590-G River Hwy Mooresville NC   704-660-0444
Your licensed and well-behaved leashed dog is allowed in the store.

Parks
Lake Norman State Park 159 Inland Sea Lane Troutman NC   704-528-6350
This park provides a variety of water activities, interpretive programs, hiking trails, and a myriad of recreational opportunities. Dogs are allowed for no additional fee. Dogs may not be left unattended at any time, and they must be leashed and cleaned up after at all times. Pets are to be brought in at night, and they are not allowed in any park buildings, swimming areas, group campsites, or on the boat rentals. Dogs must be quiet, well behaved, and be current with vaccinations and rabies inoculations.

Outdoor Restaurants
Fuel Pizza 402 S Main Street Davidson NC   704-655-3835
Dogs on leash are allowed at the outdoor tables.
Fox and Hound Pub and Grill 8711 Lindholm Drive Huntersville NC   704-895-4504
http://www.fhrg.com/
Guests will enjoy an attractive, casual ambiance here where quality food, drinks, and entertainment are the focus; they also offer outside dining. Dogs are allowed at the outside tables; they must be leashed and under owner's control/care at all times.

Laurinburg

Accommodations
Hampton Inn 115 Hampton Circle Laurinburg NC   910-277-1516
Dogs up to 50 pounds are allowed. There is a pet policy to sign at check in and there are no additional pet fees. There are only 2 non-smoking pet rooms available, and dogs are not allowed in the lobby between 6 & 10 AM.

Lenoir

Accommodations
Days Inn Lenoir 206 Blowing Rock Blvd Lenoir NC   828-754-0731 (800-329-7466)
Dogs of all sizes are allowed. There is a $5 per night pet fee per pet.

Lincolnton

Accommodations
Days Inn Lincolnton 614 Clark Drive Lincolnton NC   704-735-8271 (800-329-7466)
Dogs of all sizes are allowed. There is a $10 per night pet fee per pet.

Lumberton

Accommodations
Best Western Inn at Lumberton 201 Jackson Ct Lumberton NC   910-618-9799 (800-780-7234)
Dogs are allowed for an additional fee of $10 per night per pet.
Days Inn Lumberton Outlet Mall 3030 N Roberts Ave Lumberton NC   910-738-6401 (800-329-7466)
Dogs of all sizes are allowed. There is a $10 per night pet fee per pet.
Motel 6 - Lumberton 2361 Lackey Road Lumberton NC   910-738-2410 (800-466-8356)
One well-behaved family pet per room. Guest must notify front desk upon arrival. Guest is liable for any damages. In consideration of all guests, pets must never be left unattended in the guest rooms.
Quality Inn and Suites 3608 Kahn Drive Lumberton NC   910-738-8261 (877-424-6423)
Dogs are allowed for an additional pet fee of $25 per night per room.
Super 8 Lumberton 150 Jackson Court Lumberton NC   910-671-4444 (800-800-8000)
Dogs of all sizes are allowed. There is a $5 per night pet fee per pet. Smoking and non-smoking rooms are available for pet rooms.

Marion

Accommodations
Super 8 Marion 4281 Hwy 221 South Marion NC   828-659-7940 (800-800-8000)
Dogs of all sizes are allowed. There is a $20 one time per pet fee per visit. Smoking and non-smoking rooms are available for pet rooms.

Campgrounds and RV Parks
Buck Creek Campground 2576 Toms Creek Road Marion NC   828-724-4888
http://www.buckcreekcampground.com
Dogs up to 100 pounds are allowed. There are no additional pet fees. Dogs may not be left unattended outside, and they must be leashed and cleaned up after. There are some breed restrictions. This RV park is closed during the off-season. There is a dog walk area at the campground.
Jellystone Park at Hidden Valley Campground 1210 Deacon Drive Marion NC   828-652-7208
http://www.jellystonemarion.com/
Dogs of all sizes are allowed. There are no additional pet fees. Dogs must be leashed and cleaned up after. This RV park is closed during the off-season. The camping and tent areas also allow dogs. There is a dog walk area at the campground.

Minnesott Beach

Transportation Systems
North Carolina Ferry-Minnesott Beach Point Road/H 306 Minnesott Beach NC   800-BY FERRY (293-3779)
These vehicle and passenger transport ferries are run by the state and provide service every day of the year on all routes; however weather conditions can influence travel. Dogs are allowed on all ferries for no additional fee; they must be kept in the vehicle or leashed when out of the vehicle. Dogs must be under owner's control/care at all times.

Mocksville

Accommodations
Quality Inn 1500 Yadkinville Road Mocksville NC   336-751-7310 (877-424-6423)

Dogs up to 70 pounds are allowed for an additional one time pet fee of $25 per room.

Morganton

Accommodations
Comfort Inn and Suites 1273 Burkmount Avenue Morganton NC   828-430-4000 (877-424-6423)
Dogs are allowed for an additional one time fee of $25 per pet.
Holiday Inn 2400 South Sterling St Morganton NC   828-437-0171 (877-270-6405)
Dogs of all sizes are allowed for an additional one time pet fee of $25 per room.

Mount Airy

Accommodations
Quality Inn (formally-Comfort Inn) 2136 Rockford Street Mount Airy NC   336-789-2000 (877-424-6423)
Dogs are allowed for an additional one time pet fee of $25 per room.

Murphy

Accommodations
Best Western of Murphy 1522 Andrews Rd Murphy NC   828-837-3060 (800-780-7234)
Dogs up to 20 pounds are allowed for an additional fee per night per pet of $10; $15 for dogs 21 to 39 pounds, and $20 for dogs from 40 to 60 pounds.
Smoky Mountain Hideaway Mary King Mountain Murphy NC   727-864-0526
Dogs of all sizes are allowed. There is a $100 refundable pet deposit per room.

New Bern

Accommodations
Broad Creek Guest Quarters Resort 6229 Harbourside Dr. (Fairfield Harbour) New Bern NC   252-474-5329
This B&B welcomes your dog or cat and offers complimentary pet sitting. There is a $20 per night pet fee and dogs of all sizes are welcome.
Sheraton New Bern Hotel & Marina 100 Middle Street New Bern NC   252-638-3585 (888-625-5144)
Dogs of all sizes are allowed. There are no additional pet fees. Pets are limited to rooms on the first floor only. Dogs are not allowed to be left alone in the room.

Campgrounds and RV Parks
Croatan National Forest 141 E Fisher Street New Bern NC   252-393-7352
This park, called the "Land of Many Ecosystems", has various habitats providing for some unusual plant life and a wide range of birds and wildlife. The park also provides interpretive trails, hiking trails and recreational pursuits. Dogs may not be left unattended, and they must be leashed and cleaned up after. Dogs are allowed on the trails. The camping and tent areas also allow dogs. There is a dog walk area at the campground.
New Bern 1565 B Street New Bern NC   252-638-2556 (800-562-3341)
http://www.koa.com
Dogs of all sizes are allowed. There are no additional pet fees. Dogs must be leashed and cleaned up after. There are 2 fenced in areas for off lead. There are some breed restrictions. The camping and tent areas also allow dogs. There is a dog walk area at the campground. Dogs are allowed in the camping cabins.

Stores
Art of the Wild 218 Middle Street New Bern NC   252-638-8806
Specializing in animal and bird sculptures of the wild, and made from a variety of natural products, this store also carries many items from local artisans. Your pooch is allowed to come into the store, but they ask that you let them know first before bringing in the pet as there is a dog on site. Dogs must be well behaved, under owner's

control/care, and leashed at all times.
Williams Farm and Garden Center 1309 Old Cherry Point Road New Bern NC 252-638-1983
This farm supply and garden center will allow pets to check out the store with their owners, and they also carry pet foods and supplies. Dogs must be well behaved, under owner's control/care, and on no more than a 4½ foot leash at all times.

Outer Banks

Accommodations
Comfort Inn South Oceanfront 8031 Old Oregon Inlet Road Nags Head NC   252-441-6315 (877-424-6423)
Dogs are allowed for an additional fee of $10 per night per pet.

Vacation Home Rentals
Twiddy & Company Realtors Call to Arrange Corolla NC 252-457-1100 (866-457-1190)
http://www.twiddy.com
Over 150 pet-friendly homes are available for rent in Corolla and Duck on the North Carolina Outer Banks. There are no additional pet fees.
Paramount Destinations Call to Arrange Corolla and Duck NC 866-753-3045
http://www.paramountdestinations.com
This vacation home rental management company has many dog-friendly rentals in the Corolla and Duck areas. A $100 or more non-refundable pet fee is charged. Other pets beside dogs require special homeowner approval.
Outer Banks Blue Realty Call to Arrange Duck NC 888-623-2583
http://www.outerbanksblue.com
This realtor has a large number of pet-friendly vacation rentals in the North Carolina Outer Banks areas of Duck, KIll Devil Hills, Nags Head and Corolla. Call them for more information.
www.weloveobx.com Beach Vacation Rental Homes Duck NC 252-261-7911
http://www.weloveobx.com
Three vacation rentals, with 4 to 6 bedrooms each, are located near the beach. Dogs are welcome to join you in these rentals.
Joe Lamb Jr. & Associates 5101 N. Croatan Hwy Kitty Hawk NC 252-261-4444 (800-552-6257)
http://joelambjr.com
This company manages over 75 pet friendly vacation homes ranging in size from 3 to 7 bedrooms.
Village Realty 5301 South Croatan Highway Nags Head NC 800-548-9688
http://www.villagerealtyobx.com
Many of the homes represented by Village Realty will allow pets for a $75 non-refundable pet cleaning fee. Up to two well-behaved pets are allowed.

Transportation Systems
North Carolina Ferry-Currituck Courthouse Road Currituck NC 800-BY FERRY (293-3779)
These vehicle and passenger transport ferries are run by the state and provide service every day of the year on all routes; however weather conditions can influence travel. Dogs are allowed on all ferries for no additional fee; they must be kept in the vehicle or leashed when out of the vehicle. Dogs must be under owner's control/care at all times.

Attractions
Currituck Beach Lighthouse H 12 Corolla NC 252-453-4939
http://www.currituckbeachlight.com/
This beautifully restored and maintained lighthouse and keeper's house is maintained by the North Carolina's Outer Banks Association and has resulted in them being granted ownership of this historic site. Dogs are allowed throughout the grounds; they are not allowed in the buildings. Dogs must be under owner's control, leashed, and cleaned up after at all times.
Weeping Radish Brewery 6810 Caratoke Road/H 158 Jarvisburg NC 252-491-5205
http://www.weepingradish.com/
Specializing in handcrafted ales made in old country tradition, this award winning brewery is also the state's oldest microbrewery. Dogs are allowed on the grounds; they are not allowed in the buildings. Dogs must be well behaved, leashed, and cleaned up after at all times.

Shopping Centers
Tanger Outlet 7100 S Croatan H/H 158 Nags Head NC 252-441-5634

http://www.tangeroutlet.com/center/NGH
There are more than 23 brand name outlets and services at this center. Dogs are allowed in the common areas; it is up to individual stores whether they are allowed inside. Dogs must be well behaved, leashed, and cleaned up after at all times.

Stores

The Cyberdog USA 3105 N Croatan H/H 158 Kill Devil Hills NC   252-449-0331
http://thecyberdogusa.com/
Dedicated to all that's pet healthy, this holistic pet supply store also provide their own human grade formulas and products in addition to pre-packaged high quality foods, and they carry a long line of pet specialty items and accessories. Dogs are allowed in the store; they must be well behaved, under owner's control/care, and leashed at all times.
Salty Paws Biscuits 3723 N Croatan H/H 158 Kitty Hawk NC   252-480-2284
http://www.saltypawsbiscuits.com/
This bakery specializes in healthy, hand-crafted treats; they can also attend to pooches that need special diets, and they are host to a variety of fun events throughout the year. Well behaved dogs are welcome in the store; they must be leashed and under owner's control/care at all times.

Beaches

Corolla Beaches Ocean Trail Corolla NC   252-232-0719
http://www.outerbanks.com/
Dogs are allowed on the beaches in and around the Corolla area year round; they must be leashed and cleaned up after at all times.
Duck Beach H 12 Duck NC   252-255-1234
http://www.townofduck.com/
Dogs are welcome to romp on the beach here, and they may be off leash if they are under good voice control. Dogs must be licensed, have current rabies tags, be under owner's control, and cleaned up after at all times. Dogs must be on no more than a 10 foot leash when off the beach.
Kill Devil Hills Beaches N Virginia Dare Trail Kill Devil Hills NC   252-449-5300
http://www.kdhnc.com/
From May 15th to September 15th dogs are not allowed on the beaches between 9 AM and 6 PM. When dogs are allowed on the beach, they must be licensed, have current rabies tags, be under owner's control, on no more than a 10 foot leash, and cleaned up after at all times.
Kitty Hawk Beaches Virginai Dare Trail/H 12 Kitty Hawk NC   252-261-3552
http://www.townofkittyhawk.org/
Between 10 am and 6 pm from the Friday before Memorial Day until the day after Labor Day, dogs may be on the beach on a maximum 6 foot leash; for all other times they may be on a retractable leash up to 12 feet. Well trained dogs may be off-lead from Labor Day to the Friday before Memorial Day if they are under strict voice control and never more than 30 feet from the owner. Resident dogs must display a county registration tag plus a valid rabies tags, and non-resident dogs must have a valid rabies tag. Dogs must be under owner's control and cleaned up after at all times.
Nags Head Beaches N Vriginia Dare Trail/H 12 Nags Head NC   252-441-5508
http://www.townofnagshead.net/
The beaches here consist mostly of open spaces and low-density building. Dogs are allowed on the beaches year round; they must be licensed, have current rabies tags, be under owner's control, on no more than a 10 foot leash, and cleaned up after at all times.
Southern Shores Beaches H 12 Southern Shores NC   252-261-2394
From May 15th to September 15th dogs are not allowed on the beaches. Dogs must be licensed, have current rabies tags, be under owner's control, on no more than a 10 foot leash, and cleaned up after at all times. A parking permit is required for parking in town and can be obtained at the Town Hall, 5375 N. Virginia Dare Trail.

Parks

The Duck Trail H 12 Duck NC   252-255-1234
http://www.townofduck.com/ducktrail.htm
This scenic paved walk is a great place for walking pets. Dogs must be licensed, have current rabies tags, be under owner's control, leashed, and cleaned up after at all times.
Jockey's Ridge State Park Carolista Drive/Milepost 12 of H 158 Bypass Nags Head NC   252-441-7132
http://www.jockeysridgestatepark.com/
Home to the tallest natural sand dunes in the Eastern US, this park also has a 384 foot long boardwalk ending in a stunning view of the ridge from the overlook, a wide range of land, water, and airborne activities, a visitor center, museum, and picnicking areas. Dogs of all sizes are allowed on the grounds and trails; they are not allowed in the buildings. Dogs must be under owner's control, on no more than a 6 foot leash, and cleaned up after at all times.

Outdoor Restaurants

Duck's Cottage Coffee and Books 1240 Duck Road/H 12 Duck NC   252-261-5510
http://www.duckscottage.com/
This café bar offers all the favorite coffee drinks, pastries, and a book and gift store all in one. Dogs are allowed on the porch and at the picnic tables; they are not allowed inside the store. Dogs must be under owner's control/care and leashed at all times.
Fatboyz Ice Cream and Grill 7208 S Virginia Dare Trail Nags Head NC   252-441-6514
http://www.nagsheadguide.com/fatboyz/
Serving all American favorites, this eatery also serves up delectable home-made ice cream and offers outside dining-weather permitting. Dogs are allowed at the outer tables; they must be under owner's control/care and leashed at all times.
Sonic Drive-in 5205 S Croatan H/H 158 Nags Head NC   252-441-9030
This drive-thru serves up all the American favorites and offer outside dining, weather permitting. Dogs are allowed at the outer tables; they must be under owner's control/care and leashed at all times.

Raleigh

Accommodations

Best Western Cary Inn & Extended Stay 1722 Walnut Street Cary NC   919-481-1200 (800-780-7234)
Dogs are allowed for an additional one time fee of $125 per pet.
Comfort Suites 350 Ashville Avenue Cary NC   919-852-4318 (877-424-6423)
Dogs up to 20 pounds are allowed for an additional one time pet fee of $50 per room; the fee is $75 for dogs over 20 pounds, and a 2nd pet (any size) is an additional one time fee of $25.
La Quinta Inn & Suites Raleigh Cary 191 Crescent Commons Cary NC   919-851-2850 (800-531-5900)
Dogs of all sizes are allowed. There are no additional pet fees. Dogs must be leashed, cleaned up after, and crated when left alone in the room.
Red Roof Inn - Raleigh Southwest - Cary 1800 Walnut Street Cary NC   919-469-3400 (800-RED-ROOF)
One well-behaved family pet per room. Guest must notify front desk upon arrival. Guest is liable for any damages. In consideration of all guests, pets must never be left unattended in the guest rooms.
Residence Inn by Marriott 2900 Regency Parkway Cary NC   919-467-4080
Dogs of all sizes are allowed. There is a $75 one time fee and a pet policy to sign at check in.
TownePlace Suites Raleigh Cary/Weston Pkwy 120 Sage Commons Way Cary NC   919-678-0005
Dogs of all sizes are allowed. There is a $75 one time pet fee per visit.
Sleep Inn 105 Commerce Parkway Garner NC   919-772-7771 (877-424-6423)
Dogs are allowed for an additional one time fee of $25 per pet.
Residence Inn by Marriott 2020 Hospitality Court Morrisville NC   919-467-8689
Dogs of all sizes are allowed. There is a $75 one time fee and a pet policy to sign at check in.
Staybridge Suites 1012 Airport Blvd Morrisville NC   919-468-0180 (877-270-6405)
Dogs of all sizes are allowed for an additional one time pet fee of $150 per room.
Best Western Raleigh North 2715 Capital Boulevard Raleigh NC   919-872-5000 (800-780-7234)
Dogs up to 80 pounds are allowed for an additional pet fee of $50 per night per room; a 3rd dog would be another $25 per night.
Candlewood Suites 1020 Buck Jones Road Raleigh NC   919-468-4222 (877-270-6405)
Dogs up to 80 pounds are allowed for an additional pet fee of $12 per night per room.
Candlewood Suites 4433 Lead Mine Road Raleigh NC   919-789-4840 (877-270-6405)
Dogs up to 40 pounds are allowed. There is a $75 one time pet fee per visit. Only non-smoking rooms are used for pets.
Holiday Inn 2805 Highwoods Blvd Raleigh NC   919-872-3500 (877-270-6405)
Dogs of all sizes are allowed for an additional one time pet fee of $35 per room.
Holiday Inn 4100 Glenwood Ave Raleigh NC   919-782-8600 (877-270-6405)
A dog up to 50 pounds is allowed for an additional one time fee of $50.
La Quinta Inn Raleigh 1001 Aerial Center Parkway Raleigh NC   919-481-3600 (800-531-5900)
Dogs of all sizes are allowed. There are no additional pet fees. Dogs must be well behaved, leashed, and cleaned up after.
Motel 6 - Raleigh Northwest 3921 Arrow Drive Raleigh NC   919-782-7071 (800-466-8356)
One well-behaved family pet per room. Guest must notify front desk upon arrival. Guest is liable for any damages. In consideration of all guests, pets must never be left unattended in the guest rooms.
Motel 6 - Raleigh Southwest - Cary 1401 Buck Jones Road Raleigh NC   919-467-6171 (800-466-8356)
One well-behaved family pet per room. Guest must notify front desk upon arrival. Guest is liable for any damages. In consideration of all guests, pets must never be left unattended in the guest rooms.

Quality Suites 4400 Capital Blvd Raleigh NC 919-876-2211
Dogs up to 50 pounds are allowed. The fee for 2 pets is $25 for the first night and $10 for each night after; 3 dogs would be $35 for the first night and $20 for each additional night.
Red Roof Inn - Raleigh Downtown NCSU 1813 South Saunders Street Raleigh NC 919-833-6005 (800-RED-ROOF)
One well-behaved family pet per room. Guest must notify front desk upon arrival. Guest is liable for any damages. In consideration of all guests, pets must never be left unattended in the guest rooms.
Red Roof Inn - Raleigh East (New Bern Avenue) 3520 Maitland Drive Raleigh NC 919-231-0200 (800-RED-ROOF)
One well-behaved family pet per room. Guest must notify front desk upon arrival. Guest is liable for any damages. In consideration of all guests, pets must never be left unattended in the guest rooms.
Residence Inn by Marriott 1000 Navaho Drive Raleigh NC 919-878-6100
Dogs of all sizes are allowed. There is a $100 one time fee and a pet policy to sign at check in.
Residence Inn by Marriott 2200 Summit Park Lane Raleigh NC 919-279-3000
Dogs of all sizes are allowed. There is a $75 one time fee and a pet policy to sign at check in.

Campgrounds and RV Parks

Jordan Lake State Park 280 State Park Road Apex NC 919-362-0586
Rich in ancient American history and home to one of the largest Summer homes of the bald eagle, this park offers educational and interpretive programs, a variety of trails, and various recreation. Dogs of all sizes are allowed at no additional fee. Dogs may not be left unattended, and they must be on no more than a 6 foot leash, and cleaned up after. The camping and tent areas also allow dogs. There is a dog walk area at the campground.
William B. Umstead State Park 8801 Glenwood Avenue Raleigh NC 919-571-4170
Offering educational and recreational opportunities, this 5,577 acre park has 2 sections with easy access from I 40 and H 70, and provides a "natural" respite from city life. The park is open year round but campers are only allowed from mid-March to mid-December, Thursday 8 am through Monday at 1 pm. Dogs are allowed throughout the park for no additional fee; they are not allowed in boats, buildings, or group camps. Dogs must be on no more than a 6 foot leash and cleaned up after at all times. Campsites are first come first served and offer shaded sites with tables and grills, and drinking water, restrooms, and showers are nearby. This RV park is closed during the off-season. The camping and tent areas also allow dogs. There is a dog walk area at the campground. There are no electric or water hookups at the campgrounds.
Falls Lake State Park 13304 Creedmoor Road (H 50) Wake Forest NC 919-676-1027
This park of 26,000 acres of woodlands with a 12,000-acre lake offers educational and interpretive programs, trails with access to the Mountains-to-Sea Trail, and a variety of land and water activities and recreation. Dogs of all sizes are allowed at no additional fee. Dogs may not be left unattended, and they must be on no more than a 6 foot leash, and cleaned up after. Dogs are not allowed in swim areas or in buildings, however, they are allowed on the trails. The camping and tent areas also allow dogs. There is a dog walk area at the campground.

Attractions

Art Space 201 E Davie Street Raleigh NC 919-821-2723
http://www.artspacenc.org/
This visual art center started as a way to provide a quality, open studio environment for outreach and educational programs as well as to present upscale exhibitions. Dogs are welcome; they must be well behaved, under owner's control/care, and leashed at all times.
Raleigh Little Theatre Rose Garden 301 Pogue Street Raleigh NC 919-821-4579
Located behind the Raleigh Little Theater, this garden is ablaze with color and fragrance from late May until autumn with a large variety of roses, seasonal flowers, shrub, and trees. Dogs are allowed throughout the grounds; they must be leashed and picked up after.

Shopping Centers

Cameron Village Shopping Center 1900 Cameron Street Raleigh NC 919-821-1350
http://www.shopsofcameronvillage.com/
In the genre of an authentic hometown village shopping center with tree lined streets, this shopping area offers an eclectic array of unique shops, eateries, sidewalk cafés, and services. Dogs are allowed in the common areas of the center; they must be under owner's control/care and leashed at all times.
City Market Person and Martin Streets Raleigh NC 919-821-1350
http://www.citymarketraleigh.com/
This bustling entertainment, dining, and shopping Mecca is also a celebration of art, music, and sociability with many special events throughout the year and free concerts every Friday. Dogs are allowed on the city streets and common areas of the mall; it is up to individual stores whether they are allowed inside. Dogs must be well behaved, under owner's control, leashed, and cleaned up after at all times.

Stores

PetSmart Pet Store 1031 Beaver Creek Commons Apex NC   919-363-4056
Your licensed and well-behaved leashed dog is allowed in the store.
Three Dog Bakery 756 W Williams Street/H 55 Apex NC   919-367-2890
http://www.threedog.com
Three Dog Bakery provides cookies and snacks for your dog as well as some boutique items. You well-behaved, leashed dog is welcome.
PetSmart Pet Store 2430 Walnut St Cary NC   919-858-5442
Your licensed and well-behaved leashed dog is allowed in the store.
PetSmart Pet Store 2550 Timber Dr Garner NC   919-661-0690
Your licensed and well-behaved leashed dog is allowed in the store.
PetSmart Pet Store 265 Shenstone Blvd Garner NC   919-773-0376
Your licensed and well-behaved leashed dog is allowed in the store.
Petco Pet Store 6231 Triangle Plantation Dr Raleigh NC   919-877-9608
Your licensed and well-behaved leashed dog is allowed in the store.
Petco Pet Store 7811 Alexander Promenade Place Raleigh NC   919-596-8838
Your licensed and well-behaved leashed dog is allowed in the store.
PetSmart Pet Store 2800 Millbrook Rd Raleigh NC   919-873-0544
Your licensed and well-behaved leashed dog is allowed in the store.
PetSmart Pet Store 8111 Brier Creek Pkwy Raleigh NC   919-544-9902
Your licensed and well-behaved leashed dog is allowed in the store.
Unleashed 1025 Blue Ridge Road (N.C. State Fairgrounds Marketplace) Raleigh NC   919-673-7476
Located at the flea market-making for a nice doggy stroll day, this store offers high quality pet foods, supplies, and sturdy toys and leashes. Dogs must be well behaved, leashed, and under owner's control/care at all times.
Wag Pet Boutique 7414 Creedmoor Road/H 50 Raleigh NC   919-841-5093
http://www.wagpets.com/
Whether its funky toys, awesome pet accessories, tasty treats, good nutrition, or unique gifts, Wag has all that and a lot more. Dogs are allowed throughout the store; they must be well behaved and under owner's control/care at all times.
PetSmart Pet Store 11835 Retail Dr Wake Forest NC   919-554-6938
Your licensed and well-behaved leashed dog is allowed in the store.

Parks

Hemlock Bluffs Nature Preserve 2616 Kildaire Farm Road Cary NC   919-387-5980
Popular for the excellent bird and wildlife viewing, this park also features about 3 miles of wooded hiking trails and scenic observation platforms, plus it is home to the Stevens Nature Center where they have an outdoor educational shelter, a native wildflower garden, and a hands-on educational exhibit hall. Dogs are allowed throughout the preserve on the trails only. Dogs must be leashed and picked up after, and they are not allowed in buildings.
Mordecai Historic Park One Mimosa Street Raleigh NC   919-857-4364
This historic park allows visitors to experience a glimpse of colonial village life with the structures, gardens, special events, and guided tours. Dogs of all sizes are allowed throughout the park; they are not allowed in any of the buildings or on the trolley. Dogs must be leashed and cleaned up after at all times.
Pullen Park 520 Ashe Avenue Raleigh NC   919-831-6468
This beautiful 63 acre park has the distinction of having a TV Land tribute statue of Opie and Andy Taylor honoring the Andy Griffith Show, as well as a number of attractions, gaming fields, playgrounds, and picnic areas. Dogs are allowed throughout the park unless otherwise noted; they are not allowed in buildings, on the train, or on the carousel. Dogs may not be left alone at any time, and they must be under owner's control, leashed and cleaned up after at all times.
William B. Umstead State Park 8801 Glenwood Avenue Raleigh NC   919-571-4170
Offering educational and recreational opportunities, this 5,577 acre park has 2 sections with easy access from I 40 and H 70, and provides a "natural" respite from city life. The park is open year round but campers are only allowed from mid-March to mid-December, Thursday 8 am through Monday at 1 pm. Dogs are allowed throughout the park for no additional fee; they are not allowed in boats, buildings, or group camps. Dogs must be on no more than a 6 foot leash and cleaned up after at all times.

Off-Leash Dog Parks

Millbrook Exchange Off Leash Dog Park 1905 Spring Forest Road Raleigh NC   919-872-4156
This park is the home of the fenced Millbrook Exchange Off Leash Dog Park, and it is double-gated to prevent dogs from wandering off. When dogs are not in the off-leash area they must be on lead.

Outdoor Restaurants

The Coffee Mill and Flipside Restaurant 105 S Lombard Street Clayton NC   919-550-0174
http://www.rudinospizza.com/
There are 2 restaurants in one here; a coffee/smoothie bar that also offers a light breakfast and a full service
restaurant that offers lunch, dinner, a bar, and live music. There is also a wine and tapas bar and outside table
seating. Dogs are allowed at the outside tables; they must be leashed and under owner's control/care at all
times.
Armadillo Grill 439 Glenwood Avenue Raleigh NC   919-546-0555
http://www.armadillogrill.com/
This Tex-Mex eatery offers a margarita bar, fresh made to order food (even the tortillas), and outside dining-
weather permitting. Dogs are allowed at the outer tables; they must be under owner's control/care and leashed at
all times.
Bella Monica Restaurant 3121 Edwards Mill Road Raleigh NC   919-881-9778
http://www.bellamonica.com/
Specializing in pizza, pasta, and wines, this eatery also offers catering and shaded patio dining. Dogs are
allowed at the outer tables; they must be under owner's control/care at all times.
Ben's Place 8511-105 Cantilever Way Raleigh NC   919-782-5900
http://www.bensplacepub.com/
This fine dining steak and seafood restaurant also features a full bar and alfresco dining. Dogs are allowed at the
outer tables; they must be under owner's control/care and leashed at all times.
Cloos' Coney Island 2233 Avent Ferry Road #102 Raleigh NC   919-834-3354
This short-order grill features hamburgers, sandwiches, and Coney Island hot dogs; there is outdoor seating-
weather permitting. Dogs are allowed at the outer tables; they must be under owner's control/care at all times.
Flying Saucer Draught Emporium 328 W Morgan St Raleigh NC   919-821-7468
This restaurant serves American food. Dogs are allowed at the outdoor tables. Water is provided for your pet.
MoJoe's Burger Joint 620 Glenwood Avenue Raleigh NC   919-832-6799
In addition to serving up burgers, beer, and good music, this fun eatery also has outside seating-weather
permitting. Dogs are allowed at the outer tables; they must be under owner's control/care at all times.
New World Coffee House 4112 Pleasant Valley Road #124 Raleigh NC   919-782-5900
http://www.newworldcoffeehouse.com/
While popular for their coffee and artistic surroundings, this café also draws the crowd for their handcrafted
soups, California wraps, pastries/muffins/bagels, their delectable deserts, free WiFi, and outdoor seating. Dogs
are allowed at the outer tables; they must be well behaved, under owner's control/care and leashed at all times.
Porter's Tavern 2412 Hillsborough Street/H 54 Raleigh NC   919-821-2133
Fine dining, a full bar, special event venues, and alfresco dining are all available at this tavern. Dogs are allowed
at the outer tables; they must be under owner's control/care and leashed at all times.
The Players Retreat 105 Oberlin Road Raleigh NC   919-755-9589
http://www.playersretreat.net/
This popular eatery/sports bar offers an extensive beer and wine list, hand-crafted foods and steaks, daily
specials, free WiFi, special events, and outside dining. Dogs are allowed at the outer tables, and there are rings
in the wall by the tables to tie pets. They also provide treats and water bowls for their canine visitors. Dogs must
be under owner's control/care at all times.
The Village Draft House 428 Daniels Street Raleigh NC   919-833-1373
http://village.mydrafthouse.com/
Although this is a state-of-the-art draft house with 99 brews on tap, and they have widescreen TV/satellite feeds
throughout for all the sports, the real draw at this tavern is their all-American favorite comfort foods. Seasonal
outside dining is available. Dogs are allowed at the outside tables; they must be leashed and under owner's
control/care at all times.

Day Kennels
PetsHotel by PetsMart Day Kennel 2430 Walnut St. Cary NC   919-858-0449
http://www.petsmart.com/PETsHOTEL/
This PetSmart pet store offers day care, day camp and overnight care. You may drop off and pick up your dog
during the hours the store is open seven days a week. Dogs must have proof of current rabies, DPP and
Bordatella vaccinations.
PetsHotel by PetsMart Day Kennel 2800 Millbrook Rd. Raleigh NC   919-874-6198
http://www.petsmart.com/PETsHOTEL/
This PetSmart pet store offers day care, day camp and overnight care. You may drop off and pick up your dog
during the hours the store is open seven days a week. Dogs must have proof of current rabies, DPP and
Bordatella vaccinations.

Roaring Gap

Campgrounds and RV Parks
Stone Mountain State Park 3042 Frank Parkway Roaring Gap NC 336-957-8185
Designated as a National Natural Landmark in 1975, this park is home to a magnificent 600-foot granite dome, 16 miles of scenic trails, and a variety of recreational pursuits. Dogs of all sizes are allowed at no additional fee. Dogs may not be left unattended, and they must be on no more than a 6 foot leash at all times, and cleaned up after. Dogs are not allowed in buildings, however, they are allowed on the trails. The camping and tent areas also allow dogs. There is a dog walk area at the campground.

Rocky Mount

Accommodations
Howard Johnson Inn 7568 NC 48 Battleboro NC 252-977-9595 (800-446-4656)
Dogs of all sizes are welcome. There is a $5 per day pet fee.
Best Western Inn I-95/Gold Rock 7095 Rte 4 Rocky Mount NC 252-985-1450 (800-780-7234)
Dogs are allowed for an additional fee of $20 per night per pet.
Best Western Rocky Mount Inn 1921 N Wesleyan Boulevard Rocky Mount NC 252-442-8101 (800-780-7234)
Dogs are allowed for an additional fee of $20 per night per pet.
Comfort Inn 200 Gateway Blvd Rocky Mount NC 252-937-7765 (877-424-6423)
Dogs are allowed for an additional one time pet fee of $25 per room.
Comfort Inn North 7048 H 4 Rocky Mount NC 252-972-9426 (877-424-6423)
Dogs are allowed for an additional fee of $10 per night per pet.
Red Roof Inn - Rocky Mount 1370 North Wesleyan Boulevard Rocky Mount NC 252-984-0907 (800-RED-ROOF)
One well-behaved family pet per room. Guest must notify front desk upon arrival. Guest is liable for any damages. In consideration of all guests, pets must never be left unattended in the guest rooms.
Residence Inn by Marriott 230 Gateway Blvd Rocky Mount NC 252-451-5600
Dogs of all sizes are allowed. There is a $75 one time fee and a pet policy to sign at check in.
Super 8 Rocky Mount/Mosley Court Area 307 Mosley Court Rocky Mount NC 252-977-2858 (800-800-8000)
Dogs of all sizes are allowed. There is a $5 per night pet fee per pet. Smoking and non-smoking rooms are available for pet rooms.

Stores
Petco Pet Store 1100 N. Wesleyan Blvd Rocky Mount NC 252-442-1317
Your licensed and well-behaved leashed dog is allowed in the store.
PetSmart Pet Store 1462 Jeffreys Rd Rocky Mount NC 252-451-5200
Your licensed and well-behaved leashed dog is allowed in the store.

Rowland

Accommodations
Days Inn Rowland 14723 US Hwy 301 Rowland NC 910-422-3366 (800-329-7466)
Dogs of all sizes are allowed. There are no additional pet fees.

Rutherfordton

Campgrounds and RV Parks
Four Paws Kingdom 335 Lazy Creek Drive Rutherfordton NC 828-287-7324
http://www.4pawskingdom.com
Dogs of all sizes are allowed, however some breeds are not. There are no additional pet fees, and dogs must be cleaned up after. There are 2 park areas where your dog can run off leash; one for the large dogs and one for the smaller dogs. There is a pond dedicated for dogs and a bath house with a dog grooming area. The camping and tent areas also allow dogs. There is a dog walk area at the campground. Dogs are allowed in the camping cabins.

Salisbury

Accommodations
Hampton Inn 1001 Klumac Road Salisbury NC   704-637-8000
Dogs of all sizes are allowed. There are no additional pet fees. Dogs are not allowed to be left alone in the room.
Holiday Inn 530 Jake Alexander Blvd South Salisbury NC   704-637-3100 (877-270-6405)
Dogs up to 25 pounds are allowed for an additional one time fee of $15 per pet.

Outdoor Restaurants
Outback Steakhouse 1020 E Innes St Salisbury NC 704-637-1980
This restaurant serves Australian/American food. Dogs are allowed at the outdoor tables.

Sanford

Attractions
House in the Horseshoe 288 Alston House Road Sanford NC 910-947-2051
Rich in colonial history, this 18th century plantation features various exhibits, reenactments, and events telling of its era. This day use park also provides picnic tables and restroom areas. Dogs are allowed on the property; they are not allowed in any buildings and they must be leashed and cleaned up after.

Shopping Centers
TOP 200 PLACE **Fearrington Village** 2000 Fearrington Village Center Pittsboro NC 919-542-2121
http://www.fearrington.com/village/
In addition of offering a number of unique and eclectic varieties of shops, dining choices, and special events, this shopping center resides in farm country and comes complete with farm animals, folk art, and beautiful gardens that are open daily. Leashed, well behaved dogs are welcome.

Sapphire

Campgrounds and RV Parks
Gorges State Park 17762 Rosman H Sapphire NC 828-966-9099
Although a fairly new park still in development, there is much to enjoy, including waterfalls plunging through rocky river gorges, overlooks, a temperate rain forest, and easy to difficult trails. Primitive backpack camping is available with a 2.7 mile hike to the camp area. Dogs are allowed throughout the park and on the trails. Dogs may not be left unattended, and they must be on no more than a 6 foot leash, and cleaned up after. The camping and tent areas also allow dogs. There is a dog walk area at the campground. There are no electric or water hookups at the campgrounds.

Scaley Mountain

Accommodations
Fire Mountain Inn On H 106 Scaley Mountain NC   828-526-4446 (800-775-4446)
One dog up to 80 pounds is allowed, however they may accept 2 dogs if they are small. This place takes dogs only (no cats) and they must be over a year old and well house trained. There is a $25 per night per pet fee plus a $150 refundable deposit and a pet policy to sign at check in. Dogs are allowed in the cabins only.

Smithfield

Accommodations
Super 8 Motel 735 Industrial Park Drive Smithfield NC   919-989-8988 (800-800-8000)
Dogs of all sizes are allowed. There is a $6 per night per pet additional fee. Dogs must be leashed, cleaned up after, and a contact number left with the front desk if they are in the room alone.

Carolina Premium Outlets

Campgrounds and RV Parks
Selma/Smithfield KOA 428 Campground Road Selma NC   919-965-5923 (800-562-5897)
http://www.koa.com
Dogs of all sizes are allowed. There are no additional pet fees. Dogs may not be left unattended outside, and they must be in at night. Dogs must be quiet, leashed, and cleaned up after. The camping and tent areas also allow dogs. There is a dog walk area at the campground.

Attractions
Bentonville Battlefield State Historic Site 5466 Harper House Road Four Oaks NC   910-594-0789
In addition to being one of the best preserved battlefields of the Civil War, this also marks the site of the last major offensive by the Confederate Army, and with a mission to preserve and tell of its history they offer a number of special events, living history programs, and exhibits (including one with fiber-optics). Dogs are allowed on most of the grounds; they are not allowed in buildings. Dogs must be leashed and cleaned up after at all times.

Shopping Centers
Carolina Premium Outlets 1025 Industrial Park Drive Smithfield NC   919-989-8757
This outlet mall is an easy place to stop while driving I-95. There are more than 80 brand name outlets and services at this center. Dogs are allowed in the common areas; it is up to individual stores whether they are allowed inside. Dogs must be well behaved, leashed, and cleaned up after at all times.

Southern Pines

Accommodations

Motel 6 - Pinehurst - Aberdeen 1408 North Sandhills Boulevard Aberdeen NC   910-944-5633 (800-466-8356)
One well-behaved family pet per room. Guest must notify front desk upon arrival. Guest is liable for any damages. In consideration of all guests, pets must never be left unattended in the guest rooms.
Hampton Inn 1675 H 1S Southern Pines NC   910-692-9266
Dogs of all sizes are allowed. There is a $10 per night additional pet fee.
Residence Inn by Marriott 105 Bruce Wood Road Southern Pines NC   910-693-3400
Dogs of all sizes are allowed. There is a $50 one time fee and a pet policy to sign at check in.

Attractions

Weymouth Woods-Sandhills Nature Preserve 1024 Ft. Bragg Road Southern Pines NC   910-692-2167
Dedicated to protecting, preserving, and educating visitors about this unique ecosystem, this 898 acre, limited use, natural preserve affords visitors a glimpse of nature indigenous to the area. Dogs are allowed; they must be on no more than a 6 foot leash, and please pick up after your pet.

Stores

PetSmart Pet Store 11088 N US Hwy 15 501 Ste 600 Aberdeen NC   910-246-1587
Your licensed and well-behaved leashed dog is allowed in the store.
The Country Bookshop 140 NW Broad Street Southern Pines NC   910-692-3211
In operation for more than 50 years, this bookstore will allow your well behaved pooch inside, and they will probably be welcomed with doggy treats too.

Sunset Beach

Campgrounds and RV Parks

Shallotte/Brunswick Beaches KOA 7200 KOA Drive Sunset Beach NC   910-579-7562 (888-562-4240)
http://www.koa.com
Dogs of all sizes are allowed. There are no additional pet fees. Dogs may not be left unattended, and they must be up to date on shots, leashed, and cleaned up after. The camping and tent areas also allow dogs. There is a dog walk area at the campground.

Vacation Home Rentals

Sunset Properties 419 S. Sunset Blvd Sunset Beach NC   910-579-9900 (888-339-2670)
http://www.sunsetbeachnc.com
Some of these vacation rentals on Sunset Beach are pet-friendly. Those that are pet-friendly require a $150 non-refundable one time pet fee.

Swan Quarter

Transportation Systems

North Carolina Ferry-Swan Quarter Swan Quarter Ferry Road Swan Quarter NC   800-BY FERRY (293-3779)
These vehicle and passenger transport ferries are run by the state and provide service every day of the year on all routes; however weather conditions can influence travel. Dogs are allowed on all ferries for no additional fee; they must be kept in the vehicle or leashed when out of the vehicle. Dogs must be under owner's control/care at all times.

Parks

Mattamuskeet National Wildlife Refuge 2 Mattamuskeet Road Swan Quarter NC   252-926-4021
Covering some 50,000 acres of woodlands, marshes, and water and home to a shallow 18 mile long/7 mile wide lake, this refuge is home to over 800 species of birds and wildlife. It is known for being a place of quiet, serene beauty. Dogs are welcome on the trails of the refuge; they are not allowed to disturb wildlife in any way. Dogs must be under owner's control, leashed, and cleaned up after at all times.

Swannanoa

Campgrounds and RV Parks
Asheville East KOA 2708 H 70 E Swannanoa NC   828-686-3121 (800-562-5907)
http://www.koa.com/where/nc/33116/
Dogs of all sizes are allowed. There are no additional pet fees. Dogs may not be left unattended, and they must be quiet, leashed, and cleaned up after. The camping and tent areas also allow dogs. There is a dog walk area at the campground. Dogs are allowed in the camping cabins.
Mama Gerties Hideaway Campground 15 Uphill Road Swannanoa NC   828-686-4258
http://www.mamagerties.com
Dogs of all sizes are allowed, and there are no additional pet fees for tent or RV sites. There is a $5 per night per pet additional fee for the cabins. Dogs may not be left unattended, and they must be quiet, well behaved, leashed, and cleaned up after. There are some breed restrictions. The camping and tent areas also allow dogs. There is a dog walk area at the campground. Dogs are allowed in the camping cabins.

Tabor City

Campgrounds and RV Parks
Yogi Bear's Jellystone Park Resort @ Daddy Joe's 626 Richard Wright Road Tabor City NC   910-653-2155 (877-668-8586)
http://www.taborcityjellystone.com
Dogs of all sizes are allowed. There are no additional pet fees. Dogs must be leashed and cleaned up after. The camping and tent areas also allow dogs. There is a dog walk area at the campground.

Topsail Beach

Vacation Home Rentals
Idyll-by-the-Sea Two 134 Ocean View Lane North Topsail Beach NC   603-524-4000
This large vacation rental has 8 bedrooms and can sleep up to 18 people. It is almost 6000 square feet in size. Well behaved dogs of all sizes are welcome. You may contact the owners to make reservations at relax@idyll-by-the-sea.com or at 603-524-4000 or 240-238-4050 during business hours (ET).
Topsail Realty 712 S. Anderson Blvd. Topsail Beach NC   910-328-5241 (800-526-6432)
This realty company manages a few dog-friendly rentals in the Topsail Beach area. Dogs must be over 12 months old to stay in any of the properties and each has different pet terms.

Beaches
Topsail Beach Ocean Blvd Topsail Beach NC   910-328-5841
http://www.topsailbeach.org/
There are about 20 public accesses to the beaches in this town. From May 15th to September 30th dogs must be leashed when on the beach; otherwise dogs may be off lead if they are under strict adult voice control. Dogs must be cleaned up after at all times and always be leashed when not on the beach.

Troy

Campgrounds and RV Parks
Uwharrie National Forest 789 H 24/27E Troy NC   910-576-6391
http://www.cs.unca.edu/nfsnc/
This forest's diverse ecosystems support a large variety of plants, fish, mammals, bird species, trails, and recreation. Dogs of all sizes are allowed at no additional fee. Dogs may not be left unattended, and they must be leashed and cleaned up after. Dogs are not allowed in buildings. Dogs are allowed on the trails. The camping and tent areas also allow dogs. There is a dog walk area at the campground. There are no water hookups at the campground.

Attractions
Town Creek Indian Mound 509 Town Creek Mound Road Mount Gilead NC   910-439-6802
Rich in Native American history and culture, this site (with mounds and rebuilt structures) was once a key habitation area to a collection of tribes where major religious and clan activities took place. it is registered on the National Register of Historic Sites. Dogs are allowed on the grounds; they are not allowed in buildings, and they must be leashed and picked up after.

Weldon

Accommodations
Motel 6 - Roanoke Rapids 1911 Julian Alsbrook Highway Roanoke Rapids NC   252-537-5252 (800-466-8356)
One well-behaved family pet per room. Guest must notify front desk upon arrival. Guest is liable for any damages. In consideration of all guests, pets must never be left unattended in the guest rooms.
Days Inn Weldon 1611 Roanoke Rapids Rd Weldon NC   252-536-4867 (800-329-7466)
Dogs of all sizes are allowed. There is a $6 per night pet fee per pet.

Williamston

Accommodations
Holiday Inn US 17-64 Box 711 Williamston NC   252-792-3184 (877-270-6405)
Dogs up to 50 pounds are allowed for no additional fee.

Wilmington

Accommodations
Camellia Cottage Bed and Breakfast 118 S. 4th Street Wilmington NC   910-763-9171
http://www.camelliacottage.net/
Well-behaved dogs are welcome in the Crane Suite at this bed and breakfast inn. The pet-friendly room is located next to the front door, on the first floor. There are no pet fees.
Days Inn Wilmington 5040 Market St Wilmington NC   910-799-6300 (800-329-7466)
Dogs of all sizes are allowed. There is a $15 per night pet fee per pet. Pet must be kept in kennel when left alone.
Motel 6 - Wilmington 2828 Market Street Wilmington NC   910-762-0120 (800-466-8356)
One well-behaved family pet per room. Guest must notify front desk upon arrival. Guest is liable for any damages. In consideration of all guests, pets must never be left unattended in the guest rooms.
Residence Inn by Marriott 1200 Culbreth Drive Wilmington NC   910-256-0098
Dogs of all sizes are allowed. There is a $75 one time fee and a pet policy to sign at check in.
Waterway Lodge 7246 Wrightsville Avenue Wilmington NC   910-256-3771 (800-677-3771)
http://www.waterwaylodge.com
The Waterway Lodge offers standard motel rooms as well as one bedroom condo units with full kitchens. It is located on the Intercoastal Waterway, and a short walk to numerous shops, restaurants, marinas and the beach.

Stores
Coastal K9 Bakery 5905 Carolina Beach Road/H 421 Wilmington NC   910-794-4014
http://www.coastalk9bakery.com/
Using only the finest natural and organic ingredients, this bakery provides tasty human grade quality treats for their canine guests. Dogs are welcome in the store to try some treats and toys. Dogs must be well behaved, under owner's control/care, and leashed at all times.
Dog Gone Crazy 20 Market Street Wilmington NC   910-815-6670
This pet boutique carries a wide variety of pet supplies and accessories. Dogs are allowed in the store; they must be well behaved, under owner's control/care, and leashed at all times.
Petco Pet Store 324 S. College Rd Wilmington NC   910-799-2472
Your licensed and well-behaved leashed dog is allowed in the store.

PetSmart Pet Store 4715 E New Center Dr Wilmington NC   910-452-4422
Your licensed and well-behaved leashed dog is allowed in the store.
The Cotton Exchange Mall 321 N Front Street Wilmington NC   910-343-9896
http://www.shopcottonexchange.com/
Once one of the biggest and busiest cotton exporters, this shop area is still a bustling arena with 30 unique shops and eateries contained in 8 beautifully restored buildings that connect to each other by a series of walkways and open air courtyards. Dogs are allowed in the common areas of the mall; it is up to individual stores whether they are allowed inside. Dogs must be under owner's control, leashed, and cleaned up after at all times.

Off-Leash Dog Parks
Wilmington Dog Park at Empie Independence Blvd at Park Avenue Wilmington NC   910-341-3237
This fenced dog park is located on two acres in Empie Park. The dog park is open during daylight hours.

Outdoor Restaurants
Airlie Seafood Company 1410 Airlie Road Wilmington NC   910-256-3693
This eatery serves up beautiful waterfront dining, casual atmosphere, fresh seafood, and alfresco dining-weather permitting. Dogs are allowed at the outer tables; they must be under owner's control, leashed, and cleaned up after at all times.
Fat Tony's Italian Pizza 131 N Front Street Wilmington NC   910-343-8881
http://www.fattonysitalianpub.com/
In addition to offering 2 dozen draft beers, a good variety of fine wines, and homemade Italian food, this eatery also has ongoing weekly activities, themed and special events, and alfresco dining-weather permitting. Dogs are allowed at the outer tables; they must be under owner's control, leashed, and cleaned up after at all times.
Flaming Amy's Burrito Barn 4002 Oleander Drive/H 76 Wilmington NC   910-799-2919
In addition to a long list of specialty burritos, this eatery also offers such specialties as the Godzilladilla (their idea of a taco salad), logo items, and outside dining-weather permitting. Dogs are allowed at the outer tables; they must be under owner's control, leashed, and cleaned up after at all times.
The Caffe Phoenix 9 S Front Street Wilmington NC   910-343-1395
http://www.thecaffephoenix.com/
Specializing in fresh, local seafood, produce, and Mediterranean fare, this eatery also serves as a gallery for local artists, will cater casual to elegant affairs, and offers alfresco dining-weather permitting. Dogs are allowed at the outer tables; they must be under owner's control, leashed, and cleaned up after at all times.

Wilson

Accommodations
Best Western La Sammana 817-A Ward Blvd Wilson NC   252-237-8700 (800-780-7234)
Dogs are allowed for an additional fee of $10 per night per pet.
Holiday Inn Express Hotel and Suites 2308 Montgomery Dr Wilson NC   252-246-1588 (877-270-6405)
Dogs up to 65 pounds are allowed for an additional one time fee of $20 per pet. Dogs may not be left alone in the room at any time.

Winston - Salem

Accommodations
Days Inn Winston - Salem Convention Cntr 3330 Silas Creek Pkwy Winston - Salem NC   336-760-4770 (800-329-7466)
Dogs of all sizes are allowed. There is a $10 per night pet fee per pet.
Motel 6 - Winston - Salem 3810 Patterson Avenue Winston - Salem NC   336-661-1588 (800-466-8356)
One well-behaved family pet per room. Guest must notify front desk upon arrival. Guest is liable for any damages. In consideration of all guests, pets must never be left unattended in the guest rooms.
BW Salem Inn & Suites 127 S Cherry Street Winston-Salem NC   336-725-8561
Dogs are allowed for an additional one time pet fee of $25 per room.
La Quinta Inn & Suites Winston-Salem 2020 Griffith Road Winston-Salem NC   336-765-8777 (800-531-5900)
Dogs of all sizes are allowed. There are no additional pet fees. Dogs must be leashed, cleaned up after, and a contact number left with the front desk if there is a pet in the room alone.

Residence Inn by Marriott 7835 North Point Blvd Winston-Salem NC   336-759-0777
Dogs up to 75 pounds are allowed. There is a $75 one time fee and a pet policy to sign at check in.

Campgrounds and RV Parks
Hanging Rock State Park State Road 2015 Danbury NC   336-593-8480
Picturesque cascades and waterfalls, high rock cliffs, 18 miles of trails, and spectacular views are all located
here. In addition, the park hosts an interactive interpretive center and a variety of land and water activities and
recreation. Dogs of all sizes are allowed at no additional fee. Dogs may not be left unattended, and they must be
on no more than a 6 foot leash, and be cleaned up after. Dogs are not allowed in swim areas or in buildings.
Dogs are allowed on the trails. The camping and tent areas also allow dogs. There is a dog walk area at the
campground. There are no electric or water hookups at the campground.
Lake Meyers RV Resort 2862 H 64W Mocksville NC   336-492-7736
http://www.rvinthesun.com
Dogs of all sizes are allowed. There are no additional pet fees. Dogs may not be left unattended outside, and
they must be quiet, leashed, and cleaned up after. The camping and tent areas also allow dogs. There is a dog
walk area at the campground.
Pilot Mountain State Park 1792 Pilot Knob Park Road Pinnacle NC   336-352-2355
Dedicated as a National Natural Landmark, this park offers a wide variety of land and water recreational
activities. In addition, it has educational and interpretive programs and many miles of scenic hiking trails. Dogs of
all sizes are allowed at no additional fee. Dogs may not be left unattended, and they must be on no more than a
6 foot leash, and cleaned up after. Dogs are allowed on the trails. This campground is closed during the off-
season. The camping and tent areas also allow dogs. There is a dog walk area at the campground. There are no
electric or water hookups at the campground.

Attractions
TOP 200 PLACE **Old Salem** 601 Old Salem Road Salem NC   336-721-7350
http://www.oldsalem.org/
Old Salem is a living history town with restored buildings and costumed interpreters. Dogs are not allowed in the
buildings but you can still get a good flavor of the place and most of the buildings are small so you can take a
quick look inside if someone can watch the dog.

Old Salem

Bethabara Park 2147 Bethabara Road Winston-Salem NC   336-924-2580
http://www.bethabarapark.org/maphome.htm
Dedicated to obtaining, preserving, and educating visitors about the historic culture of this Moravian 1753
religious center and trading outpost, this 175 acre wildlife preserve (a National Historic Landmark) offers a living
history program complete with a reconstructed village, a visitor center, and nature trails.

Stores
Petco Pet Store 2080 S. Main St Kernersville NC   336-993-4982

Your licensed and well-behaved leashed dog is allowed in the store.
PetSmart Pet Store 950 Hanes Mall Blvd Winston-Salem NC   336-659-1995
Your licensed and well-behaved leashed dog is allowed in the store.
PetSmart Pet Store 438 E Hanes Mill Rd Winston-Salem NC   336-377-2399
Your licensed and well-behaved leashed dog is allowed in the store.
Piedmont Craftsmen Inc. 601 N Trade Street Winston-Salem NC   336-725-1516
http://piedmontcraftsmen.org/
This art/craft gallery will allowed well behaved, leashed dogs to explore the store with their owners. Dogs must be well trained and under owner's control/care at all times.

Parks

Tanglewood Park 4061 Clemmons Road Clemmons NC   336-778-6300
http://www.forsyth.cc/tanglewood/
A year round recreation destination, this park features gardens, gaming areas, green pastures, wooded areas, and waterways. Dogs are allowed on leash, and they must be picked up after.

Outdoor Restaurants

Celtic Cafe 201 S Stratford/H 158 Winston-Salem NC   336-703-0641
This café, known as a worldwide community for Celtic Culture, will allow dogs at their seasonal outside tables. Dogs must be under owner's control/care at all times.
Foothills Brewing 638 W 4th Street Winston-Salem NC   336-777-3348
http://www.foothillsbrewing.com/
Fresh, hand-crafted ales and food are the specialty here. Dogs are allowed at the other tables when weather permits. Dogs must be under owner's control/care at all times.

Yanceyville

Accommodations

Days Inn Yanceyville 1858 NC Hwy 86 North Yanceyville NC   336-694-9494 (800-329-7466)
Dogs of all sizes are allowed. There is a $10 per night pet fee per pet.

Chapter 17

South Carolina
Dog Travel Guide

Aiken

Accommodations
Holiday Inn Express 155 Colony Pkwy - Whiskey Rd Aiken SC   803-648-0999 (877-270-6405)
Dogs of all sizes are allowed for an additional one time pet fee of $45 per room.
Howard Johnson Express Inn 1936 Whiskey Road South Aiken SC   803-649-5000 (800-446-4656)
Dogs of all sizes are welcome. There is a $11.10 per day pet fee.
Quality Inn 110 E Frontage Road Aiken SC   803-502-0900 (877-424-6423)
Dogs are allowed for an additional one time pet fee of $15 per room.
Quality Inn and Suites 3608 Richland Avenue W Aiken SC   803-641-1100 (877-424-6423)
Dogs are allowed for an additional fee of $10 per night per pet.

Attractions
Hopeland Gardens 135 Dupree Place Aiken SC   803-642-7630
Fourteen acres of gardens, wetlands, historic sites, a beautiful gazebo, scenic paths, fountains, amphitheaters
and more can be found at this tranquil garden park. Dogs are allowed throughout the park; they must be leashed
and under owner's control/care at all times.

Stores
PetSmart Pet Store 2527 Whiskey Rd Aiken SC   803-643-8626
Your licensed and well-behaved leashed dog is allowed in the store.

Anderson

Accommodations
Country Inns & Suites by Carlson 116 Interstate Blvd Anderson SC   864-622-2200
Dogs of all sizes are allowed. There is a $15 one time additional pet fee.
Days Inn Anderson 1007 Smith Mill Rd Anderson SC   864-375-0375 (800-329-7466)
Dogs of all sizes are allowed. There is a $10 per night pet fee per pet.
La Quinta Inn Anderson 3430 Clemson Blvd. Anderson SC   864-225-3721 (800-531-5900)
Dogs of all sizes are allowed. There are no additional pet fees. Dogs may not be left unattended, and they must
be leashed and cleaned up after. Dogs may not be left unattended, unless they will be quiet and well behaved.
MainStay Suites 151 Civic Center Blvd Anderson SC   864-226-1112
Dogs are allowed for an additional one time pet fee of $35 per room.
Super 8 Anderson/Clemson Area 3302 Cinema Ave Anderson SC   864-225-8384 (800-800-8000)
Dogs of all sizes are allowed. There is a $25 one time per pet fee per visit. Smoking and non-smoking rooms are
available for pet rooms.

Campgrounds and RV Parks
Anderson/Lake Hartwell KOA 200 Wham Road Anderson SC   864-287-3161 (800-562-5804)
http://www.koa.com
Dogs of all sizes are allowed. There are no additional pet fees. Dogs may not be left unattended, and they must
be quiet, well behaved, leashed, and cleaned up after. The camping and tent areas also allow dogs. There is a
dog walk area at the campground. Dogs are allowed in the camping cabins.

Stores
PetSmart Pet Store 3523 Clemson Blvd Anderson SC   864-224-0436
Your licensed and well-behaved leashed dog is allowed in the store.

Barnwell

Stores
Little Red Barn Pottery 12080 H 278 Barnwell SC   803-541-7900
This cooperative of artists have brought together an eclectic array of unique, hand-crafted items ranging from soaps, herbal remedies, folk art, paintings, weavings, and a wide variety of numerous other items. They are normally open Wednesday through Saturday, and other times by appointment. Well behaved dogs that are cat friendly are welcome throughout the site. Dogs must be leashed and under owner's control/care at all times.

Beaufort

Accommodations
Howard Johnson Express Inn 3651 Trask Parkway, US Hwy 21 Beaufort SC   843-524-6020 (800-446-4656)
Dogs of all sizes are welcome. There is a $25 one time pet fee.

Campgrounds and RV Parks
Hunting Island State Park 2555 Sea Island Parkway Hunting Island SC   843-838-2011 (866-345-PARK (7275))
The state's most popular recreation destination, there is an abundance of wildlife, plenty of water and land fun, a maritime forest, tidal creeks, a saltwater lagoon, an historic publicly accessible lighthouse, and one of the longest public beaches in the low country at this 5,000 acre semi-tropical barrier island park. Dogs are allowed throughout the park, on the beach, and at campground; they are not allowed in the cabin areas. Dogs must be on no more than a 6 foot leash and cleaned up after. The camp area offers a day use area, fire rings, picnic tables, showers, restrooms, a playground, store, concessionaires, a laundry, and a dump station. The camping and tent areas also allow dogs. There is a dog walk area at the campground.

Beaches
Hunting Island State Park 2555 Sea Island Parkway Hunting Island SC   843-838-2011
This park offers over 4 miles of beach. Dogs on a 6 foot or less leash are allowed on the beach and on the trails at this state park. People need to clean up after their pets.

Parks
Hunting Island State Park 2555 Sea Island Parkway Hunting Island SC   843-838-2011 (866-345-PARK (7275))
The state's most popular recreation destination, there is an abundance of wildlife, plenty of water and land fun, a maritime forest, tidal creeks, a saltwater lagoon, an historic publicly accessible lighthouse, and one of the longest public beaches in the low country at this 5,000 acre semi-tropical barrier island park. Dogs are allowed throughout the park, on the beach, and at campground; they are not allowed in the cabin areas. Dogs must be on no more than a 6 foot leash and cleaned up after.

Outdoor Restaurants
Hemmingway's Bistro 920 Bay St Beaufort SC   843-521-4480
This restaurant serves American food. Dogs are allowed at the outdoor tables.

Beech Island

Attractions
Redcliffe Plantation State Historic Site 181 Redcliffe Road Beech Island SC   803-827-1473
Rich in colonial history, this beautifully landscaped estate greets visitors with an entry lane of 145 year old magnolia trees, an 1859 Greek Revival home, an heirloom garden, and several other out buildings. Dogs are allowed throughout the grounds; they are not allowed in the mansion or other buildings. Dogs must be on no more than a 6 foot leash and be under owner's control/care at all times.

Blackville

Campgrounds and RV Parks
Barnwell State Park 223 State Park Road Blackville SC   803-284-2212 (866-345-PARK (7275))
Although popular for its great fishing and recreation center, this 307 acre park also features a 1½ mile
interpretive trail with signage on many of the plants and trees. Dogs are allowed throughout the park, on the
beach, and at the campground; they are not allowed in the cabin areas. Dogs must be on no more than a 6 foot
leash and cleaned up after. The campground has about 25 sites with restrooms, hot showers, and a dump
station on site. The camping and tent areas also allow dogs. There is a dog walk area at the campground.

Parks
Barnwell State Park 223 State Park Road Blackville SC   803-284-2212 (866-345-PARK (7275))
Although popular for its great fishing and recreation center, this 307 acre park also features a 1½ mile
interpretive trail with signage on many of the plants and trees. Dogs are allowed throughout the park, on the
beach, and at the campground; they are not allowed in the cabin areas. Dogs must be on no more than a 6 foot
leash and cleaned up after.

Calhoun Falls

Campgrounds and RV Parks
Calhoun Falls State Park 46 Maintenance Shop Road Calhoun Falls SC   864-447-8269 (866-345-PARK
(7275))
This park, located on one of the state's most popular fishing lakes, also provides a scenic trail, nature study
opportunities, and a variety of recreation. Dogs of all sizes are allowed at no additional fee. Dogs may not be left
unattended, and they must be on no more than a 6 foot leash, and be cleaned up after in camp areas. Dogs are
not allowed in buildings or on the beach. Dogs are allowed on the trails. The camping and tent areas also allow
dogs. There is a dog walk area at the campground.

Charleston

Accommodations
Best Western Charleston Downtown 250 Spring Street Charleston SC   843-722-4000 (800-780-7234)
http://www.CharlestonBestWestern.com
Dogs of all sizes are allowed at this downtown Charleston hotel. There is a $25.00 nightly pet fee per pet.
Indigo Inn Maiden Lane Charleston SC   843-577-5900 (800-845-7639)
There is a $20 per day pet fee.
La Quinta Inn Charleston Riverview 11 Ashley Pointe Drive Charleston SC   843-556-5200 (800-531-5900)
Dogs of all sizes are allowed. There are no additional pet fees. Dogs must be declared at the time of check in,
and there is a pet waiver to sign. Dogs must be leashed, cleaned up after, and the Do Not Disturb sign put on the
door if there is a pet in the room alone.
Motel 6 - Charleston South 2058 Savannah Highway Charleston SC   843-556-5144 (800-466-8356)
One well-behaved family pet per room. Guest must notify front desk upon arrival. Guest is liable for any
damages. In consideration of all guests, pets must never be left unattended in the guest rooms.
Quality Suites Convention Center 5225 N Arco Lane Charleston SC   843-747-7300
Dogs up to 50 pounds are allowed for an additional one time fee of $49 per pet.
Residence Inn by Marriott 90 Ripley Point Drive Charleston SC   843-571-7979
Dogs of all sizes are allowed. There is a $75 one time fee and a pet policy to sign at check in.
Days Inn Charleston/Goose Creek 1430 Redbank Rd Goose Creek SC   843-797-6000 (800-329-7466)
Dogs of all sizes are allowed. There is a $10 per night pet fee per pet. Reservations are recommended due to
limited rooms for pets.
Quality Inn 103 Red Bank Road Goose Creek SC   843-572-9500 (877-424-6423)
Dogs are allowed for an additional one time pet fee of $25 per room.
Days Inn Charleston Patriots Point 261 Johnnie Dodds Blvd Mount Pleasant SC   843-881-1800 (800-329-
7466)
Dogs of all sizes are allowed. There is a $10 per night pet fee per pet.
MainStay Suites 400 McGrath Darby Blvd. Mount Pleasant SC   843-881-1722
We are a 71 suite hotel with a designated dog walk area, treats from our staff in the lobby and lots of hugs from
all. A $10 fee per day is charged plus any damages will be repaired and charged at cost to the guest.
Masters Inn 300 Wingo Way Mount Pleasant SC   843-884-2814

There is a $5 per day pet fee.

Red Roof Inn - Charleston - Mt Pleasant, SC 301 Johnnie Dodds Boulevard Mount Pleasant SC   843-884-1411 (800-RED-ROOF)
One well-behaved family pet per room. Guest must notify front desk upon arrival. Guest is liable for any damages. In consideration of all guests, pets must never be left unattended in the guest rooms.

Residence Inn by Marriott Isle of Palms Connector Mount Pleasant SC   843-881-1599
Dogs of all sizes are allowed. There is a $75 one time fee and a pet policy to sign at check in.

Candlewood Suites I-26 @ Northwoods Mall 2177 Northwoods Blvd North Charleston SC   843-797-3535 (877-270-6405)
Dogs of all sizes are allowed, but there may only be 1 large or 2 dogs per room. There is an additional pet fee of $12 per night for up to 11 nights; 12 nights and over is a maximum fee of $150.

Motel 6 - Charleston North 2551 Ashley Phosphate Road North Charleston SC   843-572-6590 (800-466-8356)
One well-behaved family pet per room. Guest must notify front desk upon arrival. Guest is liable for any damages. In consideration of all guests, pets must never be left unattended in the guest rooms.

Quality Inn 7415 Northside Drive North Charleston SC   843-572-6677 (877-424-6423)
Dogs up to 65 pounds are allowed for an additional one time fee of $15 per pet.

Red Roof Inn - Charleston North, SC 7480 Northwoods Boulevard North Charleston SC   843-572-9100 (800-RED-ROOF)
One well-behaved family pet per room. Guest must notify front desk upon arrival. Guest is liable for any damages. In consideration of all guests, pets must never be left unattended in the guest rooms.

Residence Inn by Marriott 7645 Northwoods Blvd North Charleston SC   843-572-5757
Dogs up to 60 pounds are allowed. There is a $75 one time fee and a pet policy to sign at check in.

Sheraton Hotel North Charleston Convention Center 4770 Goer Dr. North Charleston SC   843-747-1900 (888-625-5144)
Dogs of all sizes are allowed for an additional one time pet fee of $40 per room. Dogs may not be left alone in the room.

Comfort Inn 1005 Jockey Court Summerville SC   843-851-2333 (877-424-6423)
Large dogs are allowed for an additional one time fee of $35 per pet, and small dogs for $25 per pet.

Holiday Inn Express 120 Holiday Inn Drive, I-26 Exit 199A Summerville SC   843-875-3300 (877-270-6405)
Quiet dogs of all sizes are allowed for no additional pet fee.

Campgrounds and RV Parks

James Island County Park Campground 871 Riverland Drive Charleston SC   843-795-7275
http://www.ccprc.com
Dogs of all sizes are allowed. There are no additional pet fees. Dogs may not be left unattended outside, and may only be left inside an RV if there is temperature control. Dogs must be quiet during quiet hours, leashed, and cleaned up after. There is an fenced in Dog Park where dogs may run off lead. The camping and tent areas also allow dogs. There is a dog walk area at the campground.

Oak Plantation Campground 3540 Savannah H Charleston SC   843-766-5936
http://www.oakplantationcampground.com
Dogs of all sizes are allowed. There are no additional pet fees. Dogs may not be left unattended outside, they must be leashed at all times, and cleaned up after. There is a large fenced in dog run where dogs may run off lead. There is a dog walk area at the campground.

Lake Aire RV Park Campground 4375 H 162 Hollywood SC   843-571-1271
http://www.lakeairerv.com
Dogs of all sizes are allowed. There are no additional pet fees. Dogs may not be left unattended, and may only be left in the RV if there is tempurature control. Dogs must be well behaved, friendly, leashed, and cleaned up after. There is a dog walk area at the campground.

Charleston KOA 9494 H 78 Ladson SC   843-797-1045 (800-562-5812)
http://www.koa.com
Dogs of all sizes are allowed. There are no additional pet fees. Dogs may not be left unattended, and they must be leashed and cleaned up after. The camping and tent areas also allow dogs. There is a dog walk area at the campground. Dogs are allowed in the camping cabins.

Mt Pleasant/Charleston KOA 3157 H 17 Mount Pleasant SC   843-849-5177 (800-562-5769)
http://www.koa.com
Dogs of all sizes are allowed. There are no additional pet fees. Dogs may not be left unattended outside, and they must be leashed and cleaned up after. The camping and tent areas also allow dogs. There is a dog walk area at the campground. Dogs are allowed in the camping cabins.

Vacation Home Rentals

Charleston Cottage Call to Arrange Charleston SC   207-342-5444
http://www.landworkswaterfront.com

Located on the corner of East Bay and Tradd, this vacation rental is one block from the waterfront park and diagonally across the street from the dog park. Restaurants, historic spots of interest, fine shopping, galleries and the Battery are all within walking distance.

Attractions

Battery and White Point Gardens East Battery Street and Murray Blvd. Charleston SC   843-853-8000
A rich cultural and military history can be seen throughout this park. Dogs are allowed in the park; they must be leashed and under owner's control/care at all times.

Carolina Polo and Carriage Company 181 Church St (In lobby of Doubletree Hotel) and 16 Hayne St Charleston SC   843-577-6767
http://www.cpcc.com/
Rich with stories and sites of the Charleston area, visitors will get more than the average tour with this carriage company that have tour guides with familial ties dating back to the 1600's. Dogs are allowed on the carriage tours for no additional fee if they are small enough not to take up a seat; otherwise for a medium to large dog, the fee is the child's fee of $12. Dogs must be well mannered, leashed and under owner's control/care at all times.

Charleston Strolls 115 Meeting Street Charleston SC   843-766-2080
http://www.tours@charlestonstrolls.com
Tour where carriages and motorcoaches are not allowed as you take a fascinating stroll revealing Charleston's rich history. The tour is about 2 hours long and only 20 at a time can go, so reservations in advanced are needed. Well behaved and leashed dogs are allowed.

Magnolia Plantation and Gardens 3550 Ashley River Road Charleston SC   843-571-1266
www.magnoliaplantation.com
Magnolia Plantation and Gardens offers the oldest major public garden in America and possibly America's oldest man-made attraction. They are open 365 days a year, including all major holidays. From March through October, they are open from 8 am until dusk, with ticket sales ending at 5:30 pm. Call for November through February hours, as they vary slightly. Dogs on leash are allowed on the grounds but not in the buildings.

Palmetto Carriage Works 40 N Market Street Charleston SC   843-723-8145
http://www.carriagetour.com/splash.asp
Offering a blend of humor, history, and years of accumulated knowledge, this carriage company starts the tours at the Red Barn located in the Market area and takes visitors throughout the historic district. Dogs are allowed on the carriage tours for no additional fee if they are small enough not to take up a seat; otherwise for a medium to large dog, the fee is the child's fee. Dogs must be quiet, well mannered, leashed and under owner's control/care at all times.

Taylored Tours 375 Meeting Street/H 52 Charleston SC   888-449-TOUR (8687)
http://www.toursofcharleston.com/
This tour company will be glad to "tailor" make tours for guests, and they offer a variety of tour lengths, sights, and areas of interest. Dogs are allowed on the mini-bus for no additional fee if no one objects or private tours for $60 per hour (2 hour minimum) are available. Dogs must be quiet, well mannered, leashed and under owner's control/care at all times. Very large dogs are not allowed.

The Original Charleston Walks and Ghost Tours 58 1/2 Broad Street Charleston SC   843-577-3800
http://www.charlestonwalks.com
This guided walking tour is through the historic district of Charleston. Reservations in advance are needed. They are open daily year round from 9 am to 9:30pm. Dogs must be quiet, well behaved, and leashed. Dogs are not allowed on the Historic Homes Walk, but they are on all other tours. Tours are about 2 hours, and the Ghost Tour is about 1 1/2 hours.

TOP 200 PLACE **Tour Charleston Ghost Tours** 45 Broad Street Suite 200 Charleston SC   843-577-3800
(800-729-3420)
http://www.tourcharleston.com
This ghost tour company not only welcomes dogs on their ghost tours, they have dogs of their own who may be joining the tour from time to time. Other tours may be available as well.

Barrier Island Ecotours 50 41st Avenue Isle of Palms SC   843-886-5000
The ecotours are on large catamarans from 2 1/2 to 3 1/2 hours with a stop on an island, and they run year round. Although not a common request, 1 well behaved, leashed dog is allowed on the tour. Please bring clean up bags for your pet.

Boone Hall Plantation and Gardens 1235 Long Point Road Mount Pleasant SC   843-571-1266
http://boonehallplantation.com
Amazing, centuries old, moss draped oak trees form a canopy of greeting across the road as visitors come to visit this 1743 living history, southern plantation museum; also known as America's most photographed plantation. Dogs are allowed throughout the grounds; they are not allowed in buildings. Dogs must be leashed and under owner's control/care at all times.

Cap'n Richards ACE Basin Kayak Rentals 514B Mill Street Mount Pleasant SC   843-884-7684
http://www.coastalexpiditions.com
Dogs are not allowed on the guided tours, however they can go on a kayak, which can be rented. Open all year.

Fort Moultrie National Historic Site 1214 Middle Street Sullivan Island SC 843-883-3123
http://www.nps.gov/fosu
This place has the distinction of being the site where the American Civil War began, and for many decades past it held military influence. Dogs are allowed throughout the grounds; they are not allowed in the fort. Dogs must be leashed and under owner's control/care at all times.

Stores

Three Dog Bakery 430 King Street Charleston SC 843-937-9895
https://www.threedog.com/Default.aspx
Specializing in providing treats that are tasty and healthy, this bakery makes their treats free of artificial ingredients or harsh substances. Well behaved, leashed dogs are welcome in the store.
Palmentto Paws 1739 Maybank H, Suite A8/H 700 James Island SC 843-971-2039
http://www.palmettopaws.com/
Specializing in human grade, healthy ingredients for their pet foods and treats, they also offer a do-it-yourself dog washing station and a full line of pet supplies, toys, apparel, holiday themed items, gifts, and more. Dogs must be people and pet friendly, leashed, and under owner's control/care at all times.
Palmetto Paws 976 Houston Northcutt Blvd Mount Pleasant SC 843-216-3995
http://www.palmettopaws.com/
Specializing in human grade, healthy ingredients for their pet foods and treats, they also offer a do-it-yourself dog washing station and a full line of pet supplies, toys, apparel, holiday themed items, gifts, and more. Dogs must be people and pet friendly, leashed, and under owner's control/care at all times.
PetSmart Pet Store 676 Long Point Rd Mount Pleasant SC 843-884-1419
Your licensed and well-behaved leashed dog is allowed in the store.
PetSmart Pet Store 470 Azalea Square Blvd Summerville SC 843-821-7043
Your licensed and well-behaved leashed dog is allowed in the store.

Beaches

Folly Beach County Park Ashley Avenue Folly Beach SC 843-588-2426
http://www.beachparks.com/follybeach.htm
Dogs are only allowed during the off-season at this beach. They are not allowed from May 1 through September 30. But the rest of the year, dogs on leash are allowed on the beach during park hours. People are required to clean up after their pets. The park is located on the west end of Folly Island. On the island, turn right at Ashley Avenue stoplight and go to the end of the road.
TOP 200 PLACE Isle of Palms County Park Beach 14th Avenue Isle of Palms SC 843-886-3863
Dogs on leash are allowed year-round at this beach. People are required to clean up after their pets. The park is located on the Isle of Palms, on 14th Ave., between Palm Blvd. and Ocean Blvd. Then coming to Isle of Palms from 517, continue straight at the Palm Blvd intersection and then take the next left at the park gate.
Beachwalker County Park Beachwalker Drive Kiawah SC 843-768-2395
Dogs on leash are allowed year-round at this beach. People are required to clean up after their pets. The park is located on the west end of Kiawah Island. Take Bohicket Road to the island. Just before the island security gate, turn right on Beachwalker Drive. Follow the road to the park.
Sullivan Island Beach Atlantic Avenue Sullivan's Island SC 843-883-3198
http://www.sullivansisland-sc.com/
Dogs are allowed off leash on this barrier island beach from 5 AM to 10 AM April through October, and from 5 AM to 12 Noon November 1st to March 31st; this does not include walkways or access paths to the area where they must be leashed (no longer than 10 feet). A pet permit is required that can be obtained at the Town Hall at 1610 Middle Street-proof of vaccinations and rabies required. Dogs are not allowed on the beach, paths, or the adjacent waters at any time from 10 AM to 6 PM from April 1st to October 31st; however they are allowed at these areas on a leash from 6 PM to 5 AM, April 1st to October 31st, and from 12 Noon to 5 AM from November 1st to March 31st. Dogs must be under owner's control/care at all times. Dogs must be leashed when not in designated off-lead areas.

Parks

Audubon Swamp Garden 3550 Ashley River Road/H 61 Charleston SC 843-571-1266
Boardwalks, bridges, boats, and dikes take visitors through this unique inner world where there is a tremendous diversity of plant, animal, and bird life living among the black swamp waters, forests, and floating islands. Dogs are allowed throughout the park; they must be leashed and under owner's control/care at all times.
Charles Towne Landing State Historic Site 1500 Old Town Road Charleston SC 843-852-4200
This park reopened in the Fall of 2006 with a few new interesting features such as a re-built replica of an 18th-century trading ship (The Adventure), a new visitors center--complete with a museum and archaeology lab, an interpretive trail, and an Animal Forest. Dogs of all sizes are allowed at no additional fee. Dogs may not be left unattended, and they must be on no more than a 6 foot leash at all times, and be cleaned up after. Pets are not

allowed in buildings, the Animal Forest, and on the Adventure, however, they are allowed in most other outdoor areas while on lead. The park is open daily from 8:30 am to 5 pm.
Hampton Park corner of Rutledge and Grove Charleston SC
http://www.charlestoncity.info
This park has a fenced dog run for your pet. Dogs must be on leash when not in the dog run.
James Island County Park 871 Riverland Drive Charleston SC   843-795-7275
http://www.ccprc.com
James Island County Park is a 643 acre nature-oriented park for family and group use, with many additional activities and facilities. There is tidal creek fishing, peddle boat and kayak rentals, paved trails for walking, biking, skating, a children's Funyard playground, a Spray Play Fountain area (seasonal), a picnic center, and an Off-Leash pet area. Dogs must be leashed when entering and exiting the Dog Park and at all times when outside of the designated off-leash area, and dogs must be current on rabies vaccinations and wear current tags.
Waterfront Park corner of Vedue Range and Concord Charleston SC   843-724-7321
This park is used to a lot of dog traffic. They have doggy fountains and provide clean up bags. Dogs must be on leash.
White Point Gardens On Murray Street at the end of E Bay Street Charleston SC   843-724-7327
The park is open daily from dawn to dusk. Dogs on leash are allowed.
Charles Pincheny National Historic Site 1254 Long Point Road Mount Pleasant SC 843-881-5516
http://www.nps.gov/chpi
The historic site was established to show Charles Pinckney's plantation named Snee Farm, his role in the development of the United States Constitution and the transition of the United States from a group of colonies to a young nation. Dogs on leash are allowed on the grounds but not in the house. They are open all year from 9:00 a.m. to 5:00 p.m.
Palmetto Island County Park 444 Needle Rush Parkway Mount Pleasant SC   843-884-0832
http://www.ccprc.com
Palmetto Islands County Park is a nature-oriented, 943 acre park designed for family and group use. It is built in a tropical setting, with bike paths, boardwalks and picnic sites located throughout the park. There are fishing and crabbing docks, an observation tower with play area, a nature island, seasonal waterpark, and more, Dogs on leash are allowed at this park, but not in the buildings or on the playgrounds.

Off-Leash Dog Parks
Hampton Park Off-Leash Dog Park corner of Rutledge and Grove Charleston SC
http://www.charlestoncity.info
This park has a fenced dog run for your pet. Dogs must be on leash when not in the dog run area.
James Island County Park Dog Park 871 Riverland Drive Charleston SC   843-795-PARK (7275)
Located in the 643 acre James Island County Park, this is the only off leash dog area in town that also has lake access. There is drinking water for humans and pooches, water hoses for cooling/cleaning off, and bag stations with collection cans on site. The dog park is closed here each Wednesday from 7 to 9 AM for regular maintenance. Dogs must be sociable, current on all vaccinations, and under owner's control/care at all times. Dogs must be leashed when not in designated off-lead areas.
Isle of Palms Dog Park 29th Ave behind Rec Center Isle of Palms SC   843-886-8294
This fenced dog park is open from sunrise to sunset. The park is closed on Wednesdays from 10 am - 12 noon for cleaning. Children under 12 are not allowed into the dog park.
Palmetto Islands County Park Dog Park 444 Needlerush Parkway Mount Pleasant SC   843-572- PARK (7275)
This off lead area is located in the lush, tropical setting of the 943 acre Mount Pleasant Palmetto Islands County Park, and provides drinking water for humans and pooches, water hoses for cooling/cleaning off, and bag stations with collection cans. Dogs must be sociable, current on all vaccinations, and under owner's control/care at all times. Dogs must be leashed when not in designated off-lead areas.
Wannamaker County Park Dog Park 8888 University Blvd North Charleston SC   843-572- PARK (7275)
Located in the 1,015 acre Wannamaker County Park, a scenic experience of woodlands and wetlands with miles of trails to enjoy the natural surroundings, this off lead area provides drinking water for humans and pooches, water hoses for cooling/cleaning off, and bag stations with collection cans. Dogs must be sociable, current on all vaccinations, and under owner's control/care at all times. Dogs must be leashed when not in designated off-lead areas.

Outdoor Restaurants
39 Rue de Jean 39 John Street Charleston SC   843-722-8881
http://www.39ruedejean.com/
This French café and bar provides a casual elegant setting and classic Brasserie cuisine. Outside seating is available; dogs are allowed at the outer tables. They must be leashed and under owner's control/care at all times.
Port City Java 372 King St Charleston SC 843-577-4075

This coffee shop will allow dogs at the outdoor tables.
The Bubba Gump Shrimp Co. Restaurant & Market 99 S Market St Charleston SC   843-723-5665
This restaurant and bar serves seafood and American. Dogs are allowed at the outdoor tables.
Dog and Duck 624 Long Point Rd Unit A Mount Pleasant SC   843-881-3056
http://www.dogandduckpubs.com/
This sandwich shop offers a casual atmosphere and outside dining. Dogs are allowed at the outer tables; they
must be leashed and under owner's control/care at all times.
Red's Ice House 98 Church St Mount Pleasant SC   843-388-0003
This restaurant serves American and seafood. Dogs are allowed at the outdoor tables.
Sticky Fingers BBQ 341 Johnnie Dodds Blvd Mount Pleasant SC   843-856-8970
http://www.stickyfingersonline.com
This restaurant serves barbecue food. Dogs are allowed at the outdoor tables.
Poe's Tavern 2210 Middle Street Sullivan's Island SC   843-883-0083
http://www.poestavern.com/
Located only a 100 yards from the ocean in the heart of Sullivan's Island where Edgar Allen Poe spent 13
months during his service in the Army, this tavern celebrates and preserves this literary giant as well as providing
a number of all American favorites on the menu and a selection of beer and wines. Outside seating is available;
dogs are allowed at the outer tables. They must be leashed and under owner's control/care at all times.
Dog and Duck 1580-J Old Trolley Road Summerville SC   843-821-3056
http://www.dogandduckpubs.com/
This sandwich shop offers a casual atmosphere and outside dining. Dogs are allowed at the outer tables; they
must be leashed and under owner's control/care at all times.

Charlotte Area

Accommodations
Motel 6 - Charlotte Carowinds 255 Carowinds Boulevard Fort Mill SC   803-548-9656 (800-466-8356)
One well-behaved family pet per room. Guest must notify front desk upon arrival. Guest is liable for any
damages. In consideration of all guests, pets must never be left unattended in the guest rooms.
Super 8 Richburg/Chester Area 3085 Lancaster Hwy Richburg SC   803-789-7888 (800-800-8000)
Dogs of all sizes are allowed. There is a $5 per night pet fee per pet. Smoking and non-smoking rooms are
available for pet rooms.
Quality Inn and Suites 2625 Cherry Road Rock Hill SC   803-329-3121 (877-424-6423)
Dogs are allowed for an additional fee of $10 per night per pet.
Days Inn York 1568 Alexander Love Hwy York SC   803-684-2525 (800-329-7466)
Dogs of all sizes are allowed. There is a $5 per night pet fee per pet.

Attractions
Charlotte Knights-Dog Day Game Gold Hill Road (Exit 88 off I-77) Fort Mill SC   704-357-8071
Once a year, the Charlotte Knights minor league baseball team invites four-legged fans to attend their Dog Day
Game. This dog-friendly game is usually in August. Dogs are welcome to sit with their owners at any seat
throughout the ballpark. If your pooch is itching to walk around, dogs are also welcome on the concourse. Just
remember to clean up after your pooch!
Glencairn Garden 725 Crest St Rock Hill SC   803-329-5620
There are 6 scenic, fragrant acres at this lush garden that offers an Oriental influence, a tiered fountain,
picturesque trails, hundreds of flowers/leaf plants, and more than 3,000 azaleas. Dogs are allowed throughout
the garden. They must be kept leashed and picked up after at all times.

Stores
PetSmart Pet Store 1110 Hospitality Dr Rock Hill SC   803-817-6610
Your licensed and well-behaved leashed dog is allowed in the store.

Parks
Landsford Canal State Park 2051 Park Drive Catawba SC   803-789-5800
Rich in natural, cultural, and colonial history, this riverside park still has an intact mill site, locks, and a home
from the early 1800's plus interpretive signage. Favorite pastimes here include wildlife viewing, hiking, fishing,
and in late May and early June to watch the spectacular blooms of the white spider lily flowers. Dogs are allowed
throughout the park; they must be on no more than a 6 foot leash and under owner's control/care at all times.

Cheraw

Accommodations

Days Inn Cheraw 820 Market St Cheraw SC 843-537-5554 (800-329-7466)
Dogs of all sizes are allowed. There is a $5 per night pet fee per pet.

Clemson

Campgrounds and RV Parks

Lake Hartwell State Rec Area 19138 A H 11S Fair Play SC 864-972-3352 (866-345-PARK (7275))
Sports enthusiasts, campers, and nature lovers all like the easy access to this park with 14 miles of Lake Hartwell shoreline. Dogs of all sizes are allowed at no additional fee. Dogs may not be left unattended outside, and may only be left inside if they will be quiet, well behaved, and comfortable. Dogs must be on no more than a 6 foot leash, and be cleaned up after. Dogs are allowed on the trails. The camping and tent areas also allow dogs. There is a dog walk area at the campground.
Lake Hartwell Camping and Cabins 400 Ponderosa Point Townville SC 888-427-8935
http://www.lakehartwell.com
Dogs of all sizes are allowed, and there are no additional pet fees for tent or RV sites. There is a $25 one time pet fee for the cabins. Dogs must be leashed and cleaned up after. There are some breed restrictions. The camping and tent areas also allow dogs. There is a dog walk area at the campground.
Crooked Creek RV Park 777 Arvee lane West Union SC 864-882-5040
http://www.crookedcreekrvpark.com
Dogs of all sizes are allowed. There are no additional pet fees. Dogs are not allowed in the buildings or the pool area, and they must be leashed and cleaned up after. The camping and tent areas also allow dogs. There is a dog walk area at the campground.

Attractions

TOP 200 PLACE **South Carolina Botanical Gardens** Perimeter Road Clemson SC 864-656-3405
http://www.clemson.edu/scbg/
This 295 acre site offers a number of attractions and activities; there is a beautiful waterfall flowing into a serene pond of bright Koi fish, 70 acres of demonstration and display gardens, more than 90 acres of woods and waterways with some great hiking trails. Plus they offer a 40 acre arboretum, diverse habitats and their inhabitants, and native plants for sale. Dogs are allowed throughout the park; they are not allowed in buildings. Dogs must be leashed and under owner's control/care at all times.

Parks

Pendleton Village Green 125 E Queen Street Pendleton SC 864-646-3782
Located in one of the largest historic districts in America (50+ pre-1850 buildings) and listed on the National Register of Historic Places, the Village Green is home to the landmark Pendleton Farmers Society Hall from whose beginnings brought about the Clemson University. You can also find a hall with a very large collection of the area's history and genealogy and an active business district of eateries and various shops. Dogs are allowed throughout the town; they are not allowed in buildings (unless invited). Dogs must be leashed and under owner's control/care at all times.

Columbia

Accommodations

Carolinian Hotel 7510 Two Notch Rd, I-20 & US-1 Columbia SC 803-736-3000
There is a $25 one time pet fee. Pets must be leashed when they are not in your room.
Days Inn Columbia 133 Plumbers Rd Columbia SC 803-754-4408 (800-329-7466)
Dogs of all sizes are allowed. There is a $8 per night pet fee per pet.
La Quinta Inn Columbia NE/Fort Jackson 1538 Horseshoe Drive Columbia SC 803-736-6400 (800-531-5900)
Dogs of all sizes are allowed. There are no additional pet fees. Dogs must be crated if left alone in the room.

Dogs are not allowed in the breakfast area, and they must be leashed and cleaned up after.
Motel 6 - Columbia East 7541 Nates Road Columbia SC 803-736-3900 (800-466-8356)
One well-behaved family pet per room. Guest must notify front desk upon arrival. Guest is liable for any damages. In consideration of all guests, pets must never be left unattended in the guest rooms.
Motel 6 - Columbia West 1776 Burning Tree Road Columbia SC 803-798-9210 (800-466-8356)
One well-behaved family pet per room. Guest must notify front desk upon arrival. Guest is liable for any damages. In consideration of all guests, pets must never be left unattended in the guest rooms.
Red Roof Inn - Columbia East, SC 7580 Two Notch Road Columbia SC 803-736-0850 (800-RED-ROOF)
One well-behaved family pet per room. Guest must notify front desk upon arrival. Guest is liable for any damages. In consideration of all guests, pets must never be left unattended in the guest rooms.
Red Roof Inn - Columbia West, SC 10 Berryhill Road Columbia SC 803-798-9220 (800-RED-ROOF)
One well-behaved family pet per room. Guest must notify front desk upon arrival. Guest is liable for any damages. In consideration of all guests, pets must never be left unattended in the guest rooms.
Residence Inn by Marriott 150 Stoneridge Drive Columbia SC 803-779-7000
Well behaved dogs of all sizes are allowed. There is a $50 one time fee on the first night. Starting the second night is a $10 per night fee, and there will be a pet policy to sign at check in.
TownePlace Suites Columbia 350 Columbiana Drive Columbia SC 803-781-9391
Dogs of all sizes are allowed. There is a $75 one time pet fee per visit.
Quality Inn & Suites 328 W Main Street Lexington SC 803-359-3099 (877-424-6423)
Dogs totaling no more than 60 pounds are allowed for an additional fee of $50 per night per pet.

Campgrounds and RV Parks
Francis Marion and Sumter National Forests 4931 Broad River Road Columbia SC 803-561-4000
http://www.fs.fed.us/r8/fms/
Four ranger districts oversee more than 600,000 acres of forest lands rich with diverse ecosystems that support a large variety habitats and wildlife, cultural history, and recreational opportunities. There is also an environmental education center with numerous activities and programs, a 36 mile trail that goes from the mountains to the sea, and many other sites of interest. Dogs are allowed throughout the forest and campground areas; they must be leashed and under owner's control/care at all times. There are a variety of camp sites in numerous settings each with their own special features. Campsites may have all or some of the following: flush or vault toilets, restrooms, showers, tables, grills, lantern holders, drinking water, and a dump station. The camping and tent areas also allow dogs. There is a dog walk area at the campground. There are no electric or water hookups at the campgrounds.
Sesquicentennial State Park 9564 Two Notch Road Columbia SC 803-788-2706
A major recreation destination, this scenic 1,419 acre park offers a long list of amenities, activities, a 30 acre lake, interpretive nature programs, and much more. This park is also home to a 2 acre, double sectioned, off-leash dog park. For the dog park permits are required; they are available at the park office by the year or by the day. Dogs must be there for their photo, and proof of license, spayed/neutered, rabies, parvo and kennel cough are required. Dogs must be sociable, under owner's control/care at all times, and be on no more than a 6 foot leash when not in designated off-lead areas. The camp area offers picnic tables, a playground, playing fields/courts, showers, restrooms, and a dump station. The camping and tent areas also allow dogs. There is a dog walk area at the campground. There are special amenities given to dogs at this campground.
Barnyard RV Park 201 Oak Drive Lexington SC 803-957-1238
http://www.barnyardrvpark.com
Dogs of all sizes are allowed. There are no additional pet fees. Dogs must be leashed and cleaned up after. There is a dog walk area at the campground.
River Bottom Farms 357 Cedar Creek Road Swansea SC 803-568-4182
http://www.riverbottomfarms.com
Dogs of all sizes are allowed. There are no additional pet fees. Dogs must be well behaved, leashed, and cleaned up after. There are some breed restrictions. The camping and tent areas also allow dogs. There is a dog walk area at the campground. Dogs are allowed in the camping cabins.

Attractions
Adventure Carolina 1107 State Street/H 2 Cayce SC 803-796-4505
http://www.adventurecarolina.com/
This adventure and outfitting company will allow pooches aboard their canoes and kayaks or rent a bike for some bikjoring; they are not allowed on tours. Dogs must be under owner's control/care at all times.
African-American Historical Museum 1100 Gervais Street Columbia SC 803-734-2430
Located at the State Preservation Office, this museum details the history of African-Americans since colonial times. Dogs are not allowed in the building, but they are allowed on the grounds that offer garden areas and scenic picnic spots. Dogs must be leashed and under owner's control/care at all times.
Historic Columbia Foundation Tours Main Street Columbia SC 803-252-1770, ext. 24
Tours are available of this historic city each Tuesday at 6:30 PM from March through November, and other tours

can be made by appointment. People friendly, well behaved dogs are allowed on the walking tours; there is one building they are not allowed to go in. Dogs must be leashed and under owner's control/care at all times.
River Runner Outdoor Center 905 Gervais Street/H 1/378 Columbia SC 803-771-0353
http://www.riverrunner.us/#
This adventure and outfitting company will allow pooches aboard their rentals and on some of the tours. Dogs must be leashed and under owner's control/care at all times.
Congaree Swamp Canoe Tours 100 National Park Road Hopkins SC 803-776-4396
http://www.nps.gov/cosw
This floodplain forest has one of the highest canopies in the world with massive hardwoods and soaring pines that are some of the tallest trees in America. There is also an abundance of marine,birds and wildlife. Dogs are allowed to go on the canoe tours which are held every other Sunday (weather permitting) and reservations must be made at least 2 weeks in advance. Dogs must be well behaved, leashed, and under owner's control/care at all times.

Stores
PetSmart Pet Store 246 Harbison Blvd Columbia SC 803-781-6339
Your licensed and well-behaved leashed dog is allowed in the store.
PetSmart Pet Store 10136 Two Notch Rd Ste 109C Columbia SC 803-419-1342
Your licensed and well-behaved leashed dog is allowed in the store.

Parks
Congaree National Park 48 Old Bluff Road Columbia SC 803-776-4396
http://www.nps.gov/cosw
This 22,200-acre park protects the largest contiguous tract of old-growth bottomland hardwood forest still in the US. The park's floodplain forest has one of the highest canopies and some of the tallest trees in the eastern US. Enjoy hiking, primitive camping, birdwatching, picnicking, canoeing, kayaking, Ranger guided interpretive walks, canoe tours, nature study, and environmental education programs. Open all year; Monday to Thursday from 8:30 am to 5 pm, and Friday to Sunday from 8 am to 7 pm. To walk the trails after hours park outside the gate. Well behaved dogs on leash are allowed on the trails and the outside guided tours, but they are not allowed on the Boardwalk or in the buildings.
Finlay Park 930 Laurel Street Columbia SC 803-545-3100
A beautiful green oasis in the mist of the city, this 18 acre park offers daily recreation and repose, and it is also host to several special events and festivals throughout the year. Dogs are allowed throughout the park; they must be leashed and under owner's control/care at all times.
Francis Marion and Sumter National Forests 4931 Broad River Road Columbia SC 803-561-4000
http://www.fs.fed.us/r8/fms/
Four ranger districts oversee more than 600,000 acres of forest lands rich with diverse ecosystems that support a large variety habitats and wildlife, cultural history, and recreational opportunities. There is also an environmental education center with numerous activities and programs, a 36 mile trail that goes from the mountains to the sea, and many other sites of interest. Dogs are allowed throughout the forest and campground areas; they must be leashed and under owner's control/care at all times.
Saluda Shoals Park 5605 Bush River Road Columbia SC 803-731-5208
http://www.icrc.net
Located along the banks of the Saluda River, this 300 acre regional park offers many amenities such as paved and unpaved trails for hiking, biking and horseback riding, a river observation deck, accommodations for canoeing and kayaking as well as a boat launch, picnic areas and shelters, a fish cleaning station and more. The park is open daily from dawn to dusk. Dogs on leash are allowed at the park but not in the canoes. There is also an off-leash area in the park.
Sesquicentennial State Park 9564 Two Notch Road Columbia SC 803-788-2706
A major recreation destination, this scenic 1,419 acre park offers a long list of amenities, activities, a 30 acre lake, interpretive nature programs, and much more. This park is also home to a 2 acre, double sectioned, off-leash dog park. Permits are required for use of the dog park; they are available at the park office by the year or by the day. Dogs must be there for their photo, and proof of license, spayed/neutered, rabies, parvo and kennel cough are required. Dogs must be sociable, under owner's control/care at all times, and be on no more than a 6 foot leash when not in designated off-lead areas.
Towpath Trail and Park Laurel at Huger Street Columbia SC 803-545-3100
In addition to being the location of the world's first electrically operated textile mill and home to the state's oldest, and still operating, hydroelectric plant, this 167 acre park offers an amphitheater, and a great liner walking trail that follows along the canal and Congaree River. Dogs are allowed throughout the park; they must be leashed and under owner's control/care at all times.

Off-Leash Dog Parks
Sesqui Dog Park 9564 Two Notch Rd Columbia SC 803-788-2706

An annual permit of $25 per dog or a day permit of $4 per dog is required to use the dog park which is located in Sesquicentennial State Park. More information about the dog park is listed in the Sesquicentennial section above. Contact the park office for additional information.

Outdoor Restaurants
Rosewood Market & Deli 2803 Rosewood Drive Columbia SC   803-765-1083
Dogs are allowed at the outdoor tables.
Saluda's 751 Saluda Avenue Columbia SC   803-799-9500
http://www.saludas.com/
This steak and seafood restaurant offers fine wining and dining with handcrafted dinners and a brunch every Sunday. Outdoor dining is available, weather permitting. Dogs are allowed at the outer tables when it is not real busy; they are not allowed on Friday and Saturdays. Dogs must be leashed and under owner's control/care at all times.

Darlington

Attractions
TOP 200 PLACE **Kalmia Gardens** 1624 W Carolina Avenue/H 151 Hartsville SC   843-383-8145
http://www.coker.edu/Kalmia/index.html
An historic 1820's home and a 35 acre private botanical garden have put his amazingly beautiful location on the National Register of Historic Places. There are trails and boardwalks here that lead visitors to the Black Creek floodplain below with all its unique habitats and inhabitants. Dogs are allowed throughout the park and on the boardwalks; they are not allowed to go swimming in the pond. Dogs must be leashed and under owner's control/care at all times.

Dillon

Accommodations
Best Value Inn 904 Redford Blvd Dillon SC   843-774-5111
There is a $12 per day additional pet fee.
Deluxe Inn 818 Radford Blvd Dillon SC   843-774-6041
Dogs of all sizes are allowed. There is a $8 per night pet fee per small pet and $12 for large pet.
South of the Border Motor Inn H 301/501 Dillon SC   843-774-2411 (800-845-6011)
http://pedroland.com/hotels_camping.html
This South-of-the-Border themed stop offers lodging, campgrounds, shopping, dining, entertainment, and more. Dogs are allowed throughout the grounds, in the inn and at the campgrounds for no additional pet fee; they are not allowed in most of the park buildings or in food service areas. Dogs must be leashed and under owner's control/care at all times.
Super 8 Dillon 1203 Radford Blvd Dillon SC   843-774-4161 (800-800-8000)
Dogs of all sizes are allowed. There is a $5 per night pet fee per small pet or $10 per large pet. Smoking and non-smoking rooms are available for pet rooms.

Campgrounds and RV Parks
Little Pee Dee State Park 1298 State Park Road Dillon SC   843-774-8872 (866-345-PARK (7275))
The serene setting of this 835 acre park has made it a popular relaxation, fishing, and nature viewing area. Dogs are allowed throughout the park, on the beach, and at campground; they are not allowed in park buildings. Dogs must be on no more than a 6 foot leash and cleaned up after. There are about 50 sites in the campground with restrooms, hot showers, and a dump station on site. The camping and tent areas also allow dogs. There is a dog walk area at the campground.
South of the Border Campgrounds H 301/501 Dillon SC   843-774-2411 (800-845-6011)
http://pedroland.com/hotels_camping.html
This South-of-the-Border themed stop offers lodging, campgrounds, shopping, dining, entertainment, and more. Dogs are allowed throughout the grounds, in the inn and at the campgrounds for no additional pet fee; they are not allowed in most of the park buildings or in food service areas. Dogs must be leashed and under owner's control/care at all times. The camping and tent areas also allow dogs. There is a dog walk area at the campground.

Attractions

South of the Border

South of the Border H 301 N Dillon SC   843-774-2411
http://www.pedroland.com/
This South-of-the-Border themed stop offers shopping, dining, entertainment, and more. Dogs are allowed throughout the grounds; they are not allowed in most of the buildings. Dogs must be leashed and under owner's control/care at all times.

Parks
Little Pee Dee State Park 1298 State Park Road Dillon SC   843-774-8872 (866-345-PARK (7275))
The serene setting of this 835 acre park has made it a popular relaxation, fishing, and nature viewing area. Dogs are allowed throughout the park, on the beach, and at campground; they are not allowed in park buildings. Dogs must be on no more than a 6 foot leash and cleaned up after.

Edisto Beach

Campgrounds and RV Parks
Edisto Beach State Park 8377 State Cabin Road Edisto Island SC 843-671-2810
In addition to its popularity for its palmed beach and great shelling, this 1,255 acre oceanfront park is also home to an environmental education center, well-developed handicapped-friendly trails and facilities, a dense maritime forest, and an extensive salt march. Dogs are allowed throughout the park, on the beach, and at campground; they are not allowed in the cabin areas. Dogs must be on no more than a 6 foot leash and cleaned up after. The camp area offers 113 sites with a day use area, fire rings, picnic tables, showers, restrooms, a playground, store, concessionaires, a laundry, and a dump station. The camping and tent areas also allow dogs. There is a dog walk area at the campground.

Vacation Home Rentals
Atwood Vacations Call To Arrange Edisto Island SC   843-869-2151 (866-713-5214)
http://www.atwoodvacations.com
Located 45 miles south of Charleston, this vacation rental management company has many pet friendly rentals.

Beaches
Edisto Beach State Park 8377 State Cabin Road Edisto Island SC   843-869-2756
Sunbathe, beachcomb or hunt for seashells on this 1.5 mile long beach. This park also has a 4 mile nature trail that winds through a maritime forest with great vistas that overlook the salt marsh. Dogs on a 6 foot or less leash are allowed on the beach and on the trails. People need to clean up after their pets.

Parks
Edisto Beach State Park 8377 State Cabin Road Edisto Island SC   843-671-2810
In addition to its popularity for its palmed beach and great shelling, this 390 acre memorial park provides special programs and guided tours about this area's significance during the Civil War, and they feature a ¾ mile self-guided Battlefield Interpretive Trail. Dogs are allowed throughout the park, on the beach, and at campground; they are not allowed in the cabin areas. Dogs must be on no more than a 6 foot leash and cleaned up after.

Ehrhardt

Parks
Rivers Bridge State Historic Site 325 State Park Road Ehrhardt SC   803-267-3675
Listed on the National Register of Historic Places, this 390 acre memorial park provides special programs and guided tours about this area's significance during the Civil War, and they feature a ¾ mile self-guided Battlefield Interpretive Trail. Dogs are allowed throughout the park; they must be on no more than a 6 foot leash and under owner's control/care at all times.

Florence

Accommodations
Comfort Inn 1916 W Lucas Street Florence SC   843-665-4558 (877-424-6423)
Dogs are allowed for an additional fee of $10 per night per pet.
Days Inn Florence North/I-95 2111 W Lucas St Florence SC   843-665-4444 (800-329-7466)
Dogs of all sizes are allowed. There are no additional pet fees.
Days Inn Florence South/I-95 3783 W Palmetto St Florence SC   843-665-8550 (800-329-7466)
Dogs of all sizes are allowed. There is a $10 per night pet fee per pet.
Econo Lodge 1811 W Lucas St Florence SC   843-665-8558
There is a $6 per day additional pet fee.
Holiday Inn Hotel & Suites Florence Sc @ I-95 & Us Hwy 52 1819 Lucas St Florence SC   843-665-4555 (877-270-6405)
Dogs of all sizes are allowed for an additional one time pet fee of $25 per room.
Motel 6 - Florence 1834 West Lucas Street Florence SC   843-667-6100 (800-466-8356)
One well-behaved family pet per room. Guest must notify front desk upon arrival. Guest is liable for any damages. In consideration of all guests, pets must never be left unattended in the guest rooms.
Red Roof Inn - Florence, SC 2690 David McLeod Boulevard Florence SC   843-678-9000 (800-RED-ROOF)
One well-behaved family pet per room. Guest must notify front desk upon arrival. Guest is liable for any damages. In consideration of all guests, pets must never be left unattended in the guest rooms.
Thunderbird Motor Inn 2004 W Lucas St Florence SC   843-669-1611
There are no additional pet fees.
Young's Plantation Inn US 76 and I-95 Florence SC   843-669-4171
There is a $4 per day pet fee.

Campgrounds and RV Parks
Florence KOA 1115 E Campground Road Florence SC   843-665-7007 (800-562-7807)
http://www.koa.com
Dogs of all sizes are allowed. There are no additional pet fees. Dogs may not be left unattended, even at the dog pen area. Dogs must be leashed and cleaned up after. The camping and tent areas also allow dogs. There is a dog walk area at the campground. Dogs are allowed in the camping cabins.

Gaffney

Accommodations

Peach Tree Inn 136 Peachoid Rd Gaffney SC 864-489-7172
Dogs of all sizes are allowed. There are no additional pet fees.
Quality Inn 143 Corona Drive Gaffney SC 864-487-4200 (877-424-6423)
Dogs are allowed for an additional pet fee of $10 per night per room.
Red Roof Inn - Gaffney 132 New Painter Road Gaffney SC 864-206-0200 (800-RED-ROOF)
One well-behaved family pet per room. Guest must notify front desk upon arrival. Guest is liable for any damages. In consideration of all guests, pets must never be left unattended in the guest rooms.

Campgrounds and RV Parks

Kings Mountain State Park 1277 Park Road Blacksburg SC 803-222-3209 (866-345-PARK (7275))
Rich in American history, this picturesque park offers self guided tours of a living history farm in addition to various land and water recreation. Dogs of all sizes are allowed at no additional fee. Dogs may not be left unattended unless they will be quiet and well behaved, and they must be on no more than a 6 foot leash, and cleaned up after. Dogs are allowed on the trails. The camping and tent areas also allow dogs. There is a dog walk area at the campground.

Attractions

Overmountain Victory National Historic Trail 2635 Park Road Blacksburg SC 864-936-3477
http://www.nps.gov/ovvi/index.htm
Dogs must be on leash and must be cleaned up after. You must follow the rules and pet policies of the state parks and other National Parks that the trail goes through. The trail goes through North Carolina, South, Carolina, Tennessee, and Virginia. Activities include auto touring, camping, boating, fishing, hiking, whitewater rafting and more. The trail was used during the American Revolution war to travel to the Kings Mountain Battlesite.
Cowpens National Battlefield 4001 Chesnee H/H 11 Gaffney SC 864-461-2828
http://www.nps.gov/cowp
Known for a successful military tactic that has only been used a few times in history, this site marks the turn the tactic took for the American Revolution. There are picnicking areas, miles of trails, and they are also host to a variety of special events throughout the year. Dogs are allowed throughout the park; they are not allowed in buildings. Dogs must be leashed and under owner's control/care at all times.

Shopping Centers

Prime Outlets 1 Factory Shops Blvd Gaffney SC 864-902-9900
This shopping center offers easy access and more than 80 name brand stores. Dogs are allowed throughout the common areas of the mall with the exception of the food court. It is up to individual stores whether a dog is permitted inside or not. Dogs must be leashed and under owner's control/care at all times.

Georgetown

Accommodations

Best Western Hammock Inn 7903 Ocean Hwy Pawleys Island SC 843-237-4261 (800-780-7234)
Dogs are allowed for an additional one time fee of $10 per pet.

Attractions

Captain Sandy's Tours 343 Ida Drive Georgetown SC 843-527-4106
Whether for a casual sightseeing trip or a custom tour, there is sure to be a bit of the cultural and natural history, local folklore, and an abundance of wildlife along the way. The 16 passenger boat will pick up passengers where they are located. Dogs are allowed on board; they must be people and pet friendly and well mannered. Dogs should remain leashed and they must be under owner's control/care at all times.
TOP 200 PLACE Swamp Fox Tours 600 Front Street Georgetown SC 843-527-1112
http://www.swampfoxtours.com
These trollies and tram will take you on a guided tour of Georgetown's historic heritage. Tours depart from 1001

Front Street in front of the Georgetown Chamber of Commerce building. Tours are offered on the hour daily and are about one hour long. The Tram departs on the hour Monday through Friday, 10 AM to 4 PM. Dogs must be well behaved and leashed.

Greenville

Accommodations
Days Inn Spartanburg Airport 1386 E Main St Duncan SC 864-433-1122 (800-329-7466)
Dogs of all sizes are allowed. There is a $25 one time per pet fee per visit.
Holiday Inn Express Hotel & Suites Greenville-Spartanburg(Duncan) Hwy 290 & I-85 Duncan SC 864-486-9191 (877-270-6405)
Dogs of all sizes are allowed for an additional one time pet fee of $35 per room
Days Inn Easley 121 Days Inn Drive Easley SC 864-859-9902 (800-329-7466)
Dogs of all sizes are allowed. There is a $10 per night pet fee per pet.
Best Western Greenville Airport Inn 5009 Pelham Road Greenville SC 864-297-5353 (800-780-7234)
Dogs are allowed for an additional pet fee of $10 per night per room.
Comfort Inn Executive Center 540 N Pleasantburg Drive Greenville SC 864-271-0060 (877-424-6423)
Dogs are allowed for an additional one time pet fee of $15 per room.
Comfort Inn Executive Center 540 N Pleasantburg Drive Greenville SC 864-963-2777 (877-424-6423)
Dogs of all sizes are allowed. There is a $15 one time additional pet fee per room.
Crowne Plaza 851 Congaree Rd Greenville SC 864-297-6300 (877-270-6405)
Dogs of all sizes are allowed for an additional fee of $50 per room.
Days Inn Greenville Conference Cntr 2756 Laurens Rd Greenville SC 864-288-6900 (800-329-7466)
Dogs of all sizes are allowed. There is a $10 per night pet fee per pet.
Greenville Airport Inn 5009 Pelham Rd Greenville SC 864-297-5353
There is a $10 per day pet fee.
Holiday Inn 4295 Augusta Rd, I-85 Exit 46A Greenville SC 864-277-8921 (877-270-6405)
Dogs of all sizes are allowed for an additional one time pet fee of $30 per room.
La Quinta Inn & Suites Greenville Haywood 65 W. Orchard Park Drive Greenville SC 864-233-8018 (800-531-5900)
Dogs of all sizes are allowed. There are no additional pet fees. Dogs must be leashed and cleaned up after.
La Quinta Inn Greenville Woodruff Rd 31 Old Country Rd. Greenville SC 864-297-3500 (800-531-5900)
Dogs of all sizes are allowed. There are no additional pet fees. Dogs may not be left unattended, and they must be leashed and cleaned up after.
MainStay Suites Pelham Road 2671 Dry Pocket Road Greenville SC 864-987-5566
Dogs are allowed for an additional fee of $10 per night per pet.
Motel 6 - Greenville 224 Bruce Road Greenville SC 864-277-8630 (800-466-8356)
One well-behaved family pet per room. Guest must notify front desk upon arrival. Guest is liable for any damages. In consideration of all guests, pets must never be left unattended in the guest rooms.
Quality Inn and Suites 1314 Pleasantburg Drive Greenville SC 864-770-3737 (877-424-6423)
Dogs are allowed for an additional one time pet fee of $25 per room.
Red Roof Inn - Greenville, SC 2801 Laurens Road Greenville SC 864-297-4458 (800-RED-ROOF)
One well-behaved family pet per room. Guest must notify front desk upon arrival. Guest is liable for any damages. In consideration of all guests, pets must never be left unattended in the guest rooms.
Residence Inn by Marriott 120 Milestone Way Greenville SC 864-627-0001
Dogs of all sizes are allowed. There is a $75 one time fee and a pet policy to sign at check in.
Sleep Inn Palmetto Expo Center 231 N Pleasantburg Drive Greenville SC 864-240-2006 (877-424-6423)
Dogs are allowed for an additional one time pet fee of $20 per room.
Staybridge Suites Greenville/Spartanburg 31 Market Point Drive Greenville SC 864-288-4448 (877-270-6405)
Dogs of all sizes are allowed for an additional pet fee of $50 for 1 to 7 days; $75 for 8 to 13 days; $100 for 14 to 30 days, and a $150 fee for 31 or more days.
TownePlace Suites Greenville Haywood Mall 75 Mall Connector Rd Greenville SC 864-675-1670
Dogs of all sizes are allowed. There is a $100 one time pet fee per visit.
Holiday Inn Express Hotel and Suites 2681 Dry Pocket Road Greer SC 864-213-9331 (877-270-6405)
Dogs of all sizes are allowed for an additional one time pet fee of $20 per room.
Days Inn Greenville/Simpsonville 45 Ray East Talley Court Simpsonville SC 864-963-7701 (800-329-7466)
Dogs of all sizes are allowed. There is a $10 per night pet fee per pet.
Motel 6 - Greenville - Simpsonville 3706 Grandview Drive Simpsonville SC 864-962-8484 (800-466-8356)
One well-behaved family pet per room. Guest must notify front desk upon arrival. Guest is liable for any damages. In consideration of all guests, pets must never be left unattended in the guest rooms.
Sleep Inn 110 Hawkins Road Travelers Rest SC 864-834-7040 (877-424-6423)

Quiet dogs are allowed for an additional pet fee of $15 per night per room.

Campgrounds and RV Parks

Table Rock State Park 158 E Ellison Lane Pickens SC 864-878-9813 (866-345-PARK (7275))
Popular since its construction by the Civilian Conservation Corps (CCC) in the 1930's for its recreational activities, lakes, and natural beauty, this almost 3100 acre park is now listed on the National Register of Historic Places, and it is home to an extensive trail system that takes hikers through a variety of habitations. Dogs are allowed throughout the park, on the beach, and at campground; they are not allowed in the cabin areas. Dogs must be on no more than a 6 foot leash and cleaned up after. There are 2 camping areas with more than 90 sites available; they provide restrooms, hot showers, a laundry, and a dump station. The camping and tent areas also allow dogs. There is a dog walk area at the campground.
Scuffletown USA 603 Scuffletown Road Simpsonville SC 864-967-2276
http://www.scuffletownusa.com
Dogs of all sizes are allowed. There are no additional pet fees. Dogs must be leashed and cleaned up after. The camping and tent areas also allow dogs. There is a dog walk area at the campground.

Stores

Petco Pet Store 3270 N Pleasantburg Dr Greenville SC 864-232-7340
Your licensed and well-behaved leashed dog is allowed in the store.
PetSmart Pet Store 2449 Laurens Rd Greenville SC 864-627-1165
Your licensed and well-behaved leashed dog is allowed in the store.
PetSmart Pet Store 1125 Woodruff Rd Greenville SC 864-284-6398
Your licensed and well-behaved leashed dog is allowed in the store.
Petco Pet Store 1931 East Main Street Spartansburg SC 864-542-2350
Your licensed and well-behaved leashed dog is allowed in the store.
PetSmart Pet Store 6019 Wade Hampton Blvd Taylors SC 864-968-2024
Your licensed and well-behaved leashed dog is allowed in the store.

Parks

Table Rock State Park 158 E Ellison Lane Pickens SC 864-878-9813 (866-345-PARK (7275))
Popular since its construction by the CCC in the 1930s for its recreational activities, lakes, and natural beauty, this almost 3100 acre park is now listed on the National Register of Historic Places, and it is home to an extensive trail system that takes hikers through a variety of sites/habitations. Dogs are allowed throughout the park, on the beach, and at campground; they are not allowed in the cabin areas. Dogs must be on no more than a 6 foot leash and cleaned up after.

Off-Leash Dog Parks

Cleveland Park Dog Park Woodland Way Greenville SC 864-271-5333
This is a fenced off-leash dog park. It is located in Cleveland Park across from the horse stables and the Cleveland Park Animal Hospital. The dog park is open during daylight hours. Small children are not permitted in the dog park.
Six Wags of Greer K-9 Fun Park 3669 North Highway 14 Greer SC
http://www.upstatedogtraining.com
This is a private dog park with three play yards. Dogs are divided by how they get along with each other. There is also an area for people who want to run their dogs without other dogs and a one mile nature trail. Agility equipment is also available. There is a $5 a day pass to use the facility. Kennel and training services are also available.

Outdoor Restaurants

Overlook Grill 601 S Main Street/H 124 Greenville SC 864-271-9700
http://www.overlookgrill.com/index1.htm
This grill offers a full bar; all-American favorite foods, and alfresco dining on the patio where guest can relax to the sound of the local river. Dogs are allowed at the outer tables; they must be leashed and cleaned up after at all times.
Smoke on the Water 1 Augusta Street Greenville SC 864-232-9091
http://www.saucytavern.com/about_us.php
Specializing in an extensive menu reflecting the regional cuisine and southern comfort foods, this eatery also offers a full bar and alfresco seating for beer and wine only. Dogs are allowed at the outer tables; they must be leashed and under owner's control/care at all times.
Strossner's Bakery and Cafe 21 Roper Mountain Road Greenville SC 864-233-3996
http://www.strossners.com/

From a small bakery corner bakery, to a modern café and bakery with catering, flowers, and gifts now on the menu too, they are also happy to do special requests. When the weather permits, they offer outdoor seating. Dogs are allowed at the outer tables; they must be leashed and under owner's control/care at all times.

Day Kennels

PetsHotel by PetsMart Day Kennel 1125 Woodruff Rd. Greenville SC   864-289-0175
http://www.petsmart.com/PETsHOTEL/
This PetSmart pet store offers day care, day camp and overnight care. You may drop off and pick up your dog during the hours the store is open seven days a week. Dogs must have proof of current rabies, DPP and Bordatella vaccinations.

Greenwood

Campgrounds and RV Parks

Lake Greenwood State Rec Area 302 State Park Road Ninety-Six SC   864-543-3535 (866-345-PARK (7275))
This 914-acre park covers five peninsulas on beautiful Lake Greenwood offering ample fishing, hiking, lake shore camping, and an interactive educational center. Dogs of all sizes are allowed at no additional fee. Dogs may not be left unattended unless for a short time, and only if they will be quiet and well behaved. Dogs must be leashed at all times, and cleaned up after. Dogs are not allowed in any of the buildings, but they are allowed on the trails. The camping and tent areas also allow dogs. There is a dog walk area at the campground.

Attractions

Emerald Farm 409 Emerald Farm Road Greenwood SC   864-223-2247
http://www.emeraldfarm.com/
In addition to being a working dairy farm and soap factory, visitors can get a "hands on experience" in addition to goat milk which is available in the Natural Food store on site that offers holistic medicines, herbal nutrition plus lots more. Visit the hobby and train shops, stroll the herb garden, or just picnic and relax by the pond. Dogs are allowed throughout the grounds, and only dogs that can be carried are allowed in the buildings. Dogs must be leashed and under owner's control/care at all times.

Parks

Lake Greenwood State Recreation Area 302 State Park Road Ninety-Six SC   864-543-3535 (866-345-PARK (7275))
History and an abundance of land and water recreation blend together here, allowing for educational activities as well as fun at this 914 acre park with 212 miles of shoreline and a more than an 11,000 acre lake. Dogs are allowed throughout the park, on the beach, and at campground. Dogs must be on no more than a 6 foot leash and cleaned up after.
Ninety Six National Historic Site 1103 H 248 Ninety-Six SC   864-543-4968
http://www.nps.gov/nisi/
Being the home of two Revolutionary War battles, the beautiful woods and countryside at this park belie the battles that occurred here; however, the cultural and colonial history is preserved through exhibits, special events, interpretive trails, and reenactments. Dogs are allowed throughout the park; they are not allowed in buildings. Dogs must be leashed and under owner's control/care at all times.

Hardeeville

Accommodations

Comfort Inn Box 544 Hardeeville SC   843-784-2188 (877-424-6423)
Dogs are allowed for an additional fee of $10 per night per pet.
Days Inn Hardeeville US Highway 17 & I 95 Hardeeville SC   843-784-2281 (800-329-7466)
Dogs of all sizes are allowed. There is a $7 per night pet fee per pet.
Quality Inn and Suites 19000 Whyte Hardee Blvd Hardeeville SC   843-784-7060
Dogs are allowed for an additional fee of $10 per night per pet.
Sleep Inn I 95 & H 17 Hardeeville SC   843-784-7181 (877-424-6423)
Dogs are allowed for an additional fee of $20 per night per pet.

Hilton Head Island

Accommodations

Beachwalk Hotel & Condominiums 40 Waterside Drive Hilton Head Island SC 843-842-8888 (888-843-4136)
http://www.hiltonheadbeachwalkhotel.com
This hotel on Hilton Head Island near the beach allows up to 2 dogs. There is a $40 non-refundable one time pet fee.

TOP 200 PLACE **Daufuskie Island Resort & Breathe Spa** 421 Squire Pope Rd Hilton Head Island SC 800-648-6778
http://www.daufuskieislandresort.com
Daufuskie Island is a family friendly island golf and spa resort located a short ferry boat cruise from Hilton Head Island. They have a "Deluxe Doggie package" for your best friends for $35 per night per dog. They provide a Canine goodie bag at check - in, which includes doggie treats, chew toy, doggie pick-up bags, a Daufuskie Island Resort & Breathe Spa dog tag with phone number and a "Dog Guest in residence" door hanger. Awaiting your friend in the room is a doggie bed, extra towels, food and water bowl with bottled water. The resort has two 18 hole championship golf courses.
Motel 6 - Hilton Head 830 William Hilton Parkway Hilton Head Island SC 843-785-2700 (800-466-8356)
They allow small and medium sized dogs but will accept a large well-behaved, trained dog. There are no additional pet fees.
Red Roof Inn - Hilton Head Island 5 Regency Parkway Hilton Head Island SC 843-686-6808 (800-RED-ROOF)
One well-behaved family pet per room. Guest must notify front desk upon arrival. Guest is liable for any damages. In consideration of all guests, pets must never be left unattended in the guest rooms.

Campgrounds and RV Parks

Hilton Head Island Motor Coach Resort 133 L Street Hilton Head Island SC 800-722-2365
Dogs of all sizes are allowed. There are no additional pet fees. Dogs must be leashed at all times and cleaned up after. This is an RV only, Class A resort. There is a dog walk area at the campground.

Vacation Home Rentals

Hilton Head Rentals & Golf   Hilton Head SC 843-785-8687 (800-445-8664)
http://www.hiltonheadvacation.com
Hilton Head Rentals features one, two, and three bedroom pet-friendly vacation homes, villas, and condos. Some of the properties include fenced in yards and all rentals are near the beach, dog walks, and parks. There are no additional pet fees.

Attractions

Calibogue Cruises to Daufuskie Island Broad Creek Marina, Mathews Dr. Hilton Head SC 843-342-8687
At the Calibogue Club you'll find a great spot for boat rentals, nature tours, and visits to Daufuskie Island. All guests visiting Daufuskie Island must make reservations for the ferry tour in advance of arrival. Dogs are allowed on the ferry, and after arrival to Daufuskie Island, a golf cart can be rented for you and your pet to self-explore the island. Tours of the island are from 2 1/2 to 4 hours, and they are open year round. Dogs are not allowed to take the tour bus on the island. Dogs must be well behaved and leashed at all times.
Adventure Cruises Inc 1 Shelter Cove Lane Hilton Head Island SC 843-785-4558
Whether fishing, crabbing, marine viewing, or just cruising, breathtaking scenery of the ocean and of the east coast's 2nd largest barrier island awaits cruisers here, and they will also allow your pooch aboard for no additional fee. Dogs must be leashed and under owner's control/care at all times.
Runaway Charters Hudson Road (Charley's Crab Restaurant Docks) Hilton Head Island SC 843-689-2628 or cell # 843-384-6511
This fishing charter company sails the waters of the Atlantic Ocean and around the Hilton Head Island area, and Captain Bill shares his more than 30 years of experience and knowledge. One well behaved dog is allowed to come aboard for no additional fee. Dogs must be under owner's control/care at all times.
Vagabond Cruise 149 Lighthouse Road Hilton Head Island SC 843-342-2345
http://www.vagabondcruise.com/
This charter company will allow pooches to come aboard for public or private charters; they offer a variety of cruise options, and dogs are not allowed on the dinner cruises. Dogs must be leashed and under owner's control/care at all times.

Shopping Centers

Tanger Factory Outlet Center 1414 Fording Island Rd # B9 Bluffton SC 843-689-6767
http://www.tangeroutlet.com/hiltonhead
Offering more than 85 brand name manufacturers and designer outlets, there are a variety of shopping, dining, and entertainment opportunities. Dogs are allowed in the common areas of the mall; it is up to individual stores whether they allow a dog inside. Dogs must be well behaved, leashed, and under owner's control/care at all times.

Stores

PetSmart Pet Store 30 Malphrus Rd Bluffton SC 843-836-2020
Your licensed and well-behaved leashed dog is allowed in the store.
Petco Pet Store 1007 Fording Island Rd Bluffton SC 843-757-9081
Your licensed and well-behaved leashed dog is allowed in the store.

Beaches

Alder Lane Beach Access S. Forest Beach Drive Hilton Head Island SC 843-341-4600
This beach has restricted seasons and hours for dogs. During the Summer, from the Friday before Memorial Day through the Tuesday after Labor Day, dogs can only be on the beach before 10am and then after 5pm (they are not allowed from 10am to 5pm). Pets must be leashed. During the off-season and Winter months, from April 1 through the Thursday before Memorial Day, dogs must be on a leash between 10am and 5pm. From the Tuesday after Labor Day through September 30, dogs again must be on a leash between 10am and 5pm. At all other times, dogs may be off-leash, but must be under direct, positive voice control. People are required to clean up after their pets. There are 22 metered spaces for beach parking. The cost is a quarter for each 15 minutes.
Coligny Beach Park Coligny Circle Hilton Head Island SC 843-341-4600
This beach has restricted seasons and hours for dogs. During the Summer, from the Friday before Memorial Day through the Tuesday after Labor Day, dogs can only be on the beach before 10am and then after 5pm (they are not allowed from 10am to 5pm). Pets must be leashed. During the off-season and Winter months, from April 1 through the Thursday before Memorial Day, dogs must be on a leash between 10am and 5pm. From the Tuesday after Labor Day through September 30, dogs again must be on a leash between 10am and 5pm. At all other times, dogs may be off-leash, but must be under direct, positive voice control. People are required to clean up after their pets. There are 30 metered spaces for beach parking. The cost is a quarter for each 15 minutes. A flat fee of $4 is charged at the parking lot on Fridays through Sundays and holidays.
Folly Field Beach Park Folly Field Road Hilton Head Island SC 843-341-4600
This beach has restricted seasons and hours for dogs. During the Summer, from the Friday before Memorial Day through the Tuesday after Labor Day, dogs can only be on the beach before 10am and then after 5pm (they are not allowed from 10am to 5pm). Pets must be leashed. During the off-season and Winter months, from April 1 through the Thursday before Memorial Day, dogs must be on a leash between 10am and 5pm. From the Tuesday after Labor Day through September 30, dogs again must be on a leash between 10am and 5pm. At all other times, dogs may be off-leash, but must be under direct, positive voice control. People are required to clean up after their pets. There are 52 metered spaces for beach parking. The cost is a quarter for each 15 minutes.
Hilton Head Island Beaches Hilton Head Island SC 800-523-3373
Dogs are welcome on the beaches of the island during certain times/days: They are not permitted on the beach between 10 AM and 5 PM from the Friday before Memorial Day through Labor Day; they may be on the beach between 10 AM and 5 PM from April 1st to the Thursday before Memorial Day, and between 10 AM and 5 PM the Tuesday after Labor Day through September 30th. Dogs must be leashed and picked up after at all times.

Off-Leash Dog Parks

Best Friends Dog Park Off Hwy 40 Hilton Head SC
http://www.hiltonhead360.com
Dogs are allowed unleashed in the dog park and leashed outside on the beaches. There is a water and cleanup stations for your pets.

Outdoor Restaurants

Crazy Crab 104 N H 278 Hilton Head SC 843-681-5021
http://www.thecrazycrab.com/
Specializing in Low Country recipes with the freshest possible ingredients, this seafood house also offers alfresco dining. Dogs are allowed at the outer tables; they must be leashed and under owner's control/care at all times.
Hinchey's Chicago Bar and Grill 2 N Forest Beach Drive Hilton Head Island SC 843-686-5959
Serving up American favorites, this eatery also serves up a fun atmosphere with a theme of the town of Chicago and outside dining options. Dogs are allowed at the outer tables; they must be leashed and under owner's

control/care at all times.
Skillet's 1 N Forest Beach Drive #J 11 Hilton Head Island SC 843-785-3131
http://www.skilletscafe.com/
Steaks, seafood, and all American comfort foods are the specialty here; they also offer live music, a full bar, TVs for sports and news, and a large outdoor patio. Dogs are allowed at the outer tables; they must be leashed and under owner's control/care at all times.
Stack's Pancakes Restaurant 2 Regency Parkway Hilton Head Island SC 843-341-3347
http://www.stackspancakes.com/
A comfortable environment, fresh baked breads/vegetables, home-style cooking, and outdoor dining are some of the popularities of this restaurant. Dogs are allowed at the outer tables; they must be leashed and under owner's control/care at all times.

Lancaster

Campgrounds and RV Parks
Andrew Jackson State Park 196 Andrew Jackson Park Road Lancaster SC 803-285-3344 (866-345-PARK (7275))
This park is popular for the blending of its history to the present with a museum of President Jackson's life here, art/community activities, and a living history museum. There are also annual festivals, a fishing lake, picnic areas, a campground, and plenty of hiking trails at this 360 acre site. Dogs are allowed in most of the outdoor areas; they must be on a leash no longer than 6 feet and under owner's control/care at all times. The campground can accommodate RVs up to 30 feet, and there are restrooms, hot showers, and a dump station on site. The camping and tent areas also allow dogs. There is a dog walk area at the campground.

Parks
Andrew Jackson State Park 196 Andrew Jackson Park Road Lancaster SC 803-285-3344 (866-345-PARK (7275))
This park is popular for the blending of its history to the present with a museum of President Jackson's life here, art/community activities, and a living history museum. There are also annual festivals, a fishing lake, picnic areas, a campground, and plenty of hiking trails at this 360 acre site. Dogs are allowed in most of the outdoor areas; they must be on a leash no longer than 6 feet and under owner's control/care at all times.

Landrum

Accommodations
The Red Horse Inn 310 N Campbell Road Landrum SC 864-895-4968
Dogs up to 75 pounds are allowed in their 1 pet friendly cottage. There is a $25 one time fee per pet and a pet policy to sign at check in. A credit card must be on file. No ex-large or drooling dogs are allowed.

Lugoff

Accommodations
Sunrise Inn 529 Hwy 601 Lugoff SC 803-438-6990
Dogs of all sizes are allowed. There is a $6 per night pet fee per pet.

Manning

Accommodations
Best Western Palmetto Inn 2825 Paxville Hwy Manning SC 803-473-4021 (800-780-7234)
Dogs under 20 pounds are allowed for an additional pet fee of $5 per night per pet; the fee is $10 per night per pet for dogs over 20 pounds.
Comfort Inn 3031 Paxville H Manning SC 803-473-7550 (877-424-6423)

Dogs are allowed for an additional one time pet fee of $9 per room

McClellanville

Campgrounds and RV Parks
Francis Marion National Forest 1015 Pinckney McClellanville SC   843-887-3257 (877-444-6777)
http://www.fs.fed.us/r8/fms/
This forest's diverse ecosystems support a large variety of plants, fish, mammals, bird species, and recreation.
Dogs of all sizes are allowed at no additional fee. Dogs may not be left unattended, and they must be leashed
and cleaned up after. On the trails, dogs must be under verbal or physical restraint at all times; keep in mind they
are multi-use trails and use a leash when populated. The camping and tent areas also allow dogs. There is a dog
walk area at the campground. There are no water hookups at the campground.

Parks
Hampton Plantation State Historic Site 1950 Rutledge Road McClellanville SC   843-546-9361
Listed as a National Historic Landmark, this park offers interpretive programs, tours, a 2 mile nature trail, fishing,
and a 19th century plantation. Dogs of all sizes are allowed at no additional fee. Dogs may not be left unattended
at any time, and they must be on no more than a 6 foot leash, and be cleaned up after. Dogs are not allowed in
the villas, buildings, or on tours. Dogs must be quiet and well behaved, and they are allowed to walk the trails.
From Memorial to Labor Day the park grounds are open daily from 9am-6pm. The remainder of the year, the
park is open Th-M 9am-6pm. From Memorial Day to Labor Day, the mansion is open from 11 a.m. to 4 p.m. The
remainder of the year, hours are Thursday through Monday, 1 to 4 p.m.

McCormick

Campgrounds and RV Parks
Baker Creek State Park 863 Baker Creek Road McCormick SC   864-443-2457 (866-345-PARK (7275))
Although popular for all the common land and water recreational activities, this 1305 acre park also has a 10
mile mountain bike skill trail. Dogs are allowed throughout the park, on the beach, and at campground; they are
not allowed in the cabin areas. Dogs must be on no more than a 6 foot leash and cleaned up after. There are two
50 site lakeshore camp areas with picnic tables, hot showers, restrooms, and a dump station. The camping and
tent areas also allow dogs. There is a dog walk area at the campground.

Parks
Baker Creek State Park 863 Baker Creek Road McCormick SC   864-443-2457 (866-345-PARK (7275))
Although popular for all the common land and water recreational activities, this 1305 acre park also has a 10
mile mountain bike skill trail. Dogs are allowed throughout the park, on the beach, and at campground; they are
not allowed in the cabin areas. Dogs must be on no more than a 6 foot leash and cleaned up after.

Moncks Corner

Attractions
Cypress Gardens 3030 Cypress Gardens Road/H 9 Moncks Corner SC   843-553-0515
http://www.cypressgardens.info/
Although pets are not allowed on the swamp boats or in most of the buildings, they are allowed on the trails that
offer amazingly beautiful scenery, gardens and old growth trees, bridges, and an abundance of wildlife along the
way. Dogs are allowed on the trails only; they must be leashed and under owner's control/care at all times.
Blackwater Adventures 1944 Pinopolis Road/H 5 Pinopolis SC   843-761-1850
http://www.blackwateradventure.com/
Whether enjoying an informative tour or exploring coastal South Carolina on your own, this watercraft rental
company will allow your pooch to come along. Dogs must be kept out of the water at all times, and they must be
leashed and under owner's control/care at all times.

Parks

TOP 200 PLACE **Old Santee Canal Park** 900 Stony Landing Road Moncks Corner SC   843-899-5200
http://www.oldsanteecanalpark.org
In addition to the natural beauty of this 195 acre park, it shares a long cultural, military and natural history, an 1843 plantation home, many scenic trails and waterways, 4 miles of boardwalks, trails, several monthly events, and a museum/heritage center featuring over 12,000 years of the area's past. Dogs are allowed throughout the park and on the boardwalks; they must be leashed and under owner's control and care at all times. Dogs are not allowed in buildings.

Mountain Rest

Campgrounds and RV Parks
Oconee State Park 624 State Park Road Mountain Rest SC   864-638-5353 (866-345-PARK (7275))
Developed by the Civilian Conservation Corps (CCC) in the 1930's, this 1165 acre park has since been a popular recreation destination offering a wide variety of water and land recreation and an 80 mile wilderness hike. Dogs are allowed throughout the park, on the beach, and at campground; they are not allowed in the cabin areas. Dogs must be on no more than a 6 foot leash and cleaned up after. The camp area offers more than 150 sites with picnic tables, restrooms/hot showers, laundry facilities, and a dump station. The camping and tent areas also allow dogs. There is a dog walk area at the campground.

Parks
Oconee State Park 624 State Park Road Mountain Rest SC   864-638-5353 (866-345-PARK (7275))
Developed by the CCC in the 1930's, this 1165 acre park has since been a popular recreation destination offering a wide variety of water and land recreation and an 80 mile wilderness hike. Dogs are allowed throughout the park, on the beach, and at campground; they are not allowed in the cabin areas. Dogs must be on no more than a 6 foot leash and cleaned up after.

Myrtle Beach

Accommodations
La Quinta Inn & Suites Myrtle Beach 1561 21st Avenue North Myrtle Beach SC   843-916-8801 (800-531-5900)
Dogs of all sizes are allowed. There are no additional pet fees. Dogs must be quiet, well behaved, leashed and cleaned up after. Dogs may not be left alone in the room for long periods.
Mariner Motel 7003 N Ocean Blvd Myrtle Beach SC   843-449-5281
Dogs only are allowed and of all sizes. There is a $9 per night per pet additional fee.
Red Roof Inn - Myrtle Beach 2801 South Kings Highway Myrtle Beach SC   843-626-4444 (800-RED-ROOF)
One well-behaved family pet per room. Guest must notify front desk upon arrival. Guest is liable for any damages. In consideration of all guests, pets must never be left unattended in the guest rooms.
Sportsman Motor Inn 1405 South Ocean Blvd Myrtle Beach SC 800-334-5547
This ocean front hotel allows pets. For information on rules and fees contact the hotel.
Staybridge Suites 3163 Outlet Blvd Myrtle Beach SC   843-903-4000 (877-270-6405)
Dogs up to 50 pounds are allowed for an additional fee of $20 per night per room to a maximum fee of $100.
The Sea Mist Resort 1200 S Ocean Blvd Myrtle Beach SC   843-448-1551
http://www.seamist.com/
There is a $50 pet fee per stay (per week).
Red Roof Inn - North Myrtle Beach 1601 US 17 N North Myrtle Beach SC   843-280-4555 (800-RED-ROOF)
One well-behaved family pet per room. Guest must notify front desk upon arrival. Guest is liable for any damages. In consideration of all guests, pets must never be left unattended in the guest rooms.
Holiday Inn Oceanfront @ Surfside Beach 1601 N Ocean Blvd Surfside Beach SC   843-238-5601 (877-270-6405)
Dogs of all sizes are allowed for an additional one time pet fee of $125 per room.

Campgrounds and RV Parks
Big Cypress Lake RV Park 6531 Browns Way Shortcut Road Conway SC   843-397-1800
http://www.bigcypressfishing.com
Dogs of all sizes are allowed. There are no additional pet fees. Dogs must be quiet, well behaved, leashed, and cleaned up after. The camping and tent areas also allow dogs. There is a dog walk area at the campground.

Willow Tree Resort 520 Southern SIghts Drive Longs SC   866-207-2267
http://www.willowtreerv.com
Dogs of all sizes are allowed. There are no additional pet fees. Dogs may not be left unattended outside, and they must be leashed and cleaned up after. The camping and tent areas also allow dogs. There is a dog walk area at the campground.
Huntington Beach State Park 16148 Ocean H Murrells Inlet SC   843-237-4440 (866-345-PARK (7275))
In addition to a number of recreational pursuits, this 2,500 acre park also offers an environmental center with ongoing programs, an abundance of wildlife, a beautiful Moorish-style home owned by the benefactors of the park, an interpretive trail, and several boardwalks through a freshwater lagoon and the salt marshes. Dogs are allowed throughout the park, on the beach, and at campground; they are not allowed in the cabin areas or in park buildings. Dogs must be kept on no more than a 6 foot leash and cleaned up after at all times. The camp area offers a wonder sea breeze in addition to the normal amenities; restrooms, showers, a camp store, and a dump station. The camping and tent areas also allow dogs. There is a dog walk area at the campground.
Apache Family Campground 9700 Kings Road Myrtle Beach SC   843-449-7323
http://www.apachefamilycampground.com
Dogs of all sizes are allowed. There are no additional pet fees. Dogs must be leashed and cleaned up after. There are some breed restrictions. The camping and tent areas also allow dogs. There is a dog walk area at the campground.
Myrtle Beach KOA 613 5th Avenue S Myrtle Beach SC   843-448-3421 (800-562-7790)
http://www.koa.com
Dogs of all sizes are allowed. There are no additional pet fees. Dogs must be quiet, well behaved, leashed, and cleaned up after. There are some breed restrictions. The camping and tent areas also allow dogs. There is a dog walk area at the campground.
Myrtle Beach State Park 4401 South Kings H Myrtle Beach SC   843-238-5325 (866-345-PARK (7275))
A major recreation area, this park also offers a nature center with ongoing programs, a wooded oceanfront camp area, and it is home to one of the state's last strands of accessible maritime forest. Dogs are allowed throughout the park and at campground; they are not allowed in the cabin areas or in park buildings. Dogs are not allowed on the beach between the hours of 8 Am to 5 PM from May 15th to September 15th, (effective on all public beaches in Horry County). Dogs must be well behaved, kept on no more than a 6 foot leash, and cleaned up after at all times. There are well over 300 camp sites, and restrooms, hot showers, a laundry, camp store, and dump station are nearby. The camping and tent areas also allow dogs. There is a dog walk area at the campground.
Myrtle Beach Travel Park 10108 Kings Road Myrtle Beach SC   843-449-3714
http://www.myrtlebeachtravelpark.com
Dogs of all sizes are allowed. There are no additional pet fees. Dogs must be quiet, well behaved, leashed, and cleaned up after. The camping and tent areas also allow dogs. There is a dog walk area at the campground.
Pirateland Family Campground 5401 S Kings Road Myrtle Beach SC   843-238-5155
http://www.pirateland.com
Dogs of all sizes are allowed. There are no additional pet fees. Dogs may not be left unattended at any time, and they must be on no more than a 6 foot leash, and be cleaned up after. There are some breed restrictions. The camping and tent areas also allow dogs. There is a dog walk area at the campground.

Vacation Home Rentals
Booe Realty 7728 N. Kings Hwy Myrtle Beach SC   800-845-0647
http://www.booerealty.com
Serving the Myrtle Beach and Grand Strand area for more than 31 years, Booe Realty offers many properties (condos and houses) that are pet friendly.
The Palm House - Dog Friendly Vacation Rental P O Box 51165 Myrtle Beach SC   843-236-6623
This dog-friendly vacation rental home offers a fenced in yard and a central location.
Retreat Myrtle Beach 500 Main Street North Myrtle Beach SC   843-280-3015 (800-645-3618)
http://www.retreatmyrtlebeach.com
Vacation rentals for all groups and travelers with pets! Properties range from ocean front luxury condos to rustic family beach bungalows. All rentals are equipped to provide the comforts of home and meet basic resort rental standards. Pet fees range from $50 to $100 for the stay.

Shopping Centers
Hammock Shop Complex 9600 N Kings H/H 17 Myrtle Beach SC   843-237-9122
Dogs are allowed in the common areas of this shopping center; it is up to individual stores whether a dog is allowed inside. There is a pet store in the complex. Dogs must be leashed and under owner's control/care at all times.
TOP 200 PLACE Barefoot Landing 4898 H 17S North Myrtle Beach SC   843-272-8349
http://www.bflanding.com/index.html
In addition to over 100 retail and specialty shops, this waterside shopping and entertainment district offers

dozens of attractions and activities, plus there is a pet boutique and a pet bakery on site. A crowd favorite is the authentic remake of a Barnum and Bailey carousel with 41 animals cast from the original molds. Dogs are allowed throughout boardwalk and dock; it is up to individual stores whether a pet may enter. Dogs must be under owner's control, leashed, and cleaned up after at all times.

Stores
PetSmart Pet Store 1301 Oak Forest Lane Myrtle Beach SC   843-626-2164
Your licensed and well-behaved leashed dog is allowed in the store.

Beaches
Huntington Beach State Park 16148 Ocean Highway Murrells Inlet SC   843-234-4440
This beach is the best preserved beach on the Grand Strand. Dogs on a 6 foot or less leash are allowed on the beach. People need to clean up after their pets.
Myrtle Beach City Beaches off Interstate 73 Myrtle Beach SC   843-281-2662
There are certain restrictions for pets on the beach. Dogs are not allowed on the right of way of Ocean Blvd. (part of I-73), between 21st Avenue North and 13th Avenue South during March 1 through September 30. From Memorial Day weekend through Labor Day weekend, leashed dogs are allowed on Myrtle Beach city beaches before 9am and after 5pm. During off-season, leashed dogs are allowed on the city beaches anytime during park hours. People need to clean up after their pets.
Myrtle Beach State Park 4401 South Kings Highway Myrtle Beach SC   843-238-5325
This is one of the most popluar public beaches on the South Carolina coast. It is located in the heart of the Grand Strand. During the Summer, dogs are only allowed during certain hours. From June through August, dogs are only allowed on the beach after 4pm. For all other months of the year, dogs are allowed on the beach anytime during park hours. Dogs must be on leash at all times. People are required to clean up after their pets.

Parks
Huntington Beach State Park 16148 Ocean H Murrells Inlet SC   843-237-4440 (866-345-PARK (7275))
In addition to a number of recreational pursuits, this 2,500 acre park also offers an environmental center with ongoing programs, an abundance of wildlife, a beautiful Moorish-style home owned by the benefactors of the park, an interpretive trail, and several boardwalks through a freshwater lagoon and the salt marshes. Dogs are allowed throughout the park, on the beach, and at campground; they are not allowed in the cabin areas or in park buildings. Dogs must be kept on no more than a 6 foot leash and cleaned up after at all times.
Myrtle Beach State Park 4401 South Kings H Myrtle Beach SC   843-238-5325 (866-345-PARK (7275))
A major recreation area, this park also offers a nature center with ongoing programs, a wooded oceanfront camp area, and it is home to one of the state's last strands of accessible maritime forest. Dogs are allowed throughout the park and at campground; they are not allowed in the cabin areas or in park buildings. Dogs are not allowed on the beach between the hours of 8 Am to 5 PM from May 15th to September 15th, (effective on all public beaches in Horry County). Dogs must be well behaved, kept on no more than a 6 foot leash, and cleaned up after at all times.

Off-Leash Dog Parks
Myrtle Beach Barc Parc Kings Hwy at Mallard Lake Drive Myrtle Beach SC   843-918-1000
This is an especially nice fenced dog park of 11 acres. There is a large pond in the park for swimming. There is even a doggy shower at the park. The park is located in the former Air Force Base area just south of the city. Take Kings Hwy south just out of the city and turn left on Mallard Lake Drive. The park is the only area in Myrtle Beach where a dog is allowed to be off-leash.

Newberry

Accommodations
Comfort Inn 105 Trade Street Clinton SC   864-833-5558 (877-424-6423)
Quiet dogs are allowed for no additional pet fee.
Days Inn Newberry 50 Thomas Griffin Rd Newberry SC   803-276-2294 (800-329-7466)
Dogs up to 75 pounds are allowed. There is a $10 per night pet fee per pet. Reservations are recommended due to limited rooms for pets.

Campgrounds and RV Parks
Dreher Island State Recreation Area 3677 State Park Road Prosperity SC   803-364-4152 (866-345-PARK

(7525))
Although a popular hiking and fishing destination, there are a lot of activities to enjoy at this lakeshore 348 acre recreational park; the park is actually 3 islands linked to shore. Dogs are allowed throughout the park and campground; they are not allowed in the villas or the villa areas. Dogs must be on no more than a 6 foot leash and cleaned up after. There are 2 lakeside camps offering easy access and great views of the lake, more than 100 sites, picnic tables, hot showers, and restrooms. The camping and tent areas also allow dogs. There is a dog walk area at the campground.

Attractions
Musgrove Mill State Historic Site 398 State Park Road Clinton SC 864-938-0100
Rich in colonial history and local lore, this park offers a visitor center with an interpretive exhibit about the state's pivotal role in the Revolutionary War and about the Battle of Musgrove Mill. There is also a scenic nature trail that takes visitors to Horseshoe Falls and along other waterways. Dogs are allowed on the grounds; they must be leashed and under owner's control/care at all times.

Parks
Dreher Island State Recreation Area 3677 State Park Road Prosperity SC 803-364-4152 (866-345-PARK (7525))
Although a popular hiking and fishing destination, there are a lot of activities to enjoy at this lakeshore 348 acre recreational park; the park is actually 3 islands linked to shore. Dogs are allowed throughout the park and campground; they are not allowed in the villas or the villa areas. Dogs must be on no more than a 6 foot leash and cleaned up after.

Orangeburg

Accommodations
Days Inn Orangeburg Industrail Park Rte 2 Box 215 Orangeburg SC 803-534-0500 (800-329-7466)
Dogs of all sizes are allowed. There is a $7 per night pet fee per pet. Reservations are recommended due to limited rooms for pets.
Days Inn Orangeburg North 3691 St Mathews Rd Orangeburg SC 803-531-2590 (800-329-7466)
Dogs of all sizes are allowed. There is a $10 per night pet fee per pet.
Quality Inn and Suites 1415 John C Calhoun Drive Orangeburg SC 803-531-4600 (877-424-6423)
Dogs are allowed for an additional one time fee of $10 per pet.
Super 8 Orangeburg 610 John C Calhoun Dr Orangeburg SC 803-531-1921 (800-800-8000)
Dogs of all sizes are allowed. There is a $5 per night pet fee per pet. Smoking and non-smoking rooms are available for pet rooms.

Attractions
Edisto Memorial Gardens 250 Riverside Drive SW Orangeburg SC 803-533-6020
http://www.orangeburg.sc.us/gardens/
Visitors will enjoy a number of themes and commemoratives throughout this memorial garden that is 1 of only 23 official rose test gardens in America. In addition to the more than 4000 rose plants (75+ varieties), there is an abundance of azaleas and other flora and fauna. Dogs are allowed throughout the garden, but they must be kept leashed and picked up after at all times.

Plum Branch

Campgrounds and RV Parks
Hamilton Branch State Rec Area 111 Campground Road Plum Branch SC 864-333-2223 (866-345-PARK (7275))
This 731 acre park takes up almost an entire peninsula, allowing for ample fishing, hiking, and lakeside camping. Dogs of all sizes are allowed at no additional fee. Dogs must be on no more than a 6 foot leash and be cleaned up after. Dogs are allowed on the trails. The camping and tent areas also allow dogs. There is a dog walk area at the campground.

Ridgeland

Accommodations
Comfort Inn 200 James F Taylor Blvd Ridgeland SC   843-726-2121 (877-424-6423)
Dogs are allowed for an additional one time pet fee of $10 per room.
Days Inn Ridgeland 516 East Main Street Ridgeland SC   843-726-5553 (800-329-7466)
Dogs of all sizes are allowed. There is a $7 per night pet fee per pet.

Saint George

Accommodations
Comfort Inn 139 Motel Drive Saint George SC   843-563-4180 (877-424-6423)
Dogs are allowed for an additional fee of $10 per night per pet.
Days Inn St George 128 Interstate Dr Saint George SC   843-563-4027 (800-329-7466)
Dogs of all sizes are allowed. There is a $5 per night pet fee per pet.
Quality Inn 6014 W Jim Bilton Blvd Saint George SC   843-563-4581 (877-424-6423)
Dogs are allowed for an additional one time pet fee of $10 per night per room.
Super 8 St George 114 Winningham Road Saint George SC   843-563-5551 (800-800-8000)
Dogs of all sizes are allowed. There is a $5 per night pet fee per pet. Smoking and non-smoking rooms are available for pet rooms.

Santee

Accommodations
Days Inn Santee 9074 Old Hwy 6 Santee SC   803-854-2175 (800-329-7466)
Dogs of all sizes are allowed. There is a $6 per night pet fee per pet.
Howard Johnson Express Inn I-95 Ex 102, Rd 400 Santee SC   803-478-7676 (800-446-4656)
There is an additional $10 per day pet fee.

Campgrounds and RV Parks
Santee State Park 251 State Park Road Santee SC   803-854-2408 (866-345-PARK (7275))
A popular recreational destination, this 2,500 acre park offers an array of activities and 2 lakes that cover over 170,000 acres for lots of great fishing. Dogs are allowed throughout the park, on the beach, and at campground; they are not allowed in the cabin areas. Dogs must be on no more than a 6 foot leash and cleaned up after. There are more than 150 sites in the camp area with restrooms, hot showers, a laundry, and a dump station on site. The camping and tent areas also allow dogs. There is a dog walk area at the campground.

Parks
Santee State Park 251 State Park Road Santee SC   803-854-2408 (866-345-PARK (7275))
A popular recreational destination, this 2,500 acre park offers an array of activities and 2 lakes that cover over 170,000 acres for lots of great fishing. Dogs are allowed throughout the park, on the beach, and at campground; they are not allowed in the cabin areas. Dogs must be on no more than a 6 foot leash and cleaned up after.

Seabrook Island

Attractions
Bohicket Boat - Adventure and Tour Co. 2789 Cherry Point Road Wadmalaw Island SC   843-559-3525
http://www.bohicketboat.com/
Departuring and returning boats are located at an authentic commercial fishing pier and working shrimp dock, so there is always activity around. This company offers watercraft rentals plus a variety of tours through the various scenic waterways. Dogs are allowed on the rentals; they are not allowed on tours. Dogs must be well mannered,

leashed, and under owner's control/care at all times.

Sheldon

Attractions

Oyotunji Village 56 Bryant Lane Sheldon SC   843-846-8900
http://www.oyotunjiafricanvillage.org/
This authentic African village is dedicated to preserving and educating visitors about the Yoruba Orisa culture-their past, present, and future views, and about their deep spiritual practices and lineage. Dogs are allowed throughout the village; they are not allowed in buildings. Dogs must be leashed and under owner's control/care at all times.

Spartanburg

Accommodations

Campus Place/Extended Stay 1050 Charisma Drive Spartanburg SC   864-699-1088
Dogs of all sizes are allowed. There is a $20 one time per small pet fee per visit and $25 for large pet.
Days Inn Spartanburg 115 Rogers Commerce Blvd Spartanburg SC   864-814-0560 (800-329-7466)
Dogs of all sizes are allowed. There is a $10 per night pet fee per pet. Dogs are not allowed to be left alone in the room. Reservations are recommended due to limited rooms for pets. Only non-smoking rooms are used for pets.
Motel 6 - Spartanburg 105 Jones Road Spartanburg SC   864-573-6383 (800-466-8356)
One well-behaved family pet per room. Guest must notify front desk upon arrival. Guest is liable for any damages. In consideration of all guests, pets must never be left unattended in the guest rooms.

Stores

PetSmart Pet Store 150 E Blackstock Rd Ste A Spartanburg SC   864-576-8868
Your licensed and well-behaved leashed dog is allowed in the store.

Turbeville

Accommodations

Days Inn Lake City 170 S Ron McNair Blvd Lake City SC   843-394-3269 (800-329-7466)
Dogs of all sizes are allowed. There is a $10 per night pet fee per pet.
Days Inn Turbeville 378 Mydher Beach Hwy Turbeville SC   843-659-8060 (800-329-7466)
Dogs of all sizes are allowed. There are no additional pet fees.

Parks

Woods Bay State Natural Area 11020 Woods Bay Road Olanta SC   843-659-4445
Registered as a Heritage Trust Site, and complete with a nature center and boardwalk, the unique geology here creates diverse ecosystems that support a large variety of plants, fish, mammals, bird species, and recreation. Dogs of all sizes are allowed at no additional fee. Dogs may not be left unattended at any time, they must be on no more than a 6 foot leash, and be cleaned up after. Dogs are not allowed in buildings, but they are allowed on the trails. The park is open daily from 9 am to 6 pm.

Union

Attractions

Rose Hill Plantation State Historic Site 2677 Sardis Road Union SC   864-427-5966
Rich in colonial culture and history, this elegant plantation gives visitors a glimpse of the grandeur and strife of an era past, and now the beautiful grounds and gardens make it a popular site for special events and holiday programs throughout the year. There is also a nice walking path down to the river. Dogs are allowed throughout

the grounds; they are not allowed in buildings. Dogs must be on no more than a 6 foot leash and under owner's control/care at all times.

Walhalla

Parks
Oconee Station State Historic Site 500 Oconee Station Road Walhalla SC   864-638-0079
In addition to its historic significance as a military outpost in the late 1700's, then as a trading post in the early 1800's (still 2 buildings on site), this 210 acre park offers a fishing pond and a 1½ mile nature trail that leads into a National forest and ends at a beautiful 60 foot waterfall. Dogs are allowed throughout the park; they must be on no more than a 6 foot leash and under owner's control/care at all times.

Walterboro

Accommodations
Best Western Walterboro 1428 Sniders Highway Walterboro SC   843-538-3600 (800-780-7234)
Dogs are allowed for an additional fee of $15 per night per pet.
Econo Lodge 1145 Sniders Hwy Walterboro SC   843-538-3830
There are no additional pet fees.
Howard Johnson Express Inn 1120 Sniders Hwy. Walterboro SC   843-538-5473 (800-446-4656)
Dogs of all sizes are welcome. There is a $8 per day pet fee.
Rice Planters Inn I-95 and SR 63 Walterboro SC   843-538-8964
There is a $5 per day additional pet fee.
Super 8 Walterboro 1972 Bells Hwy Walterboro SC   843-538-5383 (800-800-8000)
Dogs of all sizes are allowed. There is a $5 per night pet fee per pet. Reservations are recommended due to limited rooms for pets. Smoking and non-smoking rooms are available for pet rooms.

Stores
Petco Pet Store 2098 Bell Hwy Walterboro SC   843-538-7387
Your licensed and well-behaved leashed dog is allowed in the store.

Whitmeyer

Campgrounds and RV Parks
Sumter National Forest H 66 Whitmeyer SC   803-276-4810 (877-444-6777)
http://www.fs.fed.us/r8/fms/
This forest's diverse ecosystems support a large variety of plants, fish, mammals, bird species, and recreation. Dogs of all sizes are allowed at no additional fee. Dogs may not be left unattended, and they must be leashed and cleaned up after. On the trails, dogs must be under verbal or physical restraint at all times; keep in mind they are multi-use trails and use a leash when populated. The camping and tent areas also allow dogs. There is a dog walk area at the campground. There are no electric or water hookups at the campground.

Winnsboro

Accommodations
Days Inn Winnsboro 1894 US Hwy 321 Bypass Winnsboro SC   803-635-1447 (800-329-7466)
Dogs up to 60 pounds are allowed. There is a $7.50 per night pet fee per pet.

Campgrounds and RV Parks
Lake Wateree State Rec Area 881 State Park Road Winnsboro SC   803-482-6401 (866-345-PARK (7275))
This 238 acre park along a more than a 13,000 acre lake provides premier fishing, lake shore camping, hiking,

and a variety of recreational pursuits. Dogs of all sizes are allowed at no additional fee. Dogs may not be left unattended at any time, and they must be on no more than a 6 foot leash, and be cleaned up after. Dogs are not allowed in the swim areas or in buildings. Dogs are allowed on the trails. The camping and tent areas also allow dogs. There is a dog walk area at the campground.

Yemassee

Accommodations
Days Inn Point South/Yemassee 3196 Point South Dr Yemassee SC   843-726-8156 (800-329-7466)
Dogs of all sizes are allowed. There is a $10 per night pet fee per pet.
Holiday Inn Express 40 Frampton Drive Yemassee SC   843-726-9400 (877-270-6405)
Dogs of all sizes are allowed for an additional one time fee of $20 per pet.
Super 8 Yemassee 409 Yemassee Hwy Yemassee SC   843-589-2177 (800-800-8000)
Dogs of all sizes are allowed. There is a $3 per night pet fee per pet. Smoking and non-smoking rooms are available for pet rooms.

Campgrounds and RV Parks
Point South KOA 14 Campground Road Yemassee SC   843-726-5733 (800-562-2948)
http://www.pointsouthkoa.com
Dogs of all sizes are allowed. There are no additional pet fees. Dogs may not be left unattended, and they must be leashed and cleaned up after. There are some breed restrictions. The camping and tent areas also allow dogs. There is a dog walk area at the campground. Dogs are allowed in the camping cabins.

Chapter 18

Georgia
Dog Travel Guide

Acworth

Accommodations
Red Roof Inn - Atlanta Acworth 5320 Cherokee Street Acworth GA   770-974-5400 (800-RED-ROOF)
One well-behaved family pet per room. Guest must notify front desk upon arrival. Guest is liable for any damages. In consideration of all guests, pets must never be left unattended in the guest rooms.
Super 8 Acworth 4970 Cowan Rd Acworth GA   770-966-9700 (800-800-8000)
Dogs of all sizes are allowed. There is a $8 per night pet fee per pet. Smoking and non-smoking rooms are available for pet rooms.

Campgrounds and RV Parks
Holiday Harbor 5989 Groover's Landing Acworth GA   770-974-2575
Dogs of all sizes are allowed. There are no additional pet fees. Dogs must be leashed and cleaned up after. This is an RV only park with cabin rentals, but there is only one pet friendly cabin. The camping and tent areas also allow dogs. There is a dog walk area at the campground. Dogs are allowed in the camping cabins.

Adairsville

Accommodations
Comfort Inn 107 Princeton Blvd Adairsville GA   770-773-2886 (877-424-6423)
Dogs are allowed for an additional fee of $10 per night per pet.

Campgrounds and RV Parks
Harvest Moon RV Park 1001 Poplar Springs Road Adairsville GA   770-773-7320
http://www.harvestmoonrvpark.us
Dogs of all sizes are allowed. There are no additional pet fees. Dogs may not be left unattended outside, and they must be leashed and cleaned up after. There are some breed restrictions. There is a dog walk area at the campground.

Adel

Accommodations
Days Inn Adel 1200 W 4th St Adel GA   229-896-4574 (800-329-7466)
Dogs of all sizes are allowed. There is a $5 per night pet fee per pet.
Hampton Inn 1500 W Fourth Street Adel GA   229-896-3099
Dogs of all sizes are allowed on the 3rd floor rooms. There is a $10 per night per pet fee.
Super 8 Adel/I-75 1103 W 4th Street Adel GA   229-896-2244 (800-800-8000)
Dogs of all sizes are allowed. There is a $5 per night pet fee per pet. Smoking and non-smoking rooms are available for pet rooms.

Albany

Accommodations
Best Western Albany Mall Inn & Suites 2729 Pointe North Boulevard Albany GA   229-446-2001 (800-780-7234)
Dogs are allowed for an additional fee of $10 per night per pet.
Holiday Inn - Albany Mall 2701 Dawson Rd Albany GA   229-883-8100 (877-270-6405)
Dogs of all sizes are allowed for an additional one time pet fee of $25 per room.
Knights Inn 1201 Schley Avenue Albany GA   229-888-9600 (800-843-5644)
There is a $10 one time pet charge.

Motel 6 - Albany 201 South Thornton Drive Albany GA   229-439-0078 (800-466-8356)
One well-behaved family pet per room. Guest must notify front desk upon arrival. Guest is liable for any damages. In consideration of all guests, pets must never be left unattended in the guest rooms.

Americus

Accommodations
Holiday Inn Express 1607 Hwy 280 East Americus GA   229-928-5400 (877-270-6405)
Dogs of all sizes are allowed for an additional one time pet fee of $15 per room.

Appling

Campgrounds and RV Parks
Mistletoe State Park 3723 Mistletoe Road Appling GA   706-541-0321 (800-864-PARK (7275))
This 1,920 acre peninsula park on a 7,200 acre lake offers a wide variety of land and water activities and recreation. Dogs of all sizes are allowed at no additional fee. Dogs may not be left unattended, and they must be leashed and cleaned up after. Dogs are not allowed around the cabin areas, however, they are allowed on the trails. The camping and tent areas also allow dogs. There is a dog walk area at the campground.

Ashburn

Accommodations
Days Inn Ashburn 823 E Washington Ave Ashburn GA   229-567-3346 (800-329-7466)
Dogs of all sizes are allowed. There is a $5 per night pet fee per pet.

Athens

Accommodations
Comfort Suites 255 North Avenue Athens GA   706-995-4000 (877-424-6423)
Dogs up to 60 pounds are allowed for an additional fee of $25 per night per pet.

Off-Leash Dog Parks
Memorial Park Dog Park 293 Gran Ellen Drive Athens GA   706-613-3580
This fenced, 1.5 acre off-leash dog park is located on the hillside near the lake in the 72 acre park. Dogs must be leashed when outside of the off-leash area.
Sandy Creek Park Dog Parks 400 Bob Holman Rd Athens GA   706-613-3800
http://www.sandycreekpark.com
There are actually 4 two to three acre fenced off-leash areas in Sandy Creek Park. One is a standard dog park where anyone may bring their dogs free of charge. The other three are by reservation only and there is a charge for this reservation of $1.00 per hour per dog. They can be used for private groups, training and other purposes. Dogs must be leashed in the park outside of the off-leash areas.
Southeast Clarke Park Dog Park 4440 Lexington Road Athens GA   706-613-3871
This fenced, 2 acre off-leash dog park is located on the Whit Davis Rd side of the park. There are separate areas for small and large dogs. Dogs must be leashed when outside of the off-leash area.

Atlanta

Accommodations
Airport Drury Inn & Suites 1270 Virginia Avenue Atlanta GA   404-761-4900 (800-378-7946)
Dogs of all sizes are permitted. Pets are not allowed in the breakfast area of the hotel. Pets are not to be left

unattended, and each guest must assume liability for damage of property or other guest complaints. There is a limit of one pet per room.

Best Western Granada Suite Hotel - Midtown 1302 W Peachtree Street NW Atlanta GA   404-876-6100 (800-780-7234)
Dogs are allowed for an additional pet fee per room of $50 for each 1 to 7 days.

Doubletree 3400 Norman Berry Drive Atlanta GA   404-763-1600
Dogs up to 50 pounds are allowed. There is a $50 one time fee per pet.

Hawthorn Suites 1500 Parkwood Circle Atlanta GA   770-952-9595
There is a $100 one time pet fee and there is a 2 dog limit per room. There is also a $50 refundable pet deposit.

Hilton 255 Courtland Street NE Atlanta GA   404-767-9000
Dogs are allowed for no additional pet fee.

Holiday Inn - Airport North 1380 Virginia Ave Atlanta GA   404-762-8411 (877-270-6405)
Dogs of all sizes are allowed for an additional one time fee of $50 per room.

Holiday Inn Atlanta Northeast Doraville 2001 Clearview Ave. Atlanta GA   770-455-3700 (877-270-6405)
Dogs of all sizes are allowed for an additional pet fee of $25 per night per room.

Holiday Inn Select-Atlanta Perimeter 4386 Chamblee-Dunwoody Rd. Atlanta GA   770-457-6363 (877-270-6405)
Dogs of all sizes are allowed for an additional one time pet fee of $75 per room.

TOP 200 PLACE **Hotel Indigo** 683 Peachtree St NE Atlanta GA   404-874-9200 (800-HOLIDAY)
Dogs of all sizes are allowed for no additional fee. This is an especially pet-friendly and high end hotel. The hotel has a weekly Canine Cocktail hour on Tuesdays from 5 to 8 pm. The hotel also provides a doggy menu as well. Please check with the hotel for the day and time and seasonal schedules.

La Quinta Inn & Suites Atlanta Perimeter Medical 6260 Peachtree Dunwoody Atlanta GA   770-350-6177 (800-531-5900)
Dogs of all sizes are allowed. There are no additional pet fees. Dogs must be well behaved, leashed, and cleaned up after. Dogs must be crated if left unattended in the room.

Laurel Hill 1992 McLendon Avenue Atlanta GA   404-377-3217
Well behaved and friendly dogs of all sizes are allowed. There is a $25 one time fee per room and pets must be leashed and kept out of the food areas.

Motel 6 - Atlanta Northeast 2820 Chamblee - Tucker Road Atlanta GA   770-458-6626 (800-466-8356)
One well-behaved family pet per room. Guest must notify front desk upon arrival. Guest is liable for any damages. In consideration of all guests, pets must never be left unattended in the guest rooms.

Red Roof Inn - Atlanta Airport North 1200 Virginia Avenue Atlanta GA   404-209-1800 (800-RED-ROOF)
One well-behaved family pet per room. Guest must notify front desk upon arrival. Guest is liable for any damages. In consideration of all guests, pets must never be left unattended in the guest rooms.

Red Roof Inn - Atlanta Druid Hills 1960 North Druid Hills Road Atlanta GA   404-321-1653 (800-RED-ROOF)
One well-behaved family pet per room. Guest must notify front desk upon arrival. Guest is liable for any damages. In consideration of all guests, pets must never be left unattended in the guest rooms.

Residence Inn by Marriott 2960 Piedmont Road NE Atlanta GA   404-239-0677
Pets of all sizes are allowed. There is a $75 one time fee per pet and a pet policy to sign at check in.

Residence Inn by Marriott 2220 Lake Blvd Atlanta GA   404-467-1660
Pets up to 70 pounds are allowed. There is a $75 one time fee and a pet policy to sign at check in.

Residence Inn by Marriott 1041 W Peachtree Street Atlanta GA   404-872-8885
Pets of all sizes are allowed. There is a $75 one time fee and a pet policy to sign at check in.

Residence Inn by Marriott 1365 Peachtree Street Atlanta GA   404-745-1000
Pets up to 75 pounds are allowed. There is a $75 one time fee and a pet policy to sign at check in.

Residence Inn by Marriott 6096 Barfield Road Atlanta GA   404-252-5066
Pets of all sizes are allowed. There is a $75 one time fee per pet and a pet policy to sign at check in.

Residence Inn by Marriott 1901 Savoy Drive Atlanta GA   770-455-4446
Pets of all sizes are allowed. There is a $75 one time fee and a pet policy to sign at check in.

Sheraton Atlanta Hotel 165 Courtland Street at International Blvd. Atlanta GA   404-659-6500 (888-625-5144)
Dogs up to 80 pounds are allowed. There are no additional pet fees. Dogs are not allowed to be left alone in the room.

Sheraton Buckhead Hotel Atlanta 3405 Lenox Road NE Atlanta GA   404-261-9250 (888-625-5144)
Dogs up to 80 pounds are allowed. There are no additional pet fees. Dogs are not allowed to be left alone in the room.

Sheraton Gateway Hotel Atlanta Airport 1900 Sullivan Road Atlanta GA   770-997-1100 (888-625-5144)
Dogs up to 80 pounds are allowed for no additional pet fee. There is a pet agreement to sign at check in, and dogs may not be left alone in the room.

Staybridge Suites - Atlanta Buckhead 540 Pharr Road NE Atlanta GA   404-842-0800 (877-270-6405)
Dogs of all sizes are allowed for an additional one time fee of $150 per pet.

Staybridge Suites - Perimeter 4601 Ridgeview Rd Atlanta GA   678-320-0111 (877-270-6405)
Dogs of all sizes are allowed for an additional one time pet fee of $150 per room.

The Westin Atlanta Airport 4736 Best Road Atlanta GA   404-762-7676 (888-625-5144)

Dogs of all sizes are allowed. There are no additional pet fees. Dogs are not allowed to be left alone in the room.
The Westin Atlanta Perimeter North 7 Concourse Pkwy Atlanta GA   770-395-3900 (888-625-5144)
Dogs of all sizes are allowed for a $25 refundable deposit, and there is a pet agreement to sign at check in. Dogs may not be left alone in the room.
TownePlace Suites Atlanta Northlake 3300 Northlake Parkway Atlanta GA   770-938-0408
Dogs of all sizes are allowed. There is a $75 one time pet fee per visit.
Days Inn Decatur 4300 Snapfinger Woods Drive Decatur GA   770-981-5670 (800-329-7466)
Dogs up to 60 pounds are allowed. There is a $25 one time per pet fee per visit.
Best Western Diplomat Inn 6187 Dawson Boulevard Norcross GA   770-448-8686 (800-780-7234)
Dogs are allowed for no additional pet fee with a credit card on file; there is a $50 refundable deposit if paying cash.
Days Inn Atlanta NE 5990 Western Hills Dr Norcross GA   770-368-0218 (800-329-7466)
Dogs of all sizes are allowed. There is a $10 per night pet fee per pet.
La Quinta Inn Norcross 5945 Oakbrook Parkway Norcross GA   770-368-9400 (800-531-5900)
Dogs of all sizes are allowed. There is a $10 refundable deposit per room. There is a pet waiver to sign at check in. Dogs may not be left unattended, and they must be quiet, well behaved, leashed, and cleaned up after.
Motel 6 - Atlanta Northeast - Norcross 6015 Oakbrook Parkway Norcross GA   770-446-2311 (800-466-8356)
One well-behaved family pet per room. Guest must notify front desk upon arrival. Guest is liable for any damages. In consideration of all guests, pets must never be left unattended in the guest rooms.
Northeast Drury Inn & Suites 5655 Jimmy Carter Blvd Norcross GA   770-729-0060 (800-378-7946)
Dogs of all sizes are permitted. Pets are not allowed in the breakfast area of the hotel. Pets are not to be left unattended, and each guest must assume liability for damage of property or other guest complaints. There is a limit of one pet per room.
Red Roof Inn - Atlanta - Peachtree Industrial Boulevard 5395 Peachtree Industrial Boulevard Norcross GA   770-446-2882 (800-RED-ROOF)
One well-behaved family pet per room. Guest must notify front desk upon arrival. Guest is liable for any damages. In consideration of all guests, pets must never be left unattended in the guest rooms.
Red Roof Inn - Atlanta Indian Trail 5171 Brook Hollow Parkway Norcross GA   770-448-8944 (800-RED-ROOF)
One well-behaved family pet per room. Guest must notify front desk upon arrival. Guest is liable for any damages. In consideration of all guests, pets must never be left unattended in the guest rooms.
Residence Inn by Marriott 5500 Triangle Drive Norcross GA   770-447-1714
Pets are allowed to the total of 75 pounds. There is a $75 one time fee per pet and a pet policy to sign at check in.
TownePlace Suites Atlanta Norcross/Peachtree Corners 6640 Bay Circle Norcross GA   770-447-8446
Dogs of all sizes are allowed. There is a $75 one time pet fee per visit.

Campgrounds and RV Parks
Stone Mountain Park H 78E Stone Mountain GA   800-385-9807
http://www.stonemountainpark.com
Dogs of all sizes are allowed. There are no additional pet fees. Dogs are not allowed on the lazer lawn, walk up trails, posted areas, nor at any of the attractions or special events. Dogs may not be left unattended, and they must be leashed and cleaned up after. The camping and tent areas also allow dogs. There is a dog walk area at the campground.

Transportation Systems
MARTA Regional Atlanta GA   404-848-4900
http://www.itsmarta.com
Small dogs carried in a closed pet carrier that fits on your lap are allowed on the buses and trains.

Attractions
Atlanta Preservation Center 327 Saint Paul Ave Se Atlanta GA   404-876-2041
The preservation center has 7 tours, and only 2 of the tours do not allow dogs; the Downtown and Fox Theater Tours. They are allowed on the other 5 outdoor tours. Dogs must be well behaved and on leash.
Bark in the Park Piedmont Park Atlanta GA   404-733-5000
http://www.atlantasymphony.org
Once a year, normally in August, the Atlanta Symphony Orchestra holds a Bark in the Park concert. It is usually located in Piedmont Park. So if you, or even your pooch loves the symphony, come for an evening of free music outdoors.
Centennial Olympic Park 265 Park Avenue West Atlanta GA   404-222-PARK
http://www.centennialpark.com/
Come enjoy this 21 acre park which highlights and commemorates the 1996 Olympics that where held in Atlanta.

Thousands of visitors come to this park every year. The park features both man-made and natural points of interest. During hot Summer days and nights, the five-ring water fountain is a popular spot to cool off. Pets must be leashed and remember to clean up after your pet. Dogs are normally not allowed in concerts at this park. The park is bordered by Marietta Street, Baker Street, Centennial Olympic Park Drive and Andrew Young International Blvd.

Stone Mountain Park Highway 78 Stone Mountain GA   770-498-5600
http://www.stonemountainpark.com
Dogs are not allowed in most of this park which includes the attractions and many public areas. However, dogs are allowed on the Cherokee Trail which goes around the base of the mountain, and the Nature Trail and Gardens. You and your pooch will also be able to see the Memorial Carving on the mountain which depicts three Confederate heroes of the Civil War; President Jefferson Davis, General Robert E. Lee, and Lt. General Thomas "Stonewall" Jackson. Admission to the park is just under $20 per adult and less for children and seniors. The price includes the attractions, but unless you take turns watching the pooch, you will not be able to take advantage of the attractions. Dogs are also allowed at the campground and RV park. Pets must be leashed throughout the park. Dogs are not allowed at the Lasershow Lawn, the Walk Up Trail or Special Events Areas. The park is located 16 miles east of downtown Atlanta. To get there, take exit 39B off I-285 and go east on Highway 78 to exit 8, the Stone Mountain Park Main Entrance.

Shopping Centers

Stone Mountain Village Main Street Stone Mountain GA   770-879-4971
http://www.stonemountainvillage.com/
Listed in the National Register of Historic Places, this destination-reminiscent of another era, offers guests a variety of dining, unique shopping, and special event opportunities. Dogs are allowed throughout the village; it is up to individual stores whether they allow a dog inside. Dogs must be well behaved, leashed, and under owner's control/care at all times. There is also an off leash dog park (Red Dog Park) located behind the visitor center off Main Street.

Stores

Junkman's Daughter Store 464 Moreland Avenue Atlanta GA   404-577-3188
This novelty store allows well-behaved leashed dogs inside.
PetSmart Pet Store 650 Ponce De Leon Ave Atlanta GA   404-872-2363
Your licensed and well-behaved leashed dog is allowed in the store.
PetSmart Pet Store 3221 Peachtree Rd Atlanta GA   404-266-0402
Your licensed and well-behaved leashed dog is allowed in the store.
PetSmart Pet Store 128 Perimeter Center W Atlanta GA   770-481-0043
Your licensed and well-behaved leashed dog is allowed in the store.
Petco Pet Store 1267 Caroline St NE Atlanta GA   404-521-1762
Your licensed and well-behaved leashed dog is allowed in the store.
Petco Pet Store 5938 Roswell Rd NE Sandy Springs GA   404-255-6544
Your licensed and well-behaved leashed dog is allowed in the store.

Parks

Chattahoochee River National Recreation Area 1978 Island Ford Parkway Atlanta GA   770-399-8070
http://www.nps.gov/chat
Dogs are allowed, but must be kept on a leash and under control at all times. Please clean up after your pooch. There are many separate areas or units that make up this park. One of the more popular trails starts near the Park Headquarters at the Island Fort Unit. The Cochran Fitness Trail follows the Chattahoochee River and is a great place to walk or run. For a map and more details, call or visit the Park Headquarters at the Island Ford Unit at 1978 Island Ford Parkway. Take Highway 400/19 and exit Northridge Road. The park is located about 15 minutes north of downtown Atlanta.
Grant Park 840 Cherokee Ave., SE Atlanta GA   404-875-7275
This park has over 125 acres and miles of scenic trails. While dogs are not allowed in the Zoo or in the Atlanta Cyclorama, they can walk with you around this park. Dogs must be leashed and pet owners must clean up after their dogs.
Piedmont Park 400 Park Drive Northeast Atlanta GA   404-875-7275
Located in Midtown is the popular Piedmont Park, which consists of 185 acres. The park offers many paths for walking or running. Dogs must be leashed, except for the designated off-leash area located north of the Park Drive bridge. Dog owners are required to clean up after their dogs. Dogs are not allowed in the lake, in the botanical gardens, on the tennis courts, ball fields or playgrounds. Of special interest to dog lovers, is the Atlanta Symphony Orchestra's Annual Bark in the Park event. The event usually takes place in August and is held in Piedmont Park. To get to the park, take I-85/75 north and take exit 101 (10th Street). Go straight to the first light, then turn right on 10th Street. Turn left at Piedmont and the park entrance will be on the right.

Off-Leash Dog Parks

Piedmont Park Off Leash Dog Park Park Drive Atlanta GA   404-875-7275
Dogs can run leash-free only in this designated area of Piedmont Park. The dog park is just over 1.5 acres. To get there, take I-85/75 north and take exit 101 (10th Street). Go straight to the first light, then turn right on 10th Street. Go past Piedmont Park, then turn left onto Monroe Drive. At the first light, turn left onto Park Drive. The dog park is below the bridge on the north side.
Henry Jones Dog Park 4770 N. Peachtree Rd Dunwoody GA   404-371-2631
This four acre and fenced dog park is located in Brook Run Park in the Atlanta/Dunwoody area on Peachtree and just south of Peeler Rd. There are no water fountains. The park is open during daylight hours.
Graves Dog Park 1540 Graves Rd Norcross GA   770-822-8840
This two acre fenced dog park has separate areas for large dogs and small dogs.
Red Dog Park 3rd and 4th Streets Stone Mountain GA   770-879-4971
There are 2 separate sections for large and small dogs at this off lead area. There are benches and shady areas plus a pathway that leads from the off lead area into the Stone Mountain Park. Dogs must be sociable, current on all vaccinations and license, and under owner's control/care at all times. Dogs must be leashed when not in designated off-lead areas.

Outdoor Restaurants

Anis Cafe and Bistro 2974 Grandview Avenue Atlanta GA   404-233-9889
This French bistro allows dogs at their outdoor tables. The cafe offers a variety of foods including soups, salads, lamb, chicken, raviolis and more.
Baja Fresh Mexican Grill 5992 Roswell Rd NE Atlanta GA   404-256-5187
This restaurant serves Mexican food. Dogs are allowed at the outdoor tables.
Brewhouse Cafe 401 Moreland Avenue NE Atlanta GA   404-525-7799
http://www.brewhousecafe.com/pub.html
In addition to their freshly prepared soups, sandwiches, and variety of tasty accompaniments, this is the city's only international and domestic sports bar. Outside seating is available. Dogs must be leashed and under owner's control/care at all times.
Broadway Cafe 2168 Briarcliff Rd Atlanta GA   404-329-0888
This restaurant serves kosher and vegetarian food. Dogs are allowed at the outdoor tables. Closed on Friday nights and all day Saturday.
Corner Bakery Cafe 3368 Peachtree Rd. NE Atlanta GA   404-816-5100
This cafe is open for breakfast, lunch and afternoon dining. Dogs are allowed at the outdoor tables.
Lush Restaurant and Bar 913 Bernina Ave NE Atlanta GA   404-223-9292
This restaurant and bar serves American cuisine. Dogs are allowed at the outdoor tables.
Mellow Mushroom Pizza Bakers 931 Monroe Dr NE Atlanta GA   404-874-2291
This restaurant serves Italian and pizza type food. Dogs are allowed at the outdoor tables.
Mellow Mushroom Pizza Bakers 4058 Peachtree Rd NE Atlanta GA   404-266-1661
This restaurant serves Italian and pizza type food. Dogs are allowed at the outdoor tables.
Mick's Restaurant 2110 Peachtree Rd Atlanta GA   404-351-6425
Dogs are allowed on the lower level patio.
Nancy G's Cafe 4920 Roswell Road, Suite 55/H 19/9 Atlanta GA   404-705-8444
http://www.nancygscafe.com/
This neighborhood restaurant also offers a full bar and patio dining. Dogs must be leashed and under owner's control/care at all times.
Park Tavern 500 10th St NE Atlanta GA   404-249-0001
This restaurant serves American. Dogs are allowed at the outdoor tables. Water is provided for your pet.
Raging Burrito 1529 B Piedmont Ave Atlanta GA   404-885-9922
This restaurant serves Mexican food. Dogs are allowed at the outdoor tables.
Raging Burrito 141 Sycamore Street Atlanta GA   404-377-3311
This restaurant serves Mexican food. Dogs are allowed at the outdoor tables.
Vermont Mustard Company 2355 Cumberland Parkway, Suite 110 Atlanta GA   770-333-9119
http://www.vermontmustardcompany.com/
Offering an all natural menu from Vermont cheeses, meats, and spreads, this restaurant also offers catering and a couple of tables outside for visitors traveling with their pets. Dogs must be leashed and under owner's control/care at all times.
Margie's Pantry 653 East Lake Drive Decatur GA   404-377-3818
http://www.margiespantry.com/
Dogs are allowed at the outdoor tables. This cafe is a European style bakery that serves brunch, lunch and dinner. They are not open for dinner on Sundays.
Mo Jo Pizza 659 East Lake Drive Decatur GA   404-373-1999
Dogs are allowed at the outdoor tables.
Universal Joint 906 Oakview Road Decatur GA   404-373-6260

http://www.ujointbar.com/
This neighborhood eatery offers a relaxed bar scene, all American favorite foods, and lots of outdoor seating. Dogs are allowed at the outer tables; they must be leashed and under owner's control/care at all times.

Day Kennels
PetsHotel by PetsMart Day Kennel 128 Perimeter Center W. Atlanta GA
http://www.petsmart.com/PETsHOTEL/
This PetSmart pet store offers day care, day camp and overnight care. You may drop off and pick up your dog between the hours of 7 am - 9 pm M-S, Sundays 7 am - 7pm. Dogs are required to have proof of up to date rabies, DPP and bordatella vaccinations.
PetsHotel by PetsMart Day Kennel 3630 Peachtree Parkway Atlanta GA   770-476-0181
http://www.petsmart.com/PETsHOTEL/
This PetSmart pet store offers day care, day camp and overnight care. You may drop off and pick up your dog 7 am - 9 pm M-S, Sunday 7 am - 7 pm. Dogs must have current proof of rabies, DPP and bordatella vacinations.

Atlanta Area

Accommodations
La Quinta Inn & Suites Atlanta Alpharetta 1350 North Point Dr. Alpharetta GA   770-754-7800 (800-531-5900)
Dogs of all sizes are allowed. There are no additional pet fees. Dogs must be leashed and cleaned up after, and removed or crated for housekeeping.
Residence Inn by Marriott 1325 North Point Drive Alpharetta GA   770-587-1151
Pets of all sizes are allowed. There is a $75 one time fee and a pet policy to sign at check in.
Residence Inn by Marriott 5465 Windward Parkway West Alpharetta GA   770-664-0664
Pets of all sizes are allowed. There is a $75 one time fee and a pet policy to sign at check in.
TownePlace Suites Atlanta Alpharetta 7925 Westside Parkway Alpharetta GA   770-664-1300
Dogs of all sizes are allowed. There is a $75 one time pet fee per visit.
Days Inn Atlanta Airport 4505 Best Road College Park GA   404-767-1224 (800-329-7466)
Dogs of all sizes are allowed. There is a $10 per night pet fee per pet.
Days inn Atlanta West 4979 Old National Hwy College Park GA   404-669-8616 (800-DAYS-INN)
Dogs of all sizes are allowed. There is a $20 one time per pet fee per visit.
Holiday Inn Express Atlanta Airport-College Park 4601 Best Road College Park GA   404-761-6500 (877-270-6405)
Dogs up to 50 pounds are allowed for an additional one time fee of $50 per pet.
Howard Johnson Express Inn 2480 Old National Pkwy. College Park GA   404-766-0000 (800-446-4656)
Dogs of all sizes are welcome. There is a $10 per day pet fee.
Motel 6 - Atlanta Airport South 2471 Old National Parkway College Park GA   404-761-9701 (800-466-8356)
One well-behaved family pet per room. Guest must notify front desk upon arrival. Guest is liable for any damages. In consideration of all guests, pets must never be left unattended in the guest rooms.
Hampton Inn 1340 Dogwood Drive Conyers GA   770-483-8838
Dogs of all sizes are allowed. There is a $25 one time fee and a pet policy to sign at check in.
La Quinta Inn & Suites Atlanta Conyers 1184 Dogwood Dr. Conyers GA   770-918-0092 (800-531-5900)
Dogs of all sizes are allowed. There are no additional pet fees. Dogs may not be left unattended, and they must be well behaved, leashed, and cleaned up after.
Candlewood Suites - Atlanta 3665 Shackleford Road Duluth GA   678-380-0414 (877-270-6405)
Dogs of all sizes are allowed for an additional pet fee of $75 for 1 to 6 days, and $150 for 7 days or more.
Days Inn Atlanta/Duluth 1920 Pleasant Hill Rd Duluth GA   770-476-8700 (800-329-7466)
Dogs of all sizes are allowed. There is a $10 per night pet fee per pet.
Extended Stay Deluxe Atlanta - Gwinnett Place 3390 Venture Parkway Duluth GA   770-623-6800
There is a one time pet fee of $25.00 for one night stays, $50.00 for two night stays, and $75.00 for any stay of three nights or longer.
Hampton Inn 1725 Pineland Road Duluth GA   770-931-9800
Dogs of all sizes are allowed. There is a $75 one time fee per pet and a pet policy to sign at check in.
Holiday Inn - Gwinnett Center 6310 Sugarloaf Parkway Duluth GA   770-476-2022 (877-270-6405)
Dogs of all sizes are allowed for an additional one time fee of $25 per pet.
Holiday Inn Express Atlanta-Gwinnett Mall 3670 Shackleford Rd. Duluth GA   770-935-7171 (877-270-6405)
Dogs of all sizes are allowed; however there is only 1 large dog or 2 small dogs permitted per room. There is a $50 one time fee per pet.
Studio 6 - Atlanta Gwinnett Place 3525 Breckinridge Boulevard Duluth GA   770-931-3113 (800-466-8356)
One well-behaved family pet per room. Guest must notify front desk upon arrival. Guest is liable for any

damages. In consideration of all guests, pets must never be left unattended in the guest rooms.
Super 8 Forest Park/Stadium/Atlanta Area 410 Old Dixie Way Forest Park GA   404-363-8811 (800-800-8000)
Dogs of all sizes are allowed. There is a $7 per night pet fee per pet. Smoking and non-smoking rooms are available for pet rooms.
Residence Inn by Marriott 3401 International Blvd Hapeville GA   404-761-0511
Pets of all sizes are allowed. There is a $100 one time fee and a pet policy to sign at check in.
Best Western Kennesaw Inn 3375 Busbee Dr Kennesaw GA   770-424-7666 (800-780-7234)
Dogs are allowed for an additional fee of $10 per night per pet.
La Quinta Inn Kennesaw 2625 George Busbee Parkway NW Kennesaw GA   770-426-0045 (800-531-5900)
Dogs of all sizes are allowed. There are no additional pet fees. There is a pet waiver to sign at check in. Dogs must be leashed and cleaned up after.
Red Roof Inn - Atlanta Town Center Mall 520 Roberts Court Northwest Kennesaw GA   770-429-0323 (800-RED-ROOF)
One well-behaved family pet per room. Guest must notify front desk upon arrival. Guest is liable for any damages. In consideration of all guests, pets must never be left unattended in the guest rooms.
Residence Inn by Marriott 3443 Busbee Drive NW Kennesaw GA   770-218-1018
Pets of all sizes are allowed. There is a $75 one time pet fee and a pet policy to sign at check in.
TownePlace Suites Atlanta Kennesaw 1074 Cobb Place Blvd NW Kennesaw GA   770-794-8282
Dogs of all sizes are allowed. There is a $75 one time pet fee per visit.
Motel 6 - Atlanta East - Panola Road 2859 Panola Road Lithonia GA   770-981-6411 (800-466-8356)
One well-behaved family pet per room. Guest must notify front desk upon arrival. Guest is liable for any damages. In consideration of all guests, pets must never be left unattended in the guest rooms.
Comfort Inn 2100 Northwest Parkway Marietta GA   770-952-3000 (877-424-6423)
Dogs up to 50 pounds are allowed for an additional one time pet fee of $25 per room.
Crowne Plaza Hotel Atlanta-Marietta 1775 Parkway Place Se Marietta GA   770-428-4400 (877-270-6405)
Dogs of all sizes are allowed for an additional one time pet fee of $75 per room.
Days Inn Atlanta/Marietta 753 N Marietta Parkway Marietta GA   678-797-0233 (800-329-7466)
Dogs of all sizes are allowed. There is a $15 one time per pet fee per visit.
La Quinta Inn Atlanta Marietta 2170 Delk Rd. Marietta GA   770-951-0026 (800-531-5900)
Dogs of all sizes are allowed. There are no additional pet fees. Dogs must be leashed and cleaned up after.
Motel 6 - Atlanta Northwest - Marietta 2360 Delk Road Marietta GA   770-952-8161 (800-466-8356)
One well-behaved family pet per room. Guest must notify front desk upon arrival. Guest is liable for any damages. In consideration of all guests, pets must never be left unattended in the guest rooms.
Studio 6 - Atlanta - Marietta 2360 Delk Road Marietta GA   770-952-2395 (800-466-8356)
One well-behaved family pet per room. Guest must notify front desk upon arrival. Guest is liable for any damages. In consideration of all guests, pets must never be left unattended in the guest rooms.
Comfort Inn 80 H 81W McDonough GA   770-954-9110 (877-424-6423)
Dogs are allowed for an additional fee of $10 per night per pet.
Days Inn Atlanta/McDonough 744 Highway 155 S McDonough GA   770-957-5261 (800-329-7466)
Dogs of all sizes are allowed. There is a $7 per night pet fee per pet.
Quality Inn and Suites 930 H 155 S McDonough GA   770-957-5291 (877-424-6423)
Dogs are allowed for an additional fee of $10 per night per pet.
Super 8 McDonough 1170 Hampton Rd McDonough GA   770-957-2458 (800-800-8000)
Dogs of all sizes are allowed. There is a $5 per night pet fee per pet. Smoking and non-smoking rooms are available for pet rooms.
Best Western Southlake Inn 6437 Jonesboro Rd Morrow GA   770-961-6300 (800-780-7234)
Dogs are allowed for an additional fee of $10 per night per pet.
Extended StayAmerica Atlanta - Morrow 2265 Mt. Zion Pkwy. Morrow GA   770-472-0727
There is a one time pet fee of $25.00 for one night stays, $50.00 for two night stays, and $75.00 for any stay of three nights or longer.
Quality Inn and Suites Southlake 6597 Joneboro Road Morrow GA   770-960-1957 (877-424-6423)
Dogs are allowed for an additional fee of $10 per night per pet.
Red Roof Inn - Atlanta South 1348 Southlake Plaza Drive Morrow GA   770-968-1483 (800-RED-ROOF)
One well-behaved family pet per room. Guest must notify front desk upon arrival. Guest is liable for any damages. In consideration of all guests, pets must never be left unattended in the guest rooms.
Sleep Inn 2185 Mt Zion Parkway Morrow GA   770-472-9800 (877-424-6423)
Dogs are allowed for an additional fee of $10 per night per pet.
South Drury Inn & Suites 6520 S. Lee Street Morrow GA   770-960-0500 (800-378-7946)
Dogs of all sizes are permitted. Pets are not allowed in the breakfast area of the hotel. Pets are not to be left unattended, and each guest must assume liability for damage of property or other guest complaints. There is a limit of one pet per room.
Holiday Inn Hotel & Suites - Peachtree City 203 Newgate Rd Peachtree City GA   770-487-4646 (877-270-6405)
Dogs of all sizes are allowed for an additional $20 per night per pet.

Studio 6 - Atlanta Roswell 9955 Old Dogwood Road Roswell GA   770-992-9449 (800-466-8356)
One well-behaved family pet per room. Guest must notify front desk upon arrival. Guest is liable for any damages. In consideration of all guests, pets must never be left unattended in the guest rooms.
Holiday Inn Express Atlanta/Smyrna-Cobb Galleria 2855 Spring Hill Parkway Smyrna GA   770-435-4990 (877-270-6405)
Dogs of all sizes are allowed for an additional one time pet fee of $25 per room.
Red Roof Inn - Atlanta North Windy Hill 2200 Corporate Plaza Smyrna GA   770-952-6966 (800-RED-ROOF)
One well-behaved family pet per room. Guest must notify front desk upon arrival. Guest is liable for any damages. In consideration of all guests, pets must never be left unattended in the guest rooms.
Residence Inn by Marriott 2771 Cumberland Blvd Smyrna GA   770-433-8877
Pets of all sizes are allowed. There is a $75 one time fee and a pet policy to sign at check in.
Motel 6 - Stone Mountain 1819 Mountain Industrial Boulevard Tucker GA   770-496-1317 (800-466-8356)
One well-behaved family pet per room. Guest must notify front desk upon arrival. Guest is liable for any damages. In consideration of all guests, pets must never be left unattended in the guest rooms.
Red Roof Inn - Atlanta Tucker Northeast 2810 Lawrenceville Highway Tucker GA   770-496-1311 (800-RED-ROOF)
One well-behaved family pet per room. Guest must notify front desk upon arrival. Guest is liable for any damages. In consideration of all guests, pets must never be left unattended in the guest rooms.
Studio 6 - Atlanta Northlake 1795 Crescent Centre Boulevard Tucker GA   770-934-4040 (800-466-8356)
One well-behaved family pet per room. Guest must notify front desk upon arrival. Guest is liable for any damages. In consideration of all guests, pets must never be left unattended in the guest rooms.

Campgrounds and RV Parks
Brookwood RV Park 1031 Wylie Road SE Marietta GA   877-727-5787
http://www.atlantarvpark.com
Dogs of all sizes are allowed. There are no additional pet fees. Dogs must be leashed and cleaned up after. There is a dog walk area at the campground.
Atlanta South RV Resort 281 Mount Olive Road McDonough GA   770-957-2610
http://www.atlantasouthrvresort.com
Dogs of all sizes are allowed. There are no additional pet fees. Dogs must be leashed and cleaned up after. The camping and tent areas also allow dogs. There is a dog walk area at the campground.

Attractions
TOP 200 PLACE **Kennesaw Mountain National Battlefield Park** 900 Kennesaw Mountain Drive Kennesaw GA   770-427-4686
http://www.nps.gov/kemo
This 2,888 acre National Battlefield preserves an 1864 Civil War battleground. Kennisaw Mountain stood between a large Union force and and a Confederate railroad and manufacturing center. There are many trails, monuments and living history demonstrations and exhibits. This is a very dog-friendly park. Dogs are welcome on the park grounds on a six foot leash. Please clean up after your dog with the "mutt mits" that are provided at the park.

Stores
PetSmart Pet Store 6370 North Point Pkwy Alpharetta GA   770-343-8511
Your licensed and well-behaved leashed dog is allowed in the store.
Petco Pet Store 10980 State Bridge Rd Alpharetta GA   678-297-0673
Your licensed and well-behaved leashed dog is allowed in the store.
PetSmart Pet Store 1370 Dogwood Dr SE Conyers GA   770-922-1772
Your licensed and well-behaved leashed dog is allowed in the store.
PetSmart Pet Store 3803 Venture Dr Duluth GA   770-813-8400
Your licensed and well-behaved leashed dog is allowed in the store.
Petco Pet Store 2131 Pleasant Hill Rd Duluth GA   678-475-1147
Your licensed and well-behaved leashed dog is allowed in the store.
PetSmart Pet Store 3665 Marketplace Blvd East Point GA   404-344-0773
Your licensed and well-behaved leashed dog is allowed in the store.
PetSmart Pet Store 860 Cobb Place Blvd Kennesaw GA   770-424-5226
Your licensed and well-behaved leashed dog is allowed in the store.
Top Dogs Pet Boutique 2615 George Busbee Parkway Suite 17 Kennesaw GA   770-218-0602
http://www.topdogs.net/
In addition to providing a wide variety of pet supplies/gifts, breed-specific items, care products, clothing items, doggy car seats, and fresh bakery items, this store also offers a number of special events throughout the year. Dogs must be current on vaccines, be leashed, and under owner's control/care at all times.

Petco Pet Store 8164 Mall Parkway Lithonia GA 770-482-1565
Your licensed and well-behaved leashed dog is allowed in the store.
PetSmart Pet Store 1285 Johnsons Ferry Marietta GA 770-971-3010
Your licensed and well-behaved leashed dog is allowed in the store.
Petco Pet Store 50 Ernest Barrett Parkway, Ste 500 Marietta GA 770-218-6201
Your licensed and well-behaved leashed dog is allowed in the store.
PetSmart Pet Store 1950 Jonesboro Rd McDonough GA 678-583-0287
Your licensed and well-behaved leashed dog is allowed in the store.
PetSmart Pet Store 1986 Mt Zion Rd Morrow GA 770-478-0860
Your licensed and well-behaved leashed dog is allowed in the store.
Petco Pet Store 1892 Mount Zion Rd Morrow GA 770-477-0839
Your licensed and well-behaved leashed dog is allowed in the store.
Beau Tye's Pet Spa and Collectibles 325 Senoia Road Peachtree City GA 770-486-TRIM (8746)
http://www.beau-tyes.com/
For the totally pampered pooch, this spa and gift boutique offers a variety of services and unique items for dogs
and the home. Dogs must be well mannered, current on all vaccines for their age (bring copies), be on a flea and
tick preventative treatment program, and dogs over 7 months old must be either spayed or neutered to receive
spa services.
PetSmart Pet Store 625 Crossville Rd Roswell GA 678-352-8138
Your licensed and well-behaved leashed dog is allowed in the store.
Petco Pet Store 2340 Holcomb Bridge Rd Roswell GA 770-649-6360
Your licensed and well-behaved leashed dog is allowed in the store.
Top Dogs Pet Boutique 900 Mansell Road Suite 13 Roswell GA 770-641-8620
http://www.topdogs.net/
In addition to providing a wide variety of pet supplies/gifts, breed-specific items, care products, clothing items,
doggy car seats, and fresh bakery items, this store also offers a number of special events throughout the year.
Dogs must be current on vaccines, be leashed, and under owner's control/care at all times.
Petco Pet Store 5938 Roswell Rd NE Sandy Springs GA 404-255-6544
Your licensed and well-behaved leashed dog is allowed in the store.
PetSmart Pet Store 2540 B Hargrove Rd SE Smyrna GA 770-432-8250
Your licensed and well-behaved leashed dog is allowed in the store.
PetSmart Pet Store 4023 Lavista Rd Tucker GA 770-414-5126
Your licensed and well-behaved leashed dog is allowed in the store.

Off-Leash Dog Parks
Waggy World Dog Park 175 Roswell Street Alpharetta GA 678-297-6100
This 1.5 acre fenced off-leash dog park is managed by the city parks department. It is open 8 am to sunset daily.
There are separate areas for large and small dogs. The park features water and benches.
Ronald Reagan Dog Park 2777 Five Forks Trickum Rd Lawrenceville GA
This is a two acre fenced dog park. It is managed by Gwinnett County and is located just north of Ronald Reagan
Parkway on 5 Forks Trickum Rd.
Sweat Mountain Dog Park 4346 Steinhauer Road Marietta GA 770-591-3160
http://prca.cobbcountyga.gov/DogPark.htm
This off-leash park has separate fenced areas for small and large dogs. The park is open from dawn until dusk
daily except for Wednesday mornings when it is closed for maintenance.
Wolf Brook Private Dog Park and Club 13665 New Providence Rd Milton GA 770-772-0440
http://www.wolfbrook.com
This private club requires a temperment test and prior approval. It has 8 acres of off-leash area, dog day care, a
club building with dog supplies, dog sports and other activities.
Leila Thompson Dog Park 1355 Woodstock Rd Roswell GA 770-641-3760
http://www.ci.roswell.ga.us
This fenced off-leash park is located near the Arts Center building in Leila Thompson Park. There is a second
fenced area for smaller dogs.
Burger Dog Park 680 Glendale Pl Smyrna GA 770-431-2842
This off-leash park is fenced and has separate areas for small and large dogs. The park is located west of S.
Cobb Drive and and south of WIndy Hill Rd.

Outdoor Restaurants
Baja Fresh Mexican Grill 7291 N Point Parkway Alpharetta GA 678-461-8410
This restaurant serves Mexican food. Dogs are allowed at the outdoor tables.
Pet Tasties Pet Cafe 3050 Windward Plaza Alpharetta GA 770-667-8525
This is a gourmet pet bakery where pets are allowed inside and out.

Day Kennels

PetsHotel by PetsMart Day Kennel 3803 Venture Dr. Duluth GA 770-813-8753
http://www.petsmart.com/PETsHOTEL/
This PetSmart pet store offers day care and overnight care. You may drop off and pick up your dog 7am - 7 pm M-S, Sunday 9am - 7 pm. Dogs are required to have proof of current rabies, DPP and bordatella vaccinactions.
PetsHotel by PetsMart Day Kennel 2540B Hargrove Rd. SE Smyrna GA 770-432-8895
http://www.petsmart.com/PETsHOTEL/
This PetSmart pet store offers day care, day camp and overnight care. You may drop off and pick up your dog during the hours of 7 am - 9 pm M-S, Sunday 7 am - 7 pm. Dogs are required to have proof for current up to date rabies, DPP and bordatella vaccinations.

Augusta

Accommodations

Comfort Inn Medical Center Area 1455 Walton Way Augusta GA 706-722-2224 (877-424-6423)
Dogs are allowed for an additional one time pet fee of $25 per room.
Country Inns & Suites Riverwalk Three Ninth Street Augusta GA 706-774-1400
Dogs up to 50 pounds are allowed. There are no additional pet fees.
Holiday Inn 2155 Gordon Hwy Augusta GA 706-737-2300 (877-270-6405)
Dogs of all sizes are allowed for an additional pet fee of $35 per room for each 1 to 7 days stay.
La Quinta Inn Augusta 3020 Washington Rd. Augusta GA 706-733-2660 (800-531-5900)
Dogs of all sizes are allowed. There are no additional pet fees. Dogs must be crated if left alone in the room, be leashed at all times, and cleaned up after.
Red Roof Inn - Augusta 4328 Frontage Road Augusta GA 706-228-3031 (800-RED-ROOF)
One well-behaved family pet per room. Guest must notify front desk upon arrival. Guest is liable for any damages. In consideration of all guests, pets must never be left unattended in the guest rooms.
The Partridge Inn 2110 Walton Way Augusta GA 706-737-8888 (800-476-6888)
Designated a Historic Hotel of America, this has been a full service hotel for business and leisure travelers for more than a hundred years. They have added a full complement of state of the art renovations to blend its rich past with all the modern comforts and amenities you would expect of a luxury retreat. Some of the amenities/features include the award winning Verandah Grill and the Bamboo Room and Piano Bar with live music, large meeting rooms, event planners/caterers for conferences or social affairs, a great Sunday brunch, richly furnished rooms/studios/suites, a secluded courtyard pool, room service, and more than a ¼ mile of verandahs and balconies. Dogs of all sizes are allowed. There is a $25 one time fee for one dog, and a second dog would be an additional $10 one time fee. Dogs may not be left alone in the room at any time, and they must be leashed and cleaned up after.

Stores

PetSmart Pet Store 217 Robert C Daniels Pky Augusta GA 706-738-0414
Your licensed and well-behaved leashed dog is allowed in the store.
Petco Pet Store 4209 Washington Rd Evans GA 706-869-0737
Your licensed and well-behaved leashed dog is allowed in the store.

Outdoor Restaurants

The Pizza Joint 1245 Broad Street/H 25 Augusta GA 706-774-0037
http://www.thepizzajoint.net/
Fresh and baked to order is the order of the day for this pizzeria, and they also offer dozens of brews and outdoor dining. Dogs are allowed at the outside tables; they must be leashed and under owner's control/care at all times.

Blairsville

Accommodations

Misty Mountain Inn 4376 Town Creek Road Blairsville GA 706-745-4786 (888-MISTY MN (647-8966))
http://www.jwww.com/misty/
Although dogs are not allowed in the Victorian farmhouse, they are allowed in any of the 6 cottages that are nestled in the woods along the mountainside. There is a $20 one time fee per pet. Dogs must be well behaved,

leashed, and under owner's care.

Campgrounds and RV Parks
Trackrock Campground and Cabins 4887 Trackrock Camp Road Blairsville GA   706-745-2420
http://www.trackrock.com
Dogs of all sizes are allowed. There are no additional pet fees. Dogs must be quiet, leashed, and cleaned up after. The camping and tent areas also allow dogs. There is a dog walk area at the campground.
Vogel State Park 7485 Vogel State Park Road Blairsville GA   706-745-2628 (800-864-7275)
http://www.gastateparks.org/info/vogel/
This 233 acre park with a 20 acre lake is one of the oldest and most popular parks in the state. It offers a museum, 17 miles of hiking trails with access to the Appalachian Trail nearby, and a variety of land and water recreation. Dogs of all sizes are allowed at no additional fee. Dogs may not be left unattended, and they must be leashed and cleaned up after. Dogs are not allowed in public swim areas or in buildings. Dogs are allowed on the trails. The camping and tent areas also allow dogs. There is a dog walk area at the campground.

Vacation Home Rentals
A Toccoa Riverfront Cabin Vacation Call to Arrange. Blairsville GA   478-862-9733
http://www.toccoa-riverfront-cabin.com
This is a mountain cabin on the Toccoa River that welcomes pets. There is fenced acreage and a barn for visiting horses.

Blue Ridge

Accommodations
Douglas Inn and Suites 1192 Windy Ridge Road Blue Ridge GA   706-258-3600 (877-416-3664)
http://www.douglasinn.com/blueridge.html
There are 1 and 2 bedroom suites offered at this inn. Dogs are allowed for an additional fee of $10 for the first night per pet, and $5 per night per pet after. Dogs must be leashed and under owner's care.

Vacation Home Rentals
My Mountain Cabin Rentals P.O. Box 388 Blue Ridge GA   800-844-4939
http://www.1MyMountain.com
These are rental cabins in the beautiful Blue Ridge area of North Georgia. Pets are allowed in most of the cabins for a $10 per night fee per pet and a $150 refundable damage deposit. Please notify the management that you are bringing a pet when making reservations.
Avenair Mtn Cabin Rentals North Georgia 1862 Old Highway 76 Blue Ridge GA   706-632-0318 (800-MTN-CABINS)
http://www.avenairmtncabins.com
These cabin rentals are located in Georgia's Blue Ridge Mountains about 1 1/2 hours from Atlanta. Many, but not all, of the cabins are pet-friendly.
Black Bear Cabin Rentals 21 High Park Drive Ste 7 Blue Ridge GA   706-632-4794 (888-902-2246)
http://www.blackbearcabinrentals.com
Black Bear Cabin Rentals are available with mountain views, water access and forests all around. Pets are allowed with a pet fee.
Tica Cabin Rentals Inc. 699 East Main Street Blue Ridge GA   706-632-4448 (800-871-8422)
http://www.ticacabins.com
There are a number of pet-friendly vacation rentals some with excellent views and various amenities. From one to five bedrooms are available. Call them for more information or to reserve the cabins.

Braselton

Accommodations
Best Western Braselton Inn 303 Zion Church Rd Braselton GA   706-654-3081 (800-780-7234)
Dogs are allowed for an additional fee of $10 per night per pet.
Holiday Inn Express 2069 Highway 211 Braselton GA   770-867-8100 (877-270-6405)
Dogs of all sizes are allowed for an additional one time pet fee of $20 per room.

Bremen

Accommodations
Days Inn Bremen 35 Price Creek Rd Bremen GA   770-537-4646 (800-329-7466)
Dogs of all sizes are allowed. There is a $5 per night pet fee per pet.

Brunswick

Accommodations
La Quinta Inn & Suites Brunswick 165 Warren Mason Blvd Brunswick GA   912-265-7725 (800-531-5900)
A dog up to 60 pounds is allowed. There are no additional pet fees. Dogs may not be left unattended, and they must be leashed at all times, and cleaned up after.
Motel 6 - Brunswick 403 Butler Drive Brunswick GA   912-264-8582 (800-466-8356)
One well-behaved family pet per room. Guest must notify front desk upon arrival. Guest is liable for any damages. In consideration of all guests, pets must never be left unattended in the guest rooms.
Red Roof Inn - Brunswick I-95 25 Tourist Drive Brunswick GA   912-264-4720 (800-RED-ROOF)
One well-behaved family pet per room. Guest must notify front desk upon arrival. Guest is liable for any damages. In consideration of all guests, pets must never be left unattended in the guest rooms.
Super 8 Brunswick/St Simons Island Area 5280 New Jesup Hwy Brunswick GA   912-264-8800 (800-800-8000)
Dogs of all sizes are allowed. There is a $10 per night pet fee per pet. Smoking and non-smoking rooms are available for pet rooms.

Campgrounds and RV Parks
Blythe Island Regional Park 6616 Blythe Island H (H 303) Brunswick GA   912-279-2812
This is a marina park that is close to other attractions and offers a variety of land and water recreation. Dogs of all sizes are allowed at no additional fee. Dogs may not be left unattended, and they must be leashed and cleaned up after. Dogs are not allowed on the beaches or in buildings. Dogs are allowed on the trails. The camping and tent areas also allow dogs. There is a dog walk area at the campground.

Buckhead

Day Kennels
PetsHotel by PetsMart Day Kennel 3221 Peachtree Rd Buckhead GA   404-266-0402
http://www.petsmart.com/PETsHOTEL/
This PetSmart pet store offers doggie day camp only. You may drop off and pick up your dog during the hours the store is open seven days a week. Dogs must have proof of current rabies, DPP and Bordatella vaccinations.

Buford

Stores
PetSmart Pet Store 1705 Mall of Georgia Blvd Buford GA   678-482-7449
Your licensed and well-behaved leashed dog is allowed in the store.
Petco Pet Store 3264 Buford Drive #110 Buford GA   678-714-8048
Your licensed and well-behaved leashed dog is allowed in the store.

Cairo

Accommodations

Days Inn Cairo 35 US Hwy 84 E Cairo GA   229-377-4400 (800-329-7466)
Dogs of all sizes are allowed. There is a $10 per night pet fee per pet.

Calhoun

Accommodations
Days Inn Calhoun 1220 Redbud Rd Calhoun GA   706-629-8877 (800-329-7466)
Dogs of all sizes are allowed. There is a $5 per night pet fee per pet.
Quality Inn 915 H 53E Calhoun GA   706-629-9501 (877-424-6423)
Dogs are allowed for an additional fee of $8 to $10 depending on length of stay and size of pet.
Super 8 Calhoun/Dalton Area 1446 US Hwy 41 North Calhoun GA   706-602-1400 (800-800-8000)
Dogs of all sizes are allowed. There is a $5 per night pet fee per pet. Smoking and non-smoking rooms are available for pet rooms.

Campgrounds and RV Parks
Calhoun KOA 2523 Redbud Road NE Calhoun GA   706-629-7511 (800-562-7512)
http://www.koa.com
Dogs of all sizes are allowed. There are no additional pet fees. Dogs may not be left unattended outside or in the cabins, and they must be quiet, leashed, and cleaned up after. The camping and tent areas also allow dogs. There is a dog walk area at the campground. Dogs are allowed in the camping cabins.

Carrollton

Accommodations
Crossroads Hotel 1202 S. Park Street Carrollton GA   770-832-2611
There is a $25 one time pet fee.
Days Inn Carrollton 180 Centennial Rd Carrollton GA   770-214-0037 (800-329-7466)
Dogs of all sizes are allowed. There is a $6 per night pet fee per pet.
Quality Inn and Suites 160 Centennial Drive Carrollton GA   770-832-2611 (877-424-6423)
Dogs are allowed for an additional fee of $20 per night per pet.

Cartersville

Accommodations
Days Inn Cartersville 5618 Hwy 20 SE Cartersville GA   770-382-1824 (800-329-7466)
Dogs of all sizes are allowed. There is a $10 per night pet fee per pet.
Holiday Inn I-75 and US 411, Exit 293 Cartersville GA   770-386-0830 (877-270-6405)
Dogs up to 50 pounds are allowed for an additional $10 per night per pet.
Howard Johnson Express Inn 25 Carson Loop NW Cartersville GA   770-386-0700 (800-446-4656)
Dogs of all sizes are welcome. There is a $5 per day pet fee.
Motel 6 - Cartersville 5657 Highway 20 Cartersville GA   770-386-1449 (800-466-8356)
One well-behaved family pet per room. Guest must notify front desk upon arrival. Guest is liable for any damages. In consideration of all guests, pets must never be left unattended in the guest rooms.
Quality Inn 235 S Dixie Avenue Cartersville GA   770-386-0510 (877-424-6423)
One dog is allowed for an additional pet fee of $5.60 per night.
Super 8 Cartersville 41 SR 20 Spur SE Cartersville GA   770-382-8881 (800-800-8000)
Dogs of all sizes are allowed. There is a $5 per night pet fee per pet. Smoking and non-smoking rooms are available for pet rooms.

Campgrounds and RV Parks
Allatoona Landing Marine Resort 24 Allatoona Landing Road Cartersville GA   770-974-6089
http://www.allatoonalandingmarina.com/
Dogs of all sizes are allowed. There are no additional pet fees. Dogs may not be left unattended outside, and they must be leashed and cleaned up after. There are some breed restrictions. The camping and tent areas also allow dogs. There is a dog walk area at the campground.

Carterville/Cassville-White KOA 800 Cass-White Road NW Cartersville GA   770-382-7330 (800-562-2841)
http://www.koa.com
Dogs of most sizes are allowed; extra-large dogs are not. There are no additional pet fees. Dogs must be leashed and cleaned up after. There are some breed restrictions. The camping and tent areas also allow dogs. There is a dog walk area at the campground.
Red Top Mountain State Park 50 Lodge Road Cartersville GA   770-975-4226 (800-864-PARK (7275))
http://www.gastateparks.org/info/redtop/
This popular park of 1,562 acres along the 12,000-acre Lake Allatoona offers over 15 miles of hiking trails, an interpretive center, and a wide variety of land and water recreation. Dogs of all sizes are allowed at no additional fee. Dogs may not be left unattended, and they must be leashed and cleaned up after. Dogs are not allowed in public swim areas or in buildings. Dogs are allowed on the trails. The camping and tent areas also allow dogs. There is a dog walk area at the campground.

Cleveland

Campgrounds and RV Parks
Leisure Acres Campground 3840 W Moreland Road Cleveland GA   888-748-6344
http://www.leisureacrescampground.com
Dogs of all sizes are allowed. There are no additional pet fees. Dogs must be leashed and cleaned up after. The camping and tent areas also allow dogs. There is a dog walk area at the campground.

Columbus

Accommodations
Holiday Inn Columbus-North I-185 2800 Manchester Expressway Columbus GA   706-324-0231 (877-270-6405)
Dogs of all sizes are allowed for an additional one time fee of $25 per pet.
La Quinta Inn Columbus 3201 Macon Rd, Suite 200 Columbus GA   706-568-1740 (800-531-5900)
Dogs of all sizes are allowed. There are no additional pet fees. Dogs must be crated if left alone in the room, be leashed, and cleaned up after.
La Quinta Inn Columbus State University 2919 Warm Springs Road Columbus GA   706-323-4344 (800-531-5900)
Dogs of all sizes are allowed. There are no additional pet fees. There is a pet waiver to sign at check in, and they request dogs be taken to the designated pet area to due their business. Dogs may not be left unattended, and they must be leashed and cleaned up after.
Motel 6 - Columbus 3050 Victory Drive Columbus GA   706-687-7214 (800-466-8356)
One well-behaved family pet per room. Guest must notify front desk upon arrival. Guest is liable for any damages. In consideration of all guests, pets must never be left unattended in the guest rooms.
Residence Inn by Marriott 2670 Adams Farm Road Columbus GA   706-494-0050
Dogs of all sizes are allowed. There is a $75 one time fee and a pet policy to sign at check in.

Stores
PetSmart Pet Store 1591 Bradley Park Dr Columbus GA   706-323-6788
Your licensed and well-behaved leashed dog is allowed in the store.

Commerce

Accommodations
Admiral Benbow Inn 30747 Hwy 441 S. Commerce GA   706-335-5183
There is a $15 one time pet fee per pet per visit.
Comfort Inn 165 Eisenhower Drive Commerce GA   706-335-9001 (877-424-6423)
Dogs are allowed for an additional fee of $10 per night per pet.
Howard Johnson Inn 148 Eisenhower Drive Commerce GA   706-335-5581 (800-446-4656)
Dogs of all sizes are welcome. There is a $10 one time pet fee.
Red Roof Inn - Commerce 157 Eisenhower Drive Commerce GA   706-335-3640 (800-RED-ROOF)

One well-behaved family pet per room. Guest must notify front desk upon arrival. Guest is liable for any damages. In consideration of all guests, pets must never be left unattended in the guest rooms.
Super 8 Commerce 152 Eisenhower Dr Commerce GA   706-336-8008 (800-800-8000)
Dogs of all sizes are allowed. There is a $10 per night pet fee per pet. Smoking and non-smoking rooms are available for pet rooms.

Cordele

Accommodations
Best Western Colonial Inn 1706 East 16th Avenue Cordele GA   229-273-5420 (800-780-7234)
Dogs are allowed for an additional one time fee of $10 per pet.
Super 8 Cordele 1618 E 16th Ave Cordele GA   229-273-2456 (800-800-8000)
Dogs of all sizes are allowed. There are no additional pet fees. Smoking and non-smoking rooms are available for pet rooms.

Campgrounds and RV Parks
Cordele KOA 373 Rockhouse Road E Cordele GA   229-273-5454 (800-562-0275)
http://www.koa.com
Dogs of all sizes are allowed, and there are no additional pet fees for tent or RV sites. There is a limit of 1 dog under 15 pounds for the cabins. Dogs must be leashed, cleaned up after, and in at night. The camping and tent areas also allow dogs. There is a dog walk area at the campground. Dogs are allowed in the camping cabins.
Veterans Memorial State Park 2459A H 280W Cordele GA   229-276-2371 (800-864-PARK (7275))
http://gastateparks.org/info/georgiavet/
This park of more than 1,300 acres on Lake Blackshear was established as a memorial to U.S. veterans, featuring a museum with artifacts from the Revolutionary War through the Gulf War. The park offers a variety of activities and recreation. Dogs of all sizes are allowed at no additional fee. Dogs may not be left unattended, and they must be on no more than a 6 foot leash, and be cleaned up after. Dogs are allowed on the trails. The camping and tent areas also allow dogs. There is a dog walk area at the campground.

Cornelia

Accommodations
Comfort Inn 2965 J Warren Road Cornelia GA   706-778-9573 (877-424-6423)
Dogs up to 50 pounds are allowed for an additional one time pet fee of $50 per room.

Campgrounds and RV Parks
Moccasin Creek State Park 3655 H 197 Clarkesville GA   706-947-3194 (800-864-PARK (7275))
This scenic 32 acre park along the 2,800-acre Lake Burton offers a wildlife observation tower, trails with access to the Appalachian Trail, and a variety of land and water activities and recreation. Dogs of all sizes are allowed at no additional fee. Dogs may not be left unattended, and they must be on no more than a 6 foot leash, and cleaned up after. Dogs are not allowed in public swim areas or in buildings. Dogs are allowed on the trails. The camping and tent areas also allow dogs. There is a dog walk area at the campground.

Cumming

Stores
PetSmart Pet Store 1020 Market Place Blvd Cumming GA   678-513-1689
Your licensed and well-behaved leashed dog is allowed in the store.

Off-Leash Dog Parks
Windermere Dog Park 3355 Windermere Parkway Cumming GA   770-781-2215
This fenced dog park is located in Windermere Park and is run by the County of Forsyth. There are separate areas for large and small dogs. The park is open from 8 am until sunset daily.

Dahlonega

Accommodations

Bend of the River Cabins and Chalets 319 Horseshoe Lane Dahlonega GA   706-219-2040
Dogs of all sizes are allowed. There is a $10 per night per pet additional fee. Dogs are not allowed on the beds and must be kept leashed when out.

Dalton

Accommodations

Motel 6 - Dalton 2200 Chattanooga Road Dalton GA   706-278-5522 (800-466-8356)
One well-behaved family pet per room. Guest must notify front desk upon arrival. Guest is liable for any damages. In consideration of all guests, pets must never be left unattended in the guest rooms.

Campgrounds and RV Parks

Fort Mountain State Park 181 Fort Mountain Park Road Chatsworth GA   706-422-1932 (800-864-7275)
http://www.gastateparks.org/info/fortmt/
There is a myriad of recreational activities available at this 3,712 acre park that is also home to interesting ancient sites, some of the most scenic trails in the state, and a seasonal mountain lake. Dogs are allowed throughout the park and in the campground (2+ dogs) for no additional fee. There is a $40 one time fee per pet for the cabin, and only 2 dogs are allowed. Dogs must be current on all vaccinations, licensed, flea/tick free, and in good health. Dogs must be on no more than a 6 foot leash, cleaned up after, and may not be left unattended. The campground offers about 80 campsites, picnic tables, grills, and restrooms. The camping and tent areas also allow dogs. There is a dog walk area at the campground. Dogs are allowed in the camping cabins.

Parks

Fort Mountain State Park 181 Fort Mountain Park Road Chatsworth GA   706-422-1932 (800-864-7275)
http://www.gastateparks.org/info/fortmt/
There is a myriad of recreational activities available at this 3,712 acre park that is also home to interesting ancient sites, some of the most scenic trails in the state, and a seasonal mountain lake. Dogs are allowed throughout the park and in the campground (2+ dogs) for no additional fee. There is a $40 one time fee per pet for the cabin, and only 2 dogs are allowed. Dogs must be current on all vaccinations, licensed, flea/tic free, and in good health. Dogs must be on no more than a 6 foot leash, cleaned up after, and may not be left unattended.

Darien

Accommodations

Comfort Inn 703 Frontage Road Darien GA   912-437-4200 (877-424-6423)
Dogs are allowed for an additional fee of $10 per night per pet.
Super 8 Darien/I-95 Highway 251 & I 95 Darien GA   912-437-6660 (800-800-8000)
Dogs of all sizes are allowed. There is a $10 per night pet fee per pet. Smoking and non-smoking rooms are available for pet rooms.

Dawsonville

Accommodations

Best Western Dawson Village Inn 76 North Georgia Ave Dawsonville GA   706-216-4410 (800-780-7234)
Dogs are allowed for an additional fee of $10 per night per pet.
Comfort Inn 127 Beartooth Parkway Dawsonville GA   706-216-1900 (877-424-6423)
Dogs up to 60 pounds are allowed for an additional fee of $15 per night per pet.

Campgrounds and RV Parks

TOP 200 PLACE **Amicalola Falls State Park and Lodge** 418 Amicalola Falls State Park Road Dawsonville GA   706-265-4703 (800-864-7275)
True to its Cherokee word meaning "tumbling waters", the 729 foot falls at this park are the highest cascading falls east of the Mississippi, and there are numerous trails for exploring this beautiful mountain recreational destination. The park is also host to many special events throughout the year. Dogs are allowed throughout the park and in the campground (2+ dogs) for no additional fee. There is a $40 one time fee per pet for the cabin, and only 2 dogs are allowed. They are not allowed in the Lodge or in any park buildings. Dogs must be leashed and under owner's control/care at all times. The camp area offers 24 sites, 14 cottages (2-pet friendly), picnic areas, restrooms, concessionaires, and a dump station. The camping and tent areas also allow dogs. There is a dog walk area at the campground. Dogs are allowed in the camping cabins.

Shopping Centers

North Georgia Premium Outlets 800 H 400 South Dawsonville GA   706-216-3609
There are a variety of dining, shopping, and entertainment opportunities at this 140 store outlet center. Dogs are allowed in the common areas of the mall; it is up to individual stores whether they allow a dog inside. Dogs must be well behaved, leashed, and under owner's control/care at all times.

Parks

Amicalola Falls State Park and Lodge 418 Amicalola Falls State Park Road Dawsonville GA   706-265-4703 (800-864-7275)
True to its Cherokee word meaning "tumbling waters", the 729 foot falls at this park are the highest cascading falls east of the Mississippi, and there are numerous trails for exploring this beautiful mountain recreational destination. The park is also host to many special events throughout the year. Dogs are allowed throughout the park and in the campground (2+ dogs) for no additional fee. There is a $40 one time fee per pet for the cabin, and only 2 dogs are allowed. They are not allowed in the Lodge or in any park buildings. Dogs must be leashed and under owner's control/care at all times.

Dillard

Campgrounds and RV Parks

River Vista Mountain Village 960 H 246 Dillard GA   888-850-PARK (7275)
http://www.rvmountainvillage.com/
Up to 3 dogs of all sizes are allowed. There are no additional pet fees for tent or RV sites. There is a $10 per night per pet additional fee for the cabins, and only 2 dogs are allowed. Dogs may not be left unattended outside or in the cabins. Dogs must be on no more than a 6 foot leash and cleaned up after. The camping and tent areas also allow dogs. There is a dog walk area at the campground. Dogs are allowed in the camping cabins.

Donalsonville

Parks

Seminole State Park 7870 State Park Dr Donalsonville GA   229- 861--3137
http://www.gastateparks.org
Dogs on leash are allowed in this state park. They are allowed in some of the cabins for an additional fee of $40 per pet (limit 2). They are also allowed in the campgrounds. This park features canoeing, hiking, swimming, fishing, boating, and more.

Dublin

Accommodations

Best Western Executive Inn and Suites 2121 Hwy 441 South Dublin GA   478-275-2650 (800-780-7234)
Dogs are allowed for an additional one time fee of $15 for 1 pet; $25 for 2 pets, and $40 for 3 pets.

Elberton

Campgrounds and RV Parks

Bobby Brown State Park 2509 Bobby Brown State Park Road Elberton GA   706-213-2046 (800-864-PARK (7275))
Rich in natural and cultural history, this 655 acre park, on the shores of the 70,000-acre Clarks Hill Lake, offers a variety of land and water recreation. Dogs of all sizes are allowed at no additional fee. Dogs may not be left unattended except for short periods, they must be on no more than a 6 foot leash, and be cleaned up after. Dogs are not allowed in the yurt area, however, they are allowed on the trails. The camping and tent areas also allow dogs. There is a dog walk area at the campground.

Elko

Campgrounds and RV Parks

Twin Oaks RV Park 305 H 26E Elko GA   478-987-9361
http://www.twinoaksrvpark.com
Dogs of all sizes are allowed. There are no additional pet fees. Dogs must be leashed and cleaned up after. The camping and tent areas also allow dogs. There is a dog walk area at the campground.

Ellijay

Vacation Home Rentals

Serenity Cabin Rentals Call to Arrange Ellijay GA   706-889-0163 (800-MTN-MEMS)
http://www.myserenitycabins.com
Pets are welcome at a number of these rental cabins. There is a $10 per pet per night additional pet fee.
Sliding Rock Cabins 177 Mossy Rock Lane Ellijay GA   706-636-5895
http://www.slidingrockcabins.com
Located midway between Ellijay and Blue Ridge, Sliding Rock Cabins offers beautifully decorated full log and rustic style cabins with large hot tubs. Pets always stay free and Sliding Rock Cabins provides a large bed for them along with food and water bowls, all natural treats, toys, and towels for the water loving dogs.

Fargo

Campgrounds and RV Parks

TOP 200 PLACE **Stephen C. Foster State Park** 17515 H 177 Fargo GA   912-637-5274 (800-864-7275)
Some of the most interesting and breathtaking scenery can be found at this park with its moss-laced cypress trees canopying the black waters below, and in addition to a range of recreational activities and the 1.5 mile Trembling Earth Nature Trail, there are environmental and educational programs provided. Dogs are allowed throughout the park and in the campground (2+ dogs) for no additional fee. There is a $40 one time fee per pet for the cabin, and only 2 dogs are allowed. Dogs are not allowed in buildings or on the boats. Dogs should not be close to the edge of waterways because of alligators. The campground offers 66 sites, restrooms, an amphitheater, a dump station, and some food, drinks, and ice can be obtained at the park office. The camping and tent areas also allow dogs. There is a dog walk area at the campground. Dogs are allowed in the camping cabins.

Parks

Stephen C. Foster State Park 17515 H 177 Fargo GA   912-637-5274 (800-864-7275)
Some of the most interesting and breathtaking scenery can be found at this park with its moss-laced cypress trees canopying the black waters below, and in addition to a range of recreational activities and the 1.5 mile Trembling Earth Nature Trail, there are environmental and educational programs provided. Dogs are allowed throughout the park and in the campground (2+ dogs) for no additional fee. There is a $40 one time fee per pet for the cabin, and only 2 dogs are allowed. Dogs are not allowed in buildings or on the boats. Dogs should not be

close to the edge of waterways because of alligators.

Fayetteville

Stores
PetSmart Pet Store 101 Pavilion Pkwy Fayetteville GA 770-719-4444
Your licensed and well-behaved leashed dog is allowed in the store.

Folkston

Accommodations
Relax Inn 1201 S 2nd St Folkston GA   912-496-2514 (800-DAYS-INN)
Dogs of all sizes are allowed. There is a $4 per night pet fee per pet.

Parks
Suwanee Canal Recreation Area Route 2, Box 3325 Folkston GA   912-496-7156
http://www.okefenokeeadventures.com/
Visitors can experience a bit of what swamp living was like at the turn of the century at this uniquely landscaped region; there are knowledgeable docents, original buildings, an 8 mile auto/walking tour, educational programs, café, gift shop, and visitor center. Dogs are allowed on the grounds; they are not allowed on the boat rentals. Dogs must be leashed and cleaned up after at all times. Dogs must be kept away from the water's edge/walkways because of alligators.

Forsyth

Accommodations
Best Western Hilltop Inn 951 Highway 42 North Forsyth GA   478-994-9260 (800-780-7234)
One dog is allowed for an additional per night fee of $15 for 1 or 2 nights; 3 or more nights is $30 per night. Add an additional $5 per night for a 2nd dog. Dogs may not be left alone in the room.
Comfort Inn 333 Harold G Clark Parkway Forsyth GA   478-994-3400 (877-424-6423)
Dogs are allowed for an additional fee of $10 per night per pet.
Days Inn Forsyth 343 N Lee St Forsyth GA   478-994-2900 (800-329-7466)
Dogs up to 60 pounds are allowed. There is a $10 per night pet fee per pet.
Hampton Inn 520 Holiday Circle Forsyth GA   478-994-9697
Dogs of all sizes are allowed, however there can only be one large or 2 to 3 medium to small dogs per room. There are no additional pet fees.
Holiday Inn 480 Holiday Circle Forsyth GA   478-994-5691 (877-270-6405)
Dogs of all sizes are allowed for an additional one time pet fee of $10 per room.
Holiday Inn Express Forsyth 520 Holiday Circle Forsyth GA   478-994-9697 (877-270-6405)
Dogs of all sizes are allowed for an additional one time pet fee of $10 per room.

Campgrounds and RV Parks
Forsyth KOA 414 S Frontage Road Forsyth GA   478-994-2019 (800-562-8614)
http://www.koa.com
Dogs of all sizes are allowed. There are no additional pet fees. Dogs may not be left unattended outside, and they must be leashed, cleaned up after, and inside at night. The camping and tent areas also allow dogs. There is a dog walk area at the campground. Dogs are allowed in the camping cabins.

Gainesville

Accommodations
Motel 6 - Gainesville 1585 Monroe Drive Gainesville GA   770-532-7531 (800-466-8356)

One well-behaved family pet per room. Guest must notify front desk upon arrival. Guest is liable for any damages. In consideration of all guests, pets must never be left unattended in the guest rooms.

Campgrounds and RV Parks
Chattahoochee-Oconee National Forest 1755 Cleveland H Gainesville GA 770-297-3000
http://www.fs.fed.us/conf/
This forest has 7 district offices, 2 visitor centers, almost 900,000 acres, and diverse ecosystems that support a large variety of plants, fish, mammals, bird species, and year round recreation. Dogs of all sizes are allowed at no additional fee. Dogs may not be left unattended, and they must be leashed at all times, and be cleaned up after. The camping and tent areas also allow dogs. There is a dog walk area at the campground.

Stores
PetSmart Pet Store 842 Dawsonville Hwy Gainesville GA 770-503-1964
Your licensed and well-behaved leashed dog is allowed in the store.

Off-Leash Dog Parks
Laurel Park Dog Park 3100 Old Cleveland Hwy Gainesville GA 770-535-8280
This fenced dog park has two areas; one for small dogs and one for large dogs. There are quite a few trees in the dog park.

Grovetown

Accommodations
Motel 6 - Grovetown - Augusta 459 Park West Drive Grovetown GA 706-651-8300 (800-466-8356)
One well-behaved family pet per room. Guest must notify front desk upon arrival. Guest is liable for any damages. In consideration of all guests, pets must never be left unattended in the guest rooms.

Hartwell

Accommodations
Best Western Lake Hartwell Inn & Suites 1357 E Franklin Street Hartwell GA 706-376-4700 (800-780-7234)
Dogs under 25 pounds are allowed for an additional one time pet fee per room; the fee is $40 for dogs over 25 pounds.

Campgrounds and RV Parks
Hart State Park 330 Hart State Park Road Hartwell GA 706-376-8756 (800-864-PARK (7275))
http://www.gastateparks.org/info/hart/
This scenic park of 147 acres on Lake Hartwell offers a variety of land and water activities and recreation. Dogs of all sizes are allowed at no additional fee. Dogs must be on no more than a 6 foot leash, and be cleaned up after. Dogs are allowed on the trails. The camping and tent areas also allow dogs. There is a dog walk area at the campground.

Helen

Campgrounds and RV Parks
Unicoi State Park 1788 H 356 Helen GA 706-878-3982 (800-864-PARK (7275))
http://www.gastateparks.org/info/unicoi/
This park offers programs that focus on its historical, natural, cultural, and recreational resources. Dogs of all sizes are allowed at no additional fee. Only 2 dogs are allowed in the cabins. Dogs may not be left unattended outside, and they must be on no more than a 6 foot leash, and be cleaned up after. Dogs are allowed on the trails, but not in the lodge. The camping and tent areas also allow dogs. There is a dog walk area at the campground. Dogs are allowed in the camping cabins.

Attractions
Charlemagne's Kingdom 8808 North Main St Helen GA 706-878-2200
Dogs on leash are allowed in this alpine model railroad museum.

Hiawassee

Campgrounds and RV Parks
Georgia Mountain 1311 Music Hall Road Hiawassee GA 706-896-4191
http://www.georgia-mountain-fair.com
Dogs of all sizes are allowed. There are no additional pet fees. Dogs are not allowed in the fair area, and they must be leashed and cleaned up after. The RV sites are open all year, but the tent sites are seasonal. The camping and tent areas also allow dogs. There is a dog walk area at the campground.

Hinesville

Accommodations
Days Inn Hinesville 738 Oglethorpe Hinesville GA 912-368-4146 (800-329-7466)
Dogs of all sizes are allowed. There is a $15 one time per pet fee per visit.

Hiram

Stores
PetSmart Pet Store 4749 Jimmy Lee Smith Pkwy 108 Hiram GA 678-567-0583
Your licensed and well-behaved leashed dog is allowed in the store.

Hogansville

Accommodations
Garden Inn and Suites 1630 Bass Cross Rd Hogansville GA 706-637-5400 (800-DAYS-INN)
Dogs of all sizes are allowed. There is a $10 per night pet fee per pet.

Jackson

Campgrounds and RV Parks
Indian Springs State Park 678 Lake Clark Road Flovilla GA 770-504-2277 (800-864-PARK (7275))
http://www.gastateparks.org/info/indspr/
Thought to be the oldest state park in the nation, and home to a "healing" spring, this park offers a variety of land and water recreation. Dogs of all sizes are allowed at no additional fee. Dogs must be on no more than a 6 foot leash, and be cleaned up after. Dogs are not allowed in buildings or in the cabin area, however, they are allowed on the trails. The camping and tent areas also allow dogs. There is a dog walk area at the campground.
High Falls State Park 76 High Falls Park Drive Jackson GA 478-993-3053 (800-864-7275)
Steeped in American history, this 1,050 acre park with 650 lake acres offers waterfalls, scenic trails, and a variety of land and water recreation. Dogs of all sizes are allowed at no additional fee. Dogs must be on no more than a 6 foot leash, and be cleaned up after. The camping and tent areas also allow dogs. There is a dog walk area at the campground.

Jekyll Island

Accommodations

Buccaneer Beach Resort 85 S. Beachview Dr. Jekyll Island GA   912-635-2261
There is a pet fee of $10 per day.
Jekyll Oceanfront Resort 975 North Benchview Drive Jekyll Island GA   912-635-2531 (800-431-5190)
http://www.jekyllinn.com/
This 15 acre resort is the largest oceanfront resort hotel in Jekyll Island. The resort is also home to the largest
public golf course in Georgia. Amenities include an outdoor pool, playground and more. All guest rooms are non-
smoking and have either one king bed or two double beds. Rollaways, cribs, microwaves and refrigerators are
also available for a minimal fee. Or you can stay in one of the Villas, which are two-level townhouses that come
with a separate bedroom, kitchen, dining area, living room, bathrooms, and private patio. There is a $25 per
night per pet charge plus tax. Dogs up to 50 pounds are allowed.
Oceanside Inn and Suites 711 Beachview Dr. Jekyll Island GA   912-635-2211 (800-228-5150)
This beachfront motel's amenities include a playground and room service. There is a $10 per day pet charge.
Quality Inn and Suites 700 N Beachview Drive Jekyll Island GA   912-635-2202 (877-424-6423)
Dogs up to 50 pounds are allowed for an additional fee of $10 per night per pet.

Campgrounds and RV Parks

Jekyll Island Campground 1197 Riverview Drive Jekyll Island GA   866-658-3021
Dogs of all sizes are allowed. There are no additional pet fees. Dogs must be leashed and cleaned up after. The
camping and tent areas also allow dogs. There is a dog walk area at the campground.

Attractions

Amazing Spaces Tour

TOP 200 PLACE **Amazing Spaces Tour** History Center Jekyll Island GA   912-635-4036
If you want to learn more about Jekyll Island including its history and highlights, you and your pooch can ride the
Amazing Spaces Tour. The tram will take you on a forty-five minute narrated tour through the Historic District for
a venture into the past. Your pooch can sit on the bench next to you. Because of physical space limitations on
the tram, they can only take a dog up to about the size of a lab or golden retriever. Well-behaved leashed dogs
are allowed. The tour is offered year round.
Mini Golf Beachview Drive Jekyll Island GA   912-635-2648
This mini golf course is located across the street from the beach. Well-behaved, leashed dogs are usually

Georgia   - Please always call ahead to make sure that an establishment is still dog-friendly

allowed on the course.

Victoria's Carriages

Jekyll Island Beaches and Trails

Victoria's Carriages Stable Road Jekyll Island GA   912-635-9500
This horse and carriage ride will take you and your dog on a thirty-five to forty-five minute narrated tour through

the Historic District of Jekyll Island. Adults and children need to pay, but pets ride for free. Well-behaved, leashed dogs are welcome. The tours are available year round.

Beaches
TOP 200 PLACE Jekyll Island Beaches and Trails off SR 520 Jekyll Island GA 877-453-5955
These beaches look like a Caribbean island setting. It is hard to believe that you just drove here over a causeway. Dogs on leash are welcome year round on the beach and the paved and dirt trails. There are about 10 miles of beaches and 20 miles of inland paved and dirt trails. It is recommended that your pooch stay on the paved trails instead of the dirt trails during the warm Summer months because there are too many ticks along the dirt trails. On warmer days you might choose a beach walk rather than the inland trails anyway because of the cooler ocean breezes.

Outdoor Restaurants
Latitude 31 1 Pier Road Jekyll Island GA 912-635-3800
http://www.latitude-31.com
This restaurant serves seafood including raw and steamed oysters. Well-behaved, leashed pets are welcome at the "Rah" Bar's outdoor seats.
SeaJays Waterfront Cafe and Pub 1 Harbor Rd Jekyll Island GA 912-635-3200
http://www.seajays.com
This cafe serves a variety of entrees including Brunswick Stew and the world famous "Low Country Boil" shrimp stew. Well-behaved, leashed pets are welcome at the outdoor tables.
Zach's Eats and Treats 44 Beachview Drive Jekyll Island GA 912-635-2040
Zach's serves sandwiches, soups, pizza and ice cream. Well-behaved, leashed pets are welcome at the outdoor picnic tables.

La Fayette

Accommodations
Days Inn Lafayette 2209 North Main Street La Fayette GA 706-639-9362 (800-329-7466)
Dogs of all sizes are allowed. There is a $5 per night pet fee per small pet and $10 per large pet.

LaGrange

Accommodations
Days Inn LaGrange 2606 Whitesville Rd LaGrange GA 706-882-8881 (800-329-7466)
Dogs of all sizes are allowed. There is a $10 per night pet fee per pet.

Lake Park

Accommodations
Days Inn Valdosta/Lake Park 4913 Timber Dr Lake Park GA 229-559-0229 (800-329-7466)
Dogs of all sizes are allowed. There is a $4 per night pet fee per pet.

Campgrounds and RV Parks
Eagle's Roost RV Resort 5465 Mill Store Road Lake Park GA 229-559-5192
http://www.eaglesroostresort.com
Dogs of all sizes are allowed. There are no additional pet fees. Dogs must be leashed and cleaned up after. The camping and tent areas also allow dogs. There is a dog walk area at the campground.
Valdosta/Lake Park KOA 5300 Jewel Futch Road Lake Park GA 229-559-9738 (800-562-2124)
http://www.koa.com
Dogs of all sizes are allowed, and there are no additional pet fees for tent or RV sites. There is a $25 one time additional pet fee for the cabin and park models. Dogs may not be left unattended outside or in rentals, and they must be leashed and cleaned up after. The camping and tent areas also allow dogs. There is a dog walk area at

the campground. Dogs are allowed in the camping cabins.

Lavonia

Accommodations
Best Western Regency Inn & Suites 13705 Jones Street Lavonia GA   706-356-4000 (800-780-7234)
Dogs are allowed for an additional one time fee of $15 per pet.
Super 8 Lavonia 14227 Jones St Lavonia GA   706-356-8848 (800-800-8000)
Dogs up to 60 pounds are allowed. There is a $10 per night pet fee per pet or $25 per visit per pet. Reservations are recommended due to limited rooms for pets. Smoking and non-smoking rooms are available for pet rooms.

Parks
Tugaloo Park 1763 Tugaloo State Park Rd Lavonia GA   706- 356--4362
http://www.gastateparks.org
Dogs on leash are allowed in this state park. They are allowed in some of the cabins for a fee of $40 per pet (limit 2 dogs). They are also allowed in the campgrounds. This park features canoeing, saltwater fishing, hiking, picnicing, swimming, and more.

Lawrenceville

Accommodations
Days Inn Lawrenceville 731 Duluth Hwy Lawrenceville GA   770-995-7782 (800-329-7466)
Dogs of all sizes are allowed. There is a $20 per night pet fee per pet.

Stores
PetSmart Pet Store 875 Lawrenceville-Suwanee Rd Lawrenceville GA   770-995-2449
Your licensed and well-behaved leashed dog is allowed in the store.
Petco Pet Store 2160 Riverside Parkway, Ste 134/135 Lawrenceville GA   770-995-9394
Your licensed and well-behaved leashed dog is allowed in the store.

Lilburn

Stores
PetSmart Pet Store 2150 Paxton Dr Lilburn GA   770-985-0469
Your licensed and well-behaved leashed dog is allowed in the store.

Lincolnton

Campgrounds and RV Parks
Elijah Clark State Park 2959 McCormick H Lincolnton GA   706-359-3458 (800-864-PARK (7275))
http://www.gastateparks.org/info/elijah/
Rich in American history, this 447 acre park with a 70,000 acre lake offers a variety of land and water recreation. Dogs of all sizes are allowed at no additional fee. Dogs may not be left unattended unless quiet and well behaved; they must be on no more than a 6 foot leash, and cleaned up after. Dogs are not allowed in buildings or on the beaches. Dogs are allowed on the trails. This campground is closed during the off-season. The camping and tent areas also allow dogs. There is a dog walk area at the campground.

Lithia Springs

Accommodations
Motel 6 - Atlanta - Lithia Springs 920 Bob Arnold Boulevard Lithia Springs GA   678-945-0606 (800-466-8356)
One well-behaved family pet per room. Guest must notify front desk upon arrival. Guest is liable for any damages. In consideration of all guests, pets must never be left unattended in the guest rooms.

Stores
PetSmart Pet Store 2940 Chapel Hill Rd Douglasville GA   770-942-3326
Your licensed and well-behaved leashed dog is allowed in the store.
Petco Pet Store 9559 Highway 5 #401 Douglasville GA   770-942-5442
Your licensed and well-behaved leashed dog is allowed in the store.

Locust Grove

Accommodations
Red Roof Inn - Locust Grove, GA 4832 Bill Gardner Parkway Locust Grove GA   678-583-0004 (800-RED-ROOF)
One well-behaved family pet per room. Guest must notify front desk upon arrival. Guest is liable for any damages. In consideration of all guests, pets must never be left unattended in the guest rooms.

Lumpkin

Parks
Providence Canyon State Park Route 1, Box 158/On H 39C Lumpkin GA   229-838-6202
In addition to a several events throughout the year and a number of recreational activities, the strikingly beautiful colors of their "little Grand Canyon" is only upstaged by its display of wildflowers and greenery. Dogs are allowed throughout the 1,003 acre park on no more than a 6 foot leash and cleaned up after at all times.

Macon

Accommodations
Best Western Riverside Inn 2400 Riverside Drive Macon GA   478-743-6311 (800-780-7234)
Dogs up to 10 pounds are allowed for an additional pet fee of $10 per night; the fee is $25 per night for dogs over 10 pounds.
Comfort Inn and Suites 3935 Arkwright Road Macon GA   478-757-8688 (877-424-6423)
Dogs up to 10 pounds are allowed for an additional pet fee of $15 per night per room; the fee is $20 per night per room for dogs over 10 pounds.
La Quinta Inn & Suites Macon 3944 River Place Dr. Macon GA   478-475-0206 (800-531-5900)
Housetrained dogs of all sizes are allowed. There are no additional pet fees. A contact number must be left with the front desk if your pet is in the room alone. Dogs must be leashed, cleaned up after, and crated or removed for housekeeping.
Motel 6 - Macon 4991 Harrison Road Macon GA   478-474-2870 (800-466-8356)
One well-behaved family pet per room. Guest must notify front desk upon arrival. Guest is liable for any damages. In consideration of all guests, pets must never be left unattended in the guest rooms.
Red Roof Inn - Macon 3950 River Place Drive Macon GA   478-477-7477 (800-RED-ROOF)
One well-behaved family pet per room. Guest must notify front desk upon arrival. Guest is liable for any damages. In consideration of all guests, pets must never be left unattended in the guest rooms.
Residence Inn by Marriott 3900 Sheraton Drive Macon GA   478-475-4280
Pets of all sizes are allowed. There is a $75 one time fee and a pet policy to sign at check in.
Sleep Inn 140 Plantation Inn Drive Macon GA   478-476-8111 (877-424-6423)
Dogs up to 20 pounds are allowed for an additional fee of $10 per night per pet; the fee is $20 to $25 per night per pet for dogs over 20 pounds.

Stores

PetSmart Pet Store 4551 Billy Williamson Drive Macon GA   478-476-9564
Your licensed and well-behaved leashed dog is allowed in the store.

Parks
Ocmulgee National Monument 1207 Emery Highway Macon GA   478-752-8257
http://www.nps.gov/ocmu
Dedicated to preserving, protecting, and educating visitors and future generations of the significance of this unique memorial, the park has preserved more than its 12,000 years of diverse history and culture. Dogs are allowed throughout the grounds; they must be leashed and under owner's control/care at all times.

Off-Leash Dog Parks
Macon Dog Park Chestnut and Adams Macon GA   478-742-5084
http://www.macondogpark.org
This fully fenced dog park is open from sunrise to sunset. The Dog Park is just off of I-75 at the Forsyth Street exit. It is located one block north of Tatnall Square at the corner of Chestnut Street and Adams Street.

Madison

Accommodations
Days Inn Madison 2001 Eatonton Hwy Madison GA   706-342-1839 (800-329-7466)
Dogs of all sizes are allowed. There is a $10 per night pet fee per pet.
Red Roof Inn - Madison 2080 Eatonton Road Madison GA   706-342-3433 (800-RED-ROOF)
One well-behaved family pet per room. Guest must notify front desk upon arrival. Guest is liable for any damages. In consideration of all guests, pets must never be left unattended in the guest rooms.
Super 8 Madison 2091 Eatonton Rd Madison GA   706-342-7800 (800-800-8000)
Dogs of all sizes are allowed. There is a $10 per night pet fee per pet. Smoking and non-smoking rooms are available for pet rooms.

Manchester

Accommodations
Days Inn Manchester 2546 Roosevelt Hwy Manchester GA   706-846-1247 (800-329-7466)
Dogs of all sizes are allowed. There is a $10 per night pet fee per pet.
Best Western White House Inn 2526 White House Parkway Warm Springs GA   706-655-2750 (800-780-7234)
Dogs are allowed for an additional fee of $15 per night per pet.

Milledgeville

Accommodations
Days Inn Milledgeville 2551 N Columbia St Milledgeville GA   478-453-8471 (800-329-7466)
Dogs of all sizes are allowed. There is a $10 per night pet fee per pet.
Holiday Inn Express Hotel & Suites 1839 North Columbia Street Milledgeville GA   478-454-9000 (877-270-6405)
Dogs of all sizes are allowed for an additional one time fee of $25 per pet.

Millington

Campgrounds and RV Parks
Meeman-Shelby State Park 910 Riddick Road Millington GA   901-876-5215
Dogs of all sizes are allowed, and there are no additional pet fees for tent or RV sites. There is a $10 per night per pet additional fee for the 1 pet friendly cabin. Dogs may not be left unattended outside or in the cabin, and

they must be leashed and cleaned up after. The camping and tent areas also allow dogs. There is a dog walk area at the campground. Dogs are allowed in the camping cabins.

Montezuma

Accommodations
Traveler's Rest 318 N Dody Street Montezuma GA   478-472-0085
Well behaved dogs of all sizes are allowed. There is a pet policy to sign at check in and there are no additional pet fees.

Newnan

Accommodations
La Quinta Inn Newnan 600 Bullsboro Drive Newnan GA   770-502-8430 (800-531-5900)
Dogs of all sizes are allowed. There are no additional pet fees. There is a pet waiver to sign at check in. Dogs are not allowed in dining areas, and they may not be left unattended in the room. Dogs must be leashed and cleaned up after.
Motel 6 - Newnan 40 Parkway North Newnan GA   770-251-4580 (800-466-8356)
One well-behaved family pet per room. Guest must notify front desk upon arrival. Guest is liable for any damages. In consideration of all guests, pets must never be left unattended in the guest rooms.
Super 8 Newnan 1455 Hwy 29 South Newnan GA   770-683-0089 (800-800-8000)
Dogs of all sizes are allowed. There is a $10 per night pet fee per pet. Smoking and non-smoking rooms are available for pet rooms.

Stores
PetSmart Pet Store 1072 Bullsboro Dr Newnan GA   770-251-8086
Your licensed and well-behaved leashed dog is allowed in the store.

Nicholls

Campgrounds and RV Parks
General Coffee State Park 46 John Coffee Road Nicholls GA   912-384-7082 (800-864-PARK (7275))
Rich in agricultural history, and host to a cypress swamp of rare and endangered plants, this park offers an amphitheater, history and nature programs, and a variety of land and water recreation. Dogs of all sizes are allowed at no additional fee. Dogs may not be left unattended, and they must be on no more than a 6 foot leash, and be cleaned up after in camp areas. Dogs are not allowed in the buildings, however, they are allowed on the trails. The camping and tent areas also allow dogs. There is a dog walk area at the campground.

Oakwood

Accommodations
Country Inns & Suites by Carlson 4535 Oakwood Road Oakwood GA   770-535-8080
Dogs of all sizes are allowed. There is a $10 per day additional pet fee.

Ochlocknee

Campgrounds and RV Parks
Sugar Mill Plantation RV Park 4857 McMillan Road Ochlocknee GA   229-227-1451
Dogs of all sizes are allowed. There are no additional pet fees. Dogs may not be left unattended outside, and they must be leashed and cleaned up after. There are some breed restrictions. The camping and tent areas also

allow dogs. There is a dog walk area at the campground.

Perry

Accommodations
Days Inn Perry 201 Lect Dr Perry GA   478-987-8777 (800-329-7466)
Dogs of all sizes are allowed. There is a $10 per night pet fee per pet. There is a $20 per night pet fee per pet for dog shows.
New Perry Hotel & Motel 800 Main Street Perry GA   478-987-1000
Dogs of all sizes are allowed. There is a $10 per night per pet fee if the pet is under 45 pounds, and there is a $15 per night per pet fee if the dog is over 45 pounds. There is a pet policy to sign at check in.
Quality Inn 1504 Sam Nunn Blvd Perry GA   478-987-1345 (877-424-6423)
Dogs are allowed for an additional pet fee of $10 per night per room.
Super 8 Perry 102 Plaza Drive Perry GA   478-987-0999 (800-800-8000)
Dogs of all sizes are allowed. There is a $10 per night pet fee per pet. Smoking and non-smoking rooms are available for pet rooms.

Pine Mountain

Accommodations
Callaway Gardens Resort 17800 H 27 Pine Mountain GA   706-663-2281
http://www.callawaygardens.com/
Each season brings it owns celebration to this "blooming" resort with its award-winning gardens, a butterfly center, 2 lush golf courses, the luxury accommodations, and for their colorful festivals. Dogs up to 50 pounds are allowed for an additional one time pet fee of $35 per room. Dogs must be leashed and cleaned up after at all times.
White Columns Motel 524 S Main Avenue/Hwy 27 Pine Mountain GA   706-663-2312 (800-722-5083)
http://www.whitecolumnsmotel.com/
Offering meticulously landscaped grounds and a number of amenities, this motel is also near a number of restaurants, shops, historic sites, and several recreational activities. Small dogs are allowed for an additional fee of $5 per night per pet, and large dogs are $10 per night per pet. Dogs must be leashed and under owner's control/care at all times.

Campgrounds and RV Parks
Pine Mountain Campground 8804 Hamilton Road Pine Mountain GA   706-663-4329
http://www.camppinemountain.com
Dogs of all sizes are allowed. There are no additional pet fees. Dogs may not be left unattended, and they must be leashed and cleaned up after. There are some breed restrictions. The camping and tent areas also allow dogs. There is a dog walk area at the campground.
Roosevelt State Park 2970 H 190E Pine Mountain GA   706-663-4858 (800-864-PARK (7275))
http://www.gastateparks.org/info/fdr/
This historical park of 9,049 acres offers spectacular views, 37 miles of hiking trails, an amphitheater and a wide variety of recreational pursuits. Dogs of all sizes are allowed at no additional fee. Dogs may not be left unattended, and they must be on no more than a 6 foot leash, and cleaned up after. Dogs are not allowed in the cottage area, at the group camp, or at the pool. Dogs are allowed on the trails. The camping and tent areas also allow dogs. There is a dog walk area at the campground.

Attractions
Pine Mountain Wild Animal Safari Kennels 1300 Oak Grove Road Pine Mountain GA   706-663-8744
http://www.animalsafari.com/
Parks such as this one are rare in the world where visitors can see up front and personal animals from almost every continent; visitors can take pictures, touch, observe, and feed some of the animals from their own car or from one of the parks Zebra Vans. Dogs are not allowed out of the vehicle at any time, so they offer a free kennel/crate service-kennels are secured outside, and the crated animals they keep in the office.

Plains

Attractions
Jimmy Carter National Historic Site 300 North Bond Street Plains GA   229-824-4104
http://www.nps.gov/jica/
This site does tribute to President and Mrs. Carter for their tremendous efforts for the sake of others; there is a library, museum, several historic sites of interest, and a community church where President Carter still does Sunday service during certain times of the year. Dogs are allowed on the grounds; they are not allowed in buildings. Dogs must be leashed and under owner's control/care at all times.

Richland

Accommodations
Days Inn Richland 46 Nicholson St Richland GA   229-887-9000 (800-329-7466)
Dogs of all sizes are allowed. There is a $5 per night pet fee per pet.

Rincon

Accommodations
Days Inn Rincon 582 Columbia Ave Rincon GA   912-826-6966 (800-329-7466)
Dogs of all sizes are allowed. There is a $10 per night pet fee per pet.

Rising Farm

Campgrounds and RV Parks
Cloudland Canyon State Park 122 Cloudland Canyon Park Road Rising Farm GA   706-657-4050 (800-864-7275)
Rugged geology and beautiful vistas make this one of the most scenic parks in the state, and a variety of trails and recreation are available for your use. Dogs of all sizes are allowed at no additional fee. Dogs may not be left unattended, and they must be quiet, well behaved, leashed and cleaned up after. Dogs are not allowed in buildings. Dogs are allowed on the trails. The camping and tent areas also allow dogs. There is a dog walk area at the campground.

Rockmart

Accommodations
Days Inn Rockmart 105 GTM Parkway Rockmart GA   770-684-9955 (800-329-7466)
Dogs of all sizes are allowed. There is a $5 per night pet fee per pet.

Rome

Accommodations
Howard Johnson Express Inn 1610 Martha Berry Blvd. Rome GA   706-291-1994 (800-446-4656)
Dogs of all sizes are welcome. There is a $5 per day pet fee.

Rossville

Campgrounds and RV Parks

Holiday Trav-L-Park 1653 Mack Smith Road Rossville GA 706-891-9766
http://www.chattacamp.com
Dogs of all sizes are allowed. There are no additional pet fees. Dogs may not be left unattended outside, must be on no more than a 6 foot leashed, and be cleaned up after. The camping and tent areas also allow dogs. There is a dog walk area at the campground.

Rutledge

Campgrounds and RV Parks

Hard Labor Creek State Park Knox Chaple Road Rutledge GA 706-557-3001 (800-864-PARK (7275))
Although best known for its golf course, there are a wide variety of land and water activities and recreation offered at this state park. Dogs of all sizes are allowed at no additional fee. Dogs must be leashed, and cleaned up after in camp areas. Dogs are not allowed in or around cottage areas or on the beach. Dogs are allowed on the trails. The camping and tent areas also allow dogs. There is a dog walk area at the campground.

Savannah

Accommodations

Econo Lodge 500 E. US 80 Pooler GA 912-748-4124 (888-econo-50)
http://www.econolodge-savannah.com
There is a $10 additional pet fee. Pets are allowed in the pet rooms on the ground floor. The hotel offers free cable w/HBO, a continental breakfast, free local calls, an outdoor pool, and in-room coffee. The hotel is located 11 miles from downtown Savannah near Interstate 95.
Quality Inn 301 Govenor Treutlen Drive Pooler GA 912-748-6464 (877-424-6423)
Dogs up to 50 pounds are allowed for an additional fee of $15 per night per pet.
Red Roof Inn - Savannah Airport 20 Mill Creek Circle Pooler GA 912-748-0370 (800-RED-ROOF)
One well-behaved family pet per room. Guest must notify front desk upon arrival. Guest is liable for any damages. In consideration of all guests, pets must never be left unattended in the guest rooms.
Days Inn Savannah/Richmond Hill 3926 HIGHWAY 17 Richmond Hill GA 912-756-3371 (800-329-7466)
Dogs of all sizes are allowed. There is a $5 per night pet fee per pet.
Motel 6 - Savannah - Richmond Hill 4071 US 17 Richmond Hill GA 912-756-3543 (800-466-8356)
One well-behaved family pet per room. Guest must notify front desk upon arrival. Guest is liable for any damages. In consideration of all guests, pets must never be left unattended in the guest rooms.
Clarion Inn and Suites 16 Gateway Blvd Savannah GA 912-920-3200 (877-424-6423)
Dogs are allowed for an additional fee of $35 per night per pet.
Clubhouse Inn and Suites 6800 Abercorn/H 204 Savannah GA 912-356-1234 (800-CLUB-INN (258-2466))
http://www.clubhouseinn.com
Convenient location, a free breakfast buffet, and a seasonal pool are just some of the popularities of this inn. Dogs are allowed for an additional fee of $10 per night per pet. Dogs must be leashed and under owner's care.
East Bay Inn 225 E Bay Street/H 25 Savannah GA 912-0238-1225 (800-500-1225)
http://www.eastbayinn.com/
Offering a blend of old and new world, this beautiful inn also has a restaurant on site, a wine and hors d' oeuvres reception each evening, and a number of comforts for the business or leisure traveler. Dogs are allowed for an additional one time pet fee of $35 per room. Dogs are not allowed in the common areas, and a contact number must be left with the front desk if there is a pet alone in the room. Dogs must be leashed and under owner's care.
Holiday Inn 7100 Abercorn St Savannah GA 912-352-7100 (877-270-6405)
Dogs of all sizes are allowed: There is an additional one time fee of $25 per pet for dogs 25 pounds and under, and $35 per pet for dogs over 25 pounds.
Joan's on Joan 17 W Jones Street Savannah GA 912-234-3863 (888-989-9806)
This stately Victorian inn gives the feel of a different era, but with all the modern conveniences. One medium to large dog or 2 very little dogs are allowed per room for an additional one time pet fee of $50 per room. Dogs must be quiet, well mannered, leashed and under owners care.
La Quinta Inn Savannah I-95 6 Gateway Blvd. South Savannah GA 912-925-9505 (800-531-5900)
Dogs of all sizes are allowed. There are no additional pet fees. Dogs must be well behaved, leashed, and cleaned up after.
La Quinta Inn Savannah Midtown 6805 Abercorn St. Savannah GA 912-355-3004 (800-531-5900)
Dogs of all sizes are allowed. There are no additional pet fees; however, a credit card must be on file. Dogs must

be leashed and cleaned up after. A contact number must be left with the front desk if the pet is in the room alone.
La Quinta Inn Savannah Southside 8484 Abercorn Street Savannah GA   912-927-7660 (800-531-5900)
Dogs of all sizes are allowed. There are no additional pet fees. Dogs may only be left in the room alone if they will be quiet, well behaved, and you have informed the front desk. Dogs must be kept leashed.
Olde Harbour Inn 508 E Factors Walk Savannah GA   912-234-4100 (800-553-6533)
http://www.oldeharbourinn.com/
In addition to being a beautiful riverfront inn with large suites that overlook the river and plenty of modern conveniences, they are also centrally located to numerous recreational activities, a monthly arts/crafts festival and various annual celebrations on the waterfront, shopping, and dining. One medium to large dog or 2 very little dogs are allowed per room for an additional one time pet fee of $35 per room; they must be declared at the time of reservations. Dogs must be quiet, well mannered, leashed and under owners care.
Quality Inn 3 Gateway Blvd Savannah GA   912-925-2770 (877-424-6423)
Dogs up to 50 pounds are allowed for an additional fee of $10 per night per pet.
Red Roof Inn - Savannah 405 Al Henderson Boulevard Savannah GA   912-920-3535 (800-RED-ROOF)
One well-behaved family pet per room. Guest must notify front desk upon arrival. Guest is liable for any damages. In consideration of all guests, pets must never be left unattended in the guest rooms.
Residence Inn by Marriott 5710 White Bluff Road Savannah GA   912-356-3266
Dogs of all sizes are allowed. There is a $75 one time fee and a pet policy to sign at check in.
Southern Chic Guesthouse 418 East Charlton Street Savannah GA   678-859-0674
http://www.southern-chic.com
Located in historic district of Savannah, Georgia. There are no additional pet fees.
Staybridge Suites Savannah Airport One Clyde E. Martin Dr. Savannah GA   912-965-1551 (877-270-6405)
Dogs of all sizes are allowed for an additional one time pet fee per room of $25 for the first night; $50 for 2 or 3 nights, and $150 for 4 or more nights.
Staybridge Suites Savannah Historic District 301 East Bay Street Savannah GA   912-721-9000 (877-270-6405)
Dogs of all sizes are allowed for an additional one time pet fee of $75 per room.
The Manor House Bed & Breakfast 201 West Liberty Street Savannah GA   912-233-9597 (800-462-3595)
There are no pet fees. There are no designated smoking or non-smoking rooms.
TownePlace Suites Savannah Midtown 11309 Abercom Street Savannah GA   912-920-9080
Dogs of all sizes are allowed. There is a $75 one time pet fee per visit.

Campgrounds and RV Parks

Brookwood RV Park Rt 5, Box 3107; on Pulaski Excelsior Metter GA   888-636-4616
http://www.bkwdrv.com
Dogs of all sizes are allowed. There are no additional pet fees. Dogs must be leashed and cleaned up after. There is a dog walk area at the campground.
Fort McAllister State Historic Park 3894 Fort McAllister Road Richmond Hill GA   912-727-2339 (800-864-PARK (7275))
This park, rich in American history and along the Colonial Coast Birding Trail, offers a Civil War museum, an Earthwork Fort, and a variety of recreational pursuits. Dogs of all sizes are allowed at no additional fee. Dogs may not be left unattended, and they must be on no more than a 6 foot leash, and be cleaned up after. Dogs are not allowed in any of the buildings, however, they are allowed on the trails. The camping and tent areas also allow dogs. There is a dog walk area at the campground.
Savannah South KOA 4915 H 17 Richmond Hill GA   912-765-3396 (800-562-8741)
http://www.koa.com
Dogs of all sizes are allowed. There are no additional pet fees. Dogs must be leashed and cleaned up after. The camping and tent areas also allow dogs. There is a dog walk area at the campground. Dogs are allowed in the camping cabins.
Waterway RV Park 70 H 17 Richmond Hill GA   912-756-2296
Dogs up to 75 pounds are allowed. There are no additional pet fees. Dogs may not be left unattended, and they must be leashed and cleaned up after. Dogs are not allowed to swim in the river because of alligators. There are some breed restrictions. There is a dog walk area at the campground.
Skidaway Island State Park 52 Diamond Causeway Savannah GA   912-598-2300 (800-864-PARK (7275))
This 588 acre barrier island park along the Colonial Coast Birding Trail, offers observation towers, an interpretive center, and a variety of recreational pursuits. Dogs of all sizes are allowed at no additional fee. Dogs may not be left unattended, and they must be leashed and cleaned up after. Dogs are not allowed in buildings or in the pool area. The camping and tent areas also allow dogs. There is a dog walk area at the campground.

Attractions

Fort Pulaski National Monument On H 80E Fort Pulaski GA   912-786-5787
http://www.nps.gov/fopu/
Rich in military history, the bombardment of this island fort, and it subsequent surrender as a result of destruction

from cannon fire, caused the cessation of building forts with masonry. There are interpretive programs, miles of lush walking trails through more than 5000 acres of coastal marshlands, a 150 year old lighthouse, and an abundance of wildlife. Dogs are allowed throughout the grounds; they must be leashed and under owner's control/care at all times.

TOP 200 PLACE **Ghost Talk** On Abercorn between Congress and Bryan Savannah GA   912-233-3896
http://www.savannahgeorgia.com/ghosttalk
This is a narrated tour of the ghostly stories and legends of Savannah. The meeting place is at the 20 foot statue of John Wesley in Reynolds's Square. Tours depart at dusk, and times vary through the year. Please call for reservations and departure times. A quiet, well behaved dog on leash is allowed.

Old Fort Jackson 1 Fort Jackson Road Savannah GA   912-232-3945
http://www.chsgeorgia.org/jackson/
Listed on the National Register of Historic Sites, this fort shares a rich colonial and military history; it is only 1 of 8 such forts in America; it has daily demonstrations of cannon fire during the Summer, and it is the only historic fort in America that still cannon salutes military vessels as they sail by. People friendly, well behaved dogs are allowed throughout the grounds. Dogs must be leashed and under owner's control/care at all times.

Shopping Centers

Savannah Riverfront Area

Savannah Riverfront Area River Street Savannah GA   912-644-6400
http://www.savannahchamber.com
This nine block shopping district lies along the river and offers nearly 100 shops, restaurants, boutiques and other establishments. There are often numerous street performers. Dogs on leash are allowed.

Stores

E. Shaver Bookstore 326 Bull Street Savannah GA   912-234-7257
Well behaved, quiet, and housebroken dogs on a leash are allowed at this book store.
PetSmart Pet Store 11132 Abercorn St Savannah GA   912-925-1116
Your licensed and well-behaved leashed dog is allowed in the store.

Off-Leash Dog Parks

Savannah Dog Park 41st and Drayton St Savannah GA
http://www.savannahdogpark.com/
This dog park is located in the Starland Area at 41st and Drayton St. The park is shaded and fenced.

Outdoor Restaurants
Bonna Bella Yacht Club 2740 Livingston Avenue Savannah GA   912-352-3134
http://www.bbyachtclub.net/
Whether coming by boat or car, for a special event or just to enjoy the bar and grill, visitors will also enjoy the ambiance at this waterside eatery. Outside dining is available. Dogs are allowed at the outer tables; they must be leashed and under owner's control/care at all times.
Vinnie VanGoGo's 317 W Bryan Street Savannah GA   912-233-6394
http://www.vinnievangogo.com/
Think "fine-dining" fast food to take out or to have on site, plus they provide an ever-changing menu for some great variety. Outside seating is available; dogs are allowed at the outer tables. They must be leashed and under owner's control/care at all times.
Wild Wing Cafe 27 Barnard Street Savannah GA   912-790-9464
http://www.wildwingcafe.com/
This café really is "wild" about chicken wings with 33 tasty flavors; they also have a full bar and outside dining. Dogs are allowed at the outer tables; they must be leashed and cleaned up after at all times.

Snellville

Stores
Petco Pet Store 1630 Scenic Highway SW Snellville GA   770-972-9995
Your licensed and well-behaved leashed dog is allowed in the store.

Springfield

Campgrounds and RV Parks
Dynasty Canine Training Facility and RV Park 3554 H 21N Springfield GA   912-754-4834
http://www.dynastyrvpark.com
Dogs of all sizes are allowed. There are no additional pet fees. Dogs may not be left unattended outside, and they must be in at dusk. Dogs must be quiet, well behaved, leashed, and cleaned up after. The Park provides wading pools for your pets in the Summer, and there are 2 fenced in areas where dogs can be off lead. The camping and tent areas also allow dogs. There is a dog walk area at the campground. There are special amenities given to dogs at this campground.

St Marys

Accommodations
Best Western Kings Bay Inn 1353 Hwy 40 East Kingsland GA   912-729-7666 (800-780-7234)
Dogs are allowed for an additional fee of $9 per night per pet.
Comfort Inn 111 Edenfield Road Kingsland GA   912-729-6979 (877-424-6423)
Dogs are allowed for an additional fee of $10 per night per pet.
Super 8 Kingsland/Kings Bay Area 120 Edenfield Dr Kingsland GA   912-729-6888 (800-800-8000)
Dogs of all sizes are allowed. There is a $5 per night pet fee per pet. Smoking and non-smoking rooms are available for pet rooms.

Campgrounds and RV Parks
Jacksonville N/Kingsland KOA 2970 Scrubby Buff Road Kingsland GA   912-729-3232 (800-562-5220)
http://www.koa.com
Dogs of all sizes are allowed. There are no additional pet fees. Dogs may not be left unattended outside, and they must be leashed and cleaned up after. The camping and tent areas also allow dogs. There is a dog walk area at the campground. Dogs are allowed in the camping cabins.

Attractions
Crooked River State Park 6222 Charlie Smith Sr. Highway St Marys GA   912- 882--5256

http://www.gastateparks.org
Dogs on leash are allowed in this state park. They are allowed in some of the cabins for a fee of $40 per pet (limit 2 dogs). They are also allowed in the campgrounds. The park features canoeing, saltwater fishing, hiking, picnicing, swimming, and more.

Parks
Cumberland Island National Seashore P. O. Box 806 St Marys GA   912-882-4336 ext. 254
http://www.nps.gov/cuis/
The 50+ miles of hiking trails on this beautiful forested island takes visitors through a variety of natural habitats abundant with marine/bird/wildlife, historic areas, open fields, and by various waterways and beaches. Dogs are allowed on the island; however, they are not allowed in campgrounds or on the ferry to the island. Dogs are not allowed in buildings or swimming areas; they must be on no more than a 6 foot leash at all times; they may not be left unattended at any time, and they must be cleaned up after.

St Simons Island

Vacation Home Rentals
Beachview House 537 Beachview Drive St Simons Island GA   603-524-4000
http://www.beachviewhouse.com/
This historic 1892 House on Cumberland Island offers a fully fenced in yard, 3 bedrooms, 4 baths and sleeps up to 9. Pets are welcome with prior approval.

Attractions
Fort Frederica National Monument 6515 Frederica Road St Simons GA   912-638-3639
http://www.nps.gov/fofr/
There are a variety of special events, activities, and educational programs provided at this historic 1700's fort, and it was at this site that the Spanish claim to Georgia ended. Dogs are allowed throughout the grounds; they are not allowed in buildings. Dogs must be leashed and under owner's control/care at all times.

Beaches
Little St. Simons Island Beaches off U.S. 17 St Simons Island GA   912-554-7566
Dogs are allowed, but only during certain hours in the Summer. From Memorial Day through Labor Day, dogs are allowed on the beach before 9:30am and after 4pm. During the rest of the year, dogs are allowed anytime during park hours. Dogs must be on leash and people need to clean up after their pets.
St. Simons Island Beaches off U.S. 17 St Simons Island GA   912-554-7566
Dogs are allowed, but only during certain hours in the Summer. From Memorial Day through Labor Day, dogs are allowed on the beach before 9:30am and after 4pm. During the rest of the year, dogs are allowed anytime during park hours. Dogs must be on leash and people need to clean up after their pets.

Statesboro

Accommodations
Best Western University Inn 1 Jameson Ave Statesboro GA   912-681-7900 (800-780-7234)
Dogs are allowed for an additional fee of $20 per night per pet.

Stockbridge

Accommodations
Motel 6 - Atlanta South - Stockbridge 7233 Davidson Parkway Stockbridge GA   770-389-1142 (800-466-8356)
One well-behaved family pet per room. Guest must notify front desk upon arrival. Guest is liable for any damages. In consideration of all guests, pets must never be left unattended in the guest rooms.
Red Roof Inn - Atlanta Southeast 637 SR 138 West Stockbridge GA   678-782-4100 (800-RED-ROOF)
One well-behaved family pet per room. Guest must notify front desk upon arrival. Guest is liable for any

damages. In consideration of all guests, pets must never be left unattended in the guest rooms.

Suwanee

Accommodations
Best Western Gwinnett Inn 77 Gwinco Boulevard Suwanee GA   770-271-5559 (800-780-7234)
Dogs up to 20 pounds are allowed for an additional pet fee of $15 per night per room; the fee is $20 per night per pet for dogs over 20 pounds.
Comfort Inn 2945 H 317 Suwanee GA   770-945-1608 (877-424-6423)
Dogs are allowed for an additional one time pet fee of $25 per room.
Motel 6 - Suwanee 3103 Lawrenceville Suwanee Road Suwanee GA   770-945-8372 (800-466-8356)
One well-behaved family pet per room. Guest must notify front desk upon arrival. Guest is liable for any damages. In consideration of all guests, pets must never be left unattended in the guest rooms.
Red Roof Inn - Atlanta Suwanee 77 Gwinco Boulevard Suwanee GA   770-271-5559 (800-RED-ROOF)
One well-behaved family pet per room. Guest must notify front desk upon arrival. Guest is liable for any damages. In consideration of all guests, pets must never be left unattended in the guest rooms.

Stores
PetSmart Pet Store 3630 Peachtree Pkwy Suwanee GA   770-814-8723
Your licensed and well-behaved leashed dog is allowed in the store.

Swainsboro

Accommodations
Best Western Bradford Inn 688 S Main Street Swainsboro GA   478-237-2400 (800-780-7234)
Dogs are allowed for an additional fee of $10 per night per pet.

Tallulah Falls

Campgrounds and RV Parks
Tallulah Gorge State Park 338 Jane Hurt Yarn Drive Tallulah Falls GA   706-754-7970 (800-864-7275)
At 2 miles long and about 1000 feet wide, there is some spectacular scenery to view from the many trails and gorge lookouts at this 2,689 acre park; there are interpretive programs, a gift shop, a 63 acre seasonal lake with beaches, and a variety of special events held throughout the year. Dogs are allowed throughout the park and in the campground for no additional fee. Dogs are not allowed on the gorge floor, on any trails accessing the gorge, or on the bridge up to (or on) the Suspension Bridge; they are allowed on the rim trails. Dogs must be leashed and cleaned up after at all times. The camp area offers 50 sites, picnic tables, gaming areas, restrooms, and a dump station. This RV park is closed during the off-season. The camping and tent areas also allow dogs. There is a dog walk area at the campground.

Parks
Tallulah Gorge State Park 338 Jane Hurt Yarn Drive Tallulah Falls GA   706-754-7970 (800-864-7275)
At 2 miles long and about 1000 feet wide, there is some spectacular scenery to view from the many trails and gorge lookouts at this 2,689 acre park; there are interpretive programs, a gift shop, a 63 acre seasonal lake with beaches, and a variety of special events held throughout the year. Dogs are allowed throughout the park and in the campground for no additional fee. Dogs are not allowed on the gorge floor, on any trails accessing the gorge, or on the bridge tup o (or on) the Suspension Bridge; they are allowed on the rim trails. Dogs must be leashed and cleaned up after at all times.

Thomaston

Accommodations

Best Western Thomaston Inn 1207 Hwy 19 N Thomaston GA   706-648-2900 (800-780-7234)
Dogs are allowed for an additional fee of $5 to $10 per night per pet depending on the pet's size.

Thomasville

Accommodations
Comfort Inn 14866 H 19S Thomasville GA   229-228-5555 (877-424-6423)
Dogs are allowed for a $30 refundable deposit.
Days Inn Thomasville 15375 US 19 S Thomasville GA   229-226-6025 (800-329-7466)
Dogs of all sizes are allowed. There is a $10 per night pet fee per pet. Reservations are recommended due to limited rooms for pets.

Thomson

Accommodations
Best Western White Columns Inn 1890 Washington Thomson GA   706-595-8000 (800-780-7234)
Dogs are allowed for an additional fee of $10 per night per pet.
Days Inn Thomson 2658 Cobbham Rd Thomson GA   706-595-2262 (800-329-7466)
Dogs of all sizes are allowed. There is a $10 per night pet fee per pet.

Tifton

Accommodations
Days Inn Tifton 1199 Hwy 82 W Tifton GA   229-382-8505 (800-329-7466)
Dogs of all sizes are allowed. There is a $6 per night pet fee per pet.
Hampton Inn 720 H 319S Tifton GA   229-382-8800
Well behaved dogs of all sizes are allowed. There are no additional pet fees.
Holiday Inn I-75 & US 82W Tifton GA   229-382-6687 (877-270-6405)
Dogs of all sizes are allowed for no additional fee.
Motel 6 - Tifton 579 Old Omega Road Tifton GA   229-388-8777 (800-466-8356)
One well-behaved family pet per room. Guest must notify front desk upon arrival. Guest is liable for any damages. In consideration of all guests, pets must never be left unattended in the guest rooms.
Super 8 Tifton I-75 and W 2nd Street Tifton GA   229-382-9500 (800-800-8000)
Dogs of all sizes are allowed. There is a $5 per night pet fee per pet. Smoking and non-smoking rooms are available for pet rooms.

Campgrounds and RV Parks
Agirama RV Park 1392 Windmill Road Tifton GA   229-386-3344 (800-767-1875)
http://www.agrirama.com
Dogs of all sizes are allowed. There are no additional pet fees. Dogs may not be left unattended outside, and they must be leashed and cleaned up after. This park is along side an 1870's working village. Dogs are not allowed in any of the Museum of Agriculture or village buildings. There is a dog walk area at the campground.
Amy's South Georgia RV Park 4632 Union Road Tifton GA   229-386-8441
http://www.amysrvpark.com
Dogs of all sizes are allowed. There are no additional pet fees. Dogs may not be left unattended outside, and they must be in at night, leashed, and cleaned up after. The camping and tent areas also allow dogs. There is a dog walk area at the campground.

Townsend

Accommodations
Days Inn Townsend RR 4 Box 3130M Townsend GA   912-832-4411 (800-329-7466)

Dogs of all sizes are allowed. There is a $10 per night pet fee per pet.

Trenton

Campgrounds and RV Parks
Lookout Mountain/Chattanooga West KOA 930 Mountain Shadows Drive Trenton GA   706-657-6815 (800-562-1239)
http://www.lookoutmountainkoa.com
Dogs of all sizes are allowed. There are no additional pet fees. Dogs must be leashed and cleaned up after. There are some breed restrictions. The camping and tent areas also allow dogs. There is a dog walk area at the campground. Dogs are allowed in the camping cabins.

Tybee Island

Campgrounds and RV Parks
River's End Campground 915 Polk Street Tybee Island GA   912-786-5518
http://www.riversendcampground.com
Dogs of all sizes are allowed. There are no additional pet fees. Dogs may not be left unattended, or at the beach at any time, and they must be leashed and cleaned up after. The camping and tent areas also allow dogs. There is a dog walk area at the campground.

Off-Leash Dog Parks
Memorial Park Dog Park Butler Avenue/H 80 Tybee Island GA   912-786-4573
http://www.tybeeisland.com/parks.shtml
There is a section set aside at Memorial Park for pets to run off leash. Dogs must be sociable, current on all vaccinations, licensed, and under owner's control/care at all times. Dogs must be leashed when not in designated off-lead areas.

Union City

Accommodations
Motel 6 - Atlanta Airport - Union City 3860 Flatshoals Road Union City GA   770-969-0110 (800-466-8356)
One well-behaved family pet per room. Guest must notify front desk upon arrival. Guest is liable for any damages. In consideration of all guests, pets must never be left unattended in the guest rooms.
Red Roof Inn - Atlanta Union City 6710 Shannon Parkway Union City GA   770-306-7750 (800-RED-ROOF)
One well-behaved family pet per room. Guest must notify front desk upon arrival. Guest is liable for any damages. In consideration of all guests, pets must never be left unattended in the guest rooms.

Valdosta

Accommodations
Best Western King of the Road 1403 N Saint Augustine Road Valdosta GA   229-244-7600 (800-780-7234)
Dogs up to 50 pounds are allowed for an additional pet fee of $10 per night per room.
Days Inn Valdosta Conference Cntr 1827 West Hill Ave Valdosta GA   229-249-8800 (800-329-7466)
Dogs of all sizes are allowed. There is a $5 per night pet fee per pet.
Howard Johnson Express Inn 1330 St. Augustine Rd. Valdosta GA   229-249-8900 (800-446-4656)
Dogs up to 65 pounds are allowed. There is a $5 per day pet fee.
La Quinta Inn & Suites Valdosta 1800 Clubhouse Drive Valdosta GA   229-247-7755 (800-531-5900)
Dogs of all sizes are allowed. There are no additional pet fees. Dogs must be quiet, well behaved, leashed and cleaned up after. Dogs may not be left unattended in the room for long periods, and they are not allowed in the lobby or pool area.
Motel 6 - Valdosta - University 2003 West Hill Avenue Valdosta GA   229-333-0047 (800-466-8356)

One well-behaved family pet per room. Guest must notify front desk upon arrival. Guest is liable for any damages. In consideration of all guests, pets must never be left unattended in the guest rooms.
Quality Inn South 1902 W Hill Avenue Valdosta GA   229-244-4520 (877-424-6423)
Dogs up to 50 pounds are allowed for an additional fee of $8 per night per pet.
Super 8 Valdosta/Conf Center Area 1825 W Hill Ave Valdosta GA   229-249-8000 (800-800-8000)
Dogs of all sizes are allowed. There is a $5 per night pet fee per pet. Smoking and non-smoking rooms are available for pet rooms.

Stores
PetSmart Pet Store 1700 Norman Dr Ste 200 Valdosta GA   229-244-0856
Your licensed and well-behaved leashed dog is allowed in the store.

Vidalia

Accommodations
Days Inn Vidalia 1503 Lyons Hwy 280 East Vidalia GA   912-537-9251 (800-329-7466)
Dogs of all sizes are allowed. There is a $5 per night pet fee per pet.
Holiday Inn Express 2619 E First Street Vidalia GA   912-537-9000 (877-270-6405)
Dogs of all sizes are allowed for no additional fee, and they must be crated when left alone in the room.

Warner Robins

Accommodations
Best Western Inn and Suites 101 Dunbar Rd Byron GA   478-956-3056 (800-780-7234)
Dogs are allowed for an additional fee of $10 per night per pet.
Comfort Inn and Suites 95 S H 247 Warner Robins GA   478-922-7555 (877-424-6423)
Dogs are allowed for an additional one time pet fee of $25 per room.

Stores
PetSmart Pet Store 2730 Watson Rd Warner Robins GA   478-971-3700
Your licensed and well-behaved leashed dog is allowed in the store.

Warner-Robins

Attractions
TOP 200 PLACE **Museum of Aviation** 247 Russell Parkway Warner-Robins GA   478-923-6600
http://www.museumofaviation.org/home.htm
Sitting on 51 scenic acres, this is the 2nd largest museum of Aviation in the US Air Force with hundreds of exhibits and aircraft, plus it is also home to Freedom Park-a beautiful park/play area dedicated to those who have given the ultimate cost for America's freedom. Although dogs are not allowed inside the buildings, there is a large display of aircraft throughout the grounds. Dogs are allowed on leash; they must be well mannered and picked up after.

Washington

Attractions
Callaway Plantation 2160 Lexington Road Washington GA   706-678-7060
http://www.kudcom.com/www/att01.html
This complex of buildings date back to the late 1700's and has well preserved items of life back in those times. It is also rare in that the same family still has control of the estate surrounding the section bequeathed to the city. Dogs are allowed throughout the grounds; they are not allowed in the buildings. Dogs must be leashed and

under owner's control/care at all times.

Waycross

Accommodations
Holiday Inn 1725 Memorial Drive Waycross GA   912-283-4490 (877-270-6405)
Dogs of all sizes are allowed for an additional one time fee of $15 per room.

Woodstock

Stores
PetSmart Pet Store 142 Woodstock Square Ave Woodstock GA   678-445-2741
Your licensed and well-behaved leashed dog is allowed in the store.

Chapter 19

Florida
Dog Travel Guide

Amelia Island

Accommodations

Florida House Inn 22 South 3rd Street Amelia Island FL   800-258-3301 (800-258-3301)
http://www.floridahouseinn.com/
Built in 1857, this registered historic bed and breakfast is located in the heart of the Fernandina Beach Historic District. This dog-friendly inn offers nine comfortable bedrooms and two suites, all with private baths. Six rooms have working fireplaces, two have old fashioned claw-footed tubs and two have large Jacuzzi tubs. All accommodations are air-conditioned and offer access to their spacious porches, perfect for rocking and relaxing. They are located near the Victorian seaport village. Walk through the 30 block historic district. Browse a variety of quaint stores, antique shops and restaurants along Centre Street, the main thoroughfare. There is a $15 per day pet fee. Dogs must be on a flea program.

Campgrounds and RV Parks

Fort Clinch State Park 2601 Atlantic Avenue Fernandina Beach FL   904-277-7274 (800-326-3521)
This park is home to one of the most well preserved 19th century forts in America, and offers deep woods, white sandy beaches, a living history program, and a variety of recreation and trails. Dogs of all sizes are allowed at no additional fee. Dogs may not be left unattended, and they must have current rabies and shot records. Dogs must be on no more than a 6 foot leash, and be cleaned up after. Dogs are not allowed in buildings or on the beaches, but they are allowed on the trails. The camping and tent areas also allow dogs. There is a dog walk area at the campground.

Vacation Home Rentals

Amelia Island Oceanfront Condo 1323 Beach Walker Road Amelia Island FL   904-642-5563
This pet-friendly condo with 1500 square feet is located on the ocean and a few miles from Fernandina Beach.

Beaches

Fernandina City Beach 14th St at the Atlantic Ocean Fernandina Beach FL   904-277-7305
The Fernandina City Beaches allow dogs on leash. The beach is about 2 miles long. Please make sure that you pick up after your dog.

Apalachicola

Accommodations

Rancho Inn 240 Hwy 98 Apalachicola FL   850-653-9435
There is a $6 per day pet charge.
The Gibson Inn Market St and Avenue C Apalachicola FL   850-653-2191
http://www.gibsoninn.com/
Restored in 1983, this historic country inn overlooks the water and St. George Island. Rooms are furnished in period, with four-poster beds, ceiling fans, antique armoires, brass and porcelain bathroom fixtures, and claw-foot tubs. There is a $15 to $25 per night pet fee.

Attractions

St.Vincent Island - Shuttle Services Indian Pass Boat Launch, Hwy C-30B Gulf County FL   850-229-1065
http://www.stvincentisland.com/
Dogs of all sizes are welcome on the Gulf and Bay pleasure cruises. The shuttle is a 24 foot pontoon boat. The shuttle operates daily and is located just west of Apalachicola .

Outdoor Restaurants

Steamer's Raw Bar 518 H 98 W Apalachicola FL   850-653-3474
http://www.steamersrawbar.com/
Steamer's is situated right on the Apalachicola Bay, and they feature a huge array of locally caught fresh seafood. Your pet is welcome to join you at one of the outside tables. Dogs must be well behaved, trained, and

leashed.

Arcadia

Accommodations
Best Western Arcadia Inn 504 South Brevard Ave Arcadia FL   863-494-4884 (800-780-7234)
Dogs are allowed for an additional pet fee of $15 per night per room.

Bonita Springs

Accommodations
Hyatt Regency Coconut Point Resort & Spa 5001 Coconut Road Bonita Springs FL   239-444-1234
Stay at this pet-friendly resort along the south Florida western Gulf Coast. The resort is situated on 26 acres and has a championship golf course, tennis course and numerous swimming pools, bars and restaurants. Dogs up to 50 pounds are welcome to accompany you. There is a $100 reservation fee for pets and a $50 per day additional pet fee. You must provide proof of your dogs rabies, distemper and parvo vaccinations.

Off-Leash Dog Parks
Dog Beach County Road 865 Bonita Beach FL   239-461-7400
Brought about by public demand, this off lead beach area is located at Lover's Key State Park, and only 2 dogs per person at a time are allowed. (Children under 15 are not allowed in the off lead area at any time) Dogs must be friendly to other pets, people, and wildlife. Dogs must be sociable, current on all vaccinations and license, and under owner's control/care at all times. Sanitary stations are on site. Dogs must be leashed when not in designated off-lead areas.

Brooksville

Accommodations
Best Western Brooksville I-75 30307 Cortez Blvd Brooksville FL   352-796-9481 (800-780-7234)
Dogs are allowed for an additional one time fee of $25 per pet.
Days Inn Brooksville 6320 Windmere Rd Brooksville FL   352-796-9486 (800-329-7466)
Dogs of all sizes are allowed. There is a $10 one time per pet fee per visit.

Cape San Blas

Vacation Home Rentals
Cape San Blas - Uncrowded, Pet Friendly Beach & Rentals. Barrier Dunes: Gulf Front, Gated Neighborhood. Cape San Blas FL   770-569-9215
http://www.TheCapeEscape.com
These six vacation rentals are located on a dog-friendly white sandy beach. The vacation rentals are in the gated Barrier Dunes with access to pools, tennis courts and fishing ponds.

Attractions
TOP 200 PLACE **Port St Joe Marina** 340 Marina Drive Port St Joe FL   850-227-9393
http://www.psjmarina.com/
There are some nice walking areas around this marina for you and your pet. There are pontoon boat rentals that dogs are allowed on, or they may join you on the patio at the restaurant, or even in the Ship Store. Dogs must be well behaved, and leashed and cleaned up after at all times.
Seahorse Water Safaris 340 Marina Drive Port St Joe FL   850-227-1099
http://www.seahorsewatersafaris.com/

This company offers tours and boat rentals. Dogs are not allowed on the tours, but they may join you on the pontoon boat rentals. There is no additional fee for the dog. They must be well behaved, leashed, and cleaned up after-please bring your own supplies.

Beaches
TOP 200 PLACE Cape San Blas Barrier Dunes   Cape San Blas FL
This is one of the nicer pet-friendly beaches in Florida. Leashed dogs are allowed year round on the beach which has a number of stations with clean up bags. Please clean up after your dog.

Outdoor Restaurants
Dockside Cafe 342 Marina Drive Port St Joe FL   850-229-52300
This restaurant is located on the waterfront in the Port St Joe Marina, and they are known for featuring the freshest in Gulf seafood. Your pet is welcome to join you at one of the outside tables. Dogs must be well behaved, trained, and leashed. There are also some nice areas for walks around the marina.

Carrabelle

Beaches
Carrabelle Beach Carrabelle Beach Rd Carrabelle FL   850-697-2585
Dogs are allowed on this beach, but the following rules apply. Dogs must be on leash when near sunbathers. In areas where there are no sunbathers, dogs can be off-leash, but must be under direct voice control. Picnic areas and restrooms are available. The beach is located 1.5 miles west of town.

Chattahoochee

Campgrounds and RV Parks
Chattahoochee/Tallahassee W KOA 2309 Flat Circle Road Chattahoochee FL   850-442-6657 (800-562-2153)
http://www.koa.com
Dogs of all sizes are allowed. There are no additional pet fees. Dogs may not be left unattended outside, and they must be well behaved, leashed, and cleaned up after. There are some breed restrictions. The camping and tent areas also allow dogs. There is a dog walk area at the campground. Dogs are allowed in the camping cabins.

Chiefland

Parks
Lower Suwannee National Wildlife Refuge C.R. 347 Chiefland FL   352-493-0238
This 50,000+ acre refuge is home to over 90 species of birds. The park consists of mostly wetlands and has miles of dog-friendly trails. Dogs must be leashed. There are alligators around, so be careful! The park is located about an hour southwest of Gainesville.

Chipley

Accommodations
Super 8 Chipley 1700 Main Street Chipley FL   850-638-8530 (800-800-8000)
Dogs of all sizes are allowed. There is a $5 per night pet fee per pet. Dogs are not allowed to be left alone in the room. Reservations are recommended due to limited rooms for pets. Smoking and non-smoking rooms are available for pet rooms.

Campgrounds and RV Parks

Falling Waters State Rec Area 1130 State Park Road Chipley FL   850-638-6130 (800-326-3521)
Features of this park are the Sink Hole Trail that takes you along a boardwalk to Florida's highest waterfall, the butterfly garden, and interpretive programs held in their amphitheater. Well behaved dogs of all sizes are allowed at no additional fee. Dogs must have current rabies and shot records, be on no more than a 6 foot leash, and be cleaned up after. Dogs are not allowed in buildings, in the lake, or on the boardwalk to the waterfall. The camping and tent areas also allow dogs. There is a dog walk area at the campground.

Parks
Falling Waters State Park 1130 State Park Rd Chipley FL   850-638-6130
http://www.floridastateparks.org
Dogs on leash are allowed in this park. This park is open 8am-sundown all year round. Dogs are allowed everywhere but on the public beaches and in the bathhouses. The park features a waterfall, butterfly garden, lake, picnic areas, and camping for a fee.

Clearwater

Accommodations
Candlewood Suites 13231 49th Street North Clearwater FL   727-573-3344 (877-270-6405)
Dogs up to 80 pounds are allowed for an additional one time fee of $75 per pet; for dogs over 80 pounds the fee is $150 per pet.
Residence Inn by Marriott 5050 Ulmerton Road Clearwater FL   727-573-4444
Dogs of all sizes are allowed. There is a $75 one time fee per pet and a pet policy to sign at check in.
Super 8 Clearwater/St Pete Airport 13260 34th Street Clearwater FL   727-572-8881 (800-800-8000)
Dogs of all sizes are allowed. There is a $10 per night pet fee per pet. Reservations are recommended due to limited rooms for pets. Smoking and non-smoking rooms are available for pet rooms.
TownePlace Suites St Petersburg Clearwater 13200 49th Street North Clearwater FL   727-299-9229
Dogs of all sizes are allowed. There is a $75 one time pet fee per visit.

Stores
PetSmart Pet Store 26277 US Hwy 19 N Clearwater FL   727-799-3311
Your licensed and well-behaved leashed dog is allowed in the store.
PetSmart Pet Store 2625 Gulf To Bay Clearwater FL   727-725-3755
Your licensed and well-behaved leashed dog is allowed in the store.

Off-Leash Dog Parks
Sand Key Park Paw Playground 1060 Gulf Blvd. Clearwater FL   727-588-4852
This leash free dog park is fully fenced with amenities like cooling stations complete with showers and dog-level water fountains. People need to clean up after their pets and all dogs must be on a leash when outside of the Paw Playground area. Sand Key Park is located south of Cleveland Street, on Gulf Blvd.

Clermont

Accommodations
Howard Johnson Inn & Even Par Pub 20329 US Hwy 27 Clermont FL   352-429-9033 (800-446-4656)
Dogs of all sizes are welcome. There is a $25 per visit pet fee.

Campgrounds and RV Parks
Lake Louisa State Park 7305 H 27 Clermont FL   352-394-3969 (800-326-3521)
Lake Louisa has 6 lakes, is a part of a chain of 13 lakes connected by the Palatlakaha River, has over 20 miles of hiking trails and a variety of land and water activities. Dogs of all sizes are allowed at no additional fee. Dogs must have current rabies and shot records, be on no more than a 6 foot leash, and be cleaned up after. Dogs are not allowed in or around buildings, but they are allowed on the trails. The camping and tent areas also allow dogs. There is a dog walk area at the campground.

Vacation Home Rentals

Secluded Sunsets 10616 South Phillips Road Clermont FL   352-429-0512 (866-839-2180)
http://www.secludedsunsets.com
This is a pet friendly duplex on Pine Island Lake. It has a two bedroom unit sleeping up to 6 adults and 3 pets and a one bedroom unit sleeping up to 4 adults and 2 pets overlooking a central Florida spring fed lake. Pet fees are $5 per pet per night. Amenities include a Hot tub, 4 person paddle boat, 2 person canoe, gas and charcoal grills, fire pit area for evening campfires, swimming, fishing, satellite TV and fully furnished kitchens.

Crestview

Accommodations
Days Inn Crestview 4255 S Ferdon Blvd Crestview FL   850-682-8842 (800-329-7466)
Dogs of all sizes are allowed. There is a $10 per night pet fee per pet.
Super 8 Crestview 3925 S Ferdon blvd Crestview FL   850-682-9649 (800-800-8000)
Dogs of all sizes are allowed. There is a $5 per night pet fee per pet. Smoking and non-smoking rooms are available for pet rooms.

Crystal River

Accommodations
Best Western Crystal River Resort 614 NW Hwy 19 Crystal River FL   352-795-3171 (800-780-7234)
Dogs are allowed for an additional fee of $3 per night per pet. Dogs may not be left alone in the room.
Days Inn Crystal River 2380 NW Hwy 19 Crystal River FL   352-795-2111 (800-329-7466)
Dogs of all sizes are allowed. There is a $10 per night pet fee per pet.
Park Inn Homosassa Springs 4076 S Suncoast Blvd Homosassa FL   352-628-4311
Dogs of all sizes are allowed. There is a $15 per day additional pet fee.

Campgrounds and RV Parks
Rock Crusher Canyon Park 275 S Rock Crusher Road Crystal River FL   352-795-1313
http://www.rccrvpark.com
Dogs of all sizes are allowed. There are no additional pet fees. Dogs must be leashed and cleaned up after. The camping and tent areas also allow dogs. There is a dog walk area at the campground.

Attractions
Crystal River State Archeological Site 3400 N. Museum Point Crystal River FL   352-795-3817
This six-mound complex was built by a cultural group called the pre-Colombian mound builders. It is considered one of the longest continually occupied sites in Florida. For 1,600 years, beginning around 200 B.C., these 14 acres were an imposing prehistoric ceremonial center for Florida's Native Americans. Dogs are not allowed in the visitor center or on the mounds, but they are allowed on the paved trail. Dogs must be leashed. This archeological site is located on the west coast of Florida.
Sunshine River Boat Tours 10330 West Yulce Dr Homosassa FL   866-645-5727
http://www.sunshinerivertours.com
Well-behaved leashed dogs are allowed on the boat tours. Open 7 days a week year round. boats tour the Crystal River, which is filled with manatees that you may be able to pet.

Parks
Crystal River Archaeological State Park 3400 N. Museum Point Crystal River FL   352-795-3817
This park is open from 8 a.m. until sundown, 365 days a year. Visitor center/museum hours are 9:00 a.m. to 5:00 p.m. daily. Designated a National Historic Landmark, this 61-acre, pre-Colombian, Native American site has six burial mounds, temple/platform mounds, a plaza area, and the site contains domestic refuse and ancient household artifacts, indicative of long-term human occupation. The park also sits on the edge of an expansive coastal marsh for saltwater and freshwater fishing, and it is part of the Great Florida Birding Trail. Dogs of all sizes are allowed at no additional fee. Dogs must be on a 6 foot leash or a retractable leash, and they must be cleaned up. Dogs on lead are allowed on the trails.
Crystal River Preserve State Park 3266 Sailboat Avenue Crystal River FL   352-563-0450
A place of exceptional natural beauty, this park is especially cherished by nature lovers and photographers. You can hike or bicycle along nine miles of trails or enjoy the two-and-a-half mile interpretive trail. They have very active interpretive/education programs and will continue to expand this in addition to adding new exhibits to the

visitors' center. Dogs of all sizes are allowed at no additional fee. Dogs must be on no more than a 6 foot leash at all times, and cleaned up after. Dogs are allowed on the trails, but they are not allowed anywhere by the water due to alligators.

Daytona Beach

Accommodations
La Quinta Inn Daytona Beach 2725 International Speedway Daytona Beach FL   386-255-7412 (800-531-5900)
Dogs of all sizes are allowed. There are no additional pet fees. Dogs must be leashed and cleaned up after.
Quality Inn Ocean Palms 2323 S Atlantic Avenue Daytona Beach FL   386-255-0476 (877-424-6423)
Dogs are allowed for an additional pet fee of $10 per night per room.
Super 8 Daytona Beach/Speedway Area 2992 W International Speedway Blvd Daytona Beach FL   386-253-0643 (800-800-8000)
Dogs of all sizes are allowed. There is a $10 per night pet fee per pet. Reservations are recommended due to limited rooms for pets. Smoking and non-smoking rooms are available for pet rooms.
Sand Castle Motel 3619 S Atlantic Avenue Daytona Beach Shores FL   386-767-3182
There is only one dog friendly room and dogs of all sizes are allowed. There is a $15 per room additional pet fee.
Holiday Inn 350 International Speedway Blvd Deland FL   386-738-5200 (877-270-6405)
Dogs up to about 65 pounds are allowed for an additional one time pet fee of $25 per room. Dogs must be crated or removed for housekeeping.
Howard Johnson Express Inn 2801 E. New York Ave. Deland FL   386-736-3440 (800-446-4656)
Dogs of all sizes are welcome. There is a $10 per day pet fee.
Days Inn Daytona/Ormond Beach 1608 N US Hwy 1 Ormond Beach FL   386-672-7341 (800-329-7466)
Dogs of all sizes are allowed. There is a $5 per night pet fee per pet.

Campgrounds and RV Parks
Bulow Plantation RV Resort 3345 Old Kings Road S Flagler Beach FL   800-782-8569
http://www.rvonthego.com
Dogs of all sizes are allowed. There are no additional pet fees. Dogs must be quiet, well behaved, leashed, and cleaned up after. There are some breed restrictions. The camping and tent areas also allow dogs. There is a dog walk area at the campground.
Daytona North RV Resort 1701 H 1 Ormond Beach FL   877-277-8737
http://www.rvonthego.com
Dogs of all sizes are allowed. There are no additional pet fees. Dogs must be leashed and cleaned up after. The camping and tent areas also allow dogs. There is a dog walk area at the campground.
Tomoka State Park 2099 N Beach Street Ormond Beach FL   386-676-4050 (800-326-3521)
This park protects a variety of wildlife habitats and endangered species and over 160 bird species. It boasts a nature trail, a museum, and a variety of land and water recreation. Dogs of all sizes are allowed at no additional fee. Dogs may not be left unattended, and they must have current rabies and shot records. Dogs must be on no more than a 6 foot leash, and be cleaned up after. Dogs are not allowed in buildings or on the beach. Dogs are allowed on the trails. The camping and tent areas also allow dogs. There is a dog walk area at the campground.
Daytona Beach Campground 4601 Clyde Morris Blvd Port Orange FL   386-761-2663
http://www.rvdaytona.com
Dogs of all sizes are allowed. There are no additional pet fees. Dogs may not be left unattended outside or in tents, and they must be quiet, leashed, and cleaned up after. There is a dog walk area just outside of the park. There are some breed restrictions. The camping and tent areas also allow dogs.

Vacation Home Rentals
EastWind Villas   New Smyrna Beach FL   386-428-1387
http://www.newsmyrnabeachvillas.com
Five pet-friendly vacation rentals are available near the beach . High speed Internet access is available in the rentals. There are no weight restrictions for dogs and each vacation rental allows up to two pets. Dogs must be on a flea program.

Stores
PetSmart Pet Store 1900 W International Speedway Blvd Daytona Beach FL   386-254-7555
Your licensed and well-behaved leashed dog is allowed in the store.
Petco Pet Store 2500 West International Speedway B #900 Daytona Beach FL   386-239-7191
Your licensed and well-behaved leashed dog is allowed in the store.

Beaches
Smyrna Dunes Park Highway 1 New Smyrna Beach FL   386-424-2935
Dogs are not allowed on the ocean beach, but are allowed almost everywhere else, including on the inlet beach and river. Bottle-nosed dolphins are typically seen in the inlet as well as the ocean. Dogs must be leashed and people need to clean up after their pets. The park is located on the north end of New Smyrna Beach.
Lighthouse Point Park A1A Ponce Inlet FL   386-239-7873
You might see some dolphins along the shoreline at this park. The park is also frequented by people watching a space shuttle launch out of Cape Canaveral. If you go during a shuttle launch, be sure to hold on tight to your pooch, as the shuttles can become very, very noisy and loud. Dogs on leash are allowed at the park and on the beach. Please clean up after your dog. This park is located at the southern point of Ponce Inlet.

Off-Leash Dog Parks
Barkley Square Dog Park 1010 N Ridgewood Avenue Deland FL   386-736-5953
http://www.volusia.org/parks/barkley.htm
There are 14 acres at this off lead area with separate areas for large and small dogs, training events, and time out spaces. There are shade trees and a pond in the large dog area as well as benches, watering stations, and restrooms. Dogs must be sociable, current on all vaccinations and license, and under owner's control/care at all times. Dogs must be leashed when not in designated off-lead areas.

Outdoor Restaurants
Lighthouse Landing 4940 S Peninsula Ponce Inlet FL   386-761-9271
This restaurant serves American and seafood. Dogs are allowed at the outdoor tables.

De Funiak Springs

Accommodations
Days Inn De Funiak Springs 472 Hugh Adams Rd De Funiak Springs FL   850-892-6115 (800-329-7466)
Dogs of all sizes are allowed. There is a $10 per night pet fee per pet.
Super 8 De Funiak Springs 402 Hugh Adams Rd De Funiak Springs FL   850-892-1333 (800-800-8000)
Dogs of all sizes are allowed. There is a $10 per night pet fee per small pet and $25 per large pet. Smoking and non-smoking rooms are available for pet rooms.

Destin

Accommodations
Days Inn Destin 1029 Hwy 98 E Destin FL   850-837-2599 (800-329-7466)
Dogs of all sizes are allowed. There is a $20 per night pet fee per pet.
Extended StayAmerica Destin - US 98 - Emerald Coast Pkwy. 4615 Opa Locka Lane Destin FL   850-837-9830
There is a one time pet fee of $25.00 for one night stays, $50.00 for two night stays, and $75.00 for any stay of three nights or longer.
Motel 6 - Destin 405 Highway 98 E #A Destin FL   850-837-0007 (800-466-8356)
One well-behaved family pet per room. Guest must notify front desk upon arrival. Guest is liable for any damages. In consideration of all guests, pets must never be left unattended in the guest rooms.
Fairway Inn 203 Miracle Strip Pkwy. Fort Walton Beach FL   850-244-8663
There is a $25 one time pet fee.
Rodeway Inn 314 Miracle Strip Parkway Fort Walton Beach FL   850-243-6162
Dogs of all sizes are allowed. There is a $10 plus tax per night per pet additional fee.
Comfort Inn 101 H 85N Niceville FL   850-678-8077 (877-424-6423)
Dogs of all sizes are allowed. There is a $10 per night per pet fee and a pet policy to sign at check in.

Campgrounds and RV Parks
Camping on the Gulf 1005 Emerald Coast Parkway Destin FL   877-226-7485
http://www.campgulf.com
Dogs of all sizes are allowed. There are no additional pet fees. Dogs may not be left unattended outside, and

they must be leashed and cleaned up after. There is a large fine levied for dogs on the beach. The camping and tent areas also allow dogs. There is a dog walk area at the campground.
Destin RV Beach Resort 362 Miramar Beach Drive Destin FL   877-737-3529
http://www.destinrvresort.com
Dogs of all sizes are allowed. There are no additional pet fees. Dogs must be leashed and cleaned up after. The dogs may be walked on the grass just outside of the park.
Henderson Beach State Park 17000 Emerald Coast Parkway Destin FL   850-837-7550 (800-326-3521)
Land and water recreation is offered here with about 6000 feet of white sandy beaches, a boardwalk, and nature trails. Quiet and well behaved dogs of all sizes are allowed at no additional fee. Dogs may not be left unattended at any time, and they must have current rabies and shot records. Dogs must be on no more than a 6 foot leash, and be cleaned up after. Dogs are not allowed in buildings, on the beach, or on the Boardwalk. Dogs are allowed on all the trails. The camping and tent areas also allow dogs. There is a dog walk area at the campground.

Stores
PetSmart Pet Store 34940 Emerald Coast Pkwy Unit 160 Destin FL   850-650-3145
Your licensed and well-behaved leashed dog is allowed in the store.

Dog Island

Beaches
Dog Island Park Dog Island FL 850-697-2585
This island is a small remote island that is accessible only by boat, ferry or airplane. Dogs are allowed on the beach, but must be on leash. There are some areas of Dog Island that are within a nature conservancy and dogs are not allowed in these areas. Dog owners will be fined in the nature conservatory. This island is south of Carrabelle.

Dunnellon

Parks
Rainbow Springs State Park 19158 Southwest 81st Place Rd Dunnellon FL   352-465-8555
http://www.floridastateparks.org
Dogs on leash are allowed in this park. They are not allowed in public beach areas or bathhouses. Open 8am-sundown all year round. There is a fee for this park which features picnic tables, boating, tubing, and more.

Elkton

Accommodations
Comfort Inn 2625 H 207 Elkton FL   904-829-3435 (877-424-6423)
Dogs are allowed for an additional pet fee of $10 per night per room.

Flagler Beach

Accommodations
Topaz Motel 1224 S Oceanshore Blvd Flagler Beach FL   386-439-3301
Dogs of all sizes are allowed. Cats are not allowed. There is a $10 per stay per room additional pet fee.
Whale Watch Motel 2448 S Oceanshore Blvd Flagler Beach FL   386-439-2545
There is a $10 per day pet fee. They have a few non-smoking pet rooms.

Campgrounds and RV Parks
Beverly Beach Campground 2816 N Ocean Shore Blvd Flagler Beach FL   800-255-2706
http://www.beverlybeachcampground.com
Dogs of all sizes are allowed. There are no additional pet fees. Dogs must be quiet, leashed, and cleaned up

after. Dogs may not be left unattended outside. They ask that dogs be walked just outside of the park, and they are allowed at the beach. The camping and tent areas also allow dogs.

Gamble Rogers Memorial State Recreation Area 3100 S A1A (Ocean Shore Blvd) Flagler Beach FL 386-517-2086 (800-326-3521)
This park is tucked between the Intra-coastal Waterway and the Atlantic Ocean with the beach being the popular draw, and there is also a nature trail and boat ramp. Dogs of all sizes are allowed at no additional fee. Dogs may not be left unattended, and they must have current rabies and shot records. Dogs must be on no more than a 6 foot leash, and be cleaned up after. Dogs are not allowed in buildings or on the beach, but they are allowed on the trails. The camping and tent areas also allow dogs. There is a dog walk area at the campground.

Beaches
Flagler Beach A1A Flagler Beach FL 386-517-2000
Dogs are allowed north of 10th Street and south of 10th Street. They are not allowed on or near the pier at 10th Street. Dogs must be on leash and people need to clean up after their dogs.

Fort Myers

Accommodations
Quality Hotel Nautilus 1538 Cape Coral Parkway Cape Coral FL 239-542-2121
Dogs up to 50 pounds are allowed for an additional pet fee of $16.65 per night per room.
Best Western Springs Resort 18051 South Tamiami Trail Hwy 41 Fort Myers FL 239-267-7900 (800-780-7234)
One dog is allowed for a pet fee of $15 per night; a 2nd dog is an additional $5 per night.
Country Inns & Suites by Carlson 13901 Shell Point Plaza Fort Myers FL 239-454-9292
Dogs of all sizes are allowed. There is a $10 per day additional pet fee up to a maximum of $50 per stay.
Econolodge North 13301 N Cleveland Fort Myers FL 239-995-0571
Dogs of all sizes are allowed. There is a $5.35 per night per pet fee and a pet policy to sign at check in.
Holiday Inn Fort Myers Downtown Historic 2431 Cleveland Ave. Fort Myers FL 239-332-3232 (877-270-6405)
Dogs of all sizes are allowed for an additional one time pet fee of $75 per room.
Howard Johnson Express Inn 13000 North Cleveland Ave. Fort Myers FL 239-656-4000 (800-446-4656)
Dogs of all sizes are welcome. There is a $10 per day pet fee per pet.
Howard Johnson Inn 4811 Cleveland Ave. Fort Myers FL 239-936-3229 (800-446-4656)
Dogs of all sizes are welcome. There is a $25 pet fee every 3 days.
La Quinta Inn Fort Myers 4850 S. Cleveland Ave. Fort Myers FL 239-275-3300 (800-531-5900)
One dog of any size is allowed. There are no additional pet fees. Dogs may not be left unattended, and they must be leashed and cleaned up after.
Motel 6 - Ft Myers 3350 Marinatown Lane Fort Myers FL 239-656-5544 (800-466-8356)
One well-behaved family pet per room. Guest must notify front desk upon arrival. Guest is liable for any damages. In consideration of all guests, pets must never be left unattended in the guest rooms.
Residence Inn by Marriott 2960 Colonial Blvd Fort Myers FL 239-936-0110
Pets of all sizes are allowed. There is a $75 one time fee and a pet policy to sign at check in.

Campgrounds and RV Parks
Koreshan State Historic Site Corner of H 41 and Corkscrew Road Estero FL 239-992-0311 (800-326-3521)
Guided or self-guided tours are offered here as well as a variety of recreational pursuits. Dogs of all sizes are allowed at no additional fee. Dogs may not be left unattended for more than 15 minutes if outside, and they must have current rabies and shot records. Dogs must be on no more than a 6 foot leash, and be cleaned up after. Dogs are not allowed in buildings, but they are allowed on the trails. The camping and tent areas also allow dogs. There is a dog walk area at the campground.
Indian Creek RV Resort 17340 San Carlos Blvd Fort Myers Beach FL 800-828-6992
http://www.sunresorts.com
Dogs of all sizes are allowed. There are no additional pet fees. Dogs may not be left unattended outside, and they must be leashed and cleaned up after. There are some breed restrictions. There is a dog walk area at the campground.
North Fort Myers RV Resort (Pioneer Village) 7974 Samville Road North Fort Myers FL 239-543-3303 (877-897-3757)
http://www.rvonthego.com
Dogs of all sizes are allowed. There are no additional pet fees. Dogs must be leashed and cleaned up after. The camping and tent areas also allow dogs. There is a dog walk area at the campground.

Fort Myers/Pine Island KOA 5120 Stringfellow Road St James City FL   239-283-2415 (800-562-8505)
http://www.pineislandkoa.com
Dogs of all sizes are allowed. There is a $5 per night per pet additional fee. Dogs may not be left unattended outside, and only inside if they will be quiet and well behaved. Dogs must be leashed and cleaned up after. The camping and tent areas also allow dogs. There is a dog walk area at the campground. Dogs are allowed in the camping cabins.

Attractions

TOP 200 PLACE Manatee World Boat Tours 5605 Palm Beach Blvd Fort Myers FL 239-693-1434
http://www.manateeworld.com/
These excursions take you on a narrated ecological cruise into a natural wildlife habitat featuring many of Florida's most beautiful birds, plants, and animals in their native surroundings, with focus on the endangered manatees. Up to 2 well behaved, friendly, dogs are allowed for no additional fee. Dogs must be leashed. The tours usually run through the Winter months, and not through the Summer when the manatees are not visible.

Stores

PetSmart Pet Store 8006 Mediterranean Dr Bldg 13 Estero FL   239-948-3581
Your licensed and well-behaved leashed dog is allowed in the store.
PetSmart Pet Store 5013 S Cleveland Ave Fort Myers FL   239-277-9890
Your licensed and well-behaved leashed dog is allowed in the store.
Petco Pet Store 13741 South Tamiami Trail Unit 2 Fort Myers FL   239-466-3737
Your licensed and well-behaved leashed dog is allowed in the store.

Beaches

TOP 200 PLACE Dog Beach Estero Blvd/H 865 Fort Myers Beach FL   239-461-7400
Located just north of the New Pass Bridge, this barrier island beach offers a perfect off-leash area for beach-lov'in pups.This beach is actually in Bonita Beach on the city line with Fort Myers Beach. Dogs are allowed in designated areas only, and they must be licensed, immunized, and non-aggressive to people, other pets, or wildlife. Dogs may not be left unattended at any time, and they must be under owner's control/care at all times; clean-up stations are provided. Two healthy dogs are allowed per person over 15 years old. Dogs on Fort Myers Beach must be leashed at all times.
Fort Myers Dog Beach 3410 Palm Beach Blvd Fort Myers Beach FL   239-461-7400
Dogs are allowed off leash on this section of the beach. Cleanup stations are provided. Must have a copy of health records with you at all times. The beach is run by Lees County Parks and Recreation.
Lee County Off-Leash Dog Beach Park Route 865 Fort Myers Beach FL
Dogs are allowed off-leash at this beach. Please clean up after your dog and stay within the dog park boundaries. Dog Beach is located south of Ft. Myers Beach and north of Bonita Beach on Route 865. Parking is available near New Pass Bridge.

Off-Leash Dog Parks

Estero Community Dog Park 9200 Corkscrew Palms Blvd Estero FL   239-498-0415
Although dogs are not allowed in the rest of the park, they can have a lot of fun at this fenced play area. There are separate sections for large and small dogs. Dogs must be sociable, current on all vaccinations, licensed, and cleaned up after at all times. Dogs must be leashed when not in designated off-lead areas.
K-9 Corral at Estero Park 9200 Corkscrew Palms Blvd Estero FL   239-498-0415
This fenced, 2 acre off lead area is located at the southeast corner of the park and there 2 separate areas for small and large dogs, water fountains, large trees for shade, and disposal stations. The dog park is open during regular park hours. Dogs must be sociable, current on all vaccinations and license, and under owner's control/care at all times. Dogs must be leashed when not in designated off-lead areas.
Buckingham Community Park and Barkingham Dog Park 9800 Buckingham Rd Fort Myers FL   239-338-3288
http://www.leeparks.org/
In addition to the community park providing a long list of recreational opportunities, this was the county's first off lead dog area. The off lead area has park benches, watering holes, a doggie shower, agility equipment, a separate small dog area, a disposal station, and shaded areas. Dogs are allowed throughout the rest of the park on leash unless otherwise noted; they are not allowed in the ponds. Dogs may not be left alone at any time, and they must be well behaved, under owner's control at all times, licensed, vaccinated, and cleaned up after.
Pooch Park 1297 Driftwood Drive North Fort Myers FL   239-656-7748
Located in Judd Park, this fenced off lead area has 2 separate areas for small and large dogs, water for hounds and humans, and disposal stations. The dog park is open during regular park hours. Dogs must be sociable, current on all vaccinations and license, and under owner's control/care at all times. Dogs must be leashed when

not in designated off-lead areas.

Outdoor Restaurants
Parrot Key Caribbean Grill 2500 Main Street Fort Myers Beach FL 239-463-3257
http://www.myparrotkey.com/
Specializing in a variety of Caribbean cuisine, this restaurant also provides live entertainment, a full bar, and outside dining. Dogs are allowed at the outer tables; they must be leashed and under owner's control/care at all times.

Fort Pierce

Accommodations
Motel 6 - Ft Pierce 2500 Peters Road Fort Pierce FL 772-461-9937 (800-466-8356)
One well-behaved family pet per room. Guest must notify front desk upon arrival. Guest is liable for any damages. In consideration of all guests, pets must never be left unattended in the guest rooms.
Royal Inn 222 Hernando Street Fort Pierce FL 561-464-0405
http://www.royalinnbeach.com
There are no additional pet fees. Pets must be well-behaved. The hotel has limited pet rooms. Please call ahead to reserve a pet room.

Beaches
Fort Pierce Inlet State Park 905 Shorewinds Drive Fort Pierce FL 772-468-3985
Dogs are not allowed on the ocean beach, but they are allowed on the cove beach. Pets must be leashed and people need to clean up after their pets. The park is located four miles east of Ft. Pierce, via North Causeway.

Parks
Heathcote Botanical Gardens 210 Savannah Rd Fort Pierce FL 772-464-4672
Well-behaved leashed dogs are welcome to walk with you on the self-guided tour of the botanical gardens. The 3.5 acre garden has orchid trees, over 40 species of palm trees, beds of ornamental annuals and an herb garden. Just remember to clean up after your pooch!

Gainesville

Accommodations
Best Western Gateway Grand 4200 NW 97th Blvd Gainesville FL 352-331-3336 (800-780-7234)
Dogs are allowed for an additional pet fee of $20 per night per room.
Comfort Inn 2435 SW 13th Street Gainesville FL 352-373-6500 (877-424-6423)
Dogs are allowed for an additional fee of $10 per night per pet.
Days Inn Gainesville/I-75 7516 Newberry Rd Gainesville FL 352-332-3033 (800-329-7466)
Dogs of all sizes are allowed. There is a $7 per night pet fee per pet.
La Quinta Inn Gainesville 920 N.W. 69th Terrace Gainesville FL 352-332-6466 (800-531-5900)
Dogs of all sizes are allowed. There are no additional pet fees. Dogs must be leashed and cleaned up after. Dogs must be crated or removed for housekeeping.
Magnolia Plantation Bed and Breakfast 305 SE 7th Street Gainesville FL 352-375-6653 (800-201-2379)
http://www.magnoliabnb.com
The Magnolia Plantation has 6 private historic cottages located within walking distance of downtown Gainesville. It is surrounded by 1.5 acres of lush gardens. They have no pet fees or weight restrictions, and only require that pets be kept on a leash while wandering around the property. Pets are not permitted in the main house but are allowed in one of the six cottages.
Motel 6 - Gainesville - Univ. of Florida 4000 SW 40th Boulevard Gainesville FL 352-373-1604 (800-466-8356)
One well-behaved family pet per room. Guest must notify front desk upon arrival. Guest is liable for any damages. In consideration of all guests, pets must never be left unattended in the guest rooms.
Red Roof Inn - Gainesville, FL 3500 SW 42nd Street Gainesville FL 352-336-3311 (800-RED-ROOF)
One well-behaved family pet per room. Guest must notify front desk upon arrival. Guest is liable for any damages. In consideration of all guests, pets must never be left unattended in the guest rooms.

Stores
PetSmart Pet Store 3736 SW Archer Rd Gainesville FL   352-380-0112
Your licensed and well-behaved leashed dog is allowed in the store.
Petco Pet Store 6869 West Newberry Rd Gainesville FL   352-331-2504
Your licensed and well-behaved leashed dog is allowed in the store.

Hobe Sound

Campgrounds and RV Parks
Jonathan Dickinson State Park 16450 SE Federal H (H 1) Hobe Sound FL   772-546-2771 (800-326-3521)
This park is Florida's first federally designated Wild and Scenic River, and is home to abundant wildlife in 13
natural communities. Dogs of all sizes are allowed at no additional fee. Dogs may not be left unattended, and
they must have current rabies and shot records. Dogs must be on no more than a 6 foot leash, and be cleaned
up after. Dogs are not allowed in buildings or any public swimming areas. The camping and tent areas also allow
dogs. There is a dog walk area at the campground.

Holt

Campgrounds and RV Parks
Blackwater River State Park 7720 Deaton Bridge Road Holt FL   850-983-5363 (800-326-3521)
This park was certified as a Registered State Natural Feature for their preserving and representation of the
natural history of Florida. Dogs of all sizes are allowed at no additional fee. Dogs may not be left unattended, and
they must have current rabies and shot records. Dogs must be on no more than a 6 foot leash, and be cleaned
up after. Dogs are not allowed in buildings or at the beaches. Dogs are allowed on the trails, including the Chain
O'Lakes Trail. The camping and tent areas also allow dogs. There is a dog walk area at the campground.

Islamorada

Attractions
Theatre of the Sea 84721 H 1, MM 84.5 H 1 Islamorada FL   305-664-2431
This educational and entertaining marine animal park is a pioneer in animal interactive programs, where
performances are up close, and where marine animals live in natural salt-water lagoons, and lush, tropical
gardens. Theater of the Sea is open 365 days a year. The ticket counter opens at 9:30 a.m. EST daily. Dogs of
any size are allowed for no additional fee, and they must be well behaved, leashed at all times, and cleaned up
after. Dogs may not go anywhere near the parrots or the Parrot Theater.

Jacksonville

Accommodations
Candlewood Suites 4990 Belfort Road Jacksonville FL   904-296-7785 (877-270-6405)
Dogs of all sizes are allowed for an additional pet fee of $75 for 1 to 14 nights, and $150 for 15 or more nights
per room.
Hampton Inn 1170 Airport Entrance Road Jacksonville FL   904-741-4980
Well behaved dogs of all sizes are allowed. There are no additional pet fees.
Homewood Suites 8737 Baymeadows Rd Jacksonville FL   904-733-9299 (800-555-0807)
There is a $75 one time pet fee.
La Quinta Inn Jacksonville Airport North 812 Dunn Ave. Jacksonville FL   904-751-6960 (800-531-5900)
Dogs of all sizes are allowed. There are no additional pet fees. Dogs are not allowed to go through the lobby
during food service hours. Dogs may only be left unattended if they are crated and will be quiet. Dogs must be
leashed and cleaned up after.
La Quinta Inn Jacksonville Baymeadows 8255 Dix Ellis Trail Jacksonville FL   904-731-9940 (800-531-5900)
Dogs of all sizes are allowed. There are no additional pet fees. Dogs must be leashed and cleaned up after.

La Quinta Inn Jacksonville Orange Park 8555 Blanding Blvd Jacksonville FL   904-778-9539 (800-531-5900)
Dogs of all sizes are allowed. There are no additional pet fees. Dogs must be leashed and cleaned up after, and removed or crated for housekeeping.
Motel 6 - Jacksonville - Orange Park 6107 Youngerman Circle Jacksonville FL   904-777-6100 (800-466-8356)
One well-behaved family pet per room. Guest must notify front desk upon arrival. Guest is liable for any damages. In consideration of all guests, pets must never be left unattended in the guest rooms.
Motel 6 - Jacksonville Airport 10885 Harts Road Jacksonville FL   904-757-8600 (800-466-8356)
One well-behaved family pet per room. Guest must notify front desk upon arrival. Guest is liable for any damages. In consideration of all guests, pets must never be left unattended in the guest rooms.
Motel 6 - Jacksonville Southeast 8285 Dix Ellis Trail Jacksonville FL   904-731-8400 (800-466-8356)
One well-behaved family pet per room. Guest must notify front desk upon arrival. Guest is liable for any damages. In consideration of all guests, pets must never be left unattended in the guest rooms.
Ramada Inn 3130 Hartley Road Jacksonville FL   904-268-8080
Dogs of all sizes are allowed. There is a $100 refundable deposit plus a $50 one time fee per pet and a pet policy to sign at check in.
Red Roof Inn - Jacksonville - Orange Park 6099 Youngerman Circle Jacksonville FL   904-777-1000 (800-RED-ROOF)
One well-behaved family pet per room. Guest must notify front desk upon arrival. Guest is liable for any damages. In consideration of all guests, pets must never be left unattended in the guest rooms.
Red Roof Inn - Jacksonville - Southpoint 6969 Lenoir Avenue East Jacksonville FL   904-296-1006 (800-RED-ROOF)
One well-behaved family pet per room. Guest must notify front desk upon arrival. Guest is liable for any damages. In consideration of all guests, pets must never be left unattended in the guest rooms.
Red Roof Inn - Jacksonville Airport 14701 Airport Entrance Road Jacksonville FL   904-741-4488 (800-RED-ROOF)
One well-behaved family pet per room. Guest must notify front desk upon arrival. Guest is liable for any damages. In consideration of all guests, pets must never be left unattended in the guest rooms.
Residence Inn by Marriott 1310 Airport Road Jacksonville FL   904-741-6550
Dogs of all sizes are allowed. There is a $75 one time fee and a pet policy to sign at check in.
Residence Inn by Marriott 8365 Dix Ellis Trail Jacksonville FL   904-733-8088
Dogs of all sizes are allowed. There is a $75 one time fee and a pet policy to sign at check in. Nearby is Dogwood Park, a 25 acre doggy play area complete with an array of treats and toys, and special digging, running and playing areas.
Residence Inn by Marriott 10551 Deerwood Park Blvd Jacksonville FL   904-996-8900
Dogs of all sizes are allowed. There is a $75 one time fee and a pet policy to sign at check in.
Studio 6 - Jacksonville - Baymeadows 8765 Baymeadows Road Jacksonville FL   904-731-7317 (800-466-8356)
One well-behaved family pet per room. Guest must notify front desk upon arrival. Guest is liable for any damages. In consideration of all guests, pets must never be left unattended in the guest rooms.
Days inn MacClenny 1499 S 6th St MacClenny FL   904-259-5100 (800-DAYS-INN)
Dogs of all sizes are allowed. There is a $10 per night pet fee per pet. Reservations are recommended due to limited rooms for pets.
Comfort Inn 341 Park Avenue Orange Park FL   904-644-4444 (877-424-6423)
Dogs are allowed for an additional fee of $30 per pet for each 1 to 3 days stay.
Sawgrass Marriott Resort, Spa, and Villas 1000 PGA TOUR Blvd Ponte Vedra Beach FL   904-285-7777 (800-457-GOLF (4653))
Dogs of all sizes are allowed at the villas, which are 1 bedroom. There is a $25 per night per pet additional fee or $75 per pet by the week. Dogs must be quiet, leashed, cleaned up after, and a contact number left with the front desk if they are in the room alone. Dogs must be removed or accompanied for housekeeping.

Campgrounds and RV Parks
Little Talbot Island State Park 12157 Heckscher Drive Jacksonville FL   904-251-2320 (800-326-3521)
This park has scenic, historical, biological, and geological sites to explore. They have introduced a new interpretive program of a self-guided auto tour of the area. Dogs of all sizes are allowed at no additional fee. Dogs may not be left unattended, and they must have current rabies and shot records. Dogs must be on no more than a 6 foot leash, and be cleaned up after. Dogs are not allowed in buildings, on beaches, or in the waterways. Dogs are allowed on the trails. The camping and tent areas also allow dogs. There is a dog walk area at the campground.
Flamingo Lake RV Resort 3640 Newcomb Road N Jacksonville FL   904-766-0672
http://www.flamingolake.com
Dogs of all sizes are allowed. There are no additional pet fees. Dogs may not be left unattended outside, and they must be leashed and cleaned up after. There are some breed restrictions. There is a dog walk area at the campground.

Attractions

TOP 200 PLACE Fort Caroline National Memorial 12713 Ft. Caroline Road Jacksonville FL   904-641-7155
http://www.nps.gov/foca/
Fort Caroline National Memorial is located within the Timucuan Ecological and Historic Preserve. The memorial commemorates the short-lived French presence in sixteenth century Florida. French settlers established a colony which comprised of a village, and a small earthen and timber fortification. There are no remains of the original fort, but there is a near full-scale interpretive rendering of the fort which provides information on the history of the French colony. Leashed dogs are allowed in the fort area and on the one mile self-guided loop trail (Hammock Trail) which has interpretive placards along the way that focus on the natural and cultural history of the site. Fort Caroline is located in Jacksonville (Duval County), Florida about 14 miles northeast of downtown.
Playtime Drive-In Theatre Flea Market 6300 Blanding Blvd Jacksonville FL   904-771-9939
Well-behaved, leashed dogs are allowed in the flea market area and the theatre area. Check local ads for movie showings. Open Wednesday-Sunday.

Stores

PetSmart Pet Store 10261 River Marsh Dr Suite 143 Jacksonville FL   904-997-1335
Your licensed and well-behaved leashed dog is allowed in the store.
PetSmart Pet Store 6000 Lake Gray Blvd Jacksonville FL   904-779-4944
Your licensed and well-behaved leashed dog is allowed in the store.
PetSmart Pet Store 356 Monument Rd Jacksonville FL   904-724-4600
Your licensed and well-behaved leashed dog is allowed in the store.
PetSmart Pet Store 8801 Southside Blvd Ste 3 Jacksonville FL   904-519-8878
Your licensed and well-behaved leashed dog is allowed in the store.
PetSmart Pet Store 13141 City Station Dr Unit 113 Jacksonville FL
Your licensed and well-behaved leashed dog is allowed in the store.
Petco Pet Store 11900 Atlantic Blvd #213-218 Jacksonville FL   904-997-8441
Your licensed and well-behaved leashed dog is allowed in the store.
Petco Pet Store 950 Marsh Landing Parkway #145 Jacksonville FL   904-273-0964
Your licensed and well-behaved leashed dog is allowed in the store.

Beaches

Dogwood Park Lake Bow Wow 7407 Salisbury Rd South Jacksonville FL   904-296-3636
http://www.jaxdogs.com
This dog park and beach is great for any size canine. It has 25 acres that are fenced in a 42 acre park. Dogs can be off leash in any part of the park. The park offers picnic tables, a pond for small dogs, a pond for large dogs (Lake Bow Wow), shower for dogs, warm water for dog baths, tennis balls and toys for play, a playground with games for your dogs, trails to walk on, and bag stations for cleanup. Locals can become members for the year for about $24.00 per month or out-of-town visitors can pay about $11 for a one time visit.
Huguenot Memorial Park 10980 Hecksher Drive Jacksonville FL   904-251-3335
Dogs are allowed in the park and on the beach. Dogs must be leashed and people need to clean up after their dogs. The park is located off A1A.
Katheryn Abby Hanna Park Beach 500 Wonderland Dr Jacksonville FL   904-249-4700
http://www.coj.net
Dogs are allowed in this park for camping, hiking, picnics and on the dog friendly beach.

Parks

Katheryn Abby Hanna Park 500 Wonderland Dr Jacksonville FL   904-249-4700
http://www.coj.net
Dogs are allowed in this park for camping, hiking, picnics and on the dog friendly beach.
Timucuan Ecological and Historic Preserve 12713 Fort Caroline Rd Jacksonville FL   904-641-7155
http://www.nps.gov/timu/index.htm
Dogs on leash are allowed in this Historic Preserve. Open year round 9 am-5 pm. The preserve features hiking, fishing, and more.

Off-Leash Dog Parks

Dogwood Park 7407 Salisbury Rd South Jacksonville FL   904-296-3636
http://www.jaxdogs.com
This dog park is great for any size canine. It has 25 acres that are fenced in a 42 acre park. Dogs can be off leash in any part of the park. The park offers picnic tables, a pond for small dogs, a pond for large dogs (Lake

Bow Wow), shower for dogs, warm water for dog baths, tennis balls and toys for play, a playground with games for your dogs, trails to walk on, and bag stations for cleanup. Locals can become members for the year for about $24.00 per month or out-of-town visitors can pay about $11 for a one time visit.
Paws Park Penman Road S Jacksonville Beach FL   904-513-9240
Open year round from dawn to dusk (except during maintenance on Thursdays), this off leash area has separate small/large dog areas, automatic watering bowls, benches, rinsing areas, clean up bag dispensers, and shaded areas. Dogs must be sociable, current on all vaccinations and license, and under owner's control/care at all times. Dogs must be leashed when not in designated off-lead areas.

Outdoor Restaurants
Joseph's Pizza 30 Ocean Blvd Atlantic Beach FL   904-270-1122
http://www.josephsitalian.com/
Fresh ground meats, homemade sauces/dressings, no preservatives, and stone baked handcrafted breads and crusts have all helped to make this a popular dining destination. They also offer outside dining. Dogs are allowed at the outer tables; they must be under owner's control/care at all times.
The Brick Restaurant 3585 St Johns Avenue/H 211 Jacksonville FL   904-387-0606
http://www.thebrickrestaurant.com/
In addition to enjoying upscale dining in a relaxed atmosphere, this restaurant offers live music Monday, Friday, and Saturday and alfresco dining. Dogs are allowed at the outer tables; they must be under owner's control/care at all times.
Caribbee Key Island Grille and Cruzan Rum Bar 100 First Street Neptune Beach FL   904-270-8940
http://www.caribbeekey.com/
Specializing in "Ameri-Caribbean" foods with the ambiance of the islands, this eatery also offers a full bar, ongoing entertainment and events, and outside dining. Well behaved dogs are allowed at the outer tables; they must be under owner's control/care at all times.

Jasper

Accommodations
Days Inn Jasper 8182 SR 6 West Jasper FL   386-792-1987 (800-329-7466)
Dogs of all sizes are allowed. There is a $10 per night pet fee per pet.

Key West

Accommodations
Ambrosia House Tropical Lodging 622 Fleming Street Key West FL   305-296-9838 (800-535-9838)
http://www.ambrosiakeywest.com/
This inn, located on almost two private acres, offers a variety of rooms, suites, town houses and a cottage, all with private baths. The inn is located in the heart of historic Old Town. There is a one time non-refundable pet fee of $25. There is no weight limit or limit to the number of pets.
Atlantic Shores (adults only) 510 South Street Key West FL   305-296-2491
Dogs of all sizes are allowed. There is a $10 one time additional pet fee per room.
Avalon 1317 Duval Street Key West FL   305-294-8233
One dog of any size is allowed. There is a pet policy to sign at check in and there are no additional fees.
Banana Bay Resort and Marina 2319 N. Roosevelt Blvd/H 1 Key West FL   305-296-6925 (866-566-6688)
http://www.bananabayresortkeywest.com/
Offering a paradisiacal setting, this elite adult oceanfront resort offers a number of amenities, plus is sits only minutes from all that the Keys have to offer. Well mannered dogs are allowed for no additional pet fee. (Children and Spring breakers are not allowed.)
Chelsea House 707 Truman Avenue Key West FL   305-296-2211 (800-845-8859)
There is a $15 per day pet charge.
Courtney's Place 720 Whitmarsh Lane Key West FL   305-294-3480 (800-869-4639)
http://www.keywest.com/courtney.html
This inn has historic guest cottages. There are no designated smoking or non-smoking cottages.

Francis Street Bottle Inn

Francis Street Bottle Inn 535 Francis Street Key West FL   305-294-8530 (800-294-8530)
http://www.bottleinn.com
Dogs are allowed, including well-behaved large dogs. There is a $25 one time pet fee.
Key West's Center Court - Bed and Breakfast and Cottages 1075 Duval St Key West FL   800-797-8787
http://www.centercourtkw.com/
Special doggy treats are available upon check-in. Pets are welcome in the suites, cottages, condos and homes.
Additional amenities include 4 pools and most suites offer private Jacuzzis. There is a $10 per pet per night
charge. Dogs of all sizes and breeds are welcome.
Key West's Travelers Palm - Inn and Cottages 915 Center Street Key West FL   800-294-9560
http://www.travelerspalm.com/
Special dog treats upon check-in. Dogs are welcome in the suites and cottages. Amenities include premier Old
Town locations and 3 heated pools. Dogs of all sizes and breeds are welcome.
Pelican Landing Resort and Marina 915 Eisenhower Drive Key West FL   305-296-9976
http://www.keywestpelican.com
Waterfront condos each with 2 bedrooms and 2 baths. A boat slip comes with each condo. The Subtropic Dive
Center is located next door. There is a heated swimming pool and all well-behaved dogs and cats are welcome.
Sheraton Suites Key West 2001 S. Roosevelt Blvd. Key West FL   305-292-9800 (888-625-5144)
Dogs of all sizes are allowed. There are no additional pet fees. Dogs are not allowed to be left alone in the room.
Sunrise Suites Resort 3685 SeaSide Drive Key West FL   305-296-6661 (888-723-5200)
http://sunrisekeywest.com/
All the amenities, the rich island ambiance, and luxury accommodations are only some of the enjoyments of the
area; they are also only moments from beaches and a number of recreational pursuits. Dogs up to 60 pounds
are allowed for an additional pet fee of $35 per night per room.

Campgrounds and RV Parks
Boyd's Key West Campground 6401 Maloney Avenue Key West FL   305-294-1465
http://www.boydscampground.com
Dogs of all sizes are allowed. There are no additional pet fees. Dogs may not be left unattended outside, and
they must be leashed and cleaned up after. There are some breed restrictions. The camping and tent areas also
allow dogs. There is a dog walk area at the campground.

Vacation Home Rentals
At Home In Key West, Inc. 905 Truman Avenue Key West FL   305-296-7975 (888-459-9378)
http://www.athomekeywest.com
Rent a pet-friendly condo or cottage in Key West. Call the property for prices and availability.
Key West Vacation Rentals 1075 Duval Street Key West FL   800-797-8787
http://www.vacationrentalskeywest.com
Special doggy treats are available upon check-in. Pets are welcome in suites, cottages, condos and homes.
Amenities include 4 pools and most suites offer private Jacuzzis. Specializing in weddings, honeymoons, and

romantic escapes. There is a $10 per pet per night charge. Dogs of all sizes and breeds are welcome.

Attractions

Duval Street Shopping District

Duval Street Shopping District Duval Street Key West FL
This street has a number of dog-friendly specialty shops.

Key West Aquarium

TOP 200 PLACE Key West Aquarium 1 Whitehead St Key West FL   305-296-2051
http://www.keywestaquarium.com/
This aquarium is the only one we know of that allows you to take your pup along on leash. It has a large
unfenced shark tank so please keep your pup under good control. You and your dog will see all sorts of marine
life.
Lazy Dog Outfitters, Kayaks and Boat Charters 5114 Overseas Highway Key West FL   305-293-9550
http://www.lazydogadventure.com/
This dog friendly store, kayak and boat charter has everything for someone planning on a day on the water. The
Lazy Dog brand was inspired by Camillo, the original Lazy Dog. Lazy Dog offers kayak tours and rentals. Single

and Double kayaks are available. Lazy Dog's 26 foot charter boat will take you out to fish the waters around Key West. Dogs are welcome on the kayak tours, rentals and on the boat charters. Lazy Dog is located at the Hurricane Hole Marina at mile marker 4 on the Overseas Highway.

Mallory Square

TOP 200 PLACE **Mallory Square** 1 Whitehead St Key West FL   305-296-4557
http://www.mallorysquare.com
You and your leashed dog can join other Key West party goers for the Key West Sunset Celebration at Mallory Square. There are numerous street performers, food, drinks, arts and crafts exhibitors, psychics and a lot more. The celebration begins about two hours before sunset nightly. Mallory square is also open for walks or congregating for the rest of the day and evening.
No Worries Charters Eisenhower Drive, Garrison Bight Marina Key West FL   305-393-2402
http://www.noworriescharters.com/
This charter company's owner, born and raised in the Keys, offers a variety of trips for snorkeling, fishing, kayaking, touring, marine viewing and more, plus they will also customize a combination of several activities for one tour. Very friendly dogs are allowed on board for no additional fee, but they must have their own properly fitting life-vest. Dogs must be under owner's control/care at all times.

Southernmost Point Monument

Southernmost Point Monument Whitehead St and South Street Key West FL
You and your pup can stand next to the monument at the southernmost point in the United States. This monument stands only ninety miles from Cuba.

Stephen Huneck Art Gallery

Stephen Huneck Art Gallery 218 Whitehead St Key West FL   305-295-7616
http://www.huneck.com/
This art gallery contains art about dogs and your well-behaved, leashed dog is very welcome to accompany you to the gallery.

Stores
Dog Thirty 1025 White Street Key West FL   305-296-4848
This pet boutique specializes in organic and holistic products, and they offer a line of gourmet treats and doggy accessories. Well behaved, leashed dogs are allowed in the store.

Beaches
Dog Beach Vernon Ave and Waddell Ave Key West FL
This tiny stretch of beach is the only beach we found in Key West where a dog can go into the water.

Parks
Dry Tortugas National Park PO Box 6208 Key West FL   305-242-7700
http://www.nps.gov/drto/index.htm
This set of Islands is 70 miles west of Key West in the Gulf of Mexico. Dogs must be on leash and must be cleaned up after on this island. Dogs are not allowed on the ferry but they can come over by private boat or charter from Key West. The park features picnicking, camping, fishing, swimming and more. Open year round.
Fort Zachary Taylor State Park Truman Annex Key West FL   305-292-6713
A National Historic Landmark, this oceanside park offers a long rich cultural and military history in addition to a wide array of recreational and educational activities. Dogs are allowed in all the common areas of the park; they are not allowed on the beach, playgrounds, buildings, or concession areas. Dogs must be well behaved, on no more than a 6 foot leash, and under owner's control/care at all times.

Off-Leash Dog Parks
Higgs Beach Dog Park White Street and Atlantic Blvd Key West FL   305-809-3765
http://www.keywestdogpark.org/
Located across from Higgs Beach this off leash area offers pets a fenced area with plenty of shade, water fountains, 2 separate areas for large and small dogs, and lots of play room. Dogs must be sociable, current on all vaccinations and license, and under owner's control/care at all times. Dogs must be leashed when not in designated off-lead areas.

Outdoor Restaurants

Blue Heaven 729 Thomas St Key West FL   305-296-8666
This restaurant serves American seafood. Dogs are allowed at the outdoor tables.
Bo's Fish Wagon 801 Caroline St Key West FL   305-294-9272
This is an outdoor restaurant that "appears" indoors and your dog is welcome where you order and where you sit.
Casablanca Bogart 904 Duval St Key West FL   305-296-0815
Dogs are allowed at the outdoor seats. This is a bar that serves some snacks as well as drinks.
Conch Republic Seafood Company 631 Greene St Key West FL   305-294-4403
There is live entertainment here often.
El Meson de Pepe's 410 Wall Street Key West FL   305-295-2620
http://www.elmesondepepe.com/index.htm
Family owned and operated, this eatery specializes in foods of the Cuban-Conch heritage, and every evening at
dusk guests are entertained by a popular Salsa band. Dogs are allowed at the outer tables; they must be
leashed and under owner's control/care at all times.
Grand Cafe Key West 314 Duval Street Key West FL   305-292-4740
http://www.grandcafekeywest.com/
Set in a beautiful Victorian mansion with lush gardens and wrap around verandas, this café offers a variety of
fine foods, a full bar, and alfresco dining. They are also host to a number of special events throughout the year.
Well mannered dogs are allowed at the outer tables; they must be under owner's control/care at all times.
Half Shell Raw Bar 231 Margaret Street Key West FL   305-294-8744
http://www.halfshellrawbar.com/
This casual beach Raw Bar offers outdoor seating. Dogs are allowed at the outer tables; they must be well
mannered, leashed, and under owner's control/care at all times.
Harpoon Harry's 832 Caroline Street Key West FL   305-294-8744
This eatery and tavern will allow dogs at their outer tables both during the day for food service and at night when
only the bar is open. Dogs must be under owner's control/care at all times.
Hogs Breath Saloon 400 Front Street Key West FL   305-296-4222
http://www.hogsbreath.com/key-west/
This is a popular eatery for good food, drink, and lots of fun with ongoing entertainment, contests, and special
events. They also offer outdoor dining, and dogs are allowed at the outer tables during the day only; they must be
leashed and under owner's control/care at all times.
Hurricane Joe's Seafood Bar and Grill Hurricane Hole Marina Mile Marker 4 Key West FL   305-294-0200
http://www.hurricanejoeskeywest.com/
This seafood restaurant at the Hurrican Hole Marina allows dogs at the outdoor seats. The restaurant is open
from 11 am to 10 pm.
Kelly's Restaurant 301 Whitehead Street Key West FL   305-293-8484
http://www.kellyskeywest.com/
Known as the birthplace of Pan-Am Airways, this Caribbean bar, grill, and micro-brewery, is located in one of the
most historic setting in Key West, plus they offer a large tropical garden dining area. Dogs are allowed at the
outer tables; they must be leashed and under owner's control/care at all times.
Limbo At Mangoes 700 Duval St Key West FL   305-292-4606
http://www.mangoeskeywest.com/
Dogs are allowed at the outdoor tables.
New York Pizza Cafe 1075 Duval St Key West FL   305-292-1991
This restaurant serves American food. Dogs are allowed at the outdoor tables.
Old Town Mexican Cafe 609 Duval St Key West FL   305-296-7500
Dogs are allowed at the outdoor tables.
Outback Steakhouse 3230 N Roosevelt Blvd/H1 Key West FL   305-292-0667
http://www.outbacksteakhouse.com/
Big, bold flavors, and fresh made-from-scratch soups/salads/sauces is the specialty at this steak house; they
also offer 4 outdoor dining tables. Dogs are allowed at the outer tables; they must be leashed and under owner's
control at all times. They just ask that someone come in and let someone at the host-stand know you are there.
Pepe's Cafe and Steakhouse 806 Caroline Street Key West FL   305-294-7192
Well-behaved leashed dogs are allowed at the outdoor tables. Thanks to one of our readers for recommending
this dog-friendly restaurant.
Schooner Wharf Bar 202 William Street Key West FL   305-292-9520
http://www.schoonerwharf.com/
This open air waterfront bar and grill offers soups, salads, sandwiches, plates like chicken or mahi-mahi and
more. This restaurant also regularly offers live musical entertainment. Well-behaved leashed dogs are allowed at
the outdoor tables. Thanks to one of our readers for recommending this dog-friendly restaurant.
Turtle Kraals Restaurant and Bar 231 Margaret Street Key West FL   305-294-2640
http://www.turtlekraals.com/
This waterfront diner features breakfast, lunch, and dinner with a wide variety of choices including fresh seafood,
a raw bar, steaks, southern specialties, a full service bar, and outside dining. Dogs are allowed at the outer

tables; they must be well mannered, leashed, and under owner's control/care at all times.

Keys

Campgrounds and RV Parks
Sunshine Key RV Resort 38801 Overseas H Big Pine Key FL   305-872-2217 (800-852-0348)
Dogs of all sizes are allowed. There are no additional pet fees. Dogs must be leashed and cleaned up after. The camping and tent areas also allow dogs. There is a dog walk area at the campground.
John Pennekamp Coral Reef State Park H 1, MM 102.5 Key Largo FL   305-451-1202 (800-326-3521)
http://www.pennekamppark.com/
This campground is located at America's first undersea park where they offer boat tours, rentals, guided nature walks, and 47 full service tent and RV sites with restrooms and hot showers. Dogs are not allowed in buildings or on the boat tours. Dogs of all sizes are allowed at no additional fee. Dogs may not be left unattended outside the camping unit, and they must be quiet, well behaved, leashed and cleaned up after. Dogs are not allowed at this park for day use because they may not be left in vehicles in the parking lot. The camping and tent areas also allow dogs. There is a dog walk area at the campground.
Sugarloaf Key/Key West KOA 251 H 939 Sugarloaf Key FL   305-745-3549 (800-562-7731)
http://www.koa.com
Dogs of all sizes are allowed. There are no additional pet fees. Dogs may not be left unattended outside, and they must be leashed and cleaned up after. The camping and tent areas also allow dogs. There is a dog walk area at the campground. Dogs are allowed in the camping cabins.

Attractions
National Key Deer Refuge 175-179 Key Deer Blvd Big Pine Key FL   305-872-0774
http://www.fws.gov/nationalkeydeer/
Dogs are allowed at this scenic, environmentally educational refuge where several endangered species are protected. Dogs must be kept on a short leash at all times and cleaned up after. They are not allowed in the back country islands in the turtle refuge area. Dogs must also be kept away from the water's edge because of the danger of alligators.

Beaches
Veteran's Memorial Park Highway 1 Duck Key FL   305-872-2411
Dogs on leash are allowed at this park and on the beach. People need to clean up after their pets. The park is located near mile marker 40, off Highway 1.
Anne's Beach Highway 1 Islamorada FL
Dog on leash are allowed at this beach. Please clean up after your dog. The beach is located around mile markers 72 to 74. There should be a sign.

Outdoor Restaurants
Key Largo Coffee House 100211 Overseas H Key Largo FL   305-532-0700
This coffee shop and cyber café allows dogs at the outside tables; they must be leashed and under owner's control/care at all times.

Lake City

Accommodations
Best Western Inn 3598 US Hwy 90 West Lake City FL   386-752-3801 (800-780-7234)
Dogs are allowed for an additional fee of $10 (plus tax) per night per pet. There may be one average sized dog or 2 very small dogs per room.
Days Inn Lake City 3430 North US Hwy 441 Lake City FL   386-758-4224 (800-329-7466)
Dogs of all sizes are allowed. There is a $10 per night pet fee per pet.
Motel 6 - Lake City 3835 US 90 Lake City FL   386-755-4664 (800-466-8356)
One well-behaved family pet per room. Guest must notify front desk upon arrival. Guest is liable for any damages. In consideration of all guests, pets must never be left unattended in the guest rooms.
Super 8 Lake City I-75 and Hwy 47 Lake City FL   386-752-6450 (800-800-8000)
Dogs of all sizes are allowed. There is a $5 per night pet fee per pet under 10 pounds and $10 per pet over 10 pounds. Reservations are recommended due to limited rooms for pets. Smoking and non-smoking rooms are

available for pet rooms.

Campgrounds and RV Parks

Stephen Foster Folk Culture Center State Park P. O. Drawer G/ US 41 N White Springs FL   386-397-2733 (800-326-3521)
This beautiful recreational nature park offers a museum, a Craft Square, miles of trails, and special events throughout the year. Dogs of all sizes are allowed at no additional fee. Dogs may not be left unattended, and they must have current rabies and shot records. Dogs must be on no more than a 6 foot leash, and be cleaned up after. Dogs are not allowed in buildings, but they are allowed on the trails. The camping and tent areas also allow dogs. There is a dog walk area at the campground.
Suwannee Valley Campground 786 N W Street White Springs FL   866-397-1667
http://www.suwanneevalleycampground.com
Dogs of all sizes are allowed, and there are no additional pet fees for tent or RV sites. There is a $50 one time pet fee for cabins. Dogs must have up to date shot records, and be leashed and cleaned up after. The camping and tent areas also allow dogs. There is a dog walk area at the campground. Dogs are allowed in the camping cabins.

Attractions

Olustee Battlefield State Historic Site U.S. 90 Olustee FL   386-758-0400
Leashed dogs are allowed on this historic battlefield. There is a one-mile walking trail which educates visitors about Florida's biggest Civil War battle. The battlefield is located about 1 hour from Jacksonville. Dogs are not allowed during the Olustee Battle Re-enactment Event.

Lake Placid

Campgrounds and RV Parks

SunShine R.V. Resort 303 St. Rt. 70 East Lake Placid FL   863-465-4815
http://www.SunShineRVResorts.com
Dogs up to 40 pounds are allowed. There are no additional pet fees. There are some breed restrictions.

Lake Wales

Accommodations

Super 8 Lake Wales 541 W Central Ave Lake Wales FL   863-676-7925 (800-800-8000)
Dogs of all sizes are allowed. There are no additional pet fees. Smoking and non-smoking rooms are available for pet rooms.

Leesburg

Accommodations

Super 8 Leesburg 1392 N Blvd West Leesburg FL   352-787-6363 (800-800-8000)
Dogs of all sizes are allowed. There is a $10 per night pet fee per pet. Smoking and non-smoking rooms are available for pet rooms.
Days Inn Wildwood 551 E SR 44 Wildwood FL   352-748-7766 (800-329-7466)
Dogs of all sizes are allowed. There is a $10 per night pet fee per pet.

Live Oak

Campgrounds and RV Parks

Suwannee River State Park 20185 County Road 132 Live Oak FL   386-362-2746 (800-326-3521)
Rich in scenery, history, and recreation, this park offers 5 different trails and panoramic views of the great river. Dogs of all sizes are allowed at no additional fee. Dogs may not be left unattended, and they must have current

rabies and shot records. Dogs must be on no more than a 6 foot leash, and be cleaned up after. Dogs are not allowed in buildings or public swim areas, but they are allowed on the trails. The camping and tent areas also allow dogs. There is a dog walk area at the campground.

Madison

Campgrounds and RV Parks
Jellystone Park 1051 SW Old St. Augustine Road Madison FL   800-347-0174
http://www.jellystoneflorida.com
Dogs of all sizes are allowed. There are no additional pet fees. Dogs must be leashed and cleaned up after. Dogs are not allowed in public areas or the beach. The camping and tent areas also allow dogs. There is a dog walk area at the campground.

Marianna

Accommodations
Best Western Marianna Inn 2086 Highway 71 Marianna FL   850-526-5666 (800-780-7234)
Dogs up to 50 pounds are allowed for an additional fee of $10 per night per pet.
Quality Inn 2175 H 71S Marianna FL   850-526-5600 (877-424-6423)
Dogs are allowed for an additional pet fee of $7 per night per room for smoking rooms, and $12 per night per room for non-smoking rooms.

Campgrounds and RV Parks
Florida Caverns State Park 3345 Caverns Road (H 166) Marianna FL   850-482-9598 (800-326-3521)
As well as having a variety of year round recreational activities, this park offers the only guided cave tours in Florida. Dogs of all sizes are allowed at no additional fee. Dogs may not be left unattended, and they must have current rabies and shot records. Dogs must be on no more than a 6 foot leash, and be cleaned up after. Dogs are not allowed in buildings, any public swimming areas, or on the cave tours. The camping and tent areas also allow dogs. There is a dog walk area at the campground.

Melbourne

Accommodations
Hilton 200 Rialto Place Melbourne FL   321-768-0200
Dogs up to 70 pounds are allowed for no additional pet fee with a credit card on file; there is a $50 refundable deposit required if paying cash.
La Quinta Inn & Suites Melbourne 7200 George T. Edwards Drive Melbourne FL   321-242-9400 (800-531-5900)
Dogs of all sizes are allowed. There are no additional pet fees. Dogs must be leashed and cleaned up after.
Motel 6 - Palm Bay 1170 Malabar Road SE Palm Bay FL   321-951-8222 (800-466-8356)
One well-behaved family pet per room. Guest must notify front desk upon arrival. Guest is liable for any damages. In consideration of all guests, pets must never be left unattended in the guest rooms.
Howard Johnson Inn 4431 West New Haven Ave. West Melbourne FL   321-768-8439 (800-446-4656)
Dogs up to 50 pounds are allowed. There is a $20 one time per day pet fee.

Campgrounds and RV Parks
Sebastian Inlet State Park 9700 S A1A Melbourne Beach FL   321-984-4852 (800-326-3521)
This park offers premier saltwater fishing, 3 miles of beaches, a boat dock, and a variety of land and water recreation. Dogs of all sizes are allowed at no additional fee. Dogs may not be left unattended, and they must have current rabies and shot records. Dogs must be on no more than a 6 foot leash, and be cleaned up after. Dogs are not allowed in buildings, on the beaches, on the jetty, or catwalks. Dogs are allowed on the trails, and there is a small area at the cove where they may go in the water as long as they are still on lead. The camping and tent areas also allow dogs. There is a dog walk area at the campground.

Vacation Home Rentals
Beach Bungalow Call to Arrange Melbourne Beach FL   321-984-1330
http://1stbeach.com
The Beach Bungalow is 3 large, luxurious 2 bedroom oceanfront villas with private gardens in a small beach town. Dogs of any size are allowed with a $50 cleaning fee. The private gardens are entirely fenced and the floors are tile and hardwood.

Stores
PetSmart Pet Store 1800 Evans Rd Melbourne FL   321-722-3190
Your licensed and well-behaved leashed dog is allowed in the store.
Petco Pet Store 7201 Shoppes Drive #109 Melbourne FL   321-637-0282
Your licensed and well-behaved leashed dog is allowed in the store.

Off-Leash Dog Parks
Satellite Beach Off-leash Dog Park Satellite Beach Sports & Rec Park Satellite Beach FL   321-777-8004
The dog park is 1.5 acres and fully fenced. The park offers water, tables and benches. There is a separate area for small dogs. The park is open daily from 8 am to 8 pm except for Mondays and Thursdays from 12 - 3 pm for maintenance. The park is next to the Satellite Beach Library which is at 751 Jamaica Blvd.

Outdoor Restaurants
Moe's Southwest Grill 630 E Eau Gallie Blvd Indian Harbour Beach FL   321-777-6351
http://www.moes.com/
This eatery specializes in southwestern grill and offer catering and an outdoor covered patio. Dogs are allowed at the outer tables; they must be under owner's control/care at all times.

Miami

Accommodations
Residence Inn by Marriott 19900 W. Country Club Drive Aventura FL   786-528-1001
Well behaved dogs of all sizes are allowed. There is a $75 one time fee per pet and a pet policy to sign at check in.
Residence Inn by Marriott 2835 Tigertail Avenue Coconut Grove FL   305-285-9303
Dogs of all sizes are allowed. There is a $75 one time fee and a pet policy to sign at check in.
Howard Johnson Hotel 7707 NW 103 St. Hialeah Gardens FL   305-825-1000 (800-446-4656)
There is a $100 one time additional pet fee.
Extended StayAmerica Miami - Airport - Doral 8655 NW 21 Terrace Miami FL   786-331-7717
There is a one time pet fee of $25.00 for one night stays, $50.00 for two night stays, and $75.00 for any stay of three nights or longer.
Extended StayAmerica Miami - Coral Gables 3640 SW 22nd Street Miami FL   305-443-7444
There is a one time pet fee of $25.00 for one night stays, $50.00 for two night stays, and $75.00 for any stay of three nights or longer.
Hampton Inn 2500 Brickell Avenue Miami FL   305-854-2070
Well behaved dogs of all sizes are allowed. There are no additional pet fees.
Homestead Village-Miami Airport 8720 NW 33rd Street Miami FL   305-436-1811 (888-782-9473)
There is a $75 one time pet charge.
La Quinta Inn & Suites Miami Airport West 8730 NW 27th St. Miami FL   305-436-0830 (800-531-5900)
One large dog (over 50 pounds) or two medium to small dogs are allowed. There are no additional pet fees. Dogs must be leashed and cleaned up after.
Quality Inn South at the Falls 14501 S Dixie H (H1) Miami FL   305-251-2000 (877-424-6423)
Dogs are allowed for an additional pet fee of $10 per night per room.
Red Roof Inn - Miami Airport 3401 Northwest LeJeune Road Miami FL   305-871-4221 (800-RED-ROOF)
One well-behaved family pet per room. Guest must notify front desk upon arrival. Guest is liable for any damages. In consideration of all guests, pets must never be left unattended in the guest rooms.
Residence Inn by Marriott 1212 NW 82nd Avenue Miami FL   305-591-2211
Dogs of all sizes are allowed. There is a $75 one time fee and a pet policy to sign at check in.
Staybridge Suites 3265 NW 87th Avenue Miami FL   305-500-9100 (877-270-6405)
Dogs of all sizes are allowed for an additional one time pet fee of $125 per pet.
TownePlace Suites Miami Airport West/Doral Area 10505 NW 36th Street Miami FL   305-718-4144
Dogs of all sizes are allowed. There is a $75 one time pet fee per visit.

571

TownePlace Suites Miami Lakes/Miramar Area 8079 NW 154 Street Miami FL   305-512-9191
Dogs of all sizes are allowed. There is a $75 one time pet fee per visit.
Wellesley Inn Miami Lakes 7925 NW 154th Street Miami FL   305-821-8274 (800-531-5900)
Dogs of all sizes are allowed. There is a $10 per night per room additional pet fee. Dogs must be leashed,
cleaned up after, and crated when left alone in the room.
Brigham Gardens Guesthouse 1411 Collins Avenue Miami Beach FL   305-531-1331
http://www.brighamgardens.com
This guesthouse offers hotel Rooms, Studios and one Bedroom Apartments.Pets are welcome for a nightly fee
of $6.00.
Hotel Leon 841 Collins Avenue Miami Beach FL   305-673-3767
http://www.hotelleon.com/
This hotel is a stone's throw from the beach and in the heart of the Art Deco District of Miami Beach.
Hotel Ocean 1230 Ocean Drive Miami Beach FL   800-783-1725
http://hotelocean.com
Pets are welcome in this Miami Beach boutique hotel. They have created a special package that includes a bed,
treats, and walking service for only $19.95 per pet per day. The regular pet fee is $15.00 per pet per day.
Loews Miami Beach Hotel 1601 Collins Avenue Miami Beach FL   305-604-1601
All well-behaved dogs of any size are welcome. This upscale hotel offers their "Loews Loves Pets" program
which includes special pet treats, local dog walking routes, and a list of nearby pet-friendly places to visit. While
pets are not allowed in the pool, they are welcome to join you at the side of the pool or at the pool bar. There are
no pet fees.
South Beach Marriott 161 Ocean Drive Miami Beach FL   305-536-7700 (800-228-9290)
Dogs up to 100 pounds are allowed. There is a $150 one time additional pet fee per room. Dogs must be
leashed, cleaned up after, and the Do Not Disturb sign put on the door if they are in the room alone.
Residence Inn by Marriott 14700 SW 29th Street Miramar FL   954-450-2717
Pets of all sizes are welcome. There is a $75 one time fee and a pet policy to sign at check in.

Transportation Systems
Miami/Dade Transit South of SW 216 Street Miami FL   305-770-3131
www.co.miami-dade.fl.us/transit/
A small dog in an enclosed, escape proof carrier are allowed on Metro-rail and Metro buses at no additional fee.

Attractions
Coopertown Airboat Tours US-41 Coopertown FL   305-226-6048
Some of the boat drivers will allow dogs, but not all will. However, there are a number of them here at any time.
The airboats are noisy. Only take a dog that is experienced with noisy boats and rides. A large dog may go on
the tour only if the boat is not full with passengers. These boat tours are about an hour from the city.
Club Nautica 4000 Crandon Blvd Key Biscayne FL   305-361-9217
You can charter any number of fishing boats for a half day or entire day or you can rent a powerboat.
Monty's Marina 2560 S Bayshore Dr Miami FL   305-854-7997
You and your dog can rent a boat here at Club Nautica or charter a fishing boat as well.
Art Deco Self-Guided Walking Tour 1001 Ocean Drive Miami Beach FL   305-672-2014
Audio tapes for a self-guided walking tour of Miami Beach's Art Deco District are available at the Welcome
Center. The Welcome Center is located at 1001 Ocean Drive. The cost is $10 per person for the audio rental.
Club Nautico Power Boat Rentals 300 Alton Rd Ste 112 Miami Beach FL   305-858-6258
http://www.clubnauticousa.com/index.htm
Enjoy a day on the water with Club Nautico Power Boat Rentals. Dogs are welcome on the rented boats. Choose
from 10 different boats and many different types of packages.
Wings Over Miami Air Museum 14710 128th Street SW Tamiami FL   305-233-5197
http://www.wingsovermiami.com
Well-behaved, well-trained dogs are allowed at this museum, around the grounds, and in the buildings. Dogs
must be on leash and cleaned up after. They are open from 10 am to 5 pm Thursday through Sunday.

Shopping Centers
Village of Merrick Park Shopping Plaza 358 Avenue San Lorenzo Coral Gables FL   305-529-0200
http://www.villageofmerrickpark.com
Well-behaved leashed dogs are allowed at this outdoor mall and inside many of the stores including Nordstrom,
Athropologie, Crabtree & Evelyn, and Williams-Sonoma. Several restaurants also allow dogs at their outdoor
tables, including Cafe Ibiza, Java of Merrick Park and Pescado.

Florida - Please always call ahead to make sure that an establishment is still dog-friendly

Art Deco Self-Guided Walking Tour

Bal Harbour Shopping Center

Bal Harbour Shopping Center 9700 Collins Ave Miami FL   305-866-0311
http://www.balharbourshops.com/
An upscale outdoor shopping center where your dog is welcome in some of the stores and the outdoor restaurants.
Lincoln Road Shops Lincoln Road Miami Beach FL   305-531-3442
This pedestrian-only street mall in Miami beach has a number of dog-friendly establishments for eating and shopping.

Stores

PetSmart Pet Store 21095 Biscayne Blvd Aventura FL   305-682-8858
Your licensed and well-behaved leashed dog is allowed in the store.
Anthropologie 330 San Lorenzo Avenue Coral Gables FL   305-443-0021
This store offers women's clothing and household items. They are located in the dog-friendly Village of Merrick Park shopping plaza. Well-behaved leashed dogs are allowed inside the store.
Crabtree & Evelyn 320 San Lorenzo Avenue Coral Gables FL   305-448-4077
This bath and skincare store allows well-behaved leashed dogs inside. They are located in the dog-friendly

Village of Merrick Park shopping plaza.
Nordstrom 4310 Ponce De Leon Blvd. Coral Gables FL   786-999-1313
This department allows well-behaved leashed dogs inside the store. They are located in the dog-friendly Village of Merrick Park shopping plaza.
Williams-Sonoma 350 San Lorenzo Avenue Coral Gables FL   305-446-9421
This store offers specialty packaged foods, appliances, cookbooks, tableware, and kitchen products. They allow well-behaved leashed dogs inside and are located in the dog-friendly Village of Merrick Park shopping plaza.
Petco Pet Store 1635 NW 107th Avenue Doral FL   305-468-9012
Your licensed and well-behaved leashed dog is allowed in the store.
PetSmart Pet Store 8241 W Flagler St Ste 101 Miami FL   786-275-8300
Your licensed and well-behaved leashed dog is allowed in the store.
PetSmart Pet Store 13621 S Dixie Hwy Miami FL   305-253-5943
Your licensed and well-behaved leashed dog is allowed in the store.
PetSmart Pet Store 14025 SW 88th St Miami FL   305-382-9911
Your licensed and well-behaved leashed dog is allowed in the store.
Petco Pet Store 12014 SW 88th St Miami FL   305-412-0244
Your licensed and well-behaved leashed dog is allowed in the store.
Petco Pet Store 8675 SW Coral Way St Miami FL   305-265-1093
Your licensed and well-behaved leashed dog is allowed in the store.
Petco Pet Store 6200 South Dixie Highway South Miami FL   305-665-7335
Your licensed and well-behaved leashed dog is allowed in the store.

Beaches

Rickenbacker Causeway Beach Rickenbacker Causeway Miami FL
This beach extends the length of the Rickenbacker Causeway from Downtown Miami to Key Biscayne. Dogs are allowed on the entire stretch. There are two types of beach, a Tree lined Dirt beach and a standard type of sandy beach further towards Key Biscayne. Dogs should be leashed on the beach.

Parks

Barnacle State Historic Site

Barnacle State Historic Site 3485 Main Highway Coconut Grove FL   305-448-9445
Dogs are allowed in the outdoor areas of the park. Dogs must be leashed at all times.
Biscayne National Park 9700 SW 328 Street Homestead FL   305-230-7275
http://www.nps.gov/bisc/index.htm
Biscayne National Park displays the coral reefs that thrive in the Miami area. Dogs are allowed in the developed areas of Elliott Key and Convoy Point on the mainland. They must be leashed and attended at all times and are not allowed in the buildings or swimming area. Pets are not allowed at all on the islands of Boca Chita Key or Adams Key or even in boats docked at the islands. Dogs may camp with you at Elliott Key.
Everglades National Park 40001 State Road 9336 Homestead FL   305-242-7700

http://www.nps.gov/ever/index.htm
Dogs on leash are allowed in the parking lot and campgrounds of Everglades National park. They are not allowed on trails or wilderness areas. Open year round this is the only subtropical preserve in North America. In the campgrounds and anywhere throughout this region where pets are allowed, pay close attention to them as alligators and snakes are always a danger. For more freedom to hike with your pet, try the Big Cypress National Preserve nearby.
Bill Baggs State Park 1200 S. Crandon Blvd Key Biscayne FL   305-361-5811
Dogs are allowed on leash. This park has trails and a lighthouse (to view from outside). Dogs are not allowed on the beach near the lighthouse.
Lummas Park Ocean Drive Miami Beach FL
This park borders the ocean in the Art Deco district of Miami Beach. Dogs must be leashed in the park.
Oleta River State Park 3400 N.E. 163rd Street North Miami FL
This park has hiking, jogging, and waterfront on the Biscayne Bay. Dogs are allowed on leash.
Big Cypress National Preserve 33100 Tamiami Trail East Ochopee FL   239-695-1201
http://www.nps.gov/bicy/index.htm
Dogs must be on leash and must be cleaned up after in this National preserve. Open year round 9am-4:30pm except Christmas. The park features auto touring, camping, hiking, boating, and more. The park does not recommend taking pets near lakes or areas where wildlife are present for their safety in this Alligator preservation. This park is about one hour from the city.

Off-Leash Dog Parks
Dog Chow Dog Park 2400 S Bayshore Drive Coconut Grove FL   954-570-9507
Located at Kennedy Park, this off leash area offers human and canine visitors lots of shade trees, benches, and water; plus there is a separate section for small dogs, and restrooms are on site. Dogs must be sociable, current on all vaccinations, licensed, and under owner's control/care at all times. Dogs must be leashed when not in designated off-lead areas.
Amelia Earhart Park Bark Park 401 East 65th Street Miami FL   305-755-7800
http://www.geocities.com/ameliabarkpark/
This 5 acre dog park is completely fenced and has a separate area for small dogs. There are paved walkways, benches, shade, and water. The dog park is open from sunrise to sunset. The Bark Park is located in Amelia Earhart Park.
Flamingo Bark Park 13th Street and Michigan Avenue Miami Beach FL   305-673-7224
This popular pooch play yard offers landscaped grounds, skill and training equipment, water fountains for hounds and humans, and waste stations. Dogs must be sociable, current on all vaccinations, licensed, and cleaned up after at all times. Dogs must be leashed when not in designated off-lead areas.

Outdoor Restaurants
Beverly Hills Cafe 5544 S. Flamingo Road Cooper City FL   954-434-2220
Menu categories for this restaurant include Munchies, Soups & Combos, Eggs, On The Healthy Side, Salads, Burgers, Chicken Grills, Sandwich Favorites, Mexican, Pastas & Stir-Frys, Specialties, Favorites, Kid's Menu, Brunch and Desserts. Well-behaved leashed dogs are allowed at the outdoor tables.
Java of Merrick Park 380 San Lorenzo Ave Coral Gables FL   305-461-1113
This cafe offers freshly roasted coffee and pastries. Well-behaved leashed dogs are allowed at the outdoor tables. They are located in the dog-friendly Village of Merrick Park shopping plaza.
Bayside Seafood Restaurant 3501 Rickenbacker Causeway Key Biscayne FL   305-361-0808
This restaurant serves Seafood. Dogs are allowed at the outdoor tables.
Bal Harbour Bistro 9700 Collins Ave Miami FL   305-861-4544
This restaurant is in the Bal Harbour shopping center.
TOP 200 PLACE **Catalina Hotel and Beach Club** 1732-1756 Collins Avenue Miami FL   305-674-1160
Summer brings about a weekly "Must Love Dogs" brunch every Sunday from 10:30 AM to 2:30 PM where pampered pups may dine alfresco with their human companions. Dogs get personal water bowls and a selection of gourmet treats to make any discerning pup happy. Dogs are not allowed in the hotel. Dogs must be well mannered and under owner's control/care at all times.
Groovy's Pizza 3030 Grand Ave Miami FL   305-476-6018
It's really an outside only restaurant. You order and sit down.
Johnny Rockets 3036 Grand Ave Miami FL   305-444-1000
Dogs are allowed at the outdoor tables.
Mambo Cafe 3105 Commodore Plz Miami FL   305-448-2768
Dogs are allowed at the outdoor tables.
Senor Frog's 3008 Grand Ave Miami FL   305-448-0999
This patio restaurant is in the Coconut Grove area of Miami.
Tutto Pasta 1751 SW 3rd Ave Miami FL   305-857-0709
This restaurant serves Italian food. Dogs are allowed at the outdoor tables.

Cafeteria 546 Lincoln Road Miami Beach FL   305-672-3663
This restaurant serves American cuisine. Dogs are allowed at the outdoor tables. This restaurant is open 24hrs/7 days a week.
Fratelli la Bufala 437 Washington Avenue Miami Beach FL   305-532-0700
Specializing in providing natural, high quality foods produced by means of biological agriculture, this Italian restaurant offers unique Mediterranean dishes from Buffalo meats and cheeses. They also offer alfresco dining. Dogs are allowed at the outer tables; they must be under owner's control/care at all times.
Les Deux Fontaines 1230 Ocean Drive Miami Beach FL   305-672-7878
This restaurant serves seafood. Dogs are allowed at the outdoor tables.
Nexxt Cafe 700 Lincoln Road Miami Beach FL   305-532-6643
This large sidewalk cafe offers salads, sandwiches, seafood and other entrees. Well-behaved leashed dogs are allowed at the outdoor tables.
Sushi Rock Cafe 1351 Collins Ave Miami Beach FL   305-532-4639
Dogs are allowed at the outdoor tables.
Taste Bakery Cafe 900 Alton Road Miami Beach FL   305-695-9930
http://tastebakerycafe.com
The food served here is hormone and pesticide free and totally organic when possible. The cafe is open for breakfast, lunch and dinner. For breakfast, try a smoothie, speciality coffee, tea, a breakfast sandwich, or bread with spread. For lunch or dinner, they offer wraps, rolls, sandwiches, salads, soups and baked goodies. Well-behaved leashed dogs are welcome to join you at the outdoor tables.
Van Dyke Cafe 1641 Jefferson Ave Miami Beach FL   305-534-3600
Dogs are allowed at the outdoor tables.
World Resources Cafe 719 Lincoln Rd Miami Beach FL   305-535-8987
Dogs are allowed at the outdoor tables.
Beverly Hills Cafe 7321 Miami Lakes Drive Miami Lakes FL   305-558-8201
Menu categories for this restaurant include Munchies, Soups & Combos, Eggs, On The Healthy Side, Salads, Burgers, Chicken Grills, Sandwich Favorites, Mexican, Pastas & Stir-Frys, Specialties, Favorites, Kid's Menu, Brunch and Desserts. Well-behaved leashed dogs are allowed at the outdoor tables.

Naples

Accommodations
La Quinta Inn Naples Airport 185 Bedzel Circle Naples FL   239-352-8400 (800-531-5900)
Dogs of all sizes are allowed. There are no additional pet fees. Dogs may not be left unattended in the rooms except for a short time, and they must be well behaved and kept on leash.
Red Roof Inn - Naples 1925 Davis Boulevard Naples FL   239-774-3117 (800-RED-ROOF)
One well-behaved family pet per room. Guest must notify front desk upon arrival. Guest is liable for any damages. In consideration of all guests, pets must never be left unattended in the guest rooms.
Residence Inn by Marriott 4075 Tamiami Trail N Naples FL   239-659-1300
Dogs of all sizes are allowed. There is a $75 one time fee and a pet policy to sign at check in. Please kennel your pet if you are out of the room.
Staybridge Suites 4805 Tamiami Trail North Naples FL   239-643-8002 (877-270-6405)
Dogs of all sizes are allowed for an additional one time pet fee of $150 per room.

Campgrounds and RV Parks
Collier-Seminole State Park 20200 E Tamiami Trail Naples FL   239-394-3397 (800-326-3521)
This park displays wildlife and vegetation typical of the Everglades, a forest of tropical trees, and is a National Historic Mechanical Engineering Landmark site. Dogs of all sizes are allowed at no additional fee. Dogs may not be left unattended outside, and they must have current rabies and shot records. Dogs must be on no more than a 6 foot leash, and be cleaned up after. Dogs are not allowed in buildings, on canoe rentals, or on any of the trails. Dogs may be walked around the camp area. The camping and tent areas also allow dogs. There is a dog walk area at the campground.
Hitching Post RV Resort 100 Barefoot Williams Road Naples FL   239-774-1259
Dogs of all sizes are allowed. There are no additional pet fees. Dogs must be quiet, leashed, and cleaned up after. This RV park is closed during the off-season. The camping and tent areas also allow dogs. There is a dog walk area at the campground.
Lake San Marino RV Resort 1000 Wiggins Pass Naples FL   239-597-4202
http://www.lakesanmarino.com
Dogs of all sizes are allowed. There are no additional pet fees. Dogs may not be tied up or left unattended outside, and they must be leashed and cleaned up after. They do have an off lead dog park on site. This a 55 years or older park. There are some breed restrictions. There is a dog walk area at the campground. There are

special amenities given to dogs at this campground.

Attractions
Collier-Seminole State Park Boat Tours 20200 E. Tamiami Trail Naples FL   941-642-8898
Dogs under 50 pounds are allowed on the pontoon boat tours. The tours last about an hour and include a narration about the early settlers and Everglade animals and plants. The cost is $8.50 per person and dogs ride free.

Stores
PetSmart Pet Store 2255 Pine Ridge Rd Naples FL   239-598-9889
Your licensed and well-behaved leashed dog is allowed in the store.
Petco Pet Store 6424 Naples Blvd Ste 401 Naples FL   239-254-0263
Your licensed and well-behaved leashed dog is allowed in the store.

Beaches
Delnor-Wiggins Pass State Park 11100 Gulfshore Drive Naples FL   239-597-6196
Dogs are not allowed on the beaches in this park, but they can take dip in the water at the boat and canoe launch only. Dogs must be on leash. Please clean up after your dog. This park is located six miles west of Exit 17 on I-75.

Ocala

Accommodations
Comfort Inn 4040 W Silver Springs Blvd Ocala FL   352-629-8850 (877-424-6423)
Dogs are allowed for an additional fee per night per pet of $5 for dogs up to 10 pounds; $10 for 11 to 20 pounds, and $20 for 21 to 50 pound dogs.
Days Inn 3811 NW Bonnie Heath Rd Ocala FL   352-629-7041 (800-329-7466)
Dogs of all sizes are allowed. There is a $5 per night pet fee per pet.
Days Inn Ocala 3620 W Silver Springs Blvd Ocala FL   352-629-0091 (800-329-7466)
Dogs of all sizes are allowed. There is a $10 per night pet fee per pet.
Hilton 3600 Southwest 36th Avenue Ocala FL   352-854-1400
Dogs are allowed for an additional one time pet fee of $50 per room. They have a treat package for each of their canine guests.
Howard Johnson Inn 3951 NW Blitchton Rd. Ocala FL   352-629-7021 (800-446-4656)
Dogs of all sizes are welcome. There is a $20 per day pet fee.
La Quinta Inn & Suites Ocala 3530 S.W. 36th Ave. Ocala FL   352-861-1137 (800-531-5900)
Dogs of all sizes are allowed. There are no additional pet fees. Dogs must be leashed, cleaned up after, and removed or attend to the pet for housekeeping. Dogs must be leashed and cleaned up after.
Red Roof Inn - Ocala 120 NW 40th Avenue Ocala FL   352-732-4590 (800-RED-ROOF)
One well-behaved family pet per room. Guest must notify front desk upon arrival. Guest is liable for any damages. In consideration of all guests, pets must never be left unattended in the guest rooms.
Days Inn Ocala/East 5001 E Silver Springs Blvd Silver Springs FL   352-236-2891 (800-329-7466)
Dogs of all sizes are allowed. There is a $10 per night pet fee per pet.

Campgrounds and RV Parks
Silver River State Park 1425 NE 58th Avenue Ocala FL   352-236-7148 (800-326-3521)
This park has dozens of springs, 15 miles of trails, 14 distinct natural communities, a pioneer cracker village, the Silver River Museum and an Environmental Education Center. Dogs of all sizes are allowed at no additional fee. Dogs may not be left unattended, and they must have current rabies and shot records. Dogs must be on no more than a 6 foot leash, and be cleaned up after. Dogs are not allowed in or around any buildings, and dogs should not be down by the river because of alligators. The camping and tent areas also allow dogs. There is a dog walk area at the campground.
Ocala National Forest 17147 E H 40 Silver Springs FL   352-625-2520 (877-444-6777)
This National Forest offers interesting geological and historical sites to explore, a wide abundance of land and water recreation, and a variety of trails, including a portion of the Florida National Scenic Trail. Dogs of all sizes are allowed at no additional fee. Dogs may not be left unattended, they must have current rabies and shot records, be on no more than a 6 foot leash, and be cleaned up after. Dogs are not allowed in public swim areas, buildings, or any day use areas. Dogs are allowed on all the trails except for the short interpretive trails. The camping and tent areas also allow dogs. There is a dog walk area at the campground.

Stores
PetSmart Pet Store 3500 SW College Rd Ocala FL   352-237-0700
Your licensed and well-behaved leashed dog is allowed in the store.

Ochopee

Campgrounds and RV Parks
Big Cypress National Preserve 521005 Tamiami Trail E/ H 41 (Vistor's Center) Ochopee FL   239-695-2000
(877-444-6777)
http://www.nps.gov/bicy/
This park is known for it's biological diversity and provides a wide variety of scenic, biological, and geological
sites to explore in addition to the recreational pursuits. Dogs are allowed at no additional fee. Dogs may not be
left unattended, and they must be leashed and cleaned up after. Dogs are not allowed in the back country or on
the boardwalks. The camping and tent areas also allow dogs. There is a dog walk area at the campground.
There are no water hookups at the campground.
Big Cypress National Preserve 33100 Tamiami Trail East Ochopee FL   239-695-1201
http://www.nps.gov/bicy/index.htm
This recreational paradise offers day use, camping, canoeing, kayaking, hiking, bird-watching opportunities,
interpretive programs, and self guided nature walks. Dogs of all sizes are allowed for no additional fee. Dogs
must be leashed at all times and cleaned up after. Dogs are allowed anywhere in the front country and the
campgrounds, but they are not allowed on trails or on any of the boardwalks. The camping and tent areas also
allow dogs. There is a dog walk area at the campground. There are no water hookups at the campgrounds.

Parks

Big Cypress National Preserve

Big Cypress National Preserve 33100 Tamiami Trail Ochopee FL   239-695-1107
This recreational paradise offers day use, camping, canoeing, kayaking, hiking, bird-watching opportunities,
interpretive programs, self guided nature walks, and a visitors' center. Dogs of all sizes are allowed for no
additional fee. Dogs must be leashed at all times and cleaned up after. Dogs are allowed anywhere in the front
country and the campgrounds, but they are not allowed on trails or on any of the boardwalks.

Orange Lake

Campgrounds and RV Parks

Grand Lake RV & Golf Resort 4555 W H 318 Orange Lake FL   352-591-3474
http://www.grandlakeresort.com
Dogs of all sizes are allowed. There are no additional pet fees. Dogs must be leashed when walking around the resort and cleaned up after, but may be off lead on own site if well behaved and under voice command. The camping and tent areas also allow dogs. There is a dog walk area at the campground.

Orlando

Accommodations

Candlewood Suites 644 Raymond Avenue Altamonte Springs FL   407-767-5757 (877-270-6405)
A dog up to 50 pounds is allowed for an additional one time pet fee of $75 for 1 to 6 days, and $150 for 7or more days.
Embassy Suites Hotel Orlando - North 225 Shorecrest Drive Altamonte Springs FL   407-834-2400
Dogs of all sizes are allowed. There is a $20 per night pet fee per pet. Dogs are not allowed to be left alone in the room.
Homestead Hotels Orlando - Altamonte Springs 302 Northlake Blvd. Altamonte Springs FL   407-332-9300
There is a one time pet fee of $25.00 for one night stays, $50.00 for two night stays, and $75.00 for any stay of three nights or longer.
Howard Johnson Express Inn 1317 S. Orange Blossom Trail Apopka FL   407-886-1010 (800-446-4656)
Dogs of all sizes are welcome. There is a $10 per day pet fee. The hotel has two pet rooms, one smoking and one non-smoking.
Best Western Maingate South 2425 Frontage Road Davenport FL   863-424-2596 (800-780-7234)
Dogs are allowed for no additional pet fee.
Hampton Inn 44117 H 27 Davenport FL   863-420-9898
Dogs of all sizes are allowed. There is a $25 per day per room fee and a pet policy to sign at check in.
Best Western Maingate East Hotel & Suites 4018 W Vine Street Kissimmee FL   407-870-2000 (800-780-7234)
Dogs are allowed for an additional pet fee per room of $75 for each 1 to 7 days.
Days Suites Orlando/Maingate East 5820 W Irlo Bronson Hwy Kissimmee FL   407-396-7900 (800-DAYS-INN)
Dogs of all sizes are allowed. There is a $10 per night pet fee per pet. Reservations are recommended due to limited rooms for pets.
Homewood Suites Orlando-Disney Resort 3100 Parkway Blvd. Kissimmee FL   407-396-2229 (800-225-5466)
There is a $250 pet deposit and $200 of the deposit is refundable. ($50 pet charge)
Howard Johnson Hotel 8660 W. Irlo Bronson Memorial Hwy Kissimmee FL   407-396-4500 (800-446-4656)
Dogs up to 50 pounds are allowed. There is a $25 per week pet fee.
La Quinta Inn & Suites Orlando/Maingate 3484 Polynesian Isle Blvd Kissimmee FL   407-997-1700 (800-531-5900)
Dogs of all sizes are allowed. There are no additional pet fees. Dogs must be leashed and cleaned up after. A call number must be left with the front desk, and the Do Not Disturb sign placed on the door if there is a pet inside alone. Make arrangements with housekeeping if you need your room serviced.
Larson's Family Inn 6075 West U.S. Hwy. 192 Kissimmee FL   407-396-6100
There is a $150 refundable pet deposit and a $10 per day pet charge. Dogs up to 50 pounds are allowed.
Motel 6 - Orlando-Kissimmee Main Gate East 5731 W Irlo Bronson Highway Kissimmee FL   407-396-6333 (800-466-8356)
One well-behaved family pet per room. Guest must notify front desk upon arrival. Guest is liable for any damages. In consideration of all guests, pets must never be left unattended in the guest rooms.
Motel 6 - Orlando-Kissimmee Main Gate West 7455 W Irlo Bronson Highway Kissimmee FL   407-396-6422 (800-466-8356)
One well-behaved family pet per room. Guest must notify front desk upon arrival. Guest is liable for any damages. In consideration of all guests, pets must never be left unattended in the guest rooms.
Park Inn & Suites Maingate East 6075 W Irlo Bronson Hwy Kissimmee FL   407-396-6100
Dogs of all sizes are allowed. There is a $10 per day additional pet fee and a $150 refundable pet deposit.
Radisson Resort Worldgate 3011 Maingate Lane Kissimmee FL   407-396-1400
Dogs up to 50 pounds are allowed. There is a $75 one time additional pet fee.

Red Roof Inn - Kissimmee 4970 Kyngs Heath Road Kissimmee FL   407-396-0065 (800-RED-ROOF)
One well-behaved family pet per room. Guest must notify front desk upon arrival. Guest is liable for any damages. In consideration of all guests, pets must never be left unattended in the guest rooms.
Comfort Inn 8442 Palm Parkway Lake Buena Vista FL   407-996-7300 (877-424-6423)
Dogs up to 50 pounds are allowed for an additional fee of $10 per night per pet.
Candlewood Suites 1130 Greenwood Blvd Lake Mary FL   407-585-3000 (877-270-6405)
Dogs up to 60 pounds are allowed for an additional fee of $12 per night per pet for 1 to 14 days; it is $150 one time fee for 15 or more days per pet.
La Quinta Inn & Suites Orlando Lake Mary 1060 Greenwood Blvd. Lake Mary FL   407-805-9901 (800-531-5900)
Dogs of all sizes are allowed. There are no additional pet fees. Dogs must be leashed and cleaned up after. A cell number must be left with the front desk and the Do Not Disturb sign on the door, if pets are in the room alone.
Red Roof Inn - Orlando West 11241 Colonial Drive Ocoee FL   407-347-0140 (800-RED-ROOF)
One well-behaved family pet per room. Guest must notify front desk upon arrival. Guest is liable for any damages. In consideration of all guests, pets must never be left unattended in the guest rooms.
Comfort Inn 445 S Volusia Avenue Orange City FL   386-775-7444 (877-424-6423)
Dogs are allowed for an additional fee of $10 per night per pet.
Celebration World Resort 7503 Atlantis Way Orlando FL   407-997-7421
Dogs up to 40 pounds are allowed as long as they have proof of up to date shots. There is a $50 one time pet fee per room.
Comfort Suites Universal South 9350 Turkey Lake Road Orlando FL   407-351-5050 (877-424-6423)
Dogs up to 50 pounds are allowed for an additional one time pet fee of $49 per room.
Country Inns & Suites by Carlson 5440 Forbes Place Orlando FL   407-856-8896
Dogs up to 75 pounds are allowed. There is a $150 one time pet fee.
Days Inn Orlando North 2500 W 33rd St Orlando FL   407-841-3731 (800-329-7466)
Dogs of all sizes are allowed. There is a $10 per night pet fee per pet.
Extended StayAmerica Orlando - Convention Center - Westwood Blvd. 6451 Westwood Blvd. Orlando FL 407-352-3454
There is a one time pet fee of $25.00 for one night stays, $50.00 for two night stays, and $75.00 for any stay of three nights or longer.
Extended StayAmerica Orlando - Universal Studios 5620 Major Blvd. Orlando FL   407-351-1788
There is a one time pet fee of $25.00 for one night stays, $50.00 for two night stays, and $75.00 for any stay of three nights or longer.
Hard Rock Hotel 5800 Universal Blvd Orlando FL   407-503-2000 (800-BEASTAR (232-7827))
This full service resort has many extras such as a 12,000 square foot pool with a sand beach, an underwater sound system, interactive fountains, and a water slide, a variety of planned activities and recreation, and express access and transportation to the Universal Orlando Theme Park. Dogs of all sizes are welcome for an additional one time pet fee of $25 per room. Guests must have a health certificate for each pet obtained within 10 days prior to arrival. Dogs must be quiet, well behaved, leashed, cleaned up after, and removed for housekeeping. Dogs must be walked in designated areas only, and they are not allowed in pool/lounge, or restaurant areas. Dogs are not allowed in Club rooms.
Holiday Inn Express Lake Buena Vista 8686 Palm Pkwy. Orlando FL   407-239-8400 (877-270-6405)
Dogs of all sizes are allowed for an additional one time fee of $50 per pet.
Holiday Inn Hotel & Suites Main Gate Universal Studios 5905 Kirkman Road Orlando FL   407-351-3333 (877-270-6405)
Quiet dogs of all sizes are allowed for an additional one time pet fee of $50 per room.
La Quinta Inn & Suites Orlando Airport North 7160 N. Frontage Rd. Orlando FL   407-240-5000 (800-531-5900)
Dogs of all sizes are allowed. There are no additional pet fees. Dogs may not be left unattended, and they must be leashed and cleaned up after. Dogs must be removed or crated for housekeeping.
La Quinta Inn & Suites Orlando Convention Center 8504 Universal Blvd. Orlando FL   407-345-1365 (800-531-5900)
Dogs of all sizes are allowed. There are no additional pet fees. Dogs must be leashed and cleaned up after. Dogs must be crated if left alone in the room.
La Quinta Inn & Suites Orlando UCF 11805 Research Pkwy. Orlando FL   407-737-6075 (800-531-5900)
Dogs of all sizes are allowed. There are no additional pet fees. Dogs must be leashed and cleaned up after. A call number must be left at the front desk, and the Do Not Disturb sign left on the door, if there is a pet alone inside.
La Quinta Inn Orlando Airport West 7931 Daetwyler Dr. Orlando FL   407-857-9215 (800-531-5900)
Dogs of all sizes are allowed. There are no additional pet fees. Dogs must be leashed and cleaned up after. Dogs may not be left unattended unless they will be quiet and well behaved.
La Quinta Inn Orlando International Dr 8300 Jamaican Court Orlando FL   407-351-1660 (800-531-5900)
Dogs of all sizes are allowed. There are no additional pet fees. Dogs must be leashed and cleaned up after. Dogs must be well behaved, and the Do Not Disturb must be on the door if there is a pet alone inside.

La Quinta Inn Orlando South 2051 Consulate Drive Orlando FL   407-240-0500 (800-531-5900)
Dogs of all sizes are allowed. There are no additional pet fees. Dogs may not be left unattended, and they must be leashed and cleaned up after.
Motel 6 - Orlando - International Drive 5909 American Way Orlando FL   407-351-6500 (800-466-8356)
One well-behaved family pet per room. Guest must notify front desk upon arrival. Guest is liable for any damages. In consideration of all guests, pets must never be left unattended in the guest rooms.
Motel 6 - Orlando - Winter Park 5300 Adanson Road Orlando FL   407-647-1444 (800-466-8356)
One well-behaved family pet per room. Guest must notify front desk upon arrival. Guest is liable for any damages. In consideration of all guests, pets must never be left unattended in the guest rooms.
TOP 200 PLACE Portofino Bay Hotel 5601 Universal Blvd Orlando FL   407-503-1000 (800-BEASTAR (232-7827))
Built to resemble an Italian Riviera seaside village, this beautiful bay hotel features 3 themed swimming pools, special privileges to the area's best golf courses, and express access and transportation to the Universal Orlando Theme Park. Dogs of all sizes are welcome for an additional one time pet fee of $25 per room. Guests must have a health certificate for each pet obtained within 10 days prior to arrival. Dogs must be quiet, well behaved, leashed and cleaned up after, and removed for housekeeping. Dogs are walked in designated areas only, and they are not allowed in the pool/lounge or restaurant areas. Dogs are not allowed in Club rooms.
Quality Inn Plaza 9000 International Drive Orlando FL   407-996-8585 (877-424-6423)
Dogs up to 50 pounds are allowed for an additional fee of $10 per night per pet.
Red Roof Inn - Orlando Convention Center 9922 Hawaiian Court Orlando FL   407-352-1507 (800-RED-ROOF)
One well-behaved family pet per room. Guest must notify front desk upon arrival. Guest is liable for any damages. In consideration of all guests, pets must never be left unattended in the guest rooms.
Residence Inn SeaWorld 11000 Westwood Blvd. Orlando FL   407-313-3600 (800-331-3131)
http://www.residenceinnseaworld.com/
There is a $150 one time pet fee.
Residence Inn by Marriott 11651 University Blvd Orlando FL   407-513-9000
Well behaved dogs of all sizes are allowed. There is a $25 plus tax per night fee up to 5 nights, not to exceed $125 per stay. There is a pet policy to sign at check in and they ask that you do not leave your pet unattended unless you leave a number where you can be reached or a cell number.
Residence Inn by Marriott 11450 Marbella Palm Court Orlando FL   407-465-0075
Dogs of all sizes are allowed. There is a $75 one time fee and a pet policy to sign at check in.
Royal Pacific Resort 6300 Hollywood Way Orlando FL   407-503-3000 (800-BEASTAR (232-7827))
Nestled in a lush lagoon setting, this full service family resort features such extras as authentic luaus with entertainment, a large pool with a sandy beach and interactive water play area, and express access and transportation to the Universal Orlando Theme Park. Dogs of all sizes are welcome for an additional one time pet fee of $25 per room. Guests must have a health certificate for each pet obtained within 10 days prior to arrival. Dogs must be quiet, well behaved, leashed and cleaned up after, and removed for housekeeping. Dogs must be walked in designated areas only, and they are not allowed in pool/lounge, or restaurant areas. Dogs are not allowed in Club rooms.
The Safari Hotel & Suites Lake Buena Vista 12205 S. Apopka Vineland Road Orlando FL   407-239-0444
Dogs up to 80 pounds are allowed. There are no additional pet fees. Dogs are not allowed to be left alone in the room.
TownePlace Suites Orlando East/UCF 11801 High Tech Avenue Orlando FL   407-243-6100
Dogs of all sizes are allowed. There is a $75 one time pet fee per visit.
Travelodge Orlando Centroplex 409 N. Magnolia Ave. Orlando FL   407-423-1671 (800-578-7878)
There is a $10 per day pet charge. Dogs up to 50 pounds are allowed.
Days Inn Sanford 4650 West SR 46 Sanford FL   407-323-6500 (800-329-7466)
Dogs of all sizes are allowed. There is a $10 per night pet fee.
Super 8 Sanford 4750 SR 46 West Sanford FL   407-323-3445 (800-800-8000)
Dogs of all sizes are allowed. There is a $10 returnable deposit required per room. Smoking and non-smoking rooms are available for pet rooms.

Campgrounds and RV Parks
Wekiwa Springs State Park 1800 Wekiwa Circle Apopka FL   407-884-2008 (800-326-3521)
There are many water and land activities year round at this park, and they have interpretive programs at their amphitheater, a nature center, and 13 miles of multi-use trails. Dogs of all sizes are allowed at no additional fee. Dogs may not be left unattended, and they must have current rabies and shot records. Dogs must be on no more than a 6 foot leash, and be cleaned up after. Dogs are not allowed in buildings, at the beach, the springs, the top of the slope, or on the boardwalk trails. Dogs are allowed on the other trails. The camping and tent areas also allow dogs. There is a dog walk area at the campground.
Florida Camp Inn 48504 H 27 Davenport FL   863-424-2494
Dogs of all sizes are allowed. There are no additional pet fees. Dogs may not be left unattended, and they must be leashed and cleaned up after. The camping and tent areas also allow dogs. There is a dog walk area at the

campground.

Encore Tropical Palms 2650 Holiday Trail Kissimmee FL 800-647-2567
Dogs of all sizes are allowed. There are no additional pet fees. Dogs must be quiet, well behaved, leashed, and cleaned up after. There is a dog walk area at the campground.

Kissimmee KOA 2643 Happy Camper Place Kissimmee FL   407-396-2400 (800-562-7791)
http://www.kissorlando.com
Dogs of all sizes are allowed. There are no additional pet fees. Dogs may not be left unattended outside, and they must be quiet, leashed, and cleaned up after. The camping and tent areas also allow dogs. There is a dog walk area at the campground.

Blue Spring State Park 2100 W French Avenue Orange City FL 386-775-3663 (800-326-3521)
Blue Spring, a scenic recreation area, is also a designated manatee refuge because the warm waters in Winter create a perfect habitat for the growing population of West Indian Manatees. Dogs of all sizes are allowed at no additional fee. Dogs may not be left unattended for more than 30 minutes at a time, and they must have current rabies and shot records. Dogs must be on no more than a 6 foot leash, and be cleaned up after. Dogs are not allowed in buildings or on the beaches. Dogs are allowed on the trails. The camping and tent areas also allow dogs. There is a dog walk area at the campground.

Deland/Orange City KOA 1440 E Minnesota Avenue Orange City FL 386-775-3996 (800-562-7857)
http://www.theockoa.com
Dogs of all sizes are allowed. There are no additional pet fees. Dogs may not be left unattended, and they must be leashed and cleaned up after. There are some breed restrictions. The camping and tent areas also allow dogs. There is a dog walk area at the campground.

Orlando SE/Lake Whippoorwill KOA 12345 Narcoossee Road Orlando FL   407-277-5075 (800-562-3969)
http://www.koa.com
Dogs of all sizes are allowed. There are no additional pet fees. Dogs may not be left unattended, and they must be leashed and cleaned up after. The camping and tent areas also allow dogs. There is a dog walk area at the campground.

Vacation Home Rentals

Caribbean Villas Privately Owned Condo near Disney Call to Arrange Kissimmee FL   407-973-8924
http://www.myfloridacondorental.com
This 2 bedroom, 2 bath condominium vacation rental is located in Carribbean Villas in Kissimmee. There are no additional pet fees.

Sun N Fun Vacation Homes Bear Path Kissimmee FL   407-932-4079 (800-874-3660)
These vacation Homes are located just 5 minutes to Disney and very close to other area attractions. All homes have private screened pools and fenced yards. Most homes welcome well-behaved pets and their families. There is a pet fee of $30 per pet, per week plus a $300 security deposit, which is refundable assuming there is no damage.

The Idyll Mouse One 8092 Roaring Creek Kissimmee FL   603-524-4000
2 Vacation Home Rentals near Disney World. Each house has many luxuries. One house is a 7 bedroom , four bath. The other is a 4 bedroom, 3 bath.

Transportation Systems

LYNX Regional Orlando FL   407-841-5969
http://www.golynx.com
Small dogs in carriers that fit on your lap are allowed on the buses.

Attractions

Celebration US 192 and I-4 Celebration FL
Celebration is a town created by Disney. It has dog-friendly walking trails, outdoor cafes, and stores. Also check for events at Celebration as there are a number of annual events, street fairs and even pet events.

Walt Disney's Animal Kingdom - Kennels Walt Disney World Exit Lake Buena Vista FL   407-842-4321
Dogs aren't allowed inside the theme park, but Disney offers day kennels located at the main entrance. The kennels are air conditioned, attended, indoor pens. You are welcome to exit the park and walk your dog. Just be sure to get your hand stamped so you can re-enter the park. The kennels are open 1 hour before the park opens to 1 hour after the park closes. Proof of vaccinations are required. There is a $10 per day kennel charge.

Florida   - Please always call ahead to make sure that an establishment is still dog-friendly

Celebration

Walt Disney's Epcot Center - Kennels Walt Disney World Exit Lake Buena Vista FL   407-842-4321
Dogs aren't allowed inside the theme park, but Disney offers day kennels located at the main entrance. The
kennels are air conditioned, attended, indoor pens. You are welcome to exit the park and walk your dog. Just be
sure to get your hand stamped so you can re-enter the park. The kennels are open 1 hour before the park opens
to 1 hour after the park closes. Proof of vaccinations are required. There is a $10 per day kennel charge.
Walt Disney's MGM Studios - Kennels Walt Disney World Exit Lake Buena Vista FL   407-842-4321
Dogs aren't allowed inside the theme park, but Disney offers day kennels located at the main entrance. The
kennels are unattended, locked, outdoor pens. You are welcome to exit the park and walk your dog. Just be sure
to get your hand stamped so you can re-enter the park. The kennels are open 1 hour before the park opens to 1
hour after the park closes. Proof of vaccinations are required. There is a $10 per day kennel charge.
Walt Disney's Magic Kingdom - Kennels Walt Disney World Exit Lake Buena Vista FL   407-842-4321
Dogs aren't allowed inside the theme park, but Disney offers day kennels located at the main entrance. The
kennels are air conditioned, attended, indoor pens. You are welcome to exit the park and walk your dog. Just be
sure to get your hand stamped so you can re-enter the park. The kennels are open 1 hour before the park opens
to 1 hour after the park closes. Proof of vaccinations are required. There is a $10 per day kennel charge.
Sea World - Kennel 7007 Sea World Drive Orlando FL   888-800-5447
http://www.seaworld.com
There is a pet care center in the parking area that will take care of your pet in a temperture control and manned
facility for $6 per day. Owners need to bring the pet food and also owners are responsible for walking their
animals.
Hip Dog Canine Aquatic Rehabilitation and Fitness Ctr. P. O. Box 793/4965 N Palmetto Avenue Winter
Park FL   407-628-1476
http://www.hipdog.net/
All the benefits of hydrotherapy, including just for fun, can be found for your canine companion here. This is a
safe environment, with trained professionals, where you can be with your pet in or out of the water. There are 1
hour fitness and fun swim times also available; call for availability.
Winter Park Shopping District Park Avenue and Osceola Ave Winter Park FL
This is a dog-friendly shopping district with outdoor cafes. Many of the stores will allow a well behaved, leashed
dog inside.

Stores

PetSmart Pet Store 380 S State Rd 434 Altamonte Springs FL   407-682-7220
Your licensed and well-behaved leashed dog is allowed in the store.
PetSmart Pet Store 4510 S US 17-92 Casselberry FL   407-331-8991
Your licensed and well-behaved leashed dog is allowed in the store.
PetSmart Pet Store 4550 W Lake Mary Blvd Lake Mary FL   407-804-1901
Your licensed and well-behaved leashed dog is allowed in the store.
PetSmart Pet Store 9585 W Colonial Dr Ocoee FL   407-297-8110
Your licensed and well-behaved leashed dog is allowed in the store.
PetSmart Pet Store 6134 E Colonial Dr Orlando FL   407-658-7710

Your licensed and well-behaved leashed dog is allowed in the store.
PetSmart Pet Store 8219 S John Young Pkwy Orlando FL   407-351-2336
Your licensed and well-behaved leashed dog is allowed in the store.
PetSmart Pet Store 731 N Alfaya Trail Orlando FL   407-275-0799
Your licensed and well-behaved leashed dog is allowed in the store.
Petco Pet Store 7649 West Colonial Drive Ste 130 Orlando FL   407-296-2422
Your licensed and well-behaved leashed dog is allowed in the store.
Petco Pet Store 4616 Millenia Plaza Way Orlando FL   407-370-9119
Your licensed and well-behaved leashed dog is allowed in the store.
Petco Pet Store 2410 East Colonial Drive Orlando FL   407-228-4340
Your licensed and well-behaved leashed dog is allowed in the store.
Petco Pet Store 1778 West Sandlake Rd Orlando FL   407-251-4211
Your licensed and well-behaved leashed dog is allowed in the store.
PetSmart Pet Store 1115 Vidina Place Oviedo FL   407-365-1029
Your licensed and well-behaved leashed dog is allowed in the store.

Parks

Wekiwa Springs State Park Wekiwa Springs Road at SR-434 Apopka FL   407-884-2008
Dogs are allowed in the park but are not allowed in the springs. Dogs must be leashed in the park.
Blue Spring State Park 2100 West French Avenue Orange City FL   386-775-3663
At this park, you and your dog can view an endangered species, the manatee (sea cow). Leashed dogs are
allowed on some of the manatee viewing platforms, and on some of the park's hiking trails. There will be signs
posted where pups are not allowed. The manatee season is from mid-November to mid-March. The park is
located about 40 minutes from Orlando.
Cady Way Trail Bennett Rd and Corrine Dr. Orlando FL   407-836-6200
http://parks.onetgov.net/6Cadyway.htm
There is a 3.5 mile paved bike and hiking trail which links Winter Park and Orlando. Dogs on leash are allowed.

Lake Eola Park

Lake Eola Park Rosalind and Washington St Orlando FL   407-246-2827
This is a downtown urban park with a 1 mile jogging trail, grassy areas and a lake. The park has outdoor
entertainment periodically. Dogs are allowed on leash.
Lake Jessup Park South end of Sanford Ave Sanford FL
This is a small park for walking or picnicing. Dogs must be leashed in this park.
Lower Wekiva River State Preserve S.R. 46 Sanford FL   407-884-2008

Dogs are allowed on the trails but are not allowed in the camping areas. Dogs must be leashed in this park.

Off-Leash Dog Parks
Gemini Springs Dog Park 37 Dirksen Drive Debary FL 386-736-5953
There are 4.5 acres at this off lead area with separate areas for large and small dogs; there are shade trees, benches, watering stations, dog wash stations, and picnic tables. Dogs must be sociable, current on all vaccinations and license, and under owner's control/care at all times. Dogs must be leashed when not in designated off-lead areas.
Mount D.o.r.a. Dog Park East end of 11th Avenue Mount Dora FL 352-735-7183
Located right past the Ice House Theater, this large, fenced off-leash area has separate sections for small, medium, and large dogs, plus a water station with bowls, waste stations, and benches. Dogs must be sociable, current on all vaccinations, licensed, and cleaned up after at all times. Dogs must be leashed when not in designated off-lead areas.
Downey Dog Park 10107 Flowers Avenue Orlando FL 407-249-6195
There are separate sections for large and small dogs, water fountains, and doggy sanitary stations. Dogs must be sociable, current on all vaccinations and license, and under owner's control/care at all times. Dogs must be leashed when not in designated off-lead areas.
Dr. Phillips Dog Park 8249 Buenavista Woods Blvd Orlando FL 407-254-9037
This park is located off of S. Apopka-Vineland Road south of Sandlake Road. Dogs must be sociable, current on all vaccinations and license, and under owner's control/care at all times. Dogs are leashed when not in designated off-lead areas.
Paw Park of Historic Sanford 427 S. French Avenue Sanford FL 407-330-5688
http://www.pawparksanford.org
This off-leash dog park is located in the historic district of Sanford. The fenced park has a dog water fountain and dog shower. It is located south of State Route 46, off Highway 17-92 at East 5th Street.
West Orange Dog Park 12400 Marshall Farms Road Winter Garden FL 407-656-3299
This off lead area can also be accessed through West Orange Park (150 Windermere Road). There are separate sections for large and small dogs, water fountains, and doggy sanitary stations. Dogs must be sociable, current on all vaccinations and license, and under owner's control/care at all times. Dogs must be leashed when not in designated off-lead areas.
TOP 200 PLACE Fleet Peeples Park Dog Park South Lakemont Avenue Winter Park FL 407-740-8897
http://www.ffpp.org/
This park is a fenced dog park with a pond for swimming. Dogs are allowed off-leash within the park. There is shade, water, and bags for cleanup. The park is open to Winter Park residents as well as the public at large. The dog park is located in Fleet Peeples Park on South Lakemont Avenue.

Outdoor Restaurants
Yellow Dog Eats Cafe 1236 Hempel Ave Gotha FL 407-296-0609
This cafe serves deli-type food. Dogs are allowed at the outdoor tables.
Dexter's of Lake Mary 950 Promenade Avenue Lake Mary FL 407-805-3090
http://www.dexwine.com/
This award winning eatery has 3 locations, each offering a monthly changing menu and an extensive list of wines, champagne, ports, and sherries. Live music and cutting edge artwork on display adds to the ambiance. They prefer that visitors do not bring their dogs when they are their busiest on Friday and Saturday nights. Dogs are permitted at the outdoor tables, and they also have water bowls for your pet. Dogs must be quiet, well behaved, under owner's control, and leashed and cleaned up after at all times.
Cafe Bravissimo 337 N Shine Avenue Orlando FL 407-898-7333
http://www.cafebravissimo.com/
This award winning restaurant offers a warm comfortable atmosphere, Italian food, an impressive list of wines, and outdoor dining. Dogs are permitted at the outdoor tables. Dogs must be well behaved, under owner's control, and leashed and cleaned up after at all times.
Casey's on Central 50 East Central Blvd Orlando FL 407-648-4218
This bar allows dogs at their outdoor tables. Water and treats are provided for your pet.
Central City Market 617 E Central Blvd Orlando FL 407-849-9779
This award-winning neighborhood market, deli, café, and grill features a wide variety of foods, both for dining in and for take out. There is amiable seating in either the back garden area or out in front, and dogs are permitted at the outdoor tables. They are not allowed inside buildings. Dogs must be well behaved, under owner's control, and leashed and cleaned up after at all times.
Dexter's of Thornton Park 808 Washington Street Orlando FL 407-629-1150
http://www.dexwine.com/
This award winning eatery has 3 locations, each offering a monthly changing menu and an extensive list of wines, champagne, ports, and sherries. Live music and cutting edge artwork on display adds to the ambiance. Dogs are not allowed when they are their busiest on Friday and Saturday nights, and on Sunday afternoons.

Dogs are permitted at the outdoor tables, and they also have water bowls for your pet. Dogs must be well behaved, under owner's control, and leashed and cleaned up after at all times.

Julie's Waterfront 4201 S Orange Avenue Orlando FL   407-240-2557
This popular eatery offers lakeside dining and a well rounded menu of seafood and American favorites. The outdoor seating has a tropical feel to it, and dogs are permitted at the outdoor tables. Dogs must be well behaved, under owner's control, and leashed and cleaned up after at all times.

K Restaurant Wine Bar 2401 Edgewater Drive Orlando FL   407-872-2332
http://www.krestaurantwinebar.com/#
This upscale dining eatery features a seasonally changing menu that incorporates flavor influences from all around the world. Dogs are permitted at the outdoor tables. Dogs must be well behaved, under owner's control, and leashed and cleaned up after at all times.

Panera Bread 227 N Eola Dr Orlando FL   407-481-1060
This restaurant serves deli-type food. Dogs are allowed at the outdoor tables.

Quiznos 719 Good Homes Road Orlando FL   407-822-0102
Dogs are allowed at the outdoor tables. The restaurant has outdoor tables only in the Summer.

Quiznos 12515 H 535 Orlando FL   407-827-1110
Dogs are allowed at the outdoor tables.

Quiznos 7583 W Sandlake Road Orlando FL   407-226-2644
Dogs are allowed at the outdoor tables.

Sam Sneads Downtown Restaurant

TOP 200 PLACE Sam Snead's Downtown Restaurant 301 East Pine Street Orlando FL   407-999-0109
http://www.samsneadsdowntown.com/
This is the restaurant that became the epicenter of the doggie dining legislation and bill in 2006. It is here that a Florida state health inspector threatened fines for dogs on the patio while dogs were happily dining on patios throughout the state. The restaurant's complaint to the city resulted in governor Jeb Bush signing the doggy dining bill at this restaurant. Now your dog can join you here with his own Furry Friends menu including meals like the Buddy Boy's Burger, Chicken and Kibble, Bow Wow Pizza and other items. The items are served on a complimentary frisbee. We recommend that people who travel with dogs to Orlando as well as locals visit Sam Snead's and show your support as well as enjoy a dog-friendly atmosphere.

The Greek Corner 1600 N Orange Avenue Orlando FL   407-228-0303
This eatery specializes in genuine Greek cuisine. Their outside dining area affords visitors a picturesque view of Lake Ivanhoe. Dogs are permitted at the outdoor tables. Dogs must be well behaved, under owner's control, and leashed and cleaned up after at all times. Dogs are not allowed to be on the chairs; they must remain on the floor.

White Wolf Cafe 1829 N Orange Avenue Orlando FL   407-895-5590

http://www.whitewolfcafe.com/
This eatery features a Bohemian atmosphere, live performances and an outdoor patio area. Dogs are permitted at the outdoor tables. Dogs must be well behaved, under owner's control, and leashed and cleaned up after at all times.
Wildside BBQ and Grill 700 E Washington Street Orlando FL   407-872-8665
This popular barbecue eatery roasts and smokes their meat in a large pit smoker out back. They also offer terrace dining, and are usually very busy on the weekends when bands perform. Dogs are permitted at the outdoor tables. Dogs must be well behaved, under owner's control, and leashed and cleaned up after at all times.
Angelo's Pizzaria 107 W 1st St Sanford FL   407-320-0799
Dogs are allowed at the outdoor tables.
Blue Dahlia Restaurant and Wine Bar 112 E First Street Sanford FL   407-688-4745
http://bluedahliasanford.com/
This eatery hosts special events and live entertainment throughout the year, features a seasonally changing menu and a selection of fine wines. They offer indoor or outdoor dining service. Dogs are permitted at the outdoor tables. Dogs must be well behaved, under owner's control, and leashed and cleaned up after at all times.
Dalli's Riverwalk Pizzeria 350 E. Seminole Blvd Sanford FL   407-328-0018
http://www.riverwalkpizzeria.com/
This pizzeria offers live entertainment on Saturday nights and alfresco dining. Dogs are allowed at the outer tables; they must be under owner's control/care at all times.
Hollerbach's Willow Tree Cafe 205 E First Street Sanford FL   407-321-2204
http://www.willowtreecafe.com/
This eatery specializes in authentic German foods. In addition to traditional German foods, they also offer American favorites, original menu creations, and daily and seasonal chef specials. Dogs are permitted at the outdoor tables. Dogs must be well behaved, under owner's control, and leashed and cleaned up after at all times.
Tin Lizzie Tavern 111 W 1st St Sanford FL   407-321-1908
Dogs are allowed at the outdoor tables.
Bosphorous 108 Park Avenue S Winter Park FL   407-644-8609
This eatery specializes in fine Turkish cuisine, offering lunch and dinner, a good selection of beer and wine, and outdoor dining. Dogs are permitted at the outdoor tables. Dogs must be well behaved, under owner's control, and leashed and cleaned up after at all times.
Chef Justin's Park Plaza Gardens 319 Park Ave South Winter Park FL   407-645-2475
http://www.parkplazagardens.com/
This popular eatery features seasonal specials and gourmet cuisine with indoor or outdoor dining. The chef here has also created a tasty doggy menu that would satisfy any pooch. Dogs are permitted at the outdoor tables. Dogs must be well behaved, under owner's control, and leashed and cleaned up after at all times.
Dexter's of Winter Park 558 W New England Avenue Winter Park FL   407-629-1150
http://www.dexwine.com/
This award winning eatery has 3 locations, each offering a monthly changing menu and an extensive list of wines, champagne, ports, and sherries. They are their busiest on Friday and Saturday nights, and suggest that may not be the best time to bring your pet. Dogs are permitted at the outdoor tables, and they also have water bowls for your pet. Dogs must be well behaved, under owner's control, and leashed and cleaned up after at all times.
Hot Olives Restaurant 463 W New England Avenue Winter Park FL   407-629-1030
http://www.hotolivesrestaurant.com/
This popular eatery features seasonal specials and gourmet cuisine with indoor or outdoor garden dining. There is also a market here that offers home replacement meals, quick lunches, gourmet foods, wines, gifts, and more. Dogs are permitted at the outdoor tables. Dogs must be well behaved, under owner's control, and leashed and cleaned up after at all times.
Luma on Park 290 Park Avenue Winter Park FL   407-599-4111
http://www.lumaonpark.com/
This upscale restaurant offers American cuisine. Dogs are permitted at the outdoor tables. Just tell the host at the door on the New England Street side that you would like to dine outside as you have your pup with you, and they will service your table and provide water for your pet. Dogs must be well behaved, under owner's control, and leashed and cleaned up after at all times.
Three Ten Park South 310 S Park Ave Winter Park FL   407-647-7277
Dogs are allowed at the outdoor tables.
Wazzabi Sushi 1408 Gay Road Winter Park FL   407-647-8744
http://www.wazzabisushi.com/
This Japanese steakhouse and fresh-to-order sushi bar also has a full liquor bar and outdoor patio seating. Dogs are permitted at the outdoor tables, and a water bowl is also made available for them. Dogs must be well behaved, under owner's control, and leashed and cleaned up after at all times.

Palatka

Parks

Ravine State Gardens Twigg Street Palatka FL   386-329-3721
This park has long been famous for its extensive plantings of azaleas and other ornamental plants. Leashed dogs are allowed on the nature trails throughout this 80+ acre park. Dogs are not allowed in the picnic areas. The park is located about a one hour drive from St. Augustine.

Panama City Beach

Accommodations

La Quinta Inn & Suites Panama City 1030 East 23rd Street Panama City FL   850-914-0022 (800-531-5900)
Dogs of all sizes are allowed. There are no additional pet fees. Dogs must be quiet, well behaved, leashed and cleaned up after. A call number must be left at the front dest, and the Do Not Disturb sign left on the door, if there is a pet alone inside.

Campgrounds and RV Parks

Emerald Coast RV Beach Resort 1957 Allison Avenue Panama City Beach FL   800-232-2478
http://www.rvresort.com
Dogs of all sizes are allowed. There are no additional pet fees. Dogs may not be left unattended outside, and they must be leashed and cleaned up after. Dogs are not allowed in any of the buildings. There are some breed restrictions. There is a dog walk area at the campground.
Raccoon River Campground 12209 Hutchison Blvd Panama City Beach FL   877-234-0181
http://www.floridacamping.com
Dogs of all sizes are allowed. There are no additional pet fees. Dogs must be leashed and cleaned up after. There are some breed restrictions. There is a dog walk area at the campground.

Stores

PetSmart Pet Store 849 E 23rd St Panama City FL   850-522-4122
Your licensed and well-behaved leashed dog is allowed in the store.

Pensacola

Accommodations

Red Roof Inn - Pensacola East - Milton 2672 Avalon Boulevard Milton FL   850-995-6100 (800-RED-ROOF)
One well-behaved family pet per room. Guest must notify front desk upon arrival. Guest is liable for any damages. In consideration of all guests, pets must never be left unattended in the guest rooms.
Comfort Inn 3 New Warrington Road Pensacola FL   850-455-3233 (877-424-6423)
Dogs under 50 pounds are allowed for an additional one time pet fee of $25 per room. The fee is $25 per pet per night for dogs over 50 pounds.
Days Inn Pensacola/Historic Downtown 710 N Palafox St Pensacola FL   850-438-4922 (800-329-7466)
Dogs of all sizes are allowed. There is a $10 per night pet fee per pet.
La Quinta Inn Pensacola 7750 North Davis Hwy. Pensacola FL   850-474-0411 (800-531-5900)
Dogs up to 50 pounds are allowed. There are no additional pet fees. Dogs must be leashed and cleaned up after.
Motel 6 - Pensacola East 7226 Plantation Road Pensacola FL   850-474-1060 (800-466-8356)
One well-behaved family pet per room. Guest must notify front desk upon arrival. Guest is liable for any damages. In consideration of all guests, pets must never be left unattended in the guest rooms.
Motel 6 - Pensacola North 7827 N Davis Highway Pensacola FL   850-476-5386 (800-466-8356)
One well-behaved family pet per room. Guest must notify front desk upon arrival. Guest is liable for any damages. In consideration of all guests, pets must never be left unattended in the guest rooms.
Quality Inn 6550 Pensacola Blvd Pensacola FL   850-477-0711 (877-424-6423)
Dogs of all sizes are allowed. There is a $25 one time fee if the dog is under 40 pounds, and there is a $50 one time fee if the dog is over 40 pounds.

Red Roof Inn - Pensacola University Mall 7340 Plantation Road Pensacola FL   850-476-7960 (800-RED-ROOF)
One well-behaved family pet per room. Guest must notify front desk upon arrival. Guest is liable for any damages. In consideration of all guests, pets must never be left unattended in the guest rooms.
Super 8 Pensacola/Davis Hwy 7220 Plantation Rd Pensacola FL   850-476-8038 (800-800-8000)
Dogs of all sizes are allowed. There is a $20 per night pet fee per pet. Smoking and non-smoking rooms are available for pet rooms.

Attractions
Fort Barrancas Pensacola Navel Air Station Pensacola FL   850-455-5167
Although dogs are not allowed in the fort or other buildings, this historic place offers great scenery, hiking, picnicking, and restrooms. Dogs of all sizes are allowed at no additional fee. Dogs must always be attended, leashed at all times, and cleaned up after. Dogs are allowed on the nature trail and in picnic areas. They are open all year; from March-October they are open from 9:30am-5:00pm, and from November-February they are open from 8:30am-4:00pm.

Stores
PetSmart Pet Store 6251 N Davis Hwy Pensacola FL   850-476-7375
Your licensed and well-behaved leashed dog is allowed in the store.

Beaches
Bayview Dog Beach In Bayou Texar off E Lloyd Street Pensacola FL   850-436-5511
This water park for dogs offers pets beach and water fun, and there are benches, picnic tables, trash cans, pooper scooper stations, and a washing station on site. Dogs must be sociable, current on all vaccinations, licensed, and under owner's control/care at all times. Dogs must be leashed when not in designated off-lead areas.

Parks
Gulf Islands National Seashore 1801 Gulf Breeze Parkway Gulf Breeze FL   850-934-2600
http://www.nps.gov/guis/index.htm
Dogs must be on leash and must be cleaned up after in the camping and trail areas. Dogs are not allowed on beaches or in buildings. This park features hiking, camping, 19th Century forts, and more. Located in Florida and Mississippi.
TOP 200 PLACE Milton Canoe Adventures 8974 Tomahawk Landing Road Milton FL   850-623-6197
http://www.adventuresunlimited.com/
Whether you take two hours or many days, you can experience canoeing here with your dog. The spring fed rivers flow at an average depth of two feet over a soft, sandy bottom. Your pet and you can enjoy a canoe trip together for an additional $10 for the dog. Dogs must be kept leashed at all times, and cleaned up after. They are open year round.

Off-Leash Dog Parks
Scott Complex Dog Park Summit Blvd Pensacola FL   850-436-5511
About an acre in size, this off leash doggy play area offers water fountains for hounds and humans, a pooper scooper station, benches, and picnic tables. Dogs must be sociable, current on all vaccinations, licensed, and under owner's control/care at all times. Dogs must be leashed when not in designated off-lead areas.

Perry

Accommodations
Days Inn Perry 2277 S Bryon Butler Pkwy Perry FL   850-584-5311 (800-329-7466)
Dogs up to 20 pounds are allowed. There is a $10 one time per pet fee per visit.

Port Charlotte

Accommodations

Motel 6 - Punta Gorda 9300 Knights Drive Punta Gorda FL   941-639-9585 (800-466-8356)
One well-behaved family pet per room. Guest must notify front desk upon arrival. Guest is liable for any damages. In consideration of all guests, pets must never be left unattended in the guest rooms.

Outdoor Restaurants
Patera's Bistro 24150 Tiseo Blvd #4 Port Charlotte FL   941-743-0626
This bistro offers a variety of pizzas, and American and Italian cuisine, plus they have take out, catering, and outside dining. Dogs are allowed at the outer tables; they must be leashed and under owner's control/care at all times.

Port Richey

Accommodations
Comfort Inn 11810 H 19 Port Richey FL   727-863-3336 (877-424-6423)
Dogs are allowed for an additional fee of $10 per night per pet.

Port St Lucie

Accommodations
Holiday Inn - Port St. Lucie 10120 S. Federal Highway Port St Lucie FL   772-337-2200 (877-270-6405)
Dogs of all sizes are allowed for an additional pet fee of $50 for each 1 to 7 days per room.

Reddick

Campgrounds and RV Parks
Encore RV Resort 16905 NW H 225 Reddick FL   352-591-1723
Dogs of all sizes are allowed. There are no additional pet fees. Dogs may not be left unattended outside, and they must be leashed and cleaned up after. The camping and tent areas also allow dogs. There is a dog walk area at the campground.

Sanibel Island

Accommodations
Tropical Winds Motel & Cottages 4819 Tradewinds Drive Sanibel Island FL   239-472-1765
Dogs of all sizes are allowed. There is a $15 per night per pet additional fee. Puppies are not allowed to be left alone in the room, and adult dogs for short periods.

Vacation Home Rentals
Signal Inn 1811 Olde Middle Gulf Drive Sanibel FL   800-992-4690
http://www.signalinn.com
Signal Inn, situated in a quiet, peaceful and casual atmosphere on the Gulf, consists of 19 furnished elevated beach houses. The pet fee (per pet) is $80 per week or $55 for 3 nights. Only particular units allow pets so please inquire about pets when contacting the inn.

Beaches
Algiers Beach Algiers Lane Sanibel FL   239-472-6477
This beach is located in Gulfside City Park. Dogs on leash are allowed and people need to clean up after their pets. Picnic tables and restrooms are available. There is an hourly parking fee. This beach is located about midway on the island. From the Sanibel causeway, turn right onto Periwinkle Way. Turn left onto Casa Ybel Rd and then left on Algiers Lane.
Bowman's Beach Bowman Beach Road Sanibel FL   239-472-6477

Walk over a bridge to get to the beach. Dogs on leash are allowed and people need to clean up after their pets. Picnic tables are available. This beach is located on the west side of the island, near Captiva. From the Sanibel causeway, turn right on Periwinkle Way. Turn right on Palm Ridge Rd and then continue on Sanibel-Captiva Road. Turn left onto Bowman's Beach Rd.

Lighthouse Park Beach Periwinkle Way Sanibel FL 239-472-6477
This park offers a long thin stretch of beach. Dogs on leash are allowed and people need to clean up after their pets. Picnic tables are available. This park is located on the east end of the island. From Causeway Road, turn onto Periwinkle Way.

Tarpon Bay Road Beach Tarpon Bay Road Sanibel FL 239-472-6477
Take a short walk from the parking lot to the beach. Dogs on leash are allowed and people need to clean up after their pets. Picnic tables and restrooms are available. There is an hourly parking fee. This beach is located mid-way on the island. From the Sanibel causeway, turn right onto Periwinkle Way. Then turn left onto Tarpon Bay Road.

Parks
JN Darling National Wildlife Refuge 1 Wildlife Drive Sanibel FL 239-472-1100
http://www.fws.gov/dingdarling/
Enjoy a 4 1/2 mile nature and wildlife scenic tour by car, as well as the other recreational activities offered here. This park is known for it's migratory bird population. If you stop to look or take pictures, park on the right and stay on the pavement. The refuge is closed Friday, and open Saturday through Thursday from 7:30 am to sunset. Dogs are allowed at no additional fee, and they must be leashed and cleaned up after.

Sarasota

Accommodations
Howard Johnson Express Inn 6511 14th St. W (US 41) Bradenton FL 941-756-8399 (800-446-4656)
Dogs of all sizes are welcome. There is a $5 per day pet fee for pets under 20 pounds, $10 per day pet fee for pets over 20 pounds.
Motel 6 - Bradenton 660 67th Street Circle E Bradenton FL 941-747-6005 (800-466-8356)
One well-behaved family pet per room. Guest must notify front desk upon arrival. Guest is liable for any damages. In consideration of all guests, pets must never be left unattended in the guest rooms.
Shoney's Inn-Bradenton 4915 17th Street East Ellenton FL 941-729-0600
There is a $10 one time pet charge.
Banana Bay Club 8254 Midnight Pass Road Siesta Key FL 941-346-0113
Dogs of all sizes are allowed. There is a $25 one time additional pet fee per room.
Siesta Holiday House 1011-1015 Cresent Street Siesta Key FL 941-312-9882
Dogs of all sizes are allowed. There is a $100 refundable deposit. Small non-hairy dogs are free, otherwise there is a maximum fee of $25 per room per stay. The fee also depends on the breed, how much hair and how large the dog is.
Turtle Beach Resort 9049 Midnight Pass Road Siesta Key FL 941-349-4554
http://www.turtlebeachresort.com/
This resort was featured in the Florida Living Magazine as one of the best romantic escapes in Florida. There is a pet charge added, which is about 10% of the daily room rate.

Campgrounds and RV Parks
Horseshoe Cove RV Resort 5100 60th Street & Caruso Road Bradenton FL 941-758-5335
Dogs up to about 75 pounds are allowed. There are no additional pet fees. Dogs must be leashed and cleaned up after. There are some breed restrictions. There is a dog walk area at the campground.
Lake Manatee State Park 20007 H 64E Bradenton FL 941-741-3028 (800-326-3521)
This park,set along 3 miles of lake shoreline, offers both land and water recreation. Well behaved dogs of all sizes are allowed at no additional fee. Dogs may not be left unattended for more than 30 minutes at a time, and they must have current rabies and shot records. Dogs must be on no more than a 6 foot leash, and be cleaned up after. Dogs are not allowed in buildings, public swimming areas, or by the boat ramps. Dogs are allowed on the trails. The camping and tent areas also allow dogs. There is a dog walk area at the campground.
Sarasota North Resort 800 K Road Bradenton FL 800-678-2131
Dogs of all sizes are allowed. There are no additional pet fees. Dogs must be leashed and cleaned up after. The camping and tent areas also allow dogs. There is a dog walk area at the campground.

Attractions

TOP 200 PLACE **De Soto National Memorial** P. O. Box 15390 Bradenton FL   941-792-0458
http://www.nps.gov/deso/
This memorial commemorates the Spanish explorer Hernando de Soto, who landed on the southwest Florida
coast in 1539. He brought with him 600 soldiers and was under orders from the King of Spain to explore,
colonize and pacify the Indians of the area known as "La Florida". The park depicts 16th century Spanish cultural
values and the clash with the native cultures that the expedition encountered. From late December to early April,
there is a reproduction of the 16th Century Indian village with park rangers dressed in period costume. They give
demonstrations of blacksmithing, cooking, armor repair and military weapons. Dogs are not allowed in the
buildings, but they are allowed on the one half mile self-guiding interpretive trail which leads through mangrove
and coastal environments. Dogs need to be on a 6 foot leash.
Hunsader U-Pick Farms 5500 C.R. 675 Bradenton FL   941-322-2168
http://www.hunsaderfarms.com/
Bring your pup and pick your own strawberries, tomatoes, peppers, eggplant, beans and more at this farm.
Produce seasons vary, but the the u-pick area is open from mid-September through mid-June. They also have a
picnic area.

Stores
PetSmart Pet Store 4425 14th St West Bradenton FL   941-753-2201
Your licensed and well-behaved leashed dog is allowed in the store.

Beaches
De Soto National Memorial Beach Area PO Box 15390 Bradenton FL   941-792-0458
http://www.nps.gov/deso/index.htm
Dogs must be on leash and must be cleaned up after in this park. Leashed dogs are allowed in the beach area,
which is past a hut following a shell path.

Off-Leash Dog Parks
Happy Tails Dog Park 51st Street W Bradenton FL   941-742-5923
Located at the G.T. Bray Park, this 3 acre fenced doggy play area offers a separate area for small or young
dogs, a water fountain, and waste disposal bags. Dogs must be sociable, current on all vaccinations, licensed,
and cleaned up after at all times. Dogs must be leashed when not in designated off-lead areas.
Happy Trails Canine Park 5502 33rd Avenue Drive W Bradenton FL   941-742-5923
http://www.manateechamber.com/parks.asp
Located at one of the county's largest parks with 140 acres of recreational opportunities with an emphasis on
sporting activities, this 3 acre, fenced doggy play area has a separate section for small dogs, a drinking fountain,
and free waste disposal bags. Dogs must be sociable, current on all vaccinations, licensed, and under owner's
control/care at all times. Dogs must be leashed when not in designated off-lead areas.

Outdoor Restaurants
The Dry Dock 412 Gulf of Mexico Dr Longboat Key FL   941-383-0102
This restaurant and bar serves American and seafood. Dogs are allowed at the outdoor tables.
Old Salty Dog 1601 Ken Thompson Pkwy Siesta Key FL   941-388-4311
This restaurant and bar serves American and seafood. Dogs are allowed at the outdoor tables.

Sebring

Accommodations
Quality Inn and Suites Conference Center 6525 H 27 N Sebring FL   863-385-4500 (877-424-6423)
Dogs are allowed for an additional fee of $20 per night per pet.

Campgrounds and RV Parks
Buttonwood Bay RV Resort 10001 H 27S Sebring FL   863-655-1122
http://www.buttonwoodbay.com
Dogs of all sizes are allowed. There are no additional pet fees. Dogs must be leashed and cleaned up after.
There are some breed restrictions. There is a dog walk area at the campground.
Highlands Hammock State Park 5931 Hammock Road Sebring FL   863-386-6094 (800-326-3521)
This park offers a variety of recreational pursuits, nine trails, special events, and an elevated boardwalk that
traverses an old-growth cypress swamp. Dogs of all sizes are allowed at no additional fee. Dogs may not be left

unattended, and they must have current rabies and shot records. Dogs must be on no more than a 6 foot leash, and be cleaned up after. Dogs are not allowed in buildings or on any of the elevated boardwalk trails. Dogs are allowed on the other trails. The camping and tent areas also allow dogs. There is a dog walk area at the campground.

Stores
Dog Designs Groom and Board 701 Thunderbird Hill Road Sebring FL   863-314-9883
http://www.dogdesignsbydana.com/
Although popular for their large off leash area, this pet resort is by membership only and they have a full-service pet day care center, a pet taxi, complete grooming services, a pet spa, and training facility - all on 5 scenic acres. Call for the first appointment. Dogs must be sociable, and owners must have proof of pet's vaccinations and license, and produce a wellness assessment from the vet. Dogs must be leashed when not in designated off-lead areas.

Sopchoppy

Campgrounds and RV Parks
Ochlockonee River State Park 429 State Park Road Sopchoppy FL   850-962-2771 (800-326-3521)
This park is where the Ochlockonee and Dead rivers intersect and flow into the Gulf of Mexico. This allows a variety of year round recreation including both freshwater and saltwater fishing. Dogs of all sizes are allowed at no additional fee. Dogs may not be left unattended outside at any time, and can only be left in your camping unit for no more than 30 minutes. Dogs must have current rabies and shot records, be on no more than a 6 foot leash, and be cleaned up after. Dogs are not allowed in buildings, in swim areas, or in the water. Dogs are allowed on the trails. The camping and tent areas also allow dogs. There is a dog walk area at the campground.

South Florida

Accommodations
Homestead Hotels Boca Raton - Commerce 501 N.W. 77th St. Boca Raton FL   561-994-2599
There is a one time pet fee of $25.00 for one night stays, $50.00 for two night stays, and $75.00 for any stay of three nights or longer.
Residence Inn by Marriott 525 NW 77th Street Boca Raton FL   561-994-3222
Pets of all sizes are allowed. There is a $75 one time pet policy to sign at check in.
TownePlace Suites Boca Raton 5110 NW 8th Avenue Boca Raton FL   561-994-7232
Dogs of all sizes are allowed. There is a $75 one time pet fee per visit.
La Quinta Inn Ft. Lauderdale Coral Springs 3701 University Dr. Coral Springs FL   954-753-9000 (800-531-5900)
Dogs of all sizes are allowed. There are no additional pet fees. Dogs may not be left unattended unless they will be quiet and well behaved. Dogs must be leashed and cleaned up after.
Studio 6 - Ft Lauderdale - Coral Springs 5645 University Drive Coral Springs FL   954-796-0011 (800-466-8356)
One well-behaved family pet per room. Guest must notify front desk upon arrival. Guest is liable for any damages. In consideration of all guests, pets must never be left unattended in the guest rooms.
Wellesley Inn Coral Springs 3100 N. University Drive Coral Springs FL   954-344-2200 (800-531-5900)
Dogs of all sizes are allowed. There are no additional pet fees. Dogs must be leashed and cleaned up after.
Motel 6 - Dania Beach 825 E Dania Beach Boulevard Dania FL   954-921-5505 (800-466-8356)
One well-behaved family pet per room. Guest must notify front desk upon arrival. Guest is liable for any damages. In consideration of all guests, pets must never be left unattended in the guest rooms.
Sheraton Fort Lauderdale Airport Hotel 1825 Griffin Rd. Dania FL   954-920-3500 (888-625-5144)
Dogs up to 75 pounds are allowed for no additional fees; there is a pet agreement to sign at check in. Dogs may not be left alone in the room.
Comfort Inn 50 S Ocean Drive Deerfield Beach FL   954-428-0650 (877-424-6423)
Dogs are allowed for an additional one time fee per pet of $25 for dogs 25 pounds or under; the fee is $40 per pet for dogs over 25 pounds.
Comfort Suites 1040 Newport Center Drive Deerfield Beach FL   954-570-8887 (877-424-6423)
Dogs are allowed for an additional fee of $10 per night per pet.
La Quinta Inn Ft. Lauderdale Deerfield Beach 351 W Hillsboro Blvd. Deerfield Beach FL   954-421-1004 (800-531-5900)

Dogs of all sizes are allowed. There are no additional pet fees. Dogs must be leashed and cleaned up after. Dogs must be attended to or crated for housekeeping.

Residence Inn by Marriott 1111 E Atlantic Avenue Delray Beach FL   561-276-7441
Pets of all sizes are allowed. There is a $75 one time fee and a pet policy to sign at check in.

Candlewood Suites Ft. Lauderdale Air/ Seaport 1120 W. State Road 84 Fort Lauderdale FL   954-522-8822 (877-270-6405)
Dogs up to 80 pounds are allowed for an additional one time pet fee of $75 per room; it's a one time fee of $150 for dogs over 80 pounds.

Embassy Suites Hotel Ft. Lauderdale 17th Street 1100 Southeast 17th Street Fort Lauderdale FL   954-527-2700
Dogs of all sizes are allowed. There are no additional pet fees. Dogs are not allowed to be left alone in the room.

Hampton Inn 2301 SW 12th Avenue Fort Lauderdale FL   954-524-9900
Dogs of all sizes are allowed. There is a an additional $50 per stay per room.

La Quinta Inn Ft. Lauderdale Cypress Creek I-95 999 West Cypress Creek Rd. Fort Lauderdale FL   954-491-7666 (800-531-5900)
Dogs of all sizes are allowed. There are no additional pet fees. Dogs must be leashed and cleaned up after. Dogs must be attended to or crated for housekeeping.

La Quinta Inn Ft. Lauderdale Tamarac East 3800 W. Commercial Boulevard Fort Lauderdale FL   954-485-7900 (800-531-5900)
Dogs of all sizes are allowed. There are no additional pet fees. Dogs may not be left unattended, and they must be leashed and cleaned up after.

Motel 6 - Ft Lauderdale 1801 SR 84 Fort Lauderdale FL   954-760-7999 (800-466-8356)
One well-behaved family pet per room. Guest must notify front desk upon arrival. Guest is liable for any damages. In consideration of all guests, pets must never be left unattended in the guest rooms.

Sheraton Yankee Clipper Hotel 1140 Seabreeze Blvd. Fort Lauderdale FL   954-524-5551 (888-625-5144)
Dogs up to 70 pounds are allowed for no additional pet fee. Dogs may not be left alone in the room.

TownePlace Suites Fort Lauderdale West 3100 Prospect Rd Fort Lauderdale FL   954-484-2214
Dogs of all sizes are allowed. There is a $75 one time pet fee per visit.

Days Inn Fort Lauderdale/Airport South 2601 N 29th Ave Hollywood FL   954-923-7300 (800-329-7466)
Dogs of all sizes are allowed. There is a $10 per night pet fee per pet. Reservations are recommended due to limited rooms for pets.

Sun Cruz Inn 340 Desoto St. Hollywood FL   954-925-7272
http://www.suncruzinn.com
This 17 unite motel and apartment building has studios and efficiencies. Pet walking is available for a fee. There is a deposit and other pet fees. Call the hotel for more information.

Holiday Inn Express-North Palm Beach 13950 US Hwy 1 Juno Beach FL   561-622-4366 (877-270-6405)
Dogs of all sizes are allowed for an additional pet fee of $10 per night per room in the Standard Building, and $20 per night per room for the Executive Building.

Motel 6 - Lantana 1310 W Lantana Road Lantana FL   561-585-5833 (800-466-8356)
One well-behaved family pet per room. Guest must notify front desk upon arrival. Guest is liable for any damages. In consideration of all guests, pets must never be left unattended in the guest rooms.

Red Roof Inn - Ft Lauderdale 4800 Powerline Road Oakland Park FL   954-776-6333 (800-RED-ROOF)
One well-behaved family pet per room. Guest must notify front desk upon arrival. Guest is liable for any damages. In consideration of all guests, pets must never be left unattended in the guest rooms.

Heart of Palm Beach 160 Royal Palm Way Palm Beach FL   561-655-5600
There is a $100 non-refundable pet fee. Pet owners must sign a pet waiver.

Plaza Inn 215 Brazilian Avenue Palm Beach FL   561-832-8666 (800-233-2632)
http://www.plazainnpalmbeach.com/
This pet friendly hotel has accommodated dogs up to 100 lbs. This inn, located on the Island of Palm Beach, is a historic 50 room hotel which has been fully renovated with warm textures of lace, polished wood, antiques and quality reproductions. Take a look at their website for pictures of this elegant inn. There are no pet fees.

The Chesterfield Hotel 363 Cocoanut Row Palm Beach FL   561-659-5800
You are allowed to have 2 to 3 pets up to 40 to 50 pounds, and it will depend on the size of the room. There is a $75 one time fee per room and a pet policy to sign at check in.

400 Avenue of Champions 400 Avenue of Champions Palm Beach Gardens FL   800-633-9150
http://www.pgaresort.com/
A luxury, waterside golf resort, there are 339 richly decorated guest rooms and suites, meticulously manicure landscaping, and a number of recreational activities available. Dogs up to 30 pounds are allowed for an additional fee of $150 per pet. Pets may only be left for a maximum of 2 hours in the room and they must be kenneled. Proof of current vaccinations/rabies is required. Dogs must be leashed or crated at all times when not in the room.

Best Western Plantation - Sawgrass 1711 N University Drive Plantation FL   954-556-8200 (800-780-7234)
Dogs up to 60 pounds are allowed for an additional fee per pet of $25 for each 1 to 7 days.

Holiday Inn 1711 N. University Dr Plantation FL   954-472-5600 (877-270-6405)
Dogs of all sizes are allowed for an additional one time pet fee of $25 per room.

Staybridge Suites 410 North Pine Island Rd Plantation FL   954-577-9696 (877-270-6405)
Dogs of all sizes are allowed for an additional one time pet fee of $100 per room.
Days Inn Pompano Beach 1411 NW 31st Ave Pompano Beach FL   954-972-3700 (800-329-7466)
Dogs up to 60 pounds are allowed. There is a $25 per night pet fee per pet. Reservations are recommended due to limited rooms for pets.
Motel 6 - Pompano Beach 1201 NW 31st Avenue Pompano Beach FL   954-977-8011 (800-466-8356)
One well-behaved family pet per room. Guest must notify front desk upon arrival. Guest is liable for any damages. In consideration of all guests, pets must never be left unattended in the guest rooms.
Pirates Cove Resort and Marina 4307 S.E. Bayview Street Stuart FL   772-287-2500
There are no additional pet fees. Pets must be well-behaved. The hotel has limited pet rooms. Please call ahead to reserve a pet room.
La Quinta Inn Sunrise/Sawgrass Mills 13651 N.W. 2nd Street Sunrise FL   954-846-1200 (800-531-5900)
Dogs may not be left unattended, and they must be leashed and cleaned up after. Dogs must be well behaved and housebroken. Dogs may not be left unattended, and they must be leashed and cleaned up after.
Wellesley Inn Sunrise at Sawgrass Mills 13600 Northwest 2nd Street Sunrise FL   954-845-9929 (800-531-5900)
A dog up to 60 pounds is allowed. There is a $10 per night additional pet fee. Dogs may not be left unattended, and they must be leashed and cleaned up after.
Wellesley Inn Fort Lauderdale-Tamarac 5070 North State Road 7 Tamarac FL   954-484-6909 (800-531-5900)
Dogs of all sizes are allowed. There are no additional pet fees. Dogs must be leashed and cleaned up after.
Days Inn West Palm Beach North 2300 45th St West Palm Beach FL   561-689-0450 (800-329-7466)
Dogs of all sizes are allowed. There is a $10 per night pet fee per pet.
Hibiscus House Bed & Breakfast 501 30th Street West Palm Beach FL   561-863-5633 (800-203-4927)
http://www.hibiscushouse.com/
This bed and breakfast was ranked by the Miami Herald as one of the ten best in Florida. The owner has a dog, and there are no pet charges. Large dogs usually stay in the cottage.
La Quinta Inn & Suites West Palm Beach 1910 Palm Beach Lakes Boulevard West Palm Beach FL   561-689-8540 (800-531-5900)
Dogs of all sizes are allowed. There are no additional pet fees. Dogs must be leashed, cleaned up after, and a contact number left with the front desk if there is a pet in the room alone.
La Quinta Inn West Palm Beach 5981 Okeechobee Blvd West Palm Beach FL   561-697-3388 (800-531-5900)
Dogs of all sizes are allowed. There are no additional pet fees. Dogs must be leashed and cleaned up after. Dogs must be crated if left alone in the room.
Radisson Suite Inn Palm Beach Airport 1808 South Australian Avenue West Palm Beach FL   561-689-6888
Dogs of all sizes are allowed. There is a $75 one time pet fee.
Red Roof Inn - West Palm Beach 2421 Metrocentre Boulevard East West Palm Beach FL   561-697-7710 (800-RED-ROOF)
One well-behaved family pet per room. Guest must notify front desk upon arrival. Guest is liable for any damages. In consideration of all guests, pets must never be left unattended in the guest rooms.
Residence Inn by Marriott 2461 Metrocentre Blvd West Palm Beach FL   561-687-4747
Pets of all sizes are allowed. There is a $75 one time fee per pet and a pet policy to sign at check in.
Residence Inn by Marriott 2605 Weston Road Weston FL   954-659-8585
Dogs of all sizes are allowed. There is a $75 one time fee and a pet policy to sign at check in.
TownePlace Suites Fort Lauderdale Weston 1545 Three Village Rd Weston FL   954-659-2234
Dogs of all sizes are allowed. There is a $75 one time pet fee per visit.

Campgrounds and RV Parks

Juno Ocean Walk RV Resort 900 Juno Ocean Walk Juno Beach FL   561-622-7500
http://www.junobeachrvresort.com
Dogs of all sizes are allowed. There is a $3 per night per pet additional fee. Dogs must be friendly, well behaved, leashed, and cleaned up after. There is a dog walk area at the campground.
John Prince County Park 6th Ave and Congress Lake Worth FL   877-992-9925
This is a very nice public campground with water and electric hookups. The campground is in a much larger public park and is surrounded on most sides by water. Dogs of all sizes are allowed. There are no additional pet fees. Dogs may not be left unattended outside at any time, and they must be well behaved, leashed, and cleaned up after.
Paradise Island RV Resort 2121 NW 29th Court Oakland Park FL   954-485-1150
http://www.paradiserv.com
Dogs of all sizes are allowed. There are no additional pet fees. Dogs may not be left unattended outside at any time, and they must be well behaved, leashed, and cleaned up after. There is also a Bark Park about 20 minutes from the resort. There are some breed restrictions. There is a dog walk area at the campground.

Highland Woods 850/900 NE 48th Street Pompano Beach FL   866-340-0649
http://www.mhchomes.com
Dogs of all sizes are allowed. There are no additional pet fees. Dogs may not be left unattended, and they must be leashed and cleaned up after. There is a dog walk area at the campground.
Markham Park 16001 W H 84 Sunrise FL   954-389-2000
http://www.broward.org/parks/mk.htm
Home to a series of interlocking lakes have made this a popular park for a number of recreational activities. The park also has a swimming pool complex, concessionaires, gaming fields/courts, multi-use trails, an observatory, model airplane field, target range, and more. Dogs are allowed for no additional fee, but they must be registered at the time of check-in. Dogs must be on no more than a 6 foot leash, be cleaned up after at all times, and they are not allowed in designated swim areas, on the athletic fields, or where otherwise posted. There are 86 tent and RV sites available at the camp area, and they offer 24 hour security, modern restrooms and showers, picnic tables, and grills. The camping and tent areas also allow dogs. There is a dog walk area at the campground.

Vacation Home Rentals

Hollywood - Ft. Lauderdale Oceanfront Rental South Ocean Drive Hollywood Beach FL   786-208-7004
http://www.AptTherapist.com
This two bedroom, two bathroom condo near the beach allows dogs up to 80 pounds.

Transportation Systems

Broward County Transit (BCT) 3201 W Cobans Road Pompano Beach FL   954-357-8400
http://www.broward.org/bct
A small dog in a carrier is allowed on the trains or buses at no additional fee.

Attractions

Club Nautico 801 Seabreeze Blvd Fort Lauderdale FL   954-467-6000
You can rent powerboats here for use on the inland waterways.
Fort Lauderdale Riverwalk 2nd St and 4th Ave Fort Lauderdale FL   954-761-5784
http://www.goriverwalk.com/map/map.htm
Leashed dogs are allowed at the Riverwalk which is a promenade that follows the river for about 1.5 miles. The walk is located along the New River's north bank and links together many historical landmarks. The walk starts near the Stranahan House and ends near the Broward Center for the Performing Arts at 201 S.W. Fifth Ave. There is an outdoor Jazz brunch on the first Sunday of each month where you can take you dog with you. There are nearby outdoor restaurants on Las Olas Blvd.
Las Olas District Las Olas Blvd and Federal Hwy Fort Lauderdale FL
This shopping district has a large number of outdoor restaurants. It is near the Riverwalk so you and your pup can make a day of it here.
Hoffman Chocolate Shop and Gardens 5190 Lake Worth Rd Lake Worth FL   561-433-GIFT
There is a nice garden to explore while you munch on chocolates and your dog sniffs the garden. You will have to go inside to order the chocolates without the pup, however.
Worth Avenue Shopping District Worth Avenue Palm Beach FL
This is a high end outdoor shopping district in Palm Beach. Many of the stores will welcome your well behaved dog, but as always we suggest that you ask.

Stores

PetSmart Pet Store 20861 State Rd 7 Boca Raton FL   561-470-8085
Your licensed and well-behaved leashed dog is allowed in the store.
Petco Pet Store 9960 Glades Rd Boca Raton FL   561-852-2016
Your licensed and well-behaved leashed dog is allowed in the store.
Three Dog Bakery 5250 Town Center Circle Boca Raton FL   561-347-8771
http://www.threedog.com
Three Dog Bakery provides cookies and snacks for your dog as well as some boutique items. You well-behaved, leashed dog is welcome.
PetSmart Pet Store 335 N Congress Ave Boynton Beach FL   561-738-4966
Your licensed and well-behaved leashed dog is allowed in the store.
PetSmart Pet Store 4151 Turtle Creek Dr Coral Springs FL   954-753-0740
Your licensed and well-behaved leashed dog is allowed in the store.
PetSmart Pet Store 4101 Oakwood Blvd Hollywood FL   954-920-7658
Your licensed and well-behaved leashed dog is allowed in the store.
Woof Gang Bakery 5500 Military Trail, Suite 12/H 809 Jupiter FL   561-630-5800
http://www.woofgangbakery.com/
Offering the best in pet care, this store provides well-balanced foods, frozen treats, natural supplements, hand-

made doggy treats, and more. Dogs must be well behaved, leashed, and under owner's control at all times
Petco Pet Store 1009 East Commercial Blvd Oakland Park FL   954-351-4244
Your licensed and well-behaved leashed dog is allowed in the store.
PetSmart Pet Store 11950 Pines Blvd Pembroke Pines FL   954-441-7005
Your licensed and well-behaved leashed dog is allowed in the store.
Petco Pet Store 12251 Pines Blvd Pembroke Pines FL   954-499-7755
Your licensed and well-behaved leashed dog is allowed in the store.
PetSmart Pet Store 12051 W Sunrise Blvd Plantation FL   954-916-8771
Your licensed and well-behaved leashed dog is allowed in the store.
Three Dog Bakery 236 S University Drive Plantation FL   954-424-3223
http://www.threedog.com
Three Dog Bakery provides cookies and snacks for your dog as well as some boutique items. You well-behaved,
leashed dog is welcome.
PetSmart Pet Store 531 N State Rd 7 Royal Palm Beach FL   561-793-2858
Your licensed and well-behaved leashed dog is allowed in the store.
PetSmart Pet Store 2435 NW Federal Hwy Stuart FL   772-692-8609
Your licensed and well-behaved leashed dog is allowed in the store.
Petco Pet Store 5837 North University Drive Tamarac FL   954-722-0142
Your licensed and well-behaved leashed dog is allowed in the store.
PetSmart Pet Store 2505 Okeechobee Blvd West Palm Beach FL   561-689-8777
Your licensed and well-behaved leashed dog is allowed in the store.
Petco Pet Store 1951-C N Military Trail West Palm Beach FL   561-683-4340
Your licensed and well-behaved leashed dog is allowed in the store.
Petco Pet Store 920 S State Rd 7 Wellington FL   561-333-5714
Your licensed and well-behaved leashed dog is allowed in the store.

Beaches

TOP 200 PLACE **Canine Beach** East End of Sunrise Blvd Fort Lauderdale FL   954-761-5346
There is a 100 yard stretch of beach which dogs can use. Dogs must be on leash when they are not in the water.
The beach is open to dogs only on Friday, Saturday and Sundays. In Winter, the hours are 3 pm - 7 pm and the
Summer hours are 5 pm - 9 pm. A permit is required to use the Canine Beach. There are annual permits
available for $25 for residents of the city or $40 for non-residents or you can get a one weekend permit for $5.65.
Permits can be purchased at Parks and Recreation Department, 1350 W. Broward Boulevard. Call (954) 761-
5346 for permit information.
Dog Swim at Snyder Park 3299 SW 4th Avenue Fort Lauderdale FL   954-828-4343
There is a $1 park admission fee for entering the park for the doggy swim area; it is available on Saturdays and
Sundays from 10AM to 5PM (closed Christmas/New Years). Dogs must be sociable, current on all vaccinations
and license, and under owner's control/care at all times. Dogs must be leashed when not in designated off-lead
areas.
TOP 200 PLACE **Jupiter Beach** A1A at Xanadu Road Jupiter FL
This is a wide, nice, white sandy beach that stretches 2 miles along the Atlantic Coast. It is one of the nicer
beaches that allow dogs in South Florida. Please follow the dog rules requiring leashes and cleaning up after
your dog.
Hobe Sound National Wildlife Refuge North Beach Road Jupiter Island FL   772-546-6141
http://hobesound.fws.gov/
This refuge has sea turtle nesting areas and endangered species like the scrub jay and gopher tortoise. Dogs on
leash are allowed at the beach. The leash law is enforced and people need to clean up after their pets. The park
headquarters is located 2 miles south of SR 708 (Bridge Road) on U.S. 1. The beach is located 1.5 miles north
of Bridge Road on North Beach Road.

Parks

South County Regional Park 11200 Park Access Rd Boca Raton FL   561-966-6600
Dogs must be leashed in the park.
Tree Tops Park 3900 S.W. 100th Ave Davie FL   954-370-3750
http://www.co.broward.fl.us/pri02100.htm
Dogs must be leashed in the park.
Quiet Waters Park 401 S. Powerline Rd Deerfield Beach FL   954-360-1315
http://www.co.broward.fl.us/pri01800.htm
Dogs must be leashed in the park.
Bike Trail - Fort Lauderdale along A1A near the beach Fort Lauderdale FL
This trail follows A1A through the Fort Lauderdale beach area. Dogs must be leashed on the trail.
Hugh Taylor Birch State Park 3109 East Sunrise Boulevard Fort Lauderdale FL   954-564-4521

Dogs must be leashed in this park near the ocean. Dogs are not allowed on any of the beaches nearby except for the Canine Beach.

Snyder Park 3299 SW 4th Avenue Fort Lauderdale FL 954-828-4585
Offering 93 oasis-like acres, this park offers nature trails, 2 spring-fed lakes, gaming fields/courts/rentals, and an off leash area that can accommodate large and small pets in separate 1 acre lots. Dogs must be sociable, current on all vaccinations and license, and under owner's control/care at all times. Dogs must be leashed when not in designated off-lead areas. Although there is no additional fee for the off leash doggy area, there is a fee for Snyder Park; annual passes are available at 954-828-DOGS (3647).

John Prince Park 2700 6th Ave. S Lake Worth FL
Dogs must be leashed in the park.

Easterlin Park 1000 N.W. 38th St Oakland Park FL 954-938-0610
http://www.co.broward.fl.us/pri01300.htm
Dogs must be leashed in the park.

Lake Trail Sunset Ave and Bradley Palm Beach FL
This is a 3 1/2 mile paved trail along the intercoastal waterway. Dogs must be leashed on the trail.

Markham Park 16001 W H 84 Sunrise FL 954-389-2000
http://www.broward.org/parks/mk.htm
Home to a series of interlocking lakes have made this a popular park for a number of recreational activities. The park also has a swimming pool complex, concessionaires, gaming fields/courts, multi-use trails, an observatory, model airplane field, target range, and more. Dogs are allowed for no additional fee, but they must be registered at the time of check-in. Dogs must be on no more than a 6 foot leash, be cleaned up after at all times, and they are not allowed in designated swim areas, on the athletic fields, or where otherwise posted.

Markham Park 16001 W. State 84 Sunrise FL 954-389-2000
http://www.co.broward.fl.us/pri01600.htm
This park is at the edge of the Everglades. Dogs must be leashed in the park.

Off-Leash Dog Parks

Boca Raton Dog Park 751 Banyan Trail Boca Raton FL 561-393-7821
There are 3 separate sections at this park; 1 each for small, medium, and large dogs. Benches, water fountains, wash stations, and 6 doggie waste stations are on site. Dogs must be sociable, current on all vaccinations, licensed, and under owner's control/care at all times. Dogs must be leashed when not in designated off-lead areas, and they must be cleaned up after at all times.

Dr. Paul's Pet Care Center Dog Park 2575 Sportsplex Drive Coral Springs FL 954-346-4428
http://www.sportsplexatcs.com/
Located in a 180+ acre regional park, this 2 acre, fenced doggy play area offers large and small dog areas, an obstacle course, exercise and play equipment, benches, picnic shelters, water fountains, and asphalt pathways. Dogs must be sociable, current on all vaccinations and license, and under owner's control/care at all times. Dogs must be leashed when not in designated off-lead areas.

Sportsplex Dog Park 2575 Sportsplex Drive Coral Springs FL 954-346-4428
http://www.sportsplexatcs.com/
A major recreation destination with several attractions and recreational opportunities, this park also holds major community events and festivals here, plus there is a 2 acre, fenced off leash dog park on site. Dogs must be sociable, current on all vaccinations and license, and under owner's control/care at all times. Dogs must be leashed when not in designated off-lead areas.

Lake Ida Dog Park 2929 Lake Ida Road Delray Beach FL 561-966-6600
Located in a park with a variety of land and water recreation, this doggy off leash park offers lots of play room, shaded areas, benches, waste bags/receptacles, and a water fountain, plus they have a paved dog washing section. Dogs must be sociable, current on all vaccinations, licensed, and under owner's control/care at all times. Dogs must be leashed when not in designated off-lead areas.

Bark Park At Snyder Park 3299 S.W. 4th Avenue Fort Lauderdale FL 954-828-3647
This fully fenced dog park has separate areas for small dogs and large dogs. There are benches, water, and pickup bags. Dogs must be on leash when outside the Bark Park. To get to Bark Park from I-95, exit at State Road 84 and head east to S.W. 4th Avenue. Turn right into Snyder Park. The Bark Park will be on your right.

Poinciana Dog Park 1301 S 21st Avenue Hollywood FL 954-921-3404
This popular off lead area has plenty of grassy and treed places with lots of play room, a paved pathway, fountains, pools, and a dog wash area. Dogs must be sociable, current on all vaccinations, licensed, and under owner's control/care at all times. Dogs must be leashed when not in designated off-lead areas.

Pembroke Pines Dog Park 9751 Johnson Street Pembroke Pines FL 954-435-6525
There are large and small sections for pets at this off leash area; there are kiddie pools for the pooches, water, obstacles, and benches on site. Dogs must be sociable, current on all vaccinations and licensed, and under owner's control/care at all times. Dogs must be leashed when not in designated off-lead areas.

Happy Tails Dog Park at Seminole Park 6600 SW 16th Street Plantation FL 954-452-2510
Located in Seminole Park, this off lead 5 acre site has 3 separate sections; one each for large and small dogs, and an exercise area that can be used for agility training, plus they are home to a variety of canine happenings

held throughout the year. A pavilion, picnic area, and restrooms are on site. Dogs must be sociable, current on all vaccinations and license, and under owner's control/care at all times. Dogs must be leashed when not in designated off-lead areas.
Barkham at Markham Park 16001 W H 84 Sunrise FL   954-389-2000
http://www.broward.org/parks/dogpark.htm
Located in a large county park, this off leash area covers about 3 acres of landscaped grounds with divided sections for large and small pooches. Some of the amenities include lush Bermuda sod grass, wide walking paths, 3 shelter rest areas-2 have refrigerated water for pet owners, doggy watering fountains, a common wash area, plus an additional wash area in the large dog section. Dogs must be sociable, current on all vaccinations and license, and cleaned up after at all times. Dogs must be on no more than a 6 foot leash when not in designated off-lead areas.
Dog Park 2975 Greenbriar Blvd Wellington FL   561-791-4005
Located at Greenbriar Park, this 3 acre dog park is open from dawn to dusk and gives plenty of run room. Dogs must be sociable, current on all vaccinations, licensed, and under owner's control/care at all times. Dogs must be leashed when not in designated off-lead areas.
Pooch Park 7715 Forest Hill Blvd/H 882 West Palm Beach FL   561-966-6600
There are 5 acres of play area for pooches here with 2 large dog sections and 1 small dog section. A paved doggy wash station, fountains, dog bag dispensers, plenty of shady areas, and benches are on site. Dogs must be sociable, current on all vaccinations, licensed, and cleaned up after at all times. Dogs must be leashed when not in designated off-lead areas.

Outdoor Restaurants
Bangkok in Boca 500 Via De Palmas Boca Raton FL   561-394-6912
Dogs are allowed at the outdoor tables.
Brasserie Mon Ami 1400 Glades Road Boca Raton FL   561-394-2428
This restaurant and bar serves American food. Small dogs are allowed at the outdoor tables.
Cheeburger Cheeburger 200 S Federal Hwy Boca Raton FL   561-392-1969
This restaurant serves American fast food. Dogs are allowed at the outdoor tables.
Courtyard Cafe 2650 North Military Trail Boca Raton FL   561-994-5210
This restaurant serves American food. Dogs are allowed at the outdoor tables.
Doc's 3rd Base Bar & Grill SE 1st Street and Mizner Blvd Boca Raton FL   561-362-8362
Dogs are allowed at the outdoor tables. The restaurant has outdoor tables only in the Summer.
Einstein Bros Bagels 9795 Glades Rd Boca Raton FL   561-477-0667
Dogs are allowed at the outdoor tables.
Ichiban Japanese Restaurant 8841 Glades Rd Boca Raton FL   561-451-0420
Dogs are allowed at the outdoor tables.
Jamba Juice 1400 Glades Rd Boca Raton FL   561-620-8895
This smoothie shop allows dogs at the outdoor tables.
Lion and Eagle English Pub 2401 N Federal Hwy Boca Raton FL   561-447-7707
Dogs are allowed at the one outdoor table.
Pacific Grill 1610 S Federal Hwy Boynton Beach FL   561-733-8988
This restaurant and bar serves American/Asian food. Dogs are allowed at the outdoor tables. Water is provided for your pet.
Muddy Waters 2237 W Hillsboro Blvd Deerfield Beach FL   954-428-8446
This restaurant serves American and seafood. Dogs are allowed at the outdoor tables.
City Oyster 213 E Atlantic Ave Delray Beach FL   561-272-0220
Dogs are allowed at the outdoor tables.
Cheeburger Cheeburger 708 East Las Olas Fort Lauderdale FL   954-524-8824
This restaurant serves American food. Dogs are allowed at the outdoor tables.
China Yung Restaurant 1201 North Highway 1 Fort Lauderdale FL   954-761-3388
Dogs are allowed at the outdoor tables.
Einsteins Bagel 3200 N Federal Hwy Fort Lauderdale FL   954-565-2155
This cafe serves deli-type food. Dogs are allowed at the outdoor tables.
Grill Room On Las Olas 620 E Las Olas Blvd Fort Lauderdale FL   954-467-2555
Dogs are allowed at the outdoor tables.
Indigo Restaurant 620 E Las Olas Blvd Fort Lauderdale FL   954-467-0045
Dogs are allowed at the outdoor tables.
Japanese Steak House 350 E. Las Olas Blvd Fort Lauderdale FL   954-525-8386
Dogs are allowed at the outdoor tables.
Samba Room 350 E Las Olas Blvd Fort Lauderdale FL   954-468-2000
Dogs are allowed at the outdoor tables.
Shizen 716 Los Olas Blvd Fort Lauderdale FL   954-763-8163
Dogs are allowed at the outdoor tables.
Starbucks 6781 W Broward Blvd Fort Lauderdale FL   954-791-7265

This coffee shop serves coffee and pastries. Dogs are allowed at the outdoor tables.
Stromboli Pizza 801 S University Dr Fort Lauderdale FL   954-472-2167
Dogs are allowed at the outdoor tables.
Zona Fresca 1635 N Federal Hwy Fort Lauderdale FL   954-566-1777
This restaurant serves Mexican food. Dogs are allowed at the outdoor tables.
Dave's Last Resort and Raw Bar 632 Lake Ave Fort Worth FL   561-588-5208
This restaurant and bar serves American and seafood. Dogs are allowed at the outdoor tables.
Beverly Hills Cafe 4000 N 46th Ave Hollywood FL   954-963-5220
This cafe serves deli-type food. Dogs are allowed at the outdoor tables.
Harrison Street Sushi Jazz 1902 Harrison St Hollywood FL   954-927-8474
Dogs are allowed at the outdoor tables.
Nakorn Japanese and Thai Restaurant 2039 Hollywood Blvd Hollywood FL   954-921-1200
This restaurant serves Japanese/Thai food. Dogs are allowed at the outdoor tables.
Friendly's 1001 H 7 Royal Palm Beach FL   561-333-5757
http://www.friendlys.com/index.aspx
Originally opened as an ice creamery, this eatery grew to add breakfast, specialty burgers, Super-melts, and more. There is outdoor seating, but no table service, so they ask that visitors go inside to order and they will bring it out. Dogs are allowed at the outer tables, they must be leashed and under owner's control/care at all times.
Buddy's Cafe and Deli 2431 Beach Ct West Palm Beach FL   561-848-1506
Dogs are allowed at the outdoor tables.
Mediterranean 200 Clematis St West Palm Beach FL   561-837-6633
Dogs are allowed at the outdoor tables.
Outback Steakhouse 871 Village Blvd West Palm Beach FL   561-683-1011
Dogs are allowed at the outdoor tables.
Rooney's Public House 213 Clematis St West Palm Beach FL   561-833-7802
http://www.rooneyspub.com
Dogs are allowed at the outdoor tables.
Cheeburger Cheeburger 1793 Bell Tower Lane Weston FL   954-659-1115
This restaurant serves American food. Dogs are allowed at the outdoor tables.

Space Coast

Accommodations
Best Western Cocoa Inn 4225 West King St Cocoa FL   321-632-1065 (800-780-7234)
Dogs up to 80 pounds are allowed for an additional fee of $10 per night per pet.
Holiday Inn 1300 N. Atlantic Ave Cocoa Beach FL   321-783-2271 (877-270-6405)
Dogs up to 50 pounds are allowed for an additional fee of $10 per night per pet with a $50 deposit; $25 is refundable.
La Quinta Inn Cocoa Beach 1275 N. Atlantic Avenue Cocoa Beach FL   321-783-2252 (800-531-5900)
Dogs of all sizes are allowed. There are no additional pet fees. There is a pet waiver to sign at check in. Dogs must be leashed and cleaned up after. Dogs may not be left unattended unless they will be quiet and well behaved.
Motel 6 - Cocoa Beach 3701 North Atlantic Avenue Cocoa Beach FL   321-783-3103 (800-466-8356)
All well-behaved dogs are welcome, just let the hotel know that you have a pet.
Quality Suites 3655 N Atlantic Avenue Cocoa Beach FL   321-783-6868
A dog up to 50 pounds is allowed for a $100 refundable pet deposit.
Surf Studio Beach Resort 1801 S. Atlantic Ave. Cocoa Beach FL   321-783-7100
There is a $25 per day pet charge. There are no designated smoking or non-smoking rooms, but they keep the rooms very clean.
Comfort Inn 3655 Cheney H Titusville FL   321-269-7110 (877-424-6423)
Dogs are allowed for an additional fee of $10 per night per pet.
Days Inn Space Coast/Titusville 3755 Cheney Hwy Titusville FL   321-269-4480 (800-329-7466)
Dogs of all sizes are allowed. There is a $10 per night pet fee per pet. Reservations are recommended due to limited rooms for pets.
Hampton Inn 4760 Helen Hauser Blvd Titusville FL   321-383-9191
Dogs of all sizes are allowed. There is a $25 one time fee per pet.
Riverside Inn 1829 Riverside Drive Titusville FL   321-267-7900
This inn was formerly the Howard Johnson Lodge. There is a $5 per day additional pet fee.

Attractions

Kennedy Space Center Tours - Kennels S.R. 405 Cape Canaveral FL   407-452-2121
http://www.kennedyspacecenter.com/
Dogs are not allowed on the tours, but there are free kennels available. The kennels are indoor and not air conditioned. They have fans to cool the room. The kennels are unattended and locked. Just press the buzzer to get an attendant to unlock the kennels.

Space Shuttle and Rocket Launches

Space Shuttle and Rocket Launches Kennedy Space Center Titusville FL   321-867-4636
http://www.ksc.nasa.gov
You and your dog can view a shuttle or rocket launch from along Highway 1 or other various locations around Titusville. Check the phone number or the web site for schedule information. Kennedy Space Center is about 1 hour from Orlando. These launches are unbelievably loud so consider the noise in deciding to bring your dog.

Outdoor Restaurants
Kelsey's Pizzeria and Restaurant 8699 Astronaut Blvd Cape Canaveral FL   321-783-9191
This restaurant serves American and Italian food. Dogs are allowed at the outdoor tables.
And All That Jazz Cafe 1641 N Cocoa Blvd Cocoa FL   321-636-3232
This restaurant serves American food. Dogs are allowed at the outdoor tables.
Dogs R Us 7025 N Cocoa Blvd Cocoa FL   321-638-0619
This restaurant serves American food. Dogs are allowed at the outdoor tables.
Kelsey's Pizzeria and Restaurant 6811 N Cocoa Blvd Cocoa FL   321-639-3333
This restaurant serves Italian and American food. Dogs are allowed at the outdoor tables.
Paradise Alley Cafe 234 Brevard Ave Cocoa FL   321-639-2515
This restaurant serves American food. Dogs are allowed at the outdoor tables.
Florida's Seafood Bar and Grill 480 W Cocoa Beach Crossway Cocoa Beach FL   321-784-0892
This restaurant and bar serves American and seafood. Dogs are allowed at the outdoor tables.
Sonny's Real Pit BBQ 2005 N Atlantic Ave Cocoa Beach FL   321-868-1000
This restaurant and bar serves barbecue. Dogs are allowed at the outdoor tables.
Bruster's Ice Cream 855 Cheney Hwy Titusville FL   321-385-0400
This ice cream shop allows dogs at the outdoor tables.
Dog R Us 4200 S Washington Ave Titusville FL   321-269-9050
This restaurant serves American food. Dogs are allowed at the outdoor tables.

St Augustine

Accommodations

Best Western St Augustine I-95 2445 SR 16 St Augustine FL   904-829-1999 (800-780-7234)
Dogs are allowed for an additional pet fee of $10 per night per room.
Days Inn St Augustine/Outlet Center Mall 2560 SR 16 St Augustine FL   904-824-4341 (800-329-7466)
Dogs of all sizes are allowed. There is a $10 per night pet fee per pet.
Howard Johnson Express Inn 137 San Marco Ave. St Augustine FL   904-824-6181 (800-446-4656)
Dogs of all sizes are welcome. There is a $10 per day pet fee.
Inn at Camachee Harbor 201 Yacht Club Dr. St Augustine FL   904-825-0003 (800-688-5379)
http://www.camacheeinn.com
Fourteen of the nineteen rooms at this inn are pet friendly. The inn is located at the Camachee Harbor only about
five minutes from historic St Augustine. You will need to get special permission from management to leave a pet
alone in the room.
Ocean Blue Motel 10 Vilano Road St Augustine FL 904-829-5939
Dogs of all sizes are allowed. There is a $10 per night per pet additional fee, and a credit card needs to be on
file.
Holiday Inn - St Augustine Beach 860 A1A Beach Blvd St Augustine Beach FL 904-471-2555 (877-270-
6405)
Dogs up to 60 pounds are allowed for an additional fee of $20 per night per pet.

Campgrounds and RV Parks

Anastasia State Park Campgrounds Anastasia Park Drive St Augustine FL 904-461-2033
This campsite offers electric and water hookups at each camp site. RVs under 40 feet can be accommodated.
Pets are allowed at the campground, in day use areas and on the 1/2 mile nature trail and the old quarry walk.
Pets are not allowed on the beach, in playgrounds, bathing areas, cabins, park buildings, or concession facilities.
Pets cannot be tied to trees, tables, bushes, or shelter facilities. Dogs tied at a campsite cannot be left
unattended for more than 30 minutes. Dogs must be on a 6 foot or less leash and people are required to clean
up after their pets. During the park's quiet hours, usually from 11pm to 8am, your pets must be inside your
camping unit. To get there from I-95, take exit 311 (old exit 94). Go east on State Road 207. Turn right on State
Road 312. Turn left on A1A. Go about 1.5 miles north to the main park entrance, which is on the right after your
pass The Surf Station.
North Beach Camp Resort 4125 Coastal Highway St Augustine FL 904-824-1806 (800-542-8316)
http://www.northbeachcamp.com
This campground is located between the Intercoastal waterway and the ocean about 5 -10 minutes from St
Augustine. It has oak trees covered with Spanish moss and is walking distance from a St. Augustine beaches
which allow dogs on leash. There is a restaurant that has a dog-friendly area next door to the campground. Dogs
of all sizes are allowed. There are full hookups available.
St. Augustine Beach KOA 525 West Pope Road St Augustine FL 904-471-3113
http://www.koa.com/where/fl/09205/
This campground is located on Anastasia Island. Both RV and tent sites are available. Campground amenities
include a year round swimming pool, fishing, bicycle rentals, maximum length pull through of 70 feet, Cable TV,
modem dataport, and 50 amp service available. Pets are welcome at the campground but not in the cabins.
There is no extra pet fee. This KOA has a dog walk area. The campground is open year round.

North Beach Camp Resort

Attractions

Fountain of Youth

TOP 200 PLACE **Fountain of Youth** 11 Magnolia Ave. St Augustine FL   904-829-3168
http://www.fountainofyouthflorida.com/
Tradition has it that The Fountain of Youth is the exact spot where the Spanish Explorer Ponce de Leon landed
on April 2, 1513. He met the Timucuan Indians who at the time had an unusually long life span that averaged
about 90 years. The Spanish at the time had a much shorter life span average. The water that the Indians drank
became known as the "fountain of youth". Of course, the Indians longer life span could have had something to
do with their healthy seafood diet and their active lifestyle. Today this park offers exhibits of early Timucuan
Indians and Sixteenth Century Spaniards. At the park you can stroll along the gardens, explore excavations, view
exhibits, presentations and a planetarium. In the Spring House, both people and pets can take a sip of the
famous "Fountain of Youth" water. A guide will hand out samples of the water in little paper cups. The water has
a very strong mineral taste. Well-behaved leashed pets are welcome both outside and inside the buildings.
Ghost Walk - Spirits of St. Augustine St. George Street St Augustine FL   904-829-2391
http://www.staugustinetransfer.com
You and your well-behaved leashed dog can take a guided tour of the most haunted sites in St. Augustine. This
entertaining 1.5 hour walk will go along the streets of historic downtown and pass by two cemeteries. There is a
$10 per person fee and free for children under six. The tours begin at 8pm at the Columbia Restaurant on St.
George Street near Hypolita Street. These tours are offered by the St. Augustine Transfer Co. If you take one of
their carriage rides first, sometime during your visit to St. Augustine, they will give you a coupon for a free Ghost
Walk tour.
Ghostly Encounters Walking Tour 3 Aviles Street St Augustine FL   800-404-2531
This guided walking ghost tour will take you through dark and narrow streets of historic St. Augustine. Tours
begin at 8pm and take about 1.5 hours. Well-behaved leashed dogs are allowed except for the beginning of the
tour which goes inside the Spanish Military Hospital Museum. The fee is $10 for adults and free for children
under six. You can purchase tickets at 1 King Street. The tour starts at the Spanish Military Hospital Museum,
located at 3 Aviles Street.

St Augustine Scenic Cruise

TOP 200 PLACE St Augustine Scenic Cruise St Augustine Municipal Marina St Augustine FL   904-824-1806 (800-542-8316)
http://www.scenic-cruise.com/
The Victory III departs daily from the Marina in downtown St Augustine for a one hour and fifteen minute scenic cruise. View the historic St Augustine area from the water and bring your well-behaved, leashed dog with you.

St. Augustine Transfer Co. Carriages

St. Augustine Transfer Co. Carriages Avenida Menendez and Hypolita St. St Augustine FL   904-829-2391
http://www.staugustinetransfer.com/
Take a carriage ride through the historic downtown area. They can give you a narrated tour and at night they can
even give you a ghost tour of the city. Well-behaved leashed pets are welcome at the driver's discretion. Pets are
allowed on the floor of the carriage, but not on the seats. Costs for a private carriage are about $80. The
carriages seat four people. If there are just two in your party, the carriage ride can be about $40 if you find
another couple to share the carriage ride. The rides are located along the waterfront on Avenida Menendez, near
Hypolita Street.
St. Augustine Historic Downtown St. George St St Augustine FL
This unique more than 400 year old city, also known as America's Oldest City, was founded in 1565 and is the
oldest continuously occupied European settlement in the continental United States. The city of St. Augustine was
founded 55 years before the Pilgrims landed at Plymouth Rock and 42 years before the English colonized
Jamestown. Ponce de Leon is credited with the discovery of Florida back in 1513. The narrow streets and
houses reflect the city's Spanish origins. Today there are many restaurants and stores located throughout the
historic district. Dogs are welcome to walk with you along the streets and are also welcome at some of the
outdoor restaurants.

Beaches

Fort Matanzas National Monument 8635 A1A South St Augustine FL   904-471-0116
http://www.nps.gov/foma/index.htm
Dogs on 6 ft leash are allowed in this National monument. Dogs are allowed in the park, on the beach, and on
the trails. They are not allowed in the visitor center, boats, or fort.
St Augustine Lighthouse and Museum 81 Lighthouse Avenue St Augustine FL   904-829-0745
Dogs on leash are allowed on the grounds of the lighthouse and beach area. There are some tables for picnics
or bring a blanket. There is a fee to enter the lighthouse grounds.

St Augustine Beach

St Augustine Beach Most Beaches St Augustine Beach FL   904-209-0655
The St. Augustine Beach allows leashed dogs. Owners must clean up after their pets. This policy extends to
most of the beaches in St John's County but other rules will apply to beaches in State Parks, many of which don't
allow dogs.

Stores

Petco Pet Store 430 Cbl Drive St Augustine FL   904-824-8520
Your licensed and well-behaved leashed dog is allowed in the store.

Parks

Castillo de San Marcos National Monument A1A, near historic downtown St Augustine FL   904-829-6506, ext 234
http://www.nps.gov/casa/
This park is situated on 25 acres along the waterfront. The historic fort was built from 1672 to 1695 and it served primarily as the Spanish Empire post which guarded St. Augustine. Its secondary purpose was to protect the sea route for Spanish treasure ships. Even though this fort served many different nations, it was never taken by force. The United States purchased the fort from the Spanish in 1821 and in 1924 the fort was declared a national monument. Pets are welcome on the park grounds, but need to be on a 6 foot or less leash. Pets are not allowed inside the fort. The park is located between the waterfront and downtown, off Castillo Drive near Fort Alley.

Outdoor Restaurants

Florida Cracker Cafe 81 St. George Street St Augustine FL   904-829-0397
This restaurant serves seafood, salads, chicken, steak, pasta, sandwiches and more. Well-behaved leashed dogs are allowed at the outdoor tables. Next door is Savannah Sweets which offers a wide variety of chocolate goodies (dogs are not allowed inside).
Harry's Seafood Bar Grille 46 Avenida Menendez St Augustine FL   904-824-7765
http://www.hookedonharrys.com/
This restaurant serves New Orleans style seafood. They are located along the waterfront and are open for lunch and dinner. Well-behaved leashed dogs are allowed at the outdoor seats.
La Pentola 58 Charlotte Street St Augustine FL   904-824-3282
http://www.lapentolarestaurant.com/
This restaurant offers continental cuisine infused with a Mediterranean ambiance. You can order seafood, steaks, wild game, pasta, salads and desserts. Well-behaved leashed dogs are welcome at the outdoor seats. The restaurant is open Tuesday for dinner, Wednesday through Saturday for lunch and dinner, and Sunday for brunch and dinner.

Scarlett O'Hara's Bar and Restaurant

Scarlett O'Hara's Bar and Restaurant 70 Hypolita Street St Augustine FL   904-824-6535
http://www.scarlettoharas.net
This restaurant is in a historic 1879 building. The menu includes sandwiches, seafood, salads and barbecue entrees. They are open for lunch and dinner. The outdoor seats are on a wooden porch. Well-behaved leashed dogs are allowed at the outdoor tables.

The Pizza Garden 21 Hypolita Street St Augustine FL   904-825-4877
This restaurant serves pizzas, salads, soups and more. They are open daily for lunch and dinner. Well-behaved leashed dogs are welcome at the outdoor courtyard seats.

St George Island

Accommodations
An Angel's Dream 2008 E Pelican Court St George Island FL   850-927-3520
Dogs of all sizes are allowed. There are no additional pet fees.
Collins Vacation Rentals 60 E Gulf Beach Drive St George Island FL   850-927-2900
Dogs of all sizes are allowed. There is a pet policy to sign at check in and there are no additonal pet fees.

Beaches
St George Island Beaches St George Island FL 850-927-2111
St. George Island beaches have been consistently ranked as one of the top 10 beaches in America. One third of the island is Florida State park land which does not allow dogs. But the rest of the island offers Franklin County public beaches, which do allow dogs on a 6 foot leash or off-leash and under direct voice control.

Outdoor Restaurants
Ocean Front Cafe 68 W Gorrie Dr #A St George Island FL 850-927-2987
This restaurant serves American and seafood. Dogs are allowed at the outdoor tables.

Starke

Accommodations
Best Western Motor Inn 1290 North Temple Avenue Starke FL   904-964-6744 (800-780-7234)
Dogs are allowed for an additional fee of $11.10 per night per pet.
Days Inn Starke 1101 N Temple Starke FL   904-964-7600 (800-329-7466)
Dogs of all sizes are allowed. There is a $10 per night pet fee per pet.

Tallahassee

Accommodations
Best Western Pride Inn and Suites 2016 Apalachee Pkwy Tallahassee FL   850-656-6312 (800-780-7234)
Dogs are allowed for an additional fee of $10 per night per pet.
Doubletree 101 S Adams Street Tallahassee FL   850-224-5000
Dogs of all sizes are allowed. There is a $200 one time fee per pet and a pet policy to sign at check in.
Econo Lodge 2681 N. Monroe St. Tallahassee FL   850-385-6155 (800-55-ECONO)
There is a $10 per day pet fee.
Holiday Inn Tallahassee-Capitol-East 1355 Apalachee Parkway Tallahassee FL   850-877-3171 (877-270-6405)
Dogs up to 90 pounds are allowed for an additional one time pet fee of $35 per room.
La Quinta Inn Tallahassee North 2905 North Monroe Tallahassee FL   850-385-7172 (800-531-5900)
Dogs of all sizes are allowed. There are no additional pet fees. Dogs must be leashed and cleaned up after. Dogs may not be left unattended unless they will be quiet and well behaved.
La Quinta Inn Tallahassee South 2850 Apalachee Pkwy. Tallahassee FL   850-878-5099 (800-531-5900)
Dogs of all sizes are allowed. There are no additional pet fees. Dogs must be leashed and cleaned up after. Dogs may not be left unattended unless they will be quiet and well behaved, and they need to be attended to or removed for housekeeping.
Motel 6 - Tallahassee - Downtown 1027 Apalachee Parkway Tallahassee FL   850-877-6171 (800-466-8356)
One well-behaved family pet per room. Guest must notify front desk upon arrival. Guest is liable for any damages. In consideration of all guests, pets must never be left unattended in the guest rooms.
Motel 6 - Tallahassee North 1481 Timberlane Road Tallahassee FL   850-668-2600 (800-466-8356)
One well-behaved family pet per room. Guest must notify front desk upon arrival. Guest is liable for any damages. In consideration of all guests, pets must never be left unattended in the guest rooms.

Motel 6 - Tallahassee West 2738 N Monroe Street Tallahassee FL   850-386-7878 (800-466-8356)
One well-behaved family pet per room. Guest must notify front desk upon arrival. Guest is liable for any damages. In consideration of all guests, pets must never be left unattended in the guest rooms.
Red Roof Inn - Tallahassee 2930 Hospitality Street Tallahassee FL   850-385-7884 (800-RED-ROOF)
One well-behaved family pet per room. Guest must notify front desk upon arrival. Guest is liable for any damages. In consideration of all guests, pets must never be left unattended in the guest rooms.
Residence Inn by Marriott 1880 Raymond Diehl Road Tallahassee FL   850-442-0093
Pets of all sizes are allowed. There is a $75 one time fee and a pet policy to sign at check in.
Staybridge Suites Tallahassee I-10 East 1600 Summit Dr. Tallahassee FL   850-219-7000 (877-270-6405)
Dogs of all sizes are allowed for an additional pet fee of $50 per room for 1 to 5 nights, and each night thereafter is $10 per night per room.
TownePlace Suites Tallahassee North/Capital Circle 1876 Capital Circle NE Tallahassee FL   850-219-0122
Dogs of all sizes are allowed. There is a $75 one time pet fee per visit.

Campgrounds and RV Parks
Apalachicola National Forest 11152 NW State Road 20 Tallahassee FL   850-643-2282 (877-444-6777)
This National Forest offers a wide variety of year round land and water recreation, interpretive exhibits, and 85 miles of various types of trails. Dogs of all sizes are allowed at no additional fee. Dogs may not be left unattended, and they must have current rabies and shot records. Dogs must be on no more than a 6 foot leash, and be cleaned up after in the camp area. Dogs are allowed on the trails. The camping and tent areas also allow dogs. There is a dog walk area at the campground. There are no water hookups at the campground.
Big Oak RV Park 4024 N Monroe Street Tallahassee FL   850-562-4660
http://www.bigoakrvpark.com
Dogs of all sizes are allowed. There are no additional pet fees. Dogs must be quiet, well behaved, leashed, and cleaned up after. There is a dog walk area at the campground.

Stores
PetSmart Pet Store 3220 Capital Circle NE Tallahassee FL   850-297-1500
Your licensed and well-behaved leashed dog is allowed in the store.
Petco Pet Store 1624 Governors Square Blvd Tallahassee FL   850-656-0395
Your licensed and well-behaved leashed dog is allowed in the store.

Parks
Edward Ball State Park 550 Wakulla Park Drive Wakulla Springs FL   850-224-5950
Listed on the Natural Register of Historic Places and designated as a National Natural Landmark, this park is home of one of the largest and deepest freshwater springs in the world, and is host to an abundance of wildlife, including alligators, turtles, deer, and birds. They provide daily guided riverboat tours, various interpretive programs, swimming, picnicking, and a nature trail. Dogs of all sizes are allowed at no additional fee. Dogs are not allowed in buildings, boats, the beach, or any waterfront area due to alligators. Dogs must be leashed at all times, and cleaned up after. They are open year round from 8 am to sunset.

Outdoor Restaurants
Food,Glorious Food 1950 Thomasville Rd Tallahassee FL   850-224-9974
This restaurant and bar serves American food. Dogs are allowed at the outdoor tables.

Tampa Bay

Accommodations
La Quinta Inn & Suites Tampa Bay Brandon 310 Grand Regency Blvd. Brandon FL   813-643-0574 (800-531-5900)
Dogs of all sizes are allowed. There are no additional pet fees. There is a pet policy to sign at check in. Dogs must be housetrained, and a cell number left with the front desk if the dog is in the room alone. Please put the Do Not Disturb sign on the door. Dogs must be leashed and cleaned up after.
Sea Spray Inn 331 Coronado Drive Clearwater Beach FL   727-442-0432
http://www.clearwaterbeach.com/seaspray/
Sea Spray Inn is just a one minute walk to the Gulf of Mexico. There are 6 rooms, 4 with full kitchens, 2 rooms have refrigerators. There are microwaves in rooms, cable TV and a swimming pool.
Changing Tides Cottages 225 Boca Ciega Dr Madeira Beach FL   727-397-7706

http://www.changingtidescottages.com
These one and two bedroom cottages are located near Boca Ciega Bay. They are fully equiped. There are no cleaning fees but there is a pet fee of $5 per day or $25 per week.
Snug Harbor Inn Waterfront Bed and Breakfast 13655 Gulf Blvd Madeira Beach FL   727-395-9256 (866-395-9256)
http://www.snugharborflorida.com
This bed and breakfast offers a location on the waterfront, continental breakfast, and a boat slip. Pets are welcome with prior approval.
Best Western Palm Harbor Hotel 37611 US Highway 19 N Palm Harbor FL   727-942-0358 (800-780-7234)
Dogs are allowed for an additional fee of $10 per night per pet.
Red Roof Inn - Clearwater - Palm Harbor 32000 US 19 North Palm Harbor FL   727-786-2529 (800-RED-ROOF)
One well-behaved family pet per room. Guest must notify front desk upon arrival. Guest is liable for any damages. In consideration of all guests, pets must never be left unattended in the guest rooms.
Howard Johnson 9359 US Hwy 19 N Pinellas Park FL   727-577-3838 (800-446-4656)
Dogs of all sizes are allowed. There is a $10 per night pet fee per pet.
La Quinta Inn Tampa Bay Pinellas Park Clearwater 7500 Hwy 19 North Pinellas Park FL   727-545-5611 (800-531-5900)
Dogs of all sizes are allowed. There are no additional pet fees. Dogs must be leashed and cleaned up after. Dogs must be healthy; tick and flea free, and be removed for housekeeping.
Calais Motel Apartments 1735 Stickney Point Road Sarasota FL   941-921-5797 (800-822-5247)
http://www.thecalais.com/
There is a $15 per day pet charge and there are no designated smoking or non-smoking rooms.
Coquina On the Beach Resort 1008 Ben Franklin Drive Sarasota FL   941-388-2141 (800-833-2141)
http://www.coquinaonthebeach.com/
There is a $30 one time pet charge. There are no designated smoking or non-smoking rooms.
Quality Inn and Suites 4800 N Tamiami Trail Sarasota FL   941-355-7091 (877-424-6423)
Dogs are allowed for an additional fee of $20 per night per pet.
Residence Inn by Marriott 1040 University Parkway Sarasota FL   941-358-1468
Pets of all sizes are allowed. There is a $75 one time fee and a pet policy to sign at check in.
TradeWinds Island Grand 5500 Gulf Blvd St Pete Beach FL   727-363-2380
This 4 diamond resort offers water sports, paddleboats, water trykes, WiFi connections and business center computers. There are five restaurants on site, five swimming pools, two whirlpools, concierge service and a kids activity center. Up to 2 pets are allowed per room up to 80 pounds each. There is a $30 per pet per day additional pet fee.
La Quinta Inn Tampa Bay St. Petersburg 4999 34th Street North St Petersburg FL   727-527-8421 (800-531-5900)
Dogs of all sizes are allowed. There are no additional pet fees. Dogs must be leashed and cleaned up after, and they request that you use the dog walk area. Dogs may not be left unattended unless they will be quiet and well behaved. They do not allow aggressive breeds.
Valley Forge Motel 6825 Central Avenue St Petersburg FL   727-345-0135
There is a $5 per day pet charge or a fee of $25 per week for a pet.
Best Western Brandon Hotel and Conf Cntr 9331 Adamo Dr Tampa FL   813-621-5555 (800-780-7234)
One dog up to 50 pounds is allowed for an additional one time $25 pet fee.
Best Western Tampa 734 S Dale Mabry Highway Tampa FL   813-490-2378 (800-780-7234)
Dogs are allowed for an additional fee of $10 per night per pet.
Comfort Inn Airport at RJ Stadium 4732 N Dale Mabry Tampa FL   813-874-6700 (877-424-6423)
Dogs are allowed for an additional one time pet fee of $25 per room.
Hampton Inn 5628 W Waters Avenue Tampa FL   813-901-5900
Dogs of all sizes are allowed. There is a $10 per night pet fee.
Holiday Inn Express Hotel & Suites Tampa-Fairgrounds-Casino 8610 Elm Fair Boulevard Tampa FL   813-490-1000 (877-270-6405)
Dogs of all sizes are allowed for an additional fee of $10 per night per pet.
Holiday Inn Express Hotel and Suites 8310 Galbraith Road Tampa FL   813-910-7171 (877-270-6405)
Dogs of all sizes are allowed for an additional pet fee of $50 for each 1 to 7 days stay.
La Quinta Inn & Suites USF (Near Busch Gardens) 3701 East Fowler Ave. Tampa FL   813-910-7500 (800-531-5900)
Dogs of all sizes are allowed. There are no additional pet fees. Dogs may be alone in the room if they will be quiet, well behaved, a contact number is left with the front desk, and the Do Not Disturb sign is left on the door. Dogs must be leashed and cleaned up after.
La Quinta Inn Tampa Brandon West 602 S. Falkenburg Road Tampa FL   813-684-4007 (800-531-5900)
Dogs of all sizes are allowed. There are no additional pet fees. Dogs may not be left unattended at any time, and they must be quiet, well behaved, leashed, and cleaned up after.
La Quinta Inn Tampa East-Fairgrounds 4811 U.S. Highway 301 N. Tampa FL   813-626-0885 (800-531-5900)

Dogs of all sizes are allowed. There are no additional pet fees. There is a pet waiver to sign at check in. Dogs may not be left unattended, and they must be leashed and cleaned up after.
Motel 6 - Tampa Downtown 333 E Fowler Avenue Tampa FL 813-932-4948 (800-466-8356)
One well-behaved family pet per room. Guest must notify front desk upon arrival. Guest is liable for any damages. In consideration of all guests, pets must never be left unattended in the guest rooms.
Motel 6 - Tampa East - Fairgrounds 6510 US 301 Tampa FL 813-628-0888 (800-466-8356)
One well-behaved family pet per room. Guest must notify front desk upon arrival. Guest is liable for any damages. In consideration of all guests, pets must never be left unattended in the guest rooms.
Red Roof Inn - Tampa Brandon 10121 Horace Avenue Tampa FL 813-681-8484 (800-RED-ROOF)
One well-behaved family pet per room. Guest must notify front desk upon arrival. Guest is liable for any damages. In consideration of all guests, pets must never be left unattended in the guest rooms.
Red Roof Inn - Tampa Busch 2307 East Busch Boulevard Tampa FL 813-932-0073 (800-RED-ROOF)
One well-behaved family pet per room. Guest must notify front desk upon arrival. Guest is liable for any damages. In consideration of all guests, pets must never be left unattended in the guest rooms.
Red Roof Inn - Tampa Fairgrounds 5001 North US 301 Tampa FL 813-623-5245 (800-RED-ROOF)
One well-behaved family pet per room. Guest must notify front desk upon arrival. Guest is liable for any damages. In consideration of all guests, pets must never be left unattended in the guest rooms.
Residence Inn by Marriott 101 E. Tyler Street Tampa FL 813-221-4224
Pets of all sizes are allowed. There is a $75 one time fee and a pet policy to sign at check in.
Residence Inn by Marriott 4312 Boy Scout Blvd Tampa FL 813-877-7988
Pets of all sizes are allowed. There is a $75 one time fee and a pet policy to sign at check in.
Sheraton Riverwalk Hotel 200 North Ashley Dr. Tampa FL 813-223-2222 (888-625-5144)
Dogs up to 80 pounds are allowed. There are no additional pet fees. Dogs are not allowed to be left alone in the room.
Sheraton Suites Tampa Airport 4400 West Cypress St. Tampa FL 813-873-8675 (888-625-5144)
Dogs up to 50 pounds are allowed. There are no additional pet fees. Dogs are not allowed to be left alone in the room.
TownePlace Suites Tampa North/I-75 Fletcher 6800 Woodstork Rd Tampa FL 813-975-9777
Dogs of all sizes are allowed. There is a $75 one time pet fee per visit.
Residence Inn by Marriott 13420 North Telecom Parkway Temple Terrace FL 813-972-4400
Pets of all sizes are allowed. There is a $75 one time fee and a pet policy to sign at check in.
A Whisper of Treasure Island 279 104th Avenue Treasure Island FL 727-363-0800 (888-987-2673)
http://www.whispersresort.com
Watch the dolphins swim by from this resort on the Gulf of Mexico. One dog of any size or two smaller dogs are allowed in guestrooms. There is a $75 per week pet fee per dog.
Lorelei Resort Motel 10273 Gulf Blvd Treasure Island FL 727-360-4351
Dogs of all sizes are allowed. There is no additional fee for up to 2 pets. If you have more than 2 pets the fee is $10 per night per pet.
Days Inn Venice 1710 S Tamiami Trail Venice FL 941-493-4558 (800-329-7466)
Dogs of all sizes are allowed. There is a $15 one time small pet or $30 large per pet fee per visit.
Holiday Inn Venice-Sarasota Area 455 US Highway 41 Bypass North Venice FL 941-485-5411 (877-270-6405)
Dogs of all sizes are allowed for an additional one time pet fee of $30 per room.
Motel 6 - Venice 281 US 41 Bypass North Venice FL 941-485-8255 (800-466-8356)
One well-behaved family pet per room. Guest must notify front desk upon arrival. Guest is liable for any damages. In consideration of all guests, pets must never be left unattended in the guest rooms.

Campgrounds and RV Parks
Oscar Scherer State Park 1843 S Tamiami Trail Osprey FL 941-483-5956 (800-326-3521)
Special events, campfire programs, guided tours, and 15 miles of trails add to the year round recreation offered here. Dogs of all sizes are allowed at designated pet sites for no additional fee. Dogs may not be left unattended, and they must have current rabies and shot records. Dogs must be leashed, and cleaned up after. Dogs are not allowed by the creek, but they are allowed on the trails. The camping and tent areas also allow dogs. There is a dog walk area at the campground.
Clearwater/Tarpon Springs KOA 37061 H 19N Palm Harbor FL 727-937-8412 (800-562-8743)
http://www.koa.com
Dogs of all sizes are allowed. There are no additional pet fees. Dogs may not be left unattended outside, and they must be well behaved, leashed, and cleaned up after. There are some breed restrictions. There is a dog walk area at the campground. Dogs are allowed in the camping cabins.
Hillsborough River State Park 15402 H 301 N Thonotosassa FL 813-987-6771 (800-326-3521)
Take a tour of a replica of an 1837 fort from the Second Seminole War, walk The Wetlands Restoration Trail, or enjoy the variety of land and water recreation at this park. Dogs of all sizes are allowed at no additional fee. Dogs may not be left unattended, and they must have current rabies and shot records. Dogs are not allowed in buildings, at the pool, or on canoe rentals. Dogs are allowed on the trails but they must be in designated dog

areas at all times. The camping and tent areas also allow dogs. There is a dog walk area at the campground.

Vacation Home Rentals
Barrett Beach Bungalows 19646 Gulf Blvd Indian Shores FL 727-455-2832
http://www.barrettbeachbungalows.com
Beachfront bungalows plus a cottage in the heart of picturesque Indian Shores. One, two and three bedroom bungalows and a pool. Any number and size of pets welcome. Private dog runs with each bungalow. Enjoy sunsets, volleyball and barbecues in your own backyard.
Vacation Shores 19742 Gulf Blvd Indian Shores FL 727-593-7164 (866-714-2588)
http://vacationshores.com
This beachfront vacation rental property has six units. There is a $100 pet fee for each pet.
Island Paradise Cottages & Apartments of Madeira Beach 13215 2nd Street East Madeira Beach FL 727-395-9751
http://www.islandparadise.com
Some of these vacation rentals allow dogs with prior approvals. Call them to make reservations.
Dog-Friendly Fenced Vacation Home near Tampa/Disney. 1 mile East of I-75, 1/4 mile off of I-4 Seffner FL 866-980-1234
This pet-friendly vacation rental sits on one fenced acre near I-75 and I-4.

Attractions
Florida Botanical Gardens 12175 125th Street N Largo FL 727-582-2100
http://www.flbg.org
There are educational classes, nature tours, beauty, and more depending on the time of year. Dogs are allowed at no additional fee. Dogs may not be left unattended at any time, and they must be leashed and cleaned up after. The gardens are open year round from 7 am to dusk, except in December when all the lights are up, they stay open until 10 pm.
TOP 200 PLACE **Heritage Village** 11909 125th Street N Largo FL 727-582-2123
http://www.pinellascounty.org/heritage/
Dogs are allowed at this open-air historical village and museum at no additional fee. There is an art and historical museum, botanical gardens, a gift shop and much more. Dogs must be leashed and cleaned up after, and they are not allowed in the buildings. The village is open Tuesday through Saturday from 10 am to 4 pm, and on Sunday from 1 to 4 pm. They are closed on Monday and major holidays.
Adventure Island - Kennel 4500 Bougainvillea Avenue Tampa FL 888-800-5447
http://www.buschgarden.com
There is a pet care center in the parking area, also shared by the Busch Gardens, that will take care of your pet in a temperature controlled and manned facility for $5 per day. Owners need to bring the pet food and also owners are responsible for walking their animals.
Busch Gardens - Kennel 3605 Bougainvillea Avenue Tampa FL 888-800-5447
http://www.buschgardens.com
There is a pet care center in the parking area, also shared by Adventure Island, that will take care of your pet in a temperature controlled and manned facility for $5 per day. Owners need to bring the pet food and also owners are responsible for walking their animals.
St Nicholas Boat Line 693 Dodecanese Blvd Tarpon Springs FL 727-942-6225
In addition to the boat tours, they also have a store with a rather large variety of Sponge. This is the area where they used to harvest sponge. The tours are 1/2 hour long and are from 11:30 am until there are no more passengers, and they are open all year except for some major holidays. A well behaved dog on lead is allowed at no additional fee.

Stores
PetSmart Pet Store 1051 Brandon Blvd West Brandon FL 813-689-4814
Your licensed and well-behaved leashed dog is allowed in the store.
PetSmart Pet Store 11331 Causeway Blvd Brandon FL 813-689-3378
Your licensed and well-behaved leashed dog is allowed in the store.
Petco Pet Store 2434 West Brandon Blvd Brandon FL 813-571-0120
Your licensed and well-behaved leashed dog is allowed in the store.
PetSmart Pet Store 10500 Ulmerton Rd Largo FL 727-518-2600
Your licensed and well-behaved leashed dog is allowed in the store.
PetSmart Pet Store 4942 S Tamiami Trail Sarasota FL 941923-7899
Your licensed and well-behaved leashed dog is allowed in the store.
PetSmart Pet Store 3993 Tyrone Blvd St Petersburg FL 727-343-7900
Your licensed and well-behaved leashed dog is allowed in the store.
PetSmart Pet Store 7777 Dr Martin Luther King St N St Petersburg FL 727-577-9935

Your licensed and well-behaved leashed dog is allowed in the store.
PetSmart Pet Store 2816 E Fletcher Av Tampa FL 813-971-0367
Your licensed and well-behaved leashed dog is allowed in the store.
PetSmart Pet Store 12835 Citrus Plaza Dr Tampa FL 813-926-7488
Your licensed and well-behaved leashed dog is allowed in the store.
PetSmart Pet Store 1540 N Dale Mabry Hwy Tampa FL 813-875-9721
Your licensed and well-behaved leashed dog is allowed in the store.
Petco Pet Store 13127 North Dale Mabery Highway Tampa FL 813-968-9361
Your licensed and well-behaved leashed dog is allowed in the store.
Petco Pet Store 136 South Westshore Blvd, Building 138 Tampa FL 813-282-3224
Your licensed and well-behaved leashed dog is allowed in the store.
PetSmart Pet Store 2920 Little Rd Trinity FL 727-375-9973
Your licensed and well-behaved leashed dog is allowed in the store.
Petco Pet Store 1231 Bruce B. Downs Blvd Wesley Chapel FL 813-973-9067
Your licensed and well-behaved leashed dog is allowed in the store.

Beaches
Honeymoon Island State Park 1 Causeway Blvd. Dunedin FL 727-469-5942
Dogs on a 6 foot or less leash are allowed on part of the beach. Please ask the rangers for details when you
arrive at the park. The park is located at the extreme west end of SR 586, north of Dunedin

Horses bathing on the causeway

Gandy Bridge Causeway Gandy Bridge east end St Petersburg FL
This stretch of beach allows dogs to run and go swimming. We even saw a horse here. Dogs should be leashed
on the beach.
Pinellas Causeway Beach Pinellas Bayway St Petersburg FL
This stretch of beach is open to humans and dogs. Dogs should be on leash on the beach.
Davis Island Dog Park Severn Ave and Martinique Ave Tampa FL
http://www.davisislanddogs.com
This dog beach is fenced and offers a large parking area and even a doggie shower. To get there go towards
Davis Island and head for the Peter Knight Airport. Loop around until you reach the water (the airport should be
on the left). Thanks to one of our readers for the updated information.

Tampa causeways have areas of beach where dogs are allowed

Parks

Flatwoods Wilderness Park Morris Bridge Road Hillsborough FL
There are a number of hiking trails here. Dogs are allowed on leash.
North Shore Park North Shore Dr and 13th Ave St Petersburg FL
Dogs must be leashed in the park.
Lake Park 17302 N. Dale Mabry Tampa FL   813-264-3806
Here your leashed dog will have to share the trails with horses and people. The park is 600 acres. There is an off-leash area in the park.

Upper Tampa Bay County Park

Upper Tampa Bay County Park 8001 Double Branch Road Tampa FL   813-855-1765
Dogs must be leashed in this park with boardwalks and trails that skirt the upper part of the bay.

Off-Leash Dog Parks

Walsingham Park Paw Playground 12615 102nd Avenue North Largo FL 727-549-6142
This leash free dog park is fully fenced with amenities like cooling stations complete with showers and dog-level water fountains. People need to clean up after their pets and all dogs must be on a leash when outside of the Paw Playground area. Walsingham Park is located south of Highway 688, on 102nd Avenue N near 125th Street.
Chestnut Park Paw Playground 2200 East Lake Road Palm Harbor FL 727-669-1951
This leash free dog park is fully fenced with amenities like cooling stations complete with showers and dog-level water fountains. People need to clean up after their pets and all dogs must be on a leash when outside of the Paw Playground area. Chestnut Park is located on East Lake Road, between Keystone Road and Highway 580.
Mango Dog Park 11717 Claypit Road Seffner FL 813-975-2160
There are 5 acres at this off lead doggy play area offering lots of run room, shade trees, swim areas, picnic tables, 2 pavilions, a doggy wash station, drinking fountains for hounds and humans, and waste dispenser stations. Dogs must be sociable, current on all vaccinations, licensed, and cleaned up after at all times. Dogs must be leashed when not in designated off-lead areas.
Boca Ciega Park Paw Playground 12410 74th Ave. N Seminole FL 727-588-4882
This leash free dog park is fully fenced with amenities like cooling stations complete with showers and dog-level water fountains. People need to clean up after their pets and all dogs must be on a leash when outside of the Paw Playground area. Boca Ciega Park is located south of Park Blvd, on 74th Avenue N. near 125th Street N.
Al Lopez Dog Park 4810 North Himes Tampa FL 813-274-8615
There is a 1.5 acre fenced dog park for larger dogs and an 8000 square foot park for small dogs. There is a double gated entry area, benches, water and pickup bags are available. The dog park is located on the west side of Al Lopez Park.
Davis Islands Dog Park 1002 Severn Tampa FL 813-274-8615
There are two fenced dog parks at the south end of Davis Islands. One of the parks is entirely fenced and is about one acre. The other park is a 1 1/2 acre beach front park with over 200 feet of waterfront available for dogs. There is water, double gated entry, and pickup bags available.
Palma Ceia San Miguel & Marti Tampa FL 813-274-8615
The dog park is about 3/4 acres and is entirely fenced. It has a double gated entry, water, and pickup bags available. The park is located on the northeast corner of the park at West San Miguel & Marti.
Anderson Park Paw Playground 39699 U.S. Highway 19 North Tarpon Springs FL 727-943-4085
This leash free dog park is fully fenced with amenities like cooling stations complete with showers and dog-level water fountains. People need to clean up after their pets and all dogs must be on a leash when outside of the Paw Playground area. Anderson Park is located off Highway 19, north of Klosterman Road.
Fort DeSoto Park Paw Playground 3500 Pinellas Bayway South Tierra Verde FL 727-582-2267
This leash free dog park is fully fenced with amenities like cooling stations complete with showers and dog-level water fountains. People need to clean up after their pets and all dogs must be on a leash when outside of the Paw Playground area. Fort DeSoto Park is located at the southern end of the Pinellas Bayway.

Outdoor Restaurants

Café Dufrain 707 Harbour Post Drive Harbour Island FL 813-275-9701
http://www.cafedufrain.com/
Imparting an international flavor to contemporary American cuisine offers guests a unique and tasty dining experience at this waterfront bistro. They also offer dining on their patio. Dogs are allowed at the outer tables; they must be leashed and under owner's control/care at all times.
Barnacle Bill's Seafood 1526 Main Street Sarasota FL 941-365-6800
http://www.barnaclebillsseafood.com/
The specialties here are freshly prepared seafood, steaks, and fowl with enough wines to balance out any meal. They also offer outdoor dining. Dogs are allowed at the outer tables; they must be leashed and under owner's control/care at all times.
Columbia Restaurant 411 St Armands Circle Sarasota FL 941-388-3987
http://www.columbiarestaurant.com/
Specializing in old traditional Spanish recipes, they also offer a variety of wines to pair with meals and alfresco dining. Dogs are allowed at the outer tables; they must be under owner's control/care at all times.
Old Salty Dog 5023 Ocean Blvd Sarasota FL 941-349-0158
This restaurant and bar serves American and seafood. Dogs are allowed at the outdoor tables.
The Purple Onion 10525 Park Blvd/H 694 Seminole FL 727-394-0064
http://www.purpleonionseminole.com/
In addition to providing substantial sandwiches and fare, they also cater, deliver, and offer outside dining. Dogs are allowed at the outer tables; they must be under owner's control/care at all times.
Buffy's Southern Pit Bar-b-que 3911 49th North St Petersburg FL 727-522-0088
This restaurant and bar serves barbecue. Dogs are allowed at the outdoor tables.
Captain Al's Waterfront Grill and Bar 800 2nd Avenue NE St Petersburg FL 727-898-5800
http://www.captainalsrestaurant.com/
In addition to a variety of homemade Italian, fresh seafood, and American cuisines, they offer a beautiful on-the-

bay setting, a full bar with daily specials, live music, and a large dining deck. Dogs are allowed at the outer tables; they must be leashed and under owner's control/care at all times. Dogs are also allowed out on the pier.
Corned Beef Corner 4040 Park St North St Petersburg FL 727-347-3921
This restaurant serves deli-type food. Dogs are allowed at the outdoor tables.
Dogwater Cafe 8300 Bay Pines Blvd St Petersburg FL 727-347-6190
This cafe serves American food. Dogs are allowed at the outdoor tables.
Foxy's Cafe 160 107th Ave St Petersburg FL 727-363-3699
Dogs are allowed at the outdoor tables.
Pizze Rustica 1003 4th Street N St Petersburg FL 727-895-3050
Dogs are allowed at the outdoor tables.
Bagels Plus 2706 E Fletcher Ave Tampa FL 813-971-9335
This bagel shop closes at 5 pm each day. Dogs on leash may join you at the outdoor tables.
Bernini Restaurant 1702 E 7th Ave Tampa FL 813-248-0099
Dogs are allowed at the outdoor tables.
Gaspar's Grotto 1805 E 7th Avenue Tampa FL 813-248-5900
http://www.gasparsgrotto.com/
In addition to serving up an array of foods, this eatery is home to one of the largest collection of fine Rums in the state, there are numerous large TVs throughout, music, and pirate wear/merchandise for sale. They also offer outdoor dining. Dogs are allowed at the outer tables; they must be leashed and under owner's control/care at all times.
Mad Dogs and Englishmen 4115 S Macdill Ave Tampa FL 813-832-3037
Dogs are allowed at the outdoor tables.
Rick's Italian Cafe 214 E Davis Blvd Tampa FL 813-253-3310
Dogs are allowed at the outdoor tables.
Thai House 3200 W Bay To Bay Blvd Tampa FL 813-839-4995
Dogs are allowed at the outdoor tables.
Costa's 521 Athens Street Tarpon Springs FL 727-938-6890
Dogs are allowed at the outdoor tables.
Mama's Greek Cuisine 735 Dodecanese Blvd # 40 Tarpon Springs FL 727-944-2888
This restaurant serves Greek food. Dogs are allowed at the outdoor tables.

Winter Haven

Accommodations
Howard Johnson Inn 33224 US Hwy. 27 South Haines City FL 863-422-8621 (800-446-4656)
Dogs of all sizes are welcome. There is a $10 pet fee for the first night and $5 for the second night.
La Quinta Inn & Suites Lakeland 1024 Crevasse St. Lakeland FL 863-859-2866 (800-531-5900)
Dogs of all sizes are allowed. There are no additional pet fees. Dogs must be leashed and cleaned up after. Dogs may not be left unattended unless they will be quiet and well behaved.
Motel 6 - Lakeland 3120 US 98 North Lakeland FL 863-682-0643 (800-466-8356)
One well-behaved family pet per room. Guest must notify front desk upon arrival. Guest is liable for any damages. In consideration of all guests, pets must never be left unattended in the guest rooms.
Residence Inn by Marriott 3701 Harden Blvd Lakeland FL 863-680-2323
Dogs of all sizes are allowed. There is a $75 one time fee and a pet policy to sign at check in.
Days Inn Plant City 301 S Frontage Rd Plant City FL 813-752-0570 (800-329-7466)
Dogs of all sizes are allowed. There is a $20 per first night and $15 for each additional night pet fee per pet.

Campgrounds and RV Parks
Greenfield Village RV Park 1015 H 542W Dundee FL 863-439-7409
Dogs of all sizes are allowed. There are no additional pet fees. Dogs may not be left unattended outside, and they must be leashed and cleaned up after. This is a 55 years or older park. There are some breed restrictions. There is a dog walk area at the campground.
Sanlan Ranch Campground 3929 H 98S Lakeland FL 863-665-1726
http://www.sanlan.com
Dogs of all sizes are allowed. There is $.50 per night per pet additional fee. Dogs may not be left unattended outside, and they must be leashed and cleaned up after. Dogs must stay out of the water because of alligators. The camping and tent areas also allow dogs. There is a dog walk area at the campground.
East Haven RV Park 4320 Dundee Road Winter Haven FL 863-324-2624
http://www.easthavenrvpark.com
One dog of any size is allowed. There are no additional pet fees. Dogs may not be left unattended, and they must be leashed and cleaned up after. There are some breed restrictions. The camping and tent areas also allow dogs. There is a dog walk area at the campground.

Attractions

Dinosaur World 5145 Harvey Tew Road Plant City FL   813-717-9865
http://www.dinoworld.net
Dogs on leash are allowed in this park. Open 9am-dusk all year round. There is a fee. The park offers a museum, outside sculptures, picnic areas, and more.

Chapter 20

Eastern Canadian Cities
Dog Travel Guide

Niagara Falls

In 2005, Ontario passed legislation banning Pit Bulls and "similar" dogs entirely from the province, which includes the Canadian side of Niagara Falls and Toronto. For more information on this see www.dogfriendly.com/server/newsletters/bslontario.shtml

Accommodations

Niagara Parkway Court Motel 3708 Main Street Niagara Falls ON 905-295-3331
http://www.goniagarafalls.com/npcm/
There is a $10 per day additional pet fee. The hotel only has one pet room so make your reservations early.
Sheraton Fallsview Hotel and Conference Center 6755 Fallsview Blvd Niagara Falls ON 905-374-1077 (888-625-5144)
This 4-diamond hotel offers guests a 5-star view of the Niagara Falls and it is also central to numerous other nearby recreational pursuits. Dogs are allowed on the 3rd floor only for an additional $25 per night per pet, and there is a pet waiver to sign at check in. If there is more than 1 dog, they may not exceed a combined weight of 80 pounds. Dogs may not be left unattended in the room, and they must be leashed and cleaned up after at all times.
Sheraton on the Falls Hotel 5875 Falls Avenue Niagara Falls ON 905-374-4445 (888-625-5144)
Positioned directly across the street from the Niagara Falls in the largest hotel and entertainment complex in North America, this 4-diamond is also home to the largest state-of-the-art conference facility in Niagara. Dogs up to 80 pounds are allowed for no additional pet fee; there is a pet waiver to sign at check in. Dogs may not be left alone in the room, and they must be leashed and cleaned up after at all times.
Holiday Inn St Catharines 2 N Service Rd St Catharines ON 905-934-8000 (877-270-6405)
http://www.holidayinnstcath.com/
Dogs of all sizes are allowed for an additional pet fee of $15 per night per room.
Comfort Inn 870 Niagara Street Welland ON 905-732-4811 (877-424-6423)
Dogs are allowed for an additional pet fee of $10 per night per room.

Campgrounds and RV Parks

Campark Resort 9387 Lundy's Lane Niagara Falls ON 877-226-7275
http://www.campark.com
Dogs of all sizes are allowed. There are no additional pet fees. Dogs may not be left outside unattended or be at the pool area. Dogs must be leashed and cleaned up after. This RV park is closed during the off-season. The camping and tent areas also allow dogs. There is a dog walk area at the campground. Due to Ontario law Pit Bulls and similar dogs are not allowed.
Jellystone Park 8676 Oakwood Drive Niagara Falls ON 905-354-1432
http://www.jellystoneniagara.ca
One dog of any size is allowed. There are no additional pet fees. Dogs are not allowed in rentals or tents. Dogs may not be left unattended, must be leashed, and cleaned up after. Due to Ontario law Pit Bulls and similar dogs are not allowed. This RV park is closed during the off-season. There is a dog walk area at the campground.
King Waldorf's Tent and Trailer Park 9015 Stanley S Avenue Niagara Falls ON 905-295-8191
http://www.marinelandcanada.com
Dogs of all sizes are allowed. There are no additional pet fees. Dogs may not be left unattended, must be leashed, and cleaned up after. This RV park is closed during the off-season. The camping and tent areas also allow dogs. There is a dog walk area at the campground. Due to Ontario law Pit Bulls and similar dogs are not allowed.
Niagara Falls KOA 8625 Lundy's Lane Niagara Falls ON 905-356-2267 (800-562-6478)
http://www.niagarakoa.com
Dogs of all sizes are allowed. There are no additional pet fees. Dogs must be well behaved, may not be left unattended, and must be leashed and cleaned up after. Dogs are not allowed in the rentals or the buildings. There are some breed restrictions. This RV park is closed during the off-season. The camping and tent areas also allow dogs. There is a dog walk area at the campground.

Attractions

Niagara Falls off Queen Elizabeth Way Niagara Falls ON 800-563-2557
http://www.discoverniagara.com
You and your pooch can stroll along the walkways to view the falls. Pets are not allowed on any of the Niagara attractions like the boat rides, but you will still be able to enjoy great views of Niagara Falls along the paths and walkways. You can also take your dog into Queen Victoria Park which is next to the falls. Dogs need to be leashed and cleaned up after.

Author Tara Kain and dog Toby in Niagara Falls

Toronto

In 2005, Ontario passed legislation banning Pit Bulls and "similar" dogs entirely from the province, which includes the Canadian side of Niagara Falls and Toronto. For more information on this see www.dogfriendly.com/server/newsletters/bslontario.shtml

Accommodations
Howard Johnson Hotel Toronto-Markham 555 Cochrane Drive Markham ON 905-479-5000 (800-446-4656)
http://www.hojomarkham.com
Dogs of all sizes are allowed.
Novotel - Toronto North York 3 Park Home Avenue North York ON 416-733-2929
Novotel Hotels welcome a maximum of 2 animals (cats and dogs) per room and never require a fee. Each guest checking in with a pet will be given a Royal Canine/Novotel Pet Welcome Kit.
Beaches Bed and Breakfast Inn 174 Waverley Road Toronto ON 416-699-0818
http://members.tripod.com/beachesbb/
This B&B, located in The Beaches neighborhood, is just 1.5 blocks from the beach. Pets and children are welcome at this bed and breakfast. Most of the rooms offer private bathrooms. The owner has cats on the premises.
Delta Toronto Airport Hotel 801 Dixon Rd West Toronto ON 416-675-6100
There are no additional pet fees.
Fairmont Royal York 100 Front Street Toronto ON 416-368-2511 (800-257-7544)
http://www.fairmont.com/royalyork/
Located in Canada's largest city metropolis, this grand hotel is a great location to explore the numerous activities and attractions of the area. Dogs are allowed for an additional pet fee of $ 25 per night per room. Dogs may not be left alone in the room at any time, and they must be leashed and cleaned up after.
Four Seasons Hotel Toronto 21 Avenue Road Toronto ON 416-964-0411
Dogs of all sizes are allowed for no additional pet fee. Dogs may not be left alone in the room; pet sitting services are available.
Hilton 145 Richmond Street West Toronto ON 416-869-3456

Dogs up to 50 pounds are allowed for a $50 refundable pet deposit.

Holiday Inn Express Toronto-Downtown 111 Lombard Street Toronto ON   416-367-5555 (877-270-6405)
One dog of any size is allowed for no additional pet fee. Dogs may not be left alone in the room.

Holiday Inn Toronto-Midtown 280 Bloor St. West Toronto ON   416-968-0010 (877-270-6405)
One dog of any size is allowed for an additional pet fee of $25 per night.

Holiday Inn on King (Downtown) 370 King Street West Toronto ON   416-599-4000 (877-270-6405)
http://www.hiok.com/
One dog up to 50 pounds is allowed for an additional one time pet fee of $35.

International Plaza Hotel and Conference Centre 655 Dixon Rd Toronto ON   416-244-1711
You must sign a pet waiver for your dog. There are no additional pet fees.

Novotel - Toronto Center 45 The Esplanade Toronto ON   416-367-8900
Novotel Hotels welcome a maximum of 2 animals (cats and dogs) per room and never require a fee. Each guest checking in with a pet will be given a Royal Canine/Novotel Pet Welcome Kit.

Novotel - Toronto Mississauga 3670 Hurontario Street Toronto ON   905-896-1000
Novotel Hotels welcome a maximum of 2 animals (cats and dogs) per room and never require a fee. Each guest checking in with a pet will be given a Royal Canine/Novotel Pet Welcome Kit.

Sheraton Centre Toronto Hotel 123 Queen Street W Toronto ON   416-361-1000 (888-625-5144)
The centerpiece of this hotel is the 2½ acres of gardens and terraces complete with waterfalls. Dogs up to 80 pounds are allowed for no additional fee, and they are greeted with a Pet Welcome kit and a Sweet Sleeper doggy bed. There is a pet policy to sign at check in. Dogs may not be left alone in the room, and they must be leashed and cleaned up after at all times.

Sheraton Gateway Hotel in Toronto International Airport Terminal 3, Toronto AMF Toronto ON   905-672-7000 (888-625-5144)
This is the only hotel located in the airport and there is a climate controlled skywalk connecting the hotel and Terminal 3. Dogs of all sizes are allowed for no additional fee. Dogs may only be left for a short time, and they request that the front desk be informed when they are alone in the room. Dogs must be well behaved, leashed, and cleaned up after.

The Westin Bristol Place Toronto Airport 950 Dixon Road Toronto ON   819-778-6111 (888-625-5144)
Offering comfort and a central, convenient location makes this an attractive destination for the business or leisure traveler. Dogs up to 80 pounds are allowed for no additional fee, and there is a pet waiver to sign at check in. A pet care amenity package is available when noted at the time of reservations. Dogs may not be left alone in the room, and they must be leashed and cleaned up after. Dogs may not be in food or beverage areas.

Travelodge Hotel 925 Dixon Road Toronto ON   416-674-2222
There are no additional pet fees.

Author Len Kain and dog Toby in downtown Toronto

Campgrounds and RV Parks
Glen Rouge Campground 7450 Kingston Road Toronto ON   416-338-2267

Dogs of all sizes are allowed. There are no additional pet fees. Dogs may not be left unattended, must be leashed, and cleaned up after. This RV park is closed during the off-season. The camping and tent areas also allow dogs. There is a dog walk area at the campground. There are some breed restrictions.

Transportation Systems
TTC Regional Toronto ON 416-393-INFO
http://www.city.toronto.on.ca/ttc
Both small and large dogs are allowed on the subway, buses, and streetcars. The driver has the discretion to decide whether or not pets are allowed if it is too crowded, there are too many pets onboard or if you have a very large dog. Pets must be on a leash or in a carrier.

Attractions
Black Creek Pioneer Village 1000 Murray Ross Parkway Toronto ON 416-736-1733
Leashed dogs are allowed in this 1860's village. The village shows how people lived in Upper Canada through the 1860's. Enjoy over 35 restored homes and shops, as well as costumed people who will demonstrate how the inhabitants lived during this time period.
Centreville Amusement Park Centre Island Toronto ON 416-203-0405
http://www.centreisland.ca/
Leashed dogs are allowed at this amusement park, but they are not allowed on any of the rides. The park offers over 30 rides and attractions and 14 food outlets. While there are no admission fees to enter the park, you will need to buy ride tickets if you plan on going on any rides. An average price for ride tickets for a family of four might cost about $72. The park is open daily from mid-May to the beginning of September and then open weekends only in May and September, weather permitting. The park is closed the rest of the year. To get there, you will have to take the ferry which departs from Queens Quay and Bay Street in downtown Toronto. Ferry prices are about $5 per person and less for children.
City Walks Guided Tours Call to arrange. Toronto ON 416-966-1550
Take a guided walking tour of historic Toronto and bring your pooch along. Learn about Toronto's history and architecture plus hear stories and get tips about the culture. There are many tours to choose from and they are normally held on the weekends. Tours are approximately 2 hours long. The cost is $12 Canadian per adult and free for children under 12 years old and pets. Reservations are required. Call 416-966-1550 between 8am and 10pm to reserve a space.
Great Lakes Schooner Company Queen's Quay Toronto ON 416-203-2322
http://www.greatlakesschooner.com/
Take a Toronto boat tour onboard a large schooner (sailboat). Your well-behaved, leashed dog is allowed on the tours. Enjoy great views of Toronto's skyline from the water. Tours run from June to September and are about 1 to 2 hours long, depending on the tour. The cost is just under $20 per adult and less for children and seniors. Dogs ride for free. The tours depart off Queen's Quay, between Rees Street and Lower Simcoe Street.
Harbourfront Centre York and John Quays Toronto ON 416-973-3000
http://www.harbourfront.on.ca/
Dogs are not allowed inside any buildings, but are allowed outside and at outdoor events. Dogs must be leashed. Located on Toronto's waterfront, this 10 acre centre provides entertaining and educational events and activities. Your pooch is welcome to join you at the summer outdoor concerts and festivals. Even if there are no outdoor events, you can enjoy a walk along the waterside. The centre is located on York Quay and John Quay, south of Queens Quay West (near University Avenue).
Toronto Islands Park Toronto ON 416-392-8186
These islands, located less than 10 minutes from downtown via ferries, have over 600 park acres with walking paths. Dogs on leash are allowed on the islands. Centre Island is home to the dog-friendly Centreville amusement park (no dogs on rides). The only way to the islands is via the ferries. Ferry prices for adults are about $5 per person, less for children and free for dogs.

Stores
Three Dog Bakery 2014 Queen Street E Toronto ON 800-752-2172
http://www.threedog.com
Three Dog Bakery provides cookies and snacks for your dog as well as some boutique items. You well-behaved, leashed dog is welcome.

Parks
Bluffer's Park Brimley Road South Toronto ON 416-397-8186
Leashed dogs are allowed in the park and on the beach. This 473 acre park is located east of the Toronto Harbour and The Beaches neighborhood. The park offers a beach and scenic overlooks from the bluffs. It is located at Brimley Road South and Kingston Road.
Dog Beach - Kew Gardens 2075 Queen Street Toronto ON

Located in The Beaches neighborhood, dogs are allowed to run leash-free on this section of the beach. Dogs can run leash-less 24 hours a day. The dog beach area is located at the foot of Kew, on Beach, between snow fence and Lake.

High Park 1873 Bloor Street West Toronto ON   416-397-8186
Leashed dogs are allowed in this park. The park covers almost 400 acres and offers many nature hiking trails and a picnic area. High Park is located west of the Toronto Harbour.

Kortright Centre 9550 Pine Valley Drive Woodbridge ON   416-661-6600
http://www.kortright.org/
Dogs on leash are allowed, but must be cleaned up after and are not allowed in the Visitor's Center. This 800 acres of green space offers about 10 miles of nature trails, a river valley, marshes, meadows, forests, and more. The park also focuses on promoting green energy. It is located about 10 minutes north of Toronto. To get there, take Highway 400 north to Major Mackenzie Drive. Follow Major Mackenzie Drive about 2 km west to Pine Valley Drive. Follow Pine Valley Drive south 1 km to Kortright.

Off-Leash Dog Parks

Dog Park - High Park 1873 Bloor Street Toronto ON   416-397-8186
Dogs can run leash-free at the open area located west of the Dream Site and the allotment Gardens, and northeast of the Grenadier Restaurant. The dog park area is open 24 hours a day, except for 6pm to 10pm during stage productions at the Dream Site. The park is located at Bloor Street and Parkside Drive.

Outdoor Restaurants

Carmelina 7501 Woodbine Avenue Markham ON   905-477-7744
Dogs are allowed at the outdoor tables.

Black Dog Pub 87 Island Road Toronto ON   416-286-4544
http://www.blackdogpub.com
Dogs are allowed at the outdoor tables. The restaurant has outdoor tables only in the summer.

Charlotte Room Restaurant 19 Charlotte Street Toronto ON   416-598-2882
http://www.charlotteroom.com/
Well-behaved, leashed dogs are allowed at the outdoor tables. Thanks to one of our readers for recommending this restaurant.

Erl's Bistro and Bar 700 University Avenue Toronto ON   416-595-0700
Dogs are allowed at the outdoor perimeter or corner tables.

Foster's on Elm 31 Elm Street Toronto ON   416-581-1037
This British pub allows dogs at their outdoor tables.

McSorley's Saloon and Grill 1544 Bayview Avenue Toronto ON   416-932-0655
http://www.mcsorleys.ca/
In addition to American favorites, this eatery also offers a number of ethnic flavors, special events, and entertainment. Dogs are allowed at the outer tables; they must be leashed and under owner's control/care at all times.

Mitzi's Cafe and Gallery 100 Sorauren Avenue Toronto ON   416-588-1234
Dogs are allowed at the outdoor tables.

Reds Wine Country Bistro and Bar 77 Adelaide West Toronto ON   416-862-7337
http://www.redsbistro.com
Dogs are allowed at the outdoor tables.

Sassafraz Restaurant 100 Cumberland Street Toronto ON   416-964-2222
http://www.cafesassafraz.com
Dogs are allowed at the outdoor tables. This restaurant, located in the posh Yorkville area, offers both French and California cuisine.

The Longest Yard Restaurant and Bar 535 Mount Pleasant Road Toronto ON   416-480-9273
This sports bar, rich in thematic paraphernalia, offers a variety of American favorites as well as a bit of the exotic, and they open up outside dining in the summer months. Dogs are allowed at the outer tables; they must be leashed and under owner's control/care at all times.

Whistler's Grille and Cafe Bar 995 Broadview Avenue Toronto ON   416-421-1344
Dogs are allowed, but need to be tied to the fence. They can sit right next to you on the same side of the fence.

Jakes on Main 202 Main Street Unionville ON   905-470-6955
Dogs are allowed at the outdoor tables.

Windy O'Neill's Irish Pub 50 Interchange Way Vaughan ON   905-760-9366
http://www.windyoneill.com
Dogs are allowed at the outdoor tables. Choose from a variety of entrees as well as fine stouts.

Montreal

Accommodations

Auberge du vieux-port 97 rue de la Commune Est Montreal PQ   514-876-0081
http://aubergeduvieuxport.com
The Auberge du vieux-port is located across from the Old Port of Montreal in Old Montreal. Dogs of all sizes are allowed. There is a $7 per pet per night pet fee for small dogs and a $14 per pet per night pet fee for larger dogs. You need to leave a cell phone number if you are leaving a dog alone in the room. One dog is allowed in the rooms but up to two dogs may be allowed in the studio lofts.

Chateau Versailles 1659 Sherbrooke Street West Montreal PQ   514-933-8111 (888-933-8111)
This hotel is located in the downtown area. There is a $17.25 nightly pet fee per pet. Dogs must be leashed on the premises and may not be left alone in the room.

Delta Montreal 475 avenue Président-Kennedy Montreal PQ   514-286-1986
There is a 30.00 pet fee.

Four Points by Sheraton Montreal Centre-Ville 475 Sherbrooke Street West/H 138 Montreal PQ   514-842-3961 (888-625-5144)
The prime location of this hotel gives visitors a good starting point for numerous activities and recreational opportunities. Dogs of all sizes are allowed for no additional fee. Dogs may not be left alone in the room, and they must be leashed and cleaned up after at all times.

Holiday Inn 420 Sherbrooke St W. Montreal PQ   514-842-6111 (877-270-6405)
Dogs of all sizes are allowed for an additional one time pet fee of $35 per room.

Holiday Inn - Airport 6500 Cote de Liesse Montreal PQ   514-739-3391 (877-270-6405)
Dogs of all sizes are allowed for an additional one time fee of $35 per pet.

Hotel Godin 10 Sherbrooke Ouest Montreal PQ   514-843-6000 (866-744-6346)
http://hotelgodin.com
This boutique hotel allows dogs of all sizes. There is a special doggy menu on the room service menu and they can provide a doggy bed if requested. There is a $50 one time additional pet fee.

Hotel Le Germain 2050, rue Mansfield Montreal PQ   514-849-2050 (877-333-2050)
http://hotelgermain.com
This boutique hotel is located in the downtown district of the city. Dogs of all sizes are allowed. There is a $30 per night additional pet fee. Dogs may only be left in the rooms for very short times.

Hotel Maritime Plaza 1155 rue Guy Montreal PQ   514-932-1411
http://www.hotelmaritime.com/
There is a $35 per night fee for the pet.

Hotel Travelodge Montreal Centre 50 boul Rene-Levesque ouest Montreal PQ   514-874-9090
There is a $20 per night pet fee.

Intercontinental Montreal 360 Saint Antoine Street Ouest Montreal PQ   514-987-9900
Dogs up to 45 pounds are allowed for an additional one time pet fee of $35 per room.

Le Saint-Sulpice 414 rue St-Sulpice Montreal PQ   514-288-1000 (877-SUL-PICE)
http://www.lesaintsulpice.com/
This Old Montreal boutique hotel allows dogs of any size. You need to declare pets at the time that you make reservations. There is a $30 one time pet fee.

Loews Hotel Vogue 1425 Rue De La Montagne Montreal PQ   514-285-5555
All well-behaved dogs of any size are welcome. This upscale hotel offers their "Loews Loves Pets" program which includes special pet treats, local dog walking routes, and a list of nearby pet-friendly places to visit. There are no pet fees.

Novotel - Montreal Center 1180 Rue de la Montagne Montreal PQ   514-861-6000
Novotel Hotels welcome a maximum of 2 animals (cats and dogs) per room and never require a fee. Each guest checking in with a pet will be given a Royal Canine/Novotel Pet Welcome Kit.

Quality Hotel Dorval Aeroport 7700 Cote de Liesse Montreal PQ   514-731-7821
One dog is allowed for an additional one time pet fee of $25 per room.

Residence Inn by Marriott 2045 Peel Street Montreal PQ   514-982-6064
Dogs of all sizes are allowed, however there can only be one large or two medium to small dogs per room. There is a $250 one time fee plus tax and a pet policy to sign at check in.

Residence Inn by Marriott 2170 Lincoln Avenue Montreal PQ   514-935-9224
Dogs of all sizes are allowed. There is a $105 plus tax one time fee and a pet policy to sign at check in.

Ritz-Carlton Montreal 1228 Sherbrooke Street West Montreal PQ   514-842-4212 (800-363-0366)
http://www.ritzmontreal.com
The Ritz-Carlton is located in the Golden Square Mile area in downtown. Dogs of all sizes are allowed. There is a $150 one time additional pet fee. The Ritz-Carlton also offers in house pet-sitting for $15 per hour.

Sheraton Four Points 475 rue Sherbrooke ouest Montreal PQ   514-842-3961 (888-625-5144)

There are no additional pet fees.

Novotel - Montreal Center

Campgrounds and RV Parks

Camping de Compton 24 Chemin De La Station Compton PQ   800-563-5277
Dogs of all sizes are allowed. There are no additional pet fees. Dogs must be leashed and cleaned up after. This RV park is closed during the off-season. The camping and tent areas also allow dogs. There is a dog walk area at the campground.

Montreal West KOA 171 H 338 Coteau du Lac PQ   450-763-5625 (800-562-9395)
http://www.koa.com
Dogs of all sizes are allowed. There are no additional pet fees. Dogs must be quiet, well behaved, leashed, and cleaned up after. This RV park is closed during the off-season. The camping and tent areas also allow dogs. There is a dog walk area at the campground.

Camping Lac LaFontaine 110 Boul Grand Heron PQ   450-431-7373
http://www.laclafontaine.ca
Dogs of all sizes are allowed. There is a $3 per stay per pet additional fee. Dogs must be leashed and cleaned up after. This RV park is closed during the off-season. The camping and tent areas also allow dogs. There is a dog walk area at the campground.

Camping Alouette 3449 L'Industrie Saint-Mathieu-de-beloeil PQ   450-464-1661
http://www.campingalouette.com
Dogs of all sizes are allowed. There is a $1 per night per pet additional fee. Dogs must be leashed and cleaned up after. This RV park is closed during the off-season. The camping and tent areas also allow dogs. There is a dog walk area at the campground.

Transportation Systems

Atlas Taxi   Montreal PQ   514-485-8585
Well-behaved, leashed dogs may ride in Montreal taxis with you. However, in winter you must provide a cover for the seats and you must report that you have a dog when calling for a taxi to avoid additional fees.

Metro (Subway) Throughout the Region Montreal PQ   514-786-4636
http://www.stm.info
Small dogs in carriers are allowed. There is no fee for the dog but they may not take up a seat.

Unitaxi   Montreal PQ   514-482-3000
Well-behaved, leashed dogs may ride in Montreal taxis with you. However, in winter you must provide a cover for the seats and you must report that you have a dog when calling for a taxi to avoid additional fees.

Attractions

Horse and Carriage Rides often leave from in front of Notre-Dame

Caleche Andre Boisrt St Lawrence Blvd at De La Commune Montreal PQ   450-653-0751
This horse and carriage company will take you, your party and your pup on a horse and carriage tour of Montreal. You can call them at 450-653-0751 to arrange pickup or they may be picking people up in front of the Imax Theater at St Lawrence Blvd and De La Commune. If one driver does not want to take dogs usually another driver will. It is usually a good idea to bring a blanket, towel or cover for the dog.
Caleche Lucky Luc   Montreal PQ   514-934-6105
http://www.calechesluckyluc.com
This horse and carriage transportation company will pick you up with a horse and carriage for an event or a tour of the city. The drivers have been known to sometimes bring their own dogs along as well. You can call them at 514-934-6105 to arrange where to meet or find out if they are giving public rides.
Circuit des Fantoms du Vieux Ghost Tours 469 Francis Xavier Montreal PQ   514-868-0303 (877-868-0303)
http://phvm.qc.ca
You and your well-behaved, leashed dog can join in after dark spooky fun on these ghost tours of Montreal. They have a number of tours such as the "New France Ghost Hunt", "Montreal's Historical Crime Scene" and others.
Guidatour Walking Tours of Montreal Sulpice at Notre Dame Street Montreal PQ   514-844-4021 (800-363-4021)
http://www.guidatour.qc.ca/en/profil.htm
This touring company offers walking tours of Old Montreal. Well-behaved, leashed dogs are allowed on the tours but may not be able to enter some buildings during the tour. The tours meet at the corner of Sulpice and Notre Dame Streets. Their offices are at 477, Saint-François-Xavier Street, Suite 300.
Lachine Canal National Historic Site East to West across Montreal Montreal PQ   514-283-6054 (888-773-8888)
The Lachine Canal was the main ship transportation route through Montreal until the St. Lawrence Seaway was built. The canal closed in 1970. Now it is a historical site with a 14 km trail for hiking, biking and other activities. The park starts at the Old Port and goes to Lake Saint-Louis. There are also boating activities on the canal. Dogs are allowed on most of the trail but between 6th and 23rd Avenues there are currently discussions about whether dogs will be allowed on this section. So it is best to use the section east of 6th Avenue. Dogs are not allowed in any parks in the District of Lachine except designated dog parks.

Lachine Canal National Historic Site

Place Jacques Cartier and Vieux Montreal Rue St-Paul E at Place Jacques Cartier Montreal PQ
This cobblestone plaza is closed to automobile traffic and offers an area for artists, singers, photographers and
other booths and shops. Around the plaza is the old Montreal area which has many shops and restaurants. Dogs
on leashes are welcome and it is up to individual shops as to whether dogs are allowed inside.
Tours Kaleidoscope 6592, Chateaubriand Montreal PQ 514-990-1872
http://tourskaleidoscope.com
This company conducts walking tours of Montreal. Tours are available in the old town (Vieux-Montreal) and other
quarters of the city. The regular tours are in French. You can get private tours for $115 for a two hour tour in
English. Well-behaved, leashed dogs are allowed to accompany you on most tours.
Geordie Charters 20 Westwood Drive Pointe-Claire Pointe-Claire PQ 514-695-2552
http://www.geordiecharters.com
These boat charters stand ready to take you and your dog on an unforgettable water tour of Montreal and nearby
areas. Tours of the Old Port, Lachine Canal, the Locks and other areas are available. Fishing trips are also
available. The boat dock is located at Highway 40 (20) at St. Johns Road. The charters can have up to 4 people
and a dog on most boats.
Santa Claus Village 987 Marin Val-David PQ 819-322-2146 (800-287-NOEL)
http://noel.qc.ca
Only very well-behaved dogs on leash are allowed on most of the premises of this theme park. The park is
located north of Montreal. To get there from Montreal take Autoroute 15, Exit 76 then follow the blue signs on
Route 117.

Stores

Club K-9 6004 Club Sherbrooke West Montreal PQ 514-489-4004
Well-behaved, leashed dogs may accompany you to this pet boutique.
Le Reveil du Maitre Boutique 1720 Av. Laurier E Montreal PQ 514-509-1430
This interesting pet boutique allows you to sip on a cappuccino while your dog snacks on a dog snack. Also the
boutique carries unique dog products from around the world. Well-behaved dogs are allowed.
Le Reveil du Maitre Boutique and Dog Cafe 5377 Boul. Saint-Laurent Montreal PQ 514-490-0202
This interesting pet boutique allows you to sip on a cappuccino while your dog snacks on a dog snack. Also the
boutique carries unique dog products from around the world. Well-behaved dogs are allowed.
Le Reveil du Maitre Boutique 1461 Van Horne Outremont PQ 514-948-0202
This interesting pet boutique allows you to sip on a cappuccino while your dog snacks on a dog snack. Also the
boutique carries unique dog products from around the world. Well-behaved dogs are allowed.
Le Reveil du Maitre Boutique and Dog Cafe 4850 Boul. Saint-Jean Pierrefonds PQ 514-696-2228

This interesting pet boutique allows you to sip on a cappuccino while your dog snacks on a dog snack. Also the boutique carries unique dog products from around the world. Well-behaved dogs are allowed.

Parks

Sentier de la Presqu'île (Trail) 2001 Jean-Pierre Le Gardeur PQ   450-585-0121
Only 30 minutes from Montreal is this family-oriented trail that has a network of four, well marked hiking trails that wander through forest and country field settings. There are picnic tables, ponds, and in spring, maple sugar shacks, to be found along the way. Dogs are welcome here, and if they are well behaved and respond to voice command, they can even be off lead. Dogs must be cleaned up after at all times.
Lafontaine Park Sherbrook at Papineau Montreal PQ   514-872-9800
This 100 acre park in the Plateau Mont-Royal area offers two ponds, interesting landscaping and fountains and waterfalls. Dogs on leash are allowed. Dogs must be cleaned up after at all times.
McGill University Campus 859 rue Sherbrooke Ouest Montreal PQ   514-398-4455
http://www.mcgill.ca
The McGill University Campus has a lot of open areas. Well-behaved, leashed dogs are allowed in the outside areas of the campus.

Montreal from Mont-Royal Park

Mont-Royal Park 1260, Chemin Remembrance Montreal PQ   514-843-8240
Many Montreal visitors come to this park for the view of Montreal. Functioning both as an environmentally educational park and a great get-a-way spot, there are a wide variety of activities, special events, year round water and land recreational opportunities, guided tours, and more to enjoy at this beautiful day use park. Some of the features and amenities include the historical Smith House (a testament to the area's past), rental equipment, look-out points, multi-use trails, a bird feeding route, picnic sites, a playground, a café and a snackbar, and restrooms. Access to the park is free; parking is $2.50 per hour to a total cost of $6 for the day. Dogs are allowed for no additional fee. Dogs must be under owner's control, leashed, and cleaned up after at all times.
Parc Jean-Drapeau Ile Notre-Dame Montreal PQ 514-872-6120
http://parcjeandrapeau.com
This island park sits on the islands of Ile Ste-Helene and Ile Notre-Dame in the St Lawrence River. There are green areas, flower gardens, and the Old Fort. Dogs on leash are allowed at the outside areas of the park. They are not allowed on the beaches.

Off-Leash Dog Parks

Autoroute 20 at 55e Avenue Off-Leash Area Autoroute 20 at 55e Avenue Lachine Borrough PQ   514-637-7587

This is one of several parks that have off-leash areas. Dogs are not allowed at all in other Lachine Borrough parks except for these dog parks. You must clean up after your dog. The park is located at Autoroute 20 and 55e Avenue.

Promendade du rail Off-Leash Area rue Victoria between 10e and 15e Lachine Borrough PQ 514-637-7587
This is one of several parks that have off-leash areas. Dogs are not allowed at all in other Lachine Borrough parks except for these dog parks. You must clean up after your dog. The park is located at Promenade du rail between 10e and 15e Avenues and between rue Victoria and rue William-MacDonald.

Rue Victoria and 28e Avenue Off-Leash Area Rue Victoria and 28e Avenue Lachine Borrough PQ 514-637-7587
This is one of several parks that have off-leash areas. Dogs are not allowed at all in other Lachine Borrough parks except for these dog parks. You must clean up after your dog.

Rue Victoria and 40e Avenue Off-Leash Area Rue Victoria and 40e Avenue Lachine Borrough PQ 514-637-7587
This is one of several parks that have off-leash areas. Dogs are not allowed at all in other Lachine Borrough parks except for these dog parks. You must clean up after your dog.

Rue des Erables Off-Leash Area Rue des Erables at Rue Emile-Pominville Lachine Borrough PQ 514-637-7587
This is one of several parks that have off-leash areas. Dogs are not allowed at all in other Lachine Borrough parks except for these dog parks. You must clean up after your dog.

Stoney Point River Park Off-Leash Area Between 45e and 56e Avenues Lachine Borrough PQ 514-637-7587
This is one of several parks that have off-leash areas. Dogs are not allowed at all in other Lachine Borrough parks except for these dog parks. You must clean up after your dog. The off-leash hours are from 6 am to 10 am and from 6 pm to 10 pm. The area that allows dogs off-leash is from 45e to 56e Avenues in the park.

Notre-Dame-de-Grace Park Girouard and Sherbrooke West Montreal PQ 514-637-7587
This off-leash dog run is open from 7 am to 10 pm on weekdays and on weekends from 9 am to 10 pm.

King George Park Off-Leash Area Cote St. Antoine and Murray Westmount PQ 514-989-5200
This off-leash dog run is located east of the tennis courts in King George Park. The area is off-leash 24 hours a day.

Outdoor Restaurants

Bistro Cote Soleil 3979, rue Saint-Denis Montreal PQ 514-282-8037
Well-behaved, leashed dogs are allowed at the outside tables in the front of the restaurant.

Brioche Lyonnaise 1593 St. Denis Street Montreal PQ 514-842-7017
Well-behaved, leashed dogs can accompany you at the outer tables of the restaurants outdoor seating area.

Guy and Dodo Morali 1445, Peel Street Montreal PQ 514-842-3636
http://www.guyetdodo.com
Well-behaved, leashed dogs are allowed at the outside tables at this chic Mont-Royal French restaurant.

Jardin Asean Garden 5828 Sherbrooke West Montreal PQ 514-487-8868
http://www.aseangarden.ca
This Chinese restaurant will allow well-behaved, leashed dogs on their outside seats.

La Iguana 51 Roy Est at St-Dominique Montreal PQ 514-844-0893
The restaurant is open from 5 pm. Well-behaved and leashed dogs are allowed at some outdoor tables.

Quebec

Accommodations

Clarion Hotel 3125 Hochelaga Blvd Quebec PQ 418-653-4901 (877-424-6423)
Dogs are allowed for no additional pet fee.

Days Inn Quebec West 3145 Avenue des Hotels Quebec PQ 418-653-9321 (800-329-7466)
Dogs of all sizes are allowed. There are no additional pet fees.

Delta Quebec Hotel 690 Boul Rene-Levesque E Quebec PQ 418-647-1717
The Delta Quebec Hotel is located in the heart of the walled city of Quebec. There is a $35 one time additional pet fee. One large dog is allowed. Two smaller dogs may be allowed. Dogs must be well-behaved and leashed at all times.

Fairmont Le Château Frontenac 1 rrue des Carrieres Quebec PQ 418-692-3861 (800-257-7544)
http://www.fairmont.com/frontenac/
This regal heritage hotel looks out over the St Lawrence River and historic old Quebec, a United Nations World Heritage Site. One dog of any size is welcome for an additional $25 per night. Dogs may not be left alone in the room at any time, and they must be leashed and cleaned up after.

Hilton 1100 Rene-Levesque East Quebec PQ 418-647-2411

Dogs are allowed for an additional one time pet of $25 per room.
Hotel Dominion 1912 126 St Pierre Quebec PQ   418-692-2224
http://www.hoteldominion.com
Dogs of any size are allowed at this boutique hotel in Quebec City. Many of the rooms have views of Old Quebec
or the St Lawrence River. Up to two dogs are allowed. There is a $30 one time additional pet fee per dog. Dogs
must be leashed at all times.
L'Hotel du Vieux Quebec 1190 rue St-Jean Quebec PQ   418-692-1850
http://www.hvq.com/
There are no additional pet fees.
Quality Suites 1600 Rue Bouvier Quebec PQ   418-622-4244
Dogs are allowed for an additional one time pet fee of $25 per room.
Loews Le Concorde Hotel 1225 Cours Du General De Montcalm Quebec City PQ   418-647-2222
All well-behaved dogs of any size are welcome. This upscale hotel offers their "Loews Loves Pets" program
which includes room service for pets, special pet treats, local dog walking routes, and a list of nearby pet-friendly
places to visit. There are no pet fees.
Days Inn Ste-Helene-de-Bagot 410 Couture Ste-Helene-de-Bagot PQ   450-791-2580 (800-329-7466)
Dogs of all sizes are allowed. There is a $5.75 per night pet fee per pet.
Comfort Inn Airport 7320 Boul Wilfrid-Hamel Ste. Foy PQ   418-872-5038 (877-424-6423)
Dogs are allowed for an additional one time pet fee of $25 per room.

Campgrounds and RV Parks

Camping Plage Fortier 1400 Lucen Francoes L'ange-Gardien PQ   888-226-7387
http://www.campingplagefortier.ca
Dogs of all sizes are allowed. There are no additional pet fees. Dogs may not be left unattended, must be
leashed, and cleaned up after. This RV park is closed during the off-season. The camping and tent areas also
allow dogs. There is a dog walk area at the campground.
Camping Aeroport 2050 Aeroport Quebec City PQ   800-294-1574
http://www.campingaeroport.com
Dogs of all sizes are allowed. There are no additional pet fees. Dogs must be quiet, well behaved, leashed, and
cleaned up after. This RV park is closed during the off-season. The camping and tent areas also allow dogs.
There is a dog walk area at the campground.
Camping Parc Beaumont 432 Fleuve Quebec City PQ   418-837-3787
Dogs of all sizes are allowed. There are no additional pet fees. Dogs must be leashed and cleaned up after. This
RV park is closed during the off-season. The camping and tent areas also allow dogs. There is a dog walk area
at the campground.

Vacation Home Rentals

Chalets-Village Mont-Sainte-Anne Call to Arrange Quebec City PQ   418-826-3331 (800-461-2030)
http://www.chaletsvillage.ca
Pet-friendly country villas for rent at the base of Mnt-Sainte-Anne. There are houses for families and up to 9
bedrooms for a large group.

Transportation Systems

Quebec - Levis Ferry Rue Dalhousie, Lower Town Quebec PQ   418-644-3704
For a fabulous view of Quebec from the river take the ferry from the Lower Town to Levis. The ferry ride takes
about ten minutes each way and they leave about every 30 minutes throughout the day and evening. Well-
behaved, leashed dogs are allowed for no additional fee. You can take the ferry for the views or if you need
transportation to Levis.
Taxi Coop de Quebec Throughout the city Quebec PQ   418-525-5191
Pets are allowed on the taxis in Quebec. They must be leashed or in a carrier at all times. People planning to
take a pet on a taxi need to call ahead to get a pet-friendly cab driver.
Taxi Quebec Throughout the city Quebec PQ   418-522-2001
Pets are allowed on the taxis in Quebec. They must be leashed or in a carrier at all times. People planning to
take a pet on a taxi need to call ahead to get a pet-friendly cab driver.

Attractions

Parc de la Chute-Montmorency 2490, avenue Royale Beauport PQ   418-663-3330
http://www.bonjourquebec.com/qc-fr/fiches/en/attraits/3197018.html
This 270 foot waterfall is actually higher than its more famous cousin at Niagara. You and your leashed dog may
take a cablecar ride up to the top of the falls, take a short 1/4 mile walk to the falls and walk across a narrow
bridge at the head of the falls. There is a great view from the bridge. Dogs on leash are allowed on the cablecar
and at all outdoor areas and trails in the park. This was definitely a highlight of our most recent trip to the area.

Parc de la Chute-Montmorency

Fortifications of Québec National Historic Site

Association des guides touristiques de Quebec   Quebec PQ   418-624-2851
You can call this Association of tour guides to get a private car tour or walking tour. The car tours are usually

done in your own car. If your dog is well-behaved they will probably be able to accommodate you on the private walking or driving tours.

CSA Historical Walking Tour 4, rue Toussaint Quebec PQ   418-692-3033
This company takes groups on walking tours of Quebec. Most of the tour is outside except for a visit to the Catholic Church. Well-behaved, leashed dogs may accompany you on all outdoor sections of the tour. Someone will have to stay outside with the dog while the tour is in the Church.

Fortifications of Québec National Historic Site 100 Saint-Louis St. Quebec PQ   418-648-7016
Quebec is the only fortified city in North America. It boasts a 4.5 km (3 mile) wall around the old city area. Fortifications of Quebec National Historic Site offers the visitor to Quebec the opportunity to walk this wall and see exhibits about the wall and the history of the city. You can take a self-guided or a guided tour. Dogs on leash are allowed to accompany you in all outdoor areas of the park. They are not allowed in any buildings. Dogs may walk the outside areas of the wall or the park. Dogs must be cleaned up after and be well-behaved.

Horse and Carriage Tours Place d'Armes or rue d'Auteuil Quebec PQ   418-683-9222
Take a carriage ride through the historical streets of Quebec. Well-behaved, leashed dogs are allowed on the tours. Please call ahead to make sure that you can get a reservation for you and your pet. Tours start at Place d'Armes or on rue d'Auteuil. With a dog, you can probably have 2 or 3 people on a carriage tour.

Le Promenade des Ecrivains (Writer's Walking Tour) 1588, avenue Bergemont Quebec PQ   418-264-2772
http://www.promenade-ecrivains.qc.ca/
These tours explore the Old City of Quebec from the writings of the region's famous authors. The tours are given twice a week and are usually on Wednesday and Saturday. The tours last for about two hours and cost $15. Well-behaved, leashed dogs are allowed on the tours.

Parc Nautique de Cap-Rouge Boat Rentals 4155, chemin de la Plage-Jacques-Cartier Quebec PQ   418-641-6148
Rent a canoe, kayak, rowboat or other marine craft at the Nautical Park. Your well-behaved, leashed dog can accompany you on your rental. They are located at the St Lawrence and Cap-Rouge rivers.

Quebec - Levis Ferry Rue Dalhousie, Lower Town Quebec PQ   418-644-3704
For a fabulous view of Quebec from the river take the ferry from the Lower Town to Levis. The ferry ride takes about ten minutes each way and they leave about every 30 minutes throughout the day and evening. Well-behaved, leashed dogs are allowed for no additional fee. You can take the ferry for the views or if you need transportation to Levis.

Rue du Tresor Open Air Artist District Rue du Tresor Quebec PQ   418-259-7453
http://www.ruedutresor.qc.ca
The Rue du Tresor is an open-air art gallery. Art from over 30 artists is available for viewing or sale on the street. Well-behaved, leashed dogs may stroll the street with you looking at the artwork. It is up the individual stores on the street if a dog may go inside.

The Old City of Quebec

Voir Quebec Walking Tours 12, rue Ste-Anne Quebec PQ   418-694-2001
http://www.toursvoirquebec.com
Voir Quebec leads historical walking tours of Quebec. The regular tour is a two hour walking tour that begins at
12, rue Ste-Anne in the Upper Town. Private tours are also available should you prefer a customized tour. Dogs
are allowed on the walking tours if they are well-behaved, leashed and cleaned up after. You need to call ahead
the night before to arrange your reservation.
Ghost Tours of Quebec 85, rue St-Louis Quebec City PQ   418-692-9770
http://www.ghosttoursofquebec.com
Well-behaved, leashed and quiet dogs are allowed to accompany you on most of this after dark ghost tour of the
old city of Quebec. The dog must be well-behaved, calm and quiet so as not to disturb the other tourists. Also,
the final ghost story is told in the Cathedral and your dog will not be able to enter the Cathedral. So someone will
have to remain outside with the dog.

Shopping Centers
Le Promenades du Vieux-Quebec 43, rue De Buade Quebec PQ   418-692-6000
This small shopping area with a dozen boutique stores is located in the center of Old Quebec. Dogs on leash
may join you but it is up to the individual store owners whether dogs may enter the shops.
Place del la Cite Shopping Area Boulevard Laurier Quebec PQ   418-659-6920
This shopping district is along Boulevard Laurier. This area has the largest concentration of boutique shopping in
the city with over 150 shops and boutiques. Leashed, well-behaved dogs may accompany you while shopping,
although it is up to the individual stores whether your dog can enter the store.

Parks

Artillery Park Heritage Site

Artillery Park Heritage Site 2 D'Auteuil Street Quebec PQ   418-648-4205 (888-773-8888)
This park is located at the site of four historical buildings that were used to defend the city in the 17th century.
Dogs on leash are allowed in the park but they are not allowed in the buildings or the museums.
Battlefield Park 835 Wilfrid-Laurier Avenue Quebec PQ   418-648-3506
Battlefield Park consists of 270 acres on the heights overlooking the St Lawrence River. The Plains of Abraham
within the park was the location of a battle between the English and French on September 13, 1759. Throughout
the park there are a number of monuments to generals from the past and a collection of ordinances from famous
battles. Dogs on leash are allowed in the park. They must be cleaned up after and are not allowed in buildings.
Cartier - Brebeuf National Historic Site 175 l'Espinay Street Quebec PQ   418-648-4038 (888-773-8888)
This historical site commemorates the travels and the arrival in Quebec of Jacques Cartier. Located on the north

shore of the Saint-Charles River, the park has parkland, monuments and an exhibit on the voyages of Jacques Cartier, the Jesuits and the native Indians. Dogs on leash are allowed. There may be water bowls for thisty pups. Please clean up after your dog.

Domaine Maizerets 2000, boulevard Montmorency Quebec PQ   418-641-6335
http://www.sracquebec.ca/maizerets.html
This historic site has fabulous landscaped gardens and a historic chateau. The chateau contains an exhibition on the history of the site. Well-behaved, leashed dogs are allowed in the outdoor areas. They are not allowed in any buildings. A bicycle and foot path sets out from the location. The area is used for cross-country skiing in the winter.

Dufferin Terrace at Chateau Frontenac Quebec PQ
This terraced park, built in 1838, provides an excellent view of the city and the St Lawrence River, Ile Orleans, the Old-Port and the Chateau Frontenac. Dogs on leash may accompany you in the park but not inside buildings.

Saint-Louis Forts and Chateaux National Historic Site 2 D'Auteuil Street Quebec PQ   418-648-7016 (888-773-8888)
The site is the location of the Saint-Louis forts and the chateaux that served as the governor's residence. Dogs on leash are allowed in the outdoor areas. They must be cleaned up after and are not allowed in buildings.

Outdoor Restaurants

Bistrot Le Pape Georges 8, rue Cul-de-Sac Quebec PQ   418-692-1320
http://www.papegeorges.com
Well-behaved, leashed dogs are allowed at some of the outdoor tables.

Chez Rabelais 2, rue du Petit-Champlain Quebec PQ   418-694-9460
Well-behaved, leashed dogs are allowed at some of the outdoor tables. They need to be kept out of the pathway so that people may walk through.

Il Teatro 972 Saint Jean Quebec PQ   418-694-9996
Dogs are allowed at the outdoor tables.

L'Ardoise 71, rue St-Paul Quebec PQ   418-694-0213
When it is not crowed your well-behaved, leashed dog may accompany you at the outdoor tables. The dog needs to be kept out of the pathway.

L'Inox Brewery 37, Quai Saint-André Quebec PQ   418-692-2877
This brewery in Old Quebec may have the largest terrace in the city. Well-behaved, leashed dogs may accompany you at some of the outdoor tables.

Le Buffet de l'Antiquaire 95 rue Saint-Paul Quebec PQ   418-692-2661
This restaurant is located in the antiques district of Quebec. Well-behaved, leashed dogs may join you at some of the outdoor tables.

Restaurant Paris-Brest 590 Grande Allee E Quebec PQ   418-529-2243
Well-behaved, leashed dogs may join you at some of the outdoor tables. Please make sure that your dog is out of the pathway so that people can get by.

Chapter 21

Highway Guides

Interstate 10 Accommodation Listings

Louisiana Listings (Interstate 10)   Dogs per Room

Sulphur			
Days Inn Sulphur	337-312-0108	2654 Hwy 108 - Exit 23 Sulphur LA	2
La Quinta Inn Sulphur	337-527-8303	2600 South Ruth - Exit 20 Sulphur LA	3+
Lake Charles			
Best Suites of America	337-439-2444	401 Lakeshore Drive Lake Charles LA	1+
Days Inn Lake Charles	337-433-1711	1010 Martin Luther King Hwy - Hwy 171 Exit Lake Charles LA	2
La Quinta Inn Lake Charles	337-436-5998	1320 MLK Hwy 171 N - Exit H 171 Lake Charles LA	3+
Crowley			
La Quinta Inn Crowley	337-783-6500	9565 Egan Highway - Exit 80 Crowley LA	3+
Lafayette			
Holiday Inn Express	337-667-8913	2942 H Grand Point Hwy - Exit 115/Henderson Breaux Bridge LA	3+
Best Western Posada Ana Inn-Lafayette	337-289-9907	126 Alcide Dominique - Exit 101 Lafayette LA	3+
Comfort Inn	337-232-9000	1421 SE Evangeline Thruway - Exit Exi t 103A Lafayette LA	2
Days Inn Lafayette	337-237-8880	1620 N University - Exit 101 Lafayette LA	2
Holiday Inn Lafayette-Us167	337-233-6815	2032 Ne Evangeline Thruway - Exit 103A Lafayette LA	3+
La Quinta Inn & Suites Lafayette	337-291-1088	1015 West Pinhook Road - Exit West Pinhook Road Lafayette LA	3+
La Quinta Inn Lafayette	337-233-5610	2100 NE Evangeline Thruway - Exit 103A Lafayette LA	2
Motel 6 - Lafayette	337-233-2055	2724 NE Evangeline Thruway Lafayette LA	1+
Quality Inn	337-234-0383	2216 NE Evangeline Thruway - Exit 103A Lafayette LA	2
Red Roof Inn - Lafayette, LA	337-233-3339	1718 North University Avenue Lafayette LA	1+
Howard Johnson Express Inn	337-593-0849	103 Nibor Lane Lafayette/Scott LA	1+
Breaux Bridge			
Best Western Of Breaux Bridge	337-332-1114	2088-B Rees St - Exit 109 Breaux Bridge LA	2
Port Allen			
Super 8 Port Allen/W Baton Rouge Area	225-381-9134	821 Lobdell Hwy - Exit 151 Port Allen LA	2
Baton Rouge			
La Quinta Inn Baton Rouge	225-924-9600	2333 S. Acadian Thruway - Exit Acadian Thruway Baton Rouge LA	3+
Residence Inn by Marriott	225-293-8700	10333 N Mall Drive - Exit 163/Siegen Lane Baton Rouge LA	3+
TownePlace Suites Baton Rouge South	225-819-2112	8735 Summa Avenue - Exit 162 Baton Rouge LA	2
University Inn & Conference Center	225-236-4000	2445 S. Acadian Thruway - Exit 157B Baton Rouge LA	2
Kenner			
La Quinta Inn New Orleans Airport	504-466-1401	2610 Williams Blvd. - Exit Williams Blvd Kenner LA	3+
Motel 6 - New Orleans - Airport	504-466-9666	2830 Loyola Drive Kenner LA	1+
New Orleans			
La Quinta Inn New Orleans Causeway	504-835-8511	3100 I-10 Service Rd. - Exit 228 Metairie LA	3+
La Quinta Inn New Orleans Veterans	504-456-0003	5900 Veterans Memorial Blvd - Exit Veterans Memorial Blvd Metairie LA	3+
Best Western St. Christopher Hotel	504-648-0444	114 Magazine Street - Exit Canal Street New Orleans LA	3+
Drury Inn & Suites	504-529-7800	820 Poydras Street New Orleans LA	1+
Holiday Inn	504-529-7211	124 Royal Street - Exit 235 A/Orleans Street New Orleans LA	2
La Quinta Inn New Orleans Bullard	504-246-3003	12001 I-10 Service Rd. - Exit 245/Bullard Road New Orleans LA	3+
Loews Hotel	504-595-3300	300 Poydras Street - Exit 235B/Canal Street New Orleans LA	3+
Residence Inn by Marriott	504-522-1300	345 St. Joseph - Exit Poydras Street New Orleans LA	3+
Windsor Court Hotel	504-523-6000	300 Gravier Street - Exit 234 New Orleans LA	2

Mississippi Listings (Interstate 10)   Dogs per Room

Gulfport			
Best Western Seaway Inn	228-864-0050	9475 US Hwy 49 and I-10 - Exit 34A Gulfport MS	2
Biloxi			
Biloxi Beachfront Hotel	228-388-3551	2400 Beach Blvd Biloxi MS	1+
Breakers Inn	228-388-6320	2506 Beach Blvd Biloxi MS	1+
Motel 6 - Biloxi	228-388-5130	2476 Beach Boulevard Biloxi MS	1+
Ocean Springs			
Days Inn Biloxi	228-872-8255	7305 Washington Ave - Exit 50 Ocean Springs MS	2

Alabama Listings (Interstate 10)   Dogs per Room

Mobile			
Best Western Battleship Inn	251-432-2703	2701 Battleship Prkwy - Exit 27 Mobile AL	3+

| Days Inn Mobile/Tillmans | 251-661-8181 | 5480 Inn Drive - Exit 15b Mobile AL | 2 |

Florida Listings (Interstate 10)   Dogs per Room

Pensacola			
Comfort Inn	850-455-3233	3 New Warrington Road - Exit H 90 Pensacola FL	2
Days Inn Pensacola/Historic Downtown	850-438-4922	710 N Palafox St - Exit 4 Pensacola FL	2
La Quinta Inn Pensacola	850-474-0411	7750 North Davis Hwy. - Exit 13 Pensacola FL	3+
Quality Inn	850-477-0711	6550 Pensacola Blvd - Exit Pensacola Blvd Pensacola FL	3+
Super 8 Pensacola/Davis Hwy	850-476-8038	7220 Plantation Rd - Exit 13 Pensacola FL	2
Crestview			
Days Inn Crestview	850-682-8842	4255 S Ferdon Blvd - Exit 56 Crestview FL	2
Super 8 Crestview	850-682-9649	3925 S Ferdon blvd - Exit 56 Crestview FL	2
De Funiak Springs			
Days Inn De Funiak Springs	850-892-6115	472 Hugh Adams Rd - Exit 85 De Funiak Springs FL	2
Super 8 De Funiak Springs	850-892-1333	402 Hugh Adams Rd - Exit 85 De Funiak Springs FL	2
Chipley			
Super 8 Chipley	850-638-8530	1700 Main Street - Exit 120 Chipley FL	2
Marianna			
Quality Inn	850-526-5600	2175 H 71S - Exit 142 Marianna FL	3+
Tallahassee			
Best Western Pride Inn and Suites	850-656-6312	2016 Apalachee Pkwy - Exit 199 Tallahassee FL	3+
Doubletree	850-224-5000	101 S Adams Street - Exit 199 Tallahassee FL	3+
Holiday Inn Tallahassee-Capitol-East	850-877-3171	1355 Apalachee Parkway - Exit 199 Tallahassee FL	2
La Quinta Inn Tallahassee North	850-385-7172	2905 North Monroe - Exit 199 Tallahassee FL	3+
Residence Inn by Marriott	850-442-0093	1880 Raymond Diehl Road - Exit 203 Tallahassee FL	3+
Staybridge Suites Tallahassee I-10 East	850-219-7000	1600 Summit Dr. - Exit 209B Tallahassee FL	2
TownePlace Suites Tallahassee North/Capital Circle	850-219-0122	1876 Capital Circle NE - Exit 203 Tallahassee FL	2
Lake City			
Best Western Inn	386-752-3801	3598 US Hwy 90 West Lake City FL	2
Days Inn Lake City	386-758-4224	3430 North US Hwy 441 - Exit 303 Lake City FL	2
Motel 6 - Lake City	386-755-4664	3835 US Hwy 90 Lake City FL	1+
Super 8 Lake City	386-752-6450	I-75 and Hwy 47 Lake City FL	2
Jacksonville			
Days inn MacClenny	904-259-5100	1499 S 6th St - Exit 48 MacClenny FL	2

Interstate 40 Accommodation Listings

Tennessee Listings (Interstate 40)   Dogs per Room

Memphis			
Baymont Inn & Suites Memphis East	901-377-2233	6020 Shelby Oaks Drive - Exit 12C Memphis TN	3+
East Drury Inn & Suites	901-373-8200	1556 Sycamore View Memphis TN	1+
Sleep Inn	901-312-7777	2855 Old Austin Peay H - Exit 8 N Memphis TN	2
Super 8 Memphis/East/Macon Cove Area	901-373-4888	6015 Macon Cove Rd - Exit 12 Memphis TN	2
Lakeland			
Days Inn Memphis East	901-388-7120	9822 Huff N Puff Rd - Exit 20 Lakeland TN	2
Brownsville			
O'Bannon Signature Hotel	731-772-4030	120 Sunny Hill Cave - Exit 56 Brownsville TN	2
Jackson			
Days Inn Jackson/N Hollywood	731-668-4840	2239 N Hollywood Dr - Exit 79 Jackson TN	2
La Quinta Inn Jackson	731-664-1800	2370 N. Highland - Exit 82A Jackson TN	3+
Super 8 Jackson	731-668-1145	2295 N Highland - Exit 82a Jackson TN	2
Wildersville			
Best Western Crossroads Inn	731-968-2532	21045 Hwy 22 North - Exit 108 Wildersville TN	2
Holladay			
Days Inn Holladay	731-847-2278	13845 Hwy 641 North - Exit 126 Holladay TN	2
Hurricane Mills			
Best Western of Hurricane Mills	931-296-4251	15542 Hwy 13 South - Exit 143 Hurricane Mills TN	3+
Days Inn Hurricane Mills	931-296-7647	15415 Hwy 13 South - Exit 143 Hurricane Mills TN	2
Super 8 Hurricane Mills/Buffalo Area	931-296-2432	15470 Hwy 13 South - Exit 143 Hurricane Mills TN	2

636

Dickson

Best Western Executive Inn of Dickson	615-446-0541	2338 Hwy 46 South - Exit 172 Dickson TN	3+
Comfort Inn	615-441-5252	1025 E Christi Drive - Exit 172 Dickson TN	2
Days Inn Dickson	615-446-7561	2415 Hwy 46 South - Exit 172 Dickson TN	2
Super 8 Dickson	615-446-1923	150 Suzanne Dr - Exit 172 Dickson TN	2

Kingston Springs

Best Western Harpeth Inn	615-952-3961	116 Luyben Hills Rd - Exit 188 Kingston Springs TN	3+

Nashville

Best Western Music Row	615-242-1631	1407 Division St - Exit 209B Nashville TN	3+
Comfort Inn	615-255-9977	1501 Demonbreun Street - Exit 209B Nashville TN	2
Days Inn Nashville Downtown	615-327-0922	1800 W End Ave - Exit 209a or 209b Nashville TN	2
Days Inn Nashville West	615-356-9100	269 White Bridge Rd - Exit 204 Nashville TN	2
Drury Inn & Suites	615-902-0400	555 Donelson Pike Nashville TN	1+
La Quinta Inn Nashville Airport	615-885-3100	531 Donelson Pike - Exit 216C Nashville TN	3+
Quality Inn	615-367-9150	981 Murfreesboro Road - Exit 213 Nashville TN	3+
Super 8 Nashville/West	615-356-6005	6924 Charlotte Pike - Exit 201 Nashville TN	2

Mount Juliet

Quality Inn and Suites	615-773-3600	1000 Hershel Drive - Exit 226 Mount Juliet TN	3+

Lebanon

Comfort Inn	615-444-1001	829 S Cumberland Street/H 231 - Exit 238 to H 231 N Lebanon TN	3+

Cookeville

Alpine Lodge & Suites	931-526-3333	2021 E. Spring St. Cookeville TN	1+
Best Western Thunderbird Motel	931-526-7115	900 South Jefferson Ave - Exit 287 and H 136 Cookeville TN	3+
Hampton Inn	931-520-1117	1025 Interstate Drive - Exit 287 Cookeville TN	3+

Crossville

Days Inn Crossville	931-484-9691	305 Executive Dr - Exit 317 Crossville TN	2

Harriman

Super 8 Harriman	865-882-6600	1867 South Roane St - Exit 347 Harriman TN	2

Knoxville

Best Western West of Knoxville	865-675-7666	500 Lovell Rd - Exit 374 Knoxville TN	3+
Candlewood Suites	865-777-0400	10206 Parkside Dr - Exit 374/Lovell Road Knoxville TN	2
Crowne Plaza Knoxville	865-522-2600	401 West Summit Hill Drive - Exit 388 Knoxville TN	2
Holiday Inn	865-584-3911	1315 Kirby Road - Exit 383 Knoxville TN	3+
Holiday Inn Express Knoxville-Strawberry Plains	865-525-5100	730 Rufus Graham Road - Exit 398 Knoxville TN	2
Holiday Inn Select	865-693-1011	304 N Cedar Bluff Road - Exit N Cedar Bluff Road Knoxville TN	3+
La Quinta Inn Knoxville West	865-690-9777	258 North Peters Road - Exit 378 Knoxville TN	3+
Residence Inn by Marriott	865-539-5339	Langley Place at North Peters Road - Exit 378A L Knoxville TN	3+
Super 8 Knoxville/Downtown/West	865-584-8511	6200 Papermill Rd - Exit 383 Knoxville TN	1+
Super 8 Knoxville/West	865-675-5566	11748 Snyder Rd - Exit 373 Knoxville TN	2

Kodak

Comfort Inn Interstate	865-933-1719	155 Dumplin Valley Road - Exit 407/H 66 S Kodak TN	3+
Holiday Inn Express & Suites	865-933-9448	2863 Winfield Dunn Parkway - Exit 407 Kodak TN	2

Sevierville

Comfort Inn River Suites	865-428-5519	860 Winfield Dunn Parkway - Exit 407/H 66 S Sevierville TN	3+

Dandridge

Comfort Inn	865-397-2090	620 Green Valley Drive - Exit 417 Dandridge TN	3+

Newport

Comfort Inn	423-623-5355	1149 Smokey Mountain Lane - Exit 432B Newport TN	3+
Holiday Inn	423-623-8622	1010 Cosby Hwy - Exit 435 Newport TN	3+
Motel 6 - Newport	423-623-1850	255 Heritage Boulevard Newport TN	1+

North Carolina Listings (Interstate 40)   Dogs per Room

Asheville

Comfort Suites Biltmore Square Mall	828-665-4000	890 Brevard Road - Exit 46-A Asheville NC	3+
Days Inn Asheville Biltmore East	828-298-4000	1435 Tunnel Road - Exit 55 Asheville NC	2
Days Inn Asheville Patton Ave	828-254-9661	120 Patton Ave - Exit 50 Asheville NC	2
Holiday Inn - Blue Ridge Parkway	828-298-5611	1450 Tunnel Rd Asheville NC	1+
Sleep Inn West	828-670-7600	1918 Old Haywood Road - Exit 44/H 19-23/Smoky Park H Asheville NC	2
Super 8 Asheville/East	828-298-7952	1329 Tunnel Rd - Exit 55 Asheville NC	2
Super 8 Black Mountain	828-669-8076	101 Flat Creek Rd - Exit 64 or 65 Black Mountain NC	2
Days Inn Asheville West	828-667-9321	2551 Smoky Park Hwy - Exit 37 Candler NC	2
Suzanne's Farm and Gardens	828-670-5248	31 Toms Road - Exit 44 Candler NC	3+

Marion

Super 8 Marion	828-659-7940	4281 Hwy 221 South - Exit 85 Marion NC	2

Morganton

Comfort Inn and Suites	828-430-4000	1273 Burkmount Avenue - Exit 103 Morganton NC	3+

Holiday Inn	828-437-0171	2400 South Sterling St - Exit 105 Morganton NC	3+
Hickory			
Holiday Inn Express	828-328-2081	2250 Highway 70 SE Hickory NC	2
Red Roof Inn - Hickory	828-323-1500	1184 Lenoir Rhyne Boulevard Hickory NC	1+
Greensboro			
Candlewood Suites	336-454-0078	7623 Thorndike Rd - Exit 210 Greensboro NC	2
Clarion Hotel Greensboro Airport	336-299-7650	415 Swing Road - Exit 213 Greensboro NC	2
Days Inn Greensboro Airport	336-668-0476	501 S Regional Rd - Exit 210 Greensboro NC	2
Drury Inn & Suites	336-856-9696	3220 High Point Road Greensboro NC	1+
Holiday Inn Express Greensboro-(I-40 @ Wendover)	336-854-0090	4305 Big Tree Way - Exit 214 Greensboro NC	2
La Quinta Inn & Suites Greensboro	336-316-0100	1201 Lanada Road - Exit 214 Greensboro NC	3+
Residence Inn by Marriott	336-294-8600	2000 Veasley Street - Exit 217 Greensboro NC	3+
Burlington			
Days Inn Burlington	336-227-3681	978 Plantation Dr Burlington NC	2
La Quinta Inn Burlington	336-229-5203	2444 Maple Ave. - Exit 145 Burlington NC	3+
Motel 6 - Burlington	336-226-1325	2155 Hanford Road Burlington NC	1+
Red Roof Inn - Burlington, NC	336-227-1270	2133 West Hanford Road Burlington NC	1+
Durham			
Comfort Inn University	919-490-4949	3508 Moriah Road - Exit 270/H 15/501 Durham NC	3+
Holiday Inn Express Hotel & Suites Research Triangle Park	919-474-9800	4912 South Miami Blvd - Exit 281 Durham NC	2
Residence Inn by Marriott	919-361-1266	201Residence Inn Blvd - Exit 278 Durham NC	3+
Sleep Inn	919-993-3393	5208 New Page Road - Exit 282 Durham NC	1
Raleigh			
TownePlace Suites Raleigh Cary/Weston Pkwy	919-678-0005	120 Sage Commons Way - Exit 287 Cary NC	2
Sleep Inn	919-772-7771	105 Commerce Parkway - Exit 312/H 42 Garner NC	2
Residence Inn by Marriott	919-467-8689	2020 Hospitality Court - Exit 284A Morrisville NC	2
Staybridge Suites	919-468-0180	1012 Airport Blvd - Exit 284 Morrisville NC	3+
Candlewood Suites	919-468-4222	1020 Buck Jones Road - Exit 293A Raleigh NC	3+
La Quinta Inn Raleigh	919-481-3600	1001 Aerial Center Parkway - Exit 284 Raleigh NC	3+
Wilmington			
Camellia Cottage Bed and Breakfast	910-763-9171	118 S. 4th Street Wilmington NC	1+
Days Inn Wilmington	910-799-6300	5040 Market St Wilmington NC	2
Motel 6 - Wilmington	910-762-0120	2828 Market Street Wilmington NC	1+
Residence Inn by Marriott	910-256-0098	1200 Culbreth Drive Wilmington NC	3+
Waterway Lodge	910-256-3771	7246 Wrightsville Avenue Wilmington NC	1+

Interstate 64 Accommodation Listings

Indiana Listings (Interstate 64)   Dogs per Room

Evansville			
Comfort Inn	812-867-1600	19622 Elpers Road - Exit 25A to H 41S Evansville IN	2
Dale			
Motel 6 - Dale	812-937-2294	1334 North Washington Street Dale IN	1+
Corydon			
Capitol Inn	812-738-4192	St Rd 135 & I-64, PO Box 773 Corydon IN	1+
Super 8 Corydon	812-738-8887	168 Pacer Dr - Exit 105 Corydon IN	2

Kentucky Listings (Interstate 64)   Dogs per Room

Louisville			
Candlewood Suites	502-261-0085	11762 Commonwealth Drive - Exit 17 Louisville KY	2
Clarion Hotel and Conf Center	502-491-4830	9700 Bluegrass Parkway - Exit 15/Hurstbourne Lane S Louisville KY	3+
Days Inn Louisville Airport	502-425-8010	9340 Blairwood Rd - Exit 15c Louisville KY	2
Drury Inn & Suites	502-326-4170	9501 Blairwood Road Louisville KY	1+
Holiday Inn	502-426-2600	1325 S. Hurstbourne Pkwy - Exit 15C Louisville KY	3+
Staybridge Suites	502-244-9511	11711 Gateworth Way - Exit 17 Louisville KY	1
Shelbyville			
Best Western Shelbyville Lodge	502-633-4400	115 Isaac Shelby Dr - Exit 32 Shelbyville KY	3+
Holiday Inn Hotel & Suites	502-647-0109	110 Club House Drive - Exit 35 Shelbyville KY	3+
Frankfort			
Americas Best Value Inn	502-875-3200	1225 U.S. Highway 127 S. Frankfort KY	3+
Lexington			
Days Inn Lexington	859-299-1202	1987 North Broadway Lexington KY	2

Days Inn Lexington South	859-263-3100	5575 Athens-Boonesboro Rd Lexington KY	2
Four Points by Sheraton Lexington	859-259-1311	1538 Stanton Way Lexington KY	1+
Hampton Inn	859-299-2613	2251 Elkhorn Road Lexington KY	3+
Holiday Inn	859-263-5241	5532 Athens-Boonesboro Rd Lexington KY	2
Holiday Inn Express Hotel & Suites Lexington-Downtown/University	859-389-6800	1000 Export Street Lexington KY	2
Motel 6 - Lexington East	859-293-1431	2260 Elkhorn Road Lexington KY	1+
Red Roof Inn - Lexington	859-293-2626	1980 Haggard Court Lexington KY	1+
Red Roof Inn - Lexington South	859-277-9400	2651 Wilhite Drive Lexington KY	1+
Red Roof Inn - Lexington Southeast	859-543-1877	100 Canebrake Drive Lexington KY	1+
Residence Inn by Marriott	859-231-6191	1080 Newtown Pike Lexington KY	3+
Residence Inn by Marriott	859-263-9979	2688 Pink Pigeon Parkway Lexington KY	3+
Sleep Inn	859-543-8400	1920 Plaudit Place - Exit 108 Lexington KY	3+
Super 8 Lexington/Dwtn	859-231-6300	925 Newtown Pike - Exit 115 Lexington KY	2
Super 8 Lexington/Winchester Road	859-299-6241	2351 Buena Vista Rd Lexington KY	2
Rose Hill Inn Bed & Breakfast	859-873-5957	233 Rose Hill Versailles KY	1+

Winchester

Best Western Country Squire	859-744-7210	1307 West Lexington Ave Winchester KY	3+
Quality Inn and Suites	859-737-3990	960 Interstate Drive - Exit 96A Winchester KY	2

Mount Sterling

Days Inn Mt Sterling	859-498-4680	705 Maysville Rd - Exit 110 Mount Sterling KY	2

Morehead - Cave Run Lake

Comfort Inn and Suites	606-780-7378	2650 H 801N - Exit 133/H 801 Morehead KY	3+
Holiday Inn Express	606-784-5796	110 Toms Drive - Exit 137 Morehead KY	3+

Ashland

Best Western River Cities	606-326-0357	31 Russell Plaza Dr Ashland KY	2
Days Inn Ashland	606-928-3600	12700 SR 180 - Exit 185 Ashland KY	2
Holiday Inn Express Hotel & Suites Ashland	606-929-1720	13131 Slone Court - Exit 185 Ashland KY	3+

West Virginia Listings (Interstate 64)   Dogs per Room

Huntington

Comfort Inn	304-733-2122	249 Mall Road - Exit Mall Road Barboursville WV	3+
Econo Lodge	304-529-1331	3325 US 60 E. Huntington WV	1+
Red Roof Inn - Huntington, WV	304-733-3737	5190 US Route 60 E Huntington WV	1+
Stone Lodge	304-736-3451	5600 U.S. Route 60 East Huntington WV	1+

Charleston

Charleston Marriott Town Center	304-345-6500	200 Lee Street E - Exit Washington St/Civic Center Charleston WV	3+
Comfort Suites	304-925-1171	107 Alex Lane Charleston WV	2
Country Inns & Suites by Carlson	304-925-4300	105 Alex Lane Charleston WV	1+
Motel 6 - Charleston East	304-925-0471	6311 MacCorkle Ave SE Charleston WV	1+
Residence Inn by Marriott	304-345-4200	200 Hotel Circle Northgate Business Park Charleston WV	3+
Comfort Inn West	800-798-7886	102 Racer Drive - Exit 47 Cross Lanes WV	2
Motel 6 - Charleston West -Cross Lanes	304-776-5911	330 Goff Mountain Rd Cross Lanes WV	1+
Red Roof Inn - Charleston West - Hurricane, WV	304-757-6392	500 Putnam Village Drive Hurricane WV	1+
Super 8 Hurricane	304-562-3346	419 Hurricane Creek Rd - Exit 34 Hurricane WV	2
Red Roof Inn - Charleston - Kanawha City, WV	304-925-6953	6305 MacCorkle Avenue SE Kanawha City WV	1+

Beckley

Best Western Four Seasons Inn	304-252-0671	1939 Harper Road Beckley WV	3+
Comfort Inn	304-255-2161	1909 Harper Road - Exit 44 E Beckley WV	3+
Super 8 Beckley	304-253-0802	2014 Harper Rd Beckley WV	2
Quality Inn New River Gorge	304-574-3443	103 Elliotts Way - Exit H 19 N Fayetteville WV	3+

Virginia Listings (Interstate 64)   Dogs per Room

Ashland

Days Inn Ashland	804-798-4262	806 England St Ashland VA	2
Quality Inn and Suites	804-798-4231	810 England Street Ashland VA	2
Days Inn Carmel Church	804-448-2011	24320 Rogers Clark Blvd Carmel Church VA	2
Best Western Kings Quarters	804-876-3321	16102 Theme Park Way Doswell VA	3+
Howard Johnson Express Inn	804-448-2499	23786 Rogers Clark Blvd. Ruther Glen VA	1+
Red Roof Inn - Ruther Glen - Carmel Church	804-448-2828	23500 Welcome Way Drive Ruther Glen VA	1+

Covington

Best Value Inn	540-962-7600	908 Valley Ridge Drive Covington VA	1+
Best Western Mountain View	540-962-4951	820 E Madison Street - Exit 16 Covington VA	3+

Lexington

1780 Stone House, rental #1350	540-463-2521	218 S Main Street/H 11 Lexington VA	2
Applewood Inn	540-463-1962	242 Tarn Beck Lane Lexington VA	1
Best Western Inn at Hunt Ridge	540-464-1500	25 Willow Springs Rd Lexington VA	3+
Best Western Lexington Inn	540-458-3020	850 N Lee Highway Lexington VA	3+
Days Inn Lexington	540-463-2143	325 West Midland Trail Lexington VA	2
Howard Johnson Inn	540-463-9181	2836 N. Lee Hwy. Lexington VA	1+
Super 8 Lexington	540-463-7858	1139 North Lee Hwy - Exit 55 Lexington VA	2
Fox Hill Bed & Breakfast & Cottage	540-377-9922	4383 Borden Grant Trail Lexington/Fairfield VA	1+

Staunton

Best Western Staunton Inn	540-885-1112	92 Rowe Rd Staunton VA	3+
Comfort Inn	540-886-5000	1302 Richmond Avenue Staunton VA	2
Days Inn Staunton	540-248-0888	273 D Bells Lane Staunton VA	2
Days Inn Staunton/Blue Ridge	540-337-3031	372 White Hill Rd Staunton VA	2
Holiday Inn	540-248-6020	152 Fairway Lane Staunton VA	2
Quality Inn	540-248-5111	96 Baker Lane Staunton VA	3+
Sleep Inn	540-887-6500	222 Jefferson H Staunton VA	2
Super 8 Staunton	540-886-2888	1015 Richmond Rd Staunton VA	2
Twelfth Night Inn	540-885-1733	402 E Beverly Staunton VA	2

Charlottesville

Comfort Inn	434-293-6188	1807 Emmet Street - Exit 118B Charlottesville VA	3+
Days Inn Charlottesville/University	434-293-9111	1600 Emmet St Charlottesville VA	2
Holiday Inn	434-977-5100	1200 5th Street - Exit 120 Charlottesville VA	3+
Quality Inn	434-971-3746	1600 Emmet Street Charlottesville VA	3+
Red Roof Inn - Charlottesville	434-295-4333	1309 West Main Street Charlottesville VA	1+
Residence Inn by Marriott	434-923-0300	1111 Millmont Street - Exit 118B Charlottesville VA	1+
Sleep Inn and Suites Monticello	434-244-9969	1185 5th Street SW - Exit 120 Charlottesville VA	3+
Montfair Resort Farm	434-823-5202	2500 Bezaleel Drive Crozet VA	1+

Louisa

Ginger Hill	540-967-3260	47 Holly Springs Drive - Exit 143 Louisa VA	3+

Richmond

Candlewood Suites	804-364-2000	4120 Brookriver Drive - Exit 178A Glen Allen VA	3+
TownePlace Suites Richmond	804-747-5253	4231 Park Place Court - Exit 178b Glen Allen VA	2
Quality Inn West End	804-346-0000	8008 W Broad Street - Exit 183C Richmond VA	1
Residence Inn by Marriott	804-762-9852	3940 Westerre Parkway - Exit 180B Richmond VA	3+
Days Inn Richmond Airport	804-222-2041	5500 Williamsburg Rd - Exit 197a Sandston VA	2

Williamsburg

Quarterpath Inn	757-220-0960	620 York Street - Exit 242-A East Williamsburg VA	2
Days Inn Williamsburg/Colonial	757-229-5060	902 Richmond Rd - Exit 238 Williamsburg VA	2
Four Points by Sheraton Williamsburg Historic District	757-229-4100	351 York St. Williamsburg VA	1+
Motel 6 - Williamsburg	757-565-3433	3030 Richmond Road Williamsburg VA	1+
Red Roof Inn - Williamsburg	757-259-1948	824 Capitol Landing Rd Williamsburg VA	1+
Residence Inn by Marriott	757-941-2000	1648 Richmond Road Williamsburg VA	3+
Woodlands Cascades Motel	757-229-1000	105 Visitor Center Drive Williamsburg VA	2
Candlewood Suites	757-952-1120	329 Commonwealth Drive - Exit 256B Yorktown VA	3+
Marl Inn	757-898-3859	220 Church Street - Exit 250B (Ft. Eustis/Yorktown) Yorktown VA	1+
TownePlace Suites Newport News/Yorktown	757-874-8884	200 Cybernetics Way - Exit 256b Yorktown VA	2

Virginia Beach Area

TownePlace Suites Chesapeake	757-523-5004	2000 Old Greenbrier Road - Exit 289a Chesapeake VA	2
Days Inn Norfolk Marina/Beachfront	757-583-4521	1631 Bayville St - Exit 272 Norfolk VA	2
Quality Suites Lake Wright	757-461-6251	6280 Northampton Blvd - Exit 282/Northampton Blvd Norfolk VA	3+
Residence Inn by Marriott	757-333-3000	1590 N Military Highway - Exit 282 Norfolk VA	3+
Sleep Inn Lake Wright	757-461-1133	6280 Northampton Blvd - Exit 282/Northampton Blvd Norfolk VA	3+
Days Inn Virginia Beach Oceanfront	757-428-7233	3107 Atlantic Ave - Exit Hwy 60 Virginia Beach VA	2
TownePlace Suites Virginia Beach	757-490-9367	5757 Cleveland St - Exit 284B Virginia Beach VA	2

Interstate 70 Accommodation Listings

Indiana Listings   (Interstate 70)   Dogs per Room

Terre Haute

Drury Inn	812-238-1206	3040 South US Hwy 41 Terre Haute IN	1+
Pear Tree Inn	812-234-4268	3050 South US Hwy 41 Terre Haute IN	1+

Plainfield

Days Inn Indianapolis Plainfield	317-839-5000	2245 Hadley Rd - Exit SR 267 Plainfield IN	2

Indianapolis

Quality Inn and Suites	317-462-7112	2270 N State Street - Exit 104 Greenfield IN	2
Candlewood Suites Indianapolis Airport	317-241-9595	5250 W. Bradbury Street - Exit 75/ Airport Expressway Indianapolis IN	3+

Candlewood Suites Indianapolis City Centre	317-536-7700	1152 N White River Pkwy, West Drive - Exit 39A/West Street Indianapolis IN	2
Days Inn Indianapolis	317-899-2100	2150 N Post Road - Exit 91 Indianapolis IN	2
Days Inn Indianapolis East	317-359-5500	7314 E 21st Street - Shadeland Exit Indianapolis IN	2
Holiday Inn	317-359-5341	6990 E. 21st St - Exit 89 Indianapolis IN	2
La Quinta Inn Indianapolis East	317-359-1021	7304 East 21st Street - Exit 89/Shadeland Avenue Indianapolis IN	3+
La Quinta Inn Indianapolis East - Post Drive	317-897-2300	2349 Post Drive - Exit 91 Indianapolis IN	3+
Super 8 Indianapolis/East	317-895-5402	8850 E 21st Street - Exit 91 Indianapolis IN	2
New Castle			
Budget Inn	765-987-8205	5243 South SR 3 - Exit 123 New Castle IN	2
Richmond			
Days Inn Richmond	765-966-4900	5775 National Rd East - Exit 156a Richmond IN	2
Super 8 Richmond	765-962-7576	2525 Chester Blvd - Exit 151 Richmond IN	2

Ohio Listings (Interstate 70)   Dogs per Room

Dayton			
Dayton Marriott	937-223-1000	1414 S Patterson Blvd - Exit I 75 S Dayton OH	2
Howard Johnson Express Inn	937-454-0550	7575 Poe Avenue Dayton OH	1+
Super 8 Englewood	937-832-3350	15 Rockridge Rd - Exit 29 Englewood OH	2
Springfield			
Holiday Inn - Springfield South	937-323-8631	383 East Leffel Lane - Exit 54 Springfield OH	3+
Columbus			
Doubletree	614-228-4600	50 S Front Street - Exit 100 A Columbus OH	2
Knight's Inn	614-275-0388	1559 W Broad St - Exit 97 Columbus OH	2
Residence Inn by Marriott	614-864-8844	2084 S Hamilton Road - Exit Hamilton Road S Columbus OH	3+
Buckeye Lake			
Super 8 Buckeye Lake	740-929-1015	I-70 and SR 79 - Exit 129a Buckeye Lake OH	2
Hebron			
Red Roof Inn - Columbus - Hebron	740-467-7663	10668 Lancaster Road Southwest Hebron OH	1+
Zanesville			
Best Western B. R. Guest	740-453-6300	4929 East Pike - Exit 160 Zanesville OH	3+
Econo Lodge	740-452-4511	135 N 7th St - Exit 155 Zanesville OH	2
Holiday Inn	740-453-0771	4645 East Pike - Exit 160 Zanesville OH	2
Red Roof Inn - Zanesville	740-453-6300	4929 East Pike Zanesville OH	1+
Super 8 Zanesville	740-455-3124	2440 National Rd - Exit 152 Zanesville OH	2
Cambridge			
Best Western Cambridge	740-439-3581	1945 Southgate Parkway - Exit 178 Cambridge OH	3+
Comfort Inn	740-435-3200	2327 Southgate Parkway - Exit 178 Cambridge OH	3+
Days Inn Cambridge	740-432-5691	2328 Southgate Pkwy - Exit 178 Cambridge OH	2
St Clairsville			
Red Roof Inn - St Clairsville	740-695-4057	68301 Red Roof Lane St Clairsville OH	1+
Super 8 St Clairsville OH/Wheeling WV Area	740-695-1994	68400 Matthews Dr - Exit 218 St Clairsville OH	2

Pennsylvania Listings (Interstate 70)   Dogs per Room

Washington			
Motel 6 - Washington, PA	724-223-8040	1283 Motel 6 Drive Washington PA	1+
Red Roof Inn - Washington	724-228-5750	1399 West Chestnut Street Washington PA	1+
New Stanton			
Howard Johnson Inn	724-925-3511	112 W. Byers Ave. New Stanton PA	1+
Quality Inn	724-925-6755	110 N Main - Exit New Stanton New Stanton PA	3+
Somerset			
Best Western Executive Inn of Somerset	814-445-3996	165 Waterworks Rd Somerset PA	3+
Days Inn Somerset	814-445-9200	220 Waterworks Rd - Exit 110 Somerset PA	2
Holiday Inn	814-445-9611	202 Harmon St - Exit 110 Somerset PA	2
Quality Inn	814-443-4646	215 Ramada Road - Exit 110 Somerset PA	2
Super 8 Somerset	814-445-8788	125 Lewis Dr - Exit 110 Somerset PA	2
Warfordsburg			
Days Inn Breezewood	814-735-3860	9648 Old 126 - Exit 156 Warfordsburg PA	2

Maryland Listings (Interstate 70)   Dogs per Room

Hancock			
Super 8 Hancock	301-678-6101	118 Limestone Rd - Exit 1b Hancock MD	2
Hagerstown			

Econo Lodge	301-791-3560	18221 Mason Dixon Rd Hagerstown MD	1+
Motel 6 - Hagerstown	301-582-4445	11321 Massey Boulevard Hagerstown MD	1+
Quality Inn	301-733-2700	1101 Dual H - Exit 32B Hagerstown MD	2
Sleep Inn and Suites	301-766-9449	18216 Colonel H K Douglas Drive - Exit 29 or 29A Hagerstown MD	3+
Super 8 Halfway/Hagerstown Area	301-582-1992	16805 Blake Rd Hagerstown MD	2
Red Roof Inn - Hagerstown - Williamsport	301-582-3500	310 East Potomac Street Williamsport MD	1+

Frederick

Comfort Inn	301-668-7272	7300 Executive Way Frederick MD	3+
Holiday Inn - Frederick	301-662-5141	999 W Patrick St Frederick MD	3+
Holiday Inn - Holidome	301-694-7500	5400 Holiday Dr Frederick MD	2
Holiday Inn Express	301-695-2881	5579 Spectrum Dr Frederick MD	3+
Mainstay Suites	301-668-4600	7310 Executive Way Frederick MD	3+
Residence Inn by Marriott	301-360-0010	5230 Westview Drive Frederick MD	3+
Travelodge	301-663-0500	200 E Walser Drive Frederick MD	3+

Interstate 75 Accommodation Listings

Michigan Listings (Interstate 75)   Dogs per Room

Sault Ste Marie

Best Value Inn	906-635-9190	3411 I-75 Business Spur - Exit I 75 BS Sault Ste Marie MI	2
Holiday Inn Express	906-632-3999	1171 Riverview Way - Exit 394 Sault Ste Marie MI	2
Best Western Sault Ste. Marie	906-632-2170	4281 I-75 Business Spur - Exit 392 Sault Ste. Marie MI	2
Comfort Inn	906-635-1118	4404 I 75 Business Spur - Exit 392 Sault Ste. Marie MI	3+
Quality Inn and Suites Conference Center	906-635-6918	3290 I 75 Business Spur - Exit 392 Sault Ste. Marie MI	2
Super 8 Sault Sainte Marie	903-632-8882	3826 I-75 Business Spur - Exit 392 Sault Ste. Marie MI	2

Mackinaw City

Holiday Inn Express Mackinaw City	231-436-7100	364 Louvingney - Exit 339 Mackinaw City MI	3+
Ramada Inn	231-436-5535	450 S Nicolet - Exit 329 Mackinaw City MI	3+
Quality Inn	906-643-9700	913 Boulevard Drive - Exit 344B Saint Ignace MI	3+
Hotel Dupont	906-643-9700	913 Boulevard Dr St Ignace MI	1+

Gaylord

Best Western Alpine Lodge	989-732-2431	833 West Main St - Exit 282 Gaylord MI	2
Quality Inn	989-732-7541	137 West Street - Exit 282 Gaylord MI	3+
Red Roof Inn - Gaylord	989-731-6331	510 S Wisconsin Ave Gaylord MI	1+

Grayling

Super 8 Grayling	989-348-8888	5828 NA Miles Parkway - Exit 251 Grayling MI	2
Holiday Inn Express	989-422-7829	200 Cloverleaf Lane - Exit 227 Houghton Lake MI	3+
Super 8 Houghton Lake	989-422-3119	9580 W Lake City Rd Houghton Lake MI	2
East Bay Lakefront Lodge	989-366-5910	125 Twelfth Street Prudenville MI	2
Super 8 West Branch	989-345-8488	2596 Austin Way - Exit 212 West Branch MI	2

Saginaw

Drury Inn & Suites	989-652-2800	260 South Main Frankenmuth MI	1+
Best Western Saginaw	989-755-0461	1408 S Outer Drive - Exit 149B Saginaw MI	3+

Flint

Best Western of Birch Run/Frankenmuth	989-624-9395	9087 Birch Run Rd - Exit 136 Birch Run MI	2
Days Inn Flint	810-239-4681	2207 W Bristol Rd - Bristol Rd Exit Flint MI	2
Holiday Inn Express	810-238-7744	1150 Longway Blvd Flint MI	2
Howard Johnson Express Inn	810-733-5910	G-3277 Miller Road Flint MI	1+

Detroit

Candlewood Suites	248-373-3342	1650 Opdyke Rd - Exit 79/University Auburn Hills MI	2
Staybridge Suites	248-322-4600	2050 Featherstone Rd - Exit 79/University Auburn Hills MI	2
Holiday Inn Express Detroit-Birmingham	248-642-6200	35270 Woodward Ave. - Exit 69 Birmingham MI	2
Best Western Palace Inn	248-391-2755	2755 S Lapeer Road - Exit 81 Lake Orion MI	3+
Residence Inn by Marriott	248-583-4322	32650 Stephenson Highway - Exit 14 Mile Road W Madison Heights MI	3+
Residence Inn by Marriott	248-858-8664	3333 Centerpoint Parkway - Exit 75/Square Lake Road Pontiac MI	3+
Clarion Hotel Detroit Metro Airport	734-728-7900	8600 Merriman Road - Exit I 275 to I 94E Romulus MI	2
La Quinta Inn Detroit/Southgate	734-374-3000	12888 Reeck Road - Exit 37 Southgate MI	3+
Candlewood Suites	248-269-6600	2550 Troy Center Drive - Exit W Big Beaver Troy MI	2
Drury Inn	248-528-3330	575 W. Big Beaver Road Troy MI	1+
Holiday Inn	248-689-7500	2537 Rochester Court - Exit 67/Rodchester Road Troy MI	2
Quality Inn and Suites	586-264-0100	32035 Van Dyke - Exit I 696E Warren MI	2

Ohio Listings (Interstate 75)   Dogs per Room

Highway Guides - Please always call ahead to make sure that an establishment is still dog-friendly

Toledo

Red Roof Inn - Toledo - Holland	419-866-5512	1214 Corporate Drive Holland OH	1+
Residence Inn by Marriott	419-867-9555	6101 Trust Drive Holland OH	3+
Comfort Inn West	419-893-2800	1426 S Reynolds Road - Exit I 475/H23 Maumee OH	3+
Days Inn Toledo/Maumee	419-897-6900	1704 Tollgate Dr Maumee OH	2
Red Roof Inn - Toledo - Maumee	419-893-0292	1570 Reynolds Road Maumee OH	1+
Days Inn Toledo/Perrysburg	419-874-8771	10667 Fremont Pike - Exit 193/80/90 Perrysburg OH	2
Howard Johnson Inn	419-837-5245	I-280 & Hanley Road Perrysburg OH	1+
La Quinta Inn Toledo/Perrysburg	419-872-0000	1154 Professional Drive - Exit 193 Perrysburg OH	3+
Motel 6 - Toledo	419-865-2308	5335 Heatherdowns Boulevard Toledo OH	1+
Radisson Hotel	419-241-3000	101 North Summit Street Toledo OH	1+
Red Roof Inn - Toledo - University	419-536-0118	3530 Executive Parkway Toledo OH	1+
Super 8 Toledo/Perrysburg Area	419-837-6409	3491 Latcha Rd Toledo OH	2

Bowling Green

Days Inn Bowling Green	419-352-5211	1550 E Wooster - Exit 181 Bowling Green OH	2
Quality Inn and Suites	419-352-2521	1630 E Wooster Street - Exit 181/BGSU Bowling Green OH	3+

Findlay

Quality Inn	419-423-4303	1020 Interstate Court - Exit 159 Findlay OH	3+
Red Roof Inn - Findlay, OH	419-424-0466	1951 Broad Avenue Findlay OH	1+
Super 8 Findlay	419-422-8863	1600 Fox St - Exit 159 Findlay OH	2
TownePlace Suites Findlay	419-425-9545	2501 Tiffin Avenue - Exit 161 Findlay OH	2

Lima

Days Inn Lima	419-227-6515	1250 Neubrecht Rd - Exit 127b or 127 Lima OH	2
Holiday Inn	419-222-0004	1920 Roschman Ave - Exit 125A/H309 Lima OH	2
Motel 6 - Lima	419-228-0456	1800 Harding Hwy Lima OH	1+

Wapakoneta

Days Inn Lima Area	419-738-2184	1659 Bellefontaine St - Exit 111 Wapakoneta OH	2
Super 8 Wapakoneta	419-738-8810	1011 Lunar Dr - Exit 111 Wapakoneta OH	2

Sidney

Comfort Inn	937-492-3001	1959 W Michigan Avenue - Exit 92/H 47 Sidney OH	2
Days Inn Sidney	937-492-1104	420 Folkerth Ave - Exit 92 Sidney OH	2
Holiday Inn Sidney	937-492-1131	400 Folkerth Avenue - Exit 92 Sidney OH	2

Piqua

Comfort Inn	937-778-8100	987 E Ash Street - Exit 82/H 36W Piqua OH	3+
La Quinta Inn Piqua	937-615-0140	950 East Ash Street - Exit 82 Piqua OH	3+

Troy

Econo Lodge	937-335-0013	1210 Brukner Drive Troy OH	1+
Holiday Inn Express Hotel and Suites	937-332-1700	60 Troy Town Drive - Exit 74 Troy OH	3+
Knights Inn	937-339-1515	30 Troy Town Drive Troy OH	1+
Residence Inn by Marriott	937-440-9303	87 Troy Town Drive Troy OH	3+

Vandalia

Super 8 Vandalia/Dayton Intl Airport	937-898-7636	550 E National Rd - Exit 63 Vandalia OH	2

Dayton

Residence Inn by Marriott	937-427-3914	2779 Fairfield Commons Beavercreek OH	3+
Dayton Marriott	937-223-1000	1414 S Patterson Blvd - Exit 51/Edwin Moses Blvd Dayton OH	2
Holiday Inn Hotel and Suites	937-294-1471	2455 Dryden Road - Exit 50A Dayton OH	3+
Howard Johnson Express Inn	937-454-0550	7575 Poe Avenue Dayton OH	1+
Motel 6 - Dayton North	937-898-3606	7130 Miller Ln Dayton OH	1+
Red Roof Inn - Dayton - Englewood	937-836-8339	9325 North Main Street Dayton OH	1+
Red Roof Inn - Dayton North	937-898-1054	7370 Miller Lane Dayton OH	1+
Motel 6 - Dayton Airport - Englewood	937-832-3770	1212 S Main St Englewood OH	1+
Super 8 Englewood	937-832-3350	15 Rockridge Rd Englewood OH	2
Holiday Inn Dayton/Fairborn 1-675	937-426-7800	2800 Presidential Dr Fairborn OH	2
Homewood Suites-Fairborn	937-429-0600	2750 Presidential Drive Fairborn OH	1+
Red Roof Inn - Dayton East - Fairborn	937-426-6116	2580 Colonel Glenn Highway Fairborn OH	1+
Doubletree	937-436-2400	300 Prestige Place - Exit 44 Miamisburg OH	3+
Holiday Inn	937-434-8030	31 Prestige Plaza Dr Miamisburg OH	3+
Red Roof Inn - Dayton South - Miamisburg	937-866-0705	222 Byers Road Miamisburg OH	1+
Studio 6 - Dayton - Miamisburg	937-434-8750	8101 Springboro Pike Miamisburg OH	1+
Super 8 Moraine/Dayton Area	937-298-0380	2450 Dryden Rd - Exit 50a Moraine OH	2

Franklin

Best Western Regency Inn	513-424-3551	6475 Culbertson Road - Exit 32 Franklin OH	2
Quality Inn	937-743-8881	2000 William C Goode Blvd - Exit 36 Franklin OH	3+

Middletown

Manchester Inn	513-422-5481	1027 Manchester Avenue - Exit 32 Middletown OH	3+

Cincinnati

La Quinta Inn & Suites Sharonville	513-771-0300	11029 Dowlin Drive - Exit Sharonville Cincinnati OH	3+

| Residence Inn by Marriott | 513-771-2525 | 11689 Chester Road - Exit 15/Sharon Road Cincinnati OH | 3+ |

Kentucky Listings (Interstate 75)   Dogs per Room

Fort Mitchell
| Super 8 Fort Mitchell KY/Cincinnati | 859-341-2090 | 2350 Royal Drive - Exit 186 Fort Mitchell KY | 2 |

Florence
Best Western Inn Florence	859-525-0090	7821 Commerce Dr - Exit 181 Florence KY	1+
La Quinta Inn & Suites Cincinnati Airport/Florence	859-282-8212	350 Meijer Drive - Exit 182/Turf Way Road Florence KY	3+
Motel 6 - Cincinnati South - Florence	859-283-0909	7937 Dream Street Florence KY	1+
Quality Inn and Suites	859-371-4700	7915 H 42 - Exit 180/Florence Union Florence KY	2
Red Roof Inn - Cincinnati Airport - Florence, KY	859-647-2700	7454 Turfway Rd Florence KY	1+
Super 8 Florence KY/Cincinnati OH Area	859-283-1228	7928 Dream St Florence KY	2

Walton
| Ivy Lodge | 859-485-2200 | 11177 Frontage Rd - Exit 175 Walton KY | 2 |

Dry Ridge
| Holiday Inn Express | 859-824-7121 | 1050 Fashion Ridge Rd - Exit 159 Dry Ridge KY | 2 |

Georgetown
Days Inn Georgetown North	502-863-5000	385 Cherry Blossom Way - Exit 129 Georgetown KY	2
Hotel Ivy	502-867-1648	250 Outlet Center Drive - Exit 126 Georgetown KY	2
Motel 6 - Lexington North - Georgetown	502-863-1166	401 Cherry Blossom Way Georgetown KY	1+

Lexington
Days Inn Lexington	859-299-1202	1987 North Broadway - Exit 113 Lexington KY	2
Days Inn Lexington South	859-263-3100	5575 Athens-Boonesboro Rd - Exit 104 Lexington KY	2
Hampton Inn	859-299-2613	2251 Elkhorn Road - Exit 110/H 60 Lexington KY	3+
Holiday Inn	859-263-5241	5532 Athens-Boonesboro Rd - Exit 104 Lexington KY	2
Holiday Inn Express Hotel & Suites Lexington-Downtown/University	859-389-6800	1000 Export Street - Exit 113 Lexington KY	2
Residence Inn by Marriott	859-231-6191	1080 Newtown Pike - Exit 115/Newtown Pike S Lexington KY	3+
Residence Inn by Marriott	859-263-9979	2688 Pink Pigeon Parkway - Exit 108 Lexington KY	3+
Super 8 Lexington/Dwtn	859-231-6300	925 Newtown Pike - Exit 115 Lexington KY	2
Super 8 Lexington/Winchester Road	859-299-6241	2351 Buena Vista Rd - Exit 110 Lexington KY	2

Richmond
Comfort Suites	859-624-0770	2007 Colby Taylor Drive - Exit 87 Richmond KY	3+
Holiday Inn Express Hotel & Suites	859-624-4055	1990 Colby Taylor Drive - Exit 87 Richmond KY	3+
La Quinta Inn Richmond	859-623-9121	1751 Lexington Rd. - Exit 90A Richmond KY	3+
Red Roof Inn - Lexington - Richmond	859-625-0084	111 Bahama Ct Richmond KY	1+

Berea
Boone Tavern Hotel	606-986-9358	100 Main Street Berea KY	1+
Days Inn Berea	859-986-7373	1029 Cooper Dr - Exit 77 Berea KY	2
Super 8 Berea	859-986-8426	196 Prince Royal Dr - Exit 76 Berea KY	2

London
Budget Host Westgate Inn	606-878-7330	254 W Daniel Boone Parkway London KY	1+
Days Inn London	606-864-7331	2035 W 192 Bypass - Exit 38 London KY	2
Holiday Inn Express Hotel & Suites	606-862-0077	506 Minton Drive - Exit 38 London KY	3+
Red Roof Inn - London I-75	606-862-8844	110 Melcon Lane London KY	1+
Super 8 London	606-878-9800	285 W Highway 80 - Exit 41 London KY	2

Corbin
| Best Western Corbin Inn | 606-528-2100 | 2630 Cumberland Falls Rd - Exit 25 Corbin KY | 3+ |
| Days Inn Corbin | 606-528-8150 | 1860 Cumberland Falls Rd - Exit 25 Corbin KY | 2 |

Williamsburg
| Super 8 Williamsburg | 606-549-3450 | 30 W Hwy 92 - Exit 11 Williamsburg KY | 2 |

Tennessee Listings (Interstate 75)   Dogs per Room

Jellico
| Holiday Plaza | 423-784-7241 | I-75 Exit 160 - Exit 160 Jellico TN | 2 |

Caryville
| Super 8 Caryville/Cove Lake | 423-562-8476 | 200 John Mcghee Blvd - Exit 134 Caryville TN | 2 |

Lake City
| Days Inn Knoxville/Lake City | 865-426-2816 | 221 Colonial Lane - Exit 129 Lake City TN | 2 |

Knoxville
| Best Western Knoxville Suites | 865-687-9922 | 5317 Pratt Road - Exit 108 Knoxville TN | 3+ |
| Days Inn Knoxville West | 865-966-5801 | 326 Lovell Rd - Exit 374 Knoxville TN | 2 |

Highway Guides - Please always call ahead to make sure that an establishment is still dog-friendly

Holiday Inn	865-584-3911	1315 Kirby Road - Exit 383 Knoxville TN	3+
La Quinta Inn Knoxville West	865-690-9777	258 North Peters Road Knoxville TN	3+
Quality Inn	865-689-6600	6712 Central Avenue Pike - Exit 110 Knoxville TN	2
Residence Inn by Marriott	865-539-5339	Langley Place at North Peters Road - Exit 378A L Knoxville TN	3+
Super 8 Knoxville/Downtown/West	865-584-8511	6200 Papermill Rd - Exit 383 Knoxville TN	1+
TownePlace Suites Knoxville Cedar Bluff	865-693-5216	205 Langley Place - Exit 378a Knoxville TN	2
Lenoir City			
Days Inn Knoxville/Lenoir City	865-986-2011	1110 Hwy 321 North - Exit 81 Lenoir City TN	2
Loudon			
Super 8 Loudon	865-458-5669	12452 Hwy 72 North - Exit 72 Loudon TN	2
Sweetwater			
Best Western Sweetwater	423-337-3541	1421 Murray's Chapel Rd - Exit 60 Sweetwater TN	3+
Comfort Inn	423-337-6646	731 S Main Street - Exit 60 Sweetwater TN	2
Days Inn Sweetwater	423-337-4200	229 Hwy 68 - Exit 60 Sweetwater TN	2
Quality Inn and Suites	423-337-4900	1116 H 68 - Exit 60 Sweetwater TN	3+
Athens			
Days Inn Athens	423-745-5800	2541 Decatur Pike - Exit 49 Athens TN	2
Motel 6 - Athens	423-745-4441	2002 Whitaker Road Athens TN	1+
Cleveland			
Days Inn Cleveland	423-476-2112	2550 Georgetown Rd - Exit 25 Cleveland TN	2
Quality Inn & Suites	423-478-5265	153 James Asbury Drive - Exit 27 Cleveland TN	2
Chattanooga			
Best Western Royal Inn	423-821-6840	3644 Cummings Highway Chattanooga TN	2
Comfort Inn Hixson	423-877-8388	4833 Hixson Pike Chattanooga TN	2
Days Inn Chattanooga Downtown	423-267-9761	101 E 20th St Chattanooga TN	2
Holiday Inn Chattanooga-Choo Choo	423-266-5000	1400 Market St Chattanooga TN	3+
Howard Johnson Plaza Hotel	423-892-8100	6700 Ringgold Rd. Chattanooga TN	1+
La Quinta Inn Chattanooga	423-855-0011	7017 Shallowford Rd. - Exit 5 Chattanooga TN	3+
MainStay Suites	423-485-9424	7030 Amin Drive - Exit 5 Chattanooga TN	1
Motel 6 - Chattanooga Downtown	423-265-7300	2440 Williams Street Chattanooga TN	1+
Motel 6 - Chattanooga East	423-892-7700	7707 Lee Highway Chattanooga TN	1+
Quality Inn & Suites	423-821-1499	3109 Parker Lane Chattanooga TN	3+
Red Roof Inn - Chattanooga Airport	423-899-0143	7014 Shallowford Road Chattanooga TN	1+
Residence Inn by Marriott	423-266-0600	215 Chestnut Street Chattanooga TN	3+
Sheraton Read House Hotel at Chattanooga	423-266-4121	827 Broad St. Chattanooga TN	1+
Staybridge Suites	423-267-0900	1300 Carter Street Chattanooga TN	3+
Super 8 Chattanooga/Lookout Mtn Area	423-821-8880	20 Birmingham Rd Chattanooga TN	2

Georgia Listings (Interstate 75)   Dogs per Room

Dalton			
Motel 6 - Dalton	706-278-5522	2200 Chattanooga Road Dalton GA	1+
Calhoun			
Days Inn Calhoun	706-629-8877	1220 Redbud Rd - Exit 315 Calhoun GA	2
Quality Inn	706-629-9501	915 H 53E - Exit 312/H 53E Calhoun GA	2
Super 8 Calhoun/Dalton Area	706-602-1400	1446 US Hwy 41 North - Exit Exi t318 Calhoun GA	2
Adairsville			
Comfort Inn	770-773-2886	107 Princeton Blvd - Exit 306 Adairsville GA	3+
Cartersville			
Days Inn Cartersville	770-382-1824	5618 Hwy 20 SE - Exit 290 Cartersville GA	2
Holiday Inn	770-386-0830	I-75 and US 411, Exit 293 - Exit 293 Cartersville GA	2
Howard Johnson Express Inn	770-386-0700	25 Carson Loop NW Cartersville GA	1+
Motel 6 - Cartersville	770-386-1449	5657 Highway 20 Cartersville GA	1+
Quality Inn	770-386-0510	235 S Dixie Avenue - Exit 288 Cartersville GA	1
Super 8 Cartersville	770-382-8881	41 SR 20 Spur SE - Exit 290 Cartersville GA	2
Atlanta Area			
Super 8 Forest Park/Stadium/Atlanta Area	404-363-8811	410 Old Dixie Way - Exit 235 Forest Park GA	2
Best Western Kennesaw Inn	770-424-7666	3375 Busbee Dr - Exit 271 Kennesaw GA	3+
La Quinta Inn Kennesaw	770-426-0045	2625 George Busbee Parkway NW - Exit 269 Kennesaw GA	3+
Residence Inn by Marriott	770-218-1018	3443 Busbee Drive NW - Exit Chastain Road Kennesaw GA	3+
TownePlace Suites Kennesaw	770-794-8282	1074 Cobb Place Blvd NW - Exit 269 Kennesaw GA	2
Comfort Inn	770-952-3000	2100 Northwest Parkway - Exit Delk Road Marietta GA	2
Crowne Plaza Hotel Marietta	770-428-4400	1775 Parkway Place Se - Exit 263 Marietta GA	3+
Days Inn Atlanta/Marietta	678-797-0233	753 N Marietta Parkway - Exit 265 Marietta GA	2
La Quinta Inn Atlanta Marietta	770-951-0026	2170 Delk Rd. - Exit 261 Marietta GA	3+
Comfort Inn	770-954-9110	80 H 81W - Exit 218 McDonough GA	2

Highway Guides - Please always call ahead to make sure that an establishment is still dog-friendly

Name	Phone	Address	Dogs per Room
Days Inn Atlanta/McDonough	770-957-5261	744 Highway 155 S - Exit 216 McDonough GA	2
Quality Inn and Suites	770-957-5291	930 H 155 S - Exit 216 McDonough GA	3+
Super 8 McDonough	770-957-2458	1170 Hampton Rd - Exit 218 McDonough GA	2
Best Western Southlake Inn	770-961-6300	6437 Jonesboro Rd - Exit 233 Morrow GA	3+
Quality Inn and Suites Southlake	770-960-1957	6597 Jonebaro Road - Exit 233 Morrow GA	2
Sleep Inn	770-472-9800	2185 Mt Zion Parkway - Exit 231 Morrow GA	3+
South Drury Inn & Suites	770-960-0500	6520 S. Lee Street Morrow GA	1+

Atlanta

Name	Phone	Address	Dogs per Room
Airport Drury Inn & Suites	404-761-4900	1270 Virginia Avenue Atlanta GA	1+
Best Western Granada Suite Hotel - Midtown	404-876-6100	1302 W Peachtree Street NW - Exit 250 Atlanta GA	2
Hotel Indigo	404-874-9200	683 Peachtree St NE - Exit 259 Atlanta GA	3+
Laurel Hill	404-377-3217	1992 McLendon Avenue - Exit Freedom Parkway Atlanta GA	3+

Stockbridge

Name	Phone	Address	Dogs per Room
Motel 6 - Atlanta South - Stockbridge	770-389-1142	7233 Davidson Parkway Stockbridge GA	1+
Red Roof Inn - Atlanta Southeast	678-782-4100	637 SR 138 West Stockbridge GA	1+

Locust Grove

Name	Phone	Address	Dogs per Room
Red Roof Inn - Locust Grove, GA	678-583-0004	4832 Bill Gardner Parkway Locust Grove GA	1+

Forsyth

Name	Phone	Address	Dogs per Room
Best Western Hilltop Inn	478-994-9260	951 Highway 42 North - Exit 188 Forsyth GA	2
Comfort Inn	478-994-3400	333 Harold G Clark Parkway - Exit 185 Forsyth GA	3+
Days Inn Forsyth	478-994-2900	343 N Lee St - Exit 187 Forsyth GA	2
Hampton Inn	478-994-9697	520 Holiday Circle - Exit 186 Forsyth GA	1+
Holiday Inn	478-994-5691	480 Holiday Circle Forsyth GA	3+
Holiday Inn Express Forsyth	478-994-9697	520 Holiday Circle - Exit 186 Forsyth GA	3+

Macon

Name	Phone	Address	Dogs per Room
Best Western Riverside Inn	478-743-6311	2400 Riverside Drive - Exit 167 Macon GA	2
Comfort Inn and Suites	478-757-8688	3935 Arkwright Road - Exit Arkwright Road Macon GA	3+
La Quinta Inn & Suites Macon	478-475-0206	3944 River Place Dr. - Exit 169 Macon GA	3+
Residence Inn by Marriott	478-475-4280	3900 Sheraton Drive - Exit 169 Macon GA	3+

Warner Robins

Name	Phone	Address	Dogs per Room
Best Western Inn and Suites	478-956-3056	101 Dunbar Rd - Exit 149 Byron GA	3+
Comfort Inn and Suites	478-922-7555	95 S H 247 - Exit 144 E on Russell Pkwy Warner Robins GA	2

Perry

Name	Phone	Address	Dogs per Room
Days Inn Perry	478-987-8777	201 Lect Dr - Exit 135 Perry GA	2
New Perry Hotel & Motel	478-987-1000	800 Main Street - Exit 135 or 136 Perry GA	3+
Quality Inn	478-987-1345	1504 Sam Nunn Blvd - Exit 136 Perry GA	3+
Super 8 Perry	478-987-0999	102 Plaza Drive - Exit 136 Perry GA	2

Cordele

Name	Phone	Address	Dogs per Room
Best Western Colonial Inn	229-273-5420	1706 East 16th Avenue - Exit 101 Cordele GA	2
Super 8 Cordele	229-273-2456	1618 E 16th Ave - Exit 101 Cordele GA	2

Tifton

Name	Phone	Address	Dogs per Room
Days Inn Tifton	229-382-8505	1199 Hwy 82 W - Exit Hwy 82 Tifton GA	2
Hampton Inn	229-382-8800	720 H 319S - Exit 62 Tifton GA	3+
Holiday Inn	229-382-6687	I-75 & US 82W - Exit 62 Tifton GA	3+
Motel 6 - Tifton	229-388-8777	579 Old Omega Road Tifton GA	1+
Super 8 Tifton	229-382-9500	I-75 and W 2nd Street - Exit 63a Tifton GA	2

Adel

Name	Phone	Address	Dogs per Room
Days Inn Adel	229-896-4574	1200 W 4th St - Exit 39 Adel GA	2
Hampton Inn	229-896-3099	1500 W Fourth Street - Exit H 37W Adel GA	3+
Super 8 Adel/I-75	229-896-2244	1103 W 4th Street - Exit 39 Adel GA	2

Valdosta

Name	Phone	Address	Dogs per Room
Best Western King of the Road	229-244-7600	1403 N Saint Augustine Road - Exit 18 Valdosta GA	2
Days Inn Valdosta Conference Cntr	229-249-8800	1827 West Hill Ave - Exit 16 Valdosta GA	2
Howard Johnson Express Inn	229-249-8900	1330 St. Augustine Rd. Valdosta GA	1+
La Quinta Inn & Suites Valdosta	229-247-7755	1800 Clubhouse Drive - Exit 18/St Augustine Road Valdosta GA	3+
Motel 6 - Valdosta - University	229-333-0047	2003 West Hill Avenue Valdosta GA	1+
Quality Inn South	229-244-4520	1902 W Hill Avenue - Exit 16/H 84 Valdosta GA	2
Super 8 Valdosta/Conf Center Area	229-249-8000	1825 W Hill Ave - Exit 16 Valdosta GA	2

Lake Park

Name	Phone	Address	Dogs per Room
Days Inn Valdosta/Lake Park	229-559-0229	4913 Timber Dr - Exit 5 Lake Park GA	2

Florida Listings (Interstate 75)   Dogs per Room

Jasper

Name	Phone	Address	Dogs per Room
Days Inn Jasper	386-792-1987	8182 SR 6 West - Exit 460 Jasper FL	2

Lake City

Name	Phone	Address	Dogs per Room
Best Western Inn	386-752-3801	3598 US Hwy 90 West - Exit 427 Lake City FL	2
Days Inn Lake City	386-758-4224	3430 North US Hwy 441 Lake City FL	2

Motel 6 - Lake City	386-755-4664	3835 US 90 Lake City FL	1+
Super 8 Lake City	386-752-6450	I-75 and Hwy 47 - Exit 423 Lake City FL	2
Gainesville			
Best Western Gateway Grand	352-331-3336	4200 NW 97th Blvd - Exit 390 Gainesville FL	3+
Comfort Inn	352-373-6500	2435 SW 13th Street - Exit 382 Gainesville FL	3+
Days Inn Gainesville/I-75	352-332-3033	7516 Newberry Rd - Exit SR 26 Gainesville FL	2
La Quinta Inn Gainesville	352-332-6466	920 N.W. 69th Terrace - Exit 387 Gainesville FL	3+
Ocala			
Comfort Inn	352-629-8850	4040 W Silver Springs Blvd - Exit 352/H 40 Ocala FL	2
Days Inn	352-629-7041	3811 NW Bonnie Heath Rd - Exit 354 Ocala FL	2
Days Inn Ocala	352-629-0091	3620 W Silver Springs Blvd - Exit 352 Ocala FL	2
Hilton	352-854-1400	3600 Southwest 36th Avenue - Exit 350 Ocala FL	2
Howard Johnson Inn	352-629-7021	3951 NW Blitchton Rd. Ocala FL	1+
La Quinta Inn & Suites Ocala	352-861-1137	3530 S.W. 36th Ave. - Exit 350 Ocala FL	3+
Days Inn Ocala/East	352-236-2891	5001 E Silver Springs Blvd - Exit 69 Silver Springs FL	2
Brooksville			
Best Western Brooksville I-75	352-796-9481	30307 Cortez Blvd - Exit 301 Brooksville FL	2
Days Inn Brooksville	352-796-9486	6320 Windmere Rd - Exit 301 Brooksville FL	2
Port Richey			
Comfort Inn	727-863-3336	11810 H 19 - Exit H 52W Port Richey FL	3+
Tampa Bay			
Quality Inn and Suites	941-355-7091	4800 N Tamiami Trail - Exit 213 W Sarasota FL	3+
Residence Inn by Marriott	941-358-1468	1040 University Parkway - Exit University Parkway/#213 Sarasota FL	3+
Best Western Brandon Hotel	813-621-5555	9331 Adamo Dr - Exit 257 Tampa FL	1
Holiday Inn Express Hotel / Suites	813-910-7171	8310 Galbraith Road - Exit 270 Tampa FL	3+
La Quinta Inn & Suites USF	813-910-7500	3701 East Fowler Ave. - Exit East Fowler Avenue Tampa FL	3+
La Quinta Inn Tampa Brandon West	813-684-4007	602 S. Falkenburg Road - Exit 257/H 60 Tampa FL	3+
TownePlace Suites Tampa North/I-75 Fletcher	813-975-9777	6800 Woodstork Rd - Exit 266 Tampa FL	2
Residence Inn by Marriott	813-972-4400	13420 North Telecom Parkway - Exit 266 Temple Terrace FL	3+
Days Inn Venice	941-493-4558	1710 S Tamiami Trail - Exit 195 Venice FL	2
Sarasota			
Banana Bay Club	941-346-0113	8254 Midnight Pass Road - Exit 205 Siesta Key FL	3+
Siesta Holiday House	941-312-9882	1011-1015 Cresent Street - Exit 205 Siesta Key FL	2
Fort Myers			
Quality Hotel Nautilus	239-542-2121	1538 Cape Coral Parkway - Exit 136 Cape Coral FL	2
Econolodge N	239-995-0571	13301 N Cleveland - Exit 143 Fort Myers FL	3+
Howard Johnson Inn	239-936-3229	4811 Cleveland Ave. Fort Myers FL	1+
La Quinta Inn Fort Myers	239-275-3300	4850 S. Cleveland Ave. - Exit 136 Fort Myers FL	1
Residence Inn by Marriott	239-936-0110	2960 Colonial Blvd - Exit 136 Fort Myers FL	3+
Bonita Springs			
Hyatt Regency Coconut Point Resort & Spa	239-444-1234	5001 Coconut Road Bonita Springs FL	1+
Naples			
La Quinta Inn Naples Airport	239-352-8400	185 Bedzel Circle - Exit 101 Naples FL	3+
Staybridge Suites	239-643-8002	4805 Tamiami Trail North - Exit 107/Pine Ridge Street Naples FL	2
South Florida			
Residence Inn by Marriott	954-659-8585	2605 Weston Road - Exit Weston Road Weston FL	3+

Interstate 77 Accommodation Listings

Ohio Listings (Interstate 77)   Dogs per Room

Akron			
Days Inn Akron South	330-644-1204	3237 S Arlington Rd - Exit 120 Akron OH	2
Motel 6 - Akron North	330-666-0566	99 Rothrock Road Akron OH	1+
Red Roof Inn - Akron South	330-644-7748	2939 South Arlington Road Akron OH	1+
Residence Inn by Marriott	330-666-4811	120 Montrose West Avenue Akron OH	3+
Sheraton Suites Akron/Cuyahoga Falls	330-929-3000	1989 Front Street Cuyahoga Falls OH	1+
Canton			
Courtyard by Marriott	330-494-6494	4375 Metro Circle NW Canton OH	1+
Residence Inn by Marriott	330-493-0004	5280 Broadmoor Circle NW - Exit 109/Everhard Road Canton OH	3+
Super 8 Canton/North	330-492-5030	3950 Convenience Circle NW - Exit 109 or 109a Canton OH	2
Motel 6 - Canton	330-494-7611	6880 Sunset Strip Ave NW North Canton OH	1+
Red Roof Inn - Canton	330-499-1970	5353 Inn Circle Court Northwest North Canton OH	1+
New Philadelphia			
Hampton Inn	330-339-7000	1299 W High Avenue - Exit 81 E New Philadelphia OH	1
Motel 6 - New Philadelphia	330-339-6446	181 Bluebell Dr SW New Philadelphia OH	1+

Highway Guides - Please always call ahead to make sure that an establishment is still dog-friendly

| Schoenbrunn Inn | 330-339-4334 | 1186 West High Avenue   New Philadelphia OH | 1+ |
| Super 8 New Philadelphia | 330-339-6500 | 131 1/2 Bluebell Drive SW - Exit 81 New Philadelphia OH | 2 |

Cambridge

Best Western Cambridge	740-439-3581	1945 Southgate Parkway Cambridge OH	3+
Comfort Inn	740-435-3200	2327 Southgate Parkway Cambridge OH	3+
Days Inn Cambridge	740-432-5691	2328 Southgate Pkwy Cambridge OH	2
Holiday Inn	740-432-7313	2248 Southgate Pkwy Cambridge OH	3+

Marietta

Best Western Marietta	740-374-7211	279 Muskingum Dr - Exit 6 Marietta OH	2
Comfort Inn	740-374-8190	700 Pike Street - Exit 1 Marietta OH	3+
Super 8 Marietta	740-374-8888	46 Acme St - Exit 1 Marietta OH	2

West Virginia Listings (Interstate 77)   Dogs per Room

Parkersburg

Blennerhassett Hotel	304-422-3131	Fourth and Market Streets Parkersburg WV	1+
Expressway Motor Inn	304-485-1851	6333 Emerson Ave Parkersburg WV	1+
Motel 6 - Parkersburg	304-424-5100	3604 1/2 East 7th Street Parkersburg WV	1+
Red Roof Inn - Parkersburg	304-485-1741	3714 East 7th Street Parkersburg WV	1+

Ripley

| Best Western McCoys Inn & Conference Center | 304-372-9122 | 701 Main Street W - Exit 138 Ripley WV | 3+ |
| Holiday Inn Express | 304-372-5000 | One Hospitality Drive - Exit 138 Ripley WV | 3+ |

Charleston

Charleston Marriott Town Center	304-345-6500	200 Lee Street E Charleston WV	3+
Comfort Suites	304-925-1171	107 Alex Lane - Exit 95 E Charleston WV	2
Country Inns & Suites by Carlson	304-925-4300	105 Alex Lane Charleston WV	1+
Motel 6 - Charleston East	304-925-0471	6311 MacCorkle Ave SE Charleston WV	1+
Residence Inn by Marriott	304-345-4200	200 Hotel Circle Northgate Business Park Charleston WV	3+
Comfort Inn West	800-798-7886	102 Racer Drive Cross Lanes WV	2
Motel 6 - Charleston West-Cross Lanes	304-776-5911	330 Goff Mountain Rd Cross Lanes WV	1+
Red Roof Inn - Charleston West - Hurricane, WV	304-757-6392	500 Putnam Village Drive Hurricane WV	1+
Super 8 Hurricane	304-562-3346	419 Hurricane Creek Rd Hurricane WV	2
Red Roof Inn - Charleston - Kanawha City, WV	304-925-6953	6305 MacCorkle Avenue SE Kanawha City WV	1+

Beckley

Best Western Four Seasons Inn	304-252-0671	1939 Harper Road - Exit 44 Beckley WV	3+
Comfort Inn	304-255-2161	1909 Harper Road Beckley WV	3+
Super 8 Beckley	304-253-0802	2014 Harper Rd - Exit 44 Beckley WV	2
Quality Inn New River Gorge	304-574-3443	103 Elliotts Way Fayetteville WV	3+

Virginia Listings (Interstate 77)   Dogs per Room

Wytheville

Super 8 Ft Chiswell/Max Meadows Area	276-637-4141	194 Ft Chiswell Rd - Exit 80 Max Meadows VA	2
Best Western Wytheville Inn	276-228-7300	355 Nye Rd - Exit 41 Wytheville VA	3+
Comfort Inn	276-637-4281	2594 East Lee H Wytheville VA	3+
Days Inn Wytheville	276-228-5500	150 Malin Dr - Exit 73 Wytheville VA	2
Motel 6 - Wytheville	276-228-7988	220 Lithia Road Wytheville VA	1+
Super 8 Wytheville	276-228-6620	130 Nye Circle - Exit 41 Wytheville VA	2

North Carolina Listings (Interstate 77)   Dogs per Room

Charlotte

Candlewood Suites	704-529-7500	5840 Westpark Drive - Exit 5 Charlotte NC	2
Comfort Inn Executive Park	704-525-2626	5822 Westpark Drive - Exit 5/Tyvola Road Charlotte NC	3+
Comfort Suites	704-547-0049	7735 University City Blvd - Exit 18 E/Harris Blvd to H49/UNCC Charlotte NC	3+
Days Inn Charlotte Central	704-333-4733	601 N Tryon - Exit 11a or 11 Charlotte NC	2
Holiday Inn	704-523-1400	321 W Woodlawn Road - Exit 60 Charlotte NC	3+
Quality Inn	704-525-0747	440 Griffith Road - Exit 5 Charlotte NC	2
Staybridge Suites	704-527-6767	7924 Forest Pine Drive Charlotte NC	3+
Summerfield Suites	704-525-2600	4920 S Tryon Street - Exit 6B/Billy Graham Parkway Charlotte NC	2
Super 8 Charlotte/Sunset Road	704-598-7710	4930 Sunset Road - Exit 16a Charlotte NC	2
TownePlace Suites Charlotte Arrowood	704-227-2000	7805 Forest Point Blvd - Arrowood Rd Exit Charlotte NC	2
TownePlace Suites Charlotte University Research Park	704-548-0388	8710 Research Drive - Exit 18 Charlotte NC	2

South Carolina Listings (Interstate 77)   Dogs per Room

Rock Hill

Quality Inn and Suites	803-329-3121	2625 Cherry Road - Exit 82-B/Rock Hill Rock Hill SC	3+

Winnsboro

Days Inn Winnsboro	803-635-1447	1894 US Hwy 321 Bypass - Exit 34 Winnsboro SC	2

Columbia

Carolinian Hotel	803-736-3000	7510 Two Notch Rd, I-20 & US-1 Columbia SC	1+

Interstate 80 Accommodation Listings

Indiana Listings (Interstate 80)   Dogs per Room

Hammond

Motel 6 - Hammond - Chicago Area	219-845-0330	3840 179th Street Hammond IN	1+

Portage

Comfort Inn	219-763-7177	2300 Willowcreek Road - Exit 23/Portage Portage IN	3+
Super 8 Portage	219-762-8857	6118 Melton Rd Portage IN	2

South Bend

Comfort Suites	574-272-1500	52939 H 933 N - Exit 77/N on H 31/33/933 South Bend IN	3+
Motel 6 - South Bend	574-272-7072	52624 US 31 North South Bend IN	1+
Quality Inn University	574-272-6600	515 N Dixieway - Exit 77 South Bend IN	3+
Residence Inn by Marriott	574-289-5555	716 N Niles Avenue South Bend IN	3+
Sleep Inn	574-232-3200	4134 Lincolnway West South Bend IN	1+

Elkhart

Candlewood Suites Elkhart	574-262-8600	300 North Pointe Blvd. Elkhart IN	2
Red Roof Inn - Elkhart	574-262-3691	2902 Cassopolis Street Elkhart IN	1+
Super 8 Elkhart	574-264-4457	345 Windsor Ave - Exit 92 Elkhart IN	2

Shipshewana

Super 8 Shipshewana	260-768-4004	740 S Van Buren - Exit 107 Shipshewana IN	2

Howe

Super 8 Howe	260-562-2828	7333 N State Rte 9 - Exit 121 Howe IN	2

Ohio Listings (Interstate 80)   Dogs per Room

Wauseon

Best Western Del Mar	419-335-1565	8319 SH 108 - Exit Mile Post 34 Wauseon OH	3+

Toledo

Days Inn Toledo/Maumee	419-897-6900	1704 Tollgate Dr - Exit 59 Maumee OH	2
Howard Johnson Inn	419-837-5245	I-280 & Hanley Road Perrysburg OH	1+

Lake Erie Island Region

Comfort Inn and Suites	419-355-9300	840 Sean Drive - Exit 91 to H 53S Fremont OH	3+
Holiday Inn	419-334-2682	3422 Port Clinton Road - Exit 91 Fremont OH	3+

Cleveland

Comfort Inn	440-324-7676	739 Leona Street - Exit 145/H 57N Elyria OH	3+
Holiday Inn	440-324-5411	1825 Lorain Blvd - Exit 145 Elyria OH	3+

Richfield

Quality Inn	330-659-6151	4742 Brecksvillle Road/H 21 - Exit 173 Richfield OH	2

Leavittsburg

Comfort Inn	330-393-1200	136 N Park Avenue Warren OH	2

Austintown

Comfort Inn and Suites	330-792-9740	5425 Clarkins Drive - Exit 223 Austintown OH	3+
Motel 6 - Austintown	330-793-9305	5431 Seventy Six Drive Austintown OH	1+

Youngstown

Days Inn Youngstown South	330-758-2371	8392 Market St Boardman OH	2
Microtel	330-758-1816	7393 South Avenue Boardman OH	1+
Best Western Meander Inn	330-544-2378	870 North Canfield-Niles Rd - Exit 223 Youngstown OH	3+
Super 8 Youngstown/Airport	330-759-0040	4250 Belmont Ave - Exit 229 Youngstown OH	2

Pennsylvania Listings (Interstate 80)   Dogs per Room

Clarion

Holiday Inn	814-226-8850	I-80 Rt 68 - Exit 62 Clarion PA	2
Quality Inn and Suites	814-226-8682	24 United Drive - Exit 62 Clarion PA	3+
Super 8 Clarion	814-226-4550	135 Hotel Road - Exit 62 Clarion PA	2

Highway Guides - Please always call ahead to make sure that an establishment is still dog-friendly

Brookville			
Days Inn Brookville	814-849-8001	230 Allegheny Blvd - Exit 78 Brookville PA	2
Holiday Inn Express	814-849-8381	235 Allegheny Blvd - Exit 78 Brookville PA	3+
DuBois			
Best Western Inn & Conference Center	814-371-6200	82 N Park Place - Exit 97 or 101 DuBois PA	2
Clearfield			
Comfort Inn	814-768-6400	1821 Industrial Park Road - Exit 120/H 879W Clearfield PA	3+
Days Inn Clearfield	814-765-5381	14451 Clearfield Shawville Hwy - Exit 120 Clearfield PA	2
Super 8 Clearfield	814-768-7580	14597 Clearfield/Shawville Hwy - Exit 120 Clearfield PA	2
Victorian Loft	814-765-4805	216 S Front Street - Exit 120 Clearfield PA	2
Bloomsburg			
Quality Inn & Suites	570-275-5100	15 Valley West Road - Exit 224 Danville PA	2
Red Roof Inn - Danville	570-275-7600	300 Red Roof Road Danville PA	1+
Super 8 Mifflinville	570-759-6778	450 WEST 3RD STREET - Exit 242 Mifflinville PA	1
Hazleton			
Best Western Genetti Lodge	570-454-2494	Route 309, RR2 - Exit 262 Hazleton PA	3+

New Jersey Listings (Interstate 80)   Dogs per Room

I-80 Corridor			
Days Inn Lake Hopatcong	973-347-5100	1691 Route 46 - Exit 27 to Rt 46 Ledgewood NJ	2

Interstate 81 Accommodation Listings

New York Listings (Interstate 81)   Dogs per Room

Watertown			
Best Western Carriage House Inn and Conf Cntr	315-782-8000	300 Washington St - Exit 44 TO 232n to 11N Watertown NY	2
Syracuse			
BN on 7th North	315-451-1511	400 7th North St - Exit 25 Liverpool NY	2
Doubletree	315-457-4000	6701 Buckley Road - Exit 7thN N Syracuse NY	2
Comfort Inn	315-437-0222	6491 Thompson Road - Exit 25A to I 90E Syracuse NY	3+
Finger Lakes			
Comfort Inn	607-272-0100	356 Elmira Road - Exit H 13/Homer Ithaca NY	2
Cortland			
Holiday Inn Cortland	607-756-4431	2 River Street - Exit 11 Cortland NY	3+
Quality Inn	607-756-5622	188 Clinton Avenue - Exit 11 Cortland NY	3+
Binghamton			
Clarion Collection: The Grand Royal Hotel	607-722-0000	80 State Street - Exit 4S/H 7S Binghamton NY	2
Quality Inn and Suites	607-722-5353	1156 Front Street - Exit 6 Binghamton NY	3+
Super 8 Binghamton/Front Street	607-773-8111	650 Old Front St - Exit 5 Binghamton NY	2

Pennsylvania Listings (Interstate 81)   Dogs per Room

Hazleton			
Best Western Genetti Lodge	570-454-2494	Route 309, RR2 - Exit 145 Hazleton PA	3+
Hazelton Motor Inn	570-459-1451	615 E Broad Street - Exit 141, 143, or 145 Hazleton PA	3+
Comfort Inn	570-455-9300	58 H 93 - Exit 145/H 93 S West Hazleton PA	3+
Jonestown			
Days Inn Lebanon	717-865-4064	3 Everest Lane - Exit 90 Jonestown PA	2
Chambersburg			
Best Western Chambersburg	717-262-4994	211 Walker Rd - Exit 16 Chambersburg PA	2
Comfort Inn	717-263-6655	3301 Black Gap Road - Exit 20 Chambersburg PA	2
Days Inn Chambersburg	717-263-1288	30 Falling Spring Rd - Exit 16 Chambersburg PA	2
Comfort Inn	717-597-8164	50 Pine Drive - Exit 3 Greencastle PA	3+
Best Western Shippensburg Hotel	717-532-5200	125 Walnut Bottom Road - Exit 29 Shippensburg PA	3+

Maryland Listings (Interstate 81)   Dogs per Room

Hagerstown			
Econo Lodge	301-791-3560	18221 Mason Dixon Rd Hagerstown MD	1+
Motel 6 - Hagerstown	301-582-4445	11321 Massey Boulevard Hagerstown MD	1+
Quality Inn	301-733-2700	1101 Dual H - Exit 6A Hagerstown MD	2
Sleep Inn and Suites	301-766-9449	18216 Colonel H K Douglas Drive Hagerstown MD	3+

Highway Guides - Please always call ahead to make sure that an establishment is still dog-friendly

Super 8 Halfway/Hagerstown Area	301-582-1992	16805 Blake Rd - Exit 5b Hagerstown MD	2
Red Roof Inn - Hagerstown - Williamsport	301-582-3500	310 East Potomac Street Williamsport MD	1+

West Virginia Listings (Interstate 81)   Dogs per Room

Martinsburg
Holiday Inn Express North	304-274-6100	1220 TJ Jackson Drive - Exit 20 Falling Waters WV	3+
Days Inn Martinsburg	304-263-1800	209 Viking Way - Exit 13 Martinsburg WV	2
Holiday Inn	304-267-5500	301 Foxcroft Avenue - Exit 20 Martinsburg WV	3+
Knights Inn	304-267-2211	1599 Edwin Miller Blvd Martinsburg WV	1+

Virginia Listings (Interstate 81)   Dogs per Room

Winchester
Super 8 Middletown/Winchester Area	540-868-1800	2120 Reliance Rd - Exit 302 Middletown VA	2
Comfort Inn	540-869-6500	167 Town Run Lane - Exit 307/H 277E Stephens City VA	2
Best Value Inn	540-662-2521	2649 Valley Avenue - Exit 310 Winchester VA	2
Best Western Lee-Jackson Motor Inn	540-662-4154	711 Millwood Ave - Exit 313B Winchester VA	3+
Candlewood Suites Winchester	540-667-8323	1135 Millwood Pike - Exit 313 Winchester VA	2
Days Inn Winchester	540-667-1200	2951 Valley Ave - Exit 310 Winchester VA	2
Holiday Inn	540-667-3300	1017 Millwood Pike - Exit 313 or 313A Winchester VA	2
Red Roof Inn - Winchester	540-667-5000	991 Millwood Pike Winchester VA	1+
Super 8 Winchester	540-665-4450	1077 Millwood Pike - Exit 313 or 313a Winchester VA	2

Mount Jackson
The Widow Kip's Country Inn	540-477-2400	355 Orchard Drive - Exit 273/Mt Jackson Mount Jackson VA	2

New Market
Days Inn New Market	540-740-4100	9360 George Collins Pkwy - Exit 264 New Market VA	2
Quality Inn Shenandoah Valley	540-740-3141	162 W Old Cross Road - Exit 264/H 211E New Market VA	2

Harrisonburg
Candlewood Suites Harrisonburg	540-437-1400	1560 Country Club Road - Exit 247A Harrisonburg VA	3+
Comfort Inn	540-433-6066	1440 E Market Street - Exit 247-A onto H 33/E Market St. Harrisonburg VA	3+
Days Inn Harrisonburg	540-433-9353	1131 Forest Hill Rd - Exit 245 Harrisonburg VA	2
Motel 6 - Harrisonburg	540-433-6939	10 Linda Lane Harrisonburg VA	1+
Super 8 Harrisonburg	540-433-8888	3330 S Main - Exit 243 Harrisonburg VA	2

Staunton
Best Western Staunton Inn	540-885-1112	92 Rowe Rd - Exit 222 Staunton VA	3+
Comfort Inn	540-886-5000	1302 Richmond Avenue - Exit 222/H 250W Staunton VA	2
Days Inn Staunton	540-248-0888	273 D Bells Lane - Exit 225 Staunton VA	2
Days Inn Staunton/Blue Ridge Mountains	540-337-3031	372 White Hill Rd - Exit 217 Staunton VA	2
Holiday Inn	540-248-6020	152 Fairway Lane - Exit 225 Staunton VA	2
Quality Inn	540-248-5111	96 Baker Lane - Exit 225/H 275 E Staunton VA	3+
Sleep Inn	540-887-6500	222 Jefferson H - Exit 222 Staunton VA	2
Super 8 Staunton	540-886-2888	1015 Richmond Rd - Exit 222 Staunton VA	2
Twelfth Night Inn	540-885-1733	402 E Beverly - Exit 225 Staunton VA	2

Raphine
Days Inn Raphine	540-377-2604	584 Oakland Cr - Exit 205 Raphine VA	2

Lexington
1780 Stone House, rental #1350	540-463-2521	218 S Main Street/H 11 Lexington VA	2
Applewood Inn	540-463-1962	242 Tarn Beck Lane Lexington VA	1
Best Western Inn at Hunt Ridge	540-464-1500	25 Willow Springs Rd - Exit 191W to Ex 55 Lexington VA	3+
Best Western Lexington Inn	540-458-3020	850 N Lee Highway - Exit 191 Lexington VA	3+
Days Inn Lexington	540-463-2143	325 West Midland Trail - Exit 188B Lexington VA	2
Howard Johnson Inn	540-463-9181	2836 N. Lee Hwy. Lexington VA	1+
Super 8 Lexington	540-463-7858	1139 North Lee Hwy - Exit 191 Lexington VA	2
Fox Hill Bed & Breakfast & Cottage Suites	540-377-9922	4383 Borden Grant Trail Lexington/Fairfield VA	1+

Natural Bridge
1926 Caboose Vacation Rental	540-463-2521	218 S Main Street/H 11 Natural Bridge VA	1+
Natural Bridge Hotel	540-291-2121	15 Appledore Lane - Exit 175/H 11N Natural Bridge VA	2

Roanoke
Comfort Inn Airport	540-527-2020	5070 Valley View Road - Exit 143/I 581 Roanoke VA	3+
Days Inn Roanoke Airport	540-366-0341	8118 Plantation Rd - Exit 146 Roanoke VA	2
Quality Inn Roanoke Airport	540-366-8861	6626 Thirlane Road - Exit 143/Roanoke Roanoke VA	3+

Christiansburg
Days Inn Christiansburg	540-382-0261	2635 Roanoke St - Exit 118c Christiansburg VA	2
Howard Johnson Express Inn	540-381-0150	100 Bristol Drive Christiansburg VA	1+

Quality Inn	540-382-2055	50 Hampton Blvd - Exit 118C Christiansburg VA	3+
Super 8 Christiansburg/Blacksburg Area	540-382-5813	55 Laurel Street NE - Exit 118b Christiansburg VA	2
Super 8 Christiansburg/East	540-382-7421	2780 Roanoke St - Exit 118c Christiansburg VA	2
Pulaski			
Comfort Inn	540-674-1100	4424 Cleburne Blvd - Exit 98 Dublin VA	2
Days Inn Pulaski	540-980-2230	3063 Old Rt 100 Rd - Exit 94 or 94a Pulaski VA	2
Best Western Radford Inn	540-639-3000	1501 Tyler Avenue - Exit 109 Radford VA	3+
Super 8 Radford	540-731-9355	1600 Tyler Ave - Exit 109 Radford VA	2
Wytheville			
Super 8 Ft Chiswell/Max Meadows Area	276-637-4141	194 Ft Chiswell Rd - Exit 80 Max Meadows VA	2
Best Western Wytheville Inn	276-228-7300	355 Nye Rd - Exit 72 to 41 Wytheville VA	3+
Comfort Inn	276-637-4281	2594 East Lee H - Exit 80 Wytheville VA	3+
Days Inn Wytheville	276-228-5500	150 Malin Dr - Exit 73 Wytheville VA	2
Motel 6 - Wytheville	276-228-7988	220 Lithia Road Wytheville VA	1+
Super 8 Wytheville	276-228-6620	130 Nye Circle - Exit 72 to Exit 41 Wytheville VA	2
Bristol			
Days Inn Abingdon	276-628-7131	887 Empire Drive - Exit 19 Abingdon VA	2
Holiday Inn Express Abingdon	276-676-2829	940 E. Main St - Exit 19 Abingdon VA	2
Super 8 Abingdon	276-676-3329	298 Town Centre Dr - Exit 17 Abingdon VA	2
Motel 6 - Bristol	276-466-6060	21561 Clear Creek Road Bristol VA	1+
Super 8 Bristol	276-466-8800	2139 Lee Hwy - Exit 5 Bristol VA	2

Tennessee Listings (Interstate 81)   Dogs per Room

Bristol			
Days inn Bristol	423-968-9119	3281 W State St - Exit 74a Bristol TN	3+
Kingsport			
Comfort Inn	423-378-4418	100 Indian Center Court - Exit 57B/R on H 93N Kingsport TN	3+
La Quinta Inn Kingsport Tri-Cities Airport	423-323-0500	10150 Airport Parkway - Exit 63 Kingsport TN	3+
Sleep Inn	423-279-1811	200 Hospitality Place - Exit 63 Kingsport TN	3+
Bulls Gap			
Best Western Executive Inn	423-235-9111	50 Speedway Ln - Exit 23 Bulls Gap TN	2
Super 8 Bulls Gap/Greenville Area	423-235-4112	90 Speedway Lane - Exit 23 Bulls Gap TN	2
Greeneville			
Comfort Inn	423-639-4185	1790 E Andrew Johnson H - Exit 23 Greeneville TN	2
Morristown			
Comfort Suites	423-585-4000	3660 W Andrew Johnson H - Exit 12/H 160N Morristown TN	3+
Super 8 Morristown/South	423-318-8888	5400 S Davey Crockett Parkway - Exit 8 Morristown TN	2
White Pine			
Days Inn White Pine	865-674-2573	3670 Roy Messer Hwy - Exit 4 White Pine TN	2

Interstate 85 Accommodation Listings

Virginia Listings (Interstate 85)   Dogs per Room

Petersburg			
Days Inn Petersburg/Walthall	804-520-1010	2310 Indian Hill Rd Colonial Heights VA	2
Candlewood Suites	804-541-0200	5113 Plaza Drive Hopewell VA	2
Days Inn Petersburg/Fort Lee South	804-733-4400	12208 S Crater Rd Petersburg VA	2
Quality Inn	804-732-2900	11974 S Crater Road Petersburg VA	3+
Hampton Inn	434-246-5500	10476 Blue Star H Stony Creek VA	2
Sleep Inn	434-246-5100	11019 Blue Star H Stony Creek VA	2

North Carolina Listings (Interstate 85)   Dogs per Room

Durham			
Best Western Skyland Inn	919-383-2508	5400 US Hwy 70 West - Exit 170 Durham NC	3+
Holiday Inn Express Durham	919-313-3244	2516 Guess Road - Exit 175/Guess Road Durham NC	3+
Super 8 Durham/University Area	919-286-7746	2337 Guess Rd - Exit 175 Durham NC	2
Burlington			
Days Inn Burlington	336-227-3681	978 Plantation Dr - Exit Rt 49 Burlington NC	2
La Quinta Inn Burlington	336-229-5203	2444 Maple Ave. Burlington NC	3+
Motel 6 - Burlington	336-226-1325	2155 Hanford Road Burlington NC	1+
Red Roof Inn - Burlington, NC	336-227-1270	2133 West Hanford Road Burlington NC	1+
Salisbury			

Highway Guides - Please always call ahead to make sure that an establishment is still dog-friendly

Hampton Inn	704-637-8000	1001 Klumac Road - Exit 75 Salisbury NC	3+
Holiday Inn	704-637-3100	530 Jake Alexander Blvd South - Exit 75 Salisbury NC	2

Charlotte

Candlewood Suites	704-598-9863	8812 University East Drive - Exit 45A Charlotte NC	2
Comfort Inn UNCC	704-598-0007	5111 Equipment Drive - Exit 41/Sugar Creek Road Charlotte NC	2
Comfort Suites	704-547-0049	7735 University City Blvd - Exit 45A/Harris Blvd to H49/UNCC Charlotte NC	3+
Days Inn Charlotte North	704-597-8110	1408 W Sugar Creek Rd - Exit 41 Charlotte NC	2
Drury Inn & Suites	704-593-0700	415 West W.T. Harris Blvd. Charlotte NC	1+
La Quinta Inn Charlotte Airport	704-393-5306	3100 Queen City Drive - Exit 33 Charlotte NC	3+
Residence Inn by Marriott	704-547-1122	8503 N Tryon Street - Exit Harris Blvd Charlotte NC	3+
TownePlace Suites Charlotte University Research Park	704-548-0388	8710 Research Drive - Exit 45b Charlotte NC	2
Days Inn Concord	704-786-9121	5125 Davidson Hwy - Exit 55 Concord NC	2
Super 8 Concord	704-786-5181	1601 US 29 North - Exit 58 Concord NC	2
Holiday Inn Express Gastonia	704-884-3300	1911 Broadcast Drive - Exit 17 Gastonia NC	3+

South Carolina Listings (Interstate 85)   Dogs per Room

Gaffney

Peach Tree Inn	864-489-7172	136 Peachoid Rd - Exit 92 Gaffney SC	2
Quality Inn	864-487-4200	143 Corona Drive - Exit H 11/92 Gaffney SC	3+
Red Roof Inn - Gaffney	864-206-0200	132 New Painter Road Gaffney SC	1+

Spartanburg

Campus Place/Extended Stay	864-699-1088	1050 Charisma Drive - Exit 69 to Exit 4 Spartanburg SC	2
Days Inn Spartanburg	864-814-0560	115 Rogers Commerce Blvd - Exit 75 Spartanburg SC	2
Motel 6 - Spartanburg	864-573-6383	105 Jones Road Spartanburg SC	1+

Greenville

Holiday Inn Express Hotel & Suites Greenville-Spartanburg(Duncan)	864-486-9191	Hwy 290 & I-85 - Exit 63 Duncan SC	2
Days Inn Easley	864-859-9902	121 Days Inn Drive - Exit 40 Easley SC	2
Best Western Greenville Airport Inn	864-297-5353	5009 Pelham Road - Exit 54 Greenville SC	3+
Comfort Inn Executive Center	864-271-0060	540 N Pleasantburg Drive - Exit I 385N Greenville SC	3+
Days Inn Greenville Conference Cntr	864-288-6900	2756 Laurens Rd - Exit 48b Greenville SC	2
Holiday Inn	864-277-8921	4295 Augusta Rd, I-85 Exit 46A - Exit 46A Greenville SC	3+
La Quinta Inn Greenville Woodruff Rd	864-297-3500	31 Old Country Rd. - Exit 51A/Woodruff Road Greenville SC	3+
MainStay Suites Pelham Road	864-987-5566	2671 Dry Pocket Road - Exit 54 Greenville SC	3+
Quality Inn and Suites	864-770-3737	1314 Pleasantburg Drive - Exit 46 Greenville SC	2
Residence Inn by Marriott	864-627-0001	120 Milestone Way - Exit 54/Pelham Road W Greenville SC	3+
Sleep Inn Palmetto Expo Center	864-240-2006	231 N Pleasantburg Drive - Exit 51 to I 385N Greenville SC	3+
Staybridge Suites Greenville/Spartanburg	864-288-4448	31 Market Point Drive - Exit 51C/Woodruff Road Greenville SC	3+
TownePlace Suites Greenville Haywood Mall	864-675-1670	75 Mall Connector Rd - Exit 51 Greenville SC	2
Holiday Inn Express Hotel and Suites	864-213-9331	2681 Dry Pocket Road - Exit 54 Greer SC	2

Anderson

Days Inn Anderson	864-375-0375	1007 Smith Mill Rd - Exit 19a Anderson SC	2
La Quinta Inn Anderson	864-225-3721	3430 Clemson Blvd. - Exit 19A Anderson SC	3+
MainStay Suites	864-226-1112	151 Civic Center Blvd - Exit 19A/H 76 E Anderson SC	2
Super 8 Anderson/Clemson Area	864-225-8384	3302 Cinema Ave - Exit 19a Anderson SC	2

Georgia Listings (Interstate 85)   Dogs per Room

Lavonia

Best Western Regency Inn & Suites	706-356-4000	13705 Jones Street - Exit 173 Lavonia GA	2
Super 8 Lavonia	706-356-8848	14227 Jones St - Exit 173 Lavonia GA	2

Commerce

Admiral Benbow Inn	706-335-5183	30747 Hwy 441 S. Commerce GA	1+
Comfort Inn	706-335-9001	165 Eisenhower Drive - Exit 149 Commerce GA	3+
Super 8 Commerce	706-336-8008	152 Eisenhower Dr - Exit 149 Commerce GA	2

Braselton

Best Western Braselton Inn	706-654-3081	303 Zion Church Rd - Exit 129 Braselton GA	2
Holiday Inn Express	770-867-8100	2069 Highway 211 - Exit 126 Braselton GA	3+

Suwanee

Best Western Gwinnett Inn	770-271-5559	77 Gwinco Boulevard - Exit 111 Suwanee GA	2
Comfort Inn	770-945-1608	2945 H 317 - Exit 111 Suwanee GA	2

Lawrenceville

Days Inn Lawrenceville	770-995-7782	731 Duluth Hwy - Exit 107 Lawrenceville GA	2

Atlanta

Airport Drury Inn & Suites	404-761-4900	1270 Virginia Avenue Atlanta GA	1+
Hilton	404-767-9000	255 Courtland Street NE - Exit 73/Virgina Avenue Atlanta GA	2
Holiday Inn - Airport North	404-762-8411	1380 Virginia Ave - Exit 73 or 73B/Virginia Avenue W Atlanta GA	2
Holiday Inn Atlanta Northeast Doraville	770-455-3700	2001 Clearview Ave. - Exit 32 Atlanta GA	3+
Residence Inn by Marriott	404-239-0677	2960 Piedmont Road NE - Exit 86 Atlanta GA	3+
Residence Inn by Marriott	404-467-1660	2220 Lake Blvd - Exit 89 Atlanta GA	2
Residence Inn by Marriott	404-872-8885	1041 W Peachtree Street - Exit Tenth Street Atlanta GA	2
Residence Inn by Marriott	404-745-1000	1365 Peachtree Street - Exit 10th/14th (#250) Atlanta GA	2
Staybridge Suites - Atlanta Buckhead	404-842-0800	540 Pharr Road NE - Exit H 400 Atlanta GA	2
Best Western Diplomat Inn	770-448-8686	6187 Dawson Boulevard - Exit 99/Jimmy Carter Blvd Norcross GA	3+
Days Inn Atlanta NE	770-368-0218	5990 Western Hills Dr - Exit 99 Norcross GA	2
Northeast Drury Inn & Suites	770-729-0060	5655 Jimmy Carter Blvd Norcross GA	1+

Atlanta Area

TownePlace Suites Atlanta Alpharetta	770-664-1300	7925 Westside Parkway - Exit 87 Alpharetta GA	2
Days Inn Atlanta Airport	404-767-1224	4505 Best Road - Exit 71 College Park GA	2
Days inn Atlanta West	404-669-8616	4979 Old National Hwy - Exit 69 College Park GA	2
Howard Johnson Express Inn	404-766-0000	2480 Old National Pkwy. College Park GA	1+
Candlewood Suites - Atlanta	678-380-0414	3665 Shackleford Road - Exit 104 Duluth GA	2
Days Inn Atlanta/Duluth	770-476-8700	1920 Pleasant Hill Rd - Exit 104 Duluth GA	2
Hampton Inn	770-931-9800	1725 Pineland Road - Exit 104/Pleasant Hill Road R Duluth GA	3+
Residence Inn by Marriott	404-761-0511	3401 International Blvd - Exit Virginia Avenue Hapeville GA	3+

Newnan

La Quinta Inn Newnan	770-502-8430	600 Bullsboro Drive - Exit 47 Newnan GA	3+
Motel 6 - Newnan	770-251-4580	40 Parkway North Newnan GA	1+
Super 8 Newnan	770-683-0089	1455 Hwy 29 South - Exit 41 Newnan GA	2

Hogansville

Garden Inn and Suites	706-637-5400	1630 Bass Cross Rd - Exit 28 Hogansville GA	2

Alabama Listings (Interstate 85)   Dogs per Room

Opelika

Motel 6 - Opelika	334-745-0988	1015 Columbus Parkway Opelika AL	1+

Auburn

Comfort Inn	334-821-6699	2283 S College Street - Exit 51 Auburn AL	3+

Shorter

Days Inn Shorter	334-727-6034	450 Main St - Exit 22 Shorter AL	2

Montgomery

Best Inns	334-270-9199	5135 Carmichael - Exit 6 Montgomery AL	3+
Best Western Monticello Inn	334-277-4442	5837 Monticello Dr - Exit 6 Montgomery AL	3+
Days Inn Montgomery Midtown	334-269-9611	2625 Zelda Rd - Ann Street Exit Montgomery AL	2
La Quinta Inn Montgomery	334-271-1620	1280 East Blvd. - Exit 6 Montgomery AL	3+
Residence Inn by Marriott	334-270-3300	1200 Himar Court - Exit 6 (East Blvd), Turn right on East Blvd to Carmichael Road, turn left Montgomery AL	1+
TownePlace Suites Montgomery	334-396-5505	5047 Carmichael Drive - Exit 6 Montgomery AL	2

Interstate 87 Accommodation Listings

New York Listings (Interstate 87)   Dogs per Room

Adirondacks

Comfort Inn	518-523-9555	2125 Saranac Avenue/H 86 - Exit H 9 Lake Placid NY	3+
Hilton	518-523-4411	One Mirror Lake Drive - Exit 30 Lake Placid NY	2
Best Western The Inn at Smithfield	518-561-7750	446 Route 3 - Exit 37 Plattsburgh NY	3+
Super 8 Plattsburgh	518-562-8888	7129 Route 9 North - Exit 39 Plattsburgh NY	2
Super 8 Queensbury/Glen Falls Area	518-761-9780	191 Corinth Rd - Exit 18 Queensbury NY	2

Saratoga

Super 8 Saratoga Springs	518-587-6244	17 Old Gick Rd - Exit 15 Saratoga Springs NY	2
Union Gables	518-584-1558	55 Union Avenue - Exit 14 Saratoga Springs NY	3+

Albany

Comfort Inn and Suites	518-869-5327	1606 Central Avenue - Exit 2/Northway Albany NY	2
Quality Inn	518-785-5891	611 Troy-Schenectady RoadH 7 - Exit 6/H 7 W Latham NY	2

Hudson Valley

Quality Inn and Conference Center	518-943-5800	704 H 23 - Exit 21 Catskill NY	2
Holiday Inn	845-338-0400	503 Washington Ave - Exit 19 Kingston NY	3+

Audrey's Farmhouse	845-895-3440	2188 Brunswyck Road - Exit 18 Wallkill NY	3+
Best Western New Baltimore Inn	518-731-8100	12600 Route 9 W - Exit 21B West Coxsackie NY	3+
New York Area North			
Days Inn Nanuet	845-623-4567	367 Rte 59 - Exit 14 Nanuet NY	2
Holiday Inn Suffern	845-357-4800	#3 Executive Blvd - Exit 14B Suffern NY	2

Interstate 90 Accommodation Listings
(From Chicago to Cleveland see Highway 80 Listings)

Ohio Listings (Interstate 90) Dogs per Room

Cleveland			
Residence Inn by Marriott	216-443-9043	527 Prospect Avenue - Exit E 9th Street Cleveland OH	3+
Residence Inn by Marriott	440-892-2254	30100 Clemens Road - Exit 156/Crocker Drive Cleveland OH	3+
Holiday Inn	440-324-5411	1825 Lorain Blvd - Exit 145A to Rt 57S Elyria OH	3+
Days Inn Cleveland/Lakewood	216-226-4800	12019 Lake Ave - Exit /west 117St Lakewood OH	2
Best Western Lawnfield Inn & Suites	440-205-7378	8434 Mentor Avenue - Exit 195/H 615 (Center Street) Mentor OH	3+
Super 8 Mentor/Cleveland Area	440-951-8558	7325 Palisades Parkway - Exit 193 Mentor OH	2
Holiday Inn Cleveland-West (Westlake)	440-871-6000	1100 Crocker Rd - Exit 156 Westlake OH	3+
TownePlace Suites Cleveland Westlake	440-892-4275	25052 Sperry Drive - Exit 159 Westlake OH	2
Conneaut			
Days Inn Conneaut	440-593-6000	600 Days Blvd - Exit 241 Conneaut OH	2

Pennsylvania Listings (Interstate 90) Dogs per Room

Erie			
Best Western Erie Inn and Suites	814-864-1812	7820 Perry Highway - Exit 27 Erie PA	3+
Days Inn Erie	814-868-8521	7415 Schultz Rd - Exit 27 Erie PA	2
Residence Inn by Marriott	814-864-2500	8061 Peach Street - Exit 24S Erie PA	3+
Super 8 Erie/I-90	814-864-9200	8040 Perry Hwy - Exit 27 Erie PA	2

New York Listings (Interstate 90) Dogs per Room

Dunkirk			
Best Western Dunkirk and Fredonia	716-366-7100	3912 Vineyard Dr - Exit 59 Dunkirk NY	3+
Comfort Inn	716-672-4450	3925 Vineyard Drive - Exit 59 Dunkirk/Fredonia Dunkirk NY	2
Fredonia			
Brookside Manor	716-672-7721	3728 Route 83 - Exit H 60 Fredonia NY	3+
Buffalo			
Comfort Inn University	716-688-0811	1 Flint Road - Exit I 290 Amherst NY	2
Clarion Hotel	716-648-5700	S-3950 McKinley Parkway - Exit 56 Blasdell NY	1
Residence Inn by Marriott	716-892-5410	107 Anderson Road - Exit 52/W Waldon Avenue Buffalo NY	2
Asa Ransom House	716-759-2315	10529 Main Street - Exit 48A or 49 Clarence NY	2
Comfort Inn and Suites	716-648-2922	3615 Commerce Place - Exit 57/H 75S-Camp Road Hamburg NY	3+
Holiday Inn	716-649-0500	5440 Camp Road (NY 75) - Exit 57 Hamburg NY	3+
Super 8 Kenmore/Buffalo/Niagara Falls Area	716-876-4020	1288 Sheridan Drive - Exit 53 Kenmore NY	2
Residence Inn by Marriott	716-623-6622	100 Maple Road - Exit 50/290W Williamsville NY	3+
Batavia			
Comfort Inn	585-344-9999	4371 Federal Drive - Exit 48 (after Toll-H 98 N) Batavia NY	3+
Days Inn Batavia	585-343-6000	200 Oak St - Exit 48 Batavia NY	2
Quality Inn and Suites	585-344-7000	8200 Park Road - Exit 48 Batavia NY	3+
Rochester			
Comfort Inn West	585-621-5700	1501 W Ridge Road - Exit I 390N Rochester NY	3+
Comfort Suites	585-334-6620	2085 Hylan Drive - Exit H 390N Rochester NY	2
Syracuse			
Days Inn Auburn	315-252-7567	37 William Street - Exit 40 Auburn NY	2
Super 8 Auburn/Finger Lakes Area	315-253-8886	19 McMaster St - Exit 40 Auburn NY	2
Holiday Inn	315-437-2761	6555 Old Collamer Rd South - Exit 35 East Syracuse NY	2
BN on 7th North	315-451-1511	400 7th North St - Exit 36 Liverpool NY	2
Doubletree	315-457-4000	6701 Buckley Road - Exit 36/Buckley N Syracuse NY	2
Candlewood Suites	315-432-1684	6550 Baptist Way - Exit 35 Syracuse NY	3+
Comfort Inn	315-437-0222	6491 Thompson Road - Exit 35 to Thompson Road S Syracuse NY	3+
Comfort Inn Fairgrounds	315-453-0045	7010 Interstate Island Road - Exit 39/I 690 Syracuse NY	3+
Holiday Inn	315-457-8700	100 Farrell Rd Syracuse NY	3+

Utica

Best Western Gateway Adirondack Inn	315-732-4121	175 N Genesee St - Exit 31 Utica NY	3+
Super 8 Utica	315-797-0964	309 N Genesee St - Exit 31 Utica NY	2

Little Falls

Best Western Little Falls Motor Inn	315-823-4954	20 Albany St - Exit 29A Little Falls NY	3+

Schenectady

Super 8 Schenectady/Albany Area	518-355-2190	3083 Carman Rd - Exit 25 Schenectady NY	2

Albany

Best Western Sovereign Hotel - Albany	518-489-2981	1228 Western Avenue - Exit 24 Albany NY	3+
Comfort Inn and Suites	518-869-5327	1606 Central Avenue - Exit 24/I 87 Albany NY	2
Cresthill Suites Hotel	518-454-0007	1415 Washington Avenue - Exit 2/Washington Avenue Albany NY	3+
TownePlace Suites Albany SUNY	518-435-1900	1379 Washington Avenue - Exit 2 Albany NY	2

Massachusetts Listings (Interstate 90)   Dogs per Room

Springfield

Quality Inn	413-592-6171	463 Memorial Drive - Exit 5 Chicopee MA	3+
Quality Inn	413-739-7261	1150 Riverdale Street - Exit 4 to H 5S West Springfield MA	2

Sturbridge

Vienna Restaurant and Historic Inn	508-764-0700	14 South Street Southbridge MA	1
Comfort Inn and Suites Colonial	508-347-3306	215 Charlton Road - Exit 9 to Exit 3A Sturbridge MA	3+
Days Inn Sturbridge	508-347-3391	66-68 Haynes St Sturbridge MA	2
Publick House Historic Inn	508-347-3313	On the Common, Route 131 Sturbridge MA	1+
Sturbridge Host Hotel	508-347-7393	366 Main Street Sturbridge MA	3+
Super 8 Sturbridge	508-347-9000	358 Main Street Sturbridge MA	3+

Worcester

Comfort Inn	508-832-8300	426 Southbridge Street - Exit 10 to H 12N Auburn MA	2
Comfort Inn	508-366-0202	399 Turnpike Road - Exit 11A/I 495N Westborough MA	3+

Boston Area

Best Western Historic Concord	978-369-6100	740 Elm St - Exit 495N to RT 2E Concord MA	3+

Boston

Doubletree	617-783-0090	400 Soldiers Field Road - Exit 18 Boston MA	3+
Hilton	617-568-6700	85 Terminal Road - Exit 24 toward Logan Airport Boston MA	2
Nine Zero Hotel	617-772-5800	90 Tremont Street - Exit 22 Boston MA	3+
Taj Boston	617-536-5700	15 Arlington Street - Exit Storrow Drive Boston MA	2

Interstate 91 Accommodation Listings

Vermont Listings (Interstate 91)   Dogs per Room

Newport

Lady Pearl's Inn and Lodging	802-334-6748	1724 E Main Street Newport VT	3+

St Johnsbury

Inn at Maplemont	802-633-4880	2742 H 5S Barnet VT	3+
Aime's Motel	802-748-3194	RR 1, Box 332 St Johnsbury VT	1+
Fairbanks Inn	802-748-5666	401 Western Avenue St Johnsbury VT	1+

Springfield

Holiday Inn Express Springfield	802-885-4516	818 Charlestown Road Springfield VT	1

Bellows Falls

Everyday Inn	802-463-4536	593 Rockingham Road Bellows Falls VT	2

Massachusetts Listings (Interstate 91)   Dogs per Room

Springfield

Motel 6 - Springfield - Chicopee	413-592-5141	36 Johnny Cake Hollow Rd. Chicopee MA	1+
Park Inn	413-739-7311	450 Memorial Drive Chicopee MA	1+
Quality Inn	413-592-6171	463 Memorial Drive Chicopee MA	3+
Holiday Inn	413-781-0900	711 Dwight St Springfield MA	3+
Sheraton Springfield Monarch Place Hotel	413-781-1010	One Monarch Place Springfield MA	1+
Candlewood Suites West Springfield	413-739-1122	572 Riverdale St. West Springfield MA	2
Hampton Inn	413-732-1300	1011 Riverdale Street West Springfield MA	3+
Quality Inn	413-739-7261	1150 Riverdale Street West Springfield MA	2
Red Roof Inn - West Springfield	413-731-1010	1254 Riverdale Street West Springfield MA	1+
Residence Inn by Marriott	413-732-9543	64 Border Way West Springfield MA	3+

Interstate 95 Accommodation Listings

Maine Listings (Interstate 95)   Dogs per Room

Medway			
Gateway Inn	207-746-3193	Route 157 - Exit 244 Medway ME	3+
Bangor			
Best Western White House Inn	207-862-3737	155 Littlefield Ave - Exit 44 Bangor ME	3+
Comfort Inn	207-942-7899	750 Hogan Road - Exit Hogan Road Bangor ME	3+
The Phenix Inn	207-947-0411	20 Broad Street Bangor ME	1+
Best Western Black Bear Inn and Conf Cntr	207-866-7120	4 Godfrey Dr - Exit 193 Orono ME	3+
Waterville			
Holiday Inn	207-873-0111	375 Main Street - Exit 130 Waterville ME	3+
Belfast			
Comfort Inn Ocean's Edge	207-338-2090	159 Searsport Avenue/H 1 - Exit 113 Belfast ME	2
Augusta			
Augusta Hotel and Suites	207-622-6371	390 Western Avenue Augusta ME	1+
Best Western Senator Inn and Spa	207-622-5804	284 Western Ave @Turnpike 95 - Exit 109 Augusta ME	3+
Comfort Inn Civic Center	207-623-1000	281 Civic Center Drive - Exit 112/H 27N Augusta ME	3+
Holiday Inn	207-622-4751	110 Community Drive - Exit 112A Augusta ME	3+
Freeport Area			
Best Western Freeport Inn	207-865-3106	31 US Rt 1 - Exit 17 Freeport ME	3+
Harraseeket Inn	207-865-9377	162 Main Street - Exit 22 Freeport ME	2
Portland			
Holiday Inn	207-774-5601	81 Riverside St - Exit 48 Portland ME	2
Howard Johnson Plaza Hotel	207-774-5861	155 Riverside Portland ME	1+
The Inn at St John	207-773-6481	939 Congress Street - Exit H 295N Portland ME	2
Residence Inn by Marriott	207-883-0400	800 Roundwood Drive - Exit 6 Scarborough ME	3+
TownePlace Suites Portland Scarborough	207-883-6800	700 Roundwood Drive - Exit 6 Scarborough ME	2
Best Western Merry Manor Inn	207-774-6151	700 Main St - Exit 45 South Portland ME	3+
Comfort Inn Airport	207-775-0409	90 Maine Mall Road - Exit 46 South Portland ME	3+
Holiday Inn Express Hotel & Suites South Portland	207-775-3900	303 Sable Oaks Drive - Exit 46 South Portland ME	3+
Howard Johnson Hotel	207-775-5343	675 Main St. South Portland ME	1+
Portland Marriott at Sable Oaks	207-871-8000	200 Sable Oaks Drive - Exit 7 South Portland ME	3+
Old Orchard Beach			
Hampton Inn	207-282- 7222	48 Industrial Park Road - Exit 36 Saco ME	3+
Kennebunk			
Arundel Meadows Inn	207-985-3770	1024 Portland Road Arundel ME	2
The Hounds Tooth Inn	207-985-0117	82 Summer Street Kennebunk ME	3+
Captain Jefferds Inn	207-967-2311	5 Pearl Street Kennebunkport ME	1+
Lodge At Turbat's Creek	207-967-8700	Turbats Creek Rd at Ocean Avenue Kennebunkport ME	1+
The Colony Hotel	207-967-3331	140 Ocean Avenue - Exit 25/Bidderford Kennebunkport ME	3+
The Yachtsman Lodge and Marina	207-967-2511	Ocean Avenue - Exit 19 Kennebunkport ME	2
York			
Enchanted Nights	207-439-1489	29 Wentworth Street - Exit 2 Kittery ME	3+

New Hampshire Listings (Interstate 95)   Dogs per Room

Portsmouth			
Meadowbrook Inn	603-436-2700	Portsmouth Traffic Circle - Exit H 1 Portsmouth NH	2

Massachusetts Listings (Interstate 95)   Dogs per Room

Boston Area			
Staybridge Suites	781-221-2233	11 Old Concord Rd - Exit 32B Burlington MA	2
Staybridge Suites	781-221-2233	11 Old Concord Road - Exit 32B Burlington MA	3+
TownePlace Suites Boston North Shore/Danvers	978-777-6222	238 Andover Street - Exit 44b Danvers MA	2
Quality Inn and Suites	781-861-0850	440 Bedford Street - Exit 31B Lexington MA	2
Holiday Inn Mansfield-Foxboro Area	508-339-2200	31 Hampshire Street - Exit 7A Mansfield MA	3+
Holiday Inn Hotel & Suites Boston-Peabody	978-535-4600	Us 1 North & Us 128 North - Exit 44A Peabody MA	3+
Homestead Village	781-890-1333	52 Fourth Ave Waltham MA	1+
Holiday Inn Select Boston-Woburn	781-935-8760	15 Middlesex Canal Park Road - Exit 35 Woburn MA	2

Highway Guides - Please always call ahead to make sure that an establishment is still dog-friendly

Providence Area

Motel 6 - Providence - Seekonk	508-336-7800	821 Fall River Avenue Seekonk MA	1+

Rhode Island Listings (Interstate 95)

Dogs per Room

Providence

Providence Marriott Downtown	401-272-2400	One Orms Street - Exit 23 Providence RI	1
Crowne Plaza	401-732-6000	801 Greenwich Ave - Exit 12 Warwick RI	3+
Hampton Inn	401-739-8888	2100 Post Road - Exit 13/TF Green Airport Warwick RI	3+
Holiday Inn Express & Suites	401-736-5000	901 Jefferson Blvd - Exit Airport Road Warwick RI	3+
Residence Inn by Marriott	401-737-7100	500 Kilvert Street - Exit 13 Warwick RI	1+

Southern Rhode Island

The Kings' Rose	401-783-5222	1747 Mooresfield Road - Exit H 138 South Kingston RI	2

Connecticut Listings (Interstate 95)

Dogs per Room

Stonington

High Acres	860-887-4355	222 NW Corner Road North Stonington CT	2

New London - Mystic

Abbey's Lantern Hill Inn	860-572-0483	780 Lantern Hill Road - Exit 92/H 2 Ledyard CT	2
Residence Inn by Marriott	860-536-5150	40 Whitehall Avenue - Exit 90 Mystic CT	3+

Old Lyme - Connecticut River

Copper Beach Inn	860-767-0330	46 Main Street - Exit H 9N Ivoryton CT	2
Old Lyme Inn	860-434-2600	85 Lyme Street - Exit 70 Old Lyme CT	2

New Haven

Premiere Hotel and Suites	203-777-5337	3 Long Wharf Drive - Exit 46 New Haven CT	3+
Residence Inn by Marriott	203-926-9000	1001 Bridgeport Avenue - Exit 27-A N to Exit 11 Shelton CT	3+

Bridgeport

Holiday Inn	203-334-1234	1070 Main Street - Exit 27A Bridgeport CT	2
Residence Inn by Marriott	203-283-2100	62 Rowe Ave - Exit 35 Milford CT	3+

Stamford

Delmar Greenwich Harbor Hotel	203-661-9800	500 Steamboat Road - Exit 3 Greenwich CT	2
Sheraton Stamford Hotel	203-359-1300	2701 Summer Street Stamford CT	1+
Stamford Marriott Hotel and Spa	203-357-9555	Two Stamford Forum - Exit 8 Stamford CT	3+

New York Listings (Interstate 95)

Dogs per Room

New York Area North

Residence Inn by Marriott	914-636-7888	35 Le Count Place - Exit 16 New Rochelle NY	3+

New Jersey Listings (Interstate 95)

Dogs per Room

Newark - NYC Area

Residence Inn by Marriott	908-352-4300	83 Glimcher Realty Way - Exit Jersey Gardens Blvd W Elizabeth NJ	3+
Candlewood Suites Jersey City	201-659-2500	21 Second Street - Exit 14C Jersey City NJ	1

New Brunswick

Somerset Hills Hotel	908-647-6700	200 Liberty Corner Road Bridgewater NJ	2
Motel 6 - East Brunswick	732-390-4545	244 Route 18 East Brunswick NJ	1+
Studio 6 - East Brunswick	732-238-3330	246 Rt 18 East Brunswick NJ	1+
Red Roof Inn - Edison	732-248-9300	860 New Durham Road Edison NJ	1+
Sheraton Edison Hotel Raritan Center	732-225-8300	125 Raritan Center Parkway Edison NJ	1+
Sheraton Woodbridge Place Hotel	732-634-3600	515 US Highway 1S Iselin NJ	1+
Embassy Suites Hotel Piscataway - Somerset	732-980-0500	121Centennial Avenue Piscataway NJ	1+
Motel 6 - Piscataway	732-981-9200	1012 Stelton Road Piscataway NJ	1+
Candlewood Suites Somerset	732-748-1400	41 Worlds Fair Drive Somerset NJ	3+
Holiday Inn	732-356-1700	195 Davidson Ave Somerset NJ	3+
Qualilty Inn	732-469-5050	1850 Easton Avenue Somerset NJ	1
Residence Inn by Marriott	732-627-0881	37 Worlds Fair Drive Somerset NJ	3+
Staybridge Suites	732-356-8000	260 Davidson Ave Somerset NJ	1

Princeton

Staybridge Suites	609-409-7181	1272 South River Road - Exit 8A Cranbury NJ	3+
Clarion Hotel Palmer Inn	609-452-2500	3499 Route 1 S - Exit 67/H 1 N Princeton NJ	2

Camden Area

Clarion Hotel and Conference Center	856-428-2300	H 70 and I 295 - Exit 34B/H 70W Cherry Hill NJ	2
Best Western Burlington Inn	609-261-3800	2020 Rt 541, RD 1 - Exit 5 Mount Holly NJ	3+
Staybridge Suites Philadelphia-Mt. Laurel	856-722-1900	4115 Church Road - Exit 4 Mount Laurel NJ	2

Highway Guides - Please always call ahead to make sure that an establishment is still dog-friendly

TownePlace Suites Mt Laurel	856-778-8221	450 Century Parkway - Exit 4 Mount Laurel NJ	2

Delaware Bridge Area

Holiday Inn Express Hotel and Suites	856-351-9222	506 Pennsville-Auburn Rd - Exit 2B Carneys Point NJ	3+
Wellesley Inn & Suites Carneys Point	856-299-3800	517 S. Pennsville-Auburn Road - Exit 2B Penns Grove NJ	3+

Delaware Listings (Interstate 95)

Dogs per Room

Wilmington

Quality Inn Skyways	302-328-6666	147 N Dupont H - Exit 5A New Castle DE	3+
Best Western Brandywine Valley Inn	302-656-9436	1807 Concord Pike - Exit 8 Wilmington DE	3+
Days Inn Wilmington	302-478-0300	5209 Concord Pike - Exit 8 Wilmington DE	2

Newark

Days Inn Newark	302-368-2400	900 Churchmans Rd - Exit 4b Newark DE	2
Howard Johnson Inn	302-368-8521	1119 South College Avenue Newark DE	1+
Quality Inn University	302-368-8715	1120 S College Avenue - Exit H 896 Newark DE	2
Residence Inn by Marriott	302-453-9200	240 Chapman Road - Exit 3 Newark DE	3+

Maryland Listings (Interstate 95)

Dogs per Room

North East

Knights Inn	410-392-6680	262 Belle Hill Rd Elkton MD	1+
Motel 6 - Elkton	410-392-5020	223 Belle Hill Road Elkton MD	1+

Aberdeen - Havre de Grace

Four Points Hotels by Sheraton	410-273-6300	980 Hospitality Way Aberdeen MD	1+
Best Western Invitation Inn	410-679-9700	1709 Edgewood Rd - Exit 77A Edgewood MD	2
Super 8 Havre de Grace	410-939-1880	929 Pulaski Hwy - Exit 89 Havre De Grace MD	2

Baltimore

Residence Inn by Marriott	410-933-9554	4980 Mercantile Road - Exit 67B Baltimore MD	3+

BWI Airport Area

TownePlace Suites Baltimore Fort Meade	301-498-7477	120 National Business Pkwy - National Business Pkwy Exit Annapolis Junction MD	2
Residence Inn by Marriott	410-799-7332	7035 Arundel Mills Circle - Exit H 100E to Exit 10A Hanover MD	1
Candlewood Suites Linthicum	410-850-9214	1247 Winterson Rd. - Exit H 295 Linthicum MD	2
Holiday Inn	410-859-8400	890 Elkridge Landing Road - Exit W Nursery Road Linthicum MD	3+
Staybridge Suites Baltimore BWI	410-850-5666	1301 Winterson Road - Exit W Nursery Road Linthicum MD	3+
Comfort Suites BWI Airport	410-691-1000	815 Elkridge Landing Road - Exit 195E Linthicum Heights MD	3+
Homestead Hotel - BWI	410-691-2500	939 International Drive Linthicum Heights MD	1+

Washington Suburbs

Days Inn Andrews AFB	301-423-2323	5001 Mercedes Blvd - Exit 7b Camp Springs MD	2

Virginia Listings (Interstate 95)

Dogs per Room

Northern Virginia

Comfort Inn Gunston Corner	703-643-3100	8180 Silverbrook Road - Exit 163 Lorton VA	3+
Comfort Inn	703-922-9000	6560 Loisdale Court - Exit 169A Springfield VA	2
Hampton Inn	703-924-9444	6550 Loisdale Court - Exit 169A Springfield VA	3+
Quality Inn	703-494-0300	1109 Hormer Road - Exit 160/Woodbridge Woodbridge VA	3+
Residence Inn by Marriott	703-490-4020	14301 Crossing Place - Exit 158B/Prince William County Parkway Woodbridge VA	3+

Fredericksburg

Best Western Fredericksburg	540-371-5050	2205 William St - Exit 130A Fredericksburg VA	3+
Days Inn Fredericksburg North	540-373-5340	14 Simpson Rd - Exit 133 Fredericksburg VA	2
Days Inn Fredericksburg South	540-898-6800	5316 Jefferson Davis Hwy - Exit 126 Fredericksburg VA	2
Holiday Inn	540-371-5550	564 Warrenton Rd - Exit 133/Warrington Fredericksburg VA	3+
Quality Inn	540-373-0000	543 Warrenton Road - Exit 133/H 17 N Fredericksburg VA	3+
TownePlace Suites Fredericksburg	540-891-0775	4700 Market Street - Exit 126 Fredericksburg VA	2
Holiday Inn Express	540-657-5566	28 Greenspring Drive - Exit 143B Stafford VA	2
Quality Inn	540-582-1097	6409 Danbell Lane - Exit 118/Thornburg Thornburg VA	3+

Ashland

Days Inn Ashland	804-798-4262	806 England St - Exit 92 or 92b Ashland VA	2
Quality Inn and Suites	804-798-4231	810 England Street - Exit 92/H 54W Ashland VA	2
Days Inn Carmel Church	804-448-2011	24320 Rogers Clark Blvd - Exit 104 Carmel Church VA	2
Best Western Kings Quarters	804-876-3321	16102 Theme Park Way - Exit 98 Doswell VA	3+
Howard Johnson Express Inn	804-448-2499	23786 Rogers Clark Blvd. Ruther Glen VA	1+
Red Roof Inn - Ruther Glen - Carmel Church	804-448-2828	23500 Welcome Way Drive Ruther Glen VA	1+

Richmond

Highway Guides - Please always call ahead to make sure that an establishment is still dog-friendly

Days Inn Chester	804-748-5871	2410 W Hundred Rd - Exit 61b Chester VA	2
Candlewood Suites	804-271-0016	4301 Commerce Road - Exit 69 Richmond VA	3+
Days Inn Richmond	804-745-7100	6910 Midlothian Turnpike - Exit 67 Richmond VA	2
Quality Inn West End	804-346-0000	8008 W Broad Street - Exit 79/I 64W Richmond VA	1
Super 8 Richmond/Midlothian Tnpk	804-320-2823	8260 Midlothian Turnpike - Exit 67b Richmond VA	2
Petersburg			
Days Inn Petersburg/Walthall	804-520-1010	2310 Indian Hill Rd - Exit 58 or 58b Colonial Heights VA	2
Days Inn Petersburg/Fort Lee South	804-733-4400	12208 S Crater Rd - Exit 45 Petersburg VA	2
Quality Inn	804-732-2900	11974 S Crater Road - Exit 45 Petersburg VA	3+
Hampton Inn	434-246-5500	10476 Blue Star H - Exit 33 Stony Creek VA	2
Sleep Inn	434-246-5100	11019 Blue Star H - Exit 33 Stony Creek VA	2
Emporia			
Best Western Emporia	434-634-3200	1100 West Atlantic ST - Exit 11B Emporia VA	3+
Comfort Inn	434-348-3282	1411 Skippers Road - Exit 8/H 301 Emporia VA	3+
Hampton Inn	434-634-9200	1207 W Atlantic Street - Exit 11B Emporia VA	3+

North Carolina Listings (Interstate 95)   Dogs per Room

Weldon			
Motel 6 - Roanoke Rapids	252-537-5252	1911 Julian Alsbrook Highway Roanoke Rapids NC	1+
Days Inn Weldon	252-536-4867	1611 Roanoke Rapids Rd - Exit 173 Weldon NC	2
Rocky Mount			
Howard Johnson Inn	252-977-9595	7568 NC 48 Battleboro NC	1+
Best Western Inn I-95/Gold Rock	252-985-1450	7095 Rte 4 - Exit 145 Rocky Mount NC	3+
Comfort Inn	252-937-7765	200 Gateway Blvd - Exit 138/H64E Rocky Mount NC	2
Comfort Inn North	252-972-9426	7048 H 4 - Exit 145/H 4 Rocky Mount NC	2
Super 8 Rocky Mount/Mosley Court	252-977-2858	307 Mosley Court - Exit 138 Rocky Mount NC	2
Wilson			
Best Western La Sammana	252-237-8700	817-A Ward Blvd - Exit 121 Wilson NC	3+
Holiday Inn Express Hotel and Suites	252-246-1588	2308 Montgomery Dr Wilson NC	2
Kenly			
Days Inn Kenly	919-284-3400	1139 Johnston Pkwy - Kenly Exit Kenly NC	2
Benson			
Days Inn Benson	919-894-2031	202 N Honeycutt St - Exit 79s Benson NC	2
Fayetteville			
Best Western Fayetteville-Ft Bragg	910-485-0520	2910 Sigman St - Exit 46B Fayetteville NC	3+
Comfort Inn	910-323-8333	1957 Cedar Creek Road - Exit 49 Fayetteville NC	3+
Comfort Inn Cross Creek	910-867-1777	1922 Skibo Road Fayetteville NC	2
Days Inn Fayetteville East of Ft Bragg	910-483-0431	333 Person St - Exit 56 or 40 Fayetteville NC	2
Holiday Inn	910-323-1600	1944 Cedar Creek Rd - Exit 49 Fayetteville NC	3+
Motel 6 - Fayetteville	910-485-8122	2076 Cedar Creek Road Fayetteville NC	1+
Red Roof Inn - Fayetteville, NC	910-321-1460	1569 Jim Johnson Road Fayetteville NC	1+
Days Inn Raeford	910-904-1050	115 Fayetteville Rd/115 US 401 Byp Raeford NC	2
Holiday Inn Express Hotel and Suites	910-436-1900	103 Brook Lane Spring Lake NC	2
Days Inn Fayetteville North	910-323-1255	3945 Goldsboro Hwy - Exit 58 or 61 Wade NC	2
Lumberton			
Best Western Inn at Lumberton	910-618-9799	201 Jackson Ct - Exit 22 Lumberton NC	3+
Days Inn Lumberton Outlet Mall	910-738-6401	3030 N Roberts Ave - Exit 20 Lumberton NC	2
Quality Inn and Suites	910-738-8261	3608 Kahn Drive - Exit 20 Lumberton NC	3+
Super 8 Lumberton	910-671-4444	150 Jackson Court - Exit 22 Lumberton NC	2
Rowland			
Days Inn Rowland	910-422-3366	14723 US Hwy 301 - Exit 1 Rowland NC	2

South Carolina Listings (Interstate 95)   Dogs per Room

Dillon			
Best Value Inn	843-774-5111	904 Redford Blvd Dillon SC	1+
Deluxe Inn	843-774-6041	818 Radford Blvd - Exit 193 Dillon SC	2
Super 8 Dillon	843-774-4161	1203 Radford Blvd - Exit 193 Dillon SC	2
Florence			
Comfort Inn	843-665-4558	1916 W Lucas Street - Exit 164 Florence SC	3+
Days Inn Florence North/I-95	843-665-4444	2111 W Lucas St - Exit 164 Florence SC	2
Days Inn Florence South/I-95	843-665-8550	3783 W Palmetto St - Exit 157 Florence SC	2
Econo Lodge	843-665-8558	1811 W Lucas St Florence SC	1+
Holiday Inn Hotel & Suites Florence	843-665-4555	1819 Lucas St - Exit 164 Florence SC Sc @ I-95 & Us Hwy 52	3+
Thunderbird Motor Inn	843-669-1611	2004 W Lucas St Florence SC	1+
Young's Plantation Inn	843-669-4171	US 76 and I-95 Florence SC	1+

Highway Guides - Please always call ahead to make sure that an establishment is still dog-friendly

Turbeville
Days Inn Lake City	843-394-3269	170 S Ron McNair Blvd - Hwy 52 Exit Lake City SC	2
Days Inn Turbeville	843-659-8060	378 Mydher Beach Hwy - Exit 135 Turbeville SC	2

Manning
Best Western Palmetto Inn	803-473-4021	2825 Paxville Hwy - Exit 119 Manning SC	2
Comfort Inn	803-473-7550	3031 Paxville H - Exit 119 Manning SC	2

Santee
Days Inn Santee	803-854-2175	9074 Old Hwy 6 - Exit 96 Santee SC	2
Howard Johnson Express Inn	803-478-7676	I-95 Ex 102, Rd 400 Santee SC	1+

Walterboro
Best Western Walterboro	843-538-3600	1428 Sniders Highway - Exit 53 Walterboro SC	3+
Econo Lodge	843-538-3830	1145 Sniders Hwy Walterboro SC	1+
Rice Planters Inn	843-538-8964	I-95 and SR 63 Walterboro SC	1+
Super 8 Walterboro	843-538-5383	1972 Bells Hwy - Exit 57 Walterboro SC	2

Yemassee
Days Inn Point South/Yemassee	843-726-8156	3196 Point South Dr - Exit 33 Yemassee SC	2
Holiday Inn Express	843-726-9400	40 Frampton Drive Yemassee SC	3+
Super 8 Yemassee	843-589-2177	409 Yemassee Hwy - Exit 38 Yemassee SC	2

Ridgeland
Comfort Inn	843-726-2121	200 James F Taylor Blvd - Exit 21/H 336 Ridgeland SC	3+
Days Inn Ridgeland	843-726-5553	516 East Main Street - Exit 21 Ridgeland SC	2

Hardeeville
Comfort Inn	843-784-2188	Box 544 - Exit 5 Hardeeville SC	3+
Days Inn Hardeeville	843-784-2281	US Highway 17 & I 95 - Exit 5 Hardeeville SC	2
Quality Inn and Suites	843-784-7060	19000 Whyte Hardee Blvd - Exit 5/H 17N Hardeeville SC	3+
Sleep Inn	843-784-7181	I 95 & H 17 - Exit 5/H 17 Hardeeville SC	1+

Georgia Listings (Interstate 95)   Dogs per Room

Rincon
Days Inn Rincon	912-826-6966	582 Columbia Ave - Exit 109 Rincon GA	2

Savannah
Econo Lodge	912-748-4124	500 E. US 80 Pooler GA	1+
Quality Inn	912-748-6464	301 Govenor Treutlen Drive - Exit 102 Pooler GA	2
Days Inn Savannah/Richmond Hill	912-756-3371	3926 HIGHWAY 17 - Exit 87 Richmond Hill GA	2
La Quinta Inn Savannah I-95	912-925-9505	6 Gateway Blvd. South - Exit 94 Savannah GA	3+
Quality Inn	912-925-2770	3 Gateway Blvd - Exit 94 Savannah GA	2
Residence Inn by Marriott	912-356-3266	5710 White Bluff Road - Exit 94 ,go R 10 miles Savannah GA	2
Staybridge Suites Savannah Airport	912-965-1551	One Clyde E. Martin Dr. - Exit 104 Savannah GA	2
TownePlace Suites Savannah Midtown	912-920-9080	11309 Abercom Street - Exit 94 Savannah GA	2

Townsend
Days Inn Townsend	912-832-4411	RR 4 Box 3130M - Exit 58 Townsend GA	2

Darien
Comfort Inn	912-437-4200	703 Frontage Road - Exit 49 Darien GA	3+
Super 8 Darien/I-95	912-437-6660	Highway 251 & I 95 - Exit 49 Darien GA	2

Brunswick
Embassy Suites Hotel	912-264-6100	500 Mall Blvd Brunswick GA	1+
La Quinta Inn & Suites Brunswick	912-265-7725	165 Warren Mason Blvd - Exit 36A Brunswick GA	2
Super 8 Brunswick/St Simons Island Area	912-264-8800	5280 New Jesup Hwy - Exit 36b Brunswick GA	2

Jekyll Island
Buccaneer Beach Resort	912-635-2261	85 S. Beachview Dr. Jekyll Island GA	1+
Quality Inn and Suites	912-635-2202	700 N Beachview Drive - Exit 29/H 17N Jekyll Island GA	2

St Marys
Best Western Kings Bay Inn	912-729-7666	1353 Hwy 40 East - Exit 3 Kingsland GA	3+
Comfort Inn	912-729-6979	111 Edenfield Road - Exit 3 Kingsland GA	3+
Super 8 Kingsland/Kings Bay Area	912-729-6888	120 Edenfield Dr - Exit 3 Kingsland GA	2

Florida Listings (Interstate 95)   Dogs per Room

Jacksonville
Candlewood Suites	904-296-7785	4990 Belfort Road - Exit 344/John Butler Blvd Jacksonville FL	3+
Hampton Inn	904-741-4980	1170 Airport Entrance Road - Exit 363 Jacksonville FL	3+
Homewood Suites	904-733-9299	8737 Baymeadows Rd Jacksonville FL	1+
La Quinta Inn Jacksonville Airport N	904-751-6960	812 Dunn Ave. - Exit 360 Jacksonville FL	3+
La Quinta Inn Jacksonville Baymeadows	904-731-9940	8255 Dix Ellis Trail - Exit Bay Meadows Road Jacksonville FL	3+
Residence Inn by Marriott	904-741-6550	1310 Airport Road - Exit 363 Jacksonville FL	3+
Residence Inn by Marriott	904-733-8088	8365 Dix Ellis Trail - Exit Baymeadows Road W Jacksonville FL	3+

Comfort Inn	904-644-4444	341 Park Avenue - Exit 10 Orange Park FL	3+
St Augustine			
Best Western St Augustine I-95	904-829-1999	2445 SR 16 - Exit 318 St Augustine FL	2
Days Inn St Augustine/Outlet Center	904-824-4341	2560 SR 16 - Exit 95 St Augustine FL	2
Howard Johnson Express Inn	904-824-6181	137 San Marco Ave. St Augustine FL	1+
Inn at Camachee Harbor	904-825-0003	201 Yacht Club Dr. St Augustine FL	1+
Ocean Blue Motel	904-829-5939	10 Vilano Road St Augustine FL	3+
Holiday Inn - St Augustine Beach	904-471-2555	860 A1A Beach Blvd St Augustine Beach FL	2
Elkton			
Comfort Inn	904-829-3435	2625 H 207 - Exit 311/H 207 Elkton FL	3+
Flagler Beach			
Topaz Motel	386-439-3301	1224 S Oceanshore Blvd - Exit A1A/H 100 Flagler Beach FL	3+
Whale Watch Motel	386-439-2545	2448 S Oceanshore Blvd Flagler Beach FL	1+
Daytona Beach			
La Quinta Inn Daytona Beach	386-255-7412	2725 International Speedway - Exit 261 Daytona Beach FL	3+
Quality Inn Ocean Palms	386-255-0476	2323 S Atlantic Avenue - Exit 261 E on H 92 Daytona Beach FL	3+
Super 8 Daytona Beach/Speedway Area	386-253-0643	2992 W International Speedway Blvd - Exit 87 or 87b Daytona Beach FL	2
Days Inn Daytona/Ormond Beach	386-672-7341	1608 N US Hwy 1 - Exit 89 Ormond Beach FL	2
Space Coast			
Best Western Cocoa Inn	321-632-1065	4225 West King St - Exit 201 Cocoa FL	2
Holiday Inn	321-783-2271	1300 N. Atlantic Ave - Exit 205 Cocoa Beach FL	2
Quality Suites	321-783-6868	3655 N Atlantic Avenue - Exit 520 Cocoa Beach FL	1
Comfort Inn	321-269-7110	3655 Cheney H - Exit 215 Titusville FL	2
Days Inn Space Coast/Titusville	321-269-4480	3755 Cheney Hwy - Exit 215 Titusville FL	2
Hampton Inn	321-383-9191	4760 Helen Hauser Blvd - Exit 215 Titusville FL	3+
Melbourne			
Hilton	321-768-0200	200 Rialto Place - Exit 180 Melbourne FL	2
La Quinta Inn & Suites Melbourne	321-242-9400	7200 George T. Edwards Drive - Exit 191 Melbourne FL	3+
Howard Johnson Inn	321-768-8439	4431 West New Haven Ave. West Melbourne FL	1+
South Florida			
Residence Inn by Marriott	561-994-3222	525 NW 77th Street - Exit 50 Boca Raton FL	3+
TownePlace Suites Boca Raton	561-994-7232	5110 NW 8th Avenue - Exit 48 Boca Raton FL	2
Comfort Inn	954-428-0650	50 S Ocean Drive - Exit 42/Hillsboro Blvd Deerfield Beach FL	2
Comfort Suites	954-570-8887	1040 Newport Center Drive - Exit 41W Deerfield Beach FL	3+
La Quinta Inn Deerfield Beach	954-421-1004	351 W Hillsboro Blvd. - Exit 42 Deerfield Beach FL	3+
Residence Inn by Marriott	561-276-7441	1111 E Atlantic Avenue - Exit 52E Delray Beach FL	3+
Candlewood Suites Ft. Lauderdale	954-522-8822	1120 W. State Road 84 - Exit Marina Mile Road Fort Lauderdale FL	2
Hampton Inn	954-524-9900	2301 SW 12th Avenue - Exit 25E Fort Lauderdale FL	3+
La Quinta Inn Ft. Lauderdale	954-491-7666	999 West Cypress Creek Rd. - Exit 33B Fort Lauderdale FL	3+
La Quinta Inn Ft. Lauderdale	954-485-7900	3800 W. Commercial Blvd - Exit Commercial Blvd Fort Lauderdale FL	2
TownePlace Suites Fort Lauderdale	954-484-2214	3100 Prospect Rd - Exit 33 Fort Lauderdale FL	2
Days Inn Fort Lauderdale/Airport	954-923-7300	2601 N 29th Ave - Exit 49 Hollywood FL	2
The Chesterfield Hotel	561-659-5800	363 Cocoanut Row - Exit 70/Okeechobee Palm Beach FL	1+
Holiday Inn	954-472-5600	1711 N. University Dr - Exit Broward Blvd Plantation FL	2
Days Inn Pompano Beach	954-972-3700	1411 NW 31st Ave - Exit 34 Pompano Beach FL	2
Days Inn West Palm Beach North	561-689-0450	2300 45th St - Exit 74 West Palm Beach FL	2
La Quinta Inn West Palm Beach	561-697-3388	5981 Okeechobee Blvd - Exit Okeechobee Blvd West Palm Beach FL	3+
Residence Inn by Marriott	561-687-4747	2461 Metrocentre Blvd - Exit 74/75 West Palm Beach FL	3+
TownePlace Suites Fort Lauderdale Weston	954-659-2234	1545 Three Village Rd - Exit 595 Weston FL	3+
Miami			
Hampton Inn	305-854-2070	2500 Brickell Avenue - Exit 1A Miami FL	3+

Interstate 95 Campground Listings

Maine Campground Listings (Interstate 95)   Dogs per Room

Medway			
Katahdin Shadows Campground and Cabins	207-746-9349	H 157 - Exit 244 Medway ME	3+
Bangor			
Paul Bunyan Campground	207-941-1177	1862 Union Street - Exit 184 Bangor ME	1+
Pumpkin Patch	207-848-2231	149 Billings Road - Exit 180 Hermon ME	3+
Old Orchard Beach			
Wild Acres Family Camping Resort	207-934-2535	179 Saco Avenue - Exit 36 Old Orchard Beach ME	3+
Kennebunk			
Hemlock Grove Campground	207-985-0398	1299 Portland Road Arundel ME	2
Red Apple Campground	207-967-4927	111 Sinnott Road Kennebunkport ME	3+

Highway Guides - Please always call ahead to make sure that an establishment is still dog-friendly

Sea-Vu Campground	207-646-7732	1733 Post Road Wells ME	3+
Well Beach Resort	207-646-7570	1000 Post Road Wells ME	3+

York
Libby's Oceanside Camp	207-363-4171	725 York Street York Harbor ME	2

New Hampshire Campground Listings (Interstate 95)   Dogs per Room

Portsmouth
Wakeda Campground	603-772-5274	294 Exeter Road Hampton Falls NH	3+

Massachusetts Campground Listings (Interstate 95)   Dogs per Room

Boston Area
Circle Farm	508-966-1136	131 Main Street Bellingham MA	3+
Normandy Farms	508-543-7600	72 West Street Foxboro MA	3+
Wompatuck State Park	781-749-7160	Union Street Hingham MA	3+
Boston Minuteman Campground	877-677-0042	264 Ayer Road Littleton MA	3+
KOA	508-947-6435	438 Plymouth Street Middleboro MA	3+
Winter Island Park	978-745-9430	50 Winter Island Road Salem MA	2
Rusnik Campground	978-462-9551	115 Lafayette Road Salisbury MA	3+

Rhode Island Campground Listings (Interstate 95)   Dogs per Room

Providence
Bowdish Lake	401-568-8890	40 Safari Road Glocester RI	3+
Holiday Acres Camping Resort	401-934-0780	591 Snakehill Road N Scituate RI	2

Southern Rhode Island
Burlingame State Campground	401-322-7337	Route 1 Charlestown RI	2
Whispering Pines	401-539-7011	41 Sawmill Road Hope Valley RI	3+
Fishermen's State Park and Campground	401-789-8374	1011 Point Judith Road Narragansett RI	2
Wordon Pond Family Campground	401-789-9113	416 A Worden Pond Road Wakefield RI	2
Wawaloam Campground	401-294-3039	510 Gardner Road West Kingston RI	2

Connecticut Campground Listings (Interstate 95)   Dogs per Room

Stonington
Pachaug State Forest Chapman Area	860-376-4075	H 49/ P. O. Box 5 Voluntown CT	1+

New London - Mystic
Aces High RV Park	860-739-8858	301 Chesterfield Road East Lyme CT	3+
Seaport Campground	860-536-4044	Old Campground Road Old Mystic CT	2

New Jersey Campground Listings (Interstate 95)   Dogs per Room

Newark - NYC Area
Liberty Harbor RV Park	201-387-7500	11 Marin Blvd - Exit 14C/Jersey City-Grand Street Jersey City NJ	3+

Jackson
Butterfly Camping Resort	732-928-2107	360 Butterfly Road - Exit 21/H 527 Jackson NJ	2
Tip Tam Camping Resort	877-TIP-TAM1	301 Brewer's Bridge Road Jackson NJ	2

Camden Area
Timberlane Campground	856-423-6677	117 Timberlane Road - Exit Timberlane Road Clarksboro NJ	3+

Delaware Bridge Area
Four Seasons Family Campground	856-769-3635	158 Woodstown Road Pilesgrove NJ	3+

Maryland Campground Listings (Interstate 95)   Dogs per Room

North East
Elk Neck State Park	410-287-5333	4395 Turkey Point Road North East MD	3+

Washington Suburbs
Cherry Hill Park	800-801-6449	9800 Cherry Hill Road - Exit 25 College Park MD	3+

Virginia Campground Listings (Interstate 95)   Dogs per Room

Northern Virginia
Pohick Bay Park	703-352-5900	6501 Pohick Bay Drive - Exit Hwy 1 Lorton VA	3+

Fredericksburg

Fredericksburg/Washington DC S KOA	540-898-7252	7400 Brookside Lane - Exit H 607 Fredericksburg VA	2
Richmond			
Pocohontas State Park	804-796-4255	10301 State Park Road Chesterfield VA	3+
Petersburg			
Petersburg KOA	804-732-8345	2809 Cortland Road - Exit 41 Petersburg VA	3+
Emporia			
Jellystone Park	434-634-3115	2940 Sussex Drive - Exit 17 Emporia VA	3+

North Carolina Campground Listings (Interstate 95)   Dogs per Room

Enfield			
Enfield/Rocky Mount KOA	252-445-5925	101 Bell Acres - Exit 154/Enfield Enfield NC	3+
Smithfield			
Selma/Smithfield KOA	919-965-5923	428 Campground Road - Exit 98 Selma NC	3+
Fayetteville			
Fayetteville/Wade KOA	910-484-5500	6250 Wade Stedman Road - Exit 61 Wade NC	3+

South Carolina Campground Listings (Interstate 95)   Dogs per Room

Hamer			
South of the Border Campground	843-774-2411	3346 H 301N Hamer SC	3+
Florence			
Florence KOA	843-665-7007	1115 E Campground Road - Exit 169 Florence SC	3+
Yemassee			
Point South KOA	843-726-5733	14 Campground Road - Exit 33 to H 17 Yemassee SC	3+

Georgia Campground Listings (Interstate 95)   Dogs per Room

Savannah			
Fort McAllister State Historic Park	912-727-2339	3894 Fort McAllister Road - Exit 90 to H 144 Richmond Hill GA	3+
Savannah South KOA	912-765-3396	4915 H 17 - Exit 87 @ Richmond Hill Richmond Hill GA	3+
Jekyll Island			
Jekyll Island Campground	866-658-3021	1197 Riverview Drive - Exit 29 Jekyll Island GA	3+
St Marys			
Jacksonville N/Kingsland KOA	912-729-3232	2970 Scrubby Buff Road - Exit 1 Kingsland GA	3+

Florida Campground Listings (Interstate 95)   Dogs per Room

Jacksonville			
Flamingo Lake RV Resort	904-766-0672	3640 Newcomb Road - Exit 32 N Jacksonville FL	3+
St Augustine			
Anastasia State Park	904-461-2033	1340-A A1A South St Augustine FL	3+
Anastasia State Park Campgrounds	904-461-2033	Anastasia Park Drive St Augustine FL	1+
St. Augustine Beach KOA	904-471-3113	525 West Pope Road St Augustine FL	1+
Stagecoach RV Park	904-824-2319	2711 County Road 208 - Exit H 16W St Augustine FL	3+
Flagler Beach			
Beverly Beach Campground	800-255-2706	2816 N Ocean Shore Blvd Flagler Beach FL	3+
Gamble Rogers Memorial State Recreation Area	386-517-2086	3100 S A1A (Ocean Shore Blvd) Flagler Beach FL	3+
Daytona Beach			
Bulow Plantation RV Resort	800-782-8569	3345 Old Kings Road S - Exit 278 Flagler Beach FL	3+
Daytona North RV Resort	877-277-8737	1701 H 1 - Exit H 1 Ormond Beach FL	3+
Tomoka State Park	386-676-4050	2099 N Beach Street - Exit 268 Ormond Beach FL	3+
Daytona Beach Campground	386-761-2663	4601 Clyde Morris Blvd - Exit 256 Port Orange FL	3+
Melbourne			
Sebastian Inlet State Park	321-984-4852	9700 S A1A - Exit State Road 192 Melbourne Beach FL	3+
Hobe Sound			
Jonathan Dickinson State Park	772-546-2771	16450 SE Federal H (H 1) - Exit 87A/Indiantown Road Hobe Sound FL	3+
South Florida			
Paradise Island RV Resort	954-485-1150	2121 NW 29th Court - Exit 33311 Oakland Park FL	3+
Highland Woods	866-340-0649	850/900 NE 48th Street - Exit 39/Sample Road Pompano Beach FL	3+